HOUGHTON MIFFLIN The Mathematics Experience

Teacher's Edition

Senior Authors

Mary Ann Haubner
Mount St. Joseph College
Cincinnati, Ohio

Edward Rathmell
University of Northern Iowa
Cedar Falls, Iowa

Douglas Super
Vancouver School Board
Vancouver, Canada

Senior Consulting Author

Lelon R. Capps
University of Kansas
Lawrence, Kansas

Authors

Harold Asturias
Norwood Street School
Los Angeles, California

Harry Bohan
Sam Houston State University
Huntsville, Texas

William L. Cole
Michigan State University
Lansing, Michigan

Portia C. Elliott
University of Massachusetts
Amherst, Massachusetts

Francis J. Gardella
East Brunswick Public Schools
East Brunswick, New Jersey

Ana María Golán
Santa Ana Unified School District
Santa Ana, California

Edwin McClintock
Florida International University
Miami, Florida

Jean M. Shaw
University of Mississippi
University, Mississippi

Charles Thompson
University of Louisville
Louisville, Kentucky

Leland Webb
California State University
Bakersfield, California

Barbara Elder Weller
Montclair Public Schools
Montclair, New Jersey

Alma Wright
Trotter Elementary School
Roxbury, Massachusetts

Judith S. Zawojewski
National-Louis University
Evanston, Illinois

Houghton Mifflin Company BOSTON

Atlanta   Dallas   Geneva, Illinois   Palo Alto   Princeton   Toronto

Critical Readers

Dennis Anderson
Canyon Park Junior High School
Bothell, Washington

Mary Buck
C. R. Anderson Middle School
Helena, Montana

Lorraine Cooke
Jefferson Elementary School
Bath, South Carolina

Janice Grashel
Instructional Skills Coordinator
Lawrence, Kansas

Lee Hoagland
Westlawn Elementary School
Mobile, Alabama

Charlotte Hughes
Marbrook Elementary School
Wilmington, Delaware

Terell Kaiser
Valley Elementary School
East Grand Forks, Minnesota

Rebecca Kirkland
Highland Elementary School
Dothan, Alabama

Charlene Little
Whitney Young Middle School
Detroit, Michigan

Rebecca Manning
Brant Elementary School
Brant, New York

Mark Medina
King Elementary School
Colorado Springs, Colorado

Michael Monaghan
Emerson Elementary School
Wichita, Kansas

Jill Moore
Yolanda Elementary School
Springfield, Oregon

Betty Pugh
Paris Intermediate School
Paris, Arkansas

Peter Scarano
Elijah Elementary School
Clinton, Iowa

Catherine Scott
Sandpiper Elementary School
Scottsdale, Arizona

Calvin Shilt
Shroder Middle School
Cincinnati, Ohio

Jeanie Sisson
Red Oak Elementary School
Oklahoma City, Oklahoma

Susan Stonebraker
South Central Elementary School
Canonsburg, Pennsylvania

Donald J. Sweeney
Silverhill School
Silverhill, Alabama

Robert Tate
Thomas Middle School
Philadelphia, Pennsylvania

Ann Watson
Rockefeller Elementary School
Little Rock, Arkansas

Carol Wood
Elma Elementary School
Elma, New York

Multicultural Reviewers

Gail Christopher
Americans All
Chicago, Illinois

Jane Horii
former Master Teacher
San Francisco Unified School
District
San Francisco, California

Christella D. Moody
Eastern Michigan University
Ypsilanti, Michigan

Houghton Mifflin Company wishes to acknowledge the contributions of Dr. Ernest R. Duncan to the teaching of elementary school mathematics. During his lifetime Dr. Duncan was devoted to creating new approaches for teaching and learning mathematics that were used by hundreds of thousands of school children all over the world. We are pleased to have been associated with him for the past twenty-five years.

Printed in U.S.A.

ISBN: 0-395-49420-6

BCDEFGHIJ-B-9987654321

Field Test Teachers

Adam Artis
Trotter Elementary School
Roxbury, Massachusetts

Julie Book
Edison Elementary School
Waterloo, Iowa

Barbara Costa
St. Teresa School
Cincinnati, Ohio

Carolyn Donahue
Patrick J. Kennedy School
East Boston, Massachusetts

Ruben P. Guzman
William Howard Taft
Middle School
Brighton, Massachusetts

Ann G. Hill
Nishuane School
Montclair, New Jersey

Michael R. Johnson
Wayne Van Horn School
Bakersfield, California

Terry Kawas
Forrestdale School
Rumson, New Jersey

Mary E. Leydon
William Howard Taft
Middle School
Brighton, Massachusetts

Emma Louie
Wayne Van Horn School
Bakersfield, California

Kelly J. Martin
Waverly Middle School
Lansing, Michigan

Trudy Olson
Irving Elementary School
Waterloo, Iowa

Elaine Randolph-Jacobs
Patrick J. Kennedy School
East Boston, Massachusetts

Janet Reinhart
Patrick J. Kennedy School
East Boston, Massachusetts

William J. Rudder
William Howard Taft
Middle School
Brighton, Massachusetts

Mary Sue Salzarulo
St. Teresa School
Cincinnati, Ohio

Louise Scanlon-Oberg
Trotter Elementary School
Roxbury, Massachusetts

Sally Schneider
St. Raphael School
Louisville, Kentucky

Kathleen Schweer
St. Teresa School
Cincinnati, Ohio

Henry Smith
William Howard Taft
Middle School
Brighton, Massachusetts

Jo Ann Smithmeyer
St. Teresa School
Cincinnati, Ohio

Frances M. Stuart
Patrick J. Kennedy School
East Boston, Massachusetts

Kathleen Harris Sullivan
William Howard Taft
Middle School
Brighton, Massachusetts

Susan Thompson
Sam Houston
Elementary School
Huntsville, Texas

Willard Vredenburg
South Miami Middle School
Miami, Florida

Robert Walsh
Patrick J. Kennedy School
East Boston, Massachusetts

Julie Weseman
Blackhawk Elementary School
Waterloo, Iowa

Polly Wing
Trotter Elementary School
Roxbury, Massachusetts

Components

Shaded cells (availability) are marked with ●.

Component	K	1	2	3	4	5	6	7	8
Core Components									
Student Book (consumable K-3, hardbound 3-8)	●	●	●	●	●	●	●	●	●
Teacher's Edition	●	●	●	●	●	●	●	●	●
Teacher's Professional Handbook	●	●	●	●	●	●	●	●	●
Teacher's Resource Book	●	●	●	●	●	●	●	●	●
Teacher's Resource Book Answer Key	●	●	●	●	●	●	●	●	●
Additional Components									
Practice Workbook	●	●	●	●	●	●	●	●	●
Skills Workbooks (and Teacher's Editions):									
Whole Numbers: Addition and Subtraction				●	●	●	●	●	●
Whole Numbers: Multiplication and Division				●	●	●	●	●	●
Decimals					●	●	●	●	●
Fractions					●	●	●	●	●
Equations, Ratio, Proportion and Percent						●	●		●
Problem Solving Strategies				●	●	●	●	●	●
Daily Review Booklet		●	●	●	●	●	●	●	●
Daily Review Booklet Answer Key		●	●	●	●	●	●	●	●
Multiple Choice Tests		●	●	●	●	●	●	●	●
Big Book	●								
Program Record Card	●	●	●	●	●	●	●	●	●
Cooperative Learning Resource Activities		●	●	●	●	●	●	●	●
Story Books	●	●	●						
Math America	●	●	●	●	●	●	●	●	●
MathWorks (Books A and B)	●	●	●						
Manipulatives Kit (classroom)	●	●	●	●	●	●	●	●	●
Teacher's Manipulatives Kit	●	●	●	●	●	●	●	●	●
Overhead Kit	●	●	●	●	●	●	●	●	●
TI-108 Calculators (10 pack)	●	●	●	●	●	●	●	●	●
TI-Math Explorer Calculators (10 pack)				●	●	●	●	●	●
The Educator Basic Overhead Calculator	●	●	●	●	●	●	●	●	●
The Educator Intermediate Overhead Calculator				●	●	●	●	●	●
Computer Software									
Mathematics Activities Courseware		●	●	●	●	●	●	●	●
Kindermath	●								
Computer Tutor								●	●
Easy Graph		●	●	●	●	●	●	●	●
Computational Skills Program			●	●	●	●	●	●	●
Friendly Filer				●	●	●	●	●	●
EduCalc				●	●	●	●		
Geometry Grapher								●	●
Algebra Plotter Plus								●	●
Computer Management System (Disks, Booklet, Binder)		●	●	●	●	●	●	●	●

Contents

Chapter 1   Number Sense, Numeration, and Metric Measures

Problem Solving and Reasoning are in every lesson. Look on the student pages for
Problem Solving, Think Aloud, Critical Thinking, and **Number Sense.**
Communication activities are printed in red. **Connections** are printed in blue.

---

*   Throughout the book, Cooperative Learning activities are identified by this logo or by directions that suggest discussing or working with a partner or in a small group.

Chapter 2
Addition and Subtraction: Whole Numbers and Decimals

Problem Solving and Reasoning are in every lesson. Look on the student pages for
Problem Solving, Think Aloud, Critical Thinking, and **Number Sense.**
Communication activities are printed in red. **Connections** are printed in blue.

Chapter 3
Multiplication and Division: Whole Numbers and Decimals

Problem Solving and Reasoning are in every lesson. Look on the student pages for
Problem Solving, Think Aloud, Critical Thinking, and **Number Sense.**
Communication activities are printed in red. **Connections** are printed in blue.

*   Throughout the book, Cooperative Learning activities are identified by this logo or
       by directions that suggest discussing or working with a partner or in a small group.

Chapter 4   Variables, Expressions, and Equations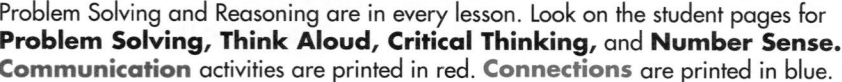

Problem Solving and Reasoning are in every lesson. Look on the student pages for
Problem Solving, Think Aloud, Critical Thinking, and **Number Sense.**
Communication activities are printed in red. **Connections** are printed in blue.

Chapter 5   Number Theory and Fraction Concepts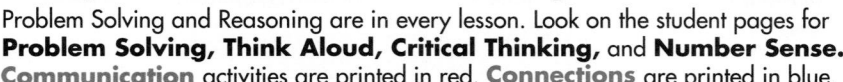

Problem Solving and Reasoning are in every lesson. Look on the student pages for
Problem Solving, Think Aloud, Critical Thinking, and **Number Sense.**
Communication activities are printed in red. **Connections** are printed in blue.

Chapter 6   Fractions: Addition and Subtraction

Problem Solving and Reasoning are in every lesson. Look on the student pages for **Problem Solving, Think Aloud, Critical Thinking,** and **Number Sense.**
Communication activities are printed in red. **Connections** are printed in blue.

* Throughout the book, Cooperative Learning activities are identified by this logo or by directions that suggest discussing or working with a partner or in a small group.

Chapter 7   Fractions: Multiplication and Division

Problem Solving and Reasoning are in every lesson. Look on the student pages for
Problem Solving, Think Aloud, Critical Thinking, and **Number Sense.**
Communication activities are printed in red. Connections are printed in blue.

Chapter 8   Geometry and Measurement

Problem Solving and Reasoning are in every lesson. Look on the student pages for
Problem Solving, Think Aloud, Critical Thinking, and **Number Sense.**
Communication activities are printed in red. Connections are printed in blue.

Chapter 9   Ratio, Proportion, and Applications

Problem Solving and Reasoning are in every lesson. Look on the student pages for
Problem Solving, Think Aloud, Critical Thinking, and **Number Sense.**
Communication activities are printed in red. **Connections** are printed in blue.

*   Throughout the book, Cooperative Learning activities are identified by this logo or by directions that suggest discussing or working with a partner or in a small group.

T10

Chapter 10   Percent

Problem Solving and Reasoning are in every lesson. Look on the student pages for **Problem Solving, Think Aloud, Critical Thinking,** and **Number Sense.** Communication activities are printed in red. Connections are printed in blue.

Chapter 11   Proportion and Percent

Problem Solving and Reasoning are in every lesson. Look on the student pages for **Problem Solving, Think Aloud, Critical Thinking,** and **Number Sense.** Communication activities are printed in red. **Connections** are printed in blue.

Chapter 12   Statistics and Probability

Problem Solving and Reasoning are in every lesson. Look on the student pages for
Problem Solving, Think Aloud, Critical Thinking, and **Number Sense.**
Communication activities are printed in red. Connections are printed in blue.

Chapter 13   Integers and Coordinate Graphing

Problem Solving and Reasoning are in every lesson. Look on the student pages for
Problem Solving, Think Aloud, Critical Thinking, and **Number Sense.**
Communication activities are printed in red. Connections are printed in blue.

* Throughout the book, Cooperative Learning activities are identified by this logo or by directions that suggest discussing or working with a partner or in a small group.

Chapter 14   Geometry and Measurement

Problem Solving and Reasoning are in every lesson. Look on the student pages for
Problem Solving, Think Aloud, Critical Thinking, and **Number Sense.**
Communication activities are printed in red. Connections are printed in blue.

Chapter 15   Statistics and Probability

Problem Solving and Reasoning are in every lesson. Look on the student pages for
Problem Solving, Think Aloud, Critical Thinking, and **Number Sense.**
Communication activities are printed in red. Connections are printed in blue.

End of Book Materials

*   Throughout the book, Cooperative Learning activities are identified by this logo or by directions that suggest discussing or working with a partner or in a small group.

Informal Assessment

DISCOVERY: ADDITION AND SUBTRACTION, WHOLE NUMBERS AND DECIMALS

Objective Assess students' skills in addition and subtraction with three- and four-digit numbers and with money and decimals.

Background This informal assessment is designed to give you flexibility in teaching the topics taught in Chapter 2. The skills in the assessment were thoroughly covered in the sixth grade. It is possible, therefore, that some of your students may know the material well. In that case, you may choose to either provide a quick review of the lessons listed in the following chart or skip the lessons entirely. If you do choose to

skip some lessons, you might still cover some of the *Number Sense, Critical Thinking,* or *Mental Math* exercises.

Using the Pages Have students complete the work on these two pages. Note how the students line up decimals to add or subtract them. If students cannot correctly line up decimals, they may not understand the concept of place value with decimals. After assessing their performance, you may wish to discuss the significance of Earth Day.

ITEM ANALYSIS OF SKILLS BEING ASSESSED				
Pages	**Items**	**Lesson**	**Pages**	**Objective**
xii	All items	2-4 2-6	40-41 46-47	Add whole number and decimals. Subtract whole numbers.
xiii	B, C, E, H, I, K, L, O	2-4	40-41	Add whole numbers and decimals.
	A, D, F, G, J, M, N	2-7	48-49	Subtract decimals.

Informal Assessment

DISCOVERY: MULTIPLICATION AND DIVISION, WHOLE NUMBERS AND DECIMALS

Objective Assess students' skills in multiplying and dividing whole numbers and decimals.

Background This informal assessment is designed to give you flexibility in teaching some of the topics taught in Chapters 1, 2, and 3. The skills in the assessment were covered thoroughly in the sixth grade. It is possible, therefore, that some of your students may know the material well. In that case, you may choose to either provide a quick review of the lessons listed in the following chart or skip the lessons entirely.

Another option is to skip the lessons but to cover *Number Sense, Critical Thinking,* and *Mental Math* exercises.

Using the Pages Have students complete the work on these two pages. Students should be able to correctly place the decimal points in their answers, and to round to the nearest tenth or hundredth. If they can not complete these activities, they may not fully understand the concept of place value with decimals.

ITEM ANALYSIS OF SKILLS BEING ASSESSED

Pages	Items	Lesson	Pages	Objective
xiv	1-9	3-3 3-4	64-65 66-67	Multiply whole numbers. Multiply decimals.
	other items	3-5 3-10 1-7	68-69 80-81 14-15	Divide whole numbers. Divide decimals by decimals. Round whole numbers and decimals.
xv	Q, R, S, T	3-6 1-7	70-71 14-15	Divide decimals by whole numbers. Round whole numbers and decimals.
	10-11	2-4	40-41	Add decimals.
	12	2-7	48-49	Subtract decimals.

Table of Numbers

Table of Numbers

	O	P	Q	R	S	T	U	V	W
A	65	38	82	49	19	77	91	24	56
B	436	903	150	539	828	671	295	747	361
C	108	94	699	75	470	274	86	562	316
D	5,239	2,430	6,771	1,121	9,036	7,329	3,615	8,484	4,418
E	1,045	6,616	789	2,318	989	5,231	3,251	832	4,119
F	0.3	0.80	0.9	0.71	0.6	0.34	0.79	0.2	0.65
G	4.8	9.7	5.3	1.1	3.5	1.6	7.2	2.9	2.4
H	1.25	2.7	8	9.58	3.9	4.5	7	4.63	8.6
I	$\frac{2}{3}$	$\frac{1}{2}$	$\frac{6}{12}$	$\frac{5}{6}$	$\frac{1}{4}$	$\frac{7}{12}$	$\frac{1}{6}$	$\frac{3}{4}$	$\frac{1}{3}$
J	$4\frac{1}{2}$	$3\frac{3}{10}$	$2\frac{3}{5}$	$1\frac{1}{10}$	7	$3\frac{3}{5}$	$4\frac{8}{10}$	5	$2\frac{4}{5}$
K	$\frac{5}{16}$	$2\frac{5}{8}$	$2\frac{1}{2}$	$\frac{7}{8}$	$4\frac{1}{16}$	$1\frac{1}{4}$	$1\frac{3}{8}$	$3\frac{3}{4}$	$4\frac{7}{16}$
L	0.2	1.5	$4\frac{3}{4}$	0.25	$\frac{3}{10}$	$\frac{1}{2}$	0.75	$2\frac{1}{4}$	$1\frac{4}{5}$
M	50%	1%	100%	25%	5%	75%	30%	200%	80%
N	-3	-5	8	0	-2	3	-1	6	-4

Ideas for using this table for estimation, mental math, and for calculator activities are found periodically in the Two Minute Math sections of the Teacher's Edition.

xvi

This table can be used for a variety of mental math, estimation, and calculator activities. You will find ideas for using it throughout the Teacher's Edition in the Two-Minute Math sections of the daily lessons.

Pacing for Students Successful with Whole Number and Decimal Computation

The informal assessment at this grade level covers addition, subtraction, multiplication and division of whole numbers and decimals. If your students were successful on the informal assessment, you may wish to implement these pacing suggestions for the following chapters.

Chapter 2   Addition and Subtraction: Whole Numbers and Decimals
Chapter Opener—Working with Data
Lesson 2-3   Problem Solving: Choosing Mental Math, Paper and Pencil, or Calculator
Lesson 2-8   Problem Solving: Reading for Understanding

Chapter 3   Multiplication and Division: Whole Numbers and Decimals
Chapter Opener—Working with Data
Lesson 3-7   Problem Solving: Looking Back
Lesson 3-8   Exploring Multiplying and Dividing Decimals
Lesson 3-12   Problem Solving: Too Much or Too Little Information

Number Sense, Numeration, and Metric Measures

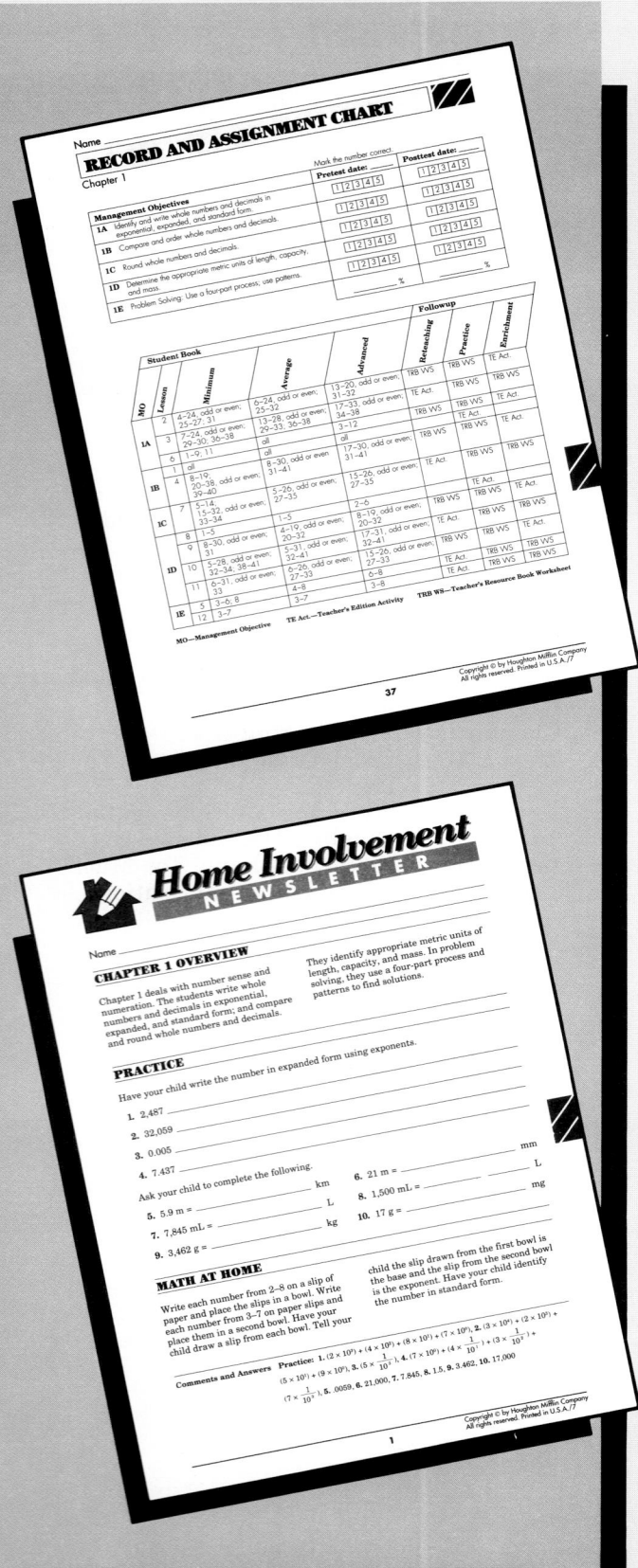

This chapter begins by developing number sense through exploring numbers in a variety of contexts. Students then review reading, writing, rounding, comparing, and ordering decimal numbers from thousandths through billions and the metric units of length, capacity, and mass. They learn to write numbers in standard form, in expanded form with exponents, and in scientific notation. Students gain an understanding of numbers and measurement, which provides them with a foundation for their work with new topics in subsequent chapters.

Management Objectives

1A Identify and write whole numbers and decimals in exponential, expanded, and standard form.
1B Compare and order whole numbers and decimals.
1C Round whole numbers and decimals.
1D Determine the appropriate metric units of length, capacity, and mass.
1E Problem Solving: Use a four-part process. Use patterns.

Assignments for different achievement levels are provided on the Record and Assignment Chart in the Teacher's Resource Book.

Vocabulary

base, exponent, page 4
factor, page 4
standard form, page 6
word form, page 6
short word form, page 6
expanded form, page 6
exponential form, page 4
perimeter, page 16
meter, centimeter, millimeter, kilometer, page 20
capacity, liter, milliliter, kiloliter, page 22
mass, gram, milligram, kilogram, page 24

Home Involvement

As you begin to teach this chapter, give each student a copy of the Home Involvement Newsletter for this chapter.

This newsletter provides parents with
■ an overview of the chapter
■ suggestions for practicing some of the skills in the chapter
■ an at-home activity to do with their child, applying the skills taught in the chapter.

Management Chart

Management Objectives	Lesson/ Pages	Student Not Successful	Student Needs More Practice	Student Successful	Pacing Range
1A Identify and write whole numbers and decimals in exponential, expanded, and standard form.	1-2/4-5	TRB/RW 1-2	TRB/PW 1-2 MAC 8 Activity 1	TE/EA 1-2 MAC 8 Activity 1	1-2 days
	1-3/6-7	TE/RA 1-3	TRB/PW 1-3 CT Unit 1 Obj. 1.3	TRB/EW 1-3	
1B Compare and order whole numbers and decimals.	1-4/8-9	TRB/RW 1-4	TRB/PW 1-4 CT Unit 1 Obj. 1.1	TE/EA 1-4	1 day
1C Round whole numbers and decimals.	1-7/14-15	TE/RA 1-7	TRB/PW 1-7 CSP Decimals Sk. 2 CT Unit 1 Obj. 1.4 CT Unit 3 Obj. 1.2	TRB/EW 1-7	1 day
1D Determine the appropriate metric units of length, capacity, and mass.	1-9/20-21	TRB/RW 1-9	TRB/PW 1-9	TE/EA 1-9	2-3 days
	1-10/22-23	TE/RA 1-10	TRB/PW 1-10	TRB/EW 1-10	
	1-11/24-25	TRB/RW 1-11	TRB/PW 1-11	TE/EA 1-11	
1E Problem Solving: Use a four-part process; use patterns	1-5/10-11	TE/RA 1-5	TRB/PW 1-5	TRB/EW 1-5	2 days
	1-12/26-27	TE/RA 1-12	TRB/PW 1-12	TRB/EW 1-12	
What Is Number Sense?	1-1/2-3			TE/CA 1-1	1 day
Greater Numbers	1-6/12-13	TRB/RW 1-6	TRB/PW 1-6	TE/EA 1-6	1 day
When Do We Estimate?	1-8/16-17			TE/CA 1-8	1 day
Chapter Checkups	18-19, 28-29				
Extra Practice	30				
Enrichment	31				
Technology	32				

TE = Teacher's Edition
TRB = Teacher's Resource Book
RW = Reteaching Worksheet
RA = Reteaching Activity
EA = Enrichment Activity
EW = Enrichment Worksheet
PW = Practice Worksheet
CA = Classroom Activity

*Other Available Items
MAC = Mathematics Activities Courseware
CSP = Computational Skills Program
CT = Computer Tutor

Manipulative Planning Guide

This is a complete list of manipulatives and materials needed for Chapter 1.

Materials for Manipulatives	TE Activities (INTRODUCE)	Student Book Lesson
Set of base ten materials to demonstrate various numbers	Lessons 1-2, 1-3	
Calculator for each student		Lesson 1-2
Number cubes, four per group		
Decimal squares		
Colored pencils and chalk		
Teaching Aid 1*, two per student	Lesson 1-7	
Newspapers/magazines	Lesson 1-8	
Scissors, one per pair	Lesson 1-12	
Paper bags		
Index cards		
Cotton balls and swabs		
Balance Scale/magazines	Lesson 1-11	
Meter stick	Lesson 1-9	
cm ruler, one per student Metric measuring tape, one per group		
200-mL juice container	Lesson 1-10	
1-L bottle/container	Lessons 1-10, 1-11	
large pail of water	Lessons 1-10, 1-11	
Metric masses	Lesson 1-11	
Small paper squares		
Plastic straw	Lesson 1-12	

*Teaching Aids are found in the Teacher's Resource Book.

Learning Stages

The concepts and skills in Chapter 1 are presented through these learning stages.

CONCRETE

Using manipulatives and verbalizing about a concept. No symbols.

Teacher Edition Activities	Student Book
At this grade level the skills of this chapter are taught at the connecting and symbolic stages.	

Enrichment/ Class Activity	Reteaching	In the Houghton Mifflin Manipulative Kit (yes/no)	In the Houghton Mifflin Overhead Kit?
		Yes	
			Available separately
Lesson 1-2, 1-6		Yes	
	Lesson 1-3	Yes	Yes
	Lesson 1-3		
	Lesson 1-10		
Lesson 1-1	Lesson 1-7		
Lesson 1-1, 1-11	Lesson 1-7		
Lesson 1-9			
		Yes	
		Yes	
Lesson 1-9		Yes	
		Yes	
	Lesson 1-12		
		Yes	

CONNECTING

5¢ 9cm^2 $\frac{1}{3}$

Making a connection between manipulatives and symbols.

Teacher Edition Activities	Student Book
Lessons 1-2, 1-3, 1-7, 1-9, 1-10	

SYMBOLIC

$.05 $A = 9\text{cm}^2$ $1 - \frac{2}{3} = \frac{1}{3}$

Using numbers or symbols. No manipulatives or pictures of manipulatives.

Teacher Edition Activities	Student Book
Lessons 1-1, 1-4, 1-5, 1-6, 1-8, 1-12	Lessons 1-1 through 1-12

CHAPTER 1

Additional Activities

COOPERATIVE LEARNING RESOURCE ACTIVITIES

Through cooperative learning activities, students learn by interacting with one another in small groups. These cooperative activities provide students with motivating settings for making connections, investigations, and problem solving situations.

The cooperative connections are interdisciplinary problem-solving projects. Each student has a particular job that helps lead the group to complete the project. For the cooperative investigations students work in pairs for investigations involving data collection and analysis. The cooperative problem solving activities encourage the sharing of ideas and information. Students work in groups of four to solve a problem. Students are each assigned a clue and work together to find a common solution.

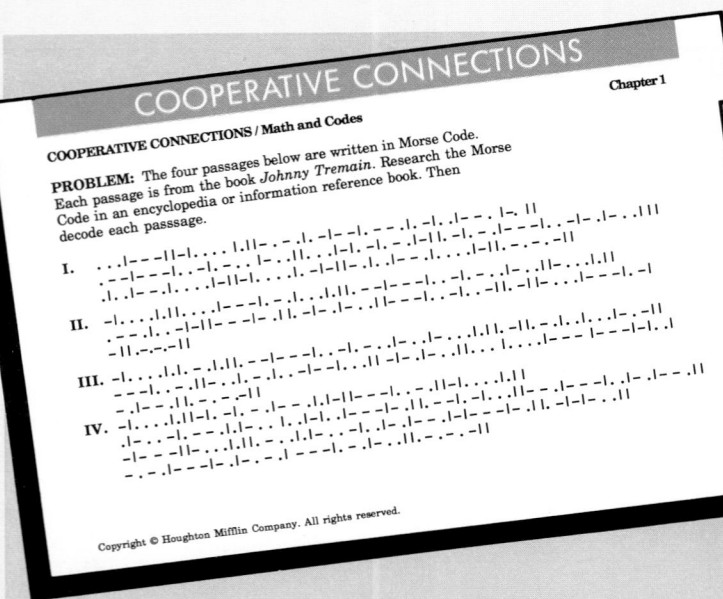

COOPERATIVE CONNECTIONS / Math and Codes

PROBLEM: The four passages below are written in Morse Code. Each passage is from the book *Johnny Tremain*. Research the Morse Code in an encyclopedia or information reference book. Then decode each passsage.

I.

II.

III.

IV.

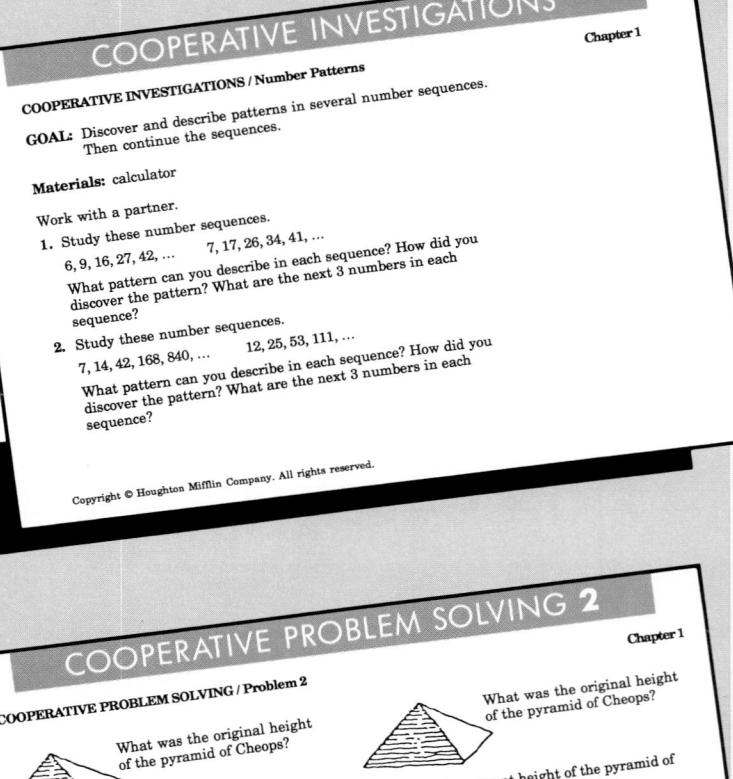

COOPERATIVE INVESTIGATIONS / Number Patterns

GOAL: Discover and describe patterns in several number sequences. Then continue the sequences.

Materials: calculator

Work with a partner.
1. Study these number sequences.

    6, 9, 16, 27, 42, ...   7, 17, 26, 34, 41, ...

    What pattern can you describe in each sequence? How did you discover the pattern? What are the next 3 numbers in each sequence?

2. Study these number sequences.

    7, 14, 42, 168, 840, ...   12, 25, 53, 111, ...

    What pattern can you describe in each sequence? How did you discover the pattern? What are the next 3 numbers in each sequence?

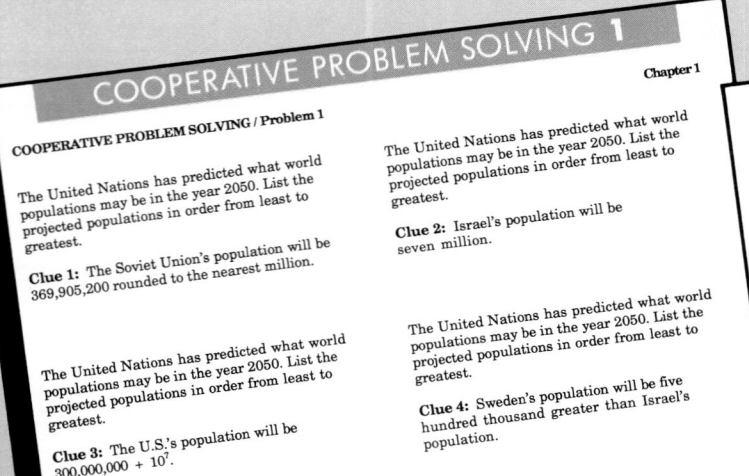

COOPERATIVE PROBLEM SOLVING / Problem 1

The United Nations has predicted what world populations may be in the year 2050. List the projected populations in order from least to greatest.

Clue 1: The Soviet Union's population will be 369,905,200 rounded to the nearest million.

The United Nations has predicted what world populations may be in the year 2050. List the projected populations in order from least to greatest.

Clue 3: The U.S.'s population will be $300,000,000 + 10^7$.

The United Nations has predicted what world populations may be in the year 2050. List the projected populations in order from least to greatest.

Clue 2: Israel's population will be seven million.

The United Nations has predicted what world populations may be in the year 2050. List the projected populations in order from least to greatest.

Clue 4: Sweden's population will be five hundred thousand greater than Israel's population.

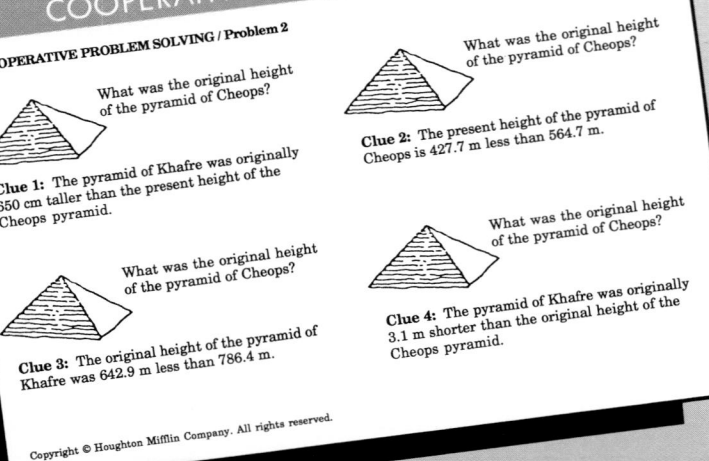

COOPERATIVE PROBLEM SOLVING / Problem 2

What was the original height of the pyramid of Cheops?

Clue 1: The pyramid of Khafre was originally 650 cm taller than the present height of the Cheops pyramid.

What was the original height of the pyramid of Cheops?

Clue 2: The present height of the pyramid of Cheops is 427.7 m less than 564.7 m.

What was the original height of the pyramid of Cheops?

Clue 3: The original height of the pyramid of Khafre was 642.9 m less than 786.4 m.

What was the original height of the pyramid of Cheops?

Clue 4: The pyramid of Khafre was originally 3.1 m shorter than the original height of the Cheops pyramid.

GAMES

RACE-A-ROUND   (For use after Lesson 1-7)

Objective: Round whole numbers and decimals.

☑ **MATERIALS CHECKLIST:** 8 index cards

Prepare eight cards, each showing a different place value from hundred thousands to thousandths. Place the cards face down in a pile. Divide the class into two teams. On the chalkboard write a number having seven whole-number places and four decimal places, for example, 4,228,764.6927. Draw a card, and read the place value. Two students (a member from each team) "race" to the board to round the given number to that place value within ten seconds. Correct responses earn one point. The student who wrote the correct answer first chooses the card for the next round.

MAKE IT EQUAL   (For use after Lesson 1-11)

Objective: Change from one unit to another in the metric system.

☑ **MATERIALS CHECKLIST:** 12 index cards for each team of 4 students

Assign students to teams of four. Have each team member write a metric measurement (length, capacity, or mass) on each of three index cards, for example, 25 cm. Players place the cards face down in a pile. The first player draws a card and displays it. The student to the player's right says "larger" or "smaller." The player must change the measurement on the card to larger or smaller units as requested. Players verify the response. A player who answers correctly keeps the card, and play moves to the right. The player with the most cards wins.

BULLETIN BOARD

Display a set of questions about one million as shown in the drawing. Have students form groups of three or four, and assign a different question to each group. Ask the groups to complete any needed research and find the answer. Groups can explain their solutions to the class and display the answers next to the questions. Challenge students to create new questions about one million for display and answering.

Alternative Assessment

In addition to the paper and pencil tests available with this program, the following items can help you assess critical thinking as well as your students' ability to solve problems in a wide variety of ways.

Open-ended Problem

$2^4 = 4^2$ and $3^4 = 9^2$. Can you assume that all other numbers follow the same pattern?

Give some examples of numbers which have a similar pattern and explain why you would agree or disagree with the assumption.

Teacher Notes

4 is the square of 2, so 4^2 equals $(2^2)^2$ which equals 2^4.

9 is the square of 3, so 9^2 equals $(3^2)^2$ which equals 3^4.

This pattern is true for all numbers a, b, given that b is the square of a. $a^4 = b^2$ if $b = a^2$ because when you substitute a^2 for b in $a^4 = b^2$, you get $a^4 = (a^2)^2$

Group Writing (General Directions)

Give each group one sheet of paper. Students will be asked to think about the topics for a couple of minutes before the activity begins. When the activity begins, the students will rotate the paper from one student to the next in the group, and each student will convey in writing, symbols, or diagrams an idea related to the topic. At the end of the specified time, each group should organize the ideas in the paper and decide what part(s) of their work they will share with the class. Students acquiring English may choose to conduct the small group activity in their native language and then share their work with the class in the common language of the classroom. After each group has shared their work, each student develops one paper which includes some or all of the ideas shared by the class (in writing, symbols, or diagrams).

Group Writing Activity

Explain how the metric system, the base ten system and our system of money are the same and how they are different.

Individual Writing Activity

How are the metric system, the base ten numerals, and our system of money related?

Portfolios

Portfolios can provide information about a student's growth in mathematical understanding over a period of time. They can help you make instructional decisions as well as become a vehicle to communicate with parents. The students' work involving the open-ended problem and writing activity suggested on this page along with work on the Critical Thinking feature on page 5, the Learning Log exercises on pages 19 and 29, and the In Your Words exercise on page 27 could be included in portfolios.

NUMBER SENSE, NUMERATION, AND METRIC MEASURES 1

DID YOU KNOW . . . ?
The fastest pitch recorded was thrown by Nolan Ryan in 1974. His record speed was 100.9 mi/h.

The ERA (earned run average) is the average number of runs a pitcher allows per 9-inning game. The graph below compares the ERAs of pitchers in the 1910s with those in the 1980s.

ERA Leaders 1917-1919 and 1987-1989

Year	Pitcher	ERA
1917	Eddie Cicotte, Chicago	1.53
	Grover Cleveland, Philadelphia	1.86
1918	Walter Johnson, Washington	1.27
	Hippo Vaughn, Chicago	1.74
1919	Walter Johnson, Washington	1.49
	Grover Cleveland, Philadelphia	1.72
1987	Jimmy Key, Toronto	2.76
	Nolan Ryan, Houston	2.76
1988	Allen Anderson, Minnesota	2.45
	Joe Magrane, St. Louis	2.18
1989	Bret Saberhagen, Kansas City	2.16
	Scott Garelts, San Francisco	2.28

National League
American League

Earned Run Average: 0.0 0.5 1.0 1.5 2.0 2.5 3.0

Years

USING DATA
- Collect
- Organize
- **Describe**
- Predict

Who has the best ERA of all pitchers in the bar graph? **Walter Johnson**

Which league had more top ERAs? **American League** Answers will vary. Suggestions given: better hitters, livelier balls, restrictions on kinds of pitches.

Why do you think ERAs are higher in more recent years?

Using the Chapter Opener

The purpose of this page is to involve students in the use of real data much like that presented in newspapers and magazines.

To use this page as you begin the chapter, direct students' attention to the data. You may wish to ask questions such as the following:

Who has the best ERA of all the National League pitchers shown on the bar graph? *(Grover Alexander of Philadelphia)*

Why do you think earned run averages are reported to 2 decimal places? *(to be able to differentiate between players with close ERAs)*

Why are there a larger space and a jagged line along the horizontal line of the graph between 1919 and 1987? *(to indicate the gap in years)*

LESSON 1-1

Lesson Organizer

Objective: Discuss number sense.

Prior Knowledge: Students should have a general knowledge of the relative magnitude of numbers in everyday usage.

Lesson Resources:
Class Activity 1-1
Daily Review 1-1

 *Two-Minute Math*

Name the next three numbers in each sequence.
4, 7, 10, 13, . . . *(16, 19, 22)*
3, 8, 13, 18, . . . *(23, 28, 33)*
2, 3, 5, 8, 12, . . . *(17, 23, 30)*

1 INTRODUCE

SYMBOLIC ACTIVITY

1. Begin a discussion of number sense by asking students to determine whether a new 19-inch color TV would cost $40, $400, or $4,000.

2. Have students work in groups of four. Ask them to list five household items and determine a "reasonable" price for each item. Give each group an opportunity to share its findings with the class.

WHEN YOUR STUDENTS ASK
★ **WHY AM I LEARNING THIS?** ★

You can connect number sense to real life problems. Suppose an ad stated that 8-inch step ladders are on sale. Could that be true? *(No, could be 8-inch step stools or 8-foot ladders.)*

2 Chapter 1 • Lesson 1-1

I *Knew* That!

What Is Number Sense?

It is important that we develop a sense for understanding and using numbers in our everyday lives.

READ ABOUT IT

If you have number sense:

You know that 365 days (d) is 1 year (yr), **BUT** 365 hours (h) has to be less than 1 yr.

You know that 78 miles (mi) is more than 72 mi, **BUT** a golf score of 72 is better than one of 78.

You know that 100 is a large number when it describes the number of years a person has lived, **BUT** 100 is small when it describes the number of minutes a person has lived.

You know that the product of 0.5 and 50 is half of 50, **BUT** the product of 5 and 50 is five times greater than 50.

You know that a car can travel greater than 50 mi in 1 h, **BUT** a person cannot run 50 mi in 1 h.

2   LESSON 1–1

2 TEACH

READ ABOUT IT   In a measurement such as 5 days or 5 weeks, when the same number is used with two different units (days, weeks), how do the units affect the measure? *(The magnitude of the measurement is affected by the unit used. The smaller unit makes the size of the measurement smaller.)*

TALK ABOUT IT   Why is the distance between two cities given in miles instead of feet? *(A smaller, more manageable measure is used with a larger unit.)*

WRITE ABOUT IT   Ask students to write about a time when they did not use number sense.

> ### Chalkboard Examples
>
> **True or false?**
> The number **15,824** is:
> close to $3 \times 5,000$ *(true)*
> closer to 16,000 than 15,000 *(true)*
> 3,100 more than 12,824 *(false)*

SUMMARIZE/ACCESS   Give an example to show how numbers have different meanings depending on the way they are used.
(Example: $\frac{1}{3}$ of a day is 8 hours, but $\frac{1}{3}$ of an hour is 20 minutes.)

Use your number sense to write *true* or *false* for each statement about 12,164.

The number **12,164** is:

1. the number of dollars you might pay for a new car. true

2. the distance in miles from New York City to Boston. false

3. close to the product of 2 × 600. false

4. close to the number of stars in the sky. false

5. less than half of 25 thousand. true

6. close to the number of minutes in $9\frac{1}{2}$ d. true

7. 2,164 more than 10,000. true

8. closer to 12,000 than to 13,000. true

9. 2,100 less than 14,264. true

10. the next counting number after 12,263. false

11. a number you can easily count to in $\frac{1}{2}$ h. false

Use your number sense to find a number in the box that matches the description.

12. the shoe size of an adult male 10

13. the amount left after you have eaten some pizza $\frac{7}{8}$

14. the number of weeks in most Februarys 4

15. the number of pages read in $1\frac{1}{2}$ h 47

WRITE ABOUT IT

16. Write a sentence explaining what you think number sense is.

MEETING INDIVIDUAL NEEDS

For Students Who Are . . .

Acquiring English Proficiency Pair each student with an English-proficient student to work through the Talk About It and Write About Sections of the lesson.

Gifted and Talented Have students work in pairs to create their own list of examples of number sense.

Today's Problem

Jerry has a set of toy blocks. The lengths of five of the blocks are 5 in., 8 in., 4 in., 11 in., and 6 in. Which blocks should he use to build a tower that is exactly 20 in. long?
(5 in. + 4 in. + 11 in. = 20 in.)

3 FOLLOW-UP

CLASS ACTIVITY 1-1

☑ **MATERIALS CHECKLIST:** Index cards, paper bag

Have the students work in groups of three. Provide each group with a paper bag containing three index cards on which you have written the following: *Whole number, Fraction, Decimal.* Have each student select a card and then brainstorm ideas for situations in which the kind of number indicated on the card is used. You may wish to help the students get started by telling them to think about the way numbers are used in sports, cooking, shopping, or science. Have the students share and discuss their work with other group members, and then have groups combine their lists to make a master list for the class.

LESSON 1-2

Lesson Organizer

Objective: Write numbers using exponents.

Prior Knowledge: Students should be able to name the product of three or more factors.

Error Analysis and Remediation: See page 29A.

Lesson Resources:
Practice Worksheet 1-2
Reteaching Worksheet 1-2
Enrichment Activity 1-2
Daily Review 1-2

 *Two-Minute Math*

$5 \times 5 \times 5$ *(125)*
$10 \times 10 \times 10 \times 10$ *(10,000)*
$3 \times 3 \times 3 \times 3$ *(81)*

1 INTRODUCE

CONNECTING ACTIVITY

☑ **MATERIALS CHECKLIST:** base-10 blocks or models

Display the following blocks:

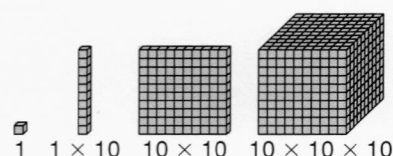

1   1×10 10×10 $10 \times 10 \times 10$

1. Write the value of each figure on the chalkboard. For example, for the hundreds square write $100 = 10 \times 10$.

2. Demonstrate how to use exponents to show $10 \times 10 = 100$ and $10 \times 10 \times 10 = 1,000$.

3. How can blocks be used to show 10^4? *(10 thousand cubes)*

4. Discuss how to model the powers of 3 with the blocks.

WHEN YOUR STUDENTS ASK
★ WHY AM I LEARNING THIS? ★

You can connect this skill to real life through biology. Biologists may use exponents to describe growth patterns of the amoeba.

Exponents

The Great Pyramid at Giza, built for King Cheops, is more than 4,500 yr old. About 100,000 workers built the pyramid. You can write the number of workers in **exponential form**.

$$100,000 = 10 \times 10 \times 10 \times 10 \times 10 = 10^5 \text{ workers.}$$

The **exponent**, 5, below tells how many times the **base**, 10, is used as a **factor**.

$$\text{base} \longrightarrow 10^5 \longleftarrow \text{exponent}$$

What patterns can you find with other powers of 10 below?

$$
\begin{array}{rcl}
10,000 = & 10 \times 10 \times 10 \times 10 & = 10^4 \\
1,000 = & 10 \times 10 \times 10 & = 10^3 \\
100 = & 10 \times 10 & = 10^2 \\
10 = & 10 & = 10^1 \\
1 = & & = 10^0
\end{array}
$$

> **Any nonzero number with an exponent of 0 is 1.**
> **Any number with an exponent of 1 is the number itself.**

Other examples:

Exponential Form		Factors	Standard Form
7^2	*seven to the second power, or seven squared*	7×7	49
6^3	*six to the third power, or six cubed*	$6 \times 6 \times 6$	216
3^4	*three to the fourth power*	$3 \times 3 \times 3 \times 3$	81

THINK ALOUD Can you write 81 another way using an exponent? 9^2 or 81^1

◼◼◼◼◼◼◼◼◼◼ **GUIDED PRACTICE** ◼◼◼◼◼◼◼◼◼◼

Give the exponent if the factors are written in exponential form.

1. $2 \times 2 \times 2 \times 2 \times 2$ 5

2. $12 \times 12 \times 12 \times 12 \times 12 \times 12 \times 12$ 7

3. **THINK ALOUD** Does 2^4 equal 4^2? Does interchanging the base and the exponent always work? Explain your answer. yes; no; $2^3 \neq 3^2$

4   LESSON 1–2

MATH AND HISTORY

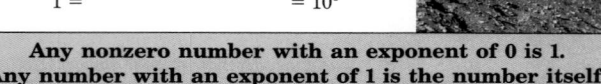

M U L T I C U L T U R A L   N O T E

The ancient Egyptians in North Africa were the first to develop and use geometric principles. See page 303B for a description of some ways that the Egyptians used geometry in the building of the pyramids.

2 TEACH

Where do you think the term *seven squared* came from? *(7^2 can be thought of as a square that is 7×7.)* **The term *six cubed*?** *(6^3 can be thought of as a cube that is $6 \times 6 \times 6$.)*

Explain why $8^1 = 8$. *(The exponent, 1, shows that 8 is used as a factor once.)* **Look at the powers of 2: 2, 4, 8, 16, 32, and so on. If you divide each power by 2, the result is the previous power. In other words, 2^5 divided by $2 = 2^4$. How does this explain why $2^0 = 1$?** *($2 \div 2 = 1$)*

> ### Chalkboard Examples
> Write in exponential form.
> $4 \times 4 \times 4$ *(4^3)*
> $10 \times 10 \times 10 \times 10$ *(10^4)*
> five cubed *(5^3)*

SUMMARIZE/ASSESS **Explain how $7 \times 7 \times 7$ can be written in exponential form and standard form.** *(The base, 7, is used as a factor three times, which is 7^3 in exponential form. In standard form $7 \times 7 \times 7$ is the product, 343.)*

The early Egyptians knew many principles of geometry, such as the right triangle relationships, and used them to construct the pyramids.

Write in exponential form.

4. $2 \times 2 \times 2 \times 2$ 2^4 **5.** $3 \times 3 \times 3 \times 3 \times 3$ 3^5

6. $8 \times 8 \times 8$ 8^3 **7.** five squared 5^2

8. four to the third power 4^3 **9.** two to the sixth power 2^6

10. seven cubed 7^3 **11.** nine squared 9^2

12. six to the zero power 6^0

Write in standard form and as a product of factors when possible.

13. 5^2 25; 5×5 **14.** 12^2 144; 12×12 **15.** 4^2 16; 4×4 **16.** 9^2 81; 9×9

17. 7^3 343; $7 \times 7 \times 7$ **18.** 10^3 1,000; $10 \times 10 \times 10$ **19.** 15^2 225; 15×15 **20.** 16^0 1

21. 2^1 2   **22.** 15^1 15   **23.** 6^2 36; 6×6 **24.** 2^3 8; $2 \times 2 \times 2$

CALCULATOR   Write in standard form.

25. 35^5 52,521,875   **26.** 29^4 707,281   **27.** 9^6 531,441

28. 12^5 248,832   *__**29.** 17^4 83,521   *__**30.** 55^3 166,375

NUMBER SENSE   Choose the correct answer.

31. Was the Great Pyramid originally 8 ft, 481 ft, or 4,810 ft tall?   **481 ft tall**

32. Does the Great Pyramid contain about 20, 200, or 2,000,000 stone blocks?   **2,000,000**

Critical Thinking

Work with a partner to discover the patterns for multiplying and dividing numbers with exponents.

$3^2 \times 3^4 = (3 \times 3) \times (3 \times 3 \times 3 \times 3) = 3^6$

$2^5 \div 2^2 = \dfrac{2 \times 2 \times 2 \times 2 \times 2}{2 \times 2} = 2 \times 2 \times 2 = 2^3$

> Are the bases the same? Compare the exponents.   **yes**

1. IN YOUR WORDS   Write rules for the product and quotient of numbers with exponents.   **Check students' work. Suggestion given below.**

2. Write the product or quotient as a number with an exponent.

a. $6^2 \times 6^3$ 6^5 **b.** $7^4 \times 7^2$ 7^6 **c.** $5^2 \times 5^6$ 5^8 **d.** $2^3 \times 2^4 \times 2^5$ 2^{12}

e. $5^7 \div 5^3$ 5^4 **f.** $8^9 \div 8^5$ 8^4 **g.** $10^{12} \div 10^3$ 10^9 **h.** $256^5 \div 256^2$ 256^3

1. The bases must be the same. For products, add exponents. For quotients, subtract.

MEETING INDIVIDUAL NEEDS

For Students Who Are . . .

Acquiring English Proficiency   Pair students with an English-proficient student to discover the patterns in the Critical Thinking exercises.

Gifted and Talented   Have students predict the next row in the powers of 10 pattern discussed on page 4. ($0.1 = 10^{-1}$)

Working 2 or 3 Grades Below Level   Have students write exercises 25–30 as products of factors before writing them in standard form.

Today's Problem

Elena bought school supplies at the beginning of the school year. She bought 2 pens for $.40 each, 3 notebooks for $.59 each, and a ruler for $.75. How much money did she spend in all if the sales tax was $.07? How much change did she receive if she paid with a five-dollar bill? *($.80 + $1.77 + $.75 + $.07 = $3.39; $5.00 − $3.39 = $1.61)*

---

3 FOLLOW-UP

Write in exponential form.

1. $2 \times 2 \times 2$ 2^3 **2.** $5 \times 5 \times 5 \times 5 \times 5$ 5^5

3. 9×9 9^2 **4.** seven squared 7^2

5. two to the zero power 2^0 **6.** eight cubed 8^3

7. four to the ninth power 4^9

Write as a product of factors when possible. Then write in standard form.

8. 6^2 $6 \times 6 = 36$ **9.** 14^2 $14 \times 14 = 196$ **10.** 3^3 $3 \times 3 \times 3 = 27$

11. 5^3 $5 \times 5 \times 5 = 125$ **12.** 8^1 8 **13.** 2^4 $2 \times 2 \times 2 \times 2 = 16$

14. 7^2 $7 \times 7 = 49$ **15.** 17^0 1 **16.** 10^2 $10 \times 10 = 100$

Solve.

17. Astronomers estimate that outside our own Milky Way galaxy there are at least 10,000,000,000 other galaxies. What is 10,000,000,000 in exponential form? 10^{10}

18. If you make 2¢ for your first day on the job, but 2¢ the next day, 2¢ the day after that, and so on, how many days will it be before you earn at least $10 a day? at least $100 a day?   *10 days; 14 days*

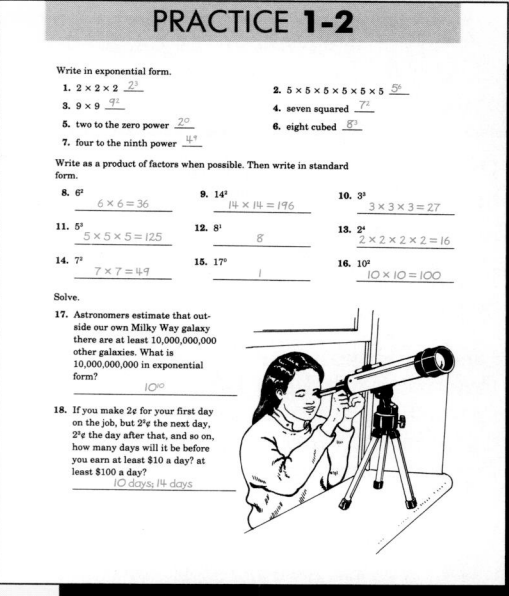

$3^0 = 1$ $3^1 = 3$ $3^2 = 3 \times 3 = 9$
$3^3 = 3 \times 3 \times 3 = 27$
$3^4 = 3 \times 3 \times 3 \times 3 = 81$

In 3^4, 3 is the **base**, and 4 is the **exponent**. The exponent tells you how many times to use the base as a factor. Remember that any nonzero number raised to the zero power is 1.

Complete the table with the correct exponential form; factors, when possible; and standard form.

	Exponential Form	Factors	Standard Form
1.	2^3	$2 \times 2 \times 2$	8
2.	5^4	$5 \times 5 \times 5 \times 5$	625
3.	10^3	$10 \times 10 \times 10$	1,000
4.	7^2	7×7	49
5.	4^4	$4 \times 4 \times 4 \times 4$	256
6.	1^8	$1 \times 1 \times 1 \times 1 \times 1 \times 1 \times 1 \times 1$	1
7.	17^1	17	17
8.	14^0	None	1
9.	2^5	$2 \times 2 \times 2 \times 2 \times 2$	32
10.	8^8	$8 \times 8 \times 8 \times 8 \times 8 \times 8 \times 8 \times 8$	16,777,216

☑ **MATERIALS CHECKLIST:** Number cubes

Have the students work in groups of four and in teams of two within each group. Teams take turns rolling two number cubes and then deciding which number will be the base and which number will be the exponent. The team that rolls the number cubes writes the standard form of the number as its score. The other team finds its score for the round by reversing the order of the numbers for base and exponent. Have the students continue in the same manner for several rounds. The team with the highest score wins.

Lesson Organizer

> **Objective:** Write expanded and standard form for whole numbers and decimals.

Prior Knowledge: Students should have a fundamental understanding of place value.

Error Analysis and Remediation: See page 29A.

Lesson Resources:
Practice Worksheet 1-3
Reteaching Activity 1-3
Enrichment Worksheet 1-3
Daily Review 1-3

 **Two-Minute Math**

In what place is the 6 in each number?
7,609 *(hundreds)*
136,481 *(thousands)*
65,034 *(ten-thousands)*

1 INTRODUCE

CONNECTING ACTIVITY

☑ **MATERIALS CHECKLIST:** base-10 blocks or models

1. Review place value of whole numbers by representing several numbers with the blocks. Review the different periods.

2. Write several larger numbers on the chalkboard. Then have students identify the periods and place values and read the numbers aloud.

3. Extend the numbers to review decimal places to thousandths. **Write one-tenth in two different ways.** *(0.1 and $\frac{1}{10}$)* **Write six hundredths in three different ways.** *(0.06, $\frac{6}{100}$, $\frac{6}{10^2}$)*

4. Have students continue the pattern below three more places.
$10^2 \quad 10^1 \quad 10^0 \quad \frac{1}{10^1} \cdots$
$100 \quad 10 \quad 1 \quad 0.1 \cdots$
$\left(\frac{1}{10^2} \quad \frac{1}{10^3} \quad \frac{1}{10^4}\right)$

WHEN YOUR STUDENTS ASK
★ WHY AM I LEARNING THIS? ★

You can connect this skill to real life situations. When writing a check, one must write the amount as a decimal and in words.

Place Value: Whole Numbers, Decimals

The largest publication in the world is the 1,112-volume set of *British Parliamentary Papers* of 1800–1900. The publication has a mass of 3,303.15 kilograms (kg).

Our number system is based on powers of ten. The value of each digit in a number depends on its place. The place value table helps you understand the different ways this mass can be written.

ten-thousands	thousands	hundreds	tens	ones		tenths	hundredths	thousandths
10^4	10^3	10^2	10^1	10^0		$\frac{1}{10^1}$	$\frac{1}{10^2}$	$\frac{1}{10^3}$
10,000	1,000	100	10	1		0.1	0.01	0.001
	3	3	0	3	.	1	5	

Standard form: 3,303.15
Word form: three thousand, three hundred three, and fifteen hundredths
Short word form: 3 thousand, 3 hundred 3, and 15 hundredths
Expanded form: $(3 \times 1,000) + (3 \times 100) + (3 \times 1) + \left(1 \times \frac{1}{10}\right) + \left(5 \times \frac{1}{100}\right)$

Expanded form with exponents: $\left(3 \times 10^3\right) + \left(3 \times 10^2\right) + \left(3 \times 10^0\right) + \left(1 \times \frac{1}{10^1}\right) + \left(5 \times \frac{1}{10^2}\right)$

THINK ALOUD One million is 10^6, or 1,000,000. Explain how you would write 1 billion in standard form and in expanded form with exponents. **1,000,000,000; 10^9**

━━━━━━━━━━ **GUIDED PRACTICE** ━━━━━━━━━━

1. **THINK ALOUD** Write 2,015 in expanded form with exponents. Why do you not need to write 0×100? **$(2 \times 10^3) + (1 \times 10^1) + (5 \times 10^0)$; Zero times any number equals zero.**

Write the number in short word form and with exponents. **See page 29b.**

2. 4,053   3. 43,000,005   4. 20.103   5. 873.52

6. **CRITICAL THINKING** Explain why 1.5 million and 1,500,000 are the same number. **$1.5 \times 1,000,000 = 1,500,000$.**

6   LESSON 1–3

2 TEACH

Why is our system called a decimal system? *(Each digit in a number is worth 10 times that of the digit to its right and one-tenth that of the digit to its left.)*

Give an example to show that this relationship continues to the right of the decimal point. *(Example: 0.04 is ten times the value of 0.004 and one-tenth the value of 0.4)*

How does a number in expanded form help you write the number in expanded form with exponents? *(The places are already separated. All that is needed is to name the place in exponential form— that is, as a power of ten.)*

> *Chalkboard Examples*
>
> Write *5,970.25* in expanded form and in expanded form with exponents.

SUMMARIZE/ASSESS **Explain how a number in standard form is written in expanded form.** *(Write the number as the sum of the value of each digit as its face value times its place value.)*

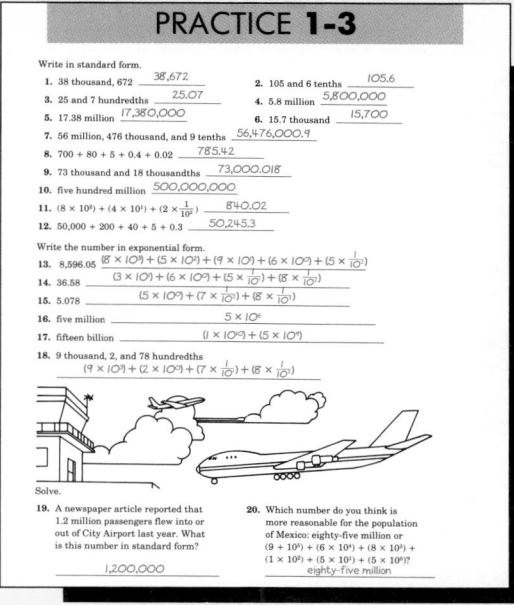 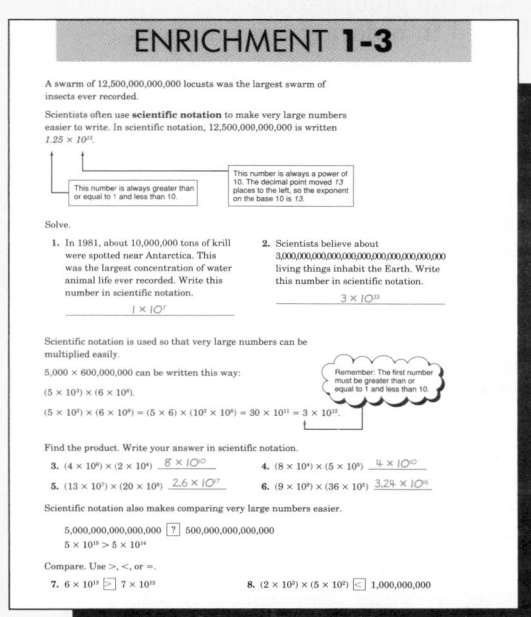

PRACTICE

Write in standard form.

7. 27 thousand, 583
27,583

8. 12 and 4 tenths
12.4

9. 751 thousand, 23
751,023

10. 17 and 3 hundredths
17.03

11. 399 and 5 tenths
399.5

12. 59 and 13 thousandths
59.013

13. 73 and 824 thousandths
73.824

14. 32 million, 352 thousand, and 6 tenths
32,352,000.6

15. $600 + 90 + 6 + 0.8$
696.8

16. $30,000 + 100 + 60 + 3 + 0.3$
30,163.3

17. $40 + 7 + 0.1 + 0.05$
47.15

18. $50,000 + 4,000 + 300 + 80 + 9 + 0.3$
54,389.3

19. a half million
500,000

20. a thousand thousand
1,000,000

21. six thousand million
6,000,000,000

22. $(6 \times 10^3) + (5 \times 10^2) + (7 \times 10^1)$
6,570

23. $(3 \times 10^2) + (5 \times 10^0) + \left(2 \times \frac{1}{10^1}\right)$
305.2

24. $(9 \times 10^2) + (5 \times 10^1) + \left(4 \times \frac{1}{10^2}\right)$
950.04

25. 2.5 thousand
2,500

26. 34.2 thousand
34,200

27. 6.8 million
6,800,000

28. 42.51 million
42,510,000

Write the number in expanded form with exponents.

29. 7,854
See below.

30. 45.42
See below.

31. 1.083
See page 29b.

32. 8,382.35
See page 29b.

33. ten million
1×10^7

34. one hundred million
1×10^8

35. ten billion
1×10^{10}

PROBLEM SOLVING

NUMBER SENSE Match the description with the number in word form.

36. the number of words in the world's longest personal letter   **b**

a. one hundred eighty-two

37. the width of *Super Book*, the world's largest book, in meters   **c**

b. one million, four hundred two thousand, three hundred forty-four

38. the number of letters in the longest word ever to appear in literature   **a**

c. two and seventy-four hundredths

29. $(7 \times 10^3) + (8 \times 10^2) + (5 \times 10^1) + (4 \times 10^0)$

30. $(4 \times 10^1) + (5 \times 10^0) + (4 \times \frac{1}{10^1}) + (2 \times \frac{1}{10^2})$

 CHAPTER 1   **7**

MEETING INDIVIDUAL NEEDS

For Students Who Are . . .

Acquiring English Proficiency   Pair students with an English-proficient student to discuss the problem-solving exercises.

Gifted and Talented   Have students write larger numbers in standard form, such as 56 billion, 49 million, 6 thousand, 8 hundred and 7 trillion, 809 billion, 99 thousand, seventeen. (56,049,006,800; 7,809,000,099,017)

Working 2 or 3 Grades Below Level   For students having difficulty with the concept of decimals use pages 4–19 of the Skills Workbook for decimals.

Today's Problem

The average child sees about 50 TV commercials per day. How many commercials per week is this? If each commercial is about $\frac{1}{2}$ minute long, about how many hours per week of commercials does the average child see? *(50 × 7 = 350; 350 × $\frac{1}{2}$ ÷ 60 = 2.91$\overline{6}$, or about 3 h)*

---

3 FOLLOW-UP

PRACTICE 1-3

Write in standard form.

1. 38 thousand, 672   38,672
2. 105 and 6 tenths   105.6
3. 25 and 7 hundredths   25.07
4. 5.8 million   5,800,000
5. 17.38 million   17,380,000
6. 15.7 thousand   15,700
7. 56 million, 476 thousand, and 9 tenths   56,476,000.9
8. $700 + 80 + 5 + 0.4 + 0.02$ 785.42
9. 73 thousand and 18 thousandths   73,000.018
10. five hundred million   500,000,000
11. $(8 \times 10^2) + (4 \times 10^1) + (2 \times \frac{1}{10^2})$ 840.02
12. $50,000 + 200 + 40 + 5 + 0.3$ 50,245.3

Write the number in exponential form.

13. 8,596.05 $(8 \times 10^3) + (5 \times 10^2) + (9 \times 10^1) + (6 \times 10^0) + (5 \times \frac{1}{10^2})$
14. 36.58 $(3 \times 10^1) + (6 \times 10^0) + (5 \times \frac{1}{10^1}) + (8 \times \frac{1}{10^2})$
15. 5.078 $(5 \times 10^0) + (7 \times \frac{1}{10^2}) + (8 \times \frac{1}{10^3})$
16. five million 5×10^6
17. fifteen billion $(1 \times 10^{10}) + (5 \times 10^9)$
18. 9 thousand, 2, and 78 hundredths $(9 \times 10^3) + (2 \times 10^0) + (7 \times \frac{1}{10^1}) + (8 \times \frac{1}{10^2})$

Solve.

19. A newspaper article reported that 1.2 million passengers flew into or out of City Airport last year. What is this number in standard form?
1,200,000

20. Which number do you think is more reasonable for the population of Mexico: eighty-five million or $(9 \times 10^6) + (6 \times 10^4) + (8 \times 10^3) + (1 \times 10^2) + (5 \times 10^1) + (5 \times 10^0)$?
eighty-five million

RETEACHING 1-3

☑ **MATERIALS CHECKLIST:** Decimal squares, colored chalk, colored pencils

Write the following numbers on the board, using one color for three of the numbers and another color for the other three: 1.3, 0.24, 0.36, 0.08, 1.09, 0.45. Have the students work in pairs. Have each partner represent three numbers using decimal squares and a matching colored pencil. For example, to represent the number **1.3,** a student would color a whole tenths square and three bars of another tenths square. Then write these numbers on the board: 36.47, 18.08, 9.63, 15.15. Have the students explain how to represent each number using decimal squares.

ENRICHMENT 1-3

A swarm of 12,500,000,000,000 locusts was the largest swarm of insects ever recorded.

Scientists often use **scientific notation** to make very large numbers easier to write. In scientific notation, 12,500,000,000,000 is written
1.25×10^{13}

This number is always greater than or equal to 1 and less than 10.

This number is always a power of 10. The decimal point moved 13 places to the left, so the exponent on the base 10 is 13.

Solve.

1. In 1981, about 10,000,000 tons of krill were spotted near Antarctica. This was the largest concentration of water animal life ever recorded. Write this number in scientific notation.
1×10^7

2. Scientists believe about 3,000,000,000,000,000,000,000,000,000,000,000 living things inhabit the Earth. Write this number in scientific notation.
3×10^{33}

Scientific notation is used so that very large numbers can be multiplied easily.

5,000 × 600,000,000 can be written this way:
$(5 \times 10^3) \times (6 \times 10^8)$

Remember: The first number must be greater than or equal to 1 and less than 10.

$(5 \times 10^3) \times (6 \times 10^8) = (5 \times 6) \times (10^3 \times 10^8) = 30 \times 10^{11} = 3 \times 10^{12}$

Find the product. Write your answer in scientific notation.

3. $(4 \times 10^6) \times (2 \times 10^4)$ 8×10^{10}
4. $(8 \times 10^4) \times (5 \times 10^5)$ 4×10^{10}
5. $(13 \times 10^7) \times (20 \times 10^{-1})$ 2.6×10^7
6. $(9 \times 10^2) \times (36 \times 10^3)$ 3.24×10^6

Scientific notation also makes comparing very large numbers easier.

5,000,000,000,000,000   **?**   500,000,000,000
$5 \times 10^{15} > 5 \times 10^{14}$

Compare. Use >, <, or =.

7. 6×10^{13} **>** 7×10^{12}
8. $(2 \times 10^5) \times (5 \times 10^3)$ **<** 1,000,000,000

 *Chapter 1 • Lesson 1-3*   **7**

Lesson Organizer

Objective: Compare and order whole numbers and decimals.

Prior Knowledge: Students should be able to locate numbers on a number line.

Error Analysis and Remediation: See page 29A.

Lesson Resources:
Practice Worksheet 1-4
Reteaching Worksheet 1-4
Enrichment Activity 1-4
Daily Review 1-4
Cooperative Problem Solving 1, Chapter 1

Two-Minute Math

List at least six different ways to make change for $1.00 using quarters, dimes, nickels. (Examples: all quarters, 2 quarters and 5 dimes)

1 INTRODUCE

SYMBOLIC ACTIVITY

Have students work in groups of four.

1. Ask each group member to write a 4-digit number.

2. Have students put the 4-digit numbers in order from least to greatest.

3. Ask the groups to list the steps they followed in ordering the numbers.

WHEN YOUR STUDENTS ASK
★ **WHY AM I LEARNING THIS?** ★

You can connect comparing numbers to real life through sports data. For example, team standings and a baseball player's batting average are expressed in comparison order to three decimal places.

Comparing and Ordering Numbers

Two birds common to many parts of the United States are the cardinal and the red-winged blackbird. These birds have similar average lengths. Which bird's average length is greater?

The number line below shows how the two lengths compare.

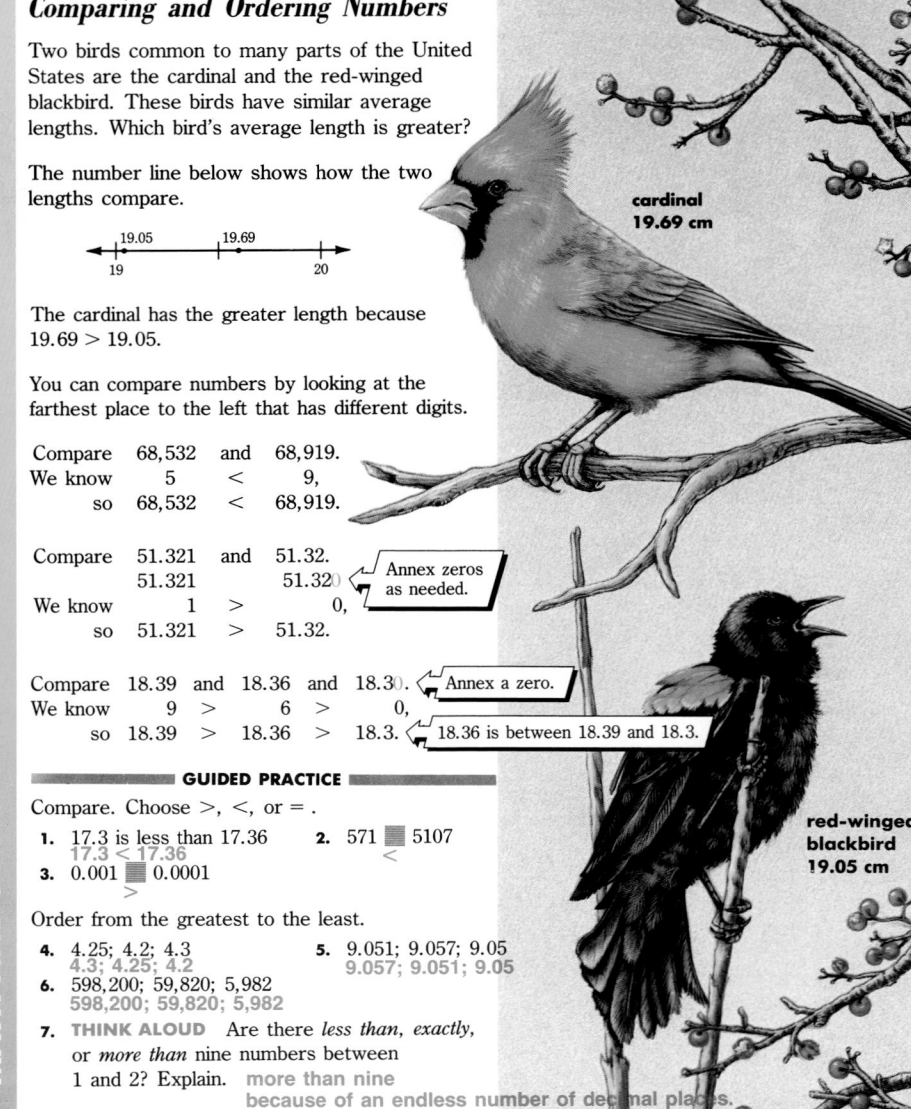

cardinal
19.69 cm

The cardinal has the greater length because $19.69 > 19.05$.

You can compare numbers by looking at the farthest place to the left that has different digits.

Compare	68,532	and	68,919.
We know	5	<	9,
so	68,532	<	68,919.

Compare 51.321 and 51.32.
51.321   51.32**0** ◁ *Annex zeros as needed.*
We know   1   >   0,
so 51.321 > 51.32.

Compare 18.39 and 18.36 and 18.3**0**. ◁ *Annex a zero.*
We know   9 >   6 >   0,
so 18.39 > 18.36 > 18.3. ◁ *18.36 is between 18.39 and 18.3.*

━━━━━ **GUIDED PRACTICE** ━━━━━
Compare. Choose >, <, or = .

1. 17.3 is less than 17.36   **2.** 571 ▇ 5107
17.3 < 17.36   <
3. 0.001 ▇ 0.0001
>

Order from the greatest to the least.

4. 4.25; 4.2; 4.3   **5.** 9.051; 9.057; 9.05
4.3; 4.25; 4.2   9.057; 9.051; 9.05
6. 598,200; 59,820; 5,982
598,200; 59,820; 5,982
7. **THINK ALOUD** Are there *less than, exactly,* or *more than* nine numbers between 1 and 2? Explain. more than nine
because of an endless number of decimal places.

8   LESSON 1–4

MATH AND SCIENCE

red-winged
blackbird
19.05 cm

2 TEACH

Why is it important to begin at the left when comparing digits in the same place? *(The digit farthest to the left in a number has the greatest value.)*

Why is the decimal with more digits not always the greater number? Give examples. *(After the decimal points are aligned, the digit with the greater value in the leftmost place determines which of two numbers has the greater value. For example, 0.4 > 0.3126)*

> ### Chalkboard Examples
> Compare. Use >, <, or =.
> 321 and 312 *(>)*
> 48.1 and 48.13 *(<)*
> 4^3 and 7^2 *(>)*

SUMMARIZE/ASSESS   **Explain how to compare two numbers.**
(First, align the decimal points. Identify the leftmost place that has different digits. The number that has the digit of greater value in that place is the greater number.)

Compare. Choose >, <, or = .

8. 456 ▨ 546 **<**   9. 935 ▨ 594 **>**   10. 1,490 ▨ 1,409 **>**

11. 0.51 ▨ 0.512 **<**   12. 0.483 ▨ 0.48 **>**   13. 0.87 ▨ 0.087 **>**

14. 10.26 ▨ 10.260 **=**   15. 192.15 ▨ 193.02 **<**   16. 43.51 ▨ 17.871 **>**

17. 0.999 ▨ 1.000 **<**   18. 0.99 ▨ 0.1 **>**   19. 658.362 ▨ 658.359 **>**

20. 3^3 ▨ 4^2 **>**   21. 27^0 ▨ 5^1 **<**   22. 3^4 ▨ 9^2 **=**

23. 1 billion ▨ 987 million **>**   24. 1 billion ▨ 1,500 million **<**

Order from the least to the greatest.

25. 3,835; 3,560; 3,480
    3,480; 3,560; 3,835
26. 0.514; 0.541; 0.554
    0.514; 0.541; 0.554
27. 0.01; 0.001; 0.1
    0.001; 0.01; 0.1
28. 5.384; 5.348; 5.843
    5.348; 5.384; 5.843
29. 12^2; 21^2; 13^2
    12^2; 13^2; 21^2
30. 17^1; 27^1; 30^1
    17^1; 27^1; 30^1

NUMBER SENSE   Match the letter with the number.

31. 0.1 *B*   32. 0.75 *C*

33. 1.3 *A*   34. 1.09 *D*

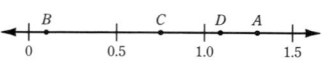

CRITICAL THINKING   Give two numbers between
the given pair of numbers. **Answers will vary. Suggestions given.**

35. 351 and 354
    352; 353
36. 99 and 100
    99.1; 99.9
37. 0.004 and 0.009
    0.005; 0.007
38. 9.528 and 9.531
    9.529; 9.530

PROBLEM SOLVING

Use the table below to solve.

39. Which birds are smaller in length than
the Baltimore oriole?
**housewren, chickadee, hummingbird,
woodpecker**

40. Outlines of a chickadee, robin, and
woodpecker are drawn to scale below.
Match the outlines to the kind of bird.
A: **woodpecker** *B:* **chickadee** *C:* **robin**

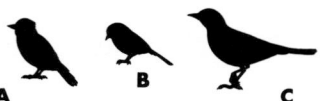

41. Copy and complete the bar graph.
Show all birds mentioned on pages 8
and 9.
Check students' work.

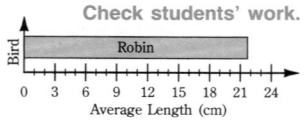

Bird	Average Length
House wren	10.08 cm
Robin	21.59 cm
Chickadee	11.43 cm
Mockingbird	22.86 cm
Baltimore oriole	15.24 cm
Hummingbird	7.62 cm
Downy woodpecker	14.61 cm

CHAPTER 1   9

MEETING INDIVIDUAL NEEDS

For Students Who Are . . .

Acquiring English Proficiency   Review the meanings of the symbols <, >, and = and the term *annex*. Pair students with an English-proficient student to complete the problem-solving exercises.

Gifted and Talented   Have students make a bar graph about birds using the information on page 8 and the data in the table on page 9.

Working 2 or 3 Grades Below Level   For students having difficulty with the concept of decimals use pages 20–27 of the Skills Workbook for decimals.

Today's Problem

Use the table to find how much each person earned at $4/h.

(Kim: $6.00;
Pat: $3.00;
Sal: $9.00)

Name	Began	Stopped
Kim	11:00 A.M.	12:30 P.M.
Pat	1:15 P.M.	2:00 P.M.
Sal	9:00 A.M.	11:15 A.M.

3 FOLLOW-UP

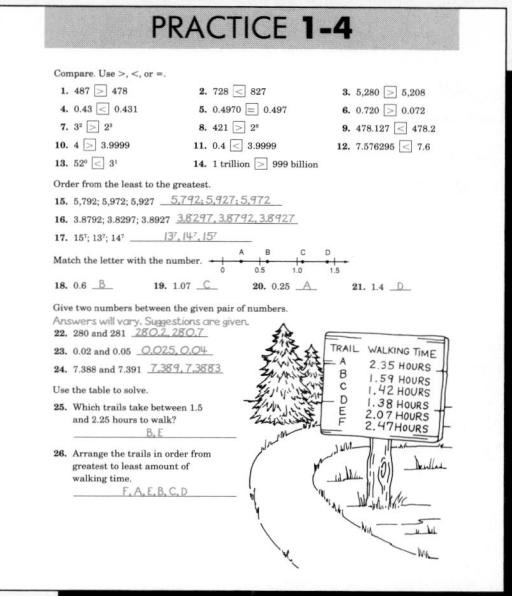

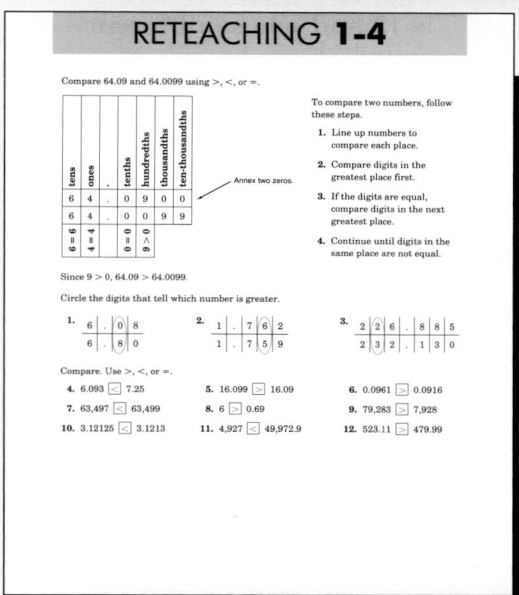

ENRICHMENT 1-4

Our number system uses base 10. Write the following chart on the board.

10^3	10^2	10^1	10^0
1,000	100	10	1

Explain how each place uses 10 as a base. Then ask students to think about using 8 as a base. Write the following chart on the board.

8^3	8^2	8^1	8^0
512	64	8	1

Explain that there is no symbol "8". The symbol "8" is written as "10". The number 64 in base 10 is written as 100 in base 8. The number 12 is written as 14 in base 8. Have students write these numbers in base 8. 14; 29; 48; 88; [16; 35; 60; 130]

Chapter 1 • Lesson 1-4   **9**

Lesson Organizer

Objective: Solve problems using a four-part process.

Prior Knowledge: Students should have a working knowledge of the four basic operations.

Error Analysis and Remediation: See page 29A.

Lesson Resources:
Practice Worksheet 1-5
Reteaching Activity 1-5
Enrichment Worksheet 1-5
Daily Review 1-5

 **Two-Minute Math**

Find two numbers whose sum is 12 and whose difference is 2. *(5 and 7)*
Find two numbers whose sum is 30 and whose difference is 4. *(17 and 13)*

1 INTRODUCE

SYMBOLIC ACTIVITY

1. On the chalkboard, list the four parts of the problem solving process. Write the following problem:

On Monday, Jake had 8 baseball cards. During the next four days, he sold 5, bought 3, sold 3, and lost 1. How many baseball cards did he then have? *(2)*

2. Have students explain how they can use each part of the four-part process to solve the problem.

3. Point out that the parts vary from problem to problem. Sometimes a part must be used several times in the same problem. **Which parts vary from problem to problem, and which remain constant?** *(For multistep problems, you must read several times, adjusting for each new piece of information. The part of making and carrying out a plan varies from problem to problem.)*

WHEN YOUR STUDENTS ASK
★ WHY AM I LEARNING THIS? ★

This skill will help you solve real-life problems by giving you a logical and systematic approach to decision making.

Problem Solving:
Four-Part Process

There are 100 floors in Chicago's John Hancock building. The elevator takes about 15 seconds (s) to go to the next floor and stop. If you stopped at each floor, about how many minutes would it take to get to the 100th floor?

MATH AND SOCIAL STUDIES

Understand the problem.	
Know what to find.	What is the question? How many minutes would it take to get to floor 100?
Read for information.	How many floors are there? 100 floors
	How long does it take to travel and stop at each floor? 15 s

Make a plan.	
Ask questions.	Would it take *more* or *less* than 100 minutes (min)? less
Decide what to do.	Find how far the elevator goes in 1 min.
	15 s ⇨ 1 floor
	60 s, or 1 min ⇨ 4 floors
	If the elevator takes 1 min to stop at 4 floors, how many minutes for 100 floors?
	$100 \div 4 = ?$

Carry out the plan.	
Work through the plan.	$100 \div 4 = 25$
	The elevator takes 25 min to stop at 100 floors.

Look back.	
Is your answer reasonable?	The answer is reasonable. In each of the 25 min, the elevator has stopped at 4 floors.
Did you answer the question?	Reread the question. Check your labels.
Can you think of another way to solve the problem?	

CRITICAL THINKING   Why do tall buildings have express elevators that go only to the top floors?

MULTICULTURAL NOTE

The word Chicago comes from the Potawatomi word *Checagou*, meaning "powerful" or "strong." The Potawatomi people were some of the earliest inhabitants of the area that is now Chicago.

2 TEACH

Why is it important to read a problem carefully? *(to determine what information is given and what you need to find out)*

What are some ways to "look back"? *(Students may suggest rereading the problem or solving it in a different way.)*

Chalkboard Example

On one subway line it takes a train about 4 min to travel from station to station. If there are 15 stations, how long does it take the train to reach the last station? *(about 56 min)*

GUIDED PRACTICE   For Exercise 2, stress the importance of making a plan and perhaps drawing a picture to help.

SUMMARIZE/ASSESS   Explain in your own words how the four-part process helps you solve problems.

Use the four-part process to solve.

1. In 1812, about 100 people lived in the Chicago area. Today, the population is about 30,000 times greater.

    a. When did about 100 people live in Chicago? **in 1812**

    b. What operation would you use to find today's population? **multiplication**

    c. About how many people live in Chicago today? **about 3,000,000 people**

2. Greg got on a Sears Tower elevator at the 1st floor. He went up 10 floors, up 5 more floors, down 8 floors, up 12 floors, down 4 floors, and got off. On which floor did Greg get off the elevator? **16th floor**

PRACTICE

Solve.

3. The Sears Tower is 1,454 ft tall. Is that *more than* or *less than* a quarter mile? (1 mi = 5,280 ft) **more than**

4. The Great Chicago Fire destroyed much of the city in 1871. How many years ago was that? **As of 1991, 120 yr**

5. There are 7,000 fish and other water animals in the John G. Shedd Aquarium. Do you think that is an exact number or an estimate? **an estimate**

6. Jean Baptiste Pointe du Sable, an African American, built a trading post on the Chicago River in the 1770s. The Du Sable Museum of African-American History is named for him. Chicago has 16 other ethnic history museums. How many ethnic history museums are in Chicago? **17**

* 7. Each different letter in *CHICAGO* has a different number value. If the sum of the numbers is 40, what number value does each letter have? **See page 29b.**

8. Chicago's Hispanic population was 247,343 in 1970, 422,061 in 1980, and 545,852 in 1990. Did it grow more from 1970 to 1980 or from 1980 to 1990? **from 1970 to 1980**

CHAPTER 1   11

MEETING INDIVIDUAL NEEDS

For Students Who Are . . .

Acquiring English Proficiency Provide assistance and check students' comprehension as they work together to solve the problems.

Gifted and Talented Have students look up additional information about Chicago and create word problems using this information.

Working 2 or 3 Grades Below Level Have students use pages 4–7 of the Skills Workbook for Problem Solving Strategies.

Having Reading Difficulties Pair each student with an able reader to discuss the problem-solving exercises.

Today's Problem

Suppose that you forgot the combination to your locker. You remember that the numbers in the combination are 5, 7, and 8 but can't remember their order. Which combinations of these three numbers could you try? *(5, 7, 8; 7, 5, 8; 8, 5, 7; 5, 8, 7; 7, 8, 5; 8, 7, 5)*

3 FOLLOW-UP

PRACTICE 1-5

Solve.

1. It takes a window washing crew 30 minutes to wash the windows on one floor of a 48-story building. How many days will it take them to wash all the windows in the building if the window washers work 8 hours every day?
   3 days

2. An architect plans to cover the steel frame of a building she is designing with slabs of granite that are 2.4 meters tall. About how tall would the building be if it would take 127 of these slabs to reach the top?
   about 305 meters

3. Of the 50 tallest buildings in the world as of 1990, 39 are located in the United States. Do you think this is the exact number or an estimate?
   the exact number

4. The first skyscraper was built in Chicago in 1883. The Sears Tower was completed 91 years later. In what year was the Sears Tower completed?
   1974

5. A law firm needs 35,000 square feet of office space. Each floor of the new CityCentre building has 28,950 square feet. How much space on a second floor of this building will the law firm need?
   6,050 square feet

RETEACHING 1-5

Some students may need to be reminded about the parts of the four-part process. Ask the following questions to guide the students through Problem 1, *Practice Worksheet 1-5:* What is the question? [How many days will it take to wash the building's windows?] How many stories are there? [48] How many minutes does it take to wash the windows on 1 floor? [30] How many minutes in 8 hours? [480] How many floors can be washed in 480 minutes? [480 ÷ 30, or 16] How will you find the number of days it will take to wash the windows on 48 floors? [divide 48 by 16] What is the answer? [3 days] Did you answer the question? [yes]

ENRICHMENT 1-5

Solve.

1. There are about 3.9 million miles of roads in the United States. What is this number in standard form?
   3,900,000 miles

2. The distance between Charlotte, North Carolina, and Dallas, Texas, is 1,058 miles. From Charlotte to Des Moines, Iowa, it is 1,061 miles. Which city is closer to Charlotte?
   Dallas

3. Matt told Mary that he knew a short-cut home. Mary drove home the regular way and recorded the distance as 13.9 miles. Matt drove home a different way and recorded the distance as 14.1 miles. Was Matt's way really a shortcut?
   no

4. In 1988, car companies in the United States sold more than 7,000,000 cars. What is this number in short word form?
   7 million

5. ABC car rental company charges $.17 for every mile one of its cars is driven. XYZ car rental company charges $.32. Which car rental company charges more for the number of miles driven?
   XYZ car rental company

6. The O'Malley family left downtown Boston for a trip to Provincetown. They drove 35 miles to the Plymouth exit and returned to Boston because they had forgotten something. Then they drove straight from Boston to Provincetown. The distance from Boston to Provincetown is 114 miles. How many miles did the O'Malleys drive in all?
   184 miles

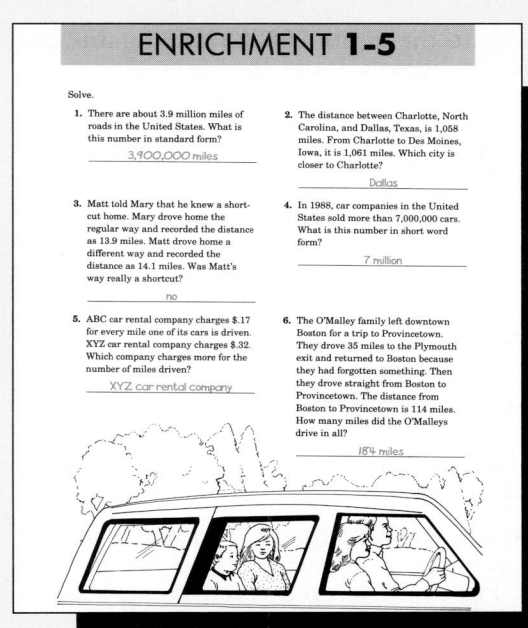

Lesson Organizer

Objective: Read and write millions and billions.

Prior Knowledge: Students should be able to read and write numbers to millions.

Lesson Resources:
Practice Worksheet 1-6
Reteaching Worksheet 1-6
Enrichment Activity 1-6
Daily Review 1-6

Two-Minute Math

Write *two million, nine hundred sixty-three thousand, forty-seven* in standard form and expanded form.
[2,963,047; (2 × 1,000,000) + (9 × 100,000) + (6 × 10,000) + (3 × 1,000) + (4 × 10) + 7]

1 INTRODUCE

SYMBOLIC ACTIVITY

1 Write *9,652,837,146* on the chalkboard. Label the periods. **What is the same about each of the periods?** *(Each has the same 3 places: hundreds, tens, ones.)*

2. Call on a volunteer to read the number aloud.

3. Write the digits 9652837146 again. Add two non-zero digits to the right of the number for a total of twelve digits. Then ask a student to:

place the commas;
indicate the periods;
read the new number aloud.

WHEN YOUR STUDENTS ASK
★ WHY AM I LEARNING THIS? ★

You can connect this skill to real life by referring to newspaper or television stories. For example, in a recent year, the total deficit of the federal budget was $129,500,000,000.

Greater Numbers

OUR SOLAR SYSTEM

MATH AND SCIENCE

Did you know that the Sun is about 5,000,000,000 yr old? This medium-sized star is now only at the halfway point of its life. As the center of our Solar System, the Sun is our nearest star. The Sun is about 93,000,000 mi away from Earth.

1. Of 500 million, 5 billion, and 5,000 million, which are short word forms of 5,000,000,000?
   5 billion; 5,000 million

2. Is 9.3 million, 93 million, or 93 hundred thousand a short word form of 93,000,000?
   93 million

3. How long is the Sun expected to live?
   10 billion years

Our Solar System spans vast distances. Use the table to solve.

Planet	Average Distance from the Sun (in million miles)
Pluto	3,675.3
Earth	93.0
Jupiter	483.8
Mercury	36.0
Saturn	887.1
Venus	67.3
Uranus	1,783.9
Mars	141.7
Neptune	2,795.5

4. Explain why it is correct to use the number 67,300,000 to describe the distance in miles between Venus and the Sun.
   $67.3 \times 10^6 = 67,300,000$

5. About how far away is Saturn from the Sun in standard form?
   887,100,000 mi

6. How much closer is Mars to the Sun than Neptune is?
   2,653,800,000 mi

7. List the planets by their distances from the Sun in order from the least to the greatest.

2 TEACH

What is the expected lifespan of the Sun expressed in exponential form? *(10^{10} years)*

What number is 100,000 more than the number of miles between Venus and the Sun? *(67.4 million)*

What is the value of $0.3 million? *($300,000)*

Chalkboard Examples

Write in standard form.
2.8 million *(2,800,000)*
456.2 million *(456,200,000)*
96.5 billion *(96,500,000,000)*

SUMMARIZE/ASSESS   How is the number 3.501 million read? How is it written in standard form? *(three million, five hundred one thousand; 3,501,000.)*

The Sun and its planets are part of the Milky Way galaxy. The Milky Way has more than 100 billion stars. There are more than 1 billion galaxies found in the universe.

8. Rewrite the numbers in the paragraph about the Milky Way in standard form.
100,000,000,000; 1,000,000,000

9. Ten thousand stars are represented by each star below. How many stars are represented in all? 560,000 stars

10. Each star in the miniature galaxy below represents 10 million stars. How many stars are represented in all?

290 million stars

Comets are very common in our Solar System. The nucleus of a comet may be up to 10 thousand miles in diameter and its tail can be as long as 28 million miles.

Halley's comet is now traveling in its orbit away from the Sun. The greatest distance the comet travels from the Sun is about 3.28 billion miles.

11. Rewrite in standard form the three large numbers in the paragraphs about comets. 10,000; 28,000,000; 3,280,000,000

12. Is the comet's tail longer than the distance between Earth and the Sun? no

MEETING INDIVIDUAL NEEDS

For Students Who Are . . .

Acquiring English Proficiency Review what it means to write a number in standard form and in short word form. Then discuss the terms *solar system, galaxy, comet,* and *nucleus.*

Gifted and Talented Have students write two more problems using the information given in the table on page 12. Then have them exchange with a partner and solve.

Working 2 or 3 Grades Below Level Have students write the numbers in the table in standard form before they do exercises 4–7.

Today's Problem

Fill in the missing numbers. Add across and down.

$$
\begin{array}{rcl}
2{,}564{,}471 \; + \; 4{,}356{,}893 \; = & (6{,}921{,}364) \\
+ \quad 23{,}420 \; + \quad 256{,}896 \; = \; + & (280{,}316) \\
(2{,}587{,}891) \; + \; (4{,}613{,}789) \; = & (7{,}201{,}680)
\end{array}
$$

3 FOLLOW-UP

PRACTICE 1-6

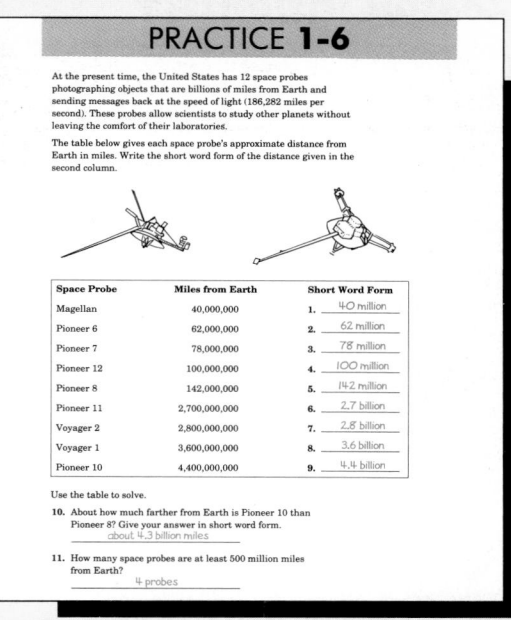

At the present time, the United States has 12 space probes photographing objects that are billions of miles from Earth and sending messages back at the speed of light (186,282 miles per second). These probes allow scientists to study other planets without leaving the comfort of their laboratories.

The table below gives each space probe's approximate distance from Earth in miles. Write the short word form of the distance given in the second column.

Space Probe	Miles from Earth	Short Word Form
Magellan	40,000,000	1. 40 million
Pioneer 6	62,000,000	2. 62 million
Pioneer 7	78,000,000	3. 78 million
Pioneer 12	100,000,000	4. 100 million
Pioneer 8	142,000,000	5. 142 million
Pioneer 11	2,700,000,000	6. 2.7 billion
Voyager 2	2,800,000,000	7. 2.8 billion
Voyager 1	3,600,000,000	8. 3.6 billion
Pioneer 10	4,400,000,000	9. 4.4 billion

Use the table to solve.

10. About how much farther from Earth is Pioneer 10 than Pioneer 8? Give your answer in short word form.
about 4.3 billion miles

11. How many space probes are at least 500 million miles from Earth?
4 probes

RETEACHING 1-6

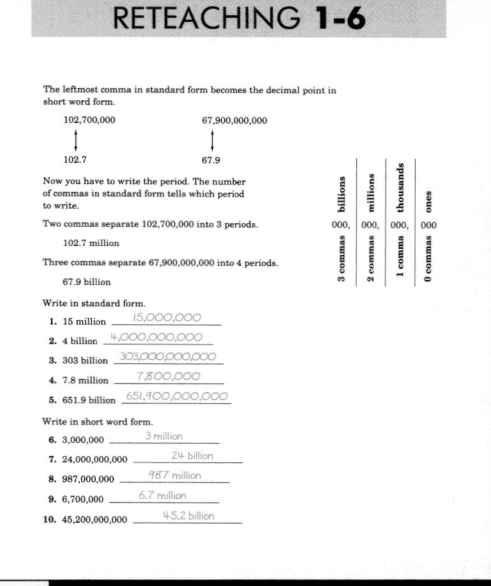

The leftmost comma in standard form becomes the decimal point in short word form.

102,700,000   67,900,000,000

102.7   67.9

Now you have to write the period. The number of commas in standard form tells which period to write.

Two commas separate 102,700,000 into 3 periods.

102.7 million

Three commas separate 67,900,000,000 into 4 periods.

67.9 billion

	billions	millions	thousands	ones
	000,	000,	000,	000
	3 commas	2 commas	1 comma	0 commas

Write in standard form.

1. 15 million   15,000,000
2. 4 billion   4,000,000,000
3. 303 billion   303,000,000,000
4. 7.8 million   7,800,000
5. 651.9 billion   651,900,000,000

Write in short word form.

6. 3,000,000   3 million
7. 24,000,000,000   24 billion
8. 987,000,000   987 million
9. 6,700,000   6.7 million
10. 45,200,000,000   45.2 billion

ENRICHMENT 1-6

☑ **MATERIALS CHECKLIST:** Number cubes, calculators

Have the students work in pairs. Provide each pair with a number cube labeled 2–7. Instruct one partner to roll the number cube and then to guess to what power this number would have to be raised to exceed 1 million. Have the other person find the answer by using a calculator, and then help the first partner guess the correct exponent for the base by responding *higher* or *lower* to each guess. Continue for several turns, with partners trading tasks each time.

Lesson Organizer

Objective: Round whole numbers and decimals.

Prior Knowledge: Students should be able to locate numbers on a number line.

Error Analysis and Remediation: See page 29A.

Lesson Resources:
Practice Worksheet 1-7
Reteaching Activity 1-7
Enrichment Worksheet 1-7
Daily Review 1-7

Two-Minute Math

Compare. Use >, <, or =.
1.63 million and 1,630,000 (=)
97.56 and 97.558 (>)
0.432 and 0.4325 (<)

1 INTRODUCE

CONNECTING ACTIVITY

☑ **MATERIALS CHECKLIST:** Teaching Aid 1, two per student

1. Have students label one number line to show 2,000, 2,500 and 3,000. Then have students locate 2,300 on the line.

Is 2,300 closer to 2,000 or to 3,000? *(2,000)* What is 2,300 rounded to the nearest thousand? *(2,000)*

2. Repeat the procedure with 2,500. *(Since 2,500 is exactly between 2,000 and 3,000, it rounds up to 3,000.)*

3. Have students label another number line to show 2.0, 2.5, and 3.0. Have them locate 2.3 and round it to the nearest whole number.

4. Repeat for 2.5, 2.4, and 2.8. *(3, 2, 3)*

WHEN YOUR STUDENTS ASK
★ WHY AM I LEARNING THIS? ★

You can connect rounding to real life situations. For example, your bike odometer may read 14.8 miles, but you usually refer to the distance as 15 miles.

Rounding Whole Numbers and Decimals

Which of these facts is easier to remember?

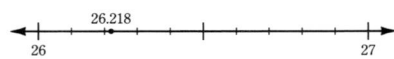

The Boston Marathon is 26.218 mi long.
The Boston Marathon is about 26 mi long.

Most people find it easier to remember a number like 26 than a number like 26.218.

The number line shows that 26.218 is close to 26.

Here's how you round 26.218 to the nearest whole number, 26.

- Mark the digit in the ones' place.
- Look at the digit to the right.   26.218
  Is it 5 or greater?
- Round down to 26, since 2 is less than 5.

THINK ALOUD What would you do if the digit to the right were 5 or greater?

Other examples:
Round 34,568 to hundreds. ➪ 34,600   Round 39.963 to tens. ➪ 40

Round 7.0834 to hundredths. ➪ 7.08   Round 0.1543 to tenths. ➪ 0.2

━━━━━━━━━━━━ GUIDED PRACTICE ━━━━━━━━━━━━
Round each number to the given place.

1. 55,789; hundreds, thousands
55,800; 56,000

2. 0.539; tenths, hundredths
0.5; 0.54

3. **NUMBER SENSE** Is 38.39 closer to 38 or 39? To which whole number would it be rounded? **38; 38**

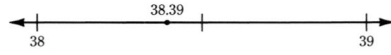

4. **CRITICAL THINKING** What is the greatest whole number that rounds to 500? **549**

MULTICULTURAL NOTE

People from all over the world race in the Boston Marathon. Some recent winners include Rosa Mota (1990) from Portugal, Ibrahim Hussein (1988 and 1991) from Kenya, and Abebe Mekonnen (1989) from Ethiopia.

2 TEACH

Which digit should you look at when rounding a decimal to the nearest whole number? *(the digit in the tenths' place)* **to the nearest hundredth?** *(the digit in the thousandths' place)*

When 7.0834 is rounded to the nearest hundredth, what happens to the digits in the thousandths' and ten-thousandths' places? *(Those digits are dropped.)*

What is the least whole number that rounds to 300? *(250)*

Chalkboard Examples

Round to the nearest ten and tenth.
248.36 *(250; 248.4)*
162.71 *(160; 162.7)*
306.25 *(310; 306.3)*
495.69 *(500; 495.7)*

SUMMARIZE/ASSESS **Explain how to round 753.861 to the nearest hundred and to the nearest tenth.** *(Because the digit in the tens' place is 5, round up to 800; because the digit in the hundredths' place is 6, round up to 753.9)*

See page 29b.

PRACTICE

Round to the nearest ten and hundred.

5. 483   **6.** 1,907   **7.** 5,864

8. 9,485   **9.** 10,079   **10.** 67,279

11. 8,006   **12.** 54,637   **13.** 100,741

14. 750,013   **15.** 995,329   **16.** 667,555

Round to the nearest tenth, hundredth, and whole number. See page 29b.

17. 3.736   **18.** 382.426   **19.** 12.996

20. 6.328   **21.** 42.4563   **22.** 18.358

23. 0.039   **24.** 0.997   **25.** 6.003

26. 5,176.15   **27.** 185.476   **28.** 8.7298

NUMBER SENSE Match each number with a letter on the number line.

29. 1,650 *D*   **30.** 1,111 *C*   **31.** 1,875 *E*

32. 591 *A*   **33.** 738.99 *B*   **34.** 2,311.51 *F*

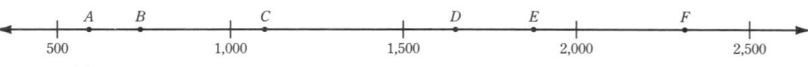

PROBLEM SOLVING

Solve.

35. What is the greatest number of runners that could have entered the Bermuda Marathon? **1,249 runners**

36. Which marathon had about 1,000 fewer runners than the Moscow Marathon? about 2,000 more? **Detroit; Kawaguchi-ko**

37. What is the least number of runners that could have run in Detroit? in Moscow?

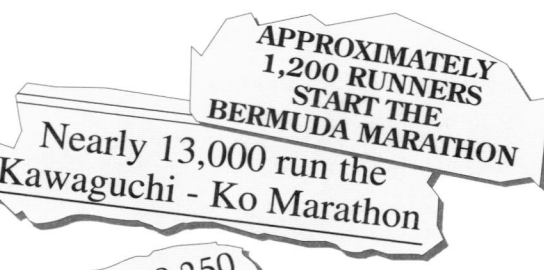

APPROXIMATELY 1,200 RUNNERS START THE BERMUDA MARATHON

Nearly 13,000 run the Kawaguchi - Ko Marathon

Close to 10,250 start the Detroit Marathon

About 11,000 begin in the Moscow Marathon

CHAPTER 1   15

---

3 FOLLOW-UP

PRACTICE 1-7

Round to the nearest ten and hundred.

		Nearest Ten	Nearest Hundred
1.	567	570	600
2.	2,305	2,310	2,300
3.	10,963	10,960	11,000
4.	152,706	152,710	152,700
5.	5,007	5,010	5,000
6.	45,014	45,010	45,000
7.	58,689	58,690	58,700
8.	655,449	655,450	655,400

Round to the nearest tenth, hundredth, and whole number.

		Nearest Tenth	Nearest Hundredth	Nearest Whole Number
9.	5.826	5.8	5.83	6
10.	15.359	15.4	15.36	15
11.	14.997	15.0	15.00	15
12.	0.999	1.0	1.00	1
13.	0.047	0.0	0.05	0
14.	90.1483	90.1	90.15	90
15.	17.0087	17.0	17.01	17
16.	3,612.255	3,612.3	3,612.26	3,612

Solve.

17. The city health department estimates that approximately 2,000 people will give blood during the annual blood drive. What is the least number of blood donors necessary for the health department's estimate to be correct?   1,500 donors

18. About 120 students made the Honor Roll at Dover Junior High School last year. What is the greatest number of students that could have made the Honor Roll?   124 students

RETEACHING 1-7

ENRICHMENT 1-7

Solve. Answers will vary. Suggestions are given.

1. Paula has $10 to spend at the store. She selects a few items, and then rounds the price of each item to estimate the total cost.

Should she round each price up or down? Why?   Up; because if she rounds down, her total might go over her $10 limit.

2. Owasu writes headlines for the *Daily News.* He knows that 55,102 tickets were sold for the championship ball game. How should he report this number in a headline? Why?   "Over 55,000 Tickets Sold"; because a headline contains general information and the actual story contains the details.

3. Kim reads in her science book that Earth is 149,600,000 kilometers from the sun. How do you know this number is rounded?   Because it would be very difficult to actually measure.

4. Ms. Gomez rounded up the price of a pen to the next dime and figured that 7 pens would cost about $3.50. What is the least each pen could have cost? $.41

5. Ben's calculator displays 0.6666666 when he divides 2 by 3. Kibo's calculator displays 0.6666667 for the same problem. Why?   Kibo's calculator rounds the last digit.

Lesson Organizer

Objective: Discuss estimation.

Prior Knowledge: Students should be able to estimate sums and differences.

Lesson Resources:
Class Activity 1-8
Daily Review 1-8

Two-Minute Math

Round 6,451.327 to the nearest thousand, hundred, tenth, and hundredth.
(6,000; 6,500; 6,451.3; 6,451.33)

1 INTRODUCE

SYMBOLIC ACTIVITY

☑ MATERIALS CHECKLIST:
newspapers, magazines

Tell students that in this lesson they will learn about estimating. Display examples of exact and estimated numbers from newspapers and magazines. Have students discuss whether each is exact or estimated. Discuss a situation, such as a newspaper headline, in which an estimate is sufficient. Ask students to identify instances when they have used estimated numbers.

WHEN YOUR STUDENTS ASK
★ WHY AM I LEARNING THIS? ★

You can connect estimation to real life with home renovations. If a general contractor is to make a profit, he or she must estimate the time it takes to do a job as well as the cost of labor and materials.

LET'S TALK MATH
Better Than a Guess

When Do We Estimate?

Many times you do not need to use your math skills to calculate an exact answer. Instead you estimate. An **estimate** is a number close enough to an exact number that permits you to make a correct decision.

■ READ ABOUT IT

We use estimates when . . .

> • an estimate is as good as an exact number.

How slow should a car be going to be driving safely in foggy conditions?

How far is it to the next town?

> • there is no way of knowing the exact number.

Milk is rich in calcium. How much calcium goes into your system when you drink a glass of milk?

How much Vitamin C is in your diet each day?

> • we could get the exact number but it is too difficult.

How many people used a ferryboat to go to work in New York City last Tuesday?

How many people were in New York City at 8:00 this morning?

> • we want to check whether an exact computation is reasonable.

The **perimeter** is the total distance around. Our backyard has a perimeter of 120 yards (yd).

$23 + 37 + 23 + 37 = 120$ yd

$36\frac{3}{4}$ yd

$36\frac{3}{4}$ yd

$23\frac{1}{4}$ yd

---

2 TEACH

READ ABOUT IT Why would an estimate be appropriate in an article about the number of people attending the opening game of the World Series? *(An exact number would be difficult to get and is unnecessary. In this instance knowing the approximate number is enough.)*

TALK ABOUT IT Have students relate their answers to Exercises 1-5 to the reasons given on page 16.

WRITE ABOUT IT Have students write one or two sentences explaining their numbers.

> ### *Chalkboard Examples*
>
> Is the number exact or estimated?
> 25,000 people watched the game. *(estimated)*
> I spent $14.52. *(exact)*
> He hit 51 home runs. *(exact)*

SUMMARIZE/ASSESS Explain how estimated answers are often used to communicate information. *(Possible answer: Bordertown is about a two-hour drive; I have about $5 in my pocket.)*

TALK ABOUT IT

1. Find each number below in the airport scene above. Decide whether it is used as an *exact number* or an *estimate*. Explain.

   a. $495.17   b. $900   c. 846 mi   d. 2nd

   e. $2.95   f. 9 runs   g. $1,200   h. $1\frac{1}{2}$ d

2. Is the number of people standing at the New York ticket counter exact or estimated? Why? exact. You can count.

3. Mr. Rivera figures the cost of two tickets to Dallas would be $495.17 + $495.17 = $990.34. Is his computation reasonable? yes

4. Would the manager of Chicago's O'Hare airport report the number of passengers inside all terminal buildings at a given time as an exact or estimated number? Why? estimate. The number is always changing as people go in and out.

5. Would the number of airplane takeoffs in one day at Seattle's Sea-Tac airport be an exact number or an estimate? Why? exact. The control tower keeps a record of each takeoff.

WRITE ABOUT IT

6. Think of an exact number not already mentioned on this page that you might see or use at an airport. Now name a number that is an estimate. Answers will vary.

3 FOLLOW-UP

CLASS ACTIVITY 1-8

Present the following situation to the students.

Jess awoke to find that she couldn't use exact numbers anymore. She knew that she had approximately 15 minutes to get dressed and that she needed to put on approximately three pairs of shoes. Jess's mom asked her how many pieces of toast she wanted, and Jess said, "About five." At school, she estimated all the answers on her math quiz and then didn't give the cashier enough money for her lunch.

Ask the students what it would be like if Jess's nightmare happened to them. Have them write a short story about how hard living without exact numbers would be.

MEETING INDIVIDUAL NEEDS

For Students Who Are . . .

Acquiring English Proficiency   Pair each student with an English-proficient student to work through the Talk About It and Write About It sections of the lesson.

Gifted and Talented   Have students work in pairs to create a list of other examples of when we use estimates. Have them use the four categories used on page 16.

Today's Problem

The average height of land above sea level is 2,757 ft. The average depth of the ocean is 12,450 ft. On the average, how many times deeper is the ocean than the height of the land?

(12,450 ÷ 2,757 = 4.515 ft; about $4\frac{1}{2}$ times deeper)

MIDCHAPTER
Checkup

The midchapter checkup provides a way for you to check students' understanding of the skills taught in the first half of the chapter.

Language and Vocabulary

Some key language and vocabulary ideas from the first half of the chapter are reinforced here.

Quick Quiz

The quiz provides a means of evaluating students' understanding of the objectives for the first half of the chapter. Page references are given so that students can check back to where the skill was taught.

Use the following guide to score the quick quiz.

Score	Percent
10	100%
9	90
8	80
7	70
6	60
5	50
4	40
3	30
2	20
1	10

Use this chart to identify the Management Objectives tested.

Items	Management Objective	Pages
1–4	**1A** Identify and write whole numbers and decimals in exponential, expanded, and standard form.	4–7; 12–13
5–7	**1B** Compare and order whole numbers and decimals.	8–9
8–9	**1C** Round whole numbers and decimals.	14–15
10	**1E** Problem Solving: Use a four-part process. Use patterns.	10–11

MIDCHAPTER CHECKUP

LANGUAGE & VOCABULARY

Tell whether you think the statement uses an *estimate* or an *exact number*. Explain your decision. Answers will vary. Suggestions given.

1. There are 45,000 people in the stadium today watching the Boston Red Sox play the Cleveland Indians.
   estimate
2. My aunt lives 12 blocks from my house.
   exact number
3. On a recent diet, Roberto lost 22 lb.
   exact number
4. The school cafeteria served 328 lunches yesterday.
   exact number

QUICK QUIZ ✓

Write in standard form. *(pages 4–7)*

1. 4^3
2. $(1 \times 10^2) + (7 \times 10^1) + (9 \times 10^0) + \left(3 \times \frac{1}{10^2}\right)$ 179.03
3. 7 million, 1 thousand, and 4 tenths
   7,001,000.4
4. 9.8 million 9,800,000

Compare. Choose >, <, or =. *(pages 8–9, 12–13)*

5. 2.5 billion ▪ 3 million
   >
6. 3^4 ▪ 9^2
   =
7. 0.666 ▪ 1.000
   <

Round the number to the given places. *(pages 14–15)*

8. 97,801; hundreds, thousands
   97,800; 98,000
9. 21.059; tenths, hundredths
   21.1; 21.06

Solve. *(pages 10–11)*

10. The Empire State Building in New York City is 1,472 ft tall. The Gateway Arch in St. Louis, Missouri, is 842 ft shorter than the Empire State Building. The Eiffel Tower in Paris, France, is 1,052 ft tall.
    a. Which of the three structures is 1,472 ft tall? Empire State Building
    b. How does the Eiffel Tower compare in size to the Empire State Building? It is shorter.
    c. How much taller is the Eiffel Tower than the Gateway Arch? 422 ft

Write the answers in your learning log.   Answers will vary. Suggestions given.

1. What do you know about a number with an exponent?   **The exponent tells how many times to use the base as a factor.**

2. How are exponents and multiplication related? Include an example in your explanation.
   Exponents represent multiplication; $3^4 = 3 \times 3 \times 3 \times 3$

3. Your friend thinks decimals with two places are always smaller than decimals with three places. Explain what is wrong with this thinking.   **Place value not the number of places tells which is greater.**

DID YOU KNOW ... ? The highest temperature ever recorded in the United States was 134°F. The lowest temperature was ⁻80°F. How do the highest and lowest temperatures ever recorded in your town compare with these temperatures?
Check students' work.

In the first round of a hopscotch game, Ellie jumped in box 1. In the second round, she jumped in boxes 1 and 2. In the third round, she jumped in boxes 1, 2, and 3, and so on. How many boxes will she have jumped in at the end of eight rounds?
36 boxes

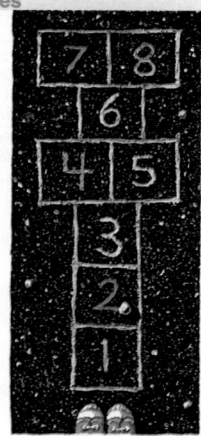

Learning Log

These are suggestions for writing about some topics taught so far in the chapter. The students keep their Learning Logs from the beginning of the school year through the end.

Math America

A mathematical skill that students have learned is related to an interesting fact about the United States.

Bonus

Students are given an opportunity to solve a challenge-type problem like a puzzle or a nonroutine problem.

Lesson Organizer

> **Objective:** Determine the appropriate metric units of length.

Prior Knowledge: Students should be able to multiply by powers of ten.

Error Analysis and Remediation: See page 29A.

Lesson Resources:
Practice Worksheet 1-9
Reteaching Worksheet 1-9
Enrichment Activity 1-9
Daily Review 1-9
Cooperative Problem Solving 2, Chapter 1

Two-Minute Math

Find each amount.
67 ten-dollar bills *($670)*
423 hundred-dollar bills *($42,300)*
57 dimes *($5.70)*
22 thousand-dollar bills *($22,000)*

1 INTRODUCE

CONNECTING ACTIVITY

☑ **MATERIALS CHECKLIST:** meter stick, centimeter rulers

1. Have students examine their centimeter rulers, identifying decimeter, centimeter, and millimeter markings. Discuss the relationships among these units. **What kinds of objects would you measure in decimeters?** *(length of a book, piece of ribbon)* **In centimeters?** *(pencil, index card)* **In millimeters?** *(paper clip, nail)*

2. Display the meter stick. Ask a volunteer to demonstrate that a meter is the same length as 10 dm, 100 cm, and 1,000 mm. **What lengths would you measure in meters?** *(length of the room, height of the door)*

3. Have students measure the length of the room, the height of the door, and the width of a desk and record their measurements.

WHEN YOUR STUDENTS ASK
★ WHY AM I LEARNING THIS? ★

You can connect metric units of length to international athletic competitions in which distances are measured in kilometers and meters.

Metric Units: Length

The metric system has standard units of measure. The **meter (m)** is the basic unit of length in the metric system.

A doorknob is about 1 m above the floor. A letter is about 1 millimeter (mm) thick. A mail carrier's little finger is about 1 centimeter (cm) wide.

The metric system is based on powers of ten. Each metric unit is ten times as great as the unit to its right and one-tenth as great as the unit to its left.

kilometer	hectometer	dekameter	meter	decimeter	centimeter	millimeter
km	hm	dam	m	dm	cm	mm
1,000 m	100 m	10 m	1 m	0.1 m	0.01 m	0.001 m

These rules are used to change metric units.

→ 1. To change from a *larger* unit to a *smaller* unit, *multiply* by a power of ten.

← 2. To change from a *smaller* unit to a *larger* unit, *divide* by a power of ten.

3.258 km = 3,258 m
rule 1; 1,000;
1,000 m = 1 km

> Which rule was used? By which number was 3.258 multiplied? Why?

437.3 cm = 4.373 m
rule 2; 100;
100 cm = 1 m

> Which rule was used? By which number was 437.3 divided? Why?

GUIDED PRACTICE

1. **NUMBER SENSE** Choose the appropriate metric unit. Use *km, m, cm,* or *mm*.
   a. the length of a thumbtack   mm
   b. the distance between towns   km

2. Change 352.73 m into kilometers, centimeters, and millimeters.   *0.35273 km; 35,273 cm; 352,730 mm*

3. **THINK ALOUD** Suppose you were asked to measure the length of a hall in your school. Would you rather measure in meters or decimeters? Explain.   *in meters because it would save time when measuring*

20   LESSON 1–9

---

2 TEACH

What is the relationship between 1 kilometer and 1 meter? *(1 km = 1,000 m; 1 m = 0.001 km)* **Between 1 meter and 1 centimeter?** *(1 m = 100 cm; 1 cm = 0.01 m)*

Which metric unit of length will give the most accurate measurement? Explain. *(Millimeters; the smaller the unit, the more precise is the measurement.)*

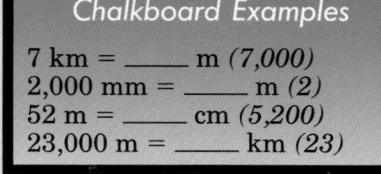

Chalkboard Examples

7 km = _____ m *(7,000)*
2,000 mm = _____ m *(2)*
52 m = _____ cm *(5,200)*
23,000 m = _____ km *(23)*

GUIDED PRACTICE   Have students justify their answer to Exercise 3.

SUMMARIZE/ASSESS   **Explain how to change from one metric unit of length to another.** *(Multiply to change from a larger unit to a smaller one; divide to change from a smaller unit to a larger one.)*

===== PRACTICE =====

NUMBER SENSE Name an appropriate unit for measuring the item.
Choose *km*, *m*, *cm*, or *mm*.

4. the height of a mountain **m**

5. the distance from Denver to Detroit
km

6. your height **cm**

7. the length of a fly **mm**

Copy and complete.

8. 7 m = ▨ cm **700**

9. 10 km = ▨ m **10,000**

10. 14 m = ▨ mm **14,000**

11. 2 m = ▨ cm **200**

12. 5 km = ▨ m **5,000**

13. 4 m = ▨ km **0.004**

14. 5.9 m = ▨ km **0.0059**

15. 3.4 cm = ▨ mm **34**

16. 0.035 km = ▨ cm **3,500**

17. 425 m = ▨ km **0.425**

18. 1.4 km = ▨ mm
1,400,000

19. 1 mm = ▨ km **0.000001**

MIXED REVIEW Compare. Choose
$>$, $<$, or $=$.

20. 0.5 million ▨ a half million **=**

21. 7^2 ▨ 4×10^1 **>**

22. 6^4 ▨ 10^3 **>**

23. 7.9 cm ▨ 3 m **<**

24. 1,800 mm ▨ 18 m **<**

25. 350 km ▨ 1,000 m **>**

Find two endpoints on the rule for each line segment length.

26. 55 mm
AB

27. 3 cm
AC

28. 0.9 cm
AD

29. 1.8 cm
CE

30. 0.003 m
CF

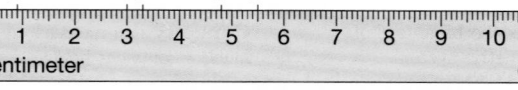

===== PROBLEM SOLVING =====

Work with a partner to solve.

31. A swimming pool
company sells three
different shapes of pools.
Find the perimeter of
(the total distance
around) each pool.
A: 24 m; B: 1,900 cm; C: 31 m

32. **IN YOUR WORDS** Draw
a pool that represents
a perimeter of 30 m.
Label the dimensions.
Compare your diagram
with a classmate's. Are the
pools the same shape?
Explain.
Check students' drawings.

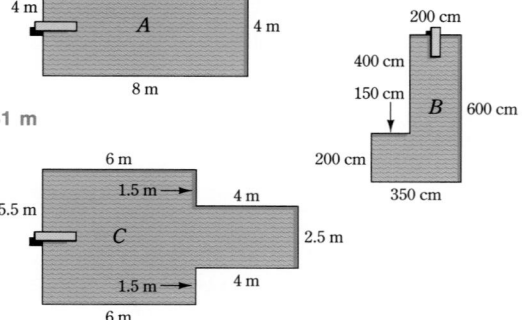

CHAPTER 1   **21**

MEETING INDIVIDUAL NEEDS

For Students Who Are . . .

Acquiring English Proficiency Pair students with an English-proficient student to discuss the number sense exercises.

Gifted and Talented Have students find all possible whole-number dimensions for exercise 32. *(1 m × 14 m; 2 m × 13 m; 3 m × 12 m; 4 m × 11 m; 5 m × 10 m; 6 m × 9 m; 7 m × 8 m)* Ask if there is a pattern. *(The dimensions must add up to $\frac{1}{2} \times 30$, or 15.)*

Working 2 or 3 Grades Below Level Have students circle the larger unit in exercises 8–19 to help them determine which rule to use.

Today's Problem

The thickness of a dime is approximately 1 mm. The height of the Statue of Liberty from base to torch is 45 m. How many dimes would it take to make a stack of this height? How much would this stack of dimes be worth?
(1,000 × 45 = 45,000; 45,000 ÷ 10 = 4,500; $4,500)

---

3 FOLLOW-UP

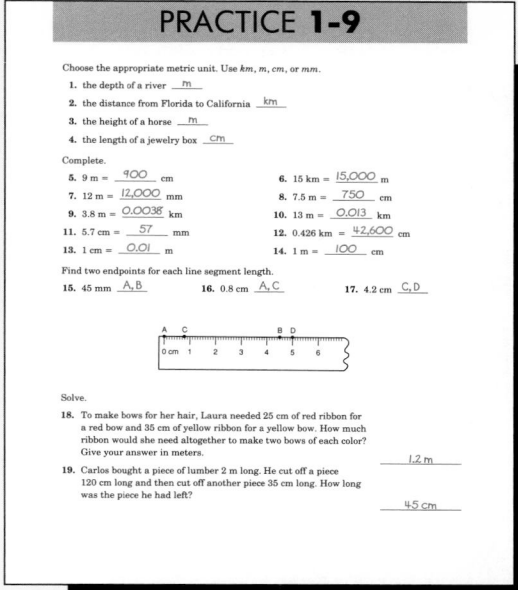

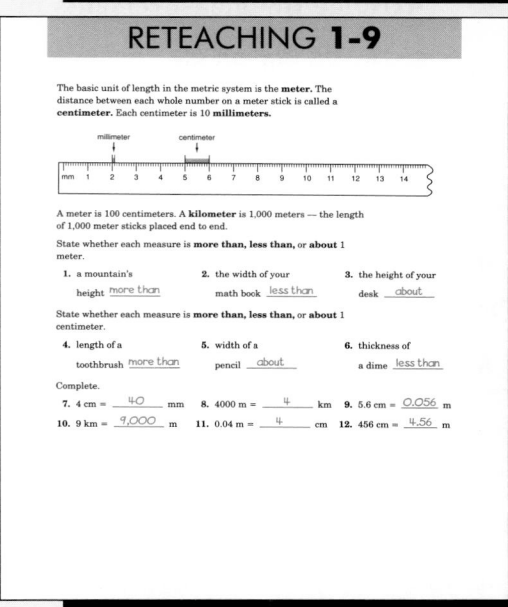

===== ENRICHMENT 1-9 =====

☑ **MATERIALS CHECKLIST:** Cotton balls, cotton swabs, metric measuring tapes

Write the following list on the board.

The Mini-Metric Olympic Events

Standing Broad Jump
Cotton Ball Shot-Put
Cotton Swab Javelin Throw
Giant Step

Have the students work in groups of four. Each group member selects an event to enter. Other members measure the distance and record it. Each team totals its distances and then compares its performance with that of other teams. The team with the highest score wins.

Lesson Organizer

Objective: Determine the appropriate metric units of capacity.

Prior Knowledge: Students should know the meanings of the metric prefixes.

Error Analysis and Remediation: See page 29A.

Lesson Resources:
Practice Worksheet 1-10
Reteaching Activity 1-10
Enrichment Worksheet 1-10
Daily Review 1-10

Two-Minute Math

Arrange the measurements in

73 cm, 73 km, 73 mm, 73 m
(73 km, 73 m, 73 cm, 73 mm)
65 cm, 6.5 mm, 6 m, 0.06 km
(0.06 km, 6 m, 65 cm, 6.5 mm)

1 INTRODUCE

CONNECTING ACTIVITY

☑ **MATERIALS CHECKLIST:** 200-mL juice container, 1 L bottle, large pail of water

1. Have volunteers determine the number of milliliters in a liter by pouring water from the juice container into the bottle. Have students record the amount of water poured each time and find the total amount used to fill the bottle.

2. Help students conclude that 1 L = 1,000 mL. **How is this relationship similar to that of meters to millimeters?** *(1 m = 1,000 mm)*

WHEN YOUR STUDENTS ASK
★ WHY AM I LEARNING THIS? ★

You can connect metric units of capacity to automobile specifications, such as the 1.6 liter engine.

Metric Units: Capacity

It is interesting to know that at peak times close to 169,800 kiloliters (kL) of water flow over Niagara Falls in 1 min.

This is the same as 169,800,000 L of water per minute.

Four glasses of water is about 1 L.

A drop of water is about 1 mL.

The **liter (L)** is the basic unit of capacity in the metric system.

Capacity is a measure of how much a container holds.

kiloliter	hectoliter	dekaliter	liter	deciliter	centiliter	milliliter
kL	hL	daL	L	dL	cL	mL
1,000 L	100 L	10 L	1 L	0.1 L	0.01 L	0.001 L

These rules are used to change metric units.

1. To change from a *larger* unit to a *smaller* unit, *multiply* by a power of ten.

2. To change from a *smaller* unit to a *larger* unit, *divide* by a power of ten.

54 mL = 0.054 L
Which rule was used? By which number was 54 divided? Explain?
rule 2; 1,000; 1,000 mL = 1 L

4.5 kL = 4,500 L
Which rule was used? By which number was 4.5 multiplied? Explain.
rule 1; 1,000; 1,000 L = 1 kL

22   LESSON 1–10

MATH AND SCIENCE

2 TEACH

What metric unit would you use to measure the capacity of a bathtub? *(L)* **A medicine bottle?** *(mL)*

Name something with the approximate capacity of a liter. *(a large bottle of juice)*

How many milliliters of water are needed to fill a 1 L bottle? *(1,000 mL)* **A 3 L bottle?** *(3,000 mL)* **A 4.5 L bottle?** *(4,500 mL)*

Chalkboard Examples

2 L = _____ mL *(2,000)*
2,500 L = _____ kL *(2.5)*
0.375 L = _____ mL *(375)*
5,850 mL = _____ L *(5.85)*

SUMMARIZE/ASSESS **Explain how metric units of capacity are related to each other.** *(Students may relate units to prefixes and discuss ways to change from one unit to another.)*

GUIDED PRACTICE

Estimate the capacity of the container.   Accept reasonable estimates. Suggestions given.

1. a small measuring cup
   250 mL
2. a toothpaste tube
   100 mL
3. a large paint can
   3 L
4. a kitchen sink
   12 L
5. an aquarium
   10 L
6. the gas tank of a car
   30 L

PRACTICE

Copy and complete.

7. 20 L = ▦ mL   **20,000**
8. 25 L = ▦ mL   **25,000**
9. 27 L = ▦ mL   **27,000**
10. 1.500 L = ▦ mL   **1,500**
11. 2.600 L = ▦ mL   **2,600**
12. 7.210 L = ▦ mL   **7,210**
13. 0.123 L = ▦ mL   **123**
14. 0.251 L = ▦ mL   **251**
15. 0.278 L = ▦ mL   **278**
16. 14.5 L = ▦ mL   **14,500**
17. 9.2 L = ▦ mL   **9,200**
18. 0.1L = ▦ mL   **100**
19. 3,000 mL = ▦ L   **3**
20. 4,000 mL = ▦ L   **4**
21. 7,000 mL = ▦ L   **7**
22. 1,200 mL = ▦ L   **1.2**
23. 1,803 mL = ▦ L   **1.803**
24. 2,315 mL = ▦ L   **2.315**
25. 700 mL = ▦ L   **0.7**
26. 634 mL = ▦ L **0.634**
27. 815 mL = ▦ L   **0.815**

Compare. Choose >, <, or =.

28. 5 L ▦ 50 mL   **>**
29. 300.5 mL ▦ 200 L   **<**
30. 0.05 L ▦ 0.005 kL   **<**
31. 0.992 mL ▦ 9 cL   **<**
32. 125 mL ▦ 1.25 L   **<**
33. 1,000 L ▦ 1 kL   **=**

MIXED REVIEW   Copy and complete. Are the units measures of *length* or *capacity*?

34. 7.5 km = ▦ m   **7,500; length**
35. 27 mL = ▦ L   **0.027; capacity**
36. 16 mm = ▦ cm   **1.6; length**
37. 33 cL = ▦ L   **0.33; capacity**
38. 0.2 m = ▦ mm   **200; length**
39. 9.1 kL = ▦ L   **9,100; capacity**

PROBLEM SOLVING

NUMBER SENSE   Match the example with the numerical expression.

40. the capacity in liters of the world's tallest water tower in New Jersey   **c**
    a. 2.260922×10^{19}

41. the capacity in kiloliters of the Pacific Ocean   **b**
    b. 7×10^{23}

42. the capacity in liters of a pelican's pouch   **d**
    c. $946,250$

43. the capacity in kiloliters of Lake Baikal, the lake with the largest amount of fresh water   **a**
    d. $(1 \times 10^1) + (1 \times 10^0) + (4 \times \frac{1}{10})$

MEETING INDIVIDUAL NEEDS

For Students Who Are . . .

Acquiring English Proficiency   Pair students with an English-proficient student to discuss the Problem Solving exercises.

Gifted and Talented   Have students research other metric units of capacity, find their equivalents, and discuss the prefixes.

Working 2 or 3 Grades Below Level   Use the following diagram to help students understand the rules for changing from one metric unit of capacity to another.

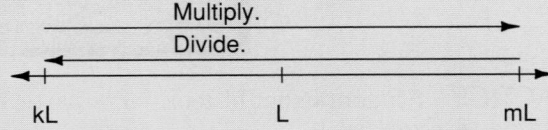

Today's Problem

The bristlecone pines of Nevada, California, and Arizona are nearly 5,000 years old. How many generations old are they if a generation is considered to be 25 years? *(5,000 ÷ 25 = 200 generations)*

PRACTICE 1-10

Complete.

1. 60 L = _60,000_ mL
2. 20 L = _0.02_ kL
3. 5.600 L = _5,600_ mL
4. 1,800 mL = _1.8_ L
5. 0.245 L = _245_ mL
6. 5,896 mL = _5.896_ L
7. 13.8 kL = _13,800_ L
8. 932 mL = _0.932_ L
9. 0.07 L = _70_ mL
10. 55 mL = _0.055_ L
11. 0.3 L = _300_ mL
12. 5,709 L = _5.709_ kL
13. 23 L = _23,000_ mL
14. 6,200 mL = _6.2_ L
15. 0.475 kL = _475_ L
16. 841 mL = _0.841_ L

Compare. Write >, <, or =.

17. 7 L ▦ 70 mL   >
18. 405.2 mL ▦ 150 L   <
19. 0.879 L ▦ 5 mL   >
20. 1,000 mL ▦ 1 L   =
21. 2.5 L ▦ 2,500 mL   =
22. 5.7 kL ▦ 570 L   >

Solve.

23. Which of the following is a reasonable estimate of the capacity in milliliters of an eyedropper?
    $(1 \times 10^0) + (5 \times \frac{1}{10})$ or $(2 \times 10^5) + (7 + 10^4)$?
    $(1 \times 10^0) + (5 \times 10^{-1})$

24. Which of the following is a reasonable estimate of the capacity of Lake Superior?
    4.168109×10^9 liters or 4.168109×10^9 kiloliters?
    4.168109×10^9 kL

RETEACHING 1-10

☑ **MATERIALS CHECKLIST:** 2-L bottle, 1-cm cube, newspapers, and magazines

Show the students a 2-L bottle and a 1-cm cube. Explain that the cube would contain 1 mL of water. Have the students work in pairs. Provide each pair with a sheet of paper on which you have written the headings *Liter* and *Milliliter*. Instruct the students to place under each heading several pictures of amounts of water that would be measured using that unit.

ENRICHMENT 1-10

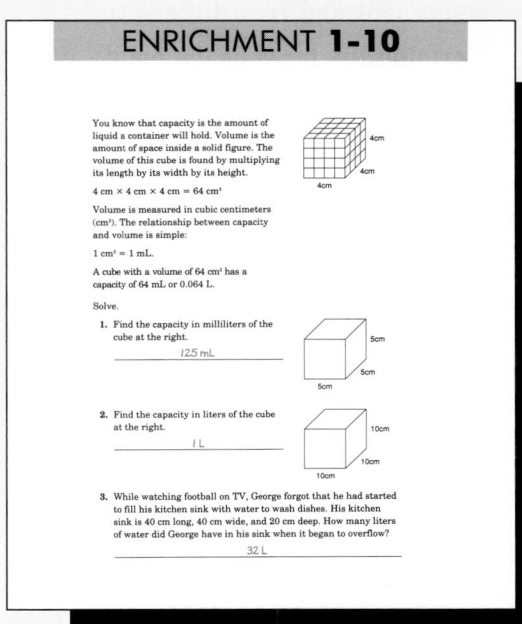

You know that capacity is the amount of liquid a container will hold. Volume is the amount of space inside a solid figure. The volume of this cube is found by multiplying its length by its width by its height.

4 cm × 4 cm × 4 cm = 64 cm³

Volume is measured in cubic centimeters (cm³). The relationship between capacity and volume is simple:

1 cm³ = 1 mL

A cube with a volume of 64 cm³ has a capacity of 64 mL or 0.064 L.

Solve.

1. Find the capacity in milliliters of the cube at the right.
   125 mL

2. Find the capacity in liters of the cube at the right.
   1 L

3. While watching football on TV, George forgot that he had started to fill his kitchen sink with water to wash dishes. His kitchen sink is 40 cm long, 40 cm wide, and 20 cm deep. How many liters of water did George have in his sink when it began to overflow?
   32 L

Lesson Organizer

Objective: Determine the appropriate metric units of mass.

Prior Knowledge: Students should know how the metric system relates to the decimal numeration system.

Error Analysis and Remediation: See page 29A.

Lesson Resources:
Practice Worksheet 1-11
Reteaching Worksheet 1-11
Enrichment Activity 1-11
Daily Review 1-11

Two-Minute Math

Compare. Use >, <, or =.
2.5 L   250 mL *(>)*
116 m   11.6 km *(<)*
125.4 cm   12,540 m *(<)*

1 INTRODUCE

CONNECTING ACTIVITY

☑ **MATERIALS CHECKLIST:** balance scale, liter container, metric masses, large pail of water

Call on volunteers to perform the following experiment and record the results.

1. Determine the mass of the empty liter container by placing it on one pan of the balance and putting metric masses on the other pan.

2. Fill the container with water. (Distilled water is preferable.)

3. Determine the mass of the water in the container.

WHEN YOUR STUDENTS ASK
★ WHY AM I LEARNING THIS? ★

You can connect this skill to real life through pharmacy. When preparing prescriptions, particularly ointments, pharmacists often measure ingredients in grams.

MATH AND SCIENCE

Metric Units: Mass

Did you know that the mass of an adult male polar bear can be more than 454 kg?

> The **kilogram (kg)** is the basic unit of mass in the metric system.

> **Mass** is a measure of the quantity of matter in an object.

When you use something you know to figure out something you do not know, you make a **MATH·CONNECTION**.

To change units of mass, make a **MATH·CONNECTION** using powers of ten as you did with metric units of length and capacity.

A polar bear at birth is just under 1 kg. A horsefly has a mass close to 1g.

1.4 kg = 1,400 g ⟵ Did you multiply or divide by a power of ten? Explain. What power of ten was used? ⟶ 45 mg = 0.045 g

multiply; 1 kg = 1,000 g   divide; 1 mg = $\frac{1}{10^3}$ g

■ **GUIDED PRACTICE** ■

1. Write the word for each abbreviation. Then copy and complete the chart.

kg	hg	dag	g	dg	cg	mg
▦ g	▦ g	▦ g	1 g	0.1 g	▦ g	▦ g
1,000	100	10			0.01	0.001

NUMBER SENSE   Which unit is appropriate to measure the mass? Choose *kg*, *g*, or *mg*.

2. an orange
g

3. a seventh grader
kg

4. a sheet of paper
mg

5. a box of cereal
g

■ **PRACTICE** ■

About how many horseflies do you need to equal the given mass?

6. 50 g   about 50   **7.** 3 kg   about 3,000   **8.** 4,000 mg   about 4

---

2 TEACH

Why do you think an astronaut's mass remains the same in space but his or her weight changes? *(The amount of matter an object contains does not change whether on Earth or the moon. Weight does change because it depends on gravity.)*

How do you change kilograms to grams? *(Multiply by 1,000)* **grams to kilograms?** *(Divide by 1,000.)*

> ### Chalkboard Examples
> 5 mg = _____ g *(0.005)*
> 2 kg = _____ g *(2,000)*
> 7,500 g = _____ kg *(7.5)*
> 60 g = _____ mg *(60,000)*

GUIDED PRACTICE   Students should look for a pattern as they complete the table in Exercise 1.

SUMMARIZE/ASSESS   **Give examples of objects whose mass could be measured in kilograms, grams, and milligrams.** *(Accept reasonable answers.)*

Copy and complete.

9. 14 kg = ■ g   14,000   **10.** 21 kg = ■ g   21,000   **11.** 35 kg = ■ g   35,000

12. 1 kg = ■ mg   1,000,000   **13.** 1 kg = ■ g   1,000   **14.** 10 kg = ■ g   10,000

15. 9 kg = ■ g   9,000   **16.** 11 g = ■ mg   11,000   **17.** 17 g = ■ mg   17,000

18. 4,600 kg = ■ mg   4,600,000,000   **19.** 1,672 g = ■ kg   1.672   **20.** 2,137 g = ■ kg   2.137

21. 800 mg = ■ g   0.8   **22.** 6 kg = ■ mg   6,000,000   **23.** 2 mg = ■ g   0.002

24. 9.15 g = ■ mg   9,150   **25.** 7 g = ■ kg   0.007   **26.** 2.5 kg = ■ mg   2,500,000

MIXED REVIEW   Write two equivalent quantities for each.   See page 29b.

27. 7 m   **28.** 0.2 g   **29.** 6.2 L   **30.** 12 cL   **31.** 0.5 km   **32.** 4,500 mg

━━━━━━━━━━━━━━━━━━━━━━━━━ **PROBLEM SOLVING** ━━━━

33. **NUMBER SENSE**   Read carefully. Then change the inappropriate units to something more commonly used.   **See page 29b.**

The length of the adult male polar bear averages between 2,400 mm and 3,400 mm. The adult female measures about 1,800 mm in length and has a mass ranging from 181,000 g to 227,000 g. Polar bear families stay together for about 730 d. Newborn polar bears have a mass of about 680,000 mg and are about 254 mm long.

Polar bears can smell food as far away as 16,000,000 mm. They can run short distances at speeds of up to 56,300 m/h.

Critical Thinking

Volume, capacity, and mass in the metric system are related for water at 4°C. The **centimeter cube (cm³)** below shows this relationship. Work with a partner to answer the questions.

1. If the capacity is 8 mL, what is the mass?   8 g

2. If the volume is 15 cm³, what is the capacity?   15 mL

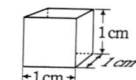

3. If the mass is 50 mg, what is the volume?   50 mm³

volume = 1 cm³
capacity = 1 mL
mass = 1 g

MEETING INDIVIDUAL NEEDS
For Students Who Are . . .

Acquiring English Proficiency   Pair students with an English-proficient student to discuss the Problem Solving and Critical Thinking exercises.

Gifted and Talented   Have students research the origins of the prefixes used in the metric system.

Working 2 or 3 Grades Below Level   Have students circle the larger unit in exercises 9–26 to help them determine which rule to use.

Today's Problem

At one time there were about 9,000,000,000 passenger pigeons. It is believed that the last one died in 1914. If the land area of the earth's surface is about 57,584,000 sq. mi, about how many passenger pigeons per square mile were there?
(9,000,000,000 ÷ 57,584,000 = 156.293; about 156 pigeons)

---

3 FOLLOW-UP

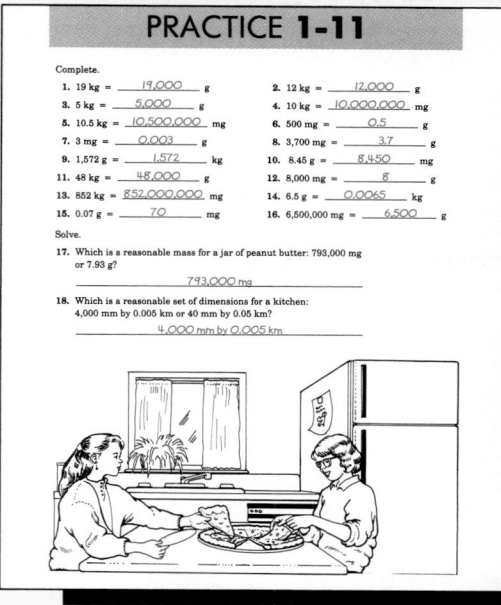

PRACTICE 1-11

Complete.

1. 19 kg = ___19,000___ g   2. 12 kg = ___12,000___ g
3. 5 kg = ___5,000___ g   4. 10 kg = ___10,000,000___ mg
5. 10.5 kg = ___10,500,000___ mg   6. 500 mg = ___0.5___ g
7. 3 mg = ___0.003___ g   8. 3,700 mg = ___3.7___ g
9. 1,572 g = ___1.572___ kg   10. 8.45 g = ___8,450___ mg
11. 48 kg = ___48,000___ g   12. 8,000 mg = ___8___ g
13. 852 kg = ___852,000,000___ mg   14. 6.5 g = ___0.0065___ kg
15. 0.07 g = ___70___ mg   16. 6,500,000 mg = ___6,500___ g

Solve.

17. Which is a reasonable mass for a jar of peanut butter: 793,000 mg or 7.93 g?
___793,000 mg___

18. Which is a reasonable set of dimensions for a kitchen: 4,000 mm by 0.005 km or 40 mm by 0.05 km?
___4,000 mm by 0.005 km___

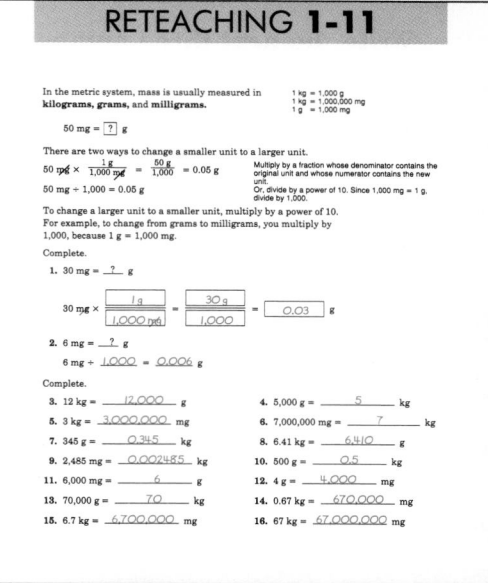

RETEACHING 1-11

In the metric system, mass is usually measured in **kilograms, grams,** and **milligrams.**

1 kg = 1,000 g
1 kg = 1,000,000 mg
1 g = 1,000 mg

50 mg = [?] g

There are two ways to change a smaller unit to a larger unit.

$50 \text{ mg} \times \dfrac{1 \text{ g}}{1,000 \text{ mg}} = \dfrac{50 \text{ g}}{1,000} = 0.05 \text{ g}$ Multiply by a fraction whose denominator contains the original unit and whose numerator contains the new unit.

50 mg ÷ 1,000 = 0.05 g   Or, divide by a power of 10. Since 1,000 mg = 1 g, divide by 1,000.

To change a larger unit to a smaller unit, multiply by a power of 10. For example, to change from grams to milligrams, you multiply by 1,000, because 1 g = 1,000 mg.

Complete.

1. 30 mg = ___?___ g

$30 \text{ mg} \times \dfrac{1 \text{ g}}{1,000 \text{ mg}} = \dfrac{30 \text{ g}}{1,000} = \boxed{0.03}$ g

2. 6 mg = ___?___ g
6 mg ÷ ___1,000___ = ___0.006___ g

Complete.

3. 12 kg = ___12,000___ g   4. 5,000 g = ___5___ kg
5. 3 kg = ___3,000,000___ mg   6. 7,000,000 mg = ___7___ kg
7. 345 g = ___0.345___ kg   8. 6.41 kg = ___6,410___ g
9. 2,485 g = ___0.002485___ kg   10. 500 g = ___0.5___ kg
11. 6,000 mg = ___6___ g   12. 4 g = ___4,000___ mg
13. 70,000 g = ___70___ kg   14. 0.67 kg = ___670,000___ mg
15. 6.7 kg = ___6,700,000___ mg   16. 67 g = ___67,000,000___ mg

---

ENRICHMENT 1-11

☑ **MATERIALS CHECKLIST:** Index cards

Have the students work in pairs. Provide each pair with several sets of cards containing three equivalent forms of some metric unit of mass, such as 1,000 g, 1 kg, and 0.001 mg. Instruct students to mix the cards and place them in rows of three, face down. In turn, partners look for the three equivalent forms by flipping over one card at a time. A turn ends when a card shows a nonequivalent measure. Matching sets are removed from the game by the person who finds them; otherwise, cards are replaced face down. The student with the most cards wins.

Lesson Organizer

> **Objective:** Solve problems using a pattern.

Prior Knowledge: Students should be able to extend simple number sequences.

Error Analysis and Remediation: See page 29A.

Lesson Resources:
Practice Worksheet 1-12
Reteaching Activity 1-12
Enrichment Worksheet 1-12
Daily Review 1-12
Cooperative Investigations, Chapter 1
Cooperative Connections, Chapter 1

Two-Minute Math

Write the next three numbers in each sequence.
11, 17, 23 *(29, 35, 41)*
4.1, 6.2, 8.3 *(10.4, 12.5, 14.6)*
11.4, 9.2, 7.0 *(4.8, 2.6, 0.4)*

1 INTRODUCE

SYMBOLIC ACTIVITY

☑ **MATERIALS CHECKLIST:** plastic straw, scissors

1. Explain that you are going to cut the straw several times. Have students record the total number of pieces that result from each cut on a chart:

Number of cuts	1	2	3	4	5	...
Number of pieces	2	3	4			

How many pieces would there be after 55 cuts? *(56)*

2. Have students state the rule that describes the pattern. *(Number of cuts plus 1 equals number of pieces.)*

WHEN YOUR STUDENTS ASK
★ WHY AM I LEARNING THIS? ★

You can connect this skill to real life situations. Suppose you want to hang some large mirrors. You can use the pattern formed by the studs in the wall to determine where to put the fastenings.

Problem Solving Strategy:
Using a Pattern

On an airline flight from Traverse City to Detroit, there was 1 empty seat for every 3 passengers. The seating capacity on the small plane is 36. How many passengers were on the flight?

This problem can be solved by finding and continuing a pattern. A table, like the one below, makes the pattern easier to see.

Empty seats	1	2	3	4	5	6	7	8	9
Passengers	3	6	9	12	15	18	21	24	27
Total seats	4	8	12	16	20	24	28	32	36

THINK ALOUD Describe the pattern for the number of passengers. Describe the pattern for the total number of seats. **3 × no. empty seats; 4 × no. empty seats** Now continue the patterns to solve the problem on your own. How many passengers were on the flight from Traverse City to Detroit? **27 passengers**

GUIDED PRACTICE

Use a pattern to solve the problem.

1. On a Lansing-Chicago flight, there were 2 empty seats for every 5 passengers. The plane can seat 42 people. How many empty seats were there? How many passengers were on board? **12 empty seats; 30 passengers**

2. A Grand Rapids–Cleveland flight had 3 empty seats for every 4 passengers. Of the 154 seats, 66 were empty. Could there have been 98 passengers on that flight? **no**

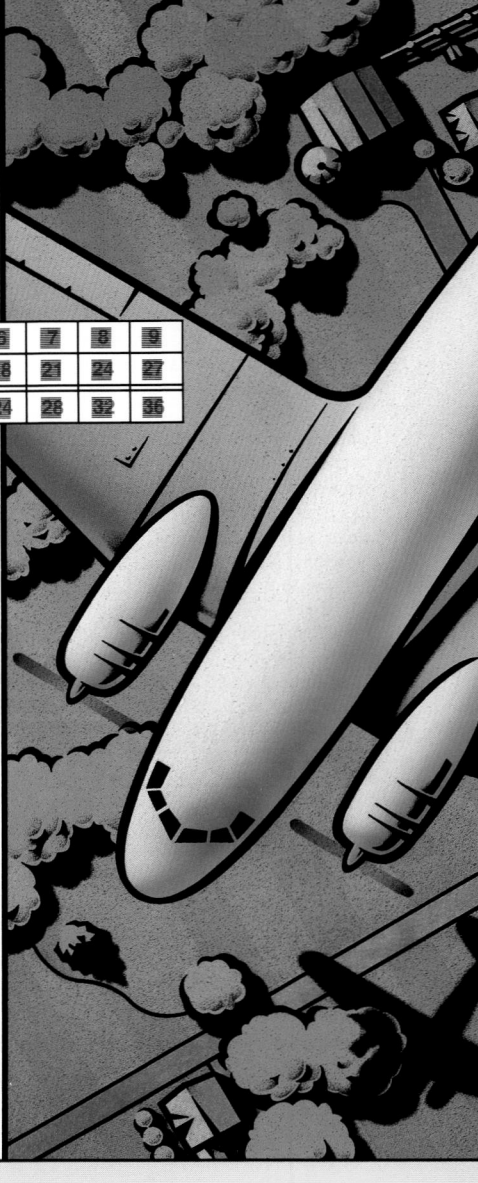

2 TEACH

Have students complete the table in the lesson problem. **How can you check that the completed table is correct?** *(Test the pattern by adding the empty seats and passenger seats to get the total number of seats.)*

How many passengers and total seats would there be if there were 12 empty seats? *(36 passengers and 48 seats)*

> ### Chalkboard Example
>
> There are 52 seats on a bus. On one trip there was 1 empty seat for every 3 passengers. How many passengers were there? *(39)*

SUMMARIZE/ASSESS **Explain when you might use a pattern to solve a problem.** *(Possible answer: If you can arrange information in a table, you may be able to identify a pattern.)*

Find a pattern to help you solve the problem.

3. An airport cafeteria has square tables that seat 4 people. When 2 tables are side by side, 6 people can be seated. How many people can be seated if 8 tables are side by side? **18 people**
Pattern: 2→6, 3→8, 4→10, . . . 8→18

4. On Monday, Sally tells 3 friends her travel plans. On Tuesday, each of her 3 friends tells 3 people. If this pattern continues, how many people other than Sally will know her travel plans after 4 d?
120 people Pattern: $3^1 + 3^2 + 3^3 + 3^4$

5. Suppose you start saving for a trip. You save $1 the 1st week, $2 the 2nd week, $4 the 3rd week, and so on. How much money would you have saved after 6 weeks (wk)?
$63 Pattern: $2^0 + 2^1 + 2^2 . . . + 2^5$

 CHOOSE Choose a strategy to solve.

6. The sum of the first 2 odd numbers (1 + 3) is 4, the first 3 is 9, the first 4 is 16, and so on. What is the sum of the first 12 odd numbers? **144 or 12^2**;
$1 + 3 = 2^2$, $1 + 3 + 5 = 3^2$, $1 + 3 + 5 + 7 = 4^2$, . . .

7. The display of cereal boxes at the right has 3 rows. If the display pattern were continued for 15 rows, how many boxes would there be altogether? **120 boxes**;
1→1, 2→3, 3→6, 4→10, . . . 15→120

8. **IN YOUR WORDS** The number pattern at the left is called Pascal's Triangle. Write the next four rows of the pattern. Describe a few patterns you see.

CHAPTER 1   27

PRACTICE 1-12

Find a pattern to help you solve the problem.

1. A train left New York City with 100 people on board. At each stop, 11 people got off and 1 person got on the train. After 9 stops, how many people were on board?
10 people

2. On Tuesday, Roberta gets her friends Alicia and Tom to promise that they will help her pick up trash around the neighborhood on Saturday. On Wednesday, both Alicia and Tom get 2 more people to help out. If this pattern continues until Friday, how many people will be helping Roberta pick up trash on Saturday?
30 people

3. The owners of Plenty O' Pets kept track of the number of customers they had during the store's first few days in business.

Day	Customers
Monday	0
Tuesday	2
Wednesday	6
Thursday	14

If the pattern continues, how many customers will they have on Sunday?
126 customers

4. This is the pattern for the seat numbers of the fans in Row V who are told to hold up a white cardboard square during the half-time show at a football game: 0, 12, 24, 36,... All the other fans are told to hold up a black square. Just before half-time, every other fan holding a white square (starting with seat number 12) is told to switch cards with the person whose seat number is 2 less than theirs. What color square should the fan in seat 204 of Row V hold up?
black

RETEACHING 1-12

☑ **MATERIALS CHECKLIST:** Small paper squares for each student

Present the following problem:

You want to tile a 12-by-15 ft room by alternating black tiles and white tiles. The tiles are one foot square. How many of each color tile do you need?

Have students work in pairs using black and white squares to represent the tiles. Let them model the pattern to find the answer to the problem. Repeat for similar and more complicated problems.

ENRICHMENT 1-12

How many squares are contained in this square?

This problem is harder than it looks at first. Not only do you have to count all the individuals squares and the large square they form, but you also have to count all the squares formed by groups of 4, 9, 16, and so on. A pattern will help you tell how many squares are in an 8 × 8 square.

1. How many squares are there in a 1 × 1 square?
_1_

2. How many 1 × 1 squares are there in a 2 × 2 square?
_4_

3. How many 1 × 1 squares are there in a 3 × 3 square?
_9_

4. How many 1 × 1 squares are there in a 4 × 4 square?
_16_

5. What pattern do you notice in the answers to Problems 1– 4? Continue the pattern for an 8 × 8 square.
_$1^2 = 1, 2^2 = 1 + 3, 3^2 = 1 + 3 + 5...; 1, 4, 9, 16, 25, 36, 49, 64$_

6. Count the _total_ number of squares for 1 × 1, 2 × 2, and 3 × 3 squares. How do these numbers compare to the numbers in the pattern you wrote in Problem 5?
1, 5, 14; each is sum of all previous squares

7. Use what you learned in Problem 6 to find the pattern that tells how many squares in all are contained in an 8 × 8 square.
1, 5, 14, 30, 55, 91, 140, 204; 204 squares

MEETING INDIVIDUAL NEEDS

For Students Who Are . . .

Acquiring English Proficiency Pair students with an English-proficient student to discuss the problems and find the patterns.

Gifted and Talented Have students do research about Blaise Pascal and how his triangle is used in mathematics.

Working 2 or 3 Grades Below Level Have students use pages 38–43 of the Skills Workbook for Problem Solving Strategies.

Having Reading Difficulties Pair each student with an able reader. Have them work together to make tables and find the patterns.

Today's Problem

Use the code A = 0, B = 1, C = 2, . . . , Z = 25, and a space = 26. Let *k* be any nonzero whole number. Code any message by substituting for each letter another letter that is *k* positions beyond it in the alphabet. If *k* = 5, decode the secret message LTTIEQZHP.
(Secret message: GOOD LUCK)

CHAPTER

Checkup

The chapter checkup provides a quick language and vocabulary review, a test for the chapter, and suggestions for student Learning Log entries.

Language and Vocabulary

Some key language and vocabulary ideas from this chapter are reinforced here.

Test

The test can be used either as a test or as a review of the chapter prior to your administering the test worksheets found in the Teacher's Resource Book.

The following guide will help you determine percentage scores.

Score	Percent	Score	Percent
22	100%	11	50%
21	95	10	45
20	91	9	41
19	86	8	36
18	82	7	32
17	77	6	27
16	73	5	23
15	68	4	18
14	64	3	14
13	59	2	9
12	55	1	5

Each test has 3 sections: concepts, skills and problem solving. These sections provide students with exposure to the formats used on standardized tests.

Use the chart on page 29 to identify the Management Objectives tested for this chapter.

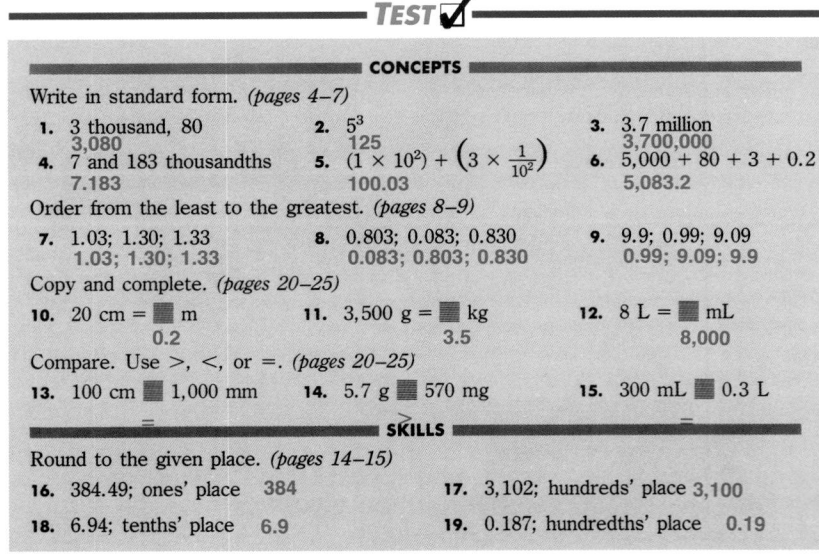

CHAPTER CHECKUP

LANGUAGE & VOCABULARY

Give the prefix. Be sure the sentence makes sense.

kilo- deci- milli- deka-

1. Ramon's fish tank holds three ____ liters. **deka**

2. Laurie measured her pencil and found it to be a little less than two ____ meters. **deci**

3. Chartia weighs about one ____ gram more when she weighs herself holding her math book than when she weighs herself without holding it. **kilo**

4. Douglas estimates the thickness of a nickel to be three ____ meters. **milli**

TEST ✓

CONCEPTS

Write in standard form. *(pages 4–7)*

1. 3 thousand, 80
   3,080
2. 5^3
   125
3. 3.7 million
   3,700,000
4. 7 and 183 thousandths
   7.183
5. $(1 \times 10^2) + \left(3 \times \frac{1}{10^2}\right)$
   100.03
6. $5,000 + 80 + 3 + 0.2$
   5,083.2

Order from the least to the greatest. *(pages 8–9)*

7. 1.03; 1.30; 1.33
   1.03; 1.30; 1.33
8. 0.803; 0.083; 0.830
   0.083; 0.803; 0.830
9. 9.9; 0.99; 9.09
   0.99; 9.09; 9.9

Copy and complete. *(pages 20–25)*

10. 20 cm = ■ m
    0.2
11. 3,500 g = ■ kg
    3.5
12. 8 L = ■ mL
    8,000

Compare. Use >, <, or =. *(pages 20–25)*

13. 100 cm ■ 1,000 mm
    =
14. 5.7 g ■ 570 mg
    >
15. 300 mL ■ 0.3 L
    =

SKILLS

Round to the given place. *(pages 14–15)*

16. 384.49; ones' place   384
17. 3,102; hundreds' place   3,100
18. 6.94; tenths' place   6.9
19. 0.187; hundredths' place   0.19

28   CHAPTER CHECKUP

CHAPTER TEST • FORM A

Write in standard form. (pp. 4–7, 12–13) I A

1. 4 thousand, 50
   4,050
2. 3^4
   81
3. $(6 \times 10^2) + (2 \times 10^0) + (5 \times \frac{1}{10^1})$
   602.5
4. 6 and 125 thousandths
   6.125
5. $6,000 + 70 + 1 + 0.6$
   6,071.6

(pp. 2–3, 8–9) I B

Order from least to greatest.

6. 1.05, 1.55, 1.15
   1.05, 1.15, 1.55
7. 0.702, 0.072, 0.720
   0.072, 0.702, 0.720

Compare. Use >, <, or =.

8. 624 _>_ 483
9. 161.25 _<_ 163.32
10. 4^3 _=_ 2^6

Round to the given place. (pp. 14–15) I C

11. 247; tens' place   250
12. 651.39; ones' place   651
13. 0.376; hundredths' place   0.38
14. 42,629; thousands' place   43,000
15. 5.209; tenths' place   5.2

Complete. (pp. 16–17, 20–25) I D

16. 6 km = _6,000_ m
17. 20,000 m = _20_ km
18. 4.5 L = _4,500_ mL
19. 16 g = _16,000_ mg
20. 7 kg = _7,000_ g

CHAPTER TEST • FORM A

Solve. (pp. 10–11, 26–27) I E

21. Jessica buys and sells stamps and coins. She paid $250 for a rare stamp. How much will she receive for the stamp if she is to make a profit of $45?
    $295

22. Five years ago one of Jessica's friends paid $125 for a coin proof set. Today the proof is valued at $220. By how many dollars has the proof set's value increased?
    $95

23. Suppose you start saving for a trip. You save $1 the first week, $4 the second week, $7 the third week, and so on. How much money would you have saved in eight weeks?
    $92

24. The first triangular number is 1, the second is 3, the third is 6, the fourth is 10, and so on. What is the tenth triangular number?
    55

25. At noon, Brenda found out she had won a trip to New Orleans. She immediately tells three friends. At 12:05 P.M. these three friends each tell 3 other people. Then at 12:10 P.M. each of them tells 3 other people. If this continues, how many will know of Brenda's trip by 12:20 P.M.?
    121 people

PROBLEM SOLVING

Solve. *(pages 10–15, 26–27)*

20. Scientists believe that the last ice age began about 2 million years ago. The earliest ice age is believed to have begun about 2.3 billion years ago.

   a. About how many years ago did the first ice age begin?   2.3 billion yr

   b. How is 2.3 billion written in standard form?   2,300,000,000

   c. How many years passed between the beginnings of the first ice age and the last ice age?   2,298,000,000

21. On an obstacle course, a runner must jump over water holes. The first hole is 3 in. across. If each hole is double the width of the previous one, how wide is the fifth hole?   48 in.

22. The Internal Revenue Service allows taxpayers to round the amount they owe to the nearest dollar. Mr. Benitez owes $384.49. For what amount can he write the check? $384

LEARNING LOG

Write the answers in your learning log.   Answers will vary.

1. What connection can you make between the metric system and place value? It is based on a system of tens. Conversion involves moving the decimal.   Suggestion given.

2. Explain why, when you change from a larger unit of measure to a smaller unit of measure, you get a greater number for an answer. It takes many small units to equal a larger unit; therefore, the answer is larger.

Note that the same numbers are used in Exercises 16 and 22.

CHAPTER TEST • FORM B

Write in standard form. *(pp. 4–7, 12–13)* | A

1. 5 thousand, 30   **2.** 2^5 **3.** $(4 \times 10^3) + (3 \times 10^1) + (2 \times \frac{1}{10^2})$
  5,030   32   4,030.02

4. 5 and 12 thousandths   **5.** 5,000 + 60 + 2 + 0.8
  5.012   5,062.8

(pp. 2–3, 8–9) | B

Order from least to greatest.

6. 9.5; 9.25; 9.3   **7.** 376,400; 37,640; 3,764
  9.25, 9.3, 9.5   3,764; 37,640; 376,400

Compare. Use >, <, or =.

8. 746 < 764   **9.** 396.65 < 396.72   **10.** 2^4 > 5^2

Round to the given place. *(pp. 14–15)* | C

11. 276; hundreds' place   300   **12.** 569.47; tenths' place   569.5

13. 0.462; hundredths' place   0.46   **14.** 53,738; thousands' place   54,000

15. 639.08; tens' place   640

Complete. *(pp. 16–17, 20–25)* | D

16. 5,000 m = 5 km   **17.** 7 km = 7,000 m

18. 2.5 L = 2,500 mL   **19.** 4,600 mg = 4.6 g

20. 9 kg = 9,000 g

CHAPTER TEST • FORM B

Solve. *(pp. 10–11, 26–27)* | E

21. Kenny buys and sells baseball cards. He paid $350 for a set of cards. How much must he receive for the set of cards if he is to make a profit of $75? $425

22. Ten years ago one of Kenny's friends bought a baseball card for $6. Today the card is valued at $400. By how many dollars has the card's value increased? $394

23. Suppose you start saving for a trip. You save $1 the first week, $3 the second week, $5 the third week, $7 the fourth week, and so on. How much money would you have saved in eight weeks? $64

24. The sum of the first two even numbers is 6, the first 3 is 12, the first 4 is 20, and so on. What is the sum of the first 20 even numbers?   420

25. At noon Eddie tells 2 friends he won a contest by guessing the number of pennies in a jar. At 12:05 P.M. his two friends each tell 2 people. Then at 12:10 P.M. each of them tells 2 other people. If this pattern continues, how many people will know of Eddie's winning by 12:30 P.M.?   255 people

---

Items	Management Objective	Pages
1–6	**1A** Identify and write whole numbers and decimals in exponential, expanded, and standard form.	4–7; 12–13
7–9	**1B** Compare and order whole numbers and decimals.	8–9
10–15	**1C** Round whole numbers and decimals.	14–15
16–19	**1D** Determine the appropriate metric units of length, capacity, and mass	20–25
20–22	**1E** Problem Solving: Use a four-part process. Use patterns.	10–11; 26–27

Problem Solving

Item 20 has 3 parts:
a. literal—this is a reading comprehension question;
b. interpretive—this involves interpretation using the facts given;
c. applied—students use a strategy or skills to find an answer.

Item 16 in the skill section and item 22 in the problem solving section use the same numbers.

This will help you informally assess how your students transfer from numerical skills to word problems.

For scoring problem solving items you may wish to use partial credit. If a student uses the correct strategy but gets a wrong answer, give the student 2 points toward the total percent score.

Learning Log

These are suggestions for writing about some topics taught in this chapter. The students keep their Learning Logs from the beginning of the school year through the end.

CHAPTER 1

Error Analysis and Remediation

Here are some common errors students make when they are writing whole numbers and decimals in various forms; comparing, ordering, and rounding whole numbers and decimals; and choosing the appropriate metric measure. The errors are listed by lesson under the appropriate management objective.

1A • IDENTIFY AND WRITE WHOLE NUMBERS AND DECIMALS IN EXPONENTIAL, EXPANDED, AND STANDARD FORM

Source of Error (Lesson 1-2)
students reverse the roles of the factor and exponent ($2^3 = 3 \times 3 = 9$); multiply the exponent by the given factor ($4^2 = 4 \times 2 = 8$); or use the base as a repeated addend instead of as a factor ($5^4 = 5 + 5 + 5 + 5 = 20$).

Remediation
Have students use graph paper to show the meaning of each number and then write the correct product.

Source of Error (Lesson 1-3)
students think that the value of a number changes when it is rewritten from one form to another.

Remediation
Demonstrate how to change from standard form to expanded form using smaller numbers. Show that multiplication occurs within parentheses and that then addition combines the values of each place to give the value of the whole number.

1B • COMPARE AND ORDER WHOLE NUMBERS AND DECIMALS

Source of Error (Lesson 1-4)
students forget to line up the decimal points when comparing decimals, or they may line up digits beginning from the right.

Remediation
Suggest that students scan two decimal numbers from left to right until they first note a place where the corresponding digits differ. Demonstrate by writing two numbers, such as 2.4365 and 2.438, on the chalkboard and covering them with a card. Slowly reveal each digit by gradually sliding away the card.

1C • ROUND WHOLE NUMBERS AND DECIMALS

Source of Error (Lesson 1-7)
when the digit to be rounded is 9, students round the 9 to 10 but neglect to increase the digit to the left

Remediation
Tell students to look at the rounded number and determine whether the answer is reasonable. For example, help students observe that when 7,496 is rounded to the nearest ten, 7,500 is a more reasonable answer than 7,400.

1D • DETERMINE THE APPROPRIATE METRIC UNITS OF LENGTH, CAPACITY, AND MASS

Source of Error (Lessons 1-9, 1-10, 1-11)
students have difficulty determining which of two units is more appropriate.

Remediation
Help students associate each unit with an estimate. For example, the width of a key on a typewriter is about a centimeter; a drop of rain is about a milliliter; and the mass of a raisin is about a gram. Lead students to see that the appropriate unit for the width of a box of cereal would be given in centimeters but the width of a store shelf would be given in meters.

1E • PROBLEM SOLVING: USE A FOUR-PART PROCESS. USE PATTERNS

Source of Error (Lesson 1-5)
Students make reading errors.

Remediation
Encourage students to read the problem several times before they make a plan. Suggest that they write down the facts as they understand them and focus on just the facts needed to solve the problem.

Source of Error (Lesson 1-12)
students have difficulty finding and continuing a pattern.

Remediation
Have students state in their own words what has been done to the first number to get the second number in the pattern. Help them continue the pattern until they reach the solution.

Answers

Page 6

2. 4 thousand, 53; $(4 \times 10^3) + (5 \times 10^1) + (3 \times 10^0)$

3. 43 million, 5; $(4 \times 10^7) + (3 \times 10^6) + (5 \times 10^0)$

4. 20 and 103 thousandths; $(2 \times 10^1) + (1 \times \frac{1}{10^1}) + (3 \times \frac{1}{10^3})$

5. 8 hundred 73 and 52 hundredths; $(8 \times 10^2) + (7 \times 10^1) + (3 \times 10^0) + (5 \times \frac{1}{10^1}) + (2 \times \frac{1}{10^2})$

Page 7

31. $(1 \times 10^0) + (8 \times \frac{1}{10^2}) + (3 \times \frac{1}{10^3})$

32. $(8 \times 10^3) + (3 \times 10^2) + (8 \times 10^1) + (2 \times 10^0) + (3 \times \frac{1}{10^1}) + (5 \times \frac{1}{10^2})$

Page 11

7. Answers will vary. Suggestions given:
   1. C = 10; H = 9; I = 5; A = 3; G = 2; O = 1
   2. C = 1; H = 10; I = 9; A = 8, G = 7; O = 4
   3. C = 4; H = 10; I = 8; A = 7; G = 6; O = 1

Page 15

5. 480; 500
6. 1,910; 1,900
7. 5,860; 5,900
8. 9,490; 9,500
9. 10,080; 10,100
10. 67,280; 67,300
11. 8,010; 8,000
12. 54,640; 54,600
13. 100,740; 100,700
14. 750,010; 750,000
15. 995,330; 995,300
16. 667,560; 667,600
17. 3.7; 3.74; 4
18. 382.4; 382.43; 382
19. 13.0; 13.00; 13
20. 6.3; 6.33; 6
21. 42.5; 42.46; 42
22. 18.4; 18.36; 18
23. 0.0; 0.04; 0
24. 1.0; 1.00; 1
25. 6.0; 6.00; 6
26. 5,176.2; 5,176.15; 5,176
27. 185.5; 185.48; 185
28. 8.7; 8.73; 9

Page 25

27. Answers will vary. Suggestion given: 7,000 mm; 0.007 km

28. Answers will vary. Suggestion given: 200 mg; 0.0002 kg

29. Answers will vary. Suggestion given: 6,200 mL; 620 cL

30. Answers will vary. Suggestion given: 0.12 L; 120 mL

31. Answers will vary. Suggestion given: 500 m; 500,000 mm

32. Answers will vary. Suggestion given: 4.5 g; 0.0045 kg

33. 2.4 m; 3.4 m; 1.8 m; 181 kg; 227 kg; 2 yr; 680 g; 25.4 cm; 16 km; 56.3 km/h

Page 27

8.
```
      1 5 10 10 5 1
     1 6 15 20 15 6 1
    1 7 21 35 35 21 7 1
   1 8 28 56 70 56 28 8 1
```
Pattern 1: 1's down the outer edges
Pattern 2: Consecutive numbers 5, 6, 7, 8, . . .
Pattern 3: Each interior number is the sum of the two numbers above it.

CHAPTER 1

Extra Practice

This page provides extra practice of all the major chapter objectives. Use this page after the chapter has been taught to reinforce the chapter skills. Page references are provided for each group of items so that students can easily look back at the appropriate lesson for additional support.

Write in standard form. *(pages 4–7)*

1. 2^0 1 **2.** 9^2 81 **3.** 10^1 10 **4.** 12^2 144 **5.** 5^3 125

6. $1,000 + 30 + 0.1 + 0.02$ 1,030.12

7. $(4 \times 10^0) + \left(6 \times \frac{1}{10^1}\right)$ 4.6

Compare. Choose >, <, or =. *(pages 8–9, 12–13)*

8. 35, 874 ▨ 35,784 > **9.** 1.000 ▨ 6^0 = **10.** 93 billion ▨ 9.3 million >

Order from the least to the greatest. *(pages 8–9)*

11. 96,094; 96,904; 96,409
96,094; 96,409; 96,904

12. 4.001; 4.010; 3.999
3.999; 4.001; 4.010

Round to the nearest hundredth, tenth, and whole number. *(pages 14–15)*

13. 2.157
2.16; 2.2; 2.0

14. 13.092
13.09; 13.1; 13

15. 456.117
456.12; 456.1; 456

16. 10.351
10.35; 10.4; 10

Copy and complete. *(pages 20–25)*

17. 3 cm = ▨ mm 30 **18.** 3,000 m = ▨ km 3 **19.** 157 cm = ▨ m 1.57

20. 2.4 L = ▨ mL 2,400 **21.** 1,500 mL = ▨ L 1.5 **22.** 0.3 L = ▨ mL 300

23. 2.3 kg = ▨ g 2,300 **24.** 10 mg = ▨ g 0.01 **25.** 1,805 g = ▨ kg 1.805

Solve. *(pages 10–11, 26–27)*

26. During one month, it rained four times. The following amounts of rain fell: 0.92 in., 1.31 in., 1.02 in., and 2.4 in. If the normal amount of rainfall for the month is 4.75 in., how much more rain than the normal amount fell?
0.9 in.

27. A square yard has been fenced using 2 fence posts on each side. Another has been fenced using 3 posts on each side. How many posts would be needed for a fence with 6 posts on each side? 20 posts

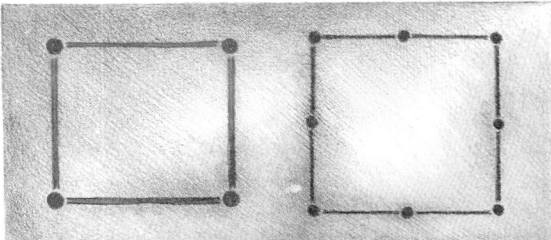

WORLD RECORDS

Select a record that interests you. It may come from the world of sports, science, music or any other field you enjoy. Try to find the following information about the record you choose:

- what the record is today and who holds it
- when the record was first set
- how many times the record has been broken
- the difference between the original record and today's record
- possible explanations for the old record being broken

For example, the world record for depth of underwater dives in a machine increased from 245 ft in 1865 to 35,802 ft in 1990. The original record was officially broken 14 times during those years.   **Check students' work.**

Measure for Measure

Work with a partner. Together write a short story of several paragraphs in which you use metric or customary measures. For example, in a story about a walk in the woods, you might write, "We froze in fear when we saw a bear just 2,000 cm to our left."

Use as many different measures as possible. You may want to read the story aloud to the rest of your class. Then ask your classmates to name the measures using other metric or customary units. For example, the bear would be 20 m away.
Check students' work.

DID YOU KNOW . . . ? The copper "skin" that protects the Statue of Liberty is about 0.2 cm thick. Is your outer layer of skin thicker or thinner than that of the Statue of Liberty?

Enrichment

This page contains activities that provide extension and enrichment for all levels of students. Depending on the needs of your students, you may wish to assign an activity from this page at certain points during the chapter, or you may wish to use this page when the entire chapter has been completed.

World Records

Refer students to various books of records found in most libraries. *The Guinness Book of Records* (Guinness Publishing Ltd.) is especially useful.

After students complete this activity, you may wish to have interested students design and illustrate a class booklet of world records.

Measure for Measure
(COOPERATIVE)

As each story is read aloud, list the different measurements on the chalkboard. After students name the other units for the measurements, discuss why one unit is more appropriate than the other.

Math America

Students will need to refer to a science book or an encyclopedia to find the thickness of the outer layer of their skin.

This activity gives students an opportunity to compare decimals in a real-life context.

Technology

This page is designed to provide calculator or computer experiences for all levels of students. The calculator or computer logo indicates the type of activity.

You may wish to assign these activities after the chapter has been taught or during the course of the chapter, depending on your needs and those of your students.

Odd Times
(COOPERATIVE)

Remind students to work carefully as they multiply or divide the number on the calculator display by 10.

How Old?

You may wish to have students use calculators to find their ages in seconds before they find Amanda's age. Remind students to consider leap years.

Last Move
(COOPERATIVE)

This activity uses Houghton Mifflin Software, found in Houghton Mifflin Math Activities Courseware, Grade 7.

After students complete the activity, have them discuss the different strategies that they used. (Exchange digits until the largest or smallest number is written; then multiply or divide by 10.)

ODD TIMES

Play this game with a partner. You will need a calculator and a number cube labeled 1–6. After entering the number 2 on your calculator, take turns rolling a number cube.

- If the number on the cube is odd, multiply by 10.
- If the number on the cube is even, divide by 10.

Continue rolling the number cube and multiplying or dividing the number on the calculator display by 10. The first player to reach 20,000 wins the game.

HOW OLD?

Mike likes to do things differently. Yesterday, he told everyone that his baby sister Amanda was about 18,489,600 s old. If Amanda was born at midnight on May 1, what was yesterday's date and how old was she? Use your calculator to find out.
December 1, 214d
How old are you in seconds?
Answers will vary.

LAST MOVE

In the computer activity *The Last Move*, you compare decimal numbers. Play this pencil and paper game with another person to sharpen your skills.

Player 1 begins with the number 0.8426 and must write a number that is greater with each turn. Player 2 begins with the number 5,791 and must write a number that is less with each turn.

You are allowed two ways to write a new number:

1. exchange two digits $\qquad$ $5,791 \rightarrow 5,719$
2. multiply or divide the number by 10 $\qquad$ $5,791 \div 10 = 579.1$

Play continues until Player 1 can no longer write a greater number obeying the rules *or* Player 2 can no longer write a number that is less obeying the rules. The player who takes the last move wins.

This game is available on computer disk in Houghton Mifflin *Mathematics Activities Courseware.*

32   TECHNOLOGY

Software Activities

activity 1 • THE SIZE OF A WHALE

MATERIALS: database program, encyclopedia

Procedure: This activity will help students see how a database file can be used to order numbers. Create a database file with the following fields: *Name, Weight,* and *Length.* Students should enter the following data into the file: Blue Whale 135 tons, 100 ft; Fin Whale, 97 tons, 88 ft; Sperm Whale, 75 tons, 63 ft. Students should first sort the file to place the weights in order from least to greatest and then sort the file to order the lengths from longest to shortest. Have students find this data for other whales, and enter it into the file. Then have students find the largest whale in the database.

Follow-up: An average human weighs 142 lb and an average elephant weighs 6.5 tons, students should find how many humans weigh the same as a Blue Whale. How many elephants weigh the same as a Blue Whale?

activity 2 • HOW ROUND IS IT?

MATERIALS: BASIC programming

Procedure: This activity will give students practice in rounding decimals. Have students type this program into the computer.

```
10 REM ROUNDS DECIMAL NUMBERS
20 PRINT "THE PROGRAM WILL ROUND
   YOUR NUMBER. WHICH ONE?"
30 PRINT: PRINT: INPUT N
40 PRINT: PRINT "TO HOW MANY PLACES
   BEYOND DECIMAL?"
50 INPUT V
60 PRINT: PRINT INT(N * 10^V
   +0.5)/10^V
70 END
```

Students should run the program using 35.097 as the number and 2 for the number of places. Have students run the program several more times to find if any limitations are present.

Follow-up: Students should identify any changes that will need to be made to have the program work for all numbers.

HOUGHTON MIFFLIN SOFTWARE

Computational Skills Program. Boston, MA: Houghton Mifflin Company, 1988. For Apple II.

EduCalc. Boston, MA: Houghton Mifflin Company, 1990. For Apple II, Commodore, IBM.

Mathematics Activities Courseware. Boston, MA: Houghton Mifflin Company, 1983. For Apple II, IBM.

Mathematics: Solving Story Problems. Levels 7–8. Boston, MA: Houghton Mifflin Company, 1985. For Apple II, IBM.

The Computer Tutor. Boston, MA: Houghton Mifflin Company, 1990. For Apple II, IBM.

OTHER SOFTWARE

AppleWorks. Santa Clara, CA: Claris Corporation, 1983–89. For Apple II.

Metrics. Fairfield, CT: Intellectual Software/Queue Software, Inc., 1989. For Apple II.

Number Munchers. St. Paul, MN: MECC, Apple II 1987, Macintosh 1990, IBM, 1990.

Rounding Up, Rounding Down. Des Plaines, IL: Looking Glass Learning, 1989, Apple II, IBM.

Order of Operations. Big Spring, TX: Gamco Industries, Inc., 1990. For Apple II, IBM.

Addition and Subtraction: Whole Numbers and Decimals

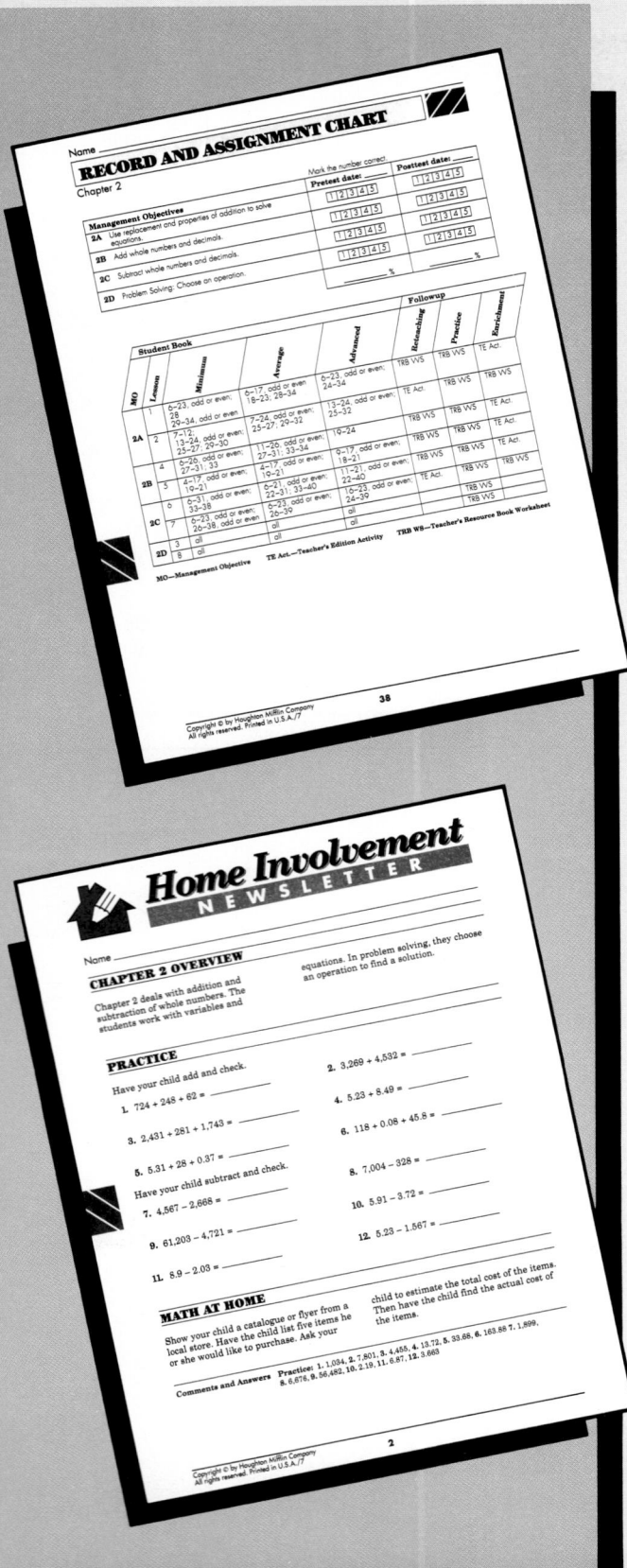

This chapter begins by introducing students to equations, variables, and the meaning of a solution to an equation. Students then learn how to add and subtract whole numbers and decimals. They use mathematical properties, math connections, number sense, estimation, and mental math strategies to facilitate their calculations. Students also learn how to read problems to identify necessary information.

Management Objectives

2A Use replacement and properties of addition to solve equations.
2B Add whole numbers and decimals.
2C Subtract whole numbers and decimals.
2D Problem Solving: Choose the operation.

Assignments for different achievement levels are provided on the Record and Assignment Chart in the Teacher's Resource Book.

Vocabulary

equation, page 34
variable, page 34
commutative property, page 36
associative property, page 36
identity property, page 36
front-end estimation, page 42

Home Involvement

As you begin to teach this chapter, give each student a copy of the Home Involvement Newsletter for this chapter.

This newsletter provides parents with
■ an overview of the chapter
■ suggestions for practicing some of the skills in the chapter
■ an at-home activity to do with their child, applying the skills taught in the chapter.

Management Chart

Management Objectives	Lesson/ Pages	Student Not Successful	Student Needs More Practice	Student Successful	Pacing Range
2A Use replacement and properties of addition to solve equations.	2-1/34-35	TRB/RW 2-1	TRB/PW 2-1	TE/EA 2-1	2 days
	2-2/36-37	TE/RA 2-2	TRB/PW 2-2	TRB/EW 2-2	
2B Add whole numbers and decimals.	2-4/40-41	TRB/RW 2-4	TRB/PW 2-4 CSP WNA CSP Dec. Sks. 5, 6	TE/EA 2-4	1-2 days
	2-5/42-43	TRB/RW 2-5	TRB/PW 2-5 MAC 7 Activity 2	TE/EA 2-5 MAC 7 Activity 2	
2C Subtract whole numbers and decimals.	2-6/46-47	TRB/RW 2-6	TRB/PW 2-6 CSP WNS CT Unit 1 Obj. 3.1, 3.2 MAC 6 Activity 1	TE/EA 2-6 MAC 6 Activity 1	1-2 days
	2-7/48-49	TE/RA 2-7	TRB/PW 2-7 CSP Dec. Sks. 7, 8 CT Unit 3 Obj. 3.1	TRB/EW 2-7	
2D Problem Solving: Choose the operation	2-3/38-39		TRB/PW 2-3		2 days
	2-8/50-51		TRB/PW 2-8		
Chapter Checkups	44-45, 52-53				
Extra Practice	54				
Enrichment	55				
Cumulative Review/ Problem Solving Review	56-57				
Technology	58				

TE = Teacher's Edition
TRB = Teacher's Resource Book
RW = Reteaching Worksheet
RA = Reteaching Activity
EA = Enrichment Activity
EW = Enrichment Worksheet
PW = Practice Worksheet
CA = Classroom Activity

*Other Available Items
MAC = Mathematics Activities Courseware
CSP = Computational Skills Program
CT = Computer Tutor

CHAPTER 2

Manipulative Planning Guide

This is a complete list of manipulatives and materials needed for Chapter 2.

Materials for Manipulatives	TE Activities (INTRODUCE)	Student Book Lesson
Balance scale	Lesson 2-1	
Gram cubes	Lesson 2-1	
Paperbag	Lesson 2-1	
10 slips of paper and small box, one set per group	Lesson 2-2	
U.S. wall map	Lesson 2-3	
Calculator for each student/pair of students		Lessons 2-3, 2-4, 2-6, 2-7
Teaching Aid 2*, one per student	Lesson 2-4	
Two different color markers for each student	Lesson 2-4	
Counters		
Different Color cubes		
Small objects, such as paper clips, pencils, and so on		
Newspapers		
Store receipts		
Number cubes, one per pair		
Decimals squares, colored pencils		
Math Connection Transparency		

*Teaching Aids are found in the Teacher's Resource Book.

Learning Stages

The concepts and skills in Chapter 2 are presented through these learning stages.

CONCRETE

Using manipulatives and verbalizing about a concept. No symbols.

Teacher Edition Activities	Student Book
At this grade level the skills of this chapter are taught at the connecting and symbolic stages.	

Enrichment	Reteaching	In the Houghton Mifflin Manipulative Kit (yes/no)	In the Houghton Mifflin Overhead Kit?
Lesson 2-1		No	
Lesson 2-1		Yes	
		No	
		No	
		No	
Lesson 2-5		No	Available separately
		No	Yes
		No	
Lesson 2-1		Yes	
Lesson 2-1	Lesson 2-2	No	
Lesson 2-1		No	
Lesson 2-4		No	
Lesson 2-5		No	
Lesson 2-6		Yes	
	Lesson 2-7	Yes	Yes
	Lesson 2-7	No	Yes

CONNECTING

5¢ $9cm^2$ $\frac{1}{3}$

Making a connection between manipulatives and symbols.

Teacher Edition Activities	Student Book
Lessons 2-1, 2-2, 2-3, 2-4	

SYMBOLIC

$.05 $A = 9cm^2$ $1 - \frac{2}{3} = \frac{1}{3}$

Using numbers or symbols. No manipulatives or pictures of manipulatives.

Teacher Edition Activities	Student Book
Lessons 2-2, 2-3, 2-5, 2-6, 2-7, 2-8	Lessons 2-1, 2-2, 2-3, 2-4, 2-5, 2-6, 2-7, 2-8

CHAPTER 2

Additional Activities

COOPERATIVE LEARNING RESOURCE ACTIVITIES

Through cooperative learning activities, students learn by interacting with one another in small groups. These cooperative activities provide students with motivating settings for making connections, investigations, and problem solving situations.

The cooperative connections are interdisciplinary problem-solving projects. Each student has a particular job that helps lead the group to complete the project. For the cooperative investigations students work in pairs for investigations involving data collection and analysis. The cooperative problem solving activities encourage the sharing of ideas and information. Students work in groups of four to solve a problem. Students are each assigned a clue and work together to find a common solution.

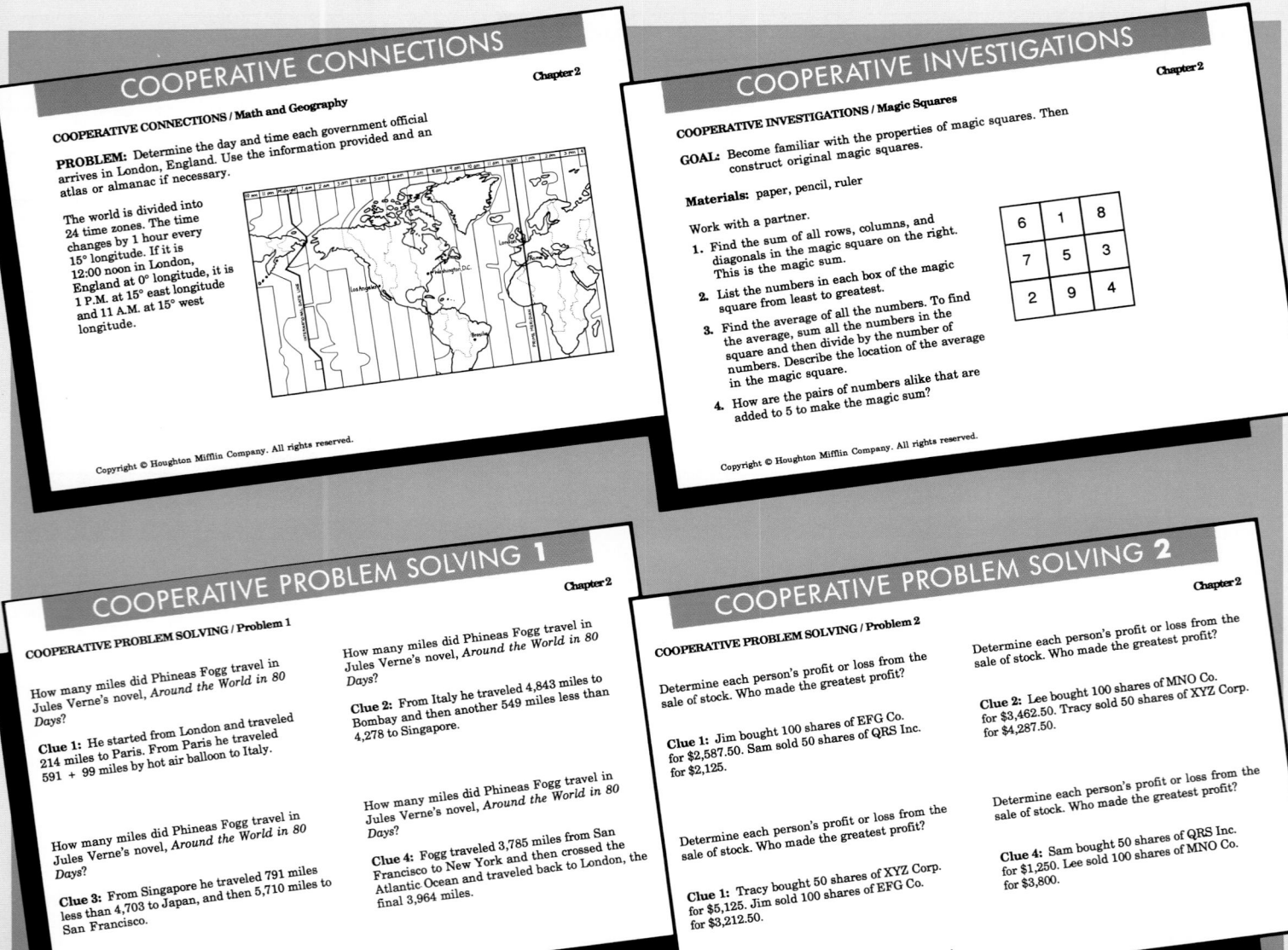

COOPERATIVE CONNECTIONS — Chapter 2

COOPERATIVE CONNECTIONS / Math and Geography

PROBLEM: Determine the day and time each government official arrives in London, England. Use the information provided and an atlas or almanac if necessary.

The world is divided into 24 time zones. The time changes by 1 hour every 15° longitude. If it is 12:00 noon in London, England at 0° longitude, it is 1 P.M. at 15° east longitude and 11 A.M. at 15° west longitude.

COOPERATIVE INVESTIGATIONS — Chapter 2

COOPERATIVE INVESTIGATIONS / Magic Squares

GOAL: Become familiar with the properties of magic squares. Then construct original magic squares.

Materials: paper, pencil, ruler

Work with a partner.

1. Find the sum of all rows, columns, and diagonals in the magic square on the right. This is the magic sum.

2. List the numbers in each box of the magic square from least to greatest.

3. Find the average of all the numbers. To find the average, sum all the numbers in the square and then divide by the number of numbers. Describe the location of the average in the magic square.

4. How are the pairs of numbers alike that are added to 5 to make the magic sum?

6	1	8
7	5	3
2	9	4

COOPERATIVE PROBLEM SOLVING 1 — Chapter 2

COOPERATIVE PROBLEM SOLVING / Problem 1

How many miles did Phineas Fogg travel in Jules Verne's novel, *Around the World in 80 Days?*

Clue 1: He started from London and traveled 214 miles to Paris. From Paris he traveled 591 + 99 miles by hot air balloon to Italy.

How many miles did Phineas Fogg travel in Jules Verne's novel, *Around the World in 80 Days?*

Clue 3: From Singapore he traveled 791 miles less than 4,703 to Japan, and then 5,710 miles to San Francisco.

How many miles did Phineas Fogg travel in Jules Verne's novel, *Around the World in 80 Days?*

Clue 2: From Italy he traveled 4,843 miles to Bombay and then another 549 miles less than 4,278 to Singapore.

How many miles did Phineas Fogg travel in Jules Verne's novel, *Around the World in 80 Days?*

Clue 4: Fogg traveled 3,785 miles from San Francisco to New York and then crossed the Atlantic Ocean and traveled back to London, the final 3,964 miles.

COOPERATIVE PROBLEM SOLVING 2 — Chapter 2

COOPERATIVE PROBLEM SOLVING / Problem 2

Determine each person's profit or loss from the sale of stock. Who made the greatest profit?

Clue 1: Jim bought 100 shares of EFG Co. for $2,587.50. Sam sold 50 shares of QRS Inc. for $2,125.

Determine each person's profit or loss from the sale of stock. Who made the greatest profit?

Clue 3: Tracy bought 50 shares of XYZ Corp. for $5,125. Jim sold 100 shares of EFG Co. for $3,212.50.

Determine each person's profit or loss from the sale of stock. Who made the greatest profit?

Clue 2: Lee bought 100 shares of MNO Co. for $3,462.50. Tracy sold 50 shares of XYZ Corp. for $4,287.50.

Determine each person's profit or loss from the sale of stock. Who made the greatest profit?

Clue 4: Sam bought 50 shares of QRS Inc. for $1,250. Lee sold 100 shares of MNO Co. for $3,800.

GAMES

ADDITION DERBY   (For use after Lesson 2-4)

Objective: Add whole numbers and decimals.

☑ **MATERIALS CHECKLIST:** index cards cut in half

Have each student write an addition exercise on each of two cards, for example, 224.5 + 99. Place all cards face down in a pile. Divide the class into four or five teams. One member from each team simultaneously chooses a card, solves the problem as quickly as possible at the chalkboard, and returns to his or her team. Every correct sum earns 5 points; the first team to finish with a correct answer earns an extra point. Any opposing team can challenge an answer and earn an additional 5 points for a corrected answer. All team members should have a turn. The team with the most points at the end is the winner.

DECIMAL DAZE   (For use after Lesson 2-7)

Objective: Add and subtract decimal numbers.

☑ **MATERIALS CHECKLIST:** 2 number cubes (0-5) and 2 number cubes (4-9) for each team, score sheets

Have each team of three students write 800 on the top of a score sheet. The first player on each team tosses all 4 cubes and forms the greatest possible number having two whole-number places and two decimal places. For example, for the digits 0, 3, 9, 7, a player would make 97.30. The second player forms a second number in the same way. The third player adds the decimal numbers and subtracts their sum from 800 on the score sheet. Players rotate positions, and the procedure is repeated. When time is called, the team with the least number on the score sheet is the winner.

BULLETIN BOARD

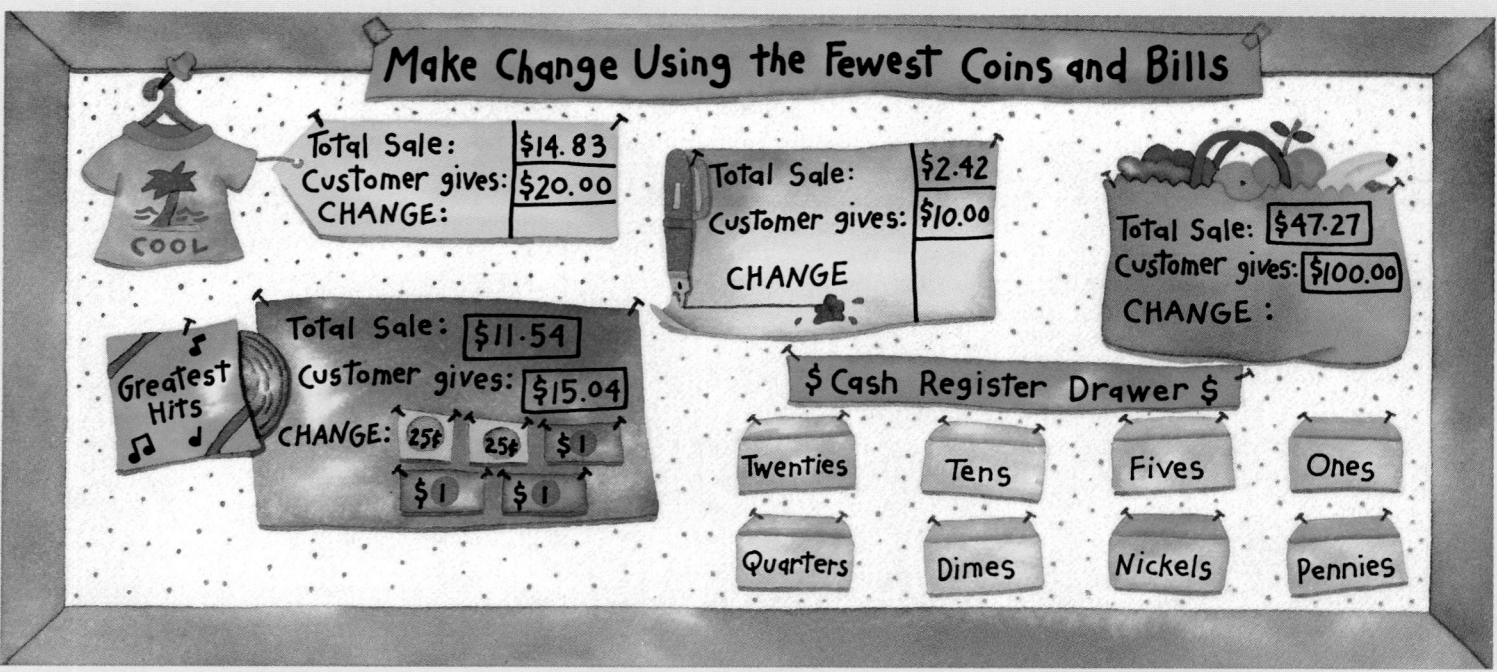

Have students collect pictures of merchandise from catalogs or magazines for use in a "store" display. Show the total sale and the amount of money the customer gives the clerk. Make "coins" and "bills" for the envelopes of the "cash register drawer." Students attach coins and bills with pushpins to show the change. Display new items regularly, and vary the number of specific coins or bills available.

Alternative Assessment

In addition to the paper and pencil tests available with this program, the following items can help you assess critical thinking as well as your students' ability to solve problems in a wide variety of ways.

Open-ended Problem

$2.63 + 1 + 0.37 + 3.5 + 2.5$
Viet used mental math to estimate the answer to the above exercise. 11 is his estimate.

He then added using paper and pencil and found 10.00 as an answer.

His friend used a calculator and got 10 for an answer.

Explain how the three answers could be correct.

Teacher Notes
In the mental math estimate Viet must have rounded 2.63 to 3, 1 to 1, 0.37 to 0, 3.5 to 4 and 2.5 to 3, thus his answer is 11.

The paper and pencil answer visually shows all the place values of the original exercise.

Calculators always add a decimal point at the end of a whole number and drop zeros after it.

All three answers are appropriate for the method used.

Group Writing Activity (See p. T24)

Let's see which group can remember more facts about how addition and subtraction of whole numbers and decimals are related.

Individual Writing Activity

Explain how you would help a third grade student understand how addition and subtraction of decimals relates to addition and subtraction of whole numbers. You may use words, diagrams, or symbols.

Portfolios

Portfolios can provide information about a student's growth in mathematical understanding over a period of time. They can help you make instructional decisions as well as become a vehicle to communicate with parents. The students' work involving the open-ended problem and writing activity suggested on this page along with work on the Write About It exercise on page 39, the Learning Log exercises on pages 45 and 53, and the Critical Thinking feature on page 49 could be included in portfolios.

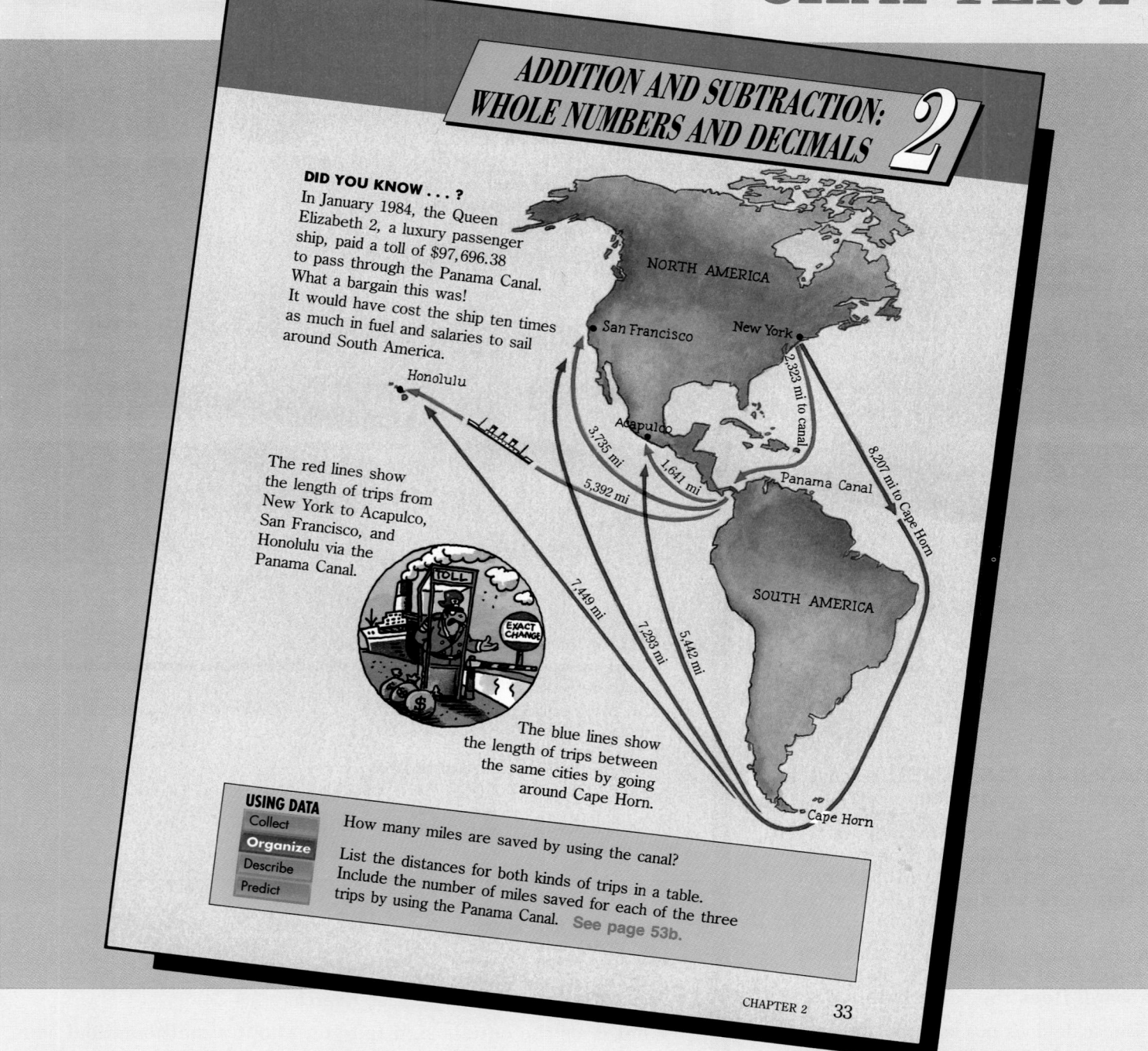

ADDITION AND SUBTRACTION:
WHOLE NUMBERS AND DECIMALS

DID YOU KNOW . . . ?
In January 1984, the Queen Elizabeth 2, a luxury passenger ship, paid a toll of $97,696.38 to pass through the Panama Canal. What a bargain this was! It would have cost the ship ten times as much in fuel and salaries to sail around South America.

NORTH AMERICA

San Francisco

New York

Honolulu

Acapulco

The red lines show the length of trips from New York to Acapulco, San Francisco, and Honolulu via the Panama Canal.

TOLL

EXACT CHANGE

3,735 mi

5,392 mi

1,641 mi

2,323 mi to canal

Panama Canal

8,207 mi to Cape Horn

7,449 mi

7,293 mi

5,442 mi

SOUTH AMERICA

The blue lines show the length of trips between the same cities by going around Cape Horn.

Cape Horn

USING DATA
Collect
Organize
Describe
Predict

How many miles are saved by using the canal?

List the distances for both kinds of trips in a table. Include the number of miles saved for each of the three trips by using the Panama Canal. See page 53b.

CHAPTER 2   33

Using the Chapter Opener

The purpose of this page is to involve the student in the use of real data much like that presented in newspapers and magazines.

To use this page as you begin the chapter, direct the students' attention to the data. You may wish to ask questions such as the following:

Which is the greater distance, New York to the Panama Canal, or San Francisco to the Panama Canal? *(San Francisco to the Panama Canal)* **How do you know?** *(2,323 < 3,735)*

What do you need to do to find the round trip mileage between New York and Honolulu by way of the Cape Horn route? *(Find the total mileage each way and double it.)*

What is the round trip mileage between New York and Honolulu by way of Cape Horn? *(31,312 miles)*

How many miles farther from the Panama Canal is San Francisco than is Acapulco? *(2,094 miles)*

In 1984, what would have been the cost of fuel and salaries for the *Queen Elizabeth II* to sail around South America? *($976,963.80)*

LESSON | 2-1

Lesson Organizer

Objective: Solve equations using replacement sets.

Prior Knowledge: Students should know basic facts and the four operations.

Error Analysis and Remediation: See page 53A.

Lesson Resources:
Practice Worksheet 2-1
Reteaching Worksheet 2-1
Enrichment Activity 2-1
Daily Review 2-1

 **Two-Minute Math**

Write the number.

5 more than 12 *(17)*

product of 4 and 6 *(24)*

36 divided by 9 *(4)*

14 decreased by 9 *(5)*

1 INTRODUCE

CONNECTING ACTIVITY

☑ **MATERIALS CHECKLIST:** balance scale, gram cubes, paper bag

1. Have a student place a number of gram cubes into the bag and put it on one side of the balance scale. Explain that n represents this unknown number of cubes, and write "$n = ?$" on the chalkboard.

2. Put five gram cubes on the other side of the scale and write "$n = 5$" on the chalkboard. **Does the scale balance?**

3. If the scale does not balance, have students guess the number of cubes that must be added (or taken away) to balance the scale. Have them record the transactions; for example, $n = 5 + 4 + 8 - 3 - 2$.

4. Discuss how an equation and a balance scale are alike.

WHEN YOUR STUDENTS ASK
★ **WHY AM I LEARNING THIS?** ★

You can connect this skill to real life through physics. Physicists write equations to explain how mechanical things work.

Variables and Equations

The scales at the right are balanced. An unknown mass called a **variable** is represented by the letter n. What is the mass in grams?

The **equation** below represents the problem.

What number added to 57 equals 95?

$$n + 57 = 95$$

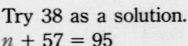

You can find the **solution** to this equation by substituting different values for n until you find one that makes the equation true.

Try 35 as a solution to the equation.
$n + 57 = 95$
$35 + 57 = 92$
$92 \neq 95$ ⟵ The two quantities are not equal.

35 is not a solution.

Try 38 as a solution.
$n + 57 = 95$
$38 + 57 = 95$
$95 = 95$ ⟵ The two quantities are equal.

So, $n = 38$. The unknown mass is 38 g. The solution to the equation is 38.

> **An equation is a mathematical sentence stating that two quantities are equal.**
>
> **The unknown number n is called the variable.**

Other examples:

4 times what number equals 36?
$4 \times k = 36$
$k = 9$ The solution is 9.

What number divided by 6 equals 8?
$b \div 6 = 8$
$b = 48$ The solution is 48.

■ GUIDED PRACTICE ■

Solve the equation.

1. What number minus 22 equals 11?
$x - 22 = 11$
$x = 33$

2. 35 divided by what number equals 5?
$35 \div p = 5$
$p = 7$

Is 4 the solution to the equation? Write *yes* or *no*.

3. $17 - x = 13$
yes

4. $b \times 6 = 21$
no

5. $8 - n = 12$
no

34   LESSON 2–1

---

2 TEACH

Pair students with partners for Exercises 28–34.

What does the equals sign tell you about a mathematical sentence? *(It states that the quantity on the right side of the equals sign is the same as the quantity on the left side.)*

How many numbers can be a solution for x in $x + 14 = 32$? *(One, 18)* **in $x + 0 = x$?** *(Any number)*

How can you tell if a number is a solution to an equation? *(Replace the variable with the number and check to see whether the statement is true.)*

> ### Chalkboard Examples
> $g + 12 = 27$ ($g = 15$)
> $x - 35 = 53$ ($x = 88$)
> $6 \times m = 42$ ($m = 7$)
> $72 \div y = 8$ ($y = 9$)

SUMMARIZE/ASSESS   **Explain how to show that 84 is a solution to $n - 46 = 38$.** *(Substitute 84 for n; since 84 makes the statement true, n = 84.)*

Is 7, 8, 9, 10, 11, or 12 a solution to the equation?

6. $24 + n = 33$ 9   **7.** $5 \times w = 45$ 9   **8.** $56 \div z = 8$ 7

9. $x - 9 = 3$ 12   **10.** $n + 14 = 25$ 11   **11.** $90 \div y = 9$ 10

Is the number in parentheses a solution? Write *yes* or *no.*

12. $17 + k = 35$ (18)   yes   **13.** $y - 13 = 28$ (15)   no   **14.** $12 \times n = 60$ (4)   no

15. $51 \div n = 3$ (17)   yes   **16.** $n \times 3 = 58$ (16)   no   **17.** $d - 34 = 19$ (53)   yes

Solve the equation.

18. $p - 14 = 6$ 20   **19.** $7 \times m = 28$ 4   **20.** $g + 15 = 23$ 8

21. $x \div 8 = 6$ 48   **22.** $r - 7 = 11$ 18   **23.** $88 = 8 \times t$ 11

*24. $23 + 7 + w = 42$ 12   ***25.** $4 \times n = 17 + 11$ 7   ***26.** $w \div 2 = 17 - 9$ 16

*27. CRITICAL THINKING The scales are *not* balanced. Name four numbers for n that allow you to keep $<$ or $>$ in the statement.
   a. $n + 5 < 8$ **b.** $n + 5 > 8$
   Answers will vary. Suggestions given.
   a. 6, 7, 8, 9   b. 14, 15, 16, 17

Work with a partner to solve.

28. Find a figure in one of the three diagrams at the right that has the same shape and direction as each of the following:
   $\vee, \triangle$, and $\sqsubset$.
   a. What number is inside each figure? 8, 7, 15 8
   b. Substituting these figures with their numbers, is the puzzle-equation $\vee + \triangle = \sqsubset$ true? yes

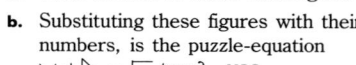

5	7
14	13

2	11	6
13	18	15
4	3	10

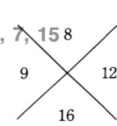

Find the unknown number using the three diagrams.

29. $> + n = <$ $n = 3$ **30.** $r \times \triangle = \sqsubset$ $r = 2$ **31.** $z \div \square = \sqcap$ $z = 12$

32. $a - \triangledown = \lrcorner$ $a = 16$ **33.** $q + \triangleright = \wedge$ $q = 3$ **34.** $m \div \llcorner = \sqcap$ $m = 18$

CHAPTER 2   **35**

MEETING INDIVIDUAL NEEDS

For Students Who Are . . .

Acquiring English Proficiency Review the meanings of *minus, divided by,* and *times,* and relate them to their mathematical symbols. For Exercises 27 and 28, pair each student with an English-proficient student.

Gifted and Talented Have students find solutions for multistep equations such as $2x + 3 = 15$ *(6)*, $3y/4 = 12$ *(16)*, and $a/5 - 1 = 6$ *(35)*.

Working 2 or 3 Grades Below Level Have students use pages 16–17 of the Skills Workbook for equations, ratio, proportion, and percent.

Today's Problem

A Fibonacci sequence is one in which each term is formed by adding the two immediately preceding terms. What are the next three terms in the following Fibonacci sequence?

1, 1, 2, 3, 5, 8, 13, . . . *(21, 34, 55)*

---

3 FOLLOW-UP

PRACTICE 2-1

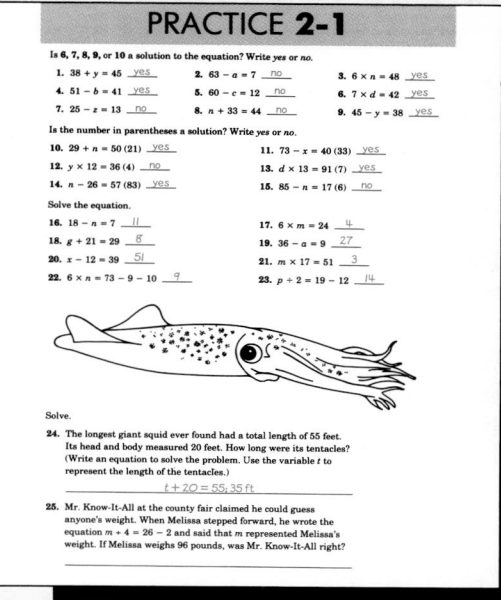

Is 6, 7, 8, 9, or 10 a solution to the equation? Write *yes* or *no.*

1. $38 + y = 45$ yes   **2.** $63 - a = 7$ no   **3.** $6 \times n = 48$ yes

4. $51 - b = 41$ yes   **5.** $60 - c = 12$ no   **6.** $7 \times d = 42$ yes

7. $25 - z = 13$ no   **8.** $n + 33 = 44$ no   **9.** $45 - y = 38$ yes

Is the number in parentheses a solution? Write *yes* or *no.*

10. $29 + n = 50$ (21) yes   **11.** $73 - x = 40$ (33) yes

12. $y \times 12 = 36$ (4) no   **13.** $d \times 13 = 91$ (7) yes

14. $n - 26 = 57$ (83) yes   **15.** $85 - n = 17$ (6) no

Solve the equation.

16. $18 - n = 7$ 11   **17.** $6 \times m = 24$ 4

18. $g + 21 = 29$ 8   **19.** $36 - a = 9$ 27

20. $x - 12 = 39$ 51   **21.** $m \times 17 = 51$ 3

22. $6 \times n = 73 - 9 - 10$ 9   **23.** $p \div 2 = 19 - 12$ 14

Solve.

24. The longest giant squid ever found had a total length of 55 feet. Its head and body measured 20 feet. How long were its tentacles? (Write an equation to solve the problem. Use the variable *t* to represent the length of the tentacles.)
$t + 20 = 55; 35\,\text{ft}$

25. Mr. Know-It-All at the county fair claimed he could guess anyone's weight. When Melissa stepped forward, he wrote the equation $m + 4 + 26 - 2$ and said that *m* represented Melissa's weight. If Melissa weighs 96 pounds, was Mr. Know-It-All right?

RETEACHING 2-1

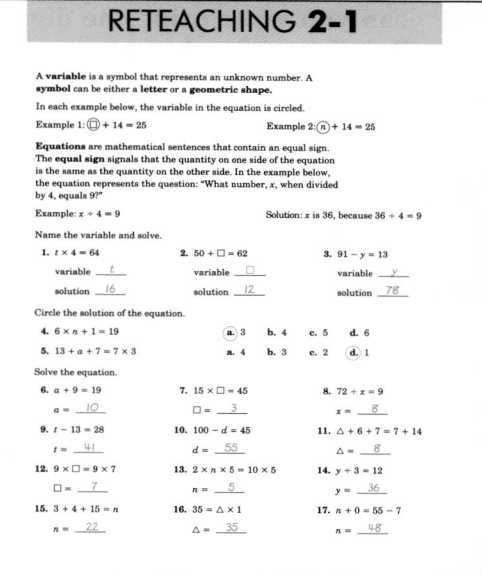

A **variable** is a symbol that represents an unknown number. A **symbol** can be either a **letter** or a **geometric shape.**

In each example below, the variable in the equation is circled.

Example 1: $\bigcirc + 14 = 25$ Example 2: $\widehat{n} + 14 = 25$

Equations are mathematical sentences that contain an equal sign. The **equal sign** signals that the quantity on one side of the equation is the same as the quantity on the other side. In the example below, the equation represents the question: "What number, x, when divided by 4, equals 9?"

Example: $x \div 4 = 9$ Solution: x is 36, because $36 \div 4 = 9$

Name the variable and solve.

1. $t \times 4 = 64$ **2.** $50 + \square = 62$ **3.** $91 - y = 13$
   variable t variable $\square$ variable y
   solution 16   solution 12   solution 78

Circle the solution of the equation.

4. $6 \times n + 1 = 19$ (a.) 3   b. 4   c. 5   d. 6

5. $13 + a + 7 = 7 \times 3$ a. 4   b. 3   c. 2   (d.) 1

Solve the equation.

6. $a + 9 = 19$ **7.** $15 \times \square = 45$ **8.** $72 \div x = 9$
   $a = $ 10 $\square = $ 3 $x = $ 8

9. $t - 13 = 28$ **10.** $100 - d = 45$ **11.** $\triangle + 6 + 7 = 7 + 14$
   $t = $ 41 $d = $ 55 $\triangle = $ 8

12. $9 \times \square = 9 \times 7$ **13.** $2 \times n \times 5 = 10 \times 5$ **14.** $y + 3 = 12$
   $\square = $ 7 $n = $ 5 $y = $ 36

15. $3 + 4 + 15 = n$ **16.** $35 = \triangle \times 1$ **17.** $n + 0 = 55 - 7$
   $n = $ 22 $\triangle = $ 35 $n = $ 48

ENRICHMENT 2-1

☑ **MATERIALS CHECKLIST:** Balance scale, gram cubes, other small objects

Have students work in pairs. Provide each pair with a balance scale. Instruct students to place 23 gram cubes on the right side of the scale. Then have them place 5 gram cubes in a bag labeled n and another 8 gram cubes on the left side. Ask students to write the equation they have modeled. [$n + 8 = 23$] Ask what they could remove from both sides of the balance to have n on one side and still balance the scale. Have students write the equations they have modeled. ($n + 8 - 8 = 23 - 8$; $n = 15$) Have them discuss how they could solve equations using inverse operations.

Lesson Organizer

Objective: Identify properties of addition.

Prior Knowledge: Students should know how to use the addition properties to compute mentally.

Error Analysis and Remediation: See page 53A.

Lesson Resources:
Practice Worksheet 2-2
Reteaching Activity 2-2
Enrichment Worksheet 2-2
Daily Review 2-2

Two-Minute Math

How many three-digit numbers can you write using the digits 0, 1, 2, and 3 only once in each number? *(18)*

1 INTRODUCE

CONNECTING ACTIVITY

☑ **MATERIALS CHECKLIST:** 10 slips of paper and small box for each group

1. Have students work in groups of four.

2. Have students write the numbers 0 through 9 on the slips of paper and place them in the box. Have each group member draw one number from the box.

3. Have students align the numbers as one-digit addends in three or four different ways and find the sum each time. **Did the sum change when you changed the order of the addends? Explain.** *(No; the order of addends does not affect the sum.)*

4. Discuss how grouping certain pairs of numbers, such as 4 and 6, make it easier to find the sum.

WHEN YOUR STUDENTS ASK
★ WHY AM I LEARNING THIS? ★

This skill will help you solve real life problems such as checking shopping receipts or keeping scores in games.

MATH AND GEOGRAPHY

Mental Math and Properties of Addition

Suppose you drive 74 mi from Baltimore to Harrisburg, 57 mi from Harrisburg to Reading, and then 43 mi from Reading to Allentown. What would be the total length of the trip?

You can find the sum mentally.

$57 + 43 = 100$ ← Look for easy combinations to add.

$74 + 100 = 174$ ← Add the rest.

The total trip is 174 mi.

Knowing the properties of addition can help you compute mentally.

THINK ALOUD Which property was used above? *associative property*

Commutative Property:
Changing the order of the addends does not change the sum.

In arithmetic: $74 + 57 = 57 + 74$ In algebra: $a + b = b + a$
  $131 = 131$

Associative Property:
Changing the grouping of the addends does not change the sum.

In arithmetic:
$(74 + 57) + 43 = 74 + (57 + 43)$
  $174 = 174$

In algebra:
$(a + b) + c = a + (b + c)$

Identity Property:
The sum of zero and any other number is that number.

In arithmetic: $74 + 0 = 74$ In algebra: $a + 0 = a$

36   LESSON 2-2

MULTICULTURAL NOTE

Lancaster, a city in southeastern Pennsylvania, is a center of Pennsylvania Dutch country, where many people live very simply. One group, the Amish, wear plain clothes and live and work as simply as possible.

2 TEACH

How can the words *commute* and *associate* help you remember the commutative and the associative property? *(Possible answer: Commute means "to go back and forth between the same two places"; associate means "to be with.")*

Is the associative property true for subtraction? Give an example to support your position. *(No, for example, [8 − 5] − 3 does not equal 8 − [5 − 3].)*

Chalkboard Examples

Add mentally.
$47 + 30 + 3$ *(80)*
$28 + 16 + 4 + 2$ *(50)*
$14 + 0 + 6 + 9$ *(29)*
$(237 + 193) + 7$ *(437)*

SUMMARIZE/ASSESS   Explain how using the addition properties makes mental addition easier. *(They help you order and group addends to add mentally.)*

Name the property shown by the equation.

1. $39 + 0 = 39$
   identity

2. $39 + 3 = 3 + 39$
   commutative

3. $(3 + 30) + 9 = 3 + (30 + 9)$
   associative

Look for tens as you add mentally. Name the property you used.

4. $13 + 19 + 17$
   49; commutative

5. $(58 + 16) + 14$
   88; associative

6. $23 + 17 + 0$
   40; identity

■ PRACTICE ■

Name the property shown by the equation.

7. $(125 + 84) + 16 = 125 + (84 + 16)$
   associative

8. $29 + 68 + 11 = 29 + 11 + 68$
   commutative

9. $0 + 1,225 = 1,225$
   identity

10. $(19 + 112) + 18 = 19 + (112 + 18)$
    associative

11. $64 + 48 + 16 = 64 + 16 + 48$
    commutative

12. $(17 + 3) + 6 = 6 + (17 + 3)$
    commutative

Use the properties to look for tens and add mentally.

13. $98 + 25 + 2$ **125**

14. $17 + 18 + 3 + 2$ **40**

15. $65 + 89 + 15$ **169**

16. $28 + (2 + 59)$ **89**

17. $(146 + 83) + 17$ **246**

18. $(26 + 91) + 9$ **126**

19. $22 + 0 + 36 + 8$ **66**

20. $(77 + 94) + 16 + 0$ **187**

21. $0 + 235 + 1,000 + 15$ **1,250**

22. $1,008 + (12 + 56)$ **1,076**

23. $164 + 119 + 106$ **389**

24. $72 + (18 + 135) + 0$ **225**

Write an equation to illustrate each addition property.   **Answers will vary. Suggestions given.**

25. commutative
    $2 + 3 = 3 + 2$

26. associative
    $(2 + 3) + 5 = 2 + (3 + 5)$

27. identity
    $23 + 0 = 23$

*28. **CRITICAL THINKING**   Evaluate the expressions.
    $(a - b) - c$ and $a - (b - c)$. Use $a = 10$, $b = 6$, and $c = 4$.
    What conclusion can you draw?   **The associative property does not hold
    for subtraction.**

■ PROBLEM SOLVING ■

Use the mileage table. Find the total distance
of each Pennsylvania driving tour mentally.

29. Reading to Philadelphia
    to Allentown to Hazelton **164 mi**

30. Scranton to Lebanon to
    Philadelphia to Allentown **247 mi**

31. Philadelphia to Allentown
    to Hazelton to Scranton **144 mi**

32. Lancaster to Reading to Allentown
    to Philadelphia to Lancaster
    195 mi

	Allentown	Philadelphia	Reading	Scranton
Allentown		54	43	74
Hazelton	48	99	53	42
Lancaster	76	66	32	127
Lebanon	63	87	31	106
Reading	43	62		95

MEETING INDIVIDUAL NEEDS

For Students Who Are . . .

Acquiring English Proficiency Discuss the meanings of *order*
and *grouping* in the definitions for the commutative and associative
properties.

Gifted and Talented Have students justify each step.

$(24 + 57) + 76$	$= (57 + 24) + 76$	(*commutative property*)
	$= 57 + (24 + 76)$	(*associative property*)
	$= 57 + 100$	(*substitution*)
	$= 157$	(*substitution*)

Working 2 or 3 Grades Below Level Have students who are having difficulty with basic addition facts use pages 4–31 of the Skills
Workbook for Whole Number Addition and Subtraction.

Today's Problem

A Fibonacci sequence is one in which each term is formed by adding
the two immediately preceding terms. What are the next three terms
in a Fibonacci sequence that begins with 1, 3? *(4, 7, 11)*

3 FOLLOW-UP

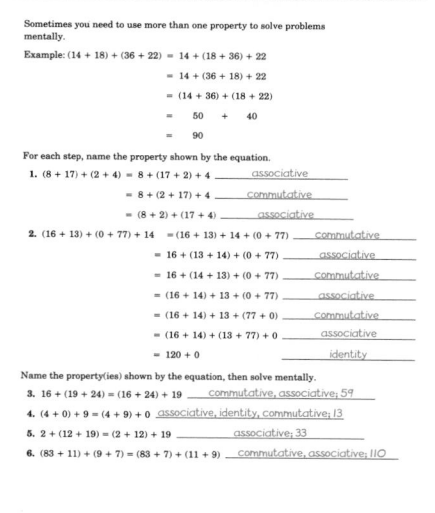
RETEACHING 2-2

☑ **MATERIALS CHECKLIST:** Color cubes

Write the following pairs of exercises on
the board: $13 + 18$ and $18 + 13$; $14 +
(6 + 5)$ and $(14 + 6) + 5$. Have the stu-
dents work in pairs to model the addends,
using different color cubes for each. Ask
the students to find the sums. [31; 31; 25;
25] Then ask them what is different about
the two exercises in each pair. [First pair:
order of addends is different; second pair:
grouping of addends is different.] Have
volunteers tell which pair illustrates the
commutative property [first] and which
pair illustrates the associative property
[second]. Ask students to use color cubes
to model additional exercises that illustrate these two properties.

Lesson Organizer

Objective: Discuss choosing mental math, paper and pencil, or calculator to solve problems.

Prior Knowledge: Students should understand how to use a calculator and apply mental math techniques.

Lesson Resources:
Practice Worksheet 2-3
Daily Review 2-3
Cooperative Problem Solving 1, Chapter 2

Two-Minute Math

Name the product of 9 × 9, 99 × 99, and 999 × 999. Then predict the product of 9,999 × 9,999.

(81; 9,801; 998,001; 99,980,001)

1 INTRODUCE

CONNECTING ACTIVITY

☑ **MATERIALS CHECKLIST:** United States wall map

Tell students that today they will read and discuss some interesting facts about a natural wonder called Rainbow Bridge. They will also decide on the best method of computation to use when solving problems. Show students the general location of Rainbow Bridge on the wall map. Ask whether any students have been to that part of the country. If so, have them describe their visit and share their impressions of southern Utah.

WHEN YOUR STUDENTS ASK
★ WHY AM I LEARNING THIS? ★

You can connect this skill to real life through advances in technology. It is important to understand when to use this advanced technology, calculators or computers, to solve problems.

Pick and Choose

Problem Solving: ***Choosing Mental Math, Paper and Pencil, or Calculator***

▮ READ ABOUT IT

Rainbow Bridge is the highest natural arch in the world. It is located on the Navajo Reservation in southern Utah.

In solving the problems in this lesson, you can use mental math, paper and pencil, or a calculator. You decide.

▮ TALK ABOUT IT

What method would you choose? Solve. **Choices will vary. Suggestions given.**

> **THINK ABOUT USING**
>
> **MENTAL MATH** when you know an easy way to compute in your head;
>
> **CALCULATOR** when the computation is complex;
>
> **PAPER AND PENCIL** when the computation is too hard for mental math and too easy for a calculator.

Rainbow Bridge spans 278 ft across a canyon. The highest point of the arch is 309 ft. The arch is 42 ft thick at the highest point.

1. What is the height of the tallest object that could fit under the bridge?
   m; 267 ft

2. How many times higher is the highest point of the arch than a 5 ft child? **c; 61.8 times**

3. How many times longer is the bridge's span than the longest side of your classroom? Measure to the nearest foot. **Answers will vary.**

4. Is it reasonable to say that the span of Rainbow Bridge is about 6 times longer than the 78 ft length of a tennis court? If *no*, explain.
   p; no; 278 ÷ 78 = 3.5

On May 30, 1910, President William Taft declared Rainbow Bridge and the 160 acres of land around it as a national monument.

5. How many years ago was this?
   m; Answers will vary. Suggestion given. Use 1991: 81 yr ago

6. How many days ago was this? (*Hint*: 1912 was a leap year.)
   c; Answers will vary. Suggestion given. Use January 1, 1991: 29,585 d ago

You can walk across the top of Rainbow Bridge, since the arch is 33 ft wide.

7. A Ping-Pong table is 5 ft wide. How many Ping-Pong tables would safely fit side-by-side across the top of the bridge? Explain.
   p; 6, because 6 × 5 = 30 ft

38   LESSON 2-3

> **MULTICULTURAL NOTE**
>
> The Navajo reservation around Rainbow Bridge is larger than Connecticut, Massachusetts, and New Jersey, combined. The Navajo traditionally called Rainbow Bridge "rainbow turned to stone."

(vertical text) MATH AND GEOGRAPHY

2 TEACH

☑ **MATERIALS CHECKLIST:** calculators

READ ABOUT IT Invite students to comment on and discuss how Rainbow Bridge was formed.

TALK ABOUT IT **What method of computation would you use to find the product of 32 and 5?** Have students give reasons for their choice of method. Point out that no one choice is "right" for everyone.

WRITE ABOUT IT Remind students that they can obtain several facts about Rainbow Bridge in Exercises 1-7 and on page 39.

SUMMARIZE/ASSESS **Explain what influences your decision to use mental math, paper and pencil, or a calculator to solve a problem.**

UTAH
Glen Canyon
Rainbow Bridge

ARIZONA

Grand Canyon

0   50 km   Flagstaff

Millions of years ago:

Now:

Bridge Creek

Rainbow Bridge is in southern Utah, about 150 mi north of Flagstaff, Arizona. Flowing water, wind, and changes in temperature over time have shaped the arch we call Rainbow Bridge. Although the bridge is

easily spotted, it is located in rough country. You can get to within a quarter mile of Rainbow Bridge via a 50-mi, or 2-h, boat ride on Bridge Creek. This creek is very small as it passes under the bridge.

▣ WRITE ABOUT IT

8. Use the information given on these two pages to write a math problem about Rainbow Bridge that can be solved using either mental math, paper and pencil, or calculator. Explain which method you chose and why. **Answers will vary. Suggestion given. How many times higher is the bridge than its span?**

---

3 FOLLOW-UP

PRACTICE 2-3

Read the passage below. To solve each problem you can use mental math, paper and pencil, or a calculator. For each problem, choose the method and solve.

The Grand Canyon is a long, wide, deep gorge in northern Arizona. It is a major tourist attraction in the southwestern United States. The canyon is about 278 mi long, and ranges in width at the top from 4 to 18 mi. At its deepest point, the canyon drops almost 6,000 ft. Grand Canyon National Park surrounds the canyon and contains approximately 645,000 acres. The United States Congress established the park in 1919.

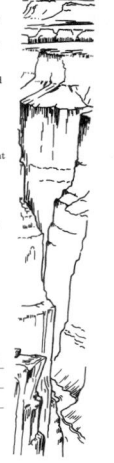

1. How tall would the tallest object that could fit in the canyon be? _____ m; 6,000 ft tall

2. How many 5-ft-tall people would it take — assuming they stand one atop another — to form a human chain from the deepest point in the canyon to the top? _____ m or p; 1,200 people

3. What is the difference between the greatest width and the shortest width of the canyon? _____ m; 14 mi

4. Is it reasonable to say that the depth of the canyon at its deepest point is about 375 times the length of a 16-ft-tall pine tree? Explain. p or c; yes; 16 × 375 = 6,000

5. Rainbow Bridge National Monument contains 160 acres. How many monuments of this size can fit inside Grand Canyon National Park? c; about 4,031 monuments

6. Use the information in the passage to write your own problem that can be solved using mental math, paper and pencil, or a calculator. Then solve your problem. Explain why you chose the method that you did.
   Answers will vary. A suggestion is given. If a horse walks 5 mi/h, how long would it take to travel the length of the canyon on horseback?

   Solution: _____ c; about 56 h

MEETING INDIVIDUAL NEEDS

For Students Who Are . . .

Acquiring English Proficiency Check students' comprehension as they choose the method and solve each problem. Make sure they understand the information about Rainbow Bridge on page 39.

Gifted and Talented Have students do library research on other natural arches. Ask students to record the lengths of spans, the heights of peaks, and other numerical data about the arches.

Working 2 or 3 Grades Below Level Have students draw a labeled diagram of Rainbow Bridge before beginning the exercises.

Having Reading Difficulties Pair each student with an able reader to discuss the problems and choose the methods.

Today's Problem

In a relay race the following times were recorded for the first three runners: 25 s, 23 s, 26 s. If the total of the times for the four runners was 98 s, what time should be recorded for the fourth runner?
$(98 - (25 + 23 + 26) = 98 - 74 = 24;\ 24\ s)$

Lesson Organizer

> **Objective:** Add whole numbers and decimals.

Prior Knowledge: Students should know basic addition facts and place value.

Error Analysis and Remediation: See page 53A.

Lesson Resources:
Practice Worksheet 2-4
Reteaching Worksheet 2-4
Enrichment Activity 2-4
Daily Review 2-4
Cooperative Investigations, Chapter 2

Two-Minute Math

Round 6,852.47 to the nearest tenth, whole number, ten, hundred, and thousand. *(6,852.5; 6,852; 6,850; 6,900; 7,000)*

1 INTRODUCE

CONNECTING ACTIVITY

☑ **MATERIALS CHECKLIST:** Teaching Aid 2, (Decimal Squares) for each student, two different colors of markers per student

Remind students that a whole decimal square equals 1.

1. Have students shade the decimal squares and write number sentences to represent these sums:

- 0.7 + 0.4 *(1.1)* (See below.)
- 35 hundredths and 25 hundredths *(0.60)*
- 0.362 + 0.145 *(0.507)*

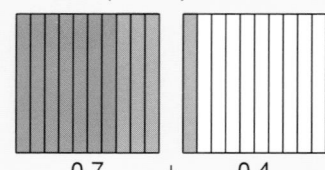

0.7   +   0.4

2. Call on students to explain their representations.

WHEN YOUR STUDENTS ASK
★ WHY AM I LEARNING THIS? ★

This skill will help you solve real life problems such as making a budget. To determine your monthly expenses, add the amounts spent for each group of items.

Adding Whole Numbers and Decimals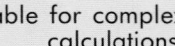

The human body needs riboflavin for growth and for healthy skin and eyes. The Recommended Daily Allowance (RDA) for riboflavin for 11- to 14-year-old boys is 1.6 mg.

Does the food listed at the right provide the daily amount of riboflavin recommended for 12-year-old boys?

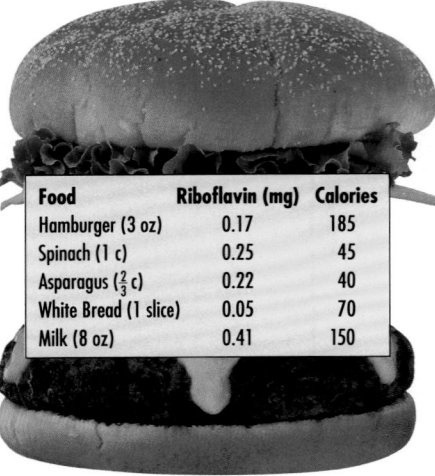

Food	Riboflavin (mg)	Calories
Hamburger (3 oz)	0.17	185
Spinach (1 c)	0.25	45
Asparagus ($\frac{2}{3}$ c)	0.22	40
White Bread (1 slice)	0.05	70
Milk (8 oz)	0.41	150

Add. Line up the decimal points.	Estimate to check your sum. Round to tenths.
1 2 0.17	0.2
0.25	0.3
0.22	0.2
0.05	0.1
+ 0.41	+ 0.4
1.10	1.2

> The estimate shows that the sum, 1.10, is reasonable.

Twelve-year-old boys need more than 1.10 mg of riboflavin each day.

Other examples:

$5,338 + 64 + 889$:

```
  5,338
     64
+   889
  6,291
```

$5.8 + 7.623 + 2$:

```
  5.800
  7.623
+ 2.000
 15.423
```
> You may need to annex zeros.

$\$15 + 28¢ + \$33.93$:

```
 $15.00
    .28
+ 33.93
 $49.21
```
> You may need to annex zeros.

THINK ALOUD How is adding whole numbers the same as adding decimals? How is it different? **For whole numbers and decimals, you line up numbers according to place value. For whole numbers, the decimal is not written.**

=== **GUIDED PRACTICE** ===

1. **THINK ALOUD** Explain how you would estimate to check the sum. **Answers will vary. Suggestions given.**

   a. $6,847 + 513$ $\approx 7,300$; Round to hundreds.
   b. $5.8 + 3.57$ ≈ 10; Round to ones.

Add. Check your answer.

2.
```
  537
+ 489
1,026
```

3.
```
 5.348
+2.769
 8.117
```

4. $72,265 + 4,892$ **77,157**
5. $16.007 + 0.19 + 30.118$ **46.315**

Calculators should be available for complex calculations.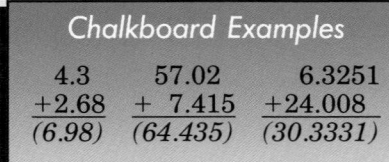

2 TEACH

☑ **MATERIALS CHECKLIST:** calculators

How can you check that your sum is reasonable? *(Round each addend to the same place and add; sum is reasonable if the estimate is close to the answer.)*

Why is it important to align decimals? *(to ensure that numbers of the same place value are added)*

Why should you estimate an answer when you are using a calculator? *(You can make errors when you enter numbers; an estimate tells you whether the answer displayed is reasonable.)*

> **Chalkboard Examples**
>
> ```
>   4.3        57.02      6.3251
> +2.68      + 7.415    +24.008
> (6.98)     (64.435)   (30.3331)
> ```

SUMMARIZE/ASSESS **Explain how to find the sum of decimal numbers in a problem written horizontally.** *(Write the numbers in a column with the decimal points aligned and annex zeros if needed.)*

Add. Use a calculator, mental math, or pencil and paper. Check your answer.

6. 5.6
    + 2.3
    ___
    7.9

7. 12.7
    + 3.2
    ___
    15.9

8. 253
    + 78
    ___
    331

9. 18
    + 7.9
    ___
    25.9

10. $1.34
    + 2.86
    _____
    $4.20

11. 8,516
    + 4,067
    _____
    12,583

12. 38.527
    + 5.964
    _____
    44.491

13. $58.48
    + 95.37
    _____
    $153.85

14. 7,530
    + 3,738
    _____
    11,268

15. 0.3
    + 2.373
    _____
    2.673

16. 5.8
    2.38
    + 4
    ____
    12.18

17. 2.136
    0.87
    + 2.64
    _____
    5.646

18. 73,591
    263,468
    + 793,244
    _____
    1,130,303

19. $32.62
    5.18
    + 21.63
    _____
    $59.43

20. $27.15
    .67
    + .52
    _____
    $28.34

21. 0.05 + 6.3 + 18 + 0.724   25.074

22. $13.07 + $6 + 72¢ + 45¢ $20.24

23. $14.34 + $17.90 + 4¢ + $20 $52.28

24. 0.0004 + 1.3 + 48.02 + 6.0006   55.321

25. a half million + 400 thousand   900,000

26. 3.4 million − 1.5 thousand   3,398,500

CALCULATOR   Use a calculator to find the sum.

27. $44.25 + $6.50 + 78¢ + $154.10 $205.63

28. $670 + $7.95 + $375.98 + $94 + 35¢ $1,148.28

NUMBER SENSE   Place decimal points in the addends to make each equation true.

29. 398 + 136 = 5.34
    3.98 + 1.36 = 5.34

30. 155 + 121 = 12.255
    0.155 + 12.1 = 12.255

31. **MENTAL MATH**   Which is greater:
    (4.2 + 3.8) + 9.7 or 9.7 + (4.1 + 3.8)?
    (4.2 + 3.8) + 9.7

*32. **CRITICAL THINKING**   What is the value of m in the equation $3.2 + 6.9 = 6 + 0.9 + m$? $m = 3.2$

PROBLEM SOLVING

CHOOSE   Choose estimation or a calculator to solve.   Choices will vary. Suggestions given.

33.   In a recent year, each person in the United States ate an average of 41.32 kg fresh vegetables, 37.29 kg canned vegetables, and 7,980 g frozen vegetables. How many kilograms of vegetables did each person average per year?
c; 86.59 kg

34.   An 11- to 14-year-old girl needs 2,200 calories daily. If a 12-year-old girl ate all the food in the table on page 40, about how many more calories would she need that day?
e; ≈1,700 calories

MEETING INDIVIDUAL NEEDS

For Students Who Are . . .

Acquiring English Proficiency   Pair students with an English-proficient student to discuss and solve Exercises 33 and 34.

Gifted and Talented   Have students solve equations such as 0.5 + 0.37 = n(0.87), n = 2.8 + 7.6 + 5(15.4), and n = 0.024 + 0.65(0.674).

Working 2 or 3 Grades Below Level   Have students use pages 32–57 of the Skills Workbook for Whole Number Addition and Subtraction and 34–39 of the Skills Workbook for Decimals.

Today's Problem

The first runner in a race finished in 5 min 48 s. The next runner came in 15 s later. What was the second runner's time?
(5 min 48 s + 15 s = 6 min 3 s)

3 FOLLOW-UP

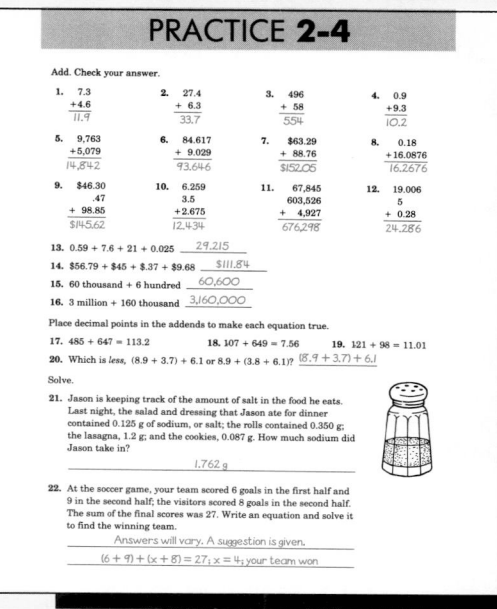

PRACTICE 2-4

Add. Check your answer.

1. 7.3
    +4.6
    ___
    11.9

2. 27.4
    + 6.3
    ____
    33.7

3. 496
    + 58
    ____
    554

4. 0.9
    +9.3
    ____
    10.2

5. 9,763
    +5,079
    _____
    14,842

6. 84.617
    + 9.029
    _____
    93.646

7. $63.29
    + 88.76
    _____
    $152.05

8. 0.18
    +16.0876
    _____
    16.2676

9. $46.30
    .47
    + 98.85
    _____
    $145.62

10. 6.259
    3.5
    +2.675
    _____
    12.434

11. 67,845
    603,526
    + 4,927
    _____
    676,298

12. 19.006
    5
    + 0.28
    _____
    24.286

13. 0.59 + 7.6 + 21 + 0.025   29.215

14. $56.79 + $45 + $.37 + $9.68 $111.84

15. 60 thousand + 6 hundred   60,600

16. 3 million + 160 thousand   3,160,000

Place decimal points in the addends to make each equation true.

17. 485 + 647 = 113.2   **18.** 107 + 649 = 7.56   **19.** 121 + 98 = 11.01

20. Which is *less*, (8.9 + 3.7) + 6.1 or 8.9 + (3.8 + 6.1)?   (8.9 + 3.7) + 6.1

Solve.

21. Jason is keeping track of the amount of salt in the food he eats. Last night, the salad and dressing that Jason ate for dinner contained 0.125 g of sodium, or salt; the rolls contained 0.350 g; the lasagna, 1.2 g; and the cookies, 0.087 g. How much sodium did Jason take in?
    1.762 g

22. At the soccer game, your team scored 6 goals in the first half and 9 in the second half; the visitors scored 8 goals in the second half. The sum of the final scores was 27. Write an equation and solve it to find the winning team.
    Answers will vary. A suggestion is given.
    (6 + 9) + (x + 8) = 27; x = 4; your team won

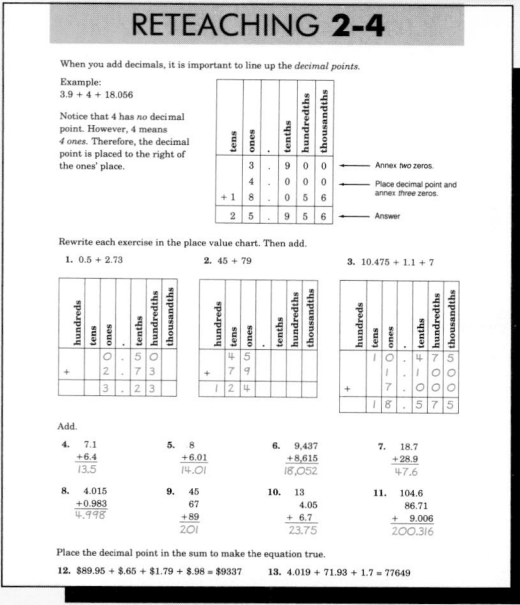

RETEACHING 2-4

When you add decimals, it is important to line up the *decimal points*.

Example:
3.9 + 4 + 18.056

Notice that 4 has *no* decimal point. However, 4 means *4 ones*. Therefore, the decimal point is placed to the right of the ones' place.

tens	ones		tenths	hundredths	thousandths	
	3	.	9	0	0	← Annex *two zeros*.
	4	.	0	0	0	← Place decimal point and annex *three zeros*.
+1	8	.	0	5	6	
2	5	.	9	5	6	← Answer

Rewrite each exercise in the place value chart. Then add.

1. 0.5 + 2.73

hundreds	tens	ones		tenths	hundredths	thousandths
		0	.	5	0	
+		2	.	7	3	
		3	.	2	3	

2. 45 + 79

hundreds	tens	ones		tenths	hundredths	thousandths
	4	5				
+	7	9				
1	2	4				

3. 10.475 + 1.1 + 7

hundreds	tens	ones		tenths	hundredths	thousandths
	1	0	.	4	7	5
		1	.	1	0	0
+		7	.	0	0	0
	1	8	.	5	7	5

Add.

4. 7.1
    +6.4
    ____
    13.5

5. 8
    +6.01
    ____
    14.01

6. 9,437
    +8,615
    _____
    18,052

7. 18.7
    +28.9
    ____
    47.6

8. 4.015
    +0.983
    _____
    4.998

9. 45
    67
    +89
    ___
    201

10. 13
    4.05
    + 6.7
    _____
    23.75

11. 104.6
    86.71
    + 9.006
    _____
    200.316

Place the decimal point in the sum to make the equation true.

12. $89.95 + $.65 + $1.79 + $.98 = $9337

13. 4.019 + 71.93 + 1.7 = 77649

ENRICHMENT 2-4

☑ MATERIALS CHECKLIST:
Newspapers

Tell the students that precipitation—rain, sleet, or snow—is measured in hundredths of inches. Have each student choose a city for which daily precipitation totals are given in the newspaper. Instruct the students to record the precipitation amounts for that city for two weeks. Then have the students record the total precipitation for the two-week period. Have students share and compare their findings.

Objective: Estimate sums using front-end estimation.

Prior Knowledge: Students should know how to add whole numbers and decimals.

Error Analysis and Remediation: See page 53A.

Lesson Resources:
Practice Worksheet 2-5
Reteaching Worksheet 2-5
Enrichment Activity 2-5
Daily Review 2-5

Two-Minute Math

Add mentally.

$3,000 + 4,000 + 5,000$ *(12,000)*

$1.5 + 0.2 + 0.3$ *(2.0)*

$900 + 200 + 70$ *(1,170)*

1 INTRODUCE

SYMBOLIC ACTIVITY

1. Write the names and prices of about ten items on the chalkboard.

2. Have students choose at least four items, round each price to the nearest dollar, and add. **Will the calculated total be greater than or less than your estimate?** *(Depends on whether all items are rounded up, all items are rounded down, or some are rounded up, some down.)*

3. Ask students to check their guesses by computation. Have students suggest ways they can improve their estimates.

WHEN YOUR STUDENTS ASK
★ WHY AM I LEARNING THIS? ★

This skill will help you solve real life estimation problems. For example, when you order items from a catalog, you can quickly determine about how much money you've spent.

Front-End Estimation

Super Sale!	Video Tape Recorder $219.45	Video Tapes $7.69 each
Double Cassette Portable Stereo $47.49	AM/FM Pocket Radios $16.29 each	Electronic Portable Typewriter $99.99
Answering Machine $59.29	Touch-Tone Phone $26.79	Compact Disc $14.95 each

Is $45 enough to buy a compact disc, a blank video tape, and an AM/FM pocket radio?

You can use **front-end estimation** to decide.

Add the front-end digits, the dollars.	Look at the cents. Find sums close to one dollar.	Add the dollars and cents.
$14.95 7.69 + 16.29 ——— $37	$14.95} about $1 7.69} about $1 + 16.29 ———— about $2	$37 + 2 —— $39

THINK ALOUD Can you tell if $45 is enough? **yes; $45 is enough.**

Other examples:

$4.58 } about $1
.39

2.16 } about $1
+ 1.91
————
$7 + about $2 ≈ $9

≈ means is about.

$42.00 } about $1
16.89

2.29 } about $1
+ .69
————
$60 + about $2 ≈ $62

━━━━━━━━━━━━━━ **GUIDED PRACTICE** ━━━━━━━━━━━━━━

Use front-end estimation to decide if the answer is reasonable.
Write *yes* or *no*.

1. Answer: $42.81
$37.98
2.88
+ 1.95
————
yes

2. Answer: $10.89
$1.36
.42
7.49
+ 3.62
————
no

3. Answer: $91.78
$74.41
3.55
.95
+ 2.87
————
no

---

2 TEACH

Would rounding each price to the nearest dollar and finding the total be as useful as the front-end method? Explain.

(It depends on the situation. Some amounts would round down, which could give an estimate that is less than the actual total.)

Chalkboard Examples

Estimate using the front-end method.
$2.58 + $.37 + $8.02 *($11)*
$71.42 + $6.56 + $.98 *($79)*
$49.94 + $18.73 + $30.29 *($99)*

SUMMARIZE/ASSESS **Explain how to use front-end estimation.** *(Find the sum of the front-end digits, look at the cents for amounts of money to find sums close to $1, and add this amount to the front-end estimate.)*

Use the front-end method to estimate.

4.	5.	6.	7.	8.
$6.24	$3.26	$50.93	$39.58	$8.44
4.81	.71	8.71	2.96	4.39
+ .98	+ 4.89	+ 30.29	+ .29	+ 5.21
≈$12	≈$9	≈$90	≈$43	≈$18

9.	10.	11.	12.	13.
$32.19	$47.92	$20.87	$73.52	$11.89
.98	31.03	6.21	3.74	7.02
6.01	.75	21.49	10.45	2.98
+ 12.76	+ 5.26	+ 4.52	+ .28	+ 28.01
≈$52	≈$85	≈$53	≈$88	≈$50

14. $4.12 + $8.79 + $8.94 + $.84 ≈$23

15. $.48 + $.39 + $.67 + $.35 ≈$2

16. $8.39 + $1.09 + $9.24 + $1.39 ≈$20

17. $74.99 + $8.98 + $2.34 + $6.67 ≈$93

*18. **CRITICAL THINKING** Round $8.45, $6.24, and $2.29 to the nearest dollar and estimate the sum. Now find the sum using the front-end method. Which answer is closer to the actual sum? Rounding method: $16; Front-end method: $17 The front-end method is closer.

PROBLEM SOLVING

Estimate. Use the prices on page 42.

19. Is $180 enough to buy 10 compact discs and 3 AM/FM pocket radios? no

20. What is the total cost of one each of the eight items on sale? ≈$500

21. You have $200 with which to buy an electronic typewriter, an answering machine, and a touch-tone phone. After purchasing these three items, do you have enough money left for a double cassette portable stereo? no

Mental Math

You can mentally check your change from the money you gave for a purchase by **counting on.** Suppose you buy a book for $7.75 and pay for it with a $10 bill:

$7.75 → $8.00 → $9; $10

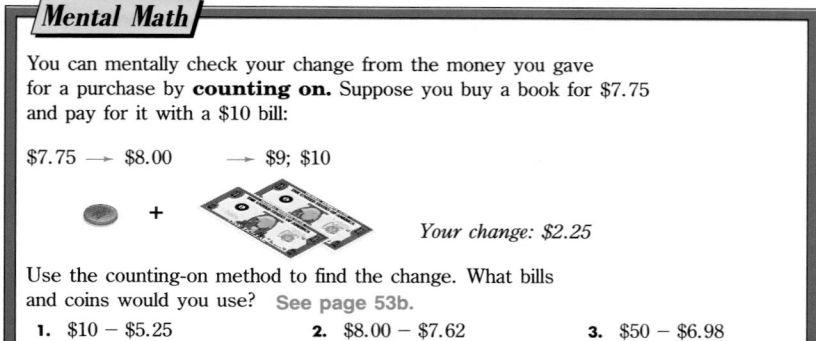

Your change: $2.25

Use the counting-on method to find the change. What bills and coins would you use? See page 53b.

1. $10 − $5.25

2. $8.00 − $7.62

3. $50 − $6.98

CHAPTER 2   43

---

3 FOLLOW-UP

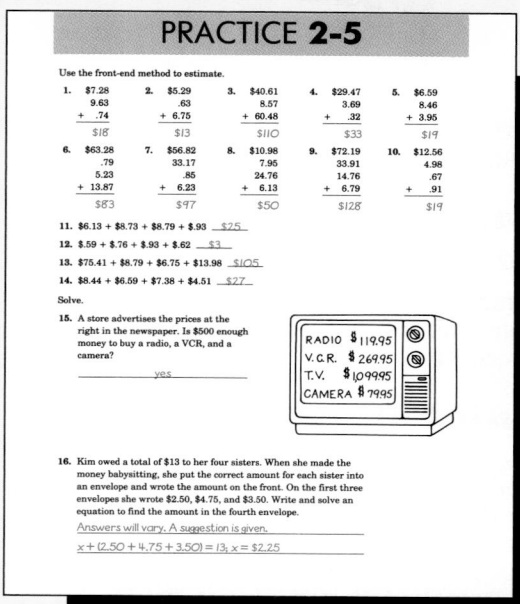

PRACTICE 2-5

Use the front-end method to estimate.

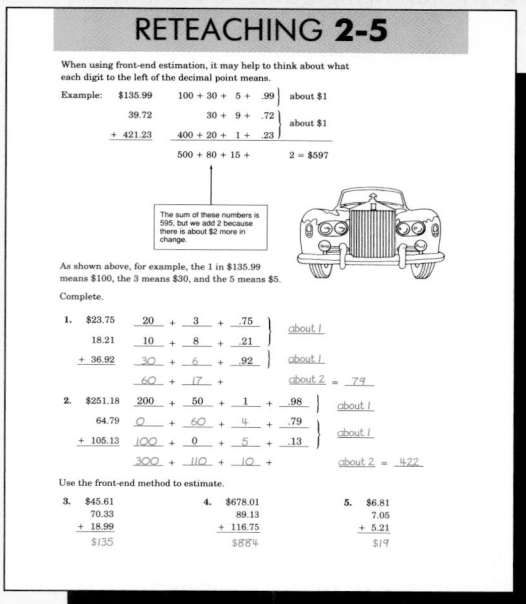

ENRICHMENT 2-5

☑ **MATERIALS CHECKLIST:** Store receipts

Have students work in groups of three or four. Cut the totals from several grocery store receipts. Give one member of each group the itemized part of a receipt. Allow 30 sec for the student to mentally estimate the total and write it down. The next student then comes up with an estimate in 30 sec. When all group members have made an estimate, provide the actual totals. Whose estimate was closest to the actual total?

MEETING INDIVIDUAL NEEDS

For Students Who Are . . .

Acquiring English Proficiency Pair students with an English-proficient student to discuss and solve the Problem Solving and Mental Math exercises.

Gifted and Talented Have students write three problems using the items and prices in the chart on page 42. Ask students to exchange papers and estimate solutions.

Working 2 or 3 Grades Below Level For Exercises 4–17 have students use braces to indicate the sums of cents that are close to one dollar, as done in the examples.

Today's Problem

The fine for not returning a carpet cleaner on time is $5 for the first day and $2 for every additional day. If a carpet cleaner is returned 5 days late, what is the fine? *(Fine: $5 + 4 × $2 = $13)*

MIDCHAPTER Checkup

The midchapter checkup provides a way for you to check students' understanding of the skills taught in the first half of the chapter.

Language and Vocabulary

Some key language and vocabulary ideas from the first half of the chapter are reinforced here.

Quick Quiz

The quiz provides a means of evaluating students' understanding of the objectives for the first half of the chapter. Page references are given so that students can check back to where the skill was taught.

Use the following guide to score the quick quiz.

Score	Percent
10	100%
9	90
8	80
7	70
6	60
5	50
4	40
3	30
2	20
1	10

Use this chart to identify the Management Objective tested.

Items	Management Objective	Pages
1–5	**2A** Use replacement and properties of addition to solve equations.	34–37
6–9	**2B** Add whole numbers and decimals.	40–41; 42–43
10	**2D** Problem Solving: Choose the method.	38–39

MIDCHAPTER CHECKUP

LANGUAGE & VOCABULARY

Decide whether the equation is always true. Write *yes* or *no*. If *yes*, tell whether the *Commutative Property*, the *Associative Property*, or the *Identity Property* proves it. If *no*, give an example that shows the equation is not true.

1. $x + 73 = 73 + x$ yes; commutative
2. $r - 18 = 18 - r$ no
3. $0 + m = m$ yes; identity
4. $(21 + b) + 97 = 21 + (b + 97)$ yes; associative

QUICK QUIZ ✓

Solve. *(pages 34–35)*
1. $18 + n = 25$ 7
2. $34 - c = 19$ 15
3. $y - 9 = 8$ 17

Use the properties to look for tens and add mentally. *(pages 36–37)*
4. $11 + 49 + 16 = \blacksquare$ 76
5. $2,608 + (64 + 12) = \blacksquare$ 2,684

Add. Check your answer. *(pages 40–41)*
6. $62.37 + .055 + 1.679 = \blacksquare$ 64.104
7. $49,365 + 4,936 + 493 = \blacksquare$ 54,794

Use the front-end method to estimate. *(pages 42–43)*   Accept reasonable estimates.
8. $\$29.23 + 2.65 + 11.08$ \$43
9. $\$109.39 + \$70.70 + \$21.98$ \$202

Solve. *(pages 38–39)*
10. The Grand Canyon in Arizona took about 8 million years to form. It is 217 mi long. The first recorded boat trip through the canyon took place in 1869.

    a. In what year did the first recorded boat trip through the Grand Canyon take place?   1869
    b. What operation would you use to find the length of time between 1869 and any other year?   subtraction
    c. How many years ago did the first recorded boat trip through the Grand Canyon take place?   Answers will vary. Suggestion given. 1992–1869 = 123 yr

Write the answers in your learning log.   Answers will vary.

1. Describe three kinds of mistakes students might make when adding decimals.

2. Which do you think is the more accurate method for estimating sums of money—rounding to the nearest dollar or front-end estimation? Explain.

DID YOU KNOW . . . ? The population of the American colonies in 1620 was 350. Compare that number with the number of people who live in your city or town.   **Check students' work.**

The symbols (in parentheses) and some spaces have been left out of the equation. Insert the symbols and add some spaces to make the equation true.

Example: $28213 = 17 \ (+,-)$
$28 + 2 - 13 = 17$

1. $92813 = 24 \ (+,-)$ $9 + 28 - 13 = 24$
2. $15311 = 56 \ (\times, +)$
   $15 \times 3 + 11 = 56$
3. $10527 = 110 \ (-,+)$ $105 - 2 + 7 = 110$
4. $426134 = 16 \ (\div, +, -)$
   $42 \div 6 + 13 - 4 = 16$

CHAPTER 2   45

Learning Log

These are suggestions for writing about some topics taught so far in the chapter. The students keep their Learning Logs from the beginning of the school year through the end.

Math America

A mathematical skill that students have learned is related to an interesting fact about the United States.

Bonus

Students are given an opportunity to solve a challenge-type problem like a puzzle or a nonroutine problem.

Lesson Organizer

Objective: Subtract whole numbers.

Prior Knowledge: Students should know basic subtraction facts and understand place value concepts.

Error Analysis and Remediation: See page 53A.

Lesson Resources:
Practice Worksheet 2-6
Reteaching Worksheet 2-6
Enrichment Activity 2-6
Daily Review 2-6
Cooperative Connections, Chapter 2

Two-Minute Math

The sum of the ages of two children is 11 years. In 5 years one child will be twice as old as the other. How old are they now? *(2 and 9)*

1 INTRODUCE

SYMBOLIC ACTIVITY

1. Write on the chalkboard: $480 - 324 = n$. Give students 15 seconds to estimate and record the answer. Have students discuss their estimates and methods.

2. Repeat the activity using these examples:

- $7,582 - 2,043 = n$
- $24,181 - 15,920 = n$
- $34,005 - 8,790 = n$

(Answers may vary.)

WHEN YOUR STUDENTS ASK
★ WHY AM I LEARNING THIS? ★

You can connect subtraction to real life situations. When retail salespeople take inventory, they must subtract the number of items sold from the number they started with.

MATH AND SCIENCE

Subtracting Whole Numbers

The diagram shows the three greatest depths in the Pacific and Atlantic oceans. How much deeper is the Mariana Trench than the Puerto Rico Trench?

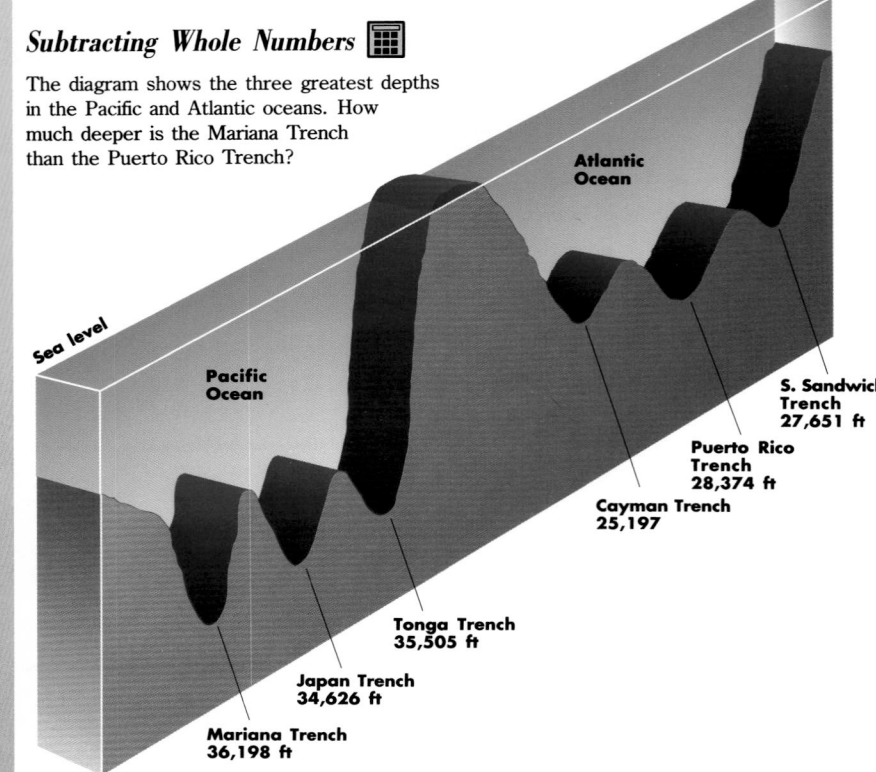

Atlantic Ocean

Pacific Ocean

Sea level

S. Sandwich Trench 27,651 ft

Puerto Rico Trench 28,374 ft

Cayman Trench 25,197

Tonga Trench 35,505 ft

Japan Trench 34,626 ft

Mariana Trench 36,198 ft

Subtract to find the difference.

$$\begin{array}{r} {\scriptstyle 2\ 15\ \ 11} \\ 3\,6\,,1\,9\,8 \\ -\ 2\,8\,,3\,7\,4 \\ \hline 7\,,8\,2\,4 \end{array}$$

Add to check.

$$\begin{array}{r} 28,374 \\ +\ 7,824 \\ \hline 36,198 \end{array}$$

The Mariana Trench is 7,824 ft deeper than the Puerto Rico Trench.

THINK ALOUD Explain how you would estimate the difference above.
Round to thousands and subtract.

Other examples:

$3,000 - 111$:

$$\begin{array}{r} {\scriptstyle 2\ \ 9\ 9\ 10} \\ 3\,,0\,0\,0 \\ -\ \ \ 1\,1\,1 \\ \hline 2\,,8\,8\,9 \end{array}$$

Check:
$$\begin{array}{r} 2,889 \\ +\ \ \ 111 \\ \hline 3,000 \end{array}$$

$7,901 - 5,832$:

$$\begin{array}{r} {\scriptstyle 8\ 9\ 11} \\ 7\,,9\,0\,1 \\ -\ 5\,,8\,3\,2 \\ \hline 2\,,0\,6\,9 \end{array}$$

Check:
$$\begin{array}{r} 2,069 \\ +\ 5,832 \\ \hline 7,901 \end{array}$$

46   LESSON 2-6

Calculators should be available for complex calculations.

2 TEACH

☑ MATERIALS CHECKLIST: calculators

Why is addition used to check subtraction; *(Addition and subtraction are inverse operations.)*

When would you check an answer by using an inverse operation as opposed to using estimation? *(When you need to know that the answer is correct, use an inverse operation. When you want to be sure an answer is reasonable, use estimation.)*

Chalkboard Examples		
48	923	202
−23	−637	− 84
(25)	(286)	(118)
$3,001 - 683$ *(2,318)*		

SUMMARIZE/ASSESS   **When do you rename in subtraction?**
(When the value of the digit in the position you are subtracting from is less than the value of the digit you are subtracting)

Find the difference. Check your answer.

1.   4,387
        − 159
        4,228

2.   16,000
        − 2,729
        13,271

3.   8,751 − 5,326
         3,425

4.   10,002 − 3,908
         6,094

5. What is the difference if 4 thousands and 5 tens are subtracted from 83,456?
79,406

Subtract and check. Use a calculator, mental math, or pencil and paper.

6.   874   **7.**   754   **8.**   930   **9.**   530   **10.** 6,482
        − 58   − 86   − 483   − 207   − 3,294
        816   **668**   **447**   **323**   **3,188**

11. 4,002   **12.** 5,306   **13.** 17,352   **14.** 52,003   **15.** 800,000
        − 3,581   − 3,094   − 5,795   − 15,265   − 752,804
        421   **2,212**   **11,557**   **36,738**   **47,196**

16. 415 − 98 **317**   **17.** 700 − 289 **411**   **18.** 4,052 − 208 **3,884**

19. 21,014 − 9,038 **11,976**   **20.** 8,009 − 4,968 **3,041**   **21.** 287,351 − 9,882 **277,469**

MIXED REVIEW Compute.

22. 45 + 3.55   **23.** 2,456 + 398   **24.** 5,006 − 359   **25.** 0.7 + 95.6   **26.** 0.93 + 4.2
     48.55   **2,854**   **4,647**   **96.3**   **5.13**
27. 85 + 699   **28.** 3,214 − 78   **29.** 956 + 788   **30.** 2.3 + 4.78   **31.** 872 − 345
     784   **3,136**   **1,744**   **7.08**   **527**

***32. CRITICAL THINKING** If 6,482 − 3,294 is 3,188,
what is 7,482 − 4,294? **3,188**

ESTIMATE Estimate the difference. **Answers will vary. Suggestions given.**

33. 2,148 − 966 **≈1,000**   **34.** 18,253 − 6,836   **35.** 45,238 − 32,657
                                      ≈ 11,000   **≈12,000**

36. CALCULATOR Explain how you can find the difference
between 38,320,574,731 and 24,879,397,856 with a calculator.
Split the 2 numbers before the millions and subtract in 2 parts.

 Use the graph on page 46.   **Choices will vary. Suggestions given.**
Choose estimation or a calculator to solve.

37. There are 5,280 ft in 1 mi. Is the
Mariana Trench about 6 mi
or 7 mi deep? **e; ≈7 mi**

38. How many feet deeper is the Tonga
Trench than the Sandwich Trench?
                        c; 7,854 ft

39. Mt. Everest is 29,028 ft high. If it
were on the bottom of the Puerto Rico
Trench, would its peak be above the
ocean's surface? If so, by how much?
        c; yes; 654 ft

40. Which is farther away from sea
level, Mt. McKinley or the Cayman
Trench? by how much?
(Mt. McKinley is 20,320 ft high.)
   c; Cayman Trench; 4,877 ft

MEETING INDIVIDUAL NEEDS

For Students Who Are . . .

Acquiring English Proficiency Explain how to read the graph on
page 46. Ask students questions such as: **What is the depth of the
Tonga Trench? Which is deeper, the Cayman Trench or the
Puerto Rico Trench?**

Gifted and Talented Assign the technology lesson on page 58.

Working 2 or 3 Grades Below Level Have students who are having difficulty with basic subtraction facts or subtraction of whole
numbers use pages 58–117 of the Skills Workbook for Whole Number Addition and Subtraction.

Today's Problem

Yaeko bought some pencils and received $.97 in change. In change
she was given 10 coins in a combination of quarters, dimes, nickels,
and pennies. How many of each denomination did Yaeko receive?
(2 quarters, 3 dimes, 3 nickels, and 2 pennies)

3 FOLLOW-UP

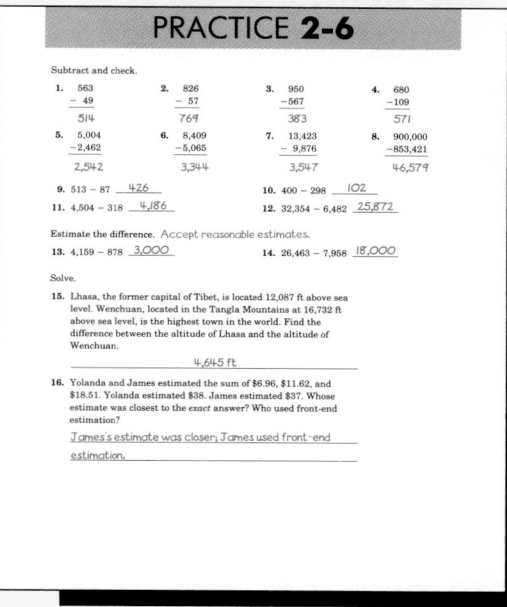

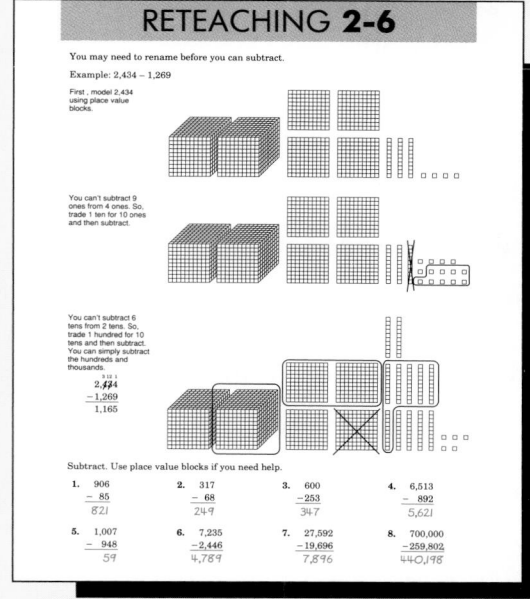

ENRICHMENT 2-6

☑ **MATERIALS CHECKLIST:** Number
cubes for each pair of students

Have students work in groups of four, and
in pairs within each group. Provide each
pair with a number cube labeled 0–5. Instruct partners to take turns rolling the
number cube four times. Students use the
numbers they roll to write the greatest
four-digit number possible and the least
four-digit number possible. Each pair then
subtracts its two numbers and compares
the difference with that of the other pair
of students in the group. The pair with
the greatest difference gets 1 point. Repeat
for other four-, five-, and, six-digit
numbers.

Lesson Organizer

Objective: Subtract decimals.

Prior Knowledge: Students should understand place value concepts and be able to subtract whole numbers.

Error Analysis and Remediation: See page 53A.

Lesson Resources:
Practice Worksheet 2-7
Reteaching Activity 2-7
Enrichment Worksheet 2-7
Daily Review 2-7
Cooperative Problem Solving 2, Chapter 2

Two-Minute Math

4 tenths + 3 hundredths =
3 tenths + □ hundredths *(13)*
1 thousandth + 4 ten-thousandths =
□ ten-thousandths *(14)*

1 INTRODUCE

SYMBOLIC ACTIVITY

1. Write: Kim had $6.00 and spent $2.75. **Did Kim have more than or less than $4 left? How do you know?** *(Less than $4; $6 less about $3 is $3.)* Have students calculate the difference. *($3.25)*

2. Repeat with $7.48 − $2.79. *(more than $4; $4.69)*

WHEN YOUR STUDENTS ASK
★ WHY AM I LEARNING THIS? ★

You can connect this skill to real life situations. Suppose you gave a clerk a $10 bill to pay for a $7.99 item. You can use subtraction with decimals to make sure you got the correct change.

(MATH AND SOCIAL STUDIES)

Subtracting Decimals

The amounts of silver mined by six countries in a recent year is represented in the bar graph. How many more kilograms of silver did Mexico mine than Canada?

If you know how to subtract whole numbers, you can make a **MATH CONNECTION** to subtract decimals.

Line up the decimal points.	Add to check.
$\overset{1}{2}.146$ $- 1.210$ $\overline{0.936}$	0.936 $+ 1.210$ $\overline{2.146}$

Mexico mined 0.936 million kilograms, or 936,000 kg, more than Canada.

THINK ALOUD Explain how to estimate the difference above. **Round to the nearest whole number and then subtract.**

Other examples:

Subtract 0.774 from 34.

Annex zeros.	Check:
$\overset{3 \quad 9\ 9\ 10}{34.000}$ $- \quad 0.774$ $\overline{33.226}$	33.226 $+ \ 0.774$ $\overline{34.000}$

59.08 − 40.29:

	Check:
$\overset{8 \quad 9\ 18}{59.08}$ $- 40.29$ $\overline{18.79}$	18.79 $+ 40.29$ $\overline{59.08}$

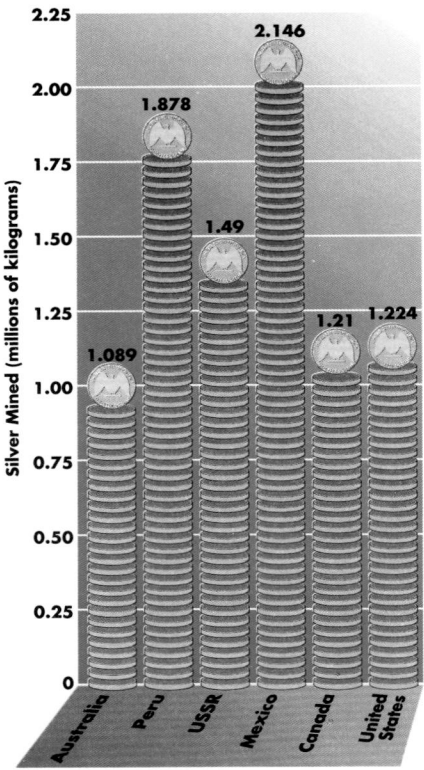

Leading Silver Mining Countries

Silver Mined (millions of kilograms)

Australia 1.089 · Peru 1.878 · USSR 1.49 · Mexico 2.146 · Canada 1.21 · United States 1.224

GUIDED PRACTICE

Subtract and check.

1. 7.64
  − 5.32
  2.32

2. $15.68
  − 3.92
  $11.76

3. 89.35 − 34.5
  54.85

4. 47 − 0.513
  46.487

5. THINK ALOUD Explain why 52 and 52.000 are the same number. 52.000 is 52 and zero thousandths.

48 LESSON 2-7

Calculators should be available for complex calculations.

2 TEACH

☑ MATERIALS CHECKLIST: calculators, Math Connection Transparency

Display the transparency. Have students fill in the spaces and discuss the math connection. (See student pages.)

How is subtracting decimals similar to subtracting whole numbers? *(Numbers in the same place are subtracted and renaming is performed when necessary.)*

How do you write a whole number as a decimal? *(Place a decimal point to the right of the ones' digit; write a zero in each decimal place as needed.)*

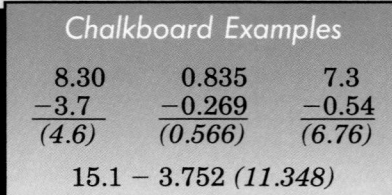

Chalkboard Examples

8.30 −3.7 *(4.6)*	0.835 −0.269 *(0.566)*	7.3 −0.54 *(6.76)*

15.1 − 3.752 *(11.348)*

SUMMARIZE/ASSESS **Explain how to subtract a number that has three decimal places from a number that has one decimal place.** *(Annex two zeros and rename to subtract.)*

Subtract and check. Use a calculator, mental math, or pencil and paper.

6.	8.94 − 4.33 4.61	**7.**	18.678 − 4.378 14.300	**8.**	74 − 0.664 73.336	**9.**	800.34 − 427.48 372.86	**10.**	8.072 − 2.685 5.387
11.	53.7 − 0.159 53.541	**12.**	$73.60 − 38.80 $34.80	**13.**	3.058 − 0.64 2.418	**14.**	21.7 − 8.52 13.18	**15.**	7.9 − 6.05 1.85
16.	0.546 − 0.159 0.387	**17.**	9 − 7.293 1.707	**18.**	$60.02 − 46.79 $13.23	**19.**	3,500 − 873.24 2,626.76	**20.**	3.00064 − 2.38476 0.61588

21. 5.7 − 2.852 **2.848**   **22.** 8.064 − 3.79 **4.274**   **23.** $7.05 − $3.28 **$3.77**

*24. 2 million − 1.2 million **0.8 million**   *25. 5 million − 2.25 million **2.75 million**

MIXED REVIEW Compute.

26. 423.8 + 1.75   **27.** 513 − 245   **28.** 99 + 864   **29.** 0.7 − 0.09
  425.55   **268**   **963**   **0.61**
30. 0.04 − 0.006   **31.** 5,246 + 999   **32.** 12.76 + 295 **33.** 12 − 3.7
  0.034   **6,245**   **307.76**   **8.3**

ESTIMATE Estimate the difference. **Answers will vary. Suggestions given.**

34. 41.852 − 3.798 ≈38   **35.** 54.6 − 0.809 ≈54   **36.** 0.14 − 0.12881 ≈ 0.01

CHOOSE Use the graph on page 48.
Choose estimation or a calculator to solve. **Choices will vary. Suggestions given.**

37. Which country mined about one and a half million kilograms of silver?
  e; USSR

38. What was the total number of million kilograms of silver mined by the six countries?
  c; 9.037 million kg

39. CREATE YOUR OWN Write a math problem about the leading silver mining countries. Give it to a friend to solve. **Check students' work.**

Critical Thinking

With a partner, think of a strategy to identify which decimals in the box were subtracted from which to obtain each difference below. **Suggestion given. Round to the nearest tenth.**

0.624	0.906
	0.83
0.468	0.682

  5. 0.682 − 0.624

1. 0.438   **2.** 0.148   **3.** 0.362   **4.** 0.282   **5.** 0.058
  0.906 − 0.468   0.83 − 0.682   0.83 − 0.468   0.906 − 0.624

6. Can you name other strategies that would work? Explain.

Answers will vary. Suggestions given. Narrow the possible pairs by examining the thousandths digits.

MEETING INDIVIDUAL NEEDS

For Students Who Are . . .

Acquiring English Proficiency Discuss how to read the bar graph on page 48. Ask: **Which country mines the most silver?** *(Mexico)* **the least?** *(Australia)* Demonstrate how the numbers in the graph are written in standard form. *(1.089 million kg = 1,089,000 kg)*

Gifted and Talented Have students solve equations with decimals such as 6.35 − 2.417 = n *(3.933)*, n = 12 − 8.309 *(3.691)*, and n = 0.7 − 0.123 *(0.577)*.

Working 2 or 3 Grades Below Level Have students use pages 40–45 of the Skills Workbook for decimals.

Today's Problem

Use estimation to solve this problem: If Theo makes $3.93 an hour and works 39 hours, will he have earned enough money to buy a stereo radio/cassette player that costs $160? *(Think: 40 h × $4.00/h = $160, so 39 h × $3.93/h would be less than $160. He will not have earned enough money.)*

---

3 FOLLOW-UP

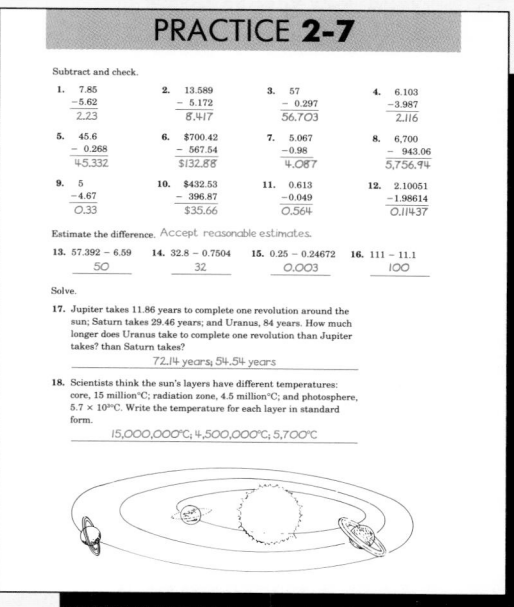

PRACTICE 2-7

Subtract and check.

1. 7.85 − 5.62 2.23	**2.** 13.589 − 5.172 8.417	**3.** 57 − 0.297 56.703	**4.** 6.103 − 3.987 2.116
5. 45.6 − 0.268 45.332	**6.** $700.42 − 567.54 $132.88	**7.** 5.067 − 0.98 4.087	**8.** 6,700 − 943.06 5,756.94
9. 5 − 4.67 0.33	**10.** $432.53 − 396.87 $35.66	**11.** 0.613 − 0.049 0.564	**12.** 2.10051 − 1.98614 0.11437

Estimate the difference. Accept reasonable estimates.

13. 57.392 − 6.59 **50**   **14.** 32.8 − 0.7504 **32**   **15.** 0.25 − 0.24672 **0.003**   **16.** 111 − 11.1 **100**

Solve.

17. Jupiter takes 11.86 years to complete one revolution around the sun; Saturn takes 29.46 years; and Uranus, 84 years. How much longer does Uranus take to complete one revolution than Jupiter takes? than Saturn takes?
  72.14 years; 54.54 years

18. Scientists think the sun's layers have different temperatures: core, 15 million°C; radiation zone, 4.5 million°C; and photosphere, 5.7 × 10³°C. Write the temperature for each layer in standard form.
  15,000,000°C; 4,500,000°C; 5,700°C

RETEACHING 2-7

☑ **MATERIALS CHECKLIST:** Decimal squares, colored pencils

Write the following exercises on the board: 5.25 − 4.30; 2.072 − 0.19. Have students work in pairs. One student represents the first number in each exercise by using a colored pencil to shade a decimal square. Using a different color pencil on the same decimal square, the other student then shows the subtraction by shading the number of squares that represent the number being subtracted. Help students see that the number of squares that have been shaded only once is the answer.

ENRICHMENT 2-7

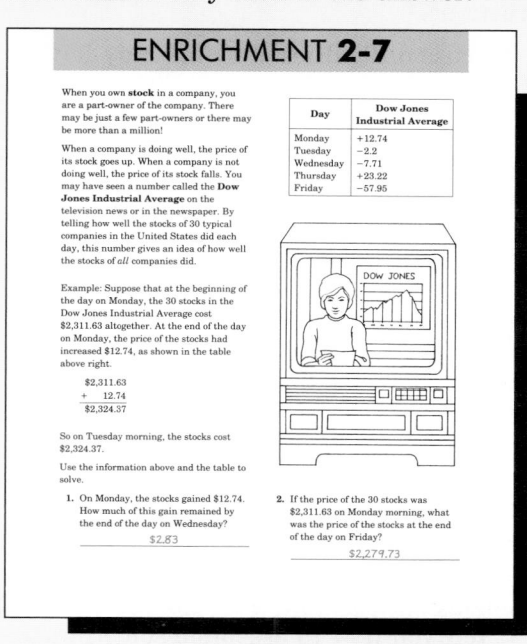

When you own **stock** in a company, you are a part-owner of the company. There may be just a few part-owners or there may be more than a million!

When a company is doing well, the price of its stock goes up. When a company is not doing well, the price of its stock falls. You may have seen a number called the **Dow Jones Industrial Average** on the television news or in the newspaper. By telling how well the stocks of 30 typical companies in the United States did each day, this number gives an idea of how well the stocks of *all* companies did.

Example: Suppose that at the beginning of the day on Monday, the 30 stocks in the Dow Jones Industrial Average cost $2,311.63 altogether. At the end of the day on Monday, the price of its stocks had increased $12.74, as shown in the table above right.

$2,311.63
+   12.74
$2,324.37

So on Tuesday morning, the stocks cost $2,324.37.

Use the information above and the table to solve.

Day	Dow Jones Industrial Average
Monday	+12.74
Tuesday	−2.2
Wednesday	−7.71
Thursday	+23.22
Friday	−57.95

1. On Monday, the stocks gained $12.74. How much of this gain remained by the end of the day on Wednesday?
  $2.83

2. If the price of the 30 stocks was $2,311.63 on Monday morning, what was the price of the stocks at the end of the day on Friday?
  $2,279.73

LESSON 2-8

Lesson Organizer

Objective: Discuss reading for understanding problems.

Prior Knowledge: Students should be familiar with the four-part problem solving process.

Error Analysis and Remediation: See page 53A.

Lesson Resources: Practice Worksheet 2-8
Daily Review 2-8

Two-Minute Math

Write answers only.

Start with 5. Add 20. Subtract 7. *(18)*

Start with (3 + 8). Subtract 4. Add 19. *(26)*

1 INTRODUCE

SYMBOLIC ACTIVITY

1. Write on the chalkboard:
Write the word *mathematics*. If it contains fewer than 9 letters or more than 4 vowels, circle the last vowel. If not, circle the consonant that precedes the second vowel. (Students should circle the consonant *h*.)

2. Tell students to read and follow the instructions.

3. Discuss difficulties students may have had following the directions. **What could you do to increase your understanding of the instructions?** *(Possible answers: Read more slowly; read several times; write down the directions step by step.)*

WHEN YOUR STUDENTS ASK
★ WHY AM I LEARNING THIS? ★

This skill will help you solve real life problems such as following instructions that tell you how to assemble something. You also need to read carefully when you follow a recipe.

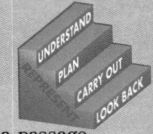

READING BETWEEN
THE LINES

Problem Solving:
Reading for Understanding

You may need to read a passage several times before you can solve a problem.

▶ READ AND TALK ABOUT IT

First read the passage quickly.

• What is it about?
the National Air and Space Museum

Now reread it carefully to solve these problems.

• In what year did the Wright Brothers invent the airplane? 1903
• Can you tell whether the *Spirit of St. Louis* is a more popular exhibit than the *Kitty Hawk*? no
• Can you tell when the National Air and Space Museum opened?
yes; 1976

Read the passage as often as necessary to answer the question.

1. Did James Smithson donate about 5 million or 0.5 million dollars?
0.5 million dollars

2. How long ago did the Wright Brothers invent the airplane?
Answer depends on current year.

3. How long ago did Lindbergh make his famous solo flight?
Answer depends on current year.

4. In what year did the Smithsonian open? 1846

MATH AND SOCIAL STUDIES

The most popular exhibits at the National Air and Space Museum in Washington, D.C. are the Wright Brothers' *Kitty Hawk* and Charles Lindbergh's *Spirit of St. Louis*. The Wright Brothers invented the airplane in 1903. Lindbergh became the first pilot to fly solo across the Atlantic 24 yr later.

The Air and Space Museum is part of the Smithsonian Institution. The Smithsonian opened in 1846 with $541,379 donated by English scientist James Smithson. The Air and Space Museum opened 130 yr later.

---

2 TEACH

READ AND TALK ABOUT IT   Why is it sometimes difficult to remember all the information in a problem after a first reading? *(Students may suggest that the problem was read too fast or that the problem contained a lot of information or information that depended on other information.)*

READ AND WRITE ABOUT IT   What mistakes can be made when a problem is not read carefully? (Accept reasonable answers.)

SUMMARIZE/ASSESS   Why is it important to read a problem for understanding? *(to be sure of the meaning of the question and the given information)*

The Library of Congress in Washington, D.C., is the national library of the United States. The library was established in 1800. Fifteen years later, Congress purchased the 6,000 books in the private library of Thomas Jefferson for the Library of Congress.

Today, the library has 84 million items, including more than 20 million books and pamphlets. Of special value are the 5,600 books that were printed after 1450 but before 1501.

READ AND WRITE ABOUT IT

Read the passage as often as necessary to answer the question.

5. How long ago was the Library of Congress established?
Answer depends on current year.

6. Which is a good estimate of the age of the library's oldest books?

    a. 440 yr   **b.** 540 yr
    b

7. In what year were books bought from the library of Thomas Jefferson?
1815

8. Can you tell the exact number of books in the Library of Congress? Explain.   no; the information given is not exact.

Solve. Use the graph below.

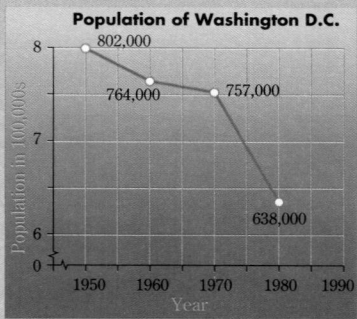

Population of Washington D.C.

802,000
764,000
757,000
638,000

9. What is the population for each year?
See below.

10. Do you think the population increased or decreased in 1990? Explain.
decrease; there has been a steady drop.

11. When looking at the graph, what did you
    a. read quickly?   Answers will vary.
    b. read first?
    c. read slowly?

9. 1950: 802,000; 1960: 764,000;
1970: 757,000; 1980: 638,000   CHAPTER 2   51

PRACTICE 2-8

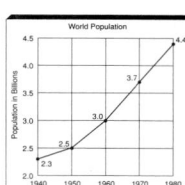

Read the passage as often as necessary to answer each question.

In 1902, Ibn Saud set out to conquer the land of the Arabian Peninsula. In 1932, his kingdom, finally complete, was called *Saudi Arabia*. Saud had 43 sons. His fourth-born son, King Fahd, is the present ruler. Saudi Arabia has 88 major tribes. About 75 of these tribes practice the religion of Islam. The population is reported to be 14.5 million, including about 4.5 million foreigners.

1. How long did it take Ibn Saud to form Saudi Arabia? 30 years

2. What is the population without foreigners? Express your answer in short word form. 10 million

3. Express your answer to Exercise 2 in standard form. 10,000,000

4. How many tribes do not practice the religion of Islam? about 13 tribes

5. How many sons of Ibn Saud were younger than King Fahd? 39 sons

6. Can you determine how long King Fahd has ruled? Explain. No, you also need to know the year he became king.

Solve. Look at the graph on the right.

7. What was the world population in 1950? 1960? 1970? 2.5 billion; 3.0 billion; 3.7 billion

8. How much larger was the population in 1960 than in 1940? 0.7 billion

World Population

MEETING INDIVIDUAL NEEDS

For Students Who Are . . .

Acquiring English Proficiency Have students tell where they found the necessary information to answer each question in Exercises 1–4.

Gifted and Talented Have students work together to find out about other exhibits at the National Air and Space Museum. Then have them write and answer questions that pertain to these exhibits.

Working 2 or 3 Grades Below Level Have students use pages 8–11 of the Skills Workbook for Problem Solving Strategies.

Having Reading Difficulties Pair each student with an able reader to read the passages and solve the problems.

Today's Problem

Information is stored in the memory of a computer in bytes. A byte is a sequence of 8 bits. How many bits are there in 8 bytes?
(8 bytes × 8 bits per byte = 64 bits)

CHAPTER

Checkup

The chapter checkup provides a quick language and vocabulary review, a test for the chapter, and suggestions for student Learning Log entries.

Language and Vocabulary

Some key language and vocabulary ideas from this chapter are reinforced here.

Test

The test can be used either as a test or as a review of the chapter prior to your administering the test worksheets found in the Teacher's Resource Book.

The following guide will help you determine percentage scores.

Score	Percent	Score	Percent
24	100%	12	50%
23	96	11	46
22	91	10	41
21	87	9	37
20	82	8	32
19	78	7	28
18	74	6	24
17	70	5	20
16	66	4	16
15	62	3	12
14	58	2	8
13	54	1	4

Each test has 3 sections: concepts, skills and problem solving. These sections provide students with exposure to the formats used on standardized tests.

Use this chart to identify additional lesson resources for this chapter.

Items	Management Objective	Pages
1–6	**2A** Use replacement and properties of addition to solve equations.	34–37
7–10; 19–21	**2B** Add whole numbers and decimals.	40–41
13–18	**2C** Subtract whole numbers and decimals.	46–49
22–24	**2D** Problem Solving: Choose the method. Choose the operation.	38–39; 50–51

CHAPTER CHECKUP

LANGUAGE & VOCABULARY

Explain how the first problem in the pair can help you find the difference in the second problem. Use math vocabulary in your explanation. **Accept reasonable answers.**

1.
$$2,943 + 8,607 = 11,550$$
$$11,550 - 2,943$$

2.
$$6,000 - 1,975 = 4,025$$
$$6,110 - 1,975$$

TEST ✔

CONCEPTS

Use the properties of addition to look for tens and compute mentally. *(pages 36 – 37)*

1. $23 + 89 + 77$ 189

2. $108 + 35 + 65$ 208

3. $(93 + 0 + 7) + 259$ 359

Is the number in parentheses the solution? Write *yes* or *no*. *(pages 34–35)*

4. $n \times 4 = 96$ (14) no

5. $3 \times r = 13 + 86 + 2$ (7) no

6. $w - 43 = 64$ (22) no

SKILLS

Add. *(pages 40–41)*

7.
$$1.8 + 4.7 = 6.5$$

8.
$$135.02 + 89.19 = 224.21$$

9.
$$\$203.98 + 67.17 = \$271.15$$

10.
$$76,809$$
$$395$$
$$+ 1,782$$
$$78,986$$

11. $0.82 + 13.7 + 15.309$ 29.829

12. 3 million + 4.7 thousand 3,004,700

Subtract. *(pages 46–49)*

13.
$$42,258 - 13,379 = 28,879$$

14.
$$2,101 - 912 = 1,189$$

15. $308 - 194$ 114

16.
$$\$40.00 - 18.53 = \$21.47$$

17.
$$76.84 - 9.679 = 67.161$$

18. $8.001 - 2.15$ 5.851

52   CHAPTER CHECKUP

CHAPTER TEST • FORM A

(pp. 34–37) 2A

Is the number in parentheses a solution? Write *yes* or *no*.

1. $n \times 6 = 96$ (16) yes

2. $4 \times r = 12 + 48 + 12$ (8) no

3. $w - 35 = 74$ (39) no

Name the property shown by the equation.

4. $(19 + 113) + 37 = 19 + (113 + 37)$ associative property

5. $0 + 1,760 = 1,760$ identity property

Add. (pp. 40–43) 2B

6.
$$3.6 + 3.5 = 7.1$$

7.
$$149.05 + 78.14 = 227.19$$

8.
$$\$301.75 + 68.19 = \$369.94$$

9.
$$65,701$$
$$289$$
$$+ 3,673$$
$$69,663$$

10. $0.75 + 14.6 + 17.209 =$ 32.559

Subtract. (pp. 46–49) 2C

11.
$$41,346 - 12,288 = 29,058$$

12.
$$3,202 - 816 = 2,386$$

13.
$$\$50.00 - 17.35 = \$32.65$$

14. $4.02 - 2.7 =$ 1.32

15. $65.73 - 8.368 =$ 57.362

CHAPTER TEST • FORM A

Solve. (pp. 38–39, 50–51) 2D

16. A VCR which regularly sells for $379.95 is on sale for $345.25. How much will you save if you buy the VCR at the sale price? $34.70

17. The price of compact discs which regularly sell for $14.95 each has been reduced by $1.45. How much would 4 compact discs cost if they were bought at this sale price? $54

18. AM/FM pocket radios have been reduced to $16.49 each. How much change would you receive from $40 if you bought two of them? $7.02

19. An answering machine is on sale for $59.29. What is the largest number of answering machines you could buy at this price if you had $200 to spend? 3 machines

20. Video tapes are on sale for $3.95 each. At the same sale CD players are on sale for $179.50. How much would two video tapes and a CD player cost at this sale? $187.40

Use the front-end method to estimate. *(pages 42–43)* **Accept reasonable estimates.**

			Suggestions
19. $42.15	**20.** $139.08	**21.** $4.32 + $8.17 + $1.53	**given.**
+ 16.89	50.89	**$14**	
$59	+ 25.98		
	$216		

━━━━━━━━━━━━━━━ **PROBLEM SOLVING** ━━━━━━━━━━━━━━━

Solve. *(pages 38–39, 46–49)*

22. The flying distance between Los Angeles and Paris, France, is 5,601 mi. The flying distance from Los Angeles to Tokyo, Japan, is 5,470 mi. **5,601 mi**

   a. What is the flying distance from Los Angeles to Paris?

   b. Would a flight from Paris to Los Angeles be *more than* or *less than* 11,000 mi? **less than**

   c. What is the total distance of a flight from Paris to Los Angeles to Tokyo? **11,071 mi**

23. An 11- to 14-year-old girl needs 2,200 calories from her daily food. How many more calories does a 13-year-old girl need to eat today if she has already eaten 1,785 calories? **415 calories**

24. Ri has $40 to spend on clothes. She spends $18.53 for a shirt. How much does she have left to spend? **$21.47**

Write the answers in your learning log. **Answers will vary. Suggestions given.**

   1. Explain how two decimals can have different numbers of places and still represent the same number. Give an example.
when only zeros are to the right of the last non-zero digit

   2. Is it more difficult for you to estimate answers to addition problems or to subtraction problems? Why do you think you answered the way you did? **Accept reasonable answers.**

Note that the same numbers are used in Exercises 16 and 24.

CHAPTER 2   53

Problem Solving

Item 22 has 3 parts:
a. literal—this is a reading comprehension question;
b. interpretive—this involves interpretation using the facts given;
c. applied—students use a strategy or skills to find an answer.

Item 16 in the skill section and item 24 in the problem solving section use the same numbers.

This will help you informally assess how your students transfer from numerical skills to word problems.

For scoring problem solving items you may wish to use partial credit. If a student uses the correct strategy but gets a wrong answer, give the student 2 points toward the total percent score.

Learning Log

These are suggestions for writing about some topics taught in this chapter. The students keep their Learning Logs from the beginning of the school year through the end.

CHAPTER TEST • FORM **B**

(pp. 34–37) 2A

Is the number in parentheses a solution? Write *yes* or *no*.

1. $n \times 5 = 75$ (15) **yes**
2. $6 \times r = 13 + 20 + 9$ (7) **yes**
3. $w - 27 = 53$ (26) **no**

Name the property shown by the equation.

4. $27 + 173 = 173 + 27$
commutative property
5. $(15 + 20) + 24 = 15 + (20 + 24)$
associative property

Add. *(pp. 40–43)* 2B

6. 1.9	**7.** 246.13	**8.** $207.48	**9.** 67,704
+ 4.5	+ 78.19	+ 56.16	483
6.4	**324.32**	**$263.64**	+ 2,972
			71,159

10. 2 million + 10.3 thousand = **2,010,300**

Subtract. *(pp. 46–49)* 2C

11. 53,147	**12.** 3,401	**13.** $60.00
− 14,288	− 835	− 27.45
38,859	**2,566**	**$32.55**

14. 607 − 281 = **326**
15. 56.81 − 7.457 = **49.353**

CHAPTER TEST • FORM **B**

Solve. *(pp. 38–39, 50–51)* 2D

16. A CD player which regularly sells for $189.95 is on sale for $154.50. How much would you save if you bought the CD player at the sale price? **$35.45**

17. The price of video tapes which regularly sell for $7.69 each has been reduced by $1.25. How much would 6 video tapes cost if they were bought at the sale price? **$38.64**

18. AM/FM pocket radios have been reduced to $17.39 each. How much change would you receive from $40 if you bought two of them? **$5.22**

19. A portable cassette player has been reduced to $47.49. What is the largest number of portable cassette players you could buy at this price if you had $250 to spend? **5 cassette players**

20. Compact discs have been reduced to $12.95 each. At the same time a VCR is on sale for $339.75. How much would two compact discs and a VCR cost at this sale? **$365.65**

Error Analysis and Remediation

Here are some common errors students make when they add and subtract whole numbers and decimals. The errors are listed by lesson under the appropriate management objective.

2A • USE REPLACEMENT AND PROPERTIES OF ADDITION TO SOLVE EQUATIONS

Source of Error (Lesson 2-1)
students substitute a subtraction fact when presented with an equation such as $x - 5 = 3$. They replace the variable with a number such as 2.

Remediation
Have students read each equation aloud. What number minus 5 equals 3? By doing this, students realize that the value of the variable must be greater than 5. *(8)*

Source of Error (Lesson 2-2)
students think that terms can be interchanged for the associative property.

Remediation
Stress that the addends remain in the same order but that the parentheses shift so that only the grouping changes.

2B • ADD WHOLE NUMBERS AND DECIMALS

Source of Error (Lesson 2-4)
students line up digits without considering the decimal point or correct place value.

Remediation
Have students use a place value chart to help them name the values of the digits and to align the decimal points.

Source of Error (Lesson 2-5)
students incorrectly adjust front-end estimates.

Remediation
Help students avoid making errors when mentally calculating the amount by which an estimate must be adjusted, by providing them with an estimate such as $30 and a group of numbers by which to correct the estimate, such as $.40, $.23, $.07, and $.75.

2C • SUBTRACT WHOLE NUMBERS AND DECIMALS

Source of Error (Lesson 2-6)
students subtract the smaller digit from the larger digit regardless of the positions of the digits in the problem or incorrectly rename across more than one zero.

Remediation
Help students avoid these errors by having them use base ten materials to model several subtraction examples.

Source of Error (Lesson 2-7)
students line up a whole number in the decimal column.

Remediation
Have students practice writing whole numbers using decimal points. Then demonstrate how to line up a decimal and a whole number.

$$35.4 - 26 \rightarrow \begin{array}{r} 35.4 \\ - \ 26.0 \\ \hline \end{array}$$

2D • PROBLEM SOLVING: CHOOSE THE OPERATION

Source of Error (Lesson 2-8)
students have difficulty understanding a problem.

Remediation
Have students break down the content of a sentence to small parts they can manage, and help them identify words or phrases that serve as clues in choosing a strategy or operation. Then have them rewrite the problem in their own words.

Answers

Page 33

Via	Acapulco	San Francisco	Honolulu
Cape Horn	13,649 mi	15,500 mi	15,656 mi
Panama Canal	3,964 mi	6,058 mi	7,715 mi
Miles saved	9,685 mi	9,442 mi	7,941 mi

Page 43

1. $4.75; 4 dollars, 3 quarters
2. $0.38; 1 quarter, 1 dime, 3 pennies
3. $43.02; 2 $20 bills, 3 $1 bills, 2 pennies

Extra Practice

This page provides extra practice of all the major chapter objectives. Use this page after the chapter has been taught to reinforce the chapter skills. Page references are provided for each group of items so that students can easily look back at the appropriate lesson for additional support.

EXTRA PRACTICE

Solve the equation. *(pages 34–35)*

1. $12 + a = 21$ **9**
2. $53 - m = 29$ **24**
3. $c + 45 = 81$ **36**
4. $64 \div d = 16$ **4**
5. $n \div 8 = 11$ **88**
6. $3 \times e = 27$ **9**

Use the properties of addition to look for tens and compute mentally. *(pages 36–37)*

7. $94 + 28 + 6$ **128**
8. $171 + 203 + 29$ **403**
9. $15 + 40 + 46$ **101**
10. $(17 + 23) + 82$ **122**
11. $(72 + 32) + 128$ **232**
12. $36 + (0 + 44)$ **80**

Use the front-end method to estimate. *(pages 42–43)* **Accept reasonable estimates.**

13.
$$\begin{array}{r} \$16.71 \\ + 25.42 \\ \hline \$42 \end{array}$$

14.
$$\begin{array}{r} \$115.35 \\ 20.57 \\ + 89.03 \\ \hline \$225 \end{array}$$

15.
$$\begin{array}{r} \$150.18 \\ 37.35 \\ + 42.44 \\ \hline \$230 \end{array}$$

Write the answer. *(pages 40–41, 46–49)*

16.
$$\begin{array}{r} 3.8 \\ + 1.9 \\ \hline 5.7 \end{array}$$

17.
$$\begin{array}{r} 18.5 \\ + 13.7 \\ \hline 32.2 \end{array}$$

18.
$$\begin{array}{r} 108.3 \\ + 62.9 \\ \hline 171.2 \end{array}$$

19.
$$\begin{array}{r} 4.9 \\ + 28 \\ \hline 32.9 \end{array}$$

20.
$$\begin{array}{r} 0.6 \\ 17.8 \\ + 9.65 \\ \hline 28.05 \end{array}$$

21.
$$\begin{array}{r} 8{,}012 \\ - 5{,}731 \\ \hline 2{,}281 \end{array}$$

22.
$$\begin{array}{r} 96{,}000 \\ - 52{,}351 \\ \hline 43{,}649 \end{array}$$

23.
$$\begin{array}{r} 67{,}312 \\ - 9{,}876 \\ \hline 57{,}436 \end{array}$$

24.
$$\begin{array}{r} 103{,}000 \\ - 25{,}671 \\ \hline 77{,}329 \end{array}$$

25.
$$\begin{array}{r} 9.83 \\ - 5.41 \\ \hline 4.42 \end{array}$$

26.
$$\begin{array}{r} 60.25 \\ - 29.37 \\ \hline 30.88 \end{array}$$

27.
$$\begin{array}{r} 14.15 \\ - 6.803 \\ \hline 7.347 \end{array}$$

28.
$$\begin{array}{r} 81 \\ - 3.92 \\ \hline 77.08 \end{array}$$

Solve. *(pages 38–39, 50–51)*

29. Auto Mart and Car World are selling the same model of car. If Auto Mart is asking $15,879 and Car World is asking $15,495 for the same model, how much money can you save if you buy the car at Car World? **$384**

30. Scientists believe that the Sun's core may reach temperatures as high as 15 million degrees Celsius. The Sun's outer atmosphere, the corona, reaches temperatures close to 3 million degrees Celsius. About what is the difference in temperature between the Sun's core and its corona? **12,000,000°C**

Plan For The Future

Work with a group. Decide on a business that you could start. Try to find answers to the kinds of questions you would face if you really were starting a business. Among the questions you need to consider are the following:

- What will you sell?
- How much do you want to earn?
- How many items do you need to sell?
- How much will you charge per item?
- Will you advertise? If so, where?
- What expenses will you have?

Once you decide on the type of business, there are many places to obtain information. You can try the following:

- business people in your community
- local manufacturers' associations
- magazines and newspapers (to find out about advertising rates and rental costs)

When you have completed your research, share your information with the rest of the class.
Check students' work.

The Bells Are Ringing

Each day you are in school, you spend most of your time doing schoolwork. However, you may be surprised to learn how much time you spend on other activities. These may include eating lunch and moving between classes. To estimate the amount of school time you spend on other activities, keep a record for several days of the number of minutes that you spend on these other activities. Then answer these questions:

- Does the number of minutes spent on other activities remain constant from day to day?
- What type of activity takes the most time away from schoolwork? Were you surprised by the results?
- Were you surprised by the results?

Check students' work.

Population Information

The United States Census is taken every 10 years. The most recent one was taken in 1990. Perhaps you helped complete a census form. You can find information on the census either in the official report at the library or in an almanac. Find the data and compare the 1980 and 1990 populations of

- the United States
- your state
- your city
- your age group

Check students' work.

Enrichment

This page contains activities that provide extension and enrichment for all levels of students. Depending on the needs of your students, you may wish to assign an activity from this page at certain points during the chapter, or you may wish to use this page when the entire chapter has been completed.

Plan for the Future
(COOPERATIVE)

After students complete the activity and share the results of their research, you may wish to have students design a bulletin board display that focuses on sources of information in your community.

The Bells Are Ringing

You may wish to have students form groups to compare their answers and discuss whether their "free" time could be spent more productively.

Population Information

You may wish to extend the activity by having students project population data for the year 2000.

CHAPTER 2

Cumulative Review

The Cumulative Review focuses on skills covered in previous chapters. All important skills are reviewed on a cyclic basis.

If students are having difficulty with particular groups of exercises, refer to the chart for follow-up work.

What is the equivalent value?

1. 6^3　c
   - a. 18
   - b. 63
   - c. 216
   - d. none of these

2. 13.8 million　b
   - a. 1,380,000
   - b. 13,800,000
   - c. 130,000,000
   - d. none of these

3. $(2 \times 10^3) + (8 \times 10^0)$　c
   - a. 2,800
   - b. 2,080
   - c. 2,008
   - d. none of these

4. 1,800 mL　a
   - a. 1.8 L
   - b. 0.18 L
   - c. 18 L
   - d. none of these

5. 49 cm　b
   - a. 4.9 m
   - b. 490 mm
   - c. 0.049 m
   - d. none of these

6. 326 g　c
   - a. 3,260 mg
   - b. 3.26 kg
   - c. 0.326 kg
   - d. none of these

What is the value of n?

7. $n + 14 = 73$　a
   - a. 59
   - b. 87
   - c. 69
   - d. none of these

8. $82 - n = 37$　b
   - a. 55
   - b. 45
   - c. 119
   - d. none of these

9. $n + 18 = 50$　d
   - a. 900
   - b. 1,000
   - c. 800
   - d. none of these

Find the answer.

10. Which number is greater than 39,763?　d
   - a. 39,673
   - b. 39,367
   - c. 39,759
   - d. none of these

11. Between which two numbers is 8.04?　c
   - a. 8.05 and 8.09
   - b. 7.95 and 8.03
   - c. 7.99 and 8.10
   - d. none of these

12. $0.08 + 9.79 =$　b
   - a. 9.77
   - b. 9.87
   - c. 10.59
   - d. none of these

13. $\begin{array}{r} \$205.69 \\ +\ \ 18.93 \end{array}$　a
   - a. $224.62
   - b. $224.52
   - c. $212.62
   - d. none of these

14. $\begin{array}{r} 3,000 \\ -\ \ 682 \end{array}$　d
   - a. 2,418
   - b. 3,682
   - c. 2,428
   - d. none of these

15. $3.5 - 1.96 =$　a
   - a. 1.54
   - b. 2.46
   - c. 1.64
   - d. none of these

Items	Management Objectives	Where Taught	Reteaching Options	Extra Practice Options
1–3	1A Identify and write whole numbers and decimals in exponential, expanded, and standard form.	pp. 4–7	TRB/RW 1-2 TE/RA 1-3	TRB/PW 1-2 and 1-3
4–6	1D Determine the appropriate metric units of length, capacity, and mass.	pp. 20–25	TRB/RW 1-9 TE/RA 1-10 TRB/RW 1-11	TRB/PW 1-9, 1-10, and 1-11
7–9	2A Use replacement and properties of addition to solve equations.	pp. 34–37	TRB/RW 2-1 TE/RA 2-2	TRB/PW 2-1, 2-2
10–11	1B Compare and order whole numbers and decimals.	pp. 8–9	TRB/RW 1-4	TRB/PW 1-4
12–13	2B Add whole numbers and decimals.	pp. 40–41	TRB/RW 2-4	TRB/PW 2-4
14–15	2C Subtract whole numbers and decimals.	pp. 46–49	TRB/RW 2-6 TE/RA 2-7	TRB/PW 2-6 and 2-7

PROBLEM SOLVING REVIEW

Problem Solving Review

This page focuses on problem solving strategies and types learned in this and previous chapters. A problem solving checklist lists some of the strategies students may use to solve the problems on this page.

Strategies may vary. Suggestions given.
Remember the strategies and types of problems you've had so far. Solve, if possible.

Problem Solving Check List

- Too much information
- Too little information
- Multistep problems
- Drawing a picture
- Using a pattern

1. A service telephone call costs $.40 for the first 3 min and $.10 for each additional 2 min.

   a. How much does a 3-min call cost?

   b. Are the first 3 min of a telephone call *cheaper* or *more expensive* than the additional minutes?

   c. How much would a 21-min telephone call cost? **multistep; $1.30**

2. Every time a certain ball hits the ground, it bounces back one-half the distance of the drop. If the ball is dropped from a height of 32 ft, how high will it bounce after it hits the ground the fourth time?
   multistep; 2 ft

3. A driver sees a road sign after driving 1 mi, another after 3 mi, another after 6 mi, and another after 10 mi. If the pattern continues, how many miles will the driver travel between the fifth and sixth road signs?
   patterns; 6 mi

4. Will earns $25/wk after school. He always spends $18 of this money and saves the rest. One week he earned an extra $12 for overtime work. If he saved the entire $12, how much did he put in the bank that week?
   multistep; $19

5. On her vacation, Sondra spent $479 on airfare and $83/d for each of the 6 d she was away. If she left on her vacation with exactly $1,000, how much money did she have left when she returned?
   multistep; $23

6. The year after Rosa's class graduated, the school's population fell to 729 students. How many of the 729 students were boys?
   too little information

7. Jet fuel costs $1.85/gal. If a jet's tank can hold 350 gal of fuel, how much does it cost to fly the jet 500 mi?
   too little information

8. Compact disks (CDs), which usually cost $11.99, are on sale for $8.99 each. Tapes, which usually cost $6.99, are selling for $5.50 each. What is the total cost of 1 CD and 1 tape on sale?
   too much information; $14.49

9. The number of students in Rosa's school increased from 684 to 743. Originally, there were 362 girls. With the increase there are 391 girls. How many new students are girls?
   multistep; 29 girls

CHAPTER 2   57

Technology

This page is designed to provide calculator or computer experiences for all levels of students. The calculator or computer logo indicates the type of activity.

You may wish to assign these activities after the chapter has been taught or during the course of the chapter, depending on your needs and those of your students.

Shopping for Three
(COOPERATIVE)

Remind students they can round the prices to the nearest dollar before they determine whether to use their calculators to find sums less than $10.

It Adds Up

Make sure students recognize that the first step is to find the sum of the decimals in the first row.

Lightning Addition
(COOPERATIVE)

Software for this activity may be found in Houghton Mifflin Math Activities Courseware, Grade 7.

After students have completed the activity once, you may wish to have them create their own sets of problem and answer cards for future rounds.

TECHNOLOGY

SHOPPING FOR THREE

Ask a friend to try this activity.

You must buy three items. You can buy more than one of an item, but you can't spend more than $10. How many different combinations of items can you buy? The person who can list the most in three minutes wins. **Answers will vary.**

Notebook	Pen	Record
$.79	$1.29	$6.89

Book	Puzzle
$3.65	$2.89

IT ADDS UP

Copy and complete the magic square so that when you add across, down, or diagonally, the sums will always be the same.

2.70	9.45	8.10
12.15	6.75	1.35
5.40	4.05	10.8

LIGHTNING ADDITION

In the computer activity *Decimal Dispatch,* you estimate decimal sums. Sharpen your number sense skills with this game. Work in pairs. You do not need a computer. **See below.**

Write the addition problems on a set of cards and the answers on another set. Shuffle the answer cards. With one player acting as a timer, the other player must match each problem with the correct answer card as quickly as possible. The timer records the time and checks the answers with a calculator. Players then switch roles. Who had the faster time? Who had more correct matches?

Problems:

A	B	C	D	E
3.467	2.314	2.813	2.749	2.047
+ 2.519	+ 3.146	+ 2.784	+ 2.856	+ 3.689

Answer cards:

5.460	5.605	5.736	5.986	5.597
B	D	E	A	C

This activity is available on computer disk in Houghton Mifflin *Mathematics Activities Courseware.*

Software Activities

activity 1 • HOURLY WAGES BY JOB TYPE

MATERIALS: database program, reference materials

Procedure: Students should create a database file using the following hourly wage information.

Type of Job	Average Hourly Wage		
	1975	1985	1989
Mining	$3.85	$9.17	$12.75
Construction	$5.24	$9.94	$13.37
Retail (Clerk)	$2.44	$4.85	$ 6.31
Finance Teller	$3.07	$5.79	$ 9.57

Using the database file, have students find the greatest and least hourly wage for each year in the file.

Follow-up: Students should find other job data and perform the same tasks to see if the new data affects their previous answers.

activity 2 • PAYING FOR PIZZA

MATERIALS: BASIC programming

Procedure: This program will tell students how much they have to pay for pizzas, depending on the number of extras purchased. Students should type the program into the computer.

```
10 PRINT "SUPER PIZZAS COST $13
   PLUS 73¢ FOR EACH EXTRA."
15 FOR I = 1 TO 7
20 PRINT: INPUT "HOW MANY PIZZAS";N
25 INPUT "HOW MANY EXTRAS IN ALL";M
30 PRINT N"PIZZAS WITH"M"EXTRAS"
35 PRINT "WILL COST
   $"(13*N)+(.73*M)
40 PRINT: PRINT "NEXT ORDER
   PLEASE!"
60 NEXT I
```

Have students run the program.

Follow-up: Ask students to identify the lines they would need to change if the cost of each extra is $0.15. They should change the program and run it to be sure the correct lines were identified.

HOUGHTON MIFFLIN SOFTWARE

Easy Graph. Boston, MA: Houghton Mifflin Company, 1987. For Apple II, Commodore, IBM.

EduCalc. Boston, MA: Houghton Mifflin Company, 1990. For Apple II, Commodore, IBM.

Friendly Filer. Boston, MA: Houghton Mifflin Company, 1989. For Apple II, Commodore, IBM.

Mathematics Activities Courseware. Boston, MA: Houghton Mifflin Company, 1983. For Apple II, IBM.

The Computer Tutor, Boston, MA: Houghton Mifflin Company, 1990. For Apple II, IBM.

OTHER SOFTWARE

Estimating & Common Sense. Kankakee, IL: Data Command, 1984. For Apple II, IBM.

Estimation: Quick Solve I and II. St. Paul, MN: MECC, 1990. For Apple II.

Fundamental Math Package: "The First Men in the Moon Math". Spinnaker Educational Software/Queue Software, Inc., Fairfield, CT: 1989, Apple II.

Guess My Rule. Fairfield, CT: HRM/Queue, 1985. For Apple II.

Integers Equations. Dimondale, MI: Hartley Courseware, 1988. For Apple II, IBM.

Microsoft Works. Redmond, WA: Microsoft Corporation, 1989. For Macintosh, IBM.

The Children's Writing and Publishing Center. Freemont, CA: The Learning Company, 1988. For Apple II.

Multiplication and Division: Whole Numbers and Decimals

This chapter reviews and extends the students' knowledge of multiplication and division of whole numbers and decimals. The multiplication and division algorithms are carefully developed along with the properties of multiplication. The important concept of estimation is used to check the reasonableness of products and quotients and to estimate the quotient before division. Students use calculators and mental math as well as paper and pencil to solve application problems. Special attention is given to Looking Back in problem solving to make sure an answer is not only reasonable but answers the question. Finally, students focus on reading carefully and learning to sort necessary information before solving a problem.

Management Objectives

3A Use properties of multiplication and order of operations.
3B Multiply and divide whole numbers.
3C Multiply and divide decimals.
3D Estimate quotients.
3E Problem Solving: Look back. Too much or too little information.

Assignments for different achievement levels are provided on the Record and Assignment Chart in the Teacher's Resource Book.

Vocabulary

commutative property, page 60
associative property, distributive property, page 60
identity property, zero property, page 60
compatible numbers, page 61
order of operations, page 62
fathom, page 70
clustering, page 71
scientific notation, page 78

Home Involvement

As you begin to teach this chapter, give each student a copy of the Home Involvement Newsletter for this chapter.

This newsletter provides parents with
■ an overview of the chapter
■ suggestions for practicing some of the skills in the chapter
■ an at-home activity to do with their child, applying the skills taught in the chapter.

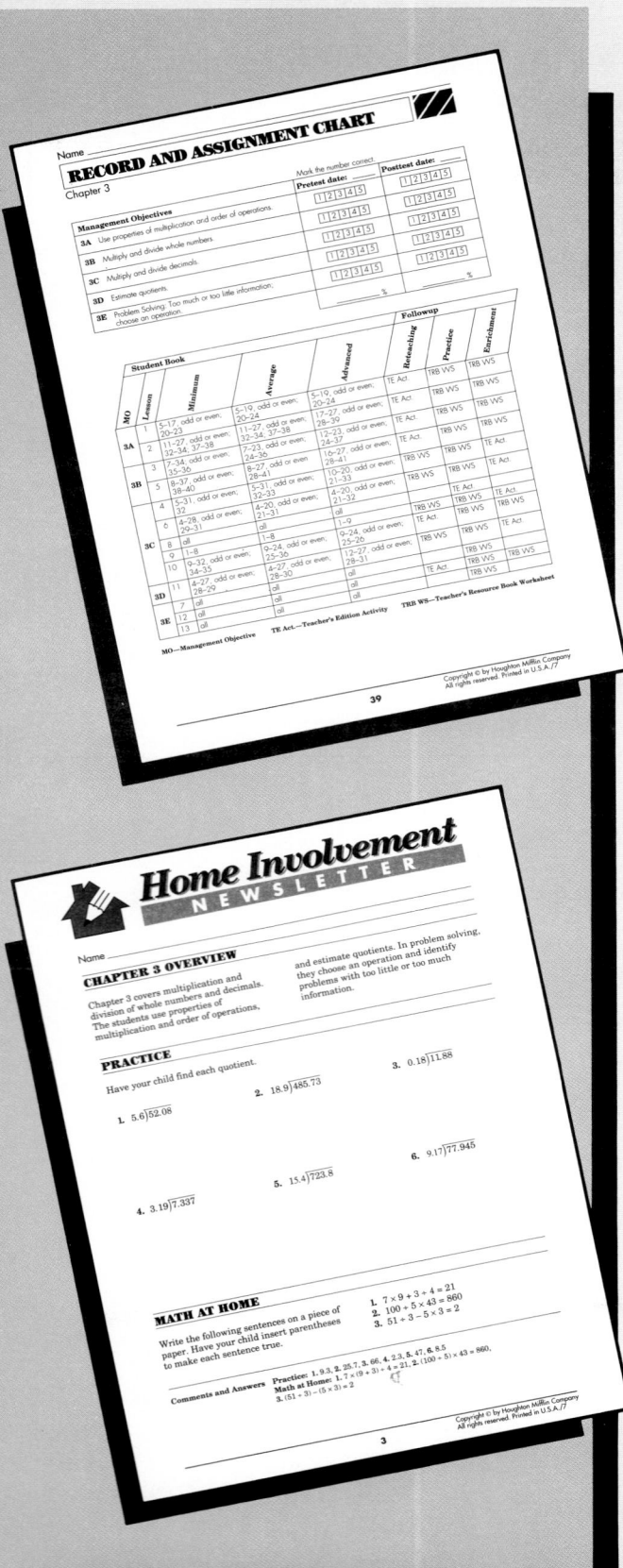

Management Chart

Management Objectives	Lesson/ Pages	Student Not Successful	Student Needs More Practice	Student Successful	Pacing Range
3A Use properties of multiplication and order of operations.	3-1/60-61	TE/RA 3-1	TRB/PW 3-1	TRB/EW 3-1	1-2 days
	3-2/62-63	TE/RA 3-2	TRB/PW 3-2 MAC 7 Activity 3	TRB/EW 3-2 MAC 7 Activity 3	
3B Multiply and divide whole numbers.	3-3/64-65	TE/RA 3-3	TRB/PW 3-3 CSP WNH CT Unit 1 Obj. 4.1	TRB/EW 3-3	1-2 days
	3-5/68-69	TE/RA 3-5	TRB/PW 3-5 MAC 7 Activity 3B	TRB/EW 3-5 MAC 7 Activity 3B	
3C Multiply and divide decimals.	3-4/66-67	TRB/RW 3-4	TRB/PW 3-4 CSP Dec. Sks. 9, 10 MAC 6 Activity 6 MAC 7 Activity 3B	TE/EA 3-4 MAC 6 Activity 6 MAC 7 Activity 3B	2-5 days
	3-6/70-71	TRB/RW 3-6	TRB/PW 3-6 CSP Dec. Sk. 11	TE/EA 3-6	
	3-8/76-77		CSP Dec. Sks. 9, 10, 11, 12	TE/CA 3-8	
	3-9/78-79	TRB/RW 3-9	TRB/PW 3-9	TE/EA 3-9	
	3-10/80-81	TE/RA 3-10	TRB/PW 3-10 CSP Dec. Sk. 12 CT Unit 3 Obj. 5.1	TRB/EW 3-10	
3D Estimate quotients.	3-11/82-83	TRB/RW 3-11	TRB/PW 3-11	TE/EA 3-11	1 day
3E Problem Solving: Looking back; too much or too little information.	3-7/72-73		TRB/PW 3-7		2 days
	3-12/84-85	TE/RA 3-12	TRB/PW 3-12	TRB/EW 3-12	
Creative Problem Solving	3-13/86-87			TE/CA 3-13	
Chapter Checkups	74-75, 88-89				
Extra Practice	90				
Enrichment	91				
Cumulative Review/ Problem Solving Review	92-93				
Technology	94				

TE = Teacher's Edition
TRB = Teacher's Resource Book
RW = Reteaching Worksheet
RA = Reteaching Activity
EA = Enrichment Activity
EW = Enrichment Worksheet
PW = Practice Worksheet
CA = Classroom Activity

*Other Available Items
MAC = Mathematics Activities Courseware
CSP = Computational Skills Program
CT = Computer Tutor

Manipulative Planning Guide

This is a complete list of manipulatives and materials needed for Chapter 3.

Materials for Manipulatives	TE Activities (INTRODUCE)	Student Book Lesson
Calculator for each student	Lesson 3-9	Lessons 3-2, 3-4, 3-5, 3-6, 3-8, 3-10
Index cards		
Different-color markers		
Base ten materials, several of each kind per group	Lessons 3-1, 3-3, 3-5, 3-8	
Counters, 50 for each student		
20 slips of paper per group	Lesson 3-6	
Counters, paper clips, or beans, handful per group	Lesson 3-6	
U.S. wall map	Lesson 3-7	
Teaching Aid 2*, one for each student	Lessons 3-4, 3-10	
Grocery store ads from newspapers		
Teaching Aid 1*, one for each student		

*Teaching Aids are found in the Teacher's Resource Book.

Learning Stages

The concepts and skills in Chapter 3 are presented through these learning stages.

CONCRETE

Using manipulatives and verbalizing about a concept. No symbols.

Teacher Edition Activities	Student Book
At this grade level the skills of this chapter are taught at the connecting and symbolic stages.	

Enrichment	Reteaching	In the Houghton Mifflin Manipulative Kit?	In the Houghton Mifflin Overhead Kit?
			Available separately
	Lessons 3-1, 3-2		
	Lesson 3-1		
		Yes	
	Lesson 3-5	Yes	
			Yes
Lesson 3-11			
	Lesson 3-10		

CONNECTING

🏛 ▦ ▭ ➡ 5¢ 9cm² $\frac{1}{3}$

Making a connection between manipulatives and symbols.

Teacher Edition Activities	Student Book
Lessons 3-1, 3-3, 3-4, 3-5, 3-6; 3-8, 3-10	

SYMBOLIC

$.05   A=9cm² $1 - \frac{2}{3} = \frac{1}{3}$

Using numbers or symbols. No manipulatives or pictures of manipulatives.

Teacher Edition Activities	Student Book
Lessons 3-2, 3-7, 3-9, 3-11, 3-12	Lessons 3-1, 3-2, 3-3, 3-4, 3-5, 3-6, 3-7, 3-8, 3-9, 3-10, 3-11, 3-12

Additional Activities

COOPERATIVE LEARNING RESOURCE ACTIVITIES

Through cooperative learning activities, students learn by interacting with one another in small groups. These cooperative activities provide students with motivating settings for making connections, investigations, and problem solving situations.

   The cooperative connections are interdisciplinary problem-solving projects. Each student has a particular job that helps lead the group to complete the project. For the cooperative investigations students work in pairs for investigations involving data collection and analysis. The cooperative problem solving activities encourage the sharing of ideas and information. Students work in groups of four to solve a problem. Students are each assigned a clue and work together to find a common solution.

COOPERATIVE CONNECTIONS

Chapter 3

COOPERATIVE CONNECTIONS / Math and Agriculture

PROBLEM: Dairy farmers who live in cold climates must plan a food supply for their livestock that will last throughout the months when grazing is not possible.

Figure out how much hay and grain are needed for one day for a farm of 100 cows. Use the facts below to help you.

- The average cow weighs about 1,200 lb.
- Each day the same cow needs about 3 lb of hay for each 100 lb of body weight.
- In addition to hay, a cow needs 1 lb of grain for every 3 lb of milk it produces. (1 gal milk = 8 lb milk)
- One cow can produce as much as 14 qt of milk each day.

COOPERATIVE INVESTIGATIONS

Chapter 3

COOPERATIVE INVESTIGATIONS / Order of Operations

GOAL: Use the order of operations and the same one-digit number four times to write a series of equations.

Work with a partner.

1. Study the equations in the box and then find the solutions.

   How are the equations alike? How are they different? What is the order of operations in each equation?

2. Study this equation: $2 \_ 2 \_ 2 \_ 2 = 6$.

   How can you use operation signs and the order of operations to make this a true equation?

3. Using for 4's, how many different equations with a solution of 1 can you write?

$(2+2) \times (2+2) = \square$

$(2+2) + (2+2) = \square$

$2+2 - (2+2) = \square$

$2+2 + 2-2 = \square$

$2+2 + (2+2) = \square$

COOPERATIVE PROBLEM SOLVING 1

Chapter 3

COOPERATIVE PROBLEM SOLVING / Problem 1

How much money should Fruits Unlimited be paid for one truckload of grapefruit?

Clue 1: A Fruits Unlimited truck, carrying 11,250 bags of grapefruit, travels from Florida to New Jersey.

How much money should Fruits Unlimited be paid for one truckload of grapefruit?

Clue 3: The average price of grapefruit in New Jersey grocery stores is $.69 a pound.

How much money should Fruits Unlimited be paid for one truckload of grapefruit?

Clue 2: Each bag of grapefruit weighs 12 lb.

How much money should Fruits Unlimited be paid for one truckload of grapefruit?

Clue 4: New Jersey grocery stores charge $.25 a pound more than the price Fruits Unlimited receives for a pound of grapefruit.

COOPERATIVE PROBLEM SOLVING 2

Chapter 3

COOPERATIVE PROBLEM SOLVING / Problem 2

Kim, Jill, Sarah, and Pam are bringing oranges to a party. How much will the oranges cost? How much will each girl pay?

Clue 1: The girls decide they will need 20 lb of oranges. They will shop for the best buy.

Kim, Jill, Sarah, and Pam are bringing oranges to a party. How much will the oranges cost? How much will each girl pay?

Clue 2: Oranges cost $2.40 for 3 lb at a local store.

Kim, Jill, Sarah, and Pam are bringing oranges to a party. How much will the oranges cost? How much will each girl pay?

Clue 3: The girls can buy 10-lb bags of oranges for $.12 less per pound at a fruit stand.

Kim, Jill, Sarah, and Pam are bringing oranges to a party. How much will the oranges cost? How much will each girl pay?

Clue 4: The girls agree to pay an equal share of the total cost of the oranges.

GAMES

ORDER, PLEASE (For use after Lesson 3-2)

Objective: Use order of operations.

☑ **MATERIALS CHECKLIST:** number cube (0-5) and number cube (5-10) for each team of four or five players

One player tosses the number cubes twice, and all players record the numbers. The object of the game is to write an expression that uses all four numbers and all four operations to make a specified number, such as the greatest number or the number closest to 25, within a time limit, say two minutes. When time is called, players check each other's expressions; the player with the winning answer scores a point. After a few rounds, vary the rules, for example, using parentheses or omitting multiplication. The player with the highest score at the end wins.

POWER NUMBERS (For use after Lesson 3-8)

Objective: Multiply and divide by powers of ten.

☑ **MATERIALS CHECKLIST:** 20 index cards, spinner

Write a whole number or decimal number on each of 20 cards. On each of six equal sections on a spinner, write one of the following: $\times 10$, $\times 100$, $\times 1000$, $\div 10$, $\div 100$, $\div 1000$. Ask students to form two teams. The first player from Team A chooses a card and spins. After reading the number and the operation by a power of ten, he or she names the product or quotient within ten seconds. Team B can challenge an incorrect answer. The team with the correct answer gets one point; a team with an unjustified challenge loses a point. Teams alternate play until everyone has a turn. The team with more points wins.

BULLETIN BOARD

Astronomical Numbers

PLANET	DIAMETER (KM)	DISTANCE TO SUN (KM)
MERCURY	4.88×10^3	5.79×10^7
VENUS	1.21×10^4	1.082×10^8
EARTH	1.2756×10^4	1.496×10^8
MARS	6.794×10^3	2.279×10^8
JUPITER	1.42984×10^5	7.783×10^8
SATURN	1.20536×10^5	1.429×10^9
URANUS	5.11×10^4	2.875×10^9
NEPTUNE	4.92×10^4	4.504×10^9
PLUTO	3.2×10^3	5.9×10^9

Ask volunteers to make a model of each planet for a bulletin-board display. Also include a large chart and a pocket for planet cards. Prepare a card for each planet that gives its diameter and its distance from the sun in standard form. A student can choose a card and write the distances in scientific notation in the chart. When the chart is complete, students can write the standard form for the scientific notation and check their answers against the cards.

Alternative Assessment

In addition to the paper and pencil tests available with this program, the following items can help you assess critical thinking as well as your students' ability to solve problems in a wide variety of ways.

Open-ended Problem

The following exercise is missing a number. Show two different methods to find the missing number. Explain why both methods work.

$$
\begin{array}{r}
34.5 \\
\times \ \ 4.2 \\
\hline
69\ 0 \\
13?0\ 0 \\
\hline
144.90
\end{array}
$$

Teacher Notes

The missing number is 8.
- Possible methods to find the missing number are:
  a) Multiply $4 \times 345 = ?$
  b) Add the column: What number plus 6 will give you an answer that ends in a 4?
  c) Subtract the first line from the final answer: $14490 - 690 = 13800$

Open-ended Problem

The answers to the following pairs of problems are the same.
$5.2 \div 0.4 = 52 \div 4$
$200 \div 100 = 20 \div 10$
$13.9 \div 0.139 = 13900 \div 139$
Explain why.

In each case one expression can be obtained from the other by multiplying or dividing both numbers by the same power of 10.

Group Writing Activity (See p. T24)

Divide the paper in half and generate the following series.
1) A series of multiplication exercises where the product is larger than the factors.
2) A series of multiplication exercises where the product is smaller than the factors.

Teacher Notes
1) The product of any 2 whole numbers is greater than either factor.
2) The product of fractions or decimals greater than 0 and less than 1 is less than either factor.

Individual Writing Activity

Explain why the product of two whole numbers is always greater than either factors but the same is not true of the product of two decimals.

Portfolios

Portfolios can provide information about a student's growth in mathematical understanding over a period of time. They can help you make instructional decisions as well as become a vehicle to communicate with parents. The students' work involving the open-ended problem and writing activity suggested on this page along with work on the Create Your Own exercise on page 63, the Write About It exercise on page 73, the Learning Log exercises on pages 75 and 89, the three In Your Words exercises (37-39) on page 77, and the Creative Problem Solving lesson on pages 86-87 could be included in portfolios.

MULTIPLICATION AND DIVISION:
WHOLE NUMBERS AND DECIMALS 3

DID YOU KNOW . . . ?

Americans buy a total of 50,000 television sets every day. If you spread the sets evenly along the roads between New York and Los Angeles, they would be about 100 yd apart—the length of a football field.

The sign below tells how many items Americans buy each day.

Buy Buy Buy

Radios	Wristwatches
120,000	**190,000**
Cars	Pencils
25,000	**4,000,000**
Books	Running shoes
5,000,000	**52,000**

USING DATA

Collect
Organize
Describe
Predict

Which of the above items do Americans buy more than 50 million of in 1 yr? **watches and books**

Organize the facts in a table. Show how many yards apart pencils, books, etc., would be from each other if they were spread evenly on the 2,800 mi from New York to Los Angeles.

See page 89b.

CHAPTER 3 59

Using the Chapter Opener

The purpose of this page is to involve the student in the use of real data much like that presented in newspapers and magazines.

To use this page as you begin the chapter, direct the students' attention to the data. You may wish to ask questions such as the following:

From examining the data, which items spread evenly along the road between New York City and Los Angeles would be about 200 yd apart? *(cars)* **How do you know?** *(There are half as many cars as television sets. Thus the distance between two cars must be twice that of the distance between two TV sets.)*

What do you need to do to decide how many yards apart from each other each radio would be if the radios were spread evenly along the road? *(Change the number of miles to yards; divide this number by the number of radios.)*

Which will be farther apart: books or pencils? *(pencils)*

If Americans bought 100,000 wristwatches instead of 190,000 each day, about how many yards apart from each other would they be? *(50 yd)*

You may wish to use the organizing and describing activities as cooperative learning situations.

Lesson Organizer

Objective: Identify properties of multiplication.

Prior Knowledge: Students should know basic multiplication facts and the addition properties.

Error Analysis and Remediation: See page 89A.

Lesson Resources:
Practice Worksheet 3-1
Reteaching Activity 3-1
Enrichment Worksheet 3-1
Daily Review 3-1

Two-Minute Math

Name the property.

$$4,813 + 0 = 4,813$$

$$75 + (25 + 39) = (75 + 25) + 39$$

$$1.7 + 2.0 + 0.3 + 0.4 = 2.4 + 2$$

1 INTRODUCE

CONNECTING ACTIVITY

☑ **MATERIALS CHECKLIST:** bundling sticks, 25 per group; rubber bands

1. Have students work in small groups to model *3 × 6* and *6 × 3*. **What is true about the two expressions?** *(The product is the same.)*

2. Have students use the sticks to show $(3 \times 2) \times 4$ and $3 \times (2 \times 4)$.

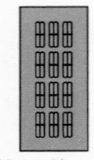 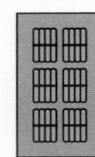

(3 × 2) × 4   3 × (2 × 4)

What effect did the parentheses have on the product? *(No effect)*

3. Have students model $2 \times (3 + 4)$ and $(2 \times 3) + (2 \times 4)$. **What is the product of each model?** *(14)*

WHEN YOUR STUDENTS ASK
★ WHY AM I LEARNING THIS? ★

You can connect this skill to real life through students' school work. Using the multiplication properties helps them organize factors for quicker computation.

Mental Math and Properties of Multiplication

A helicopter tour of Manhattan Island costs about $50 plus $3 tax per person. About how much would the tour cost for 6 passengers?

You can compute this mentally.

$$6 \times 50 = 300$$
$$6 \times 3 = 18 \qquad \text{The tour would cost about \$318.}$$

The multiplication properties can help you compute mentally.

THINK ALOUD Explain which property was used above.   distributive property

Commutative Property: Changing the order of the factors does not change the product.

In arithmetic: $50 \times 6 = 6 \times 50$ In algebra: $a \times b = b \times a$
$300 = 300$

Associative Property: Changing the grouping of the factors does not change the product.

In arithmetic: In algebra:
$(50 \times 3) \times 6 = 50 \times (3 \times 6)$ $(a \times b) \times c = a \times (b \times c)$
$150 \times 6 = 50 \times 18$
$900 = 900$

Distributive Property: The product of a factor and a sum is equal to the sum of the products.

In arithmetic: In algebra:
$6 \times (50 + 3) = (6 \times 50) + (6 \times 3)$ $a \times (b + c) = (a \times b) + (a \times c)$
$6(53) = 300 + 18$
$318 = 318$

Identity Property: The product of one and any other number is that number.

In arithmetic: $50 \times 1 = 50$ In algebra: $a \times 1 = a$

Zero Property: The product of zero and any other number is zero.

In arithmetic: $53 \times 0 = 0$ In algebra: $a \times 0 = 0$

60   LESSON 3–1

2 TEACH

What does the commutative property tell you about the order in which you multiply two numbers? *(The order does not change the product.)*

When you multiply three numbers, does it matter which two numbers you multiply first? Explain. *(No; the order and grouping can be different, but the product remains the same.)*

What two operations does the distributive property link? Give an example. *[addition and multiplication;* $4 \times 16 = (4 \times 10) + (4 \times 6)$ *]*

Chalkboard Examples

Name the property.
$9 \times 6 = 6 \times 9$ *(commutative)*
$83 \times 1 = 83$ *(identity)*
$0 \times 27 = 0$ *(zero)*

SUMMARIZE/ASSESS **Explain how the properties of multiplication can help you find products mentally.** *(Help you order and group numbers so mental computation is easier)*

GUIDED PRACTICE

THINK ALOUD Explain which multiplication property is used in each equation.

1. $34 \times 19 = 19 \times 34$
commutative property
2. $0 \times x = 0$
zero property
3. $1 \times m = m$
identity property
4. $8 \times 18 = (8 \times 10) + (8 \times 8)$
distributive property

PRACTICE

Use the multiplication properties to simplify mentally.

5. $150 \times 1 \times 4$ 600
6. $1,432 \times 0 \times 54$ 0
7. $20 \times 70 \times 5$ 7,000
8. $(30 + 7) \times 2$ 74
9. $(13 \times 25) \times 4$ 1,300
10. $6 \times (20 + 5)$ 150
11. $90 \times 1 \times 60$ 5,400
12. $250 \times 7 \times 2$ 3,500
13. $20 \times (5 \times 23)$ 2,300
14. $(9 \times 35) \times 2$ 630
15. $25 \times 83 \times 4$ 8,300
16. $92 \times 8 \times 0 \times 53$ 0
17. $(9 \times 125) \times 4$ 4,500
18. $25 \times (13 \times 4)$ 1,300
19. $(250 \times 11) \times 4$ 11,000

NUMBER SENSE Find a match that makes an equation.

20. $16 \times (35 + 16) =$ c
21. $16 \times (35 \times 88) =$ b
22. $16 \times (88 + 35) =$ a

a. $(88 + 35) \times 16$
b. $(16 \times 35) \times 88$
c. $(16 \times 35) + (16 \times 16)$

PROBLEM SOLVING

Use a property to solve mentally.

23. The water shuttle from Manhattan Island to La Guardia Airport costs about $20 per person. What is the total cost for 75 passengers?
distributive property; $1,500

24. The bus from Manhattan to JFK Airport costs about $11 per person. If the bus makes 8 trips in one day, how much money is collected if 25 seats are bought for each trip?
associative property; $2,200

Estimate

You can use **compatible numbers** to estimate a product. Compatible numbers are close to original numbers but easier to use.

$247 \Rightarrow 250$
$\times 4 \quad\quad \times 4$

250 is close to 247, but is easier to multiply.

Use a compatible number to help you estimate the product.
$\approx 24,000$
1. 495×7 $\approx 3,500$
2. 117×6 ≈ 720
3. 838×2 $\approx 1,680$
4. $2,968 \times 8$

MEETING INDIVIDUAL NEEDS

For Students Who Are . . .

Acquiring English Proficiency Write definitions of *commutative*, *associative*, and *distributive* on the chalkboard. Have students discuss how the properties relate to these definitions.

Gifted and Talented Have students prepare a written explanation of how they used mental math to solve Exercises 23 and 24.

Working 2 or 3 Grades Below Level Have students who are having difficulty with basic multiplication facts use pages 4–33 of the Skills Workbook for Whole Number Multiplication and Division.

Today's Problem

In the 1940s large computers could perform 5,000 operations per second. In the 1980s microcomputers could perform $\frac{1}{2}$ million operations per second. How much faster were the microcomputers than the computers of the 1940s? ($\frac{1}{2}$ *million = 500,000; 500,000 ÷ 5,000 = 100; 100 times faster*)

---

3 FOLLOW-UP

PRACTICE 3-1

Use the multiplication properties to simplify mentally.

1. $25 \times 5 \times 4 =$ __500__
2. $859 \times 0 \times 1 =$ __0__
3. $5 \times (6 + 7) =$ __65__
4. $200 \times (14 + 5) =$ __3,800__
5. $70 \times 1 \times 50 =$ __3,500__
6. $(4 \times 16) \times 25 =$ __1,600__
7. $(2 \times 6) \times (50 \times 4) =$ __2,400__
8. $87 \times (16 \times 7) \times 0 =$ __0__
9. $(100 \times 6) \times (8 \times 10) =$ __48,000__
10. $(40 + 5) \times 3 =$ __135__
11. $(250 \times 4) \times 18 =$ __18,000__
12. $(80 \times 1) \times 60 =$ __4,800__
13. $8 \times (30 + 8) =$ __304__
14. $(125 \times 17) \times 8 =$ __17,000__
15. $15 \times (30 \times 6) =$ __2,700__
16. $150 \times 6 \times 4 =$ __3,600__
17. $5 \times (20 \times 11) =$ __1,100__
18. $20 \times (5 \times 77) =$ __7,700__

Find a match that makes an equation.

19. $(18 \times 47) \times 29 =$ __c__
20. $18 + (47 \times 29) =$ __a__
21. $18 \times (29 + 47) =$ __b__

a. $(47 \times 29) + 18$
b. $(18 \times 47) + (18 \times 29)$
c. $18 \times (47 \times 29)$

Use compatible numbers to help you estimate the product.
800×6 110×9 $5,200 \times 10$
22. $789 \times 6 =$ __4,800__
23. $106 \times 9 =$ __990__
24. $5,201 \times 8 =$ __52,000__

Use a property to solve mentally.

25. The auditorium of the Cinema Plus movie theater has 30 rows of seats. There are 15 gray seats and 3 blue seats in each row. What is the total number of seats?
540 seats

26. There were 11 people at the first Save-the-Lake Committee meeting. There were twice as many people at the second meeting and three times the number at the third meeting as the second. How many people attended the third meeting?
66 people

RETEACHING 3-1

☑ **MATERIALS CHECKLIST:** Index cards, marking pens

Have the students work together in pairs to make their own flashcards for the multiplication properties.

Front	Back
$2 \times 3 = 3 \times 2$	Commutative Property

Ask the students to make two different cards for each property. Allow them to use their flashcards with each other as a warm-up exercise the next day.

ENRICHMENT 3-1

Name the properties illustrated in each equation. Addition and multiplication properties may be used.

1. $25 \times (16 + 0) = (25 \times 16) + (25 \times 0)$ — distributive
2. $(28 \times 16) \times 13 = 13 \times (28 \times 16)$ — commutative for multiplication
3. $4 \times (6 + 0) \times 1 = [(4 \times 6) + (4 \times 0)] \times 1$ — distributive
4. $(9 + 16 + 11) \times 3 = (3 \times 9) + (3 \times 16) + (3 \times 11)$ — distributive
5. $(18 + 29) + (2 + 31) = (18 + 2) + (29 + 31)$ — associative for addition
6. $4 \times (3 + 0 + 16) = (4 \times 3) + (0 \times 4) + (16 \times 4)$ — distributive and commutative
7. $a \times (b + c + d) = (a \times b) + (a \times c) + (a \times d)$ — distributive
8. $(3 + 4) \times y = (3 \times y) + (4 \times y)$ — distributive
9. $(a \times 1) \times 0 = a \times (0 \times 1)$ — associative for multiplication
10. $(24 \times 18) \times 1 = (24 \times 1) \times 18$ — associative for multiplication

Another way to indicate multiplication when a variable is used is to place the number next to the variable without any sign between them.

Example: $2a$ means $2 \times a$

Name the property shown by each step.

11. $4x + 8y + 3x + 16y = 4x + 3x + 8y + 16y$ — commutative for addition
$= (4 + 3)x + (8 + 16)y$ — distributive
$= 7x + 24y$

12. $16 \times (18 + 0 + 1) = 16 \times 18 + 16 \times 0 + 16 \times 1$ — distributive
$= 16 \times 18 + 0 + 16 \times 1$ — zero for multiplication
$= 16 \times 18 + 0 + 16$ — identity for multiplication
$= 16 \times 18 + 16$ — zero for addition
$= 304$

Lesson Organizer

Objective: Use order of operations.

Prior Knowledge: Students should know the properties of addition and multiplication.

Error Analysis and Remediation: See page 89A.

Lesson Resources:
Practice Worksheet 3-2
Reteaching Activity 3-2
Enrichment Worksheet 3-2
Daily Review 3-2

Two-Minute Math

Choose a one-digit nonzero number. Add 20, and multiply the sum by 100. Then add 400, divide by 10, and subtract 240. What is the result? *(Result is ten times the original number.)*

1 INTRODUCE

SYMBOLIC ACTIVITY

Write the expression $4 + 2 \times 6 = n$ on the chalkboard. **What is the value of *n* if you add first, then multiply?** *(n = 36)* **If you multiply first, then add?** *(n = 16)* Point out that there is only one correct way to simplify the expression if everyone is to get the same answer. Then explain that mathematicians have established rules that govern which operations are performed first. **Since this rule states that you multiply first, which answer is correct?** *(16)*

WHEN YOUR STUDENTS ASK
★ WHY AM I LEARNING THIS? ★

You can use this skill to solve real life problems. Suppose you want to program a VCR to record a TV show. You must follow the programming steps in the correct order to record the show.

Order of Operations

Michelle won a contest at her local grocery store. When she collected her prize, she correctly answered the skill-test question below. Which way did Michelle simplify the expression?

$5 + 8 \times (2 + 6) \div 4$	$5 + 8 \times (2 + 6) \div 4$
$13 \times (2 + 6) \div 4$	$5 + 8 \times (8) \div 4$
$13 \times 8 \div 4$	$5 + 64 \div 4$
$104 \div 4$	$5 + 16$
26	21

Which one is correct? **21**

THINK ALOUD Use the **order of operations** rules below to explain why 26 is not correct and 21 is.
21 is correct because steps 1, 3, and 4 were done in order.

Simplify in this order:

1. Do all operations within parentheses first.

2. Simplify all numbers with exponents.

3. Multiply and divide in order from left to right.

4. Add and subtract in order from left to right.

THINK ALOUD Explain the steps used to simplify.

		Order of operations: 1, 1, 2, 3
$6 \times (10 + 4) \div 2^2$	$(6 \times 10) + 4 \div 2^2$	$(6 \times 10 + 4) \div 2^2$
$6 \times 14 \div 2^2$	$60 + 4 \div 2^2$	$(60 + 4) \div 2^2$
$6 \times 14 \div 4$	$60 + 4 \div 4$	$64 \div 2^2$
$84 \div 4$	$60 + 1$	$64 \div 4$
21	61	16

Order of operations: 1, 2, 3, 3   Order of operations: 1, 2, 3, 4

GUIDED PRACTICE

Name the operation to be done first.

1. $8 + 7 \times 3$	**2.** $6^2 \div (5 - 2)$	**3.** $13 + 9^2 - 6$	**4.** $(18 - 7) \times 3$
7×3	$5 - 2$	9^2	$18 - 7$

Follow the order of operations to simplify.

5. $9 + 3 \times 6$ **27**	**6.** $(7 + 3) \times 4$ **40**	**7.** $8 - 9 \div 3^2$ **7**
8. $25 \times 2 + 4^2$ **66**	**9.** $25 \times (2 + 4)$ **150**	**10.** $9 + 2 - 6 \div 3$ **9**

Calculators should be available for complex calculations.

2 TEACH

✓ MATERIALS CHECKLIST: calculators

What is the purpose of parentheses in an expression? *(to indicate which operations(s) must be performed first.)*

What is the order of operations in simplifying the expression $4 \times 5^2 + 18$?
(Simplify 5^2; multiply by 4, finally add 18)

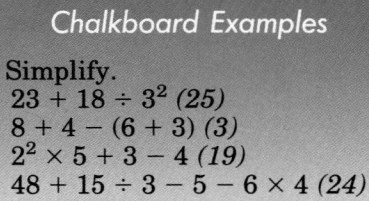

Chalkboard Examples

Simplify.
$23 + 18 \div 3^2$ *(25)*
$8 + 4 - (6 + 3)$ *(3)*
$2^2 \times 5 + 3 - 4$ *(19)*
$48 + 15 \div 3 - 5 - 6 \times 4$ *(24)*

SUMMARIZE/ASSESS **Explain how to use the order of operations to simplify the expression $4^3 \div 8 + (8 \times 3) - 12$; then find the answer.** *(First multiply 8×3 to remove the parentheses; then simplify 4^3; next divide by 8; finally add and subtract from left to right; 20)*

345

PRACTICE

Simplify the expression. Use a calculator, mental math, or pencil and paper.

11. $42 \times 2 - 16$ **68**
12. $13 + 8 \times 4$ **45**
13. $(10 - 1) \div 3$ **3**

14. $4 \times 2 + 5 - 3$ **10**
15. $14 - 6 \times 2 - 1$ **1**
16. $72 - 6 \times 1$ **66**

17. $14 - 6 \times (2 - 1)$ **8**
18. $15 \div 5 \times 9 + 2$ **29**
19. $2 + 2 \times 2 \div 2 - 2$ **2**

20. $1 \times 40 + 3$ **43**
21. $50 \times (9 - 6) \div 3$ **50**
22. $10 + 0 \div 2^2$ **10**

23. $9 + 6 \times 4 - 5 \times 3$ **18**
24. $17 + 20 \div 2 \div 2 \div 5$ **18**
25. $20 \times 4 \div 5 + 0 \times 1$ **16**

26. $(8 + 4) \div 2^2$ **3**
27. $3^2 \times (16 \div 4) \div 4$ **9**

*28. $42 + 58 + (60 - 40 \div 5)$ **152**
*29. $5^2 \times 1^3 \times (7 \div 1)$ **175**

*30. $2^2 \times 5 \div 4 + 3$ **8**
*31. $(99 \div 9 - 3 \times 2) - (7 - 4)$ **2**

CRITICAL THINKING   Insert parentheses to make
the mathematical sentence true.

32. $(19 - 16) \div 3 = 1$
33. $6 \times (4 + 8) = 72$
34. $(23 + 5) \times 4 = 112$

*35. $6 \times (4 + 8) \div 2 = 36$
*36. $(18 - 14) \times 20 \div 5 = 16$

PROBLEM SOLVING

 Choose mental math, paper and pencil,
or calculator to solve.   **Choices will vary. Suggestions given.**

37. Tim won $1,000 in a local contest.
To claim his prize, he had to find
the product of:
$5 + 12 \div 3$ and $15 - (3 \times 4)$.
What is the product?   **m; 27**

38. The answer to the skill-test question
for the Spanish Club contest is 93.
What is the question:
$(42 - 36 \div 4) \times 3$ or
$78 - 44 \div 2^2 + (4 + 22)$?
c; $78 - 44 \div 2^2 + (4 + 22)$

39. **CREATE YOUR OWN**   Write a skill-test question with five numbers
and at least three different operations that has an answer of 79.
Check students' work.

MEETING INDIVIDUAL NEEDS

For Students Who Are . . .

Acquiring English Proficiency   Pair students with an English-proficient student to discuss and solve the Problem Solving exercises.

Gifted and Talented   Challenge students to create their own methods for remembering the order of operations.

Working 2 or 3 Grades Below Level   Have students use pages 8–9 of the Skills Workbook for equations, ratio, proportion, and percent.

Today's Problem

If 25 seventh-grade students each donate $.25 to each of 25 worthy causes, how much money will they have donated all together?
$(25 \times \$.25 \times 25 = \$156.25)$

---

3 FOLLOW-UP

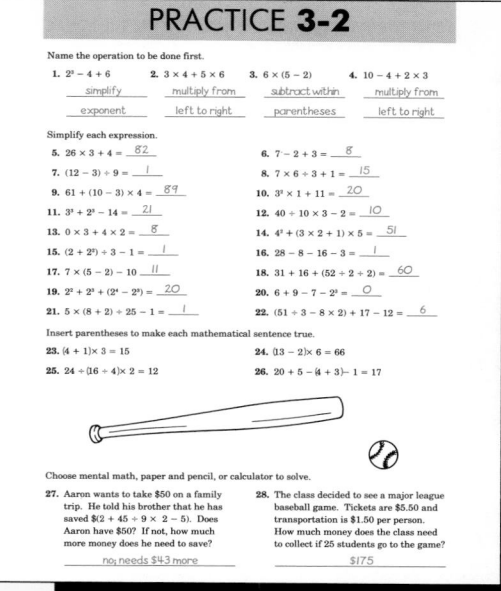

PRACTICE 3-2

Name the operation to be done first.

1. $2^3 - 4 + 6$ — simplify exponent
2. $3 \times 4 + 5 \times 6$ — multiply from left to right
3. $6 \times (5 - 2)$ — subtract within parentheses
4. $10 - 4 + 2 \times 3$ — multiply from left to right

Simplify each expression.

5. $26 \times 3 + 4 =$ **82**
6. $7 - 2 + 3 =$ **8**
7. $(12 - 3) \div 9 =$ **1**
8. $7 \times 6 + 3 + 1 =$ **15**
9. $61 + (10 - 3) \times 4 =$ **89**
10. $3^2 \times 1 + 11 =$ **20**
11. $3^3 + 2^3 - 14 =$ **21**
12. $40 + 10 \times 3 - 2 =$ **10**
13. $0 \times 3 + 4 \times 2 =$ **8**
14. $4^3 + (3 \times 2 + 1) \times 5 =$ **51**
15. $(2 + 2^3) \div 3 - 1 =$ **1**
16. $28 - 8 - 16 - 3 =$ **1**
17. $7 \times (5 - 2) - 10 =$ **11**
18. $31 + 16 + (52 \div 2 \div 2) =$ **60**
19. $2^2 + 2^3 + (2^4 - 2^3) =$ **20**
20. $6 + 9 - 7 - 2^3 =$ **0**
21. $5 \times (8 + 2) + 25 - 1 =$ **1**
22. $(51 - 3 - 8 \times 2) + 17 - 12 =$ **6**

Insert parentheses to make each mathematical sentence true.

23. $(4 + 1) \times 3 = 15$
24. $(13 - 2) \times 6 = 66$
25. $24 \div (16 + 4) \times 2 = 12$
26. $20 + 5 - (4 + 3) - 1 = 17$

Choose mental math, paper and pencil, or calculator to solve.

27. Aaron wants to take $50 on a family
trip. He told his brother that he has
saved $(2 + 45 + 9 \times 2 - 5)$. Does
Aaron have $50? If not, how much
more money does he need to save?
no; needs $43 more

28. The class decided to see a major league
baseball game. Tickets are $5.50 and
transportation is $1.50 per person.
How much money does the class need
to collect if 25 students go to the game?
$175

RETEACHING 3-2

☑ **MATERIALS CHECKLIST:** Index cards

Write the following on the board:
$15 - (2^2 \times 3) \div 6 = 13$.
Have students work in groups of four. Provide each group with these symbols on separate index cards: $=, -, +, \times, \div, (,)$, $15, 2^2, 3, 6, 13$, and several blank cards. Have students use the cards to model the mathematical sentence on the board. Group members then take turns applying one rule of the order of operations. For example, one student writes 4 on a blank card and replaces the 2^2 card, the next student writes 12 on a blank card and replaces the (4×3) cards, and so on. Have the students repeat the activity.

ENRICHMENT 3-2

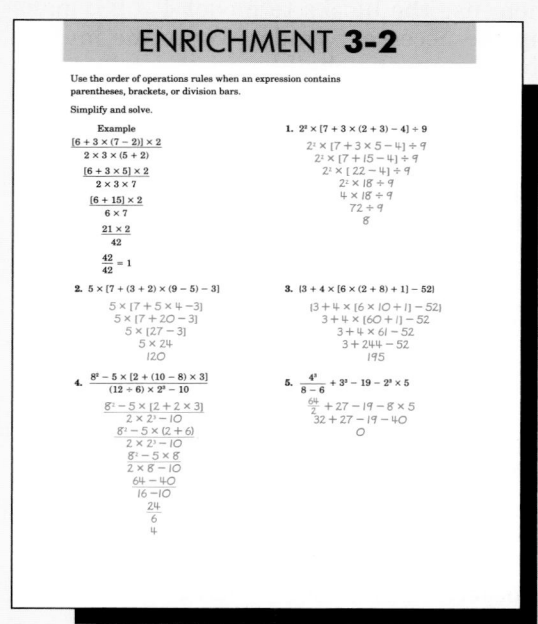

Lesson Organizer

Objective: Multiply whole numbers.

Prior Knowledge: Students should know basic multiplication facts.

Lesson Resources:
Practice Worksheet 3-3
Reteaching Activity 3-3
Enrichment Worksheet 3-3
Daily Review 3-3
Cooperative Problem Solving 1,
 Chapter 3

Two-Minute Math

Name the next three numbers in the sequence.

1, 2, 4, 8, . . .   (16, 32, 64)

3, 6, 12, 24, . . .   (48, 96, 192)

4, 20, 100, 500, . . .

(2,500, 12,500, 62, 500)

1 INTRODUCE

CONNECTING ACTIVITY

☑ **MATERIALS CHECKLIST:** base-10 blocks, several of each kind for each group of three or four students

1. Have small groups of students represent 23 using base-10 blocks. Then have them use the blocks to model 4 × 23, making the necessary trades. Write the multiplication on the chalkboard and relate the product to their model.

2. Have students use the blocks to model 14 × 23. Then write the algorithm on the chalkboard, reviewing each step in computing the product.

WHEN YOUR STUDENTS ASK
★ WHY AM I LEARNING THIS? ★

You can connect this skill to real life through catering or party planning. Caterers multiply to determine how much food to order and how many dishes, glasses, and utensils will be needed.

Multiplying Whole Numbers

Chicago's O'Hare Airport averages about 2,150 flights a day. At this rate, about how many flights would there be in February during a non-leap year?

Multiply the 2,150 flights by the 28 d (days) in February.

2,150		Estimate to check.
× 28		2,000
17 200	←2,150 × 8	× 30
43 000	←2,150 × 20	60,000
60,200		

There would be about 60,200 flights in February.

THINK ALOUD Without computing, decide whether O'Hare averages about 785,000 or 785,000,000 flights in a year. Explain. **785,000 flights; Multiply 60,000 flights by 12 mo.**

Other examples:

529	Estimate to check.	1,406	Estimate to check.
× 390	500	× 58	1,400
47 610	× 400	11 248	× 60
158 700	200,000	70 300	84,400
206,310		81,548	

--- **GUIDED PRACTICE** ---

Choose the best estimate.

1. 38 × 22 is about: a
   a. 800   b. 8,000   c. 900

2. 63 × 793 is about: b
   a. 40,000   b. 48,000   c. 4,800

Find the product. Check your answer.

3. 38
   × 25
   950

4. 63
   × 80
   5,040

5. 3,281 × 8
   26,248

6. 508 × 83
   42,164

64   LESSON 3-3

When using this lesson to review the topic, students should use calculators for computation.

2 TEACH

☑ **MATERIALS CHECKLIST:** Calculators

Demonstrate the distributive property using 15 × 445.
[15 × (400 + 40 + 5) =
15(400) + 15(40) + 15(5)]

Why should you estimate a product, even if you are using a calculator? *(It is possible to enter a number incorrectly. Estimating helps you determine if your answer is reasonable.)*

Chalkboard Examples

67 × 8 *(536)*
359 × 6 *(2,154)*
243 × 45 *(10,935)*
2,381 × 78 *(185,718)*

SUMMARIZE/ASSESS **Explain how to multiply a four-digit number by a three-digit number when the problem is written horizontally.** *(Paper and pencil: Students should mention the importance of place-value alignment and then give the steps in the algorithm. Calculator: Enter each number separated by ⊠ and followed by =.)*

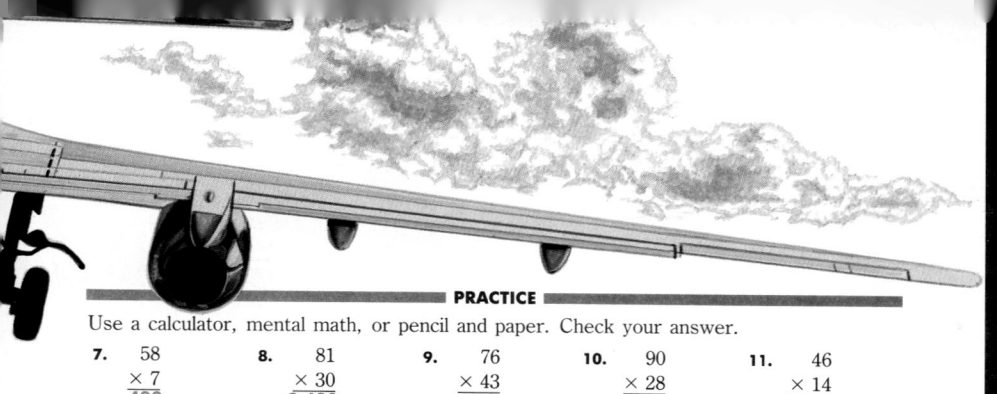

PRACTICE

Use a calculator, mental math, or pencil and paper. Check your answer.

7. 58
× 7
406

8. 81
× 30
2,430

9. 76
× 43
3,268

10. 90
× 28
2,520

11. 46
× 14
644

12. 34 × 9
306

13. 32 × 79
2,528

14. 16 × 225
3,600

15. 637 × 21
13,377

16. 205 × 70
14,350

17. 718 × 899
645,482

18. 3,060 × 83
253,980

19. 2,956 × 740
2,187,440

20. 2,005 × 507
1,016,535

21. $504 × 288
$145,152

22. $6,308 × 326
$2,056,408

23. 31 × $5,163
$160,053

MIXED REVIEW Compute.

24. 12.4 + 3.75
16.15

25. 16 × 29
464

26. 45 − 9.2
35.8

27. 185 + 46
231

28. 721 − 345
376

29. 0.4 − 0.25
0.15

30. 5 × 743
3,715

31. 3.7 + 0.5
4.2

MENTAL MATH Simplify mentally.

32. 50 × (40 × 90)
180,000

33. (47 × 250) × 8
94,000

34. (3 × 25) × 4,000
300,000

PROBLEM SOLVING

CHOOSE Choose estimation or paper and pencil to solve. Choices will vary. Suggestions are given.

Speedair Flights

Detroit to:	Plane	Seating Capacity	Departure Time	Arrival Time	Frequency
New York	757	224	9:50 P.M.	11:27 P.M.	Daily
Miami	DC10	325	8:00 A.M.	10:42 A.M.	Daily
Nassau	DC9	118	9:05 A.M.	2:00 P.M.	MTWTHF

35. Name two exact numbers and two estimates in the table.
exact: seating capacities; estimate: times

36. All Speedair flights are in the same time zone. About how many hours and minutes does each flight last?
p; to New York: 1 h 37 min; to Miami: 2 h 42 min; to Nassau: 4 h 55 min

*37. Represent the seating capacities of the three kinds of airplanes with a pictograph. Use the symbol ◆ to represent 25 seats. **See page 89b.**

MEETING INDIVIDUAL NEEDS

For Students Who Are . . .

Acquiring English Proficiency Locate Detroit, New York, Boston, and Atlanta on a U.S. wall map. Check students' understanding of *time zone* and *pictograph*. Have students work together on the Problem Solving exercises.

Gifted and Talented Have students work together to assign ticket prices for each flight in the table on page 65 and write and solve problems related to amounts of ticket sales.

Working 2 or 3 Grades Below Level Have students use pages 34–63 of the Skills Workbook for Whole Number Multiplication and Division.

Today's Problem

The product of two numbers is 315. Their sum is 36. What are the two numbers? *(The numbers are 15 and 21.)*

3 FOLLOW-UP

PRACTICE 3-3

Find the product. Check your answer.

1. 67
×8
536

2. 67
×9
603

3. 83
×46
3,818

4. 50
×46
2,300

5. 97
×46
4,462

6. 347
×85
29,495

7. 150
×25
3,750

8. 712
×85
60,520

9. 398
×659
262,282

10. 4,093
×376
1,538,968

11. $674
×808
$544,592

12. $1,057
×408
$431,256

Simplify without paper and pencil.

13. (60 × 25) × 4 = **6,000**

14. 200 × (57 × 5) = **57,000**

Choose estimation or paper and pencil to solve.

15. Mrs. West decided to buy an apple a day as an after-school snack for each of her two children. Apples are 25¢ each. If there are 22 school days this month, how much will Mrs. West spend on apples for the month? **$11.00**

16. Use exactly four 2's and addition, subtraction, multiplication, or division to express the numbers.

one **(2+2) ÷ (2+2) = 1**

three **(2 + 2 + 2) ÷ 2 = 3**

five **2 + 2 + 2 ÷ 2 = 5**

two **(2 − 2) ÷ 2 + 2 = 2**

four **2 + 2 + 2 − 2 = 4**

six **2 × 2 × 2 − 2 = 6**

RETEACHING 3-3

Have the students work in pairs. Each pair plans an imaginary party for a different number of guests. Have each pair determine how many packages of the following they will need.

Napkins: 25 per package
Noisemakers: 4 per package
Cups: 40 per package
Favors: 7 per package

What if everyone uses two napkins? three cups? *(Answers will vary depending on numbers used. Check students' work.)*

ENRICHMENT 3-3

Use multiplication to solve each problem.

1. Roberto gave half of his baseball cards to Juan, then half of what was left to Steven, and half of the remaining cards to Carl. Roberto now has 20 cards left for himself. How many cards did Roberto have when he started? **160**

How many cards did Roberto give away? **140**

2. Susan receives her allowance in dimes and quarters. She has three times more dimes than quarters. She has saved $3.30. How many dimes does she have? **18**

How many quarters does she have? **6**

3. A farmer has some cows and chickens. When the farmer counts the animals altogether, he counts 39 heads and 124 legs. How many are cows? **23**

How many are chickens? **16**

4. George earns $15 per hour for a 40-hour week. His foreman asks him to work an additional 10 hours on Saturdays. George gets "double time" for weekend work. How much money will George earn for the next three weeks? **$900 per week or $2,700**

5. A powerful microscope invented in 1981 in Switzerland magnifies objects 100,000,000 times their actual size. How many millimeters wide would a 3mm object appear to be under this magnification? **300,000,000 mm**

Convert this to meters. **300,000 m**

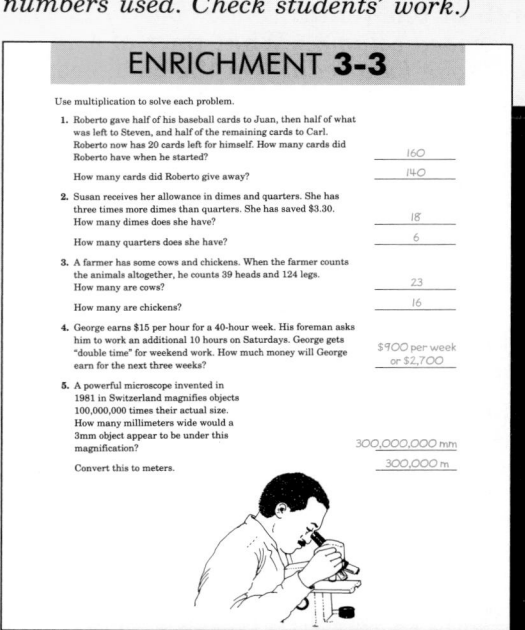

Lesson Organizer

Objective: Multiply decimals.

Prior Knowledge: Students should know how to multiply whole numbers.

Error Analysis and Remediation: See page 89A.

Lesson Resources:
Practice Worksheet 3-4
Reteaching Worksheet 3-4
Enrichment Activity 3-4
Daily Review 3-4

 *Two-Minute Math*

- 0.2 + 0.2 + 0.2 *(0.6)*
- 0.12 + 0.12 + 0.12 *(0.36)*
- 1.3 + 1.3 + 1.3 + 1.3 *(5.2)*

1 INTRODUCE

CONNECTING ACTIVITY

☑ **MATERIALS CHECKLIST:** Teaching Aid 2 (Decimal Squares) for each student

1. How can you show one-tenth on the hundredths' decimal square? *(Shade one column.)* **How can you show one-tenth of one-tenth?** *(Shade one square in the shaded column.)* **What part of 1 is this?** *(one-hundredth)* On the chalkboard, write 0.1 × 0.1 = *n*, and ask students to solve.

2. How can you show one-tenth on the thousandths' decimal square? *(Shade one column.)* **How can you show one-hundredth of a tenth?** *(Shade a single little square.)* On the chalkboard, write 0.1 × 0.01 = *n* and ask students to complete. **What is the product of tenths times hundredths?** *(thousandths)*

3. Relate this activity to the symbolic representation for decimal multiplication. Have students find these products:
0.1 × 0.3 *(0.03)*   0.26 × 0.8 *(0.208)*

WHEN YOUR STUDENTS ASK
★ WHY AM I LEARNING THIS? ★

You can connect this skill to real life through sales work. Wholesale merchants who sell case-lots of goods must multiply the number of items times the cost per item to find the total cost.

Multiplying Decimals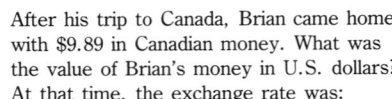

After his trip to Canada, Brian came home with $9.89 in Canadian money. What was the value of Brian's money in U.S. dollars? At that time, the exchange rate was:

$1 Canadian = $.85 U.S.

- Multiply the Canadian money ($9.89) by the U.S. exchange rate ($.85). Note how the decimal point is placed in the product.

```
      9.89  ←—2 decimal places
   ×  0.85  ←—2 decimal places
      4945
     7912
    8.4065  ←—4 decimal places
```

To the nearest cent, Brian's Canadian money was worth $8.41 in U.S. funds.

- Estimate to check the answer.
$10 × 0.85 = $8.50
$8.50 is close to $8.41.

> Other examples:
>
> What is 0.28 × 0.4?   0.28 ←—2 decimal places
>   × 0.4 ←—1 decimal place
>   0.112 ←—3 decimal places
>
> Estimate to check: 0.3 × 0.4 = 0.12

THINK ALOUD Why is the product, 0.112, smaller than 0.28 and 0.4? When a given number is multiplied by a number less than 1, the product is always less than the given number. Find the product of 2.69 and 16. On a calculator:

2.69  16 = 43.04

Estimate to check: 3 × 16 = 48

GUIDED PRACTICE

NUMBER SENSE Choose the correct product. Do not calculate.

1. 2.7 × 8   2.16, 21.6, 216
   21.6

2. 2.37 × 14   331.8, 3.318, 33.18
   33.18

Is the product *reasonable* or *unreasonable*? If *unreasonable*, find the correct product.

3. 20.5 × 3.1   635.5
   unreasonable; 63.55

4. 4.6 × 0.05   0.23
   reasonable

66   LESSON 3–4

Calculators should be available for complex calculations.

2 TEACH

☑ **MATERIALS CHECKLIST:** calculators

How does the number of decimal places in the product compare with the number of decimal places in the factors? *(It is the sum of the number of decimal places in the factors.)*

Is it always true that a product is greater than either factor? Give examples. *(When multiplying two decimals less than one, the product is less than either factor; for example, 0.3 × 0.4 = 0.12.)*

> *Chalkboard Examples*
> 24.3 × 8 *(194.4)*
> 5.78 × 3.3 *(19.074)*
> 14.58 × 0.51 *(7.4358)*
> 0.409 × 0.29 *(0.11861)*

SUMMARIZE/ASSESS **Explain how to find the product of two decimals.** *(Multiply as if both factors were whole numbers, and place the decimal point in the product.)*

Use a calculator, mental math, or pencil and paper. Check your answer.

5.	6.	7.	8.	9.
2.73	5.307	30.241	0.05	0.0053
× 2.3	× 5.8	× 0.72	× 0.03	× 0.046
6.279	**30.7806**	**21.77352**	**0.0015**	**0.0002438**

10. $3.25 × 0.04
$0.13
11. $21.15 × 0.8
$16.92
12. $70.00 × 0.004
$.28

13. 16.78 × 1,000
16,780
14. 495.2 × 10
4,952
15. 56 × 100
5,600
16. 4.5 × 3.8
17.1

17. 4.3 × 0.253
1.0879
18. 7.2 × 2.42
17.424
19. 0.42 × 0.12
0.0504
*20. 0.2 × (6 − 0.8)
1.04

MIXED REVIEW Compute.

21. 542 − 16
526
22. 6 + 5³
131
23. 0.009 × 0
0
24. 7,002 ÷ 9
778

25. 8.45 × 1³
8.45
26. 40 − 3.7
36.3
27. 9.5 × 100
950
28. 3³ + 2³
35

ESTIMATE Estimate the product.

29. $5.29 × 1.3
≈ **$5.00**
30. $698.95 × 0.6
≈ **$420.00**
31. 40¢ × 0.28
≈ **12¢**

PROBLEM SOLVING

CHOOSE Choose paper and pencil or calculator to solve. Round to cents. **Choices will vary.**

32. Bonnie changed 12,750 Mexican pesos to U.S. dollars. If 1 peso at that time was equal to $.0038 U.S., how much U.S. money did she get? **c; $48.45**

33. If 1 peso exchanges for $.0041 U.S., how much U.S. money can Bonnie get for 125,000 pesos? **p; $512.50**

Critical Thinking

The [M+] key on a calculator enters a number into memory. The [MR] key recalls the number.

Discuss how you would use a calculator's memory keys to change the Japanese yen to U.S. dollars.
Use 1 Japanese yen = $.0065 U.S.

1. 80 yen	**2.** 560 yen	**3.** 4,000 yen	**4.** 94,000 yen	**5.** 896,200 yen
$0.52	**$3.64**	**$26**	**$611**	**$5,825.30**

MEETING INDIVIDUAL NEEDS

For Students Who Are . . .

Acquiring English Proficiency Encourage students to compare their native currencies with United States currency. Pair students with an English-proficient student to complete the Critical Thinking exercises.

Gifted and Talented Have students find current exchange rates for several foreign currencies and prepare a Currency Exchange table.

Working 2 or 3 Grades Below Level Have students use pages 46–57 and pages 60–61 of the Skills Workbook for decimals.

Today's Problem

Ted's part-time job pays him $4.60 an hour. Last week he worked the following hours: 5 h 15 min, 4 h 45 min, 6 h 30 min, and 5 h. How much money did he earn last week?
(5.25 + 4.75 + 6.5 + 5) × $4.60 = $98.90)

3 FOLLOW-UP

PRACTICE 3-4

Multiply. Check your answer.

1.	2.	3.	4.
3.56	10.412	0.08	26.03
×3.6	×0.64	×0.18	×35.7
12.816	*6.66368*	*0.0144*	*929.271*

5.	6.	7.	8.
68.22	97.003	4.33	37.09
×20.01	×6.005	×0.25	×0.4
1,365.0822	*582.503015*	*1.0825*	*14.836*

9.	10.	11.	12.
$41.00	39.03	22.22	9.1
×1.05	×0.1	×1.1	×6.51
$43.05	*3.903*	*24.442*	*59.241*

Estimate the product. *Accept reasonable estimates.*

17. 7.35 × 2.8 = ___ *7.5 × 3 = 22.50*

18. $.75 × 0.75 = ___ *$.80 × .8 = $.64*

19. $105 × 10.5 = ___ *$100 × 10 = $1,000*

Choose paper and pencil or a calculator to solve.

20. The 27 students in Mr. Turner's class collected money to beautify the entrance to the school. If each student collected $.35 per day for 30 days, how much did they collect altogether? *$283.50*

21. Mrs. Anderson is taking 16 of her students to the Cincinnati Zoo. They will see the special white Bengal tigers. Viewing of this exhibit is limited to 4 people every 2 minutes. How long will it take for all the students to see it? *8 minutes*

RETEACHING 3-4

When you multiply factors with decimals, the number of decimal places in the product is equal to the sum of the decimal places in the factors.

Example:
0.36 (2 decimal places)
×0.7 + (1 decimal place)
0.252 (3 decimal places)

Check:
0.4
×0.7
0.28

Write the number of decimal places that will be in the product.

1. 0.9 × 0.04 ___ *3*
2. 1.56 × 0.7 ___ *3*
3. 1.0101 × 0.05 ___ *6*
4. 0.12005 × 6 ___ *5*
5. 13.4 × 18.7 ___ *2*
6. 7.092 × 1.45 ___ *5*

Place the decimal point in the correct place in each product. Add zeros if necessary.

7.	8.	9.	10.	11.
6.4	0.007	1.9	0.13	4.321
×0.21	×0.09	×0.8	×0.12	×1.234
1344	*0.00063*	*152*	*0.0156*	*5332114*

Compute. Estimate to check your answer.

12.	13.	14.
9.3 *9*	0.26 *0.25*	1.57 *1.5*
×0.8 *×0.8*	×0.04 *×0.04*	×0.95 *× 1*
7.44 *7.2*	*0.0104* *0.0100*	*1.4915* *1.5*

15.	16.	17.
1.004	1.2	37.3 *40*
×1.05 *×1*	×0.8 *×1*	×0.16 *×1.5*
1.05420 *1*	*0.96* *1*	*5.968* *6*

Choose the most reasonable estimate. Circle your answer.

18. 0.29 × 0.3 = ___ a. 9   b. 0.9   **c.** 0.09
19. 1.6 × 0.2 = ___ a. 4   **b.** 0.4   c. 0.04
20. 7.9 × 0.8 = ___ a. 0.64   **b.** 6.4   c. 0.064

ENRICHMENT 3-4

Explain to the students that a geometric series is one in which the next term of the series is obtained by multiplying or dividing the previous term of the series by the same number. For example, 3 [×3], 9 [×3], 27 [×3], 81 [×3], 243. . . Have the students work in pairs to develop their own geometric series using decimals. Students may then present their series to the class. If the class is unable to determine the pattern, then the student should explain it.

Lesson Organizer

> **Objective:** Divide whole numbers.

Prior Knowledge: Students should know basic division facts.

Error Analysis and Remediation: See page 89A.

Lesson Resources:
Practice Worksheet 3-5
Reteaching Activity 3-5
Enrichment Worksheet 3-5
Daily Review 3-5
Cooperative Connections, Chapter 3
Cooperative Investigations, Chapter 3

Two-Minute Math

Write at least three different pairs of factors whose product is 10. *(Examples: 2 × 5; 2.5 × 4; 20 × 0.5)*

1 INTRODUCE

CONNECTING ACTIVITY

☑ **MATERIALS CHECKLIST:** base-10 blocks, one set

1. Have a student use base-10 blocks to represent 57 on the overhead projector. **How many groups of 5 are in the tens' strips?** *(10)* **How many groups of 5 are in the unit cubes?** *(1)* **How many unit cubes are left over?** *(2)* **How many groups of 5 are there in all?** *(11)* Write 57 ÷ 5 = 11 R2 on the chalkboard. Repeat, relating the algorithmic and manipulative steps.

2. Repeat for 289 divided by 20.

3. Write 315)9,582 on the chalkboard. Have students ask the questions that must be answered in each step of the algorithm. *(For example, "How many groups of 315 (or about 300) are contained in 9,582?", and so on.)*

WHEN YOUR STUDENTS ASK
★ WHY AM I LEARNING THIS? ★

You can use this skill to solve real life problems. To find your car's gas consumption per mile, you divide the number of miles driven by the number of gallons the car used.

Dividing Whole Numbers

A year is the number of days a planet takes to orbit the Sun. One year on Mercury is equal to about 2,112 Earth hours. How many Earth days is that?

There are 24 h in 1 d. So, divide 2,112 by 24 to find the number of Earth days.

Divide 2,112 by 24.	Multiply to check.
$$\begin{array}{r} 88 \\ 24\overline{)2,112} \\ -192 \\ \hline 192 \\ -192 \\ \hline 0 \end{array}$$	$$\begin{array}{r} 88 \\ \times\ 24 \\ \hline 352 \\ 176 \\ \hline 2,112 \end{array}$$

One year on Mercury is equal to about 88 Earth days.

THINK ALOUD About how many days longer is a year on Earth than a year on Mercury? **277 d**

Another example:

What is 1,483 ÷ 37?   Check:

$$\begin{array}{r} 40\ R3 \\ 37\overline{)1,483} \\ -148 \\ \hline 03 \end{array} \qquad \begin{array}{r} 40 \\ \times\ 37 \\ \hline 1,480 \\ +\ \ \ \ 3 \\ \hline 1,483 \end{array}$$ ← Add the remainder.

═══════ **GUIDED PRACTICE** ═══════

NUMBER SENSE Choose the correct quotient. Do not calculate.

1. 39)351   9, 90   **9**   2. 62)3,100   5, 50   **50**

3. 25)1,750   7, 70   **70**   4. 192)11,520   6, 60   **60**

Divide. Check your answer.

5. 42)812   6. 19)288   7. 4,056 ÷ 78
   19 R14   **15 R3**   **52**

68   LESSON 3–5

Mercury

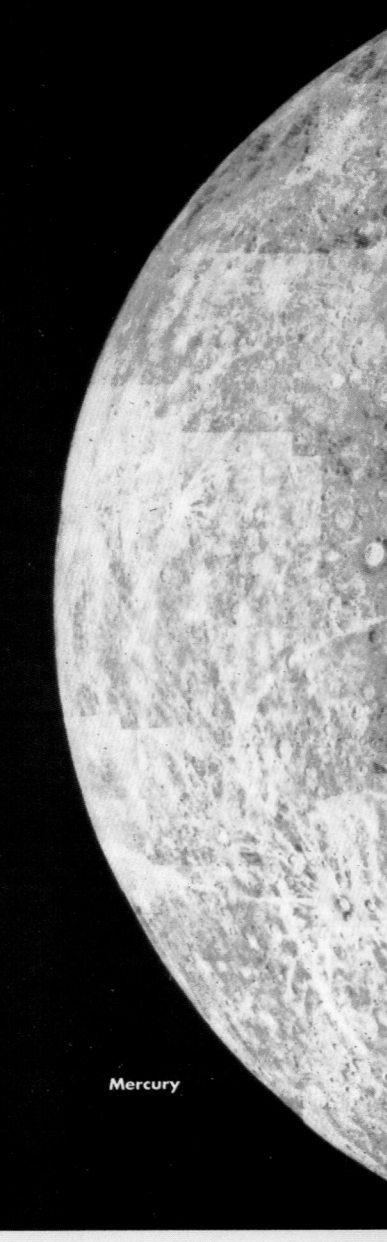

2 TEACH

☑ **MATERIALS CHECKLIST:** calculators

How do you check a quotient? *(The quotient times the divisor, plus the remainder, should equal the dividend.)*

When does estimating help in dividing? *(in obtaining the first digit in the quotient; in checking the reasonableness of the quotient.)*

If the divisor is 67, what is the greatest possible remainder? Explain. *(66; If the remainder were 67 or greater, the last digit placed in the quotient would need to be increased.)*

> ### Chalkboard Examples
> 252 ÷ 6 *(42)*
> 351 ÷ 4 *(87R3)*
> 867 ÷ 36 *(24R3)*
> 1,261 ÷ 43 *(29R14)*

SUMMARIZE/ASSESS **Explain how to divide a three-digit number by a two-digit number.** *(Students should give the steps in the algorithm: estimate, multiply, subtract, and compare.)*

PRACTICE

Divide. Check your answer.

8. $50\overline{)250}$ 5	**9.** $8\overline{)828}$ 103 R4	**10.** $4\overline{)804}$ 201	**11.** $9\overline{)210}$ 23 R3
12. $21\overline{)357}$ 17	**13.** $3\overline{)369}$ 123	**14.** $43\overline{)603}$ 14 R1	**15.** $21\overline{)2,121}$ 101
16. $382 \div 48$ 7 R46	**17.** $823 \div 24$ 34 R7	**18.** $750 \div 25$ 30	**19.** $265 \div 53$ 5
20. $85\overline{)5,149}$ 60 R49	**21.** $36\overline{)180}$ 5	**22.** $107\overline{)8,495}$ 79 R42	**23.** $231\overline{)3,812}$ 16 R116
24. $5,400 \div 54$ 100	**25.** $4,294 \div 38$ 113	**26.** $491 \div 415$ 1 R76	**27.** $35,030 \div 62$ 565

MIXED REVIEW Simplify.

28. $0.04 + 0.086$ 0.126	**29.** $500 - 7.39$ 492.61	**30.** 58×0.4 23.2	**31.** $468 \div 9$ 52
32. $0.2 - 0.19$ 0.01	**33.** $234 \div 13$ 18	**34.** $3.7 + 29.98$ 33.68	**35.** 0.6×0.07 0.042

MENTAL MATH Compare the quotients mentally. Use $>$, $<$, or $=$.

36. $480 \div 12$ ▓ $4,800 \div 120$ =

37. $180 \div 30$ ▓ $1,800 \div 30$ <

38. CALCULATOR Find each quotient. Then write the next three divisions in the pattern.

$111,111 \div 3$ ➪ $222,222 \div 6$ ➪ $333,333 \div 9$ ➪ $444,444 \div 12$ $555,555 \div 15$ $666,666 \div 18$
37,037   37,037   37,037   37,037   37,037   37,037

PROBLEM SOLVING

CHOOSE Choose paper and pencil or calculator to solve. **Choices will vary. Suggestions given.**

39. About how many hours are in 1 Earth year? Assume 1 yr is equal to 365 d. c; 8,760 h

40. One year on Venus is about 5,400 Earth hours. How many Earth days are there in 5,400 h? p; 225
p; 40,000 s, 34,800 min., 25 d

41. Order from least to greatest: 25 d, 40,000 s, 34,800 min.

MEETING INDIVIDUAL NEEDS

For Students Who Are . . .

Acquiring English Proficiency   Have pairs of students discuss and solve Exercises 38–41.

Gifted and Talented   Ask each student to choose a planet in the solar system, determine through division the distance in miles between Earth and that planet, and compare the length of the planet year with an Earth year.

Working 2 or 3 Grades Below Level   Have students who are having difficulty with basic division facts or dividing whole numbers use pages 64–125 of the Skills Workbook for Whole Number Multiplication and Division.

Today's Problem

The nation's largest state is Alaska, which has an area of 591,004 mi². The 48 mainland states have a total area of 3,021,295 mi². Approximately how many states the size of Alaska would equal the total area of the 48 mainland states?
(3,021,295 ÷ 591,004 = 5.11; about 5)

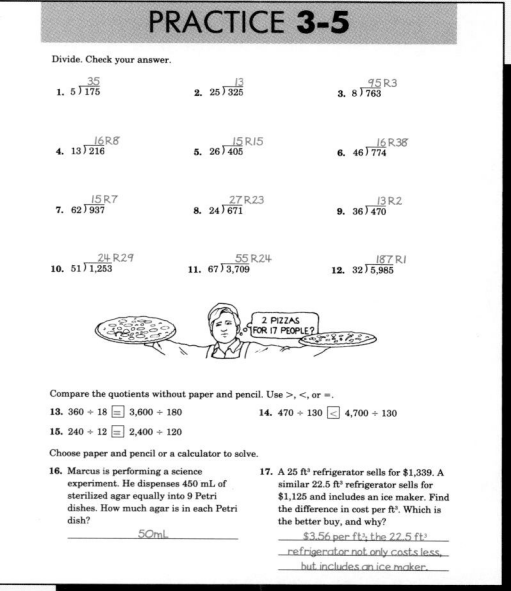

PRACTICE 3-5

Divide. Check your answer.

1. $5\overline{)175}$ 35
2. $25\overline{)325}$ 13
3. $8\overline{)763}$ 95 R3
4. $13\overline{)216}$ 16 R8
5. $26\overline{)405}$ 15 R15
6. $46\overline{)774}$ 16 R38
7. $62\overline{)937}$ 15 R7
8. $24\overline{)671}$ 27 R23
9. $36\overline{)470}$ 13 R2
10. $51\overline{)1,253}$ 24 R29
11. $67\overline{)3,709}$ 55 R24
12. $32\overline{)5,985}$ 187 R1

Compare the quotients without paper and pencil. Use >, <, or =.

13. $360 \div 18$ ▢ $3,600 \div 180$ =
14. $470 \div 130$ ▢ $4,700 \div 130$ <
15. $240 \div 12$ ▢ $2,400 \div 120$ =

Choose paper and pencil or a calculator to solve.

16. Marcus is performing a science experiment. He dispenses 450 mL of sterilized agar equally into 9 Petri dishes. How much agar is in each Petri dish? 50mL

17. A 25 ft³ refrigerator sells for $1,339. A similar 22.5 ft³ refrigerator sells for $1,125 and includes an ice maker. Find the difference in cost per ft³. Which is the better buy, and why? $3.56 per ft³; the 22.5 ft³ refrigerator not only costs less, but includes an ice maker.

RETEACHING 3-5

☑ **MATERIALS CHECKLIST:** 50 counters for each student

Remind students that division means to separate a number of objects into smaller groups with the same number in each group. Write $23 \div 4$ on the board and have students use their counters to show 23 counters divided into groups of 4 counters. Have students describe the answer as "5 groups of 4 counters with 3 counters remaining." Then have students use their counters to model the following problems: $23 \div 2$, $41 \div 3$, $18 \div 4$, $36 \div 5$.

ENRICHMENT 3-5

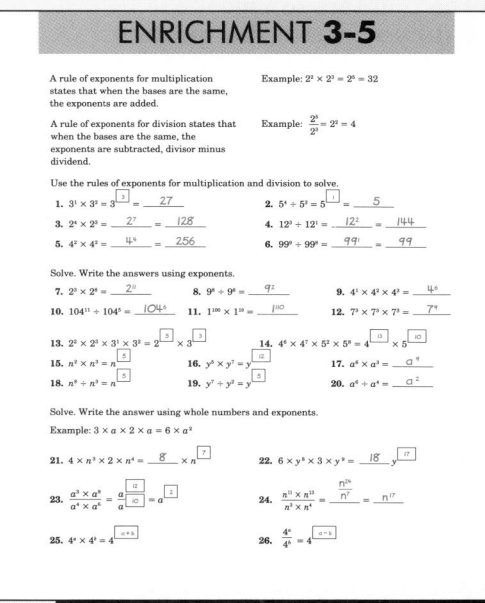

A rule of exponents for multiplication states that when the bases are the same, the exponents are added. Example: $2^3 \times 2^2 = 2^5 = 32$

A rule of exponents for division states that when the bases are the same, the exponents are subtracted, divisor minus dividend. Example: $\frac{2^3}{2^1} = 2^2 = 4$

Use the rules of exponents for multiplication and division to solve.

1. $3^1 \times 3^2 = 3^3 = 27$
2. $5^4 \div 5^3 = 5^1 = 5$
3. $2^4 \times 2^3 = 2^7 = 128$
4. $12^3 \div 12^1 = 12^2 = 144$
5. $4^2 \times 4^2 = 4^4 = 256$
6. $99^2 \div 99^1 = 99^1 = 99$

Solve. Write the answers using exponents.

7. $2^5 \times 2^4 = 2^9$
8. $9^6 \times 9^6 = 9^{12}$
9. $4^1 \times 4^2 \times 4^3 = 4^6$
10. $104^{11} \div 104^5 = 104^6$
11. $1^{100} \times 1^{10} = 1^{110}$
12. $7^3 \times 7^2 \times 7^2 = 7^4$
13. $2^2 \times 2^1 \times 3^1 \times 3^0 = 2^3 \times 3^1$
14. $4^3 \times 4^7 \times 5^2 \times 5^8 = 4^{10} \times 5^{10}$
15. $n^2 \times n^3 = n^5$
16. $y^5 \times y^7 = y^{12}$
17. $a^6 \times a^3 = a^9$
18. $n^8 \div n^7 = n^1$
19. $y^7 \div y^2 = y^5$
20. $a^6 \div a^4 = a^2$

Solve. Write the answer using whole numbers and exponents.
Example: $3 \times a \times 2 \times a = 6 \times a^2$

21. $4 \times n^3 \times 2 \times n^4 = 8 \times n^7$
22. $6 \times y^8 \times 3 \times y^9 = 18 \times y^{17}$
23. $\frac{a^3 \times a^9}{a^4 \times a^5} = \frac{a^{12}}{a^{10}} = a^2$
24. $\frac{n^{15} \times n^{13}}{n^5 \times n^6} = \frac{n^{28}}{n^{11}} = n^{17}$
25. $4^x \times 4^y = 4^{x+y}$
26. $\frac{4^x}{4^y} = 4^{x-y}$

Lesson Organizer

Objective: Divide decimals by whole numbers.

Prior Knowledge: Students should be able to divide whole numbers.

Lesson Resources:
Practice Worksheet 3-6
Reteaching Worksheet 3-6
Enrichment Activity 3-6
Daily Review 3-6

Two-Minute Math

Each letter stands for a different digit. What is each digit?

$I \times I = HI \qquad HI \times HI = MHI$

(5 × 5 = 25; 25 × 25 = 625)

1 INTRODUCE

CONNECTING ACTIVITY

☑ **MATERIALS CHECKLIST:** 20 slips of paper and a handful of counters, paper clips, or beans for each group of three or four students

Have students work in small groups.

1. Write $4\overline{)16.24}$ on the chalkboard. Tell students that one slip of paper represents one dollar and one counter represents one cent. Have students use the slips of paper and the counters to model $16.24 ÷ 4. **How do you write the quotient?** *($4.06)*

2. Have students model $1.12 ÷ 7, making the necessary trades.

3. Relate both models to the algorithm by doing the divisions on the chalkboard. Point out that when there are hundredths in the dividend, there will be hundredths in the quotient.

WHEN YOUR STUDENTS ASK
★ WHY AM I LEARNING THIS? ★

You can connect this skill to real life through unit prices. A unit price is obtained by dividing the price of the item by the number of units of measurement it contains.

MATH AND GEOGRAPHY

Dividing Decimals by Whole Numbers

A **fathom** is a unit of length that measures water depth. One fathom is 6 ft. About how many fathoms deep is Lake Erie? Round to whole numbers.

Divide 209.9 by 6 to find the depth of Lake Erie in fathoms.

If you can divide whole numbers, you can use a **MATH CONNECTION** to divide a decimal by a whole number.

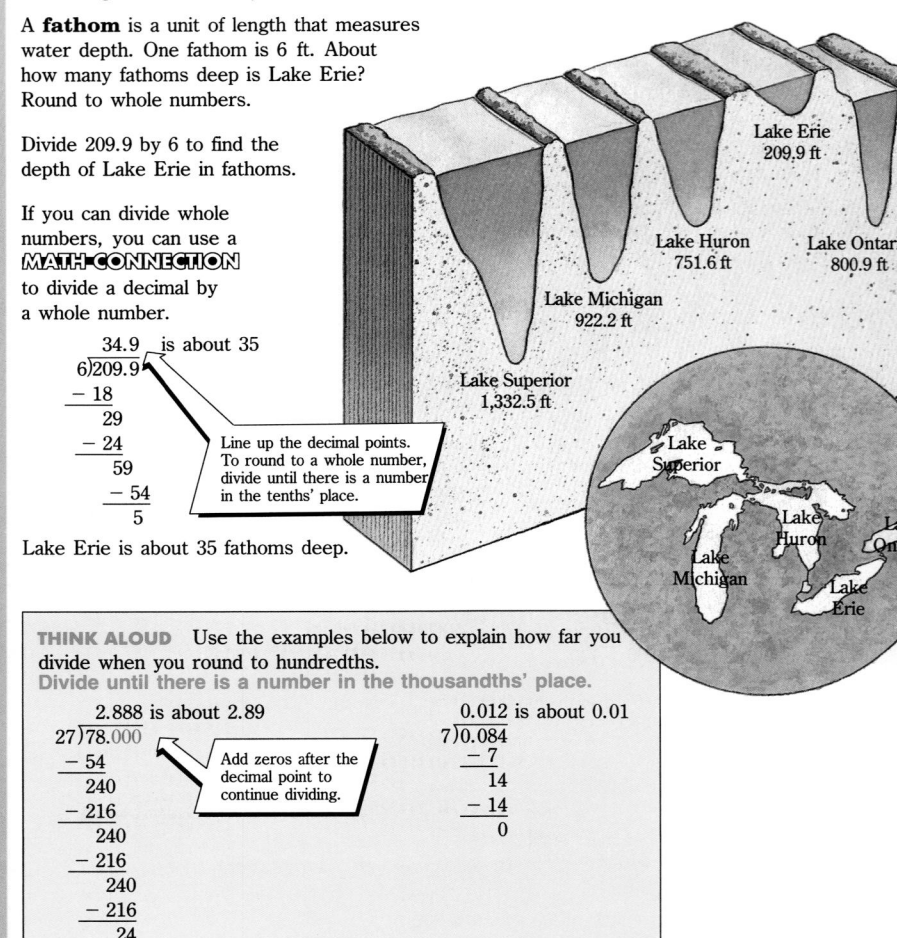

Lake Erie
209.9 ft

Lake Huron
751.6 ft

Lake Ontario
800.9 ft

Lake Michigan
922.2 ft

Lake Superior
1,332.5 ft

```
       34.9   is about 35
   6)209.9
    − 18
      29
    − 24
      59
    − 54
       5
```

Line up the decimal points. To round to a whole number, divide until there is a number in the tenths' place.

Lake Erie is about 35 fathoms deep.

THINK ALOUD Use the examples below to explain how far you divide when you round to hundredths.
Divide until there is a number in the thousandths' place.

```
        2.888 is about 2.89          0.012 is about 0.01
   27)78.000                      7)0.084
    − 54                            − 7
     240                            14
   − 216                          − 14
     240                             0
   − 216
     240
   − 216
      24
```

Add zeros after the decimal point to continue dividing.

=== GUIDED PRACTICE ===

Divide. Round to tenths.

1. 338.4 ÷ 8
42.3

2. 35.2 ÷ 14
2.5

3. 7.93 ÷ 32
0.2

70   LESSON 3–6

---

2 TEACH

☑ **MATERIALS CHECKLIST:** calculators

Why is it a good idea to place the decimal point in the quotient before you divide? *(so that the place values of the quotient align with those of the dividend.)*

Why do you have to divide to the thousandths' place when you round a quotient to the nearest hundredth?
(You use the digit in the thousandths' place to round to the hundredths' place.)

Chalkboard Examples

Divide until the remainder is zero.
$7\overline{)39.2}$ *(5.60)*
$8\overline{)3.384}$ *(0.423)*
40.59 ÷ 11 *(3.69)*
25.5 ÷ 75 *(0.34)*

SUMMARIZE/ASSESS **Explain how to divide a decimal by a whole number and when to annex zeros to the dividend.**

71

PRACTICE

Divide until there is no remainder.

4. 5)7.25 **5.** 2)7.012 **6.** 8)10.01 **7.** 60)37.68 **8.** 66)6.27
   1.45   3.506   1.25125   0.628   0.095

Divide. Round to tenths.

9. 19.12 ÷ 3 **10.** 93.5 ÷ 8 **11.** 2.3 ÷ 6 **12.** 25.49 ÷ 9
   6.4   11.7   0.4   2.8

Divide. Round to hundredths.

13. 33.52 ÷ 7 **14.** 4.32 ÷ 3 **15.** 3.17 ÷ 28 **16.** 12.98 ÷ 31
    4.79   1.44   0.11   0.42

Divide. Round to cents.

17. $45.07 ÷ 12 **18.** $6.50 ÷ 53 **19.** $2.88 ÷ 17 **20.** $18.74 ÷ 36
    $3.76 $0.12 $0.17 $0.52

MIXED REVIEW Compute. Round to cents.

21. $352 ÷ 9   **22.** $6.79 × 0.5   **23.** $2.05 ÷ 6   **24.** $704 ÷ 12
    $39.11 $3.40 $0.34 $58.67
25. $87.60 ÷ 21 **26.** $36.28 × 0.3   **27.** $9.60 ÷ 14   **28.** $82.59 × 0.1
    $4.17 $10.88 $0.69 $8.26

29. **CALCULATOR** Find each quotient.
Then write two more divisions
for the pattern.
See page 89b.

1.21 ÷ 11	1.089 × 9 ÷ 1
12.321 ÷ 111	2.178 × 8 ÷ 2
123.4321 ÷ 1,111	3.267 × 7 ÷ 3

PROBLEM SOLVING

CHOOSE Choose paper and pencil or calculator to solve.
Use the diagram on page 70. Round to tenths.

Choices will vary.

30. What are the depths in fathoms of Lake Superior,
Lake Michigan, Lake Huron, and Lake Ontario?
See below.

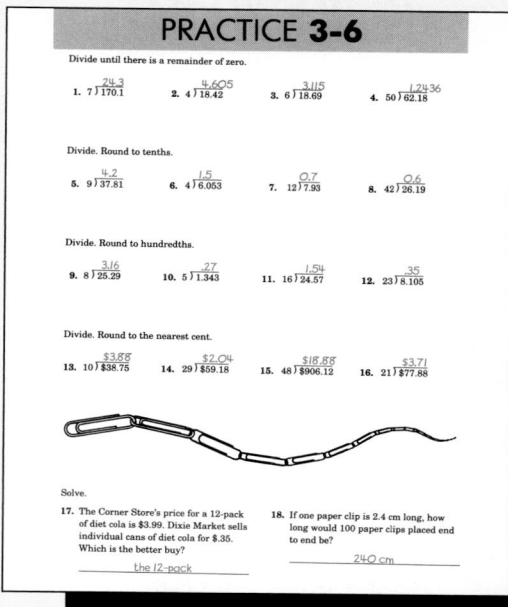

USSR

Lake Baikal

31. Lake Baikal, in the USSR, is the deepest lake
in the world, at about 886 fathoms. About how
many feet deeper is it than Lake Superior?
p; 3,983.5 ft

32. **CREATE YOUR OWN** Write a problem using the
information in the diagram. Give it to a friend to solve.
Check students' work.

Estimate

You can use **clustering** to estimate a sum.

19 + 22 + 17 + 21 + 18 + 23
     6 × 20 = 120

All numbers cluster around 20.
The sum is about 120.

Estimate the sum using the cluster method.

1. 28 + 31 + 29 + 32 + 27 ≈ 150   **2.** 12 + 9 + 11 + 8 + 13 + 7 ≈ 60

c; Lake Superior: 222.1 fathoms; Lake Michigan: 153.7 fathoms;
Lake Huron: 125.3 fathoms; Lake Ontario: 133.5 fathoms.

CHAPTER 3   71

3 FOLLOW-UP

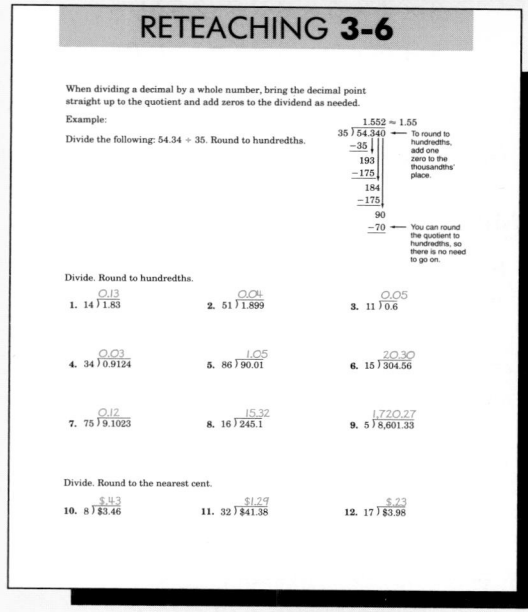

PRACTICE 3-6

Divide until there is a remainder of zero.

1. 7)170.1 **2.** 4)18.42 **3.** 6)18.69 **4.** 50)62.18
   24.3   4.605   3.115   1.2436

Divide. Round to tenths.

5. 9)37.81 **6.** 4)6.053 **7.** 12)7.93 **8.** 42)26.19
   4.2   1.5   0.7   0.6

Divide. Round to hundredths.

9. 8)25.29 **10.** 5)1.343 **11.** 16)24.57 **12.** 23)8.105
   3.16   .27   1.54   .35

Divide. Round to the nearest cent.

13. 10)$38.75 **14.** 29)$59.18 **15.** 48)$906.12 **16.** 21)$77.88
    $3.88 $2.04 $18.88 $3.71

Solve.

17. The Corner Store's price for a 12-pack
of diet cola is $3.99. Dixie Market sells
individual cans of diet cola for $.35.
Which is the better buy?
the 12-pack

18. If one paper clip is 2.4 cm long, how
long would 100 paper clips placed end
to end be?
240 cm

RETEACHING 3-6

When dividing a decimal by a whole number, bring the decimal point
straight up to the quotient and add zeros to the dividend as needed.

Example:
Divide the following: 54.34 ÷ 35. Round to hundredths.

```
        1.552 ≈ 1.55
 35)54.340          To round to
   -35                hundredths,
    193               add one
   -175               zero to the
    184               thousandths'
   -175               place.
      90          You can round
     -70           the quotient to
                   hundredths, so
                   there is no need
                   to go on.
```

Divide. Round to hundredths.

1. 14)1.83 **2.** 51)1.899 **3.** 11)0.6
   0.13   0.04   0.05

4. 34)0.9124 **5.** 86)90.01 **6.** 15)304.56
   0.03   1.05   20.30

7. 75)9.1023 **8.** 16)245.1 **9.** 5)8,601.33
   0.12   15.32   1,720.27

Divide. Round to the nearest cent.

10. 8)$3.46 **11.** 32)$41.38 **12.** 17)$3.98
    $.43 $1.29 $.23

ENRICHMENT 3-6

Have the students work in pairs. Each
pair makes a list of ten popular breakfast
cereals. Then have the students find the
price and the package size in ounces. Ask
students to find the cost per ounce for
each cereal. Then have the students determine the cereal with the best *overall value*
based on the cost per ounce.

MEETING INDIVIDUAL NEEDS

For Students Who Are . . .

Acquiring English Proficiency On a U.S. wall map, point out
each of the Great Lakes. Pair students with an English-proficient
student to discuss and solve the Problem Solving and Estimate exercises. Explain what the word *cluster* means.

Gifted and Talented Have students look in an almanac to find the
deepest lake on each continent and make a table to compare these
lakes with the deepest lake in the United States.

Working 2 or 3 Grades Below Level Have students use pages
62–67 and 70–71 of the Skills Workbook for decimals.

Today's Problem

Americans eat a lot of popcorn. About how many gallons of popcorn
would a 15-yr-old have eaten if he started eating popcorn at the age
of 8 and averaged 42 qts a year?
(15 − 8 = 7; 7 × 42 ÷ 4 = 73.5 gal)

Lesson Organizer

Objective: Discuss looking back to determine whether an answer is reasonable.

Prior Knowledge: Students should be able to identify key information from a given passage.

Lesson Resources:
Practice Worksheet 3-7
Daily Review 3-7

Two-Minute Math

$1 \times 2 \times 3 \times 4 \times 5$ *(120)*

$3 \times 4 \times 5 \times 6 \times 7$ *(2,520)*

$5 \times 6 \times 7 \times 8 \times 9$ *(15,120)*

1 INTRODUCE

SYMBOLIC ACTIVITY

☑ **MATERIALS CHECKLIST:** United States wall map

Tell students that today they will learn some interesting facts about Sequoia and Kings Canyon National Parks as well as decide whether an answer is reasonable or unreasonable. Have students locate central California on the wall map. Encourage any students who have visited these parks to describe their experiences. Tell students that as they read through this lesson they will learn some interesting facts about the natural wonders in these parks.

WHEN YOUR STUDENTS ASK
★ WHY AM I LEARNING THIS? ★

You can use this skill to solve real life problems. For example, when you plan your after-school activities, do you have enough time for sports, music lessons, and a part-time job?

Think Again!

Problem Solving:
Look Back

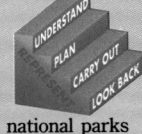

📖 READ ABOUT IT

Sequoia and Kings Canyon national parks in central California are the home of some of the oldest living things on Earth today—the giant Sequoia trees.

When solving the problems about the giant Sequoia trees, use the data on page 73 and the check list to ensure that you have reasonable answers.

REASONABLE ANSWER CHECK LIST
- ✔ Did you answer the question?
- ✔ Did you calculate correctly?
- ✔ Is your answer labeled with the right units?
- ✔ Does the answer need to be rounded to a whole number to make sense?

🗨 TALK ABOUT IT

Work with your group. Is the answer *reasonable* or *unreasonable*? If *unreasonable*, explain why and find a reasonable answer.

1. What is the approximate height of the General Sherman Tree in yards? (Hint: Recall that 3 ft = 1 yd)
   Answer: about 825 yd
   unreasonable; $274.9 \div 3 = 91.6$ yd

2. How long ago was Sequoia National Park established?
   Answer: 102 ft
   unreasonable; wrong unit; Answer depends on current year.

3. Since about what year do scientists think the General Sherman Tree has been alive?
   Answer: about 300 B.C.
   reasonable

4. About how many 6-ft adults would equal the height of the General Sherman Tree?
   Answer: 45,817 adults
   unreasonable; doesn't make sense; ≈ 46 adults

5. What is the height of the General Grant Tree?
   Answer: 267.9 yd
   unreasonable; wrong unit; 267.9 ft

6. If your arm span is 5 ft, about how many would it take to encircle the base of the General Sherman Tree?
   Answer: 30 yd
   unreasonable; 20.5 arm spans

7. Yellowstone became a national park 18 yr earlier than Sequoia National Park. In what year was Yellowstone established?
   Answer: 1872   **reasonable**

72   LESSON 3–7

MATH AND GEOGRAPHY

MULTICULTURAL NOTE

These majestic trees are named for the Cherokee leader, Sequoyah, who lived from about 1770 to 1843. Sequoyah created the Cherokee written language, which led to the first Cherokee newspaper, *The Cherokee Phoenix*.

2 TEACH

Assign students into mixed ability groups for this lesson.

READ ABOUT IT   What do the words *volume* and *circumference* on page 73 mean? *(Volume is amount of wood in the tree; circumference is distance around the tree trunk.)*

TALK ABOUT IT   Instruct each group to identify the needed data in the box before discussing whether or not an answer is reasonable.

WRITE ABOUT IT   You may wish to have group members work independently to find the answer, then get together to compare and discuss their answers.

SUMMARIZE/ASSESS   Name some ways to test the reasonableness of an answer. *(Make sure it answers the questions, is properly labeled, makes sense, has been calculated correctly.)*

Sequoia and Kings Canyon national parks are side by side in central California. The two parks are often considered as one. Sequoia became our second national park in 1890. Kings Canyon became a national park in 1940.

The oldest and most magnificent trees in the two parks are named for American generals. The General Sherman Tree, the world's biggest tree in volume of wood, is found in Sequoia National Park. It is 274.9 ft high and has a circumference at its base of 102.6 ft. Scientists estimate the tree to be between 2,000 and 2,500 yr old.

The General Grant Tree is 7 ft shorter than the General Sherman Tree but 5 ft larger in circumference.

■ WRITE ABOUT IT

8. Work with your group. Estimate how many feet of growth the General Sherman Tree has averaged each year since it has been alive. Look back to see whether your answer is reasonable.

CHAPTER 6 73

PRACTICE 3-7

Read the passages and use the data to ensure that you have reasonable answers.

Ohio

Oklahoma

Ohio was settled in 1788 and became a state on March 1, 1803. Its population is about 12,000,000. It covers 41,222 mi² and its highest point is 1,550 ft.

Oklahoma was settled in 1887, but not admitted to the Union until November 16, 1907. It covers 69,919 mi² and has a population of about 3,000,000. Its highest point is 4,973 ft.

Is the answer *reasonable* or *unreasonable*? If unreasonable, explain why and find a reasonable answer.

1. What is the highest point in Ohio in yards? Recall that 3 ft = 1 yd.
Answer: 500 yd
_____reasonable_____

2. About how long ago did Ohio become a state?
Answer: 190 ft
unreasonable; answer is labeled in
_____wrong units_____

3. What is the difference in area between Ohio and Oklahoma?
Answer: 2,800 mi²
unreasonable; should be
_____28,697 mi²_____

4. What is the total area covered by both states?
Answer: 110,010 mi²
_____reasonable_____

5. About how many miles is the highest point in Oklahoma? Recall that 5,280 ft = 1 mi.
Answer: about 1 mi
_____reasonable_____

6. About how many 6-ft adults standing head to toe would equal the highest point in Ohio?
Answer: 258.33 adults
unreasonable; cannot have part
of an adult; about 258 adults

MEETING INDIVIDUAL NEEDS

For Students Who Are . . .

Acquiring English Proficiency Define *reasonable* and point out that the prefix *un-* gives the word an opposite meaning. *(unreasonable)* Stress the importance of using the Checklist.

Gifted and Talented Have pairs of students determine a scale for models of the trees; for example, $\frac{1}{4}$ in.-10 ft. Have students round the dimension on page 73 to the nearest ten and use their scale to determine the height and circumference of each tree model.

Today's Problem

Carlo has twice as many baseball cards as Laura. Laura has 6 more cards than Harold. Together they have 38 cards. How many cards does each person have? *(Carlo: 22 cards; Laura: 11 cards; Harold: 5 cards)*

MIDCHAPTER
Checkup

The midchapter checkup provides a way for you to check students' understanding of the skills taught in the first half of the chapter.

Language and Vocabulary

Some key language and vocabulary ideas from the first half of the chapter are reinforced here.

Quick Quiz

The quiz provides a means of evaluating students' understanding of the objectives for the first half of the chapter. Page references are given so that students can check back to where the skill was taught.

Use the following guide to score the quiz.

Score	Percent
10	100%
9	90
8	80
7	70
6	60
5	50
4	40
3	30
2	20
1	10

Use this chart to identify the Management Objectives tested.

Items	Management Objective	Pages
1–3	**3A** Use properties of multiplication and order of operations.	62–63
4, 6–7	**3B** Multiply and divide whole numbers.	64–65; 68–69
5, 8–9	**3C** Multiply and divide decimals.	66–67; 70–71
10	**3E** Problem Solving: Look back. Too much or too little information.	72–73

MIDCHAPTER CHECKUP

LANGUAGE & VOCABULARY

Choose the correct answer for the exercise. Explain your choice. **Answers will vary. Suggestions given.**

1. $7 \times (40 + 8) =$ 336 or 288
   336; distributive property

2. $108 \times 1 =$ 109 or 108
   108; identity property

3. $65 \times 0 =$ 65 or 0
   0; zero property

4. $3 + 9 \times 5 =$ 48 or 60
   48; order of operations

5. $3 \times 2^2 - 6 + 5 = 11$ or 7
   11; order of operations

QUICK QUIZ ✓

Simplify. *(pages 60–63)*

1. $(80 + 3) \times 7$ **581**

2. $9 \times (8 \times 4)$ **288**

3. $4 + 3^2 \times 2 - (6 - 4)$ **20**

Multiply. *(pages 64–67)*

4. $\$3,756 \times 24$ **$90,144**

5. 8.06×3.42 **27.5652**

Divide. Write the answer, including the remainder. *(pages 68–69)*

6. $36\overline{)2,053}$ **57 R1**

7. $22\overline{)2,373}$ **107 R19**

Divide. Round to hundredths. *(pages 70–71)*

8. $16\overline{)48.8}$ **3.05**

9. $35.6 \div 22$ **1.62**

Solve.

10. Dana bought 8 paper plates and 8 napkins for a party. Each plate cost $.20, and each napkin cost $.09.

   a. How much did Dana pay for each plastic plate?   **$.20**

   b. What multiplication property would help you find the total amount Dana spent?   **distributive**

   c. How much did Dana spend altogether?   **$2.32**

74   MIDCHAPTER CHECKUP

Write the answers in your learning log.   **Answers will vary. Suggestions given.**

1. Explain how the multiplication properties in arithmetic are related to the same properties in algebra.
    See page 89b.

2. On a test Mark worked out the problem $\frac{16}{2} \times 4$ and got an answer of 2. His teacher marked it wrong. Explain Mark's mistake. **He inverted the four and multiplied.**

DID YOU KNOW . . . ? The part of Niagara Falls that is in New York State is called the American Falls. About 2.5 cm of the ledge of the falls wear away each year. About how much have the American Falls worn away in your lifetime? **Check students' work.**

BONUS

Use your knowledge of the order-of-operations rules and number properties to solve this problem.

How many expressions having a value from 0 to 5 can you create using only 4's and any operation signs you need? Here is one way to create an expression with a value of 1. **Accept reasonable answers.** $\frac{4 \times 4}{4 \times 4}$

Learning Log

These are suggestions for writing about some topics taught so far in the chapter. The students keep their Learning Logs from the beginning of the school year through the end.

Math America

A mathematical skill that students have learned is related to an interesting fact about the United States.

Bonus

Students are given an opportunity to solve a challenge-type problem like a puzzle or a nonroutine problem.

Lesson Organizer

Objective: Explore multiplying and dividing by powers of ten.

Prior Knowledge: Students should know how to multiply and divide.

Lesson Resources:
Class Activity 3-8
Daily Review 3-8

Two-Minute Math

Evaluate $n + n \times n \div n - n$ when n is equal to 4, 2, 10, 1, and 12. *(4, 2, 10, 1, 12)*

1 PREPARE

CONNECTING ACTIVITY

☑ **MATERIALS CHECKLIST:** base-10 blocks, several of each kind per group of three or four students

Have students work in small groups.

1. Have students use base-10 unit cubes to model 3, then place three tens' rods next to the three unit cubes. **By what do you multiply 3 to obtain 30?** *(10)*

2. Ask students to replace the tens' rods with three hundreds' squares. **By what do you multiply 3 to obtain 300?** *(100)*

3. Have students replace the squares with three thousands' cubes. **By what do you multiply 3 to obtain 3,000?** *(1,000)*

4. Write on the chalkboard: $3 \times 10 = 30$; $3 \times 100 = 300$; $3 \times 1,000 = 3,000$. Discuss patterns students observe. Tell students they will explore patterns with decimals in today's lesson.

WHEN YOUR STUDENTS ASK
★ WHY AM I LEARNING THIS? ★

You can connect this skill to real life problems. Suppose you need to buy a roll of one hundred 29-cent stamps. You have $20. Do you have enough money?

EXPLORE

Exploring Multiplying and Dividing Decimals

You can multiply a number by a power of 10 mentally because it follows a pattern.

Look for a pattern as you find the product.

1. 5×10 **50**
5×100 **500**
$5 \times 1,000$ **5,000**
$5 \times 10,000$ **50,000**

2. 0.4×10 **4**
0.4×100 **40**
$0.4 \times 1,000$ **400**
$0.4 \times 10,000$ **4,000**

3. 4.23×10 **42.3**
4.23×100 **423**
$4.23 \times 1,000$ **4,230**
$4.23 \times 10,000$ **42,300**

4. When you multiply a number by a whole-number power of 10, is the product *greater than* or *lesser than* the original number? **greater than**

5. **IN YOUR WORDS** What do you notice about the movement of the decimal point when multiplying by a whole-number power of 10? Describe the relation between the movement of the decimal point and the number of zeros in the power of 10. **It moves 1 place to the right. It moves right according to the number of zeros in the power of 10.**

6. **IN YOUR WORDS** Write a rule for mentally multiplying a number by a whole-number power of 10. **Move the decimal right the number of zeros in the power of 10.**

Mentally multiply the number by 10, 100, and 1,000.

7. 58   **580; 5,800; 58,000**
8. 6,238   **62,380; 623,800; 6,238,000**
9. 7.4   **74; 740; 7,400**
10. 0.04   **0.4; 4; 40**
11. 6,047   **60,470; 604,700; 6,047,000**
12. 32.08   **320.8; 3,208; 32,080**

You can also mentally divide a number by a power of 10 by using a pattern.

Look for a pattern as you find the quotient.

13. $8 \div 10$ **0.8**
$8 \div 100$ **0.08**
$8 \div 1,000$ **0.008**
$8 \div 10,000$ **0.0008**

14. $0.3 \div 10$ **0.03**
$0.3 \div 100$ **0.003**
$0.3 \div 1,000$ **0.0003**
$0.3 \div 10,000$ **0.00003**

15. $56.4 \div 10$ **5.64**
$56.4 \div 100$ **0.564**
$56.4 \div 1,000$ **0.0564**
$56.4 \div 10,000$ **0.00564**

---

2 EXPLORE

☑ **MATERIALS CHECKLIST:** calculators

Have students work in pairs to complete Exercise 1–38.

Have students compare their answer for Exercise 4 to their answer for Exercise 15, their answer to Exercise 5 to that for 16, and their answer for Exercise 6 to that for 17.

What are two different ways to obtain 0.432 if you start with 43.2? *(43.2 × 0.01 = 0.432; 43.2 ÷ 100 = 0.432)*

SUMMARIZE/ASSESS **Compare multiplying a number by 0.01 and dividing the same number by 100.** *(Answers will be the same.)*

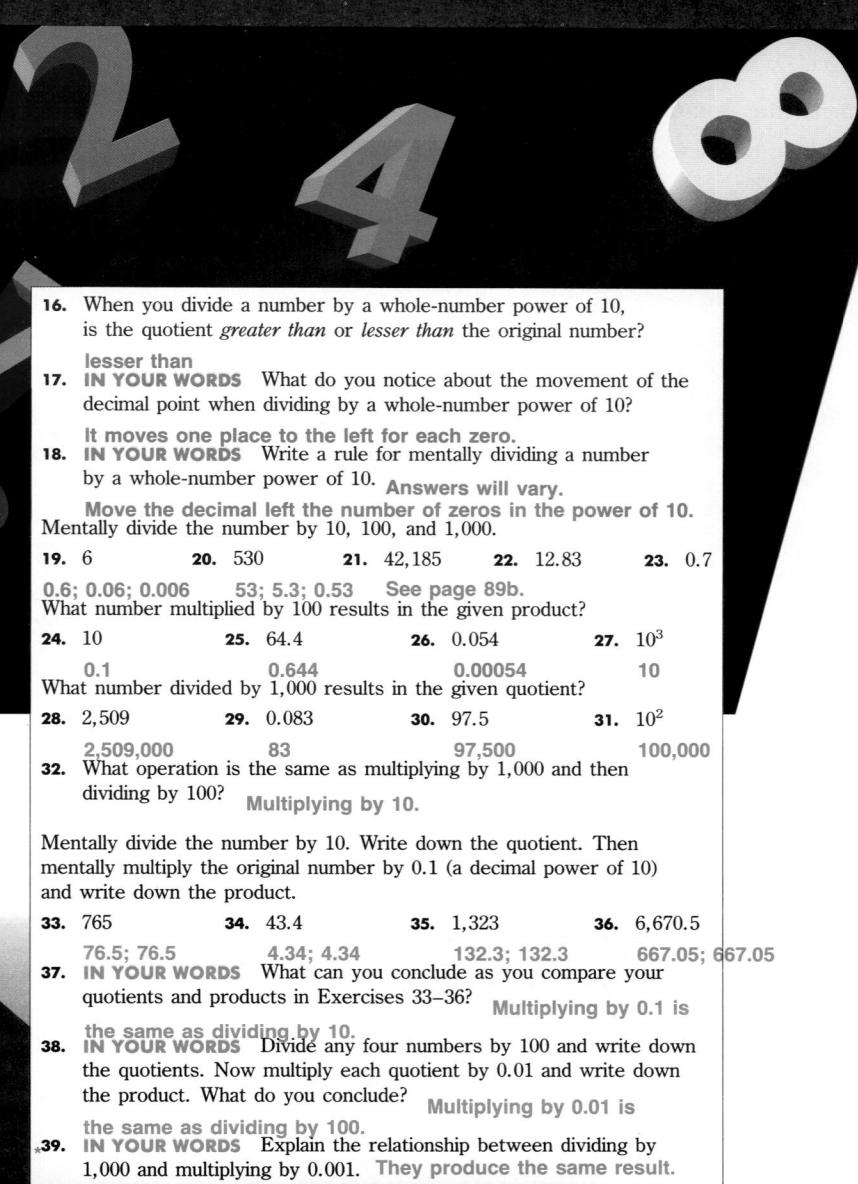

16. When you divide a number by a whole-number power of 10, is the quotient *greater than* or *lesser than* the original number?

lesser than

17. IN YOUR WORDS What do you notice about the movement of the decimal point when dividing by a whole-number power of 10?

It moves one place to the left for each zero.

18. IN YOUR WORDS Write a rule for mentally dividing a number by a whole-number power of 10. Answers will vary.

Move the decimal left the number of zeros in the power of 10.

Mentally divide the number by 10, 100, and 1,000.

19. 6   **20.** 530   **21.** 42,185   **22.** 12.83   **23.** 0.7

0.6; 0.06; 0.006   53; 5.3; 0.53   See page 89b.

What number multiplied by 100 results in the given product?

24. 10   **25.** 64.4   **26.** 0.054   **27.** 10^3

0.1   0.644   0.00054   10

What number divided by 1,000 results in the given quotient?

28. 2,509   **29.** 0.083   **30.** 97.5   **31.** 10^2

2,509,000   83   97,500   100,000

32. What operation is the same as multiplying by 1,000 and then dividing by 100?

Multiplying by 10.

Mentally divide the number by 10. Write down the quotient. Then mentally multiply the original number by 0.1 (a decimal power of 10) and write down the product.

33. 765   **34.** 43.4   **35.** 1,323   **36.** 6,670.5

76.5; 76.5   4.34; 4.34   132.3; 132.3   667.05; 667.05

37. IN YOUR WORDS What can you conclude as you compare your quotients and products in Exercises 33–36?

Multiplying by 0.1 is the same as dividing by 10.

38. IN YOUR WORDS Divide any four numbers by 100 and write down the quotients. Now multiply each quotient by 0.01 and write down the product. What do you conclude?

Multiplying by 0.01 is the same as dividing by 100.

39. IN YOUR WORDS Explain the relationship between dividing by 1,000 and multiplying by 0.001. They produce the same result.

CHAPTER 3   77

3 FOLLOW-UP

CLASS ACTIVITY 3-8

Have the students set up patterns for multiplying and dividing by 0.1, 0.01, 0.001, and 0.0001. For example, write the following multiplications and division sentences on the board:

834×0.1 $834 \div 0.1$
834×0.01 $834 \div 0.01$
834×0.001 $834 \div 0.001$
834×0.0001 $834 \div 0.0001$

Guide the students to discover that multiplication by 0.1 or $\frac{1}{10}$ is the same as division by 10, and that division by 0.1 or $\frac{1}{10}$ is the same as multiplication by 10.

MEETING INDIVIDUAL NEEDS

For Students Who Are . . .

Acquiring English Proficiency Have each student work through the lesson with an English-proficient student.

Gifted and Talented Ask students to explore Avogadro's number (6.02×10^{23}, the number of molecules in a mole of a substance) and write a short report about it.

Working 2 or 3 Grades Below Level Make sure students understand that moving the decimal point to the left decreases a number's value and moving it to the right increases a number's value.

Today's Problem

It has been estimated that smoking one cigarette shortens a person's life by 5.5 minutes. By about how many days would a person's life be shortened if he or she started smoking at age 13, is now 18 years old, and smoked 4 cigarettes a day?
($[5 \times 365 \times 4 \times 5.5] \div 60 \div 24 =$ about 28 days)

Lesson Organizer

Objective: Write numbers in scientific notation.

Prior Knowledge: Students should know how to write powers of ten in exponential form.

Lesson Resources:
Practice Worksheet 3-9
Reteaching Worksheet 3-9
Enrichment Activity 3-9
Daily Review 3-9

Two-Minute Math

Write in exponential form.

1,000   1,000,000   1,000,000,000

100,000,000   1,000,000,000,000

$(10^3; 10^6, 10^9; 10^8; 10^{12})$

1 INTRODUCE

SYMBOLIC ACTIVITY

☑ MATERIALS CHECKLIST: calculators

1. Write $800,000 \times 6,000$. Ask half the class to compute the product using paper and pencil and the other half to compute using calculators.

2. On the chalkboard write the product obtained by both forms of computation: 4,800,000,000 and the calculator display.

$$4.8 \quad 09$$

Explain that both products name the same number and that most calculators use a special abbreviated form.

3. Write 4.8×10^9. Explain that it is a third way to write the same product and is called scientific notation. Discuss any patterns students observe among the three forms of the product.

WHEN YOUR STUDENTS ASK
★ WHY AM I LEARNING THIS? ★

You can connect this skill to real life through astronomy. Astronomers use scientific notation to describe the vast distances in space.

MATH AND SOCIAL STUDIES

Scientific Notation

Scientists have developed a method for writing very large numbers. This method, called **scientific notation**, allows you to write very large numbers in an easier way. The area of the USSR is large. Scientists would write 22,402,000 as 2.2402×10^7 in scientific notation.

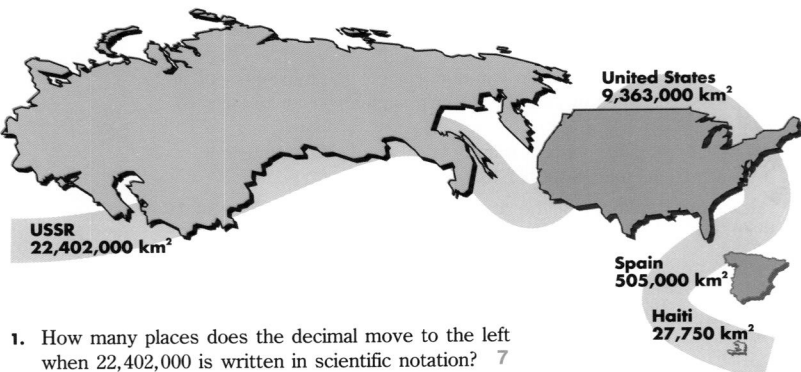

1. How many places does the decimal move to the left when 22,402,000 is written in scientific notation?   7

2. What is 10^7 in standard form?   10,000,000

There is an easy way to remember how to write numbers in scientific notation.

$$22,402,000 = 2.2402 \times 10^7$$
a number from 1 to 10   a power of 10   The decimal moved 7 places.

> A number written in scientific notation has two factors. One factor is a number greater than or equal to 1 but less than 10. The other factor is a power of 10.

3. Written in scientific notation, what is 450,000,000? 4,500,000,000? 45,000,000?
4.5×10^8; 4.5×10^9; 4.5×10^7

4. What are the areas of the United States, Spain, and Haiti in scientific notation?   See page 89b.

5. IN YOUR WORDS Explain what happens when you change 5.3×10^5 to standard form.   The decimal point moves 5 places to the right.

78   LESSON 3-9

---

2 TEACH

Describe the two factors of a number written in scientific notation? *(a number greater than or equal to 1 and less than 10; a power of ten expressed in exponential form)*

What does the exponent indicate in a number written in scientific notation? *(number of places the decimal point has been moved)*

Would you write a four-digit number in scientific notation? Explain. *(No; usually there is not reason to do so.)*

Chalkboard Examples

Write in the scientific notation.
36,000,000 (3.6×10^7)
980,000,000,000 (9.8×10^{11})
26,530,000,000
(2.653×10^{10})

SUMMARIZE/ASSESS **Explain how to write a number in scientific notation.** *(Students should describe the two factors that comprise the number.)*

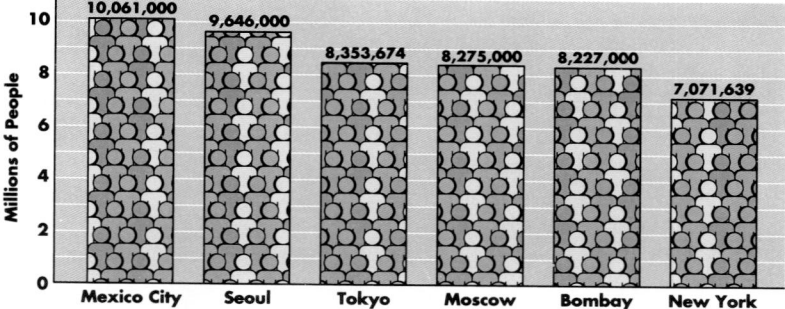

Population of World Cities

Mexico City	10,061,000
Seoul	9,646,000
Tokyo	8,353,674
Moscow	8,275,000
Bombay	8,227,000
New York	7,071,639

6. Of the populations listed above, which do you think are exact and which are estimates? Write the estimates in scientific notation.
Tokyo and New York are exact. The rest are estimates. See page 89b.

7. If you include the city's surrounding metropolitan area, Mexico City's population increases to about 1.55×10^7 people. What is this number in standard form? About how much greater is this population than the figure for Mexico City in the table above?
15,500,000; 5,439,000

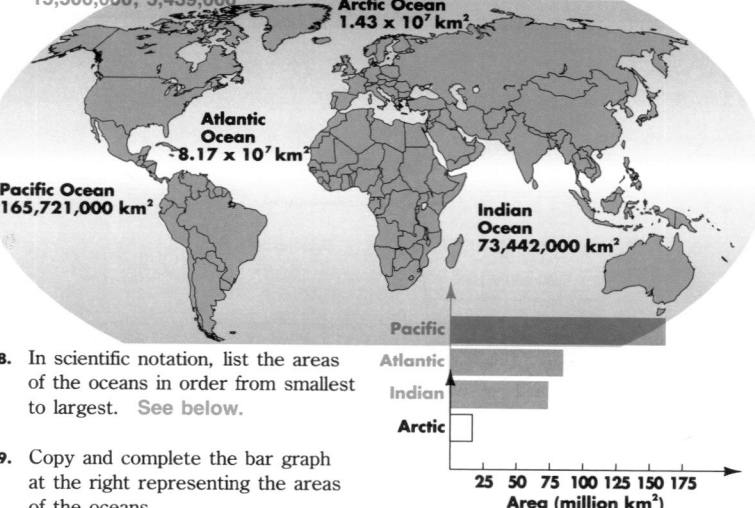

Arctic Ocean 1.43×10^7 km²

Atlantic Ocean 8.17×10^7 km²

Pacific Ocean 165,721,000 km²

Indian Ocean 73,442,000 km²

8. In scientific notation, list the areas of the oceans in order from smallest to largest. See below.

*9. Copy and complete the bar graph at the right representing the areas of the oceans.

Area (million km²)

8. Arctic Ocean: 1.43×10^7 km²; Indian Ocean: 7.3442×10^7 km²; Atlantic Ocean: 8.17×10^7 km²; Pacific Ocean: 1.65721×10^8 km²

CHAPTER 3   79

MEETING INDIVIDUAL NEEDS

For Students Who Are . . .

Acquiring English Proficiency Define *metropolitan area* as a central city and it surrounding suburbs. Pair students with an English-proficient student to discuss Exercises 6-8.

Gifted and Talented Have students list the populations of the ten most populous cities in the United States in order in scientific notation.

Today's Problem

Which continent in the Eastern Hemisphere has the greatest average population density (number of people per square mile)? *(Europe)*

Continent	Population	Area (mi²)	
Africa	350,000,000	11,673,000	*(30.0)*
Asia	2,161,110,000	17,125,641	*(126.2)*
Europe	653,956,000	4,065,654	*(160.8)*
Oceania	16,209,000	3,078,976	*(5.3)*

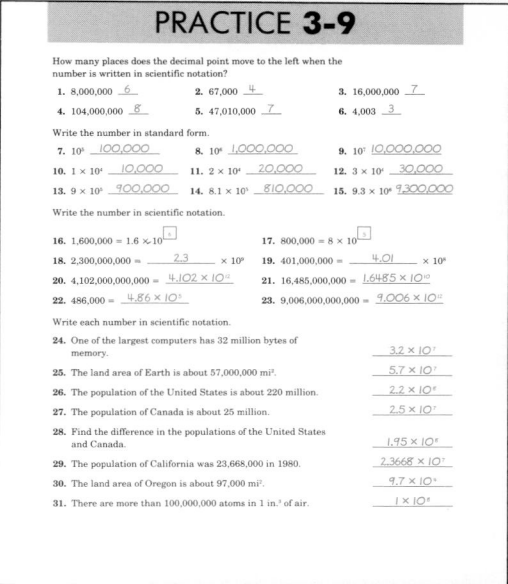

PRACTICE 3-9

How many places does the decimal point move to the left when the number is written in scientific notation?

1. 8,000,000 __6__   2. 67,000 __4__   3. 16,000,000 __7__
4. 104,000,000 __8__   5. 47,010,000 __7__   6. 4,003 __3__

Write the number in standard form.
7. 10^5 __100,000__   8. 10^6 __1,000,000__   9. 10^7 __10,000,000__
10. 1×10^4 __10,000__   11. 2×10^4 __20,000__   12. 3×10^4 __30,000__
13. 9×10^5 __900,000__   14. 8.1×10^5 __810,000__   15. 9.3×10^6 __9,300,000__

Write the number in scientific notation.
16. $1,600,000 = 1.6 \times 10^6$ 17. $800,000 = 8 \times 10^5$
18. $2,300,000,000 =$ __2.3__ $\times 10^9$ 19. $401,000,000 =$ __4.01__ $\times 10^8$
20. $4,102,000,000,000 =$ __4.102 × 10¹²__   21. $16,485,000,000 =$ __1.6485 × 10¹⁰__
22. $486,000 =$ __4.86 × 10⁵__   23. $9,006,000,000,000 =$ __9.006 × 10¹²__

Write each number in scientific notation.
24. One of the largest computers has 32 million bytes of memory. __3.2 × 10⁷__
25. The land area of Earth is about 57,000,000 mi². __5.7 × 10⁷__
26. The population of the United States is about 220 million. __2.2 × 10⁸__
27. The population of Canada is about 25 million. __2.5 × 10⁷__
28. Find the difference in the populations of the United States and Canada. __1.95 × 10⁸__
29. The population of California was 23,668,000 in 1980. __2.3668 × 10⁷__
30. The land area of Oregon is about 97,000 mi². __9.7 × 10⁴__
31. There are more than 100,000,000 atoms in 1 in.³ of air. __1 × 10⁸__

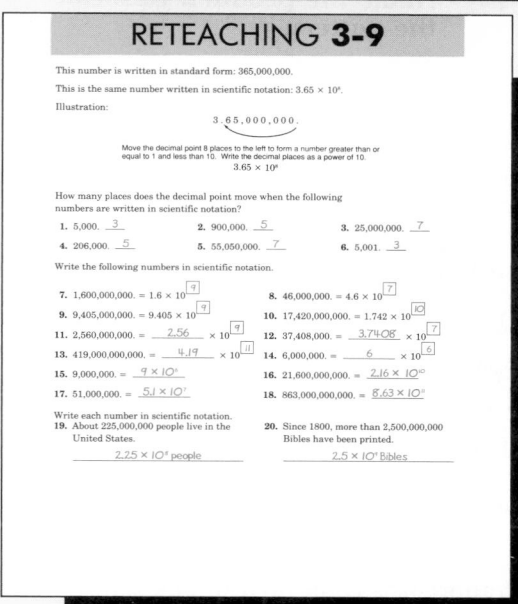

RETEACHING 3-9

This number is written in standard form: 365,000,000.
This is the same number written in scientific notation: 3.65×10^8.
Illustration:

$$3.65,000,000.$$

Move the decimal point 8 places to the left to form a number greater than or equal to 1 and less than 10. Write the decimal places as a power of 10.
3.65×10^8

How many places does the decimal point move when the following numbers are written in scientific notation?
1. 5,000. __3__   2. 900,000. __5__   3. 25,000,000. __7__
4. 206,000. __5__   5. 55,050,000. __5__   6. 5,001. __3__

Write the following numbers in scientific notation.
7. $1,600,000,000. = 1.6 \times 10^9$ 8. $46,000,000. = 4.6 \times 10^7$
9. $9,405,000,000. = 9.405 \times 10^9$ 10. $17,420,000,000. = 1.742 \times 10^{10}$
11. $2,560,000,000. =$ __2.56__ $\times 10^9$ 12. $37,408,000. =$ __3.7408__ $\times 10^7$
13. $419,000,000,000. =$ __4.19__ $\times 10^{11}$ 14. $6,000,000. =$ __6__ $\times 10^6$
15. $9,000,000. = 9 \times 10^6$ 16. $21,600,000,000. = 2.16 \times 10^{10}$
17. $51,000,000. = 5.1 \times 10^7$ 18. $863,000,000,000. = 8.63 \times 10^{11}$

Write each number in scientific notation.
19. About 225,000,000 people live in the United States. __2.25 × 10⁸ people__
20. Since 1800, more than 2,500,000,000 Bibles have been printed. __2.5 × 10⁹ Bibles__

ENRICHMENT 3-9

Have pairs of students try to determine how numbers written in scientific notation can be multiplied. Write $(4 \times 10^5) \times (8 \times 10^4)$ on the board. Let the students predict what the product is. $[3.2 \times 10^{10}]$ Then have the students suggest how to prove whether their prediction is correct. [Write each factor in standard form, multiply, and then write the product in scientific notation.] The students should see that the associative property allows them to regroup the factors in parentheses to get $(4 \times 8) \times (10^5 \times 10^4) = 32 \times 10^9 = 3.2 \times 10^{10}$.

Lesson Organizer

Objective: Divide decimals by decimals.

Prior Knowledge: Students should be able to divide decimals by whole numbers.

Error Analysis and Remediation: See page 89A.

Lesson Resources:
Practice Worksheet 3-10
Reteaching Activity 3-10
Enrichment Worksheet 3-10
Daily Review 3-10

Two-Minute Math

Name the product. Describe the pattern.

37×3 *(111)*

$15,873 \times 7$ *(111,111)*

$12,345,679 \times 9$ *(111,111,111)*

1 INTRODUCE

CONNECTING ACTIVITY

☑ **MATERIALS CHECKLIST:** Teaching Aid 2 (Decimals Squares) for each student

1. Have students shade in one-tenth on the hundredths' decimal square. **How can you find 0.1 divided by 0.01?** *(Find how many hundredths are contained in one tenth.)* Have students shade in the number of hundredths contained in one tenth. **What is $0.1 \div 0.01$?** *(10)* On the chalkboard write:
$$0.01)\overline{0.1} \to 1)\overline{10}$$
By what number were both the divisor and the dividend multiplied? *(100)*
What is the quotient? *(10)* Have students relate the quotient on the chalkboard with the one they found using the decimal bars.

2. Repeat to show $0.25)\overline{0.5} \to 25)\overline{50} = 2$.

WHEN YOUR STUDENTS ASK
★ WHY AM I LEARNING THIS? ★

You can use this skill to solve real life problems. If you want to find out how many hours you must work at $3.75 an hour to earn $100, you will have to divide by decimals.

Dividing Decimals by Decimals

A Ping-Pong ball and a golf ball are about the same size, but have different weights. A Ping-Pong ball weighs only 0.09 oz. How many Ping-Pong balls would equal the weight of 1 1.62-oz golf ball?

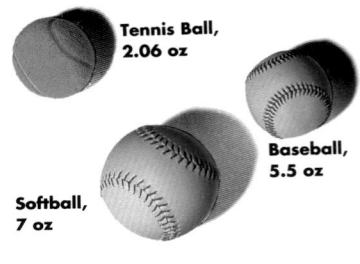

Tennis Ball, 2.06 oz

Baseball, 5.5 oz

Softball, 7 oz

How many times does 0.09 divide into 1.62?

To change the divisor to a whole number, multiply it by 100. Multiply the dividend by the same power of 10.

$$0.09)\overline{1.62} \qquad 9)\overline{162}$$
divisor × 100   × 100 dividend

Divide.	Check using the original divisor.
$\begin{array}{r} 18 \\ 9)\overline{162} \\ -9 \\ \hline 72 \\ -72 \\ \hline 0 \end{array}$	$\begin{array}{r} 18 \\ \times\, 0.09 \\ \hline 1.62 \end{array}$

Eighteen Ping-Pong balls equal the weight of one golf ball.

Volleyball, 9.88 oz

Football, 15 oz

Another example:
What is $1.57 \div 0.4$ to the nearest tenth?

$$0.4)\overline{1.5,70}$$
$$\begin{array}{r} 3.92 \\ -12 \\ \hline 37 \\ -36 \\ \hline 10 \\ -8 \\ \hline 2 \end{array}$$

rounds to 3.9

Multiply the divisor and dividend by 10 so the divisor is a whole number.

Why is the division worked to the hundredths' place?

to round to the nearest tenth

Basketball, 22.93 oz

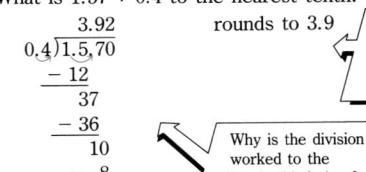

▬▬▬▬ **GUIDED PRACTICE** ▬▬▬▬

THINK ALOUD Explain how you would change the divisor to a whole number. What would you do to the dividend?

1. $0.7)\overline{4.9}$ **2.** $0.65)\overline{1.82}$ **3.** $84.21 \div 0.802$ **4.** $24 \div 0.4$
  × 10 × 10   × 100 × 100   × 1,000 × 1,000   × 10 × 10

Find the quotient. Round to tenths when necessary.

5. $0.6)\overline{8.4}$ **14**   **6.** $1.5)\overline{47.5}$ **31.7**   **7.** $0.50 \div 0.12$ **4.2**   **8.** $3.6 \div 0.09$ **40**

2 TEACH

☑ **MATERIALS CHECKLIST:** calculators

If the divisor is a decimal to the hundredths' place, how many places to the right must you move the decimal point in both the divisor and dividend? *(two)*

What is the first step when dividing by a decimal divisor? Give an example. *(Multiply both terms by a power of 10 so that the divisor becomes a whole number; $6.9 \div 2.3$ becomes $69 \div 23$ when both terms are multiplied by 10.)*

Chalkboard Examples

$2.378 \div 8.2$ *(0.29)*
$8.75 \div 12.5$ *(0.7)*
$624 \div 0.8$ *(780)*
$108.57 \div 0.231$ *(470)*

SUMMARIZE/ASSESS Explain how to determine the number of decimal places the decimal point is moved in the divisor and the dividend. *(The decimal point in both the dividend and divisor is moved the same number of decimal places as are in the divisor.)*

Divide until there is no remainder. Check your answer.

9. 0.8)7.2 9 **10.** 0.2)14.4 72 **11.** 5.5)82.5 15 **12.** 1.2)13.68 11.4

Divide. Round the quotient to the nearest tenth.

13. 2.3)3.78 1.6 **14.** 1.9)4.83 2.5 **15.** 1.7)140 82.4 **16.** 1.67)4.771 2.9

Divide. Round the quotient to the nearest cent.

17. $47.35 ÷ 6.1 **18.** $36.82 ÷ 0.83 **19.** $6.73 ÷ 3.9 **20.** $15.37 ÷ 6.4
$7.76 $44.36 $1.73 $2.40

Divide. Round the quotient to the nearest thousandth.

21. 8 ÷ 0.53 **22.** 7.836 ÷ 2.7 **23.** 0.249 ÷ 0.08 **24.** 481 ÷ 3.5
15.094 2.902 3.113 137.429

MIXED REVIEW Compute.

25. 89.7 + 128.63 **26.** 1.14 ÷ 0.06 **27.** 45.6 − 7.95 **28.** 105.6 × 4.8
218.33 19 37.65 506.88
29. 50 − 38.75 **30.** 0.9 + 0.75 **31.** 67.9 ÷ 9.7 **32.** 85.3 × 0.8
11.25 1.65 7 68.24

33. **CREATE YOUR OWN** Find the quotients. Then find the next three
quotients in the pattern. Now make up a similar division pattern. **Check students' work.**
50 ÷ 5 10 ▷ 50 ÷ 0.5 100 ▷ 50 ÷ 0.05 1,000 ▷ 50 ÷ 0.005 = 10,000
50 ÷ 0.0005 = 100,000

50 ÷ 0.00005 = 1,000,000

CHOOSE Choose estimation, paper and pencil,
or calculator to solve.

34. Estimate the number of tennis balls that would equal
the weight of a basketball. e; ≈11

35. How much more does a basketball weigh than a baseball?
p; 17.43 oz

*****36.** Make a pictograph representing the weights
of the balls shown on page 80.
Use the symbol • for 1 oz. See page 89b.

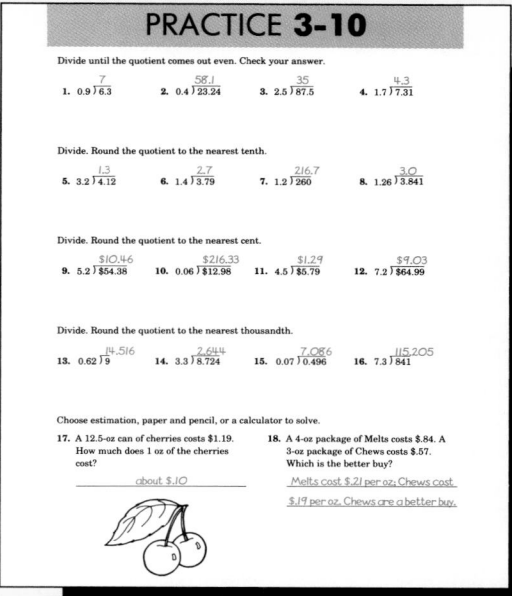

Mental Math

The three apples were cut in half, or 3 was divided by
0.5. Study how dividing by 0.5 can be done mentally.
3 ÷ 0.5 is the same as 3 × 2 ▷ 6

Now try to divide mentally.
1. 16 ÷ 0.5 32 **2.** 75 ÷ 0.5 150 **3.** 1.4 ÷ 0.5 2.8 **4.** 1.9 ÷ 0.5 3.8

MEETING INDIVIDUAL NEEDS

For Students Who Are . . .

Acquiring English Proficiency Pair students with an English-
proficient student to discuss and solve the Problem Solving and Mental Math exercises.

Gifted and Talented Have each student write a word problem that
involves dividing a decimal by a decimal. Then have students exchange papers and solve.

Working 2 or 3 Grades Below Level Have students use pages
70–77 of the Skills Workbook for decimals.

Today's Problem

The thickness of a plastic case for a compact disc is 0.75 cm. How
many compact discs in their cases would be in a stack that is
28.5 cm high? How many would be in a stack that is 47.25 cm high?
(28.5 ÷ 0.75 = 38; 47.25 ÷ 0.75 = 63)

---

3 FOLLOW-UP

PRACTICE 3-10

Divide until the quotient comes out even. Check your answer.

1. 0.9)6.3 7 **2.** 0.4)23.24 58.1 **3.** 2.5)87.5 35 **4.** 1.7)7.31 4.3

Divide. Round the quotient to the nearest tenth.

5. 3.2)4.12 1.3 **6.** 1.4)3.79 2.7 **7.** 1.2)260 216.7 **8.** 1.26)3.841 3.0

Divide. Round the quotient to the nearest cent.

9. 5.2)$54.38 $10.46 **10.** 0.06)$12.98 $216.33 **11.** 4.5)$5.79 $1.29 **12.** 7.2)$64.99 $9.03

Divide. Round the quotient to the nearest thousandth.

13. 0.62)9 14.516 **14.** 3.3)8.724 2.644 **15.** 0.07)0.496 7.086 **16.** 7.3)841 115.205

Choose estimation, paper and pencil, or a calculator to solve.

17. A 12.5-oz can of cherries costs $1.19.
How much does 1 oz of the cherries
cost?
about $.10

18. A 4-oz package of Melts costs $.84. A
3-oz package of Chews costs $.57.
Which is the better buy?
Melts cost $.21 per oz; Chews cost
$.19 per oz. Chews are a better buy.

RETEACHING 3-10

✓ **MATERIALS CHECKLIST:** Number line

Have the students refer to a number line
that is marked in tenths. Write 2.4 ÷ 0.4
on the board. Ask the students to count
the number of 4 tenths in 2.4.

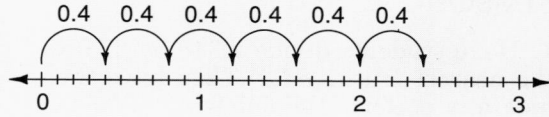

0.4 0.4 0.4 0.4 0.4 0.4

0   1   2   3

The number of 4 tenths in 2.4 is 6.

Give the students other problems in which
they must divide a decimal by a decimal.
Encourage the students to draw number
lines to check their quotients.

ENRICHMENT 3-10

The formula °C = $\frac{5 \times (°F - 32)}{9}$ converts Fahrenheit to Celsius scale temperature.

The formula °F = $\frac{9 \times °C}{5}$ + 32 converts Celsius to Fahrenheit scale temperature.

Examples:

Write 78.62°F as degrees Celsius.
°C = $\frac{5 \times (78.62 - 32)}{9}$
°C = $\frac{5 \times 46.6}{9}$
°C = $\frac{233}{9}$
°C = 25.9°

Write 31.1°C as degrees Fahrenheit.
°F = $\frac{9 \times 31.1}{5}$ + 32
°F = $\frac{279.9}{5}$ + 32
°F = 55.98 + 32
°F = 87.98°

Convert each temperature in degrees Celsius to degrees Fahrenheit.

1. 100°C **2.** 24.5°C **3.** 0°C
_212°F_ _76.1°F_ _32°F_

Convert each temperature in degrees Fahrenheit to degrees Celsius.

4. 32°F **5.** 98.6°F **6.** 136.4°F
_0°C_ _37°C_ _58°C_

Lesson Organizer

Objective: Estimate quotients using compatible numbers.

Prior Knowledge: Students should be able to round numbers to a given place.

Error Analysis and Remediation: See page 89A.

Lesson Resources:
Practice Worksheet 3-11
Reteaching Worksheet 3-11
Enrichment Activity 3-11
Daily Review 3-11

 **Two-Minute Math**

Which can be evenly divided by 90?

45,000   200   720   2,400

(45,000; 720)

1 INTRODUCE

SYMBOLIC ACTIVITY

1. Have students divide 2,348 by 27.9 to the nearest tenth. *(84.2)* Then have them mentally perform the following divisions, relating each division to the original one:

- 2,100 ÷ 30
- 2,400 ÷ 30
- 2,000 ÷ 25

2. Discuss how each related division could be used as an estimated quotient for the original problem.

3. Lead students to conclude that they can estimate a quotient by thinking of numbers close to the dividend and the divisor that are easy to divide mentally.

WHEN YOUR STUDENTS ASK
★ WHY AM I LEARNING THIS? ★

You can connect this skill to real life through conference planning. Conference planners estimate quickly how many shuttle buses are needed to transfer people between meeting places.

MATH AND SOCIAL STUDIES

Estimating Quotients

Montezuma Castle and Walnut Canyon are two national monuments in central Arizona. Montezuma Castle contains a 5-story prehistoric Native American cliff dwelling. Walnut Canyon has ancient Native American cliff dwellings built in shallow caves.

About how many times larger is the site of the Walnut Canyon National Monument than the site of the Montezuma Castle National Monument?

How many times does 858 divide into 2,249?

**Montezuma Castle, 858 acres
The Sinagua people built these dwellings and lived here from 1125 to 1400.**

Use compatible numbers to estimate this quotient.

Pick two numbers that are close to these numbers and divide easily. Estimate.

$858\overline{)2,249}$ ⇨ $900\overline{)2,700}^{\,3}$ *2,700 is easy to divide by 900.*

Walnut Canyon National Monument is about 3 times larger.

Notice that there can be more than one choice of compatible numbers when you estimate a quotient.

$4.2\overline{)46.6}$ ⇨ $4\overline{)48}^{\,12}$ $4\overline{)44}^{\,11}$ $4\overline{)40}^{\,10}$

$4\overline{)44}$; 4 and 44 are both slightly less than the given numbers.

THINK ALOUD Which estimate would you choose for the example above? Why?

Answers will vary. Suggestions given.

━━━━━━━ **GUIDED PRACTICE** ━━━━━━━

Choose a compatible number. Estimate the quotient.

1. $92\overline{)371}$ $90\overline{)\blacksquare}$ 360; ≈4

2. $31\overline{)335}$ $\blacksquare\overline{)330}$ 33; ≈10

3. $7.8\overline{)76}$ $8\overline{)\blacksquare}$ 80; ≈10

82   LESSON 3–11

MULTICULTURAL NOTE

The Sinagua people built dwellings in Walnut Canyon as well as Montezuma Castle. The Sinagua raised corn, beans, and pumpkins in what is now Arizona, but abandoned the area because of severe drought.

2 TEACH

Give an example to show how using compatible numbers is related to basic facts. *(To estimate 554 ÷ 78, you can use the basic fact 56 ÷ 8 = 7 to find the compatible numbers 560 and 80.)*

When using compatible numbers to estimate a quotient, can there be more than one correct estimate? *(Yes, since you can use different pairs of compatible numbers.)*

Chalkboard Examples

Estimate each quotient
3,701 ÷ 49   2,258 ÷ 689
7.68 ÷ 4.2   9.856 ÷ 1.97
(Possible estimates: 70; 3; 2; 5)

SUMMARIZE/ASSESS Explain how to use compatible numbers to estimate a quotient. (Change the divisor and the dividend to numbers that can be divided easily, that are close in value to the original numbers. Then divide to get the estimate.)

Walnut Canyon, 2,249 acres

━━━━━━━━━━ **PRACTICE** ━━━━━━━━━━

Use compatible numbers to estimate the quotient.   **Answers will vary. Suggestions given.**

4. $21\overline{)83}$ ≈4   **5.** $32\overline{)891}$ ≈30   **6.** $37\overline{)835}$ ≈ 20   **7.** $18\overline{)583}$ ≈30

8. $73\overline{)63.8}$ ≈0.9   **9.** $98\overline{)72.6}$ ≈0.7   **10.** $27\overline{)48.3}$ ≈2   **11.** $81\overline{)329.3}$ ≈4

12. $2.2\overline{)86}$ ≈40   **13.** $3.7\overline{)803}$ ≈200   **14.** $6.3\overline{)582}$ ≈100   **15.** $1.9\overline{)1,623}$ ≈800

16. 473 ÷ 46 ≈10   **17.** 382 ÷ 63 ≈6   **18.** 1,115 ÷ 42 ≈30   **19.** 8,237 ÷ 19 ≈400

20. 89.4 ÷ 27 ≈3   **21.** 41.2 ÷ 51 ≈0.8   **22.** 528.3 ÷ 51 ≈10   **23.** 639.2 ÷ 98 ≈6

24. 149 ÷ 2.7 ≈50   **25.** 9,578 ÷ 5.2 ≈2,000   **26.** 7,914 ÷ 1.8 ≈4,000   **27.** 4,821 ÷ 3.3 ≈1,600

━━━━━━━━━━ **PROBLEM SOLVING** ━━━━━━━━━━

CHOOSE   Choose estimation
or calculator to solve.   **Choices will vary. Suggestions given.**

28. About how many times smaller is the
land occupied by the Statue of Liberty
than by the Devil's Tower?
e; ≈20 times

29. The Timpanogos Cave and the Oregon
Caves, formed in limestone, are both
known for their great beauty.
About how many times more area
do the Oregon Caves cover than does
the Timpanogos Cave? **e; ≈2 times**

Sites of National Monuments	
Devil's Tower, WY	1,347 acres
Statue of Liberty, NY	58 acres
Oregon Caves, OR	488 acres
Timpanogos Cave, UT	250 acres
Organ Pipe Cactus, AZ	330,689 acres

30. One square mile is 640 acres. About how many square miles
is the Organ Pipe Cactus National Monument? **c; 516.7 mi²**

31. CREATE YOUR OWN   Write a question of your own that can be
solved using the facts in the table.   **Check students' work.**

CHAPTER 3   **83**

---

3 FOLLOW-UP

PRACTICE 3-11

Use compatible numbers to estimate the quotient.

1. $49\overline{)523}$
$50\overline{)500}$ 10

2. $24\overline{)748}$
$25\overline{)750}$ 30

3. $72\overline{)4.33}$
$70\overline{)4.20}$ 0.06

4. $58\overline{)54.3}$
$60\overline{)54.0}$ 0.9

5. $64\overline{)4.90}$
$60\overline{)4.80}$ 0.08

6. $45\overline{)54.4}$
$45\overline{)54.0}$ 1.2

7. $2.1\overline{)6.12}$
$2\overline{)6}$ 3

8. $4.9\overline{)78.2}$
$5\overline{)80}$ 16

9. $8.3\overline{)5.48}$
$8\overline{)5.6}$ 0.7

10. 8.43 ÷ 7.6
8 ÷ 8 = 1

11. 675 ÷ 5.8
660 ÷ 6 = 110

12. 904 ÷ 84
880 ÷ 80 = 11

13. 747 ÷ 9.9
750 ÷ 10 = 75

14. 8.99 ÷ 6.2
9 ÷ 6 = 1.5

15. 16.5 ÷ 79
16 ÷ 80 = 0.2

Choose mental math or estimation to solve.

16. Alaska has a land area of 586,412 mi²;
Ohio has an area of 41,222 mi². About
how many times bigger is Alaska than
Ohio? about 15 times bigger

17. About how much money does Judy
have left from $20 if she spends $15.98
plus $.80 tax on a sweatshirt?
about $3.20

RETEACHING 3-11

Sometimes you need an easy, close estimate instead of the exact
answer. Using compatible numbers is an easy way to get a close
estimate. A compatible number is easy to divide and close to the given
number.

Example:

Jerry needs to take a 148-mi trip. His
sports car gets 13 mi/gal of gas. He does
not want to stop for gas along the way.
What is the minimum number of gallons of
gas he should have in his gas tank before
he starts his trip?

Given numbers (the exact answer):
148 mi ÷ 13 mi/gal = 11.38 gal
Compatible numbers (close estimate):
1. 150 mi ÷ 15 mi/gal = 10 gal
2. 140 mi ÷ 14 mi/gal = 10 gal
3. 144 mi ÷ 12 mi/gal = 12 gal

1. Each compatible number pair above is easy to divide. Which pair
of compatible numbers gives the closest estimate of the exact
answer? Why?
3; it is closer to the exact answer than the other estimates.

Write the missing compatible number.

2. $63\overline{)536}$ $\boxed{60}\overline{)540}$ **3.** $49\overline{)486}$ $50\overline{)\boxed{500}}$ **4.** $5.9\overline{)499}$ $6\overline{)\boxed{480}}$ **5.** $8.7\overline{)93.8}$ $\boxed{9}\overline{)90}$ **6.** $1.2\overline{)3.815}$ $1\overline{)\boxed{3.815}}$

Write compatible numbers. Circle the appropriate estimate.

7. $9.7\overline{)29.8}$ $\boxed{10}\overline{)30}$ **a.** 3   **b.** 30   **c.** 300

8. $84\overline{)493}$ $\boxed{80}\overline{)480}$ **a.** 6   **b.** 60   **c.** 600

Use compatible numbers to estimate the quotient.

9. $46\overline{)821}$
$40\overline{)800}$ 20

10. $0.9\overline{)24.6}$
$0.9\overline{)27.0}$ 30

11. $67\overline{)3.95}$
$70\overline{)4.20}$ 0.06

12. $88\overline{)9.18}$
$90\overline{)9.0}$ 0.1

13. $6.3\overline{)96.8}$
$6\overline{)96}$ 16

14. $76\overline{)84.2}$
$80\overline{)80}$ 1

ENRICHMENT 3-11

☑ **MATERIALS CHECKLIST:** Grocery
store ads from newspapers

Challenge students to extend their use of
compatible numbers to multiplication.
Have students work in pairs to use compatible numbers to estimate bulk or unit
purchases. For example, if an ad has apples on sale for $0.79 per lb, have one stu-
dent tell how many pounds of apples he or
she wants, and then compute the exact
price. The other student then uses compatible numbers to estimate the price. If the
estimate is not close to the exact price,
have the students try to find compatible
numbers that are easy to divide (or multiply) and that are close to the given
numbers.

Chapter 3 • Lesson 3-11   **83**

Lesson Organizer

Objective: Solve problems with too much or too little information.

Prior Knowledge: Students should be able to identify the operation needed to solve a problem.

Error Analysis and Remediation: See page 89A.

Lesson Resources:
Practice Worksheet 3-12
Reteaching Activity 3-12
Enrichment Worksheet 3-12
Daily Review 3-12

Two-Minute Math

Write the missing signs.

$8,952 \square 4,861 \square 3 = 4,094$ *(−; +)*

$(9.37 \square 5.81) \square 3 = 5.06$ *(+; ÷)*

$(1,275 \square 17) \square 42 = 117$ *(÷; +)*

1 INTRODUCE

SYMBOLIC ACTIVITY

1. Have students solve this problem:
Ruth worked 2 hours after school on Monday, 3 hours on Tuesday, and 8 hours on Saturday. She earned $68.25 for the week. How many hours did she work? *(13 hours)*

2. Discuss the problem by asking:

- **How did you obtain your answer?** *(Added to find the total number of hours.)*

- **What information was not used to solve the problem?** *(the amount of money she earned)*

3. Explain to students that often they will need to sort through a problem to separate necessary from unnecessary information.

WHEN YOUR STUDENTS ASK
★ WHY AM I LEARNING THIS? ★

You can connect this skill to real life through the legal system. Judges and jurors must sort through a lot of information to obtain answers to questions.

Problem Solving: Too Much or Too Little Information

Sometimes in problem solving there are more facts than you need. Other times there are not enough facts.

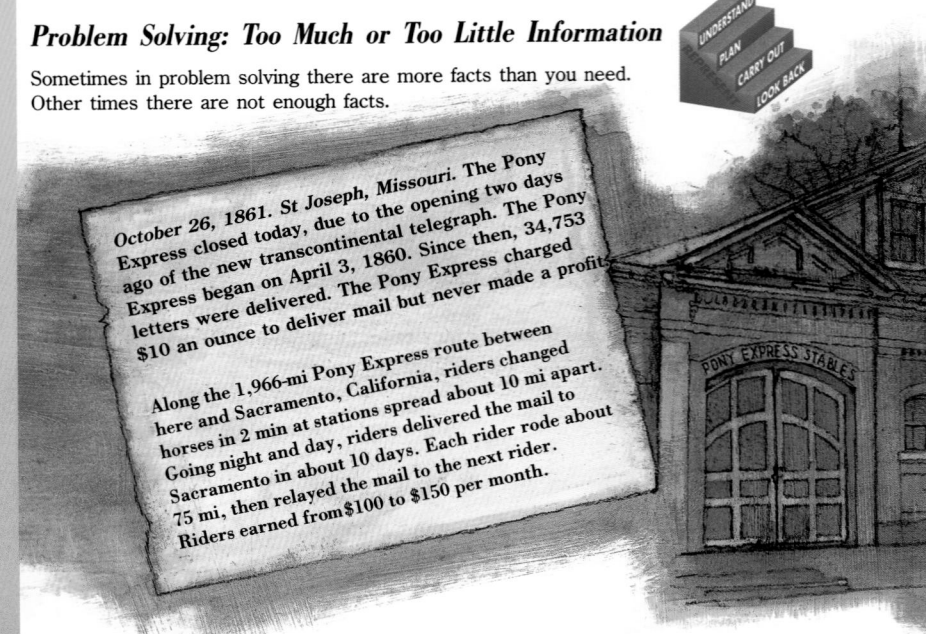

October 26, 1861. St Joseph, Missouri. The Pony Express closed today, due to the opening two days ago of the new transcontinental telegraph. The Pony Express began on April 3, 1860. Since then, 34,753 letters were delivered. The Pony Express charged $10 an ounce to deliver mail but never made a profit.

Along the 1,966-mi Pony Express route between here and Sacramento, California, riders changed horses in 2 min at stations spread about 10 mi apart. Going night and day, riders delivered the mail to Sacramento in about 10 days. Each rider rode about 75 mi, then relayed the mail to the next rider. Riders earned from $100 to $150 per month.

For about how many months was the Pony Express in operation?

- Reread the passage carefully.
- What information would you use to solve the problem? **the dates, Oct. 26, 1861**
- What information is not needed to solve the problem? **and Apr. 3, 1860; all other data**

Now solve the problem. **19 mo**

MATH AND HISTORY

━━━━━━ **GUIDED PRACTICE** ━━━━━━

1. Which question do you have enough information to answer? **b**

   a. How long did it take to deliver Lincoln's speech?
   b. If a rider reached a station at 9:23, when would he be ready to leave?
   c. What did a rider's mailbag weigh?

2. What information do you need to find the value of the mail in a Pony Express mailbag? **c**

   a. The Pony Express started on April 3, 1860.
   b. Each rider had 2 min at each stop.
   c. A mailbag carried 15 lb and mail cost $10/oz.

84   LESSON 3–12

MULTICULTURAL NOTE

George Monroe, an African American, was one of the famous Pony Express riders. He later became stagecoach driver and was ranked as the best in California and perhaps the entire West.

2 TEACH

You may wish to have students work with a partner for Exercises 3-12.

After students read the passage about the Pony Express, ask them to close their books and list all the facts given in the passage. Recall the importance of reading slowly and carefully. Then have students reread the passage to identify only the information needed to solve the problem. *(the two dates given in the passage)*

SUMMARIZE/ASSESS **How many miles did a Pony Express rider ride in a week? Explain your answer.** *(Cannot answer because there is not enough information.)*

PRACTICE

Use the information on page 84. If enough is given, solve the problem. Otherwise, state what information is needed.

3. On what date did the transcontinental telegraph open?
October 24, 1861

4. About how many stops might a rider make in 75 mi?
≈7 stops

5. How much money did the Pony Express lose? **need gross income and operating costs**

6. What was the most money a Pony Express rider could make in 1 yr?
$1,800/mo

7. How much did it cost to send a letter by telegraph? **need pricing rates**

8. About how many Pony Express stations could there have been?
≈200 stations

9. About how many miles did the mail travel in 24 h? **≈ 200 mi**

10. CREATE YOUR OWN Use the information on page 84 to write a question for a friend to solve.
Check students' work.

CHOOSE Choose a strategy to solve. **Choices will vary.**

11. On the average, about 350 letters were delivered on each trip. Use the total number of letters delivered to find about how many trips were made in all. **≈ 100 trips**

12. Before the Pony Express, it took 25 d to deliver mail by stagecoach to California. How many days less did the Pony Express take?
15 d

MEETING INDIVIDUAL NEEDS

For Students Who Are . . .

Acquiring English Proficiency Explain what the prefixes mean in the words *transcontinental* and *telegraph*. Pair students with a English-proficient student to discuss the Practice exercises.

Gifted and Talented Assign the technology lesson on page 94.

Working 2 or 3 Grades Below Level Have students use pages 108–115 of the Skills Workbook for Problem Solving Strategies.

Having Reading Difficulties Pair each student with an able reader to discuss and solve the Practice exercises, or form a group and monitor students' comprehension of the questions asked.

Today's Problem

The speed of sound is about 1,088 ft/s. The distance between the moon and Earth is about 250,000 miles. How long would it take to reach the moon if you were traveling at the speed of sound?
(250,000 mi × 5,280 ft ÷ 1,088 ft ÷ 60 s ÷ 60 min ÷ 24 h = 14; about 14 days days)

---

3 FOLLOW-UP

PRACTICE 3-12

Read the information in each problem. If enough is given, solve the problem. Otherwise, state what information is needed.

1. The combined area of Kentucky and Tennessee is 82,553 mi². The area of Kentucky is 40,409 mi², and the area of Tennessee is 42,144 mi². What is the difference in area?
1,735 mi²

2. North Carolina was the twelfth state to enter the Union. How many years ago did North Carolina become a state?
need to know when North Carolina became a state

3. The McCormick family drove 1,200 mi in 3 days so they could reach Yellowstone National Park by July 17th. On what day did they leave their home?
need to know if they left from home or from some other place

4. The first white man to see the Mississippi River was Hernando de Soto in 1541. One hundred forty years later, Robert La Salle claimed all of the Mississippi for France. In what year was La Salle's claim made? How old was he when he made it?
1681; need to know when La Salle was born

5. The state of Iowa has 5 times as many hogs as people. According to a survey in the 1980s, there were 14.3 million hogs raised in Iowa as compared to 5.6 million raised in Illinois. About how many people lived in Iowa in the 1980s?
need to know if there were 5 times as many hogs as people in the 1980s

6. North Dakota produces about 3 times as many bushels of wheat per year as Nebraska. If Nebraska produces 105 million bushels, how many does North Dakota produce?
315 million bushels

RETEACHING 3-12

☑ **MATERIALS CHECKLIST:** Reference books, world almanacs

Have pairs of students select and research one topic of interest. For example, if they choose a type of car, they might find statistics regarding price, quantities sold, mileage per gallon, size of gas tank, and trunk capacity. Then have the students write questions based on the information they gathered. Ask them to trade information and questions with other pairs of students and answer each other's questions.

ENRICHMENT 3-12

Solve the problem if there is enough information. Underline any information not needed to solve a problem. Identify missing information.

1. A home in New Jersey sold for $38,450 in 1952. Thirty-eight years later it sold for 7 times its 1952 price. How much did it sell for and in what year?
$269,150; 1990

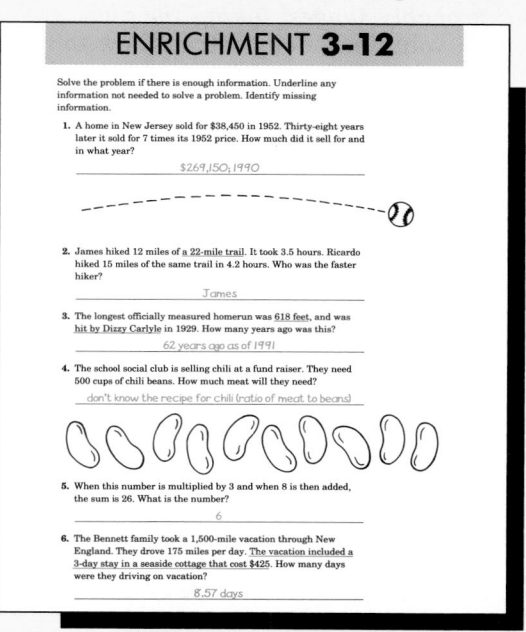

2. James hiked 12 miles of a 22-mile trail. It took 3.5 hours. Ricardo hiked 15 miles of the same trail in 4.2 hours. Who was the faster hiker?
James

3. The longest officially measured homerun was 618 feet, and was hit by Dizzy Carlyle in 1929. How many years ago was this?
62 years ago as of 1991

4. The school social club is selling chili at a fund raiser. They need 500 cups of chili beans. How much meat will they need?
don't know the recipe for chili (ratio of meat to beans)

5. When this number is multiplied by 3 and when 8 is then added, the sum is 26. What is the number?
6

6. The Bennett family took a 1,500-mile vacation through New England. They drove 175 miles per day. The vacation included a 3-day stay in a seaside cottage that cost $425. How many days were they driving on vacation?
8.57 days

Lesson Organizer

Objective: Solve problems creatively.

Prior Knowledge: Students should know how to convert seconds into minutes.

Lesson Resources:
Daily Review 3-13
Cooperative Problem Solving, Chapter 3

Two-Minute Math

Use mental math.
Write the number of seconds.
5 minutes *(300)*   9 minutes *(540)*
Write the number of minutes.
180 seconds *(3)*   420 seconds *(7)*

1 PREPARE

CONNECTING ACTIVITY

☑ **MATERIALS CHECKLIST:** stopwatch or watch with a second hand for each group

Have students work in small groups.

How many times do you think your heart beats a minute? Record your guess on a piece of paper.

How will you find the number of times your heart beats a minute? *(Students will probably suggest taking the pulse.)* With a volunteer, demonstrate how to take a pulse at the wrist.

Is it necessary to count the number of beats for an entire minute? Explain. *(Possible answer: No, count the number of beats for 15 seconds, then multiply by 4.)*

Have students practice taking their pulse. **Compare your actual pulse rate with the guess made earlier.**

WHEN YOUR STUDENTS ASK
★ **WHY AM I LEARNING THIS?** ★

You can connect this lesson to real life by considering exercise plans. Regular aerobic exercise promotes physical fitness and helps control mental or emotional stress.

CREATIVE PROBLEM SOLVING

Investigating Exercise

Running, jogging, dancing, rowing, and playing basketball or other sports are all examples of aerobic exercise. Aerobic exercise is continuous exercise for an extended period of time that makes you breathe faster. It increases the amount of oxygen your body needs.

Everyone knows that it is important to get enough exercise. But how much exercise is enough? Can there be such a thing as *too much* exercise? Get ready to find out what your heartbeat has to do with it.

Work in a small group.

1. Think of as many kinds of exercises as you can and make a list. Then write whether each kind is aerobic exercise.
   Check students' work.

2. After 30 min of aerobic exercise, most people are breathing faster than normal. Their hearts are beating faster than normal. Find out why aerobic exercise causes this to happen.
   Check students' work.

MATH AND HEALTH

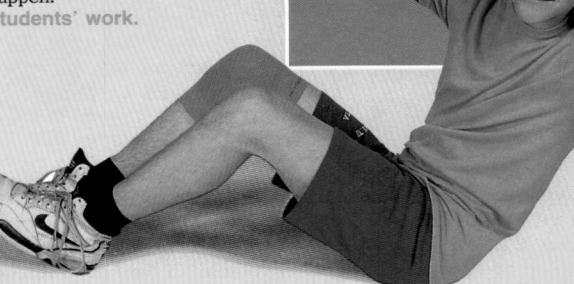

2 EXPLORE

☑ **MATERIALS CHECKLIST:** stopwatch or watch with second hand for each group, calculators

Have students work in groups of three or four for this lesson.

How many times does your heart beat in 5 minutes? in 15 minutes? in an hour? in a 24-hour period? (Use a calculator to help you answer these questions.) *(Answers will vary.)*

If your heart beats 24 times in 20 seconds, how many times does it beat in two minutes? *(144 times)*

SUMMARIZE/ASSESS   **How would you use mathematics to determine one effect of aerobic exercise on your body?** *(Possible answer: Compare the speed of the heartbeat before and after exercise.)*

3. Place the three middle fingers of one hand on the inside of your wrist close to the base of the thumb. Wait until you can feel your pulse and count the beats.
Check students' work.

4. Use a stopwatch or watch with a second hand to find out how many times your heart beats in 10 s. Record the results of all members of your group.
Check students' work.

5. Convert the 10-s information into heartbeats per minute. Discuss with your group how to do this.
Accept reasonable answers.

6. In what other ways can the heartbeat be measured?
Accept reasonable answers.

7. Predict the effect of 30 min of aerobic exercise on the rate of your heartbeat. Would the rate increase, decrease, or stay the same? Discuss some other effects that aerobic exercises could have.
increase; Accept reasonable answers.

8. Record your heartbeat rate just before and just after exercising. Report and discuss your findings with classmates.
Check students' work.

9. Why is it important to know how fast your heart beats at rest and during or after exercise? Is there value in increasing the heartbeat? What is the value of knowing your maximum heartbeat?
Accept reasonable answers.

10. Prepare a simple weekly exercise plan that a healthy student your age could follow. Should an exercise plan be checked with a doctor? Give some reasons.
Accept reasonable answers.

CHAPTER 3   87

MEETING INDIVIDUAL NEEDS

For Students Who Are . . .

Acquiring English Proficiency Discuss the meanings of *aerobic, continuous,* and *extended.* Have students use these words in original sentences.

Gifted and Talented Have students collect the at rest pulse rates of their classmates, display this information in a bar graph, and write one or two sentences describing any conclusions drawn from the data.

Working 2 or 3 Grades Below Level Review multiplying and dividing by multiples of 10.

Today's Problem

The heart pumps blood through the body at the rate of about 5 L per minute. About how many liters are pumped through the body every 24 hours? *(5 × 60 = 300 L/hr; 300 × 24 = 7,200 L every 24 h)*

3 FOLLOW-UP

CLASS ACTIVITY 3-13

☑ **MATERIALS CHECKLIST:** catalogs with exercise and sports equipment

Arrange students in groups of three or four. Tell them to imagine their school has been given a $10,000 grant to improve its sports equipment, subject to the following conditions:

1. Equipment must be available to all students.

2. Equipment must encourage good health.

Ask how they would spend this money. Have students design a plan and check prices with reference books as needed. Then have each group share results with the class.

CHAPTER Checkup

The chapter checkup provides a quick language and vocabulary review, a test for the chapter, and suggestions for student Learning Log entries.

Language and Vocabulary

Some key language and vocabulary ideas from this chapter are reinforced here.

Test

The test can be used either as a test or as a review of the chapter prior to your administering the test worksheets found in the Teacher's Resource Book.

The following guide will help you determine percentage scores.

Score	Percent	Score	Percent
35	100%	17	50%
34	98	16	48
33	95	15	45
32	93	14	42
31	90	13	39
30	87	12	36
29	84	11	33
28	81	10	30
27	78	9	27
26	75	8	24
25	72	7	21
24	69	6	18
23	67	5	15
22	64	4	12
21	62	3	9
20	59	2	6
19	56	1	3
18	53		

Each test has 3 sections: concepts, skills and problem solving. These sections provide students with exposure to the formats used on standardized tests.

Use the chart on page 89 to identify the Management Objectives tested for this chapter.

CHAPTER CHECKUP

LANGUAGE & VOCABULARY

Write *true* or *false*. If the statement is false, prove that it is false by giving an example.

1. When you evaluate an expression using the order of operations rules, you always add first.
   false; $4 + 2 \times 3 = 10$

2. When you divide, the quotient is always smaller than the dividend.
   false; $2 \div .25 = 8$

3. Multiplying a number by 100 and then dividing it by 1,000 is the same as dividing the number by 10.
   true

TEST ✓

CONCEPTS

Simplify. *(pages 60–63)*

1. $2 \times (50 \times 8)$ 800
2. $3 \times (27 + 3)$ 90
3. $29 \times 0 \times 7$ 0
4. $70 \times 1 \times 3$ 210
5. $15 \times (2 \times 5)$ 150
6. $35 \times 1 \times 8 \times 0$ 0
7. $3 + 9 \times 4$ 39
8. $25 - 3^2 + 2 \times 5$ 26
9. $6 + (2 \times 3^2) - 8$ 16

Write in scientific notation. *(pages 78–79)*

10. 3,800,000 3.8×10^6
11. 36,700,000 3.67×10^7
12. 129,000 1.29×10^5

SKILLS

Multiply. *(pages 64–67)*

13. 63×7 441
14. 95×6 570
15. 748×23 17,204
16. 608×59 35,872

17. 35.6×21 747.6
18. 40.09×3.7 148.3
19. $6,024 \times 375$ 2,259,000
20. $\$4.95 \times 100$ $495
21. 2.75×0.9 2.475
22. 87.65×3.2 280.48

88   CHAPTER CHECKUP

CHAPTER TEST • FORM A

Simplify. (pp. 60–63) 3A

1. $25 \times (4 \times 3)$ 300
2. $62 \times 1 \times 5 \times 0 =$ 0
3. $6 \times (22 + 8)$ 180
4. $15 + 2^2 + 3 \times 4$ 31
5. $24 - (3^2 \times 2) + 9$ 15

Multiply or divide. (pp. 64–65, 68–69) 3B

6. 74×8 592
7. 86×5 430
8. 639×27 17,253

9. $18 \overline{)4,410}$ 245
10. $107 \overline{)8,295}$ 77 R56

(pp. 66–67, 70–71, 76–81) 3C

Multiply or divide.

11. $25.7 \times 16 =$ 411.2
12. $5.5 \overline{)93.5}$ 17
13. $76.54 \times 4.3 =$ 329.122

Divide. Round to tenths.

14. $28 \overline{)42.74}$ 1.5
15. $65.07 + 96$ 0.7

Use compatible numbers to estimate the quotient. (pp. 82–83) 3D   Accept reasonable estimates.

16. $19 \overline{)37.53}$ 2
17. $27 \overline{)8,896}$ 300
18. $71 \overline{)34.9}$ 0.5

19. $891 \div 2.7$ 300
20. $6,513 \div 32$ 200

CHAPTER TEST • FORM A

If enough information is given, solve the problem. Otherwise, state what information is needed. (pp. 72–73, 84–85) 3E

21. The library had a surplus book and magazine sale. The books were $1.50 each and the magazines were 25¢ each. Patty spent $6 on magazines. How many magazines did she buy?
   24 magazines

22. LeRoy bought 8 books and 10 magazines. How much change did he receive?
   No solution. Need to know how much he gave the clerk.

23. The library sold $4,800 worth of books and magazines during the 16 h sale. What was the average amount of money they earned each hour?
   $300 per hour

24. A box containing 64 books weighs about 50 lb. About how much would 5 boxes of books and 6 boxes of magazines weigh?
   No solution. Need to know the weight of a box of magazines.

25. Philip made 3 round trips from his house to the library sale. He rode the city bus which cost him 35¢ each way. How much did he spend on bus fares to the library sale?
   $2.10

Divide. *(pages 68–69)*

	24 R11		10 R45		70 R19		24 R100

23. 15)371   **24.** 76)805   **25.** 44)3,099   **26.** 109)2,716

Divide. Round to tenths. *(pages 70–71, 80–81)*

27. 23)35.61 1.5   **28.** 56.08 ÷ 95 0.6   **29.** 3.2)82.63 25.8

Use compatible numbers to estimate the quotient. *(pages 82–83)* **Accept reasonable estimates.**

30. 23)409 20   **31.** 49)2,487 50   **32.** 83)71.6 0.9

========================= **PROBLEM SOLVING** =========================

Solve. *(pages 60–61, 84–85)*

33. A pottery shop has 6 large shelves that hold 60 mugs each. There are also 6 smaller display shelves with 7 mugs on each.

   a. How many mugs does each large shelf hold? **60 mugs**

   b. Since the number of large and small shelves are the same, which property can you use to solve the problem? **distributive**

   c. How many mugs altogether do the shelves hold? **402 mugs**

34. Mrs. Jackson earns $18.75 per hour as a part-time accountant. After 3 wk she has earned $1,125.00 and has deposited $875.00 in her checking account. How many hours has she worked in the past 3 wk? **60 hr**

35. A school group went on a picnic. If 371 students went on minibuses that held 15 students each, how many buses were needed? **25 buses**

LEARNING LOG

Write the answers in your learning log. **Answers will vary. Suggestions given.**

1. Explain how to multiply and divide decimals by powers of ten. **Move the decimal to the right when multiplying and to the left when dividing.**

2. Explain how to decide how many zeros to add when converting from scientific notation to standard form. **The number of spaces moved is equal to the ten's exponent.**

Note that the same numbers are used in Exercises 23 and 35.

CHAPTER 3 89

Items	Management Objectives	Pages
1–9	**3A** Use properties of multiplication and order of operations.	60–63
13–16; 23–26	**3B** Multiply and divide whole numbers.	64–65; 68–69
10–12; 17–22; 27–29	**3C** Multiply and divide decimals.	78–79; 66–67; 70–71
30–32	**3D** Estimate quotients.	82–83
33–35	**3E** Problem Solving: Look back. Too much or too little information.	72–73; 84–85

Problem Solving

Item 33 has 3 parts:
a. literal—this is a reading comprehension question;
b. interpretive—this involves interpretation using the facts given;
c. applied—students use a strategy or skills to find an answer.

Item 23 in the skill section and item 35 in the problem solving section use the same numbers.

This will help you informally assess how your students transfer from numerical skills to word problems.

For scoring problem solving items you may wish to use partial credit. If a student uses the correct strategy but gets a wrong answer, give the student 2 points toward the total percent score.

Learning Log

These are suggestions for writing about some topics taught in this chapter. The students keep their Learning Logs from the beginning of the school year through the end.

CHAPTER TEST • FORM B

Simplify. *(pp. 60–63)* 3A

1. 250 × (4 × 7) 7,000   **2.** 75 × 4 × 0 × 53 0   **3.** (40 + 5) × 8 360

4. 16 + 2² + 3 × 5 35   **5.** 3³ × 6 + 2 + 8 35

Multiply or divide. *(pp. 64–65, 68–69)* 3B

6. 65
   × 7
   455

7. 82
   × 5
   410

8. 738
   × 36
   26,568

9. 104)8,265 79 R49   **10.** 16)5,200 325

(pp. 66–67, 70–71, 76–81) 3C

Multiply or divide.

11. 27.5 × 18 = 495   **12.** 4.5)85.5 19   **13.** 65.43 × 5.9 = 386.037

Divide. Round to tenths.

14. 34)57.82 1.7   **15.** 75.06 ÷ 84 0.9

Use compatible numbers to estimate the quotient. *(pp. 82–83)* 3D Accept reasonable estimates.

16. 17)33.65 2   **17.** 29)8,864 300   **18.** 61)30.9 0.5

19. 7,568 ÷ 5.2 1,500   **20.** 1,215 ÷ 42 30

CHAPTER TEST • FORM B

If enough information is given, solve the problem. Otherwise, state what information is needed. *(pp. 72–73, 84–85)* 3E

21. The library had a surplus book and magazine sale. The books were $1.50 each and the magazines were 25¢ each. Gloria spent $9 on books. How many books did she buy?

   6 books

22. Lamar bought 6 magazines at 25¢ each. How much change did he receive?

   No solution. Need to know how much money he gave the clerk.

23. The library sold $4,800 worth of books and magazines during the 12 h sale. What was the average amount of money they earned each hour?

   $400 per hour

24. A box containing 72 books weighs about 60 lb. A box containing 125 magazines weighs about 40 lb. About how much would 6 boxes of books and 6 boxes of magazines weigh?

   600 lb

25. Paula made 3 round trips from her house to the library sale. How many miles did she travel?

   No solution. Need to know how far it is from her house to the location of the library sale.

Error Analysis and Remediation

Here are some common errors students make when they are multiplying and dividing whole numbers and decimals. The errors are listed by lesson under the appropriate management objective.

3A • USE PROPERTIES OF MULTIPLICATION AND ORDER OF OPERATIONS

Source of Error (Lesson 3-1)
students confuse the commutative and associative properties.

Remediation
Have students recall the everyday meaning of *commute*—to go back and forth, and have them relate this meaning to an example such as $3 \times 4 = 4 \times 3$. Then have students think of the general meaning of *associate* and connect this to the example $(2 \times 6) \times 5 = 2 \times (6 \times 5)$.

Source of Error (Lesson 3-2)
students do all the multiplications before doing the divisions.

Remediation
Emphasize that the operations of multiplication and division must be done together in the order in which they occur. Point out that this also applies to the operations of addition and subtraction.

3B • MULTIPLY AND DIVIDE WHOLE NUMBERS

Source of Error (Lesson 3-5)
students forget to record a zero in the quotient.

Remediation
Have students compute division problems on ruled paper that has been turned so that the rules are vertical. By using rules to separate and align each digit in the dividend and the quotient, they will notice whether a numeral is missing in the quotient.

3C • MULTIPLY AND DIVIDE DECIMALS

Source of Error (Lesson 3-4)
students count from the left instead of from the right when placing the decimal point in the answer.

Remediation
Emphasize the importance of estimating products. Have students think in terms of "less than" and "more than;" for example, 6.8×4 is more than 24 but less than 28. Therefore, the product is 27.2, not 2.72.

Source of Error (Lesson 3-10)
students move the decimal point in the divisor but not in the dividend.

Remediation
Remind students to move both decimal points and to place the decimal point in the quotient directly above the decimal point in the dividend before they begin to divide.

3D • ESTIMATE QUOTIENTS

Source of Error (Lesson 3-11)
students have difficulty naming pairs of compatible numbers.

Remediation
Encourage students to think of basic facts when choosing compatible numbers. Provide practice by giving students examples such as $7\overline{)500}$, $4\overline{)333}$, and $6\overline{)472}$, and asking them to name a compatible dividend for each divisor. ($7\overline{)490}$, $4\overline{)320}$, and $6\overline{)480}$)

3E • PROBLEM SOLVING: LOOK BACK. TOO MUCH OR TOO LITTLE INFORMATION

Source of Error (Lesson 3-12)
students try to use all the number facts given in a problem.

Remediation
Tell students to use a chart similar to the following one to keep track of the information needed to solve the problem.

Needed Information	Extra Information

Answers

Page 59

Items	Cars	Watches	Books	Radios	Pencils	Running Shoes
Distance apart (yd)	≈197	≈26	≈1	≈41	≈1.23	≈95

Page 65

37.

757		224 seats
DC 10		325 seats
DC 9		118 seats

◆ = 25 seats

Page 71

29. 0.11, 0.111, 0.1111; 9.801, 8.712, 7.623
1,234.54321 ÷ 11,111 = 0.11111
12,345.654321 ÷ 111,111 = 0.111111
4.356 × 6 ÷ 4 = 6.534
5.445 × 5 ÷ 5 = 5.445

Page 77

21. 4,218.5
421.85
42.185

22. 1.283
0.1283
0.01283

23. 0.07
0.007
0.0007

Page 75

Learning Log 1. Answers will vary. Suggestion given: The multiplication properties are the same in arithmetic and algebra, but in algebra, variables replace some of the numbers.

Page 78

4. United States: 9.363×10^6 km^2
Spain: 5.05×10^5 km^2
Haiti: 2.775×10^4 km^2

Page 79

6. Mexico City: 1.0061×10^7
Seoul: 9.646×10^6
Moscow: 8.275×10^6
Bombay: 8.227×10^6

Page 81

36.

Baseball	5.5 oz	
Basketball	22.93 oz	
Football	15.0 oz	
Golf ball	1.62 oz	
Ping Pong ball	0.09 oz	
Softball	7.0 oz	
Tennis ball	2.06 oz	
Volleyball	9.88 oz	

Weights of balls
● = 1 oz.

CHAPTER 3

Extra Practice

This page provides extra practice of all the major chapter objectives. Use this page after the chapter has been taught to reinforce the chapter skills. Page references are provided for each group of items so that students can easily look back at the appropriate lesson for additional support.

Simplify. *(pages 60–63)*

1. $60 \times (1 \times 3)$ **180**
2. $18 \times 0 \times 5$ **0**
3. $4 \times (23 + 2)$ **100**
4. $(5 \times 3) \times 6$ **90**
5. $74 \times 0 \times 1$ **0**
6. $(97 + 3) \times 5$ **500**
7. $(8 \times 30) \times 2$ **480**
8. $5 \times 16 \times 20$ **1,600**
9. $4 + 10 \times 6$ **64**
10. $23 - 7 \times (3 - 1)$ **9**
11. $25 \div 5 \times 3^2$ **45**
12. $10^2 + 3 \times 8 - 4$ **120**
13. $2^2 + (4 + 5) - 12$ **1**
14. $17 + 0 - (10 - 1)$ **8**
15. $(2^3 - 4) \div 2$ **2**

Write the answer. *(pages 64–67)*

16. $\begin{array}{r} 84 \\ \times\ 7 \\ \hline 588 \end{array}$
17. $\begin{array}{r} 307 \\ \times\ 6 \\ \hline 1,842 \end{array}$
18. $\begin{array}{r} 39 \\ \times\ 23 \\ \hline 897 \end{array}$
19. $\begin{array}{r} 567 \\ \times\ 45 \\ \hline 25,515 \end{array}$
20. $\begin{array}{r} 986 \\ \times\ 78 \\ \hline 76,908 \end{array}$
21. $\begin{array}{r} 3.45 \\ \times\ 2.5 \\ \hline 8.625 \end{array}$
22. $\begin{array}{r} 7.081 \\ \times\ 100 \\ \hline 708.1 \end{array}$
23. $\begin{array}{r} 16.684 \\ \times\ 56 \\ \hline 934.304 \end{array}$
24. $\begin{array}{r} \$.84 \\ \times\ 0.63 \\ \hline 0.5292 \end{array}$
25. $\begin{array}{r} 0.007 \\ \times\ 1.35 \\ \hline 0.00945 \end{array}$

Divide. Write the answer, including the remainder. *(pages 68–69)*

26. $6\overline{)735}$ **122 R3**
27. $21\overline{)809}$ **38 R11**
28. $29\overline{)3,099}$ **106 R25**
29. $84\overline{)7,961}$ **94 R65**

Divide. Round to hundredths. *(pages 70–71, 80–81)*

30. $4\overline{)27.63}$ **6.91**
31. $16\overline{)35.92}$ **2.25**
32. $1.7\overline{)58.08}$ **34.16**
33. $9.8\overline{)0.732}$ **0.07**

Write in standard form. *(pages 78–79)*

34. 1.87×10^5 **187,000**
35. 2.98×10^8 **298,000,000**
36. 7.653×10^7 **76,530,000**
37. 3.1×10^5 **310,000**
38. 9.082×10^6 **9,082,000**
39. 8.113×10^7 **81,130,000**

Use compatible numbers to estimate the quotient. *(pages 82–83)* **Accept reasonable estimates.**

40. $82\overline{)635}$ **8**
41. $63\overline{)1,902}$ **30**
42. $91\overline{)74.3}$ **0.8**
43. $6.3\overline{)52.9}$ **9**

If enough information is given, solve the problem. Otherwise, state what information is needed. *(pages 84–85)*

44. A television set costing $409 can be bought by making a down payment of $49 and 36 equal monthly payments. How much is each payment? **$10**

45. In a 100-m race, the winner's time was 10.17 s. The second-place runner was 2 m behind the winner at the finish line. What was the difference in their times? **too little information**

ENRICHMENT

ALPHABET SOUP

Don't look too closely or you'll miss this.

A	EF	HI	KLMN	T	VWXYZ

BCD	G	J	OPQRS	U

What rule was used in placing the letters above and below the line?
above—all straight segments; below—curved lines used

International Finance

On one day in 1990, 1 Canadian dollar could be exchanged for 0.8589 American dollars. On the same day, 1 French franc was worth 0.1905 American dollars. A Canadian traveling to France that day would get 4.509 French francs for 1 Canadian dollar (0.8589 ÷ 0.1905).

Find the foreign exchange rates in the business section of a newspaper. Pretend that you are making each trip listed below. The currency used in each country is shown in parentheses. Determine how many units of currency for the country you are visiting you can purchase with 1 unit of currency from the country you are leaving. (*Hint*: Compare the two currencies to the American dollar.)

Trip

from Australia (dollar) to Belgium (franc)

from Britain (pound) to Canada (Canadian dollar)

from Denmark (krone) to Finland (mark)

from Switzerland (Swiss franc) to Italy (lira)

from Israel (shekel) to Mexico (peso)
Check students' work.

What's My Rule?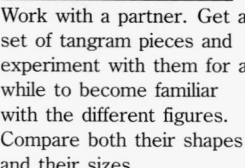

Work with a partner. Get a set of tangram pieces and experiment with them for a while to become familiar with the different figures. Compare both their shapes and their sizes.

Then sort the pieces into two groups according to a rule that you make up. Ask your partner to identify the rule you have used. Then reverse roles. Try using more than two groups.

ENRICHMENT 91

Enrichment

This page contains activities that provide extension and enrichment for all levels of students. Depending on the needs of your students, you may wish to assign an activity from this page at certain points during the chapter, or you may wish to use this page when the entire chapter has been completed.

Alphabet Soup

After students discover the rule *(letters formed by line segments in one group, all other letters in another group)*, you may wish to extend the activity by having them design alphabet patterns based on their own rules.

International Finance

Before students begin the activity, make sure they understand why they should compare the two currencies to the current value of the American dollar.

What's My Rule?
(COOPERATIVE)

After students complete the activity, you may wish to have student pairs exchange rules and use them to sort the tangram pieces into various groups.

CHAPTER 3

Cumulative Review

The Cumulative Review focuses on skills covered in previous chapters. All important skills are reviewed on a cyclic basis.

If students are having difficulty with particular groups of exercises, refer to the chart for follow-up work.

Find the answer.

1. $231 + 986$ is close to   **b**
   a. 1,100
   b. 1,200
   c. 1,300
   d. none of these

2. $19.8 + 35.4$ is closest to   **c**
   a. 50
   b. 53
   c. 55
   d. none of these

3. 17.259 rounds to   **c**
   a. 17.2
   b. 17.25
   c. 17.3
   d. none of these

4. $t \div 21 = 6$ **a**
   $t = $ ▥
   a. 126
   b. 27
   c. 15
   d. none of these

5. $41 - w + 3 = 9$ **c**
   $w = $ ▥
   a. 12
   b. 44
   c. 35
   d. none of these

6. $m \div 2 = 48 - 14$ **a**
   $m = $ ▥
   a. 68
   b. 62
   c. 96
   d. none of these

7. $(90 \times 15) \times 2 = $ **d**
   a. 270
   b. 1,352
   c. 210
   d. none of these

8. $42 - 3 \times 2^2 + 8 = $ **c**
   a. 164
   b. 14
   c. 38
   d. none of these

9. $5,003 - 749 = $ **b**
   a. 4,746
   b. 4,254
   c. 4,364
   d. none of these

10.   0.403   **b**
   $- 0.295$
   a. 0.292
   b. 0.108
   c. 0.698
   d. none of these

11. $9.007 - 8.5 = $ **a**
   a. 0.507
   b. 9.922
   c. 1.57
   d. none of these

12. $3.72 \times 10^4 = $ **c**
   a. 3,720
   b. 372,000
   c. 37,200
   d. none of these

13. $56 + 0 + 34 + 44 = $ **b**
   a. 144
   b. 134
   c. 154
   d. none of these

14. $7.31 + 12 + 9.2 = $ **a**
   a. 28.51
   b. 83.5
   c. 20.23
   d. none of these

15. $98.74   **d**
   $+ 36.89$
   a. $135.53
   b. $134.53
   c. $134.63
   d. none of these

Items	Management Objectives	Where Taught	Reteaching Options	Extra Practice Options
1–2	**2B** Add whole numbers and decimals.	pp. 42–43	TRB/RW 2-5	TRB/PW 2-5
3	**1C** Round whole numbers and decimals.	pp. 14–15	TE/RA 1-7	TRB/PW 1-7
4–6	**2A** Use replacement and properties of addition to solve equations.	pp. 34–37	TRB/RW 2-1 TE/RA 2-2	TRB/PW 2-1 and 2-2
7–8	**3A** Use properties of multiplication and order of operations.	pp. 60–63	TE/RA 3-1 and 3-2	TRB/PW 3-1 and 3-2
9–11	**2C** Subtract whole numbers and decimals.	pp. 46–49	TRB/RW 2-6 TE/RA 2-7	TRB/PW 2-6 and 2-7
12	**3C** Multiply and divide decimals.	pp. 78–79	TRB/RW 3-9	TRB/PW 3-9
13–15	**2B** Add whole numbers and decimals.	pp. 40–41	TRB/RW 2-4	TRB/PW 2-4

Remember the strategies you've learned so far. If enough information is given, solve the problem. Otherwise, state what information is needed.

Problem Solving Check List

- Too much information
- Too little information
- Multistep problems
- Drawing a picture
- Using a pattern
- Using estimation
- Using guess and check

1. The Statue of Liberty in New York occupies about 58 acres. About how many square miles does the Statue of Liberty occupy? (*Hint*: 1 square mile is 640 acres.) **0.09 mi²**

2. In a row of light bulbs, one bulb has 4 bulbs to its left, one bulb has 3 bulbs to its right, and one bulb has 2 bulbs on both sides of it. How many bulbs are in the row? **5**

4. In the figure below, the vertical, horizontal, and diagonal sums of three numbers are equal. What is *z*? **12**

6. Harriet drove 50 mi/hr for the first 6 h of a 450-mi trip along the Atlantic Coast. What was her average speed for the remainder of the trip? **need to know how long the total trip took**

8. Lenny had exactly $1 in change. He had exactly 3 times as many nickels as dimes. How many nickels and dimes did he have? **4 dimes, 12 nickels; if he only has dimes and nickels**

3. Mrs. Short assigned 3 pages of exercises for homework. She said that the pages were consecutive and that the sum of the page numbers was 996. Which pages did Mrs. Short assign? **331, 332, 333**

5. Jeff designed a game board in the shape of a rectangle. Its dimensions were 10 in. by 15 in. Jeff realized the board was too small and decided to double both dimensions.

   a. What was the shape of the game board? **rectangle**

   b. What operation would you use to find the areas of the original board and the new board? **multiplication**

   c. How many times larger is the area of the new board than the area of the original one? **4 times**

7. A stationery store sells pencils at 2 for $.25. If the pencils cost the store owner $.06 each, how much profit is made on a sale of $3 worth of pencils? **$1.56**

CHAPTER 3   93

Problem Solving Review

This page focuses on problem solving strategies and types learned in this and previous chapters. A problem solving checklist lists some of the strategies students may use to solve the problems on this page.

CHAPTER 3

Technology

This page is designed to provide calculator or computer experiences for all levels of students. The calculator or computer logo indicates the type of activity.

You may wish to assign these activities after the chapter has been taught or during the course of the chapter, depending on your needs and those of your students.

I'm Rich

Guide students by asking: What is the first step needed to solve this problem? *(Multiply 40 by 52 to find the number of hours worked in one year.)*

A-ghast

Suggest that students list the steps needed to find the total cost before they enter the operations on their calculators.

Pair-n'-theses

This activity uses Houghton Mifflin software which may be found in Houghton Mifflin Math Activities Courseware, Grade 7.

You may wish to review the order of operations before students begin this activity.

TECHNOLOGY

PAIR-N-THESES

In the computer activity *Calculator Quiz,* you evaluate equations by using the order of operations. Sharpen your skills with this activity. You do not need a computer.

Copy the equation. Then add one or two pairs of parentheses to make the equation true.

1. $8 \div (4 - 2) = 4$
2. $11 - (8 - (5 - 1)) = 7$
3. $12 - (6 + 4 - 1) = 3$
4. $12 - (12 \div (4 + 2)) = 10$
5. $(9 - 4) \times 6 \div (5 \times 3) = 2$

A-GHAST

Gas for heating is measured in therms. The Goodheat Gas Company computes each consumer's monthly bill by combining a gas supply charge of $0.3281 per therm with an additional distribution charge of $0.1402 per therm for the first 50 therms and $0.0547 per therm after the first 50 therms. If you use 254.97 therms, what would be the total charge on your bill, rounded to the nearest cent?
$101.88

I'M RICH

About how many years will it take you to earn $1,000,000 if you work 40 hours a week for 52 weeks a year and earn:

- $5 an hour • $10 an hour • $20 an hour • $40 an hour
  96 yr   48 yr   24 yr   12 yr

This game is available on computer disk in Houghton Mifflin *Mathematics Activities Courseware.*

94   TECHNOLOGY

Software Activities

Note: To leave the program, students should use the ESCAPE or QUIT command for their computers.

activity 1 • METRIC UNITS

MATERIALS: spreadsheet program

Procedure: In this activity, students create a spreadsheet which converts among the metric units. Students begin by creating the spreadsheet below; many of the cells contain values that use cell labels such as in C2 and D2. Students should complete the spreadsheet by entering expressions into the blank cells.

	A	B	C	D	E
1			km	hm	dk
2		km	+A2	+A2/10	+A2/100
3		hm	+A3*10	+A3	
4		dk	+A4*100		+A4

Follow-up: Have students expand the spreadsheet to include: deci-, centi-, and millimeters.

activity 2 • FRACTIONS TO DECIMALS

MATERIALS: BASIC programming

Procedure: This program converts a fraction that is input by the student to a decimal. Have students enter the program and run it.

```
10 PRINT "THIS PROGRAM WILL CHANGE
   A FRACTION ";
20 PRINT "TO A DECIMAL. "
30 INPUT "WHAT IS THE NUMERATOR
   ";N
40 INPUT "WHAT IS THE DENOMINATOR
   ";D
50 PRINT N "/" D " HAS THE VALUE ";
   N/D
60 PRINT: PRINT: GOTO 30
```

Follow-up: Have students try to predict what to expect for decimals when entering fractions like $\frac{1}{9}$, $\frac{2}{9}$, $\frac{1}{90}$, and $\frac{11}{90}$.

HOUGHTON MIFFLIN SOFTWARE

Computational Skills Program Boston, MA: Houghton Mifflin Company, 1988. For Apple II.

EduCalc. Boston, MA: Houghton Mifflin Company, 1990. For Apple II, Commodore, IBM.

Friendly Filer. Boston, MA: Houghton Mifflin Company, 1989. For Apple II, Commodore, IBM.

Mathematics Activities Courseware. Boston, MA: Houghton Mifflin Company, 1983. For Apple II, IBM.

Mathematics: Solving Story Problems. Levels 7–8, Boston, MA: Houghton Mifflin Company, 1985. For Apple II, IBM.

The Computer Tutor. Boston, MA: Houghton Mifflin Company, 1990. For Apple II, IBM.

OTHER SOFTWARE

Guesstimation. Danbury, CT: EME, 1987. For Apple II, Commodore.

Microsoft Works. Redmond, WN: Microsoft Corporation, 1989. For Macintosh, IBM.

More Powers to You: Exponents and Scientific Notation. Northbrook, IL: Word Associates, Inc., 1985. For Apple II, IBM.

Order of Operations. Gamco Industries, Inc., Big Spring, TX, 1990. For Apple II, IBM.

TABS: Technology and Basic Skills, "Estimation Invasion", "At the Races", "Bull's Eye". Des Plaines, IL: Looking Glass Learning, 1988. For Apple II.

Up With Math. Dallas, TX: Micro Power & Light, 1989. For Apple II.

What Do You do with a Broken Calculator? Pleasantville, NY: Sunburst Communications, 1989. For Apple II.

Variables, Expressions, and Equations

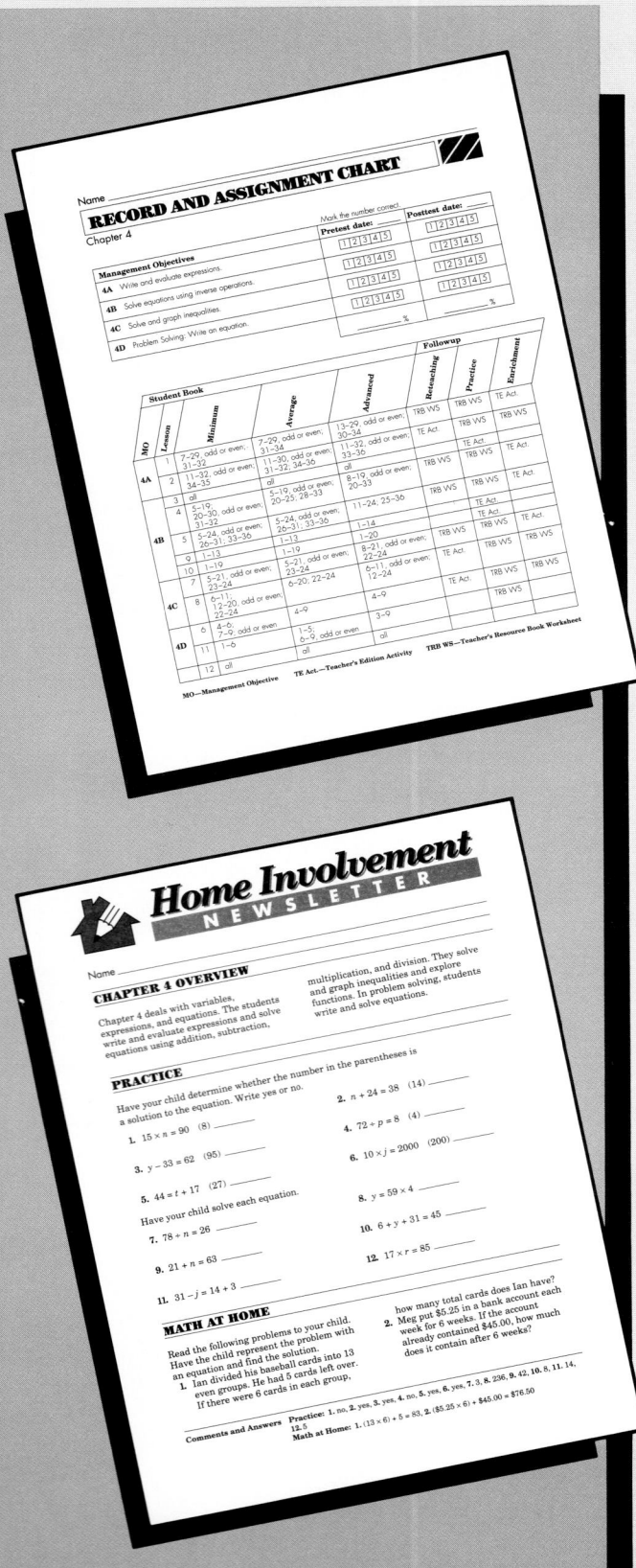

This chapter teaches students a number of important algebraic concepts. Students review basic arithmetic operations in lessons on writing and evaluating expressions; writing and solving equations; writing, solving, and graphing inequalities; and investigating functions and function rules. Problem solving is extended to include writing and solving an equation for a verbal problem and investigating the use of algebraic and graphic representations for problem situations.

Management Objectives

4A Write and evaluate expressions.
4B Solve equations using inverse operations.
4C Solve and graph inequalities.
4D Problem Solving: Write an equation.

Assignments for different achievement levels are provided on the Record and Assignment Chart in the Teacher's Resource Book.

Vocabulary

expression, page 96
evaluate, page 98
inverse operations, page 100
inequalities, page 110
function, page 114
function rule, page 116

Home Involvement

As you begin to teach this chapter, give each student a copy of the Home Involvement Newsletter for this chapter.

This newsletter provides parents with
- an overview of the chapter
- suggestions for practicing some of the skills in the chapter
- an at-home activity to do with their child, applying the skills taught in the chapter.

Management Chart

Management Objectives	Lesson/ Pages	Student Not Successful	Student Needs More Practice	Student Successful	Pacing Range
4A Write and evaluate expressions.	4-1/96-97	TRB/RW 4-1	TRB/PW 4-1	TE/EA 4-1	1-2 days
	4-2/98-99	TE/RA 4-2	TRB/PW 4-2	TRB/EW 4-2	
4B Solve equations using inverse operations.	4-3/100-101			TE/CA 4-3	4-5 days
	4-4/102-103	TRB/RW 4-4	TRB/PW 4-4 MAC 7 Act. 4A, 8 MAC 8 Activity 5	TE/EA 4-4 MAC 7 Act. 4A, 8 MAC 8 Activity 5	
	4-5/104-105	TRB/RW 4-5	TRB/PW 4-5	TE/EA 4-5	
	4-9/114-115			TE/CA 4-9	
	4-10/116-117			TE/CA 4-10	
4C Solve and graph inequalities.	4-7/110-111	TRB/RW 4-7	TRB/PW 4-7	TE/EA 4-7	1-2 days
	4-8/112-113	TE/RA 4-8	TRB/PW 4-8	TRB/EW 4-8	
4D Problem Solving: Write an equation; represent a problem.	4-6/106-107	TE/RA 4-6	TRB/PW 4-6	TRB/EW 4-6	2 days
	4-11/118-119		TRB/PW 4-11		
Creative Problem Solving	4-12/120-121			TE/CA 4-12	
Chapter Checkups	108-109, 122-123				
Extra Practice	124				
Enrichment	125				
Cumulative Review/ Problem Solving Review	126-127				
Technology	128				

TE = Teacher's Edition
TRB = Teacher's Resource Book
RW = Reteaching Worksheet
RA = Reteaching Activity
EA = Enrichment Activity
EW = Enrichment Worksheet
PW = Practice Worksheet
CA = Classroom Activity

*Other Available Items
MAC = Mathematics Activities Courseware

CHAPTER 4

Manipulative Planning Guide

This is a complete list of manipulatives and materials needed for Chapter 4.

Materials for Manipulatives	TE Activities (INTRODUCE)	Student Book Lesson
Base ten materials, several of each kind per group	Lesson 4-1	
Math Connection Transparency		Lesson 4-2
Index cards		
Balance scale	Lessons 4-4, 4-6, 4-7, 4-8	
Small objects such as counters	Lessons 4-4, 4-6, 4-7	
Blank spinners, one per group		
Gram cubes		
1-g masses		
Blank cubes, one per pair		
6 lengths of string, each 4 units long; one 24-unit length of string; one 12-unit length of string	Lesson 4-5	
Newspapers		
Counters	Lessons 4-6, 4-7, 4-8	
Envelopes	Lessons 4-4, 4-6	
Paper bag	Lesson 4-8	
Calculators		Lessons 4-3, 4-5

*Teaching Aids are found in the Teacher's Resource Book.

Learning Stages

The concepts and skills in Chapter 4 are presented through these learning stages.

CONCRETE

Using manipulatives and verbalizing about a concept. No symbols.

Teacher Edition Activities	Student Book
At this grade level the skills of this chapter are taught at the connecting and symbolic stages.	

Enrichment/ Class Activity	Reteaching	In the Houghton Mifflin Manipulative Kit?	In the Houghton Mifflin Overhead Kit?
		Yes	
			Yes
Lesson 4-1	Lesson 4-2		
Lesson 4-4			
		Yes	
	Lesson 4-2	Yes	
Lesson 4-4		Yes	
Lesson 4-4		Yes	
Lesson 4-4		Yes	
Lesson 4-9			
		Yes	
	Lesson 4-8		
			Available separately

Chapter 4 • Overview 94E

CONNECTING

5¢ 9cm² 1/3

Making a connection between manipulatives and symbols.

Teacher Edition Activities	Student Book
Lessons 4-1, 4-3, 4-4, 4-5, 4-6, 4-7, 4-8, 4-11	

SYMBOLIC

$.05   A = 9cm² $1 - \frac{2}{3} = \frac{1}{3}$

Using numbers or symbols. No manipulatives or pictures of manipulatives.

Teacher Edition Activities	Student Book
Lessons 4-2, 4-9, 4-10	Lessons 4-1 through 4-11

COOPERATIVE LEARNING
RESOURCE ACTIVITIES

Through cooperative learning activities, students learn by interacting with one another in small groups. These cooperative activities provide students with motivating settings for making connections, investigations, and problem solving situations.

The cooperative connections are interdisciplinary problem-solving projects. Each student has a particular job that helps lead the group to complete the project. For the cooperative investigations students work in pairs for investigations involving data collection and analysis. The cooperative problem solving activities encourage the sharing of ideas and information. Students work in groups of four to solve a problem. Students are each assigned a clue and work together to find a common solution.

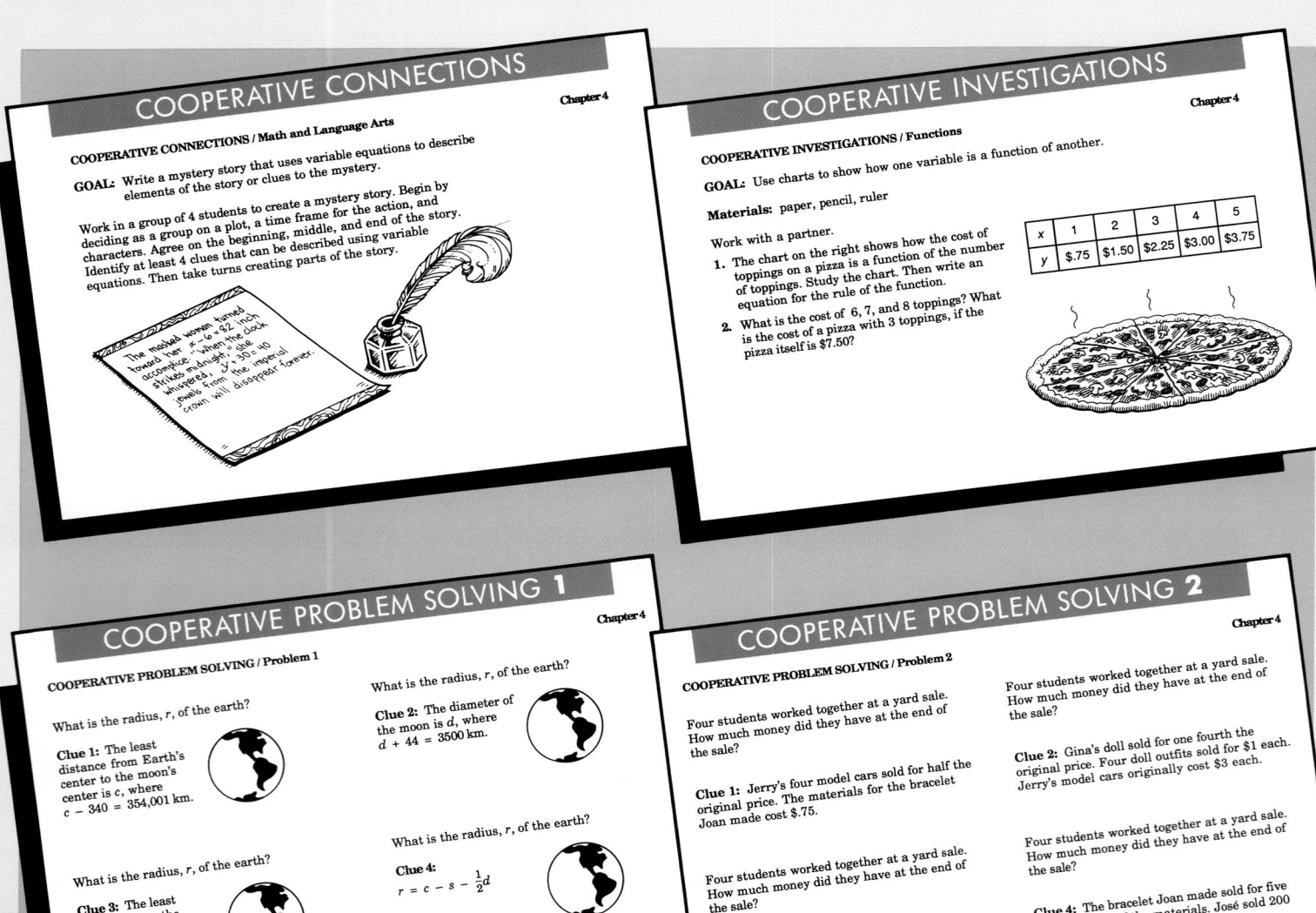

COOPERATIVE CONNECTIONS

Chapter 4

COOPERATIVE CONNECTIONS / Math and Language Arts

GOAL: Write a mystery story that uses variable equations to describe elements of the story or clues to the mystery.

Work in a group of 4 students to create a mystery story. Begin by deciding as a group on a plot, a time frame for the action, and characters. Agree on the beginning, middle, and end of the story. Identify at least 4 clues that can be described using variable equations. Then take turns creating parts of the story.

COOPERATIVE INVESTIGATIONS

Chapter 4

COOPERATIVE INVESTIGATIONS / Functions

GOAL: Use charts to show how one variable is a function of another.

Materials: paper, pencil, ruler

Work with a partner.
1. The chart on the right shows how the cost of toppings on a pizza is a function of the number of toppings. Study the chart. Then write an equation for the rule of the function.
2. What is the cost of 6, 7, and 8 toppings? What is the cost of a pizza with 3 toppings, if the pizza itself is $7.50?

x	1	2	3	4	5
y	$.75	$1.50	$2.25	$3.00	$3.75

COOPERATIVE PROBLEM SOLVING 1

Chapter 4

COOPERATIVE PROBLEM SOLVING / Problem 1

What is the radius, r, of the earth?

Clue 1: The least distance from Earth's center to the moon's center is c, where $c - 340 = 354{,}001$ km.

What is the radius, r, of the earth?

Clue 2: The diameter of the moon is d, where $d + 44 = 3500$ km.

What is the radius, r, of the earth?

Clue 3: The least distance from the moon's surface to Earth's surface is s, where $2s = 692{,}544$ km.

What is the radius, r, of the earth?

Clue 4:
$r = c - s - \frac{1}{2}d$

COOPERATIVE PROBLEM SOLVING 2

Chapter 4

COOPERATIVE PROBLEM SOLVING / Problem 2

Four students worked together at a yard sale. How much money did they have at the end of the sale?

Clue 1: Jerry's four model cars sold for half the original price. The materials for the bracelet Joan made cost $.75.

Four students worked together at a yard sale. How much money did they have at the end of the sale?

Clue 3: Ten of José's baseball cards sold for $.50. Gina's doll originally cost $20.

Four students worked together at a yard sale. How much money did they have at the end of the sale?

Clue 2: Gina's doll sold for one fourth the original price. Four doll outfits sold for $1 each. Jerry's model cars originally cost $3 each.

Four students worked together at a yard sale. How much money did they have at the end of the sale?

Clue 4: The bracelet Joan made sold for five times the cost of the materials. José sold 200 baseball cards.

GAMES

EQUATION BINGO   (For use after Lesson 4-5)

Objective: Solve equations using addition, subtraction, multiplication, and division.

☑ **MATERIALS CHECKLIST:** 4 x 4 grid, 8 index cards cut in half, about 15 markers for each pair of students

Have partners work together to prepare a game board by writing one- and two-digit numbers in the squares on the grid. On the cards partners should write equations whose solutions are the numbers on the grid, one equation per card. For example, the equation $n + 25 = 40$ could correspond to the number 15 on the grid. Have pairs exchange game boards and cards for a game of Equation Bingo. Partners in turn draw a card, solve the equation, and cover the solution on the game board. The player whose solution completes a row, column, or diagonal on the game board first is the winner.

MYSTERY NUMBER   (For use after Lesson 4-8)

Objective: Solve inequalities.

Assign students to two different teams. Select a two-digit number, say 63, and tell students that the object of the game is to guess the mystery number. Explain that you will respond to questions about your number if they are presented in the form of an inequality. Ask the first member of Team A to write an inequality on the chalkboard, for example, $x > 50$. Since your number is greater than 50, tell the player to write Yes next to the inequality; otherwise, nothing is written. Repeat with a new inequality from the first member of Team B. Continue in this manner until one team writes the equality $x = 63$.

BULLETIN BOARD

Draw a balance scale with an equals symbol on the base. Cut out pieces of colored paper that will fit on the pans of the scale, one color for variable expressions and another for numbers. Display them around the scale. Also place blank number pieces in an envelope. Form an equation by hanging an expression and a number on the pans. Ask students to write the solution on a blank piece of paper and pin it on the variable. Change the equation often.

Alternative Assessment

In addition to the paper and pencil tests available with this program, the following items can help you assess critical thinking as well as your students' ability to solve problems in a wide variety of ways.

Open-ended Problem

Look at the table of values which shows the odd numbers and their sums.

odd numbers	1	1+3	1+3+5	1+3+5+7	1+3+5+7+9
sum of odd numbers	1	4	9	16	25

Notice that the sums are generating a list of square numbers. Explain how you could prove or disprove the following statement: The sum of any group of consecutive odd numbers will always be a square number.

Teacher Notes
Students should generate more examples. A diagram may indicate that

in general, a square becomes the next largest square by adding one row, one column, (which are equal) and the corner square. Since the row and column are equal, they can be represented by $2n$. The additional square results in $2n + 1$.

Group Writing Activity (See p. T24)

Divide the paper in 3 columns. Make a list of 20 even numbers down the middle column. Then in the first column write the whole number that comes before each even number. In the last column write the whole number that comes after each even number.

Example: First Column   Middle Column   Last Column
                    13   14   15

When you complete the list each group member should write a sentence explaining how each number in the first column relates to the even number. Then write a sentence explaining how each number in the last column relates to the even number.

Teacher Notes
Since even numbers are always divisible by 2, they are usually represented by $2n$. Each number on the left is one less than the even number ($2n - 1$). Each number on the right is one more than the even number ($2n + 1$). Odd numbers can be represented by $2n + 1$ or $2n - 1$.

Individual Writing Activity

Mathematicians sometimes use the expression $(2n + 1)$ to represent an odd number and other times they use the expression $(2n - 1)$. Explain why you think odd numbers can be represented by both expressions and what is the meaning of the n in the expressions.

Portfolios

Portfolios can provide information about a student's growth in mathematical understanding over a period of time. They can help you make instructional decisions as well as become a vehicle to communicate with parents. The students' work involving the open-ended problem and writing activity suggested on this page along with work on the Create Your Own exercise on page 101, the Learning Log exercises on pages 109 and 123, the Critical Thinking feature on page 111, and the Creative Problem Solving lesson on pages 120-121 could be included in portfolios.

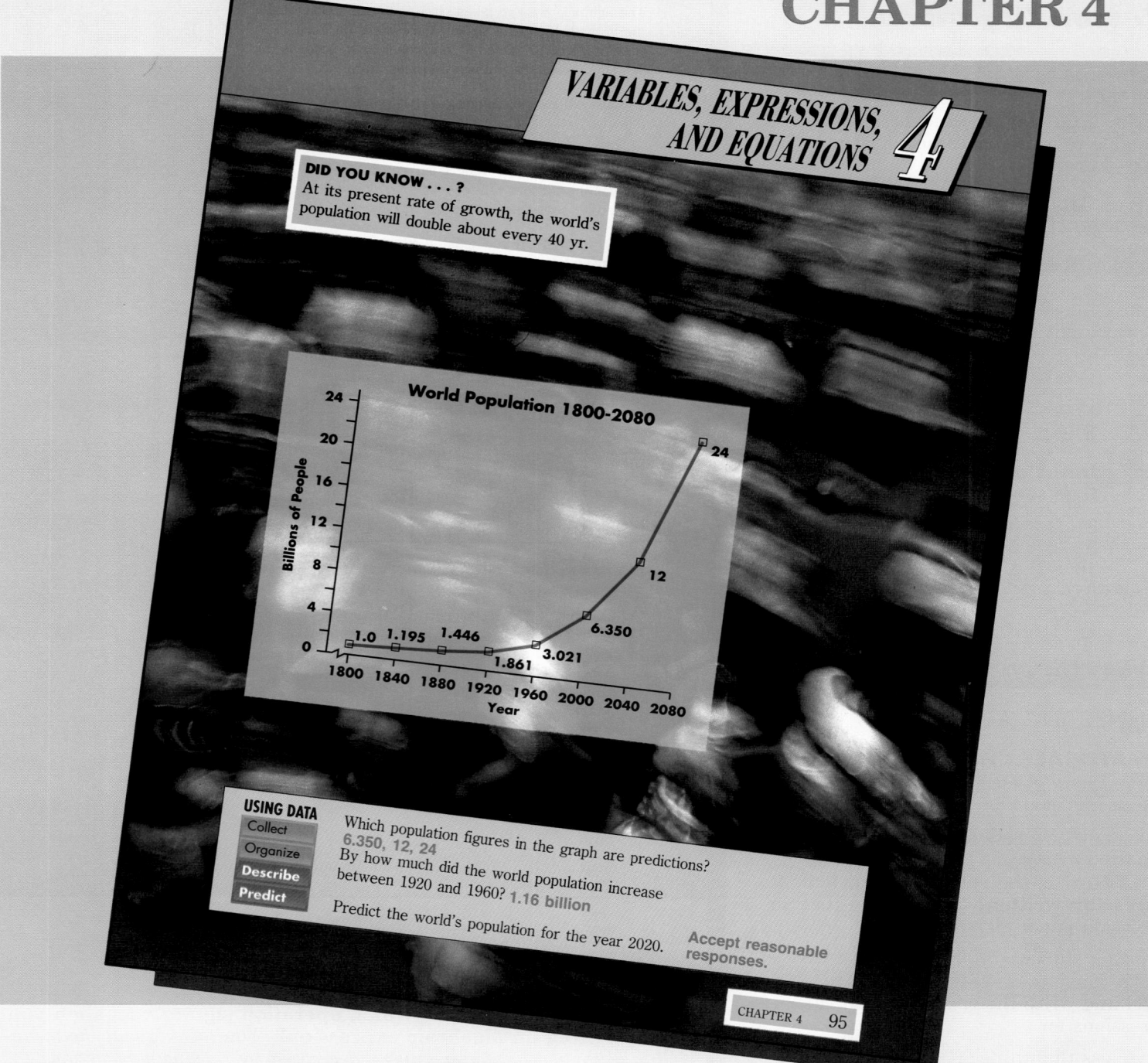

VARIABLES, EXPRESSIONS, AND EQUATIONS 4

DID YOU KNOW . . . ?
At its present rate of growth, the world's population will double about every 40 yr.

World Population 1800-2080

1.0   1.195   1.446   1.861   3.021   6.350   12   24

USING DATA

Collect

Organize

Describe

Predict

Which population figures in the graph are predictions? **6.350, 12, 24**

By how much did the world population increase between 1920 and 1960? **1.16 billion**

Predict the world's population for the year 2020. *Accept reasonable responses.*

CHAPTER 4   95

Using the Chapter Opener

The purpose of this page is to involve the students in the use of real data much like that presented in newspapers and magazines.

To use this page as you begin the chapter, direct the students' attention to the data. You may wish to ask questions such as the following:

How much greater was the world population increase between 1840 and 1880 than between 1800 and 1840? *(56 million)*
How do you know? *(1.195 − 1.000 = 0.195; 1.446 − 1.196 = 0.251; 0.251 − 0.195 = 0.056; 0.056 billion = 56 million)*

What do you need to do to estimate the world population in 1900? *(Find half of the difference between the 1880 population and the 1920 population; add to 1880 population.)* **What was the approximate world population in 1900?** *(1.654 billion)*

About how many times greater was the world population in 1960 than in 1800? *(about three times)*

What trend is shown on this graph? *(The rate of growth in the world's population has increased since 1800.)*

Lesson Organizer

Objective: Write expressions

Prior Knowledge: Students should be able to write basic facts that are stated orally.

Error Analysis and Remediation: See page 123A.

Lesson Resources:
Practice Worksheet 4-1
Reteaching Worksheet 4-1
Enrichment Activity 4-1
Daily Review 4-1

Two-Minute Math

Insert parentheses to make a true sentence.

$3 + 2 \times 8 = 40$ $[(3 + 2)]$
$8 \div 2 + 6 = 1$ $[(2 + 6)]$
$16 \div 2^2 + 3 \times 8 - 5 = 13$
$[(16 \div 2^2) \text{ and } (8 - 5)]$

1 INTRODUCE

CONNECTING ACTIVITY

☑ **MATERIALS CHECKLIST:** base 10 blocks, several of each kind per group of three or four students

1. Demonstrate how to use unit cubes to model the expression "three more than eight." **How is the related numerical expression written?** *(8 + 3)* Note that an expression is not an equation.

2. Assign students to mixed ability groups. Have them use unit cubes to model and write the related numerical expressions for

- five less than nine *(9 − 5)*
- the product of seven and three *(7 × 3)*
- the quotient of ten divided by two *(10 ÷ 2)*

3. Ask students to state each word expression in a different way. Have them record these phrases on a separate sheet of paper.

WHEN YOUR STUDENTS ASK
★ WHY AM I LEARNING THIS? ★

You can connect this skill to real life through computer science. Programmers write expressions in computer programs.

Writing Expressions

The lightning we see takes place between a cloud and the ground. Lightning strikes somewhere on Earth an average of 100 times each second. In 10 seconds (s), lightning would strike about 10 times more.

You can write an **expression** that represents this fact.

- Let *t* represent the number of seconds.
- Then $100 \times t$, or $100t$, is an expression for the number of times lightning would strike somewhere on Earth in *t* seconds.

THINK ALOUD If you counted 10 s, about how many times, on average, would lightning strike somewhere on Earth? **1,000 times**

Other examples:

Word Phrase	Algebraic Expression
thirty-seven storms decreased by *m* storms	$37 - m$
42 less than *n*	$n - 42$
eight times *z* miles	$8 \times z$ or $8z$
n sandwiches divided by twelve campers	$n \div 12$ or $\frac{n}{12}$
d seconds increased by 5	$d + 5$

MATH AND SCIENCE

━━━━━ **GUIDED PRACTICE** ━━━━━

Write as an expression.

1. the sum of 28 and a number *a*
$28 + a$

2. eighteen times a number *b*
$18 \times b$ or $18b$

3. twelve less than a number *c*
$c - 12$

4. a number *d* divided by seven
$d \div 7$ or $\frac{d}{7}$

5. a number *e* increased by 23
$e + 23$

6. twenty decreased by a number *f*
$20 - f$

96   LESSON 4–1

---

2 TEACH

How do you determine which operation sign to use when you are writing an algebraic expression? *(You think about the meaning of the words; for example, "decreased by" means subtraction.)*

When can you omit an operation sign in an expression? *(You can omit a multiplication sign when one of the factors is a variable.)*

What are some ways to write *x*/6 in words? *(Possible answers: "A number x divided by six"; "the quotient of a number x and six")*

Chalkboard Examples

Write as an expression.
2 less than a number
a number divided by 7
a number *d* increased by 5
$b - 2$ $(y \div 7)$ $(d + 5)$

SUMMARIZE/ASSESS **Explain how to write an expression for "fifteen less than a number *x*."** *(Possible answer: Rephrase to help you place the variable in the expression: "a number x minus fifteen," and then write the expression: $x - 15$.)*

PRACTICE

Write as an expression. Let x be the unknown value.

7. seven more than a number $x + 7$

8. ninety-six divided by a number $\frac{96}{x}$

9. five times a number $5x$

10. twenty-seven more than a number $x + 27$

11. a number divided by five $\frac{x}{5}$

12. 128 less than a number $x - 128$

13. a number increased by 14 $x + 14$

14. the product of a number and seven $7x$

15. twelve decreased by a number $12 - x$

16. a number divided by thirteen $\frac{x}{13}$

17. a number increased by 1,000 $x + 1,000$

18. a number multiplied by itself x^2

Write as a word phrase.   **See page 123b.**

19. $x - 18$

20. $4m$

21. $29 + q$

22. $27 \div z$

23. $n + 5$

24. $16w$

25. $z \div 12$

26. $23 - b$

27. $\frac{24}{r}$

28. $29y$

29. $\frac{q}{19}$

*30. $x - y$

PROBLEM SOLVING

Work with a partner to write the expression.

31. Let t represent the temperature before a storm.
Then ▣ represents the temperature after it drops 7°F.
$t - 7$

32. Let h represent the cost of 1 tent.
Then ▣ represents the cost of 6 tents.
$6h$

33. Let n represent any odd number.
Then ▣ represents the next larger odd number.
Then ▣ represents the next smaller even number.
$n + 2; n - 1$

34. Let w represent a whole number.
Then ▣, ▣, and ▣ represent the next
three greater whole numbers.
$w + 1; w + 2; w + 3$

Mental Math

Use mental math to match the word phrase
with an expression.

1. the number of millimeters in n centimeters   d   **a.** $n \div 1,000$

2. the number of centimeters in n millimeters   b   **b.** $n \div 10$

3. the number of meters in n centimeters   c   **c.** $n \div 100$

4. the number of kilograms in n grams   a   **d.** $10n$

CHAPTER 4   97

MEETING INDIVIDUAL NEEDS

For Students Who Are . . .

Acquiring English Proficiency Pair students with an English-proficient student to write the expressions in the Problem Solving exercises.

Gifted and Talented Have students write an expression for each phrase: nine more than twice a number $(2x + 9)$, six times the sum of a number plus three $[6(x + 3)]$, and four times a number minus three $(4x - 3)$.

Working 2 or 3 Grades Below Level Have students use pages 4–5 of the Skills Workbook for equations, ratio, proportion, and percent.

Today's Problem

Amy has a dog named Sugar. Amy is three times Sugar's age. Amy is 15 years old and Sugar is 5 years old. How many years from now will Amy be twice as old as Sugar? *(In 5 years Amy will be 20 and Sugar will be 10).*

---

3 FOLLOW-UP

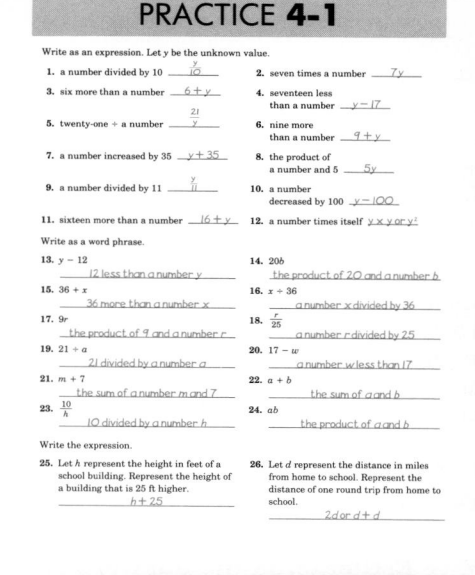

PRACTICE 4-1

Write as an expression. Let y be the unknown value.

1. a number divided by 10 $\frac{y}{10}$
2. seven times a number $7y$
3. six more than a number $6 + y$
4. seventeen less than a number $y - 17$
5. twenty-one + a number $\frac{21}{y}$
6. nine more than a number $9 + y$
7. a number increased by 35 $y + 35$
8. the product of a number and 5 $5y$
9. a number divided by 11 $\frac{y}{11}$
10. a number decreased by 100 $y - 100$
11. sixteen more than a number $16 + y$
12. a number times itself $y \times y$ or y^2

Write as a word phrase.

13. $y - 12$ 12 less than a number y
14. $20b$ the product of 20 and a number b
15. $36 + x$ 36 more than a number x
16. $x \div 36$ a number x divided by 36
17. $9r$ the product of 9 and a number r
18. $\frac{r}{25}$ a number r divided by 25
19. $21 + a$ 21 divided by a number a
20. $17 - w$ a number w less than 17
21. $m + 7$ the sum of a number m and 7
22. $a + b$ the sum of a and b
23. $\frac{10}{h}$ 10 divided by a number h
24. ab the product of a and b

Write the expression.

25. Let h represent the height in feet of a school building. Represent the height of a building that is 25 ft higher. $h + 25$
26. Let d represent the distance in miles from home to school. Represent the distance of one round trip from home to school. $2d$ or $d + d$

RETEACHING 4-1

The words on the left go with the symbol on the right.

• increased by
• more than
• sum of
• added to   +

• decreased by
• less than
• subtracted from   −

• product of
• times
• multiplied by   ×

• divided by   ÷

a number increased by 3   3 decreased by a number
n +   3   3   − n

a number multiplied by 3   3 divided by a number
n ×   3   3   ÷ n

Complete to write the word phrase as an expression.

1. 7 less than a number $n \boxed{-} 7$
2. the product of a number and 8 $n \boxed{\times} 8$
3. a number divided by 6 $n \boxed{+} 6$
4. 5 more than a number $n \boxed{+} 5$
5. a number times 22 $n \boxed{\times} 22$
6. a number decreased by 9 $n \boxed{-} 9$
7. 16 subtracted from a number $n \boxed{-} 16$
8. the sum of a number and 1 $n \boxed{+} 1$

Write as an expression. Let n be the unknown value.

9. 25 divided by a number $\frac{25}{n}$
10. the sum of a number and 348 $n + 348$
11. 34 less than a number $n - 34$
12. the product of a number and 14 $14n$

ENRICHMENT 4-1

☑ **MATERIALS CHECKLIST:** Index cards

Have the students work in groups of four, and in pairs within each group. One student in each group selects a card from a set of cards on which you have written expressions such as $\frac{r}{5} + 15$ and $47(x - 0.25)$. Each pair then writes a word problem for the expression. For example, the following problem describes the expression $\frac{r}{5} + 15$: Sarah got some money for her birthday. She gave an equal amount to 5 charities and spent $15 on a CD for herself. Have students compare their word problems.

Chapter 4 • Lesson 4-1   **97**

Lesson Organizer

Objective: Evaluate expressions.

Prior Knowledge: Students should be able to compute with whole numbers and decimals.

Lesson Resources:
Practice Worksheet 4-2
Reteaching Activity 4-2
Enrichment Worksheet 4-2
Daily Review 4-2

 *Two-Minute Math*

Estimate. Is the answer reasonable?

$87.5 - 5.3 = 34.5$ *(no)*
$53.81 \times 4.7 = 2,529.07$ *(no)*
$65.0754 \div 7.8 = 8.343$ *(yes)*

1 INTRODUCE

SYMBOLIC ACTIVITY

Play "Guess the Rule".

1. Show only the numbers in the top row in a table like the one below.

4	6	8	9	12
(7)	(9)	(11)	(12)	(15)

2. Tell students that you have a rule in mind as you write numbers in the bottom row. Have students guess the rule.

3. Write the expression $x + 3$ on the chalkboard. Discuss how the variable x represents all the numbers in the top row, and explain how you used the numbers to evaluate the expression.

4. Then write x next to the top row and $x + 3$ next to the bottom row. **How can you evaluate the expression when x equals 18?** *(21)*

WHEN YOUR STUDENTS ASK
★ **WHY AM I LEARNING THIS?** ★

You can connect this skill to real life through engineering. Engineers evaluate expressions such as volts (v) times amps (a) to answer problems about circuits.

Evaluating Expressions

A velodrome is a sports arena with an oval track used for cycling events. One lap around the track at the Marymoor Park velodrome in Redmond, Washington, is 0.4 km.

If a cyclist makes 5 laps of this track, how far has she traveled?

- Let x represent the number of laps a cyclist makes.
- Then $0.4x$ represents the distance in kilometers a cyclist travels around the track.

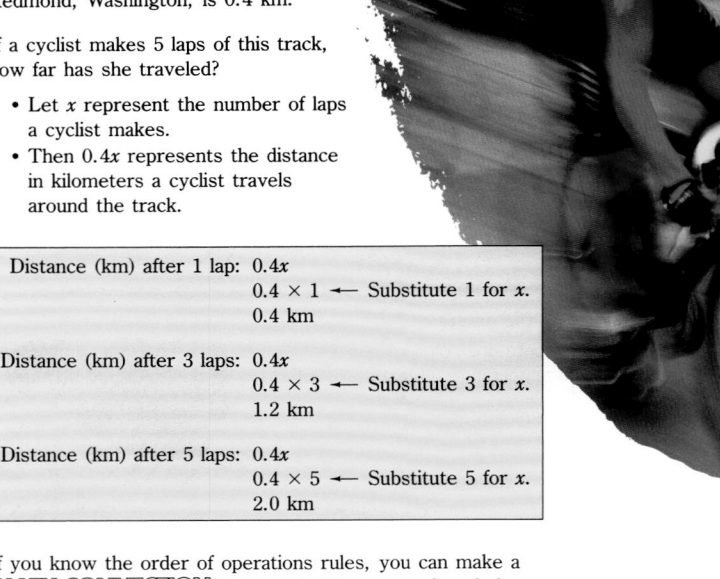

Distance (km) after 1 lap:	$0.4x$
	0.4×1 ◄— Substitute 1 for x.
	0.4 km
Distance (km) after 3 laps:	$0.4x$
	0.4×3 ◄— Substitute 3 for x.
	1.2 km
Distance (km) after 5 laps:	$0.4x$
	0.4×5 ◄— Substitute 5 for x.
	2.0 km

If you know the order of operations rules, you can make a **MATH CONNECTION** to evaluate the expressions below.

Evaluate $\frac{z}{5} + 2$. Use $z = 15$.

$$\frac{z}{5} + 2 = \frac{15}{5} + 2$$
$$= 3 + 2$$
$$= 5$$

Evaluate $a^2 - 3$. Use $a = 6$.

$$a^2 - 3 = 6^2 - 3$$
$$= 36 - 3$$
$$= 33$$

━━━━ **GUIDED PRACTICE** ━━━━

Evaluate $n + 14$ for the given value of n.

	1.	6	2.	12	3.	17	4.	8.25	5.	19.02
		20		26		31		22.25		33.02

Evaluate $\frac{24}{z} + 5$ for the given value of z.

	6.	2	7.	6	8.	4	9.	1.2	10.	0.8
		17		9		11		25		35

---

2 TEACH

☑ **MATERIALS CHECKLIST:** Transparency 1 (Math Connection)

Display the transparency. Have students fill in the spaces and discuss the math connection. *(See student pages.)*

What does a variable represent in an algebraic expression? *(the unknown number)*

What should you do first when you see parentheses in an expression? *(Do the operation within the parentheses first.)*

How many numbers can be substituted for the variable g in the expression $4g$? *(an infinite number)*

SUMMARIZE/ASSESS   **Explain how to evaluate an expression.** *(Substitute the given value for the variable in the expression; simplify the expression, using the order of operations, to get one number.)*

Evaluate. Use $x = 2$, $y = 6$, and $z = 8$.

11. $7z$ 56 **12.** $10 - y$ 4 **13.** $z \div 4$ 2 **14.** z^2 64

15. $x + 5$ 7 **16.** $3x + x - 2$ 6 **17.** $\frac{z}{2}$ 4 **18.** $x + x^2$ 6

19. $x + 3x$ 8 **20.** $\frac{28}{x}$ 14 **21.** $\frac{x+4}{3}$ 2 **22.** $(y - y) + 18$ 18

23. $\frac{z}{8} + 7$ 8 **24.** $9 \times (5 + y)$ 99 **25.** $z^2 + z^2$ 128 **26.** $24x - 10x$ 28

27. $3.2y - 1.5y$ 10.2 **28.** $\frac{z}{4} + \frac{z}{2}$ 6 **29.** $6 \times 5(4 - x)$ 60 **30.** $9 + z - x$ 15

Copy and complete.

31.
a	$5a - 2$
2	$5 \times 2 - 2 = $ ▦ 8
8	▦ 38
15	▦ 73

32.
n	$n + 5n$
12	$12 + 5 \times 12 = $ ▦ 72
18	▦ 108
45	▦ 270

*33.
x	$x^2 - 7$
9	$9^2 - 7 = $ ▦ 74
14	▦ 189
20	▦ 393

 CHOOSE Choose mental math, or pencil and paper to solve. **Choices will vary. Suggestions given.**

34. A cyclist makes 8 laps around the velodrome in Detroit. How far has the cyclist traveled? m; 2.400 km

Velodromes	
Location	Distance for 1 Lap
Portland, Oregon	0.250 km
Los Angeles, California	0.333 km
Detroit, Michigan	0.300 km
Barcelona, Spain	0.250 km

35. Who travels farther, a cyclist who makes 6 laps in Los Angeles's velodrome or a cyclist who makes 8 laps in Barcelona's velodrome?
p; the Barcelona cyclist

36. How many laps must a cyclist make to travel 1 km in Portland's velodrome? in Detroit's velodrome?
m; 4 laps; $3\frac{1}{3}$ laps

Estimate

You can use clustering to estimate the sum. $1.461 + 1.54 + 1.4992 \approx 4.5$
Each addend clusters around 1.5. $1.5 \ + 1.5 \ + 1.5 \ = 4.5$

Use clustering to estimate the sum. **Accept reasonable estimates.**
Suggestions given.
1. $4.091 + 3.94 + 3.911$ ≈ 12
2. $0.542 + 0.478 + 0.4993$ ≈ 1.5
3. $10.002 + 9.832 + 10.09 + 0.49 + 0.51$ ≈ 31

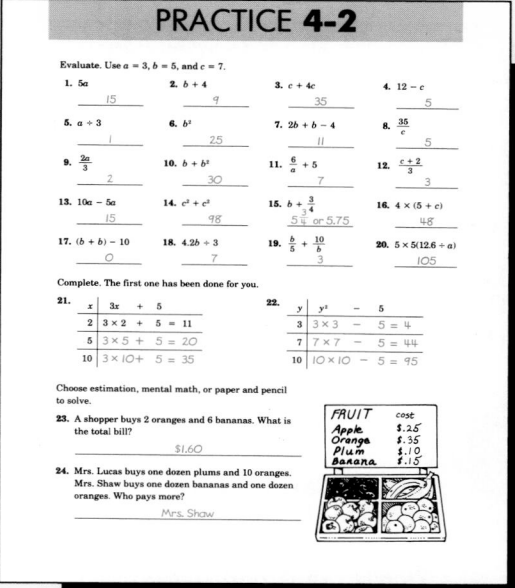

PRACTICE 4-2

RETEACHING 4-2

☑ **MATERIALS CHECKLIST:** Index cards, blank spinners

Write the following expressions on the board: $9 + a$, $\frac{20}{x} + 3$, $8b$, $w^2 - 1$. Provide each pair of students with cards on which are written the numbers **9, 20, 3, 8, 2,** and **1**; the operation signs **+** and **−**; a division bar; the variables a, x, b, and w. Each pair models one expression at a time using the cards. For each expression one partner spins a spinner labeled *1, 2, 4, 5, 10,* and *20*. Students create a new card showing the number on the spinner, and replace a variable card with the new card. Then students evaluate the expression. Continue in the same manner.

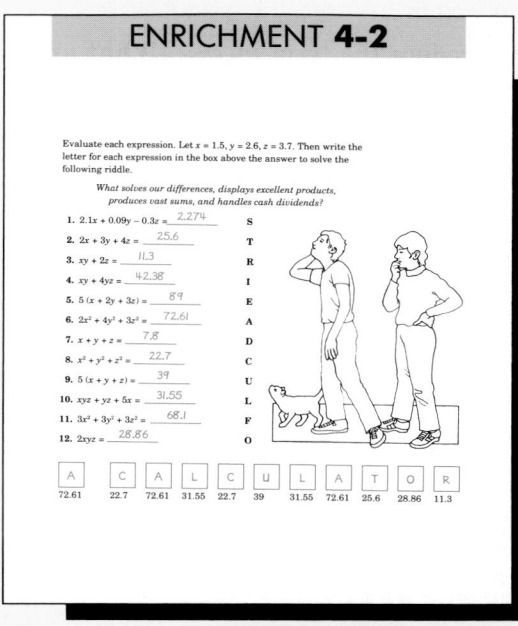

ENRICHMENT 4-2

MEETING INDIVIDUAL NEEDS

For Students Who Are . . .

Acquiring English Proficiency Discuss the meaning of *velodrome*, *expression*, and *evaluate*.

Gifted and Talented Have students evaluate these expressions using $x = 3$, $y = 5$, and $z = 6$: $x^2 + 4x + 7$ *(28)*, $2y^2 - 3y - 10$ *(25)*, $2z^2 + y^2$ *(97)*.

Working 2 or 3 Grades Below Level Have students use pages 12–13 of the Skills Workbook for equations, ratio, proportion, and percent.

Today's Problem

Rupert designs and draws personal greeting cards. It takes him about 2 hours 30 minutes per card. He works 8 hours a day, 5 days a week. How many cards could he finish in a week?
(8 h × 5 d ÷ 2.5 h = 16 cards)

Lesson Organizer

Objective: Explore inverse operations.

Prior Knowledge: Students should be able to evaluate expressions.

Lesson Resources:
Class Activity 4-3
Daily Review 4-3

Two-Minute Math

Insert parentheses to make a true sentence.

$3.5 \times 12 \div 0.3 = 140$
($3.5 \times [12 \div 0.3] = 140$)
$7^2 + 8 \times 3 = 171$
($[7^2 + 8] \times 3 = 171$)
$4 + 4 \div 4 \times 4 = 0.5$
($[(4 + 4) \div (4 \times 4) = 0.5]$)

1 PREPARE

CONNECTING ACTIVITY

1. Give a volunteer instructions (without the knowledge of the rest of the class) to undo everything you do:

- Turn off the light.
- Write something on the chalkboard.
- Close the window.

2. Ask class members to describe both kinds of actions. *(The helper's action undid your action.)*

3. Introduce the term *inverse*. **What are some other pairs of inverse actions?** *(Possible answers: walking upstairs and walking downstairs; turning on the water and turning off the water)*

WHEN YOUR STUDENTS ASK
★ WHY AM I LEARNING THIS? ★

This skill will help you solve real life problems such as finding something you have lost. You can retrace your day's activities to find the lost object.

Exploring Inverse Operations

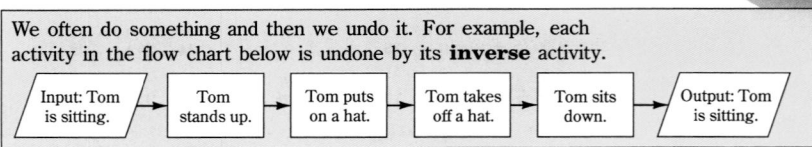

We often do something and then we undo it. For example, each activity in the flow chart below is undone by its **inverse** activity.

Input: Tom is sitting. → Tom stands up. → Tom puts on a hat. → Tom takes off a hat. → Tom sits down. → Output: Tom is sitting.

1. What inverse activity undoes "Tom stands up"?
"Tom sits down."

2. If "Tom puts on shoes" were added to the flow chart, what inverse activity would undo it? "Tom takes off shoes."

3. **IN YOUR WORDS** Is the statement "Tom does not put on a hat" an inverse of the statement "Tom puts on a hat"? Explain. No, the first statement has no action to undo.

In mathematics, when two operations undo each other, they are called **inverse operations**.

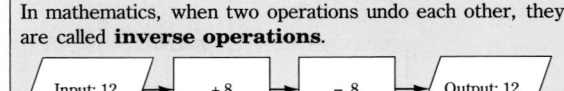

Input: 12 → + 8 → − 8 → Output: 12

4. The equation for an input of 12 is $12 + 8 - 8 = 12$.
What equation would describe the input of 6? the input of 36?
$6 + 8 - 8 = 6$; $36 + 8 - 8 = 36$

5. The number 20 is input. If $+8$ is changed to $+16$, what must also change in the flow chart to result in an output of 20?
-8 must change to -16.

6. What equation describes the input of any number *n*?
$n + 8 - 8 = n$

Some number tricks use inverse operations.

Input: Think of a number. → Multiply by 2. → Add 5. → Subtract 5. → Divide by 2. → Output: Your number is ■.

7. What is the output when we input the number 5? 5
Try inputting any three other numbers. Answers will vary.
Suggestions given: input 10, output 10; input 1, output 1; input 6, output 6

8. What will the output always be?
the input number

9. Why does the number trick work? because all the operations can be paired into inverses

---

2 EXPLORE

✓ MATERIALS CHECKLIST: calculators

If you start with an input of 5, then multiply by 8, what must you do to have an output of 5? *(Divide by 8.)*

If you start with an input of 8 then subtract 5, what must you do to have an output of 8? *(Add 5.)*

SUMMARIZE/ASSESS **Give an example to show that addition and subtraction are inverse operations and that multiplication and division are inverse operations.** *(Example: $3 + 4 = 7$; $7 - 4 = 3$; $7 \times 3 = 21$; $\frac{21}{3} = 7$)*

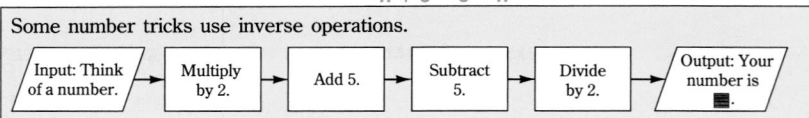

10. Of addition, subtraction, multiplication, and division, which pairs of operations are inverses? **addition and subtraction; multiplication and division**

CALCULATOR Study how the following number trick works. Then try it out.

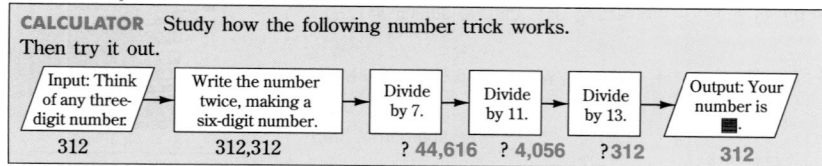

Input: Think of any three-digit number.	Write the number twice, making a six-digit number.	Divide by 7.	Divide by 11.	Divide by 13.	Output: Your number is ▦.
312	312,312	? 44,616	? 4,056	? 312	312

11. What is the output if the number 392 is input? Try 632, 759, and 104. Does the number trick work for 1,452?
392; output = input; no

12. If output from the flow chart was 761, what was the input?
761

13. In what way can you shorten the number trick?
Combine the 3 divide boxes to "Divide by 1,001."

14. For what kinds of numbers does this number trick work? Give some examples. **If zero placeholders are used, this will work for any number less than 1,000. Examples given: 111; 025; 006.**

CALCULATOR Study this number trick and try it out.

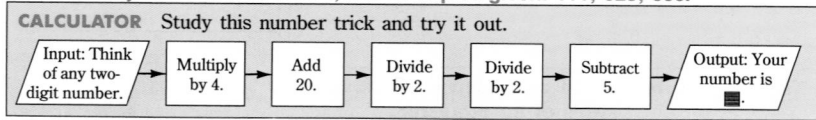

Input: Think of any two-digit number.	Multiply by 4.	Add 20.	Divide by 2.	Divide by 2.	Subtract 5.	Output: Your number is ▤.

15. Input the numbers 54, 67, 32, and 99. What is the output of each? Try this number trick on a friend.
54, 67, 32, 99

16. Try 346 and 804. Does the number trick work for three-digit numbers? **output: 346; 804; yes**

17. **CREATE YOUR OWN** Make up a number trick of your own.
Check students' work.

MEETING INDIVIDUAL NEEDS

For Students Who Are . . .

Acquiring English Proficiency Pair students with an English-proficient student to work through the lesson.

Gifted and Talented Have students write an equation to show how the number trick in the second Calculator section on page 101 works.

$$\left(\frac{4x + 20}{2 \cdot 2} - 5 = x \right)$$

Today's Problem

An operation on a whole number is defined as "Divide a number by 8, multiply the quotient by 2, and then subtract 5 from the result." What would be the inverse operation? *(Inverse operation: Add 5 to a number, divide the result by 2, and multiply the quotient by 8.)*

CLASS ACTIVITY 4-3

Write these equations on the board:
$$n \times 5 \div 24 = 1$$
$$n \times 5 \div 2 - 6 = 0$$
$$n \times 6 \div 3 \times 4 \div 5 = 8.6$$
$$n \times 8.4 \div 6 \times 1.8 \div 5 = 12$$

Ask students to find the value for *n* that makes the equation true. Then have students describe how to find the missing numbers without guessing.

Lesson Organizer

Objective: Solve equations using addition and subtraction.

Prior Knowledge: Students should recognize that addition and subtraction are inverse operations.

Error Analysis and Remediation: See page 123A.

Lesson Resources:
Practice Worksheet 4-4
Reteaching Worksheet 4-4
Enrichment Activity 4-4
Daily Review 4-4
Cooperative Problem Solving 1, Chapter 4

Two-Minute Math

Complete to write a true statement.

$28.51 + 9.8 - \square = 28.51$ *(9.8)*

$143 + \square - 53.7 = 143$ *(53.7)*

$12.1 + 7.29 - 3.5 - \square = 12.1$ *(3.79)*

1 INTRODUCE

CONNECTING ACTIVITY

☑ **MATERIALS CHECKLIST:** balance scale, envelopes, small items such as counters

1. Place an envelope containing 5 counters on one side of the balance scale. Put 9 more counters on the same side. Then put 14 counters on the other side. **Since the scale is balanced, how many counters must be in the envelope?** *(5)* Write the equation $x + 9 = 14$ on the chalkboard.

2. Show that you can remove nine counters from each pan and the scale remains balanced. Write the related equation and its solution: $x + 9 - 9 = 14 - 9$; $x = 5$.

3. Repeat the activity to model $x - 6 = 5$.

WHEN YOUR STUDENTS ASK
★ **WHY AM I LEARNING THIS?** ★

You can use equations to represent and solve real life problems. For example, you have saved $5.00. You want to buy something, but you need to have $2.05 left for lunch. Represent this idea as $5.00 - n = 2.05$.

Solving Equations Using Addition and Subtraction

The Holland and Lincoln tunnels stretch from New York to New Jersey under the Hudson River. The Lincoln Tunnel is 8,216 ft long, which is 341 ft shorter than the length of the Holland Tunnel. How long is the Holland Tunnel?

Let h represent the length in feet of the Holland Tunnel.

What length minus 341 equals 8,216?

$$h \quad - \quad 341 \quad = \quad 8,216$$

To solve the equation, you can use the operation that is the inverse of subtracting 341, that is, adding 341.

$$h - 341 = 8,216$$
$$h - 341 + 341 = 8,216 + 341 \quad \leftarrow \text{ Add 341 to both sides.}$$
$$h + 0 = 8,557$$
$$h = 8,557 \quad \leftarrow \text{ The solution is 8,557.}$$

Check: $h - 341 = 8,216$
$8,557 - 341 = 8,216$ ✔

The Holland Tunnel is 8,557 ft long.

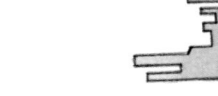

Another example:

$$5.8 + z = 10.2$$
$$5.8 - 5.8 + z = 10.2 - 5.8 \quad \leftarrow \text{ Subtract 5.8}$$
$$0 + z = 4.4 \qquad\qquad \text{from both sides.}$$
$$z = 4.4 \quad \leftarrow \text{ The solution is 4.4.}$$

Check: $5.8 + z = 10.2$
$5.8 + 4.4 = 10.2$ ✔

> **The same number can be added or subtracted on both sides of an equation.**

━━━━━━━━━━ **GUIDED PRACTICE** ━━━━━━━━━━

THINK ALOUD Which inverse operation would solve the equation? Then solve and check.

1. $x + 9 = 43$
-9; $x = 34$

2. $t - 12 = 35$
$+12$; $t = 47$

3. $15 + n = 56$
-15; $n = 41$

4. $z - 6.5 = 11.5$
$+6.5$; $z = 18$

---

2 TEACH

Why was 341 added to both sides of $h - 341 = 8,261$ in the first example? *(Adding the same number to both sides of an equation maintains equality.)*

In the second example, why was 5.8 subtracted from both sides of the equation? *(to undo the addition, leave only z on one side.)*

Why should the variable be isolated on one side of the equals sign when solving an equation? *(to determine the value of the variable)*

> *Chalkboard Examples*
>
> Solve and check.
> $a + 538 = 1,000$ *(a = 462)*
> $b - 28.9 = 51.2$ *(b = 80.1)*
> $48.3 = 9.8 + c$ *(c = 38.5)*

SUMMARIZE/ASSESS **Explain how to solve and check the equation $x + 3 = 17$.** *(Subtract 3 from both sides of the equation; x = 14. To check, substitute 14 for x in the original equation; 14 + 3 = 17, 17 = 17.)*

Lincoln Tunnel

Hudson River

Holland Tunnel

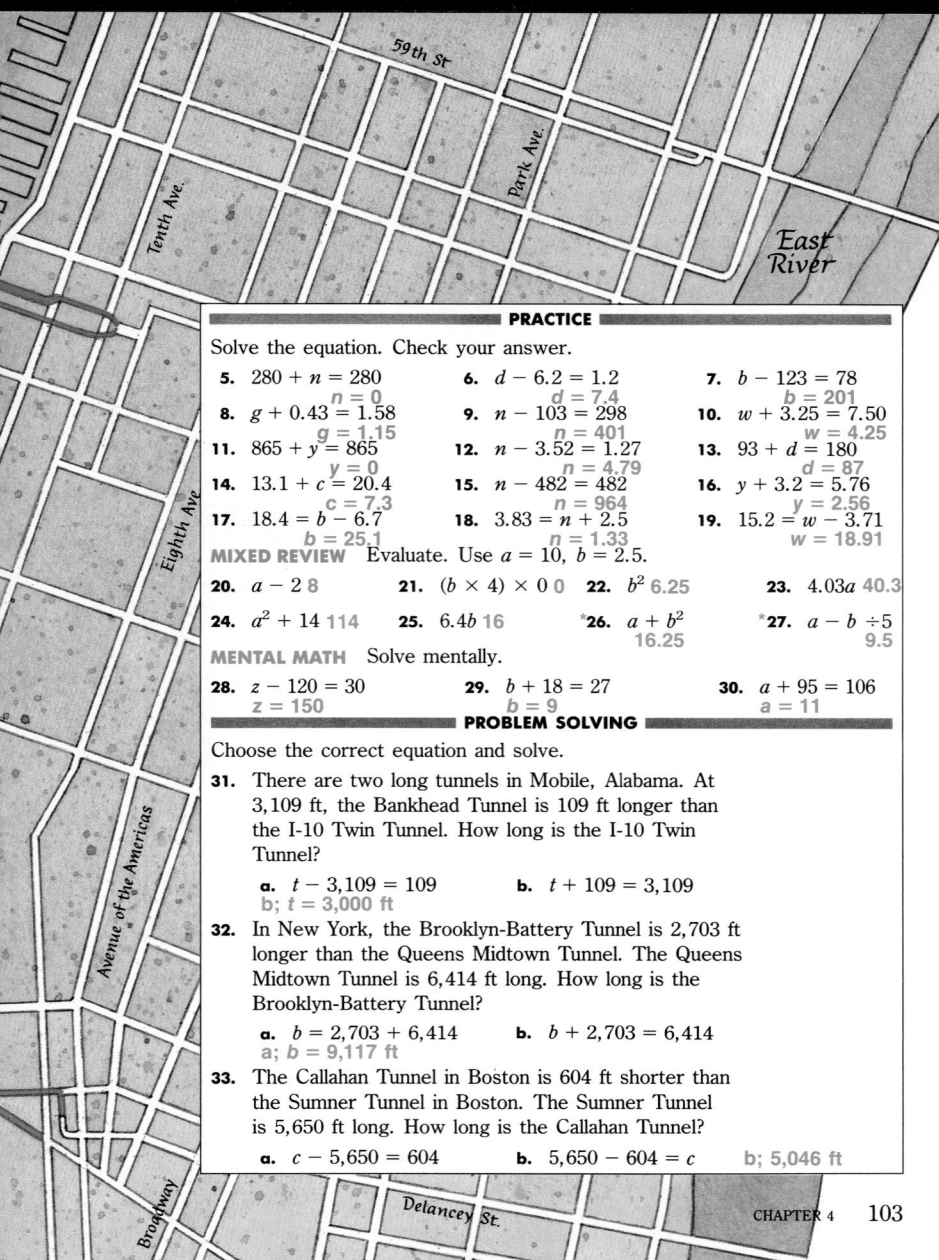

PRACTICE

Solve the equation. Check your answer.

5. $280 + n = 280$
  $n = 0$
6. $d - 6.2 = 1.2$
  $d = 7.4$
7. $b - 123 = 78$
  $b = 201$

8. $g + 0.43 = 1.58$
  $g = 1.15$
9. $n - 103 = 298$
  $n = 401$
10. $w + 3.25 = 7.50$
  $w = 4.25$

11. $865 + y = 865$
  $y = 0$
12. $n - 3.52 = 1.27$
  $n = 4.79$
13. $93 + d = 180$
  $d = 87$

14. $13.1 + c = 20.4$
  $c = 7.3$
15. $n - 482 = 482$
  $n = 964$
16. $y + 3.2 = 5.76$
  $y = 2.56$

17. $18.4 = b - 6.7$
  $b = 25.1$
18. $3.83 = n + 2.5$
  $n = 1.33$
19. $15.2 = w - 3.71$
  $w = 18.91$

MIXED REVIEW Evaluate. Use $a = 10$, $b = 2.5$.

20. $a - 2$ 8
21. $(b \times 4) \times 0$ 0
22. b^2 6.25
23. $4.03a$ 40.3

24. $a^2 + 14$ 114
25. $6.4b$ 16
*26. $a + b^2$ 16.25
*27. $a - b \div 5$ 9.5

MENTAL MATH Solve mentally.

28. $z - 120 = 30$
  $z = 150$
29. $b + 18 = 27$
  $b = 9$
30. $a + 95 = 106$
  $a = 11$

PROBLEM SOLVING

Choose the correct equation and solve.

31. There are two long tunnels in Mobile, Alabama. At 3,109 ft, the Bankhead Tunnel is 109 ft longer than the I-10 Twin Tunnel. How long is the I-10 Twin Tunnel?

  a. $t - 3,109 = 109$
  b. $t + 109 = 3,109$
  b; $t = 3,000$ ft

32. In New York, the Brooklyn-Battery Tunnel is 2,703 ft longer than the Queens Midtown Tunnel. The Queens Midtown Tunnel is 6,414 ft long. How long is the Brooklyn-Battery Tunnel?

  a. $b = 2,703 + 6,414$
  b. $b + 2,703 = 6,414$
  a; $b = 9,117$ ft

33. The Callahan Tunnel in Boston is 604 ft shorter than the Sumner Tunnel in Boston. The Sumner Tunnel is 5,650 ft long. How long is the Callahan Tunnel?

  a. $c - 5,650 = 604$
  b. $5,650 - 604 = c$
  b; 5,046 ft

CHAPTER 4 103

MEETING INDIVIDUAL NEEDS

For Students Who Are . . .

Acquiring English Proficiency Pair students with an English-proficient student to discuss and solve the Problem Solving exercises.

Gifted and Talented Have students solve equations involving fractions such as: $x + \frac{5}{8} = 3 \ (x = 2\frac{3}{8})$; $\frac{1}{3} = y - 2\frac{1}{2} \ (y = 2\frac{5}{6})$; $z - \frac{3}{4} = 1\frac{2}{5}$ $(z = 2\frac{3}{20})$.

Working 2 or 3 Grades Below Level Have students use pages 22–23 of the Skills Workbook for equations, ratio, proportion, and percent.

Today's Problem

Perfect squares are numbers like $1 \times 1 = 1$, $2 \times 2 = 4$, $3 \times 3 = 9$, and so on. What is the average of the first 10 perfect squares? $((1 + 4 + 9 + 16 + 25 + 36 + 49 + 64 + 81 + 100) \div 10 = 38.5)$

3 FOLLOW-UP

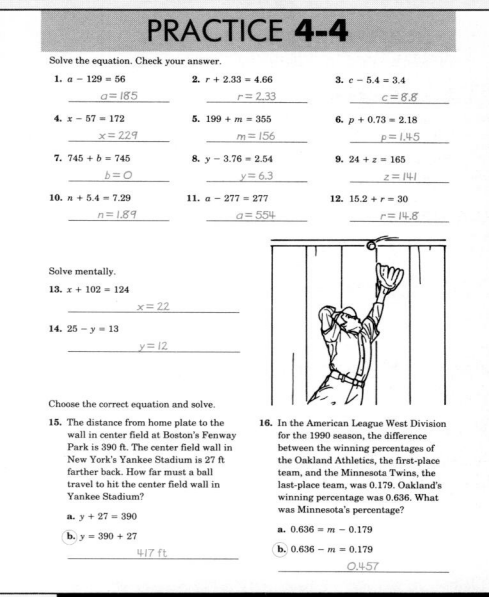

PRACTICE 4-4

Solve the equation. Check your answer.

1. $a - 129 = 56$ $a = 185$
2. $r + 2.33 = 4.66$ $r = 2.33$
3. $c - 5.4 = 3.4$ $c = 8.8$

4. $x - 57 = 172$ $x = 229$
5. $199 + m = 355$ $m = 156$
6. $p + 0.73 = 2.18$ $p = 1.45$

7. $745 + b = 745$ $b = 0$
8. $y - 3.76 = 2.54$ $y = 6.3$
9. $24 + z = 165$ $z = 141$

10. $n + 5.4 = 7.29$ $n = 1.89$
11. $a - 277 = 277$ $a = 554$
12. $15.2 + r = 30$ $r = 14.8$

Solve mentally.

13. $x + 102 = 124$ $x = 22$

14. $25 - y = 13$ $y = 12$

Choose the correct equation and solve.

15. The distance from home plate to the wall in center field at Boston's Fenway Park is 390 ft. The center field wall in New York's Yankee Stadium is 27 ft farther back. How far must a ball travel to hit the center field wall in Yankee Stadium?

  a. $y + 27 = 390$
  b. $y = 390 + 27$
  417 ft

16. In the American League West Division for the 1990 season, the difference between the winning percentages of the Oakland Athletics, the first-place team, and the Minnesota Twins, the last-place team, was 0.179. Oakland's winning percentage was 0.636. What was Minnesota's percentage?

  a. $0.636 - m = 0.179$
  b. $0.636 - 0.179 = m$
  0.457

RETEACHING 4-4

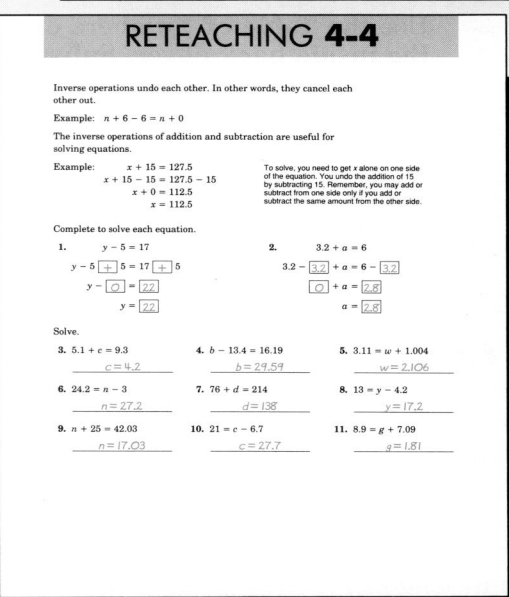

Inverse operations undo each other. In other words, they cancel each other out.

Example: $n + 6 - 6 = n + 0$

The inverse operations of addition and subtraction are useful for solving equations.

Example: $x + 15 = 127.5$
  $x + 15 - 15 = 127.5 - 15$
  $x + 0 = 112.5$
  $x = 112.5$

To solve, you need to get x alone on one side of the equation. You undo the addition of 15 by subtracting 15. Remember, you may add or subtract from one side only if you add or subtract the same amount from the other side.

Complete to solve each equation.

1. $y - 5 = 17$
  $y - 5 \boxed{+} 5 = 17 \boxed{+} 5$
  $y - \boxed{0} = \boxed{22}$
  $y = \boxed{22}$

2. $3.2 + a = 6$
  $3.2 - \boxed{3.2} + a = 6 - \boxed{3.2}$
  $\boxed{0} + a = \boxed{2.8}$
  $a = \boxed{2.8}$

Solve.

3. $5.1 + c = 9.3$ $c = 4.2$
4. $b - 13.4 = 16.19$ $b = 29.59$
5. $3.11 = w + 1.004$ $w = 2.106$

6. $24.2 = n - 3$ $n = 27.2$
7. $76 + d = 214$ $d = 138$
8. $13 = y - 4.2$ $y = 17.2$

9. $n + 25 = 42.03$ $n = 17.03$
10. $21 = c - 6.7$ $c = 27.7$
11. $8.9 = g + 7.09$ $g = 1.81$

ENRICHMENT 4-4

☑ **MATERIALS CHECKLIST:** Balance scales, gram cubes or gram masses

Have several unknown weights (multi-gram objects) prepared. Let students put an unknown weight in the left side of a balance scale. Ask students to place gram cubes on the right side of the balance scale until it balances. Then have students write an equation to represent the gram cubes in the balance scale (n = number of gram cubes)

Start with another unknown weight, x. Have students set up situations as described above, writing equations as they do. Have students compare situations and equations.

Lesson Organizer

Objective: Solve equations using multiplication and division.

Prior Knowledge: Students should be able to multiply and divide and understand that these operations are inverses of each other.

Error Analysis and Remediation: See page 123A.

Lesson Resources:
Practice Worksheet 4-5
Reteaching Worksheet 4-5
Enrichment Activity 4-5
Daily Review 4-5

Two-Minute Math

Use the Table of Numbers on the inside back cover. Substitute each number in row A for n. Evaluate $102 - n$. *(37; 64; 20; 53; 83; 25; 11; 78; 46)*

1 INTRODUCE

CONNECTING ACTIVITY

☑ **MATERIALS CHECKLIST:** six lengths of string, each 4 units long, one 24-unit length of string, one 12-unit length

1. Have students hold up the 24-unit length of string. Show one 4-unit length.

• Have other students show that six 4-unit lengths of string match the 24-unit length.

• Represent this situation: $4n = 24$. **What inverse operation would help you solve the equation?** *(Divide both sides of the equation by 4.)*

• Write the equivalent equation and the solution: $\frac{4n}{4} = \frac{24}{4}$; $n = 6$.

WHEN YOUR STUDENTS ASK
★ WHY AM I LEARNING THIS? ★

You can connect this skill to real life through the work of a florist. For example, if a florist has 50 carnations and uses 10 in each arrangement, how many arrangements can be made?

MATH AND SCIENCE

Solving Equations Using Multiplication and Division

If the average length of a triceratops was multiplied by 4, it would equal the average length of a diplodocus, which, at 88 ft, was the longest of the dinosaurs. About how long was a triceratops?

Let n represent the average length of a triceratops in feet.

Four times what number is 88?
$$4n = 88$$

Which operation is the inverse of multiplying by 4?

$$4n = 88$$
$$\frac{4n}{4} = \frac{88}{4} \quad \leftarrow \text{Divide both sides by 4.}$$
$$n = 22 \quad \leftarrow \text{The solution is 22.}$$

Check: $4n = 88$
$4 \times 22 = 88$ ✔

A triceratops averaged about 22 ft in length.

Another example:

$$\frac{d}{4} = 1.9 \qquad\qquad \text{Check: } \frac{d}{4} = 1.9$$
$$\frac{d}{4} \times 4 = 1.9 \times 4 \leftarrow \text{Multiply both sides by 4.} \qquad \frac{7.6}{4} = 1.9 \text{ ✔}$$
$$d = 7.6 \quad \leftarrow \text{The solution is 7.6.}$$

> **You can multiply or divide both sides of an equation by the same number. (Remember, you cannot divide by zero.)**

=== **GUIDED PRACTICE** ===

THINK ALOUD Explain how you would solve and check the equation.

1. $\frac{x}{6} = 9$
$6 \times \frac{x}{6} = 9 \times 6$

2. $6y = 420$
$\frac{6y}{6} = \frac{420}{6}$

3. $8w = 96$
$\frac{8w}{8} = \frac{96}{8}$

4. $\frac{k}{12} = 40$
$12 \times \frac{k}{12} = 40 \times 12$

---

2 TEACH

☑ **MATERIALS CHECKLIST:** calculators

Which inverse operation is used to solve $5n = 17$? *(division)*

Give an example of an equation that could be solved using the inverse of division. *(Possible answer: $\frac{x}{6} = 15$)*

Will $4n = 480$ and $480 = 4n$ have the same solutions? How can you tell without solving the equations? *(The equals sign expresses a balance between the two sides. It does not matter which expression is written to the left or right.)*

> **Chalkboard Examples**
>
> Solve and check.
> $9r = 108$ ($r = 12$)
> $\frac{s}{8} = 15$ ($s = 120$)
> $36 = \frac{t}{4}$ ($t = 144$)

SUMMARIZE/ASSESS **Explain how to solve and check $\frac{n}{8} = 46$.** *(Multiply both sides by 8; $n = 368$. To check, replace n with 368 and complete; $\frac{368}{8} = 46$, $46 = 46$.)*

Solve. Check your answer.

5. $3a = 48$
$a = 16$

6. $\frac{p}{6} = 8$
$p = 48$

7. $\frac{u}{12} = 5$
$u = 60$

8. $5n = 95$
$n = 19$

9. $\frac{r}{9} = 5$
$r = 45$

10. $\frac{n}{11} = 45$
$n = 495$

11. $8z = 10.4$
$z = 1.3$

12. $15z = 150$
$z = 10$

13. $\frac{n}{11} = 4$
$n = 44$

14. $\frac{x}{12} = 0$
$x = 0$

15. $1.1z = 9.9$
$z = 9$

16. $5k = 65$
$k = 13$

17. $27e = 216$
$e = 8$

18. $60x = 240$
$x = 4$

19. $4c = 6.8$
$c = 1.7$

20. $\frac{t}{21} = 14$
$t = 294$

21. $\frac{m}{0.6} = 12$
$m = 7.2$

22. $1.2x = 0.48$
$x = 0.4$

23. $3.9c = 1.56$
$c = 0.4$

24. $\frac{y}{1.6} = 2.5$
$y = 4$

*25. $6.4 = 4n$
$n = 1.6$

MIXED REVIEW Solve. Check your answer.

26. $a + 2.8 = 9.1$
$a = 6.3$

27. $\frac{m}{9} = 18$
$m = 162$

28. $g - 0.75 = 4.26$
$g = 5.01$

29. $18b = 576$
$b = 32$

30. $r - 45 = 12.2$
$r = 57.2$

31. $x + 145.7 = 320$
$x = 174.3$

*32. CALCULATOR Find three values for a in $\frac{a}{7.5}$ so that the expression is equal to a number between 1 and 3.5. **Answers will vary. Suggestions given.**
$a = 7.6,\ 15,\ 26$

PROBLEM SOLVING

Find the underlined fact. The variable represents the unknown. Select the equation that represents the problem and solve.

33. The <u>height of a tyrannosaurus in feet</u> times 2.5 equals its length of 45 ft.
b; $x = 18$ ft

a. $18 - 12 = w$

34. Two times a <u>stegosaurus's length in feet</u> is the 45 ft length of a tyrannosaurus.
d; $z = 22.5$ ft

b. $2.5x = 45$

35. A tyrannosaurus's 45-ft length divided by a <u>torosaurus's length in feet</u> is 1.5.
c; $y = 30$ ft

c. $\frac{45}{y} = 1.5$

*36. A tyrannosaurus's height minus 12 is an <u>ornitholestes's length in feet.</u>
a; $w = 6$ ft

d. $z \times 2 = 45$

MEETING INDIVIDUAL NEEDS

For Students Who Are . . .

Acquiring English Proficiency Guide students to look for words or phrases *(times, two times, minus, divided by)* in the Problem Solving exercises that will help them choose the correct equations.

Gifted and Talented Have students use the principles discussed in the lesson to solve these equations: $\frac{2}{3}x = 8$ $(x = 12)$; $10 = \frac{1}{12}y$ $(y = 120)$; $1\frac{1}{5}z = 18$ $(z = 15)$.

Working 2 or 3 Grades Below Level Have students use pages 26–27 of the Skills Workbook for equations, ratio, proportion, and percent.

Today's Problem

You have 6 chains made up of 4 links each. You want to make a large single chain of 24 links by cutting links and welding them together again. What is the fewest number of links that you can cut? *(Open 4 links on one of the chains. Use these 4 links to connect the other 5 chains. The fewest number of links is 4.)*

3 FOLLOW-UP

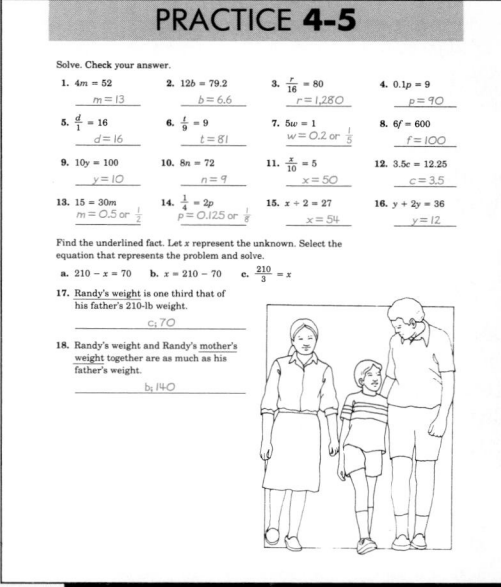
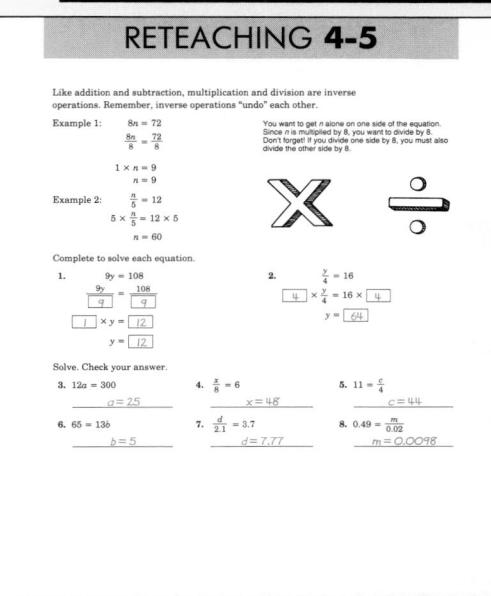
ENRICHMENT 4-5

Write the following amounts on the board: $1.60, $2.50, $1.57. Then read the following clues and have the students tell how many of each coin would be needed for each amount: For $1.60, twice as many nickels as dimes [8 dimes, 16 nickels]; for $2.50, 3 more quarters than dimes [5 dimes, 8 quarters]; for $1.57, 1 more than twice the number of dimes as pennies [7 pennies, 15 dimes]. Have the students work in pairs to develop amounts and clues of their own. Then have students trade with other groups and solve.

Lesson Organizer

Objective: Write an equation to solve a problem.

Prior Knowledge: Students should be able to write expressions and solve equations.

Error Analysis and Remediation: See page 123A.

Lesson Resources:
Practice Worksheet 4-6
Reteaching Activity 4-6
Enrichment Worksheet 4-6
Daily Review 4-6

Two-Minute Math

Match. Choose from:
$n - 12 = 14$; $\frac{1}{2}n = 14$; $n + 4 = 14$

12 less than n is 14.
Half of a number is 14.
Four more than n is 14.

1 INTRODUCE

CONNECTING ACTIVITY

☑ **MATERIALS CHECKLIST:** balance scale, counters, envelope

1. Write on the chalkboard: **Chef Charlie fixed a batch of some pancakes. Then he fixed a second batch of 7 pancakes. Altogether, there are now 15 pancakes. How many were in the first batch?**

2. Have students identify the unknown *(the number of pancakes in the first batch)* and select a variable to represent it. *(p)* **What expression represents the number of pancakes in both batches?** *(p + 7)*

3. Label an envelope p. Have students use the scale, counters, and counters in the envelope to show the equation and solution. *(p + 7 = 15; 8 + 7 = 15)*

4. Repeat with other simple situations.

WHEN YOUR STUDENTS ASK
★ WHY AM I LEARNING THIS? ★

You can connect this skill to real life through navigation. Navigators use equations to determine distances and speeds and to plan routes.

Problem Solving Strategy:
Writing and Solving Equations

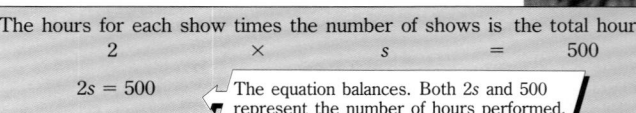

For each show at the Dance Theater of Harlem, the dancers are on stage for 2 h. After 500 h on stage, how many shows have been performed?

To solve the problem, you can represent it with an equation.

- What does the problem ask you to find? Decide on a variable to represent this.

  Let s represent the number of shows.

- Make an equation that balances.

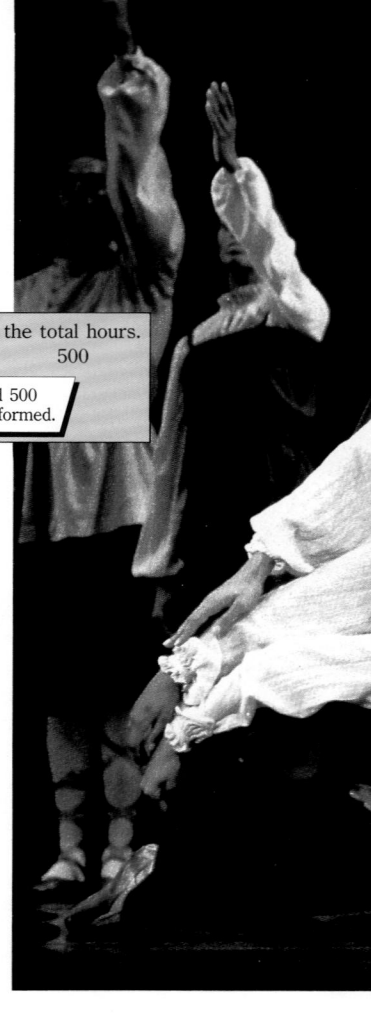

> The hours for each show times the number of shows is the total hours.
> $$2 \quad \times \quad s \quad = \quad 500$$
> $2s = 500$ — The equation balances. Both $2s$ and 500 represent the number of hours performed.

Solve the equation. Does your answer make sense?
$s = 250$ shows; yes
THINK ALOUD Can you write another equation that represents the problem?
$\frac{500}{2} = s$

━━━━━ **GUIDED PRACTICE** ━━━━━

Decide what the variable represents.
Then choose the equation that represents the problem and solve.

1. There are 18 dancers in a show. Eleven are women. How many male dancers are there?

   a. Let k represent ▓. the number of male dancers
   b. Choose: $k + 11 = 18$, $k - 11 = 18$, or $\frac{k}{11} = 18$
      $k + 11 = 18$; $k = 7$

2. Each of the 25 performances of a ballet is sold out. If the theater seats 224 people, how many people will see the ballet?

   a. Let n represent ▓. the number of people
   b. Choose: $25n = 224$, $25 \times 224 = n$, or $\frac{25}{n} = 224$
      $25 \times 224 = n$; $n = 5,600$

MULTICULTURAL NOTE

Arthur Mitchell was the first African-American male to dance with a major ballet company. He founded the Dance Theater of Harlem, in which most of the dancers are African Americans.

2 TEACH

Allow time for students to read the problem. Then ask:

- **What is the problem asking you to find?** *(the number of shows)*

- **Why is s a good choice for the variable?** *(Stands for "shows.")*

- Discuss the equation and have students solve it. **How do you check that your answer is correct?** *(Possible answers: Replace the variable with its solution and compute; ask yourself if the answers makes sense.)*

SUMMARIZE/ASSESS **Explain how writing, solving, and checking an equation is related to the four-part problem-solving process.** *(Students should relate writing an equation to the plan step, solving the equation to the solve step, and checking the equation to the look back step.)*

Decide on a variable to represent the unknown quantity. Then write an equation and solve.
Answers will vary. Suggestions given.

3. The first performance of the Dance Theater of Harlem was in 1968. How long ago was that? **y = time in years; as of 1991, y + 1968 = 1991; y = 23**

4. The Dance Theater of Harlem performs regularly at New York's Aaron Davis Hall, which has 750 seats. Performances are also given at the New York City Center, which has about 1,750 more seats. About how many seats does the City Center have? **s = number of seats; 750 + 1,750 = s; s = 2,500**

5. An amount of money is shared by 18 people to buy ballet tickets. If each ticket costs $22.50, what is the total amount of money that is shared? **d = amount shared; d ÷ 18 = 22.50; d = 405**

6. For 1 wk of performances, the Dance Theater of Harlem charges $175,000. If one performance costs $25,000, how many performances are given in 1 wk? **c = number of performances; 175,000 ÷ c = 25,000; c = 7**

CHOOSE Choose a strategy to solve, if it is possible. **Strategies will vary. Suggestions given.**

7. A 254-seat theater sells tickets at $12 each. There are eight 3-h shows put on each week, including 2 each on Saturday and Wednesday. At intermission, tea is $1 and fruit juice is $2. In 1 wk, all the shows sell out. How much money was made from ticket sales that week? **too much information; $24,384**

8. Tickets for the Dance Theater of Harlem's *Firebird* were $15 each. Props and costumes cost $20,000. What was the profit? **not enough information; need to know how many people saw the show**

9. A theater sold 214 tickets one day, 194 tickets the second day, and 210 tickets the third day. On the fourth day, the theater sold half the number of tickets sold the second day.

   a. How many tickets were sold on the second day? **194 tickets**
   b. On which of the four days were the most tickets sold? **the first day**
   c. Estimate how many tickets were sold in all. **using estimation; ≈700 tickets**

Dance Theater of Harlem

MEETING INDIVIDUAL NEEDS

For Students Who Are . . .

Acquiring English Proficiency Pair students with an English-proficient student to discuss and solve the Practice exercises.

Gifted and Talented Assign students the technology lesson on page 128.

Working 2 or 3 Grades Below Level Have students use pages 28–31 of the Skills Workbook for Problem Solving Strategies and pages 30–31 of the Skills Workbook for equations, ratio, proportion, and percent.

Today's Problem

The sum of three consecutive even whole numbers is the sum of the first four primes minus five. What are the numbers? *(The numbers are 2, 4, and 6. Solve the equation: x + (x + 2) + (x + 4) = (2 + 3 + 5 + 7) − 5; 3x + 6 = 12; x = 2)*

3 FOLLOW-UP

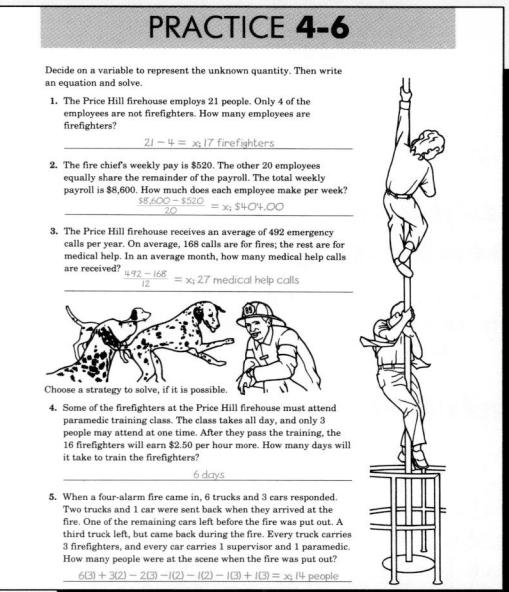

PRACTICE 4-6

Decide on a variable to represent the unknown quantity. Then write an equation and solve.

1. The Price Hill firehouse employs 21 people. Only 4 of the employees are not firefighters. How many employees are firefighters? **21 − 4 = x; 17 firefighters**

2. The fire chief's weekly pay is $520. The other 20 employees equally share the remainder of the payroll. The total weekly payroll is $8,600. How much does each employee make per week? **$8,600 − $520 / 20 = x; $404.00**

3. The Price Hill firehouse receives an average of 492 emergency calls per year. On average, 168 calls are for fires; the rest are for medical help. In an average month, how many medical help calls are received? **492 − 168 / 12 = x; 27 medical help calls**

Choose a strategy to solve, if it is possible.

4. Some of the firefighters at the Price Hill firehouse must attend paramedic training class. The class takes all day, and only 3 people may attend at one time. After they pass the training, the 16 firefighters will earn $2.50 per hour more. How many days will it take to train the firefighters? **6 days**

5. When a four-alarm fire came in, 6 trucks and 3 cars responded. Two trucks and 1 car were sent back when they arrived at the fire. One of the remaining cars left before the fire was put out. A third truck left, but came back during the fire. Every truck carries 3 firefighters, and every car carries 1 supervisor and 1 paramedic. How many people were at the scene when the fire was put out? **6(3) + 3(2) − 2(3) − 1(2) − 1(2) − 1(3) + 1(3) = x; 14 people**

RETEACHING 4-6

Present the following problem:

> An office manager's salary is $520 per week. The other 20 employees share the remainder of the $8,600 weekly payroll. How much does each employee make per week?

Have students work in groups of 2 or 3 to discuss and solve the problem. If necessary, you may wish to suggest that students use simpler numbers to help them determine how to solve the problem and then apply their plan to the original problem.

ENRICHMENT 4-6

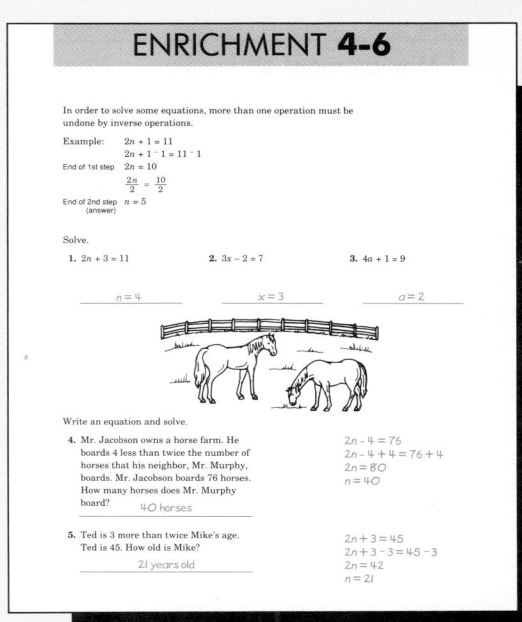

In order to solve some equations, more than one operation must be undone by inverse operations.

Example:
$2n + 1 = 11$
$2n + 1 - 1 = 11 - 1$
End of 1st step: $2n = 10$
$\frac{2n}{2} = \frac{10}{2}$
End of 2nd step: $n = 5$ (answer)

Solve.

1. $2n + 3 = 11$ 2. $3x - 2 = 7$ 3. $4a + 1 = 9$

n = 4   **x = 3**   **a = 2**

Write an equation and solve.

4. Mr. Jacobson owns a horse farm. He boards 4 less than twice the number of horses that his neighbor, Mr. Murphy, boards. Mr. Jacobson boards 76 horses. How many horses does Mr. Murphy board? **40 horses**

   2n − 4 = 76
   2n − 4 + 4 = 76 + 4
   2n = 80
   n = 40

5. Ted is 3 more than twice Mike's age. Ted is 45. How old is Mike? **21 years old**

   2n + 3 = 45
   2n + 3 − 3 = 45 − 3
   2n = 42
   n = 21

MIDCHAPTER Checkup

The midchapter checkup provides a way for you to check students' understanding of the skills taught in the first half of the chapter.

Language and Vocabulary

Some key language and vocabulary ideas from the first half of the chapter are reinforced here.

Quick Quiz

The quiz provides a means of evaluating students' understanding of the objectives for the first half of the chapter. Page references are given so that students can check back to where the skill was taught.

Use the following guide to score the quiz.

Score	Percent
10	100%
9	90
8	80
7	70
6	60
5	50
4	40
3	30
2	20
1	10

Use this chart to identify the Management Objectives tested.

Items	Management Objective	Pages
1–6	**4A** Write and evaluate expressions.	96–99
7–9	**4B** Solve equations using inverse operations.	102–105
10	**4D** Problem Solving: Write an equation.	106–107

LANGUAGE & VOCABULARY

Give an expression or equation to show that you understand the situation. Use the variable that is given. Tell whether your answer is an expression or an equation.   **Answers will vary. Suggestions given.**

1. The height h of a tree increases by 15 ft.   **$h + 15$; expression**

2. Three classes, each with the same number s of students, have a total of 78 students.   **$3s = 78$; equation**

3. When a 6-ft-long sandwich was shared equally among a number f of friends, each piece was 2 ft long.   **$2f = 6$; equation**

QUICK QUIZ

Write an expression. Let m be the unknown value. *(pages 96–97)*

1. twelve more than a number   **$m + 12$**

2. seven less than a number   **$m - 7$**

3. fifteen divided by a number   **$\dfrac{15}{m}$**

Evaluate. Use $a = 4$, $b = 11$, and $c = 8$. *(pages 98–99)*

4. $3a + 9$ **21**   5. $\dfrac{b - 5}{2}$ **3**   6. $a + c - 2$ **10**

Solve the equation. *(pages 102–105)*

7. $r + 12.4 = 23.6$ **11.2**   8. $d - 38 = 37$ **75**   9. $2.5x = 1.5$ **0.6**

Solve. *(pages 106–107)*

10. One morning, 88 planes took off from an airport. Each of the airport's 4 runways were used the same number of times.

    a. How many runways does the airport have?   **4 runways**

    b. What equation can be used to find the number of planes that took off from each runway that morning?   **4 p = 88**

    c. How many planes took off from each runway that morning?   **22 planes**

Write the answers in your learning log.   **Answers will vary. Suggestions given.**

1. Explain how an equation is different from an expression.
   expression is open ended; equation solves for one solution

2. Describe how you would evaluate the expression $2a + 3b$.
   Substitute in values for a and b and compute.

3. What does the equals sign tell you when solving an equation?
   There is an equal relationship between the sides of the equation.

DID YOU KNOW . . . ? The Flint Ridge–Mammoth Cave System in Kentucky is the longest cave system in the world. It twists and turns along more than 225 mi. What two cities in your state are about 225 mi apart?   **Check students' work.**

Work with a partner. Decide whether the given values for a, b, and c form a magic square in which all rows, columns, and diagonals have the same sum.

1. $a = 6$, $b = 4$, and $c = 8$ no
2. $a = 8$, $b = 4$, and $c = 16$ no
3. $a = 2$, $b = 4$, and $c = 8$ no

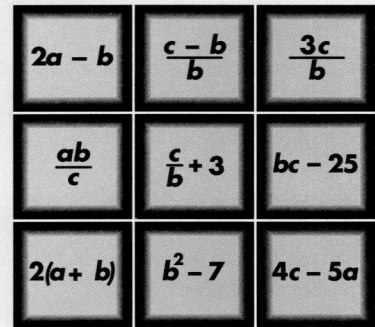

LESSON | 4-7

Lesson Organizer

Objective: Graph inequalities.

Prior Knowledge: Students should be able to graph numbers on a number line.

Error Analysis and Remediation: See page 123A.

Lesson Resources:
Practice Worksheet 4-7
Reteaching Worksheet 4-7
Enrichment Activity 4-7
Daily Review 4-7

Two-Minute Math

Use the Table of Numbers on the inside back cover. List the numbers in row H that are greater than 2.6 and less than 8.6. *(2.7; 8; 3.9; 4.5; 7; 4.63)*

1 INTRODUCE

CONNECTING ACTIVITY

☑ **MATERIALS CHECKLIST:** balance scale, counters

1. Have a student place 12 counters on one side of the scale. **What could you place on the other side that would allow 12 to be greater than the number x?** Have students experiment by placing different numbers of counters on the pan. *(any number of counters less than 12)*

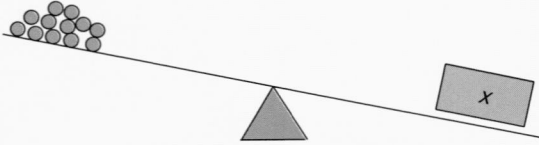

2. Write $x < 12$. Have students describe the graphs of numbers that are solutions to $x < 12$. *(They are all points to the left of 12.)*

3. Repeat the activity for $x > 7$.

WHEN YOUR STUDENTS ASK
★ WHY AM I LEARNING THIS? ★

You can connect this skill to real life through economics. For example, you may plan to buy a new car as soon as your savings account balance is greater than $14,000.

MATH AND SOCIAL STUDIES

Graphing Inequalities on a Number Line

Nearly $\frac{1}{8}$ of the world's surface is desert and receives a yearly rainfall of less than 10 in.

The yearly amount of rainfall in deserts can be represented by an inequality.

Let r represent the number of inches of yearly rainfall. The rainfall is less than 10 in.

$r \qquad < \qquad 10$ — The $<$ symbol indicates an inequality.

You can illustrate the inequality with a graph.

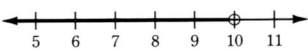

$r < 10$ The open circle indicates that 10 is not included.

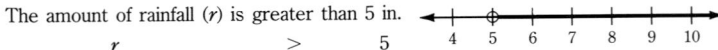

The solid line represents the numbers that are a solution to the given inequality. (Assume numbers greater than zero in the solution.)

Some solutions are 6, 8, and 9.5.

The rainfall could have been 6 in., 8 in., or 9.5 in.

THINK ALOUD Name three other possible solutions greater than zero. Include some decimal numbers. Answers will vary. Suggestions given. 0.25; 3.4; 9.999.

Another example:

The amount of rainfall (r) is greater than 5 in.

$r \qquad\qquad > \qquad 5$

Some solutions are 7, 5.5, and 90.5.

Answers will vary.
THINK ALOUD Name three other possible solutions. Suggestions given: $r = 8$, 102, 12.6

=== **GUIDED PRACTICE** ===

Name three possible solutions greater than zero for each inequality. Answers will vary. Suggestions given.

1. $x > 5$ $x = 5.01$, 6, 8.1

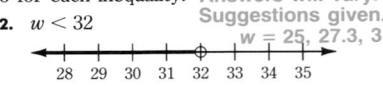

2. $w < 32$ $w = 25$, 27.3, 31

IN YOUR WORDS Explain the reason for your answer.

3. Is 5 included on the graph?

No, there is an open circle at 5.

4. Is 3.5 included on the graph?

Yes, $3.5 > 3$.

---

2 TEACH

What would be the graph for $x = 12$? *(a point at 12 on a number line)*

To graph the inequality $t > 480$, is it necessary to start the number line at zero? Explain. *(No; arrows at the ends of a number line indicate that it extends in both directions indefinitely.)*

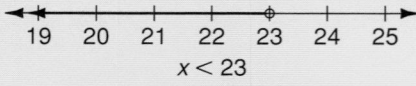

$x < 23$

Chalkboard Examples

Graph each number in the solution.

$$x > 4 \qquad x < 9$$

(graph of all numbers to right of 4; graph of all numbers to the left of 9)

SUMMARIZE/ASSESS   **Explain how to graph $x < 23$.** *(open circle at 23; shade number line left from outside of circle to arrow.)*

PRACTICE

Which of the numbers are solutions to the inequality?
$\frac{1}{3}$, 4, 6.3, 18.2, 48, 957

5. $n < 8$ $\frac{1}{3}$, 4, 6.3   **6.** $n < 17$ $\frac{1}{3}$, 4, 6.3   **7.** $n > 5$ 6.3, 18.2, 48, 957

8. $n < 81$ $\frac{1}{3}$, 4, 6.3, 18.2, 48   **9.** $n < 6.4$ $\frac{1}{3}$, 4, 6.3   **10.** $n > 18.6$ 48, 957

Match the inequality with the graph of the solution.

a. $x < 25$ **b.** $x > 11$ **c.** $x > 5.5$ **d.** $x > 2.5$

11. d

1.5   2.0   2.5   3.0   3.5   4.0

12. a

22   23   24   25   24   25   26

13. c

4.5   5.0   5.5   6.0   6.5   7.0

14. b

8   9   10   11   12   13   14

Graph the solution. **See page 123b.**

15. $n > 8$ **16.** $x < 8$ **17.** $x < 7$ **18.** $x > 73.5$

19. $n > 42$ **20.** $x > 975$ **21.** $w < 12.5$ ***22.** $x > 3 + 2$

PROBLEM SOLVING

Choose the correct inequality that represents the problem. Then graph the inequality.

23. The greatest rainfall in a 12-mo period was 1,044 in., in Cherrapunji, Meghalaya, India. What is the rainfall in a year for any other place in the world compared with Cherrapunji that year? **a**

   a. $r < 1,044$ **b.** $r < 12$ **c.** $r > 1,044$

24. The least amount of rainfall usually occurs in Arica, Chile. It receives about 0.03 in. every 12 mo. What is the rainfall in a year for any other place in the world compared with Arica? **c**

   a. $r < 0.03$ **b.** $r > 12$ **c.** $r > 0.03$

Critical Thinking

With a partner, explain the difference between the two graphs below. **Left graph: x is any number greater than 3. Right graph: x is a whole number greater than 2 and less than 8.**

2   3   4   5   6   7   2   3   4   5   6   7   8

CHAPTER 4   111

---

3 FOLLOW-UP

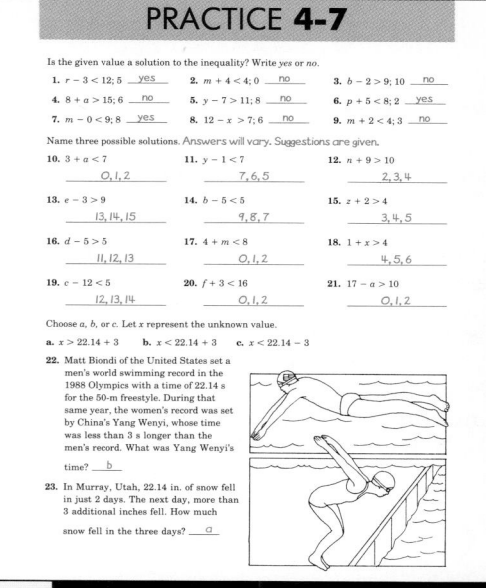

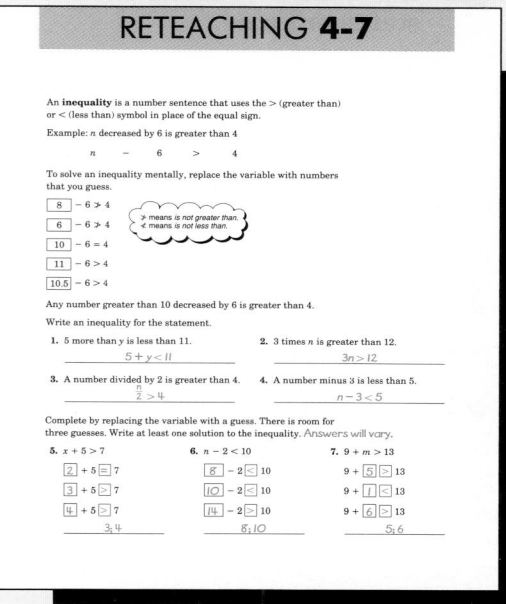

MEETING INDIVIDUAL NEEDS

For Students Who Are . . .

Acquiring English Proficiency Pair students with an English-proficient student to discuss and solve the Problem Solving and Critical Thinking exercises.

Gifted and Talented Discuss the symbols $\not>$ and $\not<$ *(not greater than, not less than)* with students. Have them graph the solutions for $x \not> 6$, $y \not< 28$, and $z \not> 9.3$.

Working 2 or 3 Grades Below Level Remind students that on the graph for "is greater than," the line goes to the right. For "is less than," the line goes to the left.

Today's Problem

Draw a coordinate plane to solve the following problem:
If you start from your home and walk 5 blocks east, 3 blocks north, 8 blocks west, 6 blocks north and end up at the point $(-4, 7)$, at which point is your home located? *$(-1, -2)$*

ENRICHMENT 4-7

Write the following inequalities on the board: $m - 3 > 10$, $t + 27 < 61$, and $12 - z = 6$. Have the students work in groups of three or four. Instruct each group to brainstorm ways that they can solve the inequalities. In their groups, have individual students prove their solutions. Let other students challenge the solutions when necessary.

Chapter 4 • Lesson 4-7   **111**

Lesson Organizer

> **Objective:** Solve inequalities using mental math.

Prior Knowledge: Students should understand what the symbols $>$ and $<$ mean.

Error Analysis and Remediation: See page 123A.

Lesson Resources:
Practice Worksheet 4-8
Reteaching Activity 4-8
Enrichment Worksheet 4-8
Daily Review 4-8

 *Two-Minute Math*

Use > or < to make each statement true.

$8 - 5 \square 2$ *(>)*

$4.7 + 7 \square 12.4$ *(<)*

$14 - 4.9 \square 10$ *(<)*

$7.6 + 9.6 \square 16.2$ *(>)*

1 INTRODUCE

CONNECTING ACTIVITY

☑ **MATERIALS CHECKLIST:** balance scale, counters, paper bag

1. Place 8 counters on one pan of a balance scale and 5 on the other pan. **Why are the pans unbalanced?** *(There are more counters on one pan than on the other.)* **Write two inequalities that represent the situation.** *(8 > 5 and 5 < 8)*

2. Put 6 counters inside a paper bag, but do not let students see. Place the bag on the right pan. **Which pan has more counters?** *(the right pan)* **Write two inequalities that represent the situation.** *(8 < n + 5 or n + 5 > 8)* **What is the fewest number of counters that could be inside the paper bag?** *(4)* **What are some solutions for this inequality?** *(all numbers greater than 3)*

WHEN YOUR STUDENTS ASK
★ WHY AM I LEARNING THIS? ★

You can relate this skill to real life through chemistry. Chemists add different quantities of a substance to neutralize an acid.

Mental Math: Solving Inequalities

Mark took 2 h to drive from Colorado Springs to Divide. From Divide he drove to Canon City on a gravel road. The entire trip took less than 7 h. How long could the drive from Divide to Canon City have lasted?

Let n be the driving time from Divide to Canon City.

2 plus what number is less than 7?

$$2 + \qquad n \qquad < 7$$

To solve the inequality mentally, cover up the variable.

$$2 + \qquad\qquad < \qquad 7$$

Try 6: Is $2 + 6 < 7$?
$\qquad\qquad 8 > 7$, so 6 is not a solution.

Try 5: Is $2 + 5 < 7$?
$\qquad\qquad 7 = 7$, so 5 is not a solution.

THINK ALOUD What can you conclude about numbers greater than or equal to 5? **They are not solutions.**

Try 4: Is $2 + 4 < 7$?
$\qquad\qquad 6 < 7$, so 4 is a solution.

THINK ALOUD What can you conclude about numbers less than 5? **They are solutions.**

Solution: any number less than 5 ($n < 5$). The drive from Divide to Canon City took less than 5 h.

---

2 TEACH

If you reversed the inequality symbol in $n + 2 < 7$, what would be the solution? *(all numbers greater than 5)*

How many whole number solutions are possible for the inequality $x - 6 < 15$? *(20 through 0 inclusive, or 21 numbers)* **Why is 21 not a solution?** *(21 results in an equality.)*

> ### *Chalkboard Examples*
>
> Name three possible solutions.
> $r + 9 > 11$ *(numbers > 2)*
> $m - 6 < 8$ *(numbers < 14)*
> $z - 1 < 3$ *(numbers < 4)*
> $y + 10 < 17$ *(numbers < 7)*

SUMMARIZE/ASSESS **Which of the inequalities—$b + 6 > 10$ or $b + 6 < 10$—has 0 as one of its solutions? Explain.** *($b + 6 < 10$; all numbers less than 4 are solutions, $0 < 4$.)*

GUIDED PRACTICE

Write an inequality for the statement.

1. 45 minus a number b is greater than 17. $45 - b > 17$

2. 1.4 plus a number p is less than 10. $1.4 + p < 10$

NUMBER SENSE Name three possible solutions. **Answers will vary. Suggestions given.**

3. $y - 5 < 9$
$y = 13, 10, 5$

4. $x - 3 > 7$
$x = 10.5, 11, 20$

5. $8 + n > 10$
$n = 2.5, 3, 8$

PRACTICE

Is the given value a solution to the inequality? Write *yes* or *no*.

6. $x - 6 > 9$; 25 **yes**

7. $a - 8 < 5$; 15 **no**

8. $y + 4 < 7$; 1 **yes**

9. $3 + b < 10$; 8 **no**

10. $a + 8 > 8$; 3 **yes**

11. $m + 0 > 12$; 14 **yes**

NUMBER SENSE Name three possible solutions. **Answers will vary. Suggestions given.**

12. $y - 2 < 8$
$y = 9, 4, 2$

13. $n - 5 > 8$
$n = 14, 15, 20$

14. $a - 7 > 4$
$a = 11.5, 12, 14$

15. $x + 8 > 8$
$x = 1, 2, 3$

16. $m + 5 > 6$
$m = 2, 3, 4$

17. $a - 12 > 5$
$a = 17.5, 18, 20$

18. $7 + a > 11$
$a = 5, 6, 9$

19. $b - 6 > 3$
$b = 10, 11, 18$

20. $c - 7 < 14$
$c = 20.5, 20, 15$

*21. **CRITICAL THINKING** The equation $x + 3 = 8$ has only one solution. How many solutions does the inequality $x + 3 > 8$ have? Explain.
Infinite. The solution is any number greater than 5.

PROBLEM SOLVING

Match the equality or the inequality with the question. Let t represent the unknown value.

22. The temperature in Denver at 9:00 A.M. was 15°C. By noon the temperature had risen to over 23°C. By how much had the temperature risen?
b

a. $15 + t = 23$

23. Twenty-three people can take a ski tram at one time. Just before the ski tram starts moving, 15 people decide to take it. How many more people can still go?
a

b. $15 + t > 23$

*24. One year, the total precipitation in Colorado was 15 in. The next year, the total precipitation was more than 23 in. What was the total precipitation for the 2 yr?
c

c. $15 + 23 < t$

MEETING INDIVIDUAL NEEDS

For Students Who Are . . .

Acquiring English Proficiency Review the symbols for "is greater than" and "is less than." Pair students with an English-proficient student to discuss and solve the Problem Solving exercises.

Gifted and Talented Have students discover how to solve inequalities without using trial and error. For example, $x - 6 > 9$ can be solved by adding 6 to both sides to obtain $x > 15$.

Working 2 or 3 Grades Below Level For Exercises 6–11, have students write the inequality and substitute the given value to determine whether it is a solution.

Today's Problem

A picture that measures 3 in. by 4 in. is placed inside a frame. The matting that surrounds the picture is 1 in. wide. What is the distance around the frame? *(The distance is (2 × 5 in.) + (2 × 6 in.) = 22 in.)*

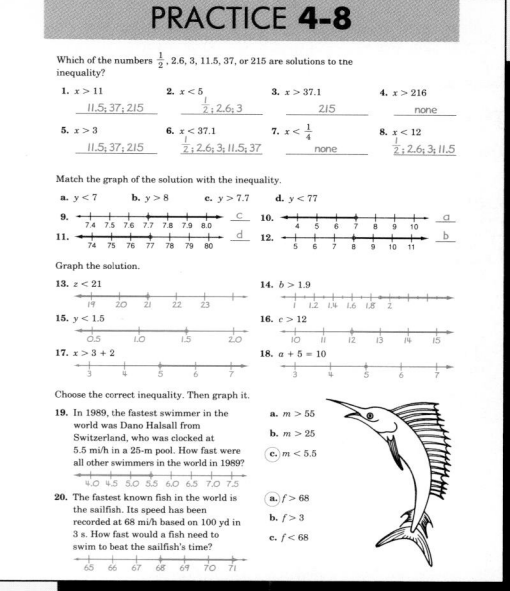

RETEACHING 4-8

Write the following on the board:

0, 1, 3, 6, 8, 9		
$x + 3 < 7$	$x - 2 > 3$	$x + 5 > 7$
(0, 1, 3)	(6, 8, 9)	(3, 6, 8, 9)

Ask students to write each of the numbers from the list above the table under the inequality which it satisfies. Numbers may be used with more than one inequality. Have students study their tables and write a summary of the results. *(Example: all numbers in the table that are 3 or less)*

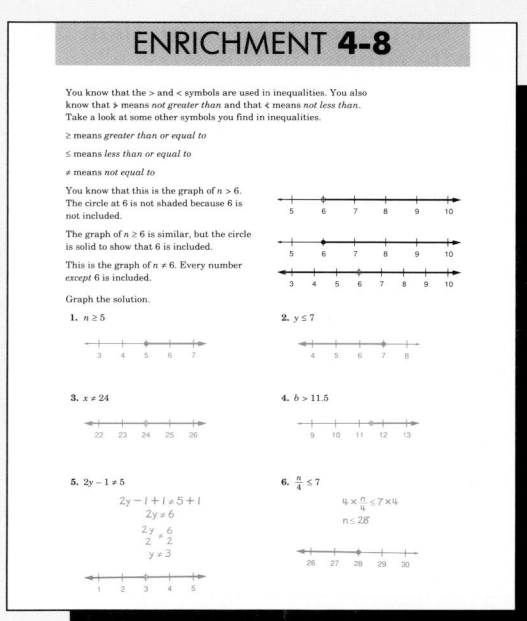

LESSON | 4-9

Lesson Organizer

Objective: Explore functions.

Prior Knowledge: Students should be able to multiply.

Lesson Resources:
Class Activity 4-9
Daily Review 4-9

Two-Minute Math

Solve for *n*.

$n \div 1{,}000 = 3.562$ *(3,562)*
$3.8 \times n = 380$ *(100)*
$58.2 \div n = 0.0582$ *(1,000)*
$n \times 10{,}000 = 4{,}823.6$ *(0.48236)*

1 PREPARE

SYMBOLIC ACTIVITY

1. Conduct a brief survey. Have each student write his or her name and single favorite school subject on piece of paper.

2. Collect papers and discuss general results of the survey. For example, which subject do most students prefer?

3. Write the names of several students in one column and list the subjects that these students chose in a second column. Draw arrows to match each student's name to a subject.

- **Can one person have more than one favorite subject in this survey?** *(no)*

- **Can more than one person have the same favorite subject?** *(yes)*

WHEN YOUR STUDENTS ASK
★ WHY AM I LEARNING THIS? ★

You can connect this skill to real life through pay scales at work. For example, a salary may be a function of hourly pay and hours worked.

Exploring Functions

A seventh grade class made a survey to find out what students liked best about their trip to the zoo. The survey had two rules for the question that asked for a favorite animal.

Rule 1: Select one animal.
Rule 2: You may not select more than one animal.

The students made these selections.

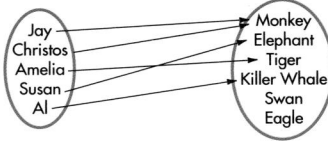

The pairing of students to favorite animals is a **function**, because one and only one animal was chosen by each student.

1. Notice that each student can select only one animal, but two students can select the same animal. Name two students who did.
   Jay and Christos

2. This is *not* a function because rule 1 does not hold. Megan did not choose an animal. How can you make it a function? **Answers will vary. Suggestion given.**

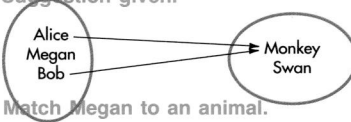

Match Megan to an animal.

3. This is *not* a function because rule 2 does not hold. Which student did not follow rule 2? **Paul**

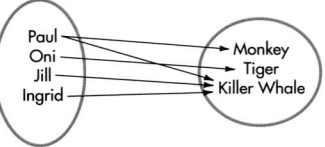

THINK ALOUD Is the statement true for a function? Explain.

4. Each student must pick one animal.
   Yes, rule 1 is satisfied.

5. Some students can pick two animals.
   No, this breaks rule 2.

6. No student can select more than one animal.
   Yes, rule 2 is satisfied.

7. Two different students can select the same animal.
   Yes, both rules are satisfied.

114   LESSON 4-9

2 EXPLORE

Describe a pairing that is a function and one that is not a function. *(Accept reasonable answers; have students check their responses against the rules on page 114.)*

SUMMARIZE/ASSESS   **Is the pairing of months to the number of days in the months a function? Explain.** *(No; February may have 28 or 29 days, and therefore does not pair with just one number.)*

8. The diagrams below show other surveys that asked students to choose a favorite animal. One diagram does *not* show a function. Which one is it? Why?   diagram 1; because Isaac broke rule 1 and Ed broke rule 2

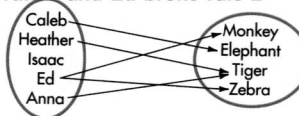 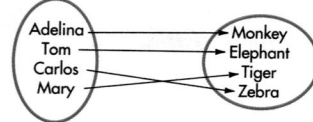

Does the diagram show a function? If not, name the rule that does not hold.

Rule 1: Each student selects one ride.
Rule 2: No student may select more than one ride.

9.   **10.**

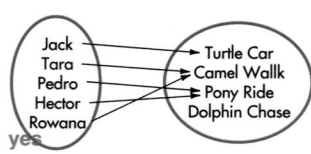 yes   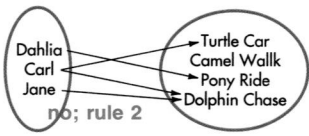 no; rule 2

Many functions pair numbers with numbers. As an example, we can pair the number of students (n) who go to the zoo with the admission cost (c) of $2.50 per student.

11. Copy and complete the diagram and the table to show a function for the number of students and the cost.

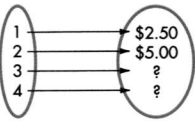

Number (n)	1	2	3	4
Cost ($) ($c$)	?	?	?	?
	$2.50	$5.00	$7.50	$10.00

12. Make a table of a function for 1 to 8 students going to the zoo when the admission is $1.75.   See page 123b.

Make a function table for n from 1 to 6.   See page 123b.

13. n = number of elephants
e = number of elephant ears

14. n = number of zoo train rides
c = cost at 75¢ each

15. CREATE YOUR OWN   Now make up two functions of your own.
Check students' work.

---

3 FOLLOW-UP

CLASS ACTIVITY 4-9

☑ **MATERIALS CHECKLIST:**
Newspapers

Have the students work in groups of three or four. Give each student a newspaper. Ask students to write down the part or parts of the newspaper that they like to read most. Have each group compile its list of names and reading choices. Ask if any group contains a student who did not choose any favorite part. **Do the group choices represent a function?** *(No; For a function, each student must choose.)* Find a group with a student choosing 2 or more articles. **Do the group choices represent a function?** *(No; For a function, no student chooses more than one.)* Find a group with each person choosing one and only one article. **Do the group choices represent a function?** *(Yes)*

MEETING INDIVIDUAL NEEDS

For Students Who Are . . .

Acquiring English Proficiency Have students work through the lesson in cooperative groups. Check their understanding of the rules and questions asked.

Gifted and Talented Have students write equations for the functions in Exercises 11–14. *($c = 2.50n$, $c = 1.75n$, $e = 2n$, $c = 0.75n$)*

Today's Problem

A function can be defined as a set of ordered pairs of two elements in which no two different second elements have the same first element of the pair. For example, if the function f("word") = number of letters in the "word," then f(BIG) = 3. What is the value of f(AMERICA)? What is the least value of f? What is the greatest value of f? *(f(AMERICA) = 7; the least value of f is 1, and the greatest value is the number of letters in the longest word.)*

Lesson Organizer

Objective: Explore function rules.

Prior Knowledge: Students should understand the concept of a function.

Lesson Resources:
Classroom Activity 4-10
Daily Review 4-10
Cooperative Connections, Chapter 4
Cooperative Investigations, Chapter 4

Two-Minute Math

Evaluate. Let $x = 5$.

$3x - 10 + 8$ *(13)*
$x^2 + 48 \div 6$ *(33)*
$4x + 3x - 45/x$ *(26)*

1 PREPARE

SYMBOLIC ACTIVITY

1. Draw the following tables on the chalkboard:

?	2	4	6	8	10
?	$.79	$1.58	$2.37	$3.16	$3.95

?	1	2	3	4	5
?	4	8	12	16	20

2. Have students suggest situations that could be represented by each table. *(Possible situations: the number of muffins to the cost of muffins; the number of chairs to chair legs)*

3. Discuss how each table shows a function. *(Each is a special way of pairing numbers, following rules described in Lesson 4–9.)*

WHEN YOUR STUDENTS ASK
★ WHY AM I LEARNING THIS? ★

You can relate this skill to real life through the stock market. The pairing of a stock name and the day's closing value is a function that is recorded daily.

Exploring Function Rules

The Central High School team is in the state football tournament. Buses are used to take the fans to games across the state.

The number of buses (b) and the number of fans that fit (f) in each bus are shown below.

Buses (b)	1	2	3	4	5
Fans (f)	35	70	105	140	175

1. Explain why the pairing of buses to fans is a function.

2. **IN YOUR WORDS** Explain how the numbers of buses and fans are related. *For each bus there are 35 fans.*

You can write a **function rule** that tells how the numbers of buses and fans are related.

number of fans	=	35 × number of buses	
f	=	$35b$	function rule

Use the function rule $f = 35b$ to answer the question.

3. How many people will 10 buses hold?
350 people

4. How many buses do you need for 595 people?
17 buses

Central High School decides to put 32 fans in each bus. The new function rule is $f = 32b$.

5. Make a table to show the function for 1 to 8 buses.
See page 123b.

6. What function rule would indicate that 60 fans fit in each of 10 buses?
For b from 1 to 10, $f = 60b$.

Copy and complete the table using the function rule.

7.

Souvenirs (s)	1	2	3	4	5	6
Cost ($) ($c$)	?	?	?	?	?	?

Function Rule: $c = 8.95s$
8.95; 17.90; 26.85; 35.80; 44.75; 53.70

8.

Players (p)	11	22	33	44	55	66
Teams (t)	?	?	?	?	?	?

Function Rule: $t = \frac{p}{11}$
1; 2; 3; 4; 5; 6

---

2 EXPLORE

What function rule tells that one pizza (p) should be ordered for every three guests (g)? ($p = \frac{g}{3}$) **Use the rule to determine how many pizzas should be ordered for 21 guests.** *(7)* **For 39 guests.** *(13)*

What could the function rule $c = 3.50t$ represent? *(Possible answer: the total cost of tickets that are $3.50 each)*

SUMMARIZE/ASSESS Make a table using the function rule $a = 3b$ for $b = 1$ to 8. What questions can be answered from the table?

$$\left(\begin{array}{c|c} b & 1\ 2\ 3 \ldots 8 \\ \hline a & 3\ 6\ 9 \ldots 24 \end{array} \right)$$

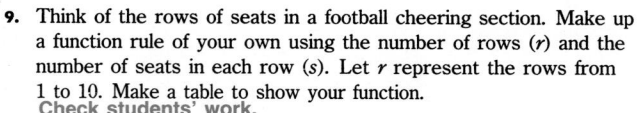

9. Think of the rows of seats in a football cheering section. Make up a function rule of your own using the number of rows (r) and the number of seats in each row (s). Let r represent the rows from 1 to 10. Make a table to show your function. **Check students' work.**

If the pairing has a function rule, write the rule. Otherwise, write *no rule*.

10.

End of quarter (q)	1	2	3	4
Minutes played (m)	15	30	45	60

$m = 15q$

11.

Number of fans (f)	1	2	3	4
Cost of tickets in dollars (t)	20	40	60	80

$t = 20f$

12.

Passes completed (p)	1	2	3	4
Pass length in yards (l)	40	5	15	32

no rule

13.

Quarter (q)	1	2	3	4
Points (p)	13	7	0	14

no rule

14.

Number of touchdowns (t)	1	2	3	4
Points from touchdowns (p)	6	12	18	24

$p = 6t$

15. Use the function in Exercise 14 to find the number of points scored for 8 touchdowns.   **48 points**

Use the given function rule to complete the table.

16. Minutes (m) per Hour (h)

h	1	2	3	4	4.5
m	60	120	180	240	270

Function Rule: $m = 60h$

17. Feet (f) per Yard (y)

y	0	5	10	15	20
f	0	15	30	45	60

Function Rule: $f = 3y$

Write the rule for the function.

18. Feet (f) per Mile (m)

m	1	2	3
f	5,280	10,560	15,840

Function Rule: $f = $ ▨ $5,280m$

19. Ounces (o) per Pound (p)

p	1	3	5	7
o	16	48	80	112

Function Rule: $o = $ ▨ $16p$

20. **CREATE YOUR OWN**   Choose a sport other than football.

   a. Make a table showing an aspect of the game that has a function rule. **Check students' work.**

   b. Make a table showing an aspect of the game that does not have a function rule.   **Check students' work.**

CLASS ACTIVITY **4-10**

☑ **MATERIALS CHECKLIST:** Calculators

Explain to the students that state and local governments use tax money to provide public services. Have the students find the sales tax rate in your area. Show them how to figure the total cost if the price of an item is $5.00. Tell the students that $t = 0.06$ is the function rule and have groups of four students figure the total cost for every price between $5.01 and $6, $6.01 and $7, $7.01 and $8, and so on. When each group has finished, read several prices such as $7.57, $6.75, and $5.99 and have the students use their "tax tables" to find the total cost of the item.

MEETING INDIVIDUAL NEEDS

For Students Who Are . . .

Acquiring English Proficiency   Pair students with an English-proficient student to work through the lesson.

Gifted and Talented   Have students choose several points on the coordinate plane and write their coordinates. Have them decide if their points make a function and explain. (*Answers will vary.*)

Today's Problem

Given: f is a function, and f "acts" on squares of various sizes. Some sample values of f are f(2-in. square) $= 8$; f(3-in. square) $= 12$; f(4-in. square) $= 16$. What is the rule of the function? (*The function of the square is its perimeter.*)

Lesson Organizer

Objective: Discuss representing problems.

Prior Knowledge: Students should understand the four-part problem-solving process.

Lesson Resources:
Practice Worksheet 4-11
Daily Review 4-11

 **Two-Minute Math**

Each letter represents a different digit. Find the value of each letter. $M \div M = A$

$$
\begin{array}{r}
M \\
M\overline{)AT} \\
\underline{AT} \\
AT
\end{array}
$$

$(A = 1, M = 4, T = 6)$

1 INTRODUCE

CONNECTING ACTIVITY

1. Have students work in small groups to determine different ways to solve the following problem. Remind students to look for methods, not solutions.
The five members of the chess club decided that each club member would play every other member one time. How many games will have to be played?

2. Students should describe these methods for solving problems:

- acting out the problem
- identifying a pattern
- making a table
- drawing a picture

3. You may wish students to use one or two of these methods to solve the problem.

WHEN YOUR STUDENTS ASK
★ WHY AM I LEARNING THIS? ★

You can use this skill to solve real life problems. For example, representations will help you solve puzzles and design winning strategies in games.

 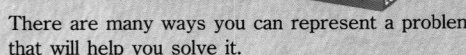

It's ShowTime!

Problem Solving:
Representing a Problem

READ ABOUT IT

There are many ways you can represent a problem that will help you solve it.

- You can represent a problem with a picture or diagram.

  Using the numerals 3, 4, and 7, how many different three-digit whole numbers can you write? **6** You can use each numeral only once in the three-digit whole number.

First digit →	3		4		7	
Second digit →	4	7	3	7	3	4
Third digit →	7	4	7	3	4	3

- A problem can be represented with an equation.

  A freshly baked loaf of bread is about 2 times higher than the unbaked dough. A baked loaf is 4.5 in. high. How high was the dough before baking? **2.25 in.**

  Let n represent the height of the unbaked dough.
  $$2n = 4.5$$

- A problem can be represented by a pattern.

  Each diagram at the right represents a triangular number. What are the next three triangular numbers?
  10, 15, 21

  1   3   6

- You can represent a problem in a table.

  What are the first four powers of 4 that when simplified have a 6 in the ones' place? $4^2, 4^4, 4^6, 4^8$

Power of 4	Simplified	Ones' Place
4^1	4	4
4^2	16	6
4^3	64	4
4^4	256	6

2 TEACH

READ ABOUT IT Make sure that students understand that the type of representation chosen often depends on the particular problem. Stress that no one representation is "correct," but that students should use the type of representation they think is most appropriate and with which they are comfortable.

TALK ABOUT IT If partners do not agree on how a problem should be represented, ask each partner to solve the problem independently. Then have partners compare solutions and discuss methods.

WRITE ABOUT IT Tell students that each problem they write must be able to be solved by the given representation.

SUMMARIZE/ASSESS **Give an example of a problem that can be represented by a pattern. Explain why the pattern is a good way to represent your problem.**

Work with a partner to show how you would represent the problem in order to solve it. Discuss the following questions.

- *Why did you represent the problem this way?*
- *Is there any other way to represent the problem?*
- *Do all the ways to represent the problem give you the same solution?*

1. Mr. Apple always cuts his homemade pies in straight cuts through the center of the pie. How many pieces would he have after 10 cuts?   **20 pieces**

2. Four students are waiting in a line to buy muffins. Ann is standing in front of Pete and behind Marie. Carl is standing in front of Marie. Who is first and who is last in line?
first: Carl; last: Pete

3. A baker's worktable has a perimeter of 12 ft. Find three different shapes that the table could be that would have a perimeter of 12 ft.   **equilateral triangle 4 ft sides; 3 ft × 3 ft, square, 2 ft × 4 ft rectangle**

4. You can go from Denver to Chicago either by plane or by train. After that, there are three ways you might go on to Minneapolis: plane, train, or bus. How many different ways are there that you might choose to go from Denver to Minneapolis?   **6 ways**

5. A school uses only two-digit numbers on its baseball uniforms. How many differently numbered uniforms can the team have using the digits 1, 2, and 3? Two of the same number can appear on a uniform.   **9 uniforms**

WRITE ABOUT IT

Write a problem that fits the representation.   **Check students' work.**

6.

Distance	30 mi	60 mi	90 mi
Time	0.5 h	1 h	1.5 h

7. $x + 34.5 = 100$

8.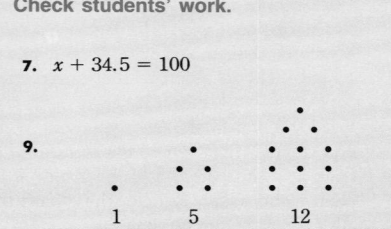

9.

```
          .
        . . .
 .    . . .  . . . . .
 1      5      12
```

3 FOLLOW-UP

PRACTICE 4-11

Represent each problem using a picture, an equation, a pattern, or a table. Then solve.

1. To send packages using the Speedee Corp. costs $1.50 for the first pound and $.75 for each additional pound. How much does it cost to send packages of 1 through 10 pounds? How much more does it cost to send one 9-lb and one 6-lb package than to send three 4-lb packages?
$1.50 more

Pounds	Cost
1	1.50
2	$1.50 + .75(2-1) = \$2.25$
3	$1.50 + .75(3-1) = \$3.00$
4	$1.50 + .75(4-1) = \$3.75$
5	$1.50 + .75(5-1) = \$4.50$
6	$1.50 + .75(6-1) = \$5.25$
7	$1.50 + .75(7-1) = \$6.00$
8	$1.50 + .75(8-1) = \$6.75$
9	$1.50 + .75(9-1) = \$7.50$
10	$1.50 + .75(10-1) = \$8.25$

2. The numbers 1, 4, and 9 are square numbers. Find the next three square numbers.
16, 25, 36

3. What is the perimeter (total distance around an object) when 20 T-shaped tiles are placed together end to end as shown?
86

4. There are 2 spinners in a game. The first spinner is labeled 1, 2, 3, 4, and 5. The second spinner has the colors red, white, and blue. How many different combinations of numbers and colors are there?
15

1, red   2, red   3, red   4, red   5, red
1, white   2, white   3, white   4, white   5, white
1, blue   2, blue   3, blue   4, blue   5, blue

5. Jackie's age is 2 less than 3 times Damon's age. Jackie is 58. How old is Damon?
Damon is 20.

n = Damon's age
3n − 2 = 58

MEETING INDIVIDUAL NEEDS

For Students Who Are . . .

Acquiring English Proficiency Pair students with an English-proficient student to determine how to represent the problems in the Talk About It section.

Gifted and Talented Have students make a table or diagram, write an equation, or draw a pattern. Then have them exchange papers and write a problem that matches the representation.

Working 2 or 3 Grades Below Level Have students use pages 12–15 of the Skills Workbook for Problem Solving Strategies.

Having Reading Difficulties Pair students with an able reader to discuss and represent the problems in the Talk About It section.

Today's Problem

Choose any four different letters, such as *DLTX*. How many four-letter combinations can you form using each letter once? *(24; students may use a list or calculate $4 \times 3 \times 2 \times 1 = 24$ combinations.)*

Lesson Organizer

Objective: Solve problems creatively.

Prior Knowledge: Students should be able to measure time and to estimate and calculate distances.

Lesson Resources:
Daily Review 4-12
Cooperative Problem Solving, Chapter 4

Two-Minute Math

If you were born in December, 1921, how old would you be today? *(Answers will vary.)*

1 PREPARE

SYMBOLIC ACTIVITY

Ask students to read the first lines of *Paul Revere's Ride* on page 120. Tell students that, according to the poem, it was 12 o'clock when Paul Revere rode into the town of Medford, 1 o'clock into Lexington, and 2 o'clock into Concord.

Based on the poem, what can you say about the distance between Medford and Lexington and the distance between Lexington and Concord? *(The distances are probably close to the same; it took Paul Revere one hour to travel from one town to the next.)*

If a person can walk about 3 mi/h, and Paul Revere's horse galloped steadily at about 2.5 times that speed, what was the approximate distance from Medford to Lexington? *(about 7.5 mi)*

WHEN YOUR STUDENTS ASK
★ WHY AM I LEARNING THIS? ★

You can connect this lesson to real life by considering the mathematical elements of poetry, such as meter.

CREATIVE PROBLEM SOLVING
Investigating Paul Revere's Ride

Listen, my children, and you shall hear
Of the midnight ride of Paul Revere,
On the eighteenth of April, in Seventy-five;
Hardly a man is now alive
Who remembers that famous day and year.

The lines above are the beginning of a famous poem called "Paul Revere's Ride" by Henry Wadsworth Longfellow. The poem tells about an important event in the history of the United States.

Work with a partner.

1. Longfellow published the poem in 1863. How old would someone have had to be at that time to "remember that famous day and year"?
   Answers will vary. Suggestion given: 93 yr
2. One account says that Paul Revere crossed the river from Boston to Charlestown where he began his ride. He traveled first to Medford, then to Arlington, and finally to Lexington. Use the map on page 121 to estimate the total distance he rode.
   Answers will vary. Suggestion given: about 14.5 mi
3. Read the stanza above to yourself. Which lines have the same end rhyme? How would this stanza be different if the ride had been at a time other than midnight? if the year of the ride had been eighty-nine? Rewrite the stanza to include these changes. Be as creative as possible.
   Check students' work.

MATH AND LITERATURE

120   LESSON 4-12

---

2 EXPLORE

Have students work with a partner.

Suppose you had been born in 1716. How old would you have been at the time of Paul Revere's ride? *(1775 − 1716 = 59 years old)*

By January of 1990, how many complete years had passed since Paul Revere's ride? *(214 complete years)*

SUMMARIZE/ASSESS   **What is another math question suggested by the poem, *Paul Revere's Ride*?** *(Questions will vary. Example: Paul Revere was about 40 years old at the time of his famous ride; in what year was he born?)*

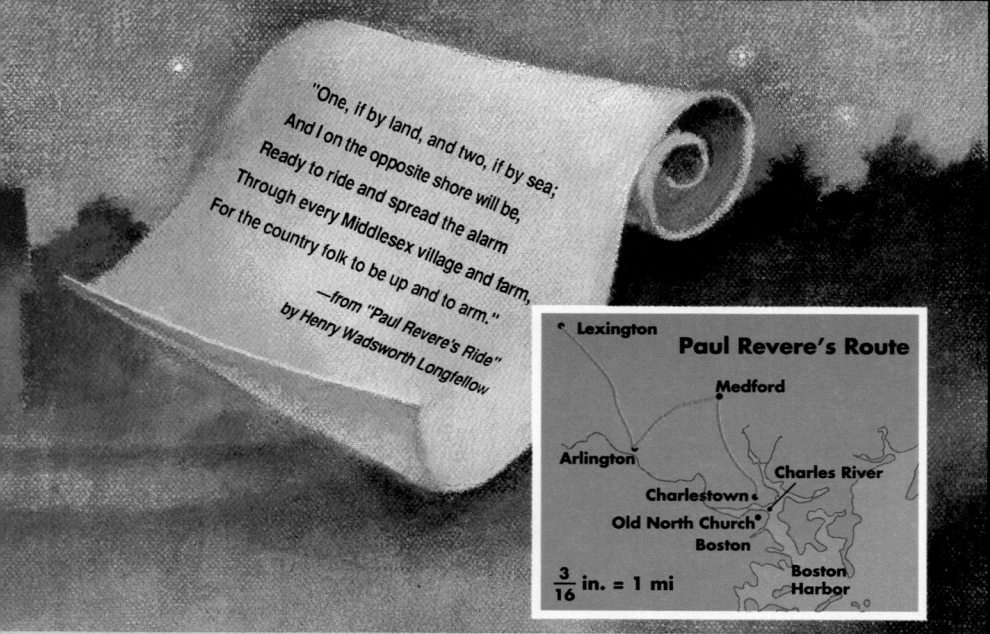

"One, if by land, and two, if by sea;
And I on the opposite shore will be,
Ready to ride and spread the alarm
Through every Middlesex village and farm,
For the country folk to be up and to arm."

—from "Paul Revere's Ride"
by Henry Wadsworth Longfellow

Paul Revere's Route

Lexington
Medford
Arlington
Charles River
Charlestown
Old North Church
Boston
Boston Harbor

$\frac{3}{16}$ in. = 1 mi

4. According to other stanzas in the poem, Revere started his ride sometime after "the moon rose over the bay." He and his horse arrived at their destination when "it was two by the village clock." If he averaged about 8 mi/h, about what time did "the moon rise over the bay"?
Answers will vary. Suggestion given: midnight

5. How many lanterns were to be hung in the tower of the Old North Church in Boston if the British troops were coming by a land route? by a water route?
1; 2

6. What river did Revere have to cross?
Charles River

7. Find the poem "Paul Revere's Ride" by Longfellow in a book of American poetry. In a short paragraph, explain what the "midnight message of Paul Revere" was.
Accept reasonable answers.

8. Think of an event that has happened in your lifetime and that involves some type of measurement (for example, distances, time, money, or weight measurements). Then write a short poem about this event. Give your poem to a classmate to read and identify the measurements.
Check students' work.

CHAPTER 4   121

MEETING INDIVIDUAL NEEDS

For Students Who Are . . .

Acquiring English Proficiency Have students work with an English-proficient student for this lesson.

Gifted and Talented Have students work together to identify popular songs or poems that have some sort of mathematical content. They can share their findings with the class, suggesting questions based on the songs or poems they have identified.

Working 2 or 3 Grades Below Level Review using a map scale to estimate distances.

Today's Problem

What three consecutive numbers less than 50 have a sum of 102?
(33 + 34 + 35 = 102)

3 FOLLOW-UP

CLASS ACTIVITY 4-12

☑ **MATERIALS CHECKLIST:** map of your city, town, or location near school

Arrange students in groups of three or four. Tell them to plan a bike trip that is the same distance as Paul Revere's ride. Give each group a map and discuss how to read mileage. Have students draw the path and determine the approximate length of time for the trip. Have groups share plans.

CHAPTER

Checkup

The chapter checkup provides a quick language and vocabulary review, a test for the chapter, and suggestions for student Learning Log entries.

Language and Vocabulary

Some key language and vocabulary ideas from this chapter are reinforced here.

Test

The test can be used either as a test or as a review of the chapter prior to your administering the test worksheets found in the Teacher's Resource Book.

The following guide will help you determine percentage scores.

Score	Percent	Score	Percent
23	100%	12	50%
22	96	11	46
21	92	10	42
20	88	9	38
19	84	8	34
18	79	7	30
17	74	6	26
16	69	5	22
15	64	4	18
14	59	3	14
13	54	2	10
		1	5

Each test has 3 sections: concepts, skills and problem solving. These sections provide students with exposure to the formats used on standardized tests.

Use this chart to identify the management objectives tested for this chapter.

Items	Management Objective	Pages
1–8	**4A** Write and evaluate expressions.	96–99
9–14	**4B** Solve equations using inverse operations.	102–105
15–20	**4C** Solve and graph inequalities.	110–113
21–23	**4D** Problem Solving: Write an equation.	106–107

122 *Chapter 4 • Chapter Checkup*

CHAPTER CHECKUP

LANGUAGE & VOCABULARY

Tell whether the price can be represented by an expression, an equation, or an inequality.

1. The price of an item plus 8% sales tax is more than $20.00.   inequality
2. the price of an item plus 8% sales tax   expression
3. The price of an item plus 8% sales tax is $10.80.   equation

TEST ✓

CONCEPTS

Write as an expression. *(pages 96–97, 100–101)*

1. a number y decreased by 31 $y - 31$
2. a number s divided by 5 $\frac{s}{5}$
3. the product of 19 and a number n $19n$
4. a number f divided by 1.3 $\frac{f}{1.3}$

Evaluate. Use $a = 4$, $b = 8$, and $c = 2$. *(pages 98–99)*

5. $9a$ 36
6. $13b - 5$ 99
7. $\frac{8c}{2}$ 8
8. $a + 3b - c$ 26

SKILLS

Solve the equation. *(pages 102–105)*

9. $d - 35 = 64$ 99
10. $203 + r = 391$ 188
11. $0.8m = 1.92$ 2.4
12. $24.26 = z - 15.1$ 39.36
13. $\frac{x}{3.1} = 19$ 58.9
14. $\frac{w}{7} = 3.25$ 22.75

Is the given value a solution to the inequality? Write *yes* or *no*. *(pages 110–111)*

15. $f + 11 < 15$; 26 no
16. $h - 3 > 12$; 17 yes
17. $k - 7 < 3$; 10 no

Graph the solution. *(pages 112–113)*   Check students' graphs.

18. $p < 9$
19. $r > 50$
20. $z < 21$

CHAPTER TEST • FORM A

(pp. 96–99) 4A

Write as an expression.

1. a number y increased by 25 $y + 25$
2. a number f divided by twelve $\frac{f}{12}$

Evaluate. Use $a = 2$, $b = 6$, and $c = 3$.

3. $5a$ 10
4. $12b - 7$ 65
5. $c + 2c - 2$ 7

Solve the equation. (pp. 100–105, 114–115) 4B

6. $d - 17 = 44$ $d = 61$
7. $165 + r = 365$ $r = 200$
8. $0.5m = 1.65$ $m = 3.3$
9. $16.4 = z - 12.6$ $z = 29$
10. $\frac{w}{6} = 4.5$ $w = 27$

Use mental math to solve the inequality. Graph the solution. (pp. 110–113) 4C

11. $p - 2 < 4$ $p < 6$

1 2 3 4 5 6 7

12. $r - 3 > 7$ $r > 10$

7 8 9 10 11 12 13

13. $z + 4 < 15$ $z < 11$

6 7 8 9 10 11 12

14. $5 + a > 9$ $a > 4$

0 1 2 3 4 5 6

15. $c - 7 < 13$ $c < 20$

15 16 17 18 19 20 21

CHAPTER TEST • FORM A

Solve. (pp. 106–107, 118–119) 4D

16. The oldest coin in a rare coin collection was minted in 1816. The coin was purchased in 1972. How old was the coin at the time of its purchase?   156 yr.

17. Last year 27,275 coins were owned by a museum. During this year 1,089 coins were added to the collection. How many coins are in the collection now?   28,364 coins

18. The museum has 8 full-time employees and 35 volunteers. Each full-time employee is paid $1,850 per month. Find the total yearly salary of the full-time employees. $177,600

19. The museum had a fund-raising picnic. The cost was $7.50 for adults and $4.00 for children. How much money was received if 240 adults and 160 children attended the picnic? $2,440

20. A football team uses only two-digit numbers on its uniforms. How many different number choices are there using only the digits 1, 2, 3, 4, and 5? Two of the same numbers can appear on a uniform.   25 choices

Solve. *(pages 102–103, 106–107)*

21. A letter carrier emptied two mailboxes on her route. She collected 173 pieces of mail from the first. From both boxes she collected 301 pieces of mail.

   a. How many pieces of mail did she collect from the first box? **173 pieces**

   b. What information is unknown? **pieces from 2nd box**

   c. Choose a variable for the unknown. Then write an equation and solve the problem. **173 + y = 301; 128**

22. Gina's backpack seemed too heavy. She removed an item that weighed 3 lb, but the pack still weighed more than 12 lb. How much did the pack weigh before she removed the item? **more than 15 lb**

Choose the correct equation and solve. *(pages 102–103)*

23. In New York City, the Lincoln Tunnel is 1,236 ft longer than the Queens Midtown Tunnel. The Queens Midtown Tunnel is 6,414 ft long. How long is the Lincoln Tunnel? **b**

   a. $l + 1{,}236 = 6{,}414$

   b. $1{,}236 + 6{,}414 = l$

Write the answers in your learning log. **Answers will vary. Suggestions given.**

1. Describe two ways an equation and an inequality are different.
   equation-one solution; inequality-solution set

2. What does it mean to solve an equation or inequality?
   find the number that makes the statement true

3. What does the open circle on the graph of an inequality mean?
   That number is not included in the solution set.

Note that the same numbers are used in Exercises 16 and 22.

CHAPTER 4   123

Problem Solving

Item 21 has 3 parts:
a. literal—this is a reading comprehension question;
b. interpretive—this involves interpretation using the facts given;
c. applied—students use a strategy or skills to find an answer.

Item 16 in the skill section and item 22 in the problem solving section use the same numbers.

This will help you informally assess how your students transfer from numerical skills to word problems.

For scoring problem solving items you may wish to use partial credit. If a student uses the correct strategy but gets a wrong answer, give the student 2 points toward the total percent score.

Learning Log

These are suggestions for writing about some topics taught in this chapter. The students keep their Learning Logs from the beginning of the school year through the end.

CHAPTER TEST • FORM **B**

(pp. 96–99) 4A

Write as an expression.

1. a number y increased by 29 $y + 29$

2. a number f multiplied by 16 $16f$

Evaluate. Use $a = 3$, $b = 12$, and $c = 4$.

3. $7a$ 21 **4.** $12b - 9$ 135 **5.** $2a + a - 2$ 7

Solve the equation. (pp. 100–105, 114–115) 4B

6. $d + 25 = 72$ $d = 47$ **7.** $108 + r = 439$ $r = 331$ **8.** $0.9m = 1.98$ $m = 2.2$

9. $23.14 = z - 13.9$ $z = 37.04$ **10.** $\frac{w}{6} = 3.5$ $w = 21$

Use mental math to solve the inequality. Graph the solution. (pp. 110–113) 4C

11. $p - 3 > 5$ $p > 8$

12. $r - 4 < 6$ $r < 10$

13. $z + 6 > 10$ $z > 4$

14. $2 + a > 7$ $a > 5$

15. $c - 9 < 11$ $c < 20$

CHAPTER TEST • FORM **B**

Solve. (pp. 106–107, 118–119) 4D

16. The oldest painting in a museum was painted in 1536. The museum purchased the painting in 1968. How old was the painting when it was purchased by the museum?   **432 yr.**

17. Last year 29,324 people visited the museum. The number of visitors this year was 3,015 more than last year. How many people visited the museum this year?   **32,339 people**

18. The museum has 6 full-time employees and 45 volunteers. The full-time employees each earn $1,750 per month. Find the total yearly salary of the full-time employees.   **$126,000**

19. The museum rented 500 chairs for use at a Memorial Day celebration. The daily rental fee on the chairs was $4 each. If the chairs were rented for two days, what was the total rental fee?   **$4,000**

20. A basketball team uses only two-digit numbers on its uniforms. How many different number choices are there using the digits 1, 2, 3, and 4? Two of the same number can appear on a uniform.   **16 choices**

Error Analysis and Remediation

Here are some common errors students make when they are writing and evaluating expressions, solving equations, and graphing and solving inequalities. The errors are listed by lesson under the appropriate management objective.

4A • WRITE AND EVALUATE EXPRESSIONS

Source of Error (Lesson 4-1)
students, given the word phrase "5 less than a number n," write the incorrect expression, "$5 - n$."

Remediation
Relate writing an expression to a real-life situation. Ask: How do you write $5 less than $15? *(15 − 5)* $5 less than n? *(n − 5)* 5 years less than 29 years? *(29 − 5)* 5 years less than n years? *(n − 5)*

4B • SOLVE EQUATIONS USING INVERSE OPERATIONS

Source of Error (Lesson 4-4)
students do not use the inverse operation to solve an equation.

Remediation
For example, students may add to solve $x + 8 = 22$ and get 30 (8 + 22 = 30). Show students that this answer is not reasonable by substituting 30 for the variable in the equation and guiding them to conclude that the inverse operation, subtraction, should be used to solve an addition equation.

Source of Error (Lesson 4-5)
students do not use the inverse operation to solve an equation.

Remediation
Write the equation $8x = 16$ on the chalkboard, and use the following number line to illustrate that division is required to solve the equation.

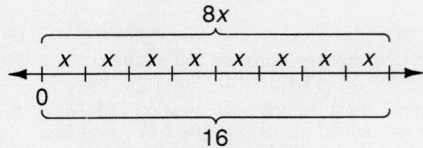

4C • SOLVE AND GRAPH INEQUALITIES

Source of Error (Lesson 4-7)
when graphing inequalities, students place the open circle to the left or to the right of the number given in the inequality.

Remediation
Stress that the open circle indicates that the number is not included as a solution. Illustrate by graphing $x > 4$ on the chalkboard. Place the open circle on 4 and the solid line to the right of 4 to represent only numbers greater than, not including, 4 are solutions.

Source of Error (Lesson 4-8)
students list numbers as solutions of inequalities.

Remediation
If, for example, students incorrectly write 5, 6, 7, 8, 9, 10, 11 as the solution to the inequality $n + 8 < 20$, ask: Is 3 a solution? *(yes)* $4\frac{1}{2}$? *(yes)* 11.48? *(yes)* Explain to students that they need to write the solution as $n < 12$ so that all possible numbers are included.

4D • PROBLEM SOLVING: WRITE AN EQUATION

Source of Error (Lesson 4-6)
students have difficulty writing an equation to represent a problem.

Remediation
Present students with this simple problem:

> A small theater has 360 seats. If there are 12 rows with the same number of seats in each row, how many seats are in each row? *(20 seats)*

Then write the equation $12s = 360$ on the chalkboard. Explain step by step how the equation represents the problem. Point out that the equation balances because both $12s$ and 360 represent the number of seats in the theater.

Answers

Page 97 For exercises 19–30, answers will vary. Suggestions given.

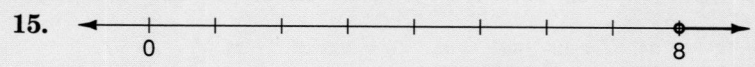
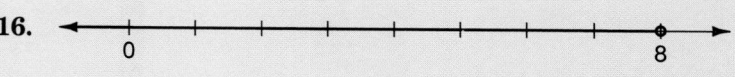
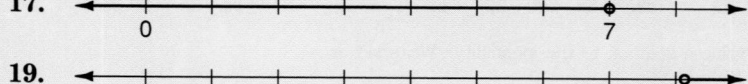
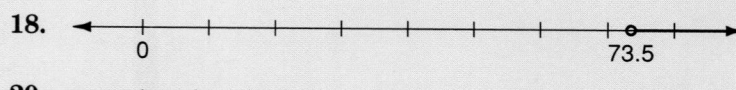

19. a number x decreased by 18

20. 4 times a number m

21. 29 increased by a number q

22. 27 divided by a number z

23. 5 more than a number n

24. the product of 16 and a number w

25. a number z divided by 12

26. a number b less than 23

27. 24 divided by a number r

28. 29 times a number y

29. a number q divided by 19

30. a number x decreased by y

Page 111

15. number line: point at 8 (open), starting at 0

16. number line: point at 8 (open), starting at 0

17. number line: point at 7 (open), starting at 0

18. number line: point at 73.5 (open), starting at 0

19. number line: point at 42 (open), starting at 0

20. number line: point at 975 (open), starting at 0

21. number line: point at 12.5 (open), starting at 0

22. number line: point at 5 (closed), starting at 0

Page 115

12.

Number (n)	1	2	3	4	5	6	7	8
Cost (c)	$1.75	$3.50	$5.25	$7.00	$8.75	$10.50	$12.25	$14.00

13.

n	1	2	3	4	5	6
e	2	4	6	8	10	12

14.

n	1	2	3	4	5	6
c	$0.75	$1.50	$2.25	$3.00	$3.75	$4.50

Page 116

5.

b	1	2	3	4	5	6	7	8
f	32	64	96	128	160	192	224	256

Extra Practice

This page provides extra practice of all the major chapter objectives. Use this page after the chapter has been taught to reinforce the chapter skills. Page references are provided for each group of items so that students can easily look back at the appropriate lesson for additional support.

Write as an expression. Let n be the unknown value. *(pages 96–97)*

1. a number plus 3 $n + 3$

2. a number divided by 8 $\frac{n}{8}$

3. a number divided by itself $\frac{n}{n}$

4. 2 increased by a number $2 + n$

5. the product of 11 and a number $11n$

6. 75 less than a number $n - 75$

7. a number added to itself $n + n$

8. a number multiplied by itself n^2

Evaluate. Use $r = 6$, $s = 8$, and $t = 10$. *(pages 98–99)*

9. $3r + 5$ 23

10. $\frac{r}{2} - 3$ 0

11. $s - 5 + t$ 13

12. $2t - 1$ 19

13. $(3 \times s) + 2$ 26

14. $\frac{(s+4)}{2}$ 6

15. s^2 64

16. $t^2 + 9$ 109

Solve. *(pages 102–105)*

17. $z + 172 = 300$ 128

18. $22 = x - 18$ 40

19. $108 = 86 + y$ 22

20. $r - 35.4 = 18.7$ 54.1

21. $45.7 = 26.8 + a$ 18.9

22. $31 = c - 13.2$ 44.2

23. $6x = 72$ 12

24. $\frac{m}{9} = 12$ 108

25. $21f = 105$ 5

26. $\frac{h}{3} = 19$ 57

27. $\frac{w}{0.9} = 8$ 7.2

28. $4.5n = 90$ 20

29. $\frac{x}{23} = 253$ 5,819

30. $3n = 22.95$ 7.65

Is the given value a solution to the inequality? Write *yes* or *no*.
(pages 112–113)

31. $r + 7 < 19$; 7 yes

32. $a - 12 > 8$; 24 yes

33. $13 + b > 24$; 15 yes

34. $d - 1 < 32$; 37 no

35. $n + 102 > 185$; 80 no

36. $m - 15 < 50$; 27 yes

Graph the solution. *(pages 110–111)* **Check students' graphs.**

37. $x > 12$

38. $y < 24$

39. $m < 8.5$

40. $c > 15.5$

Solve. *(pages 106–107, 118–119)*

41. A school had $2,070 for special events. If $345 were spent on each event the school sponsored during the year, how many events were held? **6 events or less**

42. When 3 friends stood on a scale, their total weight was 280 lb. When 2 got off, the scale showed 98 lb. If the 2 friends who got off each weighed the same amount, how much did each weigh? **91 lb**

Who Uses Functions?

Many real situations exist where you might expect a function rule to apply, but it does not. For example, a bakery might sell one bagel for $.35. If a function rule, such as "cost = $.35 times the number of bagels" were used, you could predict the cost of any number of bagels.

However, stores often charge less when more than one item is purchased. Two bagels might cost $.65. When this happens, you cannot use a function rule to determine the cost of a larger number of bagels.

Visit some stores that post the prices for different numbers of the same item. Try a bookstore, a sporting goods store, or a take-out food shop. Write the prices charged for different numbers of the same item. Then decide whether a function rule exists, and if so, what the rule is. **Check students' work.**

Writing Temperature Equations

Newspapers report temperatures in cities throughout the United States. You can use this information to practice writing and reading equations. Work with a partner to choose ten cities from the weather page of today's newspaper. Be sure that each city had a different high temperature yesterday.

Use ten index cards. For each city, write an equation that names yesterday's high temperature on the card. Then write the city's name on the back of the card. When you have completed ten cards, list each city you have used and its temperature on a sheet of paper.

For example, if the high temperature in Philadelphia was 78°F, let 78 be the variable y. You could identify Philadelphia by an equation such as $y + 12 = 90$, $y - 19 = 59$, $3y = 234$, or $\frac{y}{26} = 3$.

Exchange the cards and the list with another team. Try to decide what cities are on their list. Look at the back of the card to check. **Check students' work.**

Enrichment

This page contains activities that provide extension and enrichment for all levels of students. Depending on the needs of your students, you may wish to assign an activity from this page at certain points during the chapter, or you may wish to use this page when the entire chapter has been completed.

Who Uses Functions?

Before students begin this activity, you may wish to have them review function rules on pages 116–117. Suggest that students record the data from their visits in a table or chart.

Writing Temperature Equations
(COOPERATIVE)

Suggest that students vary their equations so that some require addition, others subtraction, multiplication, or division.

CHAPTER 4

Cumulative Review

The Cumulative Review focuses on skills covered in previous chapters. All important skills are reviewed on a cyclic basis.

If students are having difficulty with particular groups of exercises, refer to the chart for follow-up work.

Find the answer.

1. 53 **d**
   $\times$ 27
   a. 457
   b. 477
   c. 1,411
   d. none of these

2. 5.94 **b**
   $\times$ 3.6
   a. 2.1384
   b. 21.384
   c. 213.84
   d. none of these

3. 0.0072 **c**
   $\times$ 0.12
   a. 0.0864
   b. 0.00864
   c. 0.000864
   d. none of these

4. $65\overline{)3,218}$ **b**
   a. 46 R26
   b. 49 R33
   c. 44 R58
   d. none of these

5. $91\overline{)47.32}$ **a**
   a. 0.52
   b. 52
   c. 0.052
   d. none of these

6. $172.04 \div 68 =$ **c**
   a. 0.253
   b. 25.3
   c. 2.53
   d. none of these

7. $m - 5.2 = 14.9$ **b**
   $m = $ ▦
   a. 9.7
   b. 20.1
   c. 8.7
   d. none of these

8. $30x = 165$ **a**
   $x = $ ▦
   a. 5.5
   b. 55
   c. 4,950
   d. none of these

9. $\frac{w}{2.5} = 40$ **c**
   $w = $ ▦
   a. 16
   b. 0.0625
   c. 100
   d. none of these

What is the best estimate?

10. $32 \times 706 =$ **b**
    a. 2,100
    b. 21,000
    c. 210,000
    d. none of these

11. $31\overline{)1,217}$ **c**
    a. 400
    b. 4
    c. 40
    d. none of these

12. $59.8 \div 1.89 =$ **a**
    a. 30
    b. 3
    c. 0.03
    d. none of these

What is the equivalent value? Use $a = 3$, $b = 4$, and $c = 7$.

13. $5a + a + 7$ **d**
    a. 15
    b. 22
    c. 18
    d. none of these

14. $b^2 - 3$ **c**
    a. 5
    b. 15
    c. 13
    d. none of these

15. $3 \times (c + 4)$ **a**
    a. 33
    b. 25
    c. 19
    d. none of these

126   CUMULATIVE REVIEW

Items	Management Objectives	Where Taught	Reteaching Options	Extra Practice Options
1, 4, 10	**3B** Multiply and divide whole numbers.	pp. 64–65, 68–69	TE/RA 3-3 and 3-5	TRB/PW 3-3 and 3-5
2–3, 5–6	**3C** Multiply and divide decimals.	pp. 66–67, 70–71	TRB/RW 3-4 and 3-6	TRB/PW 3-4 and 3-6
7–9	**4B** Solve equations using inverse operations.	pp. 102–105	TRB/RW 4-4 and 4-5	TRB/PW 4-4 and 4-5
11–12	**3D** Estimate quotients.	pp. 82–83	TRB/RW 3-11	TRB/PW 3-11
13–15	**4A** Write and evaluate expressions.	pp. 98–99	TE/RA 4-2	TRB/PW 4-2

Strategies may vary. Suggestions given.
Remember the strategies and types of problems you have had so far. Solve, if possible.

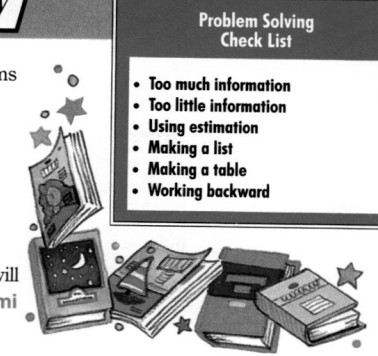

> **Problem Solving Check List**
> - Too much information
> - Too little information
> - Using estimation
> - Making a list
> - Making a table
> - Working backward

1. Sharon has been driving for 3 h. If from now on she averages 50 mi/h, she will complete her 235-mi trip in 2 more hours.

   a. How many hours has Sharon already driven? **3 h**

   b. If she can average 50 mi/h, how far will she drive during the next 2 h? **100 mi**

   c. How far has she driven during the first 3 h? **estimation; 135 mi**

2. José bought an old baseball card. During the first three years, the card increased $8 in value, then dropped $5, then increased $12. The card is now worth $27. How much did José pay for it?
working backward; $12

3. Sally bought some books costing $3 each and some magazines costing $2 each. She spent exactly $18. What combinations of books and magazines could she have bought?
list; 2 books, 6 magazines; 4 books, 3 magazines

4. Headrick has decided to wait to buy a new CD player until the bank pays him interest on his savings account. If he has 86 d to wait, about how many weeks must Headrick wait?
estimation; about 12 wk

5. Dinner for 4 friends at Jack O's Tacos cost $23.40. Tax and tip combined added 20% to the bill. To the nearest dollar, what was the total cost of the dinner?
estimation; $28

6. On the way to school, Mario lent a friend half his money. Then he spent $.50 on orange juice. If he has $.75 left, how much money did Mario have when he left home?
working backward; $2.50

7. What is the sum of all the three-digit numbers you can make using the digits 2, 3, and 4 if you do not repeat a digit in a number?
list; 1,998

8. Dorcas received $4.65 change after paying for two magazines with a $10 bill. One of the magazines cost $1.25 more than the other. What was the total cost of the two magazines?
too much information; $5.35

9. Seattle is west of Kansas City. Denver is west of Kansas City but east of Seattle. Cleveland is east of Kansas City but west of New York. What is the correct order of the cities from west to east?
table; Seattle, Denver, Kansas City, Cleveland, New York

Problem Solving Review

This page focuses on problem solving strategies and types learned in this and previous chapters. A problem solving checklist lists some of the strategies students may use to solve the problems on this page.

Technology

This page is designed to provide calculator or computer experiences for all levels of students. The calculator or computer logo indicates the type of activity.

You may wish to assign these activities after the chapter has been taught or during the course of the chapter, depending on your needs and those of your students.

A Shady Deal

Suggest that students use mental math and number sense to estimate some of the values. They can check their estimates with the calculator.

Many Times
(COOPERATIVE)

Tell students that accuracy in entering the numbers and multiplication symbols is as important as speed.

What's Your Guess?
(COOPERATIVE)

Provide a hint by asking: Since the product has a 5 in the ones' place, what does this tell you about one of the two numbers? *(It is divisible by 5.)*

Software for this activity may be found in Houghton Mifflin Math Activities Courseware, Grade 7.

A SHADY DEAL

Copy the table. Find the hidden number by shading each area in which the value of the expression is 150. **Hidden number is 4.**

Let $a = 10$, $b = 25$, and $c = 6$.

150 $5a + 10a$	$3c + a$	150 $100 + 5a$	$4a + 7c$
150 $8b - 5a$	$30a$	150 $30a - 6b$	$2a$
150 $5a + 4b$	$100 + 2b$	150 bc	150 $20a - 2b$
$10b$	$b + 5$	150 $90 + 10c$	$10b - 5c$
$7b$	$40c$	150 $25c$	$8b$

MANY TIMES

Play in pairs. At a signal, make as many true statements as you can by inserting one or more multiplication symbols between two digits. Use a calculator to check. Record your results. The player who finishes first is the winner.

1. $(2\ 2)(2\ 2)(2) = 968$

2. $(2\ 2\ 2)(2\ 2) = 4,884$

3. $(3\ 3)(3)(3)(3) = 891$

4. $(5\ 5\ 5)(5\ 5)(5) = 152,625$

WHAT'S YOUR GUESS?

In the computer game *Guess and Test*, you solve word problems by first guessing and then checking. This pencil-and-paper activity will sharpen your problem solving skills. Play with a partner. Each player makes a copy of the chart. Read the clues. Then guess and check. The player who gets the two numbers in the fewest guesses is the winner. See below.

Clues:
a. The sum of the two numbers is 112.
b. Their product is 2,775.
37 and 75

Guesses	Tests	
	Sum	Product
#1 _____		
#2 _____		

Discuss how you made your guesses.
Make clues for other numbers for your partner to solve.

This game is available on computer disk in Houghton Mifflin *Mathematics Activities Courseware.*

Software Activities

activity 1 • RUNNERS

MATERIALS: database program, calculators, almanacs

Procedure: For the data below, have students create a database file and modify the time so that it is expressed in seconds to hundredths of a second. Help students write and solve equations to see which race was the fastest. For example, to compare the speed of the 100 and 200 meter races, use: 9.92T = 100 and 19.72S = 200. Students solve the equations with a calculator. The speed is then entered into the file and sorted to order. Ask students which speed is the fastest in their file?

Racer	Country	Distance	Time (min:sec)	Speed (D/S)
C. Lewis	USA	100	9.92	
P. Mennca	Italy	200	19.72	
B. Reynolds	USA	400	43.29	
S. Coe	Great Britain	800	1:41	
S. Coe	Great Britain	1,000	2:13	

Follow-up: Have students expand the file for long distance track events. Students should perform the same calculations for the new data. **Which event had the fastest speed?**

activity 2 • EVALUATING EXPRESSIONS

MATERIALS: BASIC programming

Procedure: This program will evaluate an expression when students enter values for A, B, and C. Have students predict the value of the expression $3 \times A + 2(B + C)$ when $A = 3$, $B = 4$ and $C = 6$. Students should confirm their answer by running the program. Students should evaluate the expression using other values for the variables. They should check their answers by using the program.

```
10 PRINT "ENTER VALUES FOR A, B
   AND C ";
20 PRINT "TO EVALUATE AN
   EXPRESSION. "
30 PRINT "PUT COMMAS BETWEEN YOUR
   NUMBERS. "
40 INPUT A,B,C
50 PRINT "WHAT IS THE VALUE OF ";
60 PRINT "3 *"A "+ 2 * ("B "+"
   C ")"
70 INPUT E
80 LET V=3*A+2 * (B+C)
90 IF V=E GOTO 110
100 PRINT "TRY AGAIN ":GOTO 60
110 PRINT "CORRECT "
```

Follow-up: Have students change the expression to be evaluated and run the program several times.

HOUGHTON MIFFLIN SOFTWARE

Easy Graph. Boston, MA: Houghton Mifflin Company, 1987. For Apple II, Commodore, IBM.

EduCalc. Boston, MA: Houghton Mifflin Company, 1990. For Apple II, Commodore, IBM.

Friendly Filer. Boston, MA: Houghton Mifflin Company, 1989. For Apple II, Commodore, IBM.

Mathematics Activities Courseware. Boston, MA: Houghton Mifflin Company, 1983. For Apple II, IBM.

OTHER SOFTWARE

Algebra: Equation-Solving Skills. Northbrook, IL: Word Associates, Inc., 1986. For IBM.

AppleWorks. Santa Clara, CA: Claris Corporation, 1983–89. For Apple II.

Equation Math. St. Paul, MN: MECC, 1989. For Apple II.

Expression Writer. Fairfield, CT: HRM/Queue Software, Inc., 1983. For Apple II.

Number Capers. Fairfield, CT: Intellectual Software/Queue Software, Inc., 1989. For Apple II.

The Children's Writing and Publishing Center. Freemont, CA: The Learning Company, 1988. For Apple II.

Number Theory and Fraction Concepts

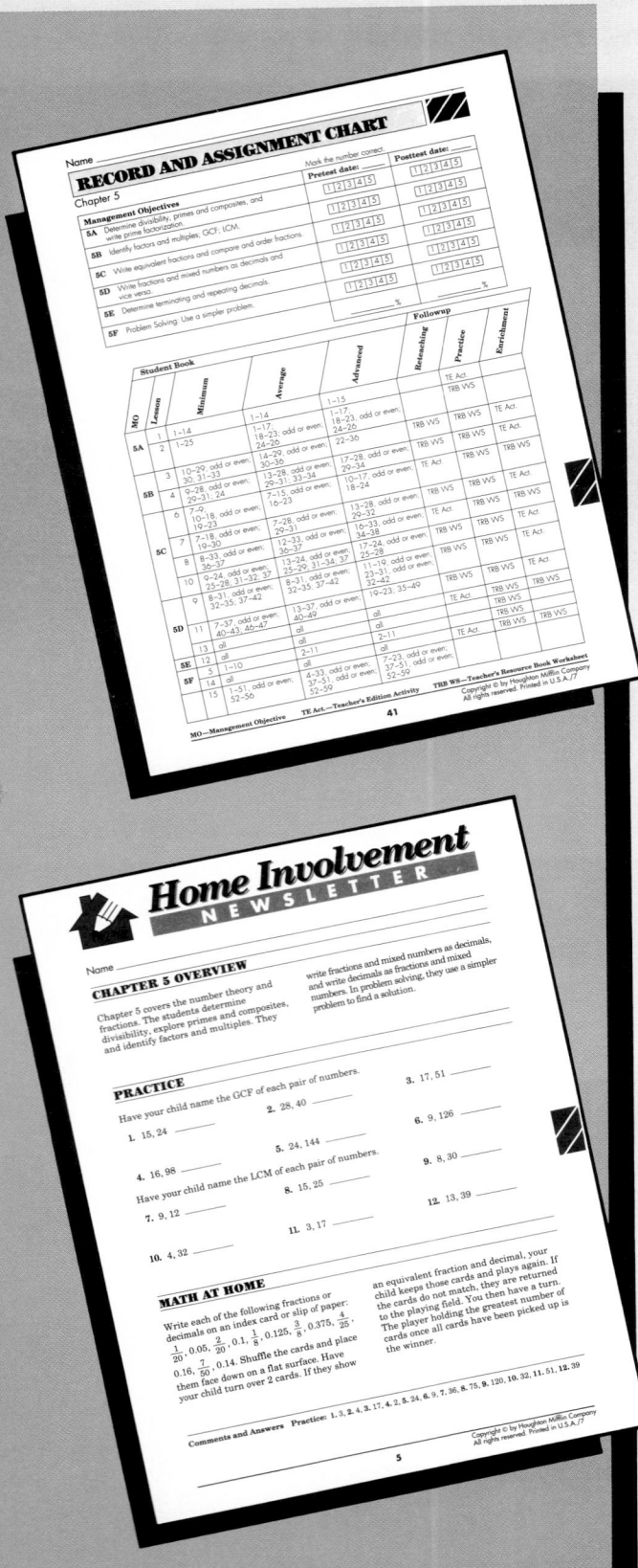

The first part of this chapter focuses on number theory. Students explore factors, divisibility rules, and prime factorization. The concepts of greatest common factor (GCF) and least common multiple (LCM) are taught to prepare students for writing equivalent fractions.

The second part of this chapter reviews the meaning of fractions and develops skills that students need to add and subtract fractions. Students are taught how to write equivalent fractions, name fractions in lowest terms, and compare and order fractions and mixed numbers. The relationship among fractions, mixed numbers, and decimals is also developed.

Problem solving is extended to include interpreting nonnumerical graphs and investigating a simpler but related problem to solve a more complex problem.

Management Objectives

5A Determine divisibility, primes and composites, and write prime factorizations.
5B Identify factors and multiples; GCF; LCM.
5C Write equivalent fractions and compare and order fractions.
5D Write fractions and mixed numbers as decimals and write decimals as fractions and mixed numbers.
5E Determine terminating and repeating decimals.
5F Problem Solving: Use a simpler problem.

Assignments for different achievement levels are provided on the Record and Assignment Chart in the Teacher's Resource Book.

Vocabulary

factors, page 130
prime, page 132
composite, page 132
prime factorization, page 133
factor tree, page 133
common factors, greatest common factor (GCF), page 134
multiple, least common multiple (LCM), page 136
equivalent fractions, page 144
lowest terms, page 146
mixed number, page 148
least common denominator (LCD), page 150
terminating decimal, page 154
repeating decimal, page 154

Home Involvement

As you begin to teach this chapter, give each student a copy of the Home Involvement Newsletter for this chapter.

This newsletter provides parents with
■ an overview of the chapter
■ suggestions for practicing some of the skills in the chapter
■ an at-home activity to do with their child, applying the skills taught in the chapter.

Management Chart

Management Objectives	Lesson/Pages	Student Not Successful	Student Needs More Practice	Student Successful	Pacing Range
5A Determine divisibility, primes and composites, and write prime factorizations.	5-1/130-131			TE/CA 5-1	2 days
	5-2/132-133		TRB/PW 5-2		
5B Identify factors and multiples; GCF; LCM.	5-3/134-135	TRB/RW 5-3	TRB/PW 5-3	TE/EA 5-3	2 days
	5-4/136-137	TRB/RW 5-4	TRB/PW 5-4 CSP FBS Sks 8, 9	TE/EA 5-4 MAC 8 Activity 3	
5C Write equivalent fractions and compare and order fractions.	5-6/142-143	TE/RA 5-6	TRB/PW 5-6	TRB/EW 5-6	4 days
	5-7/144-145	TRB/RW 5-7	TRB/PW 5-7 CT Unit 2 Obj. 3.1	TE/EA 5-7 MAC 8 Activity 7	
	5-8/146-147	TE/RA 5-8	TRB/PW 5-8	TRB/EW 5-8	
	5-10/150-151	TRB/RW 5-10	TRB/PW 5-10	TE/EA 5-10	
5D Write fractions and mixed numbers as decimals and vice versa.	5-9/148-149	TRB/RW 5-9	TRB/PW 5-9	TE/EA 5-9	3-4 days
	5-11/152-153	TRB/RW 5-11	TRB/PW 5-11 CSP FBS Sks 13-15 CSP Dec. Sks 3-4 CT Unit 2 Obj. 2.2	TE/EA 5-11 MAC 6 Activity 9	
	5-13/156-157	TE/RA 5-13	TRB/PW 5-13	TRB/EW 5-13	
5E Determine terminating and repeating decimals.	5-12/154-155		TRB/PW 5-12		1 day
5F Problem Solving: Use a simpler problem.	5-14/158-159	TE/RA 5-14	TRB/PW 5-14	TRB/EW 5-14	2 days
	5-5/138-139		TRB/PW 5-5		
Mixed Review	5-15/160-161				
Chapter Checkups	140-141, 162-163				
Extra Practice	164				
Enrichment	165				
Cumulative Review/ Problem Solving Review	166-167				
Technology	168				

TE = Teacher's Edition
TRB = Teacher's Resource Book
RW = Reteaching Worksheet
RA = Reteaching Activity
EA = Enrichment Activity
EW = Enrichment Worksheet
PW = Practice Worksheet
CA = Classroom Activity

*Other Available Items
MAC = Mathematics Activities Courseware
CSP = Computational Skills Program
CT = Computer Tutor

Manipulative Planning Guide

This is a complete list of manipulatives and materials needed for Chapter 5.

Materials for Manipulatives	TE Activities (INTRODUCE)	Student Book Lesson
Teaching Aid 2* for each student	Lesson 5-13	
Teaching Aid 3* for each student or pair	Lessons 5-1, 5-2, 5-7	Lessons 5-1, 5-2, 5-7
Teaching Aid 4* or fraction bars for each student	Lessons 5-6, 5-9	
Math Connection Transparency		Lessons 5-8, 5-10
Construction paper, 12 squares per group	Lesson 5-1	
Construction paper, one package per pair		
Calculator for each student/pair of students	Lesson 5-12	Lessons 5-1, 5-7, 5-10, 5-11, 5-12, 5-13, 5-14
Metric ruler for each student	Lessons 5-4, 5-13	Lesson 5-13
Line graph from newspaper	Lesson 5-5	
One ream of paper per pair		
Small boxes or bags of crackers, popcorn, or nuts		
Blank cubes		
Two-sided counters, 100 per group		
Index cards, 100 per group		
Counters		
Clock or watch with second hand		
Recipes, several per pair		

*Teaching Aids are found in the Teacher's Resource Book.

CONCRETE

Using manipulatives and verbalizing about a concept. No symbols.

Teacher Edition Activities	Student Book
At this grade level the skills of this chapter are taught at the connecting and symbolic stages.	

Learning Stages

The concepts and skills in Chapter 5 are presented through these learning stages.

Enrichment	Reteaching	In the Houghton Mifflin Manipulative Kit (yes/no)	In the Houghton Mifflin Overhead Kit?
			Yes
			Yes
	Lesson 5-8	Yes	Yes
			Yes
	Lesson 5-13		
Lesson 5-3			Available separately
	Lesson 5-13	Yes	
	Lesson 5-13		
Lesson 5-13			
Lesson 5-1		Yes	Yes
Lesson 5-4	Lesson 5-6	Yes	
Lessons 5-4, 5-9, 5-11			
	Lesson 5-7	Yes	
Lesson 5-9			
Lesson 5-10			

CONNECTING

5¢ 9cm² $\frac{1}{3}$

Making a connection between manipulatives and symbols.

Teacher Edition Activities	Student Book
Lessons 5-1, 5-2, 5-4, 5-6, 5-7, 5-9, 5-10, 5-13	Lessons 5-1, 5-6, 5-7

SYMBOLIC

$.05 $A=9cm²$ $1 - \frac{2}{3} = \frac{1}{3}$

Using numbers or symbols. No manipulatives or pictures of manipulatives.

Teacher Edition Activities	Student Book
Lessons 5-3, 5-5, 5-8, 5-11, 5-12, 5-14	Lessons 5-2 through 5-5, 5-7 through 5-14

CHAPTER 5

Additional Activities

COOPERATIVE LEARNING RESOURCE ACTIVITIES

Through cooperative learning activities, students learn by interacting with one another in small groups. These cooperative activities provide students with motivating settings for making connections, investigations, and problem solving situations.

The cooperative connections are interdisciplinary problem-solving projects. Each student has a particular job that helps lead the group to complete the project. For the cooperative investigations students work in pairs for investigations involving data collection and analysis. The cooperative problem solving activities encourage the sharing of ideas and information. Students work in groups of four to solve a problem. Students are each assigned a clue and work together to find a common solution.

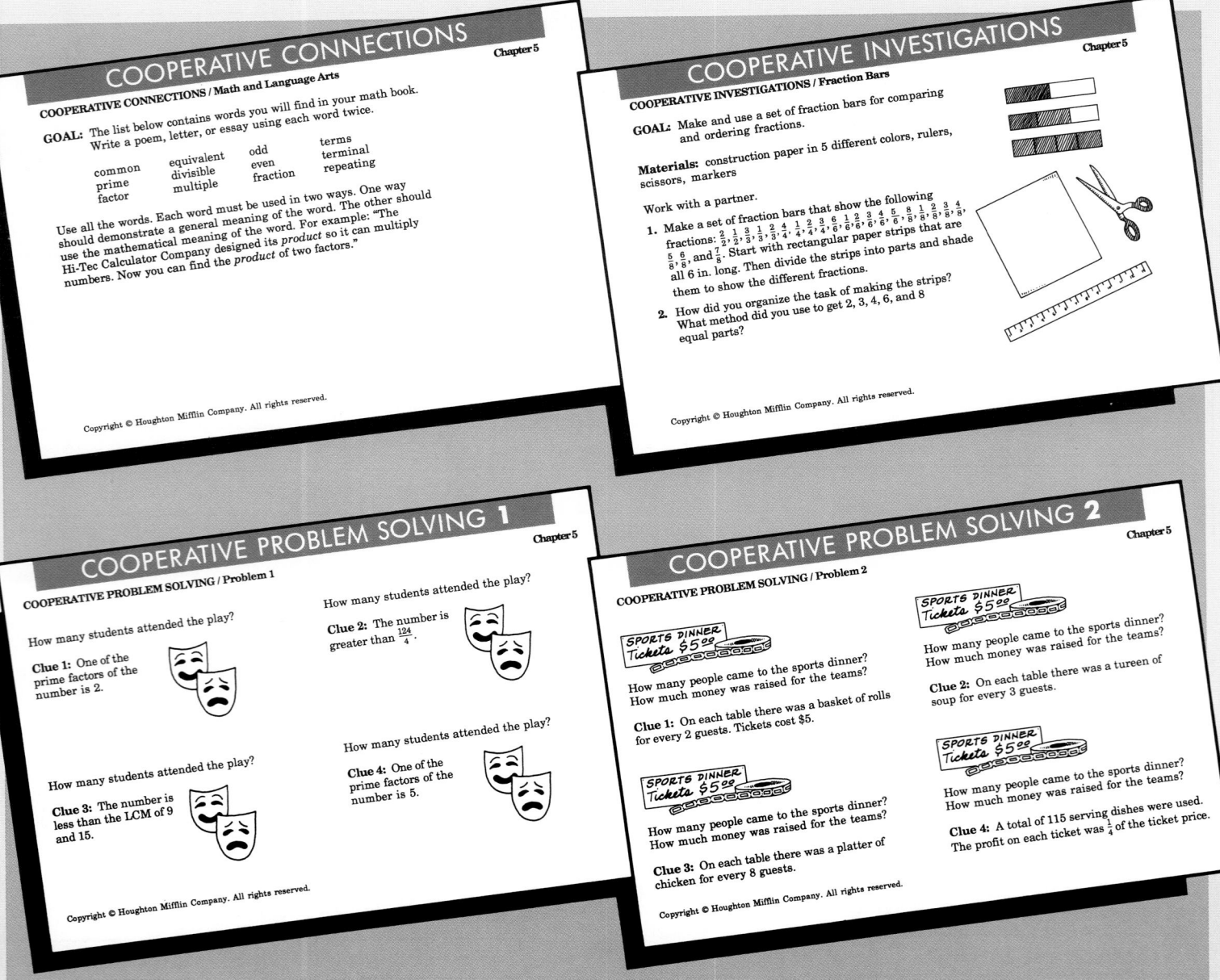

COOPERATIVE CONNECTIONS   Chapter 5

COOPERATIVE CONNECTIONS / Math and Language Arts

GOAL: The list below contains words you will find in your math book. Write a poem, letter, or essay using each word twice.

common	equivalent	odd	terms
prime	divisible	even	terminal
factor	multiple	fraction	repeating

Use all the words. Each word must be used in two ways. One way should demonstrate a general meaning of the word. The other should use the mathematical meaning of the word. For example: "The Hi-Tec Calculator Company designed its *product* so it can multiply numbers. Now you can find the *product* of two factors."

Copyright © Houghton Mifflin Company. All rights reserved.

COOPERATIVE INVESTIGATIONS   Chapter 5

COOPERATIVE INVESTIGATIONS / Fraction Bars

GOAL: Make and use a set of fraction bars for comparing and ordering fractions.

Materials: construction paper in 5 different colors, rulers, scissors, markers

Work with a partner.

1. Make a set of fraction bars that show the following fractions: $\frac{2}{2}, \frac{1}{3}, \frac{3}{3}, \frac{1}{4}, \frac{2}{4}, \frac{3}{4}, \frac{1}{6}, \frac{2}{6}, \frac{3}{6}, \frac{4}{6}, \frac{5}{6}, \frac{1}{8}, \frac{2}{8}, \frac{3}{8}, \frac{4}{8}, \frac{5}{8}, \frac{6}{8}$, and $\frac{7}{8}$. Start with rectangular paper strips that are all 6 in. long. Then divide the strips into parts and shade them to show the different fractions.

2. How did you organize the task of making the strips? What method did you use to get 2, 3, 4, 6, and 8 equal parts?

Copyright © Houghton Mifflin Company. All rights reserved.

COOPERATIVE PROBLEM SOLVING 1   Chapter 5

COOPERATIVE PROBLEM SOLVING / Problem 1

How many students attended the play?

Clue 1: One of the prime factors of the number is 2.

How many students attended the play?

Clue 2: The number is greater than $\frac{124}{4}$.

How many students attended the play?

Clue 3: The number is less than the LCM of 9 and 15.

How many students attended the play?

Clue 4: One of the prime factors of the number is 5.

Copyright © Houghton Mifflin Company. All rights reserved.

COOPERATIVE PROBLEM SOLVING 2   Chapter 5

COOPERATIVE PROBLEM SOLVING / Problem 2

SPORTS DINNER Tickets $5.00

How many people came to the sports dinner? How much money was raised for the teams?

Clue 1: On each table there was a basket of rolls for every 2 guests. Tickets cost $5.

SPORTS DINNER Tickets $5.00

How many people came to the sports dinner? How much money was raised for the teams?

Clue 3: On each table there was a platter of chicken for every 8 guests.

SPORTS DINNER Tickets $5.00

How many people came to the sports dinner? How much money was raised for the teams?

Clue 2: On each table there was a tureen of soup for every 3 guests.

SPORTS DINNER Tickets $5.00

How many people came to the sports dinner? How much money was raised for the teams?

Clue 4: A total of 115 serving dishes were used. The profit on each ticket was $\frac{1}{4}$ of the ticket price.

Copyright © Houghton Mifflin Company. All rights reserved.

GAMES

PRIME TIME   (For use after Lesson 5-2)

Objective: Identify prime numbers.

☑ **MATERIALS CHECKLIST:** number cube (1-6) and spinner for each team of three players

Form teams of three players. Each team needs a number cube and a spinner divided into six equal sections numbered 4 through 9. One player spins twice to generate two numbers and names their product. The second player tosses the number cube, then adds and subtracts the number tossed to the product to get two numbers. For example, spins of 4 and 8 result in the product 32; a toss of 3 leads to 35 (32 + 3) and 29 (32 − 3). The third player identifies any prime numbers, in this case, 29. Players check each other's work and list every new prime on a sheet of paper. The players change roles, and the process is repeated. The team with the most primes when time is called is the winner.

FRACTION ORDER   (For use after Lesson 5-10)

Objective: Compare fractions.

☑ **MATERIALS CHECKLIST:** 10 index cards cut in half for each group of four students

Have each group of four students write the following numbers on their cards, one per card: 1, 1, 2, 2, 3, 4, 5, 6, 7, 8, 9, 10, 11, 12, 14, 15, 16, 18, 20, 24. Students in each group should form two teams of two. The cards are mixed and placed face down. The players from Team A draw four cards and use them to form two fractions less than 1. For example, the numbers 2, 5, 1, and 12 could be used to form $\frac{1}{2}$ and $\frac{5}{12}$. The members from Team B must name the greater fraction. If the members of Team B answer correctly, they get one point; if not, the point goes to Team A. The teams switch roles, and the procedure is repeated. The team with more points at the end wins.

BULLETIN BOARD

Display simple treasure chests. Write five numbers on each chest, and label each chest with a letter from the word *PRIMES*. Students pick one chest at a time and identify the prime numbers. Encourage students to use divisibility rules and a guess and check strategy. (*The following numbers are primes: P-11, 71, 79; R-all; I-2, 47, 397; M-41, 131, 257; E-7, 23, 491; S-19, 523*).

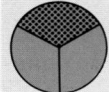

Alternative Assessment

In addition to the paper and pencil tests available with this program, the following items can help you assess critical thinking as well as your students' ability to solve problems in a wide variety of ways.

Open-ended Problem

Students were asked to write the fraction(s) represented in the drawing. One of the students wrote $\frac{1}{3}, \frac{2}{3}, \frac{1}{2}, \frac{2}{1}, \frac{3}{3}$.
Explain what you think each fraction that the student wrote represents.

Teacher Notes

$\frac{1}{3} = \frac{\text{shaded pieces}}{\text{total number of pieces}}$ $\frac{2}{3} = \frac{\text{unshaded pieces}}{\text{total number of pieces}}$

$\frac{1}{2} = \frac{\text{shaded pieces}}{\text{unshaded pieces}}$ $\frac{2}{1} = \frac{\text{unshaded pieces}}{\text{shaded pieces}}$

$\frac{3}{3} = \frac{\text{sum of shaded and unshaded pieces}}{\text{total number of pieces}}$

Group Writing Activity (See p. T24.)

A classroom has 36 individual desks. The desks can be moved so that the students can work in equal groups. List all possible grouping arrangements.

Teacher Notes

1. 2 groups of 18–each group could have 10 rulers.
2. 18 groups of 2–each group could have 1 ruler and 2 rulers would be left.
3. 3 groups of 12–each group could have 6 rulers and 2 rulers would be left.
4. 12 groups of 3–each group could have 1 ruler and 8 rulers would be left.
5. 4 groups of 9–each group could have 5 rulers.
6. 9 groups of 4–each group could have 2 rulers and 2 rulers would be left.
7. 6 groups of 6–each group could have 3 rulers and 2 rulers would be left.

Individual Writing Activity

If a classroom set of rulers has 20 rulers, which grouping arrangement of 36 desks would make it easier for 36 students to share the rulers? (Answers will vary.)

Portfolios

Portfolios can provide information about a student's growth in mathematical understanding over a period of time. They can help you make instructional decisions as well as become a vehicle for communicating with parents. The students' work involving the open-ended problem and writing activity suggested on this page along with work on the Critical Thinking feature on page 135, the Write About It exercise on page 139, the Learning Log exercises on pages 141 and 163, the Mental Math feature on page 151, and the Create Your Own exercise on page 161 could be included in portfolios.

You can use the last Teaching Aid to gain insight about your students' attitudes regarding mathematics and its relevance. This activity will be recommended again in chapters 10 and 15. It will help you establish an ongoing dialogue with your students as they progress through the school year.

NUMBER THEORY
AND FRACTION CONCEPTS 5

DID YOU KNOW . . . ?
Tennis was first played in France nearly 900 yr ago. Today, it is the most popular racket sport.

United States Racket Sport Participation in a Recent Year

Tennis

Table Tennis

Racketball

= 1 million players

USING DATA

Collect
Organize
Describe
Predict

Which racket sport is played by about 14 million people? **table tennis**

Ask 20 people which racket sports they play. Organize your data into a table. How does your survey compare to the one above? **Answers will vary.**

CHAPTER 5   129

Using the Chapter Opener

The purpose of this page is to involve the student in the use of real data much like that presented in newspapers and magazines.

To use this page as you begin the chapter, direct the students' attention to the data. You may wish to ask questions such as the following:

About how many more people played tennis than played racquetball? *(about 11 million)* **How do you know?** *(Used key to determine value of one symbol; 20 million − 9 million = 11 million)*

If about $\frac{1}{3}$ of the tennis players also played squash, another racquet sport, would there be more squash players or more racquetball players? *(More racquetball players; $\frac{1}{3}$ of 20 is a little more than 6.)*

How do you know that the data on this graph represent estimated numbers? *(Symbols represent number of players to the nearest half million.)*

You may wish to use the data collecting and comparing activities as cooperative learning situations. Some students may require two days to complete the assignment.

Lesson Organizer

Objective: Explore fractions and divisibility.

Prior Knowledge: Students should know basic multiplication facts.

Lesson Resources:
Class Activity 5-1
Daily Review 5-1
Cooperative Investigations, Chapter 5

 Two-Minute Math

List two ways you can add exactly eight odd numbers to obtain 20? You can use any odd number more than once.
(Possible answers: 1 + 1 + 1 + 1 + 1 + 1 + 1 + 13 = 20; 1 + 1 + 1 + 1 + 1 + 1 + 3 + 11 = 20)

1 PREPARE

CONNECTING ACTIVITY

☑ **MATERIALS CHECKLIST:** Teaching Aid 3 (Grid Paper) for each student, construction paper squares, 12 per group

1. Have students work in groups of three or four and arrange the squares into as many different rectangles as possible. One arrangement is shown below.

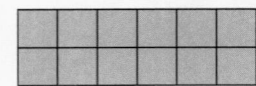

2. Ask students to draw each arrangement on grid paper.

- **How are the rectangles alike?** *(All contain exactly 12 squares.)*

- **How are the rectangles different?** *(Each has a unique length and width.)*

- **What is an easy way to find the number of squares used in each rectangle?** *(Multiply the number of squares in each row by the number in each column.)*

WHEN YOUR STUDENTS ASK
★ WHY AM I LEARNING THIS? ★

You can connect this skill to real life through party planning. If 80 guests are expected, how many seating arrangements are possible so that the same number of people sit at each table?

 EXPLORE

Exploring Factors and Divisibility

Grid paper can be used to investigate some interesting numbers.

Shade rectangular regions with the same number of squares as the three at the right on a sheet of grid paper.

1. How many small squares does each rectangle have?
24

2. There is another rectangular region that can be made with 24 squares. Shade it on your grid paper.
1 row of 24 squares

3. List all the whole numbers that can be used for the length and width of a rectangle of 24 squares.
1, 2, 3, 4, 6, 8, 12, 24
The numbers you listed are called the **factors** of 24.

> A *factor* is any of two or more numbers that are multiplied to obtain a product.

Factors of 24: 1, 2, 3, 4, 6, 8, 12, 24

4. On grid paper, draw all the possible rectangular regions using 36 squares. Then list the factors of 36. 1 by 36; 2 by 18; 3 by 12; 4 by 9; 6 by 6; factors: 1, 2, 3, 4, 6, 9, 12, 18, 36

5. Repeat Exercise 4 for rectangles made of 45 and 60 squares. List the factors of 45 and 60. Check students' drawings.
45: 1, 3, 5, 9, 15, 45; 60: 1, 2, 3, 4, 5, 6, 10, 12, 15, 20, 30, 60

6. **CRITICAL THINKING** What number is a factor of any number? Explain.
1; Any number times 1 equals the number.

7. List the factors of the number.

   a. 12   **b.** 15   **c.** 18
   1, 2, 3, 4, 6, 12   1, 3, 5, 15   1, 2, 3, 6, 9, 18
   d. 32   **e.** 50   **f.** 59
   1, 2, 4, 8, 16, 32 1, 2, 5, 10, 25, 50   1, 59

The factors of 14 are 1, 2, 7, and 14. Notice how each factor divides into 14 without a remainder. We say 14 is **divisible** by 1, 2, 7, and 14.

$$1\overline{)14} \qquad 2\overline{)14} \qquad 7\overline{)14} \qquad 14\overline{)14}$$
$$14 \qquad\quad 7 \qquad\quad 2 \qquad\quad 1$$

---

2 EXPLORE

☑ **MATERIALS CHECKLIST:** Teaching Aid 3 (Grid Paper) for each pair, calculators

Assign students into pairs for these activities.

If students do not include all possible factors for 36, 45, or 60, ask the group to describe the method used to identify rectangular regions.

What multiplication property is related to the answer to Exercise 6? *(identity for multiplication)*

Explain how you know that 59 has only two factors. *(Possible answer: Only one rectangle can be formed.)*

SUMMARIZE/ASSESS **Explain how to tell that 26 is divisible by 1, 2, 13, and 26.** *(Possible answer: Each of these numbers divides into 26 without a remainder.)*

Make a 100 chart on a sheet of grid paper.

1	2	3	4	5	6	7	8	9	10
11	12	13	14	15	16	17	18	19	20
21	22	23	24	25	26	27	28	29	30
31	32	33	34	35	36	37	38	39	40
41	42	43	44	45	46	47	48	49	50
51	52	53	54	55	56	57	58	59	60
61	62	63	64	65	66	67	68	69	70
71	72	73	74	75	76	77	78	79	80
81	82	83	84	85	86	87	88	89	90
91	92	93	94	95	96	97	98	99	100

8. Draw a circle around all numbers divisible by 2. Write a rule explaining when a number is divisible by 2.
   A number is divisible by 2 if it is even.

9. Draw a slash (/) through all numbers divisible by 5. Write a rule explaining when a number is divisible by 5. A number is divisible by 5 if the ones' digit is 5 or 0.

10. Draw a backslash (\) through all numbers divisible by 10. Write a rule explaining when a number is divisible by 10. A number is divisible by 10 if it is even and the ones' digit is 0.

11. **a. CALCULATOR** Which numbers at the right are divisible by 3?
    80,004; 847,395; 199,989

80,004	847,395	767,534	199,989

    b. Add the digits in each number in Exercise 11a that is divisible by 3. Is the sum of the digits divisible by 3?
    For example: 987 ⇨ 9 + 8 + 7 = 24 ⇨ 2 + 4 = 6, and 6 is divisible by 3.
    Now write a divisibility rule for 3.
    Yes. A number is divisible by 3 if the sum of its digits is divisible by 3.

12. **a. CALCULATOR** Which numbers in Exercise 11a are divisible by 9? 847,395; 199,989

    b. Add the digits of each number that is divisible by 9. Is the sum of the digits divisible by 9? Yes. A number is divisible Write a divisibility rule for 9. by 9 if the sum of its digits is divisible by 9.

13. **CALCULATOR** Which numbers in Exercise 11a are divisible by 6? Write a divisibility rule for 6. 80,004; A number is divisible by 6 if it is even and the sum of its digits is divisible by 3.

Your divisibility rules should look something like this.

A number is divisible by:	
2 if it is even;	6 if it is divisible by 2 and 3;
3 if the sum of the digits is divisible by 3;	9 if the sum of the digits is divisible by 9;
5 if the ones' digit is 5 or 0.	10 if the ones' digit is 0.

14. By which number(s) is the number divisible? 2, 3, 5, 6, 9, 10
    a. 102   **b.** 135   **c.** 300   **d.** 5,790   **e.** 7,146   **f.** 13,846
    2, 3, 6   3, 5, 9   2, 3, 5, 6, 10   2, 3, 5, 6, 10   2, 3, 6, 9   2

*15. **CREATE YOUR OWN** Write a divisibility rule for 4.

    A number is divisible by 4 if the number formed by the last 2 digits is divisible by 4.

3 FOLLOW-UP

CLASS ACTIVITY 5-1

☑ **MATERIALS CHECKLIST:** Blank number cubes

Have students work in groups of four, and in pairs within each group. Using a cube labeled *1–6,* each pair finds a three-digit number by rolling the cube three times. The first pair doubles the digit in the ones' place and subtracts this number from the first two digits. For example, if the rolled number is 364, students subtract 8 (4 × 2) from 36. The other pair multiplies the digit in the ones' place of their rolled number by 4, and adds this number to the first two digits. So for 273, students add 12 (3 × 4) to 27. Have the first pair divide its difference and the rolled number by 7. [28 ÷ 7 = 4; 364 ÷ 7 = 52] Have the second pair divide its sum and the rolled number by 13. [39 ÷ 13 = 3; 273 ÷ 13 = 21] Ask students to repeat the procedure and to explain how to test for divisibility by 7 and 13. [If difference found by method described above is divisible by 7 so is rolled number. If sum found by method described above is divisible by 13 so is rolled number.

MEETING INDIVIDUAL NEEDS

For Students Who Are . . .

Acquiring English Proficiency Review the meanings of *rectangle, factor, even number,* and *sum of digits.* Have students write the new words in their Learning Logs.

Gifted and Talented Have students investigate divisibility rules for 8.

Working 2 or 3 Grades Below Level Review basic facts to prepare students to find factors and test for divisibility.

Today's Problem

Carrie's aunt gave her some pennies. When Carrie put them into stacks of 5, she had one penny left over. She then put them into stacks of 3 and also had one penny left over. What is the smallest number of pennies that her aunt gave her? *(16; 16 ÷ 5 = 3R 1; 16 ÷ 3 = 5R 1)*

Lesson Organizer

Objective: Explore primes, composites, and prime factorization.

Prior Knowledge: Students should be able to name all the factors of a given number.

Lesson Resources:
Practice Worksheet 5-2
Daily Review 5-2
Cooperative Problem Solving 1,
 Chapter 5

Two-Minute Math

Find three consecutive whole numbers less than 10 whose product is five times their sum. *(3, 4, 5)*

1 PREPARE

CONNECTING ACTIVITY

☑ **MATERIALS CHECKLIST:** Teaching Aid 3, (Grid Paper) for each student

1. On the grid paper, ask students to draw all possible rectangular regions with areas of 8 and 15.

- **What are the factors of 8?** *(1, 2, 4, 8)* **of 15?** *(1, 3, 5, 15)*

2. Have students draw rectangular regions with areas of 5, 7, and 11.

- **How many rectangular regions did you draw for each number?** *(one)*

- **Describe the factors for each of these numbers.** *(only two, the number itself and 1)*

WHEN YOUR STUDENTS ASK
★ WHY AM I LEARNING THIS? ★

You can relate prime numbers to code making. Prime numbers are useful in creating and interpreting high-security codes used in several government agencies.

Exploring Primes, Composites, and Prime Factorization

You can make a chart of the factors of numbers to investigate some other interesting numbers.

1. Copy and complete the chart below on a sheet of grid paper.

Factors																					
											12							18		20	
											6				16			9		10	
					6		8		10		4		14	15	8			6		5	21
			4		3		4	9	5		3		7	5	4			3		4	7
	2	3	2	5	2	7	2	3	2	11	2	13	2	3	2	17	2	19	2	3
	1	1	1	1	1	1	1	1	1	1	1	1	1	1	1	1	1	1	1	1
	1	2	3	4	5	6	7	8	9	10	11	12	13	14	15	16	17	18	19	20	21

Counting Numbers

2. **IN YOUR WORDS** Explain why the number 0 is not included in the chart. Zero is not a counting number. Every number is a factor of 0, since $a \times 0 = 0$ for all a.

3. Which numbers in your chart have exactly two factors? 2, 3, 5, 7, 11, 13, 17, 19

> Numbers that have exactly two factors, namely *1* and the number itself, are called *prime numbers*.

4. Which numbers in your chart have more than two factors? 4, 6, 8, 9, 10, 12, 14, 15, 16, 18, 20, 21

> Numbers that have more than two factors are called *composite numbers*. The numbers *0* and *1* are neither prime nor composite.

List the factors for the number. Is the number *prime* or *composite*? See page 163b.

5. 42 — composite
6. 60 — composite
7. 59 — prime
8. 41 — prime
9. 39 — composite
10. 51 — composite

11. Which numbers less than 80 and greater than 70 are prime? 71, 73, 79

12. Which numbers less than 100 and greater than 89 are composite? 90, 91, 92, 93, 94, 95, 96, 98, 99

---

2 EXPLORE

☑ **MATERIALS CHECKLIST:** Teaching Aid 3 (Grid Paper) for each student

Have students use the grid paper for Exercise 1.

What are the prime numbers between 22 and 42? *(23, 29, 31, 37, 41)*

What composite number can be represented as $3^2 \times 5$? *(45)*
Draw three different factor trees for 48. What do you notice? *(All three result in the same prime factorization: $2^4 \times 3$.)*

SUMMARIZE/ASSESS **Explain how to tell that a number is prime.** *(A number is prime when it has only two factors, 1 and itself, or is divisible only by 1 and itself.)*

Every composite number can be written as a product of prime factors. This is called the **prime factorization** of a number.

You can use a **factor tree** to find the prime factorization of a number.

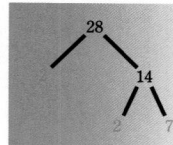

Composite number: 28

Factors: 1, 2, 4, 7, 14, 28

Prime factorization: $2 \times 2 \times 7$ ← In **exponential form,** $2 \times 2 \times 7$ is $2^2 \times 7$.

13. IN YOUR WORDS Explain why 0 and 1 are not used in prime factorizations.   Answers will vary. Suggestion given: Zero is a factor of only itself. One is a factor of every number.

Copy and complete the factor tree.

14.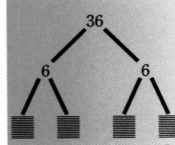

15.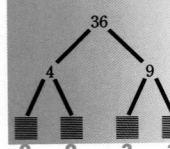

16.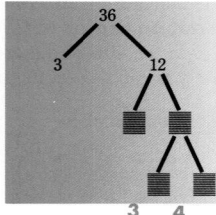

17. Did all three factor trees above result in the same prime factorization of 36? Draw another factor tree for 36 that is different from these three.   Yes. Answers will vary. Suggestion given. See page 163b.

Use a factor tree to name the prime factorization of the number.

18. 48 $2^4 \times 3$ **19.** 78 $2 \times 3 \times 13$ **20.** 45 $3^2 \times 5$ **21.** 54 2×3^3 **22.** 92 $2^2 \times 23$ **23.** 144 $2^4 \times 3^2$

24. Copy and complete the chart at the right on grid paper.

25. IN YOUR WORDS Describe the prime factors that all multiples of 10 have in common.   2 and 5

26. CREATE YOUR OWN Think of another set of numbers like the multiples of 10. Show their prime factors in a chart to discover which ones they have in common.   Answers will vary. Suggestion given: All multiples of 5 contain a factor of 5.

Prime Factors										
						5			
			5		5		2	5	5
	5	5	2	5	3	7	2	3	5
5	3	3	2	5	2	5	2	3	2
2	2	2	2	2	2	2	2	2	2
10	20	30	40	50	60	70	80	90	100

Multiples of 10

3 FOLLOW-UP

PRACTICE 5-2

List the factors for each number. Is the number *prime* or *composite*?

1. 36 composite   **2.** 52 composite   **3.** 61 prime   **4.** 57 composite
1,2,3,4,6,9,12,18,36   1,2,4,13,26,52   1,61   1,3,19,57

5. Which numbers less than 70 and greater than 60 are prime?   61, 67

6. Which numbers less than 60 but greater than 49 are composite?
50, 51, 52, 54, 55, 56, 57, 58

Complete the factor tree.

7. 24   **8.** 30   **9.** 16

10. 60   **11.** 42   **12.** 91

Make a factor tree for each number. Use the factor tree to name the prime factorization of each number. Answers will vary. Suggestions are given.

13. 56   **14.** 63   **15.** 27

16. Find the common factors for all multiples of 8 from 8 through 100. What do you observe about the common factors for the multiples of 8?
1, 2, 4, 8; all the common factors have the same prime factor: 2.

MEETING INDIVIDUAL NEEDS

For Students Who Are . . .

Acquiring English Proficiency Discuss the meaning of *composite*.

Gifted and Talented Have students find the prime numbers between 100 and 200.

Working 2 or 3 Grades Below Level Have students circle the prime numbers when they make factor trees and then check the prime factorization by multiplying all the circled numbers.

Today's Problem

The minute hand of a clock moves through $\frac{1}{2}$ of a circle in 30 minutes. What fraction of a circle does the hour hand move in one half-hour? *(It takes 12 hours for the hour hand to return to its original place. Since there are 24 half-hours in 12 hours, the hour hand moves $\frac{1}{24}$ of a circle in one half-hour.)*

Lesson Organizer

Objective: Identify factors and greatest common factor (GCF).

Prior Knowledge: Students should be able to name all the factors of a given number.

Error Analysis and Remediation: See page 163A.

Lesson Resources:
Practice Worksheet 5-3
Reteaching Worksheet 5-3
Enrichment Activity 5-3
Daily Review 5-3

Two-Minute Math

Continue the pattern for the next two numbers.

9, 18, 27, 36, □, □ *(45, 54)*
99, 1, 98, 2, 97, □, □ *(3, 96)*
2, 20, 3, 30, 4, 40, □, □ *(5, 50)*
11, 2, 12, 3, 13, 4, 14, □, □ *(5, 15)*

1 INTRODUCE

SYMBOLIC ACTIVITY

1. Have students list all factors of 32 and 80.

2. Draw two large intersecting circles that form three distinct regions and label the circles as shown:

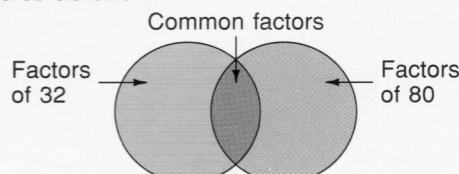

Common factors

Factors of 32   Factors of 80

3. Write each factor of 32 and 80 in the appropriate region. What are the common factors of 32 and 80? *(1, 2, 4, 8, 16)* What is the greatest common factor of 32 and 80? *(16)*

WHEN YOUR STUDENTS ASK
★ WHY AM I LEARNING THIS? ★

You can connect this skill to architecture. Architects need to be familiar with factors when selecting modular components such as windows so that the windows will be evenly spaced along the walls.

Greatest Common Factor

People in many cultures have made quilts for important occasions. Many quilts tell interesting stories. You want to make an 8 ft by 10 ft quilt. What is the size of the greatest square you can use?

You can list the factors of 8 and 10 to solve the problem.

Factors of 8:   1, 2, 4, 8
Factors of 10:   1, 2, 5, 10

The **common factors** 1 and 2 tell you the size of the squares you can use.

The number 2 is called the **greatest common factor** (**GCF**) of 8 and 10. This is the size of the greatest square that you can use on the quilt.

Another example:

What is the GCF of 18, 27, and 36?

Factors of 18: 1, 2, 3, 6, 9, 18
Factors of 27: 1, 3, 9, 27
Factors of 36: 1, 2, 3, 4, 6, 9, 12, 18, 36

Common factors of 18, 27, and 36: 1, 3, 9

The GCF of 18, 27, and 36 is 9.

THINK ALOUD Which whole number is a factor of every number?   1

The quilt was made of old wedding clothes sewn together in the Rajasthan region of north west India.

10 ft
8 ft
10 ft
8 ft

MULTICULTURAL NOTE

Developed as a way to create functional items, quilting today is considered an American folk art. The Amish in Pennsylvania are known for making beautiful quilts, which are prized throughout the United States.

2 TEACH

What do you call factors that are the same for different numbers? *(common factors)*

What do you call the greatest factor that is common to different numbers? *(the greatest common factor, or GCF)*

What factor do all numbers have in common? *(1)*

What is the greatest common factor of two numbers when one number is a factor of the other? Give an example. *(The GCF is the lesser of the two numbers; example: 4 and 8.)*

Chalkboard Examples

Find the GCF.
28 and 42 *(14)*
72 and 96 *(24)*
26, 52, and 65 *(13)*

SUMMARIZE/ASSESS **Explain how to find the GCF of two or more numbers.** *(List the factors of the numbers, identify the common factors; identify the greatest common factor.)*

List all the factors of the number.

1. 36
See page 163 b.
2. 27
1, 3, 9, 27
3. 45
1, 3, 5, 9, 15, 45
4. 72
See page 163 b.
5. 54
See page 163 b.

List the common factors. Then name the GCF.

6. 6, 9
1, 3; 3
7. 10, 15
1, 5; 5
8. 14, 56
1, 2, 7, 14; 14
9. 21, 84
1, 3, 7, 21; 21

List the common factors. Name the GCF.

10. 4, 6
1, 2; 2
11. 12, 15
1, 3; 3
12. 18, 25
1; 1
13. 14, 42
1, 2, 7, 14; 14
14. 9, 12
1, 3; 3
15. 18, 45
1, 3, 9; 9
16. 12, 16
1, 2, 4; 4
17. 24, 43
1; 1
18. 20, 35
1, 5; 5
19. 18, 32
1, 2; 2
20. 12, 20
1, 2, 4; 4
21. 22, 33
1, 11; 11
22. 21, 63
1, 3, 7, 21; 21
23. 48, 72
1, 2, 3, 4, 6, 8, 12, 24; 24
24. 15, 24
1, 3; 3
25. 40, 27
1; 1
26. 27, 81
1, 3, 9, 27; 27
27. 45, 65
1, 5; 5
28. 9, 12, 18
1, 3; 3
29. 20, 28, 36
1, 2, 4; 4

30. **CRITICAL THINKING** Which is the smallest number that has 2, 3, and 5 as factors? **30**

Find the next three numbers in the pattern.

31. 4, 8, 12, 16, ▓, ▓, ▓
20, 24, 28
32. 90, 180, 270, 360, ▓, ▓, ▓
450, 540, 630
33. 5, 13, 21, 29, ▓, ▓, ▓
37, 45, 53
34. 34, 79, 124, 169, ▓, ▓, ▓
214, 259, 304
*35. 7, 11, 10, 14, 13, ▓, ▓, ▓
17, 16, 20
*36. 2, 10, 3, 11, 4, ▓, ▓, ▓
12, 5, 13

Critical Thinking

With a partner, discuss how prime factorization can be used to name the GCF of 28 and 42.

Prime factorization of 28: 2 × 2 × 7

Prime factorization of 42: 2 × 3 × 7

> The GCF contains all the common prime factors of each number.

GCF: 2 × 7 = 14, because 2 and 7 are common prime factors.

Use prime factorization to name the GCF.

1. 12, 20 **4** **2.** 21, 56 **7** **3.** 39, 52 **13** **4.** 63, 84 **21** **5.** 18, 27, 36 **9**

CHAPTER 5 135

MEETING INDIVIDUAL NEEDS

For Students Who Are . . .

Acquiring English Proficiency Pair students with an English-proficient student to discuss the Critical Thinking exercises.

Gifted and Talented Have students use prime factorization to find the GCF of 75 and 50 *(25)*, 72 and 108 *(36)*, and 96 and 156 *(12)*.

Working 2 or 3 Grades Below Level Have students use pages 34–35 of the Skills Workbook for fractions.

Today's Problem

One number is relatively prime to another number if they have no common divisors except 1. For example, 8 and 9 are relatively prime. If *a* is relatively prime to *b* and *b* is relatively prime to *c*, must *a* be relatively prime to *c*? Demonstrate by giving an example. *(No; 8 is relatively prime to 9, 9 is relatively prime to 16, yet 8 is not relatively prime to 16.)*

3 FOLLOW-UP

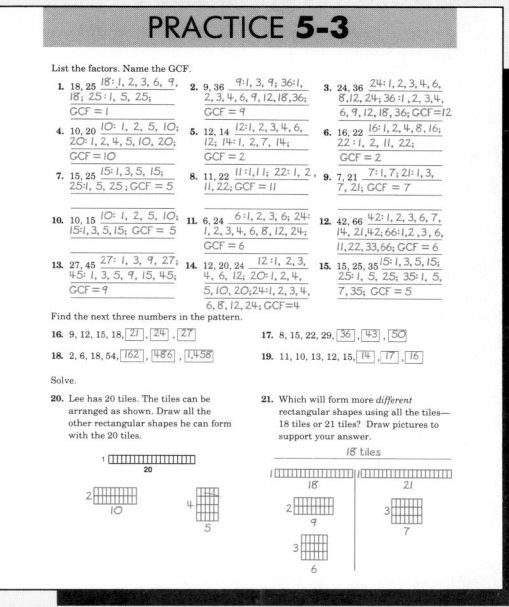

PRACTICE 5-3

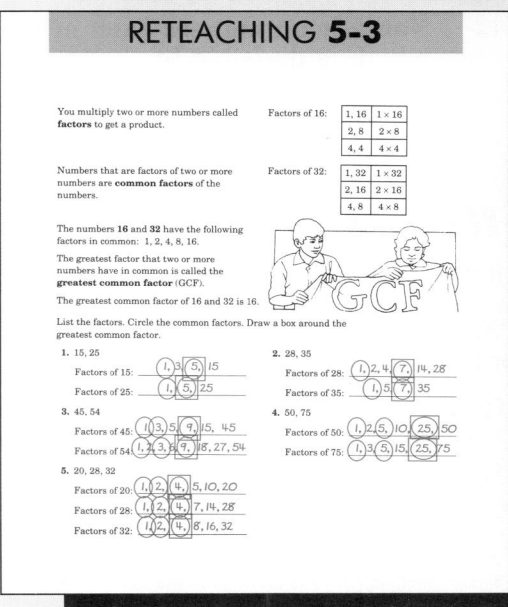

RETEACHING 5-3

ENRICHMENT 5-3

☑ **MATERIALS CHECKLIST:** Calculators

Write the following numbers on the board: 70; 836; 4,080; 5,830. Explain to the students that three of these numbers are "weird" numbers. Weird numbers are numbers whose factors cannot be added together in any combination to form the original number. Have the students work in pairs. Each pair uses a calculator to find the factors of each number. Then the partners try various combinations of factors to find the number that is not a weird number. [2040 + 1020 + 816 + 204 = 4,080]

Lesson Organizer

> **Objective:** Identify multiples and least common multiple (LCM).

Prior Knowledge: Students should know the multiplication facts.

Error Analysis and Remediation: See page 163A.

Lesson Resources:
Practice Worksheet 5-4
Reteaching Worksheet 5-4
Enrichment Activity 5-4
Daily Review 5-4
Cooperative Problem Solving 2, Chapter 5

 *Two-Minute Math*

Name two numbers each of which is divisible by 3, a multiple of 9, and a factor of 81. *(9, 27)*

1 INTRODUCE

CONNECTING ACTIVITY

☑ **MATERIALS CHECKLIST:** centimeter ruler for each student

1. Have students draw two number lines each 20 cm long on two pieces of paper.

2. **Mark off and label 3-cm intervals on one number line and 6-cm intervals on the other as shown.**

● **What multiples of 3 did you mark?** *(3, 6, 9, 12, 15, 18)*

● **What multiples of 6?** *(6, 12, 18)*

3. **What marked nonzero multiples do the number lines have in common?** *(6, 12, 18)* **What is the least common multiple?** *(6)*

WHEN YOUR STUDENTS ASK
★ **WHY AM I LEARNING THIS?** ★

You can connect this skill to publishing. Publishers of books and magazines need to know about multiples because pages are printed in signatures (multiples of 8 or 16.)

Least Common Multiple

To increase bicycle sales, a store is giving gifts to its customers. Every 4th customer gets a pair of reflectors and every 6th customer gets a water bottle. Which customer is the first to get both gifts?

The multiples of 4 and 6 help you solve the problem. A **multiple** is the product of a given number and any whole number.

Multiples of 4: 0, 4, 8, 12, 16, 20, 24, 28, 32, 36, . . .
Multiples of 6: 0, 6, 12, 18, 24, 30, 36, . . .

The 12th, 24th, 36th, . . . customers will get both gifts. The 12th customer will be the first to get both.

The number 12 is called the **least common multiple (LCM)** of 4 and 6.

What is the LCM of 4, 5, and 10?

Multiples of 4: 4, 8, 12, 16, 20, 24, 28, 32, 36, 40, . . .

Multiples of 5: 5, 10, 15, 20, 25, 30, 35, 40, . . .
Multiples of 10: 10, 20, 30, 40, 50, . . .

Some common multiples of 4, 5, and 10 are 20, 40, 60, . . . The LCM is 20.

When we find the LCM, we disregard the multiple 0 because it is a common multiple of every number.

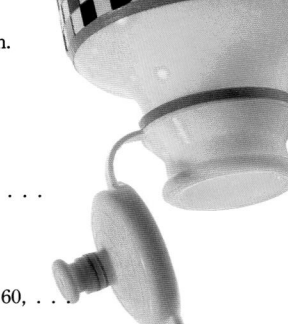

GUIDED PRACTICE

List the first six nonzero multiples of the numbers. See page 163b.

1. 3, 6   **2.** 7, 9   **3.** 11, 12   **4.** 18, 24

List enough nonzero multiples of the numbers to find the LCM.

5. 2, 3 6   **6.** 6, 8 24   **7.** 2, 12 12   **8.** 4, 6, 10 60

PRACTICE

Name the LCM.

9. 4, 6 12   **10.** 6, 5 30   **11.** 2, 6 6   **12.** 3, 4 12

13. 3, 11 33   **14.** 8, 12 24   **15.** 9, 15 45   **16.** 8, 9 72

17. 10, 15 30   **18.** 1, 14 14   **19.** 13, 39 39   **20.** 16, 1 16

136   LESSON 5–4

---

2 TEACH

What is one way to find multiples of a number? *(Multiply the number by 1, 2, 3, and so on.)*

How many multiples are there for a given number? *(an infinite number)*

Why isn't zero the LCM of a pair of numbers? *(Zero is a multiple of every number.)*

What is the LCM of any pair of prime numbers? *(their product)*

> ### Chalkboard Examples
> Find the LCM.
> 12 and 16 *(48)*
> 8 and 10 *(40)*
> 18 and 27 *(54)*
> 12 and 30 *(60)*

SUMMARIZE/ASSESS **Explain how to find the LCM of a pair of numbers.** *(Name the multiples of each number. Identify the common multiples. Select the least of the common multiples.)*

21. 25, 150 150   **22.** 20, 15 60   **23.** 9, 21 63   **24.** 50, 80 400

25. 6, 8, 12 24   **26.** 4, 5, 6 60   **27.** 9, 6, 4 36   **28.** 2, 3, 7 42

Copy and complete the table.

	Numbers	4, 14	20, 25	4, 5	8, 12	30, 10	6, 15
29.	GCF	2	5	1	4	10	3
30.	LCM	28	100	20	24	30	30
31.	Product	56	500	20	96	300	90

*32. **IN YOUR WORDS** Explain how the GCF, LCM, and product are related. Try other pairs of numbers. Does this relationship always work? **The product of two numbers equals the product of their GCF and LCM. Yes.**

PROBLEM SOLVING

CHOOSE Choose mental math or paper and pencil to solve. **Choices will vary.**

33. On an assembly line, bicycles are assembled so that every 5th bicycle has reflectors, every 6th has a bell, and every 15th has a basket. What are the first two positions in the assembly line for the bicycles with all three of these features?
p; 30th bicycle, 60th bicycle

34. Juan and Maria start cycling on a circular track at the same time but at different speeds. Maria passes Juan every 4 laps. If Maria completes 30 laps of the track, how many times has she passed Juan? m; 7 times

---

Critical Thinking 🧩

With a partner, study how prime factorization is used to name the LCM of 24 and 20.

Prime factorization of 24: $2 \times 2 \times 2 \times 3$
Prime factorization of 20: $2 \times 2 \qquad \times 5$
LCM is 120: $\qquad 2 \times 2 \times 2 \times 3 \times 5$

> The LCM contains all factors of 24 as well as those factors of 20 that are not factors of 24.

Use prime factorization to name the LCM.

1. 8, 18   **2.** 28, 40   **3.** 12, 20   **4.** 27, 36   **5.** 9, 12, 15
72   280   60   108   180

MEETING INDIVIDUAL NEEDS

For Students Who Are . . .

Acquiring English Proficiency Pair students with an English-proficient student to discuss the Problem Solving exercises.

Gifted and Talented Have students find the LCM: 8, 12, 16, 24 *(48)*, 6, 8, 15, 20 *(120)*, 9, 18, 27, 36 *(108)*, and 12, 15, 18, 24 *(360)*.

Working 2 or 3 Grades Below Level Have students use pages 50–51 of the Skills Workbook for fractions.

Today's Problem

A loaf of date-nut bread is to be sliced into equal-size pieces. What is the least number of slices that should be cut so that either 3, 4, or 6 guests can each have the same number of pieces? *(The LCM of 3, 4, and 6 is 12; 12 pieces.)*

---

3 FOLLOW-UP

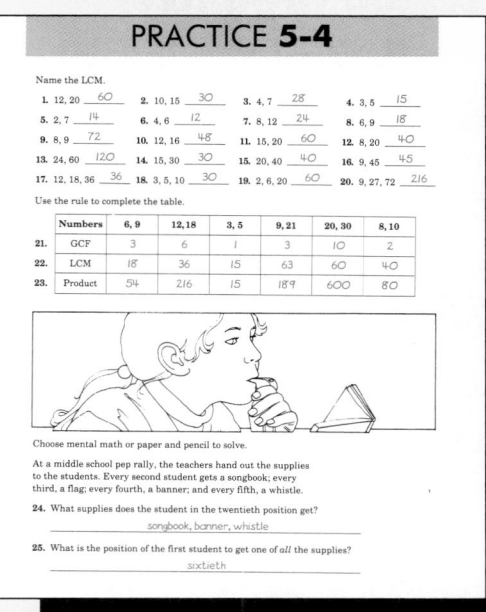
Have the students work in groups of four or five. Provide each group with 100 counters to place in a row on the floor with the same color showing on all 100 counters. Have the students "number" the counters by writing the numbers 1–100 on index cards and placing each card above the corresponding counter. One student then flips all the multiples of 2. Another flips all the multiples of 3, a third flips all the multiples of 4, and so on. Students record the number of each unturned counter and describe the pattern. [1, 4, 9, 16, 25, 36, 49, 64, 81, 100; 1^2, 2^2, 3^2, 4^2, 5^2. . .]

Lesson Organizer

Objective: Discuss non-numerical graphs.

Prior Knowledge: Students should be able to read and interpret numerical graphs.

Lesson Resources:
Practice Worksheet 5-5
Daily Review 5-5

Two-Minute Math

Use $7 \times 11 \times 13 = 1{,}001$ to name the product quickly.

$7 \times 11^2 \times 13 \times 16$ $7^2 \times 11^2 \times 13$
$7 \times 11 \times 13 \times 47$ $7^2 \times 11 \times 13$

(176,176; 77,077; 47,047; 7,007)

1 INTRODUCE

SYMBOLIC ACTIVITY

☑ **MATERIALS CHECKLIST:** line graph from a newspaper or magazine

1. Display the line graph on the overhead projector.

2. Help students interpret the data by asking questions such as:

● **What is the title of the graph?**

● **What facts does the graph describe?**
Include questions specific to the data on the graph.

WHEN YOUR STUDENTS ASK
★ **WHY AM I LEARNING THIS?** ★

You can relate this skill to real life through graphs on television news programs. For example, graphs that show stock market changes over a two-week period may show a trend without using numbers.

LET'S TALK **MATH**

Picture *This*

Problem Solving:
Reading Nonnumerical Graphs

UNDERSTAND
PLAN
CARRY OUT
LOOK BACK

▣ READ ABOUT IT

Graphs can be used to show relationships between two quantities. One quantity is represented on the horizontal axis, the other on the vertical axis.

▣ TALK ABOUT IT

Work with a partner as you read the information illustrated in the nonnumerical graphs at the right.

1. Which two quantities are represented on the graph at the right?
   distance and time

2. Match the forms of transportation to the letters on the graph. Give a reason for each matching.
   See page 163b.

3. In the graph at the right, did both runners go the same distance?
   yes

4. Which runner went farther in the early part of the race?
   runner B

5. Who ran the distance in the shortest amount of time?
   runner A

6. A cyclist travels the same route as the runners. Describe how a line representing the cyclist's distance and time might look on the graph.
   Answers will vary. Suggestion given: The line would be straighter than both A and B with a steeper slope.

138 LESSON 5–5

2 TEACH

READ ABOUT IT   Ask students to recall the kinds of graphs they have interpreted in other subjects.

TALK ABOUT IT   **What might be a title for the first graph? If you added a ship as a form of transportation, where would you put the matching letter?**

WRITE ABOUT IT   Ask students to exchange paragraphs they wrote for Exercise 11 and evaluate each other's story.

SUMMARIZE/ASSESS   **Explain how understanding nonnumerical graphs can help you interpret other kinds of graphs.** *(Possible answer: Nonnumerical graphs help me focus on the graph itself as a tool for displaying data.)*

The graph at the right represents Stella's and Fred's trips to school.

7. Stella has a short walk before and after riding a bus. Which line represents Stella's trip to school? **the solid line**

8. How do you think Fred gets to school? Explain. **By bicycle. He goes faster than Stella walking and slower than her bus.**

9. How do the distances Fred and Stella travel to school compare? **They are the same.**

10. Discuss how you would represent the following people on the graph. Then copy the graph and draw a line to represent each person. **Answers will vary.**
    • George rides to school by car. He lives twice as far from school as Fred, but he gets to school twice as fast.
    • Alicia lives only half the distance from school as Stella. Yet she takes twice as long to get to school.

■ WRITE ABOUT IT

11. The graph at the right represents a bicycle trip. Write a paragraph describing what is happening. Be sure to include a description of points *A*, *B*, *C*, *D*, and *E* in your story. **Check students' work.**

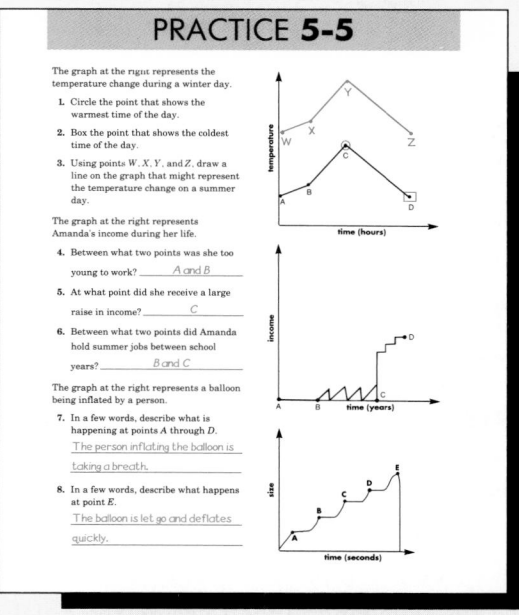

PRACTICE 5-5

The graph at the right represents the temperature change during a winter day.

1. Circle the point that shows the warmest time of the day.

2. Box the point that shows the coldest time of the day.

3. Using points *W*, *X*, *Y*, and *Z*, draw a line on the graph that might represent the temperature change on a summer day.

The graph at the right represents Amanda's income during her life.

4. Between what two points was she too young to work? ____*A and B*____

5. At what point did she receive a large raise in income? ____*C*____

6. Between what two points did Amanda hold summer jobs between school years? ____*B and C*____

The graph at the right represents a balloon being inflated by a person.

7. In a few words, describe what is happening at points *A* through *D*.
   The person inflating the balloon is
   taking a breath.

8. In a few words, describe what happens at point *E*.
   The balloon is let go and deflates
   quickly.

MEETING INDIVIDUAL NEEDS

For Students Who Are . . .

Acquiring English Proficiency Discuss the meanings of *horizontal*, *vertical*, and *axis*.

Gifted and Talented Have each student create a graph that shows the relationship between two quantities. Then have them exchange papers and write a paragraph to describe each other's graph.

Having Reading Difficulties Pair students with an able reader to discuss the graphs in Exercises 1–11.

Today's Problem

In a game of tug-of-war, Tom, George, and Paul pulled on the rope from one side, and Geraldine, Tabetha, and Marylin pulled on the rope from the other side. If Tom can pull harder than Geraldine, George can pull harder than Tabitha, and Paul can pull harder than Marylin, what can you conclude? *(The boys will win.)*

MIDCHAPTER Checkup

The midchapter checkup provides a way for you to check students' understanding of the skills taught in the first half of the chapter.

Language and Vocabulary

Some key language and vocabulary ideas from the first half of the chapter are reinforced here.

Quick Quiz

The quiz provides a means of evaluating students' understanding of the objectives for the first half of the chapter. Page references are given so that students can check back to where the skill was taught.

Use the following guide to score the quick quiz.

Score	Percent
10	100%
9	90
8	80
7	70
6	60
5	50
4	40
3	30
2	20
1	10

Use this chart to identify the Management Objectives tested.

Items	Management Objective	Pages
1–3	**5A** Determine divisibility, primes and composites, and write prime factorizations.	130–131
4–10	**5B** Identify factors and multiples; GCF: LCM.	134–137

MIDCHAPTER CHECKUP

LANGUAGE & VOCABULARY

Write a sentence for each pair of terms to show that you understand the difference between them. **Accept reasonable answers. Suggestion given.**

1. prime number, composite number **2 factors; more than 2 factors**
2. factor, prime factor **exact divisor; exact divisor that is prime**
3. factor, multiple **exact divisor; product of given number and any whole number**
4. common factor, greatest common factor **same for 2 or more numbers; greatest factor common to 2 or more numbers**
5. greatest common factor, least common multiple **greatest factor common to 2 or more numbers; least factor common to 2 or more numbers**

QUICK QUIZ

By what is each number divisible? Write *2, 3, 5, 6, 9,* or *10.* (*pages 130–131*)

1. 3,861 **3; 9**
2. 7,350 **2, 3, 5, 6, 10**
3. 17,045 **5**

List the factors. Name the GCF. (*pages 134–135*)

4. 18, 54 **18: 1, 2, 3, 6, 9, 18; 54: 1, 2, 3, 6, 9, 18, 27, 54; 18**
5. 12, 64 **12: 1, 2, 3, 4, 6, 12; 64: 1, 2, 4, 8, 16, 32, 64; 4**
6. 39, 65 **39: 1, 3, 13, 39; 65: 1, 5, 13, 65; 13**

Name the LCM. (*pages 136–137*)

7. 3, 14 **42**
8. 9, 12 **36**
9. 25, 15 **75**

Solve. (*pages 136–137*)

10. The school chorus can perform on stage in rows of either 3, 4, or 5 students with no members left over.
    a. How can the chorus members arrange themselves? **rows of 3, 4, 5**
    b. If 5 more students join the chorus, which of the arrangements would no longer be possible? **rows of 3 and 4**
    c. What is the smallest number of students that can be in the chorus? **60 students**

LEARNING LOG

Write the answers in your learning log. **Answers will vary. Suggestions given.**

1. Most numbers have an even number of factors. Describe numbers that have an odd number of factors. **numbers that use one factor twice, such as 4, 9, 25, or 36**

2. Describe numbers with more than one factor tree. **composite numbers that have two different composite numbers as factors**

3. Often students confuse GCF and LCM. Tell how you remember these two ideas. **GCF is greatest factor common to all. LCM is least multiple common to all.**

MATH AMERICA

DID YOU KNOW . . . ? The Statue of Liberty is 151 ft tall. It is about 25 times taller than life size. How tall would a statue of you be if it were 25 times your height?
Check students' work.

BONUS

A stadium seats 48,060 people for a baseball game. Extra sections are added for a football game, enabling the stadium to seat 56,700. Every section in the stadium contains the same number of seats for both sports. What is the largest number of seats that can be in each section? **540 seats**

CHAPTER 5   141

Learning Log

These are suggestions for writing about some topics taught so far in the chapter. The students keep their Learning Logs from the beginning of the school year through the end.

Math America

A mathematical skill that students have learned is related to an interesting fact about the United States.

Bonus

Students are given an opportunity to solve a challenge-type problem like a puzzle or a nonroutine problem.

Lesson Organizer

Objective: Write a fraction to represent a model.

Prior Knowledge: Students should be familiar with the meanings of fractions for this review lesson.

Lesson Resources:
Practice Worksheet 5-6
Reteaching Activity 5-6
Enrichment Worksheet 5-6
Daily Review 5-6

 *Two-Minute Math*

Use the Table of Numbers on the inside of back cover. Will the sum of the numbers in row D be odd or even? *(odd)* **Test your answer.**

1 INTRODUCE

CONNECTING ACTIVITY

☑ **MATERIALS CHECKLIST:** Teaching Aid 4 (Fraction Bars)

1. Display the following fraction bars on the overhead projector.

• **Into how many equal parts is each fraction bar divided?** *(3; 5)*

• **What fraction represents the shaded part of each fraction bar?** ($\frac{1}{3}$; $\frac{3}{5}$)

2. Ask students to shade in a fraction bar that represents the fraction $\frac{5}{8}$.

WHEN YOUR STUDENTS ASK
★ WHY AM I LEARNING THIS? ★

You can connect this skill to real life through time signatures in music. For example, in $\frac{4}{4}$ time the denominator shows that a quarter note gets a beat, and the numerator shows four beats to the measure.

Meaning of Fractions

The flag of Chad is divided into three *equal* parts. The red part is one third of the flag's area. This color can be represented with the fraction $\frac{1}{3}$.

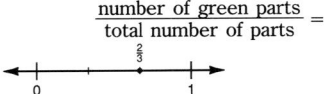

$$\frac{\text{number of red parts}}{\text{total number of parts}} = \frac{1}{3} \begin{array}{l}\longrightarrow \text{numerator} \\ \longrightarrow \text{denominator}\end{array}$$

The Nigerian flag also consists of three equal parts. Two of them are green, so two thirds of the flag is green. This color can be represented with the fraction $\frac{2}{3}$.

$$\frac{\text{number of green parts}}{\text{total number of parts}} = \frac{2}{3}$$

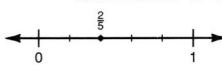

What fraction of the flags at the right have vertical stripes?

$$\frac{\text{number of flags with vertical stripes}}{\text{total number of flags}} = \frac{2}{5}$$

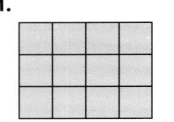

CRITICAL THINKING How would you use the flags above to find an example representing the fraction $\frac{5}{5}$? $\frac{5}{5}$ of the flags represent countries.

Chad

Austria

Nigeria

Indonesia

Netherlands

MATH AND SOCIAL STUDIES

GUIDED PRACTICE

Write the fraction for the shaded parts in the diagram.

1. $\frac{7}{12}$

2. $\frac{5}{7}$

Draw a diagram that represents the fraction.

3. a. $\frac{1}{4}$ **b.** $\frac{5}{16}$
Check students' drawings.

NUMBER SENSE Write the fraction associated with the letter.

4.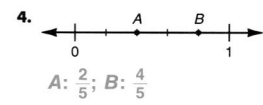
A: $\frac{2}{5}$; B: $\frac{4}{5}$

5.
A: $\frac{1}{4}$; B: $\frac{3}{4}$

6.
A: $\frac{1}{7}$; B: $\frac{4}{7}$

142 LESSON 5-6

MULTICULTURAL NOTE

Countries with a common history often have similar colors on their flags. Blue and white appear on the flags of many Central American countries which were once united. Many Middle Eastern countries use black, green, red, and white on their flags to show Arab unity.

2 TEACH

What does the numerator of a fraction describe? *(number of parts being considered)*

What does the denominator describe? *(total number of equal parts)*

Name a fraction describing each situation:

• **3 out of 8 sandwiches are cheese sandwiches.** ($\frac{3}{8}$)

• **7 out of 8 sweaters are red.** ($\frac{7}{8}$)

Chalkboard Examples

Name the fraction.
A circle divided into six equal parts with one part shaded ($\frac{1}{6}$)
Four stars with three of the stars shaded ($\frac{3}{4}$)

SUMMARIZE/ASSESS **Explain the meaning of the fraction $\frac{5}{6}$.** *(The 5 stands for the number of parts being considered; the 6 represents the total number of parts.)*

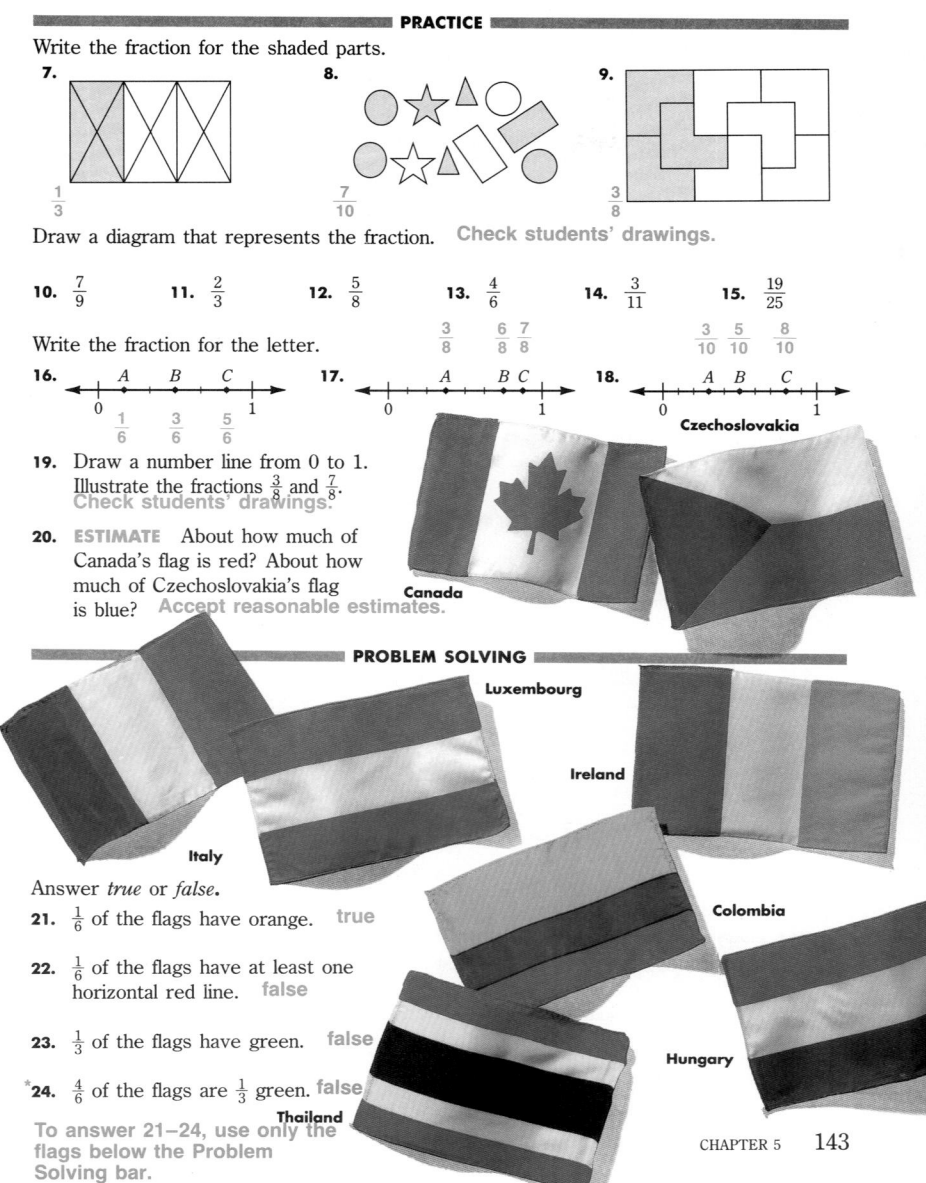

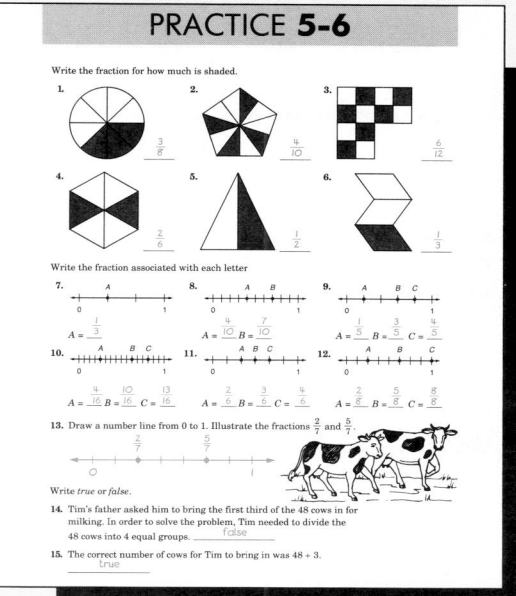

=== PRACTICE ===

Write the fraction for the shaded parts.

7.
$\dfrac{1}{3}$

8.
$\dfrac{7}{10}$

9.
$\dfrac{3}{8}$

Draw a diagram that represents the fraction.   Check students' drawings.

10. $\dfrac{7}{9}$ **11.** $\dfrac{2}{3}$ **12.** $\dfrac{5}{8}$ **13.** $\dfrac{4}{6}$ **14.** $\dfrac{3}{11}$ **15.** $\dfrac{19}{25}$

Write the fraction for the letter.

$\dfrac{3}{8}$ $\dfrac{6}{8}$ $\dfrac{7}{8}$

16. A B C $0 \quad \dfrac{1}{6} \quad \dfrac{3}{6} \quad \dfrac{5}{6} \quad 1$

17. A B C $0 \quad 1$

18. A B C $0 \quad 1$ Czechoslovakia

$\dfrac{3}{10}$ $\dfrac{5}{10}$ $\dfrac{8}{10}$

19. Draw a number line from 0 to 1. Illustrate the fractions $\dfrac{3}{8}$ and $\dfrac{7}{8}$.
Check students' drawings.

20. **ESTIMATE** About how much of Canada's flag is red? About how much of Czechoslovakia's flag is blue?   Accept reasonable estimates.

Canada

=== PROBLEM SOLVING ===

Luxembourg

Ireland

Italy

Colombia

Hungary

Thailand

Answer *true* or *false*.

21. $\dfrac{1}{6}$ of the flags have orange.   **true**

22. $\dfrac{1}{6}$ of the flags have at least one horizontal red line.   **false**

23. $\dfrac{1}{3}$ of the flags have green.   **false**

*24.** $\dfrac{4}{6}$ of the flags are $\dfrac{1}{3}$ green. **false**

To answer 21–24, use only the flags below the Problem Solving bar.

CHAPTER 5   143

MEETING INDIVIDUAL NEEDS

For Students Who Are . . .

Acquiring English Proficiency Have students read aloud the names of the countries on pages 142 and 143.

Gifted and Talented Have students research flags from other countries and write questions similar to Exercises 20–24.

Working 2 or 3 Grades Below Level Have students use pages 4–25 of the Skills Workbook for fractions.

Today's Problem

Study this sample of a Basic program in which the computer processes the commands sequentially.
What is the value of D?

```
100 LET A = 3
110 LET B = 5
120 LET C = (A + B)/2
130 IF C > 5 THEN D = 7
140 IF C < 5 THEN D = 8
```

(Since C = 4 and 4 < 5, then D = 8.)

3 FOLLOW-UP

=== PRACTICE 5-6 ===

Write the fraction for how much is shaded.

1. $\dfrac{3}{8}$ **2.** $\dfrac{4}{10}$ **3.** $\dfrac{6}{12}$

4. $\dfrac{2}{6}$ **5.** $\dfrac{1}{2}$ **6.** $\dfrac{1}{3}$

Write the fraction associated with each letter.

7. $A = \dfrac{1}{3}$ **8.** $A = \dfrac{4}{10}\; B = \dfrac{7}{10}$ **9.** $A = \dfrac{1}{5}\; B = \dfrac{3}{5}\; C = \dfrac{4}{5}$

10. $A = \dfrac{4}{16}\; B = \dfrac{10}{16}\; C = \dfrac{13}{16}$ **11.** $A = \dfrac{2}{6}\; B = \dfrac{5}{6}\; C = \dfrac{4}{6}$ **12.** $A = \dfrac{2}{8}\; B = \dfrac{5}{8}\; C = \dfrac{6}{8}$

13. Draw a number line from 0 to 1. Illustrate the fractions $\dfrac{2}{7}$ and $\dfrac{5}{7}$.

$\dfrac{2}{7}$ $\dfrac{5}{7}$

Write *true* or *false*.

14. Tim's father asked him to bring the first third of the 48 cows in for milking. In order to solve the problem, Tim needed to divide the 48 cows into 4 equal groups. false

15. The correct number of cows for Tim to bring in was 48 ÷ 3. true

=== RETEACHING 5-6 ===

☑ **MATERIALS CHECKLIST:** Counters

Have the students work in pairs. Provide each pair with several stacks of green, blue, and red counters. The stacks should be of varying sizes with mixed colors of counters. Also provide each pair with a sheet of paper on which you have drawn several "fraction frames," such as the following: $\frac{\square}{\bigcirc}$. Instruct one partner to write the total number of counters in one stack in three denominator circles. Have the other partner write the number of green, blue, and red counters in three numerator squares above the circles. Partners should repeat the activity for the other stacks.

=== ENRICHMENT 5-6 ===

Write a word that meets the conditions. Use a dictionary if you wish.
Answers will vary. Suggestions are given.

1. One half of the letters are vowels.
SEAT

2. One third of the letters are consonants.
TOE

3. One fourth of the letters are *R* or *T*.
SORE

4. Two thirds of the letters are *D, S, N,* or *W*.
SAW

5. Exactly one thirteenth of the letters of the alphabet are used.
IS

6. At least three sevenths of the letters are *R, E, L, D, G,* or *W*.
SLOWEST

Write a sentence or two using the words you wrote above. Answers will vary.
As I took my seat in the theater, I saw my friend Kim walk in. "Sorry, I'm late," she said, "but that bus was the slowest one I've ever taken, and my toe is so sore I had to walk very slowly."

Lesson Organizer

Objective: Write equivalent fractions using multiplication.

Prior Knowledge: Students should understand the meaning of fractions.

Lesson Resources:
Practice Worksheet 5-7
Reteaching Worksheet 5-7
Enrichment Activity 5-7
Daily Review 5-7

Two-Minute Math

Replace the ☐ with × or ÷.
Replace the ? with a number.

24 ☐ ? = 4   12 ☐ ? = 4.8

18 ☐ ? = 108

(÷ 6; × 0.4; × 6)

1 INTRODUCE

CONNECTING ACTIVITY

✓ **MATERIALS CHECKLIST:** Teaching Aid 3 (Centimeter Grid Paper) for each student

1. Have students enclose a rectangle 8 cm by 16 cm, divide it into four equal parts, and shade three of the parts. **What fraction represents the shaded part?** ($\frac{3}{4}$)

2. Draw another rectangle of the same size, divide it into eight equal parts, and shade six of the parts. **What fraction represents the shaded part?** ($\frac{6}{8}$)

3. Have students compare the shaded parts of their two rectangles. **Are the shaded parts the same?** (Yes.) **What can you conclude about the fractions?** (They represent the same value.)

WHEN YOUR STUDENTS ASK
★ WHY AM I LEARNING THIS? ★

You can connect equivalent fractions to real life through carpentry. Carpenters use equivalent fractions to help them determine how much material they need for a given job.

Equivalent Fractions

Who is right?

$\frac{3}{12}$ ← blue fish
$\quad$ ← fish in all

1 out of every 4 fish is blue. →

Equivalent fractions have the same value. To write an equivalent fraction, multiply the numerator and the denominator of the given fraction by the same nonzero number.

$$\frac{1}{4} = \frac{1 \times 3}{4 \times 3} = \frac{3}{12}$$

Both are right, because $\frac{1}{4}$ and $\frac{3}{12}$ are equivalent fractions.

Other examples:

$$\frac{2}{5} = \frac{2 \times 2}{5 \times 2} = \frac{4}{10} \qquad\qquad \frac{9}{10} = \frac{9 \times 4}{10 \times 4} = \frac{36}{40}$$

THINK ALOUD Name some other fractions equivalent to $\frac{2}{5}$ and to $\frac{9}{10}$.
Answers will vary. Suggestions given: $\frac{2}{5} = \frac{4}{10} = \frac{6}{15}$; $\frac{9}{10} = \frac{18}{20} = \frac{45}{50}$.

▬ GUIDED PRACTICE ▬

1. Draw a picture to show that $\frac{4}{8}$ is equivalent to $\frac{1}{2}$.
Check students' drawings.

Name two equivalent fractions for each.   Find the value of n.

2. $\frac{3}{4}$ $\frac{6}{8}, \frac{75}{100}$ 3. $\frac{5}{9}$ $\frac{10}{18}, \frac{15}{27}$ 4. $\frac{6}{7}$ $\frac{12}{14}, \frac{60}{70}$ 5. $\frac{7}{9} = \frac{n}{18}$ $n = 14$ 6. $\frac{5}{12} = \frac{15}{n}$ $n = 6$
Answers will vary. Suggestions given.

---

2 TEACH

✓ **MATERIALS CHECKLIST:** Teaching Aid 3 (Centimeter Grid Paper) for each student, calculators, fraction models

Are $\frac{2}{2}$, $\frac{4}{4}$, and $\frac{8}{8}$ **equivalent fractions? Explain or demonstrate on your grid paper.** (Yes; they each name the same number, 1.)

Explain the relationship between multiplying both the numerator and the denominator of a fraction by the same nonzero number and the identity number for multiplication.
(Possible answer: Multiplying by $\frac{2}{2}$, $\frac{3}{3}$, and so on, is the same as multiplying by 1; 1 is the identity number for multiplication.)

> ### Chalkboard Examples
>
> Name two equivalent fractions.
>
> $\frac{4}{9}$ $\qquad$ $\frac{7}{8}$ $\qquad$ $\frac{3}{7}$
>
> (Answers may vary.)

SUMMARIZE/ASSESS **Explain how to use multiplication to name equivalent fractions.** (Multiply both the numerator and the denominator by the same number.)

PRACTICE

Write three fractions equivalent to the given fraction. Use fraction models to help.
Answers will vary. Suggestions given.

7. $\frac{1}{3}$ $\frac{2}{6}, \frac{3}{9}, \frac{4}{12}$

8. $\frac{3}{4}$ $\frac{6}{8}, \frac{9}{12}, \frac{30}{40}$

9. $\frac{1}{2}$ $\frac{10}{20}, \frac{5}{10}$ $\frac{2}{4}, \frac{10}{20}$

10. $\frac{5}{9}$ $\frac{10}{18}, \frac{15}{27}, \frac{50}{90}$

11. $\frac{2}{5}$ $\frac{4}{10}, \frac{6}{15}, \frac{8}{20}$

12. $\frac{3}{11}$ $\frac{6}{22}, \frac{9}{33}, \frac{12}{44}$

13. $\frac{3}{5}$ $\frac{6}{10}, \frac{9}{15}, \frac{30}{50}$

14. $\frac{4}{7}$ $\frac{8}{14}, \frac{12}{21}, \frac{16}{28}$

15. $\frac{3}{8}$ $\frac{6}{16}, \frac{9}{24}, \frac{12}{32}$

16. $\frac{5}{16}$ $\frac{10}{32}, \frac{15}{48}, \frac{20}{64}$

17. $\frac{11}{12}$ $\frac{22}{24}, \frac{33}{36}, \frac{44}{48}$

18. $\frac{17}{20}$ $\frac{34}{40}, \frac{51}{60}, \frac{68}{80}$

Find the value of n.

19. $\frac{2}{5} = \frac{8}{n}$ $n = 20$

20. $\frac{3}{7} = \frac{n}{21}$ $n = 9$

21. $\frac{8}{15} = \frac{n}{60}$ $n = 32$

22. $\frac{5}{7} = \frac{20}{n}$ $n = 28$

23. $\frac{6}{13} = \frac{n}{52}$ $n = 24$

24. $\frac{3}{4} = \frac{n}{72}$ $n = 54$

25. $\frac{8}{9} = \frac{n}{72}$ $n = 64$

26. $\frac{12}{25} = \frac{96}{n}$ $n = 200$

27. $\frac{3}{7} = \frac{48}{n}$ $n = 112$

28. $\frac{4}{15} = \frac{n}{75}$ $n = 20$

29. Draw a picture to show that $\frac{2}{3}$ and $\frac{4}{6}$ are equivalent fractions.
Check students' drawings.

PROBLEM SOLVING

 Choose mental math or paper and pencil to solve. Choices will vary. Suggestions given.

30. Match the fraction with the kind of fish shown in the aquarium.

a. $\frac{1}{3}$ **b.** $\frac{1}{2}$ **c.** $\frac{1}{6}$

m; swordtail   m; neon tetra   m; angelfish

31. CREATE YOUR OWN Write a fraction problem about the fish in the aquarium.
Check students' work.

*32. Two more of each kind of fish are put in the tank. Write two equivalent fractions that represent what part of the fish in the aquarium are neon tetras.
p; $\frac{20}{42}, \frac{10}{21}$

Critical Thinking

Suppose you and a partner put 72 fish (guppies, neon tetras, and angelfish) in an aquarium. How many of each kind of fish would you have if the following conditions are met?

- One fourth are neon tetras.
- One half are guppies.
- More than $\frac{1}{6}$ are angelfish.

18 neon tetras, 36 guppies, 18 angel fish

CHAPTER 5   **145**

MEETING INDIVIDUAL NEEDS

For Students Who Are . . .

Acquiring English Proficiency Lead students to conclude that for Exercises 30–32 they must first find the total number of fish.

Gifted and Talented Assign students the Technology lesson on page 168.

Working 2 or 3 Grades Below Level Have students use pages 26–33 of the Skills Workbook for fractions.

Today's Problem

The numerator of a fraction is one less than its denominator. The sum of its numerator and denominator is 11. What is the fraction?
(The fraction is $\frac{5}{6}$.)

---

3 FOLLOW-UP

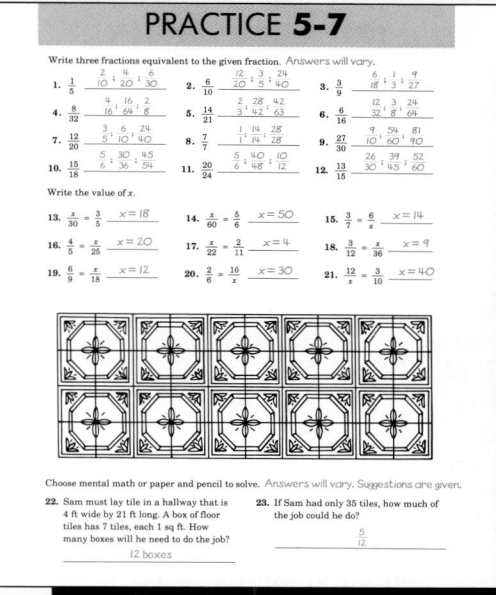

PRACTICE 5-7

Write three fractions equivalent to the given fraction. Answers will vary.

1. $\frac{1}{5}$ $\frac{2}{10}, \frac{4}{20}, \frac{6}{30}$

2. $\frac{6}{10}$ $\frac{12}{20}, \frac{3}{5}, \frac{24}{40}$

3. $\frac{3}{9}$ $\frac{6}{18}, \frac{1}{3}, \frac{9}{27}$

4. $\frac{8}{32}$ $\frac{4}{16}, \frac{16}{64}, \frac{1}{8}$

5. $\frac{14}{21}$ $\frac{2}{3}, \frac{28}{42}, \frac{42}{63}$

6. $\frac{6}{10}$ $\frac{12}{32}, \frac{3}{8}, \frac{24}{64}$

7. $\frac{12}{20}$ $\frac{3}{5}, \frac{6}{10}, \frac{24}{40}$

8. $\frac{7}{7}$ $\frac{1}{1}, \frac{14}{14}, \frac{28}{28}$

9. $\frac{27}{30}$ $\frac{9}{10}, \frac{54}{60}, \frac{81}{90}$

10. $\frac{15}{24}$ $\frac{5}{6}, \frac{10}{36}, \frac{54}{54}$

11. $\frac{20}{24}$ $\frac{5}{6}, \frac{40}{48}, \frac{10}{12}$

12. $\frac{13}{15}$ $\frac{26}{30}, \frac{39}{45}, \frac{52}{60}$

Write the value of x.

13. $\frac{x}{30} = \frac{3}{5}$ $x = 18$

14. $\frac{x}{60} = \frac{5}{6}$ $x = 50$

15. $\frac{3}{7} = \frac{6}{x}$ $x = 14$

16. $\frac{4}{5} = \frac{x}{25}$ $x = 20$

17. $\frac{x}{22} = \frac{2}{11}$ $x = 4$

18. $\frac{3}{12} = \frac{x}{36}$ $x = 9$

19. $\frac{6}{9} = \frac{x}{18}$ $x = 12$

20. $\frac{2}{6} = \frac{10}{x}$ $x = 30$

21. $\frac{12}{x} = \frac{3}{10}$ $x = 40$

Choose mental math or paper and pencil to solve. Answers will vary. Suggestions are given.

22. Sam must lay tile in a hallway that is 4 ft wide by 21 ft long. A box of floor tiles has 7 tiles, each 1 sq ft. How many boxes will he need to do the job?
12 boxes

23. If Sam had only 35 tiles, how much of the job could he do?
$\frac{5}{12}$

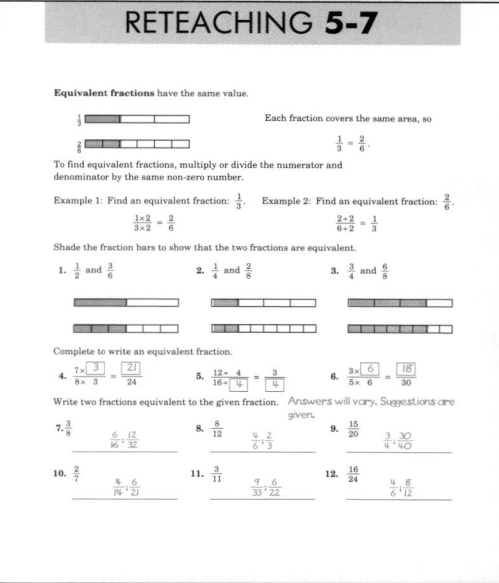

RETEACHING 5-7

Equivalent fractions have the same value.

Each fraction covers the same area, so $\frac{1}{3} = \frac{2}{6}$.

To find equivalent fractions, multiply or divide the numerator and denominator by the same non-zero number.

Example 1: Find an equivalent fraction: $\frac{1}{3}$. $\frac{1 \times 2}{3 \times 2} = \frac{2}{6}$

Example 2: Find an equivalent fraction: $\frac{2}{6}$. $\frac{2 \div 2}{6 \div 2} = \frac{1}{3}$

Shade the fraction bars to show that the two fractions are equivalent.

1. $\frac{1}{2}$ and $\frac{3}{6}$ **2.** $\frac{1}{4}$ and $\frac{2}{8}$ **3.** $\frac{3}{4}$ and $\frac{6}{8}$

Complete to write an equivalent fraction.

4. $\frac{7 \times \boxed{3}}{8 \times 3} = \frac{\boxed{21}}{24}$ **5.** $\frac{12 \div 4}{16 \div \boxed{4}} = \frac{3}{\boxed{4}}$ **6.** $\frac{3 \times \boxed{6}}{5 \times 6} = \frac{\boxed{18}}{30}$

Write two fractions equivalent to the given fraction. Answers will vary. Suggestions are given.

7. $\frac{3}{8}$ $\frac{6}{16}, \frac{12}{32}$

8. $\frac{4}{12}$ $\frac{2}{6}, \frac{1}{3}$

9. $\frac{15}{20}$ $\frac{3}{4}, \frac{30}{40}$

10. $\frac{2}{7}$ $\frac{4}{14}, \frac{6}{21}$

11. $\frac{3}{11}$ $\frac{9}{33}, \frac{6}{22}$

12. $\frac{16}{24}$ $\frac{4}{6}, \frac{8}{12}$

ENRICHMENT 5-7

☑ **MATERIALS CHECKLIST:** Counters

Provide each pair of students with several stacks of blue and red counters to arrange in patterns as shown.

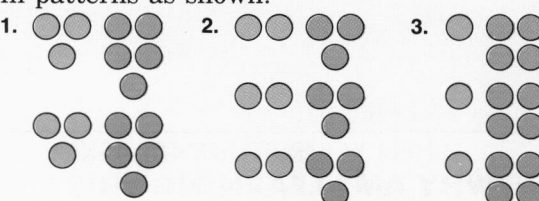

1.   **2.**   **3.**

For each pattern write the fractions:
$\frac{\text{red}}{\text{total}}$ $\frac{\text{blue}}{\text{total}}$ $\frac{\text{red}}{\text{blue}}$

Write each fraction in two ways. Explain why the pairs of fractions are equivalent. Have students make up other patterns.

LESSON | 5-8

Objective: Write equivalent fractions using division.

Prior Knowledge: Students should be able to find the GCF of two or more numbers.

Lesson Resources:
Practice Worksheet 5-8
Reteaching Activity 5-8
Enrichment Worksheet 5-8
Daily Review 5-8

Two-Minute Math

If you separate 18 nickels, 30 dimes, and 12 quarters into equal amounts, what is the maximum number of coins and money in each amount? *(6 nickels, 10 dimes, 4 quarters; $2.30)*

1 INTRODUCE

SYMBOLIC ACTIVITY

Write the fraction $\frac{18}{24}$.

1. Have students list the factors of the numerator and the denominator. **What is the GCF of 18 and 24?** *(6)*

2. Explain that the numerator and denominator can be divided by the GCF to name an equivalent fraction in lowest terms. Write the following on the chalkboard: $\frac{18 \div 6}{24 \div 6} = \frac{3}{4}$. **What is the GCF of the numerator and denominator of $\frac{3}{4}$?** *(1)*

3. Explain that a fraction is in lowest terms when the GCF of the numerator and the denominator is 1.

4. Repeat the activity with $\frac{25}{60}$ and $\frac{21}{35}$.

WHEN YOUR STUDENTS ASK
★ WHY AM I LEARNING THIS? ★

You can use this skill in real life situations. Scientists often use fractions. Chemists use fractions to see what the ratio of one number to another is in a compound.

MATH AND SCIENCE

Lowest Terms

There are 206 bones in the human body. These bones support the body, protect the internal organs, and aid in movement.

There are 32 bones in the arm and hand. Of these, 8 are found in the wrist.

Can you name the fraction equivalent to $\frac{8}{32}$ that is in **lowest terms**?

If you know how to find the GCF of 8 and 32, you can make a **MATH CONNECTION** to write a fraction in lowest terms equivalent to $\frac{8}{32}$.

Divide the numerator and denominator by the GCF of 8 and 32, 8.

$$\frac{8}{32} = \frac{8 \div 8}{32 \div 8} = \frac{1}{4} \longleftarrow \text{lowest terms}$$

THINK ALOUD What is true about a fraction if the GCF of the numerator and denominator is 1? **The fraction is in lowest terms.**
Other examples:

What is the GCF of 6 and 10?	What is the GCF of 12 and 18?
$\frac{6}{10} = \frac{6 \div 2}{10 \div 2} = \frac{3}{5}$	$\frac{12}{18} = \frac{12 \div 6}{18 \div 6} = \frac{2}{3}$

GUIDED PRACTICE

Is the fraction in lowest terms? Answer *yes* or *no*. If *no*, write the fraction in lowest terms.

1. $\frac{5}{35}$ no; $\frac{1}{7}$ **2.** $\frac{3}{16}$ yes **3.** $\frac{6}{18}$ no; $\frac{1}{3}$

4. $\frac{5}{12}$ yes **5.** $\frac{14}{20}$ no; $\frac{7}{10}$ **6.** $\frac{21}{42}$ no; $\frac{1}{2}$

7. **THINK ALOUD** If you divide the numerator and denominator of any fraction by the GCF, will the equivalent fraction always be in lowest terms? Explain. **Yes. You are dividing by the largest number they have in common.**

146   LESSON 5–8

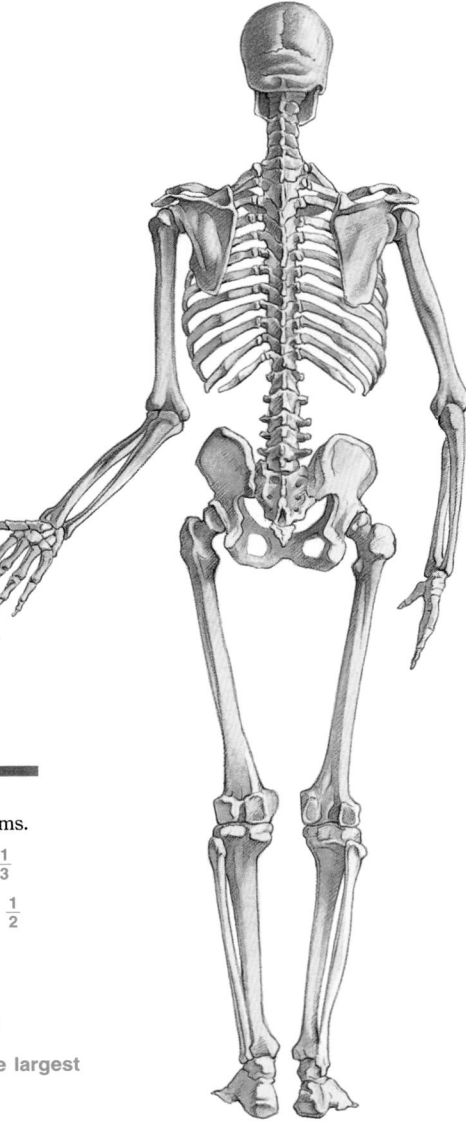

---

2 TEACH

☑ MATERIALS CHECKLIST: Math Connection Transparency

Display the transparency. Have students fill in the spaces and discuss the math connection. *(See student pages.)*

If you divide the numerator and the denominator by a common factor that is neither the GCF nor 1, will the fraction be in lowest terms? Explain. *(No, you can still divide the numerator and denominator by a factor.)*

How can you check that a fraction is in lowest terms? *(The GCF of both the numerator and denominator will be 1.)*

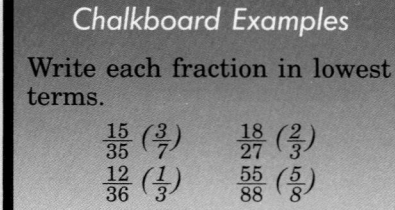

Chalkboard Examples

Write each fraction in lowest terms.

$\frac{15}{35}$ $\left(\frac{3}{7}\right)$ $\frac{18}{27}$ $\left(\frac{2}{3}\right)$

$\frac{12}{36}$ $\left(\frac{1}{3}\right)$ $\frac{55}{88}$ $\left(\frac{5}{8}\right)$

SUMMARIZE/ASSESS   **Explain how to use division to name an equivalent fraction in lowest terms.** *(Divide the numerator and denominator by the GCF.)*

Find the value of *n*.

8. $\frac{2}{16} = \frac{n}{8}$ $n = 1$ **9.** $\frac{12}{15} = \frac{4}{n}$ $n = 5$ **10.** $\frac{2}{n} = \frac{6}{9}$ $n = 3$ **11.** $\frac{48}{60} = \frac{n}{5}$ $n = 4$

12. $\frac{15}{40} = \frac{n}{8}$ $n = 3$ **13.** $\frac{18}{22} = \frac{9}{n}$ $n = 11$ **14.** $\frac{28}{36} = \frac{7}{n}$ $n = 9$ **15.** $\frac{33}{42} = \frac{n}{14}$ $n = 11$

Write the fraction in lowest terms.

16. $\frac{8}{16}$ $\frac{1}{2}$ **17.** $\frac{10}{15}$ $\frac{2}{3}$ **18.** $\frac{7}{13}$ $\frac{7}{13}$ **19.** $\frac{16}{20}$ $\frac{4}{5}$ **20.** $\frac{15}{45}$ $\frac{1}{3}$ **21.** $\frac{8}{20}$ $\frac{2}{5}$

22. $\frac{9}{21}$ $\frac{3}{7}$ **23.** $\frac{6}{27}$ $\frac{2}{9}$ **24.** $\frac{35}{50}$ $\frac{7}{10}$ **25.** $\frac{28}{32}$ $\frac{7}{8}$ **26.** $\frac{13}{28}$ $\frac{13}{28}$ **27.** $\frac{45}{81}$ $\frac{5}{9}$

28. $\frac{23}{46}$ $\frac{1}{2}$ **29.** $\frac{18}{81}$ $\frac{2}{9}$ **30.** $\frac{16}{44}$ $\frac{4}{11}$ **31.** $\frac{16}{96}$ $\frac{1}{6}$ **32.** $\frac{84}{140}$ $\frac{3}{5}$ **33.** $\frac{150}{210}$ $\frac{5}{7}$

*34. Write the phrase as a fraction in lowest terms.

   a. 20 min of an hour $\frac{1}{3}$ h   **b.** 60 d of a 365-d year $\frac{12}{73}$ yr **c.** 5 d in June $\frac{1}{6}$ d

*35. CRITICAL THINKING Find all the ways in which the numbers 3, 9, 27, and 81 can replace the variables to make equivalent fractions in the equation $\frac{a}{b} = \frac{c}{d}$. $\frac{3}{9} = \frac{27}{81}$, $\frac{9}{3} = \frac{81}{27}$, $\frac{3}{27} = \frac{9}{81}$, $\frac{27}{3} = \frac{81}{9}$, $\frac{27}{81} = \frac{3}{9}$, $\frac{81}{27} = \frac{9}{3}$, $\frac{9}{81} = \frac{3}{27}$, $\frac{81}{9} = \frac{27}{3}$

PROBLEM SOLVING

Solve.

36. Rewrite the fractions in the paragraph in lowest terms. $\frac{14}{103}$, $\frac{2}{7}$, $\frac{3}{14}$, $\frac{3}{14}$

> The skull contains $\frac{28}{206}$ of the bones in the human body. Of the skull bones, $\frac{8}{28}$ make up the cranium, which protects the brain, and $\frac{6}{28}$ are facial bones. Of the facial bones, $\frac{12}{56}$ are used to conduct sound in the ear.

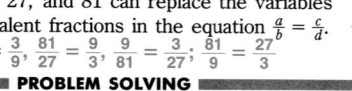

37. The bones in the two legs and feet make up $\frac{56}{206}$ of the bones in the body. The shaded region in which rectangle below represents this number of bones? **c**

  a.    **b.**    **c.**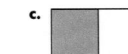

*38. Shade a region of a circle to represent the number of bones in the human body that are *not* in the legs and feet.   See page 163b.

MEETING INDIVIDUAL NEEDS

For Students Who Are . . .

Acquiring English Proficiency Pair students with an English-proficient student to discuss and answer Exercises 34–38.

Gifted and Talented Have students find the number of bones in the hand and arm and use the information to write a problem.

Working 2 or 3 Grades Below Level Have students use pages 36–39 of the Skills Workbook for fractions.

Today's Problem

Consider this sentence: "The moon is made of green cheese." What fraction represents the number of letters that are vowels (*a, e, i, o,* and *u*) in this sentence? What is an equivalent fraction? (*The fraction is 12 vowels/26 letters, or $\frac{6}{13}$.*)

---

3 FOLLOW-UP

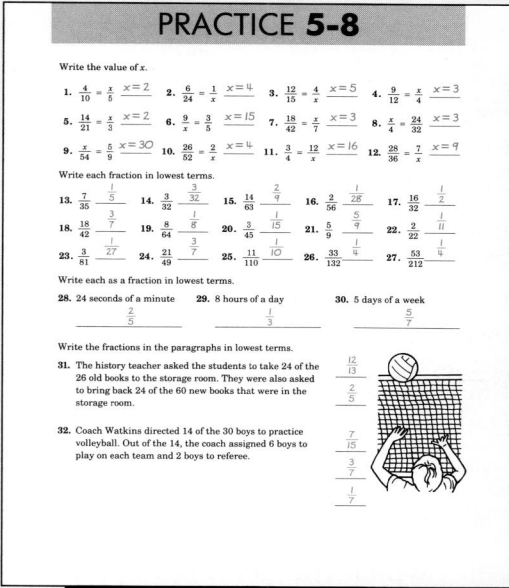

RETEACHING 5-8

☑ **MATERIALS CHECKLIST:** Fraction bars

Write the following fractions on the board: $\frac{1}{2}$, $\frac{2}{4}$, $\frac{3}{5}$, $\frac{2}{6}$, $\frac{4}{6}$, $\frac{4}{8}$, $\frac{6}{8}$, $\frac{6}{9}$, $\frac{4}{10}$, $\frac{6}{10}$, $\frac{8}{10}$, $\frac{2}{12}$, $\frac{4}{12}$, $\frac{8}{12}$, $\frac{10}{12}$. Have the students work in groups of four. Provide each student with two fraction bars from a set of fraction bars showing halves, thirds, fourths, fifths, sixths, eighths, tenths, or twelfths. Instruct the students to place their fraction bars in a column to find all the equivalent fractions for each fraction on the board by noticing how the vertical lines on the fraction bars line up. Have the students tell which fraction bar shows the fraction in lowest terms.

ENRICHMENT 5-8

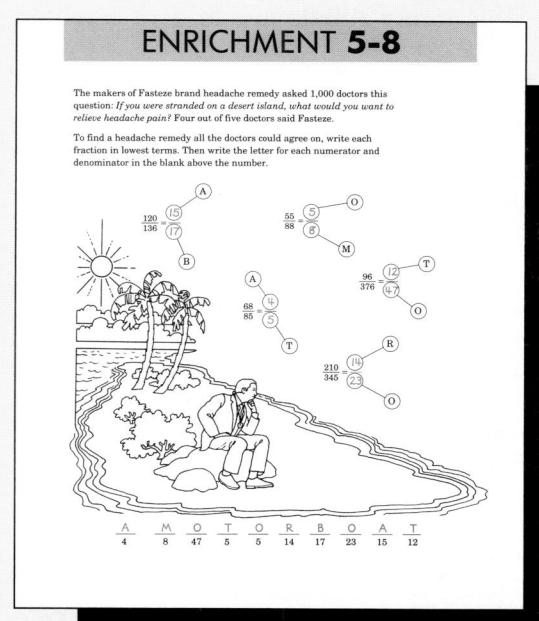

Lesson Organizer

Objective: Write fractions as mixed numbers and mixed numbers as fractions.

Prior Knowledge: Students should be able to divide whole numbers.

Error Analysis and Remediation: See page 163A.

Lesson Resources:
Practice Worksheet 5-9
Reteaching Worksheet 5-9
Enrichment Activity 5-9
Daily Review 5-9

Two-Minute Math

Which fraction does not belong in each group?

$\frac{12}{18}, \frac{10}{15}, \frac{2}{3}, \frac{2}{5} \left(\frac{2}{5}\right)$

$\frac{6}{12}, \frac{60}{72}, \frac{10}{12}, \frac{25}{30} \left(\frac{6}{12}\right)$

1 INTRODUCE

CONNECTING ACTIVITY

✔ **MATERIALS CHECKLIST:** fraction bars

1. Write $2\frac{2}{3}$ on the chalkboard and display fraction bars to represent this value.

- **How many thirds are in each whole unit?** *(3)*
- **How many thirds are in two whole units?** *(6)*
- **How many thirds are in $\frac{2}{3}$ of a whole unit?** *(2)*

How many thirds are there in all? *(8)*
Relate each step to the algorithm:
$2\frac{2}{3} = \frac{(2 \times 3)}{3} + 2 = \frac{6 + 2}{3} = \frac{8}{3}$

2. Repeat the activity using $\frac{9}{4}$.

WHEN YOUR STUDENTS ASK
★ WHY AM I LEARNING THIS? ★

You can relate this skill to real life through food preparation. Suppose there are $19\frac{3}{4}$ pizzas ready to be served in the cafeteria. Each pizza can be cut into four servings. Is there enough for 98 servings?

Fractions and Mixed Numbers

Jumbo, an elephant in P. T. Barnum's famous circus in the 1880s, weighed $6\frac{1}{2}$ t. The number $6\frac{1}{2}$ is a **mixed number**.

You can write a mixed number as a fraction. This number line shows that $6\frac{1}{2}$ is $\frac{13}{2}$.

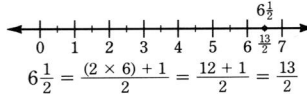

$6\frac{1}{2} = \frac{(2 \times 6) + 1}{2} = \frac{12 + 1}{2} = \frac{13}{2}$

The fraction $\frac{11}{4}$ can be written as a mixed number.

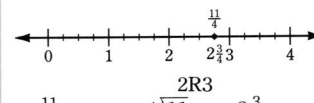

$\frac{11}{4}$ means $4\overline{)11}$ with $2R3$ or $2\frac{3}{4}$.

■■■■■ **GUIDED PRACTICE** ■■■■■

Write the mixed number as a fraction.

1. $1\frac{3}{4}$ $\frac{7}{4}$ **2.** $2\frac{3}{5}$ $\frac{13}{5}$ **3.** $3\frac{5}{6}$ $\frac{23}{6}$

Write the fraction as a mixed number in lowest terms. $2\frac{1}{3}$

4. $\frac{7}{5}$ $1\frac{2}{5}$ **5.** $\frac{11}{3}$ $3\frac{2}{3}$ **6.** $\frac{14}{6}$

7. THINK ALOUD Explain what a mixed number is. *A number that has a whole number part and a fractional part.*

MATH AND SCIENCE

148 LESSON 5-9

2 TEACH

What is true of all fractions that can be written as mixed numbers? Give examples to demonstrate your answer. *(The numerator is greater than the denominator; example: $\frac{9}{8}$.)*

In the example on page 148, why is the remainder, R3, written as $\frac{3}{4}$? *(because 3 of 4 equal parts remain)*

Chalkboard Examples
Write as a fraction.
$2\frac{5}{6} \left(\frac{17}{6}\right)$ $3\frac{3}{4} \left(\frac{15}{4}\right)$
Write as a mixed number.
$\frac{15}{2} \left(7\frac{1}{2}\right)$ $\frac{13}{5} \left(2\frac{3}{5}\right)$

SUMMARIZE/ASSESS **Explain how to write a mixed number as a fraction and a fraction as a mixed number.** *(Students should give examples to model their explanations.)*

Write the mixed number as a fraction.

8. $1\frac{3}{8}$ $\frac{11}{8}$ 9. $2\frac{5}{9}$ $\frac{23}{9}$ 10. $2\frac{3}{4}$ $\frac{11}{4}$

11. $1\frac{7}{9}$ $\frac{16}{9}$ 12. $3\frac{2}{3}$ $\frac{11}{3}$ 13. $2\frac{1}{2}$ $\frac{5}{2}$

14. $2\frac{9}{10}$ $\frac{29}{10}$ 15. $3\frac{5}{8}$ $\frac{29}{8}$ 16. $4\frac{2}{3}$ $\frac{14}{3}$

17. $9\frac{4}{5}$ $\frac{49}{5}$ 18. $9\frac{1}{6}$ $\frac{55}{6}$ 19. $5\frac{3}{4}$ $\frac{23}{4}$

Write the fraction as a whole or mixed number in lowest terms.

20. $\frac{8}{5}$ $1\frac{3}{5}$ 21. $\frac{7}{4}$ $1\frac{3}{4}$ 22. $\frac{13}{8}$ $1\frac{5}{8}$

23. $\frac{15}{7}$ $2\frac{1}{7}$ 24. $\frac{18}{9}$ 2 25. $\frac{14}{8}$ $1\frac{3}{4}$

26. $\frac{9}{2}$ $4\frac{1}{2}$ 27. $\frac{23}{5}$ $4\frac{3}{5}$ 28. $\frac{26}{7}$ $3\frac{5}{7}$

29. $\frac{18}{11}$ $1\frac{7}{11}$ 30. $\frac{21}{9}$ $2\frac{1}{3}$ 31. $\frac{29}{7}$ $4\frac{1}{7}$

NUMBER SENSE   Find the measurement in inches represented by the letter. Give the answer in lowest terms.

32. A $\frac{3}{8}$ in.   33. B $1\frac{1}{4}$ in.

34. C $2\frac{7}{8}$ in.   35. D $3\frac{3}{16}$ in.

*36. **CRITICAL THINKING**   Choose from the numbers 1, 2, 3, 5, and 7 to replace the variables in the equation. $\frac{a}{b} = n + \frac{c}{b}$ Answers will vary. Suggestion given: $\frac{5}{3} = 1 + \frac{2}{3}$.

Read carefully. Change each fraction to a mixed number in lowest terms. Use your number sense to select the missing measurements from the fractions listed.

    The elephant is the largest living land animal. The largest

37. known elephant, an African bull, measured $\frac{79}{6}$ ft tall. One $13\frac{1}{6}$

38. record-size elephant tusk is 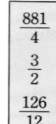 ft long. The tusk weighs about $10\frac{1}{2}$

39. 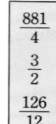 lb. On average, an elephant's tail measures about $220\frac{1}{4}$

40. $\frac{10}{3}$ ft in length. An average elephant's trunk measures about $3\frac{1}{3}$

41. 5 ft in length and can hold about 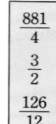 gal of water. An $1\frac{1}{2}$

42. elephant also has four back teeth, each weighing about $\frac{17}{2}$ lb. $8\frac{1}{2}$

$\frac{881}{4}$
$\frac{3}{2}$
$\frac{126}{12}$

MEETING INDIVIDUAL NEEDS

For Students Who Are . . .

Acquiring English Proficiency   Pair students with an English-proficient student to discuss and answer Exercises 37–42.

Gifted and Talented   Have each student create a problem similar to Exercise 36. Then have students trade papers and solve.

2 or 3 Grades Below Level   Have students use pages 40–43 of the Skills Workbook for fractions.

Today's Problem

What fraction of the numbers printed on a pair of number cubes are even? What fraction of the numbers printed in a single number cube are even? How are these two answers related? *(The fraction of even numbers on a pair is $\frac{6}{12}$; the fraction of even numbers on a single cube: $\frac{3}{6}$. These are equivalent fractions.)*

---

3 FOLLOW-UP

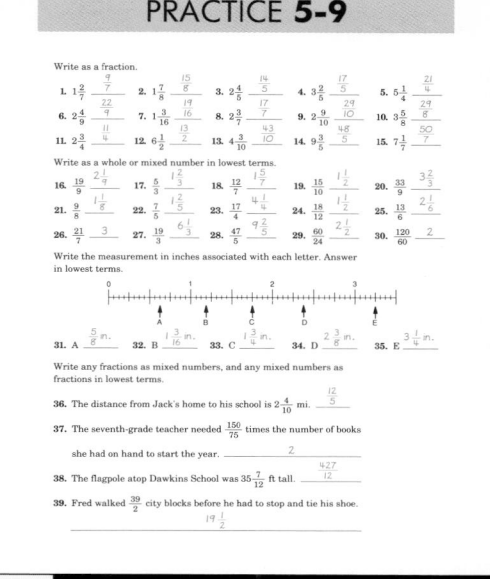

PRACTICE 5-9

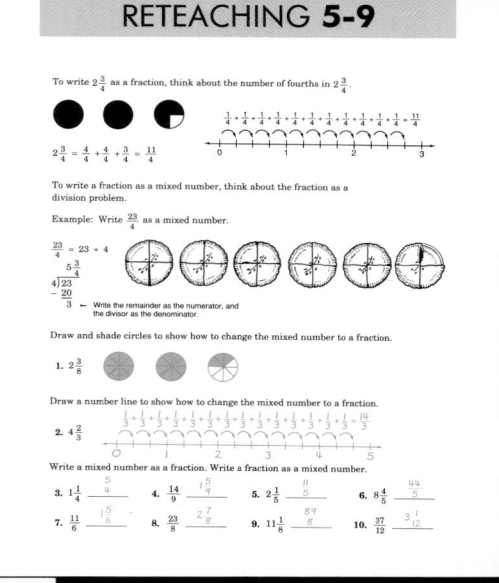

RETEACHING 5-9

ENRICHMENT 5-9

☑ **MATERIALS CHECKLIST:** Index cards, clock or watches with second hands

Have the students work in groups of four, and in pairs within each group. Provide each pair with an identical set of index cards on which you have written various amounts of time in minutes, such as 245 minutes or 525 minutes, that can be written as a whole number of hours and a fractional part of another hour. One partner works through half the cards, while the other times the work. Ask the partners to switch roles. The fastest time wins, but the students must add 10 seconds for each incorrect answer.

LESSON 5-10

Lesson Organizer

Objective: Compare and order fractions and mixed numbers.

Prior Knowledge: Students should be able to name equivalent fractions by finding the LCD.

Error Analysis and Remediation: See page 163A.

Lesson Resources:
Practice Worksheet 5-10
Reteaching Worksheet 5-10
Enrichment Activity 5-10
Daily Review 5-10

Two-Minute Math

Find the LCM.

5 and 18 *(90)*   27 and 81 *(81)*
18, 24, and 36 *(72)*

1 INTRODUCE

CONNECTING ACTIVITY

1. Display the following number line.

0 ———————————————— 1

- Label $\frac{1}{7}$, $\frac{6}{7}$, and $\frac{4}{7}$ on the number line.

- Compare the three fractions from least to greatest and from greatest to least. ($\frac{1}{7} < \frac{4}{7} < \frac{6}{7}$; $\frac{6}{7} > \frac{4}{7} > \frac{1}{7}$)

2. Write the fractions $\frac{3}{4}$ and $\frac{5}{6}$.

- **What can you do so that it will be easy to compare these fractions?** *(Rename them as equivalent fractions with a denominator of 12.)*

- **Write two inequalities to compare the original fractions $\frac{3}{4}$ and $\frac{5}{6}$.** *($\frac{3}{4} < \frac{5}{6}$ and $\frac{5}{6} > \frac{3}{4}$)*

WHEN YOUR STUDENTS ASK
★ WHY AM I LEARNING THIS? ★

You can connect this skill to real life through auto repair. If a $\frac{1}{4}$-in. wrench is too small, a mechanic must know if a $\frac{5}{16}$-in. or a $\frac{9}{32}$-in. wrench would be bigger.

Comparing and Ordering Fractions and Mixed Numbers

Did you know that copper is one of the first metals known to human beings? Its use has been traced back to 8000 B.C.

The world's top five copper mining countries produce a total of about 4,656,000 t/yr. The circle graph shows the fraction of the 4,656,000 t of copper each country mines.

Does the USSR mine more copper than Zambia?

If you know how to write an equivalent fraction, you can make a **MATH CONNECTION** to compare two fractions.

Use the **least common denominator (LCD)** to write equivalent fractions so you can compare $\frac{7}{50}$ and $\frac{3}{25}$.

$$\frac{7}{50} = \frac{7}{50} \text{ and } \frac{3}{25} = \frac{6}{50}$$

> The LCD, 50, is the least common multiple of the denominators 50 and 25.

Since $\frac{7}{50} > \frac{6}{50}$, $\frac{7}{50} > \frac{3}{25}$.

So the USSR mines more copper than Zambia.

Other examples:

Compare $\frac{7}{8}$ and $\frac{5}{6}$.

$\frac{7}{8} = \frac{21}{24}$ and $\frac{5}{6} = \frac{20}{24}$

Since $\frac{21}{24} > \frac{20}{24}$, $\frac{7}{8} > \frac{5}{6}$.

Compare $2\frac{3}{5}$ and $2\frac{2}{3}$.

$2\frac{3}{5} = \frac{13}{5} = \frac{39}{15}$ and $2\frac{2}{3} = \frac{8}{3} = \frac{40}{15}$

Since $\frac{39}{15} < \frac{40}{15}$, $2\frac{3}{5} < 2\frac{2}{3}$.

MATH AND SOCIAL STUDIES

Zambia $\frac{3}{25}$
USSR $\frac{7}{50}$
Chile $\frac{8}{25}$
Canada $\frac{4}{25}$
United States $\frac{13}{50}$

GUIDED PRACTICE

Copy and compare. Choose $>$, $<$, or $=$.

1. $\frac{1}{4}$ ▇ $\frac{1}{3}$
   <

2. $\frac{2}{3}$ ▇ $\frac{5}{8}$
   >

3. $3\frac{1}{6}$ ▇ $3\frac{2}{9}$
   <

4. $1\frac{5}{6}$ ▇ $1\frac{4}{7}$
   >

Order the fractions from the greatest to the least.

5. $\frac{2}{5}, \frac{4}{7}, \frac{2}{3}$
   $\frac{2}{3}, \frac{4}{7}, \frac{2}{5}$

6. $\frac{4}{9}, \frac{6}{11}, \frac{2}{5}$
   $\frac{6}{11}, \frac{4}{9}, \frac{2}{5}$

7. $\frac{1}{3}, \frac{2}{7}, \frac{5}{12}$
   $\frac{5}{12}, \frac{1}{3}, \frac{2}{7}$

8. $\frac{3}{4}, \frac{13}{16}, \frac{19}{24}$
   $\frac{13}{16}, \frac{19}{24}, \frac{3}{4}$

150   LESSON 5-10

> **MULTICULTURAL NOTE**
>
> People living in what is now Iraq were probably the first to use copper. The Egyptians, the Inca, the ancient Chinese, and various Native American peoples also used copper.

2 TEACH

☑ **MATERIALS CHECKLIST:** Transparency 1, calculators

Display the transparency. Have students fill in the spaces and discuss the math connection. *(See student pages.)*

What is meant by the *least common denominator (LCD)*? *(The LCD is the LCM of the denominators of two or more fractions.)*

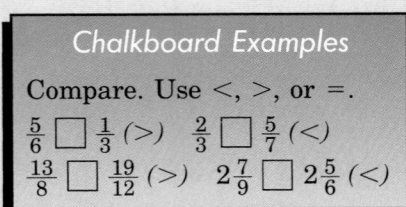

> ### Chalkboard Examples
>
> Compare. Use $<$, $>$, or $=$.
>
> $\frac{5}{6}$ ☐ $\frac{1}{3}$ *(>)* $\frac{2}{3}$ ☐ $\frac{5}{7}$ *(<)*
>
> $\frac{13}{8}$ ☐ $\frac{19}{12}$ *(>)* $2\frac{7}{9}$ ☐ $2\frac{5}{6}$ *(<)*

SUMMARIZE/ASSESS Use $\frac{3}{8}$ and $\frac{9}{10}$ to explain how to compare fractions with unlike denominators. *($\frac{3}{8} = \frac{15}{40}$; $\frac{9}{10} = \frac{36}{40}$; $\frac{36}{40} > \frac{15}{40}$)*

Copy and compare. Choose >, <, or =.

9. $\frac{5}{6}$ ■ $\frac{2}{3}$ >   10. $\frac{2}{3}$ ■ $\frac{5}{9}$ >   11. $\frac{3}{8}$ ■ $\frac{1}{4}$ >   12. $\frac{7}{12}$ ■ $\frac{3}{4}$ <

13. $\frac{1}{4}$ ■ $\frac{2}{8}$ =   14. $\frac{3}{4}$ ■ $\frac{5}{6}$ <   15. $7\frac{1}{2}$ ■ $2\frac{2}{3}$ >   16. $\frac{4}{5}$ ■ $\frac{3}{4}$ >

17. $2\frac{1}{2}$ ■ $\frac{15}{6}$ =   18. $\frac{5}{6}$ ■ $\frac{8}{9}$ <   19. $5\frac{4}{5}$ ■ $5\frac{3}{4}$ >   20. $\frac{13}{20}$ ■ $\frac{3}{4}$ <

21. $2\frac{6}{9}$ ■ $2\frac{2}{3}$ =   22. $1\frac{7}{9}$ ■ $1\frac{1}{2}$ >   23. $3\frac{7}{8}$ ■ $3\frac{11}{12}$ <   24. $\frac{18}{5}$ ■ $\frac{23}{7}$ >

CALCULATOR   Order from the least to the greatest. *See bottom of page.*

25. $2, \frac{7}{8}, \frac{3}{4}, \frac{5}{6}, \frac{2}{3}, 1$ 26. $\frac{1}{3}, 1, 2\frac{1}{3}, \frac{2}{5}, 2\frac{1}{2}, 1\frac{1}{4}$ 27. $\frac{18}{5}, 3\frac{7}{8}, \frac{21}{6}, 0.5, \frac{4}{1}, 2\frac{9}{9}$

PROBLEM SOLVING

The circle graph at right shows the top five nickel-producing countries. Use it to solve.

28. Match one of the fractions below to each of the countries represented in the circle graph.

   a. $\frac{1}{4}$ b. $\frac{1}{10}$ c. $\frac{7}{40}$
   Canada   Indonesia   Australia
   d. $\frac{1}{8}$ e. $\frac{7}{20}$
   New Caledonia   USSR

*29. One year, Canada produced about 121,800 t of nickel. About how many tons of nickel did the top five countries produce that year in all? *Accept reasonable estimates. Suggestion given.* ≈480,000 t

---

Mental Math

To compare each pair of fractions, the product of the pairs of denominators were used as common denominators.

$\frac{3}{4}$ ■ $\frac{2}{3}$ $\frac{4}{7}$ ■ $\frac{5}{8}$ $\frac{4}{9}$ ■ $\frac{3}{7}$ $\frac{4}{6}$ ■ $\frac{6}{9}$

⑨   ⑧   ㉜   ㉟   ㉘   ㉗   ㊱   ㊱

$\frac{3 \times 3}{12}$ ■ $\frac{2 \times 4}{12}$ $\frac{4 \times 8}{56}$ ■ $\frac{5 \times 7}{56}$ $\frac{4 \times 7}{63}$ ■ $\frac{3 \times 9}{63}$ $\frac{4 \times 9}{54}$ ■ $\frac{6 \times 6}{54}$

1. In each case, how were the common denominators determined?
   by multiplying the denominators

2. In each case, what will determine if the fractions are equal?
   if the numerators are equal

3. Look for a pattern to find a short cut for comparing fractions without finding the common denominator.   Use cross products: $\frac{4}{6} \diagdown \frac{6}{9}$.

$\frac{2}{3}, \frac{3}{4}, \frac{5}{6}, \frac{7}{8}, 1, 2$ $\frac{1}{3}, \frac{2}{5}, 1, 1\frac{1}{4}, 2\frac{1}{3}, 2\frac{1}{2}$ $0.5, 2\frac{9}{9}, \frac{21}{6}, \frac{18}{5}, 3\frac{7}{8}, \frac{4}{1}$ CHAPTER 5   **151**

PRACTICE 5-10

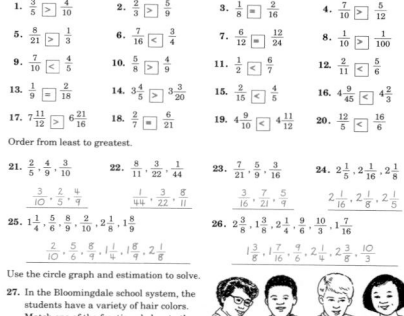

Compare. Choose >, <, or =.

1. $\frac{3}{5}$ > $\frac{4}{10}$ 2. $\frac{2}{3}$ > $\frac{5}{9}$ 3. $\frac{3}{8}$ = $\frac{6}{16}$ 4. $\frac{7}{10}$ > $\frac{5}{9}$

5. $\frac{8}{21}$ > $\frac{1}{3}$ 6. $\frac{7}{16}$ < $\frac{3}{4}$ 7. $\frac{6}{12}$ = $\frac{12}{24}$ 8. $\frac{1}{10}$ > $\frac{1}{100}$

9. $\frac{7}{10}$ < $\frac{4}{5}$ 10. $\frac{5}{8}$ > $\frac{4}{9}$ 11. $\frac{1}{2}$ < $\frac{6}{7}$ 12. $\frac{2}{11}$ < $\frac{4}{5}$

13. $\frac{1}{9}$ = $\frac{2}{18}$ 14. $3\frac{4}{5}$ > $3\frac{3}{20}$ 15. $\frac{2}{15}$ < $\frac{4}{5}$ 16. $4\frac{9}{45}$ < $4\frac{2}{3}$

17. $7\frac{11}{12}$ > $6\frac{21}{16}$ 18. $\frac{2}{7}$ = $\frac{6}{21}$ 19. $4\frac{9}{10}$ < $4\frac{11}{12}$ 20. $\frac{12}{5}$ = $\frac{10}{4}$

Order from least to greatest.

21. $\frac{2}{5}, \frac{4}{9}, \frac{3}{10}$ 22. $\frac{8}{11}, \frac{3}{22}, \frac{1}{44}$ 23. $\frac{5}{21}, \frac{9}{9}, \frac{1}{16}$ 24. $2\frac{1}{5}, 2\frac{1}{16}, 2\frac{1}{8}$

   $\frac{3}{10}, \frac{2}{5}, \frac{4}{9}$ $\frac{1}{44}, \frac{3}{22}, \frac{8}{11}$ $\frac{1}{16}, \frac{5}{21}, \frac{9}{9}$ $2\frac{1}{16}, 2\frac{1}{8}, 2\frac{1}{5}$

25. $1\frac{1}{4}, \frac{5}{6}, \frac{8}{9}, \frac{2}{10}, 1\frac{8}{9}$ 26. $2\frac{3}{10}, 1\frac{8}{3}, 2\frac{1}{4}, 1\frac{9}{6}, 2\frac{1}{16}$

   $\frac{2}{10}, \frac{5}{6}, \frac{8}{9}, 1\frac{1}{4}, 1\frac{8}{9}$ $1\frac{8}{3}, 1\frac{9}{6}, 2\frac{1}{4}, 2\frac{3}{8}, \frac{10}{3}$

Use the circle graph and estimation to solve.

27. In the Bloomingdale school system, the students have a variety of hair colors. Match one of the fractions below to the color represented in the circle graph.

   a. $\frac{7}{30}$ brown   b. $\frac{3}{45}$ red
   c. $\frac{1}{4}$ blond   d. $\frac{9}{20}$ black

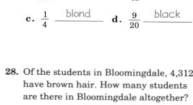

28. Of the students in Bloomingdale, 4,312 have brown hair. How many students are there in Bloomingdale altogether?
   18,480 students

RETEACHING 5-10

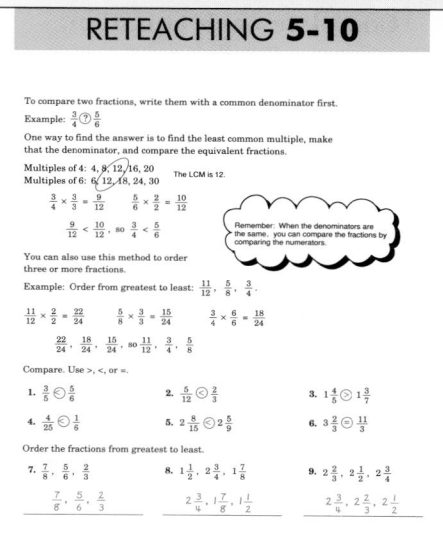

To compare two fractions, write them with a common denominator first.

Example: $\frac{3}{4}$ ⑦ $\frac{5}{6}$

One way to find the answer is to find the least common multiple, make that the denominator, and compare the equivalent fractions.

Multiples of 4: 4, 8, 12, 16, 20   The LCM is 12.
Multiples of 6: 6, 12, 18, 24, 30

$\frac{3}{4} \times \frac{3}{3} = \frac{9}{12}$ $\frac{5}{6} \times \frac{2}{2} = \frac{10}{12}$

$\frac{9}{12} < \frac{10}{12}$, so $\frac{3}{4} < \frac{5}{6}$

Remember: When the denominators are the same, you can compare the fractions by comparing the numerators.

You can also use this method to order three or more fractions.

Example: Order from greatest to least: $\frac{11}{12}, \frac{5}{8}, \frac{3}{4}$.

$\frac{11}{12} \times \frac{2}{2} = \frac{22}{24}$ $\frac{5}{8} \times \frac{3}{3} = \frac{15}{24}$ $\frac{3}{4} \times \frac{6}{6} = \frac{18}{24}$

$\frac{22}{24}, \frac{18}{24}, \frac{15}{24}$, so $\frac{11}{12}, \frac{3}{4}, \frac{5}{8}$

Compare. Use >, <, or =.

1. $\frac{3}{5}$ ◯ $\frac{5}{6}$ 2. $\frac{5}{12}$ ◯ $\frac{2}{3}$ 3. $1\frac{4}{5}$ ◯ $1\frac{3}{7}$

4. $\frac{4}{25}$ ◯ $\frac{1}{6}$ 5. $2\frac{8}{15}$ ◯ $2\frac{5}{8}$ 6. $3\frac{2}{9}$ ◯ $\frac{11}{3}$

Order the fractions from greatest to least.

7. $\frac{7}{8}, \frac{5}{6}, \frac{2}{3}$ 8. $1\frac{1}{2}, 2\frac{3}{4}, 1\frac{7}{8}$ 9. $2\frac{2}{3}, 2\frac{1}{2}, 2\frac{3}{4}$

   $\frac{7}{8}, \frac{5}{6}, \frac{2}{3}$ $2\frac{3}{4}, 1\frac{7}{8}, 1\frac{1}{2}$ $2\frac{3}{4}, 2\frac{2}{3}, 2\frac{1}{2}$

MEETING INDIVIDUAL NEEDS

For Students Who Are . . .

Acquiring English Proficiency Discuss how to read and interpret the circle graphs in the lesson and in the Problem Solving exercises.

Gifted and Talented Have students look in a current almanac to find actual data for the leading copper- and nickel-mining countries and record the data in a table.

Working 2 or 3 Grades Below Level Have students use pages 46–49 and 52–55 of the Skills Workbook for fractions.

Today's Problem

Harry, Juan, and Marva bought some pizza and juice drinks. They agreed to split the bill three ways. Harry was short of money, and so Juan agreed to pay half of Harry's share of the bill, which was $1.50. What was the total bill, and how much did each person contribute toward it? *(Juan: $1.50 + $3.00 = $4.50; Marva: $3.00; Harry: $1.50; total bill: $9.00)*

ENRICHMENT 5-10

✓ **MATERIALS CHECKLIST:** Recipes from cookbooks, magazines, or newspapers

Have the students work in pairs. Instruct each partner to find several dessert recipes. Partners then work together to order the recipes from least amount of sugar required to greatest amount of sugar required. Have the students write the amount of sugar each recipe calls for. Then instruct the students to order the recipes from least amount of salt to greatest amount of salt. Have them write the amount of salt. Finally, have pairs of students share their work so that the class can determine which recipe or recipes call for the greatest amount of sugar and salt.

LESSON | 5-11

Lesson Organizer

Objective: Write fractions and mixed numbers as decimals; write decimals as fractions and mixed numbers.

Prior Knowledge: Students should be able to divide whole numbers and decimals.

Error Analysis and Remediation: See page 163A.

Lesson Resources:
Practice Worksheet 5-11
Reteaching Worksheet 5-11
Enrichment Activity 5-11
Daily Review 5-11

 *Two-Minute Math*

Complete each equation.

$\frac{1}{2} = \square/10$ *(5)*

$\frac{3}{4} = \square/100$ *(75)*

$\frac{17}{40} = \square/1000$ *(425)*

$\frac{13}{20} = \square/100$ *(65)*

1 INTRODUCE

SYMBOLIC ACTIVITY

1. Write each of the following as a fraction and as a decimal:
   seven tenths
   fifteen hundredths
   three thousandths

2. What steps would you take to write $\frac{2}{5}$ as a decimal? *(Name it as an equivalent fraction with a denominator of 10.)* Have students write $\frac{2}{5} = \frac{4}{10} = 0.4$.

3. Repeat, naming $\frac{1}{4}$ as hundredths.

4. Explain that students can also use division to write fractions as decimals. Recall that a fraction represents a division. Have students rewrite $\frac{3}{8}$ as a division. *(3 ÷ 8)*

WHEN YOUR STUDENTS ASK
★ WHY AM I LEARNING THIS? ★

You can connect this skill to real life through baseball statistics. Batting averages are fractions written as decimals. A perfect batting average is written as 1.000.

Fractions, Mixed Numbers, and Decimals

The weights of the animals shown can be written in decimal form.

Bat, $\frac{1}{8}$ lb

Grey squirrel, $1\frac{1}{2}$ lb

Divide. On a calculator:

$$8)\overline{1.000} \quad \frac{0.125}{} \qquad 1 \div 8 = 0.125 \text{ (lb)}$$

Change $1\frac{1}{2}$ to $\frac{3}{2}$. Divide.

$$2)\overline{3.0} \quad \frac{1.5}{} \qquad 3 \div 2 = 1.5 \text{ (lb)}$$

Use a fraction with a multiple of 10 to help you change the weights of the animals below to fraction form.

Hummingbird, 0.4 oz

Canada Goose, 8.75 lb

$0.4 = \frac{4}{10} = \frac{2}{5}$ (oz)

$8.75 = 8\frac{75}{100} = 8\frac{3}{4}$ (lb)

MATH AND SCIENCE

=== GUIDED PRACTICE ===

Write the fraction as a decimal.

1. $\frac{1}{2}$ 0.5   **2.** $\frac{2}{5}$ 0.4   **3.** $\frac{4}{10}$ 0.4   **4.** $\frac{1}{4}$ 0.25   **5.** $\frac{2}{25}$ 0.08   **6.** $\frac{3}{50}$ 0.06

Write the decimal as a fraction or mixed number in lowest terms.

7. 0.3 $\frac{3}{10}$ **8.** 0.25 $\frac{1}{4}$ **9.** 6.7 $6\frac{7}{10}$ **10.** 0.3 $\frac{3}{10}$ **11.** 0.75 $\frac{3}{4}$ **12.** 4.5 $4\frac{1}{2}$

Calculators will be an effective teaching tool for this lesson.

2 TEACH

☑ **MATERIALS CHECKLIST:** calculators

Which number in a fraction is the divisor? *(denominator)*

Which of the following can be written as a mixed number: 0.523; 0.95; 1.2? Explain. *(1.2, because it represents a value greater than 1)*

Chalkboard Examples

Write as a decimal.

$\frac{3}{5}$ *(0.6)* $\frac{11}{4}$ *(2.75)*

Write as a fraction in lowest terms.

0.24 $\left(\frac{6}{25}\right)$ 0.875 $\left(\frac{7}{8}\right)$

SUMMARIZE/ASSESS   Demonstrate two ways to write $\frac{9}{5}$ as a decimal. Write 0.58 as a fraction in lowest terms. $\left(\frac{9}{5} = \frac{18}{10} = 1.8 \text{ or } 9 \div 5 = 1.8; \frac{58}{100} = \frac{29}{50}\right)$

Write the fraction or mixed number in decimal form.

13. $\frac{3}{5}$ 0.6 **14.** $\frac{5}{8}$ 0.625 **15.** $\frac{9}{20}$ 0.45 **16.** $\frac{17}{25}$ 0.68 **17.** $\frac{9}{8}$ 1.125 **18.** $\frac{7}{10}$ 0.7

19. $\frac{13}{5}$ 2.6 **20.** $\frac{13}{40}$ 0.325 **21.** $\frac{85}{100}$ 0.85 **22.** $\frac{21}{24}$ 0.875 **23.** $\frac{7}{8}$ 0.875 **24.** $\frac{3}{16}$ 0.1875

25. $\frac{9}{40}$ 0.225 **26.** $\frac{5}{16}$ 0.3125 **27.** $\frac{17}{32}$ 0.53125 **28.** $4\frac{3}{8}$ 4.375 **29.** $\frac{125}{500}$ 0.25 **30.** $\frac{30}{200}$ 0.15

Write the decimal as a fraction or mixed number in lowest terms.

31. 0.6 $\frac{3}{5}$ **32.** 0.9 $\frac{9}{10}$ **33.** 0.45 $\frac{9}{20}$ **34.** 0.125 $\frac{1}{8}$ **35.** 1.3 $1\frac{3}{10}$

36. 4.23 $4\frac{23}{100}$ **37.** 3.6 $3\frac{3}{5}$ **38.** 8.75 $8\frac{3}{4}$ **39.** 0.08 $\frac{2}{25}$ **40.** 2.32 $2\frac{8}{25}$

41. 1.125 $1\frac{1}{8}$ **42.** 0.625 $\frac{5}{8}$ **43.** 2.375 $2\frac{3}{8}$ *44. 5.004 $5\frac{1}{250}$ *45. 0.0005 $\frac{1}{2,000}$

CALCULATOR Order from the greatest to the least.

46. 1, 0.42, $\frac{3}{8}$, $\frac{2}{5}$, $\frac{9}{20}$, 2, 0.04, $\frac{11}{50}$ 2, 1, $\frac{9}{20}$, 0.42, $\frac{2}{5}$, $\frac{3}{8}$, $\frac{11}{50}$, 0.04

47. $\frac{13}{50}$, 0.38, $\frac{15}{40}$, 3.8, 0.09, 1, $\frac{1}{4}$, $\frac{39}{100}$ 3.8, 1, $\frac{39}{100}$, 0.38, $\frac{15}{40}$, $\frac{13}{50}$, $\frac{1}{4}$, 0.09

CALCULATOR Compute.

48. $4.9 + \frac{3}{8}$ 5.275 **49.** $5.6 + \frac{4}{5}$ 6.4 **50.** $8.69 + \frac{4}{5}$ 9.49 **51.** $4.6 - \frac{7}{40}$ 4.425

Copy and complete the pattern.

52. $\frac{1}{8} = 0.125$, $\frac{2}{8} = 0.250$, $\frac{3}{8} = 0.375$, $\frac{4}{8} = \blacksquare$, $\frac{5}{8} = \blacksquare$, $\frac{6}{8} = \blacksquare$, $\frac{7}{8} = \blacksquare$, $\frac{8}{8} = \blacksquare$
0.500 0.625 0.750 0.875 1.000

53. $\frac{1}{20} = 0.05$, $\frac{2}{20} = \blacksquare$, $\frac{3}{20} = 0.15$, $\frac{4}{20} = 0.20$, $\frac{5}{20} = \blacksquare$, $\frac{6}{20} = \blacksquare$, $\frac{7}{20} = \blacksquare$
0.10 0.25 0.30 0.35

54. $\frac{1}{50} = \blacksquare$, $\frac{2}{50} = 0.04$, $\frac{3}{50} = 0.06$, $\frac{4}{50} = \blacksquare$, $\frac{5}{50} = \blacksquare$, $\frac{6}{50} = 0.12$, $\frac{7}{50} = \blacksquare$
0.02 0.08 0.10 0.14

55. $\frac{1}{25} = \blacksquare$, $\frac{2}{25} = \blacksquare$, $\frac{3}{25} = 0.12$, $\frac{4}{25} = 0.16$, $\frac{5}{25} = 0.20$, $\frac{6}{25} = \blacksquare$, $\frac{7}{25} = \blacksquare$
0.04 0.08 0.24 0.28

Mental Math

Use your number sense to find a number in lowest terms that is
between the two given numbers in value. **Answers will vary. Suggestions given.**

1. $\frac{1}{2}$, $\frac{6}{8}$ $\frac{5}{8}$ **2.** $1\frac{1}{3}$, $1\frac{5}{9}$ $1\frac{4}{9}$ **3.** $\frac{7}{10}$, $\frac{1}{2}$ $\frac{3}{5}$ **4.** $2\frac{1}{16}$, $2\frac{1}{4}$ $2\frac{3}{16}$

5. $3\frac{1}{12}$, $3\frac{1}{4}$ $3\frac{1}{6}$ **6.** $\frac{7}{8}$, $\frac{15}{16}$ $\frac{29}{32}$ **7.** $9\frac{2}{3}$, $10\frac{1}{4}$ $9\frac{7}{8}$ **8.** $7\frac{5}{16}$, $7\frac{1}{2}$ $7\frac{7}{16}$

MEETING INDIVIDUAL NEEDS

For Students Who Are . . .

Acquiring English Proficiency Discuss how to change a fraction to a decimal using a calculator before students begin Exercises 40–45. Point out that $\frac{2}{5}$ means $2 \div 5$.

Gifted and Talented Have students write patterns for $\frac{1}{9}$, $\frac{2}{9}$, $\frac{3}{9}$, $\frac{4}{9}$ or $\frac{1}{7}$, $\frac{2}{7}$, $\frac{3}{7}$, $\frac{4}{7}$.

Working 2 or 3 Grades Below Level Have students use pages 82–85 of the Skills Workbook for decimals and pages 104–107 of the Skills Workbook for fractions.

Today's Problem

Yip, Flip, and Chip are puppies from the same litter. Yip weighs 2.72 lb, Flip weighs $2\frac{3}{4}$ lb, and Chip weighs $\frac{27}{10}$ lb. Which puppy weighs the most? *(Flip; 2.75 > 2.72 > 2.70)*

---

3 FOLLOW-UP

ENRICHMENT 5-11

☑ **MATERIALS CHECKLIST:** Index cards

Provide each pair of students with an identical stack of cards on which you have written, on separate cards, decimals and their fraction equivalents. Have the partners place them face down on a desk. The partners then take turns trying to match equivalent numbers by flipping over two cards at a time. If the cards show an equivalent decimal and fraction, the partner removes them and continues. Otherwise, the cards are returned face down to the desk and the other partner takes a turn. Play stops when one pair of students has matched all the cards. The pair with the most cards wins.

Lesson Organizer

Objective: Explore terminating and repeating decimals.

Prior Knowledge: Students should be able to divide with decimals.

Error Analysis and Remediation: See page 163A.

Lesson Resources:
Practice Worksheet 5-12
Daily Review 5-12
Cooperative Connections, Chapter 5

Two-Minute Math

Use the Table of Numbers on the inside back cover. Which numbers in rows A and B are divisible by both 3 and 4?
(24 and 828)

1 PREPARE

SYMBOLIC ACTIVITY

☑ **MATERIALS CHECKLIST:** calculators

Have students work with a partner.

1. Write these two groups of fractions on the chalkboard

Group 1: $\frac{4}{5}$ $\frac{7}{8}$ $\frac{9}{20}$

Group 2: $\frac{1}{3}$ $\frac{5}{9}$ $\frac{7}{15}$

2. Ask partners to use calculators to find equivalent decimals. Remind students to record the quotients. **How are the decimal equivalents in each group alike?** *(In Group 1, they all end in zero. In Group 2, they do not end but have digits that repeat.)*

3. Use students' responses to introduce and define the terms *terminating decimals* and *repeating decimals*.

WHEN YOUR STUDENTS ASK
★ WHY AM I LEARNING THIS? ★

This skill will help you in your math class. Recognizing fractions whose decimal equivalents have repeating digits can help you decide which computation method to use when you solve problems.

Terminating and Repeating Decimals

Did you know that Alaska is the largest state in the United States? California is about $\frac{3}{11}$ as large as Alaska, and Texas is about $\frac{9}{20}$ the size of Alaska.

1. Is Texas or California the second largest state? Compare $\frac{9}{20}$ and $\frac{3}{11}$ by writing equivalent fractions.
Texas; $\frac{9}{20} > \frac{3}{11}$
Another way to compare $\frac{9}{20}$ and $\frac{3}{11}$ is to change them to decimal form. You can use a calculator to do this.

2. What is the quotient of 9 ÷ 20? **0.45**

If the remainder is zero when you divide, the decimal is a **terminating decimal.**

3. What is the quotient of 3 ÷ 11? Is $\frac{3}{11}$ a terminating decimal? Describe the pattern of the digits in the quotient.
0.272727 . . . No. The digits "27" repeat forever.

If the remainder in a division never becomes zero, and the digits in the quotient repeat, the decimal is a **repeating decimal.**

4. Write a comparison statement using >, <, or = for the decimal equivalents of $\frac{9}{20}$ and $\frac{3}{11}$.
0.45 > 0.272727 . . .

Write the fraction as a terminating decimal.

5. $\frac{3}{4}$ **0.75**   **6.** $\frac{16}{25}$ **0.64**   **7.** $\frac{61}{40}$ **1.525**   **8.** $\frac{49}{80}$ **0.6125**   **9.** $\frac{27}{32}$ **0.84375**   **10.** $\frac{59}{50}$ **1.18**

California is $\frac{3}{11}$ or 0.27272727 . . . the size of Alaska. The three dots mean the digits 2 and 7 repeat forever. We can also write $0.\overline{27}$ to show that this is a repeating decimal. The repeating bar covers only those digits that are continually repeated.

Write the fraction as a repeating decimal. Place a bar over the repeating digits.

11. $\frac{5}{9}$ $0.\overline{5}$ **12.** $\frac{1}{6}$ $0.1\overline{6}$ **13.** $\frac{5}{12}$ $0.41\overline{6}$ **14.** $\frac{11}{27}$ $0.\overline{407}$ **15.** $\frac{7}{15}$ $0.4\overline{6}$ **16.** $\frac{12}{27}$ $0.\overline{4}$

17. $\frac{12}{41}$ **18.** $\frac{19}{27}$ $0.\overline{703}$ **19.** $\frac{12}{26}$ **20.** $\frac{14}{11}$ $1.\overline{27}$ **21.** $\frac{39}{37}$ $1.\overline{054}$ **22.** $\frac{25}{22}$ $1.1\overline{36}$
    $0.\overline{29268}$ $0.\overline{461538}$

(vertical text) **MATH AND GEOGRAPHY**

154   LESSON 5–12

Calculators should be available for tedious calculations.

2 EXPLORE

☑ **MATERIALS CHECKLIST:** calculators

Before students complete Exercises 1–4, ask: **Why do you think changing $\frac{3}{11}$ and $\frac{9}{20}$ to decimals is more efficient than changing them to equivalent fractions with like denominators?** *(Possible answer: The equivalent fractions would have large denominators and require cumbersome multiplications.)*

Call attention to the denominators of the fractions in Exercises 11–16. Ask: **What number is a factor of each denominator in Exercises 11–16?** *(3)* **Do you think $\frac{17}{18}$ will be a terminating or repeating decimal? Test your prediction.** *(repeating: $0.9\overline{4}$)*

SUMMARIZE/ASSESS   **Explain the difference between a terminating and a repeating decimal. Give an example of each.** *(If the remainder at some step of the division is 0, the decimal terminates; if the remainder never becomes zero and quotient digits repeat, the decimal repeats. Examples: $\frac{3}{4} = 0.75$; $\frac{1}{6} = 0.1\overline{6}$)*

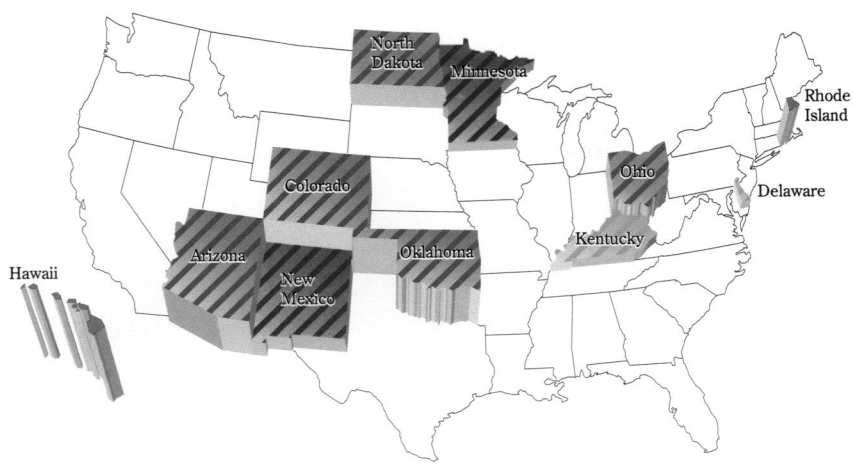

Rewrite each fraction as a decimal. State whether it is a *repeating* or a *terminating* decimal.

23. The area of the state of Delaware is about $\frac{1}{20}$ that of the state of Kentucky.
0.05; terminating

24. Ohio has about $\frac{4}{7}$ the area of North Dakota.
0.571428; repeating

25. Rhode Island, the smallest state, is about $\frac{3}{16}$ the size of Hawaii.
0.1875; terminating

26. Minnesota is about $\frac{2}{3}$ the size of New Mexico.
0.$\overline{6}$; repeating

27. Oklahoma is about $\frac{4}{11}$ the size of Arizona, and Colorado is about $\frac{10}{11}$ the area of Arizona.
0.$\overline{36}$; repeating; 0.$\overline{90}$; repeating

Write the number as a terminating or a repeating decimal.

28. $\frac{2}{5}$ 0.4 **29.** $\frac{1}{3}$ 0.$\overline{3}$ **30.** $\frac{1}{8}$ 0.125 **31.** $\frac{4}{15}$ 0.2$\overline{6}$ **32.** $\frac{2}{9}$ 0.$\overline{2}$ **33.** $\frac{17}{16}$ 1.0625

34. $2\frac{9}{11}$ 2.$\overline{81}$ **35.** $\frac{3}{50}$ 0.06 **36.** $5\frac{7}{30}$ 5.2$\overline{3}$ **37.** $\frac{1}{6}$ 0.1$\overline{6}$ **38.** $6\frac{2}{15}$ 6.1$\overline{3}$ **39.** $\frac{202}{200}$ 1.01

40. **IN YOUR WORDS** Describe a few fraction denominators that you know will be a terminating decimal. How do you know? **Answers will vary.**
Suggestion given: numbers with only 2 and 5 as factors.

41. **IN YOUR WORDS** Describe a few fraction denominators that you know will be a repeating decimal. How do you know? **Answers will vary.**
Suggestion given: numbers containing factors other than 2 and 5.

CHAPTER 5   155

PRACTICE 5-12

Write as a terminating decimal.

1. $\frac{1}{2}$ _0.5_ 2. $\frac{4}{5}$ _0.8_ 3. $\frac{13}{20}$ _0.65_ 4. $\frac{1}{8}$ _0.125_

5. $\frac{17}{25}$ _0.68_ 6. $\frac{1}{4}$ _0.25_ 7. $\frac{7}{8}$ _0.875_ 8. $\frac{23}{50}$ _0.46_

Write as a repeating decimal. Place a bar over the repeating digits.

9. $\frac{5}{6}$ _0.8$\overline{3}$_ 10. $\frac{9}{11}$ _0.8$\overline{1}$_ 11. $\frac{7}{30}$ _0.2$\overline{3}$_ 12. $\frac{5}{9}$ _0.$\overline{5}$_

13. $\frac{11}{24}$ _0.45$\overline{83}$_ 14. $\frac{1}{3}$ _0.$\overline{3}$_ 15. $\frac{5}{12}$ _0.41$\overline{6}$_ 16. $\frac{1}{6}$ _0.1$\overline{6}$_

17. $\frac{3}{11}$ _0.$\overline{27}$_ 18. $\frac{1}{12}$ _0.08$\overline{3}$_ 19. $\frac{2}{3}$ _0.$\overline{6}$_ 20. $\frac{1}{9}$ _0.$\overline{1}$_

Rewrite the fractions as decimals. State whether they are repeating (r) or terminating (t) decimals.

21. $\frac{5}{24}$ _0.208$\overline{3}$; r_ 22. $\frac{7}{32}$ _0.21875; t_ 23. $\frac{7}{9}$ _0.$\overline{7}$; r_ 24. $\frac{7}{7}$ _1.0; t_

25. $\frac{3}{8}$ _0.375; t_ 26. $\frac{10}{11}$ _0.$\overline{90}$; r_ 27. $\frac{4}{25}$ _0.16; t_ 28. $\frac{5}{16}$ _0.3125; t_

29. $\frac{7}{12}$ _0.58$\overline{3}$; r_ 30. $\frac{3}{32}$ _0.09375; t_ 31. $\frac{5}{30}$ _0.1$\overline{6}$; r_ 32. $\frac{4}{9}$ _0.$\overline{4}$; r_

Solve. Write your answer as a decimal.

33. The umpire had 25 baseballs ready for the opening day game. He used 9 of them. What portion of the 25 balls did he use?
_0.36_

34. The Tigereyes won 8 of their 15 marble games last season. What portion of their games did they win?
_0.53_

MEETING INDIVIDUAL NEEDS

For Students Who Are . . .

Acquiring English Proficiency Discuss the meanings of *terminating decimal* and *repeating decimal*.

Gifted and Talented Have students look up the areas of five other states and write statements similar to Exercises 23–27. Then have them exchange papers and write each other's fractions as decimals.

Working 2 or 3 Grades Below Level Have students work in pairs to answer Exercise 41. Help them make a table using Exercises 11–22 and 28–39 to find patterns.

Today's Problem

If $\frac{1}{11} = 0.\overline{09}$; $\frac{2}{11} = 0.\overline{18}$; and $\frac{3}{11} = 0.\overline{27}$, what are the decimals for: $\frac{4}{11}$? $\frac{8}{11}$? $\frac{12}{11}$? ($\frac{4}{11} = 0.\overline{36}$; $\frac{8}{11} = 0.\overline{72}$; $\frac{12}{11} = 1.\overline{09}$)

Lesson Organizer

> **Objective:** Read and write small numbers.

Prior Knowledge: Students should be able to measure with a centimeter ruler.

Lesson Resources:
Practice Worksheet 5-13
Reteaching Activity 5-13
Enrichment Worksheet 5-13
Daily Review 5-13

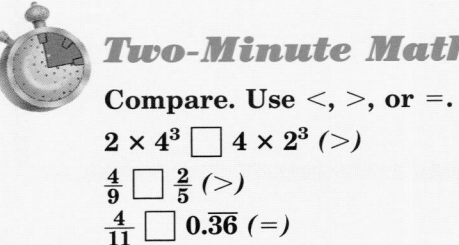

Two-Minute Math

Compare. Use $<$, $>$, or $=$.

$2 \times 4^3 \; \Box \; 4 \times 2^3 \;$ (>)

$\frac{4}{9} \; \Box \; \frac{2}{5} \;$ (>)

$\frac{4}{11} \; \Box \; 0.\overline{36} \;$ (=)

1 INTRODUCE

CONNECTING ACTIVITY

☑ **MATERIALS CHECKLIST:** Teaching Aid 2 (Decimal Squares), centimeter ruler for each student

1. Mark off a 30-by-30 square on the thousandths' decimal square and measure the length of a side with the centimeter ruler. *(2 cm)*

2. Then have students try to measure the length and width of one of the smallest units on the decimal square. Why is it more difficult to measure this unit than the larger one? *(Possible answers: It is hard to see clearly; the ruler is not marked off in units smaller than centimeters.)*

3. What are some other items that might be difficult to measure because they are so small? *(Possible answers: thickness of a sheet of paper, width of an eyelash)*

WHEN YOUR STUDENTS ASK
★ WHY AM I LEARNING THIS? ★

You can connect this skill to real life through physics. Physicists deal with very small objects including particles and subparticles such as quarks and hadons.

Smaller Numbers

Do you recognize what this photograph shows? It is a human hair, magnified 500 times by a scanning electron microscope.

Use a metric ruler for Exercises 1–10.

1. Measure the thickness of the hair in the photograph to the nearest half centimeter.
   3 cm (hair in front)

2. What would be the approximate thickness of a human hair in centimeters? in millimeters?
   0.006 cm; 0.06 mm

3. How many human hairs would equal 7 mm? 7 cm?
   ≈100; ≈1,000

4. The average thickness of human skin is 19 times greater than the average thickness of human hair. What is the approximate thickness of human skin in centimeters? Use the information from Exercise 2.
   about 0.114 cm

An electronic chip is small enough to pass through the eye of a tapestry needle.

5. Measure the length and width of the electronic chip shown. The actual length and width of the chip is about 10 times smaller than the picture. What are the approximate dimensions of the actual chip?
   8.5 cm × 5 cm; ≈0.85 cm × 0.5 cm

To see a World in a Grain of Sand,
And a Heaven in a Wild Flower,
Hold Infinity in the palm of your hand,
And Eternity in an hour.
— from "Auguries of Innocence"
by William Blake

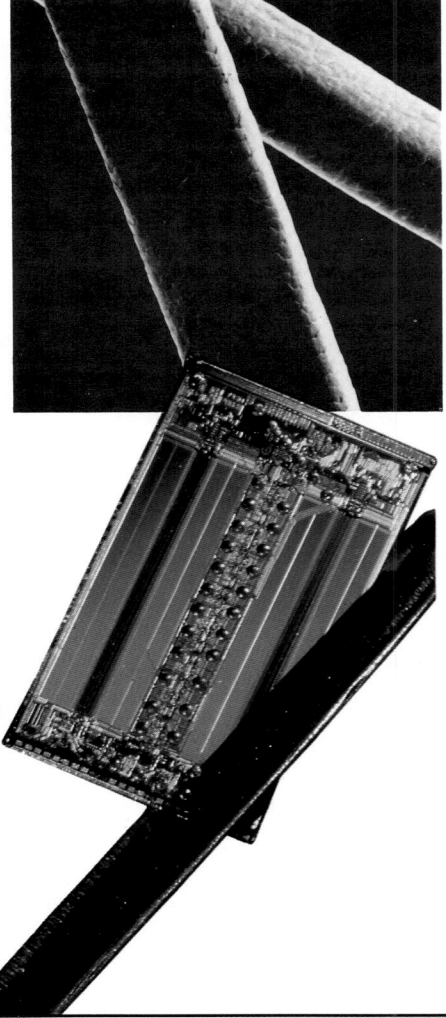

MATH AND SCIENCE

Calculators should be available for tedious calculations.

2 TEACH

☑ **MATERIALS CHECKLIST:** centimeter ruler for each student, calculators

Have students read problems 1–4. **What skills that you have studied will help you solve these problems?** *(Possible answer: choosing the appropriate unit of measure; converting between cm and mm)*

SUMMARIZE/ASSESS **Explain why it is necessary to use a powerful microscope to enlarge various items for study.** *(Possible answer: so that the items can be measured and studied in detail.)*

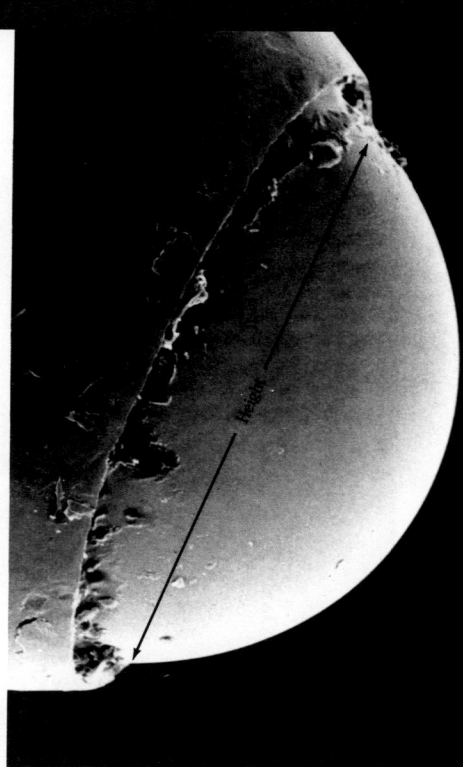

The line across the ball in this picture of the tip of a ball-point pen is about 200 times larger than the actual distance.

Accept reasonable estimates. Suggestions given.

6. Measure the line across the ball in centimeters. What is the approximate distance across the ball in a ball-point pen tip in centimeters? in millimeters?
   11.2 cm; ≈0.056 cm; ≈0.56 mm

7. About how many ball-point pen tips of this size would equal 1 cm?
   ≈ 18 pen tips

8. The ball point on a fine ball-point pen is about 1.6 times smaller than that on a medium ball-point pen. If the distance across the ball tip on a medium pen is about 0.04 cm, about what is the distance across the ball on a fine ball-point pen?
   ≈0.025 cm

9. The diameter of a nickel is about 2.2 cm. How many times smaller than the diameter of a nickel is the distance across the ball on a medium pen? Use the information in Exercise 8.
   ≈55 times

10. Only part of a fly's eye is magnified in the photograph at the left. If the entire magnification could be shown, the eye would measure 100 cm across. That is because this photograph has enlarged the fly's eye 400 times. About what would the actual length across the fly's eye be?
    ≈0.25 cm

CHAPTER 5   157

MEETING INDIVIDUAL NEEDS

For Students Who Are . . .

Acquiring English Proficiency Pair students with an English-proficient student to discuss and answer Exercises 1–10.

Gifted and Talented Have students research ways that powerful electronic imaging machines have contributed to medical advances.

Having Reading Difficulties Pair students with an able reader to work through Exercises 1–10.

Today's Problem

The diameter of a compact disc is about 12 cm. How many times smaller is a laser beam that has a diameter of 0.0002 cm?
(12 ÷ 0.0002 = 60,000; it is 60,000 times smaller.)

3 FOLLOW-UP

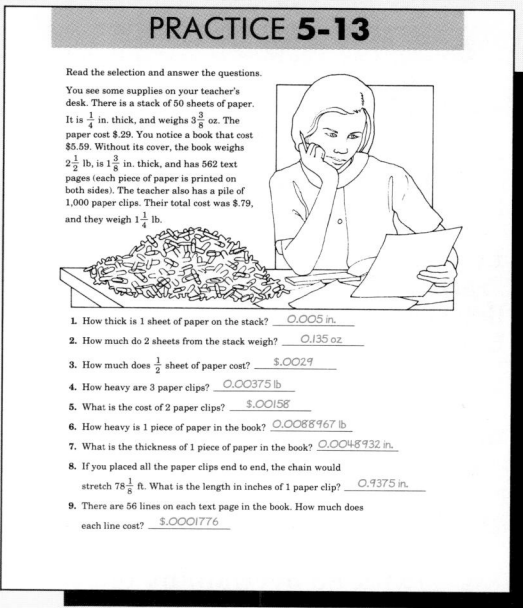

PRACTICE 5-13

Read the selection and answer the questions.

You see some supplies on your teacher's desk. There is a stack of 50 sheets of paper. It is $\frac{1}{4}$ in. thick, and weighs $3\frac{3}{8}$ oz. The paper cost $.29. You notice a book that cost $5.59. Without its cover, the book weighs $2\frac{1}{2}$ lb, is $1\frac{3}{8}$ in. thick, and has 562 text pages (each piece of paper is printed on both sides). The teacher also has a pile of 1,000 paper clips. Their total cost was $.79, and they weigh $1\frac{1}{4}$ lb.

1. How thick is 1 sheet of paper on the stack? __0.005 in.__
2. How much do 2 sheets from the stack weigh? __0.135 oz__
3. How much does $\frac{1}{2}$ sheet of paper cost? __$.0029__
4. How heavy are 3 paper clips? __0.00375 lb__
5. What is the cost of 2 paper clips? __$.00158__
6. How heavy is 1 piece of paper in the book? __0.0088967 lb__
7. What is the thickness of 1 piece of paper in the book? __0.0048932 in.__
8. If you placed all the paper clips end to end, the chain would stretch $78\frac{1}{8}$ ft. What is the length in inches of 1 paper clip? __0.9375 in.__
9. There are 56 lines on each text page in the book. How much does each line cost? __$.0001776__

RETEACHING 5-13

☑ **MATERIALS CHECKLIST:** Reams of paper, packages of construction paper, metric rulers

Have the students work in pairs. Provide each pair with a ream of paper and a package of construction paper. Instruct each pair to find the thickness of one sheet of each kind of paper by measuring the thickness of the package in centimeters and then dividing by the number of sheets. Then have the students find the cost of one sheet of paper by dividing the package price by the number of sheets.

ENRICHMENT 5-13

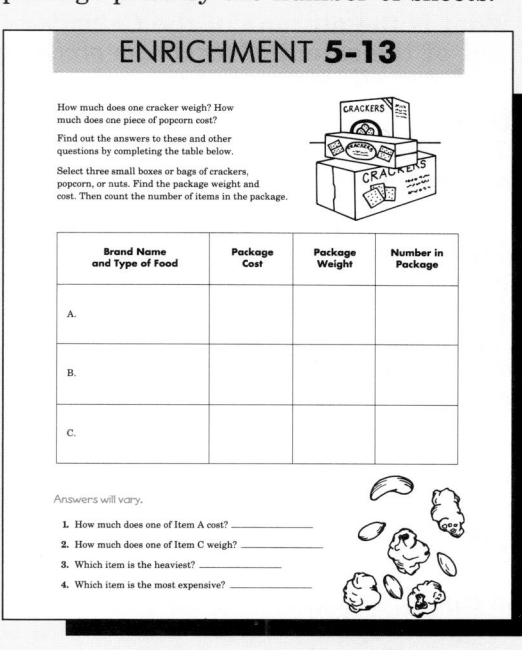

How much does one cracker weigh? How much does one piece of popcorn cost?

Find out the answers to these and other questions by completing the table below.

Select three small boxes or bags of crackers, popcorn, or nuts. Find the package weight and cost. Then count the number of items in the package.

Brand Name and Type of Food	Package Cost	Package Weight	Number in Package
A.			
B.			
C.			

Answers will vary.

1. How much does one of Item A cost? _____
2. How much does one of Item C weigh? _____
3. Which item is the heaviest? _____
4. Which item is the most expensive? _____

LESSON | 5-14

Lesson Organizer

Objective: Solve problems using a simpler problem.

Prior Knowledge: Students should be able to do the four basic operations.

Lesson Resources:
Practice Worksheet 5-14
Reteaching Activity 5-14
Enrichment Worksheet 5-14
Daily Review 5-14

 **Two-Minute Math**

What is the smallest square that can be covered evenly (with no overlap) by either a number of 9-in. squares or a number of 12-in. squares?
(36-in. square)

1 INTRODUCE

SYMBOLIC ACTIVITY

1. Read the following problem aloud.

The *Columbia* spacecraft orbits the earth at an altitude of 277,000 meters. A communications satellite orbits at an altitude of 35,800,000 meters. To the nearest tenth, how many times higher is the orbit of the satellite?

- **What is the altitude of the *Columbia* and of the satellite?** *(Students probably cannot recall large numbers.)*

- **How will you solve this problem?** *(Students probably need to hear the problem again.)*

2. Reread the problem substituting "15 miles" for the altitude of *Columbia's* orbit and "30 miles" for the altitude of the satellite's orbit. Then, ask the same questions as before. *(Answer to simpler problem: 2 times; answer to original problem: 129.2 times)*

WHEN YOUR STUDENTS ASK
★ WHY AM I LEARNING THIS? ★

You can connect this problem to real life through the space program. Simulations of actual conditions in space break down complex conditions into simpler steps, which can be more easily managed.

Problem Solving Strategy:
Using a Simpler Problem

Sometimes the numbers in a problem make it appear more difficult than it really is. If you rewrite the problem using simpler numbers, it is easier to solve.

Problem:
The research spacecraft *Helios B* came within 27 million miles of the Sun. Traveling at a speed of 124,277.6 mi/h, how many hours did *Helios B* take to get this close to the Sun, which is about 93 million miles from Earth?

- The large numbers in the problem make it appear difficult. Rewrite the problem using simpler numbers.

Simpler Problem:
Helios B came within about 30,000 mi of the Sun. Traveling at a speed of about 100 mi/h, how many hours did *Helios B* take to get this close to the Sun, which is about 90,000 mi away? **600 h**

- Which operations would you use to solve the simpler problem? **See below.**
- Now solve the original problem using the same operations. **531 h**
  subtraction, division

Helios B research space [truncated]

=== GUIDED PRACTICE ===

Solve the simpler problem first, then solve the original problem.

1. **Problem:** What is the quotient of $1 \div 500,000,000$?
   0.000000002

   Simpler Problem: What is the quotient of $1 \div 5$? **0.2**
   $1 \div 50$? $1 \div 500$? **0.02; 0.002**

2. **Problem:** How many seconds are there in 2 wk? **1,209,600 s**

   Simpler Problem: How many seconds are there in 1 min? **60 s**
   1 h? 1 d? **3,600 s; 86,400 s**

MULTICULTURAL NOTE

The first rockets were probably built in China and used there in warfare about 800 years ago. The gunpowder that the rockets burned has been used in China for more than 1,200 years.

2 TEACH

☑ **MATERIALS CHECKLIST:** calculators

After students read through the lesson, have them compare the original problem to the simplified version.

What are some advantages of using a simpler problem? *(Possible answer: A simpler problem sometimes makes choosing the operations more obvious.)*

SUMMARIZE/ASSESS **Explain why solving a simpler problem is an important strategy.** *(Possible answer: It gives you a "starting point" when the problem is very complex.)*

Solve by using a simpler problem.
Work with a partner.

3. The average height of an adult male is $5\frac{3}{4}$ ft. How
   many men of average height would equal the
   height of the *Saturn V* rocket, which was 363 ft tall?
   about 63 men

4. The *Saturn V* rocket launched the first astronauts
   to go to the Moon. This rocket burned more than
   560,000 gal of fuel during the first $2\frac{3}{4}$ min of launch.
   At that rate, how much did *Saturn V* burn in 1 s?
   3,393.93 gal/s

5. *Saturn V* launched *Apollo 11*, which put two men,
   Armstrong and Aldrin, on the Moon. This historic
   flight began on July 16, 1969, at 9:32 A.M. and ended
   on July 24, 1969, at 12:51 A.M. For how many hours
   and minutes did the flight of *Apollo 11* last?
   183 h, 19 min

6. The Earth circles the Sun at a speed of 18.5 mi/s
   (miles per second).

   a. What is Earth's speed as it circles the Sun? **18.5 mi/s**

   b. What is 18.5 mi/s in miles per minute? **1,110 mi/min**
      in miles per hour? **66,600 mi/h**

   c. How far does Earth travel in 1 d? **1,598,400 mi**

7. An athlete jogs at a pace of 9.65 km/h. About how many
   days would it take the athlete to jog a distance equal to the
   equatorial circumference of Earth, which is 40,064 km?
   about 173 d

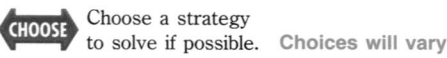 **CHOOSE** Choose a strategy
   to solve if possible. **Choices will vary.**

8. On average, a guinea pig weighs 1.54 lb. The average 25-yr
   old woman weighs about 124 lb. A 25-yr old man weighs, on
   average, about as much as 112 guinea pigs. What is the weight
   of an average 25-yr old man, to the nearest pound? **c; ≈172 lb**

9. The diameter of the Moon is about 2,100 mi. How many Moon
   diameters is the Moon away from Earth?
   There is missing information.

10. The distance from Earth to the Sun, 93 million mi, is called
    1 astronomical unit (A.U.). The planet Pluto was discovered in
    1930, and its average distance from the Sun is 39.53 A.U. About
    how many miles from the Sun is Pluto?
    ≈ 3.7 billion miles

CHAPTER 5   159

MEETING INDIVIDUAL NEEDS

For Students Who Are . . .

Acquiring English Proficiency Have students work in a group to
formulate simpler problems for Exercises 3–10.

Gifted and Talented Have students find additional information
about *Saturn V* and use the information to create problems for class
solution.

Working 2 or 3 Grades Below Level Have students use pages
88–91 of the Skills Workbook for Problem Solving Strategies.

Having Reading Difficulties Pair students with an able reader to
discuss and solve Exercises 3–10.

Today's Problem

In the theory of numbers, Hamann's conjecture suggests that every
even number from 2 to 250 can be expressed as the difference between prime numbers. Show that this is true for even numbers from
100 to 110. *(100 = 107 − 7, 102 = 107 − 5, 104 = 117 − 13, 106 =
117 − 11, 108 = 119 − 11, 110 = 117 − 7)*

---

3 FOLLOW-UP

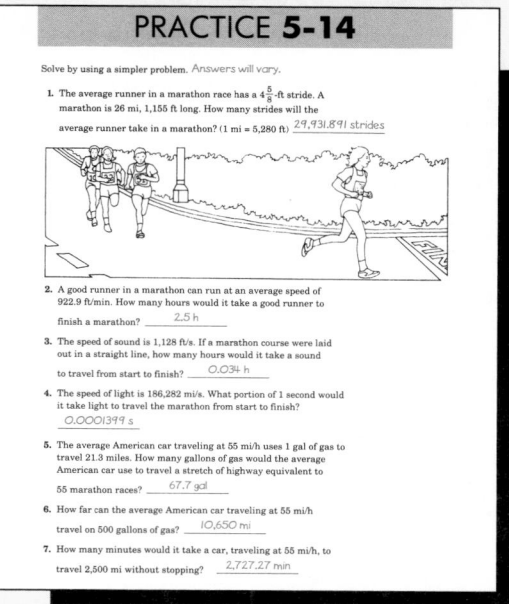

PRACTICE 5-14

Solve by using a simpler problem. Answers will vary.

1. The average runner in a marathon race has a $4\frac{5}{8}$-ft stride. A
   marathon is 26 mi, 1,155 ft long. How many strides will the
   average runner take in a marathon? (1 mi = 5,280 ft) _29,931.891 strides_

2. A good runner in a marathon can run at an average speed of
   922.9 ft/min. How many hours would it take a good runner to
   finish a marathon? _2.5 h_

3. The speed of sound is 1,128 ft/s. If a marathon course were laid
   out in a straight line, how many hours would it take a sound
   to travel from start to finish? _0.034 h_

4. The speed of light is 186,282 mi/s. What portion of 1 second would
   it take light to travel the marathon from start to finish?
   _0.0001399 s_

5. The average American car traveling at 55 mi/h uses 1 gal of gas to
   travel 21.3 miles. How many gallons of gas would the average
   American car use to travel a stretch of highway equivalent to
   55 marathon races? _67.7 gal_

6. How far can the average American car traveling at 55 mi/h
   travel on 500 gallons of gas? _10,650 mi_

7. How many minutes would it take a car, traveling at 55 mi/h, to
   travel 2,500 mi without stopping? _2,727.27 min_

RETEACHING 5-14

Some students may need help understanding how to make a difficult problem simpler. One way to solve Problem 1, *Practice
Worksheet 50*, is to ask the following questions: How long is one stride? [$4\frac{5}{8}$ ft] How
can you write $4\frac{5}{8}$ so that it is easier to
work with? [write it as a decimal—4.625]
What is the total distance a marathon
runner runs? [26 miles, 1,155 ft] How can
you write this distance so that it is easier
to work with? [change 26 miles to feet—
137,280 ft] How will you find the total
number of strides? [divide the total distance in feet—137,280 + 1,155, or
138,435—by 4.625] What is the answer?
[29,931.891 strides]

ENRICHMENT 5-14

Solve.

Gelindo Bordin of Italy won the 1990 Boston Marathon. He ran
the 26-mi, 385-yd course in 2 h 8 min 20 s and won $50,000.

1. How much money did Gelindo Bordin
   make per minute during the race?
   about $390 per min

2. How fast did he run in miles per
   hour?
   about 12.27 mi/h

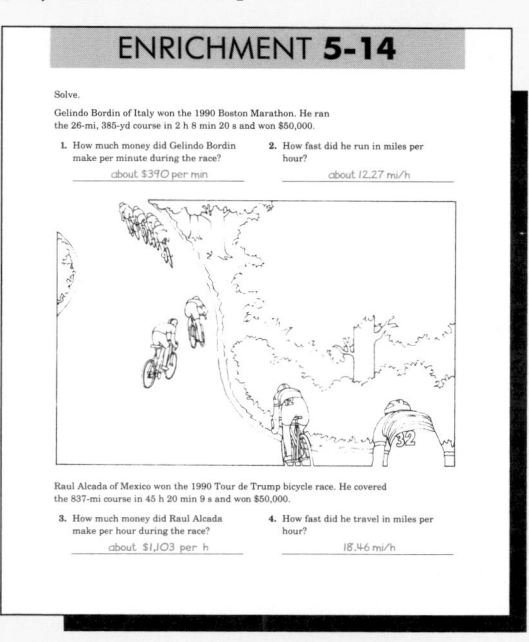

Raul Alcada of Mexico won the 1990 Tour de Trump bicycle race. He covered
the 837-mi course in 45 h 20 min 9 s and won $50,000.

3. How much money did Raul Alcada
   make per hour during the race?
   about $1,103 per h

4. How fast did he travel in miles per
   hour?
   _18.46 mi/h_

Lesson Organizer

Objective: Review operations with whole numbers and decimals.

Lesson Resource:
Daily Review 5-15

These pages provide students with a review of addition, subtraction, multiplication, and division with both whole numbers and decimals.

Remind students that these pages review skills covered in previous chapters and will help them to do a self-check to see how well they remember what they've learned.

MATH AND SOCIAL STUDIES

Mixed Review

Compute.

1. 963 + 87 1,050
2. 475 + 89 564
3. 21,356 + 4,519 25,875
4. 953 + 3,294 4,247
5. 7,246 + 978 8,224
6. 18,000 + 5,628 23,628
7. 53.4 + 19.7 73.1
8. 5.6 + 4.3 9.9
9. 1.51 + 2.7 4.21
10. 1.25 + 5.2 6.45
11. 536.2 + 66.4 602.6
12. 13.19 + 12.20 25.39
13. 567 − 438 129
14. 512 − 54 458
15. 3,766 − 1,333 2,433
16. 7,442 − 6,999 443
17. 12,574 − 10,342 2,232
18. 458,369 − 314,041 144,328
19. 9.5 − 6.3 3.2
20. 16.25 − 10.14 6.11
21. 301.56 − 150.32 151.24
22. 13.45 − 12.54 0.91
23. 34.765 − 17.532 17.233
24. 675.125 − 466.346 208.779
25. 28 × 28 784
26. 37 × 52 1,924
27. 49 × 67 3,283
28. 56 × 980 54,880
29. 631 × 876 552,756
30. 79 × 12,458 984,182
31. 587 × 4,120 2,418,440
32. 1,234 × 4,321 5,332,114
33. 398 × 19,555 7,782,890

Compute. Round the answer to the nearest tenth when necessary.

34. 78.2 × 3.5 273.7
35. 34.6 × 23.87 825.9
36. 88.88 × 11.11 987.5
37. 6.75 × 30.8 207.9
38. 898.5 × 9.2 8,266.2
39. 333.33 × 44.44 14,813.2
40. 804 ÷ 12 67
41. 2,052 ÷ 57 36
42. 5,590 ÷ 65 86
43. 23,975 ÷ 685 35
44. 18,768 ÷ 368 51
45. 227,574 ÷ 269 846
46. 18 ÷ 7.5 2.4
47. 3,209.6 ÷ 47.2 68
48. 248.45 ÷ 25.8 9.6
49. 625.6 ÷ 122.5 5.1
50. 4,815.2 ÷ 1.2 4,012.7
51. 129.73 ÷ 4.4 29.5

The French TGV Atlantique is the world's fastest train.

160 LESSON 5–15

CHOOSE Choose mental math, pencil and paper, estimation, or calculator to solve.

52. Gustave Eiffel designed both the 300-m-high Eiffel Tower in Paris and the 46.05-m-high Statue of Liberty in New York City. How much higher is the Eiffel Tower?
c; 253.95 m

53. The Arc de Triomphe was built between 1806 and 1836 to commemorate Napoleon's victories. For how long has the Arc de Triomphe been completed?
p; Answer depends on current year.

54. The world's fastest electric train runs between Paris and Lyon at an average speed of 169.9 mi/h. Its top speed is about 1.9 times faster than its average. About what is the top speed of this train?
e; ≈340 mi/h

55. Chicago's O'Hare Airport handled about 56.3 million people in a recent year, about 2.8 times more than Orly Airport in Paris. About how many people went through Orly?
e; ≈20 million people

Use the bar graph to answer the question.

56. About what is the total population of the five cities?   e; ≈4,200,000

57. Which city has about $\frac{1}{5}$ the population of Paris?   m; Lyon

58. Which two cities together have about the same population as Marseille?   m; Nice, Lyon

59. CREATE YOUR OWN   Use the information in the bar graph to write a word problem. Give it to a partner to solve.
Check students' work.

Eiffel Tower, Paris, France

Population of Five French Cities

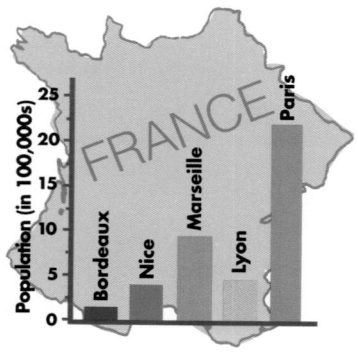

CHAPTER 5   161

CHAPTER
Checkup

The chapter checkup provides a quick language and vocabulary review, a test for the chapter, and suggestions for student Learning Log entries.

Language and Vocabulary

Some key language and vocabulary ideas from this chapter are reinforced here.

Test

The test can be used either as a test or as a review of the chapter prior to your administering the test worksheets found in the Teacher's Resource Book.

The following guide will help you determine percentage scores.

Score	Percent	Score	Percent
32	100%	16	51%
31	97	15	48
30	94	14	45
29	91	13	42
28	88	12	38
27	85	11	34
26	82	10	30
25	79	9	27
24	76	8	24
23	73	7	21
22	70	6	18
21	67	5	15
20	64	4	12
19	61	3	9
18	58	2	6
17	55	1	3

Use this chart to identify additional lesson resources for this chapter.

Items	Management Objective	Pages
1–5; 31–32	**5B** Identify factors and multiples; GCF; LCM	134–137
6–16	**5D** Write fractions and mixed numbers as decimals and write decimals as fractions and mixed numbers.	148–149 152–153
17–21	**5E** Determine terminating and repeating decimals.	154–155
22–29	**5C** Write equivalent fractions and compare and order fractions.	144–147 150–151
30	**5F** Problem Solving: Use a simpler problem.	158–159

CHAPTER CHECKUP

LANGUAGE & VOCABULARY

Explain why each statement is true. **Answers will vary. Suggestions given.**

1. $\frac{4}{8} = \frac{1}{2}$

2. $\frac{13}{3} = 4\frac{1}{3}$

3. $\frac{7}{9} > \frac{5}{10}$

4. $\frac{3}{6} < 0.65$

5. $0.\overline{18} > 0.18$

1. simplifies to $\frac{1}{2}$

2. written as a mixed number

3. $\frac{70}{90} > \frac{45}{90}$

4. $\frac{3}{6} = \frac{1}{2} = .50 < .65$ 5. $.1818 > .18$

TEST ✓

Name the GCF and LCM for the pair of numbers. *(pages 134–137)*

1. 3, 12 **3; 12** 2. 5, 20 **5; 20** 3. 6, 16 **2; 48** 4. 20, 12 **4; 60** 5. 14, 21 **7; 42**

6. Write the mixed number as a fraction. *(pages 148–149)*

a. $1\frac{8}{9}$ $\frac{17}{9}$ b. $7\frac{3}{5}$ $\frac{38}{5}$ c. $9\frac{5}{8}$ $\frac{77}{8}$

Write the prime factorization.

7. 72 8. 136

Write the fraction as a whole or mixed number in lowest terms. *(pages 146–149)*

9. $\frac{16}{4}$ **4** 10. $\frac{14}{8}$ $1\frac{3}{4}$ 11. $\frac{27}{6}$ $4\frac{1}{2}$

Write the fraction as a decimal or the decimal as a fraction. *(pages 152–153)*

12. $\frac{5}{8}$ **0.625** 13. $\frac{34}{50}$ **0.68** 14. $\frac{18}{24}$ **0.75** 15. 0.0625 16. 0.4 **0.4**
                                                                                    0.0625

Write as a terminating or repeating decimal. *(pages 154–155)*

17. $\frac{5}{6}$ $0.8\overline{3}$ 18. $\frac{7}{11}$ $0.\overline{63}$ 19. $\frac{17}{40}$ **0.425** 20. $3\frac{1}{9}$ $3.\overline{1}$ 21. $\frac{15}{16}$ **0.9375**

SKILLS

Write the value of *n*. *(pages 142–147)*

22. $\frac{4}{9} = \frac{16}{n}$ **36** 23. $\frac{7}{12} = \frac{n}{36}$ **21** 24. $\frac{15}{35} = \frac{3}{n}$ **7** 25. $\frac{n}{45} = \frac{2}{5}$ **18**

Compare. Choose >, <, or =. *(pages 150–151)*

26. $\frac{5}{6}$ ▦ $\frac{3}{4}$ **>** 27. $\frac{3}{5}$ ▦ $\frac{9}{15}$ **=** 28. $1\frac{1}{2}$ ▦ $1\frac{7}{9}$ **<** 29. $3\frac{1}{2}$ ▦ $\frac{14}{4}$ **=**

162 CHAPTER CHECKUP

CHAPTER TEST • FORM A

Write the prime factorization of each number. (pp. 130–133) 5A

1. 96 2. 65 3. 44 4. 150 5. 140

   $2^5 \times 3$ 5×13 $2^2 \times 11$ $2 \times 3 \times 5^2$ $2^2 \times 5 \times 7$

Name the GCF and LCM for each pair of numbers. (pp. 134–137) 5B

6. 2, 12 **2;12** 7. 5, 25 **5;25** 8. 8, 20 **4; 40**
9. 30, 24 **6;120** 10. 12, 18 **6;36**

(pp. 142–147, 150–151) 5C

Write the value of *n*.

11. $\frac{2}{5} = \frac{16}{n}$ $n = 40$ 12. $\frac{n}{45} = \frac{3}{5}$ $n = 27$

Compare. Choose >, <, or =.

13. $\frac{3}{4}$ **<** $\frac{7}{8}$ 14. $1\frac{1}{4}$ **<** $1\frac{3}{8}$ 15. $2\frac{1}{5}$ **=** $\frac{11}{5}$

(pp. 148–149, 152–153, 156–157) 5D

Write as a decimal.

16. $\frac{3}{8}$ **0.375** 17. $\frac{16}{20}$ **0.80** 18. $\frac{15}{25}$ **0.60**

Write as a fraction or mixed number in lowest terms.

19. 0.36 $\frac{9}{25}$ 20. 2.25 $2\frac{1}{4}$

Write as a terminating or repeating decimal. (pp. 154–155) 5E

21. $\frac{1}{6}$ 22. $\frac{3}{11}$ 23. $\frac{7}{20}$ 24. $2\frac{1}{5}$ 25. $\frac{5}{12}$

   0.16 **0.27** **0.35** **2.2** **0.416**

CHAPTER TEST • FORM A

Solve by using a simpler problem. (pp. 138–139, 158–159) 5F

26. The average height of an adult male is $5\frac{3}{4}$ ft. About how many average men would equal the height of the Empire State Building, which is 1,250 ft tall? **about 217 men**

27. The Armstrong family left for vacation on July 10, 1990, at 7:12 A.M. and returned on July 19, 1990, at 5:30 P.M. For how many hours and minutes were they gone? **226 h 18 min**

28. The Armstrong family bought 225 gal of gasoline. How many pints is this? **1,800 pints**

29. The Armstrongs drove 3 h at a steady speed of 60 mi/h. How many miles did they drive? **180 mi**

30. Anne Armstrong jogs at a pace of 9.5 km/h. At this pace, how many days and hours would it take her to jog a distance equal to a 5,073 km trip from Philadelphia to Los Angeles? **22 days 6 h**

Solve by using a simpler problem. *(pages 158–159)*

30. The planet Pluto is usually described as being farthest from the Sun, but at one point in its orbit Pluto is 4 million miles closer to the Sun than Neptune is at its closest distance to the Sun, 2 billion, 766 million miles. Even at its closest point to the Sun, Pluto is 2 billion, 670 million, 600 thousand miles farther from the Sun than Earth is at its closest point.

  a. What is the closest Neptune comes to the Sun?   **2,766,000,000 mi**

  b. What is the closest Pluto comes to the Sun?   **2,762,000,000 mi**

  c. What is the closest Earth comes to the Sun?   **91,400,000 mi**

Choose mental math or pencil and paper to solve. *(pages 136–137)*

31. On Bernie's used car lot, every 4th car has power windows, every 5th car has power locks, and every 10th car has power seat adjusters. If there are 75 cars lined up in the lot, which cars would have all three features?   **20th, 40th, 60th**

32. Larry is building a model car using a scale of $\frac{2}{5}$. If a part of the real car is 45 in. long, how long will that part be on Larry's scale model?   **18 in.**

LEARNING LOG

Write the answers in your learning log.   **Answers will vary. Suggestions given.**

1. How do you think cross products got their name? **because you cross from one numerator to the other denominator**

2. Tell where you find mixed numbers on the number line. **to the right of 1; between whole numbers**

3. Describe three ways you can decide whether two fractions are equal. **Write both with the same denominator; change both to decimals; use cross products; write both in lowest terms**

Note that the same numbers are used in Exercises 25 and 32.   CHAPTER 5   **163**

Problem Solving

Item 30 has 3 parts:
a. literal—this is a reading comprehension question;
b. interpretive—this involves interpretation using the facts given;
c. applied—students use a strategy or skills to find an answer.

Item 25 in the skill section and item 32 in the problem solving section use the same numbers.

This will help you informally assess how your students transfer from numerical skills to word problems.

For scoring problem solving items you may wish to use partial credit. If a student uses the correct strategy but gets a wrong answer, give the student 2 points toward the total percent score.

Learning Log

These are suggestions for writing about some topics taught in this chapter. The students keep their Learning Logs from the beginning of the school year through the end.

CHAPTER TEST • FORM B

Write the prime factorization of each number. (pp. 130–133) 5A

1. 42   **2.** 75   **3.** 48   **4.** 90   **5.** 136
$2 \times 3 \times 7$ 3×5^2 $2^4 \times 3$ $2 \times 3^2 \times 5$ $2^3 \times 17$

Name the GCF and LCM for each pair of numbers. (pp. 134–137) 5B

6. 3, 15 **3;15**   **7.** 4, 20 **4;20**   **8.** 6, 15 **3;30**

9. 40, 32 **8;160**   **10.** 15, 25 **5;75**

(pp. 142–147, 150–151) 5C

Write the value of *n*.

11. $\frac{3}{5} = \frac{21}{n}$ **n = 35**   **12.** $\frac{n}{40} = \frac{5}{8}$ **n = 25**

Compare. Choose >, <, or =.

13. $\frac{5}{8}$ **>** $\frac{1}{2}$ **14.** $1\frac{3}{4}$ **<** $1\frac{7}{8}$ **15.** $3\frac{1}{5}$ **=** $\frac{16}{5}$

(pp. 148–149, 152–153, 156–157) 5D

Write as a decimal.

16. $\frac{5}{8}$ **0.625**   **17.** $\frac{12}{25}$ **0.48**   **18.** $\frac{7}{20}$ **0.35**

Write as a fraction or mixed number in lowest terms.

19. 0.64 **$\frac{16}{25}$**   **20.** 3.75 **$3\frac{3}{4}$**

Write as a terminating or repeating decimal. (pp. 154–155) 5E

21. $\frac{1}{8}$ **22.** $\frac{9}{11}$ **23.** $\frac{13}{20}$ **24.** $3\frac{1}{4}$ **25.** $\frac{7}{12}$
0.125   **0.$\overline{81}$**   **0.65**   **3.25**   **0.58$\overline{3}$**

CHAPTER TEST • FORM B

Solve by using a simpler problem. (pp. 138–139, 158–159) 5F

26. The average height of an adult female is $5\frac{1}{4}$ ft. About how many average women would equal the height of the Sears Tower which is 1,154 ft tall?   **about 220 women**

27. The Morentz family left for vacation on June 12, 1990, at 8:15 A.M. and returned on June 21, 1990, at 6:20 P.M. For how many hours and minutes were they gone?   **226 h 5 min**

28. The Morentz family bought 312 gal of gasoline. How many pints is this?   **2,496 pints**

29. The Morentz family drove for 4 h at a steady speed of 55 mi/h. How many miles did they drive?   **220 mi**

30. Abbie Morentz jogs at a pace of 10 km/h. At this pace, how many days and hours would it take to jog a distance equal to the 4,870 km trip from Boston to Seattle?   **20 days 7 h**

Error Analysis and Remediation

Here are some common errors students make when they are working with fractions and mixed numbers. The errors are listed by lesson under the appropriate management objective.

5B • IDENTIFY FACTORS AND MULTIPLES: GCF; LCM

Source of Error (Lesson 5-3)
students write a common factor that is not the GCF.

Remediation
Have students write the numbers and list all the factors. Then have them circle all common factors and identify the GCF.

Example: 24: ①, ②, ③, 4 , ⑥, 8 , 12 , 24
30: ①, ②, ③, 5 , ⑥, 10 , 15 , 30

Source of Error (Lesson 5-4)
students do not examine a sufficient number of multiplies for two numbers and conclude that there are no common multiples.

Remediation
Assign students several exercises, and include for each exercise a guideline such as: List the multiples that are less than 80.

5C • WRITE EQUIVALENT FRACTIONS AND COMPARE AND ORDER FRACTIONS

Source of Error (Lesson 5-8)
students forget to divide both the numerator and the denominator by the GCF to write a fraction in lowest terms.

Remediation
Write the fraction $\frac{15}{45}$ on the chalkboard. Have students list the common factors of 15 and 45. Divide the numerator and the denominator by 3. Is the fraction $\frac{5}{15}$ in lowest terms? *(no)* Divide by 5. Is the fraction $\frac{3}{9}$ in lowest terms? *(no)* Divide by 15. Is the fraction $\frac{1}{3}$ in lowest terms? *(yes)*

Source of Error (Lesson 5-10)
students try to compare numerators when the fractions have different denominators.

Remediation
Prepare the following chart for students to use when comparing two or more fractions.

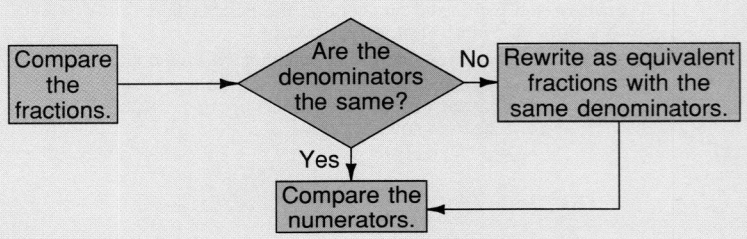

5D • WRITE FRACTIONS AND MIXED NUMBERS AS DECIMALS AND WRITE DECIMALS AS FRACTIONS AND MIXED NUMBERS

Source of Error (Lesson 5-9)
students have difficulty writing mixed numbers as fractions.

Remediation
Have students look at the fraction part of the mixed number and identify into how many parts each whole should be divided. Then have students put the new name for the whole number directly above it.

Example:
$$4\frac{1}{5} = \overset{\frac{20}{5}}{4} + \frac{1}{5} = \frac{21}{5}$$

Source of Error (Lesson 5-11)
students divide by the numerator instead of by the denominator when writing a fraction as a decimal.

Remediation
Emphasize that a number such as $\frac{4}{5}$ means "4 divided by 5," or $5\overline{)4}$.

5E • DETERMINE TERMINATING AND REPEATING DECIMALS

Source of Error (Lesson 5-12)
students do not write enough zeros in the dividend to name the full terminating decimal.

Remediation
Emphasize that students should continue dividing until the remainder is zero. Tell them that they can check that their answer is correct by multiplying the decimal quotient by the divisor; the result should equal the dividend.

Answers

5. 1, 2, 3, 6, 7, 14, 21, 42

6. 1, 2, 3, 4, 5, 6, 10, 12, 15, 20, 30, 60

7. 1, 59

8. 1, 41

9. 1, 3, 13, 39

10. 1, 3, 17, 51

Page 135

1. 1, 2, 3, 4, 6, 9, 12, 18, 36

4. 1, 2, 3, 4, 6, 8, 9, 12, 18, 24, 36, 72

5. 1, 2, 3, 6, 9, 18, 27, 54

Page 136

1. 3: 3, 6, 9, 12, 15, 18; 6: 6, 12, 18, 24, 30, 36

2. 7: 7, 14, 21, 28, 35, 42; 9: 9, 18, 27, 36, 45, 54

3. 11: 11, 22, 33, 44, 55, 66; 12: 12, 24, 36, 48, 60, 72

4. 18: 18, 36, 54, 72, 90, 108; 24: 24, 48, 72, 96, 120, 144

Page 138

2. w: plane, x: car, y: bicycle, z: skateboard
The plane travels the farthest in the least amount of time; the skateboard takes the longest time to go any distance.

Page 147

38.

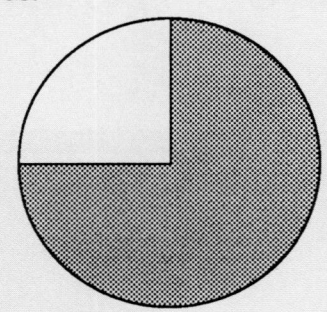

$\frac{150}{206}$ or $\approx 73\%$

73% of $360° = \approx 263°$

$\approx \frac{3}{4}$ of the circle

Page 133

17.

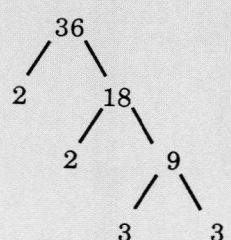

This page provides extra practice of all the major chapter objectives. Use this page after the chapter has been taught to reinforce the chapter skills. Page references are provided for each group of items so that students can easily look back at the appropriate lesson for additional support.

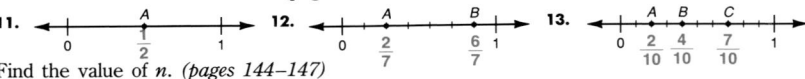

EXTRA PRACTICE

List the factors. Name the GCF. *(pages 134–135)*

1. 6, 15 **3**   **2.** 9, 21 **3**   **3.** 15, 25 **5**   **4.** 16, 40 **8**   **5.** 63, 35 **7**

Name the LCM. *(pages 136–137)*

6. 9, 7 **63**   **7.** 6, 9 **18**   **8.** 5, 11 **55**   **9.** 4, 14 **28**   **10.** 24, 30 **120**

Write a fraction for each letter. *(pages 142–143)*

11. (number line: 0, $\frac{1}{2}$, 1, with A)   **12.** (number line: 0, $\frac{2}{7}$, $\frac{6}{7}$, 1, with A, B)   **13.** (number line: 0, $\frac{2}{10}$, $\frac{4}{10}$, $\frac{7}{10}$, 1, with A, B, C)

Find the value of n. *(pages 144–147)*

14. $\frac{1}{7} = 4n$ $\frac{1}{28}$ **15.** $\frac{3}{n} = \frac{36}{48}$ **4**   **16.** $\frac{n}{24} = \frac{5}{6}$ **20**   **17.** $\frac{3}{8} = \frac{12}{n}$ **32**

Write the mixed number as a fraction. *(pages 148–149)*

18. $1\frac{2}{3}$ $\frac{5}{3}$ **19.** $2\frac{3}{4}$ $\frac{11}{4}$ **20.** $8\frac{1}{6}$ $\frac{49}{6}$

Write as a whole or mixed number in lowest terms. *(pages 148–149)*

21. $\frac{7}{5}$ $1\frac{2}{5}$ **22.** $\frac{21}{7}$ **3**   **23.** $8\frac{22}{6}$ $11\frac{2}{3}$

Compare. Choose $>$, $<$, or $=$. *(pages 150–151)*

24. $\frac{3}{7}$ ▓ $\frac{5}{8}$ $<$ **25.** $\frac{2}{9}$ ▓ $\frac{5}{18}$ $<$ **26.** $4\frac{7}{9}$ ▓ $4\frac{9}{12}$ $>$ **27.** $3\frac{12}{18}$ ▓ $3\frac{2}{3}$ $=$

Write the fraction as a decimal. *(pages 152–153)*

28. $\frac{8}{20}$ 0.4   **29.** $\frac{35}{40}$ 0.875   **30.** $\frac{12}{5}$ 2.4

Write the decimal as a fraction or mixed number in lowest terms. *(pages 152–153)*

31. 0.09 $\frac{9}{100}$ **32.** 0.875 $\frac{7}{8}$ **33.** 2.375 $2\frac{3}{8}$

Write as a terminating or repeating decimal. *(pages 154–155)*

34. $\frac{3}{5}$ 0.6   **35.** $\frac{2}{3}$ $0.\overline{6}$ **36.** $\frac{4}{9}$ $0.\overline{4}$ **37.** $2\frac{5}{6}$ $2.8\overline{3}$ **38.** $\frac{8}{11}$ $0.\overline{72}$

Solve. *(pages 158–159)*

39. Mount McKinley is 20,320 ft high. Mount Whitney is 14,491 ft. high. Mount Alverstone is 9 ft higher than Mount Whitney. What is the difference in height between Mount McKinley and Mount Alverstone? **5,820 ft**

The American Flag

The American flag has changed as new states have been admitted to the Union. At first, both a new star and stripe were added for each new state. In 1818, Congress decided to return to the original 13 stripes for the original colonies and to add only a star for each new state. The changing placement of the stars has created some interesting patterns. For example, from 1912 through 1959, the flag had 48 stars arranged in six rows of eight stars.

Find pictures of the American flag in different years. Draw a picture of one of the flags. Then write a short explanation of why the stars in that flag are arranged in the pattern you see.

At some point in the future, a 51st state may join the United States. How do you think the flag might look then? Try to design a flag with 51 stars so that the arrangement of the stars has an appealing look. Compare your ideas with others in the class.
Check students' work.

RELATIVELY PRIME NUMBERS

Whole numbers greater than 1 are either prime or composite. However, two or more composite numbers can be relatively prime. Numbers are relatively prime if the only factor they have in common is 1. For example, 25 and 36 form a pair of relatively prime numbers. No factor of 25 (1, 5, 25) is also a factor of 36 (1, 2, 3, 4, 6, 9, 12, 18, 36) except for 1. Are 49 and 54 relatively prime?

Work with a partner. Make up some pairs of numbers, some of which are relatively prime. Exchange your list with another team. Try to find the pairs that are relatively prime.
Check students' work.

ENRICHMENT   165

Enrichment

This page contains activities that provide extension and enrichment for all levels of students. Depending on the needs of your students, you may wish to assign an activity from this page at certain points during the chapter, or you may wish to use this page when the entire chapter has been completed.

The American Flag

Students can use encyclopedias to find pictures of the flag in different years. Some American history books also have this information.

Before students begin this activity, ask them to name the prime numbers between 13 and 50. *(17, 19, 23, 29, 31, 37, 41, 43, and 47)*

Relatively Prime Numbers
(COOPERATIVE)

Guide students by asking: Can you think of a quick way to determine that two numbers are *not* relatively prime? *(If both numbers are divisible by the same number, they are not relatively prime.)*

CHAPTER 5

Cumulative Review

The Cumulative Review focuses on skills covered in previous chapters. All important skills are reviewed on a cyclic basis.

If students are having difficulty with particular groups of exercises, refer to the chart for follow-up work.

Find the answer.

1. 66 is divisible **b** by
  a. 3, 5
  b. 2, 3, 6
  c. 2, 3, 6, 9
  d. none of these

2. Which of these is a **c** prime number?
  a. 57
  b. 77
  c. 71
  d. none of these

3. A prime factorization **c** of 54 is
  a. $3 \times 3 \times 6$
  b. $3 \times 3 \times 2 \times 2$
  c. $3 \times 3 \times 3 \times 2$
  d. none of these

4. A solution to **d** $x - 9 < 4$ is
  a. 15
  b. 14
  c. 13
  d. none of these

5. A solution to **c** $m + 3 > 12$ is
  a. 8
  b. 9
  c. 10
  d. none of these

6.

The graph shows **a**
  a. $x < 8$
  b. $x = 8$
  c. $x > 8$
  d. none of these

7. The GCF of 10 and 36 **a** is
  a. 2
  b. 6
  c. 10
  d. none of these

8. The LCM of 8 and 12 **b** is
  a. 16
  b. 24
  c. 36
  d. none of these

9. The LCM of 2, 3, and **c** 9 is
  a. 9
  b. 12
  c. 18
  d. none of these

10. $4 \times 4 \times 4 \times 4 \times 4 =$ **a**
  a. 4^5
  b. 5^4
  c. 20
  d. none of these

11. 5.2 million = **d**
  a. 5,000,002
  b. 52,000,000
  c. 5,002,000
  d. none of these

12. $(9 \times 10^2) + (7 \times 10^1) =$ **c**
  a. 97
  b. 907
  c. 970
  d. none of these

13. Which number is **b** between 6.904 and 6.980?
  a. 6.019
  b. 6.915
  c. 6.991
  d. none of these

14. Which number is less **a** than 378.42?
  a. 378.39
  b. 378.50
  c. 379.02
  d. none of these

15. 0.085 is between **d** which two numbers?
  a. 0.081 and 0.084
  b. 0.008 and 0.0089
  c. 0.80 and 0.90
  d. none of these

166   CUMULATIVE REVIEW

Items	Management Objectives	Where Taught	Reteaching Options	Extra Practice Options
1–3	**5A** Determine divisibility, primes and composites, and write prime factorization.	pp. 130–133		TRB/PW 5-2
4–6	**4C** Solve and graph inequalities.	pp. 110–113	TRB/RW 4-7 TE/RA 4-8	TRB/PW 4-7 and 4-8
7–9	**5B** Identify factors and multiples; GCF; LCM.	pp. 134–137	TRB/RW 5-3 and 5-4	TRB/PW 5-3 and 5-4
10–12	**1A** Identify and write whole numbers and decimals in exponential, expanded, and standard forms.	pp. 4–7	TRB/RW 1-2 TE/RA 1-3	TRB/PW 1-2 and 1-3
13–15	**1B** Compare and order whole numbers and decimals.	pp. 8–9	TRB/RW 1–4	TRB/PW 1-4

PROBLEM SOLVING REVIEW

Strategies may vary, suggestions given.
Remember the strategies and types of problems you've had so far. Solve, if possible.

Problem Solving Check List

- Too much information
- Too little information
- Multistep problems
- Using a simpler problem
- Making a list
- Making a table
- Making a chart
- Using a pattern

1. For an auto race around a $2\frac{1}{2}$-mi oval, the cars line up side by side. When the race begins, the fastest car completes 7 laps in the time the slowest car completes 6 laps.

   a. How far is it around the track? $2\frac{1}{2}$ mi

   b. How far has the fastest car traveled when it completes the first 7 laps? $17\frac{1}{2}$ mi

   c. How far will each car have traveled the next time the fastest car and the slowest car meet at the starting line?
   multistep; 35 mi vs. 30 mi

2. A mashed potato recipe makes 2 servings for each potato used. If Marietta follows the recipe how many servings can she prepare?
   too little information

3. If the pattern continues, how many dots will be in the tenth term of this sequence? **patterns; 55**

   .
   . . .
   . . . . . .
   . . . .

4. How many line segments of any length are in the figure?

   list; 18 segments

5. A baseball diamond is a square 30 yd on a side. For a football game, the diamond becomes part of the football field, a 100-yd by 53-yd rectangle. In square yards, how much of the football field is not part of the baseball diamond?
   multistep; 4,400 yd²

6. Randall paid for a $.45 drink with exact change. If he did not have any pennies, how many different combinations of coins could he have used?
   table; 8 combinations

7. Twenty-five riders started a 20 mi bicycle race. At 15 mi, 7 riders had dropped out. Everyone else completed the race. How many riders finished?
   too much information; 18 riders

8. Cornell checked in for a 12:15 P.M. flight that took off 20 minutes late. If he checked in $1\frac{1}{2}$ h before takeoff, what time did he check in?
   too much information; 11:05 A.M.

9. How many times does the digit 2 appear in the page numbers of a 128-page book?
   list; 32 times

CHAPTER 5   167

Problem Solving Review

This page focuses on problem solving strategies and types learned in this and previous chapters. A problem solving checklist lists some of the strategies students may use to solve the problems on this page.

Technology

This page is designed to provide calculator or computer experiences for all levels of students. The calculator or computer logo indicates the type of activity.

You may wish to assign these activities after the chapter has been taught or during the course of the chapter, depending on your needs and those of your students.

Prime Time Riddles

As students start solving the riddles, they should recognize that more than one answer is possible for each riddle. Encourage students to make up their own riddles.

Quick Factor
(COOPERATIVE)

When one of the partners has found the prime factorization for a number, the other partner should check by finding the product of all prime factors.

Number Detective
(COOPERATIVE)

You may wish to have a "practice run" before students begin this activity. Give clues for the number 75, such as: "My number divided by 12 has a remainder of 3."

Software for this activity may be found in Houghton Mifflin Math Activities Courseware, Grade 7.

TECHNOLOGY

PRIME TIME RIDDLES

Divide me by 3 and you get a 2-digit prime. Multiply me by 3 and you get a 2-digit composite number. Who am I?
33

We are 3-digit numbers less than 150. We are products of two 2-digit prime numbers. Who are we?
121, 143

QUICK FACTOR

Work with a partner. See who can completely write the prime factorization for each number the fastest. To get you started, one factor is given.

1. 24,840 {factor: 23} $2^3 \cdot 3^3 \cdot 5 \cdot 23$

2. 5,814 {factor: 19} $2 \cdot 3^2 \cdot 17 \cdot 19$

3. 108,108 {factor: 7} $2^2 \cdot 3^3 \cdot 7 \cdot 11 \cdot 13$

NUMBER DETECTIVE

In the computer activity *Remainder Clues,* players use clues about divisors and remainders to try to guess a mystery number. This activity for partners will help you decide whether a certain remainder is appropriate for a given divisor and dividend. You do not need a computer. See table below.

Players A and B secretly choose numbers from the table. Player A then gives Player B a clue about his or her number. For instance, a clue for 62 could be: "My number divided by 4 has a remainder of 2." Player B would then eliminate any number in the table that doesn't have a remainder of 2 when it is divided by 4.

Player B then gives a clue about his or her number and Player A checks the table. Play continues until either player guesses the other's number. Only one guess is permitted on each turn.

56	57	58	59	60	61	62
63	64	65	66	67	68	69
70	71	72	73	74	75	76

This game is available on computer disk in Houghton Mifflin *Mathematics Activities Courseware.*

168   TECHNOLOGY

Software Activities

activity 1 • CUSTOMARY UNITS OF LENGTH

MATERIALS: spreadsheet program

Procedure: In this activity, students create a spreadsheet that converts between customary units of length. Students should begin by creating the following spreadsheet and entering numbers in cells B2 and B3. They should then watch the numbers calculated in the cells in rows 2 and 3.

	B	C	D	E	F	G
1			in.	ft	yd	mi
2		in.		$+\frac{B2}{12}$	$+\frac{B2}{36}$	——
3		ft	12*B3		$+\frac{B3}{3}$	$+\frac{B3}{5280}$
4		yd	——	——		——
5		mi	——		——	

Follow-up: Have students write formulas for the dashed cells (——) and enter them into the spreadsheet. Again, they should enter numbers in column B and watch how the numbers are affected in rows 2, 3, 4, and 5.

activity 2 • NUMBER FACTORING

MATERIALS: BASIC programming

Procedure: This program will find the factors of a number. Begin by having the students type the program into the computer. Have them run it several times.

```
10 REM: THE PROGRAM FACTORS THE
   NUMBER YOU INPUT.
20 PRINT "THIS PROGRAM FACTORS A
   NUMBER FOR YOU. "
30 INPUT "FACTOR WHAT NUMBER ";N
40 FOR F= 1 TO N
50 IF N/F=INT {N/F} THEN PRINT F
   "IS A FACTOR OF "N
60 NEXT F
70 END
```

Follow-up: Help students to change the program so it counts and prints the total number of factors.

HOUGHTON MIFFLIN SOFTWARE

Computational Skills Program. Boston, MA: Houghton Mifflin Company, 1988. For Apple II.

Easy Graph. Boston, MA: Houghton Mifflin Company, 1987. For Apple II, Commodore, IBM.

Friendly Filer. Boston, MA: Houghton Mifflin Company, 1989. For Apple II, Commodore, IBM.

Mathematics Activities Courseware. Boston, MA: Houghton Mifflin Company, 1983. For Apple II, IBM.

The Computer Tutor. Boston, MA: Houghton Mifflin Company, 1990. For Apple II, IBM.

OTHER SOFTWARE

Factoring Machine. Dallas, TX: Micro Power & Light, 1981. For Apple II.

Introduction to Fractions. Big Spring, TX: Gamco Industries, Inc., 1989. For Apple II, Commodore, IBM.

Get To The Point. Pleasantville, NY: Sunburst Communications, 1985. For Apple II, IBM, Commodore.

Hands-On Math: III. Newbury Park, CA: Ventura Educational Systems, 1989. For Apple II.

More Teasers from Tobbs. Pleasantville, NY: Sunburst Communications, 1988. For Apple II.

The Children's Writing and Publishing Center. Freemont, CA: The Learning Company, 1988. For Apple II.

Adding and Subtracting Fractions; Customary Measure

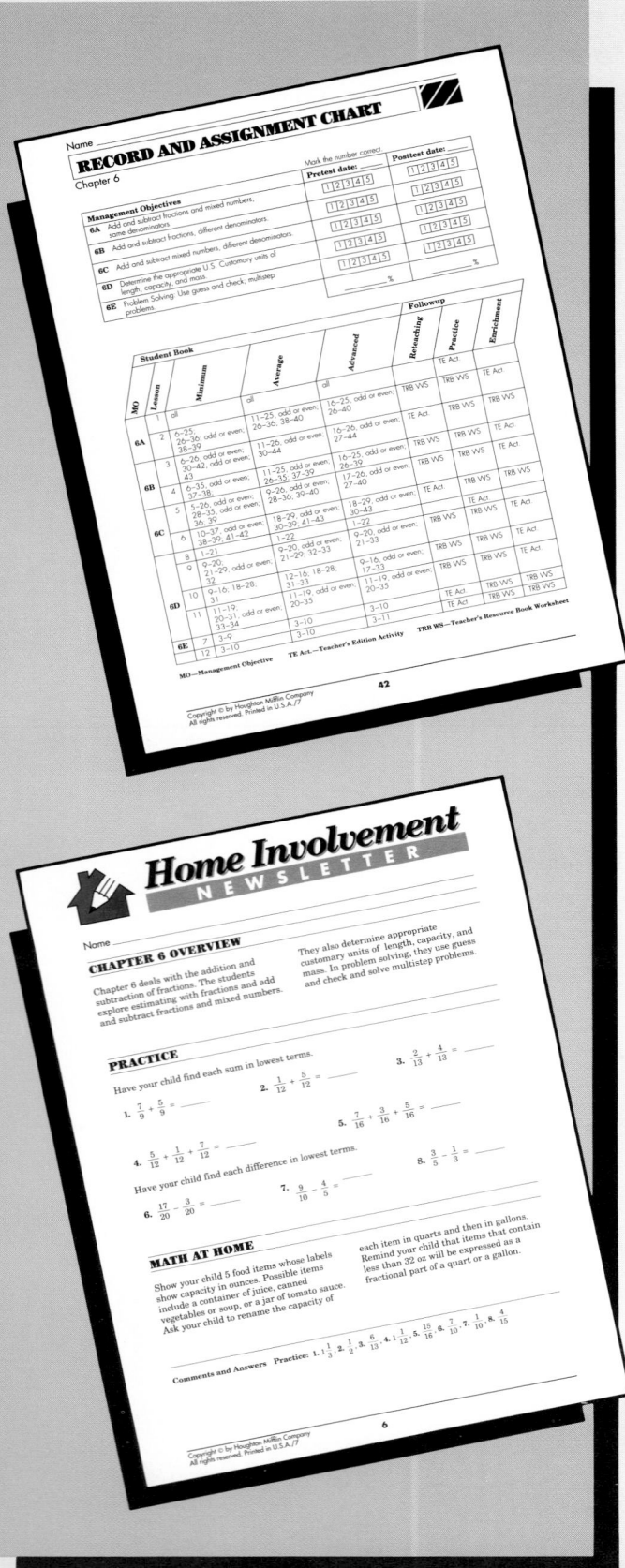

In Chapter 6 students extend their knowledge of fractions to computation and problem solving. They add and subtract fractions with same denominators and different denominators; they also add and subtract mixed numbers. In the second half of the chapter, students work with customary units of length, capacity, and weight.

Problem solving lessons highlight the strategy of guess and check. Students use this strategy to solve multistep problems.

Management Objectives

6A Add and subtract fractions and mixed numbers, same denominators.

6B Add and subtract fractions, different denominators.

6C Add and subtract mixed numbers, different denominators.

6D Determine the appropriate customary units of length, capacity, and mass.

6E Problem Solving: Use guess and check. Multistep problems.

Assignments for different achievement levels are provided on the Record and Assignment Chart in the Teacher's Resource Book.

Home Involvement

As you begin to teach this chapter, give each student a copy of the Home Involvement Newsletter for this chapter.

This newsletter provides parents with
■ an overview of the chapter
■ suggestions for practicing some of the skills in the chapter
■ an at-home activity to do with their child, applying the skills taught in the chapter.

Management Chart

Management Objectives	Lesson/Pages	Student Not Successful	Student Needs More Practice	Student Successful	Pacing Range
6A Add and subtract fractions and mixed numbers, same denominators.	6-1/170-171			TE/CA 6-1	2 days
	6-2/172-173	TRB/RW 6-2	TRB/PW 6-2 CSP FA Skill 1 CSP FS Skill 2 CT Unit 2 Obj. 4.1, 4.5	TE/EA 6-2	
6B Add and subtract fractions, different denominators.	6-3/174-175	TE/RA 6-3	TRB/PW 6-3 CSP FA Skill 4 CSP FS Skill 5 CT Unit 2 Obj. 4.2, 5.2	TRB/EW 6-3	2 days
	6-4/176-177	TRB/RW 6-4	TRB/PW 6-4 CSP FA Skills 1, 4 CSP FS Skills 1, 5 CT Unit 2 Obj. 4.1, 4.2, 5.1, 5.2	TE/EA 6-4	
6C Add and subtract mixed numbers, different denominators.	6-5/178-179	TRB/RW 6-5	TRB/PW 6-5 CSP FA Skills 3, 5 CSP FS Skills 4, 6 MAC 7 Activity 6	TE/EA 6-5 MAC 6 Activity 9 MAC 7 Activity 6	2-3 days
	6-6/180-181	TE/RA 6-6	TRB/PW 6-6 CSP FS Skill 3	TRB/EW 6-6	
6D Determine the appropriate customary units of length, capacity, and mass.	6-8/186-187			TE/CA 6-8	3 days
	6-9/188-189	TRB/RW 6-9	TRB/PW 6-9	TE/EA 6-9	
	6-10/190-191	TRB/RW 6-10	TRB/PW 6-10	TE/EA 6-10	
	6-11/192-193	TRB/RW 6-11	TRB/PW 6-11	TE/EA 6-11	
6E Problem Solving: Using guess and check. Multistep problems.	6-7/184-185	TE/RA 6-7	TRB/PW 6-7 MAC 8 Activity 9A	TRB/EW 6-7 MAC 8 Activity 9A	2 days
	6-12/194-195	TE/RA 6-12	TRB/PW 6-12	TRB/EW 6-12	
Chapter Checkups	182-183, 196-197				
Extra Practice	198				
Enrichment	199				
Cumulative Review/ Problem Solving Review	200-201				
Technology	202				

TE = Teacher's Edition
TRB = Teacher's Resource Book
RW = Reteaching Worksheet
RA = Reteaching Activity
EA = Enrichment Activity
EW = Enrichment Worksheet
PW = Practice Worksheet
CA = Classroom Activity

*Other Available Items
MAC = Mathematics Activities Courseware
CSP = Computational Skills Program
CT = Computer Tutor

Manipulative Planning Guide

This is a complete list of manipulatives and materials needed for Chapter 6.

Materials for Manipulatives	TE Activities (Introduce)	Student Book Lesson
Inch ruler, one per student	Lesson 6-1	Lesson 6-1
Tape measure or ruler, two per group	Lesson 6-9	Lesson 6-8
Containers: gallon, half-gallon, quart, pint, cup; water or sand	Lesson 6-10	
Balance scale	Lesson 6-11	
Pound and ounce weights	Lesson 6-11	
Blank cubes, two per pair		
Blank spinners, one per pair		
Tagboard		
Strips of paper, tape		
Drinking straws, tape		
Colored pencils		
Index cards		
Paper bags, two per group		
Cookbooks, one per group		
Gallon-size plastic milk jug		
Small objects such as paper clips or toothpicks, tape		
Teaching Aid 4* or fraction bars	Lessons 6-2, 6-3, 6-4	
Teaching Aid 5* for each student	Lesson 6-12	
Math Connection Transparency		Lessons 6-3, 6-4
Calculator for each student		Lessons 6-2, 6-10, 6-11

*Teaching Aids are found in the Teacher's Resource Book.

CONCRETE

Learning Stages

The concepts and skills in Chapter 6 are presented through these learning stages.

Using manipulatives and verbalizing about a concept. No symbols.

Teacher Edition Activities	Student Book
At this grade level, the skills of this chapter are taught at the connecting and symbolic stages.	

Enrichment/Class Activity	Reteaching	In the Houghton Mifflin Manipulative Kit?	In the Houghton Mifflin Overhead Kit?
Lesson 6-1		Yes	
		Yes	
Lesson 6-11			
		Yes	
Lesson 6-2		Yes	
Lesson 6-2		Yes	
Lesson 6-2			
Lesson 6-8			
Lesson 6-1			
Lesson 6-8			
Lesson 6-4			
Lesson 6-4			
Lesson 6-5			
Lesson 6-10			
Lesson 6-11			
	Lessons 6-3, 6-6		Yes
			Yes
			Available separately

CONNECTING

   5¢ 9cm² $\frac{1}{3}$

Making a connection between manipulatives and symbols.

Teacher Edition Activities	Student Book
Lessons 6-1, 6-2, 6-3, 6-4, 6-10, 6-11	Lesson 6-1

SYMBOLIC

$.05 $A = 9cm^2$ $1 - \frac{2}{3} = \frac{1}{3}$

Using numbers or symbols. No manipulatives or pictures of manipulatives.

Teacher Edition Activities	Student Book
Lessons 6-5, 6-6, 6-7, 6-8, 6-9, 6-12	Lessons 6-2, 6-3, 6-4, 6-5, 6-6, 6-7, 6-8, 6-9, 6-10, 6-11, 6-12

Additional Activities

COOPERATIVE LEARNING RESOURCE ACTIVITIES

Through cooperative learning activities, students learn by interacting with one another in small groups. These cooperative activities provide students with motivating settings for making connections, investigations, and problem solving situations.

The cooperative connections are interdisciplinary problem-solving projects. Each student has a particular job that helps lead the group to complete the project. For the cooperative investigations students work in pairs for investigations involving data collection and analysis. The cooperative problem solving activities encourage the sharing of ideas and information. Students work in groups of four to solve a problem. Students are each assigned a clue and work together to find a common solution.

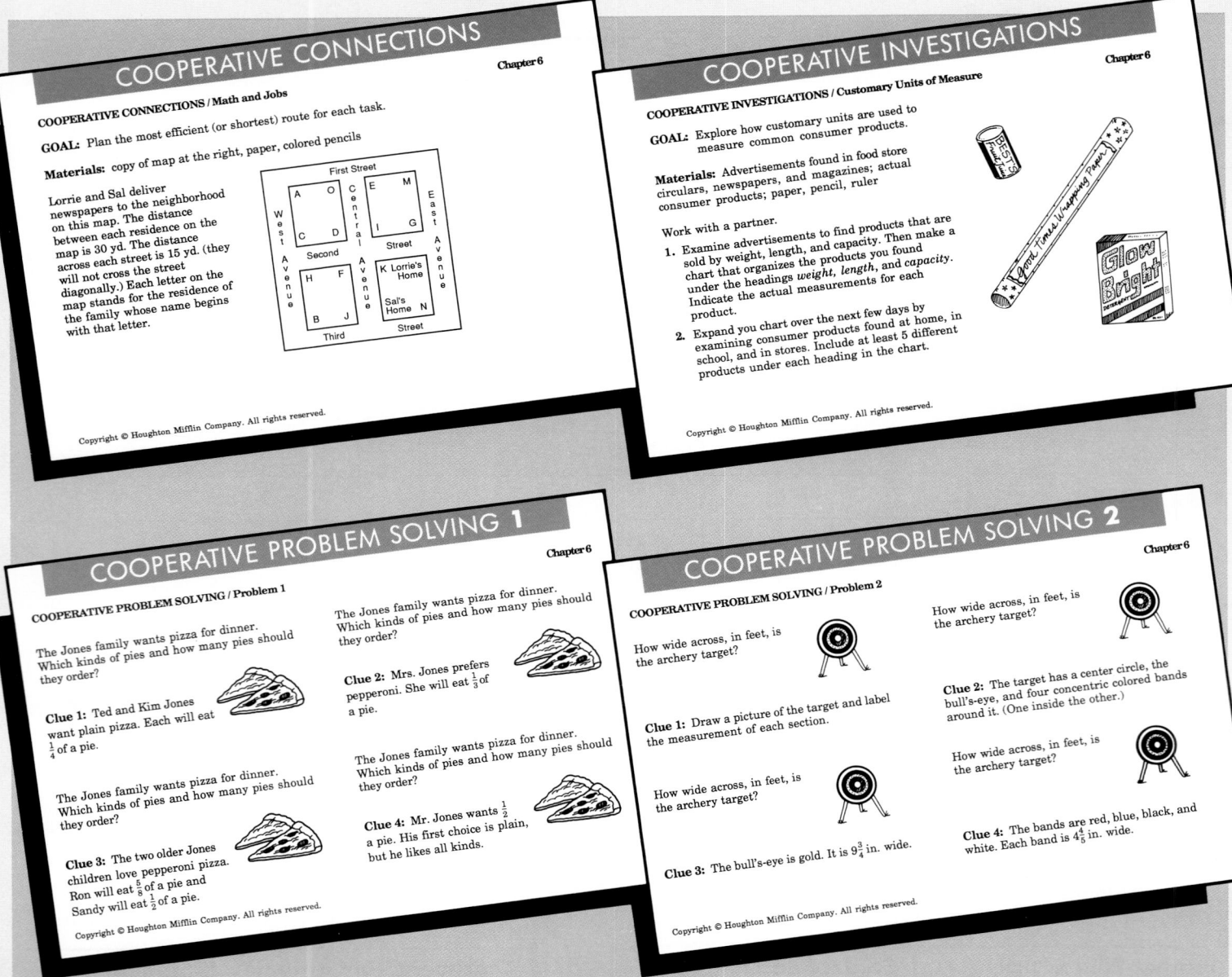

COOPERATIVE CONNECTIONS — Chapter 6

COOPERATIVE CONNECTIONS / Math and Jobs

GOAL: Plan the most efficient (or shortest) route for each task.

Materials: copy of map at the right, paper, colored pencils

Lorrie and Sal deliver newspapers to the neighborhood on this map. The distance between each residence on the map is 30 yd. The distance across each street is 15 yd. (they will not cross the street diagonally.) Each letter on the map stands for the residence of the family whose name begins with that letter.

Copyright © Houghton Mifflin Company. All rights reserved.

COOPERATIVE INVESTIGATIONS — Chapter 6

COOPERATIVE INVESTIGATIONS / Customary Units of Measure

GOAL: Explore how customary units are used to measure common consumer products.

Materials: Advertisements found in food store circulars, newspapers, and magazines; actual consumer products; paper, pencil, ruler

Work with a partner.
1. Examine advertisements to find products that are sold by weight, length, and capacity. Then make a chart that organizes the products you found under the headings *weight, length,* and *capacity.* Indicate the actual measurements for each product.
2. Expand you chart over the next few days by examining consumer products found at home, in school, and in stores. Include at least 5 different products under each heading in the chart.

Copyright © Houghton Mifflin Company. All rights reserved.

COOPERATIVE PROBLEM SOLVING 1 — Chapter 6

COOPERATIVE PROBLEM SOLVING / Problem 1

The Jones family wants pizza for dinner. Which kinds of pies and how many pies should they order?

Clue 1: Ted and Kim Jones want plain pizza. Each will eat $\frac{1}{4}$ of a pie.

The Jones family wants pizza for dinner. Which kinds of pies and how many pies should they order?

Clue 3: The two older Jones children love pepperoni pizza. Ron will eat $\frac{5}{8}$ of a pie and Sandy will eat $\frac{1}{2}$ of a pie.

The Jones family wants pizza for dinner. Which kinds of pies and how many pies should they order?

Clue 2: Mrs. Jones prefers pepperoni. She will eat $\frac{1}{3}$ of a pie.

The Jones family wants pizza for dinner. Which kinds of pies and how many pies should they order?

Clue 4: Mr. Jones wants $\frac{1}{2}$ a pie. His first choice is plain, but he likes all kinds.

Copyright © Houghton Mifflin Company. All rights reserved.

COOPERATIVE PROBLEM SOLVING 2 — Chapter 6

COOPERATIVE PROBLEM SOLVING / Problem 2

How wide across, in feet, is the archery target?

Clue 1: Draw a picture of the target and label the measurement of each section.

How wide across, in feet, is the archery target?

Clue 3: The bull's-eye is gold. It is $9\frac{3}{4}$ in. wide.

How wide across, in feet, is the archery target?

Clue 2: The target has a center circle, the bull's-eye, and four concentric colored bands around it. (One inside the other.)

How wide across, in feet, is the archery target?

Clue 4: The bands are red, blue, black, and white. Each band is $4\frac{4}{5}$ in. wide.

Copyright © Houghton Mifflin Company. All rights reserved.

GAMES

FRACTURED FRACTIONS   (For use after Lesson 6-4)

Objective: Add fractions with different denominators.

☑ **MATERIALS CHECKLIST:** two number cubes, paper, and pencils for two teams of four players each

Two teams of four players play against each other. The first player from Team A tosses both number cubes twice. On each toss, the greater number becomes the denominator of a fraction; the lesser number, the numerator. For example, a toss of 3 and 5 yields the fraction $\frac{3}{5}$, and a toss of 2 and 6 results in the fraction $\frac{2}{6}$. A toss of the same digits should be repeated. The player who made the tosses adds the fractions and expresses the sum in lowest terms; teammates may provide help. If the sum is correct, it is recorded as Team A's score. If it is incorrect, Team A scores no points. Teams alternate turns. Scoring is cumulative, and the first team to reach 15 points wins.

WHEEL OF EQUALS   (For use after Lesson 6-11)

Objective: Change from one customary unit to another.

☑ **MATERIALS CHECKLIST:** 25 index cards, a six-part spinner labeled *0, 1, 2, 3, 4, 5*

On each index card, write an exercise that involves changing from one customary unit to another, such as 2 yd = _____ ft.

Have students form teams of four players and decide on the order for team play. Place the cards face up in a pile. A player from Team A spins and plays for the number of points indicated. (On *0* the team loses its turn.) That player takes the top card and names the missing number; teammates may help. If the answer is correct, Team A scores the number of points spun. If the answer is incorrect, the next team has a chance to answer correctly and score instead. The procedure is repeated for the next team. The team with the most points at the end wins.

BULLETIN BOARD

Draw paths similar to those shown above. Avoid creating any intersections, and indicate each end of a path with a large dot. Ask students to decide which path is longer and to estimate the lengths of both paths in inches. Students should place their estimates in the "Answers" envelope. Then have students measure both paths to the nearest half-inch and also submit those totals. Declare as "winners" students who picked the longer path correctly and had the closest estimates.

Alternative Assessment

In addition to the paper and pencil tests available with this program, the following items can help you assess critical thinking as well as your students' ability to solve problems in a wide variety of ways.

Investigation

As a class project, you are going to shade portions of a square divided into 100 equal smaller squares to represent the area of each of the seven continents and the total water area of Earth. Describe how estimates, fractions, percents, etc. could be used in this activity.

Teacher Notes

The seven continents represent $\frac{1}{4}$ of the total area. Water represents the other $\frac{3}{4}$. The seven continents as fractions of Earth's land area are:

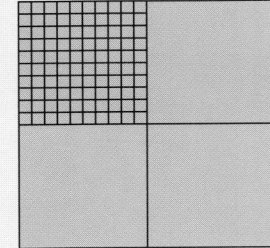

South America	$\frac{6}{50}$	Australia	$\frac{1}{20}$
North America	$\frac{4}{25}$	Europe	$\frac{7}{100}$
Africa	$\frac{1}{5}$	Asia	$\frac{3}{10}$
Antarctica	$\frac{9}{100}$		

Students may be asked to research the information above.
Students should choose what size square to use. The total land area should be $\frac{1}{4}$ of the square, so $\frac{1}{4}$ of the square may have to be subdivided into 100ths.
Students responses may include:
• a description of how they found out which portions to shade.
• a chart or graph displaying the data.
• an explanation about using fractions and percents.
• an oral or written report about the project.

Group Writing Activity (See p. T24.)

Fill each of the boxes below with one of the numbers 0, 1, 2, 3, 4, 5, 6, 7, 8, or 9 so that the sum of the fractions is less than 1. You may use each number only once in each sum. What strategy did you use?

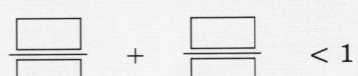

Teacher Notes

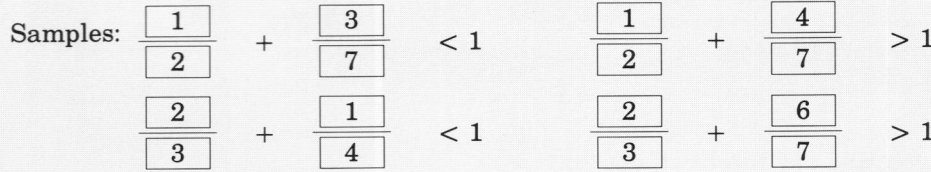

Samples:

Fractions with large denominators and small numerators will often give a sum less than 1.

Individual Writing Activity

What strategies did you use to choose the numbers so that the sum would be less than 1? How would your strategy change if the sum had to be greater than 1? Include examples to clarify your explanation.

Portfolios

Portfolios can provide information about a student's growth and help you make instructional decisions and communicate with parents. The students' work involving the investigation and writing activity suggested on this page along with work on the Learning Log exercises on pages 183 and 197 and the Create Your Own exercises on pages 187 and 191 could be included in portfolios.

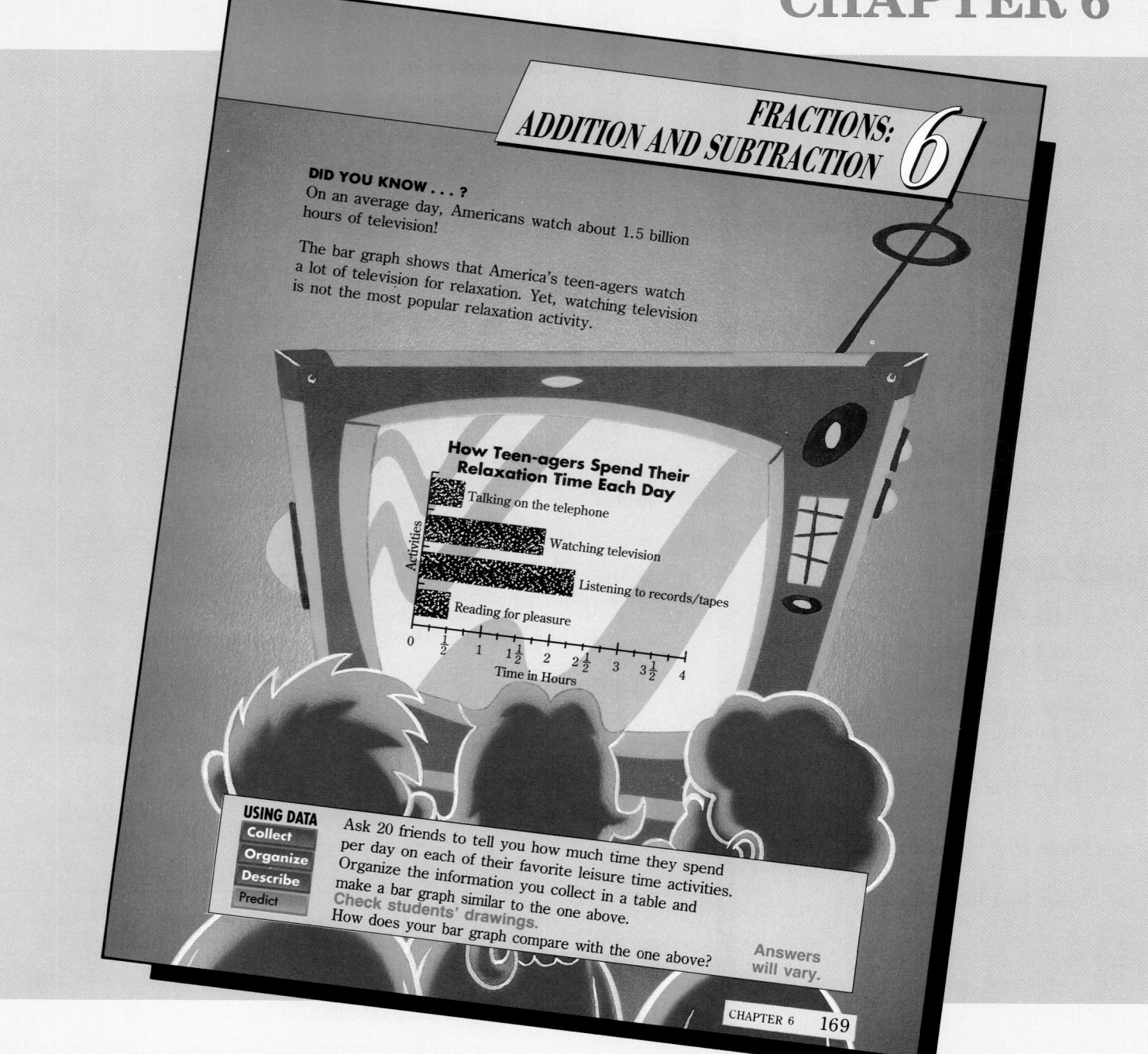

FRACTIONS:
ADDITION AND SUBTRACTION **6**

DID YOU KNOW . . . ?
On an average day, Americans watch about 1.5 billion hours of television!

The bar graph shows that America's teen-agers watch a lot of television for relaxation. Yet, watching television is not the most popular relaxation activity.

How Teen-agers Spend Their Relaxation Time Each Day

Talking on the telephone
Watching television
Listening to records/tapes
Reading for pleasure

Activities

Time in Hours
$0 \quad \frac{1}{2} \quad 1 \quad 1\frac{1}{2} \quad 2 \quad 2\frac{1}{2} \quad 3 \quad 3\frac{1}{2} \quad 4$

USING DATA
Collect
Organize
Describe
Predict

Ask 20 friends to tell you how much time they spend per day on each of their favorite leisure time activities. Organize the information you collect in a table and make a bar graph similar to the one above. Check students' drawings. How does your bar graph compare with the one above?
Answers will vary.

CHAPTER 6   169

Using the Chapter Opener

The purpose of this page is to involve the student in the use of real data much like that presented in newspapers and magazines.

To use this page as you begin the chapter, direct students' attention to the data. You may wish to ask questions such as the following:

Approximately what fractional part of a day do teenagers spend listening to records and tapes? *(about $\frac{1}{12}$)* **How do you know?** *(Two hours out of a 24-hour day is $\frac{2}{24} = \frac{1}{12}$.)*

What do you need to do to compare the amount of time teenagers spend watching television with the amount of time they spend reading for pleasure? *(Subtract the reading time—$\frac{1}{2}$ hour—from the television time—$1\frac{3}{4}$ hours.)*

How much more time do teenagers spend watching television than reading for pleasure? *($1\frac{1}{4}$ hours)*

You may wish to use the data collecting and graph-making activities as cooperative learning situations. Some students may require several days to complete the assignment.

LESSON 6-1

Lesson Organizer

Objective: Explore estimating with fractions using perimeters.

Prior Knowledge: Students should be able to measure to the nearest $\frac{1}{8}$ in.

Lesson Resources:
Class Activity 6-1
Daily Review 6-1

Two-Minute Math

Without using a ruler, draw a line to estimate each length: $\frac{5}{16}$ in., $2\frac{5}{8}$ in., $\frac{7}{8}$ in., and $3\frac{3}{4}$ in. Then measure each line to see how closely you estimated.

1 PREPARE

CONNECTING ACTIVITY

☑ **MATERIALS CHECKLIST:** inch ruler for each student

1. Tell students to measure and draw a 2-in. line and label it at points 0, 1 in., and 2 in.

2. Directly below the 2-in. line have them draw two lines: $1\frac{3}{8}$ in. and $1\frac{5}{8}$ in.

Is $1\frac{3}{8}$ in. closer to 1 in. or to 2 in.?
(1 in.)

Is $1\frac{5}{8}$ in. closer to 1 in. or to 2 in.?
(2 in.)

WHEN YOUR STUDENTS ASK
★ WHY AM I LEARNING THIS? ★

This skill will help you solve real life estimation problems. For example, when dimensions of posters are given as fractions, you can round the fractions to estimate how much wood is needed for the frame.

Exploring Estimating Perimeters

1. The diagram at the right shows the inch (in.) divided into halves, fourths, eighths, and sixteenths. Draw line segments that are $\frac{1}{2}$ in., $\frac{2}{4}$ in., $\frac{4}{8}$ in., and $\frac{8}{16}$ in. in length. What do you notice? **All are the same length.**

Is the measurement *greater than* or *less than* $\frac{1}{2}$ in.?

2. $\frac{1}{4}$ in. 3. $\frac{3}{4}$ in. 4. $\frac{1}{8}$ in. 5. $\frac{7}{8}$ in.
   less than **greater than** **less than** **greater than**

Use the diagram to help you estimate the length. Is the length closer to *0 in.* or to *1 in.*?

6. $\frac{5}{8}$ in. **1 in.** 7. $\frac{3}{8}$ in. **0 in.** 8. $\frac{2}{16}$ in. **0 in.** 9. $\frac{3}{16}$ in. **0 in.**

10. $\frac{5}{16}$ in. **0 in.** 11. $\frac{7}{16}$ in. **0 in.** 12. $\frac{9}{16}$ in. **1 in.** 13. $\frac{13}{16}$ in. **1 in.**

14. **IN YOUR WORDS** Is there a way to tell whether a fractional measurement is closer to 0 in. or to 1 in. without using the diagram? If so, describe it. **Yes**
Compare it to $\frac{1}{2}$ in. If it is less than $\frac{1}{2}$ in., it is closer to 0 in.

Use what you discovered in Exercise 14 to tell whether the fraction is closer to *0* or to *1*.

15. $\frac{9}{10}$ **1** 16. $\frac{6}{42}$ **0** 17. $\frac{8}{11}$ **1** 18. $\frac{3}{5}$ **1** 19. $\frac{4}{7}$ **1**

20. The perimeter of a plane figure is the distance around the figure. By adding the lengths of the sides, a student found the perimeter of this triangle to be $5\frac{9}{16}$ in. Estimate to see whether the answer is reasonable. Round to the nearest inch.

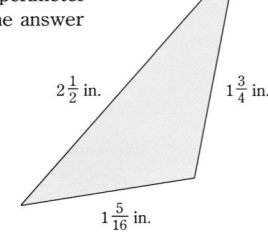

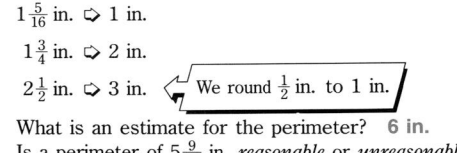

$1\frac{5}{16}$ in. ⇨ 1 in.
$1\frac{3}{4}$ in. ⇨ 2 in.
$2\frac{1}{2}$ in. ⇨ 3 in. ◁ We round $\frac{1}{2}$ in. to 1 in.

What is an estimate for the perimeter? **6 in.**
Is a perimeter of $5\frac{9}{16}$ in. *reasonable* or *unreasonable*?
reasonable

---

2 EXPLORE

☑ **MATERIALS CHECKLIST:** inch ruler for each student

What fraction of an inch do you consider when rounding to the nearest inch? $\left(\frac{1}{2}\right)$

What fractions of an inch on your ruler are equivalent to $\frac{1}{2}$ in.? $\left(\frac{2}{4}, \frac{4}{8}, and \frac{8}{16}\right)$

What is the least fraction that could be rounded to 5 in.? $\left(4\frac{1}{2} in.\right)$

SUMMARIZE/ASSESS Explain how to estimate fractions to check whether a perimeter is reasonable. *(Round each measure to the nearest inch and add to find the sum of the measures.)*

Is the given perimeter reasonable? Use estimation to decide.

21. yes

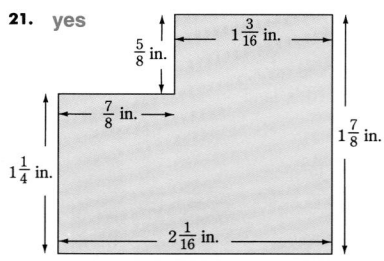

Perimeter: $7\frac{7}{8}$ in.

22. no

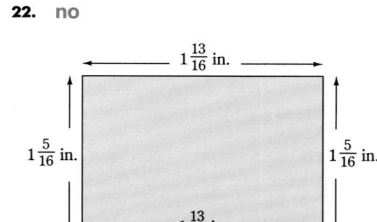

Perimeter: $9\frac{1}{4}$ in.

Use a ruler to measure. Does the perimeter fall between the measurements?

23. yes

Between: 5 in. and 7 in.

24. no

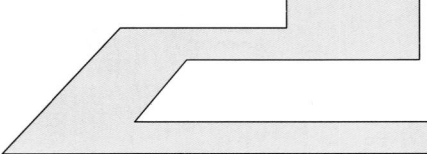

Between: 9 in. and 10 in.

25. Does Figure *A* or Figure *B* have the greater perimeter?
Use measurements and estimation to decide. Figure B

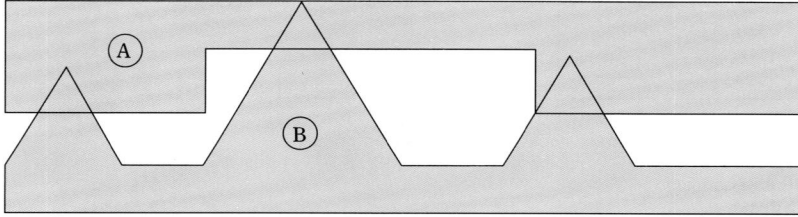

Draw the given figure so that it has a perimeter of between 8 in.
and 10 in. Label the dimensions. Check students' drawings.

26. any triangle   **27.** a square   **28.** any other figure

CLASS ACTIVITY **6-1**

☑ **MATERIALS CHECKLIST:** Drinking
straws, scissors, tape, rulers

Have the students work in pairs. Each
student cuts three drinking straws into
two or three pieces. Have the students
measure each length of straw, rounding to
the nearest $\frac{1}{16}$ inch. Then ask each student to form a polygon by taping the sections of straw to a sheet of paper. Have
the students label the length of each side.
Partners take turns showing each other
their polygons. The partner displaying the
polygon gives a perimeter for it that may
or may not be the actual perimeter. Using
estimation, the other partner guesses
whether the perimeter given is reasonable.
A correct guess is worth 1 point. Repeat
the procedure several times. The student
with the most points at the end is the
winner.

MEETING INDIVIDUAL NEEDS

For Students Who Are . . .

Acquiring English Proficiency Review the meanings of *segment*
and *perimeter*. Pair students with an English-proficient student to
discuss and answer Exercises 20–28.

Gifted and Talented Have students draw each figure so that it
has a perimeter between 15 in. and 20 in.: a rectangle, length twice
its width; an equilateral triangle; and a regular pentagon.

Working 2 or 3 Grades Below Level Review how to use cross
products to compare fractions. Remind students to compare the fractions to $\frac{1}{2}$ in Exercises 15–19.

Today's Problem

What fraction with a value less than one can be read upside down
and still have the same value? (*The fraction is $\frac{6}{9}$*)

Lesson Organizer

Objective: Add and subtract fractions and mixed numbers, same denominators.

Prior Knowledge: Students should be able to add and subtract whole numbers.

Error Analysis and Remediation: See page 197A.

Lesson Resources:
Practice Worksheet 6-2
Reteaching Worksheet 6-2
Enrichment Activity 6-2
Daily Review 6-2

Two-Minute Math

Write all mixed numbers such that: the fractions are in lowest terms; the denominators are 2, 4, or 8; the mixed numbers round to 24. ($23\frac{1}{2}$; $23\frac{3}{4}$; $23\frac{5}{8}$; $23\frac{7}{8}$; $24\frac{1}{4}$; $24\frac{1}{8}$; $24\frac{3}{8}$)

1 INTRODUCE

CONNECTING ACTIVITY

☑ **MATERIALS CHECKLIST:** Teaching Aid 4 (Fraction Bars), for each pair

1. Write $\frac{3}{6} + \frac{1}{6}$ on the chalkboard. Have pairs of students determine a way to model the addition using the fraction bars and name the sum. (*Combine the fraction bars showing sixths: $\frac{3}{6} + \frac{1}{6}$ sum is $\frac{4}{6}$.*)

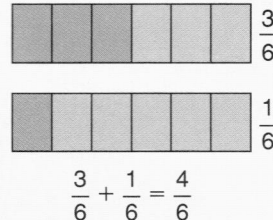

$$\frac{3}{6} + \frac{1}{6} = \frac{4}{6}$$

What is the sum in lowest terms? ($\frac{2}{3}$)

2. Repeat for $\frac{7}{12} - \frac{5}{12}$. ($\frac{2}{12} = \frac{1}{6}$)

WHEN YOUR STUDENTS ASK
★ WHY AM I LEARNING THIS? ★

You can connect this skill through bread making. Bakers add and subtract fractional amounts as they combine ingredients and adjust quantities.

Adding and Subtracting Fractions: Same Denominators

The continent of Asia covers about $\frac{3}{10}$ of the world's land area, while Africa covers about $\frac{2}{10}$. What total fraction of Earth's land area do these two continents cover?

Add to find the total area. Why is it easy to add $\frac{3}{10}$ and $\frac{2}{10}$?
because they have the same denominator

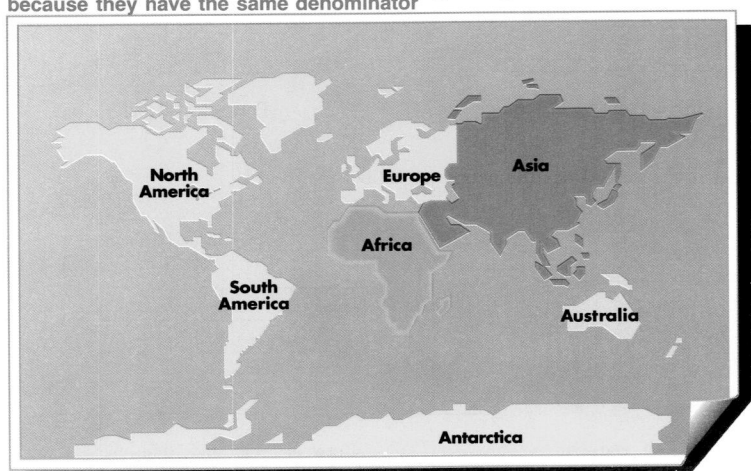

Add the numerators. Why?	Give the sum in lowest terms.
because only the numerators are different	
$\frac{3}{10}$ 3 tenths	
$+ \frac{2}{10}$ 2 tenths	
$\frac{5}{10}$ 5 tenths	$\frac{5}{10} = \frac{1}{2}$

The two continents cover about $\frac{1}{2}$ of Earth's land area.

Other examples:

$$4\frac{6}{12}$$
$$+ \frac{7}{12}$$
$$4\frac{13}{12} = 5\frac{1}{12}$$

$$\frac{7}{9}$$
$$- \frac{1}{9}$$
$$\frac{6}{9} = \frac{2}{3}$$

$$8\frac{4}{5}$$
$$- 1\frac{2}{5}$$
$$7\frac{2}{5}$$

172   LESSON 6–2

MATH AND GEOGRAPHY

---

2 TEACH

☑ **MATERIALS CHECKLIST:** calculators

In what way is adding $\frac{3}{10}$ and $\frac{2}{10}$ similar to adding 3 cars and 2 cars? How is it different? (*The 2 and 3 tell how many to add; the "tenths" and "cars" tell what you are adding. However, adding with "tenths" is adding fractional parts, while adding "cars" is like whole numbers.*)

> ### Chalkboard Examples
>
> Add or subtract. Write the answer in lowest terms.
>
> $\frac{3}{5} - \frac{1}{5}$ $\frac{4}{5} + \frac{3}{5}$
>
> $4\frac{5}{8} + 5\frac{7}{8}$ $7\frac{5}{10} - 3\frac{3}{10}$
>
> ($\frac{2}{5}$; $1\frac{2}{5}$; $10\frac{1}{2}$; $4\frac{1}{5}$)

SUMMARIZE/ASSESS **Explain how to add and subtract fractions with the same denominators.** (*Add numerators. Put the sum over the common denominator.*)

========== GUIDED PRACTICE ==========

Add or subtract. Give the answer in lowest terms.

1. $\frac{3}{5} + \frac{1}{5}$ $\frac{4}{5}$ **2.** $\frac{5}{6} - \frac{1}{6}$ $\frac{2}{3}$ **3.** $5\frac{2}{8} + 4\frac{5}{8}$ $9\frac{7}{8}$ **4.** $8\frac{7}{9} - 4\frac{4}{9}$ $4\frac{1}{3}$ **5.** $4\frac{3}{8} + 9\frac{7}{8}$ $14\frac{1}{4}$

========== PRACTICE ==========

Add or subtract. Give the answer in lowest terms.

6. $\frac{1}{5} + \frac{1}{5}$ $\frac{2}{5}$ **7.** $\frac{3}{8} + \frac{2}{8}$ $\frac{5}{8}$ **8.** $\frac{4}{6} - \frac{1}{6}$ $\frac{1}{2}$ **9.** $\frac{3}{4} + \frac{3}{4}$ $1\frac{1}{2}$ **10.** $\frac{7}{8} - \frac{5}{8}$ $\frac{1}{4}$

11. $\frac{4}{5} - \frac{2}{5}$ $\frac{2}{5}$ **12.** $\frac{2}{3} + \frac{2}{3}$ $1\frac{1}{3}$ **13.** $\frac{3}{5} + \frac{3}{5}$ $1\frac{1}{5}$ **14.** $\frac{7}{8} + \frac{1}{8}$ 1 **15.** $\frac{5}{12} - \frac{1}{12}$ $\frac{1}{3}$

16. $2\frac{2}{6} + 1\frac{5}{6}$ $4\frac{1}{6}$ **17.** $2\frac{3}{7} - 1\frac{1}{7}$ $1\frac{2}{7}$ **18.** $4\frac{2}{3} + 1\frac{2}{3}$ $6\frac{1}{3}$ **19.** $14\frac{2}{5} - 9\frac{1}{5}$ $5\frac{1}{5}$ **20.** $16\frac{2}{8} + 4\frac{7}{8}$ $21\frac{1}{8}$

21. $5\frac{8}{9} - 3\frac{4}{9}$ $2\frac{4}{9}$ **22.** $4\frac{6}{13} + 2\frac{5}{13}$ $6\frac{11}{13}$ **23.** $3\frac{7}{11} - \frac{5}{11}$ $3\frac{2}{11}$ **24.** $3\frac{1}{4} + 3\frac{1}{4}$ $6\frac{1}{2}$ **25.** $11\frac{6}{10} - 9\frac{4}{10}$ $2\frac{1}{5}$

MIXED REVIEW Compute.

26. 3.4×2 **6.8**   **27.** 5.47×10 **54.7**   **28.** $1\frac{3}{4} - \frac{1}{4}$ $1\frac{1}{2}$ **29.** $29 + 2^2$ **33**

30. $3.64 \div 1.4$ **2.6**   **31.** $\frac{5}{6} + 1\frac{1}{6}$ **2**   **32.** $18 \div 0.09$ **200**   **33.** $57 - 4^2$ **41**

MENTAL MATH Solve for n mentally.

34. $\frac{7}{8} - n = \frac{5}{8}$ **35.** $\frac{5}{9} + n = \frac{8}{9}$ **36.** $4\frac{2}{3} - n = 1\frac{1}{3}$ *37. $\frac{2}{7} + \frac{4}{7} + n = 1\frac{2}{7}$

$\frac{2}{8}$ or $\frac{1}{4}$ $\frac{3}{9}$ or $\frac{1}{3}$ $3\frac{1}{3}$ $\frac{3}{7}$

========== PROBLEM SOLVING ==========

CHOOSE Choose paper and pencil or calculator to solve.

38. Match the continent to the region in the circle graph.
p; see right.

39. Which is the largest continent?
p; Asia

40. What is the sum of all the fractions for the continents? What should it be? Give a possible reason for the difference.

c; $\frac{99}{100}$; $\frac{100}{100}$, or 1. There may be some islands that are not part of any continent.

The Seven Continents as Fractions of the World's Land Area

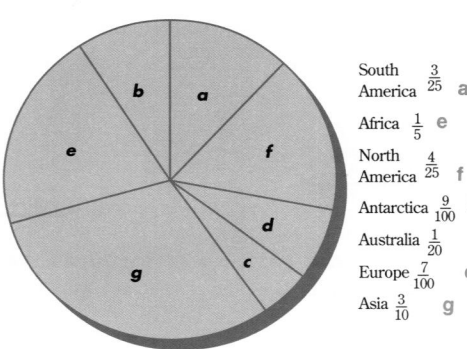

South America $\frac{3}{25}$ a
Africa $\frac{1}{5}$ e
North America $\frac{4}{25}$ f
Antarctica $\frac{9}{100}$ b
Australia $\frac{1}{20}$ c
Europe $\frac{7}{100}$ d
Asia $\frac{3}{10}$ g

CHAPTER 6   173

MEETING INDIVIDUAL NEEDS

For Students Who Are . . .

Acquiring English Proficiency Discuss how to read the circle graph in the Problem Solving section.

Gifted and Talented Have students compute: $3\frac{1}{5} + 6\frac{4}{5} + 10\frac{2}{5}$ $(20\frac{2}{5})$; $9\frac{3}{4} + \frac{1}{4} - 8$ (2); $4\frac{3}{4} + 7 - 5\frac{1}{4}$ $(6\frac{1}{2})$.

Working 2 or 3 Grades Below Level Have students use pages 56–59 of the Skills Workbook for fractions.

Today's Problem

In our decimal system we combine ten symbols—the digits 0 through 9—to form different fractions, which have decimal equivalents (for example, $\frac{1}{2} = 0.5 = 5 \times \frac{1}{10}$). In a duodecimal system we use 12 symbols—the digits 0 through 9, T = 10, E = 11. How would you represent the decimal equivalents of $\frac{1}{2}$, $\frac{1}{3}$, $\frac{1}{4}$, and $\frac{1}{6}$ in the duodecimal system? *(0.6, 0.4, 0.3, 0.2)*

3 FOLLOW-UP

PRACTICE 6-2

Add or subtract. Write the answer in lowest terms.

1. $\frac{6}{7} + \frac{1}{7} = $ __1__   **2.** $\frac{9}{10} + \frac{3}{10} = $ __$1\frac{1}{5}$__   **3.** $\frac{8}{13} - \frac{5}{13} = $ __$\frac{3}{13}$__
4. $\frac{11}{12} - \frac{3}{12} = $ __$\frac{2}{3}$__   **5.** $\frac{3}{5} + \frac{4}{5} = $ __$1\frac{2}{5}$__   **6.** $\frac{9}{15} - \frac{6}{15} = $ __$\frac{1}{5}$__
7. $\frac{10}{18} - \frac{3}{18} = $ __$\frac{4}{9}$__   **8.** $\frac{3}{4} + \frac{5}{4} = $ __2__   **9.** $\frac{7}{8} - \frac{3}{8} = $ __$\frac{1}{2}$__
10. $\frac{5}{6} + \frac{4}{6} = $ __$1\frac{1}{2}$__   **11.** $2\frac{1}{6} + 3\frac{5}{6} = $ __6__   **12.** $4\frac{2}{8} - 1\frac{2}{3} = $ __$3\frac{1}{2}$__
13. $3\frac{3}{8} + 4\frac{1}{8} = $ __$7\frac{1}{2}$__   **14.** $15\frac{9}{10} + 6\frac{3}{10} = $ __$22\frac{1}{5}$__
15. $10\frac{7}{12} - 6\frac{5}{12} = $ __$4\frac{1}{6}$__   **16.** $6\frac{13}{15} - 3\frac{8}{15} = $ __$3\frac{1}{3}$__
17. $4\frac{1}{2} + 2\frac{3}{2} = $ __8__   **18.** $8\frac{6}{25} - 1\frac{1}{25} = $ __$7\frac{1}{5}$__
19. $7\frac{11}{20} - 3\frac{6}{20} = $ __$4\frac{1}{4}$__   **20.** $4\frac{4}{10} + 9\frac{7}{10} = $ __$14\frac{1}{10}$__

Solve for n mentally.

21. $\frac{3}{4} - n = \frac{1}{4}$; $n = $ __$\frac{2}{4}$, or $\frac{1}{2}$__   **22.** $\frac{1}{6} + n = \frac{5}{6}$; $n = $ __$\frac{4}{6}$, or $\frac{2}{3}$__
23. $5\frac{5}{8} - n = 1\frac{3}{8}$; $n = $ __$4\frac{2}{8}$, or $4\frac{1}{4}$__

Choose paper and pencil or a calculator to solve. Answers will vary. Suggestions are given.

24. Joe surveyed the students in his math class and said he found $\frac{1}{8}$ owned dogs; $\frac{5}{8}$ owned cats; $\frac{2}{8}$ owned gerbils; $\frac{1}{8}$ owned fish; and $\frac{3}{8}$ owned ponies. Do the results of his survey appear to be sensible?
Yes; some people owned more than one pet.

25. Felix bought a pizza. Jill ate 0.4 of the pizza, Jim ate $\frac{3}{10}$, and Jenny ate one tenth. How much of the pizza was left?
____0.2 or $\frac{2}{10}$____

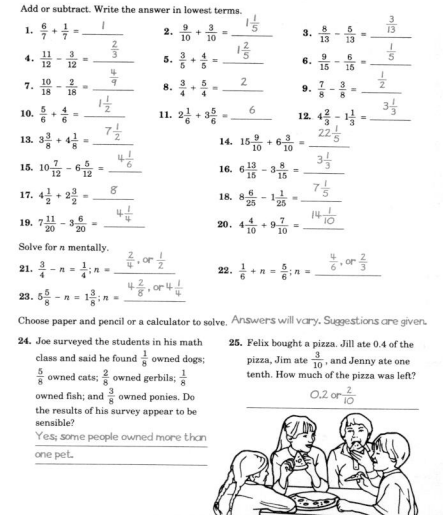

RETEACHING 6-2

When adding or subtracting fractions with the same denominator, add or subtract the numerators, write the sum or difference over the same denominator, and then write in lowest terms.

Example 1: $\frac{4}{5} + \frac{2}{5} = ?$

$\frac{4}{5} + \frac{2}{5} = \frac{6}{5} = 1\frac{1}{5}$

Use a number line if you need help.

Example 2: $3\frac{7}{8} - 1\frac{5}{8} = ?$

$3\frac{7}{8} - 1\frac{5}{8} = 2\frac{2}{8} = 2\frac{1}{4}$

Add or subtract. Write the answer in lowest terms.

1. $\frac{1}{4} + \frac{2}{4} = $ __$\frac{3}{4}$__   **2.** $\frac{5}{6} - \frac{1}{6} = $ __$\frac{2}{3}$__   **3.** $\frac{2}{7} + \frac{2}{7} = $ __$\frac{4}{7}$__
4. $\frac{11}{12} - \frac{6}{12} = $ __$\frac{5}{12}$__   **5.** $6 + 2\frac{1}{4} = $ __$8\frac{1}{4}$__   **6.** $6 + 2\frac{1}{4} = $ __$8\frac{1}{4}$__
7. $3\frac{1}{2} - 1 = $ __$2\frac{1}{2}$__   **8.** $1\frac{1}{6} + 2\frac{2}{3} = $ __$3\frac{5}{6}$__   **9.** $10\frac{9}{15} - 6\frac{3}{15} = $ __$4\frac{2}{5}$__
10. $10\frac{11}{20} + 6\frac{7}{20} = $ __$16\frac{9}{10}$__   **11.** $6\frac{11}{12} - 1\frac{7}{12} = $ __$5\frac{1}{3}$__   **12.** $5\frac{1}{6} + 5\frac{1}{6} = $ __$10\frac{1}{3}$__

ENRICHMENT 6-2

☑ **MATERIALS CHECKLIST:** Blank cubes, blank spinners, tagboard

Have the students work in groups of four, and in pairs within each group. Provide each pair with a "numerator" cube, which they label *1–6;* a "denominator" cube which they label *2, 3, 5, 8, 9, 12;* a spinner, which they label *Add* and *Subtract;* and a piece of tagboard on which you draw a row of five squares. Each student rolls the numerator cube and the denominator cube and writes a fraction. One partner spins the spinner and the partners add or subtract their fractions. The first pair to write five exercises in the squares and to complete them accurately wins.

Lesson Organizer

> **Objective:** Add and subtract fractions with denominators that are multiples.

Prior Knowledge: Students should be able to use the LCD to write equivalent fractions.

Error Analysis and Remediation: See page 197A.

Lesson Resources:
Practice Worksheet 6-3
Reteaching Activity 6-3
Enrichment Worksheet 6-3
Daily Review 6-3

Two-Minute Math

Find the missing number.

$\frac{3}{4} = \frac{\Box}{12}$ *(9)*

$\frac{5}{6} = \frac{\Box}{30}$ *(25)*

$\frac{5}{8} = \frac{\Box}{24}$ *(15)*

1 INTRODUCE

CONNECTING ACTIVITY

☑ **MATERIALS CHECKLIST:** fraction bars or Teaching Aid 4 (Fraction Bars)

1. Write $\frac{1}{2} + \frac{1}{6}$ on the chalkboard. Model the example with fraction bars on the overhead projector.

2. Ask a volunteer to use the fraction bars to show that $\frac{1}{2} = \frac{3}{6}$. Add $\frac{1}{6} + \frac{3}{6}$.

3. Repeat for other addition and subtraction examples. Call on different students to explain the procedure for each example.

WHEN YOUR STUDENTS ASK
★ WHY AM I LEARNING THIS? ★

You can use this skill to solve real life problems. Suppose your stock went up $\frac{5}{8}$ of a point this morning and down $\frac{1}{4}$ this afternoon. How did you do for the day?

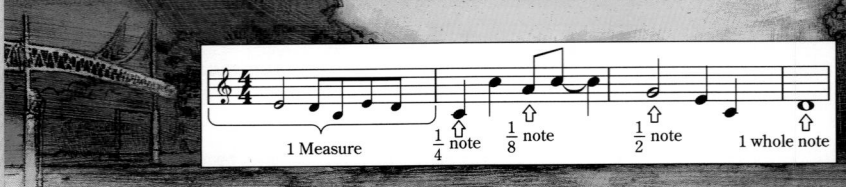

1 Measure $\frac{1}{4}$ note $\frac{1}{8}$ note $\frac{1}{2}$ note   1 whole note

MATH AND MUSIC

Adding and Subtracting Fractions: Denominators That Are Multiples

From Old Folks at Home, *by Stephen Foster. Also known as* Swanee River.

The different types of notes tell you how long to hold a note as you play the music. Find one note in the music above that is held for the same time as two $\frac{1}{8}$ notes (♪) and one $\frac{1}{4}$ (♩) note.

Add $\frac{1}{8} + \frac{1}{8} + \frac{1}{4}$ to solve this problem.

To add fractions with different denominators, you can make a **MATH CONNECTION**.

- You know how to find equivalent fractions.
- You know how to add fractions with the same denominator.

What is the lowest common denominator (LCD) of 8 and 4?

$$\begin{aligned} \frac{1}{8} &= \frac{1}{8} \\ \frac{1}{8} &= \frac{1}{8} \\ + \frac{1}{4} &= + \frac{2}{8} \\ \hline \frac{4}{8} &= \frac{1}{2} \quad \text{← lowest terms} \end{aligned}$$

One half note (♩) is held for the same time.

Other examples:

Stephen Foster, great American songwriter, wrote many songs about the beauty of the South.

$$\begin{aligned} \frac{15}{24} &= \frac{15}{24} \\ - \frac{3}{8} &= - \frac{9}{24} \\ \hline \frac{6}{24} &= \frac{1}{4} \quad \text{← lowest terms} \end{aligned}$$

What is the LCD of 8 and 24? **24**

$$\begin{aligned} \frac{3}{4} &= \frac{15}{20} \\ + \frac{17}{20} &= + \frac{17}{20} \\ \hline \frac{32}{20} &= 1\frac{3}{5} \end{aligned}$$

What is the LCD of 4 and 20? **20**

GUIDED PRACTICE

Add or subtract. Give the answer in lowest terms.

1. $\frac{3}{4} - \frac{1}{2}$ $\frac{1}{4}$ **2.** $\frac{7}{10} + \frac{2}{5}$ $1\frac{1}{10}$ **3.** $\frac{1}{4} + \frac{3}{8}$ $\frac{5}{8}$ **4.** $\frac{5}{12} - \frac{1}{6}$ $\frac{1}{4}$ **5.** $\frac{8}{9} + \frac{5}{18}$ $1\frac{1}{6}$

2 TEACH

☑ **MATERIALS CHECKLIST:** Math Connection Transparency

Display the transparency. Have students fill in the spaces and discuss the math connection. *(See student pages.)*

What is an advantage of using the LCD to write equivalent fractions? *(Possible answer: The fractions will contain the least numbers possible which are easier to add or subtract.*

Suppose you wanted to add $\frac{3}{8} + \frac{1}{2} + \frac{3}{4}$. What would you do first? *(Find the LCD of 8, 2, and 4; then write equivalent fractions.)*

> **Chalkboard Examples**
>
> Write the sum in lowest terms.
>
> $$\frac{1}{3} + \frac{1}{12} \qquad \frac{1}{4} + \frac{1}{12}$$
>
> $$\frac{3}{10} - \frac{1}{5} \qquad \frac{5}{9} - \frac{1}{3}$$
>
> $$\left(\frac{5}{12}, \frac{1}{3}, \frac{1}{10}, \frac{2}{9}\right)$$

SUMMARIZE/ASSESS **Explain how to add and subtract fractions with different denominators.** *(Use the LCD to write equivalent fractions with the same denominator and then compute.)*

PRACTICE

Add or subtract. Give the answer in lowest terms.

6. $\frac{1}{6} + \frac{1}{2}$ $\frac{2}{3}$ **7.** $\frac{1}{4} + \frac{7}{12}$ $\frac{5}{6}$ **8.** $\frac{5}{6} - \frac{1}{2}$ $\frac{1}{3}$ **9.** $\frac{2}{3} + \frac{13}{15}$ $1\frac{8}{15}$ **10.** $\frac{1}{2} - \frac{2}{4}$ 0

11. $\frac{3}{5} - \frac{11}{30}$ $\frac{7}{30}$ **12.** $\frac{11}{27} + \frac{4}{9}$ $\frac{23}{27}$ **13.** $\frac{4}{5} - \frac{3}{25}$ $\frac{17}{25}$ **14.** $\frac{5}{6} - \frac{7}{36}$ $\frac{23}{36}$ **15.** $\frac{15}{16} + \frac{1}{32}$ $\frac{31}{32}$

16. $\frac{4}{9} + \frac{1}{3}$ $\frac{7}{9}$ **17.** $\frac{4}{5} + \frac{3}{25}$ $\frac{23}{25}$ **18.** $\frac{5}{6} - \frac{7}{24}$ $\frac{13}{24}$ **19.** $\frac{13}{27} + \frac{5}{9}$ $1\frac{1}{27}$ **20.** $\frac{3}{4} - \frac{5}{12}$ $\frac{1}{3}$

21. $\frac{19}{25} - \frac{9}{50}$ $\frac{29}{50}$ **22.** $\frac{3}{4} + \frac{3}{8}$ $1\frac{1}{8}$ **23.** $\frac{6}{9} - \frac{6}{18}$ $\frac{1}{3}$ **24.** $\frac{11}{12} + \frac{20}{24}$ $1\frac{3}{4}$ **25.** $\frac{6}{7} - \frac{3}{14}$ $\frac{9}{14}$

26. $\frac{1}{2} + \frac{3}{4} + \frac{1}{2}$ $1\frac{3}{4}$ **★27.** $\frac{4}{5} - \frac{4}{10} + \frac{2}{5}$ $\frac{4}{5}$ **★28.** $\frac{3}{4} + \frac{1}{2} - \frac{3}{8}$ $\frac{7}{8}$ **★29.** $\frac{5}{6} + \frac{1}{2} - \frac{1}{3}$ 1

MIXED REVIEW Compute. Give the answer in lowest terms if necessary.

30. $5.7 + 0.45$ 6.15 **31.** $4\frac{5}{6} - \frac{1}{6}$ $4\frac{2}{3}$ **32.** $\frac{3}{8} + \frac{3}{4}$ $1\frac{1}{8}$ **33.** $8.51 - 7$ 1.51

34. $\frac{11}{12} - \frac{1}{2}$ $\frac{5}{12}$ **35.** $6 - 2.3$ 3.7 **36.** $\frac{5}{9} + 8\frac{4}{9}$ 9 **37.** $0.6 + 0.042$
0.642

Complete the function table. Give the answer in lowest terms.

38.
a	$\frac{1}{8}$	$\frac{2}{8}$	$\frac{3}{8}$	$\frac{4}{8}$	$\frac{5}{8}$
$a + \frac{1}{8}$	? $\frac{1}{4}$	? $\frac{3}{8}$	? $\frac{1}{2}$	? $\frac{5}{8}$	? $\frac{3}{4}$

39.
b	$\frac{9}{10}$	$\frac{8}{10}$	$\frac{7}{10}$	$\frac{6}{10}$	$\frac{5}{10}$
$b - \frac{1}{10}$	? $\frac{4}{5}$	? $\frac{7}{10}$	? $\frac{3}{5}$	? $\frac{1}{2}$	? $\frac{2}{5}$

MENTAL MATH Solve for n mentally.

40. $\frac{2}{7} + n = 1$ $\frac{5}{7}$ **41.** $n - \frac{2}{3} = \frac{2}{3}$ $1\frac{1}{3}$ **42.** $\frac{19}{25} - n = 0$ $\frac{19}{25}$

PROBLEM SOLVING

CHOOSE Use the music for *Swanee River* on page 174. Choices will vary.
Choose mental math or paper and pencil to solve. Suggestions given.

43. For each measure of the music for *Swanee River* shown, add
the fractions that represent each kind of note in the measure.
What is the sum in each case?
p; 1

44. The *Swanee River* music requires that a whole note (○) gets four beats.
  a. How many beats does a $\frac{1}{2}$ note get? a $\frac{1}{4}$ note? an $\frac{1}{8}$ note? m; 2 beats; 1 beat;
  b. How many beats are there in each measure of *Swanee River*? $\frac{1}{2}$ beat
  p; 4 beats

CHAPTER 6   175

---

3 FOLLOW-UP

PRACTICE 6-3

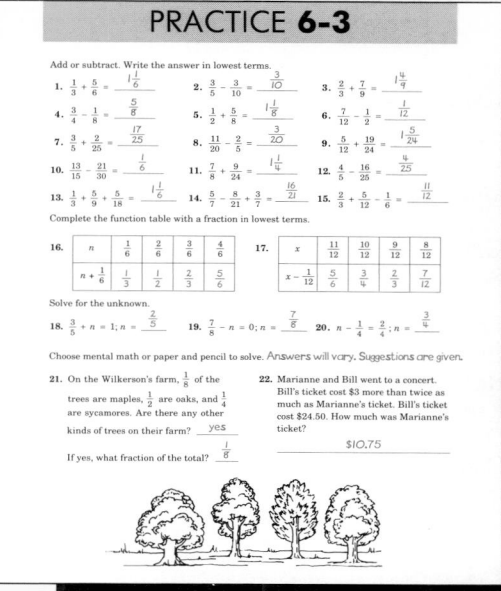

RETEACHING 6-3

☑ **MATERIALS CHECKLIST:** Fraction bars

Have the students work in pairs. Write an addition or subtraction exercise on the board. Have each student find the fraction bar that matches one of the fractions and all other colored bars that have the same amount shaded. Then have them find the common colors in each set and use those bars to find the sum or difference.

ENRICHMENT 6-3

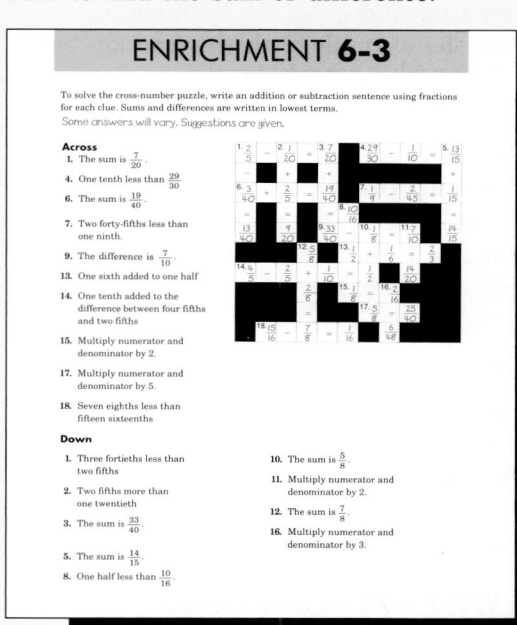

MEETING INDIVIDUAL NEEDS

For Students Who Are . . .

Acquiring English Proficiency Have students work in a group with an English-proficient student to discuss Exercises 43–44.

Gifted and Talented Have students write three bars of music in which each bar gets 4 beats. Ask them to find out what this is called. ($\frac{4}{4}$ *time*)

Working 2 or 3 Grades Below Level Have students use pages 66–69 of the Skills Workbook for fractions.

Today's Problem

Write five numbers between 7 and 9 that round to 8. (*Possible answers:* $7\frac{1}{2}$, $7\frac{3}{4}$, $8\frac{1}{3}$, $8\frac{3}{8}$, $8\frac{7}{16}$)

Chapter 6 • Lesson 6-3 **175**

Lesson Organizer

Objective: Add and subtract fractions, different denominators.

Prior Knowledge: Students should be able to use the LCD to write equivalent fractions.

Error Analysis and Remediation: See page 197A.

Lesson Resources:
Practice Worksheet 6-4
Reteaching Worksheet 6-4
Enrichment Activity 6-4
Daily Review 6-4
Cooperative Problem Solving 1, Chapter 6

Two-Minute Math

Find the LCD

$\frac{2}{3}$ and $\frac{2}{5}$ *(15)* $\frac{1}{4}$ and $\frac{3}{7}$ *(28)*

$\frac{5}{6}$ and $\frac{3}{8}$ *(24)* $\frac{9}{10}$ and $\frac{5}{6}$ *(30)*

1 INTRODUCE

CONNECTING ACTIVITY

☑ **MATERIALS CHECKLIST:** fraction bars or Teaching Aid 4 (Fraction Bars)

1. Write $\frac{2}{3}$ and $\frac{1}{2}$ on the chalkboard. Model the example with the fraction bars on the overhead projector.

2. **Use the bars to find fractions equivalent to $\frac{2}{3}$.** *(Possible answers: $\frac{4}{6}$, $\frac{8}{12}$)* **Find some fractions equivalent to $\frac{1}{2}$.** *(Possible answers: $\frac{2}{4}$, $\frac{3}{6}$)* **Which of the equivalent fractions for $\frac{2}{3}$ and $\frac{1}{2}$ have the same denominator?** *($\frac{4}{6}$ and $\frac{3}{6}$ or $\frac{8}{12}$ and $\frac{6}{12}$)*

3. Have a volunteer use the fraction bar model to demonstrate $\frac{4}{6} + \frac{3}{6}$.

4. Repeat with other addition and subtraction examples.

WHEN YOUR STUDENTS ASK
★ WHY AM I LEARNING THIS? ★

You can use this skill to solve real life problems. Suppose you are climbing a mountain, which is $\frac{7}{8}$ mi high. You climbed $\frac{1}{2}$ mi before lunch. How much further must you climb to reach the top?

Adding and Subtracting Fractions: Any Denominators

A student surveying colleges in the United States used this circle graph to get information on degrees earned at historically African American institutions of higher learning in a past year. What fraction of the enrolled students earned either a bachelor's or a master's degree?

Since you know how to write equivalent fractions and how to add fractions with the same denominator, you can make a **MATH CONNECTION** to add $\frac{3}{4} + \frac{1}{7}$.

What is the LCD of 4 and 7? **28**

$$
\begin{array}{rcr}
\frac{3}{4} & = & \frac{21}{28} \\
+ \frac{1}{7} & = & + \frac{4}{28} \\
\hline
& & \frac{25}{28}
\end{array}
$$

Almost all of the students, or $\frac{25}{28}$, received these two degrees.

CRITICAL THINKING Which degree did twice as many students receive as the associate degree? *Master's degree*

Another example:

What is the LCD of 8 and 9? **72**

$$
\begin{array}{rcr}
\frac{6}{8} & = & \frac{54}{72} \\
- \frac{5}{9} & = & - \frac{40}{72} \\
\hline
& & \frac{14}{72} = \frac{7}{36}
\end{array}
$$

lowest terms

Degrees Earned at Historically African American Institutions of Higher Learning

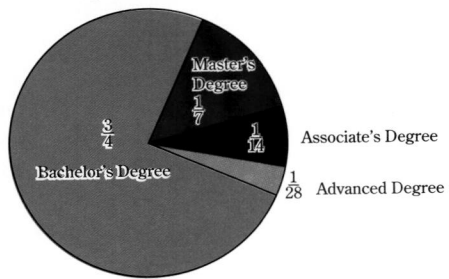

Master's Degree $\frac{1}{7}$ · Bachelor's Degree $\frac{3}{4}$ · Associate's Degree $\frac{1}{14}$ · Advanced Degree $\frac{1}{28}$

Tuskegee Institute, Tuskegee, Alabama

■ **GUIDED PRACTICE** ■

Add or subtract. Give the answer in lowest terms.

1. $\frac{3}{8} - \frac{1}{4}$ $\frac{1}{8}$
2. $\frac{2}{5} + \frac{2}{6}$ $\frac{11}{15}$
3. $\frac{7}{8} - \frac{2}{3}$ $\frac{5}{24}$
4. $\frac{1}{6} + \frac{5}{8}$ $\frac{19}{24}$
5. $\frac{4}{6} - \frac{1}{8}$ $\frac{13}{24}$

MULTICULTURAL NOTE

Tuskegee Institute began as a school for African Americans in 1881. Today, it is a university attended by people of all races; a majority of the students are African Americans.

2 TEACH

☑ **MATERIALS CHECKLIST:** Math Connection Transparency

Display the transparency. Have students fill in the spaces and discuss the math connection. *(See student pages.)*

Write $\frac{2}{5} + \frac{1}{6}$ in vertical form on the chalkboard. **What is the LCD?** *(30)* Have students write equivalent fractions with denominators of 30 and complete the addition. *($\frac{12}{30} + \frac{5}{30} = \frac{17}{30}$)*

Chalkboard Examples

Write the answer in lowest terms.

$$\frac{3}{5} + \frac{5}{6} \qquad \frac{5}{7} - \frac{1}{2}$$

$$\frac{1}{3} + \frac{5}{12} \qquad \frac{8}{9} - \frac{5}{6}$$

($1\frac{13}{30}$; $\frac{3}{14}$; $\frac{3}{4}$; $\frac{1}{18}$)

SUMMARIZE/ASSESS **Explain how to add and subtract fractions that have different denominators.** *(Write equivalent fractions with the same denominator and then compute.)*

Find the sum or the difference in lowest terms.

6. $\frac{5}{9} + \frac{1}{4}$ $\frac{29}{36}$ 7. $\frac{7}{8} - \frac{3}{5}$ $\frac{11}{40}$ 8. $\frac{2}{6} + \frac{1}{3}$ $\frac{2}{3}$ 9. $\frac{4}{8} + \frac{4}{6}$ $1\frac{1}{6}$ 10. $\frac{6}{9} + \frac{1}{3}$ 1

11. $\frac{2}{3} - \frac{2}{6}$ $\frac{1}{3}$ 12. $\frac{8}{10} - \frac{3}{4}$ $\frac{1}{20}$ 13. $\frac{5}{6} - \frac{7}{9}$ $\frac{1}{18}$ 14. $\frac{10}{12} + \frac{3}{18}$ 1 15. $\frac{1}{8} + \frac{1}{5}$ $\frac{13}{40}$

16. $\frac{3}{10} + \frac{4}{15}$ $\frac{17}{30}$ 17. $\frac{6}{9} - \frac{3}{15}$ $\frac{7}{15}$ 18. $\frac{6}{11} - \frac{2}{5}$ $\frac{8}{55}$ 19. $\frac{4}{5} - \frac{17}{24}$ $\frac{11}{120}$ 20. $\frac{7}{12} + \frac{4}{9}$ $1\frac{1}{36}$

21. $\frac{7}{8} - \frac{3}{4}$ $\frac{1}{8}$ 22. $\frac{6}{7} - \frac{5}{9}$ $\frac{19}{63}$ 23. $\frac{15}{20} + \frac{1}{5}$ $\frac{19}{20}$ 24. $\frac{6}{8} + \frac{2}{7}$ $1\frac{1}{28}$ 25. $\frac{7}{16} - \frac{2}{12}$ $\frac{13}{48}$

MIXED REVIEW   Compute.

26. $5\frac{2}{6} + 8\frac{3}{6}$ $13\frac{5}{6}$ 27. 3.524×1.8 6.3432 28. $\frac{4}{5} + \frac{5}{6}$ $1\frac{19}{30}$ 29. $6.5 \div 0.0013$ $5,000$

30. $0.08 + 0.4$ 0.48 31. $1\frac{10}{12} - \frac{3}{12}$ $1\frac{7}{12}$ 32. $0.2 - 0.06$ 0.14 33. $\frac{4}{5} - \frac{4}{15}$ $\frac{8}{15}$

MENTAL MATH   Compute mentally.

34. $\frac{2}{3} + \frac{1}{6} + \frac{1}{3}$ $1\frac{1}{6}$ 35. $\frac{5}{8} + \frac{1}{2} + \frac{3}{8}$ $1\frac{1}{2}$ 36. $\frac{7}{8} + \frac{1}{8} - \frac{1}{4}$ $\frac{3}{4}$

CHOOSE   Use the circle graph on page 176.   **Choices will vary. Suggestions given.**
Choose mental math or paper and pencil to solve.

37. What fraction of the students received a degree other than
the associate degree?   m; $\frac{13}{14}$

38. What fraction of the students earned a master's or an
advanced degree?   p; $\frac{5}{28}$

39. Ask 12 classmates which academic degree they might choose
to work toward in college. Write a fraction to show how many
of the 12 classmates made each choice.   **Check students' work.**

Critical Thinking

Work with a partner.
What is the total number
of different ways possible
to combine one class with
one after school activity?
16 combinations

Class	After School Activity
Mathematics	Basketball Team
English	Glee Club
Home Economics	Debating Team
Social Studies	Drama Club

MEETING INDIVIDUAL NEEDS

For Students Who Are . . .

Acquiring English Proficiency   Pair students with an English-proficient student to discuss and solve the Problem Solving and Critical Thinking exercises.

Gifted and Talented   Have students find the number of people that received each degree if 560 people were surveyed. (*Bachelor's, 420; Master's, 80; Associate, 40; Advanced, 20*)

Working 2 or 3 Grades Below Level   Have students use pages 70–71 of the Skills Workbook for fractions.

Today's Problem

Pi (π) is the number of times the diameter of a circle divides into the circumference, or distance around, the circle. Its value today is sometimes approximated as $3\frac{1}{7}$. The Egyptians, earlier than 1700 B.C., used $\frac{16 \times 16}{9 \times 9}$ as the value of pi. What is the difference between these values? (*The difference is $\frac{256}{81} - \frac{22}{7} = \frac{1,792}{567} - \frac{1,782}{567} = \frac{10}{567}$.*)

3 FOLLOW-UP

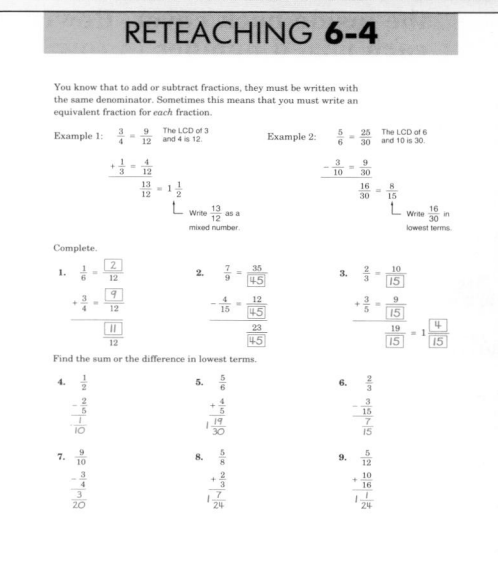

PRACTICE 6-4

Find the sum or the difference in lowest terms.

1. $\frac{3}{4} + \frac{3}{8}$ $1\frac{1}{8}$ 2. $\frac{5}{9} - \frac{1}{3}$ $\frac{2}{9}$ 3. $\frac{4}{7} + \frac{2}{3}$ $1\frac{5}{21}$

4. $\frac{5}{12} - \frac{1}{4}$ $\frac{1}{6}$ 5. $\frac{1}{2} + \frac{2}{3}$ $1\frac{1}{6}$ 6. $\frac{8}{15} - \frac{2}{5}$ $\frac{2}{15}$

7. $\frac{9}{10} + \frac{3}{8}$ $1\frac{11}{40}$ 8. $\frac{17}{20} - \frac{4}{5}$ $\frac{1}{20}$ 9. $\frac{7}{12} + \frac{2}{3}$ $1\frac{1}{4}$

10. $\frac{5}{6} - \frac{3}{4}$ $\frac{1}{12}$ 11. $\frac{5}{6} + \frac{1}{5}$ $1\frac{1}{30}$ 12. $\frac{7}{8} - \frac{1}{3}$ $\frac{13}{24}$

13. $\frac{3}{16} + \frac{5}{12}$ $\frac{29}{48}$ 14. $\frac{7}{9} - \frac{1}{6}$ $\frac{11}{18}$ 15. $\frac{11}{12} + \frac{5}{8}$ $1\frac{17}{30}$

16. $\frac{3}{8} - \frac{1}{12}$ $\frac{7}{24}$ 17. $\frac{3}{4} + \frac{3}{8}$ $\frac{7}{8}$ 18. $\frac{9}{10} - \frac{3}{4}$ $\frac{3}{20}$

19. $\frac{11}{12} + \frac{5}{8}$ $1\frac{13}{24}$ 20. $\frac{7}{8} + \frac{1}{5}$ $1\frac{3}{40}$

Use mental math to solve.

21. $\frac{5}{6} + \frac{3}{4} + \frac{1}{6}$ $1\frac{3}{4}$ 22. $\frac{2}{3} - \frac{2}{9} + \frac{1}{3}$ $\frac{7}{9}$ 23. $\frac{11}{12} + \frac{1}{12} - \frac{1}{6}$ $\frac{5}{6}$

Choose paper and pencil or estimation to solve. *Answers will vary. Suggestions are given.*

24. In a recent election, Fred Buchanan received $\frac{3}{5}$ of the votes and George Snyder received $\frac{3}{10}$ of the votes. What fraction of the votes did not go to either candidate? $\frac{1}{10}$

25. Ryan is much younger than his 50-year-old parents. The sum of the two digits of his age is 9 and the difference is 5. How old is Ryan?   27

RETEACHING 6-4

You know that to add or subtract fractions, they must be written with the same denominator. Sometimes this means that you must write an equivalent fraction for *each* fraction.

Example 1: $\frac{3}{4} = \frac{9}{12}$ The LCD of 3 and 4 is 12.

$+ \frac{1}{3} = \frac{4}{12}$
$\frac{13}{12} = 1\frac{1}{2}$ Write $\frac{13}{12}$ as a mixed number.

Example 2: $\frac{5}{6} = \frac{25}{30}$ The LCD of 6 and 10 is 30.

$- \frac{3}{10} = \frac{9}{30}$
$\frac{16}{30} = \frac{8}{15}$ Write $\frac{16}{30}$ in lowest terms.

Complete.

1. $\frac{1}{6} = \frac{2}{12}$
$+ \frac{3}{4} = \frac{9}{12}$
$\frac{11}{12}$

2. $\frac{7}{9} = \frac{35}{45}$
$- \frac{4}{15} = \frac{12}{45}$
$\frac{23}{45}$

3. $\frac{2}{3} = \frac{10}{15}$
$+ \frac{3}{5} = \frac{9}{15}$
$\frac{19}{15} = 1\frac{4}{15}$

Find the sum or the difference in lowest terms.

4. $\frac{1}{2}$
$- \frac{2}{5}$
$\frac{1}{10}$

5. $\frac{5}{6}$
$+ \frac{4}{5}$
$1\frac{19}{30}$

6. $\frac{2}{3}$
$- \frac{3}{15}$
$\frac{7}{15}$

7. $\frac{9}{10}$
$- \frac{3}{4}$
$\frac{3}{20}$

8. $\frac{5}{8}$
$+ \frac{2}{3}$
$1\frac{7}{24}$

9. $\frac{5}{12}$
$+ \frac{10}{16}$
$1\frac{1}{24}$

ENRICHMENT 6-4

☑ **MATERIALS CHECKLIST:** Index cards, paper bags

Have the students work in groups of four. Provide each group with two paper bags—the first containing cards on which you have written $\frac{5}{8}$, $\frac{7}{12}$, $\frac{2}{3}$, $\frac{7}{9}$, $\frac{5}{6}$ and the second containing cards on which you have written $-\frac{1}{5}$, $-\frac{1}{6}$, $-\frac{2}{15}$, $+\frac{1}{5}$, $+\frac{1}{6}$, $+\frac{2}{15}$, $+\frac{3}{4}$. One student draws a card from the first bag and tells the other three students to write the fraction and decide whether they want to combine the fraction with one from the second bag or stay with the original fraction. Play several times. The student who ends up with the largest fraction the most number of times wins.

Lesson Organizer

Objective: Add and subtract mixed numbers, different denominators.

Prior Knowledge: Students should be able to add and subtract fractions with different denominators.

Error Analysis and Remediation: See page 197A.

Lesson Resources:
Practice Worksheet 6-5
Reteaching Worksheet 6-5
Enrichment Activity 6-5
Daily Review 6-5

Two-Minute Math

Use the Table of Numbers on the inside back cover. Rewrite each mixed number in row K as an equivalent mixed number with a denominator of 32. $(2\frac{20}{32}; 2\frac{16}{32}; 4\frac{2}{32}; 1\frac{8}{32}; 1\frac{12}{32}; 3\frac{24}{32}; 4\frac{14}{32})$

1 INTRODUCE

SYMBOLIC ACTIVITY

Have students explain how to complete each of the following:

- $6\frac{7}{8} = 6\frac{\square}{24}$ *(21)*
- $9\frac{1}{3} = 9\frac{\square}{24}$ *(8)*
- $35\frac{3}{4} = 35\frac{\square}{24}$ *(18)*

WHEN YOUR STUDENTS ASK
★ WHY AM I LEARNING THIS? ★

You can connect this skill to real life through sports history. The winning long jump in the 1988 Olympic Games was 28 ft $7\frac{1}{4}$ in. How much short of the 1968 world record of 29 ft $2\frac{1}{2}$ in. is this?

Adding and Subtracting Mixed Numbers

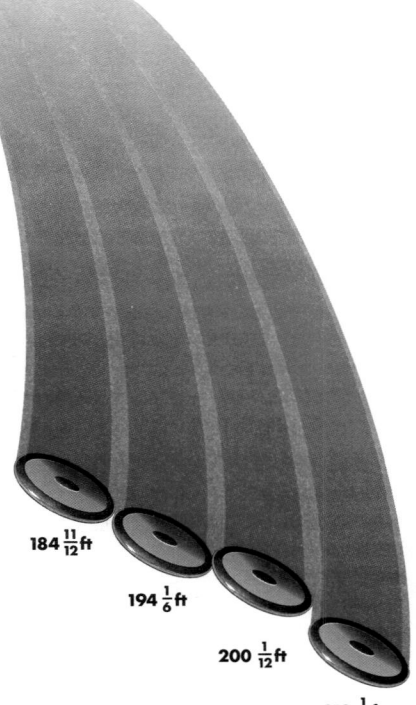

1956 1960 1964 1968

American Al Oerter won the gold medal in the discus throw in four straight Olympic games, an amazing feat.

Use the bar graph to find out how much farther Oerter threw the discus in the 1968 Olympics than in the 1964 Olympics.

Write equivalent fractions.		Subtract.
$212\frac{1}{2} =$	$212\frac{6}{12}$	$212\frac{6}{12}$
$-200\frac{1}{12} =$	$-200\frac{1}{12}$	$-200\frac{1}{12}$
		$12\frac{5}{12}$

Al Oerter threw the discus $12\frac{5}{12}$ ft farther in 1968 than in 1964.

THINK ALOUD What $12\frac{5}{12}$ ft is in feet and inches? **12 ft 5 in.**

Another example:

$$2\frac{1}{3} = 2\frac{4}{12}$$

What is the LCD of 3 and 4? **12**

$$+ 4\frac{3}{4} = + 4\frac{9}{12}$$
$$6\frac{13}{12} = 7\frac{1}{12}$$

$184\frac{11}{12}$ ft
$194\frac{1}{6}$ ft
$200\frac{1}{12}$ ft
$212\frac{1}{2}$ ft

GUIDED PRACTICE

Give the sum or difference in lowest terms.

1. $3\frac{1}{2} + 5\frac{1}{3}$ $8\frac{5}{6}$
2. $4\frac{2}{3} + 5\frac{1}{6}$ $9\frac{5}{6}$
3. $5\frac{3}{8} - 2\frac{1}{4}$ $3\frac{1}{8}$
4. $8\frac{5}{6} - 2\frac{1}{4}$ $6\frac{7}{12}$

PRACTICE

Give the sum or difference in lowest terms.

5. $1\frac{1}{2} + 1\frac{1}{4}$ $2\frac{3}{4}$
6. $5\frac{2}{3} + 4\frac{1}{9}$ $9\frac{7}{9}$
7. $7\frac{3}{4} - 7\frac{1}{2}$ $\frac{1}{4}$
8. $6\frac{1}{5} - 1\frac{1}{10}$ $5\frac{1}{10}$
9. $3\frac{2}{5} + 4\frac{5}{6}$ $8\frac{7}{30}$
10. $5\frac{3}{8} + 1\frac{1}{4}$ $6\frac{5}{8}$
11. $12\frac{1}{3} - 3\frac{1}{4}$ $9\frac{1}{12}$
12. $4\frac{7}{8} - 1\frac{1}{2}$ $3\frac{3}{8}$

2 TEACH

How much farther was the discus thrown in the 1968 Olympics than in the 1956 Olympics? $(27\frac{7}{12}$ ft$)$

What is the basic difference between adding fractions with different denominators and adding mixed numbers with different denominators? *(Possible answer: The only difference is an extra step; with mixed numbers, you must add the whole numbers, too.)*

Chalkboard Examples

Write the answer in lowest terms.

$$12\frac{1}{3} + 7\frac{1}{8} \qquad 7\frac{7}{8} - 1\frac{3}{4}$$
$$6\frac{5}{6} + 2\frac{3}{8} \qquad 13\frac{5}{6} - 8\frac{3}{4}$$
$$(19\frac{11}{24}; 6\frac{1}{8}; 9\frac{5}{24}; 5\frac{1}{12})$$

SUMMARIZE/ASSESS What math connection is used to add and subtract mixed numbers that have different denominators? *(If you know how to add and subtract fractions with different denominators and how to add and subtract whole numbers, then you can make a math connection to add and subtract mixed numbers.)*

13. $7\frac{1}{3} + 3\frac{1}{6}$ $10\frac{1}{2}$
14. $8\frac{3}{4} - 1\frac{1}{2}$ $7\frac{1}{4}$
15. $4\frac{1}{5} + 3\frac{1}{3}$ $7\frac{8}{15}$
16. $4\frac{1}{3} - 4\frac{1}{8}$ $\frac{5}{24}$

17. $5\frac{1}{4} - 1\frac{1}{6}$ $4\frac{1}{12}$
18. $4\frac{5}{6} - \frac{1}{8}$ $4\frac{17}{24}$
19. $7\frac{5}{8} + 2\frac{1}{10}$ $9\frac{29}{40}$
20. $2\frac{3}{5} + 4\frac{4}{10}$ 7

21. $6\frac{3}{4} + 3\frac{5}{6}$ $10\frac{7}{12}$
22. $5\frac{5}{12} - 4\frac{1}{3}$ $1\frac{1}{12}$
23. $6\frac{5}{12} + \frac{7}{18}$ $6\frac{29}{36}$
24. $12\frac{5}{9} - 6\frac{3}{8}$ $6\frac{13}{72}$

25. $3\frac{1}{4} + 4\frac{1}{4} + 6\frac{1}{8}$ $13\frac{5}{8}$
26. $5\frac{3}{8} + \frac{1}{16} + 3\frac{3}{4}$ $9\frac{3}{16}$
*27. $7\frac{2}{3} + \left(3\frac{3}{5} - 1\frac{1}{3}\right)$ $9\frac{14}{15}$

MIXED REVIEW Compute.

28. $4\frac{2}{9} + 3\frac{2}{6}$ $7\frac{5}{9}$
29. $14.8 - 6.5$ 8.3
30. $6\frac{4}{5} - 2\frac{6}{10}$ $4\frac{1}{5}$
31. $2.7 \div 0.3$ 9

32. $5\frac{8}{21} - 4\frac{2}{7}$ $1\frac{2}{21}$
33. $22.1 + 16.3$ 38.4
34. $50.4 \div 6.3$ 8
35. 4.2×3.1 13.02

Evaluate. Use $a = 2\frac{1}{2}$, $b = 3\frac{7}{8}$, $c = \frac{1}{5}$.

36. $3\frac{2}{3} + a + 6\frac{1}{8}$ $12\frac{7}{24}$
*37. $6\frac{7}{8} + a - c$ $9\frac{7}{40}$
*38. $(b - a) - c$ $1\frac{7}{40}$

PROBLEM SOLVING

CHOOSE Choose estimation or paper and pencil to solve.
Give the answer in lowest terms. **Choices will vary. Suggestions given.**

39. The women's discus weighs about $2\frac{3}{16}$ lb. The men's discus weighs twice this amount. About what is the weight of a men's discus?
e; $\approx 4\frac{1}{2}$ lb

40. In the 1988 Olympics, the winning throw in the men's discus was $225\frac{3}{4}$ ft. The best women's discus throw in that Olympics was $11\frac{5}{12}$ ft farther. What was that distance?
p; $237\frac{1}{6}$ ft

Mental Math

You can count on to subtract mentally.

$1 - \frac{3}{5}$

Start with $\frac{3}{5}$. Count on by $\frac{1}{5}$'s to 1.

$1 - \frac{3}{5} = \frac{2}{5}$

Count on to subtract mentally.

1. $1 - \frac{4}{5}$ $\frac{1}{5}$
2. $2 - \frac{2}{3}$ $1\frac{1}{3}$
3. $3 - \frac{1}{2}$ $2\frac{1}{2}$
4. $7 - \frac{7}{9}$ $6\frac{2}{9}$
5. $2 - \frac{3}{8}$ $1\frac{5}{8}$

MEETING INDIVIDUAL NEEDS
For Students Who Are . . .

Acquiring English Proficiency Review that 1 ft equals 12 in. Briefly describe *Olympic games, gold medal,* and *discus throw.*

Gifted and Talented Have students solve for n.
$2\frac{3}{5} + 5\frac{1}{2} = n$ $\left(8\frac{1}{10}\right)$ $n = 2\frac{1}{4} + 3\frac{7}{12} - 5\frac{1}{3}$ $\left(\frac{1}{2}\right)$
$4\frac{1}{2} - n = \frac{3}{8}$ $\left(4\frac{1}{8}\right)$ $n + 3\frac{2}{3} = 5\frac{1}{6}$ $\left(1\frac{1}{2}\right)$

Working 2 or 3 Grades Below Level Have students use pages 60–65 and 72–79 of the Skills Workbook for fractions.

Today's Problem
What is the smallest nonzero whole number that is divisible by all whole numbers 1 through 9? $(2{,}520; 2^3 \times 3^2 \times 5 \times 7)$

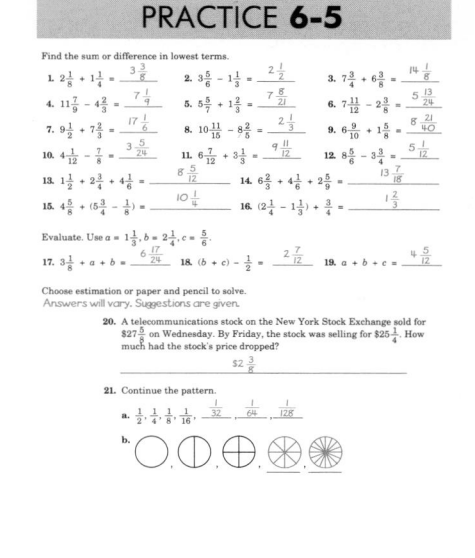

PRACTICE 6-5

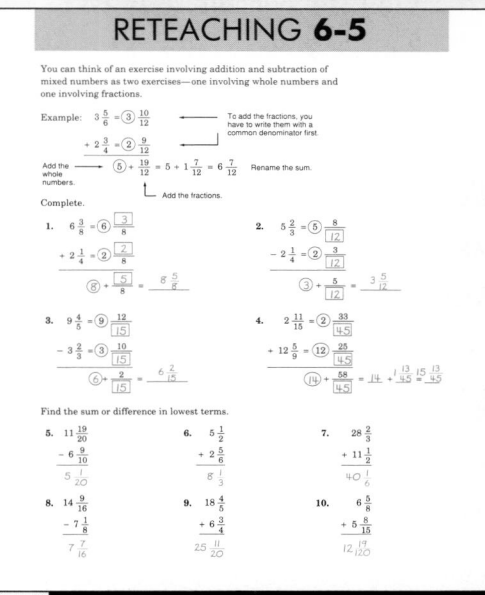

RETEACHING 6-5

ENRICHMENT 6-5

☑ **MATERIALS CHECKLIST:** Cookbooks

Have the students work in groups of four or five. Ask each student to find a recipe for a dessert that he or she would like to make. Then have the group members share their recipes. The students find the ingredients that are common to each recipe and tell how much of each ingredient is needed to make all the desserts. For example, four recipes might call for the following amounts of sugar: $1\frac{3}{4}$ c, $\frac{2}{3}$ c, $2\frac{1}{2}$ c, and $1\frac{1}{2}$ c; the amount of sugar needed would be $6\frac{5}{12}$ c. Tell the students that for some ingredients they may have to convert to a common unit of measure.

Lesson Organizer

Objective: Subtract fractions, renaming before subtracting.

Prior Knowledge: Students should be able to subtract mixed numbers that have different denominators.

Error Analysis and Remediation: See page 197A.

Lesson Resources:
Practice Worksheet 6-6
Reteaching Activity 6-6
Enrichment Worksheet 6-6
Daily Review 6-6

Two-Minute Math

Find the missing number.

$5\frac{5}{4} = \square\frac{1}{4}$ *(6)* $\qquad 8\frac{1}{2} = 7\frac{\square}{2}$ *(3)*

$6\frac{7}{8} = 5\frac{\square}{8}$ *(15)* $\qquad 4 = 3\frac{\square}{5}$ *(5)*

1 INTRODUCE

SYMBOLIC ACTIVITY

1. Write $54.34 - 28.97$ on the chalkboard. Ask a volunteer to explain the renaming and subtract. **Why is it easy to rename when subtracting decimals for whole numbers?** *(Possible answer: Each place has a value of 10 times that of the place to its right.)*

2. Write $6\frac{3}{8} - 2\frac{5}{8}$. **What problem is there in subtracting the fractions in this example?** *(There are not enough eighths to subtract $\frac{5}{8}$ from $\frac{3}{8}$.)*

Where will we get more eighths so that we can subtract the fractions? *(Rename $6\frac{3}{8}$ as $5\frac{11}{8}$.)* **Explain the steps in this renaming.:**

$$6\frac{3}{8} = 5 + 1 + \frac{3}{8}$$
$$= 5 + \frac{8}{8} + \frac{3}{8}$$
$$= 5 + \frac{11}{8}$$

WHEN YOUR STUDENTS ASK
★ **WHY AM I LEARNING THIS?** ★

You can connect this skill to real life through carpentry. For example, carpenters add and subtract mixed numbers to determine how much wood they need for a door frame.

Renaming Before Subtracting

The osprey uses its large wings to dive from great heights to catch fish. The wingspan of the osprey averages $4\frac{1}{2}$ ft. The osprey's body length averages only $1\frac{5}{6}$ ft.

How much longer is the osprey's average wingspan than its average body length?

The diagram represents the problem.

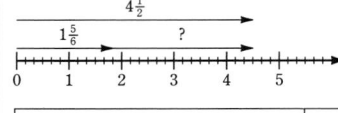

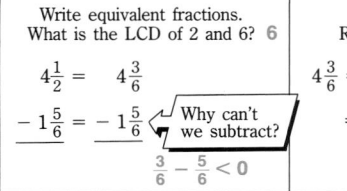

Write equivalent fractions. What is the LCD of 2 and 6? **6**	Rename.	Subtract.
$4\frac{1}{2} = \quad 4\frac{3}{6}$ $-1\frac{5}{6} = -1\frac{5}{6}$ Why can't we subtract? $\frac{3}{6} - \frac{5}{6} < 0$	$4\frac{3}{6} = 3\frac{6}{6} + \frac{3}{6}$ $= 3\frac{9}{6}$	$3\frac{9}{6}$ $-1\frac{5}{6}$ $2\frac{4}{6} = 2\frac{2}{3}$

THINK ALOUD How would you estimate the difference between $4\frac{1}{2}$ and $1\frac{5}{6}$?

$$5 - 2 = 3$$

Another example:

Rename 6 as $5\frac{4}{4}$.	Subtract.
6 $-2\frac{1}{4}$	$5\frac{4}{4}$ $-2\frac{1}{4}$ $3\frac{3}{4}$

GUIDED PRACTICE

Find the value of *n*.

1. $5\frac{1}{3} = 4\frac{n}{3}$ **2.** $7\frac{2}{5} = 6\frac{n}{5}$ **3.** $15\frac{3}{8} = 14\frac{11}{n}$ **4.** $7\frac{1}{4} = 6\frac{n}{4}$ **5.** $8\frac{5}{8} = 7\frac{13}{n}$

Give the answer in lowest terms.

6. $5\frac{1}{3} - 1\frac{2}{3}$ $\ 3\frac{2}{3}$ **7.** $7\frac{2}{5} - 2\frac{4}{5}$ $\ 4\frac{3}{5}$ **8.** $15\frac{3}{8} - 5\frac{3}{4}$ $\ 9\frac{5}{8}$ **9.** $9\frac{1}{4} - 1\frac{2}{3}$ $\ 7\frac{7}{12}$

2 TEACH

Is it necessary to rename before subtracting in the example $12\frac{7}{10} - 3\frac{3}{5}$? Explain. *(No, when equivalent fractions are written, it is possible to subtract $\frac{6}{10}$ from $\frac{7}{10}$.)*

Find the error in this example:

$16\frac{1}{7} - 5\frac{5}{7} = 15\frac{11}{7} - 5\frac{5}{7} = 10\frac{6}{7}$

($16\frac{1}{7}$ was incorrectly renamed; in this number, one whole is equal to $\frac{7}{7}$, not to $\frac{10}{7}$.)

Chalkboard Examples
Write the difference in lowest terms.
$4\frac{1}{4} - 1\frac{3}{4}\,(2\frac{1}{2})$ $5\frac{2}{3} - 2\frac{5}{6}\,(2\frac{5}{6})$
$20\frac{2}{5} - 2\frac{3}{4}\,(17\frac{13}{20})$

SUMMARIZE/ASSESS Explain the steps to follow when renaming a mixed number before subtraction. *(If necessary, write equivalent fractions. Then compare the fractions, and rename the mixed number so that there are enough fractional parts to proceed with the computation.)*

===== PRACTICE =====

Subtract. Give your answer in lowest terms.

10. $9\frac{2}{5} - 2\frac{4}{5}$ $6\frac{3}{5}$ **11.** $6\frac{3}{8} - 2\frac{7}{8}$ $3\frac{1}{2}$ **12.** $9\frac{5}{12} - 8\frac{9}{12}$ $\frac{2}{3}$ **13.** $15\frac{5}{9} - 12\frac{7}{9}$ $2\frac{7}{9}$

14. $45\frac{7}{12} - 9\frac{11}{12}$ $35\frac{2}{3}$ **15.** $40 - 7\frac{5}{12}$ $32\frac{7}{12}$ **16.** $15 - 8\frac{7}{9}$ $6\frac{2}{9}$ **17.** $10\frac{4}{6} - 4\frac{5}{6}$ $5\frac{5}{6}$

18. $34\frac{5}{8} - \frac{7}{8}$ $33\frac{3}{4}$ **19.** $30\frac{3}{9} - 19\frac{7}{9}$ $10\frac{5}{9}$ **20.** $7\frac{1}{6} - 2\frac{5}{12}$ $4\frac{3}{4}$ **21.** $5\frac{1}{8} - 1\frac{3}{4}$ $3\frac{3}{8}$

22. $50\frac{7}{12} - 18\frac{15}{24}$ $31\frac{23}{24}$ **23.** $12 - 10\frac{6}{9}$ $1\frac{1}{3}$ **24.** $7\frac{4}{5} - 2\frac{9}{10}$ $4\frac{9}{10}$ **25.** $5\frac{1}{4} - 2\frac{4}{6}$ $2\frac{7}{12}$

26. $17 - 6\frac{5}{9}$ $10\frac{4}{9}$ **27.** $9\frac{2}{9} - 8\frac{5}{8}$ $\frac{43}{72}$ **28.** $6\frac{2}{4} - 1\frac{4}{5}$ $4\frac{7}{10}$ **29.** $40 - 21\frac{9}{10}$ $18\frac{1}{10}$

MIXED REVIEW Compute.

30. 391×4.57
    $1,786.87$
31. $2\frac{5}{8} + \frac{3}{4}$ $3\frac{3}{8}$
32. $9,825 + 697$
    $10,522$
33. $3\frac{1}{6} - 2\frac{1}{2}$ $\frac{2}{3}$

34. $\frac{2}{9} + \frac{5}{9} + \frac{1}{2}$
    $1\frac{5}{18}$
35. $3,528 \div 28$ 126 **36.** $48 - 6\frac{1}{2}$
    $41\frac{1}{2}$
37. $0.179 - 0.099$
    0.08

MENTAL MATH Solve for n mentally.

38. $8\frac{4}{5} - n = 3\frac{2}{5}$ $5\frac{2}{5}$ **39.** $13\frac{2}{3} - n = 4\frac{1}{3}$ $9\frac{1}{3}$ **40.** $24\frac{3}{4} - n = 14\frac{1}{2}$ $10\frac{1}{4}$

===== PROBLEM SOLVING =====

CHOOSE Choose estimation or paper and pencil to solve.
Use the graph below.   Choices will vary. Suggestion given.

41. California condors are the largest flying bird in the United States. What is the difference between the condor's average body length and wingspan?
e; ≈6 ft

42. What is the difference between the average wingspan of the condor and the peregrine falcon?
p; $6\frac{2}{3}$ ft

43. Estimate the number of times longer the bald eagle's average wingspan is than its body length.
e; ≈$2\frac{1}{2}$ times longer

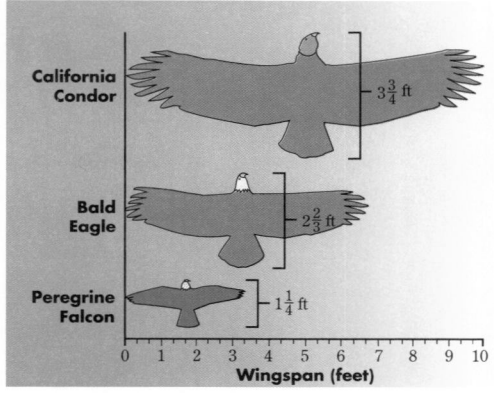

Average Body Length and Wingspan of Some Endangered Birds

California Condor — $3\frac{3}{4}$ ft

Bald Eagle — $2\frac{2}{3}$ ft

Peregrine Falcon — $1\frac{1}{4}$ ft

Wingspan (feet)
0 1 2 3 4 5 6 7 8 9 10

CHAPTER 6   181

MEETING INDIVIDUAL NEEDS
For Students Who Are . . .

Acquiring English Proficiency Discuss the meanings of *wingspan* and *endangered*. Have students work in pairs to solve Exercises 41–43.

Gifted and Talented Have students create two additional problems using the information in the graph for Exercises 41–43.

Working 2 or 3 Grades Below Level Have students use this extra step to rename: $5\frac{1}{3} = 4 + \frac{3}{3} + \frac{1}{3} = 4\frac{4}{3}$.

Today's Problem

What fraction of the different sums that can result from tossing a pair of number cubes are prime? *(The sums that are primes are 2, 3, 5, 7, and 11. They represent $\frac{5}{11}$ of the possible sums.)*

3 FOLLOW-UP

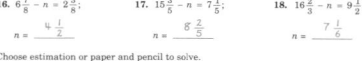

PRACTICE 6-6

Subtract. Write your answer in lowest terms.

1. $6\frac{1}{4} - 1\frac{3}{4} =$ $4\frac{1}{2}$ **2.** $7\frac{1}{6} - 4\frac{5}{6} =$ $2\frac{1}{3}$ **3.** $16 - 8\frac{7}{9} =$ $7\frac{2}{9}$

4. $11\frac{2}{9} - 6\frac{8}{9} =$ $4\frac{1}{3}$ **5.** $10 - 6\frac{2}{3} =$ $3\frac{1}{3}$ **6.** $10\frac{5}{8} - 3\frac{7}{8} =$ $6\frac{3}{4}$

7. $19\frac{2}{6} - 8\frac{2}{3} =$ $10\frac{2}{3}$ **8.** $12 - 6\frac{9}{10} =$ $5\frac{1}{10}$ **9.** $11\frac{1}{8} - 7\frac{5}{8} =$ $3\frac{1}{2}$

10. $20\frac{1}{20} - 15\frac{1}{5} =$ $4\frac{17}{20}$ **11.** $18 - 3\frac{5}{12} =$ $14\frac{7}{12}$ **12.** $8\frac{1}{7} - 6\frac{3}{21} =$ $1\frac{17}{21}$

13. $14\frac{3}{8} - 11\frac{3}{5} =$ $2\frac{31}{40}$ **14.** $24\frac{1}{6} - 19\frac{3}{5} =$ $4\frac{17}{30}$ **15.** $24\frac{2}{5} - 18\frac{1}{2} =$ $5\frac{9}{10}$

Solve for n using mental math.

16. $6\frac{7}{8} - n = 2\frac{3}{8}$;   **17.** $15\frac{3}{5} - n = 7\frac{1}{5}$;   **18.** $16\frac{2}{3} - n = 9\frac{1}{2}$;

$n =$ $4\frac{1}{2}$ $n =$ $8\frac{2}{5}$ $n =$ $7\frac{1}{6}$

Choose estimation or paper and pencil to solve.

19. Steve won a ribbon at the State Fair last year by entering a watermelon that weighed $47\frac{9}{10}$ lb. This year he has grown a watermelon that weighs $52\frac{2}{5}$ lb. How much heavier is this year's watermelon?
$4\frac{7}{10}$ lb

20. Phyllis plans to compete in the State Fair with a tomato she grew that weighs $5\frac{1}{16}$ lb. This tomato is $1\frac{3}{16}$ lb heavier than the one she entered last year. How much did last year's tomato weigh?
$3\frac{7}{8}$ lb

RETEACHING 6-6

☑ **MATERIALS CHECKLIST:** Fraction bars

Represent $3\frac{1}{3}$ with fraction bars. Use the $\frac{1}{3}$ bar to represent the fraction part and 3 bars of the same color with their non-shaded sides showing to represent the whole number part. Have students find a way to subtract $1\frac{2}{3}$. Lead them to trade one of the whole bars for the $\frac{3}{3}$ bar. Record what is left as $2\frac{4}{3}$ and subtract. Have them use the bars to find $4\frac{1}{6} - 1\frac{5}{6}$, $4\frac{3}{8} - \frac{7}{8}$, and $4\frac{1}{4} - 2\frac{5}{8}$.

ENRICHMENT 6-6

You know that computation inside parentheses must be done first according to the order of operations. This applies to fractions and mixed numbers as well as to whole numbers.

Example: Insert parentheses to make the equation true.

$$\frac{3}{4} - \frac{1}{8} + \frac{3}{8} = \frac{1}{4}$$

$$\frac{6}{8} - \frac{1}{8} + \frac{3}{8} = \frac{2}{8} \quad \text{First, write all the fractions with a common denominator.}$$

$$\frac{3}{4} - \left(\frac{1}{8} + \frac{3}{8}\right) = \frac{1}{4} \quad \text{Since } 6 - (1 + 3) = 2, \text{ you know where to put the parentheses.}$$

Insert parentheses to make the equation true. If the equation is already true without parentheses, write *true*.

1. $\frac{2}{5} + \frac{1}{4} - \frac{7}{20} = \frac{3}{10}$
true
2. $4\frac{7}{8} + 6 - 2\frac{1}{3} = 8\frac{13}{24}$
true

3. $1\frac{2}{3} + \frac{5}{9} - \frac{1}{3} + \frac{4}{9} = 2\frac{1}{3}$
true
4. $\frac{3}{5} + \frac{2}{5} - \frac{1}{5} + \frac{5}{9} = 1\frac{16}{45}$
true

5. $7 - \left(2\frac{1}{8} - 1\frac{1}{2}\right) = 6\frac{3}{8}$
6. $6\frac{1}{4} - \left(1\frac{2}{3} + \frac{5}{6}\right) = 3\frac{3}{4}$

7. $6 - \left(1\frac{1}{3} - 1\frac{1}{2}\right) - 4\frac{1}{2} = 1\frac{1}{2}$
8. $9 - \left(3 - 1\frac{6}{7}\right) = 7\frac{6}{7}$

9. $\frac{7}{8} - \frac{1}{6} + 1\frac{1}{4} - \frac{1}{3} = 1\frac{5}{8}$
true
10. $100 - 16\frac{7}{12} - \left(5\frac{2}{3} + 11\frac{3}{4}\right) = 66$

11. $\frac{1}{2} - \frac{2}{5} + \frac{11}{20} - \frac{1}{5} = \frac{9}{20}$
true
12. $2\frac{1}{2} + 1\frac{1}{2} + 3\frac{1}{2} - 4\frac{1}{2} = 3$
true

MIDCHAPTER
Checkup

The midchapter checkup provides a way for you to check students' understanding of the skills taught in the first half of the chapter.

Language and Vocabulary

Some key language and vocabulary ideas from the first half of the chapter are reinforced here.

Quick Quiz

The quiz provides a means of evaluating students' understanding of the objectives for the first half of the chapter. Page references are given so that students can check back to where the skill was taught.

Use the following guide to score the quick quiz.

Score	Percent
10	100%
9	90
8	80
7	70
6	60
5	50
4	40
3	30
2	20
1	10

Use this chart to identify the Management Objectives tested.

Items	Management Objective	Pages
1–2	**6A** Add and subtract fractions and mixed numbers, same denominators.	172–173
4–6	**6B** Add and subtract fractions, different denominators.	174–177; 180–181
7–9	**6C** Add and subtract mixed numbers, different denominators.	178–179
10	**6E** Problem Solving: Using fractions.	178–179

LANGUAGE & VOCABULARY

Explain in your own words how each pair of activities is similar and how each pair is different. **Accept reasonable answers.**

1. Adding fractions with the same denominators and adding fractions with different denominators.

2. Finding the LCM of two numbers and finding the LCD of two fractions.

3. Subtracting fractions and subtracting mixed numbers.

4. Subtracting mixed numbers without renaming and subtracting mixed numbers with renaming.

QUICK QUIZ ✓

Find the sum or difference in lowest terms. *(pages 172–181)*

1. $\frac{3}{5} + \frac{4}{5}$ $1\frac{2}{5}$

2. $12\frac{5}{6} - 7\frac{3}{6}$ $5\frac{1}{3}$

3. $\frac{7}{10} - \frac{1}{2}$ $\frac{1}{5}$

4. $\frac{3}{9} + \frac{7}{18}$ $\frac{13}{18}$

5. $\frac{2}{3} + \frac{3}{5}$ $1\frac{4}{15}$

6. $\frac{11}{12} - \frac{3}{10}$ $\frac{37}{60}$

7. $4\frac{2}{7} + 5\frac{1}{3}$ $9\frac{13}{21}$

8. $12\frac{1}{5} - 3\frac{2}{4}$ $8\frac{7}{10}$

9. $18 - 9\frac{3}{8}$ $8\frac{5}{8}$

Solve. *(pages 178–179)*

10. A 5-mi race consists of 20 laps around a $\frac{1}{4}$-mi track.

   a. How far will a runner have gone when she completes 20 laps? **5 mi**

   b. Jackie has run $3\frac{1}{4}$ mi. How can you find out how many miles she must run to complete the race? **subtract**

   c. How far must Jackie run to complete the race? $1\frac{3}{4}$ mi

LEARNING LOG

Write the answers in your learning log. **Answers will vary. Suggestions given.**

1. When will the common denominator for an addition or a subtraction problem be different than the original denominators?
   when the two numbers have different denominators

2. Your friend has trouble finding the LCD when adding fractions. You want to help him. What would you tell him to check first?
   Check to see if one is a multiple of the other.

MATH AMERICA

DID YOU KNOW . . . ? Old Faithful, a geyser in Yellowstone National Park, erupts every 73 min. If it erupted at 8:00 A.M., during what classes would it erupt for the rest of your school day? **Check students' work.**

BONUS

a. $\blacksquare \frac{\equiv}{\equiv} + \blacksquare \frac{\equiv}{\equiv} = 7\frac{5}{8}$ $4\frac{1}{8}; 3\frac{1}{2}$

b. $\blacksquare - \blacksquare \frac{\equiv}{\equiv} = 2\frac{1}{4}$ $4; 1\frac{3}{4}$

c. $\blacksquare \frac{\equiv}{\equiv} + \frac{\equiv}{\equiv} - \frac{\equiv}{\equiv} = 6\frac{9}{20}$ $6\frac{1}{5}; \frac{1}{2}; \frac{1}{4}$

d. $\blacksquare \frac{\equiv}{\equiv} - \frac{\equiv}{\equiv} = 7\frac{7}{8}$ $8\frac{3}{8}; \frac{1}{2}$

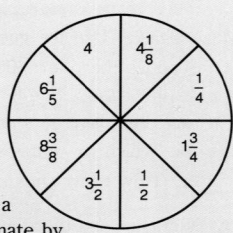

Use the fractions or mixed numbers in the circle. Work with a partner. Use estimation to fill in the boxes. Check your estimate by using a calculator.

Learning Log

These are suggestions for writing about some topics taught so far in the chapter. The students keep their Learning Logs from the beginning of the school year through the end.

Math America

A mathematical skill that students have learned is related to an interesting fact about the United States.

Bonus

Students are given an opportunity to solve a challenge-type problem like a puzzle or a nonroutine problem.

LESSON 6-7

Lesson Organizer

> **Objective:** Solve problems using guess and check.

Prior Knowledge: Students should be able to add and subtract fractions and mixed numbers.

Error Analysis and Remediation: See page 197A.

Lesson Resources:
Practice Worksheet 6-7
Reteaching Activity 6-7
Enrichment Worksheet 6-7
Daily Review 6-7

Two-Minute Math

Write *true* or *false*.
The sum of an even number and an odd number is always even. *(false)*
The sum of two odd numbers is always odd. *(false)*
The sum of three odd numbers is always even. *(false)*

1 INTRODUCE

SYMBOLIC ACTIVITY

1. Present this problem to students: **I am thinking of two numbers. Their sum is 30 and their difference is 11. What are the numbers?** *(20$\frac{1}{2}$ and 9$\frac{1}{2}$)* Have students work in groups of three or four to find the answer.

2. Ask students to describe what they did. *(Students will probably say that they tried and checked different numbers.)* **Was your first guess correct? Did your first guess help you make a better second guess?**

WHEN YOUR STUDENTS ASK
★ WHY AM I LEARNING THIS? ★

You can use this skill to solve different kinds of real life problems. When you are stuck and can't get started to solve a problem, making a guess and checking may get you going.

Problem Solving Strategy: **Guess and Check**

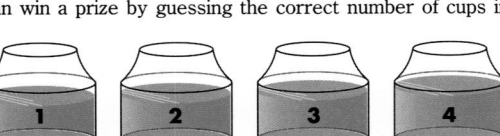

At the amusement park, there are 94 cups (c) of water in four jars. You are told each jar contains 2$\frac{1}{3}$ more cups than the jar to its left. You can win a prize by guessing the correct number of cups in jar 1.

Ask yourself questions to be sure you understand the problem.

• How many jars in all are there? **4 jars**
• How does the number of cups in each jar compare to the number of cups in the jar to its right?
  It is 2$\frac{1}{3}$ c more.

Often the best way to solve a problem is to guess and check. List your guesses in a table.

	Jar 1	Jar 2	Jar 3	Jar 4	Total
1st Guess: 8$\frac{1}{3}$	8$\frac{1}{3}$	10$\frac{2}{3}$	13	15$\frac{1}{3}$	47$\frac{1}{3}$
2nd Guess: 25	25	? 27$\frac{1}{3}$	? 29$\frac{2}{3}$	? 32	? 114

← Should the next guess be a higher number or a lower number? **higher** Should it be a mixed number? **no**

← How many cups would be in jars 2, 3, and 4? Why was 25 a good guess? Why was it bad? How can you make the next guess better? **See table; closer to 94; 25 too high. Choose between 9 and 25.**

Now make a new guess and solve the problem. **Jar 1 has 20 c.**
Be sure your answer is reasonable.

• Do the numbers add up to 94? **yes**
• Does each jar contain 2$\frac{1}{3}$ more cups than the one to its left? **yes**

━━━━━━━ **GUIDED PRACTICE** ━━━━━━━

Make a table. Use the guess and check strategy to solve.

1. Suppose there are 100 c of water in five jars. Each jar contains 2$\frac{1}{2}$ more cups of water than the jar to its left.

  a. How many jars are there? **5 jars**

  b. Which jar contains the most water? **jar 5**

  c. How many cups of water are there in jar 1? **15 c**

2. Now suppose there are 108 c of water in four jars. Each jar contains 2$\frac{2}{3}$ fewer cups of water than the jar to its left. How many cups of water are there in jar 4? **22$\frac{1}{4}$ c**

---

2 TEACH

Should your third guess be greater than or less than 25? Explain. *(It should be less than because the total from the second guess is greater than 94.)*

Why is it important to list the guesses in a table? *(Possible answer: to keep track of them; to see the results of adding 2$\frac{1}{3}$ each time)*

Suppose your third guess is 22. How does the table help you decide what to do next? *(The sum will be a whole number greater than 94. This means that the first jar must contain a whole number slightly less than 22.)*

SUMMARIZE/ASSESS
In what kinds of situations would using guess and check as a problem solving method be appropriate? *(Possible answer: Those in which a solution is not readily apparent and you can't seem to find a way to start.)*

Four Aces Amusement Park

Admission:
- Adults $8.00
- Children (under 12) $6.50
- Children (under 5) $4.75

All rides are free once you get in.

Use the guess and check strategy to solve.

3. The 4 members of the Lee family pay a total of $24 for admission to the park. How many adults, children under 12, and children under 5 are in the Lee family? **1 adult, 1 child under 12, 2 children under 5**

4. Enrique, Mario, Juana, Rita, and Rosa Sanchez paid a total of $32.50 to enter the park. How many tickets were purchased at each price? **5 tickets at $6.50**

5. Anders, Dag, Hilde, Inga, and Berta Olsen pay a total of $34 for admission to the park. How many of the five members of the Olsen family are adults? are children under 12? are children under 5? **1; 4; 0**

6. Jay bought 2 of one type of souvenir and 3 of another for a total of $19. If one type of souvenir cost a half dollar more than the other, what was the price of each? **There are two solutions: 2 at $3.50, 3 at $4 or 2 at $4.10, 3 at $3.60**

PROBLEM SOLVING

CHOOSE Choose a strategy to solve. **Choices will vary.**

7. Brigid counted 24 out-of-state license plates in the amusement-park parking lot. There were 10 from Alabama, 5 from Florida, and 3 from Tennessee. What fractional part of the out-of-state plates were not from Alabama, Florida, or Tennessee? $\frac{1}{4}$

8. **CRITICAL THINKING** In which state do you think the park was located? Defend your choice. **Georgia; it borders the 3 states in Exercise 7.**

9. Andrea bought 2 cats. She exchanged each cat for 2 dogs. Each dog was exchanged for 2 horses. Each horse was exchanged for 2 fish. If this pattern continued, how many pets would Andrea have after six exchanges? **128 pets**

10. When Greg got home from the park, he had five coins of four different types totaling $1. What coins and how many of each did he have? **one halfdollar, one quarter, two dimes, one nickel**

CHAPTER 6   185

---

3 FOLLOW-UP

PRACTICE 6-7

Use the guess and check strategy to solve.

1. Five members of the Sampson family paid a total of $17.75 for admission to the museum. How many of each kind of ticket did they purchase?
   1 at $5; 3 at $3.50; 1 at $2.25

The Lowe Museum of Art	
Admission Prices	
Museum members	$1.00
Adults	$5.00
College students, senior citizens	$3.50
Children younger than 12	$2.25

2. Bill and Betty Rizzoli take their 5 grandchildren to the museum. Mr. and Mrs. Rizzoli are both museum members. They pay $15.75 for admission. The Rizzoli grandchildren fit into which admission price categories?
   2 college; 3 under 12

3. Admission to the museum is $2.75 for adults after 5:00 P.M. on Tuesdays. A group of 8 adults go to the museum on Tuesday. One is a member. Some in the group arrive before 5:00 P.M. and some arrive after 5:00 P.M. If the group pays a total of $27 for admission, how many of each kind of ticket are bought?
   1 at $1; 3 at $5; 4 at $2.75

4. A puzzle in the museum gift shop has 4 pieces. The longest piece is $\frac{2}{3}$ in. longer than the next longest piece. Each of the remaining pieces also is $\frac{2}{3}$ in. longer than the next piece. What is the length of each puzzle piece if the total length of the pieces is 36 in.?
   10 in., $9\frac{1}{3}$ in., $8\frac{2}{3}$ in., 8 in.

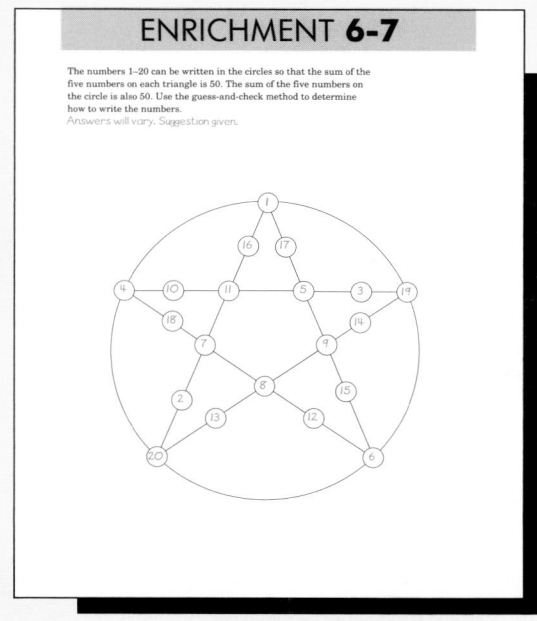

RETEACHING 6-7

Present the following problem.

Meg bought 3 of one type of pens and 2 of another type for a total of $8.00. If one pen costs twice as much as the other, what was the price of each?

Can you find the cost of the pens using numbers in the problem? [no] Suppose one type of pen costs $.50 and the other costs $1.00. What are the two possible total costs for the pens? [$3.50; $4.00] Could these be the costs of the pens? [no] How do you know? [total cost is $8] What do you need to do to try to get close to $8.00? [make the price higher] Continue questions until students guess that the prices are $1.00 and $2.00.

ENRICHMENT 6-7

The numbers 1–20 can be written in the circles so that the sum of the five numbers on each triangle is 50. The sum of the five numbers on the circle is also 50. Use the guess-and-check method to determine how to write the numbers.
Answers will vary. Suggestion given.

MEETING INDIVIDUAL NEEDS

For Students Who Are . . .

Acquiring English Proficiency Pair students with an English-proficient student to solve Exercises 3–10.

Gifted and Talented Have students create a problem similar to Exercise 5, trade papers and solve.

Working 2 or 3 Grades Below Level Have students use pages 94–101 of the Skills Workbook for Problem Solving Strategies.

Having Reading Difficulties Suggest that students draw a tree diagram for Exercise 7, and point out the word *not* in Exercise 9.

Today's Problem

Consider this sentence: "At the present time the decimal system is practically universal throughout the world." What fraction of the letters in this sentence are consonants? *(The fraction is $\frac{47}{72}$.)*

LESSON 6-8

Lesson Organizer

Objective: Explore measurement.

Prior Knowledge: Students should be familiar with the Customary units of length.

Lesson Resources:
Class Activity 6-8
Daily Review 6-8

 **Two-Minute Math**

In these two minutes, write as many different names for the number 36 as you can.

1 PREPARE

SYMBOLIC ACTIVITY

Ask students to guess how many erasers wide the chalkboard is. Have them compare their guesses. Who was the closest? Why? *(Perhaps students used benchmarks such as subdivisions of the chalkboard to help decide.)*

Explain that an eraser is a nonstandard measure of length. **Which standard units would be appropriate for measuring the width of the chalkboard?** *(foot, yard, meter)*

What are some advantages of using standard units of measure? *(Everyone understands what the unit means.)*

WHEN YOUR STUDENTS ASK
★ WHY AM I LEARNING THIS? ★

You can connect this skill to real life through history. For example, after measurement devices made it possible for a piston to fit a cylinder, the age of steam engines began.

 EXPLORE

Exploring Measurement

Measuring is comparing. The earliest humans did not need to make accurate comparisons. They could tell by looking whether a cave was large enough for a family to live in.

1. Describe a situation in which you measure this way today. **Answers will vary. Suggestion given: buying pumpkins.**

Later on, people began to use different units of measure.

• The inch we use today came from the width of a thumb.
• A foot was the length of a foot.
• A yard was the distance from the nose to the tip of the middle finger of the outstretched arm.

2. Measure the length and the width of your math book using thumb widths. **Answers will vary.**

3. About how many of your feet equal 1 yd? Measure by using the nonstandard foot and yard above. **Answers will vary.**

4. Measure the length of your classroom in your foot lengths. **Answers will vary.**

5. Measure the length of your classroom blackboard in the nonstandard yard. **Answers will vary.**

6. **IN YOUR WORDS** Compare your measurements with those of your classmates. What problems are caused by these nonstandard units of measure? **Answers will vary.**

Our system of measuring length has **standard units** that are always the same. The smallest unit is the inch. Any measurement requiring more precision must be done using fractional parts of an inch.

Use a ruler to measure the following to the nearest eighth of an inch.

7. the length of your shoe
   Answers will vary.
8. the length of a desk top
   Answers will vary.
9. the width of a pencil
   Answers will vary.
10. the length of this phrase
    $\approx 1\frac{5}{8}$ in.

186   LESSON 6-8

MATH HISTORY

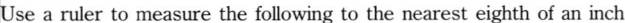

MULTICULTURAL NOTE

The ancient Egyptians were the first people to establish and use standard units of measure for length, volume, and weight. See page 303B for more information on the measures that were used by the ancient Egyptians.

2 TEACH

☑ **MATERIALS CHECKLIST:** inch rulers or tape measures, 2 per group

Assign students to work in groups of three or four.

Why do you think people used informal units of measure? *(Answers will vary.)*

About how many of your inches equal one foot, using the nonstandard inch and foot described in the lesson?

If you could, would you change the number of inches in a foot? the number of feet in a yard? the number of yards in a mile? Explain your reasoning.

SUMMARIZE/ASSESS **Explain why using the standard unit of a foot is more practical than using your own foot as a unit of measure.** *(Possible answer: Everyone understands the length represented by a standard unit foot; sizes of human feet vary.)*

11. **CRITICAL THINKING** How would you change our
measurement system to make it easier to use? **Answers will vary.**
Suggestion given: Use easier numbers so computation is easier.

The earliest known standard unit was the **cubit.** It was the distance
from the tip of the middle finger to the elbow, and it varied in length
in different parts of the ancient world. The **royal cubit,** used by the
Egyptians in building the pyramids, was $20\frac{1}{2}$ in.

12. Use a ruler to measure the cubit of your arm and a partner's
arm to the nearest eighth of an inch.
Answers will vary.

13. How do the lengths of each of your cubits compare to the $20\frac{1}{2}$ in.?
Answers will vary.

Some ancient units were smaller than the cubit.

the **span**   the **palm**   the **digit**

14. Measure the span, the palm, and the digit of your hand
and a partner's hand to the nearest eighth of an inch.
Answers will vary.

ESTIMATE Use the span, palm, and digit measurements
from Exercise 14 to estimate each length in inches.
Do not use paper and pencil. **Accept reasonable estimates. Suggestions given.**

15. the length of a calculator $\approx 5\frac{1}{2}$ in.   16. the length of a notebook ≈ 10 in.

17. the length of the word "length" $\approx \frac{1}{2}$ in.   18. the height of your chair
Answers will vary.

19. the width of a quarter ≈ 1 in.   20. the height of the classroom door
Answers will vary.

21. **IN YOUR WORDS** Describe how you can use your span
to estimate the height of the classroom ceiling.
Check students' work.

22. **CREATE YOUR OWN** Write a paragraph describing your bedroom.
Use only cubits, spans, palms, and digits when you describe
your bedroom and the size of the objects in it.
Check students' work.

☑ **MATERIALS CHECKLIST:** Strips of
paper, scissors, tape

Have the students work in groups of four.
Instruct the students to find the width of
their hand. Each student places a thumb
along the edge of a sheet of paper and
marks the distance from the edge to his or
her outstretched little finger. Each student
then makes a 12-hand-span-long measuring tape by marking, cutting, and taping
together twelve 1-hand-span-long strips of
paper. Ask the students to label their
tapes *1, 2, 3, . . . 12.* Group members then
measure various classroom objects independently, using hand spans and fractions
of hand spans as the unit of measure. Have
students compare their measurements.

MEETING INDIVIDUAL NEEDS

For Students Who Are . . .

Acquiring English Proficiency Discuss the meanings of *accurate,*
nonstandard, and *precision* in this lesson. Have students put the new
words in their learning logs.

Gifted and Talented Assign students the Technology lesson on
page 202.

Working 2 or 3 Grades Below Level Have students practice mea-
suring to the nearest $\frac{1}{2}$ in., $\frac{1}{4}$ in., and $\frac{1}{8}$ in. Make sure they place the
ruler correctly and read the right numbers.

Today's Problem

In Riverside Church in New York City one of the bells in the caril-
lon weighs 40,926 pounds. Approximately how many tons does the
bell weigh? *(40,926 ÷ 2,000 = about 21 tons)*

LESSON | 6-9

Lesson Organizer

> **Objective:** Determine the appropriate customary units of length.

Prior Knowledge: Students should be familiar with the inch, foot, yard, and mile.

Error Analysis and Remediation: See page 197A.

Lesson Resources:
Practice Worksheet 6-9
Reteaching Worksheet 6-9
Enrichment Activity 6-9
Daily Review 6-9
Cooperative Connections, Chapter 6

 **Two-Minute Math**

Look around the room closely. Name some objects you see with a length of about one inch, one foot, and one yard.

1 INTRODUCE

SYMBOLIC ACTIVITY

☑ **MATERIALS CHECKLIST:** inch rulers or tape measures for each pair of students

Have pairs of students estimate the perimeter of a rectangular desktop or tabletop. Then have them measure the length and width and add to find the perimeter.

Which unit did you use in your estimate and your measurement? Why did you choose that particular unit? (*Accept reasonable answers.*)

WHEN YOUR STUDENTS ASK
★ WHY AM I LEARNING THIS? ★

This skill will help you solve many real life problems. For example, you use a road map to compare the mileages of two different routes between two places.

Customary Units: Length

Several customary units of length are shown in the illustration. The chart below shows how they are related.

> 12 inches (in.) = 1 foot (ft)
> 36 in. = 1 yard (yd)
> 3 ft = 1 yd
> 5,280 ft = 1 mile (mi)

Why do we multiply by 12 to change from feet to inches? **because 1 ft = 12 in.**

4 ft = ▓ in. ⟨ Is the number of inches *more* or *less* than 4? 4 ft = 48 in. **more** ⟩

Why do we divide by 3 to change from feet to yards? **because 3 ft = 1 yd**

15 ft = ▓ yd ⟨ Is the number of yards *more* or *less* than 15? 15 ft = 5 yd **less** ⟩

About one ft

About one in.

About one yd

Notice how you rename as you add and subtract measures.

$$\begin{array}{r} 9 \text{ ft } 8 \text{ in.} \\ + 10 \text{ ft } 5 \text{ in.} \\ \hline 19 \text{ ft } 13 \text{ in.} \end{array}$$

⟨ **THINK ALOUD** What is the answer in yards, feet, and inches? ⟩ **6 yd 2 ft 1 in.**

$$\begin{array}{r} \overset{4}{5} \text{ yd } \overset{4}{1} \text{ ft} \\ - 3 \text{ ft} \\ \hline 4 \text{ yd } 1 \text{ ft} \end{array}\qquad \begin{array}{r} \overset{1}{2} \text{ mi } \overset{2,480}{720} \text{ yd} \\ - 1,000 \text{ yd} \\ \hline 1 \text{ mi } 1,480 \text{ yd} \end{array}$$

━━━━━━━━━━━ **GUIDED PRACTICE** ━━━━━━━━━━━

Copy and complete.

1. 9 yd = ▓ in. **324**
2. 4 yd = ▓ ft **12**
3. 360 in. = ▓ yd **10**
4. 2 mi = ▓ ft **10,560**
5. 33 ft = ▓ yd **11**
6. 33 ft = ▓ in. **396**

7. **NUMBER SENSE** What is an object whose height you would measure in inches? in feet? in yards? *Answers will vary. Suggestions given.* **chair; room; building**
8. **THINK ALOUD** Explain how you would find the difference between 1 mi and 100 yd. **1 mi = 1,760 yd; 1,760 − 100 = 1,660 yd**

188   LESSON 6-9

---

2 TEACH

Have students work with a partner for the Critical Thinking activity.

What frame of reference do you use to think about the length of a mile? (*Possible answers: 4 laps around a $\frac{1}{4}$-mi track; about 20 city blocks; a 15–20 min walk*) Have students share their ideas with other students.

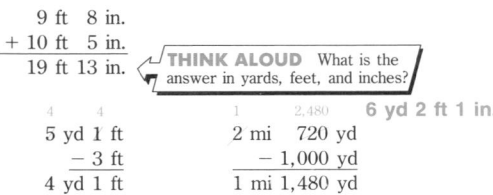

Find the error in this addition:
4 ft 9 in. + 3 ft 11 in. = 7 ft 20 in. = 9 ft 0 in.
(*When you add inches, you do not rename by 10's; you rename by 12's, because there are 12 inches in a foot.*)

> ### Chalkboard Examples
> Add or subtract.
> $$\begin{array}{r} 5 \text{ yd } 3 \text{ ft} \\ + 4 \text{ yd } 10 \text{ ft} \\ \hline (13 \text{ yd } 1 \text{ ft}) \end{array}\qquad \begin{array}{r} 8 \text{ ft } 6 \text{ in.} \\ - 2 \text{ ft } 9 \text{ in.} \\ \hline (5 \text{ ft } 9 \text{ in.}) \end{array}$$

SUMMARIZE/ASSESS **Explain how to find the difference between 100 yd and 1 ft** (*Possible answer: 100 yd = 99 yd 3 ft; 99 yd 3 ft − 1 ft = 99 yd 2 ft*)

PRACTICE

Copy and complete.

9. 12 ft = ▦ in. 144   **10.** 54 ft = ▦ yd 18   **11.** 18 ft = ▦ in. 216

12. 3 mi = ▦ ft 15,840   **13.** 3 yd = ▦ in. 108   **14.** 10 yd = ▦ in. 360

15. 4 yd = ▦ ft 12 in. 11   **16.** 5 ft = 2 ft ▦ in. 36   **17.** 4 yd = ▦ yd 9 ft 1

18. 6 yd = ▦ ft 18   **19.** 9 ft = ▦ in. 108   **20.** 2 yd 15 in. = ▦ in. 87

NUMBER SENSE Choose the best estimate.

21. the depth of a fish pond
  a. 48 yd   **b.** 48 ft   **c.** 48 in. c

22. the distance around a garage
  a. 3 ft   **b.** 30 ft   **c.** 3 mi b

23. the height of a stop sign
  a. 8 ft   **b.** 48 ft   **c.** $\frac{1}{4}$ mi a

24. the length of a toothbrush
  a. $\frac{1}{2}$ in.   **b.** 20 in.   **c.** $\frac{1}{2}$ ft c

MIXED REVIEW Compare. Choose >, <, or =.

25. 9 ft ▦ 3 yd =   **26.** 2 mi ▦ 10,400 ft >   **27.** 33 yd ▦ 100 ft <

Compute.

28.   5 ft 8 in.
    + 8 ft 9 in.
    14 ft 5 in.

29.   10 ft 4 in.
    − 6 ft 11 in.
    3 ft 5 in.

*30.   2 mi 960 yd
    + 8 mi 900 yd
    11 mi 100 yd

*31.   3 yd 2 ft 8 in.
    − 1 yd 2 ft 9 in.
    1 yd 2 ft 11 in.

PROBLEM SOLVING

 CHOOSE Use the diagram. Choose paper and pencil or calculator to solve. **Choices will vary. Suggestions given.**

32. The perimeter of Boston Common is about 2,182 yd. About how long, in yards, is the side for which no dimension is given?
p; 598 yd

33. If you walked the perimeter of Boston Common, how many miles would you walk?
c; 1.24 mi

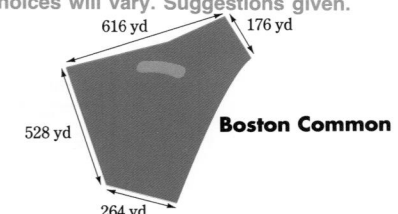

616 yd   176 yd

528 yd   **Boston Common**

264 yd

The Boston Common, established in 1634, was the first public park in the colonies.

 **Critical Thinking**

Discuss how you would change each measurement to inches.

1. $\frac{1}{4}$ yd   **2.** $\frac{1}{3}$ ft   **3.** $6\frac{1}{2}$ ft   **4.** $1\frac{2}{3}$ yd   **5.** $8\frac{1}{6}$ ft   **6.** $2\frac{3}{4}$ yd

×36   ×12   ×12   ×36   ×12   ×36

MEETING INDIVIDUAL NEEDS

For Students Who Are . . .

Acquiring English Proficiency Pair students with an English-proficient student to discuss and solve the Problem Solving and Critical Thinking exercises.

Gifted and Talented Have students do problems like these: 8 glubs = 1 blurb; 20 blurbs = 1 vlert; 36 vlerts = how many glubs? (5,760); 32 glubs = how many vlerts? ($\frac{1}{5}$)

Working 2 or 3 Grades Below Level Have students use an extra step to rename: 19 ft 13 in. = 19 ft + 12 in. + 1 in. = 20 ft 1 in.

Today's Problem

One mile of nickels has a total value of $3,696. How many nickels is that? To the nearest hundredth of an inch, how wide is a nickel? *(Number of nickels: $3,696 × 20 = 73,920; width of a nickel: 5,280 × 12 ÷ 73,920 = 0.86 in.)*

---

3 FOLLOW-UP

PRACTICE 6-9

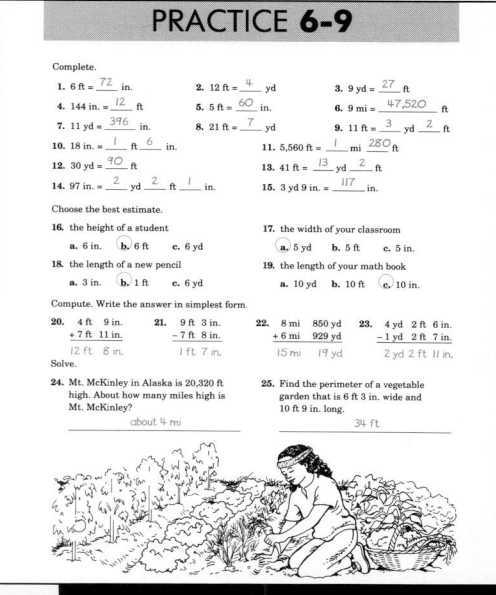

RETEACHING 6-9

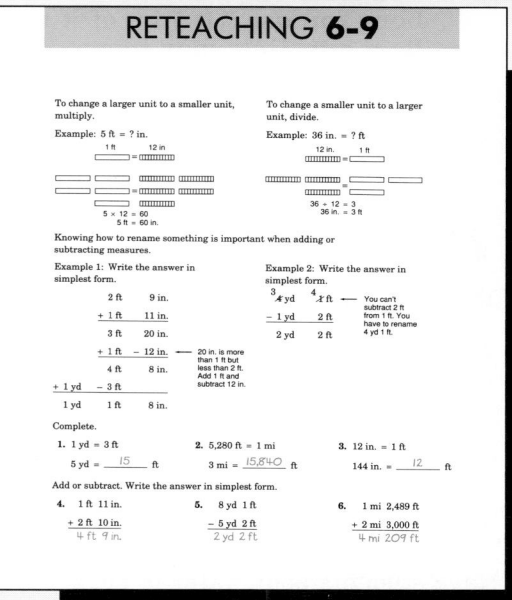

ENRICHMENT 6-9

Explain to the students that while inches, feet, yards, and miles are the most common customary units of measure in the United States, there are others. Write the following on the board: 1 chain = 66 ft; 1 fathom = 6 ft; 1 hand = 4 in.; 1 league = 3 mi; 1 rod = $16\frac{1}{2}$ ft. Have the students convert between common and nonstandard units of measure by asking questions such as, How many hands is 5 ft? [15] You may wish to extend the activity by having the students research in what situation each nonstandard unit of measure might be used.

LESSON 6-10

Lesson Organizer

> **Objective:** Determine the appropriate customary units of capacity.

Prior Knowledge: Students should be familiar with the customary units of capacity.

Error Analysis and Remediation: See page 197A.

Lesson Resources:
Practice Worksheet 6-10
Reteaching Worksheet 6-10
Enrichment Activity 6-10
Daily Review 6-10

Two-Minute Math

You have 18 yd 2 ft 5 in. of ribbon. You use 5 ft 7 in. of it to tie a gift. How may inches of ribon are left? About how many feet is this? *(610 in.; about 51 ft)*

1 INTRODUCE

CONNECTING ACTIVITY

☑ **MATERIALS CHECKLIST:** gallon, half-gallon, quart, pint, and cup containers; water or sand

1. Display the containers, identifying each by name. Brainstorm with students to determine what they know about the relationships among the units.

2. Have students pour water to show that a gallon contains:

- 2 half-gallons
- 8 pints
- 4 quarts
- 16 cups

3. Ask questions such as:

- A cup is what part of a gallon? $\left(\frac{1}{16}\right)$
- A pint is what part of a gallon? $\left(\frac{1}{8}\right)$

WHEN YOUR STUDENTS ASK
★ WHY AM I LEARNING THIS? ★

This skill will help you solve real life problems. Suppose you need 5 c of milk for a recipe. Milk is sold in pints or quarts. How many pints would you need to buy? how many quarts?

Customary Units: Capacity

The chart shows how the customary units of capacity are related.

8 fluid ounces (fl oz) = 1 cup (c)
2 c = 1 pint (pt)
2 pt = 1 quart (qt)
4 qt = 1 gallon (gal)

Why do we multiply by 2 to change from pints to cups?　　**because 1 pt = 2 c**

14 pt = ■ c　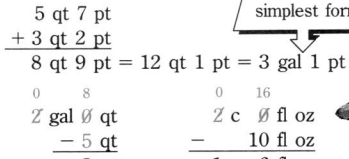　Is the number of cups *more* or *less* than 14?　14 pt = 28 c　**more**

Why do we divide by 4 to change from quarts to gallons?　　**because 4 qt = 1 gal**

48 qt = ■ gal　　Is the number of gallons *more* or *less* than 48?　48 qt = 12 gal　**less**

THINK ALOUD How would you find the number of fluid ounces in 1 pt? in 1 qt?
multiply by 16, multiply by 32
Notice how you add and subtract units of capacity.

```
   5 qt 7 pt
 + 3 qt 2 pt                    simplest form
   8 qt 9 pt = 12 qt 1 pt = 3 gal 1 pt

   0    8                  0    16
   Z gal Ø qt              Z c  Ø fl oz
 −     5 qt              −      10 fl oz
       3 qt                1 c   6 fl oz
```

=== GUIDED PRACTICE ===

Which unit of capacity is appropriate? Choose *fl oz, c, pt, qt,* or *gal.*

1. a bathtub　**gal**
2. a tube of toothpaste　**fl oz**
3. a car's gasoline tank　**gal**

Copy and complete.

4. 3 gal = ■ qt　**12**
5. 4 pt = ■ c　**8**
6. 12 qt = ■ pt　**24**
7. 36 c = ■ pt　**18**

8. **THINK ALOUD** How much of a gallon is 1 qt? 2 qt?　$\frac{1}{4}$ gal; $\frac{1}{2}$ gal

---

2 TEACH

☑ **MATERIALS CHECKLIST:** calculators

How do you change from fluid ounces to pints? *(Divide by 16.)* **from gallons to pints?** *(Multiply by 8.)*

Which unit of capacity would you use to measure the amount of soup in a bowl? *(cup or fluid ounce)* **What might you measure in pints?** *(Example: olive oil)*

Explain how you would finish this addition:
3 c 7 fl oz + 2 c 6 fl oz = 5 c 13 fl oz *(Rename 13 fl oz as 1 c 5 fl oz; add 1 c to 5 c; rename 6 c as 3 pt); answer is 3 pt 5 fl oz)*

Chalkboard Examples	
Add or subtract.	
3 c 5 fl oz	9 gal 2 qt
+ 4 c 7 fl oz	− 5 gal 3 qt
(8 c 4 fl oz)	*(3 gal 3 qt)*

SUMMARIZE/ASSESS　Explain how to find the number of cups of punch that can be poured from a 2-gal bowl. *(There are 16 c in a gal; multiply 16 by 2 to find the number of cups in 2gal.)*

Copy and complete.

9. 72 fl oz = ▦ c   9
10. 16 qt = ▦ gal   4
11. 160 pt = ▦ c   320
12. 22 pt = ▦ c   44
13. 9 gal = ▦ qt   36
14. 64 fl oz = ▦ pt   4
15. 12 c = ▦ fl oz   96
16. 100 gal = ▦ pt   800
*17. $13\frac{1}{2}$ qt = ▦ c   54

MIXED REVIEW Compare. Choose >, <, or =.

18. 5 yd ▦ 14 ft   >
19. 15,840 ft ▦ 3 mi   =
20. 200 fl oz ▦ 30 c   <

NUMBER SENSE Choose the best estimate.

21. a small fishbowl
    a. 3 qt b. 3 c c. 3 fl oz
    a
22. a bathtub
    a. 200 fl oz b. 20 qt c. 20 gal
23. a can of soup
    a. 10 c b. 10 fl oz c. 10 qt
    b
24. a bottle of dish detergent
    a. 20 pt b. $\frac{1}{2}$ c c. 20 fl oz
    c

Copy and complete. Use the appropriate unit of capacity.

25. 240 fl oz = 15 ▦ c
26. 14 gal = 112 ▦ pt
27. $4\frac{1}{2}$ qt = 18 ▦ c

Compute. Give the answer in simplest form.

28.   3 gal 2 qt
    + 1 gal 6 qt
    ―――――――――
      4 gal 8 qt
      or 6 gal

*29.   8 pt 0 c
     − 5 pt 3 c
    ―――――――――
       1 pt 1 c

*30.   1 c 9 fl oz
     + 0 c 16 fl oz
    ―――――――――――
       4 c 1 fl oz
       or 2 pt 1 fl oz

CHOOSE Choose estimation, paper and pencil, or calculator to solve. **Choices will vary. Suggestions given.**

31. Nutritionists recommend we drink 8 c of water every day. How many quarts is that in 1 wk? How many gallons is that in 4 wk?
    p; 14 qt; 14 gal

32. It takes about 150 gal of water to make the paper for just 1 Sunday newspaper. The circulation of the Sunday *New York Times* is 1,663,000. About how many gallons of water does it take to produce this many copies?
    e; ≈250,000,000 gal

33. **CREATE YOUR OWN** Each person in the United States uses an average of 70 gal of water per day. Create a math problem about this fact. Give it to a friend to solve.
    Check students' work.

MEETING INDIVIDUAL NEEDS
For Students Who Are . . .

Acquiring English Proficiency Review 7 days is 1 week and 52 weeks is 1 year before having students work in pairs to do Exercises 31–33.

Gifted and Talented Have students find newspaper ads that announce savings for buying larger quantities of items. Then have them find the amount that can be saved.

Working 2 or 3 Grades Below Level Have students list the steps they need to follow to solve Exercises 31 and 32.

Today's Problem

The largest seed in the world—the coconut—can weigh 40 pounds. The smallest seed is that of an orchid. There are 35,000,000 orchid seeds to the ounce. The coconut seed by weight is equivalent to how many orchid seeds? *(Number of orchid seeds: 35,000,000 × 16 × 40 = 22,400,000,000)*

3 FOLLOW-UP

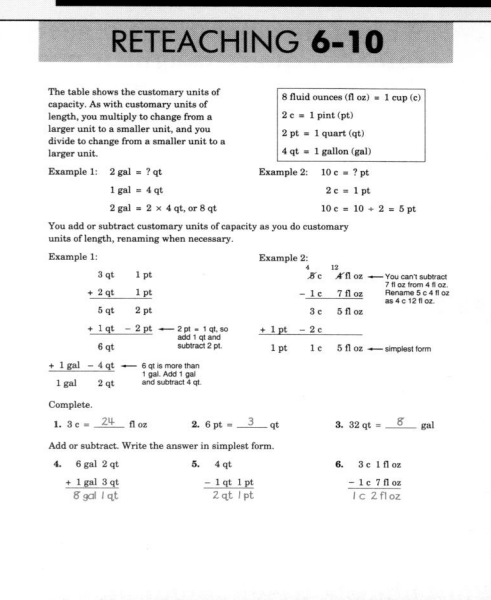

PRACTICE 6-10

Complete.
1. 56 fl oz = __7__ c
2. 7 gal = __28__ qt
3. 37 pt = __74__ c
4. 6 pt = __3__ c
5. 8 c = __64__ fl oz
6. 12 qt = __3__ gal
7. 11 qt = __2__ gal __3__ c
8. 96 fl oz = __3__ qt
9. $21\frac{1}{2}$ c = __86__ c

Choose the best estimate.
10. a can of juice
    (a.) 12 fl oz b. 12 c c. 12 pt
11. a swimming pool
    a. 10,000 fl oz b. 10,000 qt (c.) 10,000 gal
12. a container of milk in the refrigerator
    (a.) 128 fl oz b. 128 c c. 128 pt
13. a large milk shake
    a. 16 pt b. 16 c (c.) 16 oz

Complete with the appropriate unit of capacity.
14. 384 fl oz = 3 __gal__
15. 9 c = 72 __fl oz__
16. $24\frac{1}{2}$ c = 98 __c__

Compute. Write the answers in simplest form.
17.   5 gal 1 qt
    − 2 gal 3 qt
    ―――――――――
      2 gal 2 qt
18.   2 pt 1 c
    + 1 pt 2 c
    ―――――――――
       2 qt 1 c
19.   6 c 4 fl oz
    − 1 c 11 fl oz
    ―――――――――
      4 c 1 fl oz
20.   3 qt
    − 1 qt 3 pt
    ―――――――――
       1 pt
21.   2 c 9 fl oz
    + 6 c 11 fl oz
    ―――――――――
      2 qt 1 pt 4 fl oz
22.   5 gal 3 qt 1 pt
    + 1 gal 2 qt 3 pt
    ―――――――――
       7 gal 3 qt

Solve.
23. Kim made punch for her party. The recipe called for a 64-oz can of pineapple juice, 2 qt of orange juice, and 32 oz of soda water. How much punch did she make?
    __1 gal 1 qt__
24. How many 1-cup servings would Kim's punch recipe make?
    __20__

RETEACHING 6-10

The table shows the customary units of capacity. As with customary units of length, you multiply to change from a larger unit to a smaller unit, and you divide to change from a smaller unit to a larger unit.

8 fluid ounces (fl oz) = 1 cup (c)
2 c = 1 pint (pt)
2 pt = 1 quart (qt)
4 qt = 1 gallon (gal)

Example 1:   2 gal = ? qt
              1 gal = 4 qt
              2 gal = 2 × 4 qt, or 8 qt

Example 2:   10 c = ? pt
              2 c = 1 pt
              10 c = 10 ÷ 2 = 5 pt

You add or subtract customary units of capacity as you do customary units of length, renaming when necessary.

Example 1:
       3 qt   1 pt
    + 2 qt   1 pt
    ―――――――――
      5 qt   2 pt
    + 1 qt − 2 pt   2 pt = 1 qt, so add 1 qt and subtract 2 pt.
    ―――――――――
      6 qt
    + 1 gal − 4 qt   6 qt is more than 1 gal. Add 1 gal and subtract 4 qt.
    ―――――――――
      1 gal   2 qt

Example 2:
            4   12
       8 c   4 fl oz   You can't subtract 7 fl oz from 4 fl oz. Rename 5 c 4 fl oz as 4 c 12 fl oz.
    − 1 c   7 fl oz
    ―――――――――
      3 c   5 fl oz
    + 1 pt − 2 c
    ―――――――――
      1 pt   1 c   5 fl oz   simplest form

Complete.
1. 3 c = __24__ fl oz
2. 6 pt = __3__ qt
3. 32 qt = __8__ gal

Add or subtract. Write the answer in simplest form.
4.   6 gal 2 qt
    + 1 gal 3 qt
    ―――――――――
      8 gal 1 qt
5.   4 qt
    − 1 qt 1 pt
    ―――――――――
      2 qt 1 pt
6.   3 c 1 fl oz
    − 1 c 7 fl oz
    ―――――――――
      1 c 2 fl oz

ENRICHMENT 6-10

☑ **MATERIALS CHECKLIST:** 1-gal plastic milk jugs

Have the students work in groups of three or four. Instruct each group to use a 1-gal plastic milk jug to guess how many gallons it would take to fill the classroom with about 4 inches of water. Have the group discuss and record its strategy for making the estimate. For example, the students might find the length and width of the classroom in milk jugs, multiply these measurements to find the number required to cover the floor, and then divide this number by 2, since the height of a milk jug is about 8 inches.

Lesson Organizer

Objective: Determine the appropriate customary units of weight.

Prior Knowledge: Students should be familiar with customary units of weight.

Error Analysis and Remediation: See page 197A.

Lesson Resources:
Practice Worksheet 6-11
Reteaching Worksheet 6-11
Enrichment Activity 6-11
Daily Review 6-11
Cooperative Investigations, Chapter 6

Two-Minute Math

Why is this statement inaccurate? "A quart weighs a pound the world around." How could you make it accurate? *(A pint of most liquids weighs about a pound. "A pint's a pound the world around" is an old saying.)*

1 INTRODUCE

CONNECTING ACTIVITY

☑ **MATERIALS CHECKLIST:** balance scale, pound and ounce weights

1. What objects in this classroom weigh about one pound? Weigh the objects on the scale to verify.

2. What objects weigh about an ounce? If students name paper clips, show that 16 clips weigh about one ounce.

WHEN YOUR STUDENTS ASK
★ WHY AM I LEARNING THIS? ★

You can connect this skill to real life through consumer decision-making. Your favorite Quick Chili calls for $1\frac{1}{2}$ lb canned kidney beans. The beans come in 12 oz or 20 oz cans. What should you buy?

Customary Units: Weight

One of the largest rainbow trout ever caught weighed 42 lb 2 oz.

Rainbow trout usually weigh about 1 lb.

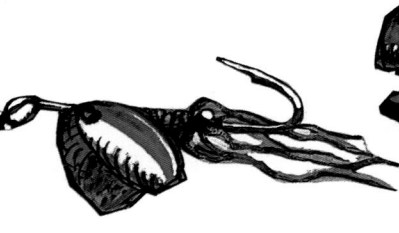

The weight tied to the fishing line is 1 oz.

> 16 ounces (oz) = 1 pound (lb)
> 2,000 lb = 1 ton (t)

Why do we multiply by 16 to change from pounds to ounces?
because 1 lb = 16 oz

4 lb = ▦ oz   Is the number of ounces *more* or *less* than 4?
                4 lb = 64 oz   **more**

Why do we divide by 2,000 to change from pounds to tons?
because 2,000 lb = 1 t

10,000 lb = ▦ t   Is the number of tons *more* or *less* than 10,000?
                    10,000 lb = 5 t   **less**

Notice how you add and subtract units of weight.

```
   4 lb   9 oz                    3    2,000
 + 3 lb   5 oz              4 t       0 lb
 ──────────────            ─        650 lb
   7 lb  14 oz  ← simplest form →  ─────────────
                                   3 t 1,350 lb
```

GUIDED PRACTICE

Find the missing number.

1. 9 lb = ▦ oz   **144**
2. 24,000 lb = ▦ t   **12**
3. 160 oz = ▦ lb   **10**
4. 7 t = ▦ lb   **14,000**
5. 5 lb = ▦ oz   **80**
6. 10 t = ▦ lb   **20,000**

---

2 TEACH

☑ **MATERIALS CHECKLIST:** calculators

A bar of soap weights 10 oz. What part of a pound is this? $\left(\frac{10}{16} = \frac{5}{8}; \frac{5}{8} \, lb\right)$

How many 8-oz servings can you get from a $9\frac{1}{2}$ lb roast? *(19)*

Trucks weighing more than 2 t are not allowed on the bridge. A 1,500-lb truck was carrying 8 cartons of bricks, each carton weighing 150 lb. Could the truck travel on the bridge? *(Yes; the bricks weigh 1,200 lb. That, plus the weight of the truck is less than 4,000 lb or 2 t.)*

Chalkboard Examples	
3 lb 9 oz	7 lb 4 oz
+ 4 lb 13 oz	− 2 lb 11 oz
(8 lb 6 oz)	*(4 lb 9 oz)*

SUMMARIZE/ASSESS   Explain how to subtract 9 oz from 6 lb 2 oz. *(Rename 6 lb 2 oz as 5 lb 18 oz; subtract; answer is 5 lb 9 oz.)*

NUMBER SENSE Name an object with the given weight.   Answers will vary. Suggestions given.

7. about 2 lb
an iron

8. about 2 oz
a pencil

9. about 2 t
a car

10. THINK ALOUD What is $7\frac{1}{2}$ lb in pounds and ounces?
7 lb 8 oz

━━━━━━━━━━━━━━━━━ **PRACTICE** ━━━━━━━━━━━━━━━━━

Copy and complete.

11. 4 t = ■ lb   8,000

12. 24 oz = ■ lb $1\frac{1}{2}$

13. 19 lb 8 oz = ■ lb $19\frac{1}{2}$

14. 16 lb = ■ oz   256

15. 12 lb 15 oz = ■ oz   207

16. 28 lb = ■ oz   448

17. 18,000 lb = ■ t   9

18. 15,000 lb = ■ t $7\frac{1}{2}$

19. $5\frac{1}{2}$ lb = ■ lb ■ oz
5; 8

MIXED REVIEW Compute.

20. 14 yd = ■ ft   42

21. 12 qt = ■ gal   3

22. 5 t = ■ lb   10,000

23. 2 lb = ■ oz   32

24. 10 pt = ■ qt   5

25. 72 in. = ■ ft   6

NUMBER SENSE Choose the best estimate.

26. a hamburger **a**
  a. 4 oz **b.** 2 lb **c.** $\frac{1}{2}$ oz

27. a dictionary **b**
  a. 12 oz **b.** 2 lb **c.** 42 lb

28. a loaded truck **b**
  a. 400 lb **b.** 2 t **c.** 40,000 oz

29. an apple **a**
  a. $\frac{1}{2}$ lb **b.** 1 lb **c.** 64 oz

Compute. Give the answer in simplest form.

30.
  12 lb 15 oz
  + 18 lb 10 oz
  ―――――――
  31 lb 9 oz

31.
  30 lb 2 oz
  − 14 lb 9 oz
  ―――――――
  15 lb 9 oz

32.
  6 t 1,400 lb
  +   1,800 lb
  ―――――――
  7 t 1,200 lb

━━━━━━━━━━━━━ **PROBLEM SOLVING** ━━━━━━━━━━━━━

 CHOOSE Choose mental math, paper and pencil, or calculator to solve.   Choices will vary. Suggestions given.

33. A record-size catch for a walleye was 25 lb. How many 25-lb walleyes would weigh a total of 1 t?
p; 80 walleyes

34. Which two record-size fish in the table differ in weight by 2 lb 7 oz?
m; lake whitefish, smallmouth bass

35. Represent the information in the table with a bar graph.
Check students' graphs.

Record Fish Catches	
Smallmouth bass	11 lb 15 oz
Lake whitefish	14 lb 6 oz
Yellow perch	4 lb 3 oz
White catfish	17 lb 7 oz
Bluegill	4 lb 12 oz
Pickerel	9 lb 6 oz

MEETING INDIVIDUAL NEEDS

For Students Who Are . . .

Acquiring English Proficiency Discuss student responses to Exercises 7–9. Make sure students are familiar with the items named in Exercises 26–29.

Gifted and Talented Have students research other customary units such as the hundred weight (*equal 100 lb*) and the long ton (*equals 2,240 lb*).

Working 2 or 3 Grades Below Level Students should be allowed to use graph paper to construct the graph. Discuss an appropriate scale for the graph like each square equals 1 lb or 8 oz.

Today's Problem

A large gold nugget, found in Australia in 1869, weighed 7,560 ounces. How many pounds was this? (*Weight in pounds: 7,560 ÷ 16 oz = $472\frac{1}{2}$*)

3 FOLLOW-UP

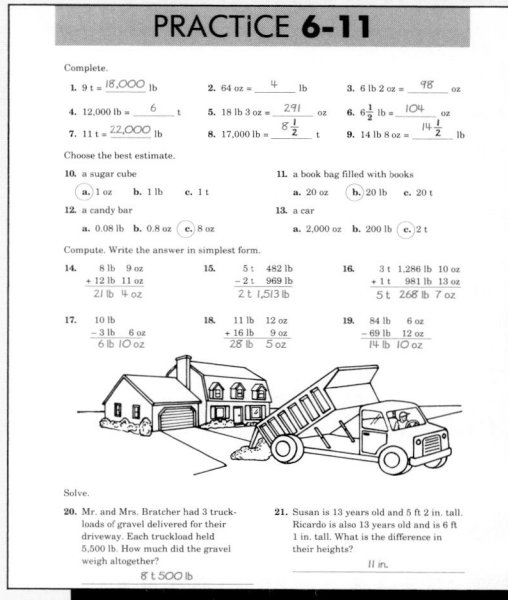

PRACTICE 6-11

Complete.

1. 9 t = _18,000_ lb

2. 64 oz = _4_ lb

3. 6 lb 2 oz = _98_ oz

4. 12,000 lb = _6_ t

5. 18 lb 3 oz = _291_ oz

6. $6\frac{1}{2}$ lb = _104_ oz

7. 11 t = _22,000_ lb

8. 17,000 lb = _$8\frac{1}{2}$_ t

9. 14 lb 8 oz = _$14\frac{1}{2}$_ lb

Choose the best estimate.

10. a sugar cube
  a. 1 oz **b.** 1 lb **c.** 1 t

11. a book bag filled with books
  a. 20 oz **b.** 20 lb **c.** 20 t

12. a candy bar
  a. 0.08 lb **b.** 0.8 oz **c.** 8 oz

13. a car
  a. 2,000 lb **b.** 200 lb **c.** 2 t

Compute. Write the answer in simplest form.

14.
  8 lb   9 oz
  + 12 lb 11 oz
  ―――――――
  21 lb 4 oz

15.
  5 t   482 lb
  − 2 t 969 lb
  ―――――――
  2 t 1,513 lb

16.
  3 t 1,286 lb 10 oz
  + 1 t 981 lb 13 oz
  ――――――――――
  5 t 268 lb 7 oz

17.
  10 lb
  − 3 lb 6 oz
  ―――――――
  6 lb 10 oz

18.
  11 lb 12 oz
  + 16 lb 9 oz
  ―――――――
  28 lb 5 oz

19.
  84 lb   6 oz
  − 69 lb 12 oz
  ―――――――
  14 lb 10 oz

Solve.

20. Mr. and Mrs. Bratcher had 3 truckloads of gravel delivered for their driveway. Each truckload held 5,500 lb. How much did the gravel weigh altogether?
8 t 500 lb

21. Susan is 13 years old and 5 ft 2 in. tall. Ricardo is also 13 years old and is 6 ft 1 in. tall. What is the difference in their heights?
11 in.

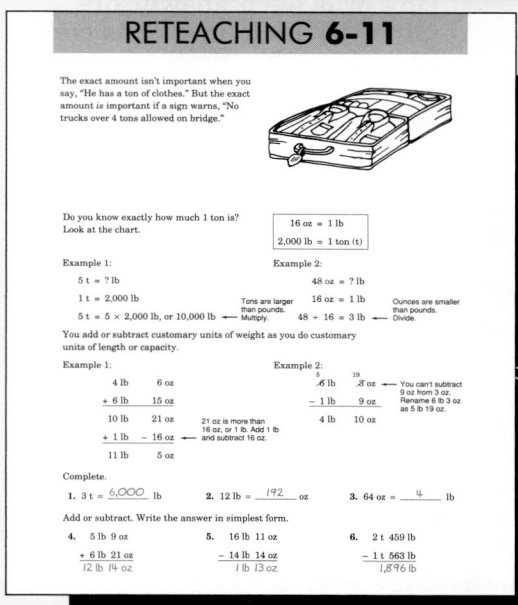

RETEACHING 6-11

The exact amount isn't important when you say, "He has a ton of clothes." But the exact amount *is* important if a sign warns, "No trucks over 4 tons allowed on bridge."

Do you know exactly how much 1 ton is? Look at the chart.

16 oz = 1 lb
2,000 lb = 1 ton (t)

Example 1:
5 t = ? lb
1 t = 2,000 lb
5 t = 5 × 2,000 lb, or 10,000 lb ← Tons are larger than pounds. Multiply.

Example 2:
48 oz = ? lb
16 oz = 1 lb
48 ÷ 16 = 3 lb ← Ounces are smaller than pounds. Divide.

You add or subtract customary units of weight as you do customary units of length or capacity.

Example 1:
  4 lb   6 oz
  + 6 lb 15 oz
  ―――――――
  10 lb 21 oz   21 oz is more than 16 oz, or 1 lb. Add 1 lb and subtract 16 oz.
  + 1 lb − 16 oz
  ―――――――
  11 lb   5 oz

Example 2:
  6 lb   8 oz   You can't subtract 9 oz from 3 oz. Rename 6 lb 3 oz as 5 lb 19 oz.
  − 1 lb 9 oz
  ―――――――
  4 lb 10 oz

Complete.

1. 3 t = _6,000_ lb

2. 12 lb = _192_ oz

3. 64 oz = _4_ lb

Add or subtract. Write the answer in simplest form.

4.
  5 lb 9 oz
  + 6 lb 21 oz
  ―――――――
  12 lb 14 oz

5.
  16 lb 11 oz
  − 14 lb 14 oz
  ―――――――
  1 lb 13 oz

6.
  2 t 459 lb
  − 1 t 563 lb
  ―――――――
  1,896 lb

ENRICHMENT 6-11

☑ **MATERIALS CHECKLIST:** Balance scales, tape, small objects such as paper clips, counters, and toothpicks

Have the students work in pairs. Instruct each pair to create their own units of weight—one for lesser weights, one for common weights, and one for greater weights. The students create a weight for the two smaller units by taping together a number of objects and tell how the unit for very heavy objects is related to these two. On a balance scale, they then weigh various classroom objects, such as an eraser or a book, using the weights they have made. Have students find the customary equivalents for their units.

LESSON 6-12

Lesson Organizer

Objective: Solve problems using two or more steps.

Prior Knowledge: Students should be able to compute with whole numbers and decimals.

Lesson Resources:
Practice Worksheet 6-12
Reteaching Activity 6-12
Enrichment Worksheet 6-12
Daily Review 6-12
Cooperative Problem Solving 2,
  Chapter 6

 *Two-Minute Math*

$3 + 4 \times 5 = 23$ $3 + 4 \times 5 = 35$
How was each answer obtained? Which answer is correct? Explain. *(Problem on left is correct because it follows order of operations.)*

1 INTRODUCE

SYMBOLIC ACTIVITY

☑ **MATERIALS CHECKLIST:** Teaching Aid 5

1. Present the following situation: **You have ordered some items from a catalog. Fill out the order form to find the total cost to buy: 3 sweaters, at $19.95 each; 1 belt, at $8.50; and 2 scarves, at $6.49 each. Do not include a state sales tax.** *(sweaters: $59.85; scarves: $12.98; belt: $8.50; Total for purchases: $81.33; Packing and shipping: $7.05; Total cost: $88.38)*

2. **Describe the steps you followed to compute the total cost.**

WHEN YOUR STUDENTS ASK
★ WHY AM I LEARNING THIS? ★

You can connect this skill to many everyday tasks. For example, planning a budget and balancing a checkbook involve multiple steps.

Problem Solving:
Multistep Problems

A jogger takes 30 min to complete 13 laps around a 0.25-mi track. If this speed is maintained, how long will it take the jogger to complete a 26-mi marathon?

This problem requires several steps to solve.

STEP 1: How many miles did the jogger run in 30 min?

> **THINK ALOUD** Why does 13×0.25 answer the question? **This gives the distance.**
> $13 \times 0.25 = 3.25$ (mi)

STEP 2: What is the jogger's speed in miles per hour?

> **THINK ALOUD** Why does multiplying 3.25 by 2 answer this question? **30 min × 2 = 1 h**
> $3.25 \times 2 = 6.5$ (mi/h)

STEP 3: At a speed of 6.5 mi/h, how long will it take to run 26 mi?

> **THINK ALOUD** Why does dividing 26 by 6.5 answer this question? Solve this last step yourself.
> **This gives the time. 4 h**

CRITICAL THINKING Is it reasonable to assume that a jogger can run at the same speed for 26 mi? Why or why not? **No. Fatigue and varied road conditions will affect the jogger.**

▬▬▬▬▬▬ **GUIDED PRACTICE** ▬▬▬▬▬▬

Use several steps to solve.

1. A jogger runs 8 laps on a 0.25-mi track in 15 min. How many hours would it take to run a 26-mi marathon if the jogger could maintain her speed? $3\frac{1}{4}$ h

2. In the 1988 Olympics, Florence Griffith-Joyner set a world record for running 200 m with the time of 21.34 s.
   a. What was the distance of this race? **200 m**
   b. Was the distance run in *more than* or *less than* than 1 min? **less than**
   c. If this pace were maintained, about how far would Griffith-Joyner run in 1 min? **≈562.3 m**

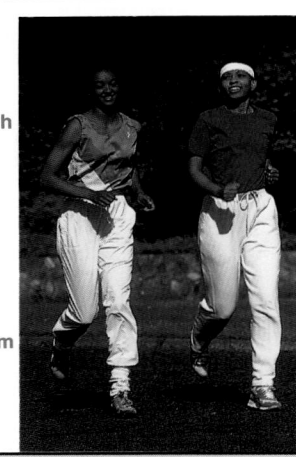

---

2 TEACH

☑ **MATERIALS CHECKLIST:** Calculators

Calculators should be available for complex computation in solving problems.

Have pairs of students discuss each step, explaining to each other both the step and the order of the steps.

Suppose you multiplied 13 × 30 for the first step. What question would the product answer? Would this answer help you solve the problem? *(The product would not mean anything and would not help find the solution.)*

Why is it important to label the answer to each step? *(to help you keep track of the steps and to provide a record of what you have found out)*

SUMMARIZE/ASSESS **Explain how to solve a multistep problem.** *(Students' responses should focus on understanding the question and planning how to solve the problem by identifying and carrying out each step.)*

Fastest Swimming Speeds	
Stroke	**Speed over 100m**
Backstroke	1.83 m/s
Breaststroke	1.62 m/s
Freestyle	2.07 m/s
Butterfly	1.89 m/s

=== PRACTICE ===

Use the information shown above to solve, if necessary.

3. **IN YOUR WORDS** A record holder swims 0.5 km in 308 s. What stroke do you think was used? **breaststroke**

4. How far would the fastest butterfly swimmer travel in 1.5 min? **170.1 m**

5. About how much longer would it take the fastest breaststroke swimmer than the fastest backstroker to swim 200 m? **≈14.2 s**

6. A dolphin can swim 16.6 m/s. By about how many seconds would a dolphin defeat a human swimming freestyle over a distance of 200 m? **≈84.6 s**

7. A downhill skier has been recorded as traveling at a speed of 2 mi/min. At this speed, how many minutes would it take to complete a 2.5-mi ski run? **1.25 min, or 1 min 15 s**

8. The record speed for roller skaters is a little more than 24 mi/h. What is this speed in miles per minute? At this speed, what distance can be skated in 40 s? **0.4 mi/min; 0.2̄6 mi**

 Choose a strategy to solve, if possible. **Choices will vary.**

9. In the 1988 Olympics, Carl Lewis ran 100 m in a record 9.92 s. At that speed, how long would it take him to complete one lap around the Olympic track? **not enough information**

10. One way to arrange the letters at the right is shown. How many different ways are possible? **6**

A   B   C

*__**11.** If you multiplied 3 by itself once, the result is 9. What would be the digit in the ones' place if 3 were multiplied by itself 10 times? **7**

MEETING INDIVIDUAL NEEDS

For Students Who Are . . .

Acquiring English Proficiency Pair students with an English-proficient student to answer Exercises 3–10.

Gifted and Talented Have each student create a multistep problem based on another Olympic record. Then have students exchange papers and solve.

Working 2 or 3 Grades Below Level Have students use pages 116–123 of the Skills Workbook for Problem Solving Strategies.

Having Reading Difficulties Pair students with an able reader to discuss and solve Exercises 3–10.

Today's Problem

If $1\frac{1}{2}$ chickens can lay $1\frac{1}{2}$ eggs in $1\frac{1}{2}$ minutes, at this rate how many eggs can 3 chickens lay in 3 minutes? *(On the average, one chicken can lay one egg every $1\frac{1}{2}$ minutes. Three chickens can lay 3 eggs in $1\frac{1}{2}$ minutes and, therefore, 6 eggs in 3 minutes.)*

---

3 FOLLOW-UP

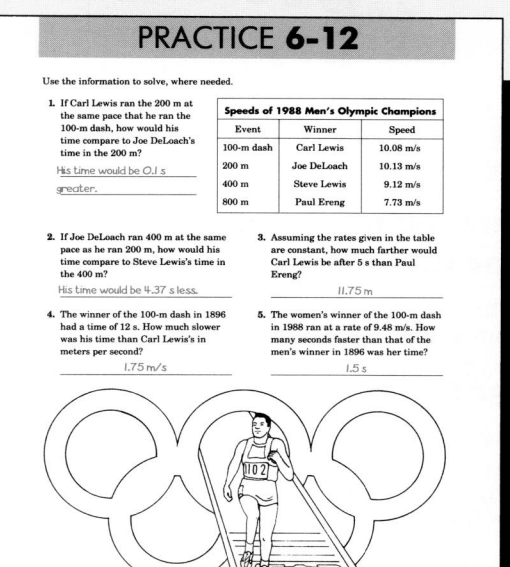

PRACTICE 6-12

Use the information to solve, where needed.

1. If Carl Lewis ran the 200 m at the same pace that he ran the 100-m dash, how would his time compare to Joe DeLoach's time in the 200 m?

His time would be 0.1 s greater.

Speeds of 1988 Men's Olympic Champions		
Event	**Winner**	**Speed**
100-m dash	Carl Lewis	10.08 m/s
200 m	Joe DeLoach	10.13 m/s
400 m	Steve Lewis	9.12 m/s
800 m	Paul Ereng	7.73 m/s

2. If Joe DeLoach ran 400 m at the same pace as he ran 200 m, how would his time compare to Steve Lewis's time in the 400 m?

His time would be 4.37 s less.

3. Assuming the rates given in the table are constant, how much farther would Carl Lewis be after 5 s than Paul Ereng?

11.75 m

4. The winner of the 100-m dash in 1896 had a time of 12 s. How much slower was his time than Carl Lewis's in meters per second?

1.75 m/s

5. The women's winner of the 100-m dash in 1988 ran at a rate of 9.48 m/s. How many seconds faster than that of the men's winner in 1896 was her time?

1.5 s

RETEACHING 6-12

Some students may have difficulty with problems whose solutions require more than one step. One way to solve Problem 1, *Practice Worksheet 6-12*, is to ask the following questions: What do you need to find? [Carl Lewis's time for 200 meters and Joe DeLoach's time] How will you find each time? [divide the 200 meters by the speed in meters per second] What are the times? [Carl Lewis: 19.84 sec, Joe DeLoach: 19.74 sec] How will you compare these times? [subtract] Which runner's time was faster? [Joe DeLoach's] By how much? [0.1 sec] Did you answer the question? [yes]

ENRICHMENT 6-12

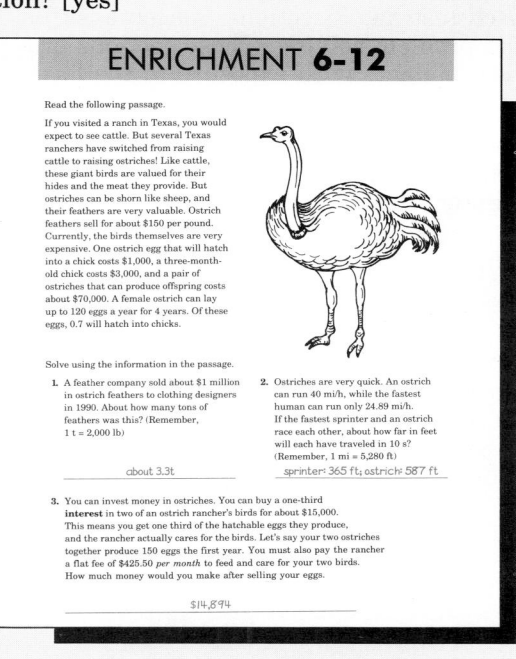

Read the following passage.

If you visited a ranch in Texas, you would expect to see cattle. But several Texas ranchers have switched from raising cattle to raising ostriches! Like cattle, these giant birds are valued for their hides and the meat they provide. But ostriches can be shorn like sheep, and their feathers are very valuable. Ostrich feathers sell for about $150 per pound. Currently, the birds themselves are very expensive. One ostrich egg that will hatch into a chick costs $1,000, a three-month-old chick costs $3,000, and a pair of ostriches that can produce offspring costs about $70,000. A female ostrich can lay up to 120 eggs a year for 4 years. Of these eggs, 0.7 will hatch into chicks.

Solve using the information in the passage.

1. A feather company sold about $1 million in ostrich feathers to clothing designers in 1990. About how many tons of feathers was this? (Remember, 1 t = 2,000 lb)

about 3.3 t

2. Ostriches are very quick. An ostrich can run 40 mi/h, while the fastest human can run only 24.89 mi/h. If the fastest sprinter and an ostrich race each other, about how far in feet will each have traveled in 10 s? (Remember, 1 mi = 5,280 ft)

sprinter: 365 ft; ostrich: 587 ft

3. You can invest money in ostriches. You can buy a one-third **interest** in two of an ostrich rancher's birds for about $15,000. This means you get one third of the hatchable eggs they produce, and the rancher actually cares for the birds. Let's say your two ostriches together produce 150 eggs the first year. You must also pay the rancher a flat fee of $425.50 *per month* to feed and care for your two birds. How much money would you make after selling your eggs?

$14,894

CHAPTER

Checkup

The chapter checkup provides a quick language and vocabulary review, a test for the chapter, and suggestions for student Learning Log entries.

Language and Vocabulary

Some key language and vocabulary ideas from this chapter are reinforced here.

Test

The test can be used either as a test or as a review of the chapter prior to your administering the test worksheets found in the Teacher's Resource Book.

The following guide will help you determine percentage scores.

Score	Percent	Score	Percent
27	100%	13	50%
26	97	12	46
25	93	11	42
24	90	10	38
23	86	9	35
22	83	8	32
21	79	7	28
20	75	6	24
19	72	5	20
18	68	4	16
17	65	3	12
16	61	2	8
15	58	1	4
14	54		

Each test has 3 sections: concepts, skills, and problem solving. These sections provide students with exposure to the formats used on standardized tests.

Use the chart on page 197 to identify the Management Objectives tested for this chapter.

CHAPTER CHECKUP

LANGUAGE & VOCABULARY

Decide whether the unit is appropriate for the measurement. Explain your decision.

1. using yards to measure a student's height   units too large
2. using feet to measure the distance between cities   units too small
3. using gallons to measure the water in a swimming pool   yes
4. using fluid ounces to measure the fuel in a car's gas tank   units too small
5. using tons to measure a horse's weight   units too large

TEST ✔

CONCEPTS

Copy and complete. *(pages 188–193)*

1. 48 ft = ▓ yd   16
2. 6 ft = ▓ in.   72
3. 2 yd 1 ft = ▓ in.   84
4. 3 pt = ▓ c   6
5. 96 fl oz = ▓ pt   6
6. 3 gal = ▓ qt   12
7. $2\frac{1}{4}$ lb = ▓ lb ▓ oz   2; 4
8. 3 lb 7 oz = ▓ oz   55
9. 212,000 lb = ▓ t   106

SKILLS

Find the sum or difference in lowest terms. *(pages 172–181)*

10. $\frac{4}{9} - \frac{1}{9}$ $\frac{1}{3}$
11. $\frac{4}{7} + \frac{5}{7}$ $1\frac{2}{7}$
12. $8\frac{3}{12} - 2\frac{1}{12}$ $6\frac{1}{6}$
13. $5\frac{2}{3} + 9\frac{2}{3}$ $15\frac{1}{3}$
14. $\frac{3}{4} + \frac{2}{12}$ $\frac{11}{12}$
15. $\frac{5}{9} - \frac{3}{18}$ $\frac{7}{18}$
16. $\frac{7}{10} + \frac{12}{30}$ $1\frac{1}{10}$
17. $\frac{5}{7} - \frac{5}{14}$ $\frac{5}{14}$
18. $\frac{8}{9} - \frac{3}{5}$ $\frac{13}{45}$
19. $\frac{5}{6} + \frac{7}{9}$ $1\frac{11}{18}$
20. $\frac{6}{11} - \frac{1}{4}$ $\frac{13}{44}$
21. $4\frac{3}{8} + 1\frac{1}{16}$ $5\frac{7}{16}$
22. $12\frac{1}{2} + 9\frac{2}{3}$ $22\frac{1}{6}$
23. $7\frac{1}{4} - 2\frac{5}{6}$ $4\frac{5}{12}$
24. $15 - 6\frac{1}{7}$ $8\frac{6}{7}$

CHAPTER TEST • FORM A

Find the sum or difference. Write the answer in lowest terms. (pp. 170–173) 6A

1. $\frac{5}{8} - \frac{3}{8}$ $\frac{1}{4}$
2. $\frac{3}{7} + \frac{2}{7}$ $\frac{5}{7}$
3. $6\frac{5}{12} - 3\frac{1}{12}$ $3\frac{1}{3}$

4. $4\frac{1}{3} + 8\frac{2}{3}$ 13
5. $5\frac{8}{9} - 2\frac{4}{9}$ $3\frac{4}{9}$

Find the sum or difference. Write the answer in lowest terms. (pp. 174–177) 6B

6. $\frac{2}{3} + \frac{7}{12}$ $1\frac{1}{4}$
7. $\frac{4}{5} - \frac{7}{15}$ $\frac{1}{3}$
8. $\frac{3}{10} + \frac{7}{20}$ $\frac{13}{20}$

9. $\frac{3}{10} - \frac{4}{15}$ $\frac{1}{30}$
10. $\frac{5}{8} + \frac{2}{5}$ $1\frac{1}{40}$

Find the sum or difference. Write the answer in lowest terms. (pp. 178–181) 6C

11. $3\frac{1}{8} + 1\frac{2}{3}$ $4\frac{19}{24}$
12. $10\frac{1}{3} - 2\frac{1}{4}$ $8\frac{1}{12}$
13. $5\frac{5}{6} - 1\frac{1}{8}$ $4\frac{17}{24}$

14. $14 - 4\frac{1}{2}$ $9\frac{1}{2}$
15. $6\frac{4}{5} - 3\frac{9}{10}$ $2\frac{9}{10}$

Complete. (pp. 186–193) 6D

16. 27 ft = 9 yd
17. 5 ft = 60 in.
18. 8,000 lb = 4 t

19. 4 lb 9 oz = 73 oz
20. 7 pt = 3 qt 1 pt

CHAPTER TEST • FORM A

(pp. 184–185, 194–195)

Solve.

21. Brigette and Anders collect 1950s records. The combined number of records they own is 260. If Anders owns 40 more than Brigette, how many does each person own?   Anders 150, Brigette 110

22. Brigette recently bought 5 records. Two were like new and 3 were in fair condition. Each of the like-new records cost $12 more than the ones which were in fair condition. If Brigette paid $64 for the 5 records, how much did each like-new record cost? $20

23. Five oranges and one banana cost $1.90. An orange and five bananas cost $2.30. How much does a banana cost? $.40

24. Mattie earns $12/h for a 40h week and $15/h for a 54 h week. How much did she earn if she worked forty 40 h weeks and eight 54 h weeks? $25,680

25. At the beginning of September, Mattie had $2,150.75 in her checking account. Before depositing her paycheck at the end of the month, she had a balance of $380.15. What was her average daily expenditure for the month? $59.02

PROBLEM SOLVING

Use the guess-and-check strategy to solve. *(pages 184–185)*

25. Two friends paid a total of $8.05 for their lunches of pizza and milk. Ben paid $.85 more than Cal. Pizza is $1.25 per slice and milk is $.70 per glass or $1.10 per container.

   a. How much in all did Ben and Cal spend on lunch? **$8.05**

   b. If they each ordered milk, what do you suppose is the largest number of pizza slices they could have ordered? **5 slices**

   c. What did each boy have for lunch? **Ben: 3 slices; glass of milk**
   Cal: 2 slices; container of milk

Use several steps to solve. *(pages 194–195)*

26. A restaurant uses an average of 3 lb 8 oz of butter per hour during the time it is open. If the restaurant is open 6 h/d every day, how much butter will be used in 2 wk? **294 lb**

Solve.

27. In a gym class competition, Jaime's two jumps were $12\frac{1}{2}$ ft and $9\frac{2}{3}$ ft. What was the combined distance of his jumps? $22\frac{1}{6}$ **ft**

LEARNING LOG

Write the answers in your learning log.   **Answers will vary. Suggestions given.**

1. Do you think a carrot would be a good standard unit of measure? Why or why not?
no; length not constant or standard

2. Study examples where you change from a smaller unit of measure to a larger unit of measure. Describe what happens and why. **The answer becomes smaller because it takes fewer large units to equal many small units.**

Note that the same numbers are used in Exercises 22 & 27.

CHAPTER 6   197

Items	Management Objective	Pages
1–9	**6D** Determine the appropriate customary units of length, capacity, and mass.	188–193
10–13	**6A** Add and subtract fractions and mixed numbers, same denominators.	172–173
14–20	**6B** Add and subtract fractions, different denominators.	174–177
21–24	**6C** Add and subtract mixed numbers, different denominators.	178–181
25–27	**6E** Problem Solving: Use guess and check. Multistep problems.	184–185; 194–195

Problem Solving

Item 25 has 3 parts:
a. literal—this is a reading comprehension question;
b. interpretive—this involves interpretation using the facts given;
c. applied—students use a strategy or skills to find an answer.

Item 22 in the skill section and item 27 in the problem solving section use the same numbers.

This will help you informally assess how your students transfer from numerical skills to word problems.

For scoring problem solving items you may wish to use partial credit. If a student uses the correct strategy but gets a wrong answer, give the student 2 points toward the total percent score.

Learning Log

These are suggestions for writing about some topics taught in this chapter. The students keep their Learning Logs from the beginning of the school year through the end.

CHAPTER TEST • FORM **B**

Find the sum or difference. Write the answer in lowest terms. (pp. 170–173) **6A**

1. $\frac{2}{9} + \frac{4}{9}$ $\frac{2}{3}$ **2.** $\frac{7}{10} - \frac{3}{10}$ $\frac{2}{5}$ **3.** $5\frac{7}{8} - 2\frac{5}{8}$ $3\frac{1}{4}$

4. $6\frac{2}{5} + 3\frac{3}{5}$ 10 **5.** $6\frac{7}{9} - 2\frac{1}{9}$ $4\frac{2}{3}$

Find the sum or difference. Write the answer in lowest terms. (pp. 174–177) **6B**

6. $\frac{3}{5} + \frac{7}{15}$ $1\frac{1}{15}$ **7.** $\frac{9}{10} - \frac{1}{4}$ $\frac{13}{20}$ **8.** $\frac{7}{10} + \frac{3}{20}$ $\frac{17}{20}$

9. $\frac{8}{15} - \frac{3}{10}$ $\frac{7}{30}$ **10.** $\frac{5}{8} + \frac{4}{5}$ $1\frac{17}{40}$

Find the sum or difference. Write the answer in lowest terms. (pp. 178–181) **6C**

11. $4\frac{1}{12} + 1\frac{3}{8}$ $5\frac{11}{24}$ **12.** $10\frac{2}{3} - 2\frac{3}{4}$ $7\frac{11}{12}$ **13.** $5\frac{1}{6} - 1\frac{5}{8}$ $3\frac{13}{24}$

14. $16 - 4\frac{7}{12}$ $11\frac{5}{12}$ **15.** $10 - 3\frac{2}{5}$ $6\frac{3}{5}$

Complete. (pp. 186–193) **6D**

16. 24 ft = 8 yd   **17.** 7 ft = 84 in.   **18.** 5 t = $10,000$ lb

19. 3 lb 10 oz = 58 oz   **20.** 11 qt = 2 gal 3 qt

CHAPTER TEST • FORM **B**

(pp. 184–185, 194–195)

Solve.

21. Doug and Leah collect video games. The combined number of games they own is 65. If Leah owns 15 more than Doug, how many video games does each person own? **Leah 40, Doug 25**

22. Yesterday Doug bought 7 video games—3 were in like-new condition and 4 were in fair condition. Each of the like-new games cost $12 more than the ones which were in fair condition. If Doug paid $92 for the 7 video games, how much did each like-new game cost? **$20**

23. 4 apples and one lemon cost $1.90. An apple and 4 lemons cost $1.60. How much does an apple cost? **$.40**

24. Last year Clint worked 8 h a day for 5 days a week and for 40 weeks. For 8 weeks in the summer he worked 9 h a day for 6 days a week. How many hours did he work last year? **2,032 h**

25. When Clint left home, the odometer on his car registered 12,691 mi. At the end of a 12h drive, it registered 13,291 mi. What was his average rate of speed for this period of time? **50 mi/h**

Error Analysis and Remediation

Here are some common errors students make when they are adding and subtracting fractions and using customary units. The errors are listed by lesson under the appropriate management objective.

6A • ADD AND SUBTRACT FRACTIONS AND MIXED NUMBERS, SAME DENOMINATORS

Source of Error (Lesson 6-2)
students add both the numerator and the denominator.
For example, $\frac{1}{3} + \frac{1}{3} = \frac{2}{6}$

Remediation
Demonstrate with fraction bars that the answer is not reasonable, emphasizing that $\frac{2}{6}$ is equivalent to $\frac{1}{3}$. Then have students use fraction bars to model several examples, including $\frac{3}{5} + \frac{3}{5}$ as example whose answer is greater than one.

6B • ADD AND SUBTRACT FRACTIONS, DIFFERENT DENOMINATORS

Source of Error (Lessons 6-3 and 6-4)
students have difficulty using the LCD to rename fractions.

Remediation
Have students list the multiples of each denominator and circle the common multiples. Emphasize that the least common multiple is the LCD for the fractions.

6C • ADD AND SUBTRACT MIXED NUMBERS, DIFFERENT DENOMINATORS

Source of Error (Lesson 6-5)
students have difficulty keeping their work in columns.
For example: $5\frac{7}{8} - 1\frac{1}{4}$

Remediation
Tell students to think of the example as two subtractions—one with whole numbers and one with fractions. Have them cover the whole numbers and subtract the fractions and then cover the fractions and subtract the whole numbers.

Source of Error (Lesson 6-6)
students make errors when renaming.

Remediation
Have students rename and show the steps next to the example before performing the subtraction.

6D • DETERMINE THE APPROPRIATE CUSTOMARY UNITS OF LENGTH, CAPACITY, AND MASS

Source of Error (Lessons 6-9, 6-10, 6-11)
students do not remember the relationships between commonly used units.

Remediation
Encourage memorization through use. Help students see the pattern of progression from smaller to larger units by showing them physical models of various units at the same time.

6E • PROBLEM SOLVING: USE GUESS AND CHECK. MULTISTEP PROBLEMS

Source of Error (Lesson 6-7)
students do not keep track of their guesses.

Remediation
Tell students to organize their information and develop a means for finding a pattern or a direction for further guesses. Emphasize that guess and check is most effective when it is systematic, not simply a series of random guesses.

Notes

Extra Practice

This page provides extra practice of all the major chapter objectives. Use this page after the chapter has been taught to reinforce the chapter skills. Page references are provided for each group of items so that students can easily look back at the appropriate lesson for additional support.

Write the answer in lowest terms. *(pages 172–181)*

1. $\frac{1}{8} + \frac{3}{8}$ $\frac{1}{2}$

2. $\frac{7}{10} - \frac{4}{10}$ $\frac{3}{10}$

3. $9\frac{3}{5} - 6\frac{1}{5}$ $3\frac{2}{5}$

4. $3\frac{5}{12} + 8\frac{4}{12}$ $11\frac{3}{4}$

5. $\frac{3}{7} - \frac{2}{14}$ $\frac{2}{7}$

6. $\frac{8}{9} + \frac{1}{18}$ $\frac{17}{18}$

7. $\frac{11}{20} + \frac{9}{40}$ $\frac{31}{40}$

8. $\frac{4}{16} + \frac{3}{8}$ $\frac{5}{8}$

9. $\frac{5}{12} + \frac{3}{6}$ $\frac{11}{12}$

10. $\frac{1}{8} + \frac{2}{4}$ $\frac{5}{8}$

11. $\frac{8}{10} - \frac{3}{5}$ $\frac{1}{5}$

12. $\frac{6}{12} + \frac{3}{4}$ $1\frac{1}{4}$

13. $\frac{4}{18} - \frac{1}{6}$ $\frac{1}{18}$

14. $\frac{5}{6} - \frac{2}{5}$ $\frac{13}{30}$

15. $\frac{1}{7} + \frac{1}{8}$ $\frac{15}{56}$

16. $\frac{4}{6} - \frac{1}{2}$ $\frac{1}{6}$

17. $\frac{6}{7} + \frac{2}{3}$ $1\frac{11}{21}$

18. $2\frac{1}{2} + 1\frac{3}{6}$ 4

19. $5\frac{2}{7} + 6\frac{1}{14}$ $11\frac{5}{14}$

20. $6\frac{3}{5} - \frac{2}{4}$ $6\frac{1}{10}$

21. $1\frac{8}{10} + 3\frac{1}{5}$ 5

22. $16 + 4\frac{1}{8}$ $20\frac{1}{8}$

23. $4\frac{4}{9} - 3\frac{1}{7}$ $1\frac{19}{63}$

24. $8\frac{1}{7} + 9\frac{1}{8}$ $17\frac{15}{56}$

25. $12 - 6\frac{1}{2}$ $5\frac{1}{2}$

26. $3 - 2\frac{5}{7}$ $\frac{2}{7}$

27. $3\frac{1}{6} - 2\frac{5}{6}$ $\frac{1}{3}$

28. $7\frac{3}{5} - 2\frac{3}{4}$ $4\frac{17}{20}$

Copy and complete. *(pages 188–193)*

29. 2 mi = ▬ ft   10,560

30. 17 ft = ▬ in.   204

31. 1 yd 11 in. = ▬ in.   47

32. 9 yd = ▬ in.   324

33. 20 pt = ▬ gal $2\frac{1}{2}$

34. 48 fl oz = ▬ pt   3

35. 32 gal = ▬ pt   256

36. 80 fl oz = ▬ c   10

37. 3 t = ▬ lb   6,000

38. 5 lb 3 oz = ▬ oz   83

39. 48 oz = ▬ lb   3

40. 16 lb = ▬ oz   256

Solve. *(pages 184–185, 194–195)*

41. Two friends compare their ages. The difference between their ages is 3 yr and the product of their ages is 238 yr. How old is the older friend?   **17 yr**

42. A fish tank is filled at the rate of $\frac{1}{2}$ gal/min. At that rate, how long will it take to put 14 gal into the tank?   **28 min**

A Stock Market Investment

Many people invest in the stock market to try to earn money. Buying shares in a company shows confidence in a company and its ability to be profitable. Because so many people have these investments, you can find daily reports on the stock market in newspapers and on radio and television.

Find the stock market news in the financial section of a newspaper. Choose five public companies to "invest" in. The stock market report will show the number of shares sold the day before, the final (closing) price of a share, and the daily change in price.

Pretend that you have bought 10 shares of stock in each company you chose at the closing price in the report. Notice that the price and change are given as fractions or mixed numbers, not decimals. Change the fraction to a decimal, rounded to the nearest hundredth.

Keep a daily record of the price of your shares for at least two weeks. Also, record the amount your stocks have gained or lost from the previous day. At the end of the two weeks, compare the price of each stock with the price when you "bought" it. Then multiply each final value by 10 for the 10 shares you "own." Did you make or lose money?
Check students' work.

NO CONNECTIONS

Copy the drawing. Use each number from 1 to 8 once. Fill the boxes so that no boxes that touch, even at corners, have consecutive numbers.
Check students' work.

MENUS OF MEALS

Plan menus for a weekend. Use cookbooks to decide what foods you need to include for balanced meals and how much of each food to buy. Make a grocery list and estimate how much the food will cost.
Check students' work.

Enrichment

This page contains activities that provide extension and enrichment for all levels of students. Depending on the needs of your students, you may wish to assign an activity from this page at certain points during the chapter, or you may want to use this page when the entire chapter has been completed.

A Stock Market Investment

Have on hand the stock market pages from several previous days. You may want to show some stock prices on the overhead projector to point out the high, low, and closing prices, along with the number of shares traded. You may wish to suggest that students select a varied portfolio of stocks to "buy"; some general types include electronics, utilities, foods, and chemicals.

Cumulative Review

The Cumulative Review focuses on skills covered in previous chapters. All important skills are reviewed on a cyclic basis.

If students are having difficulty with particular groups of exercises, refer to the chart for follow-up work.

CUMULATIVE REVIEW

Find the answer.

1. $\frac{16}{24} =$ **b**
a. $\frac{2}{4}$
b. $\frac{2}{3}$
c. $\frac{3}{4}$
d. none of these

2. $\frac{3}{5}$ is less than **a**
a. $\frac{5}{6}$
b. $\frac{3}{10}$
c. $\frac{1}{3}$
d. none of these

3. $\frac{5}{8} =$ **a**
a. 0.625
b. 1.6
c. 0.58
d. none of these

4. 3.125 = **d**
a. $3\frac{1}{4}$
b. $3\frac{1}{6}$
c. $3\frac{1}{12}$
d. none of these

5. $\frac{7}{10} - \frac{6}{12} =$ **b**
a. $\frac{1}{2}$
b. $\frac{1}{5}$
c. $\frac{1}{3}$
d. none of these

6. $\frac{3}{7} + \frac{5}{14} =$ **c**
a. $\frac{8}{14}$
b. $\frac{8}{21}$
c. $\frac{11}{14}$
d. none of these

7. 7 km = **b**
a. 700 m
b. 7,000 m
c. 0.007 m
d. none of these

8. 0.085 L = **a**
a. 85 mL
b. 850 mL
c. 8.5 mL
d. none of these

9. 1,400 g = **c**
a. 14 kg
b. 140 kg
c. 1.4 kg
d. none of these

Round to the given place.

10. 3,749 (tens) **d**
a. 3,700
b. 3,740
c. 4,000
d. none of these

11. 16,421 (hundreds) **c**
a. 16,000
b. 16,300
c. 16,400
d. none of these

12. 2.458 (tenths) **c**
a. 2.4
b. 2.46
c. 2.5
d. none of these

Items	Management Objective	Where Taught	Reteaching Options	Extra Practice Options
1–2	**5C** Write equivalent fractions and compare and order fractions.	pp. 144–147; 150–151	TE/RA 5-8 TRB/RW 5-7, 5-9 and 5-10	TRB/PW 5-7, 5-8, 5-9, and 5-10
3–4	**5D** Write fractions and mixed numbers as decimals and write decimals as fractions and mixed numbers.	pp. 152–153	TRB/RW 5-11	TRB/PW 5-11
5–6	**6B** Add and subtract fractions, different denominators.	pp. 174–177	TE/RA 6-3 TRB/RW 6-4	TRB/PW 6-3 and 6-4
7–9	**6D** Determine the appropriate customary units of length, capacity, and weight.	pp. 188–193	TRB/RW 6-9, 6-10, and 6-11	TRB/PW 6-9, 6-10, and 6-11
10–12	**1C** Round whole numbers and decimals.	pp. 14–15	TE/RA 1-7	TRB/PW 1-7

PROBLEM SOLVING REVIEW

Strategies may vary. Suggestions given.
Remember the strategies and types of problems you've had so far. Solve.

1. Three friends combine their money to buy a gift. Theresa has $2.50, Paula has $1.50, and Ann has $1\frac{1}{2}$ times as much as the other two together.

   a. How much does Paula have? **$1.50**

   b. How much does Ann have? **$6.00**

   c. How much more do they need to buy a $12.00 gift? **multistep; $2.00**

2. When John stands on the scale holding his cat, the scale shows 125 lb. John weighs 95 lb more than his cat. How much do John and his cat each weigh?
   guess and check; 110; 15

3. Three classes with 34 students each come to the auditorium. Four classes with 27 students each follow them. If the room has 600 seats, how many seats will still be empty?
   multistep; 390 seats

4. During a basketball game, 2 players drank 1.5 c of water each. The other 3 players drank 2.5 c each. How much water altogether did the players drink?
   multistep; 10.5 c

5. Mr. Jaskowiak uses the formula $C = \$3.00 + \$.12m$ to determine the cost (C) of traveling to work, where m is the distance in miles. What is the cost of a 15-mi round trip?
   formula; $4.80

6. The Pizza Palace allows the use of up to three $.55 coupons per pizza. To find the cost of a pizza, the owner uses the formula $C = \$9.00 - \$.55n$ where n is the number of coupons. What is the lowest cost for 1 pizza?
   formula; $7.35

7. Caesar can join the math club if he has a 90 average in math. His four test scores are 93, 83, 86, and 90. How much less than 90 is Caesar's average?
   multistep; 2 points

Is the answer *reasonable* or *unreasonable*? If unreasonable, explain why and find a reasonable answer.

8. Several friends had $2\frac{1}{3}$ mi to hike to reach their destination. They hiked $\frac{1}{3}$ of the way and rested. How far did they hike before resting?

   Answer: They hiked $1\frac{1}{6}$ mi.
   unreasonable; $1\frac{1}{6} \times 3 > 2\frac{1}{3}$;

   $\frac{7}{9}$

9. A dressmaker has 26 yd of fabric. If each dress requires 2.75 yd, how many dresses can be made from the fabric?

   Answer: 9 dresses
   reasonable

Problem Solving Review

This page focuses on problem solving strategies and types learned in this chapter and previous chapters. A problem solving checklist lists some of the strategies students may use to solve the problems on this page.

CHAPTER 6

Technology

This page is designed to provide calculator or computer experiences for all levels of students. The calculator or computer logo indicates the type of activity.

You may wish to assign these activities after the chapter has been taught or during the course of the chapter, depending on your needs and those of your students.

Math America

If students do not know how to begin, suggest that they need additional information: what is the cost of a ticket to the movies today?

Stack Them Up

Explain that the boxes do not need to remain in the position shown in the picture. You may wish to guide students to recognize that the problem becomes simpler to do on a calculator if the numbers are written as decimals first.

Digit Dilemma

Have students identify helpful clues; for example, the numerators in the first exercise have a sum of 7.

Although this can be considered a paper and pencil activity, software is found in Houghton Mifflin Math Activities Courseware, Grade 7.

TECHNOLOGY

DID YOU KNOW . . . ?

Admission to a movie was 25¢ in the late 1930s. How much more money would a theater that holds 125 people take in now than in the late 1930s? **Answers will vary. $718.75, if ticket costs $6.00 now.**

STACK THEM UP

The dimensions of three boxes are shown below. How can you arrange them in a stack so that the total height is $9\frac{7}{16}$ in.? $3\frac{1}{4} + 3\frac{5}{16} + 2\frac{7}{8}$

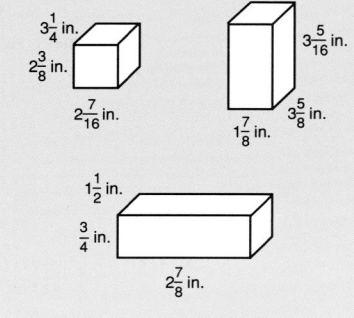

$3\frac{1}{4}$ in.
$2\frac{3}{8}$ in.
$2\frac{7}{16}$ in.

$3\frac{5}{16}$ in.
$1\frac{7}{8}$ in.
$3\frac{5}{8}$ in.

$1\frac{1}{2}$ in.
$\frac{3}{4}$ in.
$2\frac{7}{8}$ in.

DIGIT DILEMMA

In the computer activity *Fraction Challenge I,* you place the digits from 1 to 9 into the fraction equations to form true statements. For this pencil-and-paper activity, you supply missing digits to form fraction equations. See below.

Use each digit only once for the set of equations. You won't need all the digits for Set 1, but you will use all of them for Set 2. All fractions must be in lowest terms.

Digits:

1 2 3 4 5 6 7 8 9

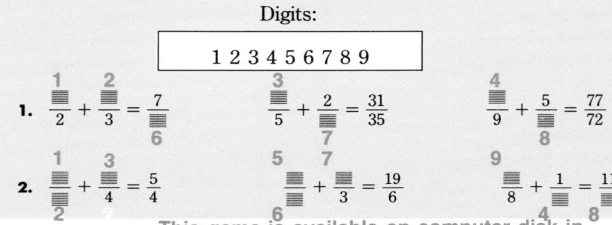

1. $\dfrac{1}{2} + \dfrac{2}{3} = \dfrac{7}{6}$ $\dfrac{3}{5} + \dfrac{2}{\square} = \dfrac{31}{35}$ $\dfrac{4}{9} + \dfrac{5}{\square} = \dfrac{77}{72}$

2. $\dfrac{1}{2} + \dfrac{3}{4} = \dfrac{5}{4}$ $\dfrac{5}{6} + \dfrac{7}{3} = \dfrac{19}{6}$ $\dfrac{9}{8} + \dfrac{1}{4} = \dfrac{11}{8}$

This game is available on computer disk in
202 TECHNOLOGY Houghton Mifflin *Mathematics Activities Courseware.*

Software Activities

Note: To leave the program, students should use the ESCAPE or QUIT command for their computers.

activity 1 • CAREER INVESTIGATIONS

MATERIALS: database, graphing, and word-processing programs

Procedure: Have students survey adults to identify the degree (often, sometimes, seldom, or never) to which academic areas such as communication skills, mathematics, and use of computers are emphasized in their professions. Students should enter their results into a database file with fields: *Profession,* and each *Academic Area.* Have students sort the file for each *Academic Area* and degree of use. Students should prepare circle graphs identifying the academic area and the percent of total responses for each degree of use.

Follow-up: Using word-processing programs, have the students interpret the data and write about the academic areas they should emphasize for their career goals.

activity 2 • SUMMING FRACTIONS

MATERIALS: BASIC programming

Procedure: This program will add fractions that are input by the student. Have students enter the program and run it several times.

```
10 PRINT "TO ADD FRACTIONS, TYPE IN
   YOUR "
20 PRINT "NUMBERS AS FOLLOWS: "
30 PRINT "1,2,3,4 FOR THE FRACTIONS
   1/2 AND 3/4 "
40 INPUT "WHAT ARE THE NUMBERS";
   A,B,C,D
50 PRINT "YOUR FRACTIONS ARE
   ";A"/"B " AND "C"/"D
60 PRINT "YOUR SUM IS
   ";(A*D+B*C);"/";(B*D)
70 PRINT: PRINT: GOTO 10
```

Follow-up: Challenge students to modify the program so that the answer is always expressed in lowest terms.

HOUGHTON MIFFLIN SOFTWARE

Easy Graph. Boston, MA: Houghton Mifflin Company, 1987. For Apple II, Commodore, IBM.

EduCalc. Boston, MA: Houghton Mifflin Company, 1990. For Apple II, Commodore, IBM.

Friendly Filer. Boston, MA: Houghton Mifflin Company, 1989. For Apple II, Commodore, IBM.

Mathematics Activities Courseware. Boston, MA: Houghton Mifflin Company, 1983. For Apple II, IBM.

The Computer Tutor. Boston, MA: Houghton Mifflin Company, 1990. For Apple II, IBM.

OTHER SOFTWARE

Conquering Fractions (+,−). St. Paul, MN: MECC, 1988. For Apple II.

Fast Track Fractions. Allen, TX: DLM, 1989. For Apple II.

Fractions: Add & Subtract. Big Spring, TX: Gamco Industries, Inc., 1989. For Apple II.

Microsoft Works. Redmond, WA: Microsoft Corporation, 1989. For Macintosh, IBM.

Partial Fractions. Pleasantville, NY: Sunburst Communications, 1986. For Apple II, Commodore, IBM.

Pizza Fractions. Fairfield, CT: HRM/Queue Software, Inc., 1989. For Apple II, IBM.

Super Paint. San Diego, CA: Silicon Beach Software, 1988. For Macintosh.

Multiplying and Dividing Fractions

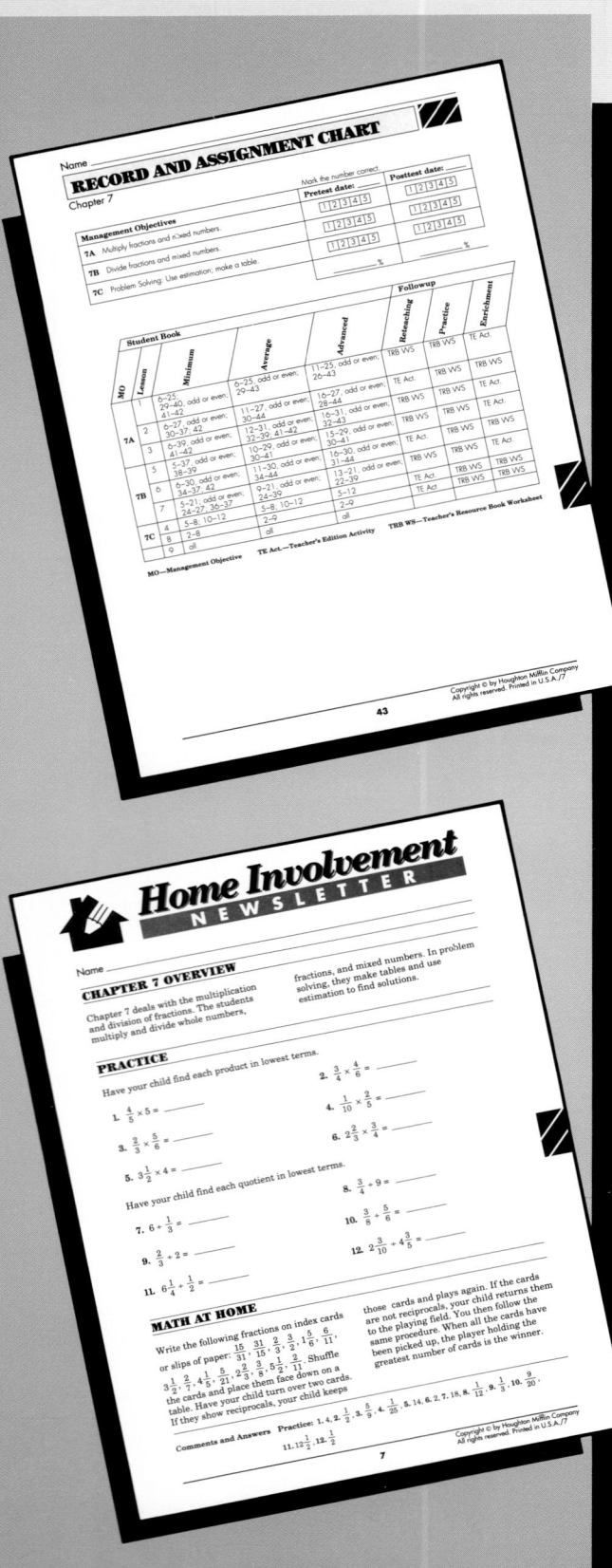

In Chapter 7, students continue to build on the fraction concepts developed thus far. They multiply and divide fractions by whole numbers, other fractions, and mixed numbers, learning to estimate answers and evaluate the reasonableness of their solutions.

Problem solving lessons stress using estimation and making a table to organize information given in a problem.

Management Objectives

7A Multiply fractions and mixed numbers.
7B Divide fractions and mixed numbers.
7C Problem Solving: Use estimation. Make a table.

Assignments for different achievement levels are provided on the Record and Assignment Chart in the Teacher's Resource Book.

Home Involvement

As you begin to teach this chapter, give each student a copy of the Home Involvement Newsletter for this chapter.

This newsletter provides parents with
■ an overview of the chapter
■ suggestions for practicing some of the skills in the chapter
■ an at-home activity to do with their child, applying the skills taught in the chapter.

Vocabulary

canceling, page 204
reciprocals, page 208

Management Chart

	Management Objectives	Lesson/ Pages	Student Not Successful	Student Needs More Practice	Student Successful	Pacing Range
7A	Multiply fractions and mixed numbers.	7-1/204-205	TRB/RW 7-1	TRB/PW 7-1 CSP FM Skills 1, 2 CT Unit 2 Obj. 6.1	TE/EA 7-1	3-4 days
		7-2/206-207	TE/RA 7-2	TRB/PW 7-2 CSP FM Skill 3	TRB/EW 7-2	
		7-3 208-209	TRB/RW 7-3	TRB/PW 7-3 CSP FM Skills 1-4 CT Unit 2 Obj. 6.2	TE/EA 7-3	
7B	Divide fractions and mixed numbers.	7-5/214-215	TRB/RW 7-5	TRB/PW 7-5 CSP FD Skills 1, 2	TE/EA 7-5	3-4 days
		7-6/216-217	TE/RA 7-6	TRB/PW 7-6 CSP FD Skill 3 CT Unit 2 Obj. 7.1	TRB/EW 7-6	
		7-7/218-219	TRB/RW 7-7	TRB/PW 7-7 CSP FD Skills 4-6 MAC 7 Activity 7 MAC 6 Activity 10	TE/EA 7-7 MAC 7 Activity 7 MAC 6 Activity 10 MAC 8 Activity 4	
7C	Problem Solving: Use estimation. Make a table.	7-4/210-211	TE/RA 7-4	TRB/PW 7-4	TRB/EW 7-4	2 days
		7-8/220-221	TE/RA 7-8 ED, FF	TRB/PW 7-8 ED, FF	TRB/EW 7-8 ED, FF	

Creative Problem Solving	222-223
Chapter Checkups	212-213; 224-225
Extra Practice	236
Enrichment	227
Cumulative Review/ Problem Solving Review	228-229
Technology	230

TE = Teacher's Edition
TRB = Teacher's Resource Book
RW = Reteaching Worksheet
RA = Reteaching Activity
EA = Enrichment Activity
EW = Enrichment Worksheet
PW = Practice Worksheet
CA = Classroom Activity

*Other Available Items
MAC = Mathematics Activities Courseware
CSP = Computational Skills Program
CT = Computer Tutor
FF = Friendly Filer
ED = EduCalc

CHAPTER 7

Manipulative Planning Guide

This is a complete list of manipulatives and materials needed for Chapter 7.

Materials for Manipulatives	TE Activities (INTRODUCE)	Student Book Lesson
Teaching Aid 3* for each student	Lessons 7-1, 7-9	
Teaching Aid 7*	Lesson 7-3	
Math Connection Transparency		Lessons 7-2, 7-3, 7-7
Calculator for each student		Lessons 7-1, 7-2, 7-3
Base-ten rods, 20 in all; rubberbands	Lesson 7-5	
Quart-size measuring container; two measuring cups; water or sand		Lesson 7-5
Teaching Aid 6*	Lesson 7-1	
Teaching Aid 4* or fraction bars for each student	Lesson 7-6	Lesson 7-6
Blank spinners		
Construction paper, one sheet for each pair	Lesson 7-7	
Inch ruler for each group	Lesson 7-7	Lesson 7-9
Index cards		
Strips of paper, four for each pair		
Colored pencils		
Teaching Aid 15*		Lesson 7-9

*Teaching Aids are found in the Teacher's Resource Book.

Learning Stages

The concepts and skills in Chapter 7 are presented through these learning stages.

CONCRETE

Using manipulatives and verbalizing about a concept. No symbols.

Teacher Edition Activities	Student Book
Lessons 7-5, 7-6	

Enrichment	Reteaching	In the Houghton Mifflin Manipulative Kit?	In the Houghton Mifflin Overhead Kit?
			Yes
			Yes
			Available separately
		Yes	
	Lesson 7-6	Yes	Yes
Lesson 7-3		Yes	
Lesson 7-5		Yes	
Lessons 7-1, 7-7			
	Lesson 7-2		
	Lesson 7-2		
Lesson 7-9		Yes	Yes

CONNECTING

    → 5¢ 9cm^2 $\frac{1}{3}$

Making a connection between manipulatives and symbols.

Teacher Edition Activities	Student Book
Lessons 7-1, 7-2, 7-3, 7-7, 7-8, 7-9	Lessons 7-1, 7-2, 7-5, 7-6

SYMBOLIC

$\$.05$ $A = 9\text{cm}^2$ $1 - \frac{2}{3} = \frac{1}{3}$

Using numbers or symbols. No manipulatives or pictures of manipulatives.

Teacher Edition Activities	Student Book
Lesson 7-4	Lessons 7-3, 7-4, 7-7, 7-8, 7-9

Additional Activities

COOPERATIVE LEARNING RESOURCE ACTIVITIES

Through cooperative learning activities, students learn by interacting with one another in small groups. These cooperative activities provide students with motivating settings for making connections, investigations, and problem solving situations.

The cooperative connections are interdisciplinary problem-solving projects. Each student has a particular job that helps lead the group to complete the project. For the cooperative investigations students work in pairs for investigations involving data collection and analysis. The cooperative problem solving activities encourage the sharing of ideas and information. Students work in groups of four to solve a problem. Students are each assigned a clue and work together to find a common solution.

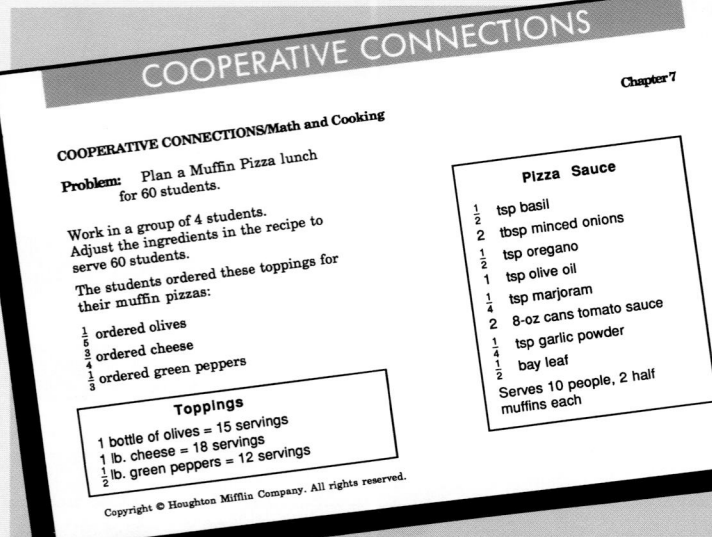

COOPERATIVE CONNECTIONS

COOPERATIVE CONNECTIONS/Math and Cooking

Chapter 7

Problem: Plan a Muffin Pizza lunch for 60 students.

Work in a group of 4 students. Adjust the ingredients in the recipe to serve 60 students.

The students ordered these toppings for their muffin pizzas:

$\frac{1}{5}$ ordered olives
$\frac{3}{4}$ ordered cheese
$\frac{1}{3}$ ordered green peppers

Toppings

1 bottle of olives = 15 servings
1 lb. cheese = 18 servings
$\frac{1}{2}$ lb. green peppers = 12 servings

Pizza Sauce

$\frac{1}{2}$ tsp basil
2 tbsp minced onions
$\frac{1}{2}$ tsp oregano
1 tsp olive oil
$\frac{1}{4}$ tsp marjoram
2 8-oz cans tomato sauce
$\frac{1}{2}$ tsp garlic powder
$\frac{1}{2}$ bay leaf
Serves 10 people, 2 half muffins each

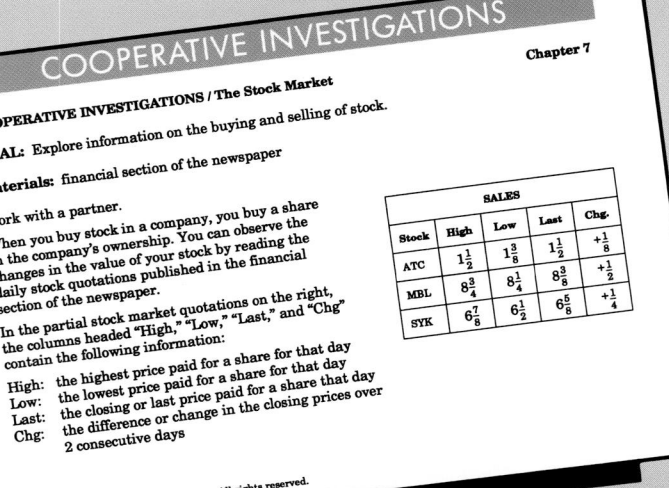

COOPERATIVE INVESTIGATIONS

COOPERATIVE INVESTIGATIONS / The Stock Market

Chapter 7

GOAL: Explore information on the buying and selling of stock.

Materials: financial section of the newspaper

Work with a partner.

When you buy stock in a company, you buy a share in the company's ownership. You can observe the changes in the value of your stock by reading the daily stock quotations published in the financial section of the newspaper.

In the partial stock market quotations on the right, the columns headed "High," "Low," "Last," and "Chg" contain the following information:

	SALES			
Stock	High	Low	Last	Chg.
ATC	$1\frac{1}{2}$	$1\frac{3}{8}$	$1\frac{1}{2}$	$+\frac{1}{8}$
MBL	$8\frac{3}{4}$	$8\frac{1}{4}$	$8\frac{3}{8}$	$+\frac{1}{2}$
SYK	$6\frac{7}{8}$	$6\frac{1}{2}$	$6\frac{5}{8}$	$+\frac{1}{4}$

High: the highest price paid for a share for that day
Low: the lowest price paid for a share for that day
Last: the closing or last price paid for a share that day
Chg: the difference or change in the closing prices over 2 consecutive days

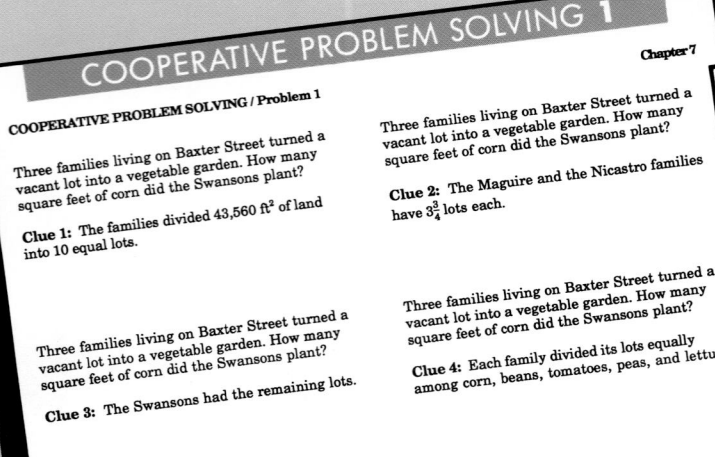

COOPERATIVE PROBLEM SOLVING 1

COOPERATIVE PROBLEM SOLVING / Problem 1

Chapter 7

Three families living on Baxter Street turned a vacant lot into a vegetable garden. How many square feet of corn did the Swansons plant?

Clue 1: The families divided 43,560 ft² of land into 10 equal lots.

Three families living on Baxter Street turned a vacant lot into a vegetable garden. How many square feet of corn did the Swansons plant?

Clue 3: The Swansons had the remaining lots.

Three families living on Baxter Street turned a vacant lot into a vegetable garden. How many square feet of corn did the Swansons plant?

Clue 2: The Maguire and the Nicastro families have $3\frac{3}{4}$ lots each.

Three families living on Baxter Street turned a vacant lot into a vegetable garden. How many square feet of corn did the Swansons plant?

Clue 4: Each family divided its lots equally among corn, beans, tomatoes, peas, and lettuce.

COOPERATIVE PROBLEM SOLVING 2

COOPERATIVE PROBLEM SOLVING / Problem 2

Chapter 7

Emil's Music Store got a shipment of CDs on Monday. What part of the shipment was still for sale on Friday?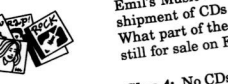

Clue 1: Emil sold $\frac{1}{3}$ of the CDs by Monday afternoon.

Emil's Music Store got a shipment of CDs on Monday. What part of the shipment was still for sale on Friday?

Clue 3: On Tuesday Emil sold $\frac{1}{2}$ of the remaining CDs.

Emil's Music Store got a shipment of CDs on Monday. What part of the shipment was still for sale on Friday?

Clue 2: On Wednesday $\frac{1}{3}$ of the CDs sold on Monday and Tuesday were returned.

Emil's Music Store got a shipment of CDs on Monday. What part of the shipment was still for sale on Friday?

Clue 4: No CDs were sold on Wednesday, but on Thursday Emil sold $\frac{2}{5}$ of his remaining supply.

GAMES

MULTIPLICATION BINGO (For use after Lesson 7-1)

Objective: Multiply fractions.

☑ **MATERIALS CHECKLIST:** 15 index cards, paper, ruler, and scissors for each student

Write these exercises on index cards, one per card:

$$\frac{1}{2}\times\frac{1}{3}=\frac{1}{6} \qquad \frac{1}{2}\times\frac{3}{4}=\frac{3}{8} \qquad \frac{5}{6}\times\frac{1}{2}=\frac{5}{12}$$

$$\frac{7}{8}\times\frac{1}{2}=\frac{7}{16} \qquad \frac{5}{6}\times\frac{1}{6}=\frac{5}{36} \qquad \frac{4}{5}\times\frac{7}{8}=\frac{7}{10}$$

$$\frac{1}{6}\times\frac{7}{8}=\frac{7}{48} \qquad \frac{1}{3}\times\frac{1}{6}=\frac{1}{18} \qquad \frac{3}{4}\times\frac{1}{6}=\frac{1}{8}$$

$$\frac{2}{3}\times\frac{5}{6}=\frac{5}{9} \qquad \frac{2}{3}\times\frac{1}{3}=\frac{2}{9} \qquad \frac{3}{4}\times\frac{2}{3}=\frac{1}{2}$$

$$\frac{4}{5}\times\frac{3}{4}=\frac{3}{5} \qquad \frac{4}{5}\times\frac{1}{3}=\frac{4}{15} \qquad \frac{7}{8}\times\frac{2}{3}=\frac{7}{12}$$

Have each player prepare a 4×4 grid and cut out small squares of paper to use as game markers. As you call out the products from the exercises and the fraction $\frac{2}{3}$, ask students to write one fraction in each space on their grids.

To begin play, place the mixed cards in a stack. Pick the top card, and read the factors. Players find the product (they may use pencil and paper), covering it on their grids. Repeat with a new card. The first player to complete a row or column correctly wins.

TARGET ZERO (For use after Lesson 7-7)

Objective: Multiply, divide, and compare fractions.

☑ **MATERIALS CHECKLIST:** two number cubes and a spinner for each group of students

This game should be played by groups of four or six students. Give each group two number cubes and a spinner divided into four equal sections showing Multiply, Divide, Multiply, Divide.

Two students play at a time. Each player tosses the number cubes twice to generate four digits to form two fractions. Then each player spins to determine his or her operation. The object of the game is to write an exercise—multiplying or dividing fractions depending on the spin—so that the result is as close as possible to zero. The other players check the results and determine which answer is closer to zero. The closer answer is worth two points; equally close answers are worth one point each; and a wrong answer earns no points. The procedure is repeated for other pairs. The player with the most points at the end is the winner.

BULLETIN BOARD

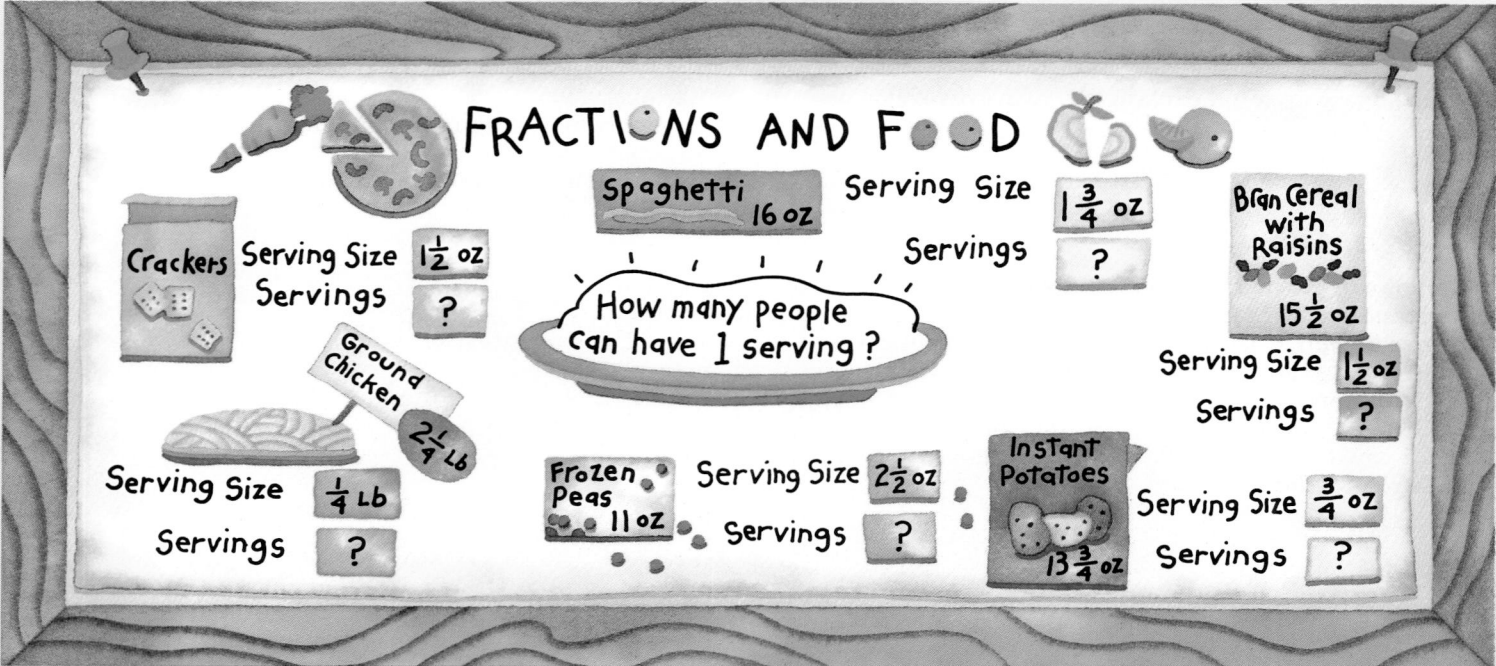

Collect empty food packaging made from cardboard or paper, and labels from cans. Make certain that the size of the product is given. Tack the packaging to the bulletin board to create a "Fractions and Food" display. List a suggested serving size, and ask students to find out how many people can be served from each product. Have students write their results on index cards and attach them to the display. Encourage students to bring in new items for the bulletin board.

Alternative Assessment

In addition to the paper and pencil tests available with this program, the following items can help you assess critical thinking as well as your students' ability to solve problems in a wide variety of ways.

Open-ended Problem

When you multiply two fractions, you can change the order and still get the same answer. For example, $\frac{1}{2} \times \frac{1}{3} = \frac{1}{6}$ and $\frac{1}{3} \times \frac{1}{2} = \frac{1}{6}$.

Explore whether the same relationship is true when you divide two fractions. Example: Does $\frac{1}{2} \div \frac{1}{3}$ equal $\frac{1}{3} \div \frac{1}{2}$? Try several examples and describe a pattern if one develops.

Teacher Notes

$\frac{1}{2} \div \frac{1}{3} = \frac{1}{2} \times \frac{3}{1} = \frac{3}{2}$ but $\frac{1}{3} \div \frac{1}{2} = \frac{1}{3} \times \frac{2}{1} = \frac{2}{3}$

When one changes the order of the fractions in a division problem, the resulting answers are the reciprocals of each other.

Group Writing Activity (See p. T24.)

These two models were used to compare the products 1.25×1.5 and $1\frac{1}{4} \times 1\frac{1}{2}$. How are the models similar? (Reproduce these drawings for the students.)

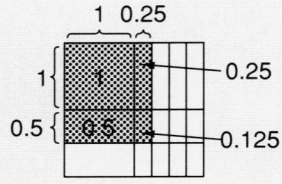
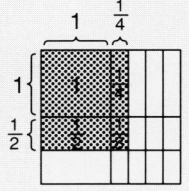

Teacher Notes

$1.875 = 1\frac{7}{8} (1 + \frac{1}{2} + \frac{1}{4} + \frac{1}{8} = 1 + \frac{4+2+1}{8} = 1\frac{7}{8})$

$1.25 = 1\frac{1}{4}$

$1.5 = 1\frac{1}{2}$

$0.25 = \frac{1}{4}$

$0.5 = \frac{1}{2}$

$0.125 = \frac{1}{8}$

Individual Writing Activity

Describe how you would explain to a fifth grader how to multiply $1\frac{1}{5} \times 1\frac{1}{2}$.

Teacher Notes

Students may explain by changing the mixed numbers to improper fractions or to decimals, by using a diagram, or by using the Distributive Property.

Portfolios

Portfolios can provide information about a student's growth in mathematical understanding over a period of time. They can help you make instructional decisions as well as become a vehicle for communicating with parents. The students' work involving the open-ended problem and writing activity suggested on this page along with work on the Critical Thinking features on pages 209 and 217, the Create Your Own exercise on page 211, the Learning Log exercises on pages 213 and 225, and the Creative Problem Solving lesson on pages 222-223 could be included in portfolios.

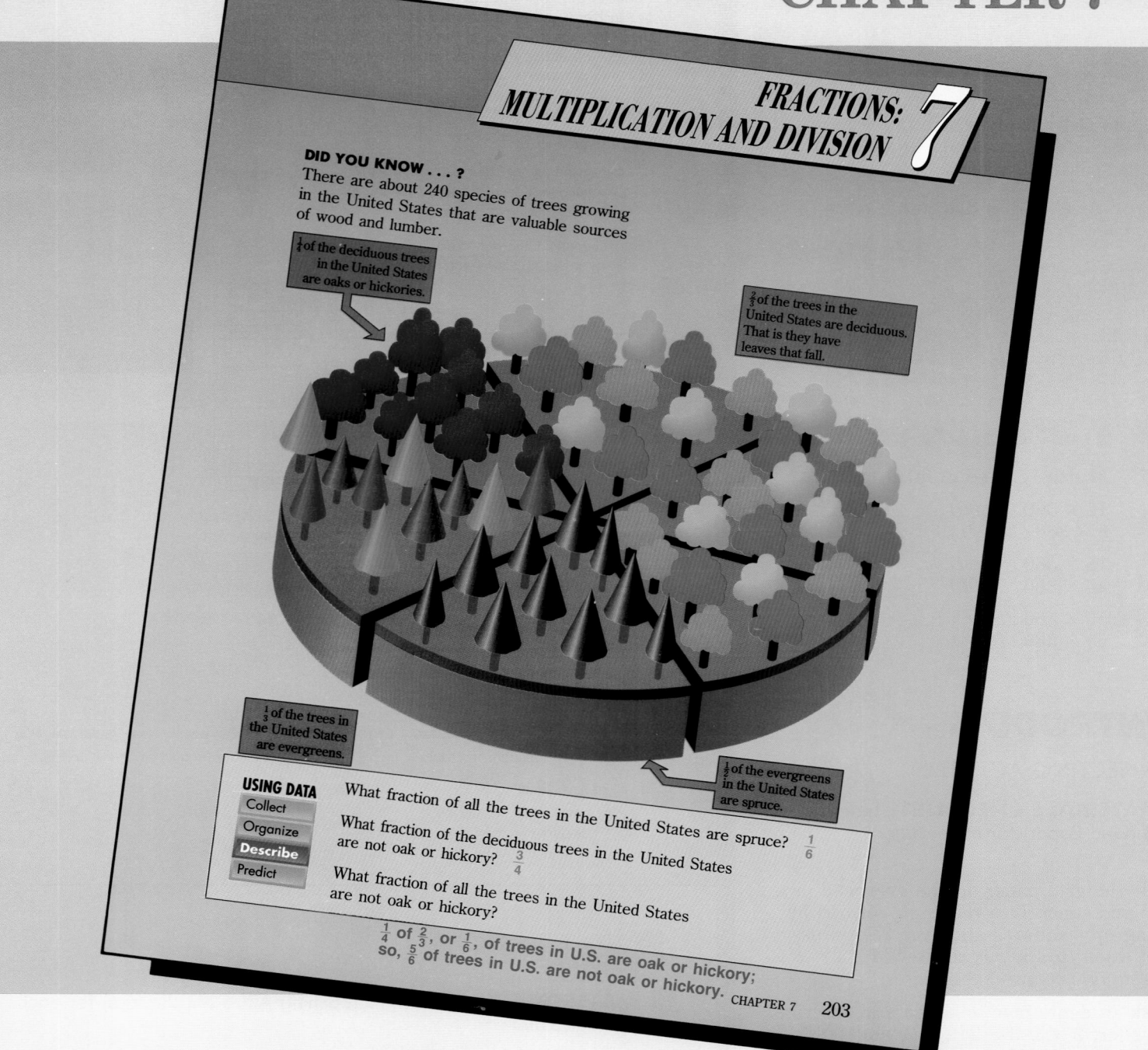

FRACTIONS:
MULTIPLICATION AND DIVISION 7

DID YOU KNOW . . . ?
There are about 240 species of trees growing
in the United States that are valuable sources
of wood and lumber.

¼ of the deciduous trees
in the United States
are oaks or hickories.

⅔ of the trees in the
United States are deciduous.
That is they have
leaves that fall.

⅓ of the trees in
the United States
are evergreens.

½ of the evergreens
in the United States
are spruce.

USING DATA

Collect

Organize

Describe

Predict

What fraction of all the trees in the United States are spruce? ⅙

What fraction of the deciduous trees in the United States
are not oak or hickory? ¾

What fraction of all the trees in the United States
are not oak or hickory?

¼ of ⅔, or ⅙, of trees in U.S. are oak or hickory;
so, ⅚ of trees in U.S. are not oak or hickory. CHAPTER 7   203

Using the Chapter Opener

The purpose of this page is to involve the student in the
use of real data much like that presented in newspapers
and magazines.

To use this page as you begin the chapter, direct students'
attention to the data. You may wish to ask questions
such as the following:

**What fraction of all the trees in the United States are
not spruce?** ($\frac{5}{6}$) **How do you know?** *(If $\frac{1}{6}$ of all the trees
are spruce, then $\frac{5}{6}$ of all the trees are not spruce.)*

**What do you need to do to determine what fraction
of all the trees in the United States are trees other
than spruce, oak, and hickory?** *(Determine the two
fractions representing spruce, oak, and hickory; add the
two fractions together, subtract the sum from 1.)*

**What fraction of all trees are trees other than spruce,
oak, and hickory?** ($\frac{2}{3}$)

**If all the evergreen trees were divided evenly among
the fifty states, what fractional part of all the trees
would be the evergreens in each state?** ($\frac{1}{150}$)

Lesson Organizer

Objective: Multiply fractions.

Prior Knowledge: Students should be able to multiply whole numbers and decimals and should understand the concept of fractions.

Error Analysis and Remediation: See page 225A.

Lesson Resources:
Practice Worksheet 7-1
Reteaching Worksheet 7-1
Enrichment Activity 7-1
Daily Review 7-1

Two-Minute Math

Multiply. Use mental math.

10×360 *(3,600)*
5×360 *(1,800)*

15×360 *(5,400)*
20×360 *(7,200)*

50×360 *(18,000)*
55×360 *(19,800)*

1 INTRODUCE

CONNECTING ACTIVITY

☑ **MATERIALS CHECKLIST:** Teaching Aid 3 (Grid Paper) for each student

1. Put the grid paper on the overhead projector and shade in a rectangle formed by moving up 4 squares and over 2 squares. **What does this array show?** *(4 × 2 = 8; the rectangle contains 8 squares.)*

2. Ask students how to shade and describe arrays for: 2 × 3; 3 × 2; 2 × 2; and 1 × 1. *(Students should describe the "up and over" movements.)*

3. How would you make an array to show $\frac{1}{6} \times \frac{3}{5}$? *(Move up $\frac{1}{6}$ of a square, then over $\frac{3}{5}$.)* **Is $\frac{1}{6} \times \frac{3}{5}$ greater than or less than 1?** *(less than 1)*

WHEN YOUR STUDENTS ASK
★ WHY AM I LEARNING THIS? ★

You can connect this skill to real life through sports. For example, $\frac{1}{3}$ of the first half of the game is over. What fractional part of the whole game is left to play?

MATH AND GEOGRAPHY

Multiplying Fractions

About three fifths of the population of South America live in Brazil and Argentina. About $\frac{1}{6}$ of the people in these two countries live in the cities of São Paulo and Buenos Aires. What fraction of the population of South America is that?

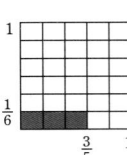

Brazil
São Paulo
Buenos Aires
Argentina

You must find $\frac{1}{6}$ of $\frac{3}{5}$, or multiply $\frac{1}{6} \times \frac{3}{5}$.

Find the product by:

- representing the total population with a square grid divided into sixths and fifths
- shading a part that is $\frac{1}{6}$ by $\frac{3}{5}$

First think about the denominators. Shade by going up sixths and over fifths.

$$\frac{1}{6} \times \frac{3}{5} = \frac{}{?}$$

Since the square has 30 parts, the denominator of the answer is 30.

Now think about the numerators. Shade by going up $\frac{1}{6}$ and over $\frac{3}{5}$.

$$\frac{1}{6} \times \frac{3}{5} = \frac{?}{30}$$

What part of the square is shaded? $\frac{1}{10}$
What is the numerator of the product? 1

$$\frac{1}{6} \times \frac{3}{5} = \frac{1 \times 3}{6 \times 5} = \frac{3}{30} = \frac{1}{10}$$

About $\frac{1}{10}$ of all South Americans live in São Paulo and Buenos Aires.

> **To multiply fractions, multiply the numerators. Then multiply the denominators. Write the resulting fraction in lowest terms.**

To save time, you can divide out common factors before multiplying. This process is called **canceling**.

$$\frac{1}{6} \times \frac{3}{5} = \frac{1}{\underset{2}{6}} \times \frac{\overset{1}{3}}{5} = \frac{1}{10}$$

━━ **GUIDED PRACTICE** ━━

Draw a square diagram for each.

1. $\frac{1}{3}$ of $\frac{1}{2}$ **2.** $\frac{2}{3} \times \frac{3}{5}$
Check students' drawings.

Multiply. Write the product in lowest terms.

3. $\frac{4}{5}$ of $\frac{5}{8}$ **4.** $\frac{2}{3} \times \frac{3}{7}$ **5.** $\frac{4}{7} \times \frac{4}{5}$
$\frac{1}{2}$ $\frac{2}{7}$ $\frac{16}{35}$

204   LESSON 7–1

---

2 TEACH

☑ **MATERIALS CHECKLIST:** Teaching Aid 6 (Big Square) for each student, calculators

Show the big square on the overhead projector. **Why can you model $\frac{1}{6} \times \frac{3}{5}$ within this square?** *(Both factors are less than 1; the answer will be less than 1.)*

Mark off the vertical side in 6 parts. **Why do you show 6 parts?** *(so you can move up $\frac{1}{6}$).* **How should you mark off the horizontal side? Explain.** *(in 5 parts, so you can move over $\frac{3}{5}$)* Shade in the part of the square that is $\frac{1}{6}$ by $\frac{3}{5}$.

Chalkboard Examples

Write the product in lowest terms.

$$\frac{3}{5} \times \frac{5}{6} \qquad \frac{5}{12} \times \frac{2}{3} \qquad \frac{3}{8} \times \frac{2}{5}$$
$$\left(\frac{1}{2}; \frac{5}{18}; \frac{3}{20}\right)$$

SUMMARIZE/ASSESS Use the Big Square to show $\frac{2}{3}$ of $\frac{1}{3}$.

━━━━━━━━━━━━━━━━ **PRACTICE** ━━━━━━━━━━━━━━━━

Write the product in lowest terms.

6. $\frac{3}{7}$ of $\frac{4}{5}$ $\frac{12}{35}$ **7.** $\frac{3}{5}$ of $\frac{2}{9}$ $\frac{2}{15}$ **8.** $\frac{5}{8} \times \frac{0}{7}$ 0   **9.** $\frac{1}{6} \times \frac{3}{5}$ $\frac{1}{10}$ **10.** $\frac{5}{10} \times \frac{7}{10}$ $\frac{7}{20}$

11. $\frac{3}{4} \times \frac{5}{6}$ $\frac{5}{8}$ **12.** $\frac{7}{8} \times \frac{5}{7}$ $\frac{5}{8}$ **13.** $\frac{5}{4} \times \frac{4}{5}$ 1   **14.** $\frac{9}{8} \times \frac{8}{9}$ 1   **15.** $\frac{7}{8} \times \frac{1}{6}$ $\frac{7}{48}$

16. $\frac{2}{5} \times \frac{3}{5}$ $\frac{6}{25}$ **17.** $\frac{7}{9} \times \frac{3}{7}$ $\frac{1}{3}$ **18.** $\frac{1}{8} \times \frac{6}{7}$ $\frac{3}{28}$ **19.** $\frac{5}{2} \times \frac{2}{5}$ 1   **20.** $\frac{4}{5} \times \frac{1}{10}$ $\frac{2}{25}$

21. $\frac{0}{4} \times \frac{5}{6}$ 0   **22.** $\frac{1}{5} \times \frac{12}{20}$ $\frac{3}{25}$ **23.** $\frac{7}{8} \times \frac{2}{14}$ $\frac{1}{8}$ **24.** $\frac{1}{10} \times \frac{50}{100}$ $\frac{1}{20}$ **25.** $\frac{0}{12} \times \frac{0}{8}$ 0

26. $\frac{1}{5} \times \frac{5}{6} \times \frac{1}{6}$ $\frac{1}{36}$ *27. $\frac{2}{3} \times \frac{1}{2} \times \frac{1}{4}$ $\frac{1}{12}$ *28. $\frac{7}{8} \times \frac{4}{5} \times \frac{1}{3}$ $\frac{7}{30}$

MIXED REVIEW Compute.

29. 95×76 7,220   **30.** $\frac{1}{3} + 6\frac{1}{2}$ $6\frac{5}{6}$ **31.** $216 \div 6$ 36   **32.** $15 - 1\frac{7}{8}$ $13\frac{1}{8}$

33. 0.4×0.11 0.044 **34.** $19 - 1.63$ 17.37 **35.** $2.4 \div 0.2$ 12   **36.** $0.24 + 0.9$ 1.14

CALCULATOR Use a calculator to solve.

37. $\frac{3}{5} \times 0.42$ 0.252   **38.** $0.09 \times \frac{7}{8}$ 0.07875   **39.** $\frac{3}{4} \times 1.36$ 1.02   **40.** $\frac{5}{8} \times 4.9$ 3.0625

━━━━━━━━━━━━━━━━ **PRACTICE** ━━━━━━━━━━━━━━━━

CHOOSE Use the circle graph. Choose mental math or paper and pencil to solve. Write your answers in lowest terms.   Choices will vary. Suggestions given.

41. About $\frac{1}{7}$ of the population of Venezuela live in the capital city of Caracas. What fraction of the population of South America is in Caracas? m; $\frac{1}{175}$

42. About $\frac{7}{20}$ of Chile's population live in the capital city of Santiago. What fraction of South Americans live in Santiago? p; $\frac{7}{400}$

43. What fraction of South America's population live in Peru, Brazil, or Venezuela? p; $\frac{61}{100}$

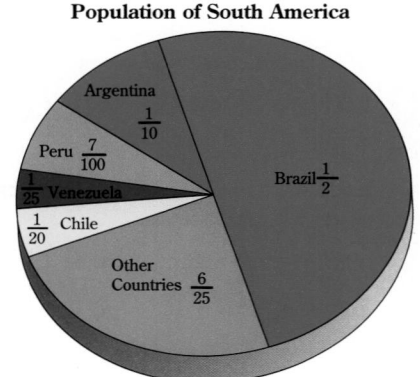

Approximate Population of South America

Argentina $\frac{1}{10}$ Peru $\frac{7}{100}$ $\frac{1}{25}$ Venezuela $\frac{1}{20}$ Chile   Brazil $\frac{1}{2}$ Other Countries $\frac{6}{25}$

CHAPTER 7   205

MEETING INDIVIDUAL NEEDS

For Students Who Are . . .

Acquiring English Proficiency Discuss the circle graph for Exercises 41–43, and have students read aloud the names of the countries.

Gifted and Talented Have students demonstrate the commutative and associative properties for multiplication of fractions.

Working 2 or 3 Grades Below Level Remind students that when they use canceling they must find common factors in the numerator and the denominator of the fractions. Have students use pages 80–85 of the Skills Workbook for fractions.

Today's Problem

Natalie fell asleep in the car when the family was halfway home. She slept for $\frac{1}{4}$ of the rest of the trip. For how much of the total trip did she sleep? ($\frac{1}{4} \times \frac{1}{2} = \frac{1}{8}$ of the total trip)

---

3 FOLLOW-UP

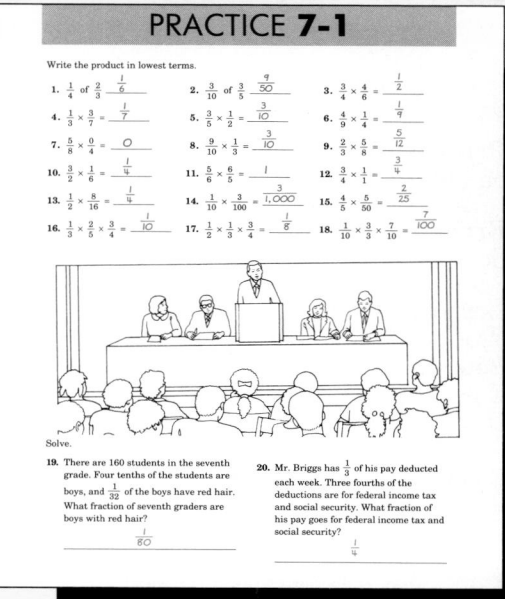

PRACTICE 7-1

Write the product in lowest terms.

19. There are 160 students in the seventh grade. Four tenths of the students are boys, and $\frac{1}{32}$ of the boys have red hair. What fraction of seventh graders are boys with red hair? $\frac{1}{80}$

20. Mr. Briggs has $\frac{1}{3}$ of his pay deducted each week. Three fourths of the deductions are for federal income tax and social security. What fraction of his pay goes for federal income tax and social security? $\frac{1}{4}$

RETEACHING 7-1

To multiply fractions, you multiply the numerators. You write this product over the product of the denominators and then write the answer in lowest terms.

Example: $\frac{3}{5} \times \frac{2}{3} = \frac{3 \times 2}{5 \times 3} = \frac{6}{15} = \frac{2}{5}$ ← lowest terms

Sometimes you can use a short cut. When a numerator and denominator have a common factor, you can divide by the common factor before you multiply.

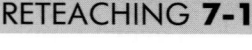

The name for this short cut is **canceling**.

ENRICHMENT 7-1

☑ **MATERIALS CHECKLIST:** Index cards

Have the students work in groups of four, and in pairs within each group. Provide each pair with a set of five cards, on which you have written the following exercises:

The product of $\frac{1}{3}$ and __ is $\frac{1}{6}$. The difference is $\frac{1}{6}$. $\cdot$ [$\frac{1}{2}$]

The product of $\frac{2}{3}$ and __ is $\frac{4}{21}$. The difference is $\frac{8}{21}$. $\cdot$ [$\frac{2}{7}$]

The product of $\frac{2}{3}$ and __ is $\frac{1}{2}$. The difference is $\frac{1}{12}$. $\cdot$ [$\frac{3}{4}$]

The product of $\frac{3}{8}$ and __ is $\frac{1}{6}$. The difference is $\frac{5}{72}$. $\cdot$ [$\frac{4}{9}$]

The product of $\frac{4}{5}$ and __ is $\frac{2}{3}$. The difference is $\frac{1}{30}$. $\cdot$ [$\frac{5}{6}$]

Instruct each pair to find the missing fraction on each card. The first pair to find all five missing fractions is the winner.

Chapter 7 • Lesson 7-1   **205**

LESSON 7-2

Lesson Organizer

> **Objective:** Multiply fractions and whole numbers.

Prior Knowledge: Students should be able to multiply fractions.

Error Analysis and Remediation: See page 225A.

Lesson Resources:
Practice Worksheet 7-2
Reteaching Activity 7-2
Enrichment Worksheet 7-2
Daily Review 7-2
Cooperative Connections, Chapter 7
Cooperative Problem Solving 1,
  Chapter 7

 *Two-Minute Math*

Find $\frac{1}{2}$ of every number in row I on the Table of Numbers on the inside back cover. Write the answer in lowest terms. ($\frac{1}{3}$; $\frac{1}{4}$, $\frac{1}{4}$, $\frac{5}{12}$, $\frac{1}{8}$, $\frac{7}{24}$, $\frac{1}{12}$, $\frac{3}{8}$, $\frac{1}{6}$)

1 INTRODUCE

CONNECTING ACTIVITY

1. Draw the following diagram on the chalkboard. Move up $\frac{1}{2}$ and over 5, and shade in the resulting rectangle.

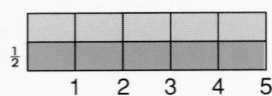

What does the model represent? ($\frac{1}{2}$ of 5) Write $\frac{1}{2} \times 5 = \frac{5}{2} = 2\frac{1}{2}$ on the chalkboard. **How can you check your answer?** (*Possible answers: by counting the number of halves; by multiplying $2 \times 2\frac{1}{2}$ to get 5*)

2. Repeat for $\frac{2}{3} \times 4$. Have students write the equation the model represents.

WHEN YOUR STUDENTS ASK
★ WHY AM I LEARNING THIS? ★

You can connect this skill to real life through interpreting newspaper articles. For example, if $\frac{2}{3}$ of 54,000 fans parked at the stadium, how many fans parked there?

Multiplying Fractions and Whole Numbers

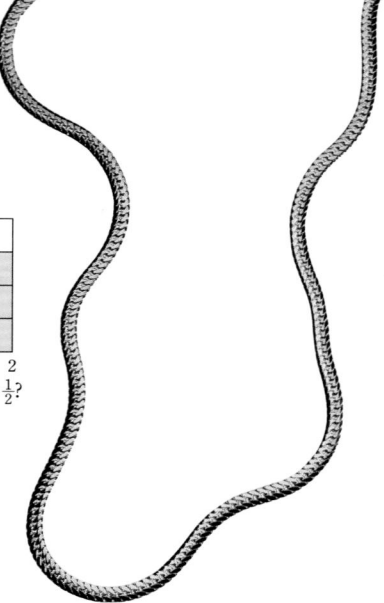

Pure gold is 24 k (karats). Gold that is 18 k is $\frac{18}{24}$, or $\frac{3}{4}$, pure gold and $\frac{1}{4}$ other metals. How many ounces of pure gold are there in an 18-k chain that weighs 2 oz?

The diagram shows $\frac{3}{4}$ of 2 squares, or $\frac{3}{4} \times 2$.

Go up $\frac{3}{4}$ and across 2.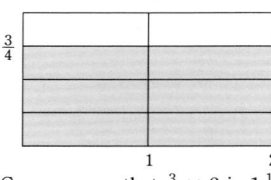

Can you see that $\frac{3}{4} \times 2$ is $1\frac{1}{2}$?

If you know that $2 = \frac{2}{1}$, you can make a **MATH CONNECTION** to multiply $\frac{3}{4} \times 2$.

$$\frac{3}{4} \times 2 \;=\; \frac{3}{\overset{}{\underset{2}{4}}} \times \frac{\overset{1}{2}}{1} = \frac{3}{2} = 1\frac{1}{2}$$

The chain contains $1\frac{1}{2}$ oz of pure gold.

> **To multiply a fraction by a whole number, write the whole number as a fraction and multiply.**

═══ GUIDED PRACTICE ═══

Explain how to find the product in lowest terms.   Accept reasonable answers.

1. $\frac{4}{5} \times 3$ $2\frac{2}{5}$
2. $\frac{7}{8} \times 4$ $3\frac{1}{2}$
3. $\frac{3}{4} \times 20$ 15
4. $12 \times \frac{1}{3}$ 4
5. $\frac{5}{6} \times 0$ 0

═══ PRACTICE ═══

Write the product in lowest terms.

6. $3 \times \frac{5}{6}$ $2\frac{1}{2}$
7. $\frac{5}{8} \times 16$ 10
8. $\frac{7}{8} \times 4$ $3\frac{1}{2}$
9. $\frac{3}{4} \times 9$ $6\frac{3}{4}$
10. $7 \times \frac{1}{3}$ $2\frac{1}{3}$

11. $\frac{2}{5} \times \frac{3}{5}$ $\frac{6}{25}$
12. $\frac{7}{8} \times 1$ $\frac{7}{8}$
13. $\frac{7}{8} \times \frac{5}{7}$ $\frac{5}{8}$
14. $5 \times \frac{2}{5}$ 2
15. $\frac{4}{5} \times \frac{5}{4}$ 1

16. $0 \times \frac{7}{8}$ 0
17. $\frac{5}{16} \times 0$ 0
18. $\frac{3}{4} \times \frac{4}{3}$ 1
19. $\frac{2}{3} \times 12$ 8
20. $16 \times \frac{1}{8}$ 2

---

2 TEACH

☑ **MATERIALS CHECKLIST:** Math Connection Transparency, calculators

Display the transparency. Have students fill in the spaces and discuss the math connection. *(See student pages.)*

After students work through the example, point out that the product of $\frac{3}{4} \times 2$ $(1\frac{1}{2})$ is greater than $\frac{3}{4}$. **Why is $1\frac{1}{2}$ a reasonable product for this example?** (*Since $\frac{3}{4} \times 1 = \frac{3}{4}$, $\frac{3}{4} \times 2$ should be twice as great or $1\frac{1}{2}$.*)

> **Chalkboard Examples**
>
> Write the product in lowest terms.
>
> $\frac{3}{5} \times 4$ $(2\frac{2}{5})$
> $6 \times \frac{2}{3}$ (4)
> $\frac{3}{8} \times 2$ $(\frac{3}{4})$

SUMMARIZE/ASSESS **Explain how to find the product of $\frac{5}{8} \times 8$.** (*Write 8 as $\frac{8}{1}$, cancel, multiply; the answer is 5. Encourage students to use a diagram to model their response.*)

21. $\frac{0}{12} \times 6$ 0   22. $\frac{7}{16} \times 8$ $3\frac{1}{2}$ 23. $25 \times \frac{3}{20}$ $3\frac{3}{4}$ 24. $0 \times \frac{0}{50}$ 0   25. $\frac{3}{32} \times 16$ $1\frac{1}{2}$

26. $\frac{3}{5} \times \frac{2}{9}$ $\frac{2}{15}$ 27. $7 \times \frac{5}{14}$ $2\frac{1}{2}$ *28. $\frac{7}{10} \times 30 \times \frac{1}{3}$ 7   *29. $\left(\frac{1}{6} + \frac{3}{4}\right) \times \frac{2}{3}$ $\frac{11}{18}$

MIXED REVIEW   Compute.

30. 14.67×53.11 **779.1237**
31. $\frac{7}{12} + \frac{3}{8}$ $\frac{23}{24}$
32. $687.09 + 54.23$ **741.32**
33. $\frac{12}{14} - \frac{5}{7}$ $\frac{1}{7}$

34. $6\frac{2}{7} + 5\frac{5}{6}$ $12\frac{5}{42}$
35. $231.76 - 230.81$ **0.95**
36. $12\frac{1}{6} - 5\frac{10}{12}$ $6\frac{1}{3}$
37. $945.73 + 34.6$ **980.33**

Use **MENTAL MATH** to solve the equation.

38. $\frac{2}{5}n = \frac{6}{35}$ $\frac{3}{7}$
39. $\frac{5}{6}n = \frac{15}{42}$ $\frac{3}{7}$
40. $\frac{3}{4}n = 1$ $\frac{4}{3}$
41. $\frac{11}{16}n = 0$ 0

PROBLEM SOLVING

 CHOOSE   Use the information on page 206.
Choose paper and pencil or calculator to solve.

42. The largest known coin was 14 k, weighed 365 lb, and was worth $1 million. How many pounds of pure gold did it contain?   p; $212\frac{11}{12}$ lb

43. At $420/oz, what is the value of the gold in a 12-k medallion that weighs $\frac{15}{16}$ oz?   p; $196.88

44. How long is a line of 1,000,000 pennies that are side by side? Each penny is $\frac{3}{4}$ in. wide.
c; 750,000 in., or 62,500 ft, or ≈11.8 mi.

Mental Math

You can use mental math to multiply a whole number by a fraction with a numerator of 1.

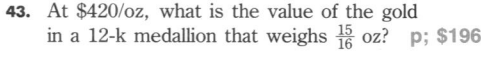

- How many coins are there in all?   **15 coins**
- What part of the coins are gold? $\frac{1}{3}$
- How many of the coins are gold?   **5 coins**

$\frac{1}{3}$ of 15 = 5 ⟹ 15 ÷ 3 = 5

Multiply mentally.

1. $\frac{1}{5}$ of 40   8
2. $\frac{1}{7} \times 42$ 6
3. $\frac{1}{3}$ of 18   6
4. $\frac{1}{10} \times 360$ 36
5. $\frac{1}{6}$ of 24   4

*6. $\frac{3}{8}$ of 24 (*Hint:* Find $\frac{1}{8}$ of 24 first.)   9   *7. $\frac{2}{5} \times 20$ 8   *8. $24 \times \frac{5}{6}$ 20

MEETING INDIVIDUAL NEEDS

For Students Who Are . . .

Acquiring English Proficiency   Discuss the meaning of *karat* and *medallion*. For the mental math, tell students that the variable represents a fraction. They may want to write it as $\frac{2}{5} \times \underline{\quad} = \frac{6}{35}$.

Gifted and Talented   Have students use the commutative and associative properties to find these products mentally: $4 \times \frac{3}{5} \times \frac{7}{2}$ $(8\frac{2}{5})$; $\frac{1}{3} \times \frac{5}{8} \times 9$ $(1\frac{7}{8})$; $8 \times \frac{4}{9} \times \frac{7}{8}$ $(3\frac{1}{9})$; $\frac{6}{7} \times 3 \times \frac{11}{12}$ $(2\frac{5}{14})$.

Working 2 or 3 Grades Below Level   Have students use pages 86–89 of the Workbook for Fractions.

Today's Problem

A cross-country skier uses about $\frac{1}{5}$ of a calorie per minute for each kilogram of body weight. If a skier weighs 55 kg, how many calories does he or she use in a second? ($\frac{calories}{minute} = \frac{1}{5} \times 55 = 11$; $\frac{calories}{second} = \frac{1}{60} \times 11 = \frac{11}{60}$)

PRACTICE 7-2

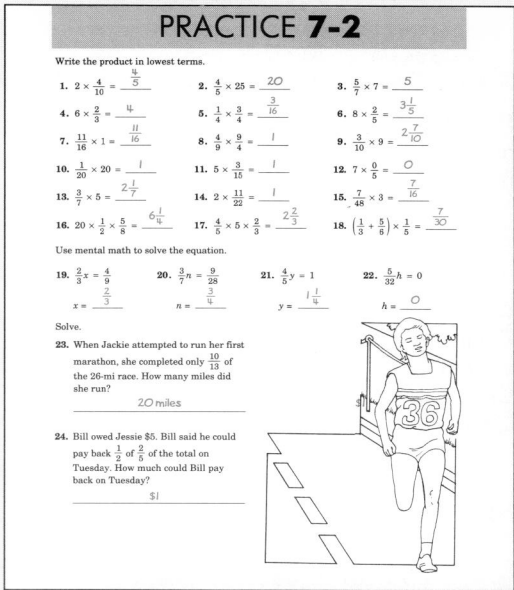

Write the product in lowest terms.

1. $2 \times \frac{4}{10} =$ $\frac{4}{5}$
2. $\frac{4}{5} \times 25 =$ 20
3. $\frac{5}{7} \times 7 =$ 5
4. $6 \times \frac{2}{3} =$ 4
5. $\frac{1}{4} \times \frac{3}{4} =$ $\frac{3}{16}$
6. $8 \times \frac{2}{5} =$ $3\frac{1}{5}$
7. $\frac{11}{16} \times 1 =$ $\frac{11}{16}$
8. $\frac{4}{9} \times \frac{9}{4} =$ 1
9. $\frac{3}{10} \times 9 =$ $2\frac{7}{10}$
10. $\frac{1}{20} \times 20 =$ 1
11. $5 \times \frac{3}{15} =$ 1
12. $7 \times \frac{0}{5} =$ 0
13. $\frac{3}{7} \times 5 =$ $2\frac{1}{7}$
14. $2 \times \frac{11}{22} =$ 1
15. $\frac{7}{48} \times 1 =$ $\frac{7}{48}$
16. $20 \times \frac{1}{2} \times \frac{5}{8} =$ $6\frac{1}{4}$
17. $\frac{4}{5} \times 5 \times \frac{2}{3} =$ $2\frac{2}{3}$
18. $\left(\frac{1}{3} + \frac{5}{6}\right) \times \frac{1}{5} =$ $\frac{7}{30}$

Use mental math to solve the equation.

19. $\frac{2}{3}x = \frac{4}{9}$
   $x =$ $\frac{2}{3}$
20. $\frac{3}{7}n = \frac{9}{28}$
   $n =$ $\frac{3}{4}$
21. $\frac{4}{5}y = 1$
   $y =$ $1\frac{1}{4}$
22. $\frac{5}{32}h = 0$
   $h =$ 0

Solve.

23. When Jackie attempted to run her first marathon, she completed only $\frac{10}{13}$ of the 26-mi race. How many miles did she run?
   20 miles

24. Bill owed Jessie $5. Bill said he could pay back $\frac{1}{2}$ of $\frac{2}{5}$ of the total on Tuesday. How much could Bill pay back on Tuesday?
   $1

RETEACHING 7-2

✓ **MATERIALS CHECKLIST:** Strips of paper, scissors, colored pencils

Write the following exercise on the board: $\frac{2}{3} \times 4$. Have students work in pairs to draw vertical lines to show thirds. Then have them shade 2 of the 3 sections to show $\frac{2}{3}$. Ask: How many fraction bars must you make to model $\frac{2}{3} \times 4$? [4] Have the students make three more fraction bars showing $\frac{2}{3}$, then have them cut them apart. Ask: How many shaded squares are there? [8] What fraction does this represent? [$\frac{8}{3}$] What mixed number can you write for the fraction? [$2\frac{2}{3}$] Repeat.

ENRICHMENT 7-2

Keep the order of operations in mind for an exercise involving fractions if the exercise contains any of the following: more than one operation, grouping symbols, or exponents.

Example: $\frac{3}{4} + \frac{2}{3} \times \left(\frac{1}{2}\right)^2 = \frac{3}{4} + \frac{2}{3} \times \frac{1}{4} = \frac{3}{4} + \frac{2}{12} = \frac{9}{12} + \frac{2}{12} = \frac{11}{12}$

Solve.

1. $\frac{3}{8} + \frac{4}{5} \times \left(\frac{1}{2}\right)^2 =$ $\frac{23}{40}$
2. $\frac{1}{4} \times \frac{2}{3} + \frac{3}{8} \times \frac{5}{6} =$ $\frac{23}{48}$
3. $\left(\frac{2}{3}\right)^2 + \left(\frac{1}{4}\right)^2 =$ $\frac{73}{144}$
4. $\frac{2}{3}\left(1 + \frac{1}{8}\right) =$ $\frac{1}{4}$
5. $\frac{3}{4} - \frac{2}{3} + \frac{5}{12} \times 4 =$ $3\frac{5}{12}$
6. $\frac{3}{4} \times \frac{8}{9} \times \frac{1}{2} \times \frac{6}{5} =$ $\frac{2}{5}$
7. $4 \times \frac{2}{3} \times 5 \times \frac{6}{8} =$ 10
8. $\frac{3}{4} \times \left(\frac{2}{5} - \frac{3}{10}\right) =$ $\frac{3}{40}$
9. $\left(\frac{2}{3}\right)^2 + \left(\frac{1}{3}\right)^2 - \left(\frac{5}{6}\right)^2 =$ 0
10. $6 - \frac{3}{4} \times \frac{3}{8} + 4 =$ $9\frac{11}{32}$
11. $\frac{3^2}{4} + \frac{1}{2} \times \frac{2}{3} =$ $2\frac{7}{12}$
12. $\left(\frac{3}{8} + \frac{1}{4}\right) \times \frac{1}{2} \div 2 =$ $2\frac{5}{16}$

Lesson Organizer

> **Objective:** Multiply mixed numbers.

Prior Knowledge: Students should be able to write mixed numbers as fractions and multiply fractions.

Lesson Resources:
Practice Worksheet 7-3
Reteaching Worksheet 7-3
Enrichment Activity 7-3
Daily Review 7-3

Two-Minute Math

You have $19.42. What is the fewest number of coins you could have, excluding fifty-cent pieces? *(81 coins)*

1 INTRODUCE

CONNECTING ACTIVITY

☑ **MATERIALS CHECKLIST:** Teaching Aid 7 (Fraction Multiplier Model)

1. Write $2\frac{1}{2} \times 3\frac{1}{3}$ on the chalkboard.

2. Display the fraction multiplier model. Call on a student to show how to go up $2\frac{1}{2}$ and over $3\frac{1}{3}$. Be sure students recognize that the array enclosed by the heavy line represents the product.

- **How do you know the product is less than 12?** *(The array covers a smaller area than the 12-square shaded part.)*

- **How do you know that the product is greater than 6?** *(The array covers a larger area than the 6-square checked part.)*

3. Use the teaching aid to show you cannot multiply the whole numbers and multiply the fractions to find the answer.

WHEN YOUR STUDENTS ASK
★ **WHY AM I LEARNING THIS?** ★

You can connect this skill to real life through surveying. When surveyors plot boundary lines to determine the area of a property, they may have to multiply mixed numbers.

Multiplying With Mixed Numbers

Devin worked $2\frac{3}{4}$ h of overtime on Monday making a patio. How many hours of regular pay did this earn him?

You need to multiply $1\frac{1}{2}$ by $2\frac{3}{4}$.

ESTIMATE You can estimate the product of $1\frac{1}{2}$ and $2\frac{3}{4}$ by rounding to whole numbers. What do you estimate the product to be? **6**

Pay Policy for Paul's Patios Inc.
- A full workweek is $37\frac{1}{2}$ h. Overtime is over $37\frac{1}{2}$ h.
- Overtime during the week or on Saturdays earns $1\frac{1}{2}$ h of regular pay per hour worked.
- Overtime on Sundays or holidays earns $1\frac{3}{4}$ h of regular pay per hour worked.

If you know how to multiply fractions and how to change mixed numbers to fractions, you can make a **MATH CONNECTION** to multiply mixed numbers.

$$1\frac{1}{2} \times 2\frac{3}{4} = \frac{3}{2} \times \frac{11}{4} = \frac{33}{8} = 4\frac{1}{8}$$

Is this answer close to your estimate?

Devin earned $4\frac{1}{8}$ h of regular pay.

Other examples:

$$\frac{3}{4} \times \frac{4}{3} = \frac{3}{\overset{1}{4}} \times \frac{\overset{1}{4}}{3} = 1 \qquad \frac{1}{2} \times 2 = \frac{1}{2} \times \overset{1}{2} = 1 \qquad \frac{2}{3} \times 1\frac{1}{2} = \frac{\overset{1}{2}}{3} \times \frac{3}{\overset{}{2}} = 1$$

CRITICAL THINKING In each of the examples above, can you multiply the first factor by a different factor and still get 1? **only if they are equivalent to $\frac{4}{3}$, 2, and $\frac{3}{2}$**

> **Two numbers whose product is 1 are called reciprocals.**

$\frac{3}{4}$ and $\frac{4}{3}$ are called reciprocals. Name some other pairs of numbers that are reciprocals. **Answers will vary. Suggestion given: $\frac{4}{5}$ and $\frac{5}{4}$**

=== **GUIDED PRACTICE** ===

Find the reciprocal of the number.   Write the product in lowest terms.

1. 7 $\frac{1}{7}$ **2.** $\frac{3}{8}$ $\frac{8}{3}$ **3.** $5\frac{1}{2}$ $\frac{2}{11}$ **4.** $1\frac{3}{5} \times 10$ **16**   **5.** $1\frac{2}{7} \times 7$ **9**

=== **PRACTICE** ===

Write the reciprocal of the number.

6. $\frac{3}{4}$ $\frac{4}{3}$ **7.** $4\frac{5}{6}$ $\frac{6}{29}$ **8.** $1\frac{1}{7}$ $\frac{7}{8}$ **9.** $\frac{1}{8}$ **8**   **10.** 6 $\frac{1}{6}$ **11.** 1   **1**

---

2 TEACH

☑ **MATERIALS CHECKLIST:** Math Connection Transparency, calculators

Have students work with a partner for the two Critical Thinking activities.

Display the transparency. Have students fill in the spaces and discuss the math connection. *(See student pages.)*

Suppose Devin worked $2\frac{3}{4}$ h of overtime on Sunday. **How many hours of regular pay would this earn him?**
($1\frac{3}{4} \times 2\frac{3}{4} = 4\frac{13}{16}$ h)

> **Chalkboard Examples**
>
> Write the product in lowest terms.
>
> $2\frac{3}{5} \times 3\frac{5}{6}$ *($9\frac{29}{30}$)*
> $4\frac{5}{12} \times 3\frac{2}{3}$ *($16\frac{7}{36}$)*
> $5\frac{3}{8} \times \frac{3}{4}$ *($4\frac{1}{32}$)*

SUMMARIZE/ASSESS **Explain how to multiply with mixed numbers.** *(Change all numbers to fractions, cancel, multiply, and write the answer in lowest terms.)*

Write the product in lowest terms. Estimate to see if your answer is reasonable.

12. $\frac{1}{4} \times 2\frac{1}{3}$ $\frac{7}{12}$ **13.** $2\frac{4}{5} \times 15$ 42 **14.** $49 \times 1\frac{2}{7}$ 63 **15.** $4\frac{4}{7} \times 3\frac{1}{2}$ 16

16. $4\frac{3}{5} \times 3$ $13\frac{4}{5}$ **17.** $6 \times 6\frac{7}{8}$ $41\frac{1}{4}$ **18.** $\frac{5}{31} \times 6\frac{1}{5}$ 1 **19.** $7\frac{1}{5} \times 0$ 0

20. $2\frac{1}{4} \times 1\frac{2}{3}$ $3\frac{3}{4}$ **21.** $\frac{3}{4} \times 1\frac{1}{3}$ 1 **22.** $10\frac{3}{4} \times \frac{2}{3}$ $7\frac{1}{6}$ **23.** $2\frac{3}{7} \times 2\frac{1}{4}$ $5\frac{13}{28}$

24. $5\frac{1}{3} \times 2\frac{5}{8}$ 14 **25.** $6\frac{3}{5} \times 1\frac{3}{4}$ $11\frac{11}{20}$ **26.** $3\frac{4}{9} \times 8\frac{1}{10}$ $27\frac{9}{10}$ **27.** $5\frac{9}{10} \times 8$ $47\frac{1}{5}$

28. $\frac{1}{4} \times 1\frac{1}{4}$ $\frac{5}{16}$ **29.** $\frac{9}{10} \times 1\frac{1}{9}$ 1 **30.** $8\frac{7}{8} \times 40$ 355 **31.** $5\frac{1}{3} \times \frac{3}{16}$ 1

MIXED REVIEW Compute.

32. $\frac{3}{8} + \frac{3}{4}$ $\frac{9}{8}$ **33.** $5 - 4\frac{2}{3}$ $\frac{1}{3}$ **34.** $1\frac{1}{4} \times 1\frac{1}{4}$ $1\frac{9}{16}$ **35.** $5\frac{1}{5} + 6\frac{4}{9}$ $11\frac{29}{45}$

36. $7 - 6\frac{3}{5}$ $\frac{2}{5}$ **37.** $\frac{4}{5} + 1\frac{1}{3}$ $2\frac{2}{15}$ **38.** $5\frac{3}{5} \times \frac{3}{7}$ $2\frac{2}{5}$ **39.** $\frac{1}{4} \times \frac{3}{5} \times \frac{8}{9}$ $\frac{2}{15}$

***40.** **CRITICAL THINKING** What number has no reciprocal? Why not?
0; $\frac{1}{0}$ is not possible

━━━━━━━━━━━━ **PROBLEM SOLVING** ━━━━━━━━━━━━

CHOOSE Use the chart on page 208.
Choose paper and pencil or calculator to solve.

41. Susan worked $5\frac{1}{2}$ h of overtime on Thanksgiving Day. How many hours of regular pay did she earn? p; $9\frac{5}{8}$ h

42. In the first week of July, Mandy worked a full workweek. Also, she worked $3\frac{1}{2}$ h on July 4th. At $8/h, what was her salary that week? c; $349

***43.** Ashley worked a full workweek plus 6 h and 20 min overtime on Saturday. What was his salary that week if he earns $8/h? p; $376

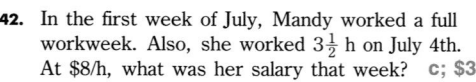

Critical Thinking

Work with a partner.

1. What are the products of:
$\frac{3}{4} \times 1$, $\frac{3}{4} \times 0$, $\frac{3}{4} \times \frac{1}{2}$, $\frac{3}{4} \times \frac{1}{4}$?
$\frac{3}{4}$ 0 $\frac{3}{8}$ $\frac{3}{16}$

2. **IN YOUR WORDS** Explain the value of the product you get when you multiply by a fraction less than 1.
It is smaller than the larger of the two factors.

MEETING INDIVIDUAL NEEDS

For Students Who Are . . .

Acquiring English Proficiency Make sure students understand the concept of overtime and the information in the chart on page 208.

Gifted and Talented Have students create a pay-policy chart and then write a problem using the information.

Working 2 or 3 Grades Below Level Have students estimate their answers to the Practice exercises first. Then tell them to change all mixed numbers to fractions, cancel, and multiply. Have students use pages 90–93 of the Skills Workbook for Fractions.

Today's Problem

Kahim usually works $8\frac{1}{2}$ hours a week. Next week he has been asked to work $1\frac{1}{2}$ times his usual hours. How many hours will he work next week? $\left(8\frac{1}{2} h \times 1\frac{1}{2} = \frac{17}{2} h \times \frac{3}{2} = \frac{51}{4} h = 12\frac{3}{4} h\right)$

---

3 FOLLOW-UP

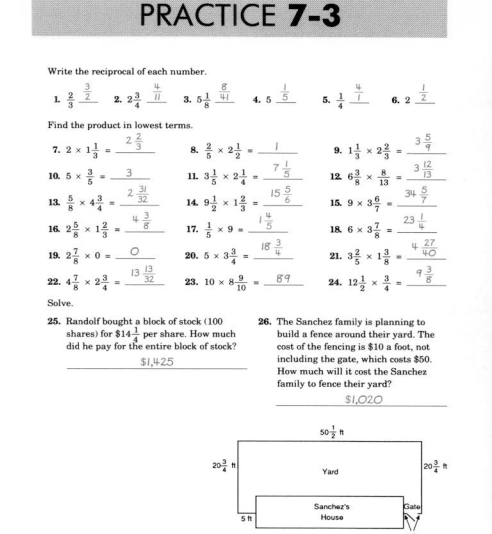

Lesson Organizer

> **Objective:** Solve problems using estimation.

Prior Knowledge: Students should be able to round numbers, multiply fractions, and compute with money.

Lesson Resources:
Practice Worksheet 7-4
Reteaching Activity 7-4
Enrichment Worksheet 7-4
Daily Review 7-4

 *Two-Minute Math*

Have pairs of students list ways in which they have used numbers in their lives so far today. Students should classify those numbers as estimates or exact numbers.

1 INTRODUCE

SYMBOLIC ACTIVITY

1. Have students share their lists from the Two-Minute Math activity.

2. Discuss general instances in which exact numbers are needed and times when estimates are sufficient.

WHEN YOUR STUDENTS ASK
★ WHY AM I LEARNING THIS? ★

You can connect this skill to many real life situations. You estimate when you ask yourself: Do I have enough time? Do I have enough money? Will there be enough ribbon to tie the gift?

Problem Solving Strategy:
Using Estimation

UNDERSTAND
PLAN
CARRY OUT
LOOK BACK

A museum was given discounted prices on the cost of several Native American crafts to aid the museum in setting up its exhibit of Native American arts and crafts.

Suppose the museum had $170 to buy 2 large baskets. Would that amount of money be enough?

An estimated answer is all that is needed to solve the problem.

- Round the cost of 1 large basket to make the calculation easier. ≈$120

- Estimate the total cost at the regular price. ≈$240

- What would you do to find the amount of the discount? multiply by $\frac{1}{3}$

- Estimate the discounted price of 2 large baskets.
$240 − ($240 × $\frac{1}{3}$) = $240 − $80 = $160

THINK ALOUD Can you estimate the discounted price in fewer steps.
yes; $\frac{2}{3}$ × $240 = $160

GUIDED PRACTICE

Estimate. Do not calculate. Answers will vary. Suggestions given.

1. The museum wants to buy a totem pole.
   a. What is the regular price? $49.99
   b. What amount close to the regular price is easy to multiply by $\frac{1}{3}$? $48
   c. Estimate the discounted price. ≈$32

2. **IN YOUR WORDS** The discounted price for 2 bear masks is about $90. Is that about right? Explain.
No, about $100 is needed.

3. Would $12 be enough to buy three bookmarks? yes

4. About how much less would the large basket and the small planter cost at the discounted price? ≈$60

210   LESSON 7-4

Price list:

$\frac{1}{3}$ off regular prices shown

large basket — $119.95
bear mask — $74.95
totem pole — $49.99
bookmark — $4.95
small planter — $62.95

$\frac{1}{4}$ off regular prices shown

drum — $265.95
Cherokee "e tsi" mother doll — $25.00

MULTICULTURAL NOTE

The baskets shown above are traditional Cherokee baskets made of river cane. The Cherokee were related to the Iroquois of the Northeast, and called themselves *Ani-yun-wiya*, which means "real people" in Iroquoian.

2 TEACH

Imagine you are in a store with a certain amount of money. You do not want to be embarrassed at the checkout counter by not having enough money, so you need to estimate the total cost of your purchases. Do you round the prices up or down? Why? *(Round up, to be sure that the estimate is more than the actual cost of each item; then add the estimates to keep the sum at less than the amount you have.)*

What are two different ways to estimate the sale price of a basket and a bookmark? *(Estimate the sale price of each, and then determine the approximate sum; determine the approximate sum and then estimate the sale price.)*

Chalkboard Example

Would $80 be enough to buy 18 bookmarks at $\frac{1}{3}$ off the regular price of $4.95 each?

SUMMARIZE/ASSESS **What kinds of problems can be solved by estimating?** *(Answers will vary.)*

Estimate. Do not calculate. **Answers will vary.**

5. How much money does the museum save by buying the drum at a discount? ≈$66

6. About what is the discounted price of the drum? ≈$198

7. Is $50 enough to buy the Cherokee "e tsi" mother doll and a totem pole at the discounted prices? **no**

8. **CREATE YOUR OWN** Write two problems using the information on these two pages. Give them to a friend to solve. **Check students' work.**

9. **IN YOUR WORDS** With a budget of $400, which discounted items from both pages would you buy for the museum? Explain and defend your choices in a paragraph. **Answers will vary. Check students' work.**

CHOOSE Choose a strategy to solve, if possible. **Choices will vary.**

10. A hiking trail near the museum starts at one marker and goes 2 mi north, then 3 mi east, 5 mi south, 4 mi east, and 3 mi north to another marker. How far apart are the two markers?
draw a diagram; The last marker is 7 mi due east of the first marker.

11. Miguel bought a bear mask at the discounted price. What was his change? **too little information**

12. How much change did Lara receive when she bought a Cherokee "e tsi" mother doll at the discounted price? She gave the clerk $20 and paid $.94 sales tax. **use percent; $.31**

CHAPTER 7   211

MEETING INDIVIDUAL NEEDS

For Students Who Are . . .

Acquiring English Proficiency Pair students with an English-proficient student to answer Exercises 5–12.

Gifted and Talented Have students find newspaper ads announcing discounts on sale items. Have them find the sale price.

Working 2 or 3 Grades Below Level Have students use pages 76–83 of the Skills Workbook for Problem Solving Strategies.

Having Reading Difficulties Have students work with an able reader to discuss and solve Exercises 5–12.

Today's Problem

Matt's times on three athletic events are $\frac{7}{8}$ min, $\frac{5}{6}$ min, and $\frac{3}{4}$ min. Michelle's times for the same events are $\frac{3}{6}$ min, $\frac{6}{8}$ min, and $\frac{7}{9}$ min. Whose total time for the three events is less? *(Since $\frac{7}{9} < \frac{7}{8}$, $\frac{3}{6} < \frac{5}{6}$, and $\frac{6}{8} = \frac{3}{4}$, Michelle's total time is less.)*

---

3 FOLLOW-UP

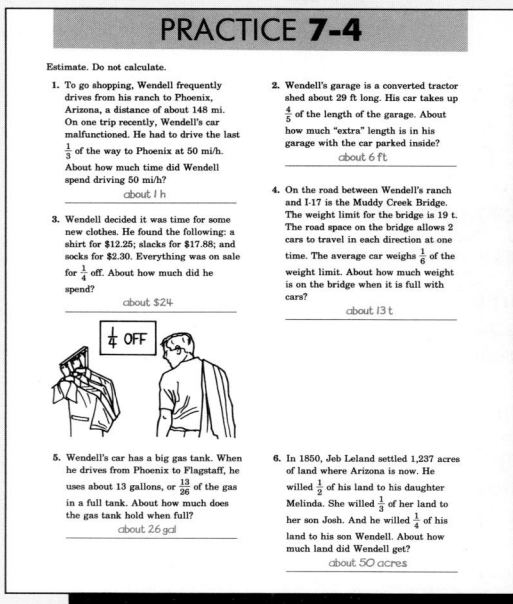

PRACTICE 7-4

Estimate. Do not calculate.

1. To go shopping, Wendell frequently drives from his ranch to Phoenix, Arizona, a distance of about 148 mi. On one trip recently, Wendell's car malfunctioned. He had to drive the last $\frac{1}{3}$ of the way to Phoenix at 50 mi/h. About how much time did Wendell spend driving 50 mi/h?
   about 1 h

2. Wendell's garage is a converted tractor shed about 29 ft long. His car takes up $\frac{4}{5}$ of the length of the garage. About how much "extra" length is in his garage with the car parked inside?
   about 6 ft

3. Wendell decided it was time for some new clothes. He found the following: a shirt for $12.25; slacks for $17.88; and socks for $2.30. Everything was on sale for $\frac{1}{4}$ off. About how much did he spend?
   about $24

4. On the road between Wendell's ranch and I-17 is the Muddy Creek Bridge. The weight limit for the bridge is 19 t. The road space on the bridge allows 2 cars to travel in each direction at one time. The average car weighs $\frac{1}{6}$ of the weight limit. About how much weight is on the bridge when it is full with cars?
   about 13 t

5. Wendell's car has a big gas tank. When he drives from Phoenix to Flagstaff, he uses about 13 gallons, or $\frac{13}{26}$ of the gas in a full tank. About how much does the gas tank hold when full?
   about 26 gal

6. In 1850, Jeb Leland settled 1,237 acres of land where Arizona is now. He willed $\frac{1}{2}$ of his land to his daughter Melinda. She willed $\frac{1}{2}$ of her land to her son Josh. And he willed $\frac{1}{4}$ of his land to his son Wendell. About how much land did Wendell get?
   about 50 acres

RETEACHING 7-4

Some students may not recognize when an estimate will be helpful in making a decision or when an estimate is all that is needed to solve a problem. One way to solve Problem 1, *Practice Worksheet 7-4*, is to ask the following questions: What is the question? [About how long did Wendell have to drive 50 mi/h?] What word tells you that an estimate is all you need? [about] How will you find the distance that Wendell was forced to drive 50 mi/h? [Find $\frac{1}{3}$ of 148 mi; $\frac{1}{3} \times 148$ is about 50, so Wendell drove 50 mi/h for about 50 mi.] At a speed of 50 mi/h, how far will Wendell travel in 1 h? [50 mi] What is the answer? [about 1 h]

ENRICHMENT 7-4

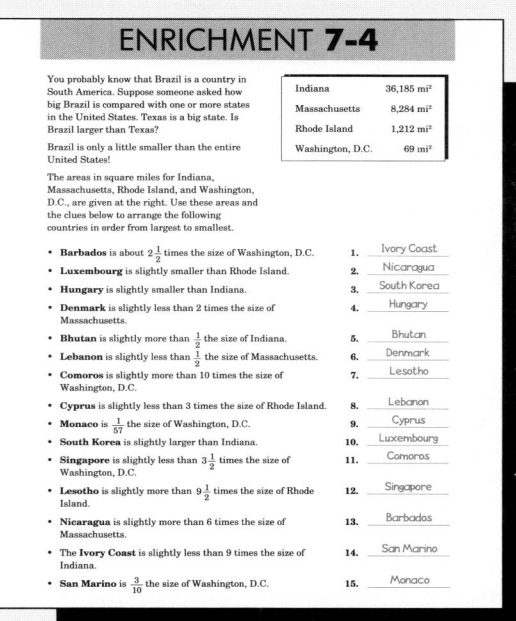

You probably know that Brazil is a country in South America. Suppose someone asked how big Brazil is compared with one or more states in the United States. Texas is a big state. Is Brazil larger than Texas?

Brazil is only a little smaller than the entire United States!

The areas in square miles for Indiana, Massachusetts, Rhode Island, and Washington, D.C., are given at the right. Use these areas and the clues below to arrange the following countries in order from largest to smallest.

Indiana	36,185 mi²
Massachusetts	8,284 mi²
Rhode Island	1,212 mi²
Washington, D.C.	69 mi²

- **Barbados** is about $2\frac{1}{2}$ times the size of Washington, D.C.
- **Luxembourg** is slightly smaller than Rhode Island.
- **Hungary** is slightly smaller than Indiana.
- **Denmark** is slightly less than 2 times the size of Massachusetts.
- **Bhutan** is slightly more than $\frac{1}{2}$ the size of Indiana.
- **Lebanon** is slightly less than $\frac{1}{2}$ the size of Massachusetts.
- **Comoros** is slightly more than 10 times the size of Washington, D.C.
- **Cyprus** is slightly less than 3 times the size of Rhode Island.
- **Monaco** is $\frac{1}{57}$ the size of Washington, D.C.
- **South Korea** is slightly larger than Indiana.
- **Singapore** is slightly less than $3\frac{1}{2}$ times the size of Washington, D.C.
- **Lesotho** is slightly more than $9\frac{1}{2}$ times the size of Rhode Island.
- **Nicaragua** is slightly more than 6 times the size of Massachusetts.
- The **Ivory Coast** is slightly less than 9 times the size of Indiana.
- **San Marino** is $\frac{3}{10}$ the size of Washington, D.C.

1.	Ivory Coast
2.	Nicaragua
3.	South Korea
4.	Hungary
5.	Bhutan
6.	Denmark
7.	Lesotho
8.	Lebanon
9.	Cyprus
10.	Luxembourg
11.	Comoros
12.	Singapore
13.	Barbados
14.	San Marino
15.	Monaco

MIDCHAPTER Checkup

The midchapter checkup provides a way for you to check students' understanding of the skills taught in the first half of the chapter.

Language and Vocabulary

Some key language and vocabulary ideas from the first half of the chapter are reinforced here.

Quick Quiz

The quiz provides a means of evaluating students' understanding of the objectives for the first half of the chapter. Page references are given so that students can check back to where the skill was taught.

Use the following guide to score the quiz.

Score	Percent
10	100%
9	90
8	80
7	70
6	60
5	50
4	40
3	30
2	20
1	10

Use this chart to identify the Management Objectives tested.

Items	Management Objectives	Pages
1–9	**7A** Multiply fractions and mixed numbers.	204–209
10	**7C** Problem Solving: Use estimation.	210–211

LANGUAGE & VOCABULARY

Decide whether the product *must be, can be,* or *cannot be* greater than at least one factor. Support your answer with at least one example. Accept reasonable examples.

1. multiplying a fraction by a fraction   cannot be
2. multiplying a fraction by a whole number   can be
3. multiplying a fraction by a mixed number   must be
4. multiplying a whole number by a mixed number   can be

QUICK QUIZ ✔

Write the product in lowest terms. *(pages 204–209)*

1. $\frac{5}{6}$ of $\frac{7}{8}$ $\frac{35}{48}$

2. $\frac{4}{5}$ of $\frac{3}{10}$ $\frac{6}{25}$

3. $\frac{0}{8} \times 7$ 0

4. $16 \times \frac{3}{8}$ 6

5. $\frac{5}{9} \times 30$ $16\frac{2}{3}$

6. $\frac{2}{3} \times 8\frac{1}{2}$ $5\frac{2}{3}$

7. $13 \times 2\frac{1}{5}$ $28\frac{3}{5}$

8. $7\frac{3}{4} \times 3\frac{2}{5}$ $26\frac{7}{20}$

9. $2\frac{1}{8} \times 5\frac{2}{3}$ $12\frac{1}{24}$

Solve. *(pages 210–211)*

10. A 247-mi car trip can be shortened by about $\frac{1}{4}$ using a short cut. Mr. and Mrs. Spence have 6 gal of gas in their tank. Their car averages 30 mi/gal.

   a. If they do not use the short cut, how far must Mr. and Mrs. Spence drive?   247 mi

   b. How can you find out the distance they must drive using the short cut?   247 ÷ 4 = a; 247 − a = distance

   c. Do they have enough gas to complete the trip either way?   no

Write the answers in your learning log.   **Answers will vary. Suggestions given.**

1. Describe the size of the answer when you multiply two mixed numbers.   **The answer is at least as big as the product of the two whole numbers.**

2. Explain how dollars and cents are like mixed numbers. **Dollars are the whole numbers and the cents are fractional parts of a dollar.**

DID YOU KNOW . . . ? In 1689, one of the colonies had 23 public schools—more than any other colony. How many public schools are there in your state? Compare the two numbers with a fractional statement.
Check students' work.

Work with a partner. Use a calculator.

A recipe for an apple dessert uses the following ingredients:

$$3 \text{ c bread crumbs}$$

$$1\frac{1}{4} \text{ c sugar}$$

$$\frac{1}{2} \text{ c butter}$$

$$\frac{1}{2} \text{ tsp cinnamon}$$

$$3 \text{ large apples}$$

$$\frac{1}{4} \text{ tsp nutmeg}$$

Directions: Bake in a 3-qt baking dish for 30 min at 375°F.

To make $1\frac{1}{2}$ times the recipe, which ingredients and directions must be changed? Write the new recipe.
$4\frac{1}{2}$ c bread crumbs; $1\frac{7}{8}$ c sugar

$\frac{3}{4}$ c butter; $\frac{3}{4}$ tsp cinnamon

$4\frac{1}{2}$ large apples; $\frac{3}{8}$ tsp nutmeg
Bake in 4.5 qt dish.

Learning Log

These are suggestions for writing about some topics taught so far in the chapter. The students keep their Learning Logs from the beginning of the school year through the end.

Math America

A mathematical skill that students have learned is related to an interesting fact about the United States.

Bonus

Students are given an opportunity to solve a challenge-type problem like a puzzle or a nonroutine problem

Lesson Organizer

Objective: Divide fractions and whole numbers.

Prior Knowledge: Students should be able to multiply fractions.

Error Analysis and Remediation: See page 225A.

Lesson Resources:
Practice Worksheet 7-5
Reteaching Worksheet 7-5
Enrichment Activity 7-5
Daily Review 7-5

Two-Minute Math

Drew has a collection of 35 half-dollars. Tomorrow he plans to get $5 worth of half-dollars. What will be the value of his collection then? *($22.50)*

1 INTRODUCE

CONCRETE ACTIVITY

☑ **MATERIALS CHECKLIST:** twenty base-10 rods, rubber bands

1. Present the following model:

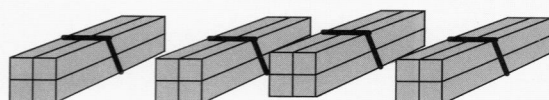

2. Pose this problem: **A recipe for dinner rolls calls for $\frac{3}{4}$ lb of margarine for each batch. How many batches can you make with 4 lb of margarine?**

3. Follow these steps to demonstrate:

• Make 5 groups of 3 rods each.

• Show the 1 left-over rod.

• Compare the 1 left-over rod with the 3-batch rod.

What part of a batch can be made with the left-over rod? $\left(\frac{1}{3}\right)$

WHEN YOUR STUDENTS ASK
★ **WHY AM I LEARNING THIS?** ★

You can use this skill to help you plan class parties. Suppose you buy 5 lb of hamburger. How many $\frac{1}{4}$-lb hamburgers can you make?

Dividing Fractions and Whole Numbers

A recipe for 1 batch of pancakes calls for $\frac{2}{3}$ c of milk. How many batches of pancakes can you make with 4 c of milk?

There are at least two ways to find out.

Use division:

• How many $\frac{2}{3}$ c are in 4 c?
$$4 \div \frac{2}{3} = ?$$

• The diagram at the right shows that 6 batches can be made with 4 c of milk.
$$4 \div \frac{2}{3} = 6$$

Use multiplication:

• First find out how many batches can be made from 1 c of milk. You can get $1\frac{1}{2}$, or $\frac{3}{2}$, batches from 1 c of milk.

• Then multiply to find out the number of batches in 4 c.
$$4 \times \frac{3}{2} = 6$$

You can make 6 batches of pancakes with 4 c of milk.

Notice that dividing 4 by $\frac{2}{3}$ has the same result as multiplying 4 by $\frac{3}{2}$. This is because $\frac{3}{2}$ is the reciprocal of $\frac{2}{3}$.

$$4 \div \frac{2}{3} = 4 \times \frac{3}{2} = 6$$

To divide by a fraction, multiply by its reciprocal.

━━━━━━━━ GUIDED PRACTICE ━━━━━━━━

Find the value of *n*.

1. $15 \div \frac{3}{5} = 15 \times n$ $\frac{5}{3}$

2. $28 \div \frac{4}{9} = 28 \times n$ $\frac{9}{4}$

Write the quotient in lowest terms.

3. $5 \div \frac{1}{4}$ 20

4. $12 \div \frac{3}{4}$ 16

2 TEACH

☑ **MATERIALS CHECKLIST:** quart measuring container, two measuring cups, water or sand

Do these activities to model $4 \div \frac{2}{3}$: Fill the quart container to the 4-c mark. Point to the $\frac{2}{3}$ c mark. **How many $\frac{2}{3}$-c batches could be poured from the 4 cups?** *(6)* Have a volunteer verify by pouring.

Fill one cup and pour it into the empty container. **How many $\frac{2}{3}$-c batches could be poured from one cup?** *($1\frac{1}{2}$, or $\frac{3}{2}$ batches)* **How can you find the number of batches that could be poured from the 4 cups?** *($4 \times 1\frac{1}{2}$)*

> ### Chalkboard Examples
>
> Write the answer in lowest terms.
>
> $4 \div \frac{1}{2}$ *(8)* $3 \div \frac{3}{4}$ *(4)*
>
> $3 \div \frac{2}{5}$ *($7\frac{1}{2}$)* $8 \div \frac{5}{6}$ *($9\frac{3}{5}$)*

SUMMARIZE/ASSESS   **Explain or use the containers to demonstrate why 6 is a reasonable answer for $3 \div \frac{1}{2}$.**

Write the quotient in lowest terms.

5. $3 \div \frac{1}{2}$ 6   **6.** $5 \div \frac{1}{3}$ 15   **7.** $4 \div \frac{1}{5}$ 20   **8.** $7 \div \frac{1}{8}$ 56   **9.** $4 \div \frac{1}{20}$ 80

10. $6 \div \frac{2}{3}$ 9   **11.** $1 \div \frac{3}{4}$ $1\frac{1}{3}$ **12.** $1 \div \frac{7}{8}$ $1\frac{1}{7}$ **13.** $3 \div \frac{3}{10}$ 10   **14.** $4 \div \frac{2}{5}$ 10

15. $9 \div \frac{9}{11}$ 11   **16.** $5 \div \frac{3}{4}$ $6\frac{2}{3}$ **17.** $7 \div \frac{3}{4}$ $9\frac{1}{3}$ **18.** $10 \div \frac{5}{6}$ 12   **19.** $3 \div \frac{11}{20}$ $5\frac{5}{11}$

20. $7 \div \frac{2}{3}$ $10\frac{1}{2}$ **21.** $15 \div \frac{1}{3}$ 45   **22.** $32 \div \frac{4}{5}$ 40   **23.** $5 \div \frac{4}{4}$ 5   **24.** $20 \div \frac{2}{5}$ 50

25. $19 \div \frac{12}{12}$ 19   **26.** $21 \div \frac{7}{8}$ 24   **27.** $32 \div \frac{16}{25}$ 50   **28.** $6 \div \frac{34}{34}$ 6   **29.** $100 \div \frac{3}{5}$ $166\frac{2}{3}$

MIXED REVIEW   Compute.

30. $18 - \frac{3}{4}$ $17\frac{1}{4}$ **31.** $18 \div \frac{3}{4}$ 24   **32.** $9\frac{1}{3} \times \frac{5}{6}$ $7\frac{7}{9}$ **33.** $9\frac{1}{3} + \frac{5}{6}$ $10\frac{1}{6}$

34. $48 \div \frac{3}{8}$ 128   **35.** $\frac{3}{8} \times 48$ 18   **36.** $4\frac{1}{3} + 1\frac{1}{2}$ $5\frac{5}{6}$ **37.** $4\frac{1}{3} - 1\frac{1}{2}$ $2\frac{5}{6}$

MENTAL MATH   Use the pattern to solve mentally.

38. If $10 \div \frac{1}{2} = 20$, what is $10 \div \frac{1}{4}$? $10 \div \frac{1}{8}$? $10 \div \frac{1}{16}$?
40;   80;   160

Solve using the Sculptor's Dough recipe.

39. Phil made an eagle using the Sculptor's Dough recipe for 6 c. If an eagle takes $\frac{3}{4}$ c of dough, how many eagles can he make from 1 batch of dough?   8

40. Cathy's model of a snowflake used about $\frac{2}{5}$ c of dough. How many snowflakes can she make from $\frac{1}{2}$ batch of dough?   7

41. How much water and salt would you use to make the dough with only 3 c of flour? $1\frac{5}{16}$ c water, $1\frac{1}{2}$ c salt

Sculptor's Dough (makes 6 cups)
1¾ c water
4c flour
2c salt
Mix all 3 ingredients together. Add more water as needed. Shape the dough into several flat designs. Bake in oven at 200°F for about 3 h.

CHAPTER 7   215

MEETING INDIVIDUAL NEEDS

For Students Who Are . . .

Acquiring English Proficiency   Make sure students understand the meaning of *batch* and how to write the reciprocal of a fraction.

Gifted and Talented   Have students show why the associative and commutative properties do not work for division of fractions.

Working 2 or 3 Grades Below Level   Remind students that when they divide a whole number by a fraction less than 1, the answer will be greater than the dividend. Have students use pages 94–97 of the Skills Workbook for Fractions.

Today's Problem

A certain game has a strategy in which each "good" move is worth $\frac{2}{3}$ of a point. If Team A currently has 2 points, how many of these moves would Team A have to make to get ahead of Team B, which has 14 points? *(Team B is 12 points ahead of Team A. $12 \div \frac{2}{3} = 18$, so Team A would have to make at least 19 "good" moves.)*

3 FOLLOW-UP

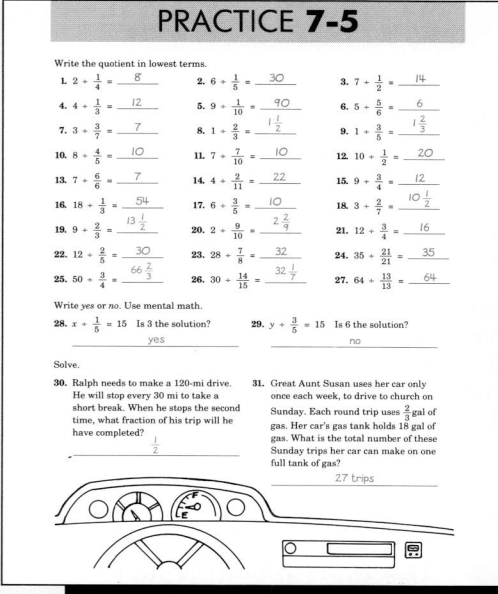

PRACTICE 7-5

Write the quotient in lowest terms.

1. $2 + \frac{1}{4} = $ 8   2. $6 + \frac{1}{5} = $ 30   3. $7 + \frac{1}{2} = $ 14
4. $4 + \frac{1}{3} = $ 12   5. $9 + \frac{1}{10} = $ 90   6. $5 + \frac{5}{6} = $ 6
7. $3 + \frac{3}{7} = $ 7   8. $1 + \frac{2}{3} = $ $1\frac{1}{2}$ 9. $1 + \frac{4}{5} = $ $1\frac{1}{4}$
10. $8 + \frac{4}{5} = $ 10   11. $7 + \frac{7}{10} = $ 10   12. $10 + \frac{1}{2} = $ 20
13. $7 + \frac{6}{7} = $ 7   14. $4 + \frac{2}{11} = $ 22   15. $9 + \frac{3}{4} = $ 12
16. $18 + \frac{1}{3} = $ 54   17. $6 + \frac{3}{5} = $ 10   18. $3 + \frac{2}{7} = $ $10\frac{1}{2}$
19. $9 + \frac{2}{3} = $ $13\frac{1}{2}$ 20. $2 + \frac{9}{10} = $ $2\frac{2}{9}$ 21. $12 + \frac{3}{4} = $ 16
22. $12 + \frac{2}{5} = $ 30   23. $28 + \frac{7}{8} = $ 32   24. $35 + \frac{21}{21} = $ 35
25. $50 + \frac{3}{4} = $ $66\frac{2}{3}$ 26. $30 + \frac{14}{15} = $ $32\frac{1}{7}$ 27. $64 + \frac{13}{13} = $ 64

Write yes or no. Use mental math.

28. $x + \frac{1}{5} = 15$ Is 3 the solution?   yes
29. $y + \frac{3}{5} = 15$ Is 6 the solution?   no

Solve.

30. Ralph needs to make a 120-mi drive. He will stop every 30 mi to take a short break. When he stops the second time, what fraction of his trip will he have completed? $\frac{1}{2}$

31. Great Aunt Susan uses her car only once each week, to drive to church on Sunday. Each round trip uses $\frac{2}{3}$ gal of gas. Her car's gas tank holds 18 gal of gas. What is the total number of these Sunday trips her car can make on one full tank of gas?   27 trips

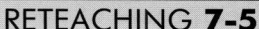

RETEACHING 7-5

Dividing by a fraction has the same result as multiplying by the reciprocal of the fraction.

Example: Find the quotient: $5 \div \frac{3}{5}$.

$5 \div \frac{3}{5} = 5 \times \frac{5}{3}$ $\frac{3}{5}$ and $\frac{5}{3}$ are reciprocals.
$\frac{3}{5} \times \frac{5}{3} = 1$

$5 \times \frac{5}{3} = \frac{5}{1} \times \frac{5}{3} = \frac{25}{3} = 8\frac{1}{3}$

Complete.

1. $6 + \frac{3}{5} = 6 \times \boxed{\frac{5}{3}}$ 2. $9 + \frac{2}{3} = 9 \times \boxed{\frac{3}{2}}$

$6 \times \boxed{\frac{5}{3}} = \frac{6}{1} \times \boxed{\frac{5}{3}} = \frac{30}{\boxed{3}} = 10$ $9 \times \boxed{\frac{3}{2}} = \frac{9}{1} \times \boxed{\frac{3}{2}} = \frac{27}{2} = 13\frac{1}{2}$

Write the quotient in lowest terms.

3. $2 + \frac{2}{3} = $ 3   4. $7 + \frac{1}{8} = $ 56   5. $1 + \frac{4}{5} = $ $\frac{5}{4}$
6. $3 + \frac{9}{10} = $ $3\frac{1}{3}$ 7. $8 + \frac{2}{5} = $ 20   8. $6 + \frac{6}{5} = $ $7\frac{1}{5}$
9. $9 + \frac{6}{7} = $ $10\frac{1}{2}$ 10. $8 + \frac{1}{3} = $ 24   11. $11 + \frac{11}{12} = $ 12
12. $12 + \frac{3}{3} = $ 12   13. $15 + \frac{8}{9} = $ $16\frac{7}{8}$ 14. $10 + \frac{3}{8} = $ $26\frac{2}{3}$

ENRICHMENT 7-5

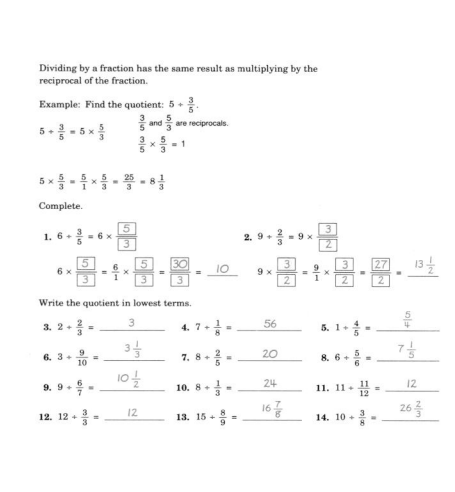

☑ **MATERIALS CHECKLIST:** Rulers

Write the following formula on the board: (foot length − 4) $\div \frac{1}{3}$ = British shoe size. Have the students measure the length of a partner's right foot with a ruler. Tell them that because the British system for sizing shoes begins with 4 in. and increases by $\frac{1}{3}$ in. for whole number sizes, they must give a measurement that consists of a whole number and one of these fractions: $\frac{1}{6}$, $\frac{1}{3}$, $\frac{1}{2}$, $\frac{2}{3}$, $\frac{5}{6}$ (for example, $9\frac{2}{3}$ in.). Partners then find each other's British shoe size using the formula. (For shoe sizes greater than or equal to 14, the students must subtract 13.)

Lesson Organizer

Objective: Divide fractions.

Prior Knowledge: Students should be able to multiply fractions and write the reciprocal of a number.

Error Analysis and Remediation: See page 225A.

Lesson Resources:
Practice Worksheet 7-6
Reteaching Activity 7-6
Enrichment Worksheet 7-6
Daily Review 7-6

 *Two-Minute Math*

Use the Table of Numbers on the inside back cover. Write the reciprocal of each number in row K.
$\left(\frac{16}{5}, \frac{8}{21}, \frac{2}{5}, \frac{8}{7}, \frac{16}{65}, \frac{4}{5}, \frac{8}{11}, \frac{4}{15}, \frac{16}{71}\right)$

1 INTRODUCE

CONCRETE ACTIVITY

✓ **MATERIALS CHECKLIST:** fraction bars or Teaching Aid 4 (Fraction Bars)

1. Show fraction bars for $\frac{5}{6}$ and $\frac{1}{6}$. **How many $\frac{1}{6}$'s are in a $\frac{5}{6}$ bar?** *(5)* Call on a volunteer to use the fraction bars to demonstrate the answer.

2. Show fraction bars for $\frac{3}{4}$ and $\frac{1}{3}$. **How many $\frac{1}{3}$'s are in a $\frac{3}{4}$ bar?** *(two and part of another)* Have a student demonstrate the answer.

3. Show fraction bars for $\frac{3}{4}$ and $\frac{2}{3}$. **How many $\frac{3}{4}$'s are in a $\frac{2}{3}$ bar?** *(less than one)* Have a student demonstrate the answer.

WHEN YOUR STUDENTS ASK
★ **WHY AM I LEARNING THIS?** ★

You can connect this skill to real life through interpreting map scales. If $\frac{1}{3}$ in. on the scale represents 1 mi on Earth, what distance would be represented by $\frac{5}{8}$ in.?

216 *Chapter 7 • Lesson 7-6*

Dividing Fractions

How many $\frac{1}{4}$-lb hamburgers can be made from $\frac{3}{4}$ lb of meat?

• How many $\frac{1}{4}$ lb are in $\frac{3}{4}$ lb?

To divide, multiply by the reciprocal of $\frac{1}{4}$.

$$\frac{3}{4} \div \frac{1}{4} = \frac{3}{4} \times \frac{4}{1} = 3$$

Do you see that three $\frac{1}{4}$-lb hamburgers can be made from $\frac{3}{4}$ lb of meat? **yes**

How many $\frac{1}{8}$-lb hamburgers can be made with the same amount of meat?

• How many $\frac{1}{8}$ lb are in $\frac{3}{4}$ lb?

Multiply by the reciprocal of $\frac{1}{8}$.

$$\frac{3}{4} \div \frac{1}{8} = \frac{3}{4} \times \frac{8}{1} = 6$$

Can you count six $\frac{1}{8}$-lb hamburgers in $\frac{3}{4}$ lb? **yes**

How can $\frac{5}{6}$ lb of meat be shared equally between Pat and Lou?

• What is $\frac{5}{6}$ divided by 2?

Multiply by the reciprocal of 2.

$$\frac{5}{6} \div 2 = \frac{5}{6} \times \frac{1}{2} = \frac{5}{12}$$

Pat's
Lou's

Do you see that Pat and Lou would get $\frac{5}{12}$ lb of meat each? **yes**

━━━━━━━━━━━ **GUIDED PRACTICE** ━━━━━━━━━━━

Write the quotient in lowest terms.

1. $\frac{7}{8} \div \frac{3}{4}$ $1\frac{1}{6}$ **2.** $\frac{3}{4} \div \frac{7}{8}$ $\frac{6}{7}$ **3.** $\frac{4}{5} \div 4$ $\frac{1}{5}$ **4.** $\frac{5}{6} \div \frac{5}{6}$ 1 **5.** $\frac{1}{6} \div 6$ $\frac{1}{36}$

━━━━━━━━━━━ **PRACTICE** ━━━━━━━━━━━

Write the quotient in lowest terms.

6. $\frac{3}{4} \div \frac{2}{3}$ $1\frac{1}{8}$ **7.** $\frac{3}{4} \div \frac{3}{4}$ 1 **8.** $\frac{4}{5} \div \frac{3}{4}$ $1\frac{1}{15}$ **9.** $\frac{3}{4} \div 1$ $\frac{3}{4}$ **10.** $\frac{3}{4} \div 3$ $\frac{1}{4}$

11. $\frac{6}{11} \div 4$ $\frac{3}{22}$ **12.** $\frac{5}{8} \div 10$ $\frac{1}{16}$ **13.** $\frac{7}{9} \div 14$ $\frac{1}{18}$ **14.** $\frac{2}{3} \div 36$ $\frac{1}{54}$ **15.** $\frac{4}{9} \div \frac{4}{5}$ $\frac{5}{9}$

216   LESSON 7-6

---

2 TEACH

┌─────────── **MULTICULTURAL NOTE** ───────────┐
Exercises 42–44. According to Chinese legends, Emperor Shen Nung was the first person to drink tea, nearly 5,000 years ago. The custom of tea drinking spread through Asia and was brought to Europe in about 1600.
└──────────────────────────────────────┘

✓ **MATERIALS CHECKLIST:** fraction bars or Teaching Aid 4 (Fraction Bars) for each student

Use the fraction bars to explain why $\frac{3}{4} \div \frac{1}{6}$ is greater than 1. *(There is more than one $\frac{1}{6}$ bars in $\frac{3}{4}$.)*

Use the fraction bars to explain why $\frac{1}{6} \div \frac{3}{4}$ is less than 1. *(There is less than one $\frac{3}{4}$ bar in $\frac{1}{6}$.)*

By what number can you divide $\frac{3}{4}$ to get an answer of 1? *(itself, $\frac{3}{4}$)*

┌─── *Chalkboard Examples* ───┐
Write the answer in lowest terms.

$\frac{3}{5} \div \frac{1}{5}$ (3) $\frac{5}{12} \div \frac{2}{3}$ $\left(\frac{5}{8}\right)$

$\frac{3}{8} \div \frac{4}{3}$ $\left(\frac{9}{32}\right)$ $\frac{5}{6} \div \frac{1}{10}$ $\left(8\frac{1}{3}\right)$
└──────────────────────────┘

SUMMARIZE/ASSESS   **Explain how to divide a fraction by a fraction.** *(Multiply the dividend by the reciprocal of the divisor, and write the answer in lowest terms.)*

16. $\frac{6}{1} \div \frac{1}{6}$ 36
17. $\frac{5}{9} \div \frac{1}{3}$ $1\frac{2}{3}$
18. $\frac{1}{16} \div 4$ $\frac{1}{64}$
19. $\frac{4}{5} \div \frac{14}{5}$ $\frac{2}{7}$
20. $\frac{18}{19} \div 12$ $\frac{3}{38}$

21. $\frac{8}{9} \div \frac{2}{3}$ $1\frac{1}{3}$
22. $\frac{9}{10} \div 45$ $\frac{1}{50}$
23. $\frac{8}{15} \div \frac{16}{25}$ $\frac{5}{6}$
24. $\frac{8}{11} \div \frac{8}{11}$ 1
25. $\frac{3}{8} \div \frac{7}{12}$ $\frac{9}{14}$

26. $\frac{4}{7} \div \frac{10}{14}$ $\frac{4}{5}$
27. $\frac{7}{9} \div 13$ $\frac{7}{117}$
28. $\frac{9}{12} \div \frac{7}{6}$ $\frac{9}{14}$
29. $\frac{8}{7} \div \frac{4}{9}$ $2\frac{4}{7}$
30. $\frac{14}{9} \div \frac{6}{4}$ $1\frac{1}{27}$

*31. $\left(\frac{2}{3} + \frac{1}{8}\right) \div \frac{1}{2}$ $1\frac{7}{12}$
*32. $\left(\frac{7}{8} - \frac{1}{4}\right) \div 4$ $\frac{5}{32}$
*33. $\left(\frac{4}{5} \times \frac{10}{20}\right) \div \frac{8}{9}$ $\frac{9}{20}$

MIXED REVIEW Compute.

34. $4\frac{1}{2} + \frac{5}{6}$ $5\frac{1}{3}$
35. $3\frac{1}{3} - \frac{7}{8}$ $2\frac{11}{24}$
36. $\frac{5}{6} \times 1\frac{1}{2}$ $1\frac{1}{4}$
37. $\frac{4}{5} \div \frac{3}{8}$ $2\frac{2}{15}$

38. $9\frac{1}{3} + 6\frac{1}{2}$ $15\frac{5}{6}$
39. $5\frac{3}{4} - 2\frac{9}{10}$ $2\frac{17}{20}$
40. $3\frac{1}{4} \times 3\frac{1}{4}$ $10\frac{9}{16}$
41. $\frac{1}{2} \div \frac{4}{5}$ $\frac{5}{8}$

═══ **PROBLEM SOLVING** ═══

CHOOSE Choose paper and pencil or mental math to solve. **Choices will vary. Suggestions given.**

42. You want to make spicy orange herbal tea but have only 1 tea bag. How much of each other ingredient would you need? **See page 225b.**

43. How many tablespoons of honey are used per cup of orange juice in this recipe?
m; 6 T

44. Suppose this is a recipe for 4 c of tea. In that case, how could you modify it to make 10 c?
p; Multiply each amount by $2\frac{1}{2}$.

"Spicy Orange Herbal Tea"
4 c boiling water
2 herbal lemon tea bags
$\frac{1}{2}$ c orange juice
3 T honey
1 in. cinnamon stick
5 whole cloves
Pour boiling water over the tea bags. Add the remaining ingredients. Let brew 5 min before serving.

$\frac{3}{4} \div \frac{1}{2} = \frac{3}{4} \times \frac{2}{1} = 1\frac{1}{2}$
This answer is weird! When you divide the answer should get smaller!

Critical Thinking

• With a partner, continue the pattern for the next three divisions.
$8 \div 8, \ 8 \div 4, \ 8 \div 2, \ 8 \div 1,$
$8 \div \frac{1}{2}, \ 8 \div \frac{1}{4}, \ \blacksquare, \ \blacksquare, \ \blacksquare$

• Explain the value of the quotient you get when you divide by a fraction less than 1. **Greater than the number that is being divided.**

$8 \div \frac{1}{8}; \ 8 \div \frac{1}{16}; \ 8 \div \frac{1}{32}$

CHAPTER 7 217

MEETING INDIVIDUAL NEEDS

For Students Who Are . . .

Acquiring English Proficiency Pair students with an English-proficient student to discuss and solve the Problem Solving and Critical Thinking exercises.

Gifted and Talented Have students simplify these fractions:

$\dfrac{\frac{9}{16}}{\frac{3}{8}} \ (1\frac{1}{2})$ $\dfrac{\frac{2}{3}}{\frac{5}{8}} \ (1\frac{1}{15})$ $\dfrac{\frac{5}{12}}{\frac{3}{16}} \ (2\frac{2}{9})$ $\dfrac{\frac{7}{8}}{\frac{5}{12}} \ (2\frac{1}{10})$

Working 2 or 3 Grades Below Level When students divide a fraction by a whole number, have them first write the whole number over 1 and then multiply by its reciprocal.

Today's Problem

The auditorium at a junior high school can seat $\frac{2}{3}$ of the student body. There are 12 classes, and each class has $\frac{1}{12}$ of the student body. How many classes can be in the auditorium at one time? *(Number of classes: $\frac{2}{3} \div \frac{1}{12} = \frac{24}{3} = 8$)*

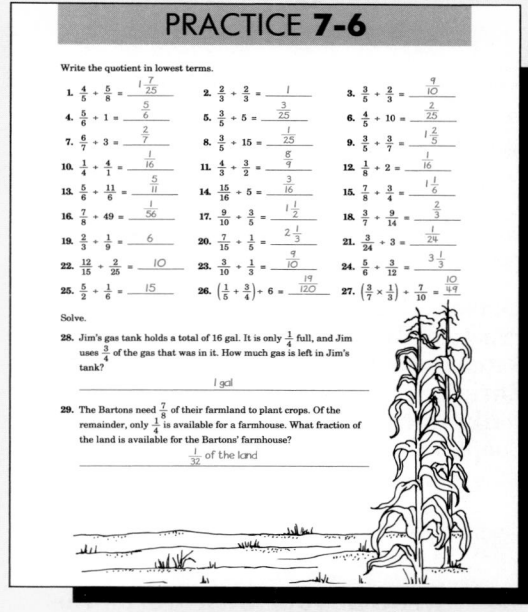

PRACTICE 7-6

Write the quotient in lowest terms.

1. $\frac{4}{5} \div \frac{5}{8} = \underline{1\frac{7}{25}}$
2. $\frac{2}{5} \div \frac{2}{5} = \underline{1}$
3. $\frac{3}{5} \div \frac{2}{3} = \underline{\frac{9}{10}}$
4. $\frac{5}{6} \div 1 = \underline{\frac{5}{6}}$
5. $\frac{3}{5} \div 5 = \underline{\frac{3}{25}}$
6. $\frac{4}{5} \div 10 = \underline{\frac{2}{25}}$
7. $\frac{6}{7} \div 3 = \underline{\frac{2}{7}}$
8. $\frac{3}{5} \div 15 = \underline{\frac{1}{25}}$
9. $\frac{3}{5} \div \frac{3}{7} = \underline{1\frac{2}{5}}$
10. $\frac{1}{4} \div \frac{4}{1} = \underline{\frac{1}{16}}$
11. $\frac{4}{3} \div \frac{3}{2} = \underline{\frac{8}{9}}$
12. $\frac{1}{8} \div 2 = \underline{\frac{1}{16}}$
13. $\frac{5}{6} \div \frac{1}{6} = \underline{5}$
14. $\frac{15}{16} \div 5 = \underline{\frac{3}{16}}$
15. $\frac{7}{8} \div \frac{3}{4} = \underline{1\frac{1}{6}}$
16. $\frac{7}{8} \div 49 = \underline{\frac{1}{56}}$
17. $\frac{9}{10} \div \frac{2}{5} = \underline{2\frac{1}{4}}$
18. $\frac{3}{7} \div \frac{2}{14} = \underline{3}$
19. $\frac{2}{3} \div \frac{1}{9} = \underline{6}$
20. $\frac{7}{5} \div \frac{1}{5} = \underline{2\frac{2}{5}}$
21. $\frac{3}{24} \div 3 = \underline{\frac{1}{24}}$
22. $\frac{12}{15} \div \frac{2}{25} = \underline{10}$
23. $\frac{3}{4} \div \frac{1}{10} = \underline{\frac{9}{10}}$
24. $\frac{5}{3} \div \frac{5}{9} = \underline{3\frac{1}{3}}$
25. $\frac{5}{2} \div \frac{1}{6} = \underline{15}$
26. $\left(\frac{1}{5} + \frac{3}{4}\right) \div 6 = \underline{\frac{19}{120}}$
27. $\left(\frac{3}{7} \times \frac{1}{3}\right) \div \frac{7}{10} = \underline{\frac{10}{49}}$

Solve.

28. Jim's gas tank holds a total of 16 gal. It is only $\frac{1}{4}$ full, and Jim uses $\frac{3}{4}$ of the gas that was in it. How much gas is left in Jim's tank?
1 gal

29. The Bartons need $\frac{7}{8}$ of their farmland to plant crops. Of the remainder, only $\frac{1}{4}$ is available for a farmhouse. What fraction of the land is available for the Bartons' farmhouse?
$\frac{1}{32}$ of the land

RETEACHING 7-6

☑ **MATERIALS CHECKLIST:** Fraction bars

Have the students work in pairs. Provide each pair with fraction bars showing halves, thirds, fourths, fifths, sixths, eighths, tenths, and twelfths. Write the following exercise on the board: $\frac{2}{3} \div \frac{1}{6}$. Ask: What does this exercise ask you to find? [the number of sixths in $\frac{2}{3}$] Have the students use equivalent fraction bars (in this case, thirds and sixths) to find the answer. [4] Repeat the activity for the following exercises: $\frac{3}{4} \div \frac{1}{12}$; $\frac{1}{2} \div \frac{1}{4}$; $\frac{3}{5} \div \frac{1}{10}$; $\frac{7}{8} \div \frac{1}{8}$, $\frac{3}{4} \div \frac{3}{8}$.

ENRICHMENT 7-6

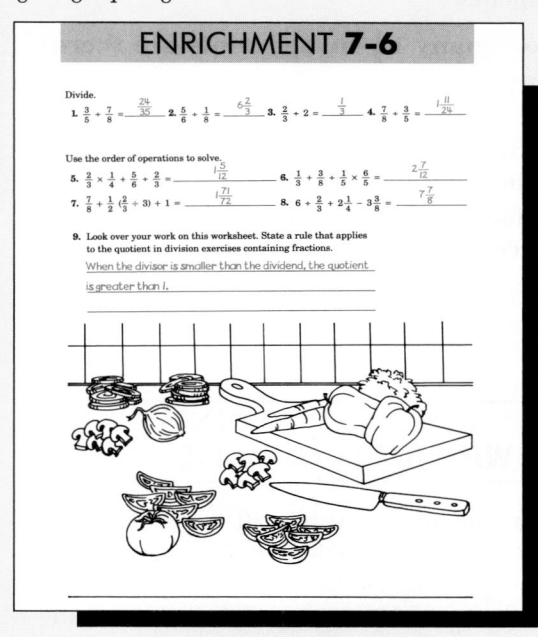

Divide.

1. $\frac{3}{5} \div \frac{7}{8} = \underline{\frac{24}{35}}$
2. $5 \div \frac{3}{4} = \underline{6\frac{2}{3}}$
3. $\frac{2}{3} \div 2 = \underline{\frac{1}{3}}$
4. $\frac{7}{8} \div \frac{3}{5} = \underline{1\frac{11}{24}}$

Use the order of operations to solve.

5. $\frac{2}{3} \times \frac{4}{5} + \frac{5}{8} \div 2 = \underline{1\frac{5}{12}}$
6. $\frac{1}{8} + \frac{3}{5} + \frac{1}{2} \times \frac{6}{5} = \underline{2\frac{7}{12}}$
7. $\frac{7}{8} + \frac{1}{2}(\frac{3}{4} \div 3) + 1 = \underline{1\frac{71}{72}}$
8. $6 \div \frac{2}{3} + 2\frac{1}{4} - 3\frac{3}{8} = \underline{7\frac{7}{8}}$

9. Look over your work on this worksheet. State a rule that applies to the quotient in division exercises containing fractions.
When the divisor is smaller than the dividend, the quotient is greater than 1.

Objective: Divide mixed numbers.

Prior Knowledge: Students should be able to change mixed numbers to fractions and multiply fractions.

Error Analysis and Remediation: See page 225A.

Lesson Resources:
Practice Worksheet 7-7
Reteaching Worksheet 7-7
Enrichment Activity 7-7
Daily Review 7-7
Cooperative Investigations, Chapter 7

 **Two-Minute Math**

Write in your own words the meaning of a math connection. Give examples if you wish.

1 INTRODUCE

CONNECTING ACTIVITY

☑ **MATERIALS CHECKLIST:** inch ruler and sheet of construction paper for each pair

Have students work with a partner.

1. Tell students to

- use a ruler to draw a 12-in. line segment.

- divide the line segment into $1\frac{1}{2}$-in. segments.

How many $1\frac{1}{2}$-in. segments are there?
(8) Write $12 \div 1\frac{1}{2} = 12 \div \frac{3}{2} = \overset{4}{\cancel{12}} \times \frac{2}{3} = 8$

2. Repeat, having students draw another 12-in. segment and divide it into $\frac{3}{4}$-in. segments. **How many $\frac{3}{4}$ in. segments are there?** *(16 segments; $12 \div \frac{3}{4} = 16$)*

WHEN YOUR STUDENTS ASK
★ **WHY AM I LEARNING THIS?** ★

You can connect this skill to real life through mass production. If a bolt of cloth contains $16\frac{1}{2}$ yd, and a manufacturer needs $2\frac{2}{3}$ yd for each garment, how many garments can be made from the bolt?

Dividing With Mixed Numbers

Two square pieces of wood measuring $5\frac{1}{8}$ in. on a side are needed for the ends of the CD (compact disk) holder at the right. Could you use a board that is 11 in. long and $5\frac{1}{8}$ in. wide for the 2 end pieces?

If you know how to divide fractions and how to change mixed numbers to fractions, you can make a 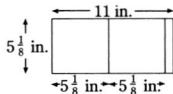 to divide 11 by $5\frac{1}{8}$.

Change $5\frac{1}{8}$ to $\frac{41}{8}$.	Multiply by the reciprocal of $5\frac{1}{8}$, or $\frac{8}{41}$.
$11 \div 5\frac{1}{8} \Rightarrow 11 \div \frac{41}{8}$	$11 \times \frac{8}{41} = \frac{88}{41} = 2\frac{6}{41}$

The 11-in. board could be used.

Another example:

$2\frac{1}{4} \div 1\frac{1}{2} = \frac{9}{4} \div \frac{3}{2} = \overset{3}{\underset{2}{\cancel{\frac{9}{4}}}} \times \overset{1}{\underset{1}{\cancel{\frac{2}{3}}}} = \frac{3}{2} = 1\frac{1}{2}$

▬ GUIDED PRACTICE ▬

Write the quotient in lowest terms.

1. $3\frac{3}{7} \div \frac{6}{7}$ 4

2. $3\frac{1}{2} \div 1\frac{1}{2}$ $2\frac{1}{3}$

3. $9\frac{3}{4} \div 1\frac{7}{8}$ $5\frac{1}{5}$

4. $6\frac{2}{3} \div 1\frac{1}{9}$ 6

▬ PRACTICE ▬

Write the quotient in lowest terms.

5. $8\frac{2}{3} \div 4\frac{1}{3}$ 2

6. $8\frac{2}{3} \div 8\frac{2}{3}$ 1

7. $4 \div 2\frac{1}{2}$ $1\frac{3}{5}$

8. $6\frac{3}{4} \div 40\frac{1}{2}$ $\frac{1}{6}$

9. $5\frac{3}{5} \div \frac{4}{7}$ $9\frac{4}{5}$

10. $\frac{16}{15} \div 3\frac{1}{5}$ $\frac{1}{3}$

11. $15\frac{3}{4} \div 15\frac{3}{4}$ 1

12. $8\frac{7}{8} \div \frac{7}{8}$ $10\frac{1}{7}$

13. $8\frac{2}{3} \div 1\frac{5}{8}$ $5\frac{1}{3}$

14. $0 \div 3\frac{4}{5}$ 0

15. $4\frac{4}{5} \div 1$ $4\frac{4}{5}$

16. $2\frac{1}{10} \div 5\frac{1}{5}$ $\frac{21}{52}$

17. $\frac{5}{6} \div 2\frac{1}{2}$ $\frac{1}{3}$

18. $6\frac{3}{4} \div 7\frac{1}{4}$ $\frac{27}{29}$

19. $13\frac{1}{2} \div 3\frac{3}{8}$ 4

20. $25\frac{1}{3} \div 3\frac{1}{6}$ 8

---

2 TEACH

☑ **MATERIALS CHECKLIST:** Math Connection Transparency

How is division with mixed numbers like division with fractions? *(After changing the mixed numbers to fractions, the division is done the same way.)*

Chalkboard Examples

Write the answer in lowest terms.

$6 \div 2\frac{1}{5} \ \left(2\frac{8}{11}\right)$
$2\frac{5}{12} \div 3\frac{2}{3} \ \left(\frac{29}{44}\right)$
$12\frac{3}{8} \div 2\frac{3}{4} \ \left(4\frac{1}{2}\right)$

SUMMARIZE/ASSESS Describe the steps to follow in dividing a mixed number by a mixed number.

(Sidebar label: MATH AND INDUSTRIAL ARTS)

21. $5\frac{1}{2} \div \frac{3}{8}$ $14\frac{2}{3}$ ***22.** $\left(4\frac{1}{2} \times \frac{2}{4}\right) \div \frac{1}{2}$ $4\frac{1}{2}$ ***23.** $\left(\frac{4}{5} - \frac{6}{10}\right) \div 1\frac{1}{2}$ $\frac{2}{15}$

MIXED REVIEW Compute.

24. $6\frac{1}{7} - \frac{5}{7}$ $5\frac{3}{7}$ **25.** $\frac{3}{8} \times \frac{4}{5}$ $\frac{3}{10}$ **26.** $2\frac{1}{2} + \frac{3}{4}$ $3\frac{1}{4}$ **27.** $2\frac{1}{4} \div 1\frac{1}{2}$ $1\frac{1}{2}$

28. $9\frac{1}{3} \times \frac{3}{4}$ 7 **29.** $\frac{5}{16} + 1\frac{1}{8}$ $1\frac{7}{16}$ **30.** $\frac{5}{6} \div \frac{5}{6}$ 1 **31.** $3 - 1\frac{2}{3}$ $1\frac{1}{3}$

NUMBER SENSE Is the quotient *greater than* or *less than* 1?

32. $6 \div 2\frac{1}{2}$
greater

33. $2\frac{3}{4} \div 11$
less

34. $5 \div \frac{3}{4}$
greater

35. $2\frac{1}{3} \div 9\frac{1}{2}$
less

=== **PROBLEM SOLVING** ===

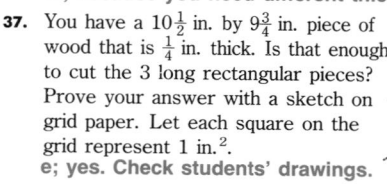 **CHOOSE** Choose mental math, estimation, or paper and pencil to solve.   Choices will vary. Suggestions given.

36. **IN YOUR WORDS** Explain why you would not want to cut all 5 pieces for the CD holder at the right from the same board.
m; because you need different thicknesses

37. You have a $10\frac{1}{2}$ in. by $9\frac{3}{4}$ in. piece of wood that is $\frac{1}{4}$ in. thick. Is that enough to cut the 3 long rectangular pieces? Prove your answer with a sketch on grid paper. Let each square on the grid represent 1 in.^{2}.
e; yes. Check students' drawings.

38. Once the CD holder is made, what is its overall height? its length?
p; $5\frac{1}{2}$ in.; $9\frac{3}{4}$ in.

*39. A single CD is about $\frac{7}{16}$ in. thick. About how many CDs could you store in this holder?   e; ≈20 CDs

$9\frac{3}{4}$ in.

$5\frac{1}{2}$ in.

$\frac{1}{4}$ in.

$\frac{1}{2}$ in.

$5\frac{1}{2}$ in.

$3\frac{1}{2}$ in.

$\frac{1}{4}$ in.

Estimate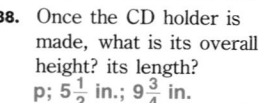

Compatible numbers can help you estimate the quotient of mixed fractions.

$43\frac{1}{2} \div 6\frac{1}{8} = ?$ ▷ $42 \div 6 = 7$ ▷   So, $43\frac{1}{2} \div 6\frac{1}{8}$ is about 7.

Accept reasonable estimates.

Use compatible numbers to estimate.   Suggestions given.

1. $58 \div 5\frac{3}{5}$ ≈ 10 **2.** $25\frac{3}{8} \div 3\frac{1}{9}$ ≈ 8 **3.** $34\frac{5}{16} \div 8\frac{2}{13}$ ≈ 4 **4.** $105\frac{1}{3} \div 8\frac{2}{3}\approx 12$

MEETING INDIVIDUAL NEEDS

For Students Who Are . . .

Acquiring English Proficiency Review how to change a mixed number to a fraction greater than one in the math connection:

$$5\frac{1}{2} \rightarrow 5 \times 2 + 1 \rightarrow \frac{11}{2}.$$

Gifted and Talented Have students simplify these fractions:

$$\frac{4\frac{1}{2} + 1\frac{1}{2}}{7\frac{1}{4} + 2\frac{5}{8}} \left(\frac{48}{79}\right) \qquad \frac{2\frac{3}{4} + 1\frac{7}{8}}{3\frac{11}{16} - \frac{1}{2}} \left(1\frac{23}{51}\right)$$

Working 2 or 3 Grades Below Level Remind students to change all mixed numbers to fractions greater than one first, then multiply by the reciprocal of the second fraction.

Today's Problem

A floor is $12\frac{1}{2}$ ft long and $10\frac{1}{2}$ ft wide. The floor is to be covered with rectangular tiles that are $1\frac{1}{4}$ ft long by $\frac{3}{4}$ ft wide. How many tiles will it take to cover the floor? *(140)*

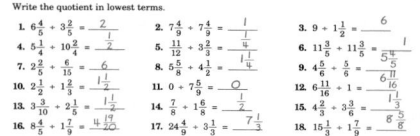

PRACTICE 7-7

Write the quotient in lowest terms.

1. $6\frac{4}{5} \div 3\frac{2}{5} = \frac{2}{1}$ **2.** $7\frac{4}{9} \div 7\frac{4}{8} = \frac{1}{1}$ **3.** $9 \div 1\frac{1}{2} = \frac{6}{1}$

4. $5\frac{1}{4} \div 10\frac{2}{4} = \frac{1}{2}$ **5.** $\frac{11}{12} \div 3\frac{2}{3} = \frac{1}{4}$ **6.** $11\frac{3}{5} \div 11\frac{3}{5} = 1$

7. $2\frac{2}{5} \div \frac{6}{15} = 6$ **8.** $5\frac{5}{8} \div 4\frac{1}{2} = 1\frac{1}{4}$ **9.** $4\frac{5}{6} \div \frac{5}{9} = 8\frac{11}{10}$

10. $2\frac{1}{3} \div 1\frac{5}{9} = 1\frac{1}{2}$ **11.** $0 \div 7\frac{5}{8} = 0$ **12.** $6\frac{11}{16} \div 1 = 6\frac{11}{16}$

13. $3\frac{3}{10} \div 2\frac{1}{5} = 1\frac{1}{2}$ **14.** $\frac{7}{8} \div 1\frac{6}{8} = \frac{1}{2}$ **15.** $4\frac{3}{8} \div 3\frac{3}{6} = 1\frac{1}{4}$

16. $8\frac{4}{5} \div 1\frac{7}{9} = 4\frac{19}{20}$ **17.** $8\frac{4}{4} \div 3\frac{1}{3} = \frac{7}{3}$ **18.** $15\frac{1}{3} \div 1\frac{7}{9} = \frac{5}{8}$

Is the quotient *greater than* or *less than* 1?

19. $7 \div 1\frac{5}{9}$ greater than   **20.** $3\frac{1}{3} \div 10$ less than   **21.** $2\frac{3}{4} \div 5\frac{7}{9}$ less than

Solve.

22. Ron has received a shipment of ball bearings in crates that weigh $12\frac{1}{8}$ lb each. He needs to use a small service elevator to get the crates up to the next floor. The weight limit on this service elevator is $60\frac{5}{6}$ lb. How many crates can Ron put on the elevator without going over the weight limit?
5 crates

23. Brian has a baseball card file box that is $10\frac{11}{16}$ in. long. Each of his packets of cards is $\frac{9}{16}$ in. thick. How many packets can Brian put in the file box?
19 packets

RETEACHING 7-7

With division involving mixed numbers, change the mixed numbers to fractions first. Then divide the fractions.

Example: $2\frac{1}{2} \div 1\frac{1}{3} = \frac{5}{2} \div \frac{4}{3} = \frac{5}{2} \times \frac{3}{4} = \frac{15}{8} = 1\frac{7}{8}$ ← lowest terms

Complete.

1. $1\frac{2}{3} \div 1\frac{5}{8} = \frac{5}{3} \div \frac{13}{8} = \frac{5}{3} \times \frac{8}{13} = \frac{40}{39} = 1\frac{1}{39}$

2. $7 \div 2\frac{2}{3} = \frac{7}{1} \div \frac{8}{3} = \frac{7}{1} \times \frac{3}{8} = \frac{21}{8} = 2\frac{3}{8}$

3. $10\frac{1}{8} \div \frac{1}{3} = \frac{81}{8} \div \frac{1}{3} = \frac{81}{8} \times \frac{3}{1} = \frac{243}{8} = 30\frac{3}{8}$

Write the quotient in lowest terms.

4. $2\frac{1}{3} \div 3\frac{2}{5} = \frac{5}{8}$ **5.** $3\frac{1}{4} \div \frac{3}{4} = 4\frac{1}{3}$ **6.** $5\frac{1}{2} \div 5\frac{1}{2} = 1$

7. $3\frac{1}{8} \div 1\frac{5}{9} = 2\frac{1}{112}$ **8.** $2\frac{3}{7} \div \frac{5}{9} = 4\frac{13}{35}$ **9.** $0 \div 4\frac{5}{7} = 0$

10. $3\frac{1}{10} \div 2\frac{1}{10} = 1\frac{10}{21}$ **11.** $7\frac{1}{2} \div 1\frac{1}{4} = 6$ **12.** $1\frac{1}{4} \div 2\frac{2}{5} = \frac{25}{48}$

ENRICHMENT 7-7

☑ **MATERIALS CHECKLIST:** Index cards

Have the students work in groups of four, and in pairs within each group. Provide each pair with a set of index cards on which you have written these exercises: $4\frac{2}{3} \div 2\frac{1}{8}$, $6\frac{2}{3} \div 5\frac{1}{9}$, $1\frac{1}{10} \div 6\frac{1}{4}$, $2\frac{1}{5} \div 1\frac{2}{3}$, $5\frac{1}{6} \div 2\frac{1}{2}$, $8\frac{1}{8} \div 3\frac{5}{16}$. One partner changes the first mixed number in each problem to a fraction. The second partner does the same to the second mixed number. Partners then divide and find the quotient in lowest terms. The first pair to complete the exercises wins.

Lesson Organizer

> **Objective:** Solve problems by making a table.

Prior Knowledge: Students should be familiar with the idea of function rules.

Error Analysis and Remediation: See page 225A.

Lesson Resources:
Practice Worksheet 7-8
Reteaching Activity 7-8
Enrichment Worksheet 7-8
Daily Review 7-8
Cooperative Problem Solving 2, Chapter 7

Two-Minute Math

What is the rule for multiplying 0.4 × 0.7? *(4 × 7 = 28, move decimal point 2 places left to get 0.28)* **Use fractions to explain why this rule works.** $\left(\frac{4}{10} \times \frac{7}{10} = \frac{28}{100} = 0.28\right)$

1 INTRODUCE

CONNECTING ACTIVITY

Explain that students are going to do a little experiment with handshakes. To keep track of the results, you will write them on the chalkboard.

1. Have two students shake hands. **How many handshakes took place?** *(1)*

2. Add another person to the group.

- **How many more handshakes are needed?** *(2)*

- **How many handshakes took place in all?** *(3)*

3. Add another person and continue, filling in a table on the chalkboard as you go.

WHEN YOUR STUDENTS ASK
★ WHY AM I LEARNING THIS? ★

You can connect this skill to real life through medical diagnosis. Doctors can organize a patient's symptoms in a table to identify patterns that indicate a particular disease.

Problem Solving Strategy:
Making A Table

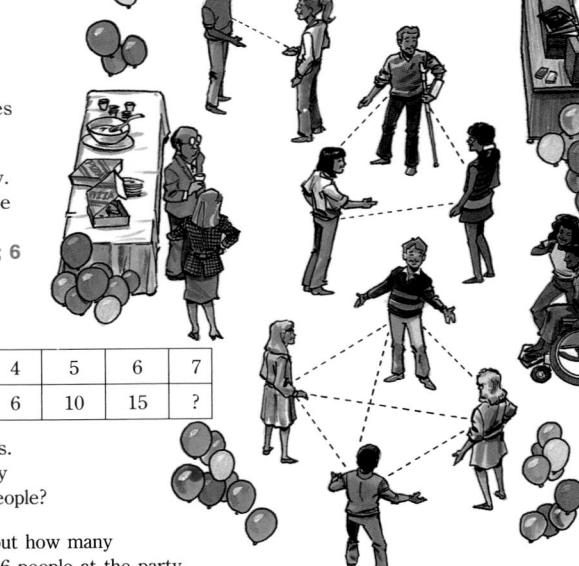

Some problems can be solved when you put the information in a table and look for a pattern.

At a party, every person shook hands with every other person once. If there were 16 people at the party, how many handshakes took place?

Think of fewer people at the party. How many handshakes would there be if there were 2 people at the party? 3 people? 4 people? **1; 3; 6**

Record what you learned from the diagrams into the table.

People	1	2	3	4	5	6	7
Handshakes	0	1	3	6	10	15	?

Look at the number of handshakes. Can you see a pattern? How many handshakes would there be for 7 people?
yes; 21 handshakes
Now, continue the pattern to find out how many handshakes took place among the 16 people at the party.
120 handshakes

GUIDED PRACTICE

Make a table to help you find a pattern that solves the problem.

1. You must choose exactly 2 ingredients on a pizza from the list shown.

   a. How many ingredients are there in all to select from? **8 ingredients**

   b. How many different combination pizzas could you choose if there were only 2 ingredients on the list? 3 ingredients? 4 ingredients? **1; 3; 6**

   c. How many different combination pizzas could you choose from the list of all 8 ingredients? **28**

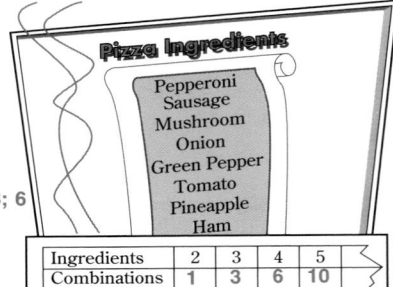

Pizza Ingredients

Pepperoni
Sausage
Mushroom
Onion
Green Pepper
Tomato
Pineapple
Ham

Ingredients	2	3	4	5	
Combinations	1	3	6	10	

220   LESSON 7–8

> **MULTICULTURAL NOTE**
>
> A handshake is used as a greeting by many cultures. Other gestures of greeting include bowing, used in Japan among other places, and kissing both cheeks, used in some European countries among other places.

2 TEACH

How did making the table help solve the problem? *(Possible answer: It provided a way to organize the data to help discover the pattern.)*

What pattern can you identify? *(Possible answer: The pattern in the handshakes is: difference of 1, difference of 2, difference of 3, and so on.)*

SUMMARIZE/ASSESS   Explain how making the table helped to solve the problem. *(Possible answer: The table organized the data so that the pattern could be seen.)*

Make a table to help you find the pattern that solves the problem.

2. If the pattern were continued, how many toothpicks would it take to make 25 squares? **76**

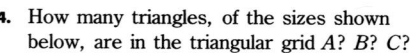

3. a. How many small triangles, , are on triangular grids A, B, and C? **4; 9; 16**

  b. How many small triangles would a triangular grid with 10 rows have? **100**

4. How many triangles, of the sizes shown below, are in the triangular grid A? B? C?

  A: 4, 1
  B: 9,3
  C: 64, 49

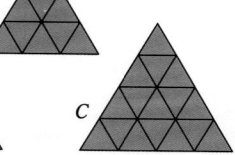

5. How many squares of the sizes shown below are on checkerboards A, B, and C?

  A: 4, 1
  B: 9, 4
  C: 64, 49

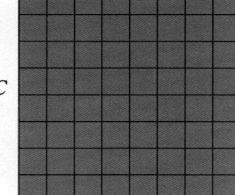

6. Find all of the different sized squares on checkerboard C. How many squares, of all different sizes are there?
64 + 49 + 36 + 25 + 16 + 9 + 4 + 1 = 204

CHOOSE Choose a strategy to solve. **Choices will vary.**

7. What is the greatest number of weekend days you can have in any month? **10**

8. It takes 5 min to saw through a log. How long will it take to cut the log into 4 pieces? **15 min**

*9. Each card has the number **12**, **15**, **18**, or **20** on its back. Use the clues to decide which number is on each card.
A: 12, B: 15, C: 20, D: 18

- The numbers on **C** and **B** are multiples of 5.
- The number on **D** is greater than that on **B**.
- The number on **A** is less than that on **C**.

MEETING INDIVIDUAL NEEDS

For Students Who Are . . .

Acquiring English Proficiency Pair students with an English-proficient student for Exercises 2–6.

Gifted and Talented Have students create a design using a pattern and then make a table to show the pattern used.

Working 2 or 3 Grades Below Level Have students use pages 58–63 of the Skills Workbook for Problem Solving Strategies.

Having Reading Difficulties Pair students with an able reader to work through Exercises 2–9. For Exercise 7, point out that weekend days are Saturday and Sunday.

Today's Problem

There are 20 students in a class. Their grades on a test are 74, 72, 80, 86, 70, 98, 85, 84, 67, 79, 65, 76, 87, 81, 84, 69, 71, 78, 76, and 79. What is the range of grades? What is the greatest difference between any two numerically successive grades? *(Range: 98 − 65 = 33; greatest difference: 98 − 87 = 11)*

---

3 FOLLOW-UP

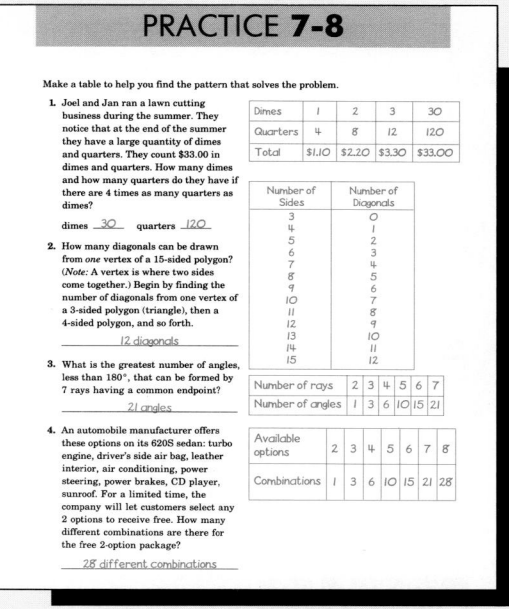

PRACTICE 7-8

Make a table to help you find the pattern that solves the problem.

1. Joel and Jan ran a lawn cutting business during the summer. They notice that at the end of the summer they have a large quantity of dimes and quarters. They count $33.00 in dimes and quarters. How many dimes and how many quarters do they have if there are 4 times as many quarters as dimes?

dimes ___30___ quarters ___120___

Dimes	1	2	3	30
Quarters	4	8	12	120
Total	$1.10	$2.20	$3.30	$33.00

2. How many diagonals can be drawn from *one* vertex of a 15-sided polygon? (*Note:* A vertex is where two sides come together.) Begin by finding the number of diagonals from one vertex of a 3-sided polygon (triangle), then a 4-sided polygon, and so forth.

___12 diagonals___

Number of Sides	Number of Diagonals
3	0
4	1
5	2
6	3
7	4
8	5
9	6
10	7
11	8
12	9
13	10
14	11
15	12

3. What is the greatest number of angles, less than 180°, that can be formed by 7 rays having a common endpoint?

___21 angles___

Number of rays	2	3	4	5	6	7
Number of angles	1	3	6	10	15	21

4. An automobile manufacturer offers these options on its 620S sedan: turbo engine, driver's side air bag, leather interior, air conditioning, power steering, power brakes, CD player, sunroof. For a limited time, the company will let customers select any 2 options to receive free. How many different combinations are there for the free 2-option package?

___28 different combinations___

Available options	2	3	4	5	6	7	8
Combinations	1	3	6	10	15	21	28

RETEACHING 7-8

Some students may not understand that making a table is an appropriate method for solving a problem. One way to solve Problem 1, *Practice Worksheet 7-8*, is to ask the following question: What is the question? [How many dimes and nickels do Joel and Jan have?] Think of a small amount. How many quarters do they have if they have 1 dime? [4] 2 dimes? [8] How much money is this? [$1.10; $2.20] How can you organize your information to find a pattern? [make a table] What pattern do you see? [The number of dimes multiplied by $1.10 gives the total amount.] How many dimes did they have? [30] How many quarters is 4 times this amount? [120]

ENRICHMENT 7-8

Solve.

1. At a factory, there are 100 electrical switches to be tested in 100 different ways. At the beginning of the testing, all 100 switches are off. For the first test, they are all turned on. Then, beginning with the second switch, every second switch is flipped. For the third test, every third switch is flipped, beginning with the third switch. This pattern continues through the 100th test. After the last test, which switches are off?

every switch is off except
1, 4, 9, 16, 25, 36, 49, 64, 81, 100

2. At a new airport, a traveler must pass through 4 security checkpoints to get to any gate. After each checkpoint, a traveler may go straight, turn left, or turn right. How many gates does the new airport have?

___81 gates___

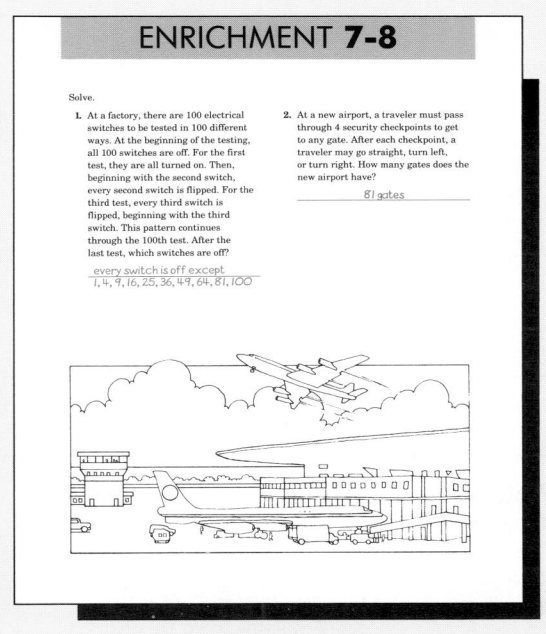

Lesson Organizer

Objective: Solve problems creatively.

Prior Knowledge: Students should understand the concepts of scale and area.

Lesson Resources:
Daily Review 7-9

Two-Minute Math

Which is greater:
$\frac{1}{2}$ **of** $\frac{1}{3}$ **of** $\frac{1}{3}$ **or** $\frac{1}{3}$ **of** $\frac{1}{2}$ **of** $\frac{1}{2}$**?**
($\frac{1}{12} > \frac{1}{18}$; $\frac{1}{3}$ of $\frac{1}{2}$ of $\frac{1}{2}$ is greater)

1 PREPARE

☑ MATERIALS CHECKLIST: Teaching Aid 3 (Grid Paper) for each group

Have students work in small groups as they follow these directions.

Enclose 24 squares on your grid paper so that you have the longest perimeter possible. *(Enclosing a single row of 24 squares will give a perimeter of 50 cm)*

Imagine that the side of each square on the grid paper represents $2\frac{1}{2}$ **ft. What perimeter is represented on your paper?** *(125 ft)*

WHEN YOUR STUDENTS ASK
★ **WHY AM I LEARNING THIS?** ★

You can connect this lesson to real life through the career of landscape design. Landscape designers often must determine the best arrangement for planting a certain number of trees in a given space.

Planning a Tree Planting Project

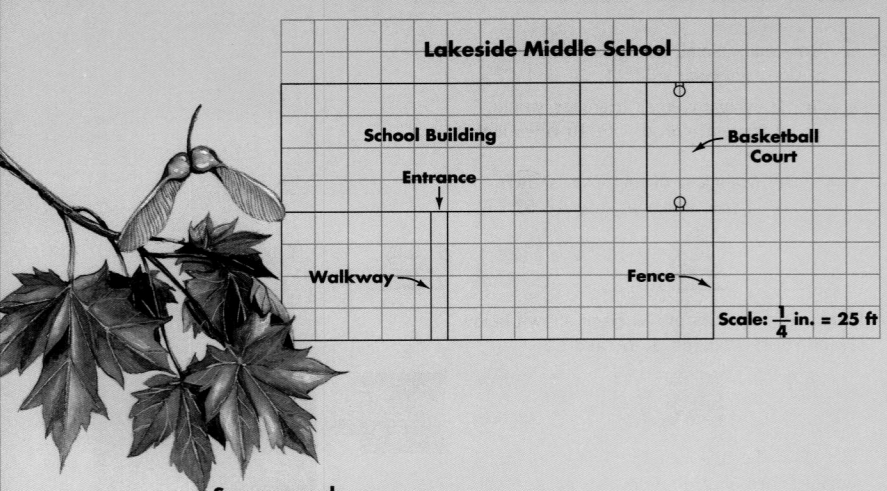

Scale: $\frac{1}{4}$ in. = 25 ft

Sugar maple

MATH AND ECOLOGY

The Lakeside Nursery is donating as many sugar maple, white ash, and red maple trees as needed for landscaping to the new Lakeside Middle School.

Pretend that you have been appointed to a task force to plan the tree-planting project. The job of your task force is to determine the number of trees needed and the number of volunteers needed to get the job done and to oversee the project.

Work in a small group.

1. Copy the scale drawing of the Lakeside School grounds. Use the scale to decide where there is room to plant the trees.
Check students' drawings.

2. Agree on the number and kind of trees that will be planted. Use the chart on page 223 to help you decide. On the scale drawing show the location of the new trees.
Check students' work.

2 EXPLORE

☑ MATERIALS CHECKLIST: inch ruler for each group, Teaching Aid

Have students work in groups of three or four for this lesson. **On the drawing, measure the distance from the school building to the basketball court. According to the scale, what real distance is represented by this distance?** *(The distance is $\frac{1}{2}$ in., which represents 5 ft.)*

Suppose it takes two workers about an hour and a half to plant each tree. If you want to plant 10 trees between 9 and 12 on Saturday morning, how many workers will you need? *(10 workers)*

SUMMARIZE/ASSESS **How did you use mathematics to help you plan the tree-planting project?** *(Answers will vary. Example: Used multiplying fractions with scale; used the strategy of drawing a picture to determine how wide a hole should be dug for each tree.)*

3. Write the Lakeside Nursery a letter stating the number of trees of each type you will need. Be sure to thank them for donating the trees. Tell them when and where the trees are to be delivered. What else might be included in your letter?
Accept reasonable answers.

Continue the planning by answering the questions.

4. Estimate that it will take 2 workers about 1 h to plant each tree. How many volunteers will you need to get the trees planted? Would you include only students on your project or also members of the community? Why?
Accept reasonable answers.

5. Each tree delivered from the nursery is about 10 to 12 ft tall. Holes need to be dug about 2 ft deep and about 1 ft wider than the ball of earth around the tree's roots. If the ball of earth is 30 in., how wide a hole should be dug for each tree?
42 in. or 3½ ft

6. What types of equipment will you need to plant the trees? How will you lift the trees? How will you dig the holes? Decide on a plan to get the equipment.
Accept reasonable answers.

7. Can the tree planting be completed in one weekend? What factors might influence the completion of the job?
Accept reasonable answers.

Congratulations! You and the tree-planting task force have done a great job.

Type of Tree	Dimensions of Full-grown Tree	Suggested Spacing Between Trees
sugar maple	60–80 ft high 40–60 ft wide	20 ft
white ash	60–80 ft high 40–60 ft wide	20 ft
red maple	50–70 ft high 30–50 ft wide	15 ft

Red maple

White ash

CLASS ACTIVITY **7-9**

☑ **MATERIALS CHECKLIST:** vegetable seeds or information about the length of germination for different kinds of vegetables and methods of planting; inch grid paper

Arrange students in groups of three or four. Tell them to plan a vegetable garden (5 ft by 5 ft). Using the information provided, have them design their own garden. Decide when each vegetable should be planted and predict when it will be ready for harvest.

MEETING INDIVIDUAL NEEDS

For Students Who Are . . .

Acquiring English Proficiency   Work with students as they read this lesson aloud through Exercise 3. Emphasize the concept of scale. For Exercises 4–7, see that students are grouped with English-proficient students.

Gifted and Talented   Have students work in a group to measure and make a scale drawing of an area around their own school they might landscape. They can plan an arrangement for planting trees in that area.

Today's Problem

Write the letters represented by each fraction. Then write the mystery message.

First $\frac{1}{4}$ of CANCELLATION

First $\frac{2}{3}$ of DOT

First $\frac{1}{3}$ of HEARTS

First $\frac{1}{2}$ of THISTLES

(CAN HE DO THIS?)

CHAPTER
Checkup

The chapter checkup provides a quick language and vocabulary review, a test for the chapter, and suggestions for student Learning Log entries.

Language and Vocabulary

Some key language and vocabulary ideas from this chapter are reinforced here.

Test

The test can be used either as a test or as a review of the chapter prior to your administering the test worksheets found in the Teacher's Resource Book.

The following guide will help you determine percentage scores.

Score	Percent	Score	Percent
28	100%	14	50%
27	96	13	46
26	93	12	43
25	89	11	39
24	86	10	36
23	82	9	32
22	79	8	29
21	75	7	25
20	72	6	22
19	68	5	18
18	65	4	15
17	61	3	11
16	58	2	8
15	54	1	4

Each test has 3 sections: concepts, skills, and problem solving. These sections provide students with exposure to the formats used on standardized tests.

Use this chart to identify the Management Objectives tested for this chapter.

Items	Management Objectives	Pages
1–17	**7A** Multiply fractions and mixed numbers.	204–209
18–25	**7B** Divide fractions and mixed numbers.	214–219
26–28	**7C** Problem Solving. Use estimation. Make a table.	210–211; 220–221

CHAPTER CHECKUP

LANGUAGE & VOCABULARY

Answers will vary. Suggestion given.
1. Explain how to find the reciprocal of a mixed number.
   Change it into an improper fraction and invert the fraction.
2. Explain how to divide $\frac{1}{8}$ by $\frac{6}{7}$.
   Invert the second fraction and multiply.

Make up one problem to fit each situation.

3. dividing a whole number by a fraction so that the quotient is greater than the whole number
   $3 \div \frac{1}{3}$
4. dividing a whole number by a fraction so that the quotient is equal to the whole number $\quad 2 \div \frac{3}{3}$

TEST ✓

CONCEPTS

Write the reciprocal of the number. *(pages 208–209)*

1. $3 \quad \frac{1}{3}$
2. $\frac{1}{7} \quad 7$
3. $2\frac{1}{4} \quad \frac{4}{9}$
4. $\frac{5}{9} \quad \frac{9}{5}$
5. $4\frac{2}{3} \quad \frac{3}{14}$

SKILLS

Write the product in lowest terms. *(pages 204–209)*

6. $\frac{1}{4}$ of $\frac{1}{3} \quad \frac{1}{12}$
7. $\frac{2}{5}$ of $\frac{5}{6} \quad \frac{1}{3}$
8. $\frac{3}{8} \times \frac{2}{3} \quad \frac{1}{4}$
9. $\frac{6}{9} \times \frac{1}{2} \quad \frac{1}{3}$
10. $2 \times \frac{3}{8} \quad \frac{3}{4}$
11. $\frac{3}{11} \times 4 \quad 1\frac{1}{11}$
12. $\frac{2}{9} \times 8 \quad 1\frac{7}{9}$
13. $28 \times \frac{3}{7} \quad 12$
14. $2\frac{1}{2} \times \frac{3}{4} \quad 1\frac{7}{8}$
15. $\frac{1}{4} \times 4\frac{1}{5} \quad 1\frac{1}{20}$
16. $1\frac{1}{3} \times 7\frac{2}{5} \quad 9\frac{13}{15}$
17. $3\frac{5}{9} \times 2\frac{1}{5} \quad 7\frac{37}{45}$

Write the quotient in lowest terms. *(pages 214–219)*

18. $7 \div \frac{2}{5} \quad 17\frac{1}{2}$
19. $25 \div \frac{2}{3} \quad 37\frac{1}{2}$
20. $9 \div \frac{3}{7} \quad 21$
21. $\frac{7}{9} \div 12 \quad \frac{7}{108}$
22. $\frac{9}{11} \div \frac{3}{5} \quad 1\frac{4}{11}$
23. $\frac{4}{8} \div \frac{1}{5} \quad 2\frac{1}{2}$
24. $8\frac{3}{5} \div \frac{1}{5} \quad 43$
25. $6\frac{2}{9} \div 2\frac{1}{3} \quad 2\frac{2}{3}$

224   CHAPTER CHECKUP

CHAPTER TEST • FORM A

Write the product in lowest terms. (pp. 204–209) 7A

1. $\frac{5}{8} \times \frac{2}{15} \quad \frac{1}{12}$
2. $\frac{2}{9} \times 18 \quad 4$
3. $\frac{3}{10} \times 40 \times \frac{1}{4} \quad 3$

4. $36 \times 1\frac{3}{4} \quad 63$
5. $2\frac{4}{5} \times 2\frac{1}{7} \quad 6$

Write the quotient in lowest terms. (pp. 214–219) 7B

6. $6 \div \frac{3}{4} \quad 8$
7. $\frac{2}{5} \div 10 \quad \frac{1}{25}$
8. $\frac{9}{10} \div \frac{18}{25} \quad 1\frac{1}{4}$

9. $\frac{5}{8} \div 2\frac{1}{2} \quad \frac{1}{4}$
10. $6\frac{3}{4} \div 2\frac{5}{8} \quad 2\frac{4}{7}$

(pp. 210–211, 220–221) 7C

Estimate to find an answer.

11. A table which usually sells for $276.50 is marked $\frac{1}{4}$ off. How much would be saved by buying the table while on sale?   about $70

12. A lamp which usually sells for $178.50 is marked $\frac{1}{3}$ off. What will be the price of the lamp?   about $120

CHAPTER TEST • FORM A

13. A planter which usually sells for $64.95 is marked $\frac{1}{3}$ off. In the same store, a $115.75 vase is marked $\frac{1}{4}$ off. How much would be saved by buying both items while on sale?   about $50

Make a table to help you find the pattern that solves the problem.

14. How many squares, of all different sizes, are in the figure?   55 squares

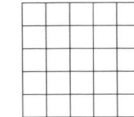

15. How many triangles, of all different sizes, are in the figure?   48 triangles

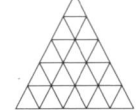

━━━━━━━━━━━━━━ **PROBLEM SOLVING** ━━━━━━━━━━━━━━

Estimate. Do not calculate. *(pages 210–211)*

Accept reasonable estimates.
Suggestions given.

26. Two bookcases, each with 7 shelves, are empty. Each shelf holds about 20 books. The library receives a shipment of 6 cartons, each containing 50 books.

    a. How many empty shelves are there? **14 shelves**

    b. About how many books can fit on the 2 bookcases? **about 280 books**

    c. About how many books in the shipment will not fit on the shelves? **about 20 books**

Solve. *(pages 220–221)*

27. Make a table to help you find the pattern that solves the problem. Square banquet tables seat 4 people, 1 on each side. If the tables are lined up as shown in the picture, what is the fewest number of tables needed to seat 25 dinner guests? **12 tables**

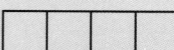

28. A 25-ft piece of timber is to be cut into pieces, each $\frac{2}{3}$ ft long. How many $\frac{2}{3}$-ft pieces can be cut? How much timber will be left? **37 pieces; $\frac{1}{2}$ ft**

LEARNING LOG

Write the answers in your learning log. **Answers will vary. Suggestions given.**

1. Your friend says $4\frac{3}{5}$ and $\frac{5}{23}$ are reciprocals. Explain this thinking.
    $4\frac{3}{5} = \frac{23}{5}$ and $\frac{23}{5}$ is the reciprocal of $\frac{5}{23}$

2. A multiplication problem with whole numbers can be checked by dividing. Explain how this method would work with fractions. Include an example. **It works the same way.**
    $\frac{1}{4} \times \frac{1}{3} = \frac{1}{12}$; $\frac{1}{12} \div \frac{1}{3} = \frac{1}{12} \times \frac{3}{1} = \frac{3}{12} = \frac{1}{4}$

Note that the same numbers are used in Exercises 19 and 28.

Problem Solving

Item 26 has 3 parts:
a. literal—this is a reading comprehension question
b. interpretive—this involves interpretation using the facts given
c. applied—students use a strategy or skills to find an answer

Item 19 in the skill section and item 28 in the problem solving section use the same numbers.

This will help you informally assess how your students transfer from numerical skills to word problems.

For scoring problem solving items you may wish to use partial credit. If a student uses the correct strategy but gets a wrong answer, give the student 2 points toward the total percent score.

Learning Log

These are suggestions for writing about some topics taught in this chapter. The students keep their Learning Logs from the beginning of the school year through the end.

CHAPTER TEST • FORM **B**

Write the product in lowest terms. (pp. 204–209) 7A

1. $\frac{5}{6} \times \frac{3}{10}$ $\frac{1}{4}$ **2.** $\frac{3}{8} \times 16$ 6   **3.** $\frac{4}{5} \times 20 \times \frac{1}{4}$ 4

4. $45 \times 1\frac{3}{5}$ 72   **5.** $2\frac{5}{8} \times 5\frac{1}{3}$ 14

Write the quotient in lowest terms. (pp. 214–219) 7B

6. $6 \div \frac{2}{5}$ 15   **7.** $\frac{3}{4} \div 12$ $\frac{1}{16}$ **8.** $\frac{4}{15} \div \frac{8}{25}$ $\frac{5}{6}$

9. $\frac{7}{10} \div 3\frac{1}{2}$ $\frac{1}{5}$ **10.** $5\frac{1}{5} \div 1\frac{3}{10}$ 4

(pp. 210–211, 220–221) 7C

Estimate to find an answer.

11. A chair which usually sells for $389.95 is marked $\frac{1}{4}$ off. How much would be saved by buying the chair while on sale?   about $100

12. A vase which usually sells for $78.95 is marked $\frac{1}{3}$ off. What will be the price of the vase?   about $50

CHAPTER TEST • FORM **B**

13. A planter which usually sells for $54.95 is marked $\frac{1}{3}$ off. In the same store, a $109.95 picture is marked $\frac{1}{4}$ off. How much would be saved by buying both items while on sale?   about $45

Make a table to help you find the pattern that solves the problem.

14. How many small squares are in an arrangement like this which is 15 steps high?   120 squares

15. How many squares, of all different sizes, are in a 9 × 9 checkerboard?   285 squares

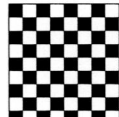

Error Analysis and Remediation

Here are some common errors students make when they are multiplying and dividing fractions and mixed numbers. The errors are listed by lesson under the appropriate management objective.

7A • MULTIPLY FRACTIONS AND MIXED NUMBERS

Source of Error (Lesson 7-1)
Students divide common factors in both numerators or both denominators.

For example:

$$\frac{\frac{1}{2}}{3} \times \frac{\frac{2}{4}}{6}$$

Remediation
Remind students that when they divide by a common factor, they are dividing by a fraction equal to 1 and that therefore they must divide both a numerator and a denominator by the common factor.

Source of Error (Lesson 7-2)
Students multiply the whole number and the denominator instead of the whole number and the numerator.

Remediation
Have students write the whole number as a fraction with a denominator of 1.

7B • DIVIDE FRACTIONS AND MIXED NUMBERS

Source of Error (Lessons 7-5 and 7-6)
Students multiply by the reciprocal of the dividend.

Remediation
Have students make the following chart, which they can keep for reference.

DIVIDING FRACTIONS

What is the reciprocal of the divisor?	Multiply the dividend by the reciprocal of the divisor.	Write the quotient.

Source of Error (Lesson 7-7)
Students try to divide the whole numbers and then divide the fractions.

Remediation
Review the steps that students should follow when they are dividing mixed numbers. Remind them that before they can divide mixed numbers they must change them to fractions.

7C • PROBLEM SOLVING: USE ESTIMATION. MAKE A TABLE.

Source of Error (Lesson 7-8)
Students have difficulty organizing the information.

Remediation
Have students read the problem aloud, sentence by sentence, and then rewrite the problem in their own words.

Answers

Page 217

42. 2 c. boiling water
$\frac{1}{4}$ c. orange juice
$1\frac{1}{2}$ T. honey
$\frac{1}{2}$ in. cinnamon stick
$2\frac{1}{2}$ cloves

CHAPTER 7

Extra Practice

This page provides extra practice of all the major chapter objectives. Use this page after the chapter has been taught to reinforce the chapter skills. Page references are provided for each group of items so that students can easily look back at the appropriate lesson for additional support.

Write the reciprocal of the number. *(pages 208–209)*

1. 6 $\frac{1}{6}$ 2. $\frac{1}{5}$ 5 3. $\frac{7}{9}$ $\frac{9}{7}$ 4. 2 $\frac{1}{2}$ 5. $9\frac{3}{8}$ $\frac{8}{75}$

6. $1\frac{1}{2}$ $\frac{2}{3}$ 7. 14 $\frac{1}{14}$ 8. $\frac{3}{11}$ $\frac{11}{3}$ 9. 10 $\frac{1}{10}$ 10. $7\frac{2}{5}$ $\frac{5}{37}$

Write the answer in lowest terms. *(pages 204–209, 214–219)*

11. $\frac{1}{3} \times \frac{0}{8}$ 0 12. $\frac{2}{5} \times \frac{3}{2}$ $\frac{3}{5}$ 13. $\frac{6}{7} \times \frac{1}{2}$ $\frac{3}{7}$ 14. $\frac{0}{9} \times \frac{0}{5}$ 0

15. $\frac{3}{7} \times 15$ $6\frac{3}{7}$ 16. $8 \times \frac{1}{5}$ $1\frac{3}{5}$ 17. $2 \times \frac{13}{12}$ $2\frac{1}{6}$ 18. $\frac{1}{9} \times 11$ $1\frac{2}{9}$

19. $\frac{1}{3} \times 2\frac{1}{5}$ $\frac{11}{15}$ 20. $2\frac{1}{2} \times \frac{4}{9}$ $1\frac{1}{9}$ 21. $3 \times 8\frac{1}{7}$ $24\frac{3}{7}$ 22. $4\frac{1}{3} \times 2\frac{3}{8}$ $10\frac{7}{24}$

23. $56 \times \frac{1}{7}$ 8 24. $3\frac{7}{9} \times 2\frac{1}{5}$ $8\frac{14}{45}$ 25. $\frac{2}{5} \times 3\frac{1}{4}$ $1\frac{3}{10}$ 26. $27 \times 1\frac{5}{6}$ $49\frac{1}{2}$

27. $8 \div \frac{1}{5}$ 40 28. $12 \div \frac{1}{5}$ 60 29. $7 \div \frac{3}{4}$ $9\frac{1}{3}$ 30. $15 \div \frac{2}{3}$ $22\frac{1}{2}$

31. $\frac{5}{9} \div 3$ $\frac{5}{27}$ 32. $\frac{1}{4} \div 11$ $\frac{1}{44}$ 33. $\frac{3}{10} \div 14$ $\frac{3}{140}$ 34. $\frac{3}{7} \div 8$ $\frac{3}{56}$

35. $\frac{1}{2} \div \frac{2}{9}$ $2\frac{1}{4}$ 36. $\frac{2}{3} \div \frac{1}{6}$ 4 37. $\frac{7}{15} \div \frac{8}{9}$ $\frac{21}{40}$ 38. $\frac{2}{5} \div \frac{4}{3}$ $\frac{3}{10}$

39. $2\frac{5}{6} \div \frac{3}{5}$ $4\frac{13}{18}$ 40. $3\frac{5}{8} \div 1\frac{1}{4}$ $2\frac{9}{10}$ 41. $\frac{7}{16} \div 1\frac{5}{9}$ $\frac{9}{32}$ 42. $4\frac{11}{12} \div 5\frac{1}{3}$ $\frac{59}{64}$

Solve. *(pages 210–211, 220–221)*

43. A roller coaster has 6 cars. Each car can hold 4 people. A ride takes 3 min and there are 150 people in line. The ride is closing in 30 min. Will all the people be able to ride?   yes

44. During a sale, you pay $10 for the first shirt you buy. If you buy 2 shirts, you pay $10 plus $\frac{1}{2}$ of $10 for the second. If you buy 3 shirts, you pay $20 plus $\frac{1}{3}$ of $10 for the third, and so on. How much would you pay for 10 shirts? $91

Multiplying with Unit Fractions ▦

The ancient Egyptians did almost all computations using unit fractions, or fractions with a numerator of 1. Although this was difficult, much of what was known several thousand years ago can still be applied today. Here are some examples.

- To double the size of any fraction whose denominator is an even number, divide the denominator by 2. Using this method for $2 \times \frac{1}{8}$ leads to thinking $8 \div 2 = 4$, so $2 \times \frac{1}{8} = \frac{1}{4}$.

- To double any fraction whose denominator is divisible by 3, divide the denominator by 3 to get a quotient q. Then write the double as $\frac{1}{2q} + \frac{1}{6q}$. To double $\frac{1}{27}$, divide 27 by 3 to get the quotient 9. Then the double of $\frac{1}{27}$ is $\frac{1}{2 \times 9} + \frac{1}{6 \times 9}$, or $\frac{1}{18} + \frac{1}{54}$.

Work with a partner. Write ten unit fractions and discuss which ones can be doubled by either method above. Work together to write the double for each of those that you can. Find out about other methods the ancient Egyptians used to perform computations. **Check students' work.**

A Shopping Spree

Choose a mail-order catalog. Pretend that you have just been given $500 and that your goal is to spend as much of it as possible on items from the catalog. In addition to deciding what you want to purchase, think about whether you have to pay sales tax and shipping charges.

You can find answers to these questions in your catalog. Remember that both sales tax and shipping charges must be deducted from the $500. How close can you come to spending exactly $500?
Check students' work.

One Line Design

Try to draw the design at the bottom without lifting your pencil from the paper and without retracing any lines. After you do this, make up other designs that can be drawn without lifting the pencil or retracing. Give them to a friend to try to draw.
Check students' work.

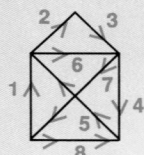

Enrichment

This page contains activities that provide extension and enrichment for all levels of students. Depending on the needs of your students, you may wish to assign an activity from this page at certain points during the chapter, or you may want to use this page when the entire chapter has been completed.

Multiplying With Unit Fractions
(COOPERATIVE)

You may wish to ask if the following fractions can be doubled the Egyptian way: $\frac{1}{13}$; $\frac{1}{25}$; $\frac{1}{45}$. Students should recognize that neither 13 nor 25 are divisible by 3 or are even numbers; 45 is divisible by 3 and can be doubled using the second method.

A Shopping Spree

To help students get started, you might wish to suggest that they start with an expensive item, then estimate how much they have left to spend.

One Line Design

If students have difficulty drawing the design, ask them to think about the way they are working; are they making progress with each attempt or just drawing at random?

Cumulative Review

The Cumulative Review focuses on skills covered in previous chapters. All important skills are reviewed on a cyclic basis.

If students are having difficulty with particular groups of exercises, refer to the chart for follow-up work.

Find the answer.

1. $3\frac{1}{8} + 2\frac{5}{6} =$ **b**

  a. $5\frac{3}{7}$

  b. $5\frac{23}{24}$

  c. $5\frac{1}{6}$

  d. none of these

2. $12 - 5\frac{3}{7} =$ **a**

  a. $6\frac{4}{7}$

  b. $7\frac{4}{7}$

  c. $6\frac{3}{7}$

  d. none of these

3. $\frac{3}{7} \times \frac{4}{9} =$ **c**

  a. $\frac{3}{4}$

  b. $\frac{7}{16}$

  c. $\frac{4}{21}$

  d. none of these

4. $2\frac{1}{7} \times 3\frac{5}{8} =$ **a**

  a. $7\frac{43}{56}$

  b. $6\frac{5}{56}$

  c. 6

  d. none of these

5. $2 \div \frac{4}{7} =$ **b**

  a. $\frac{2}{7}$

  b. $3\frac{1}{2}$

  c. $1\frac{1}{7}$

  d. none of these

6. $3\frac{5}{9} \div 1\frac{1}{5} =$ **a**

  a. $2\frac{26}{27}$

  b. $4\frac{4}{15}$

  c. $1\frac{13}{32}$

  d. none of these

Find the matching value.

7. $\frac{2}{9}$ **a**

  a. $0.\overline{2}$

  b. 0.29

  c. 0.11

  d. none of these

8. $\frac{3}{8}$ **c**

  a. 0.378

  b. 0.37

  c. 0.375

  d. none of these

9. $4\frac{9}{11}$ **b**

  a. 4.9

  b. $4.\overline{81}$

  c. 4.81

  d. none of these

10. 6 yd **a**

  a. 216 in.

  b. 12 ft

  c. 24 ft

  d. none of these

11. 9 qt, 1 pt **d**

  a. 2 gal, 1 qt

  b. 37 qt

  c. 19 c

  d. none of these

12. 4 lb, 5 oz **b**

  a. 133 oz

  b. 69 oz

  c. 20 oz

  d. none of these

Items	Management Objective	Where Taught	Reteaching Options	Extra Practice Options
1–2	**6C** Add and subtract mixed numbers, different denominators.	178–179	TRB/RW 6-5	TRB/PW 6-5
3–4	**7A** Multiply fractions and mixed numbers.	204–205; 208–209	TRB/RW 7-1 and 7-3	TRB/PW 7-1 and 7-3
5–6	**7B** Divide fractions and mixed numbers.	214–215; 218–219	TRB/RW 7-5 and 7-7	TRB/PW 7-5 and 7-7
7–9	**5D** Write fractions and mixed numbers as decimals.	152–153	TRB/RW 5-11	TRB/PW 5-11
10–12	**6D** Determine the appropriate customary units of length, capacity, and mass.	188–193	TRB/RW 6-9, 6-10, and 6-11	TRB/PW 6-9, 6-10, and 6-11

Strategies may vary. Suggestions given.
Remember the strategies and types of
problems you've had so far. Solve.

1. Ally built a number tetrahedron (figure with
   4 faces). The smallest number on a face is
   12; the largest is 30. The numbers are all
   multiples of the same number.

   a. How many faces are on the
      tetrahedron? **4 faces**

   b. How can you find the other
      numbers on the faces? **find the GCF**

   c. What is the sum of the numbers on
      the faces? **guess and check; 84**

2. The winning team scored 5 points less
   than 3 times the number of points the
   losing team scored. The winning team
   scored 40 points. How many points
   did the losing team score?
   guess and check; 15 points

3. Mark enlarged a 5-in. by 7-in. photo so
   that the short edge of the enlargement
   was $12\frac{1}{2}$ in. If the ratio of the sides
   stayed the same, how long was the
   long edge of the enlargement?
   working backward; $17\frac{1}{2}$ in.

4. Between 8 A.M. and noon, the
   temperature rose 5°F, fell 4°F, fell 3°F,
   and rose 2°F. If the temperature at
   noon was 2°F, what was the
   temperature at 8 A.M.?
   working backward; 2°F

5. A truck carrying cargo weighs
   32,365 lb when fully loaded. At
   two stops, the driver unloads 7 yd^3
   and 12 yd^3 of cargo. What is the
   weight of the truck then?
   too little information

6. Bart's school has 6 doors. Each day he
   enters through 1 door and leaves
   through a different door. How many
   days can he do this before he must
   repeat a combination?
   making a table; 30 days

7. A driver travels east for 25 mi, turns
   north and goes another 15 mi. To
   return home over the same roads, in
   what directions will she have to
   travel?
   working backward; south and west

8. On Monday the highest temperature was 80°F. On Tuesday the
   highest temperature was 15% lower than on Monday. On
   Wednesday the highest temperature reached 90% of Tuesday's
   temperature. To the nearest degree, what was Wednesday's
   highest temperature?
   working backward; 61.2°F

Problem Solving Review

This page focuses on problem solving
strategies and types learned in this chapter and previous chapters. A problem solving checklist lists some of the strategies
students may use to solve the problems on
this page.

Technology

This page is designed to provide calculator or computer experiences for all levels of students. The calculator or computer logo indicates the type of activity.

You may wish to assign these activities after the chapter has been taught or during the course of the chapter, depending on your needs and those of your students.

The Weird Series

Encourage students to estimate before finding the values of A and B. When students finish, they may wish to experiment with other similar series.

Fraction Madness

(COOPERATIVE)

Remind students that a set of keystrokes includes numbers, an operation sign, and an "is equal to" sign.

Changing and Rearranging

Remind students that they can cancel as part of the process of multiplying or dividing.

Although this is a paper and pencil activity, software that develops the same skill is found in Houghton Mifflin Math Activities Courseware, Grade 7.

TECHNOLOGY

THE WEIRD SERIES 🖩

Estimate the values of A and B.

$$\frac{9}{8} \times \frac{7}{6} \times \frac{5}{4} \times \frac{3}{2} = A \quad \frac{945}{384}$$

$$\frac{2}{3} \times \frac{4}{5} \times \frac{6}{7} \times \frac{8}{9} = B \quad \frac{384}{945}$$

What special relationship do the values of A and B have?
They are inverses.
Find the values of A and B, and write them in simplest form. Compare your estimates with the actual values of A and B.

FRACTION MADNESS 🖩

Work with a partner or in a small group to answer the problems.
Answers will vary.
1. Study the equation. Write two sets of keystrokes that will give you the answer.

$$\frac{33}{12} \times \frac{15}{27} \times \frac{36}{30} \times \frac{24}{44} = 1$$

2. Study the equation. Write a set of keystrokes that will give you the answer.
(*Hint:* Remember reciprocals.)

$$\frac{9}{24} \div \frac{6}{16} \times \frac{40}{72} \div \frac{35}{63} = 1$$

CHANGING AND REARRANGING 💻

In the computer game *Fraction Challenge II*, players find missing digits to complete fraction multiplication and division problems. This activity, which you can do with a pencil and paper, helps you develop skills at writing multiplication and division problems with fractions.
See below.
Use each group of six numbers to create fraction equations. Work with a partner to try and create as many true equations as possible. Use the models with the missing digits to help. Answers will vary. Suggestions given.

1 3 5 6 9 10 [multiplication]

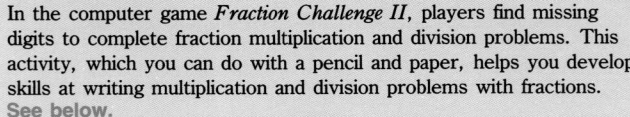

$\frac{1}{3}, \frac{9}{6}, \frac{5}{10}$

2 4 4 4 6 12 [division]

$\frac{2}{4}, \frac{4}{4}, \frac{6}{12}$

Software Activities

activity 1 • ADJUSTING RECIPE AMOUNTS

MATERIALS: spreadsheet program, students' favorite recipes

Procedure: This activity helps students to increase recipe amounts. Have students create a spreadsheet similar to the one below for their recipes.

	A	B	C
1	Recipe Name	Number Fed By	Number to Feed
2			

Have students expand the spreadsheet so each recipe ingredient, unit, and amount needed (whole number, numerator, and denominator) is included in the spreadsheet. Students should compute the ingredient amounts needed if the entire class was to be served.

Follow-up: Have students plan an activity where four of the favorite recipes will be used. Students should prepare one shopping list of all ingredients.

activity 2 • MIXED NUMBER DIVISION

MATERIALS: BASIC programming

Procedure: This program will divide mixed numbers input by the student. Have students enter the program into the computer and run it several times.

```
10  PRINT "THIS PROGRAM DIVIDES
    MIXED NUMBERS."
20  INPUT "WHAT IS THE FIRST WHOLE
    NUMBER? ";W
30  INPUT "WHAT IS THE FIRST
    NUMERATOR? ";N
40  INPUT "WHAT IS THE FIRST
    DENOMINATOR? ";D
50  INPUT "WHAT IS THE SECOND WHOLE
    NUMBER? ";H
60  INPUT "WHAT IS THE SECOND
    NUMERATOR? ";U
70  INPUT "WHAT IS THE SECOND
    DENOMINATOR? ";E
80  LET F=(W*D+N): LET S=(H*E+U)
90  PRINT "YOUR IMPROPER FRACTIONS
    ARE: ";F"/"D;
100 PRINT "AND ";S"/";E
110 X=F*E: Y=S*D
120 PRINT "YOUR QUOTIENT IS ";X"/"Y
130 PRINT "PLEASE SIMPLIFY YOUR
    ANSWER. "
```

Follow-up: Challenge students to modify the program so the answer is always given in lowest terms.

HOUGHTON MIFFLIN SOFTWARE

Easy Graph. Boston, MA: Houghton Mifflin Company, 1987. For Apple II, Commodore, IBM.

EduCalc. Boston, MA: Houghton Mifflin Company, 1990. For Apple II, Commodore, IBM.

Friendly Filer. Boston, MA: Houghton Mifflin Company, 1989. For Apple II, Commodore, IBM.

Mathematics Activities Courseware. Boston, MA: Houghton Mifflin Company, 1983. For Apple II, IBM.

OTHER SOFTWARE

Fast Facts. Berkeley, CA: Edusoft. 1984. For Apple II.

Fraction Action. Las Vegas, NV: Unicom Software, 1989. For Apple II, Commodore, IBM, Macintosh.

Math Football, Fractions. Big Spring, TX: Gamco Industries, Inc., 1989. For Apple II, Commodore, IBM, TRS-80.

Microsoft Works. Redmond, WA: Microsoft Corporation, 1989. For IBM, Macintosh.

Quarter Mile: Fraction Pack. Oakland, CA: Barnum Software, 1989. For Apple II.

Geometry and Measurement

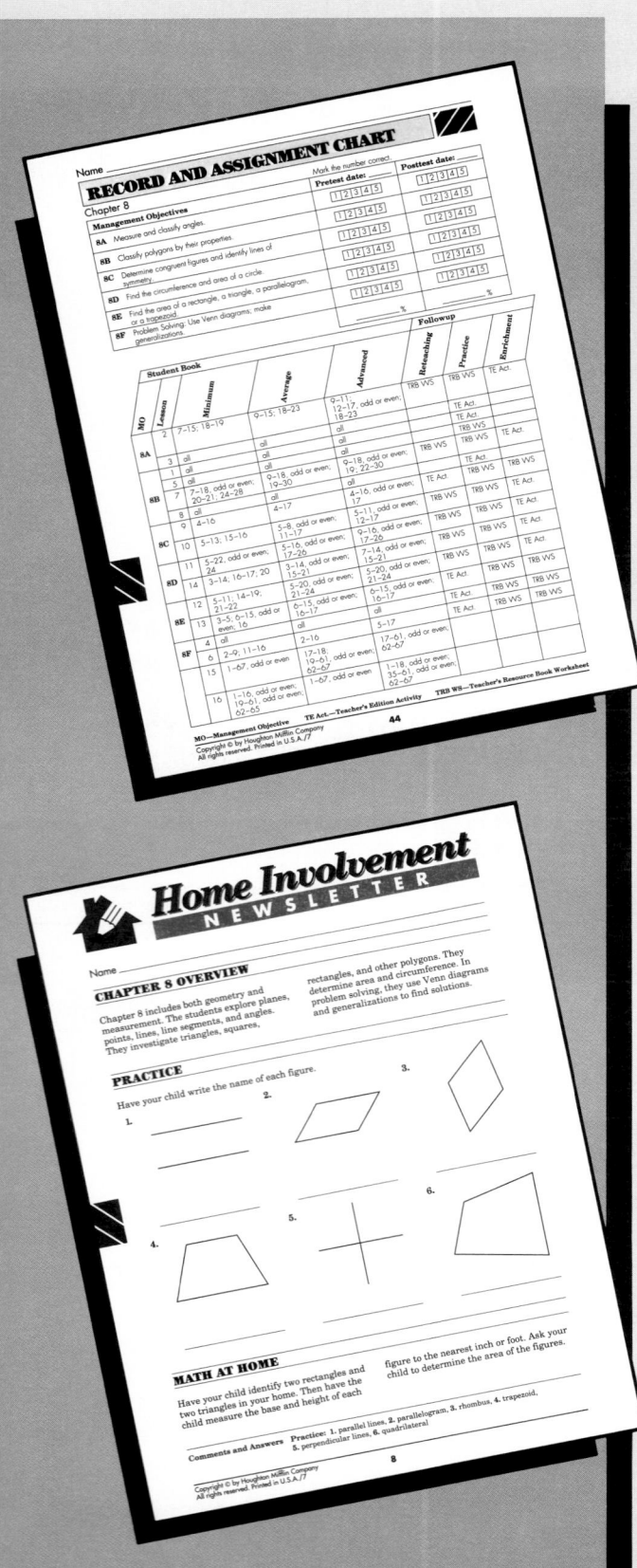

Chapter 8 focuses on basic concepts of geometry and measurement of plane figures. Students study polygons and their classifications, translations, rotations, reflections, symmetry, congruence, as well as measurement of circumference and area.

In problem solving lessons, students learns to make Venn diagrams, then use the diagrams as an aid to classifying figures. Students use the classifications as a basis for making generalizations.

Management Objectives

8A Measure and classify angles.
8B Classify polygons by their properties.
8C Determine congruent figures and identify lines of symmetry.
8D Find the circumference and area of a circle.
8E Find the area of a rectangle, a triangle, a parallelogram, or a trapezoid.
8F Problem Solving: Use Venn diagrams. Make generalizations.

Assignments for different achievement levels are provided on the Record and Assignment Chart in the Teacher's Resource Book.

Vocabulary

plane, page 232
points, page 232
line, page 232
line segment, page 232
congruent lines, page 232
parallel lines, page 233
ray, vertex, page 233
angle, page 233
perpendicular, page 233
right angle, page 234
straight angle, page 234
acute angle, page 234
obtuse angle, page 234
congruent angles, page 236
vertical angles, page 236
adjacent angles, page 236
complementary angles, page 236
supplementary angles, page 236
polygon, page 240
regular polygon, page 240
trapezoid, page 240
parallelogram, page 241

quadrilateral, page 241
square, rectangle, page 241
rhombus, 241
equilateral triangle, page 244
isoceles triangle, page 244
scalene triangle, page 244
right triangle, page 244
obtuse triangle, page 244
acute triangle, page 244
rotation, page 248
reflection, page 248
translation, page 249
tessellation, page 249
congruent figures, page 250
line symmetry, page 252
line of symmetry, page 252
diameter (d), page 254
radius (r), page 254
circumference (C), page 254
pi (π), page 254
area (A), page 256
height, page 256

Home Involvement

As you begin to teach this chapter, give each student a copy of the Home Involvement Newsletter for this chapter.

This newsletter provides parents with
■ an overview of the chapter
■ suggestions for practicing some of the skills in the chapter
■ an at-home activity to do with their child, applying the skills taught in the chapter.

Management Chart

Management Objectives	Lesson/Pages	Student Not Successful	Student Needs More Practice	Student Successful	Pacing Range
8A Measure and classify angles.	8-2/234-235	TRB/RW 8-2	TRB/PW 8-2 *MAC 6 Activity 7 *MAC 7 Activity 12	TE/EA 8-2 *MAC 6 Activity 7 *MAC 7 Activity 12	2 days
	8-3/236-237	Teacher Tool: GG	*MAC 7 Activity 12 Teacher Tool: GG	TE/CA 8-3 *MAC 7 Activity 12 Teacher Tool: GG	
8B Classify polygons by their properties.	8-1/232-233			TE/CA 8-1	3-4 days
	8-5/240-241	GG	TRB/PW 8-5 GG	GG	
	8-7/244-245	TRB/RW 8-7	TRB/PW 8-7	TE/EA 8-7	
	8-8/248-249			TE/CA 8-8 *MAC 8 Activity 14	
8C Determine congruent figures and identify lines of symmetry.	8-9/250-251	TE/RA 8-9	TRB/PW 8-9 *MAC 6 Activity 12A *MAC 7 Activity 13	TRB/EW 8-9 *MAC 6 Activity 12A *MAC 7 Activity 13	2 days
	8-10/252-253	TRB/RW 8-10	TRB/PW 8-10	TE/EA 8-10	
8D Find the circumference and area of a circle.	8-11/254-255	TRB/RW 8-11	TRB/PW 8-11	TE/EA 8-11	2 days
	8-14/260-261	TRB/RW 8-14	TRB/PW 8-14	TE/EA 8-14	
8E Find the area of a rectangle, a triangle, a parallelogram, or a trapezoid.	8-12/256-257	TRB/RW 8-12	TRB/PW 8-12	TE/EA 8-12	2 days
	8-13/258-259	TE/RA 8-13	TRB/PW 8-13 MAC 7 Activity 4B MAC 8 Activity 6	TRB/EW 8-13 MAC 7 Activity 4B MAC 8 Activity 6	
8F Problem Solving: Use Venn diagrams. Make generalizations.	8-4/238-239	TE/RA 8-4	TRB/PW 8-4	TRB/EW 8-4	2 days
	8-6/242-243	TE/RA 8-6	TRB/PW 8-6	TRB/EW 8-6	
Creative Problem Solving	262-263				
Mixed Review	264-265				
Chapter Checkups	246-247; 266-267				
Extra Practice	268				
Enrichment	269				
Cumulative Review/ Problem Solving Review	270-271				
Technology	272				

TE = Teacher's Edition
TRB = Teacher's Resource Book
RW = Reteaching Worksheet
RA = Reteaching Activity
EA = Enrichment Activity
EW = Enrichment Worksheet
PW = Practice Worksheet
CA = Classroom Activity

*Other Available Items
MAC = Mathematics Activities Courseware
GG = Using Geometry Grapher

Manipulative Planning Guide

This is a complete list of manipulatives and materials needed for Chapter 8.

Materials for Manipulatives	TE Activities (INTRODUCE)	Student Book Lesson
Paper, ruler, scissors for each student	Most lessons	Most lessons
Teaching Aid 8* or protractor for each student, Protractor transparency	Lessons 8-2, 8-3, 8-7	Lessons 8-2, 8-3
Angle Sum of Triangle transparency		Lesson 8-7
Envelopes: two for each student	Lesson 8-5	
Piece of yarn, about 4 m long with ends tied together	Lesson 8-6	
Construction paper		
Teaching Aid 11* or dot paper for each student	Lesson 8-8	Lessons 8-8, 8-9, 8-10
Teaching Aid 3* or grid paper for each student	Lesson 8-13	Lessons 8-9, 8-13
Miras or clear plastic for each student		Lesson 8-10
Circular objects or cans of different sizes, string	Lesson 8-11	
Yardstick and inch tape measure for each pair	Lesson 8-11	
Narrow strips of paper or pieces of yarn, four for each student		Lesson 8-11
Compass for each student	Lesson 8-14	Lesson 8-11
Index cards, three for each student	Lesson 8-12	
Pattern blocks for each pair		
Tracing paper, science books		
Teaching Aids 9 and 10* for each student		
Areas of Simple Polygons transparency		Lessons 8-12, 8-13

*Teaching Aids are found in the Teacher's Resource Book.

Learning Stages

The concepts and skills in Chapter 8 are presented through these learning stages.

CONCRETE

Using manipulatives and verbalizing about a concept. No symbols.

Teacher Edition Activities	Student Book
Lessons 8-1, 8-5, 8-6, 8-10, 8-12	Lessons 8-1, 8-5, 8-8

Enrichment	Reteaching	In the Houghton Mifflin Manipulative Kit?	In the Houghton Mifflin Overhead Kit?
Lessons 8-11, 8-12	Lesson 8-13	Yes	
		Yes	Yes
			Yes
	Lesson 8-6		
Lessons 8-7, 8-14	Lesson 4		
	Lesson 8-9		Yes
Lesson 8-12	Lesson 8-13		Yes
		Yes	
Lesson 8-11			
		Yes	
	Lessons 8-9, 8-13	Yes	
Lesson 8-10			
Lesson 8-11			
Lesson 8-14			Yes

CONNECTING

5¢   9cm² $\frac{1}{3}$

Making a connection between manipulatives and symbols.

Teacher Edition Activities	Student Book
Lessons 8-2, 8-3, 8-4, 8-7, 8-9, 8-11, 8-13, 8-14	Lessons 8-1, 8-2, 8-4, 8-5, 8-6, 8-8 through 8-13

SYMBOLIC

$.05 $A = 9cm^2$ $1 - \frac{2}{3} = \frac{1}{3}$

Using numbers or symbols. No manipulatives or pictures of manipulatives.

Teacher Edition Activities	Student Book
Lesson 8-15	Lessons 8-2, 8-3, 8-7, 8-11 through 8-15

Additional Activities

COOPERATIVE LEARNING RESOURCE ACTIVITIES

Through cooperative learning activities, students learn by interacting with one another in small groups. These cooperative activities provide students with motivating settings for making connections, investigations, and problem solving situations.

   The cooperative connections are interdisciplinary problem-solving projects. Each student has a particular job that helps lead the group to complete the project. For the cooperative investigations students work in pairs for investigations involving data collection and analysis. The cooperative problem solving activities encourage the sharing of ideas and information. Students work in groups of four to solve a problem. Students are each assigned a clue and work together to find a common solution.

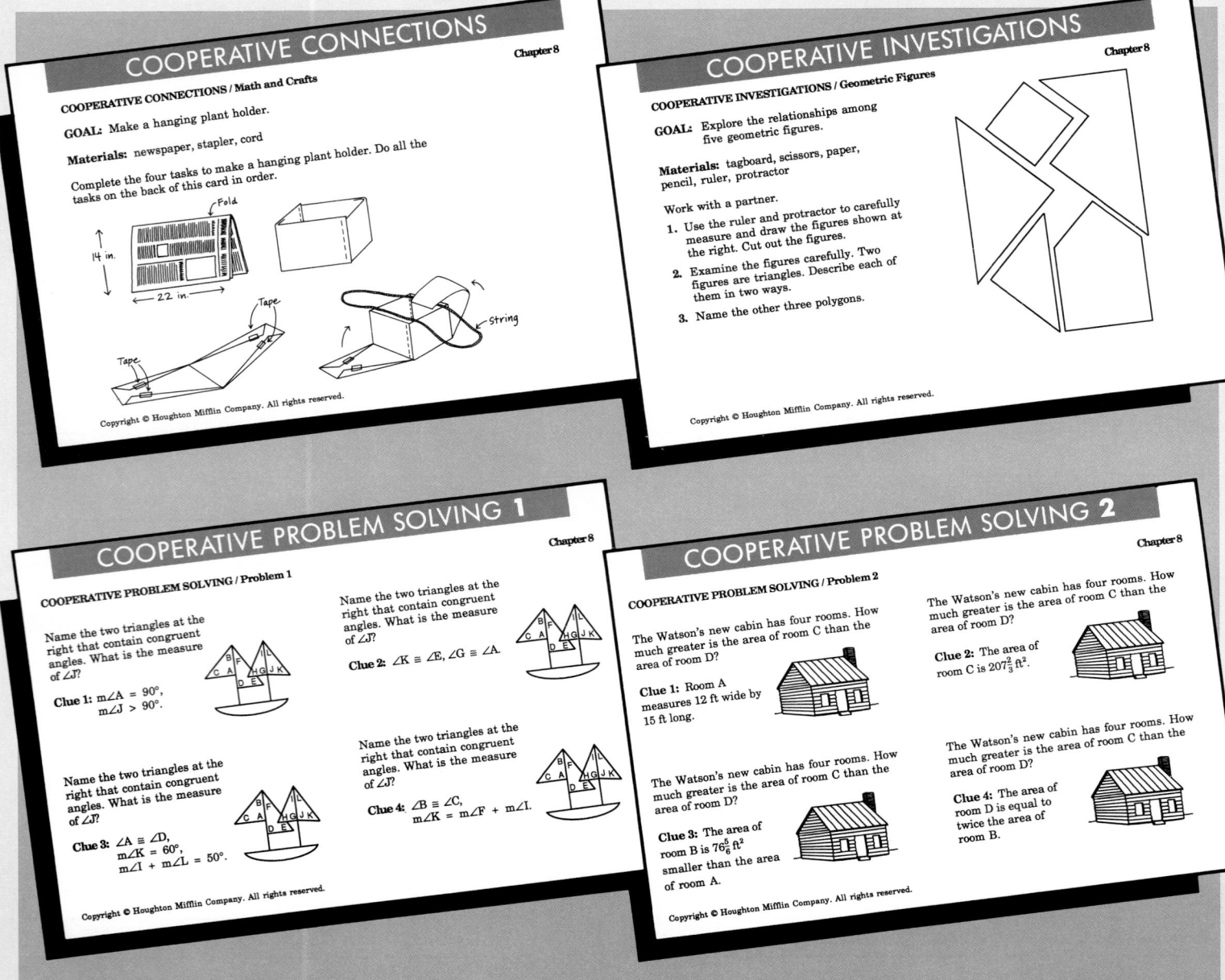

COOPERATIVE CONNECTIONS
Chapter 8

COOPERATIVE CONNECTIONS / Math and Crafts

GOAL: Make a hanging plant holder.

Materials: newspaper, stapler, cord

Complete the four tasks to make a hanging plant holder. Do all the tasks on the back of this card in order.

Copyright © Houghton Mifflin Company. All rights reserved.

COOPERATIVE INVESTIGATIONS
Chapter 8

COOPERATIVE INVESTIGATIONS / Geometric Figures

GOAL: Explore the relationships among five geometric figures.

Materials: tagboard, scissors, paper, pencil, ruler, protractor

Work with a partner.

1. Use the ruler and protractor to carefully measure and draw the figures shown at the right. Cut out the figures.

2. Examine the figures carefully. Two figures are triangles. Describe each of them in two ways.

3. Name the other three polygons.

Copyright © Houghton Mifflin Company. All rights reserved.

COOPERATIVE PROBLEM SOLVING 1
Chapter 8

COOPERATIVE PROBLEM SOLVING / Problem 1

Name the two triangles at the right that contain congruent angles. What is the measure of ∠J?

Clue 1: m∠A = 90°, m∠J > 90°.

Name the two triangles at the right that contain congruent angles. What is the measure of ∠J?

Clue 2: ∠K ≅ ∠E, ∠G ≅ ∠A.

Name the two triangles at the right that contain congruent angles. What is the measure of ∠J?

Clue 3: ∠A ≅ ∠D, m∠K = 60°, m∠I + m∠L = 50°.

Name the two triangles at the right that contain congruent angles. What is the measure of ∠J?

Clue 4: ∠B ≅ ∠C, m∠K = m∠F + m∠I.

Copyright © Houghton Mifflin Company. All rights reserved.

COOPERATIVE PROBLEM SOLVING 2
Chapter 8

COOPERATIVE PROBLEM SOLVING / Problem 2

The Watson's new cabin has four rooms. How much greater is the area of room C than the area of room D?

Clue 1: Room A measures 12 ft wide by 15 ft long.

The Watson's new cabin has four rooms. How much greater is the area of room C than the area of room D?

Clue 2: The area of room C is $207\frac{2}{3}$ ft².

The Watson's new cabin has four rooms. How much greater is the area of room C than the area of room D?

Clue 3: The area of room B is $76\frac{5}{6}$ ft² smaller than the area of room A.

The Watson's new cabin has four rooms. How much greater is the area of room C than the area of room D?

Clue 4: The area of room D is equal to twice the area of room B.

Copyright © Houghton Mifflin Company. All rights reserved.

GAMES

IT'S SUPPLEMENTARY   (For use after Lesson 8-3)

Objective: Measure angles and name the supplement of an angle.

☑ **MATERIALS CHECKLIST:** two protractors and straightedges for the chalkboard, index cards

Have each student write the measure of an angle on an index card. Collect the cards, and place them in two equal piles. Then ask students to form two teams.

The game begins when the first player from each team chooses a card from the team stack and draws an angle with the given measure on the board. After completing the angle, the player gives the protractor to the next team player, who measures the angle and names the supplement. You may want to set a time limit for these tasks. A team earns 5 points for a correctly drawn angle. A correct supplement is worth 3 additional points. The process is repeated with the next two players from each team. The team with the greater number of points after everyone has had a turn is the winner.

GEO RELAY   (For use after Lesson 8-14)

Objective: Identify geometric figures

☑ **MATERIALS CHECKLIST:** posterboard, markers, index cards, masking tape

Make a large poster, illustrating vocabulary from Chapter 8, such as ray or diameter. Write the term that corresponds to each illustration on an index card; make as many cards as students. Divide the cards into equal stacks, marking the cards in each pile with an identifying symbol, say a green or red dot.

Have students form two teams. When you signal, the first player from Team A takes a card from the team stack and quickly attaches it with masking tape to the corresponding illustration on the poster. When he or she has finished, the next player from Team A attaches a card. The procedure is repeated until all Team A players have had a turn. Note how long Team A took, and challenge Team B to beat that time as they match their cards. A correctly placed card is worth a point. The team with more points wins.

BULLETIN BOARD

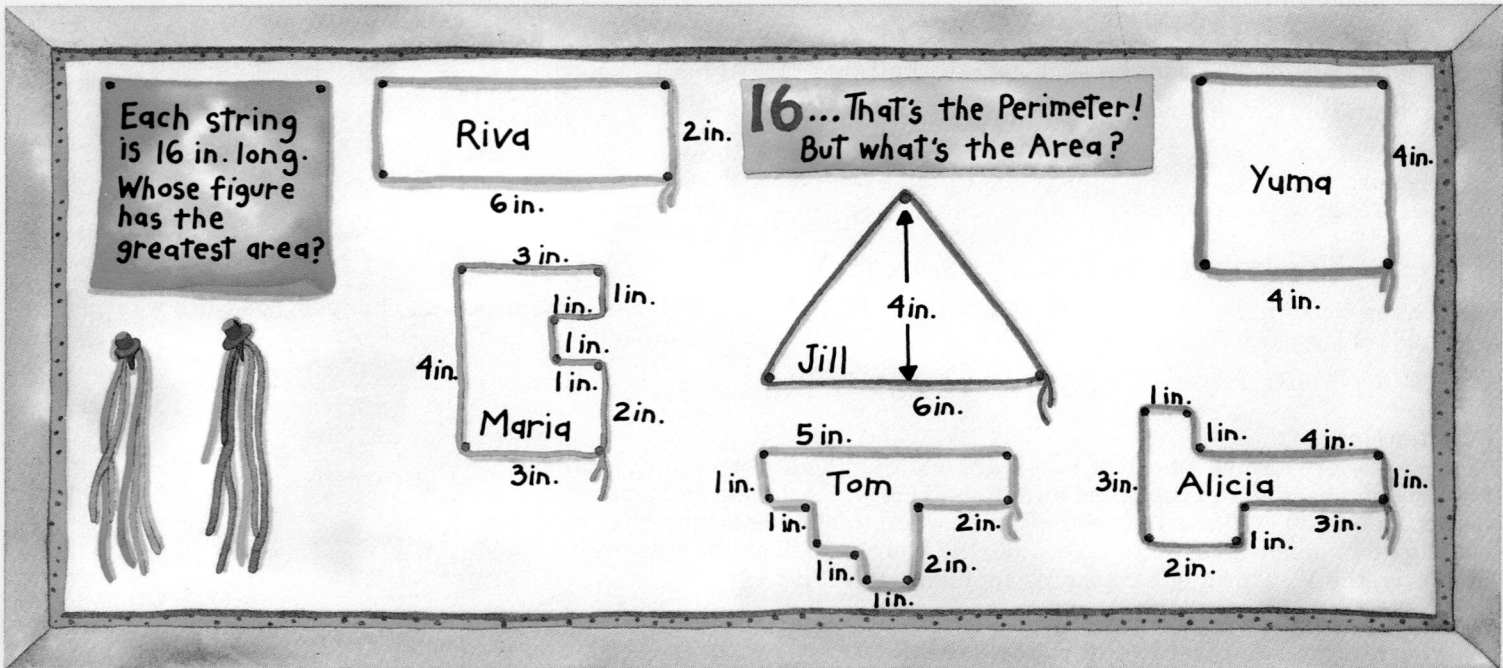

Cover the bulletin board with one-inch grid paper, or rule it with larger square units. Cut several pieces of string that are each 16 units long, and hang them on the bulletin board with pushpins. Ask students to take a string and make a polygon that has a perimeter of 16 units. Pushpins or tacks at the vertices can hold the figure in place. Then have students find the area of the figure, and display it next to the figure.

Alternative Assessment

In addition to the paper and pencil tests available with this program, the following items can help you assess critical thinking as well as your students' ability to solve problems in a wide variety of ways.

Investigation

You will need 3 push pins, a piece of string or yarn about 42 inches long, and some grid paper. On one of the pieces of grid paper, draw a rectangle and count the number of squares inside the rectangle. Measure the length and the width of the rectangle by counting how many squares it measures in each direction (across, up). With the string

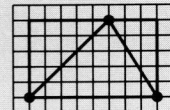

and pins you will form various triangles, as shown at right. Using two push pins, secure the string to two corners of the rectangle. Use the third pin to form the third vertex of the triangle. The third vertex could be anywhere on the side of the rectangle opposite the secured side. Pick 5 points to try. Record your results in a chart on another piece of grid paper. Each time you form a new triangle, count (or estimate) the number of squares from the grid inside the triangle.

Make a conjecture about the size of the triangles and the rectangle. What rule would you recommend one uses to find the area of a triangle? Try to verify your rule by securing a different side of the rectangle and by using other rectangles.

Teacher Notes
Students should try rectangles of different sizes.

They should compare the results by securing the pins to the length and by securing the pins to the width.

Since estimates will be needed for the area of various triangles, they will have to decide if the area of the triangles is, in general, half the area of the rectangles.

The presentation may include:

- a model
- a chart
- an oral or written report with a conclusion

Group Writing Activity (See p. T24.)

Look at the clock in the classroom. At what times will the hands of the clock form these angles?

ACUTE   OBTUSE   RIGHT   STRAIGHT

Teacher Notes
Acute angles are formed when the hands are less than 3 numbers apart. Example: 3:05, the hour hand is on the 3, the minute hand is on the 1. The angle measures approximately 60°. *Obtuse* angles are formed when the hands are more than 3 but less than 6 numbers apart. Example: 5:00, the hour hand is on the 5, the minute hand is on the 12. This angle measures approximately 150°.

Right angles are formed when the hands are exactly 3 numbers apart. Example: 9:00 *Straight* angles are formed when the hands are exactly opposite each other. Example: 6:00. The size of the clock does not change the angle measures. The hands of the clock represent the rays that form the angle.

Individual Writing Activity

Will the angle measures change if the clock is larger or smaller?

Portfolios

Portfolios can provide information about a student's growth in mathematical understanding over a period of time. They can help you make instructional decisions as well as become a vehicle for communicating with parents. The students' work involving investigation and writing activity suggested on this page along with work on the Create Your Own exercises on pages 237, 249, and 251 and the Learning Log exercises on pages 247 and 267 could be included in portfolios.

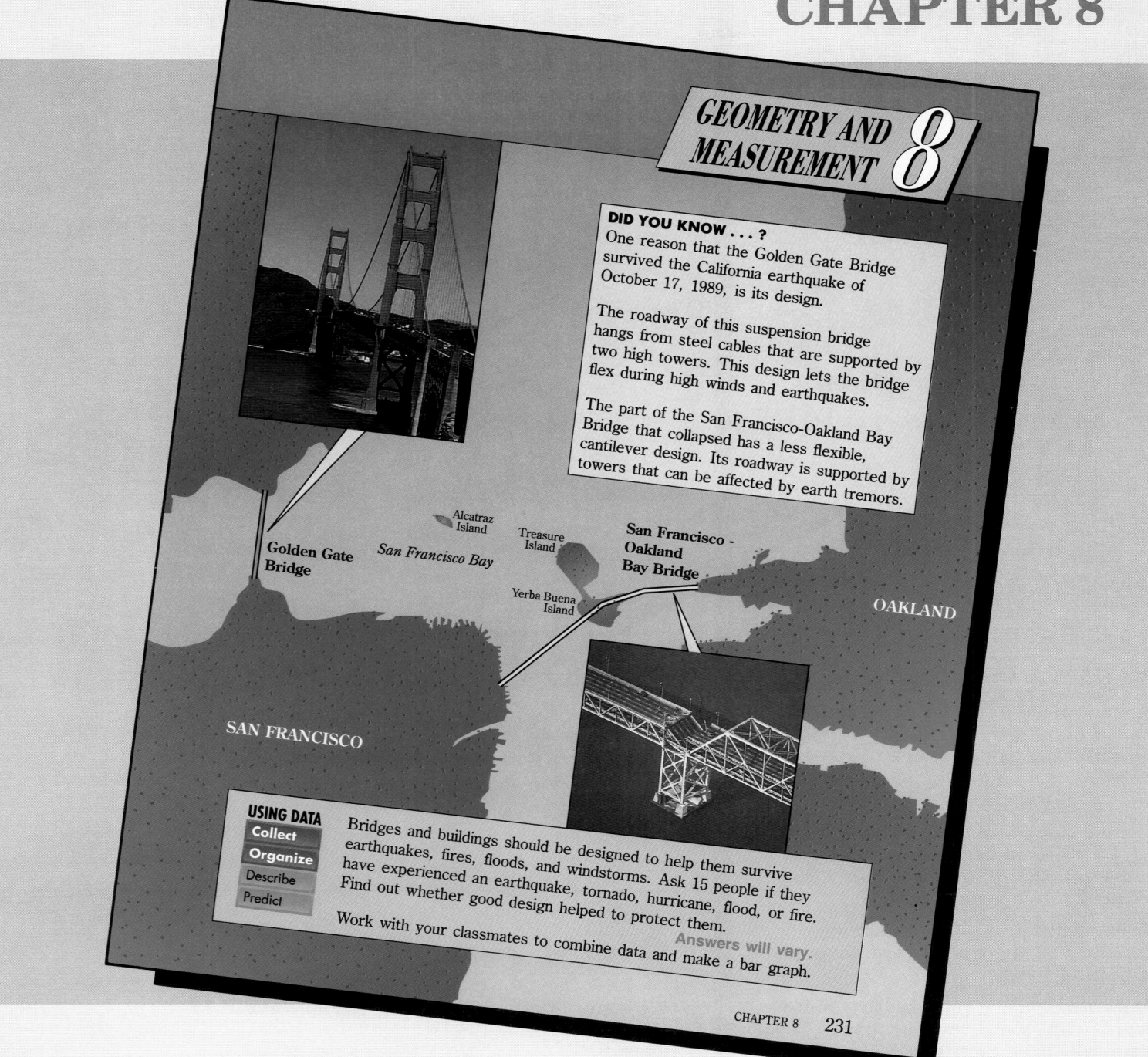

GEOMETRY AND MEASUREMENT 8

DID YOU KNOW . . . ?

One reason that the Golden Gate Bridge survived the California earthquake of October 17, 1989, is its design.

The roadway of this suspension bridge hangs from steel cables that are supported by two high towers. This design lets the bridge flex during high winds and earthquakes.

The part of the San Francisco-Oakland Bay Bridge that collapsed has a less flexible, cantilever design. Its roadway is supported by towers that can be affected by earth tremors.

Alcatraz Island

Treasure Island

San Francisco - Oakland Bay Bridge

Golden Gate Bridge

San Francisco Bay

Yerba Buena Island

OAKLAND

SAN FRANCISCO

USING DATA
Collect
Organize
Describe
Predict

Bridges and buildings should be designed to help them survive earthquakes, fires, floods, and windstorms. Ask 15 people if they have experienced an earthquake, tornado, hurricane, flood, or fire. Find out whether good design helped to protect them.

Work with your classmates to combine data and make a bar graph.

Answers will vary.

CHAPTER 8   231

Using the Chapter Opener

The purpose of this page is to involve the student in the use of real data much like that presented in newspapers and magazines.

To use this page as you begin the chapter, direct students' attention to the data in the illustrations and the map. Have students use the illustrations to compare suspension and cantilever bridges. You may wish to ask questions such as the following:

What geometric shapes do you see in the pictures of the bridges? *(Answers may include triangles, rectangles, parallelograms.)*

You may wish to use the data collecting and graph-making activities as cooperative learning situations. Be sure each group member surveys a different set of respondents so that the group has sufficient data.

Lesson Organizer

Objective: Explore basic figures.

Prior Knowledge: Students should be familiar with basic geometric ideas.

Error Analysis and Remediation: See page 267A.

Lesson Resources:
Class Activity 8-1
Daily Review 8-1

Two-Minute Math

Write the next three numbers in the pattern.

$\frac{1}{2}, \frac{1}{4}, \frac{1}{8}, \cdots \left(\frac{1}{16}, \frac{1}{32}, \frac{1}{64}\right)$

$\frac{2}{3}, \frac{3}{4}, \frac{4}{5}, \cdots \left(\frac{5}{6}, \frac{6}{7}, \frac{7}{8}\right)$

1 PREPARE

CONCRETE ACTIVITY

✔ **MATERIALS CHECKLIST:** paper, ruler

1. **Place a piece of paper representing part of a plane on your desk. How is a plane different from a piece of paper?** *(A plane goes on and on in all directions and has no thickness.)*

2. **Draw a dot on the paper. Call it a point. Draw as many segments as you can through the point. How many can you draw?** *(an infinite number)*

3. **Draw two points. How many segments can you draw that pass through both points?** *(one)*

4. **Draw three more points. How many segments can you draw that pass through all three points?** *(Most students will say none. Some may discover that a line segment can be drawn if the three points are along a straight line.)*

WHEN YOUR STUDENTS ASK
★ WHY AM I LEARNING THIS? ★

You can connect this skill to real life through language. "The point is to get in line for the plane." Many everyday words such as *point*, *line*, and *plane*, have special mathematical meanings.

Exploring Basic Figures

A **plane** is like a flat surface that goes on and on without end. It contains an infinite number of **points**, or exact locations.

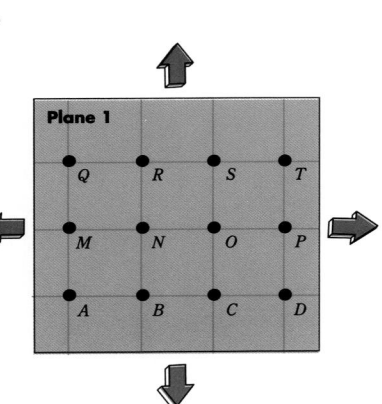

Plane

1. Name some objects that look like parts of planes. **Answers will vary. Suggestions given: floor, billboard.**

Use plane 1 at right for Exercises 2–9.

2. How many points can you see? **16**

   THINK ALOUD How many points can you not see? Explain. **an infinite number since the plane extends forever**

A **line** is a set of points that extends without end in opposite directions.

You say, "line *MP*" or "line *PM*."
You write $\overleftrightarrow{MP}$ or $\overleftrightarrow{PM}$.

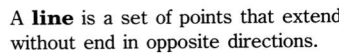

Answers will vary. $\overleftrightarrow{MN}; \overleftrightarrow{NO}; \overleftrightarrow{OP}$

4. What are three other names for $\overleftrightarrow{MP}$?

5. How many lines can be drawn through *B* and *D*? any two points? **1; 1**

6. How many lines can be drawn that connect *S* with any point shown? **7**

7. **THINK ALOUD** How many lines in the plane contain point *S*? **an infinite number**

A **line segment** is a part of a line with two endpoints.

You write $\overline{MN}$ or $\overline{NM}$.

You say "line segment *MN*" or "line segment *NM*."

8. If $\overline{ST}$ is 1 cm long, name all segments you can draw that measure 3 cm.
   $\overline{QT}; \overline{MP}; \overline{AD}$

Line segments of the same length are **congruent**.

9. Name four line segments that can be drawn congruent to $\overline{MO}$. **Answers may vary. Suggestions given.**
   Repeat for $\overline{SC}$. $\overline{MO} \rightarrow \overline{NP}; \overline{QS}; \overline{RT}; \overline{AC}; \overline{BD}$
   $\overline{SC} \rightarrow \overline{TD}; \overline{RB}; \overline{QA}$

2 EXPLORE

Why must the endpoint of a ray be read first? *(to show the direction of the ray)*

Can any two rays form an angle? Explain. *(No; only rays that have the same endpoint)*

How is ∠XYZ different from ∠YZX? *(They have different vertices and rays.)*

SUMMARIZE/ASSESS **Explain how symbols help describe some geometric figures.** *(Possible answer: The symbol for line, ↔; line segment, ⟷; ray, →; and angle, ∠; suggest characteristics of these figures.)*

10. In plane 2, do $\overleftrightarrow{HJ}$ and $\overleftrightarrow{FK}$ intersect at point J, point K, or point F?
K

Remember that lines extend without end.

11. Do $\overleftrightarrow{KF}$ and $\overleftrightarrow{GM}$ intersect at some point?
yes

12. Do $\overleftrightarrow{HK}$ and $\overleftrightarrow{GM}$ intersect at some point?
no

Parallel lines are lines that never intersect and are in the same plane.

13. Are $\overleftrightarrow{HK}$ and $\overleftrightarrow{GM}$ parallel lines? Name two other pairs of parallel lines you could draw. **yes;** **Answers may vary.**
$\overleftrightarrow{HL} \parallel \overleftrightarrow{JM}; \overleftrightarrow{JG} \parallel \overleftrightarrow{KL}$ **Suggestions given.**

A **ray** is a part of a line with one endpoint.

The endpoint is A.

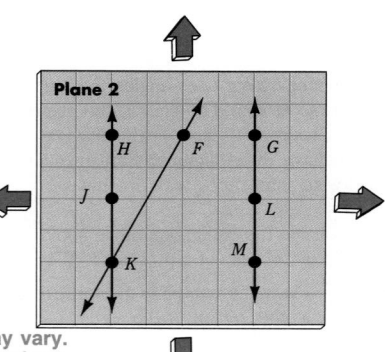

You write $\overrightarrow{AB}$.
You say, "ray AB."

14. In plane 3, what is another name for $\overrightarrow{AE}$?
$\overrightarrow{AB}$

15. Name all the rays shown in plane 3.
$\overrightarrow{AG}; \overrightarrow{AB}; \overrightarrow{AF}; \overrightarrow{AC}$

Two rays with the same endpoint form an **angle**. The common endpoint is a **vertex**.

In plane 3, ray AB and ray AC form angle BAC. You write $\angle BAC$ with the vertex in the middle.

16. Name the rays that form $\angle DAF$.
$\overrightarrow{AD}; \overrightarrow{AF}$

17. Are $\angle BAC$ and $\angle CAE$ the same angle? **yes**

18. Name all angles shown in plane 3.
$\angle CAF; \angle CAB; \angle GAC; \angle GAB; \angle GAF; \angle FAB$

19. **CREATE YOUR OWN** Use two pieces of paper to construct a model of two planes like planes 4 and 5. Where do the two planes intersect?
Check students' work.

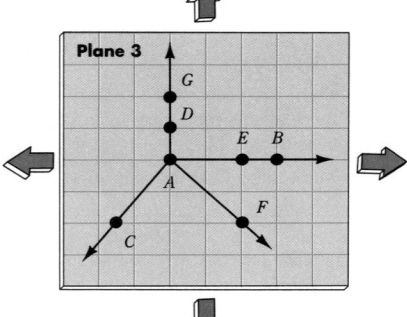

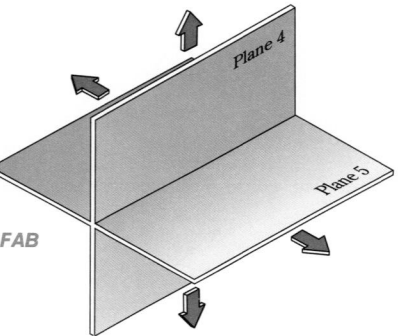

CLASS ACTIVITY **8-1**

Have the students work in groups of four. Ask each group to find objects in the classroom that illustrate: points, rays, line segments, angles, planes, intersecting and parallel lines. For example, the point of a pencil or pen could illustrate a point; a pencil or a pointer could illustrate a ray; and a piece of string or wire could illustrate a line segment. Encourage the students to use as many different objects as possible. Have each group share its work with the rest of the class and compile a master list of real-world objects that illustrate geometric figures.

MEETING SPECIAL NEEDS

For Students Who Are . . .

Acquiring English Proficiency Discuss the differences in meaning of *line, line segment,* and *ray.*

Gifted and Talented Have groups design and construct a model that has 4 or more planes. Ask each group to explain its designs to the class.

Working 2 or 3 Grades Below Level Have students draw and label examples of *planes, points, line segments, parallel lines, intersecting lines, angles, vertexes,* and *congruent line segments.*

Today's Problem

Think of two different planes in space. What figure is formed if they intersect? (a line)

Lesson Organizer

Objective: Measure angles and classify as acute, right, obtuse, and straight.

Prior Knowledge: Students should know the meaning of *angle* and *ray*.

Error Analysis and Remediation: See page 276A.

Lesson Resources:
Practice Worksheet 8-2
Reteaching Worksheet 8-2
Enrichment Activity 8-2
Daily Review 8-2
Cooperative Problem Solving 1, Chapter 8

Two-Minute Math

Write five mixed numbers and five decimals between 5 and 10. Order the numbers from least to greatest.

1 INTRODUCE

CONNECTING ACTIVITY

☑ **MATERIALS CHECKLIST:** Teaching Aid 8 (Protractor) or protractor for each student, Protractor transparency

1. Write *protractor* on the chalkboard; provide time for students to examine their protractors.

• **What is a protractor used to do?** *(Measure angles)*

• **What unit is used to measure angles?** *(degree)*

2. Ask students to brainstorm a list of characteristics or observations about the protractor. Record students' responses on the chalkboard, and refer to the list as students measure and draw various angles. *(Possible responses: Has numbers from 0 to 180; intervals of 10 are labeled; 0 and 180 line up, as do 10 and 170; 90 is in middle.)*

WHEN YOUR STUDENTS ASK
★ **WHY AM I LEARNING THIS?** ★

You can connect this skill to real life through architecture and drafting. Architects and draftspersons draw and measure angles.

Measuring Angles

A ship's navigator uses angles to stay on course at sea. The ship in the diagram is on a course 60° from north. Navigation angles have three digits and are measured clockwise from north with a compass.

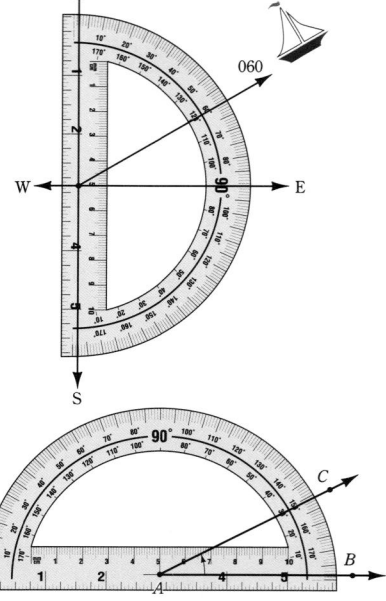

To measure the navigation angle above, use the outer scale of a protractor. Why?
measures from 0°–180°
STEPS Place the center of the protractor at the vertex of the angle.

Line up one side of the angle with 0°.

To draw an angle with a measure of 30°, use the inner scale of a protractor. Why?
measures from 0°–90°
STEPS Draw ray *AB*.

Place the protractor's center mark at the vertex, *A*. Line up 0° with ray *AB*.

Mark point *C* at 30° and draw ray *AC*.

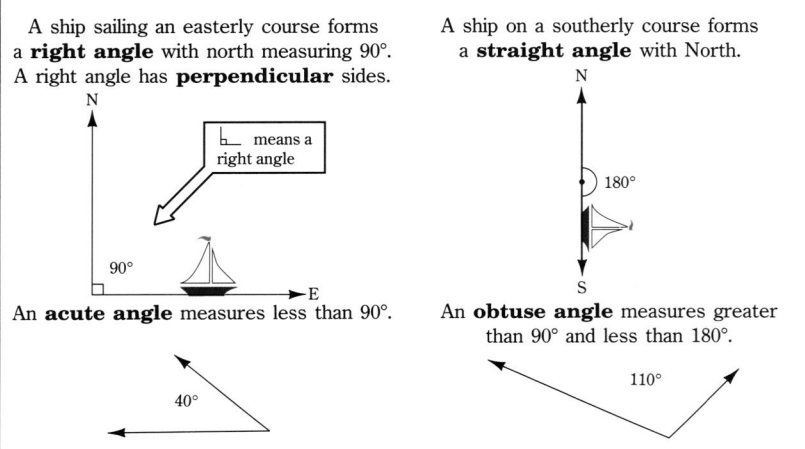

A ship sailing an easterly course forms a **right angle** with north measuring 90°. A right angle has **perpendicular** sides.

┗ means a right angle

90°

N

W ——— E

An **acute angle** measures less than 90°.

40°

A ship on a southerly course forms a **straight angle** with North.

N

180°

S

An **obtuse angle** measures greater than 90° and less than 180°.

110°

---

2 TEACH

☑ **MATERIALS CHECKLIST:** Teaching Aid 8 (Protractor) or protractor, rulers for each student, Protractor transparency

Name some objects in the classroom that have right, acute, and obtuse angles. *(Examples: corner of the room; hands of a clock)*

How can you use a protractor to draw two perpendicular lines? *(Draw a 90° angle, and extend the lines.)*

Order the types of angles studied in this lesson from those with the greatest to those with the least measures. *(straight, obtuse, right acute)*

Chalkboard Examples

Is the angle *acute, right, obtuse,* or *straight*?
180°   95°   15°   90°

SUMMARIZE/ASSESS   Demonstrate and explain how to use a protractor to measure and draw an acute angle and an obtuse angle. *(Students should explain the steps given in the lesson.)*

Is the angle *acute, right, obtuse,* or *straight*?

1. 90°   2. 137°   3. 40°   4. 120°   5. 5°   6. 180°
   right   obtuse   acute   obtuse   acute   straight

PRACTICE

Use a protractor to complete. (m∠FED means "the measure of ∠FED is")

7. m∠*FED* = ▓° 70°   8. m∠*JKL* = ▓° 25°   9. m∠*WXY* = ▓° 130°

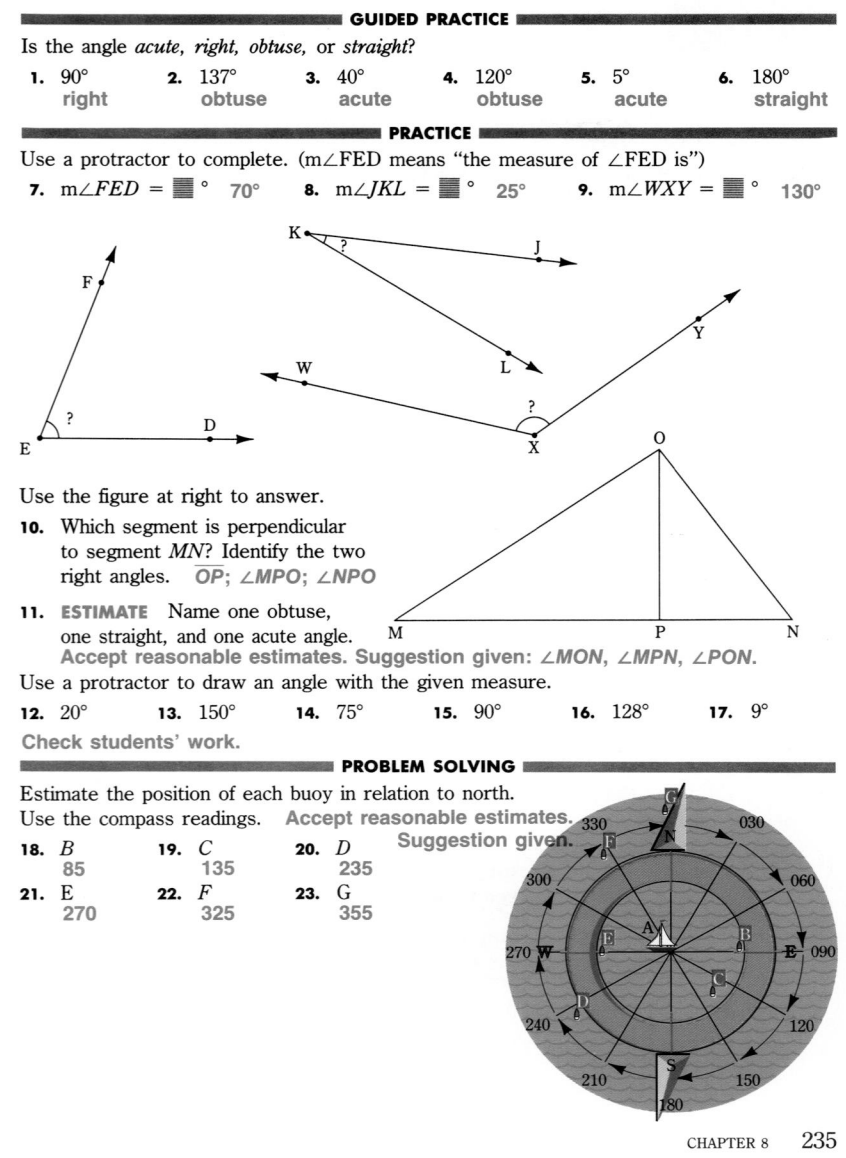

Use the figure at right to answer.

10. Which segment is perpendicular to segment *MN*? Identify the two right angles. $\overline{OP}$; ∠*MPO*; ∠*NPO*

11. **ESTIMATE** Name one obtuse, one straight, and one acute angle.
    Accept reasonable estimates. Suggestion given: ∠*MON*, ∠*MPN*, ∠*PON*.

Use a protractor to draw an angle with the given measure.

12. 20°   13. 150°   14. 75°   15. 90°   16. 128°   17. 9°
Check students' work.

PROBLEM SOLVING

Estimate the position of each buoy in relation to north.
Use the compass readings.   **Accept reasonable estimates.**
                              Suggestion given.

18. *B*   19. *C*   20. *D*
    85   135   235

21. *E*   22. *F*   23. *G*
    270   325   355

CHAPTER 8   235

PRACTICE 8-2

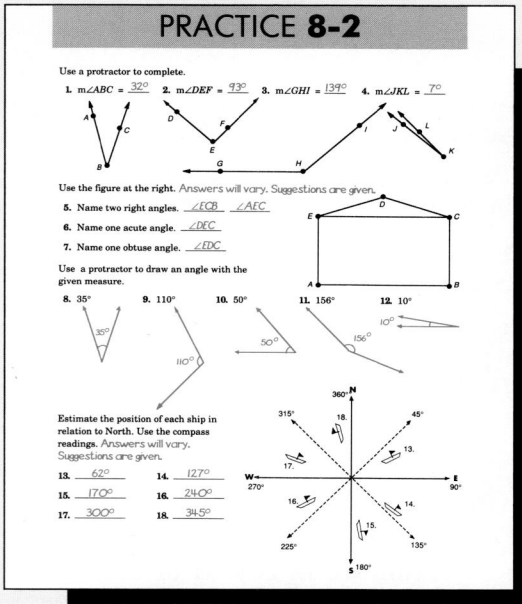

Use a protractor to complete.

1. m∠*ABC* = 32°   2. m∠*DEF* = 93°   3. m∠*GHI* = 139°   4. m∠*JKL* = 7°

Use the figure at the right. Answers will vary. Suggestions are given.

5. Name two right angles. ∠*EQB*; ∠*AEC*
6. Name one acute angle. ∠*DEC*
7. Name one obtuse angle. ∠*EDC*

Use a protractor to draw an angle with the given measure.

8. 35°   9. 110°   10. 50°   11. 156°   12. 10°

Estimate the position of each ship in relation to North. Use the compass readings. Answers will vary. Suggestions are given.

13. 62°   14. 127°
15. 170°   16. 240°
17. 300°   18. 345°

RETEACHING 8-2

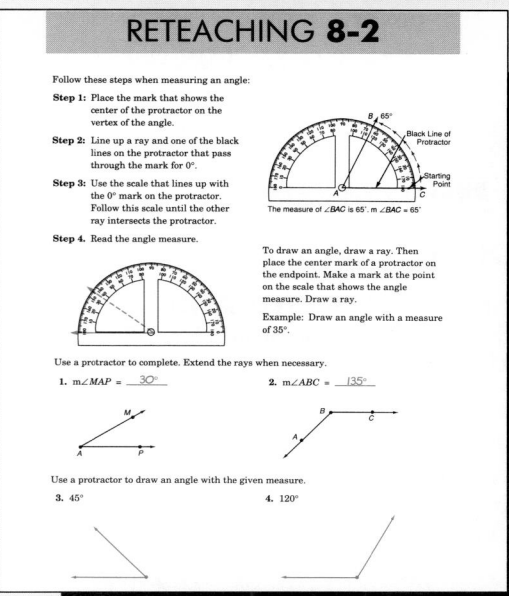

Follow these steps when measuring an angle:

Step 1: Place the mark that shows the center of the protractor on the vertex of the angle.

Step 2: Line up a ray and one of the black lines on the protractor that pass through the mark for 0°.

Step 3: Use the scale that lines up with the 0° mark on the protractor. Follow this scale until the other ray intersects the protractor.

Step 4. Read the angle measure.

The measure of ∠*BAC* is 65°. m∠*BAC* = 65°

To draw an angle, draw a ray. Then place the center mark of a protractor on the endpoint. Make a mark at the point on the scale that shows the angle measure. Draw a ray.

Example: Draw an angle with a measure of 35°.

Use a protractor to complete. Extend the rays when necessary.

1. m∠*MAP* = 30°   2. m∠*ABC* = 135°

Use a protractor to draw an angle with the given measure.

3. 45°   4. 120°

ENRICHMENT 8-2

☑ **MATERIALS CHECKLIST:** Protractors

Have the students work in groups of three or four. Instruct each group to use protractors to find angles associated with various classroom objects. For example, the students might find that the angle formed by an open pair of scissors has a measure of 135°. Or they might find that the angle formed by a light switch in the off position is approximately 40°. Have the groups share their findings with each other and compile a master list of classroom angle measurements.

MEETING SPECIAL NEEDS

For Students Who Are . . .

Acquiring English Proficiency Discuss the meaning of *navigator* and *clockwise*. Explain that in this lesson 030 is the same as 30°.

Gifted and Talented Have students solve these problems: Between 11:25 and 11:30 the hands on a clock form a straight angle. Between what five minute intervals will this first happen after 12:00? (12:30 and 12:35) after 7:00? (7:10 and 7:15) after 9:00 (9:20 and 9:25)

Working 2 or 3 Grades Below Level If students have difficulty using the protractor, have them use only the lower scale. Make sure they turn the angle so the vertex is on the left.

Having Reading Difficulties Pair students with able readers to work on the Problem Solving exercises.

Today's Problem

Decide if each of the following is or is not possible.
A triangle with two right angles. (not possible)
A triangle with two obtuse angles. (not possible)
A triangle with two acute triangles. (possible)

LESSON 8-3

Lesson Organizer

> **Objective:** Explore angle relations (adjacent, vertical, complementary, and supplementary angles).

Prior Knowledge: Students should be able to measure and draw angles.

Error Analysis and Remediation: See page 267A.

Lesson Resources:
Class Activity 8-3
Daily Review 8-3

Two-Minute Math

Subtract one-tenth from each number in row H of the Table of Numbers on the inside back cover.

(1.15; 2.6; 7.9; 9.48; 3.8; 4.4; 6.9; 4.53; 8.5)

1 PREPARE

CONNECTING ACTIVITY

✔ **MATERIALS CHECKLIST:** Teaching Aid 8 (Protractor) or protractor, ruler for each student, Protractor transparency

Draw and label $\overrightarrow{KL}$. At K, make a 45° angle. Mark point M.

Extend $\overrightarrow{KL}$ and label point N. What other angle is formed at K? *(∠NKM)*

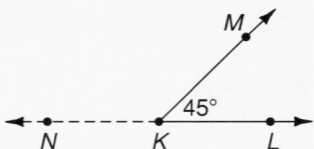

Without measuring, tell how many degrees are in ∠NKM. *(135°)* **Measure to check your answer.**
What would the measure of ∠NKM be if ∠KLM were 60°? *(120°)*

WHEN YOUR STUDENTS ASK
★ WHY AM I LEARNING THIS? ★

You can connect this skill to real life through art. Many artists, such as the Dutch painter Piet Mondrian, have created intricate compositions through repetition of related angles.

Exploring Angle Relations

Many designs for stained glass are based on relations between angles. Use a protractor to explore some angle relations in the design on page 237.

Congruent angles are angles with the same measure. Angles *HIC* and *NOG* are congruent angles. Both measure 135°.

1. Find an angle congruent to ∠*AIB*.   **Answers will vary. Suggestion given. ∠CLD**
2. What are the measures of ∠*FOG*, ∠*CLE*, and ∠*UOV*? Which two of these angles are congruent?
   45°; 90°; 45°; ∠FOG and ∠UOV

Vertical angles have rays going in opposite directions from the same point. All pairs of vertical angles are congruent. Angles *AIB* and *RIS* are vertical angles.

3. Measure ∠*CLD* and ∠*TLU*. What kind of angles are they? Are they congruent?
   vertical; yes
4. Find two other pairs of vertical angles in the design.
   Answers will vary. Suggestion given. ∠EOG and ∠UOW

Adjacent angles have a common vertex and a common side, but no interior points in common. ∠*QIR* and ∠*RIS* are adjacent angles.

5. Do ∠*TLU* and ∠*ULM* have a common vertex? a common side? What can you conclude?
   yes; yes; They are adjacent angles.
6. Find two other pairs of adjacent angles in the design.
   Answers will vary. Suggestion given. <AIB and <AIH
7. **CRITICAL THINKING**   Are pairs of adjacent angles always congruent? **no**

> **Two angles are complementary angles if the sum of their measures is 90°.**
>
> **Two angles are supplementary angles if the sum of their measures is 180°.**

8. Find two angles in the design that are: **Answers will vary. Suggestion given.**
   a. complementary   b. supplementary
   ∠AIB; ∠BIC   **∠CLD; ∠DLU**

---

2 EXPLORE

✔ **MATERIALS CHECKLIST:** Teaching Aid 8 (Protractor) or protractor, ruler for each student, Protractor transparency

Can two obtuse angles be supplementary? Explain. *(No; the sum of their measures would be greater than 180°.)*

Can two acute angles be complementary? Explain. *(Yes; the sum of their measures could be equal to 90°.)*

SUMMARIZE/ASSESS   **Draw a picture to show four rays intersecting at point P. On your picture, identify a pair of: vertical angles; adjacent angles; supplementary angles; and congruent angles.** *(Check students' drawings.)*

9. Use a protractor and ruler to draw:

   a. any angle supplementary to a 45° angle   **135° angle**

   b. any angle complementary to a 25° angle   **65° angle**

10. **CREATE YOUR OWN**   Design a stained glass window that has an example of each kind of angle relation studied in this lesson.
Check students' work.

CLASS ACTIVITY **8-3**

☑ **MATERIALS CHECKLIST:** Protractors

Have the students work in pairs. Instruct each student to construct an acute angle. Then have partners exchange papers. Each partner constructs a complementary, a supplementary, and a congruent angle to the acute angle. Have partners check each other's work. Continue by having each partner draw a line on another sheet of paper. Partners again exchange papers. This time, each student draws a line that intersects the line on the page and measures the vertical angles formed to see if they are congruent.

MEETING SPECIAL NEEDS

For Students Who Are . . .

Acquiring English Proficiency   Pair students with an English-proficient student to answer the questions in this lesson.

Gifted and Talented   Have students do library research in art books to find paintings that show different kinds of angle relations.

Working 2 or 3 Grades Below Level   Have students make cards showing different kinds of angles named on page 236.

Having Reading Difficulties   Have students name each other's angle relations in Create Your Own.

Today's Problem

If ∠A is complementary to ∠B, and ∠B is supplementary to ∠C, what is the relation of ∠A to ∠C *(Angle A is smaller than angle C.)*

LESSON 8-4

Lesson Organizer

Objective: Solve problems using Venn diagrams.

Prior Knowledge: Students should be able to use a diagram to represent a problem.

Lesson Resources:
Practice Worksheet 8-4
Reteaching Activity 8-4
Enrichment Worksheet 8-4
Daily Review 8-4

Two-Minute Math

Which months have 30 days? *(April, June, September, November)* **28 days?** *(February, except for leap years)* **31 days?** *(the rest)*

1 INTRODUCE

CONNECTING ACTIVITY

1. Organize students into two groups: those who are 12 years old and those who are 13 or older. **Is there anyone in both groups?** *(no)*

2. Ask students who are 12 years old to stand. Have students who were born in June, July, or August raise their hands. **Is there anyone standing and raising a hand? What does this mean?** *(This person is in both collections.)*

3. Draw this diagram on the chalkboard. Have a student explain it.

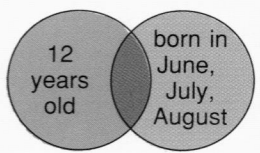

WHEN YOUR STUDENTS ASK
★ WHY AM I LEARNING THIS? ★

You can connect this skill to real life through lawmaking. Laws are often the result of compromise; that is, legislators may have different ideas, but the laws reflect intersecting points of view.

Problem Solving:
Venn Diagrams

You can use **Venn diagrams** to represent a collection of objects or events.

Days beginning with the letter S — Saturday, Sunday

When two collections have nothing in common, the figures in a Venn diagram do not overlap.

Collection 1: Days beginning with the letter S — Saturday, Sunday

Monday, Tuesday, Wednesday, Thursday, Friday

Collection 2: Days you usually go to school

THINK ALOUD How would you draw a Venn diagram representing two collections with some items in common? **linked ovals**

Try drawing a Venn diagram for collections 1 and 3.

Collection 1: days beginning with the letter S
Collection 3: days with six letters

(Hint: How many figures will you draw? What days will you use? Can figures overlap?*)*
2; Sunday, Saturday, Monday, Friday; yes

How would you draw a Venn diagram when one collection is contained entirely within another collection? Draw a Venn diagram for collections 2 and 4. **one circle inside another**

Collection 2: days you usually go to school
Collection 4: days beginning with the letter T

(Hint: Can one figure be inside the other?*)*
yes

Do your Venn diagrams look like these?

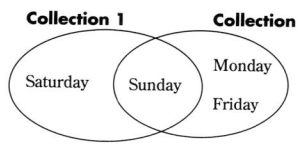

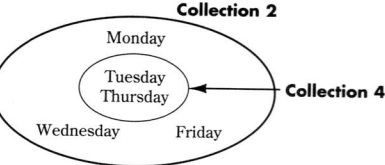

238   LESSON 8–4

---

2 TEACH

Why is the Venn diagram for Collections 1 and 3 a different configuration from the Venn diagram for Collections 2 and 4?
(Collections 1 and 3 have Sunday in common and thus have an overlap; Collection 4— Tuesday and Thursday—is contained entirely within Collection 2—school days.)

Chalkboard Examples

Draw a Venn diagram to represent two collections that have nothing in common.
(Drawing should show two ovals that do not overlap.)

SUMMARIZE/ASSESS How would you draw a Venn diagram representing one collection contained entirely within another?
(Draw a small oval within a larger oval.)

GUIDED PRACTICE

1. Look at the Venn diagram and answer the question.

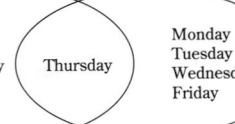

   a. What kind of objects are represented in this Venn diagram? **days of week**

   b. What are the two collections **Days with** represented in this Venn diagram? **8 letters;**

   c. Which school day has 8 letters? **school days**
   Thursday

Venn diagram labels: Saturday | Thursday | Monday Tuesday Wednesday Friday

PRACTICE

Draw a Venn diagram. **Check students' work. See page 267b for**
Use the collections at right. **diagrams 2–4.** Months of the Year:

2. A and B   **3.** B and C

4. A and G   **5.** C and D

6. C and E   **7.** A and C

8. G and C   **9.** D and F

10. C and F

A: months with exactly 30 days
B: months with 31 days
C: months beginning with the letter J
D: months that have the letters *ber*
E: months that have four letters
F: months with some summer vacation days
G: all months

Describe the collection of numbers the Venn diagram shows.

11. **even numbers 0–16 12.**   **13.** **even numbers 0–20; multiples of ten to 70**

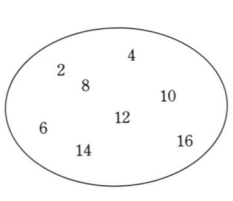

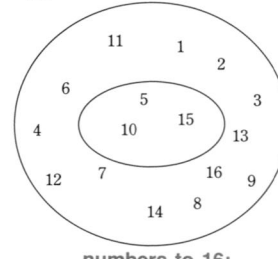

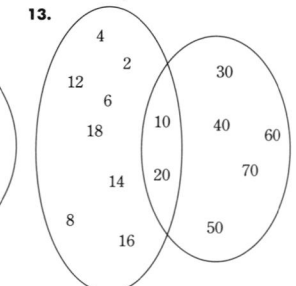

numbers to 16; multiples of 5 to 15

Critical Thinking

How would you draw a Venn diagram to represent three collections? Think about these collections. **3 linked ovals**

Collection 1: multiples of 3 that are less than 35
Collection 2: multiples of 5 that are less than 35
Collection 3: multiples of 2 that are less than 35

Draw the diagram. **See page 267b.**

CHAPTER 8   239

MEETING SPECIAL NEEDS

For Students Who Are . . .

Acquiring English Proficiency Make sure students are familiar with the months of the year and the number of days in each month.

Gifted and Talented Have each student create a problem that would use a Venn diagram to solve. Students can exchange papers and solve.

Working 2 or 3 Grades Below Level Have students make cards showing three types of Venn diagrams: all in common, some in common, none in common.

Today's Problem

In a class of 30 students, 5 take only Latin, 8 take only Spanish, 3 take only French, 4 take both Latin and French, 2 take all three languages, 6 take French and Spanish, and none take only Latin and Spanish. How many take no foreign language? (*Use a Venn diagram; two students.*)

---

3 FOLLOW-UP

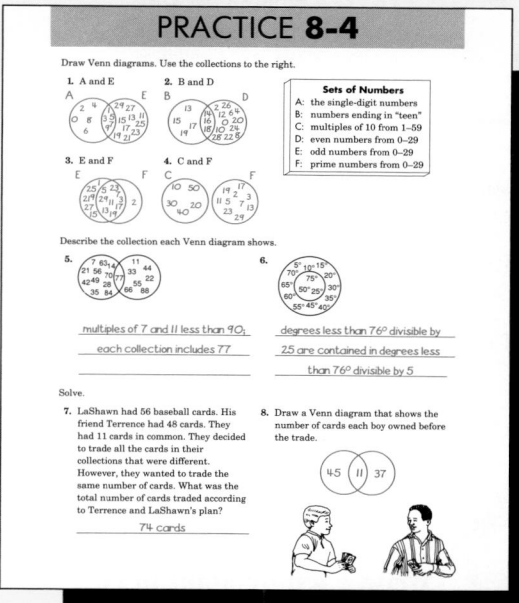

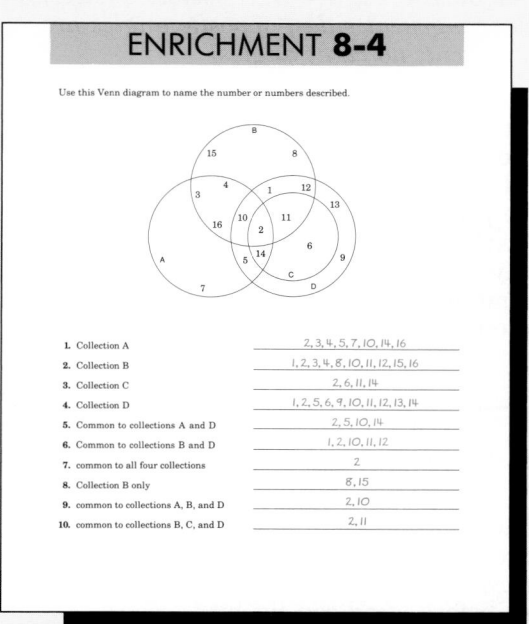

Lesson Organizer

Objective: Explore the classification of polygons by their properties.

Prior Knowledge: Students should be familiar with the different types of polygons.

Error Analysis and Remediation: See page 267A.

Lesson Resources:
Practice Worksheet 8-5
Daily Review 8-5
Cooperative Connections, Chapter 8

Two-Minute Math

Write each decimal in row L of the Table of Numbers on the inside back cover as a fraction in lowest terms.

$(\frac{1}{5};\ 1\frac{1}{2}\ or\ \frac{3}{2};\ \frac{1}{4};\ \frac{3}{4})$

1 PREPARE

CONCRETE ACTIVITY

☑ **MATERIALS CHECKLIST:** Teaching Aids 9 and 10, (Polygon Shapes and Polygon Properties) scissors, two envelopes per student

1. Ask students how they can tell whether the figures on Teaching Aid 9 have congruent sides, congruent angles, parallel sides, or right angles. Discuss the symbols key.

2 Describe Figure J. *(Possible answer: four congruent sides; opposite angles are congruent; no right angles)*

Find and identify a four-sided figure with exactly one pair of parallel sides and two right angles. *(Figure Q)* **Cut out the figures on Teaching Aid 9 and the polygon names and properties on Teaching Aid 10. Sort the figures any way you want. Explain your method to a friend.** Have students store each set of cutouts in a separate envelope.

WHEN YOUR STUDENTS ASK
★ WHY AM I LEARNING THIS? ★

You can connect this skill to real life through carpentry. A carpenter needs to know which sides and angles are congruent before wood can be cut.

Exploring Polygons

Use the workmasters with geometric figures and polygon properties.

1. A **polygon** is a closed, plane figure made from three or more line segments. Two of your **geometric figures** are *not* polygons. Write their letters.
   G and T

Polygons	Number of Sides
Triangle	3
Quadrilateral	4
Pentagon	5
Hexagon	6
Octagon	8

2. Sort the rest of the geometric figures by the number of sides they have. Which are triangles? quadrilaterals? pentagons? Is *E* or *F* a hexagon? *A, B; C, I, J, K, L, M, N, Q, P, Q, R, S; D, H; E*

3. Figures *C*, *D*, and *F* are **regular polygons**. Regular polygons have all sides and angles congruent. Name two other figures that are regular polygons. *B, E*

4. Quadrilaterals with exactly one pair of parallel sides are called **trapezoids**. They cannot have two sets of parallel sides. Name the figures that are trapezoids. *P, Q, R*

5. Place these quadrilaterals in two rows.

   Row 1: *M   K   L   N*   ➯ These are **parallelograms**.
   Row 2: *R   S   P   Q*   ➯ These are not parallelograms.

   a. Find the **polygon properties** that apply to a parallelogram. *See below.*

   b. IN YOUR WORDS Now write your own definition of a parallelogram. *Answers may vary. Suggestion given: a quadrilateral with opposite sides parallel*

240   LESSON 8–5   closed figure; plane figure; made from line segments; four sides; opposite sides parallel; opposite sides congruent

---

2 EXPLORE

Tell students to use the polygon cutouts for Exercises 1–4 and to use both the figures and the polygon properties for Exercises 5–8. Have students first arrange the figures in rows, and then find the properties to describe them.

After students complete page 240, ask them to make a general statement describing the figures in the diagram. *(All figures in the diagram are special polygons.)* Repeat this activity after completing page 241. *(All figures in the diagram are special quadrilaterals.)*

SUMMARIZE/ASSESS **Explain what you have discovered about polygons.** *(Accept reasonable responses.)*

6. Place these figures in two rows.

Row 1: *N*   *O*   *C*   ⇨ rectangles
Row 2: *I*   *J*   *K*   *L*   *M*   ⇨ all other parallelograms

CRITICAL THINKING Do rectangles have all the properties of parallelograms? Are rectangles parallelograms? What other property do rectangles have?

7. Place these figures in two rows.

Row 1: *C*   *J*   *L*   ⇨ rhombuses

Row 2: *N*   *O*   *I*   *K*   *M*   ⇨ all other parallelograms

CRITICAL THINKING Do rhombuses have all the properties of parallelograms? Are rhombuses parallelograms? What other property do rhombuses have?

8. Place these parallelograms in two rows.

Row 1:   all rectangles
Row 2:   all rhombuses

THINK ALOUD Which figure belongs in both rows? Why?

9. **IN YOUR WORDS** Tell why a square is both a rectangle and a rhombus.

10. Use the descriptions below to check your answers to Exercises 5–9.

> A parallelogram is a quadrilateral with opposite sides parallel. Notice that opposite sides are also congruent.
>
> A rhombus is a parallelogram with all sides congruent.
>
> A rectangle is a parallelogram with only right angles.
>
> A square can be described as a rectangle with all sides congruent, or as a rhombus with only right angles.

CHAPTER 8   241

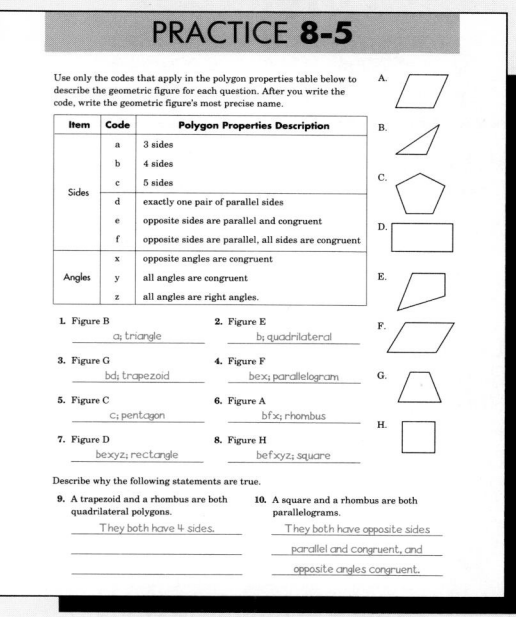

PRACTICE 8-5

Use only the codes that apply in the polygon properties table below to describe the geometric figure for each question. After you write the code, write the geometric figure's most precise name.

Item	Code	Polygon Properties Description
Sides	a	3 sides
	b	4 sides
	c	5 sides
	d	exactly one pair of parallel sides
	e	opposite sides are parallel and congruent
	f	opposite sides are parallel, all sides are congruent
Angles	x	opposite angles are congruent
	y	all angles are congruent
	z	all angles are right angles.

1. Figure B   a; triangle
2. Figure E   b; quadrilateral
3. Figure G   bd; trapezoid
4. Figure F   bex; parallelogram
5. Figure C   c; pentagon
6. Figure A   bfx; rhombus
7. Figure D   bexyz; rectangle
8. Figure H   befxyz; square

Describe why the following statements are true.

9. A trapezoid and a rhombus are both quadrilateral polygons.
They both have 4 sides.

10. A square and a rhombus are both parallelograms.
They both have opposite sides parallel and congruent, and opposite angles congruent.

MEETING SPECIAL NEEDS

For Students Who Are . . .

Acquiring English Proficiency Review the meanings of *quadrilaterals, congruent sides and angles, parallel sides,* and *rhombus*

Gifted and Talented Have students make a Venn diagram to show the relationships of the quadrilaterals on page 241.

Working 2 or 3 Grades Below Level Discuss the meaning of the prefixes of the polygons listed on page 240. Have students give examples of other words with these prefixes.

Today's Problem

A square is always a rectangle. A parallelogram is always a quadrilateral. A triangle is never a quadrilateral. A parallelogram is sometimes a rectangle. A trapezoid is always a quadrilateral. A rectangle is always a quadrilateral. A triangle is always a polygon. From this information, is a square always a quadrilateral? *(Yes; if a square is always a rectangle, a rectangle is always a quadrilateral, then a square is a quadrilateral.)*

Lesson Organizer

Objective: Solve problems by making generalizations.

Prior Knowledge: Students should know how the basic geometric figures are related.

Lesson Resources:
Practice Worksheet 8-6
Reteaching Activity 8-6
Enrichment Worksheet 8-6
Daily Review 8-6

Two-Minute Math

Draw a triangle. Write *9* in the center. Write a factor at each vertex. Find another number with exactly three factors. Show the factors on a triangle. *(squares of prime numbers, such as 4, 25, and 49)*

1 INTRODUCE

CONCRETE ACTIVITY

☑ **MATERIALS CHECKLIST:** piece of yarn about 4 m long with ends tied together

Have four students hold the yarn so that each student holds a vertex during the activity.

1. Ask students to pull the yarn to make a rhombus with two very large and two very small angles.

2 Have students gradually increase the sizes of the smaller angles and decrease the sizes of the larger angles. Stop students when the yarn has formed a square. **What type of figure is the rhombus now?** *(a square)* **Is every square a rhombus?** *(yes)* **Is every rhombus a square?** *(no)*

WHEN YOUR STUDENTS ASK
★ WHY AM I LEARNING THIS? ★

You can connect this skill to real life through medicine. Doctors must make generalizations that include and exclude information when they diagnose a patient's illness.

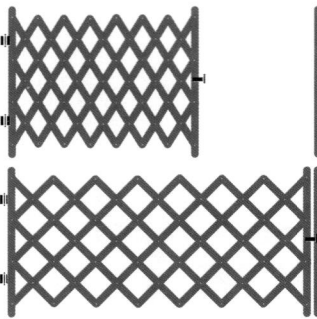

Problem Solving:
Making Generalizations

When the safety gate is partially open, many figures on it look like rhombuses. When closed, the figures look like squares.

THINK ALOUD What properties do squares and rhombuses have in common? What property does a square have that other rhombuses do not have? **both parallelograms and all sides equal; all right angles**

When we generalize, we tell how ideas or things are related. The generalization, "A square is a rhombus," says that rhombuses make up a larger class of figures than squares. A Venn diagram can be used to show generalizations.

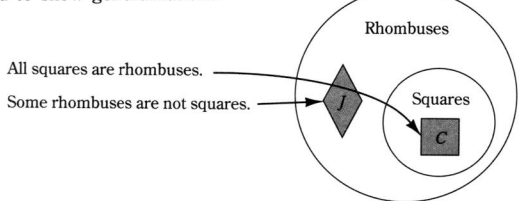

All squares are rhombuses.
Some rhombuses are not squares.

Are all properties of parallelograms also true for rhombuses? **yes**

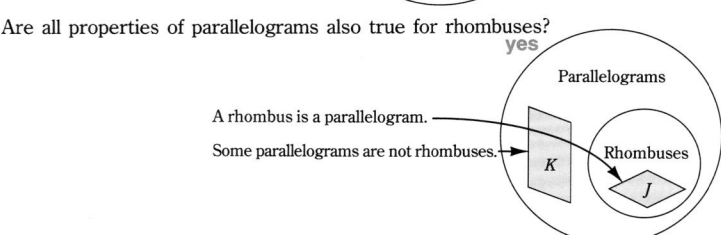

A rhombus is a parallelogram.
Some parallelograms are not rhombuses.

GUIDED PRACTICE

1. Use the Venn diagram to answer the question.
   a. What three figures are in the Venn diagram? **rhombus, square, rectangle**
   b. With what figures does a square share properties? **rhombus and rectangle**
   c. Where would you place a trapezoid? **outside the 2 circles**

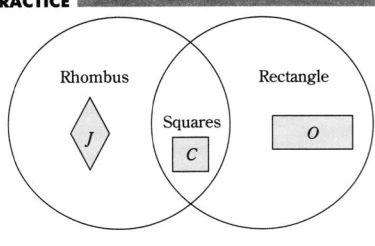

---

2 TEACH

In the first Venn diagram on page 242, why is the collection of squares shown inside the collection of rhombuses? *(All squares are rhombuses.)*

In the second Venn diagram, why is figure K placed where it is? *(It is a parallelogram but not a rhombus; all sides are not congruent.)*

In the Venn diagram in Guided Practice, why do the circles overlap? *(A square is both a rectangle and a rhombus.)*

SUMMARIZE/ASSESS **Explain how making a generalization can help you solve a problem.** *(Possible answer: A generalization helps you understand how ideas or things are related.)*

Is the generalization true? Write *yes* or *no*.

2. No trapezoid is a parallelogram.
yes

3. Some trapezoids are parallelograms.
no

4. All trapezoids are parallelograms.
no

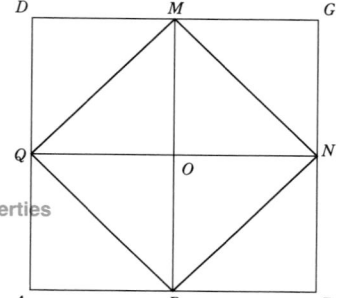

Complete each generalization with *All, Some,* or *No.*

5. **All** parallelograms are quadrilaterals.

6. **All** rectangles are parallelograms.

7. **Some** quadrilaterals are rectangles.

8. **All** rectangles are quadrilaterals.

9. **No** trapezoids are parallelograms.

10. **CRITICAL THINKING** Why is a square a special kind of rectangle, parallelogram, and quadrilateral?
It satisfies their properties.

Draw a Venn diagram. Then decide whether the generalization is *true* or *false.*

11. Some rectangles are not squares.
true

12. Some parallelograms are not rectangles.
true

13. Some trapezoids are not quadrilaterals.
false

 Choose any strategy to solve.

14. How many triangles can you find altogether? Explain your answer.
12; join some small triangles

15. Why can't you make a two-sided polygon? It wouldn't be closed or have three sides. doesn't meet properties

16. Name the vertices that identify a triangle, a square, a pentagon, a hexagon, and a seven-sided polygon.

17. **CREATE YOUR OWN** Make a drawing that contains different kinds of polygons. Ask a friend to list all the polygons.
Check students' work.

16. Answers will vary. Suggestion given.
DMQ; DMOQ; DQPNM; DQPBNM; DQPBNOM

CHAPTER 8 243

MEETING SPECIAL NEEDS

For Students Who Are . . .

Acquiring English Proficiency Discuss the meanings of *in common, generalization,* and *a larger class of figures.*

Gifted and Talented Assign the technology lesson on page 272 of this chapter.

Working 2 or 3 Grades Below Level Have students draw and label several of these figures on index cards: rectangle, parallelogram, quadrilateral, trapezoid, square and rhombus to refer to while completing the exercises.

Having Reading Difficulties Pair these students with able readers for the Practice exercises.

Today's Problem

A rectangular floor is completely covered with square tiles. There are 12 tiles along one length and 15 tiles along the other. If a diagonal is drawn from one corner to the opposite corner, how many tiles are cut in two? *(24)*

---

3 FOLLOW-UP

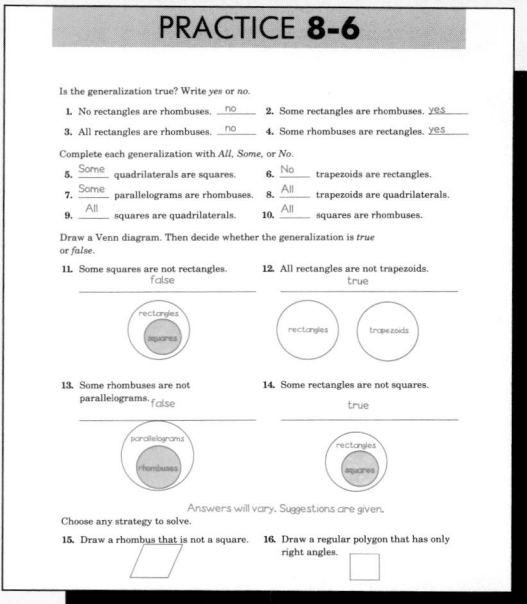

PRACTICE 8-6

Is the generalization true? Write *yes* or *no.*

1. No rectangles are rhombuses. no 2. Some rectangles are rhombuses. yes
3. All rectangles are rhombuses. no 4. Some rhombuses are rectangles. yes

Complete each generalization with *All, Some,* or *No.*

5. Some quadrilaterals are squares. 6. No trapezoids are rectangles.
7. Some parallelograms are rhombuses. 8. All trapezoids are quadrilaterals.
9. All squares are quadrilaterals. 10. All squares are rhombuses.

Draw a Venn diagram. Then decide whether the generalization is *true* or *false.*

11. Some squares are not rectangles. false 12. All rectangles are not trapezoids. true

13. Some rhombuses are not parallelograms. false 14. Some rectangles are not squares. true

Answers will vary. Suggestions are given.

Choose any strategy to solve.

15. Draw a rhombus that is not a square. 16. Draw a regular polygon that has only right angles.

RETEACHING 8-6

☑ **MATERIALS CHECKLIST:** Different sizes of envelopes

Have the students work in pairs. Provide each pair with a large envelope on which you have written *Polygon*. Inside the *Polygon* envelope is a smaller envelope labeled *Quadrilateral*. Inside the *Quadrilateral* envelope are two smaller envelopes labeled *Trapezoid* and *Parallelogram*. Inside the *Parallelogram* envelope are a *Rhombus* envelope and a *Rectangle* envelope and inside both of these is a *Square* envelope. Ask them to draw a Venn diagram using the information provided by the envelopes. Ask, Are some parallelograms trapezoids? [no] Are all squares rectangles? [yes]

ENRICHMENT 8-6

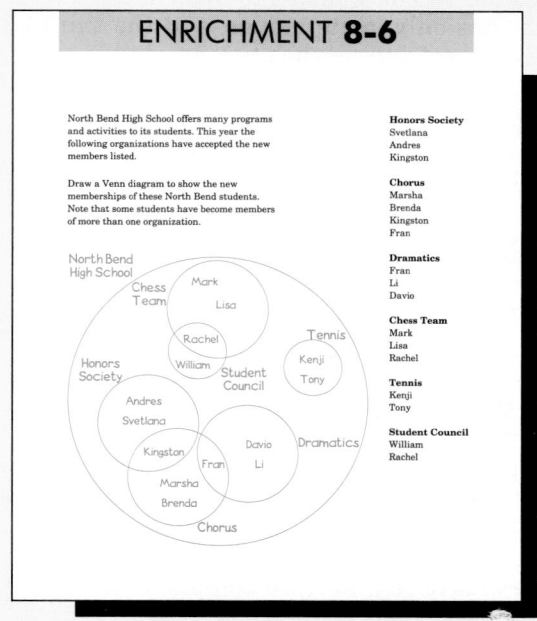

North Bend High School offers many programs and activities to its students. This year the following organizations have accepted the new members listed.

Draw a Venn diagram to show the new memberships of these North Bend students. Note that some students have become members of more than one organization.

Honors Society
Svetlana
Andres
Kingston

Chorus
Marsha
Brenda
Kingston
Fran

Dramatics
Fran
Li
Davio

Chess Team
Mark
Lisa
Rachel

Tennis
Kenji
Tony

Student Council
William
Rachel

Lesson Organizer

> **Objective:** Classify triangles by sides and angles.

Prior Knowledge: Students should have a basic visual understanding of triangles.

Error Analysis and Remediation: See page 267A.

Lesson Resources:
Practice Worksheet 8-7
Reteaching Worksheet 8-7
Enrichment Activity 8-7
Daily Review 8-7
Cooperative Investigations, Chapter 8

Two-Minute Math

On a protractor each mark represents two different degrees. What is the other degree for: 35°; 150°; 17°; 145°?
(145°; 30°; 163°; 35°)

1 INTRODUCE

CONNECTING ACTIVITY

☑ **MATERIALS CHECKLIST:** Teaching Aid 8 (Protractor) or protractor, ruler, three of each for each group, Protractor transparency

Have students work in groups of three.

1. Ask one student to draw a right triangle, the second student to draw a triangle that has only acute angles, and the third to draw a triangle that has an obtuse angle.

2. Have students use their protractors to measure the angles of each triangle and find the sum of the measures.

3. Ask group members to compare sums. **What did you discover about the sum of the measures of the angles of a triangle?** *(It is equal to 180°.)*

WHEN YOUR STUDENTS ASK
★ WHY AM I LEARNING THIS? ★

This skill will help you solve real life problems. Classifying organizes materials in a useful way. You use this skill in school when you write a paper, and outside of school when you compile a shopping list.

Classifying Triangles

With seven sticks of the lengths shown, you could make several different kinds of triangles.

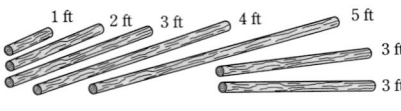

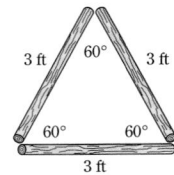

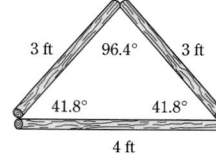

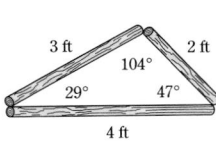

An **equilateral triangle** has all sides and angles congruent.

An **isosceles triangle** has two congruent sides and two congruent angles.

A **scalene triangle** has no congruent sides or congruent angles.

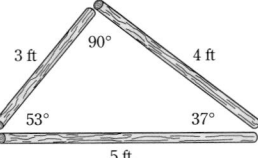

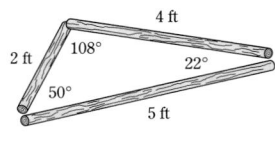

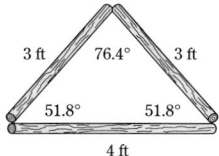

A **right triangle** has a right angle.

An **obtuse triangle** has one obtuse angle.

An **acute triangle** has all acute angles.

Add the three angle measures for each triangle above. What is the sum in each case? **180°**

> The sum of the measures of the angles of a triangle is 180°.

THINK ALOUD If you use any three of the seven sticks, will you always be able to make a triangle? Why or why not?
no; Some combinations would not be closed.

━━━━━━━━━━━ **GUIDED PRACTICE** ━━━━━━━━━━━

Name the triangle with the given property.

1. all acute angles   acute, equilateral
2. two congruent angles   isosceles
3. no congruent angles   scalene
4. one obtuse angle   obtuse

NUMBER SENSE The measures of two angles of a triangle are given. What is the measure of the third angle? Explain your answer.

5. 110°, 35°   **35°; 180 − (110 + 35)**
6. 60°, 60°   **60°; 180 − (60 + 60)**

---

2 TEACH

☑ **MATERIALS CHECKLIST:** Angle Sum of Triangle transparency

Can a triangle have two right angles? Explain. *(No; there would be no number of degrees left for the third angle.)*

In a right triangle, what is the sum of the measures of the two non-right angles? *(90°)* **How do you know?** *(180° − 90° = 90°)*

If one angle of an isosceles triangle measures 120°, what is the measure of the other two angles? *(30°; 180° − 120° = 60°; 60° ÷ 2 = 30°)*

SUMMARIZE/ASSESS **Explain how triangles are classified.** *(by the measures of their sides and angles)*

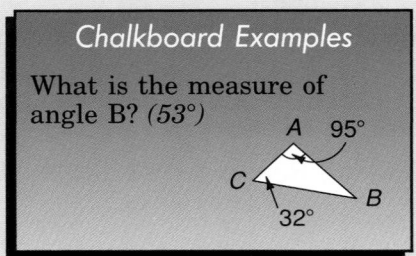

Chalkboard Examples

What is the measure of angle B? *(53°)*

PRACTICE

Is a triangle that has these side lengths or angle measures *equilateral, isosceles,* or *scalene*?

7. 5 in., 7 in., 5 in.   isosceles

8. $8\frac{1}{2}$ in., $8\frac{1}{2}$ in., $8\frac{1}{2}$ in.   equilateral

9. 2 in., 3 in., 4 in.   scalene

10. 20°, 90°, 70°   scalene

11. 60°, 60°, 60°   equilateral

12. 99.6°, 40.2°, 40.2°   isosceles

Is a triangle with these angle measures *right, obtuse,* or *acute*?

13. 40°, 40°, 100°   obtuse   **14.** 60°, 60°, 60°   acute   **15.** 110°, 10°, 60°   obtuse

16. 90°, 45°, 45°   right   **17.** 80.2°, 90°, 9.8°   right   **18.** 29.5°, 79.1°, 71.4°   acute

19. CRITICAL THINKING Can a triangle have two obtuse angles?
Explain.   no; angle sum greater than 180° and sides wouldn't be closed

The measures of two angles of a triangle are given.
What is the measure of the third angle?

20. 60°, 80°   40°   **21.** 125°, 45°   10°   **22.** 55°, 64.2°   60.8°   **23.** 90°, 30.5°   59.5°

Can you make a triangle with segments of these lengths?
Write *yes* or *no*.

24. 1 in., 3 in., 5 in.   no   **25.** 4 in., $3\frac{1}{2}$ in., 10 in.   no   **26.** 10 in., $6\frac{1}{4}$ in., 4 in.   yes

PROBLEM SOLVING

Is the generalization *true* or *false*?

27. Some right triangles can be scalene.   true

28. No equilateral triangles are right.   true

29. All scalene triangles are obtuse.   false

30. No isosceles triangles are obtuse.   false

Critical Thinking

A **diagonal** of a polygon is a line segment that joins two nonadjacent vertices. Draw the polygon and its diagonals. Complete the table.

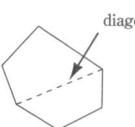
diagonal

Look for a pattern in the numbers. Then predict the number of diagonals in an octagon. Check your answer by drawing an octagon with its diagonals.   Check students' drawings.

Polygon	△	□	⬠	⬡	⬡
Number of sides	3	4			
Number of diagonals					

# of sides   3   4   5   6   7   8

# of diagonals   0   2   5   9   14   20

CHAPTER 8   **245**

MEETING SPECIAL NEEDS

For Students Who Are . . .

Acquiring English Proficiency   Have students try to draw pictures for the generalizations in the Problem Solving section.

Gifted and Talented   Have students draw Venn diagrams for the true exercises in the Problem Solving section.

Working 2 or 3 Grades Below Level   Have students use straws to experiment to find the answer for Think Aloud.

Having Reading Difficulties   Pair students with an able reader for the Critical Thinking activity.

Today's Problem

Can the triangle have the indicated angles?

	Acute	Right	Obtuse
Scalene	(yes)	(yes)	(yes)
Isosceles	(yes)	(yes)	(yes)
Equilateral	(yes)	(no)	(no)

---

3 FOLLOW-UP

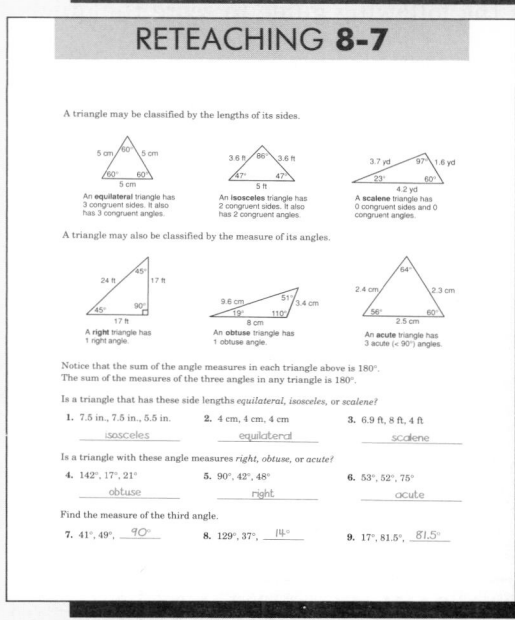

PRACTICE 8-7

RETEACHING 8-7

ENRICHMENT 8-7

☑ **MATERIALS CHECKLIST:**
Construction paper

Have the students work in pairs. Provide each pair with 25 equilateral triangles cut from construction paper—15 in one color and 10 in another color. Ask the students to arrange the triangles so that they form one large triangle. Then have them find the total number of different triangles formed. [48] Suggest to the students that they find the number of different triangles that can be formed when four small triangles are arranged to form a large triangle. [5] The students can then add one row at a time and look for a pattern.

MIDCHAPTER
Checkup

The midchapter checkup provides a way for you to check students' understanding of the skills taught in the first half of the chapter.

Language and Vocabulary

Some key language and vocabulary ideas from the first half of the chapter are reinforced here.

Quick Quiz

The quiz provides a means of evaluating students' understanding of the objectives for the first half of the chapter. Page references are given so that students can check back to where the skill was taught.

Use the following guide to score the quick quiz.

Score	Percent
10	100%
9	90
8	80
7	70
6	60
5	50
4	40
3	30
2	20
1	10

Use this chart to identify the Management Objectives tested.

Items	Management Objectives	Pages
1–4; 8–9	**8A** Measure and classify angles.	234–235; 244–245
5–7	**8B** Classify polygons by their properties.	244–245
10	**8F** Problem Solving: Use Venn diagrams. Make generalizations.	238–239, 242–243

MIDCHAPTER CHECKUP

═══ LANGUAGE & VOCABULARY ═══

For the pair of terms, write one sentence describing how the terms are the same and one sentence describing how they are different.
Accept reasonable answers. Suggestion given.

1. line—line segment
   both straight; no endpoints vs. two endpoints
2. line segment—ray
   both straight paths; two endpoints vs. one endpoint
3. intersecting line segments—parallel line segments
   both straight paths; different slopes vs. same slope
4. scalene triangle—equilateral triangle
   sum of angles is 180°; no congruent sides vs. three congruent sides
5. isosceles right triangle—isosceles obtuse triangle
   both have two congruent sides; right angle vs. obtuse angle

═══ QUICK QUIZ ✓ ═══

Is the angle *acute, right, obtuse,* or *straight?* *(pages 234–237)*

1. 92°   2. 159°   3. 17°   4. 180°
   obtuse   obtuse   acute   straight

Is a triangle with these angle measures *right, obtuse,* or *acute?*
(pages 232–233, 240–241, 244–245)

5. 60°, 71°, 49°   6. 108°, 35°, 37°   7. 13°, 90°, 77°
   acute   obtuse   right

The measures of two angles of a triangle are given. What is the measure of the third angle? *(pages 244–245)*

8. 123°, 31° **26°**   9. 68°, 72° **40°**

Solve. *(pages 238–239)*

10. All the students in class 7-152 study at least one of two languages. Sixteen study only Spanish, 9 study only French, and 3 study both languages.

    a. How many different languages are studied? **2**

    b. Does the Venn diagram at right represent the situation? **yes**

    c. How many students are in the class? **28 students**

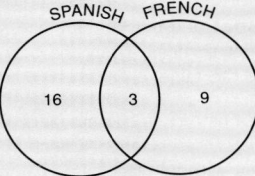

LEARNING LOG

Write the answers in your learning log. **Answers will vary. Suggestion given.**

1. How are pictures of lines, segments, and rays different from symbols of lines, segments, and rays?
   Accept reasonable answers.

2. Explain how a right angle can help identify acute and obtuse angles. **Using the right angle as a measuring device, you can say that any angle smaller is acute and any angle larger is obtuse.**

3. Your friend thinks vertical angles are adjacent. What is wrong with this thinking?
   Vertical angles share only a vertex—not a side.

MATH AMERICA

DID YOU KNOW . . . ? The game of basketball was invented and developed in the United States. A high school basketball court is 84 ft long and 50 ft wide. How many times could your classroom fit into an area that size?
Check students' work.

BONUS

The drawing shows all the exterior angles of two polygons. Trace the polygons. Measure each exterior angle with a protractor. Add the measures of the exterior angles of each polygon.

Draw some other polygons. Measure each exterior angle, and add those measures. What generalization do you think you can make about the sum of the measures of the exterior angles of any polygon?
The sum equals 360°.

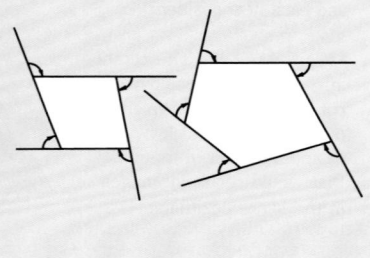

Learning Log

These are suggestions for writing about some topics taught so far in the chapter. The students keep their Learning Logs from the beginning of the school year through the end.

Math America

A mathematical skill that students have learned is related to an interesting fact about the United States.

Bonus

Students are given an opportunity to solve a challenge-type problem like a puzzle or nonroutine problem.

Lesson Organizer

Objective: Explore translations, rotations, and reflections.

Prior Knowledge: Students should know the meaning of a line segment and an angle.

Lesson Resources:
Class Activity 8-8
Daily Review 8-8

Two-Minute Math

Do this mental math activity. Have one student start with 0.7. Go around the room having each student add 0.7 until everyone has had a turn.

1 PREPARE

1. Write these words on the chalkboard: *translate, rotate,* and *reflect.* **What meanings for these words come to your mind?** *(Answers will vary.)*

2. Explain that today students will explore the geometric meanings of these words as they study three types of motions: translations, reflections, and rotations. Point out that in the lower grades, students used simpler terms to represent the same ideas:

• translate—slide

• rotate—turn

• reflect—flip

WHEN YOUR STUDENTS ASK
★ WHY AM I LEARNING THIS? ★

You can connect this skill to real life observations. Two cars in a Ferris wheel model the idea of translation; horses on a merry-go-round are like a rotation; your image in a nondistorting mirror is a reflection.

Exploring Reflections, Rotations, and Translations

Reflections, rotations, and translations are motions that change the positions of figures. These motions are often used in tiling designs.

Many designs are based on a **reflection** (flip) of an object in a line.

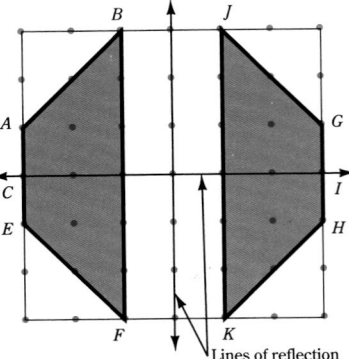

Lines of reflection

1. Notice how the figures are reflected along the vertical and horizontal lines. What are the images of $\overline{AB}$? Are the images congruent to $\overline{AB}$?
   $\overline{GJ}$; $\overline{EF}$; yes

2. $\overline{AC}$ and $\overline{CE}$ are congruent. What other segments are congruent to them?
   $\overline{GI}$; $\overline{IH}$

3. **CREATE YOUR OWN** On dot paper make a design of your own with vertical and horizontal reflections.
   Check students' work.

Designs can also be created by the **rotation** (turn) of an object about a point.

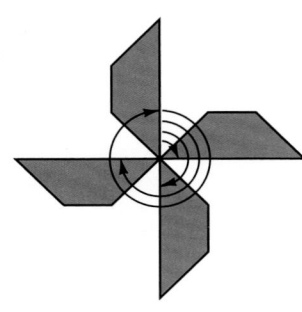

4. Cut out a trapezoid as shown. Rotate it to the four positions. How many degrees did it rotate between the original position and each new position?
   90°; 180°; 270°

5. **THINK ALOUD** The rotation images at right result from 60° rotations about the given point. Can you think of another kind of motion that would result in images in the same positions?
   Answers will vary. Suggestion given: a reflection in one side of each diamond.

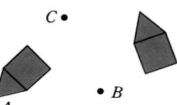

6. Is point A, point B, or point C the center of the rotation? To test a point, trace the shaded figure and the point. Rotate your paper about that point.
   B

MATH AND ART

248   LESSON 8–8

---

2 EXPLORE

☑ **MATERIALS CHECKLIST:** Teaching Aid 11 (Dot Paper), scissors, ruler for each student

What happens if you rotate a figure 180° and then rotate it 180° again around the same point? *(The figure returns to its original position.)*

Can you make a tessellation using regular pentagons? Try it and see. *(No)*

SUMMARIZE/ASSESS **Draw a scalene triangle on the dot paper. Use it to explain and demonstrate the meaning of *reflection, rotation,* and *translation.*** *(Check students' drawings.)*

A **translation** (slide) is another way to create a tiling design. During translation, the figure should not flip or turn.

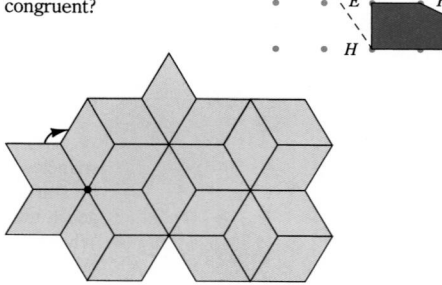

7. What is the translation image of $\overline{DC}$?
   HG

8. $\overline{DC}$ and $\overline{HG}$ are congruent. Are $\overline{AB}$ and $\overline{EF}$ congruent? Are $\overline{DH}$ and $\overline{CG}$ congruent?
   yes; yes

9. Are $\overline{DH}$ and $\overline{CG}$ parallel?
   yes

A **tessellation** fills the plane with figures that touch but do not overlap. Some tessellations, like the one at right, are made by starting with one figure and rotating it around different points.

10. Copy and cut out the triangle. Trace around the cutout on dot paper. Now rotate it 180° about the given point of rotation. Trace around the shape in its new position. What new polygon is made?
    rectangle

    • Point of rotation

11. Use your triangle to tessellate the plane using rotations. Your point of rotation can change to the midpoint of another side.
    Answers will vary.

12. **CREATE YOUR OWN** Design a tiling pattern using these ideas. Cut out a polygon. Trace around it. Then translate, reflect, or rotate it and trace again. Experiment with altering the polygon before moving it, as shown. If your polygon does not tessellate the plane, try a different polygon or use more than one figure.
    Check students' work.

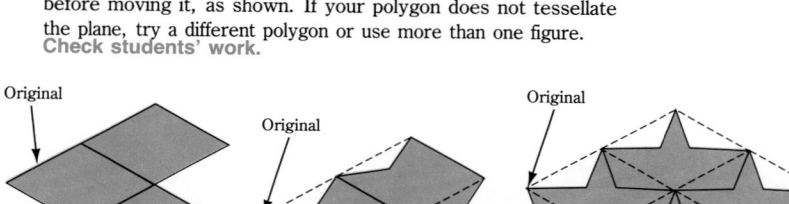

Original

Original

Original

MEETING SPECIAL NEEDS

For Students Who Are . . .

Acquiring English Proficiency Pair students with an English proficient student for Exercises 10–12.

Gifted and Talented Have students find examples of tessellations in art books to share with the class.

Having Reading Difficulties Pair students with an able reader for this lesson.

Today's Problem

Which printed capital letters in the alphabet can be rotated 180° about a point and remain unchanged in appearance? *(the letters, H, I, N, O, S, X, and Z)*

---

3 FOLLOW-UP

CLASS ACTIVITY 8-8

☑ MATERIALS CHECKLIST:
Construction paper, grid paper, blank spinners

Have the students work in pairs. Provide each pair with two small congruent polygons cut from different colors of construction paper. Have one partner line up one vertex of the polygon and one corner of a square on a sheet of grid paper. The other partner spins a spinner labeled with an equal number of *translation, rotation,* and *reflection* sections. This partner then places the second polygon on the grid paper to show the result of a translation, rotation, or reflection on the original figure. The pairs then exchange papers and guess what motion was used.

Lesson Organizer

> **Objective:** Determine congruent figures.

Prior Knowledge: Students should understand translation, reflection, and rotation.

Lesson Resources:
Practice Worksheet 8-9
Reteaching Activity 8-9
Enrichment Worksheet 8-9
Daily Review 8-9

Two-Minute Math

Add 9 to each number in row N of the Table of Numbers on the inside back cover. Then subtract 9 from each number.
(Sums: 6, 4, 17, 9, 7, 12, 8, 15, 5; Differences: −12, −14, −1, −9, −11, −6, −10, −3, −13)

1 INTRODUCE

CONNECTING ACTIVITY

1. Trace one of the purple triangles in the quilt square on page 250. Cut it out.

2. Place the cutout triangle on top of the purple triangle. Put the tip of your figure on the point of rotation. Rotate your cutout triangle to coincide with another triangle.

3. Find a point from the triangle you are now on to rotate your cutout triangle so that it coincides with still another triangle.

4. Identify two figures that are translations of each other. Draw one of them and show the translation. Repeat for reflections.

WHEN YOUR STUDENTS ASK
★ WHY AM I LEARNING THIS? ★

You can connect ideas of congruence to the work of a toolmaker. This craftsperson uses patterns to cut out congruent parts or shapes from metal.

250 *Chapter 8 • Lesson 8-9*

Congruent Figures

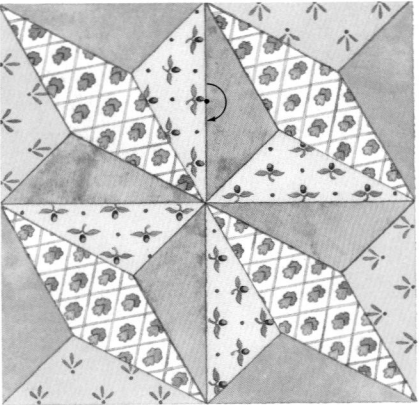

This quilt block pattern is made up of a tessellation of congruent triangles and diamonds.

Congruent figures have the same size and shape.

Translations, rotations, and reflections can be used to form congruent figures.

THINK ALOUD One pair of congruent triangles in the quilt can be formed by starting with the purple triangle and rotating it about the point shown. What other congruent figures in the quilt are formed by reflection? by translation? Answers will vary.

For congruent figures, corresponding sides and angles are congruent. Marks (|, ||, |||) are placed on corresponding sides of $\triangle ABC$ and $\triangle DEF$ to show that the sides are congruent. We write $\triangle ABC \cong \triangle DEF$, where $\cong$ means "is congruent to."

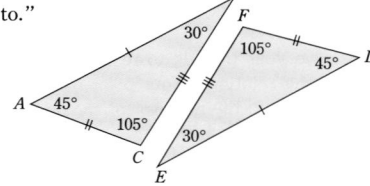

Corresponding Sides	Corresponding Angles
$\overline{AB} \cong \overline{DE}$	$\angle BAC \cong \angle EDF$
$\overline{BC} \cong \overline{EF}$	$\angle ACB \cong \angle DFE$
$\overline{AC} \cong \overline{DF}$	$\angle ABC \cong \angle DEF$

Where do corresponding sides appear in the quilt?
Answers will vary.

━━━━━━ **GUIDED PRACTICE** ━━━━━━

The triangles are congruent. Name all sets of corresponding sides and angles. See page 267b.

1.
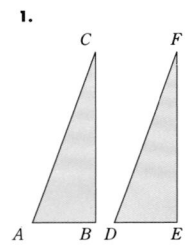

2.
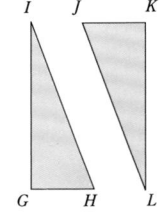

3.
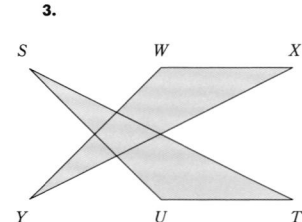

250   LESSON 8–9

---

2 TEACH

✓ **MATERIALS CHECKLIST:** Teaching Aid 3 (Grid Paper), ruler, Teaching Aid 11 (Dot Paper) for each student

How can you tell by looking at the figures that $\overline{AB}$ is congruent to $\overline{DE}$? *(Students may say that they look like they are the same length or that the same marks, ||, mean they are congruent.)*

Describe the location of the 105° angle in each triangle. *(It is located between the two sets of corresponding sides marked || and |||.)*

Will any two triangles with angles of 105°, 45°, and 30° be congruent? Explain. *(No; the sides can be of different lengths.)*

> ### Chalkboard Example
> Use $\triangle MNO$ and $\triangle PQR$ on page 251. Name all corresponding sides and angles.

SUMMARIZE/ASSESS **Explain how to determine whether two figures are congruent.** *(Two figures are congruent if their corresponding sides and angles are congruent.)*

Are the figures congruent? Did you use a translation, rotation, or reflection to decide?

4. yes; reflection **5.** yes; translation **6.** no; translation **7.** yes; rotation

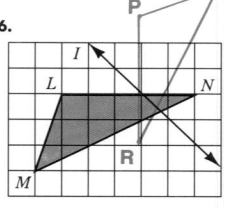

P.

$\triangle MNO$ and $\triangle PQR$ are congruent.
Find the missing measure.

8. $\overline{PR}$ **9.** $\overline{MN}$ **10.** $\overline{NO}$
  5 cm   2.5 cm   4.3 cm

11. $\angle MNO$ **12.** $\angle PRQ$ **13.** $\angle RPQ$
  90°   30°   60°

P
2.5 cm 90° R
Q   4.3 cm
N
        30° O
  60°   5 cm
M

Line I is a reflection line. Draw the figure and the reflection image on grid paper. Identify all sets of congruent sides and angles.

14.   **15.**   **16.**

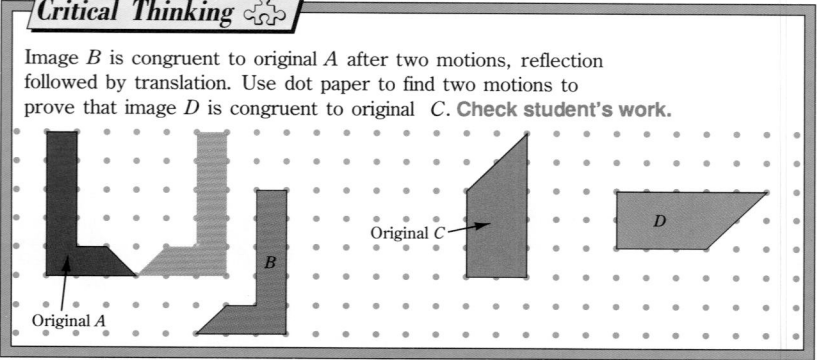

17. CREATE YOUR OWN Design a quilt block pattern.
Try to use reflection, rotation, and translation images.
Check students' work.

Critical Thinking

Image B is congruent to original A after two motions, reflection followed by translation. Use dot paper to find two motions to prove that image D is congruent to original C. **Check student's work.**

Original C
B
Original A
D

MEETING SPECIAL NEEDS

For Students Who Are . . .

Acquiring English Proficiency Review the meanings of *translations, rotations,* and *reflections.* You may wish to cut out a similar quilt pattern to show the transformations.

Gifted and Talented Have students create an original and an image similar to those in the Critical Thinking activity, exchange papers, and identify the transformations to prove the congruence.

Working 2 or 3 Grades Below Level Reinforce the idea that congruent figures will coincide if placed on top of one another. The corresponding parts will then match up.

Today's Problem

Why is "congruence" between plane figures in geometry a different kind of relationship than "less than" between numbers in arithmetic? *(Possible answer: "Congruence" has the property that shape S is "congruent" to shape S. However, the number N is not "less than" the number N.)*

---

3 FOLLOW-UP

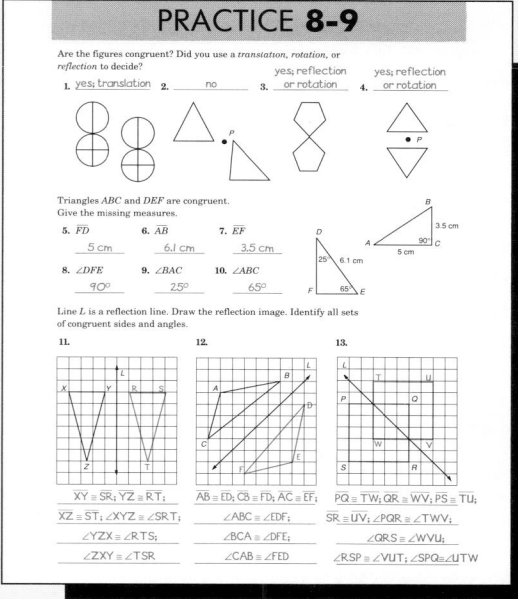

RETEACHING 8-9

☑ **MATERIALS CHECKLIST:** Pattern blocks, dot paper

Have the students work in groups of four. Provide each group with a pattern block. One student traces the figure on a sheet of dot paper. Another student slides the pattern block and traces it to show the effects of a translation on the original figure. A third student then flips and traces the block to show the effects of a reflection. Finally, a fourth student rotates the block about a point and traces it. Have the student measure the figures on the dot paper to verify that they are congruent. Repeat the activity with different pattern blocks and have the students trade roles.

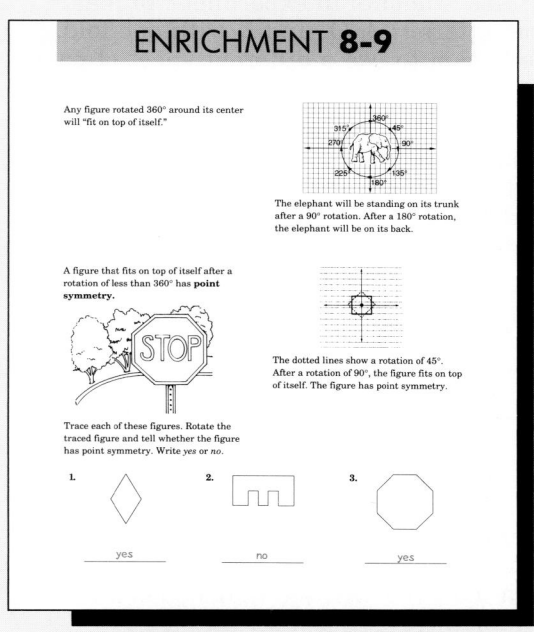

Lesson Organizer

Objective: Identify lines of symmetry.

Prior Knowledge: Students should know types of triangles and polygons.

Lesson Resources:
Practice Worksheet 8-10
Reteaching Worksheet 8-10
Enrichment Activity 8-10
Daily Review 8-10

 *Two-Minute Math*

Find the products.

$^-1 \times \, ^-1 \, (1)$ $^-1 \times \, ^-1 \times \, ^-1 \, (^-1)$

$^-1 \times \, ^-1 \times \, ^-1 \times \, ^-1 \, (1)$

$^-1 \times \, ^-1 \times \, ^-1 \times \, ^-1 \times \, ^-1 \, (^-1)$

1 INTRODUCE

CONCRETE ACTIVITY

☑ **MATERIALS CHECKLIST:** paper, ruler, scissors for each student

1. Write the capital letters V and R. **Which of these letters can you cut from paper by making one fold?** *(V)* Have students test their answers by folding and cutting.

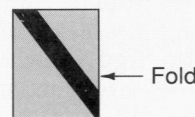
← Fold

2. Ask students to experiment to make the letters H, I, O, and X with one fold. Tell them to use a different sheet of paper for each experiment.

3. Compare the various ways students made their letters. Note the different possible positions for the fold line. *(Different fold line positions are possible because all four letters have both horizontal and vertical lines of symmetry.)*

WHEN YOUR STUDENTS ASK
★ WHY AM I LEARNING THIS? ★

You can connect symmetry to the natural world. For example, if you look carefully at a leaf, you will see that it has a line of symmetry.

Symmetry

A design that has symmetry has a harmonious balance and is pleasing to the eye. One type of symmetry is **line symmetry**.

A figure with line symmetry can be folded so that the two parts of the figure are congruent. The fold is called the **line of symmetry**.

You can use some clear plastic to check for symmetry (or to draw parts of symmetric figures).

STEPS Hold the plastic upright on the line of symmetry.

Look through the plastic to see the image.

Decide whether the parts coincide (or draw the image).

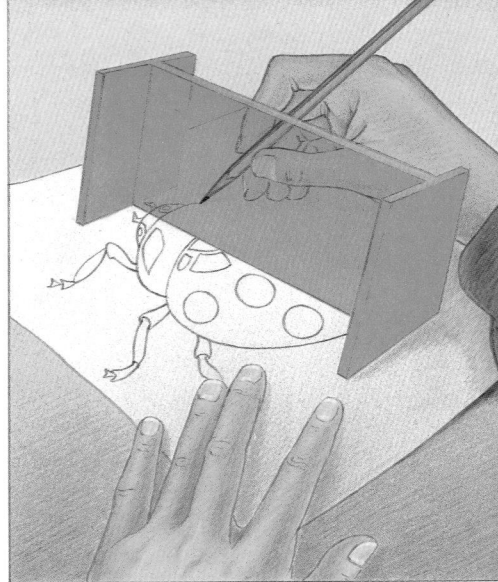

An equilateral triangle has three lines of symmetry. Trace the triangle three times, drawing a different line of symmetry on each tracing. Use clear plastic or folding to show each line is a line of symmetry.

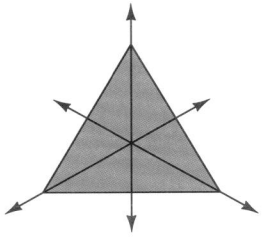

CRITICAL THINKING What types of triangles are formed by the three lines of symmetry?
right triangles

GUIDED PRACTICE

How many lines of symmetry does the figure have? To decide, draw, cut out, and fold the figure. Draw all lines of symmetry.

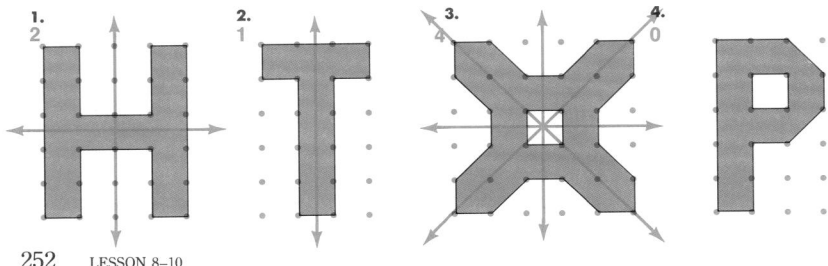

1. 2   **2.** 1   **3.** 4   **4.** 0

252   LESSON 8–10

---

2 TEACH

☑ **MATERIALS CHECKLIST:** Teaching Aid 11 (Dot Paper), scissors for each student; clear plastic or Miras for each pair

Have students work with a partner.

Which objects in the classroom have line symmetry? *(Examples: chalkboard, number 3 on some clocks)*

What kind of triangle has exactly one line of symmetry? *(isosceles triangle)* **Explain and use dot paper to demonstrate your answer.** *(When you fold along the noncongruent side, the parts match.)*

> ### *Chalkboard Examples*
>
> Which letters in the word GEOMETRY have line symmetry? *(E, O, M, T, Y)*

SUMMARIZE/ASSESS **How can you tell if a figure has line symmetry?** *(A figure has line symmetry when it can be folded to form two congruent parts.)*

Draw the figure. Then cut out and fold the figure to find the
lines of symmetry. Draw them.

5. 2 **6.** 0 **7.** 4 **8.** 2

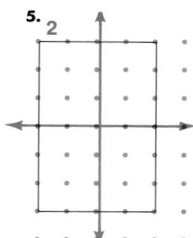 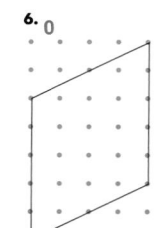 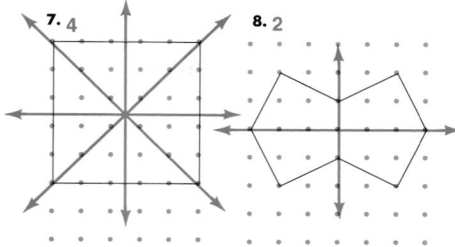

The hexagon at right shows two lines of symmetry.
Name all figures congruent to the figure.

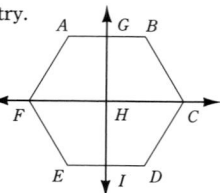

9. the pentagon with vertices *A, G, I, E, F*
BGIDC

10. the trapezoid with vertices *A, B, C, F*
EDCF

11. the trapezoid with vertices *E, F, H, I*
FHGA; CHGB; CHID

PROBLEM SOLVING

Draw a figure to solve.

12. Show all of the lines of symmetry in a regular hexagon.
Start by tracing the regular hexagon above.

13. What polygon has no lines of symmetry?
Answers will vary. Suggestion given: right trapezoid.

14. What polygon has five lines of symmetry?
regular pentagon

15. How many lines of symmetry does a circle have?
an infinite number

A design was made by folding paper as shown.
Draw the completed design. **Check student's work.**

16. 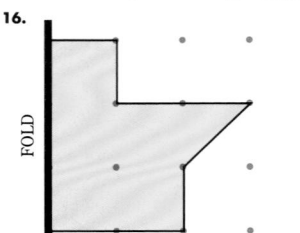   **17.**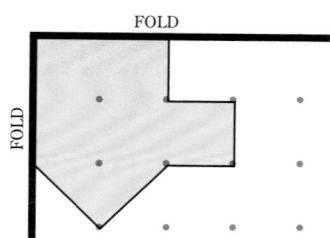

---

3 FOLLOW-UP

PRACTICE 8-10

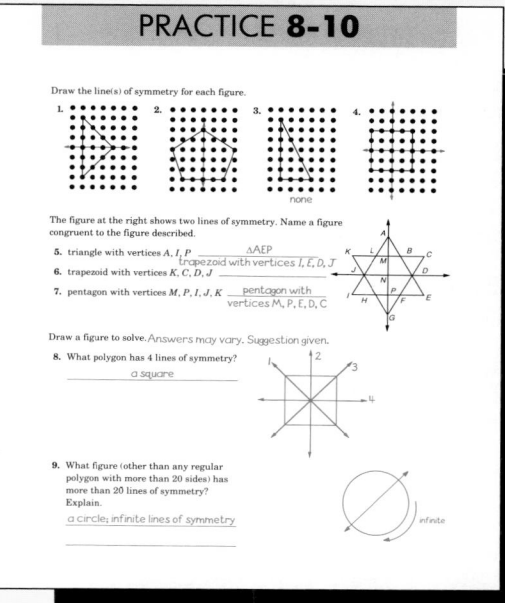

RETEACHING 8-10

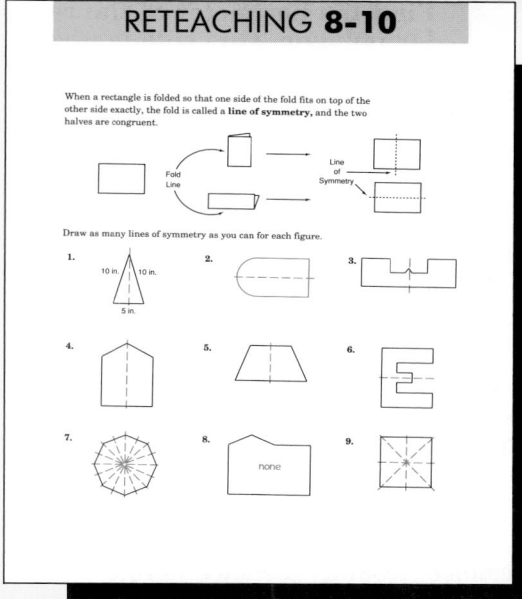

MEETING SPECIAL NEEDS

For Students Who Are . . .

Acquiring English Proficiency Discuss the meanings of *pentagon, trapezoid,* and *vertices.*

Gifted and Talented Have students find pictures of paintings that show line symmetry and share them with the class.

Having Reading Difficulties Review the meaning of *regular hexagon* in the Problem Solving exercises.

Today's Problem

Are our faces approximately symmetrical? our hands and feet? *(our faces, yes; hands and feet, no)*

ENRICHMENT 8-10

☑ **MATERIALS CHECKLIST:** Tracing paper, science books

Have the students look through science books to find several examples of symmetry in nature. For example, a student might find a picture of the cross-section of a honeycomb. Have the students trace each figure they find and indicate all lines of symmetry on the traced figure. Have them share their work with their classmates.

Lesson Organizer

Objective: Find the circumference of a circle.

Prior Knowledge: Students should know how to multiply with fractions and decimals, round decimals, and find perimeters.

Error Analysis and Remediation: See page 267A.

Lesson Resources:
Practice Worksheet 8-11
Reteaching Worksheet 8-11
Enrichment Activity 8-11
Daily Review 8-11

Two-Minute Math

Find the perimeter of the regular polygon. One side is given.

quadrilateral, 15 in. *(60 in.)*

pentagon, 20 in. *(100 in.)*

hexagon, $1\frac{1}{2}$ in. *(9 in.)*

1 INTRODUCE

CONNECTING ACTIVITY

☑ **MATERIALS CHECKLIST:** five or more circular objects of different sizes, a yardstick, and inch tape measure for each pair

1. Display the following table.

Distance Around	Distance Across Widest Part (in.)

2. Have pairs of students make the two measurements for each circular object and fill in the table. **What do you observe about the relationship between distance around and distance across the widest part of the circle?** *(Distance around is about three times the distance across.)*

WHEN YOUR STUDENTS ASK
★ WHY AM I LEARNING THIS? ★

You can use this skill to solve real life problems. For example, if you jog on a circular track, you can find the distance around it once you know the distance across it.

Circles and Circumference

Meteor Crater in Arizona has a diameter of about 1 mi. How does its radius compare to its diameter? $\frac{1}{2}$ **size**

About how many times longer is the circumference than the diameter? **about 3**

Use a piece of yarn or a narrow strip of paper to find out. Measure the circumference and the diameter in the photograph of the crater.

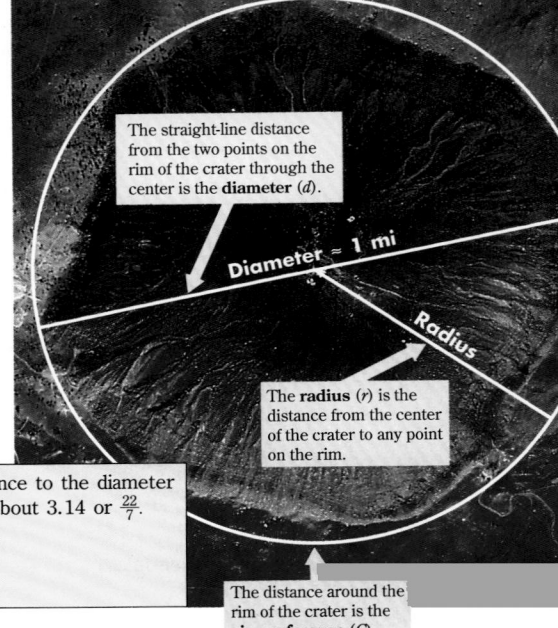

The straight-line distance from the two points on the rim of the crater through the center is the **diameter** (*d*).

Diameter = 1 mi

Radius

The **radius** (*r*) is the distance from the center of the crater to any point on the rim.

The distance around the rim of the crater is the **circumference** (*C*).

The exact ratio of the circumference to the diameter of a circle is called **pi** (π). It is about 3.14 or $\frac{22}{7}$.
You write:
$$\frac{C}{d} = \pi, \text{ or } \frac{C}{d} \approx 3.14$$
$$C = \pi d, \text{ or } C \approx 3.14 \times d$$

CRITICAL THINKING How would you write an expression for the circumference of a circle if you know its radius?
$C = 2\pi r$

Mt. Vesuvius, in Italy, is the only active volcano on the mainland of Europe. The radius of its crater rim is 1,000 ft. About what is the circumference of its crater rim?

$C = \pi \times d$ $C = \pi \times 2 \times r$
$\approx 3.14 \times 2,000 \approx 6,280$ $\approx 3.14 \times 2 \times 1,000 \approx 6,280$

$D = 2 \times r$, so
$C = \pi \times 2 \times r$

The circumference of the crater is about 6,280 ft.

GUIDED PRACTICE

Find the circumference. Use $\pi \approx 3.14$. Round to tenths.

1. 12.6 ft   2. 31.4 ft   3. 6.3 in.   4. 37.7 in.

4 ft   10 ft   1 in.   6 in.

MATH AND GEOGRAPHY

MULTICULTURAL NOTE

The Rhind Mathematical Papyrus (written about 1650 B.C.) contains problems that indicate the ancient Egyptians were aware of a constant relationship between the diameter of a circle and its area. See page 303B.

2 TEACH

☑ **MATERIALS CHECKLIST:** four pieces of yarn or narrow strips of paper, inch ruler, compass for each student

Have students place yarn or paper (needs to stand upright to bend) on the radius and then the diameter of the Meteor Crater circle. **How does the length of the radius compare with the length of the diameter?** *(Length of radius is one-half length of diameter.)*

Consider the two approximations for pi: 3.14 and $\frac{22}{7}$. How close is 3.14 to $\frac{22}{7}$?

(Named as a decimal, $\frac{22}{7}$ is 3.1428571. . . . The two forms are equal to two decimal places.)

Chalkboard Examples

Find the circumference.

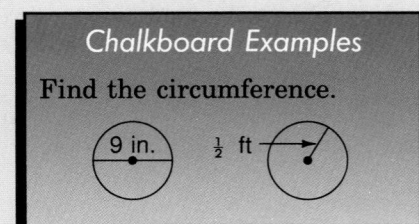

9 in. $\frac{1}{2}$ ft

SUMMARIZE/ASSESS **Explain how to find the circumference of a circle when the diameter is given and when the radius is given.** *(Multiply pi times diameter; multiply radius times 2 times pi)*

Find the circumference. Use $\pi \approx 3.14$. Round to tenths.

5. $d = 8$ in. **25.1 in. 6.** $d = 2$ yd **6.3 yd 7.** $r = 2$ yd **12.6 yd 8.** $r = 1.2$ ft **7.5 ft**

9. d = 15 in. **10.** $d = 2.5$ ft **7.9 ft 11.** $r = 0.5$ in. **12.** $r = 3.4$ in. **21.4 in.**
47.1 in.   **3.1 in.**

Find the circumference. Use $\pi \approx \frac{22}{7}$.

13. $d = \frac{7}{8}$ yd **14.** $r = 1\frac{1}{6}$ mi **15.** $d = 1{,}449$ mi **16.** $r = 4{,}200$ ft
$\frac{11}{4}$ yd $\frac{22}{3}$ mi   **4,554 mi**   **26,400 ft**

ESTIMATE About what is the perimeter of the figure? **Accept reasonable estimates.**

17. 24 in. **18.** 500 ft $d = 40$ ft **19.** 70 mi

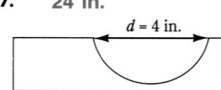 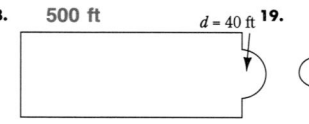

$d = 4$ in.   10 mi

Find the length of each figure. Use $\pi \approx 3.14$. *Hint:* Notice how the three figures are alike and how they are different.

20. 31.4 ft **21.** 92.8 ft **22.** 92.8 ft

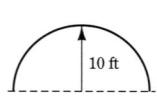

10 ft

15 ft
10 ft 10 ft
15 ft

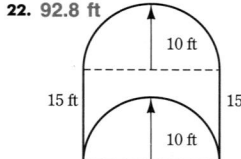

10 ft
15 ft 15 ft
10 ft

Solve. Use $\pi \approx 3.14$. Round your answer to tenths.

23. The world's largest crater on an inactive volcano is Haleakala, located in Hawaii. The circumference of the crater is about 20 mi. About what is the diameter of the crater?
6.4 mi

24. Mauna Loa, in Hawaii, is the world's largest volcano. It rises 30,000 ft from the ocean floor and has a diameter at its base of 60 mi. About what is the circumference at the base of Mauna Loa?
188.4 mi

25. On March 27, 1980, the crater of the Mount Saint Helens volcano measured 250 ft in diameter. The volcano erupted that day. Twelve days later, the crater measured 1,700 ft across. By how much did the circumference increase?
4,553 ft

26. **CREATE YOUR OWN** Use a compass and straightedge. Draw a figure with line segments and parts of circles. Ask a friend to find the length of the figure.
Check students' work.

MEETING SPECIAL NEEDS

For Students Who Are . . .

Acquiring English Proficiency Review the meanings of *diameter* and *radius*. Define the word *crater*.

Gifted and Talented Have students research other volcanoes, find the diameters of their craters, and display this information on a bar graph.

Working 2 or 3 Grades Below Level Have students measure the circumference and diameter of several circles with string. Help them generalize that the circumference is always about 3 times the diameter.

Today's Problem

If the radius of the wheels of a bicycle is 15 in., how many feet has the bicycle moved after the wheel has turned 10 times? (*distance* = $\frac{[\pi \times 30 \times 10]}{12}$ = about $\frac{22}{7} \times 30 \times \frac{10}{12} = 78\frac{4}{7}$ ft)

3 FOLLOW-UP

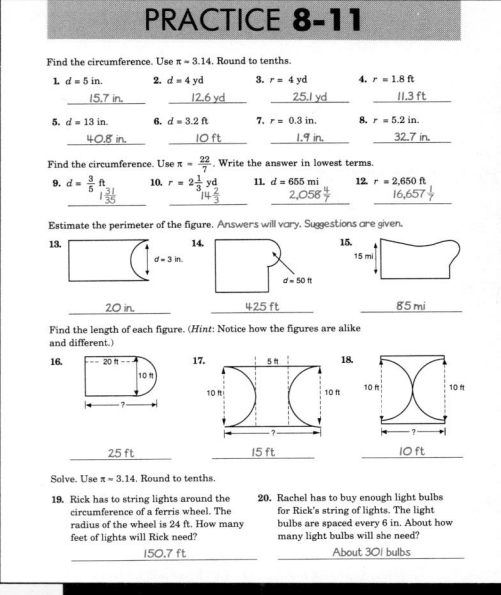

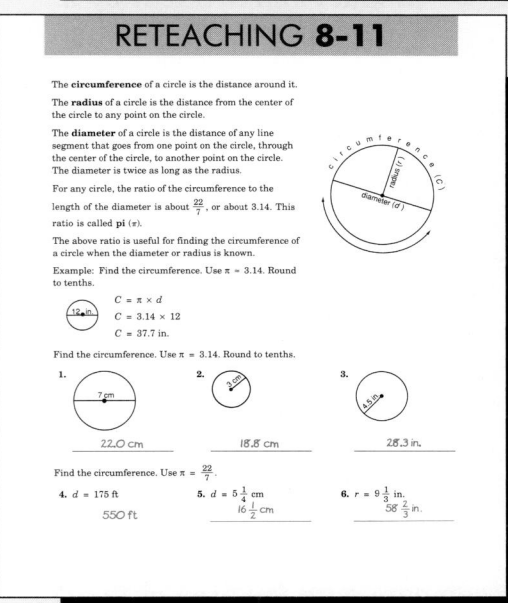

ENRICHMENT 8-11

☑ **MATERIALS CHECKLIST:** Cans and various other circular objects, string, rulers

Have the students work in pairs. Instruct each pair to verify that the ratio of the circumference of a circle to its diameter is a constant. Each pair makes a table with the headings *Object, Circumference, Diameter,* and $\frac{C}{d}$. Partners then trace several circular objects, measure each circumference with the string and a ruler, and find the diameter. When the students have completed the table, they find the average of the values they wrote $\frac{C}{d}$. Ask: Were the values of $\frac{C}{d}$ fairly constant? How close is the average to 3.14?

LESSON | 8-12

Lesson Organizer

Objective: Find the area of a rectangle and a triangle.

Prior Knowledge: Students should have a basic understanding of area.

Error Analysis and Remediation: See page 267A.

Lesson Resources:
Practice Worksheet 8-12
Reteaching Worksheet 8-12
Enrichment Activity 8-12
Daily Review 8-12

Two-Minute Math

Use mental math. Estimate the product and divide it by 2.

2.056 × 48.1   19.99 × 3.68

(Possible answers: 50; 40)

1 INTRODUCE

CONCRETE ACTIVITY

☑ **MATERIALS CHECKLIST:** 3 index cards, scissors, ruler for each student

1. Have students cut out one triangle as shown.

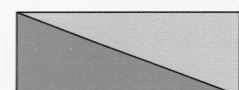

How does the area of the cutout triangle compare with the area of the rectangle? *(It is half.)*

2. Have students select any point on the longer side of another index card and use it to draw and cut out a figure as shown. Repeat the question from step 1.

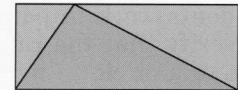

WHEN YOUR STUDENTS ASK
★ **WHY AM I LEARNING THIS?** ★

You can use this skill to solve real life problems. For example, wallpaper is often sold in square feet. To buy the right amount of wallpaper, you must know the area of the wall.

Area: Rectangles and Triangles

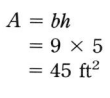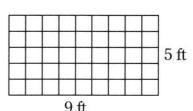

An official table for table tennis measures 9 ft by 5 ft. What is its area in square feet (ft²)?

The **area** of a plane figure measures the surface it covers. By counting squares, you can see that the area of the table is 45 ft².

You can also calculate the area using a formula.

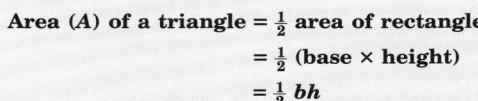

Area (A) of a rectangle = base × height = *bh*

$A = bh$
$= 9 \times 5$
$= 45$ ft²

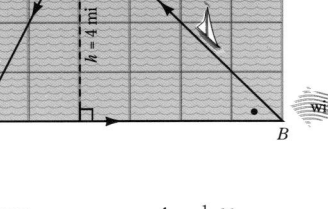

THINK ALOUD   What is the formula for the area of a square?
$A = b^2$

A triangular race course for sailboats is shown by $\triangle ABC$ in the diagram. What is the area of the race course in square miles (mi²)?
12 mi²

Count squares to find the area of the triangle and of the rectangle. Is the area of the triangle *half* the area of the rectangle?
yes

The **height** *(h)* of a triangle is the length of a segment that is perpendicular to the base *(b)*. This formula gives the area of a triangle.

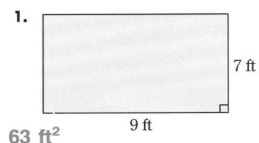

Area (A) of a triangle = ½ area of rectangle
= ½ (base × height)
= ½ *bh*

$A = \frac{1}{2} bh$
$= \frac{1}{2} \times 6 \times 4$
$= \frac{1}{2} \times 24$
$= 12$ mi²

GUIDED PRACTICE

Find the area.

1.   **2.**   **3.**

7 ft   12 in.   6 yd

63 ft² 9 ft   **144 in.²** 12 in.   **27 yd²** 9 yd

256   LESSON 8-12

---

2 TEACH

☑ **MATERIALS CHECKLIST:** Areas of Simple Polygons transparency

Consider the formulas $A = \frac{1}{2} bh$ and $A = \frac{bh}{2}$. Are these formulas different? Test your prediction by calculating both ways; let $b = 10$ mi and $h = 4$ mi. *(They are the same.)*

How can you use the formula for the area of a rectangle to find the area of a square?
(Since a square is a rectangle with all sides [s] the same length, $A = s \times s$ or $A = s^2$.)

What other names are sometimes used for the base and height of a rectangle? *(length and width)*

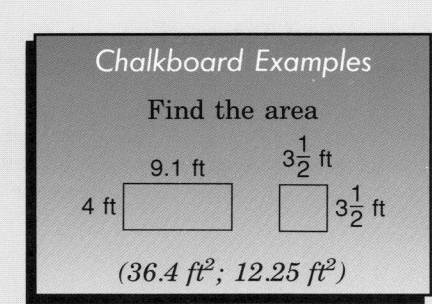

Chalkboard Examples

Find the area

9.1 ft $3\frac{1}{2}$ ft

4 ft $3\frac{1}{2}$ ft

(36.4 ft²; 12.25 ft²)

SUMMARIZE/ASSESS   Explain how to find the area of a rectangle and the area of a triangle.

4. Each square represents 1 in². Estimate the area of each figure. **See page 267b.**

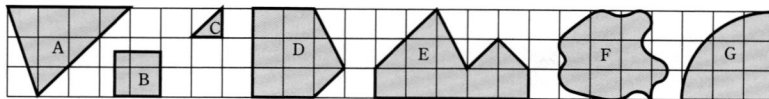

Find the area.

5. rectangle:
$b = 9$ in.; $h = 3$ in.
27 in.²

6. triangle
$b = 20$ in.; $h = 8$ in.
80 in.²

7. triangle:
$b = 6.5$ yd; $h = 9.2$ yd
29.9 yd²

8. rectangle:
$b = 10$ in.; $h = 8\frac{1}{4}$ in.
82.5 in.²

9. triangle:
$b = 30$ in.; $h = 14$ in.
210 in.²

10. rectangle:
$b = 6.5$ yd; $h = 9.2$ yd
59.8 yd²

Find the unknown dimension.

11. rectangle:
$A = 21$ ft²; $b = 2$ ft
What is the height?
10.5 ft

12. rectangle:
$A = 34.1$ in.²; $h = 5.5$ in.
What is the base?
6.2 in.

13. Triangle:
$A = 36$ yd²; $b = 8$ yd
What is the height?
9 yd

Find the area of a square with side s.   Find the length of the square.

14. $s = 12$ in.
144 in.²

15. $s = 9\frac{1}{4}$ ft
85.6 ft²

16. $A = 81$ yd²
9 yd

17. $A = 10,000$ mi²
100 mi

Find the area of the rectangle and all triangles in the figure. **See page 267b.**

18.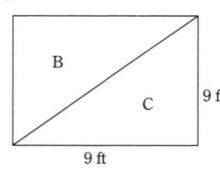

19.

20.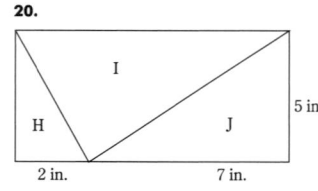

21. A football field is 360 ft by 160 ft. The playing area for field hockey is 300 ft by 180 ft. Which field is larger?
football field

22. At the half-time show for a football game, the band made a triangular formation. What area was covered by the band if the base of the triangle was 15 yd and the height was 32 yd?
240 yd²

23. A rectangular ice-skating rink has a floor with an area of 2,112 yd². The length of the floor is 66 yd. What is the width?
32 yd

24. A sailboat has a triangular sail with an area of 77 ft². If the height of the triangle is 14 ft, how many feet long is the base?
11 ft

MEETING SPECIAL NEEDS

For Students Who Are . . .

Acquiring English Proficiency Discuss the symbols used in the formulas before students do Exercises 5–20.

Gifted and Talented Have students create figures similar to Exercise 20. They can exchange papers with a partner and find the areas.

Working 2 or 3 Grades Below Level Remind students of the right angle symbol in Exercises 1–3. In Exercise 3, identify 9 yd as the base and 6 yd as the height.

Today's Problem

If you double the lengths of the sides of an equilateral triangle, how many times do you multiply its area? *(four times)*

3 FOLLOW-UP

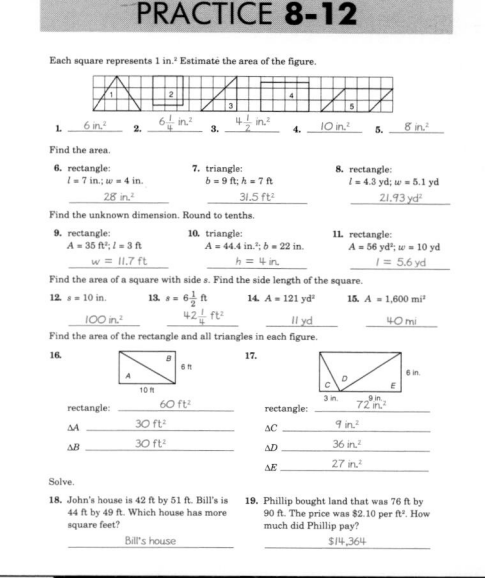

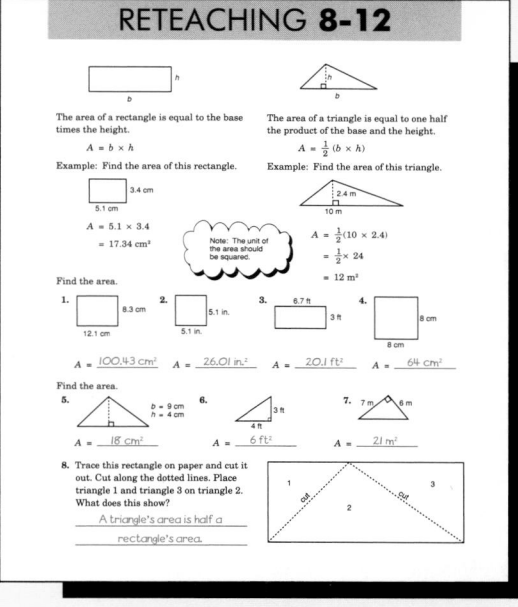

ENRICHMENT 8-12

☑ **MATERIALS CHECKLIST:** Grid paper, rulers

Have the students work in pairs. Have each pair draw rectangles on grid paper with the following areas: 24 sq units *[Possible answers: 1×24, 2×12, 3×8, 4×6]*, 15 sq units *[Possible answers: 1.5×10, 3×5]*, $3\frac{1}{2}$ sq units *[Possible answer: $2\frac{1}{3} \times 1\frac{1}{2}$]*, 53.8 sq units *[Possible answer: 8×6.72]* Have the students draw triangles on grid paper with the following areas: 30 sq units *[Possible answer: $b = 12$, $h = 5$]*, 21 sq units *[Possible answer: $b = 7$, $h = 6$]*, $1\frac{7}{8}$ sq units *[Possible answer: $b = 5$, $h = \frac{3}{4}$.]*

LESSON 8-13

Lesson Organizer

Objective: Find the area of a parallelogram and a trapezoid.

Prior Knowledge: Students should know the formula for the area of a rectangle.

Lesson Resources:
Practice Worksheet 8-13
Reteaching Activity 8-13
Enrichment Worksheet 8-13
Daily Review 8-13

 **Two-Minute Math**

Add mentally. Divide the sum by 2.

3.2 and 6.8 *(5)* $4\frac{1}{2}$ and $9\frac{1}{2}$ *(7)*

$3\frac{1}{4}$ and $7\frac{3}{4}$ $(5\frac{1}{2})$

1 INTRODUCE

CONNECTING ACTIVITY

☑ **MATERIALS CHECKLIST:** Teaching Aid 3, (Grid Paper) scissors for each student

1. Have students draw the rectangles and the trapezoids shown below.

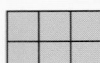 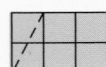 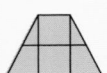 

2. Cut along the dashed line of one rectangle and rearrange the two pieces to form a parallelogram. What can you say about the area of the parallelogram? *(It is the same as the area of the rectangle.)*

3. Use the trapezoids to form a parallelogram. What can you say about the area of the trapezoid? *(It is one-half the area of the parallelogram.)*

WHEN YOUR STUDENTS ASK
★ WHY AM I LEARNING THIS? ★

You can use this skill to solve real life problems. For example, how much seed do you need to cover the yard? how much carpet to cover the floor? how much paper to wrap the gift?

Area: Parallelograms and Trapezoids

If you know how to find the area of a rectangle, you can use a **MATH CONNECTION** to find the area of a parallelogram.

Cut out a parallelogram from grid paper, as shown. Transform the parallelogram into a rectangle by cutting out a triangular piece from one end and moving it to the other end.

Are the areas of the rectangle and of the parallelogram the same?
yes

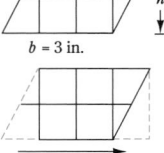

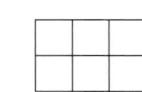

> **Area (A) of a parallelogram = base × height**
> **= bh**

$$A = bh$$
$$= 3 \times 2$$
$$= 6 \text{ in.}^2$$

You can use a similar **MATH CONNECTION** to find the area of a trapezoid.

Cut out a trapezoid from grid paper, as shown.

Trace around it. Then rotate it and trace again to form a parallelogram.

How does the area of the trapezoid compare to the area of the parallelogram? $\frac{1}{2}$

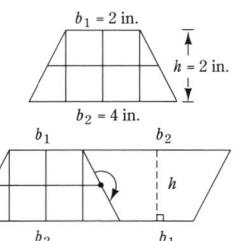

> **Area (A) of a trapezoid = $\frac{1}{2}$ area of parallelogram**
> **= $\frac{1}{2}$ (sum of bases) × height**
> **= $\frac{1}{2}$ ($b_1 + b_2$) × h**

$$A = \frac{1}{2}(b_1 + b_2) \times h$$
$$= \frac{1}{2}(2 + 4) \times 2 = 6 \text{ in.}^2$$

=== **GUIDED PRACTICE** ===

1. Find the area of the parallelogram.
75 in.²
6 in.
12.5 in.

2. Find the area of the trapezoid.
88 ft²
6 ft
8 ft
16 ft

---

2 TEACH

☑ **MATERIALS CHECKLIST:** inch grid paper, scissors for each student, Areas of Simple Polygons transparency

Where on the drawing do you see the sum of the bases from the formula ($b_1 + b_2$)? *(The base of the parallelogram is the sum of the bases of the trapezoid.)*

How do their heights compare? *(They are the same.)*

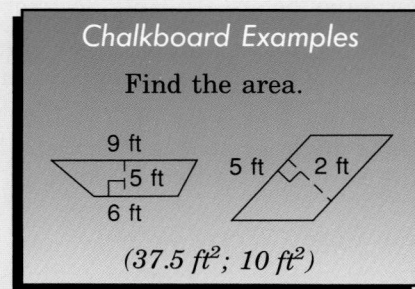

Chalkboard Examples

Find the area.

9 ft
5 ft
6 ft

5 ft   2 ft

(37.5 ft²; 10 ft²)

SUMMARIZE/ASSESS   Explain how you used a math connection to find the area of a parallelogram and the area of a trapezoid. *(Students should explain how they transformed the parallelogram into a rectangle and the trapezoid into a parallelogram.)*

Find the area.

3.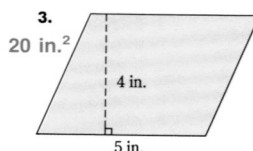
20 in.² 4 in. 5 in.

4.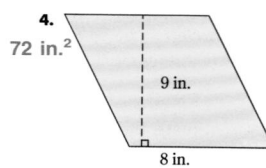
72 in.² 9 in. 8 in.

5.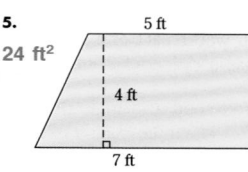
24 ft² 5 ft 4 ft 7 ft

6. parallelogram: 22.75 in.²
$b = 6\frac{1}{2}$ in., $h = 3\frac{1}{2}$ in.

7. trapezoid: 20.8 ft²
$b_1 = 5$ ft, $b_2 = 8$ ft, $h = 3.2$ ft

8. parallelogram: 128.1 in.²
$b = 10\frac{1}{4}$ in., $h = 12\frac{1}{2}$ in.

9. trapezoid: 3.4 ft²
$b_1 = 2.5$ ft, $b_2 = 1.3$ ft, $h = 1.8$ ft

10. What is the height?
parallelogram: 4 mi
$A = 16$ mi²; $b = 4$ mi

11. What is the base?
parallelogram: 2 ft
$A = 11$ ft²; $h = 5\frac{1}{2}$ ft

12. What is the height?
trapezoid: 1 ft
$A = 7$ ft²; $b_1 = 10$ ft;
$b_2 = 4$ ft

Find the area.

13. 195 ft²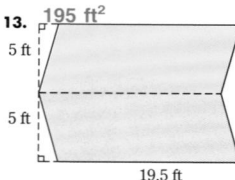
5 ft / 5 ft / 19.5 ft

14. 78 in.²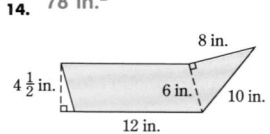
8 in. / $4\frac{1}{2}$ in. / 6 in. / 10 in. / 12 in.

15. 93 in.²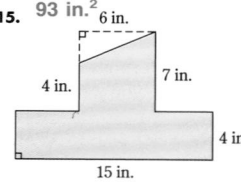
6 in. / 4 in. / 7 in. / 4 in. / 15 in.

Make drawings on inch grid paper to solve.   Check students' work.

16. Draw two different parallelograms each with an area of 9 in.².

17. Sketch three different trapezoids each with an area of 12 in.².

Critical Thinking

1. What is the area of the given polygon shown in the figure?
 a. rectangle *BDFG*   **b.** parallelogram *ABFG*   **c.** parallelogram *CEFG*
    12 ft²   12 ft²   12 ft²

2. How are these three polygon areas related? Why?
equal areas; same base and height

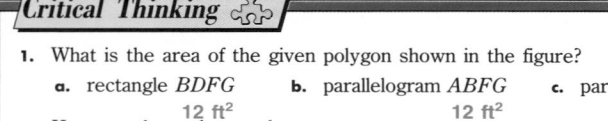
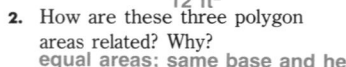
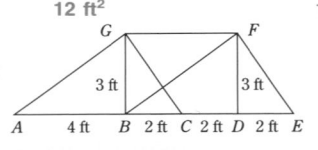

G   F
3 ft   3 ft
A   4 ft   B   2 ft   C   2 ft   D   2 ft   E

CHAPTER 8   259

---

3 FOLLOW-UP

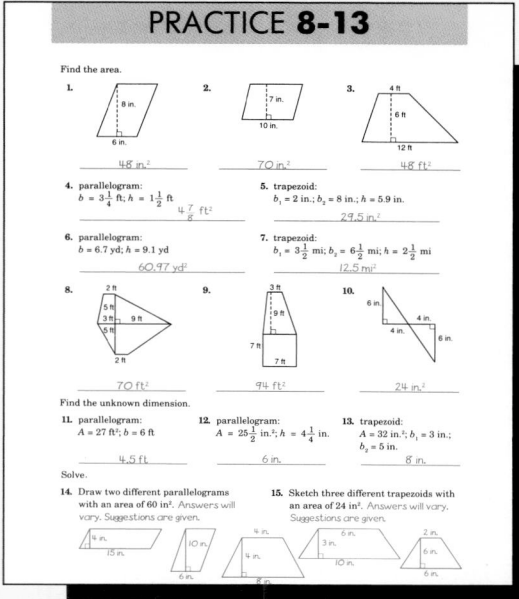
RETEACHING 8-13

☑ MATERIALS CHECKLIST: Pattern blocks, grid paper, rulers

Write these formulas on the board: *Area of parallelogram = base × height; Area of trapezoid = $\frac{1}{2}$ (sum of bases) × height.*
Have the students work in pairs. Provide each partner with either a trapezoid or a parallelogram from a set of pattern blocks. Instruct the students to trace the pattern block on grid paper. Then have them find the area of the figure by counting squares. Partners use the formulas on the board to find the area of each other's figures. Repeat the activity with larger or smaller trapezoids and parallelograms.

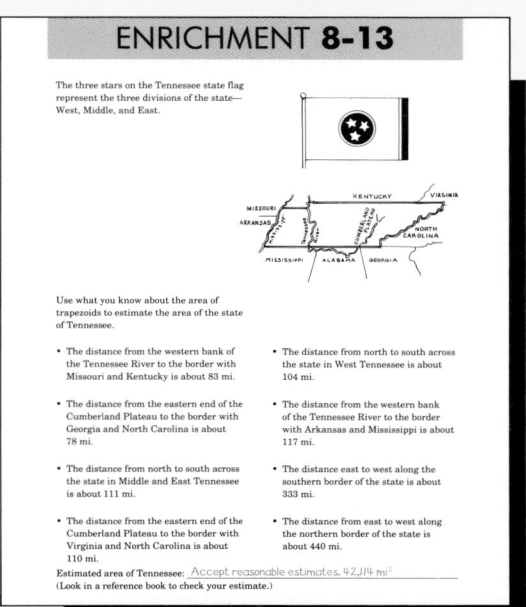

MEETING SPECIAL NEEDS

For Students Who Are . . .

Acquiring English Proficiency Review the meanings of *base* and *height* or parallelograms and trapezoids.

Gifted and Talented Have students create two original problems similar to Exercises 16–17, and exchange with a classmate to solve.

Working 2 or 3 Grades Below Level In the formula for the area of a trapezoid, remind students to do the work in parentheses first, then multiply, then add.

Today's Problem

Can a parallelogram ever be congruent to a trapezoid? *(No, a trapezoid has only one pair of parallel sides, whereas a parallelogram must have two pairs of parallel sides.)*

Lesson Organizer

Objective: Find the area of a circle.

Prior Knowledge: Students should know the meaning of π, how to square a number, and how to find the area of a square.

Error Analysis and Remediation: See page 267A.

Lesson Resources:
Practice Worksheet 8-14
Reteaching Worksheet 8-14
Enrichment Activity 8-14
Daily Review 8-14

Two-Minute Math

Square each number mentally.
Multiply the result by 3.

1   2   3   4   5   10

(3; 12; 27; 48; 75; 300)

1 INTRODUCE

CONNECTING ACTIVITY

☑ **MATERIALS CHECKLIST:** compass, ruler, scissors for each student

1. Have students follow these steps. **Draw a circle with a radius of 3 in. Draw and cut out a square that measures 1 in. on each side. Use the square inch to estimate the area of the circle.**

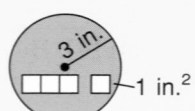

2. Have students form pairs and compare their estimates. Explain that the area of the circle is about 28 in.² Have partners discuss why one estimate might be closer than the other.

WHEN YOUR STUDENTS ASK
★ WHY AM I LEARNING THIS? ★

You can use this skill to solve real life problems such as choosing the right size cloth to cover a circular table or selecting a frame for a circular mirror.

Area: Circles

A sprinkler is rotating in a full circle to water part of a lawn. The watered circle has a radius of 2 yd. What is the area of the circle?

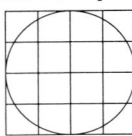

You need a formula that gives the area of a circle for which the radius is known. First, estimate the area of this circle by drawing one square outside the circle and another one inside the circle. What are the areas of these two squares?

The area of the outer square is 16 yd². Write that as $4 \times (2^2)$ yd², or $4r^2$.

The area of the inner square is 8 yd². Write that as $2 \times (2^2)$ yd², or $2r^2$.

A good estimate for the area of the circle would be between 8 yd² and 16 yd², or about 12 yd². You can write that as 3×2^2 yd², or $3r^2$.

The actual formula for the area of a circle uses the number π. In the work you just did, $3r^2$ is an approximation for πr^2.

> **Area (A) of a circle = πr^2**

The ancient Egyptians worked out a value of $4\left(\frac{8}{9}\right)^2$, or about 3.16, for π. By putting a square around a circle and marking off the corners, they formed an octagon that had almost the same area as the circle.

You can use 3.14 in the formula as an estimate for π. Using this formula for the sprinkler problem, you will find that the area of the circle is 12.6 yd².

NUMBER SENSE What is a good estimate of the area of a circle that has a radius of 1 yd?

━━━━━━━━━━━━━━━ **GUIDED PRACTICE** ━━━━━━━━━━━━━━━

1. How do you find the area of a circle that has a radius of 3 yd? What is the area rounded to tenths?

2. How do you find the area of a circle that has a diameter of 9 in.? What is the area rounded to tenths?

260   LESSON 8–14

---

2 TEACH

Relate the formula to the drawings at the top of page 260. **What is $2 \times r^2$?** *(2 × 2² or 8 yd²; the area of the inner square)* **What is $4 \times r^2$?** *(4 × 2² or 16 yd²; the area of the outer square)* **What is $3 \times r^2$?** *(3 × 2² or 12 yd²; an estimate for the area of the circle)*

Do you think the area of the circle is exactly 12 yd²? Explain.
(Possible answer: No, because the circle is curved and it is hard to get an exact answer)

Why is ≈ used instead of = when 3.14 is substituted for π? *(because this is an estimate for π)*

> ### Chalkboard Example
> What is the area (rounded to tenths) of a circle with a diameter of 17 ft?
> *(≈ 226.9 ft²)*

SUMMARIZE/ASSESS   **Explain how to find the area of a circle.**
(Use the formula $A = \pi r^2$; multiply an approximation of π by the square of the radius.)

Find the area. Use $\pi \approx 3.14$. Round the answer to tenths.

3. 254.3 in.²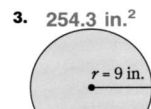
$r = 9$ in.

4. 1,256 yd²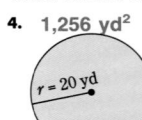
$r = 20$ yd

5. 153.9 ft²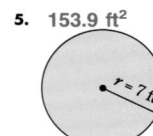
$r = 7$ ft

6. 1.8 yd²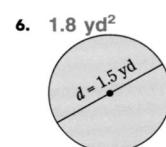
$d = 1.5$ yd

7. $r = 2.5$ ft
19.6 ft²

8. $r = 1.4$ in.
6.2 in.²

9. $d = 18$ in.
254.3 in.²

10. $d = 10$ ft
78.5 ft²

11. $r = 16$ in.
803.8 in.²

12. $r = 40$ in.
5,024 in.²

13. $d = 50$ yd
1,962.5 yd²

14. $d = 22.2$ ft
386.9 ft²

15. CRITICAL THINKING What is the radius of a circle that has an area of about 12.56 in.²? **2 in.**

Find the area of the shaded part. Use $\pi \approx 3.14$. Round to tenths.

16. 100.5 in.²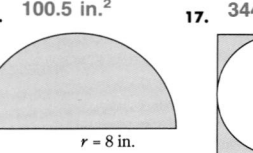
$r = 8$ in.

17. 344 in.²
40 in.

18. 546.8 in.²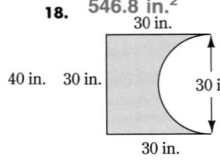
30 in.
40 in. 30 in. 30 in.
30 in.

19. 14.1 in.²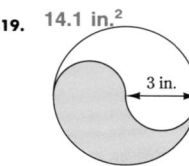
3 in.

20. Six sprinklers, with a radius of 10 yd each, are used to water a large lawn. About what is the area of the watered part of the lawn? Round the answer to tenths.
1,884 yd²

21. A rotating sprinkler swings through a 90° angle in a quarter turn. How many degrees does it swing through in a half turn? in a full turn? in three full turns?
180°; 360°; 1080°

Critical Thinking

Use these figures and draw any others you need to answer the question.

2 in.
3 in.
4 in.
6 in.

5 in.
10 in.

1. What happens to the perimeter and the area of a rectangle when the length and the width double? Explain. **perimeter doubled; area quadrupled**

2. What happens to the circumference and the area of a circle when the radius doubles? Explain.
circumference doubled; area quadrupled

MEETING SPECIAL NEEDS

For Students Who Are . . .

Acquiring English Proficiency For Exercise 21, explain that a full turn is 360°.

Gifted and Talented Have students answer these questions: What happens to the perimeter and area of a rectangle when the length is doubled? the width is doubled? when the length is tripled? the width is halved?

Working 2 or 3 Grades Below Level Review rounding decimals to tenths. Remind students that in Exercises 9, 10, 13, and 14, they must find the radius first and that $2r = d$.

Today's Problem

A square is inscribed in a circle. What fraction of the area of the circle is the area of the square? (*Let $2r$ be the diameter of the circle. The area of the square is the area of four triangles whose base is r and whose height is r. The area of the circle is $\pi \times r \times r$. The fraction then, is $\frac{(2 \times r \times r)}{(\pi \times r \times r)}$ or $\frac{2}{\pi}$ or about $\frac{2}{3}$.*)

---

3 FOLLOW-UP

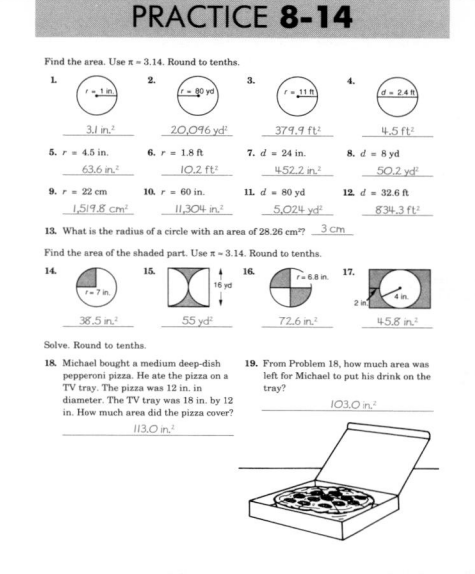

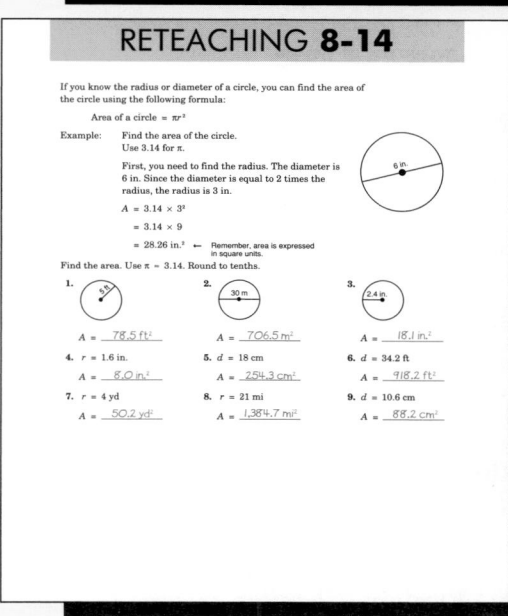

ENRICHMENT 8-14

☑ MATERIALS CHECKLIST:
Construction paper, scissors, hole punches

Have the students work in pairs. Punch holes in parallelograms and trapezoids cut from construction paper, and give several figures to each pair. Tell the students to find the area of each figure. [They will first have to find the area of the intact parallelogram or trapezoid, and then the area of each hole punched from the figure. The students then multiply to find the area of all the holes and subtract to find the area of the figure.] When the areas of all the figures have been found, have each partner take one figure and punch enough holes to reduce the area of the figure by about one half.

Lesson Organizer

Objective: Solve problems creatively.

Prior Knowledge: Students should know how to find averages.

Lesson Resources:
Daily Review 8-15
Cooperative Problem Solving, Chapter 8

Two-Minute Math

Use the Table of Numbers on the inside back cover. Find the average of the even numbers greater than 30 in row A. *(about 59)*

1 PREPARE

SYMBOLIC ACTIVITY

☑ **MATERIALS CHECKLIST:** inch ruler and yardstick for each group

Have students work in groups of three or four.

Pose this situation:

Suppose you had to pay for your ruler and your yardstick by the inch. The ruler costs $1.35, and the yardstick costs $2.90. To the nearest cent, what is the average price per inch for each? *(ruler: $11; yardstick: $.08)*

Does the fact that the yardstick is relatively cheaper mean that it is a better buy? Explain. *(Possible answer: Not necessarily; it may be too long to carry around. Accept reasonable responses.)*

WHEN YOUR STUDENTS ASK
★ WHY AM I LEARNING THIS? ★

You can connect this lesson to real life by thinking about the factors to consider when you buy something. Quality and practicality of the item as well as its price should determine the best buy.

Investigating Fasteners ▦

Many of the machines and tools that you use every day did not exist 100 yr ago. One of these inventions is the zipper.

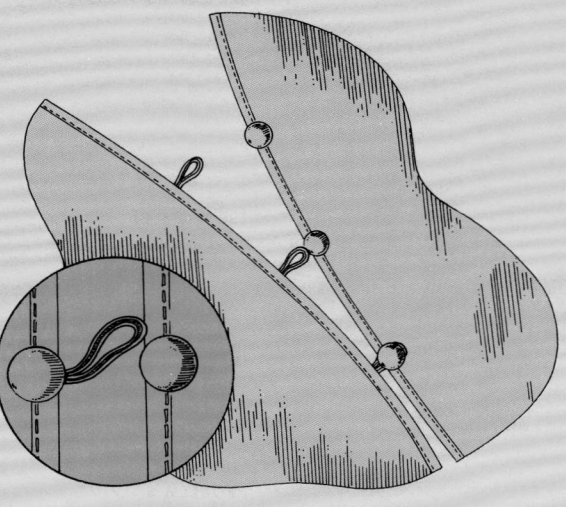

The drawings at right are similar to ones you might find in a sewing book published around 1900. They show two different kinds of fasteners used at the time.

Work with a partner.

1. Write a description of each drawing. How are the fasteners similar? How are they different?
Check students' work.

The zipper, or zip fastener, was invented in 1891 by Whitcomb L. Judson and made practical in 1913 by Gideon Sundback. At least ten more years went by before manufacturers would even consider using zippers for galoshes and even longer for ready-made clothes.

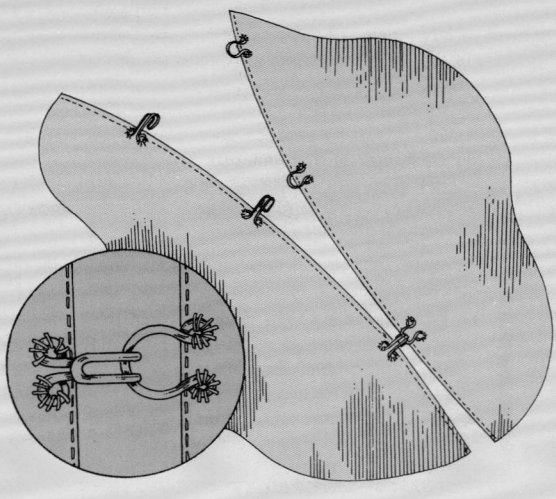

2. Compare a zipper fastener with the two fasteners shown at right. What advantages does the zipper have? disadvantages?
Accept reasonable answers.

MATH AND HISTORY

---

2 EXPLORE

☑ **MATERIALS CHECKLIST:** calculators

Have students work with a partner for this lesson.

What would be the price of a 16 in. zipper if the average price per inch were $.13? *($2.08)*

A 12 in. zipper has 18 teeth per half inch. How many teeth does the zipper have altogether? *(432)*

SUMMARIZE/ASSESS   **What mathematics skills did you use to investigate zippers?** *(Possible answer: Used classifying to devise a system to compare prices of different kinds of zippers; used division to help compute average price per inch.)*

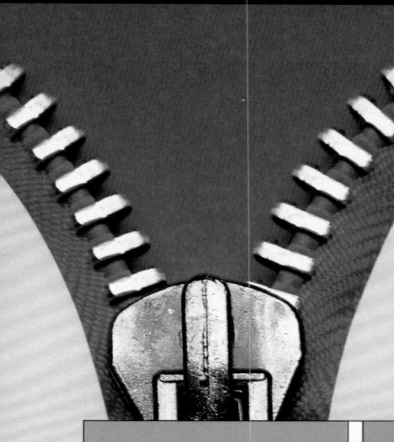

A zipper is made of three parts.
- dozens of identical metal or plastic hooks
- two strips of fabric
- a Y-shaped slider

Use the chart and a calculator to answer these questions.

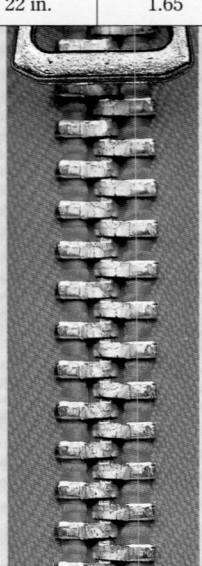

Plastic Zippers		Metal Zippers Medium-Weight		Metal Zippers Heavy-Weight	
Size	Price	Size	Price	Size	Price
7 in.	$1.20	12 in.	$1.80	6 in.	$1.25
9 in.	1.25	14 in.	1.85	7 in.	1.40
12 in.	1.35	16 in.	1.85	9 in.	1.40
16 in.	1.50	18 in.	1.85	11 in.	1.45
20 in.	1.60	20 in.	1.90		
22 in.	1.65	22 in.	2.05		

3. Why is it difficult to compare the prices of the different zippers on the chart? Answers will vary. Suggestion given: different sizes; different materials used

4. Decide on a way to compare the prices of plastic and medium-weight metal zippers. Which are more expensive? medium-weight metal zippers

5. Compare the prices of medium-weight and heavy-weight metal zippers by computing the average price per inch for each type. Round amounts to the nearest cent and organize your work in a chart. medium, 12¢; heavy, 18¢; Check students' charts.

6. What factors besides price would you consider before deciding what kind of zipper to buy? Accept reasonable answers.

7. What other fasteners have you used? How do they compare to zippers in performance? Do they cost *more than* or *less than* zippers? Accept reasonable answers.

3 FOLLOW-UP

CLASS ACTIVITY 8-15

☑ **MATERIALS CHECKLIST:** objects made from patterns like wallets, purses, shirts, briefcases, envelopes, binders; grid paper, scissors, ruler

Discuss how patterns are made as a part of the construction of an object. After patterns are made, tracings are made onto objects, cut out, and objects are formed. If possible, display the pattern for a shirt or other objects that use a fold. Talk about the fact that the fold can be used because the object has line symmetry. Arrange students in small groups. Have each group design a simple pattern for a wallet, envelope, or binder. Students may construct their objects if materials are available. After completing the designs, have groups share with one another.

MEETING INDIVIDUAL NEEDS

For Students Who Are . . .

Acquiring English Proficiency Discuss the word *fastener*. Have students explain why zippers, hooks and eyes, and buttons with button holes are called fasteners. Have students name other types of fasteners. (*Examples: snaps, laces, "velcro"*)

Gifted and Talented Have students write an original problem based on the information in the table on page 263, trade papers with a partner, and solve.

Working 2 or 3 Grades Below Level Review finding averages of money amounts.

Today's Problem

If September 3rd falls on a Sunday, on what day of the week will September 20th fall? (*Wednesday*) October 9th? (*Monday*) December 14th? (*Thursday*)

Lesson Organizer

Objective: Review addition, subtraction, and multiplication of whole numbers and fractions.

Lesson Resources:
Daily Review 8-16

These pages provide a review of whole number and fraction computation for addition, subtraction, and multiplication. Remind students that these pages review skills covered in previous chapters and will help them to do a self-check to see how well they remember what they have learned.

MATH AND SOCIAL STUDIES

Mixed Review

Write as fractions or as mixed numbers in lowest terms.

1. $\frac{9}{12}$ $\frac{3}{4}$
2. $\frac{36}{24}$ $1\frac{1}{2}$
3. 0.45 $\frac{9}{20}$
4. 6.75 $6\frac{3}{4}$
5. $5\frac{11}{7}$ $6\frac{4}{7}$
6. $7\frac{16}{6}$ $9\frac{2}{3}$

Find the missing numerator.

7. $8\frac{3}{4} = 8\frac{?}{8}$ 6
8. $8\frac{3}{5} = 7\frac{?}{5}$ 8
9. $13\frac{1}{6} = \frac{?}{6}$ 79
10. $5\frac{7}{8} = \frac{?}{8}$ 47

Write the reciprocal of the number.

11. 5 $\frac{1}{5}$
12. $\frac{5}{2}$ $\frac{2}{5}$
13. 9 $\frac{1}{9}$
14. $\frac{4}{7}$ $\frac{7}{4}$
15. 1 1
16. $2\frac{7}{8}$ $\frac{8}{23}$

17. Explain what it means for one number to be the reciprocal of another. **Their product is one.**

18. Explain how two fractions can be simplified before multiplying. **cancel common factors in numerator and denominator**

Give the answer in lowest terms.

19. $\frac{3}{5} \times \frac{2}{5}$ $\frac{6}{25}$
20. $\frac{3}{5} - \frac{2}{5}$ $\frac{1}{5}$
21. $\frac{3}{5} \div \frac{2}{5}$ $1\frac{1}{2}$
22. $\frac{3}{5} + \frac{2}{5}$ 1

23. $9 \times \frac{2}{3}$ 6
24. $\frac{5}{9} \div 25$ $\frac{1}{45}$
25. $\frac{11}{12} \times 18$ $16\frac{1}{2}$
26. $56 \div \frac{7}{8}$ 64

27. $3\frac{2}{3} - 2\frac{1}{4}$ $1\frac{5}{12}$
28. $3\frac{2}{3} \div 2\frac{1}{4}$ $1\frac{17}{27}$
29. $3\frac{2}{3} + 2\frac{1}{4}$ $5\frac{11}{12}$
30. $\frac{2}{3} \times 2\frac{1}{4}$ $1\frac{1}{2}$

31. $2\frac{1}{6} - \frac{5}{9}$ $1\frac{11}{18}$
32. $3\frac{1}{5} \times 3\frac{1}{5}$ $10\frac{6}{25}$
33. $5\frac{1}{2} \div 8.25$ $\frac{2}{3}$
34. $6\frac{1}{3} \times 0.8$ $5\frac{1}{15}$

35. $15 - 3\frac{3}{4}$ $11\frac{1}{4}$
36. $2\frac{1}{3} + 9$ $11\frac{1}{3}$
37. $84 \div \frac{1}{12}$ $1,008$
38. $95 \times \frac{3}{5}$ 57

39. $300 \div \frac{1}{2}$ 600
40. $\frac{5}{8} \times 400$ 250
41. $250 - 48\frac{5}{9}$ $201\frac{4}{9}$
42. $\frac{1}{26} \div \frac{5}{13}$ $\frac{1}{10}$

Use mental math to solve.

43. $a + 2\frac{1}{3} = 6\frac{2}{3}$ $4\frac{1}{3}$
44. $\frac{6}{7}b = 0$ 0
45. $c \div \frac{4}{5} = 1$ $\frac{4}{5}$
46. $3\frac{1}{4} \div d = 3\frac{1}{4}$ 1

47. $e - 3\frac{3}{4} = \frac{1}{4}$ 4
48. $1\frac{2}{9}f = 2\frac{4}{9}$ 2
49. $g + \frac{5}{6} = 6\frac{5}{6}$ 6
50. $h \div 3\frac{1}{2} = 2$ 7

Write as a variable expression. Use n as the variable.

51. two-thirds less than a number
$n - \frac{2}{3}$

52. a number increased by $4\frac{1}{2}$
$n + 4\frac{1}{2}$

53. $3\frac{4}{5}$ divided by some number
$3\frac{4}{5} \div n$

54. $\frac{4}{5}$ of some number
$\frac{4}{5}n$

55. a number divided by $\frac{7}{8}$
$n \div \frac{7}{8}$

56. the product of $6\frac{7}{8}$ and some number
$6\frac{7}{8}(n)$

264   LESSON 8–15

Write the variable expression in words.

57. $z - \frac{2}{9}$ **58.** $n \div \frac{3}{8}$ **59.** $\frac{4}{5} + a$ **60.** $6\frac{7}{8} - c$ **61.** $32\frac{3}{4} \div a$

━━━━━━━━━━━━━━ **PROBLEM SOLVING** ━━━━━━━━━━━━━━

 Solve. Choose mental math, estimation, pencil and paper, or calculator.

62. In 1985, Mexico's exports equaled $1\frac{4}{7}$ times its imports. If its imports in 1985 were worth $14 million, what was the value of Mexico's exports that year? **p; $22 million**

63. It has been predicted that in the year 2100 the population of Mexico will be 196 million, or about $2\frac{3}{8}$ times what it was in 1987. About what was Mexico's population in 1987? **e; about 83 million**

64. In 1987, the world's most populous country, China, had about $12\frac{4}{5}$ times as many residents as had Mexico. If Mexico's population was 82 million in 1987, what is a good estimate for China's population in 1987? **e; about 1,050,000,000**

65. Juarez, Mexico, would need $30\frac{4}{5}$ additional inches of rain each year to equal the average yearly rainfall in Seattle, Washington. If Seattle's average rainfall is $38\frac{3}{5}$ in., what is the average rainfall in Juarez? **m; 7.8 in.**

66. Approximately 15 out of every 100 Mexicans live in Mexico City. Use your answer from Exercise 63 to find the population of Mexico City in 1987. **p or e; 12.45 million**

67. The state of Texas occupies 262,000 mi^2 of land. Mexico takes up 761,000 mi^2. Is Texas about $\frac{2}{5}$, $\frac{3}{8}$, $\frac{1}{3}$, or $\frac{1}{4}$ the size of Mexico? **p; $\frac{1}{3}$**

Mexico City, Mexico

MULTICULTURAL NOTE

Mexican influence is strong in the United States, especially in the Southwest, which was part of Mexico. Among the Spanish words from Mexico that are part of the American language are *canyon, patio, rodeo,* and *corral.*

CHAPTER
Checkup

The chapter checkup provides a quick language and vocabulary review, a test for the chapter, and suggestions for student Learning Log entries.

Language and Vocabulary

Some key language and vocabulary ideas from this chapter are reinforced here.

Test

The test can be used either as a test or as a review of the chapter prior to your administering the test worksheets found in the Teacher's Resource Book.

The following guide will help you determine percentage scores.

Score	Percent	Score	Percent
24	100%	12	50%
23	96	11	46
22	92	10	42
21	88	9	38
20	83	8	33
19	79	7	29
18	75	6	25
17	71	5	21
16	67	4	17
15	63	3	13
14	58	2	8
13	54	1	4

Each test has 3 sections: concepts, skills, and problem solving. These sections provide students with exposure to the formats used on standardized tests.

Use the chart on page 267 to identify the Management Objectives tested for this chapter.

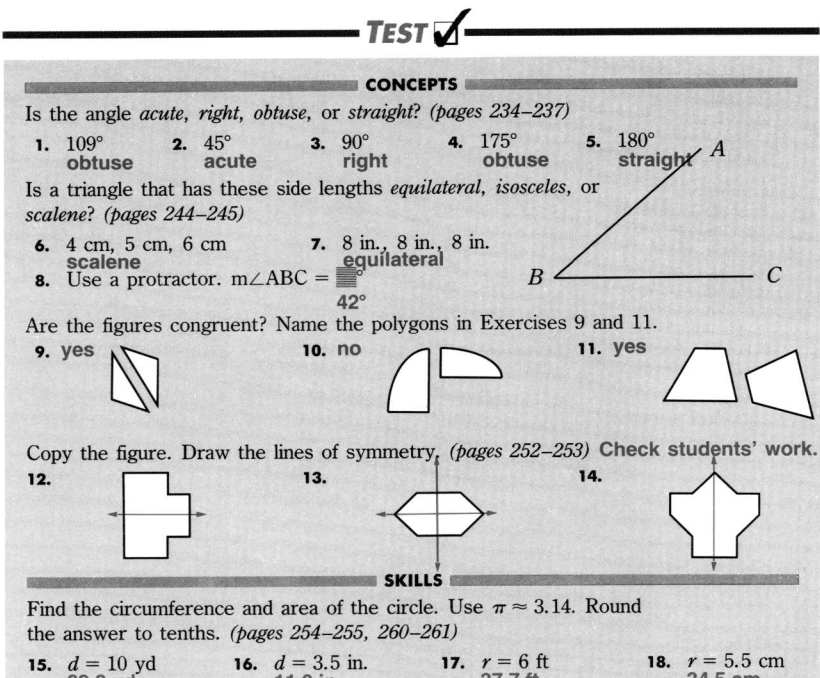

CHAPTER CHECKUP

LANGUAGE & VOCABULARY

Write a sentence to answer the question. **Answers will vary. Suggestions given.**

1. How do you know whether two figures are congruent?
same size and shape

2. How do you know whether a figure has a line of symmetry?
mirror-image; can fold to exactly match

3. How do you decide whether a figure is a parallelogram or a trapezoid?
two sets of parallel sides or only one set

TEST ✓

CONCEPTS

Is the angle *acute, right, obtuse,* or *straight? (pages 234–237)*

1. 109° **obtuse**
2. 45° **acute**
3. 90° **right**
4. 175° **obtuse**
5. 180° **straight**

Is a triangle that has these side lengths *equilateral, isosceles,* or *scalene? (pages 244–245)*

6. 4 cm, 5 cm, 6 cm **scalene**
7. 8 in., 8 in., 8 in. **equilateral**
8. Use a protractor. m∠ABC = ▦° **42°**

Are the figures congruent? Name the polygons in Exercises 9 and 11.

9. **yes**
10. **no**
11. **yes**

Copy the figure. Draw the lines of symmetry. *(pages 252–253)* **Check students' work.**

12.
13.
14.

SKILLS

Find the circumference and area of the circle. Use $\pi \approx 3.14$. Round the answer to tenths. *(pages 254–255, 260–261)*

15. $d = 10$ yd **62.8 yd**
16. $d = 3.5$ in. **11.0 in.**
17. $r = 6$ ft **37.7 ft**
18. $r = 5.5$ cm **34.5 cm**

266   CHAPTER CHECKUP

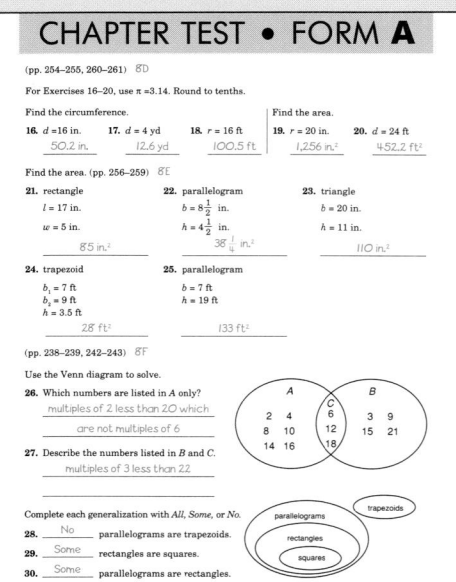

CHAPTER TEST • FORM A

(pp. 234–237) 8A
Use a protractor to complete.

1.
2.

m∠DEF = **55°**   m∠WXY = **110°**

Is the angle *acute, right, or obtuse?*

3. 12° **acute**
4. 99° **obtuse**
5. 90° **right**

(pp. 232–233, 240–241, 244–245, 248–249) 8B

Classify the polygon.

6.
7.
8.

rhombus   **parallelogram**   **rectangle**

Is a triangle with these angle measurements *right, obtuse, or acute?*

9. 35°, 35°, 110° **obtuse**
10. 39.5°, 69.2°, 71.3° **acute**

(pp. 250–253) 8C

The square shows two lines of symmetry.

Name all figures congruent to the figure.

11. triangle with vertices C, B, G **F, E, G**
12. triangle with vertices C, A, F **C, D, F**
13. trapezoid with vertices A, B, G, F **D, E, G, C**
14. rectangle with vertices A, B, E, F **C, B, E, D**
15. Name another line of symmetry for the figure. ↔**AD**

CHAPTER TEST • FORM A

(pp. 254–255, 260–261) 8D

For Exercises 16–20, use π =3.14. Round to tenths.

Find the circumference.   Find the area.

16. $d = 16$ in. **50.2 in.**
17. $d = 4$ yd **12.6 yd**
18. $r = 16$ ft **100.5 ft**
19. $r = 20$ in. **1,256 in.²**
20. $d = 24$ ft **452.2 ft²**

Find the area. (pp. 256–259) 8E

21. rectangle
$l = 17$ in.
$w = 5$ in.
85 in.²

22. parallelogram
$b = 8\frac{1}{2}$ in.
$h = 4\frac{1}{2}$ in.
38$\frac{1}{4}$ in.²

23. triangle
$b = 20$ in.
$h = 11$ in.
110 in.²

24. trapezoid
$b_1 = 7$ ft
$b_2 = 9$ ft
$h = 3.5$ ft
28 ft²

25. parallelogram
$b = 7$ ft
$h = 19$ ft
133 ft²

(pp. 238–239, 242–243) 8F

Use the Venn diagram to solve.

26. Which numbers are listed in A only? **multiples of 2 less than 20 which** **are not multiples of 6**

27. Describe the numbers listed in B and C. **multiples of 3 less than 22**

Complete each generalization with *All, Some,* or *No.*

28. **No** parallelograms are trapezoids.
29. **Some** rectangles are squares.
30. **Some** parallelograms are rectangles.

Find the area of the figure. *(pages 256–259)*

19. rectangle
$h = 8$ cm
$b = 12$ cm
96 cm²

20. triangle
$b = 2.5$ yd
$h = 3.4$ yd
4.25 yd²

21. parallelogram
$b = 7.5$ in.
$h = 4$ in.
30 in.²

22. trapezoid
$b_1 = 2$ ft; $b_2 = 3$ ft
$h = 1.5$ ft
3.75 ft²

━━━━━━━━━━━━━━ **PROBLEM SOLVING** ━━━━━━━━━━━━━━

Use a Venn diagram to solve. *(pages 238–239, 242–243)*

23. A survey showed that of 50 people asked, 22 say they read newspapers daily and 35 say they watch TV news daily.

a. How many people were questioned? **50 people**

b. Does the Venn diagram at right represent this situation? **yes**

c. Do *some, all,* or *none* of the 50 people read newspapers and watch TV news daily? **7 people**

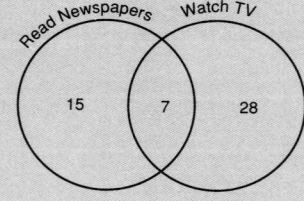

Read Newspapers   Watch TV
15   7   28

24. A roof brace for a new house is shaped like a right triangle with a base of 2.5 yd and a height of 3.4 yd. How many square yards of insulation will be needed to fill the interior of the brace? **4.25 yd²**

LEARNING LOG

Write the answers in your learning log.   **Answers will vary. Suggestions given.**

1. You know the diameter of a circle. Explain how to find the radius. $\frac{1}{2}d = r$

2. The woman working in the cafeteria tells you the two pieces of bread used to make a sandwich are congruent. What does she mean? **They are exactly the same size and shape.**

3. Explain to your friend why we use the label *square units* when finding the area of a circle. **Area is always in square units regardless what the shape of the figure is.**

Note that the same numbers are used in Exercises 20 and 24.

Items	Management Objectives	Pages
1–5	**8A** Measure and classify angles.	234–235
6–8	**8B** Classify polygons by their properties.	244–245
9–14	**8C** Determine congruent figures and identify lines of symmetry.	250–251; 252–253
15–18	**8D** Find the circumference and area of a circle.	254–255; 260–261
19–22	**8E** Find the area of a rectangle, a triangle, a parallelogram, or a trapezoid.	256–259
23–24	**8F** Problem Solving: Use Venn diagrams. Make generalizations.	238–239; 242–243

Problem Solving

Item 23 has 3 parts:

a. literal—this is a reading comprehension question
b. interpretive—this involves interpretation using the facts given
c. applied—students use a strategy or skills to find an answer

Item 20 in the skill section and item 24 in the problem solving section use the same numbers.

This will help you informally assess how your students transfer from numerical skills to word problems.

For scoring problem solving items you may wish to use partial credit. If a student uses the correct strategy but gets a wrong answer, give the student 2 points toward the total percent score.

Learning Log

These are suggestions for writing about some topics taught in this chapter. The students keep their Learning Logs from the beginning of the school year through the end.

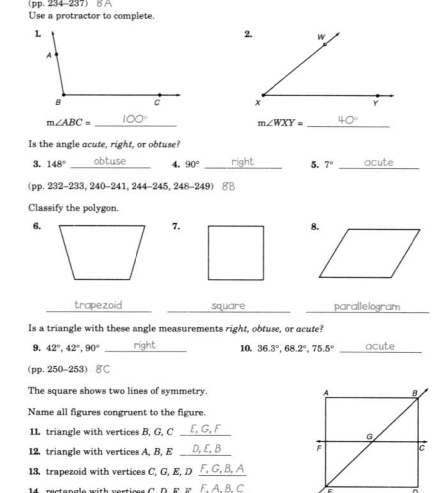

CHAPTER TEST • FORM **B**

(pp. 234–237) 8A
Use a protractor to complete.

1.
m∠ABC = ____ 100°

2.
m∠WXY = ____ 40°

Is the angle *acute, right,* or *obtuse?*

3. 148° ____ obtuse   **4.** 90° ____ right   **5.** 7° ____ acute

(pp. 232–233, 240–241, 244–245, 248–249) 8B

Classify the polygon.

6. ____ trapezoid   **7.** ____ square   **8.** ____ parallelogram

Is a triangle with these angle measurements *right, obtuse,* or *acute?*

9. 42°, 42°, 90° ____ right   **10.** 36.3°, 68.2°, 75.5° ____ acute

(pp. 250–253) 8C

The square shows two lines of symmetry.

Name all figures congruent to the figure.

11. triangle with vertices B, G, C ____ E, G, F
12. triangle with vertices A, B, E ____ D, E, B
13. trapezoid with vertices C, G, E, D ____ F, G, B, A
14. rectangle with vertices C, D, E, F ____ F, A, B, C
15. Name another line of symmetry for the figure. ____ AD

CHAPTER TEST • FORM **B**

(pp. 254–255, 260–261) 8D

For Exercises 16–20, use π = 3.14. Round to tenths.

Find the circumference.

16. $d = 12$ in. 37.7 in.
17. $d = 8$ yd 25.1 yd
18. $r = 35$ in. 219.8 in.

Find the area.

19. $r = 10$ in. 314 in.²
20. $d = 22$ yd 379.94 yd²

Find the area. (pp. 256–259) 8E

21. rectangle
$l = 15$ in.
$w = 9$ in.
135 in.²

22. parallelogram
$b = 6\frac{1}{2}$ in.
$h = 5\frac{1}{2}$ in.
$35\frac{3}{4}$ in.²

23. triangle
$b = 14$ in.
$h = 10$ in.
70 in.²

24. trapezoid
$b_1 = 9$ ft
$b_2 = 11$ ft
$h = 5.5$ ft
55 ft²

25. triangle
$b = 16$ yd
$h = 14$ yd
112 yd²

(pp. 238–239, 242–243) 8F

Use the Venn diagram to solve.

26. Which numbers are listed in *D* only?
multiples of 4 less than 33 which are not multiples of 3

D   E
4 8   F 3 6
16 20   12   9 15
28 32   24   21 27

27. Describe the numbers listed in *F.*
common multiples of 3 and 4 that are less than 33.

Complete each generalization with *All, Some,* or *No.*

quadrilaterals
trapezoids
parallelograms
rectangles

28. Some quadrilaterals are parallelograms.
29. No trapezoids are rectangles.
30. All rectangles are quadrilaterals.

Error Analysis and Remediation

Here are some common errors students make when they are working with geometry. The errors are listed by lesson under the appropriate management objective.

8A • MEASURE AND CLASSIFY ANGLES

Source of Error (Lesson 8-1)
Students name a ray by naming the point on the ray first and then the endpoint.

Remediation
Give students practice exercises that include rays in different positions. Have them label the endpoint before naming the ray.

Source of Error (Lessons 8-2 and 8-3)
Students read the wrong scale on the protractor.

Remediation
Have students note the direction in which the angle opens. If it opens from right to left, tell them to start from zero at the right and count on the appropriate scale until they reach the position where the ray crosses the protractor. Have students follow the same procedure for angles that open from left to right.

8B • CLASSIFY POLYGONS BY THEIR PROPERTIES

Source of Error (Lesson 8-5)
Students confuse the names of polygons.

Remediation
Display a large chart that shows each figure, its name, and the number of sides. Help students associate the prefixes with their meanings.
tri—3   quad—4   penta—5   hexa—6   octa—8

Source of Error (Lesson 8-7)
Students have difficulty using more than one name to classify a triangle.

Remediation
Demonstrate that some right triangles can be classified as isosceles triangles as well as scalene triangles and that obtuse triangles can be classified as scalene triangles.

8C • DETERMINE CONGRUENT FIGURES AND IDENTIFY LINES OF SYMMETRY

Source of Error (Lesson 8-9)
Students have difficulty determining corresponding sides and angles when the two figures are in different positions.

Remediation
Tell students to trace one figure in the pair and place it on the other. They can then name congruent sides and angles as corresponding sides and angles.

8D • FIND THE CIRCUMFERENCE AND AREA OF A CIRCLE

Source of Error (Lessons 8-11 and 8-14)
Students use the radius when finding the circumference and the diameter when finding the area.

Remediation
Suggest that students make a small chart to help them keep track of the correct dimensions. For example,

    radius   diameter
    6 cm   12 cm

Remind them to write the formula before finding the circumference or the area and then to substitute the correct value.

8E • FIND THE AREA OF A RECTANGLE, A TRIANGLE, A PARALLELOGRAM, OR A TRAPEZOID

Source of Error (Lessons 8-12 and 8-13)
Students confuse the height of a triangle or a parallelogram with the length of a side.

Remediation
Have students draw diagrams and represent the height by a perpendicular line segment.

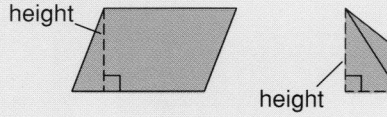

Answers

Page 239

2.

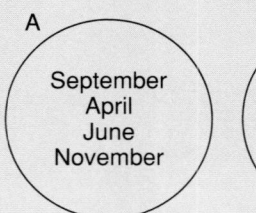

3.

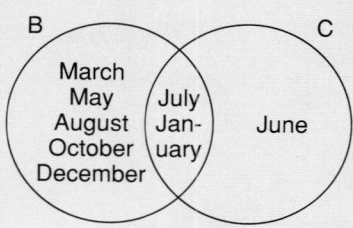

4.

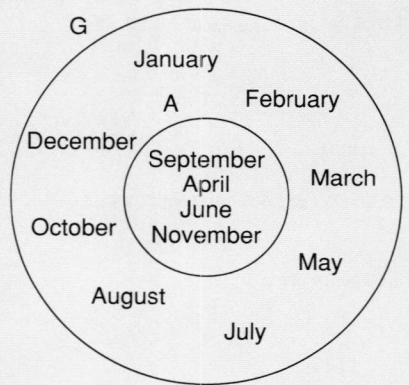

Critical Thinking

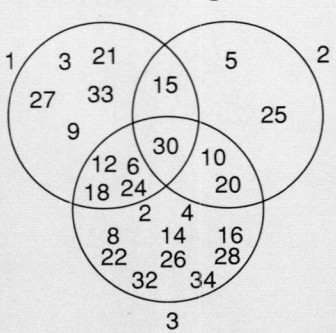

Page 250

1. $\angle CAB \cong \angle FDE$
$\angle CBA \cong \angle FED$
$\angle ACB \cong \angle DFE$
$\overline{AB} \cong \overline{DE}$
$\overline{BC} \cong \overline{EF}$
$\overline{CA} \cong \overline{FD}$

2. $\angle IGH \cong \angle LKJ$
$\angle IHG \cong \angle LJK$
$\angle GIH \cong \angle KLJ$
$\overline{GH} \cong \overline{KJ}$
$\overline{HI} \cong \overline{JL}$
$\overline{IG} \cong \overline{KL}$

3. $\angle UST \cong \angle WYX$
$\angle SUT \cong \angle YWX$
$\angle STU \cong \angle YXW$
$\overline{SU} \cong \overline{YW}$
$\overline{UT} \cong \overline{WX}$
$\overline{TS} \cong \overline{YX}$

Page 251

14. Check students'
drawings.
$\angle HFG \cong \angle CAB$
$\angle FGH \cong \angle ABC$
$\angle GHF \cong \angle BCA$
$\overline{FG} \cong \overline{AB}$
$\overline{GH} \cong \overline{BC}$
$\overline{HF} \cong \overline{CA}$

15. Check students'
drawings.
$\angle JIK \cong \angle CBA$
$\angle IJK \cong \angle BCA$
$\angle JKI \cong \angle CAB$
$\overline{IK} \cong \overline{BA}$
$\overline{KJ} \cong \overline{AC}$
$\overline{JI} \cong \overline{CB}$

16. Check students'
drawings.
$\angle LMN \cong \angle PQR$
$\angle MNL \cong \angle QRP$
$\angle NLM \cong \angle RPQ$
$\overline{LM} \cong \overline{PQ}$
$\overline{MN} \cong \overline{QR}$
$\overline{LN} \cong \overline{PR}$

Page 257

4. Accept reasonable estimates. Suggestions given:
  a. 6 in.^{2} **b.** $2\frac{1}{4}$ in.^{2}
  c. $\frac{1}{2}$ in.^{2} **d.** $7\frac{11}{2}$ in.^{2}
  e. 9 in.^{2} **f.** 7 in.^{2}
  g. 7 in.^{2}

18. Rectangle = 81 ft^2
  $\triangle B = 40.5$ ft^2
  $\triangle C = 40.5$ ft^2

19. Rectangle = 225 mi^2
  $\triangle F = 112.5$ mi^2
  $\triangle E = 112.5$ mi^2

20. Rectangle = 45 in^2
  $\triangle H = 5$ in.^{2}
  $\triangle I = 22.5$ in.^{2}
  $\triangle J = 17.5$ in.^{2}

Page 265

57. Answers will vary. Suggestion given: two-ninths less than a number.

58. Answers will vary. Suggestion given: a number increased by $\frac{3}{8}$.

59. Answers will vary. Suggestion given: $\frac{4}{5}$ more than a number.

60. Answers will vary. Suggestion given: $6\frac{7}{8}$ minus a number.

61. Answers will vary. Suggestion given: $32\frac{3}{4}$ more than a number.

CHAPTER 8

Extra Practice

This page provides extra practice of all the major chapter objectives. Use this page after the chapter has been taught to reinforce the chapter skills. Page references are provided for each group of items so that students can easily look back at the appropriate lesson for additional support.

Use a protractor to complete. *(pages 234–235)*

1. $m\angle ABC = $ ▤ 50°

2. $m\angle FGH = $ ▤ 140°

Is a triangle that has these side lengths or angle measures equilateral, isosceles, or scalene? *(pages 244–245)*

3. 7 cm, 8 cm, 10 cm
scalene

4. $9\frac{1}{2}$ in., $12\frac{1}{2}$ in., $15\frac{1}{2}$
scalene

5. 35°, 35°, 110°
isosceles

6. 103°, 39°, 38°
scalene

7. 65°, 60°, 55°
scalene

8. 7 yd, 7 yd, 7 yd
equilateral

Are the figures congruent? *(pages 250–251)*

9. yes

10. no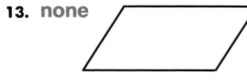

11. yes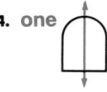

How many lines of symmetry does the figure have? Copy the figure and draw the lines of symmetry. *(pages 252–253)*

12. one

13. none

14. one

Find the circumference. Use $\pi \approx 3.14$. Round the answer to tenths. *(pages 254–255)*

15. $d = 32$ in.
100.5 in.

16. $r = 17.5$ ft
109.9 ft

17. $r = 9.2$ m
57.8 m

18. $d = 2.9$ cm
9.1 cm

Find the area. *(pages 256–259)*

19. rectangle   126 m²
$l = 7$ m
$w = 18$ m

20. parallelogram   118.5 in.²
$b = 7.5$ in.
$h = 15.8$ in.

21. trapezoid   4.93 m²
$b_1 = 2$ m
$b_2 = 3.8$ m
$h = 1.7$ m

Find the area of the circle. Use $\pi \approx 3.14$. Round to tenths. *(pages 260–261)*

22. $r = 5.4$ ft   91.6 ft²

23. $d = 25.8$ in.   522.5 in.²

24. $r = 49.7$ yd   7,756.1 yd²

Solve. *(pages 238–239, 242–243)*

25. Decide whether the generalization "Some line segments are rays" is *true* or *false*.   false

268   EXTRA PRACTICE

Circles of Cities

How many cities are within 10 mi of your city or town? You can find out this way. **Check students' work.**

1. Find a road map of your state or the part of your state that your city or town is in.

2. Locate your city or town on the map. Tape one end of a piece of string to the mark for your town.

3. Determine the number of miles represented by 1 in. on the map.

4. Calculate the number of inches of string that represents 10 mi. For example, if 1 in. on the map represents 2 mi, mark off a length of 5 in. on the string.

5. Tie a pencil to the string at the length you calculated and draw a circle with your city or town at the center.

6. Make a list of all the cities and towns inside the circle. They are all within 10 mi. of your city or town.

A Different Angle on Angle Measurement

A different way to think of angle measurement is to think of holding one ray of the angle stationary while rotating the other ray around the vertex. If the two rays begin as a single ray, like ————▶, then a 90° angle can be thought of as a $\frac{1}{4}$ turn, as shown at right.

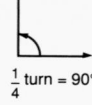

$\frac{1}{4}$ turn = 90°

Thinking of angle measurement this way relates an angle to a fractional part of 360°. Work with a partner. One person models a turn using two pencils as rays. The other writes the turn and the angle equivalent. Some turns to try are $\frac{1}{3}$, $\frac{1}{2}$, $\frac{3}{4}$, $\frac{1}{8}$, $\frac{3}{8}$, $\frac{5}{8}$, $\frac{7}{8}$, and 1 whole turn. What other fractional turns can you use that will result in an angle with a whole number of degrees? **Answers will vary. Suggestions given:**
$\frac{1}{18}$, $\frac{1}{9}$, $\frac{3}{18}$, $\frac{2}{9}$, $\frac{5}{18}$

MATH AMERICA

DID YOU KNOW . . . ?
There are 435 seats in the United States House of Representatives. Each of our states is allowed a certain number of representatives based on the state's population. What fraction of the total number of seats do your state representatives occupy?
Check students' work.

Enrichment

This page contains activities that provide extension and enrichment for all levels of students. Depending on the needs of your students, you may wish to assign an activity from this page at certain points during the chapter, or you may want to use this page when the entire chapter has been completed.

Circles of Cities

If you don't have enough roadmaps of your area, students can use maps of other places to determine the number of cities within a 10-mile radius. Be sure the map does not cover too large an area.

A Different Angle Measure
(COOPERATIVE)

Some fractional turns that will result in an angle of a whole number of degrees (such as $\frac{1}{9}$) are difficult to model with pencils; if students wish, allow them to use a protractor to show the angles. See if students can make a math connection to help them answer the question.

Cumulative Review

The Cumulative Review focuses on skills covered in previous chapters. All important skills are reviewed on a cyclic basis.

If students are having difficulty with particular groups of exercises, refer to the chart for follow-up work.

CUMULATIVE REVIEW

Find the answer.

1. circle, $d = 5$ ft **a**
circumference = ▓
Use $\pi \approx 3.14$.
  a. 15.70 ft
  b. 7.90 ft
  c. 19.63
  d. none of these

2. triangle, $b = 12$ ft **b**
$h = 15$ ft,
area = ▓
  a. 180 ft^2
  b. 90 ft^2
  c. 27 ft^2
  d. none of these

3. trapezoid, $b_1 = 10$ cm **b**
$b_2 = 14$ cm, $h = 8$ cm
area = ▓
  a. 152 cm^2
  b. 96 cm^2
  c. 192 cm^2
  d. none of these

4. $138.7 + 96.09 =$ **d**
  a. 234.16
  b. 325.69
  c. 235.79
  d. none of these

5. $\$37.95 + \$.76 =$ **b**
  a. $38.61
  b. $38.71
  c. $37.71
  d. none of these

6. $0.6 + 24.9 + 0.184 =$ **c**
  a. 246.84
  b. 27.34
  c. 25.684
  d. none of these

7. $3,000 - 1,823 =$ **a**
  a. 1,177
  b. 1,077
  c. 1,223
  d. none of these

8. $12.9 - 7.12 =$ **c**
  a. 20.02
  b. 4.97
  c. 5.78
  d. none of these

9. $0.0316 - 0.007 =$ **b**
  a. 0.0386
  b. 0.0246
  c. 0.0309
  d. none of these

Find the matching value.

10. 37.51 million **c**
  a. 37,000,051
  b. 37,051,000
  c. 37,510,000
  d. none of these

11. 97 hundredths **a**
  a. 0.97
  b. 0.097
  c. 0.0097
  d. none of these

12. $(4 \times 10^2) + (3 \times 10^0)$ **a**
  a. 403
  b. 430
  c. 4,030
  d. none of these

13. $29 \times (7 \times 6) =$ **b**
  a. 377
  b. 1,218
  c. 908
  d. none of these

14. $32 - (4 + 3^2) =$ **c**
  a. 37
  b. 25
  c. 19
  d. none of these

15. $8 \times (15 - 5) \div 8 =$ **c**
  a. 3
  b. 8
  c. 10
  d. none of these

Items	Management Objective	Where Taught	Reteaching Options	Extra Practice Options
1	**8D** Find the circumference and area of a circle.	254–255	TRB/RW 8-11	TRB/PW 8-11
2–3	**8E** Find the area of a rectangle, a triangle, a parallelogram, or a trapezoid.	256–259	TRB/RW 8-12 TE/RA 8-13	TRB/PW 8-12 TRB/PW 8-13
4–6	**2B** Add whole numbers and decimals.	40–41	TRB/RW 2-4	TRB/PW 2-4
7–9	**2C** Subtract whole numbers and decimals.	46–49	TRB/RW 2-7 TE/RA 2-7	TRB/PW 2-7
10–12	**1A** Identify and write whole numbers and decimals in exponential, expanded, and standard form.	6–7; 12–13	TE/RA 1-3 TRB/RW 1-6	TRB/PW 1-3 and 1-6
13–15	**3A** Use order of operations.	62–63	TE/RA 3-2	TRB/PW 3-2

Strategies may vary. Suggestions given.
Remember the strategies and types of
problems you've had so far. Solve.

1. Barry's lunch of an omelet and milk
cost $3.75. Bob had only a glass of milk
and spent $2.95 less than Barry. What
was their total bill?
multistep; $4.55

2. A car averages 20 mi/gal of gas. If gas
costs $1.60/gal, how much does it cost
to drive the car 400 mi?
multistep; $32.00

3. Sue bought a dress for $60 and wants
a coat that costs 2.5 times as much as
the dress. If she originally had $200,
how much more money does she need
to buy the coat?
multistep; $10

5. Steve wrote his three-number
combination in code. The first
number is a multiple of 7 whose
digits add to 8. The second is a prime
number between 55 and 60. The third
is a perfect square number with 9
factors. What is Steve's combination?
(*Hint:* All 3 numbers have 2 digits.)

guess and check; 35, 59, 100

7. A three-speed electric fan turns 900
revolutions per minute on low. It
turns $1\frac{1}{2}$ times faster on medium than
on low. It turns $1\frac{1}{2}$ times faster on
high than on medium. How fast does
the fan turn on high?
multistep; 2,025 rpm

9. A machine pays $.05 for each bottle
returned. The machine took 72 bottles
one week and 85 bottles the next
week. How much more did the
machine pay out the second week
than the first week?
multistep; $.65

Problem Solving Check List

- **Multistep problems**
- **Using an equation**
- **Using a pattern**
- **Using guess and check**

---

4. Training for a marathon, Tony ran
50 mi/wk for exactly one half year.
Altogether, how far did he run by
the end of this period?
equation; 1,300 mi

6. A lumber mill cuts planks $\frac{7}{8}$ in. thick.
The log that is being cut is exactly
9 in. thick.

   a. How thick is each plank? $\frac{7}{8}$ **in.**

   b. How many planks can be
   cut from the log? **10 planks**

   c. How thick will the
   remaining piece be? **multistep; $\frac{1}{4}$ in.**

8. Roberto studied $\frac{1}{2}$ h Monday, $\frac{3}{4}$ h
Tuesday, and 1 h Wednesday. If he
continues this pattern on Thursday
and Friday, how many hours will
he have studied for the 5 d?
pattern; 5 h

10. A ladder is leaning against the side
of a 35-ft building. If the ladder is
26 ft long and the base of the ladder
is 10 ft from the building, does the
ladder reach the top of the building?

   equation; no

Problem Solving Review

This page focuses on problem solving
strategies and types learned in this chapter and previous chapters. A problem solving checklist lists some of the strategies
students may use to solve the problems on
this page.

CHAPTER 8

Technology

This page is designed to provide calculator or computer experiences for all levels of students. The calculator or computer logo indicates the type of activity.

You may wish to assign these activities after the chapter has been taught or during the course of the chapter, depending on your needs and those of your students.

Cover It Up

If students do not know how to begin, suggest that they first determine the total area of the floor to be carpeted.

Waste Not
(COOPERATIVE)

To help students begin, you might ask students to find the area of rectangle A, then determine how much needs to be cut. Remind students that the rectangle must retain its shape.

Causing a Problem

If students cannot think of "answers," allow them to use variations of the example given.
Although this is described as a paper and pencil activity, software that develops the same skill is found in Houghton Mifflin Math Activities Courseware, Grade 7.

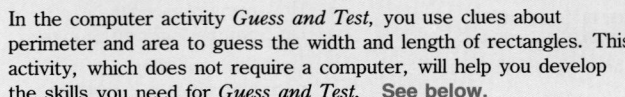

COVER IT UP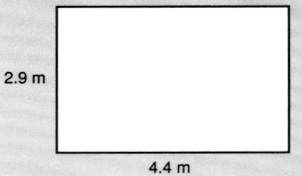

Keiko wants to carpet her room, shown below. The carpeting comes in a roll that is 1.9 m wide. What is the least amount of uncarpeted floor space Keiko will have left if she does not want to pay extra for cutting carpet to a different width? **1.74 m²**

2.9 m

4.4 m

WASTE NOT

Work in a group of three or four people. Use a metric ruler and make these rectangles.

	length	width
A→	15.2 cm	1.6 cm
B→	3.3 cm	4 cm
C→	12.5 cm	2.1 cm

Cutting from only one side, find the least amount of paper you could cut from each rectangle so that the area of each rectangle will be a whole number. Draw where you would cut. Compare your answers with other groups. **Check students' drawings.**

CAUSING A PROBLEM

In the computer activity *Guess and Test*, you use clues about perimeter and area to guess the width and length of rectangles. This activity, which does not require a computer, will help you develop the skills you need for *Guess and Test*. **See below.**

One way to write word problems is to work backward, beginning with your answers, and then creating clues.

Example:

Answer   Problem

Jorge is 13. Jan is 9. ⇨ The sum of Jorge's and Jan's ages is 22 and the product is 117. How old are Jorge and Jan?

Use this method to create two word problems. Trade papers with a classmate and try to solve each other's word problems.
Check students' work.

Software Activities

Note: To leave the program, students should use the ESCAPE or QUIT command for their computers.

activity 1 • TIME AROUND THE WORLD

MATERIALS: database program, globes, reference materials

Procedure: In this activity, students are asked to compare times in several cities. Begin by having students enter the data in the chart into a database file. Next ask students to order the times. What conclusion can they make about the times before 12 00?

City	Time		City	Time
Amsterdam	18 00		New York	12 00
Bombay	22 30		Moscow	20 00
Budapest	18 00		Paris	18 00
Cairo	19 00		Rome	18 00
Calcutta	22 30		Sydney	3 00
Cape Town	19 00		Tokyo	2 00
Lima	12 00			

Follow-up: Have students convert the times to a 12 hour clock.

activity 2 • ESTIMATING THE SQUARE ROOT

MATERIALS: BASIC programming

Procedure: In this program, students enter a number and the program identifies the two numbers the square root is between. Have the students enter the program and run it.

```
10 PRINT "WHAT IS THE NUMBER YOU
   WISH ";
20 INPUT "TO ESTIMATE THE SQUARE
   ROOT OF ";N
30 Y=SQR(N)
40 IF INT(Y)=Y THEN 80
50 PRINT "THE SQUARE ROOT IS
   BETWEEN ";INT(Y);
60 PRINT " AND ";INT(Y)+1
70 GOTO 10
80 PRINT "THE SQUARE ROOT OF "; N "
   IS ";Y
90 PRINT: GOTO 10
```

Follow-up: Challenge students to expand the program so it will print the square root as well as the two numbers.

HOUGHTON MIFFLIN SOFTWARE

Easy Graph. Boston, MA: Houghton Mifflin Company, 1987. For Apple II, Commodore, IBM.

EduCalc. Boston, MA: Houghton Mifflin Company, 1990. For Apple II, Commodore, IBM.

Friendly Filer. Boston, MA: Houghton Mifflin Company, 1989. For Apple II, Commodore, IBM.

Mathematics Activities Courseware. Boston, MA: Houghton Mifflin Company, 1983. For Apple II, IBM.

The Computer Tutor. Boston MA: Houghton Mifflin Company, 1990. For Apple II, IBM.

Using Geometry Grapher. Boston, MA: Houghton Mifflin Company, 1990. For Apple II, IBM.

OTHER SOFTWARE

Coordinate Math. St. Paul, MN: MECC, 1987. For Apple II.

Geometry Pool and Billiards. Fairfield, CT: Intellectual Software/Queue Software, Inc., 1989. For Apple II.

Microsoft Works. Redmond, WA: Microsoft Corporation, 1989. For IBM, Macintosh.

Supergraph. Newbury Park, CA: Ventura Educational Systems, 1989. For Apple II.

The Geometric presupposer. Pleasantville, NY: Sunburst Communications, 1986. For Apple II.

Ratio, Proportion, and Applications

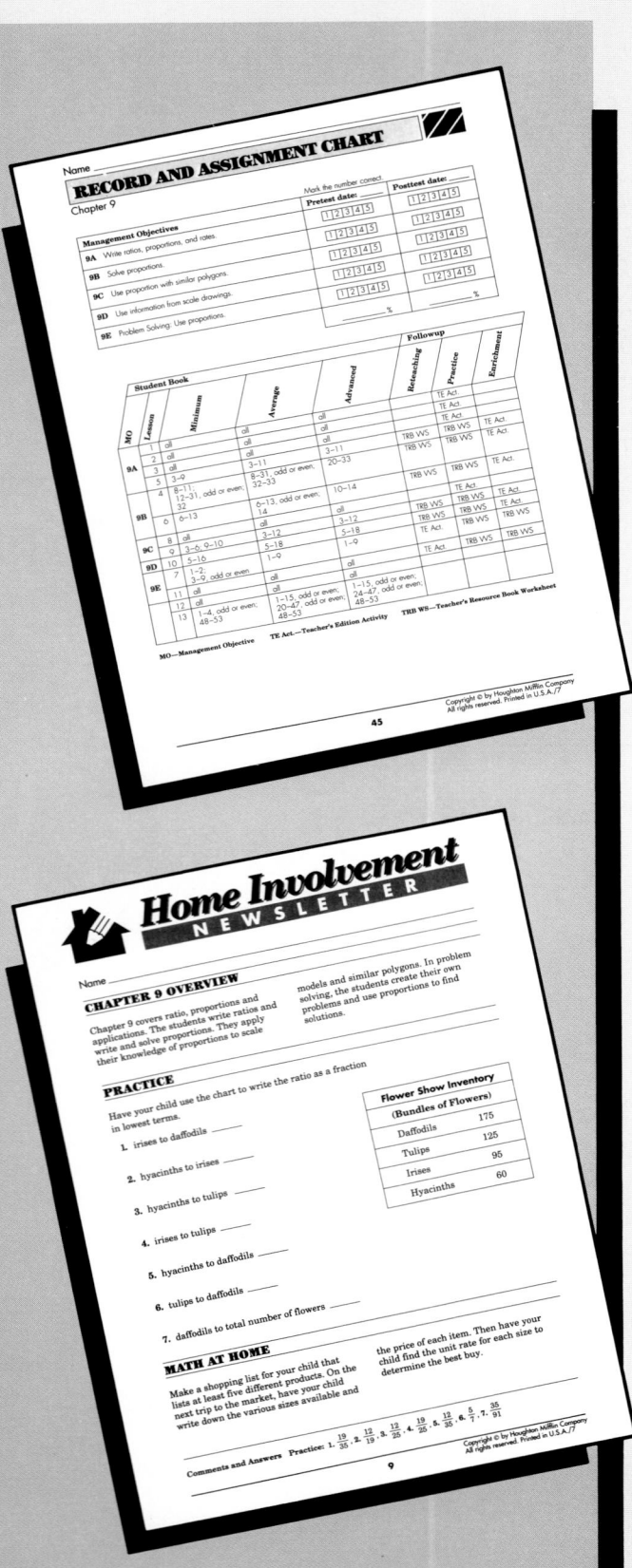

In Chapter 9, students learn to write ratios and to write and solve proportions using cross products. Students use math connections to solidify their understanding of the skills. They apply proportional thinking to finding unit rates in comparison shopping and to working with similar polygons and scale drawings. Throughout the development of the topics, mental math and estimation are stressed.

Problem solving lessons in the chapter emphasize writing problems and using proportions.

Management Objectives

9A Write ratios, proportions, and rates.
9B Solve proportions.
9C Use proportion with similar polygons.
9D Use information from scale drawings.
9E Problem Solving: Use proportions.

Assignments for different achievement levels are provided on the Record and Assignment Chart in the Teacher's Resource Book.

Vocabulary

ratio, page 274
proportion, page 277
rate, unit rate, page 279
cross products, page 280
similar, page 290

Home Involvement

As you begin to teach this chapter, give each student a copy of the Home Involvement Newsletter for this chapter.

This newsletter provides parents with
- an overview of the chapter
- suggestions for practicing some of the skills in the chapter
- an at-home activity to do with your child, applying the skills taught in the chapter.

Management Chart

Management Objectives	Lesson/Pages	Student Not Successful	Student Needs More Practice	Student Successful	Pacing Range
9A Write ratios, proportions, and rates.	9-1/274-275			TE/CA 9-1	4-5 days
	9-2/276-277			TE/CA 9-2	
	9-3/278-279			TE/CA 9-3	
	9-5/282-283	TRB/RW 9-5	TRB/PW 9-5	TE/EA 9-5	
9B Solve proportions.	9-4/280-281	TRB/RW 9-4	TRB/PW 9-4 CSP RRP Skills 5, 6 CT Unit 4 Obj. 3.1, 3.2 MAC 7 Activity 9	TE/EA 9-4 MAC 7 Activity 9	3-4 days
	9-6/284-285	TRB/RW 9-6	TRB/PW 9-6 CT Unit 4 Obj. 2.1, 2.2	TE/EA 9-6	
9C Use proportion with similar polygons.	9-8/290-291			TE/CA 9-8	2-3 days
	9-9/292-293	TRB/RW 9-9	TRB/PW 9-9	TE/EA 9-9	
9D Use information from scale drawings.	9-10/294-295	TRB/RW 9-10	TRB/PW 9-10 MAC 6 Activity 12B	TE/EA 9-10 MAC 6 Activity 12B	1 day
9E Problem Solving: Use proportions.	9-7/288-289	TE/RA 9-7	TRB/PW 9-7	TRB/EW 9-7	2 days
	9-11/296-297	TE/RA 9-11	TRB/PW 9-11 CT Unit 4 Obj. 3.3	TRB/EW 9-11	
Creative Problem Solving	298-299				
Mixed Review	300-301				
Chapter Checkups	286-287; 302-303				
Extra Practice	304				
Enrichment	305				
Cumulative Review/ Problem Solving Review	306-307				
Technology	308				

TE = Teacher's Edition
TRB = Teacher's Resource Book
RW = Reteaching Worksheet
RA = Reteaching Activity
EA = Enrichment Activity
EW = Enrichment Worksheet
PW = Practice Worksheet
CA = Classroom Activity

*Other Available Items
MAC = Mathematics Activities
    Courseware
CSP = Computational Skills Program
CT = Computer Tutor

CHAPTER 9

Manipulative Planning Guide

This is a complete list of manipulatives and materials needed for Chapter 9.

Materials for Manipulatives	TE Activities (INTRODUCE)	Student Book Lesson
Pattern blocks or Teaching Aid 12*: for each group for each student	Lessons 9-2, 9-5	Lesson 9-2
Math Connection Transparency		Lesson 9-2
Calculator for each student		Lesson 9-4, 9-6, 9-10, 9-12
Newspaper ads from different stores for same product	Lesson 9-6	
Teaching Aid 13* for each group	Lesson 9-8	
Teaching Aid 14* for each student	Lesson 9-9	
Recipes		
Teaching Aid 8* or protractor for each group		Lesson 9-8
24 counters or beans for each group	Lesson 9-12	
Adding machine tape or tape measure for each group	Lesson 9-11	
Index cards		
Blank spinners, newspapers		
Watch or clock with second hand or stopwatch		
Rulers, measuring tape or yardstick		Lessons 9-8, 9-10
Scissors	Lessons 9-2, 9-5, 9-8	Lessons 9-2, 9-8

*Teaching Aids are found in the Teacher's Resource Book.

Learning Stages

The concepts and skills in Chapter 9 are presented through these learning stages.

CONCRETE

Using manipulatives and verbalizing about a concept. No symbols.

Teacher Edition Activities	Student Book
Lesson 9-8	

Enrichment/ Class Activity	Reteaching	In the Houghton Mifflin Manipulative Kit?	In the Houghton Mifflin Overhead Kit?
		Yes	
			Yes
			Available separately
	Lesson 9-11	Yes	
			Yes
Lessons 9-2, 9-4, 9-9	Lesson 9-7	Yes	
		Yes	
Lessons 8-4, 8-9			
Lesson 8-6		Yes	
Lesson 9-3			
Lessons 9-8, 9-9		Yes	

CONNECTING

5¢ 9cm² ⅓

Making a connection between manipulatives and symbols.

Teacher Edition Activities	Student Book
Lessons 9-2, 9-5	Lessons 9-2, 9-8, 9-11, 9-12

SYMBOLIC

$.05   A=9cm² $1 - \frac{2}{3} = \frac{1}{3}$

Using numbers or symbols. No manipulatives or pictures of manipulatives.

Teacher Edition Activities	Student Book
Lessons 9-1, 9-3, 9-4, 9-6, 9-7, 9-9, 9-10	Lessons 9-1, 9-3, 9-4, 9-5, 9-6, 9-7, 9-9, 9-10, 9-11, 9-12

Additional Activities

COOPERATIVE LEARNING
RESOURCE ACTIVITIES

Through cooperative learning activities, students learn by interacting with one another in small groups. These cooperative activities provide students with motivating settings for making connections, investigations, and problem solving situations.

   The cooperative connections are interdisciplinary problem-solving projects. Each student has a particular job that helps lead the group to complete the project. For the cooperative investigations students work in pairs for investigations involving data collection and analysis. The cooperative problem solving activities encourage the sharing of ideas and information. Students work in groups of four to solve a problem. Students are each assigned a clue and work together to find a common solution.

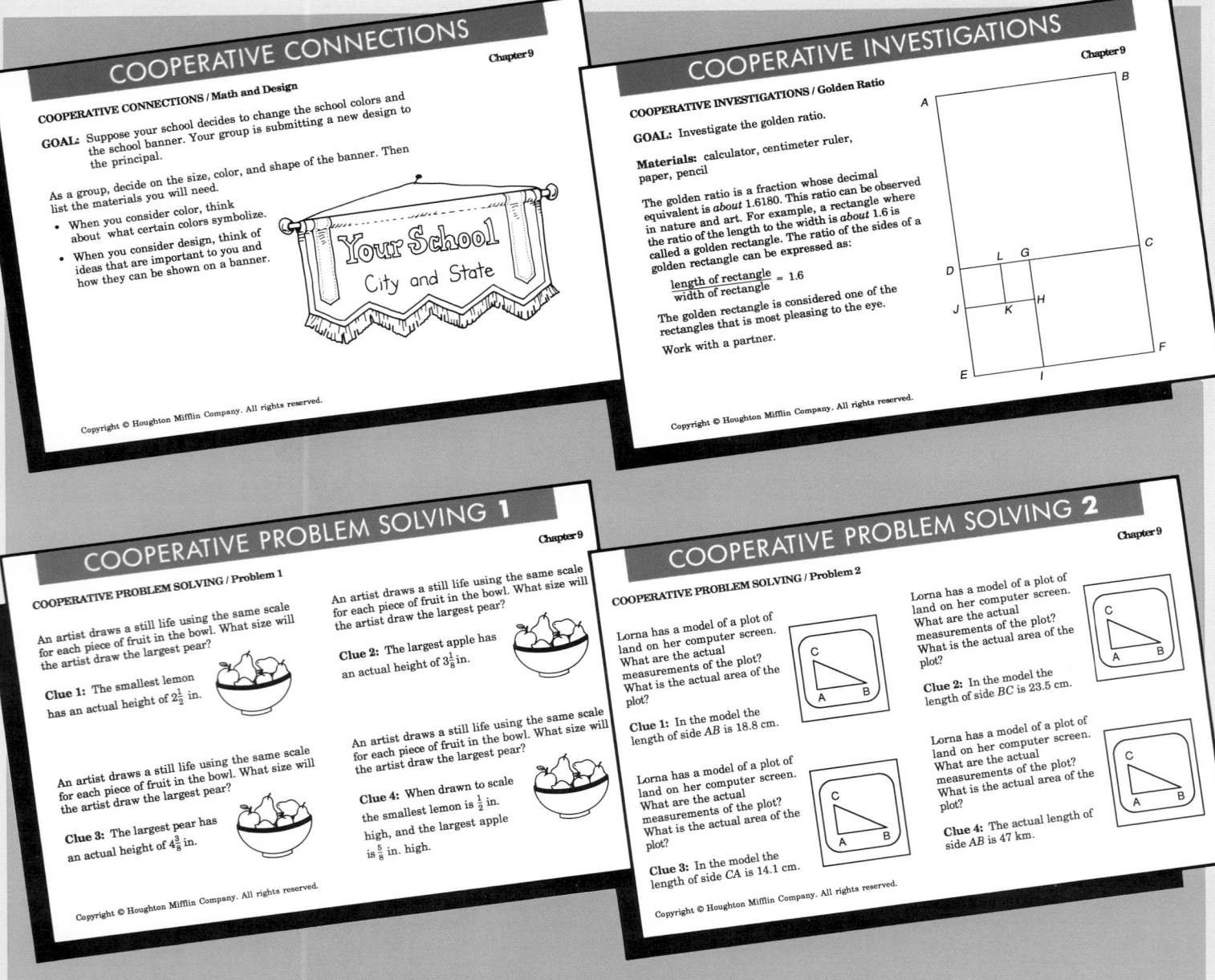

COOPERATIVE CONNECTIONS — Chapter 9

COOPERATIVE CONNECTIONS / Math and Design

GOAL: Suppose your school decides to change the school colors and the school banner. Your group is submitting a new design to the principal.

As a group, decide on the size, color, and shape of the banner. Then list the materials you will need.

- When you consider color, think about what certain colors symbolize.
- When you consider design, think of ideas that are important to you and how they can be shown on a banner.

Your School — City and State

COOPERATIVE INVESTIGATIONS — Chapter 9

COOPERATIVE INVESTIGATIONS / Golden Ratio

GOAL: Investigate the golden ratio.

Materials: calculator, centimeter ruler, paper, pencil

The golden ratio is a fraction whose decimal equivalent is *about* 1.6180. This ratio can be observed in nature and art. For example, a rectangle where the ratio of the length to the width is *about* 1.6 is called a golden rectangle. The ratio of the sides of a golden rectangle can be expressed as:

$$\frac{\text{length of rectangle}}{\text{width of rectangle}} = 1.6$$

The golden rectangle is considered one of the rectangles that is most pleasing to the eye.

Work with a partner.

COOPERATIVE PROBLEM SOLVING 1 — Chapter 9

COOPERATIVE PROBLEM SOLVING / Problem 1

An artist draws a still life using the same scale for each piece of fruit in the bowl. What size will the artist draw the largest pear?

Clue 1: The smallest lemon has an actual height of $2\frac{1}{2}$ in.

An artist draws a still life using the same scale for each piece of fruit in the bowl. What size will the artist draw the largest pear?

Clue 2: The largest apple has an actual height of $3\frac{1}{8}$ in.

An artist draws a still life using the same scale for each piece of fruit in the bowl. What size will the artist draw the largest pear?

Clue 3: The largest pear has an actual height of $4\frac{3}{8}$ in.

An artist draws a still life using the same scale for each piece of fruit in the bowl. What size will the artist draw the largest pear?

Clue 4: When drawn to scale the smallest lemon is $\frac{1}{2}$ in. high, and the largest apple is $\frac{5}{8}$ in. high.

COOPERATIVE PROBLEM SOLVING 2 — Chapter 9

COOPERATIVE PROBLEM SOLVING / Problem 2

Lorna has a model of a plot of land on her computer screen. What are the actual measurements of the plot? What is the actual area of the plot?

Clue 1: In the model the length of side AB is 18.8 cm.

Lorna has a model of a plot of land on her computer screen. What are the actual measurements of the plot? What is the actual area of the plot?

Clue 2: In the model the length of side BC is 23.5 cm.

Lorna has a model of a plot of land on her computer screen. What are the actual measurements of the plot? What is the actual area of the plot?

Clue 3: In the model the length of side CA is 14.1 cm.

Lorna has a model of a plot of land on her computer screen. What are the actual measurements of the plot? What is the actual area of the plot?

Clue 4: The actual length of side AB is 47 km.

GAMES

NAME YOUR TERMS (For use after Lesson 9-5)

Objective: Write and solve proportions.

☑ **MATERIALS CHECKLIST:** three number cubes for each group of four students

Have students form groups of four and two-player teams within each group. Distribute three number cubes to each group.

The first player on Team A tosses the cubes and uses the digits to write a proportion containing a missing term. For example, if the digits from the toss are 2, 4, and 5, a player may write $\frac{2}{5}=\frac{4}{x}$ (other proportions are possible). Players should toss again if doubles or triples appear. Then the player solves the proportion. Other group members check the result; a correct answer is worth one point. Play alternates between a player from Team A and one from Team B. The team with the greatest number of points at the end wins.

WHERE'S THE BOX? (For use after Lesson 9-10)

Objective: Make scale drawings.

☑ **MATERIALS CHECKLIST:** five different-sized boxes; ruler for each student

Choose a large classroom object, say a table, and measure its dimensions. Decide on a scale using centimeters or inches, such as 1 inch : 1 foot. Determine the size of a scale model of your object, and collect five different-sized boxes, one of which provides a good fit for the scale model. Label the boxes A, B, C, D, and E.

To begin play, divide the class into teams of three to five students. Write the name of the object, its dimensions, and the scale on the chalkboard. Display all five boxes. Explain that the goal is to determine the size of the scale model of the object and to decide which box would be the best fit for the scale model. When a team has decided on a box, a team member should present the solution to you. The first team to find the "best" box wins.

BULLETIN BOARD

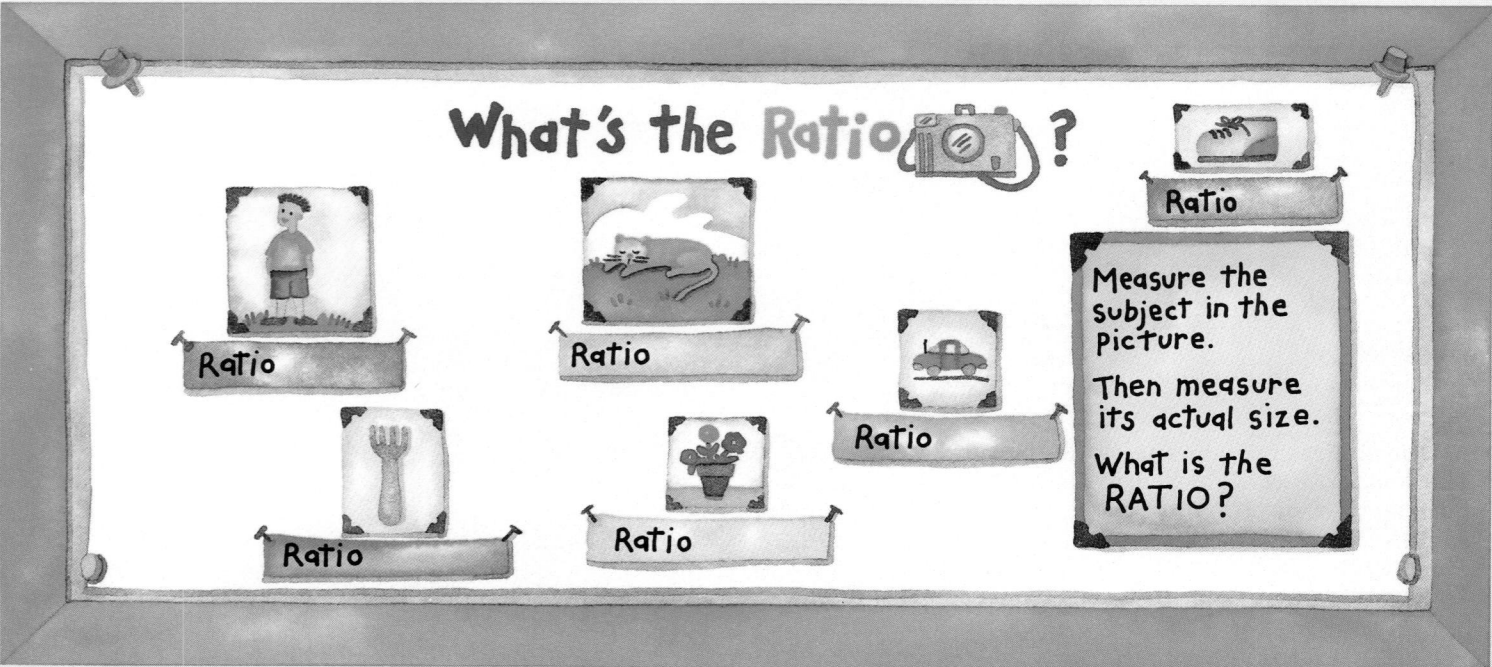

Ask students to bring in photographs. The subjects can be anything or anyone whose actual size can be measured. Tell students to choose two parts of each photo to measure, for example, the width of the face at the nose and the length of the head. Suggest that they select parts that are at least 1 cm in length in the photo. They should measure the corresponding parts on the actual subject and write a ratio comparing the size of the photo to the actual size. Form a display of the photographs and ratios.

Alternative Assessment

Open-ended Problem

The ratio of boys to girls in the Math Club was 1 to 3. There were 8 boys and 24 girls in the club. Through an increase or decrease in membership the ratio changed to 1 to 4. Fewer than 10 students moved into or out of the club. How many boys and how many girls do you think the club has now? Does the club have more or fewer members now?

Teacher Notes
A 1 to 4 ratio belongs to the following family:

$$\frac{1}{4} = \frac{2}{8} = \frac{3}{12} = \frac{4}{16} = \frac{5}{20} = \frac{6}{24} = \frac{7}{28} = \frac{8}{32} = \ldots$$

Possible explanations use one of the following forms of the ratio:

$\frac{5}{20}$, 3 boys and 4 girls left the club. $8 - 3 = 5$, $24 - 4 = 20$

$\frac{6}{24}$, 2 boys left. $8 - 2 = 6$. The number of girls did not change.

$\frac{7}{28}$, 1 boy left and 4 girls joined. $8 - 1 = 7$, $24 + 4 = 28$

$\frac{8}{32}$, The number of boys did not change, but 8 more girls joined.

Group Writing Activity

Study the two families of rectangles. How are they alike and how are they different? (Reproduce these drawings for the students.)

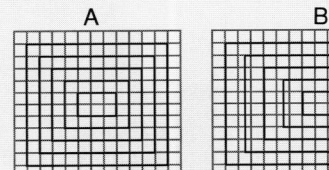

Teacher Notes
Possible observations are:

Alike
- All the angles are right angles, all the sides are perpendicular.
- The smallest rectangle measures 2 units by 3 units.
- Both families have 5 rectangles.
- All the shapes are rectangles.
- The height of each rectangle increases by 2.
- The height is always an even number. (2, 4, 6, 8, 10)

Different
- The shape in A changes to a more square form.
- The ratio of the sides in B remains constant $\left(\frac{2}{3} = \frac{4}{6} = \frac{6}{9} = \frac{8}{12} = \frac{10}{15}\right)$ but the ratio of the sides in A does not remain constant $\left(\frac{2}{3} \neq \frac{4}{5} \neq \frac{6}{7} \neq \frac{8}{9} \neq \frac{10}{11}\right)$.
- The rectangles in B are similar; the rectangles in A are not similar.

Individual Writing Activity

Create a family of squares. How can you decide if all squares are similar?

Teacher Notes
- All squares have 4 sides and 4 right angles.
- The ratio of the sides of squares remains constant. $\frac{1}{1} = \frac{2}{2} = \frac{3}{3} = \frac{4}{4}$

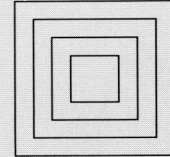

Portfolios

Portfolios can provide information about a student's growth in mathematical understanding over a period of time. They can help you make instructional decisions as well as become a vehicle for communicating with parents. The students' work involving the open-ended problem and writing activity suggested on this page along with work on the In Your Words exercises on pages 279 and 297, the Learning Log exercises on pages 287 and 303, the Write About It exercises on page 289, and the Creative Problem Solving lesson on pages 298-299 could be included in portfolios.

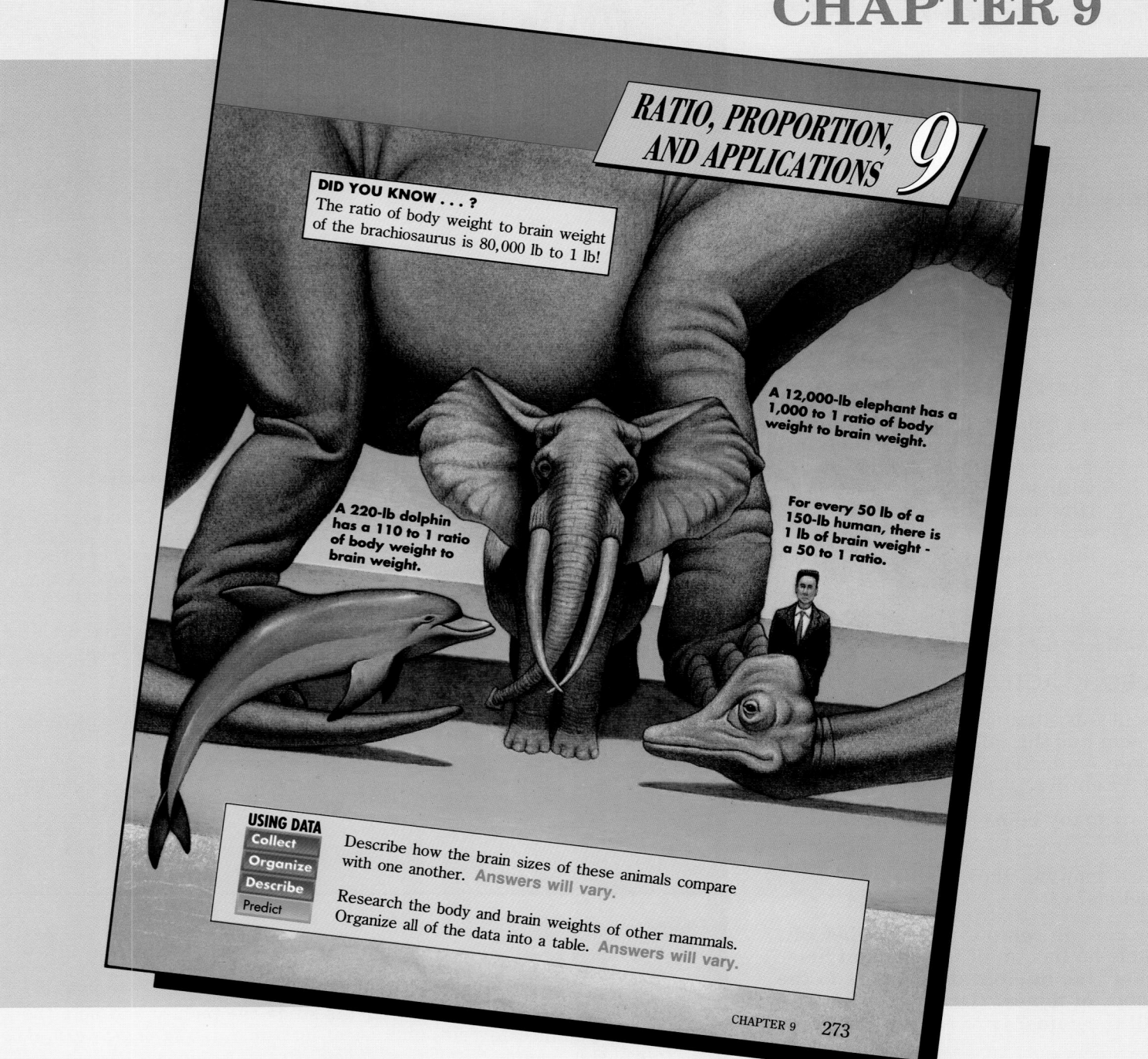

RATIO, PROPORTION, AND APPLICATIONS 9

DID YOU KNOW . . . ?
The ratio of body weight to brain weight of the brachiosaurus is 80,000 lb to 1 lb!

A 12,000-lb elephant has a 1,000 to 1 ratio of body weight to brain weight.

A 220-lb dolphin has a 110 to 1 ratio of body weight to brain weight.

For every 50 lb of a 150-lb human, there is 1 lb of brain weight - a 50 to 1 ratio.

USING DATA
Collect
Organize
Describe
Predict

Describe how the brain sizes of these animals compare with one another. Answers will vary.

Research the body and brain weights of other mammals. Organize all of the data into a table. Answers will vary.

CHAPTER 9 273

Using the Chapter Opener

The purpose of this page is to involve the student in the use of real data much like that presented in newspapers and magazines.

To use this page as you begin the chapter, direct students' attention to the data. You may wish to ask questions such as the following:

Suppose that a Brachiosaurus had weighed 40,000 lb. How much would its brain have weighed? ($\frac{1}{2}$ lb)

How much does the brain of a 220-lb dolphin weigh? (2 lb) **How do you know?** (For every 110 lb of body weight, there is 1 lb of brain weight.)

How much does the brain of a 12,000-lb elephant weigh? (12 lb) **How do you know?** (For every 1,000 lb of body weight, there is 1 lb of brain weight.)

You may wish to use the data collecting and table making activities as cooperative learning situations. Some students may require extra time to complete the assignment.

Lesson Organizer

Objective: Discuss ratio.

Prior Knowledge: Students should know basic division facts to express ratios using least possible numbers.

Error Analysis and Remediation: See page 303A.

Lesson Resources:
Class Activity 9-1
Daily Review 9-1

Two-Minute Math

A chain on a bicycle connects a small gear with 12 teeth on the wheel and a larger gear with 48 teeth on the pedals. How many times will the wheel turn for every turn of the pedals? *(4)*

1 INTRODUCE

SYMBOLIC ACTIVITY

Present this situation:
Kareem has the following coins in his pocket: 1 quarter, 3 dimes, 4 nickels, and 3 pennies.

- **How many coins does he have in all?** *(11)*

- **How many of these coins are nickels?** *(4)*

How can we compare the number of nickels he has to all the coins in his pocket? the number of quarters to the number of dimes? the number of dimes to all the coins? *(4 to 11; 1 to 3; 3 to 11)*

WHEN YOUR STUDENTS ASK
★ WHY AM I LEARNING THIS? ★

You can connect ratios to real life through advertisements. Ratios are often mentioned in advertising slogans, such as "Four out five people prefer Soapy Suds."

Comparatively Speaking

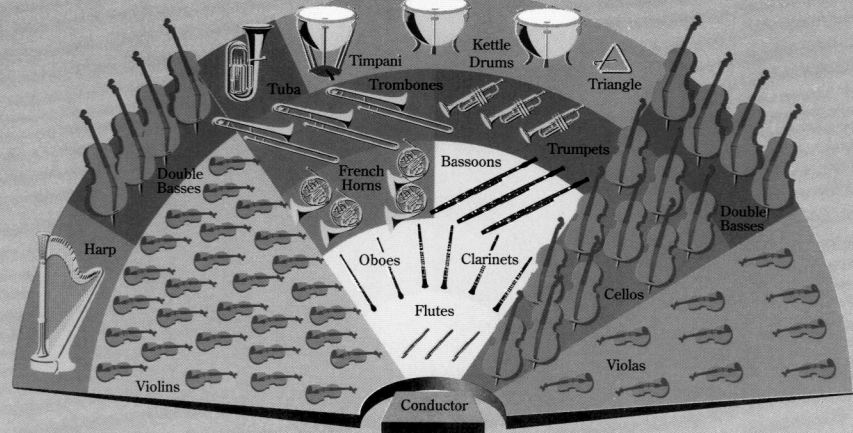

MATH AND MUSIC

What Is Ratio?

📖 READ ABOUT IT

The Boston Pops Symphony Orchestra normally has the instruments shown above.

Several ratios can be written about this orchestra. A **ratio** is a special way of comparing two numbers. Some ratios are shown at right.

Of the 84 musicians, 28 are violinists.
all musicians to violinists ➪ 84 to 28
violinists to all musicians ➪ 28 to 84

There are 3 trumpet players and 1 tuba player.
trumpet players to tuba players ➪ 3 to 1
tuba players to trumpet players ➪ 1 to 3

The cello is about twice as long as the viola.
cello length to viola length ➪ 2 to 1
viola length to cello length ➪ 1 to 2

💬 TALK ABOUT IT

Work with a partner. Use the picture above to help you answer the question.

1. What is the ratio of all the strings to all of the instruments in the orchestra?
   57:84

2. What is the ratio of violas to all of the strings other than violas?
   10:47

---

2 TEACH

READ ABOUT IT   Have students study the picture and note the four different categories of musical instruments. *(Strings: harp, double basses, violins, cellos, and violas; Brass: trombones, trumpets, tuba, and French horns; Woodwinds: bassoons, clarinets, oboes, and flutes; Percussion: timpani, kettle drums, and triangle)*

TALK ABOUT IT   Have pairs of students discuss and solve Exercises 1–11 together. **What is the ratio of woodwinds to all musical instruments using the least possible numbers?** *(1 to 7)* **What is the ratio of clarinets to woodwinds?** *(2 to 12)*

WRITE ABOUT IT   Have partners create questions about ratios for other pairs of students to answer: for example, find a situation that has a ratio of 3 to 1. *(Possible answer: number of woodwinds to number of French horns)*

SUMMARIZE/ASSESS   **In your math class, what is the ratio of students to teacher? boys to girls?** *(Answers will vary.)*

3. What is the ratio of double basses to all string instruments of any type? **8:57**

4. What is the ratio of French horns to clarinets? **4:4**

5. IN YOUR WORDS Describe a situation involving only the woodwinds that has a ratio of 2 to 3. **2 oboes to 3 flutes**

6. What is the ratio of violas to cellos? **10:10**

7. ESTIMATE What is the ratio of the length of a flute to the length of a bassoon? **≈1:3**

To make them easier to interpret, ratios are usually stated using the smallest possible numbers. An example is shown below.

Of 84 musicians, 4 play percussion instruments.
    all instruments to percussion instruments ⇨ 84 to 4
    in smallest possible numbers ⇨ 21 to 1

Solve using the smallest possible numbers.

8. There are 2 kettle drums and 4 percussion instruments in all. What is the ratio of kettle drums to all percussion instruments? **1:2**

9. Describe a situation involving the brass instruments that has a ratio of 1 to 1. **Answers will vary.**

10. What is the ratio of percussion instruments to woodwinds? **1:3**

11. ESTIMATE What is the ratio of the length of a trumpet to the length of a trombone? **≈ 1:2**

WRITE ABOUT IT

Write a paragraph about a musical group you know. Use as many ratios as you can to describe the musicians and their instruments. **Check students' work.**

CHAPTER 9   275

MEETING INDIVIDUAL NEEDS

For Students Who Are . . .

Acquiring English Proficiency Discuss the different families of instruments in an orchestra. Show pictures if possible.

Gifted and Talented Have students create ratio problems using the information at the top of page 274. Students can exchange papers with a partner and solve.

Working 2 or 3 Grades Below Level Explain that to simplify the ratio 84 to 4, one must divide each number by 4 to get 21 to 1.

Having Reading Difficulties Pair students with an able reader to write the paragraph about the musical group.

Today's Problem

A turtle crawled 60 ft during the same time that a rabbit hopped 120 yd. What is the ratio of the distance traveled by the turtle compared to the distance traveled by the rabbit? *(60 ft compared to 120 × 3 or 360 ft; the ratio is 1 to 6.)*

---

3 FOLLOW-UP

CLASS ACTIVITY **9-1**

Have the students work in pairs. Take a survey of the class to find out how many students play a musical instrument; how many play strings; how many play brass; how many play woodwinds; how many play percussion; how many sing in a choir; how many play more than one instrument; and how many neither sing nor play an instrument. Ask each pair to make a table of this information, and then to make up ratios. For example, they may make up a ratio that shows the number of students who play brass to the total number who play an instrument.

Lesson Organizer

Objective: Explore the meaning of ratio.

Prior Knowledge: Students should know what a ratio is and how to write equivalent fractions.

Lesson Resources:
Class Activity 9-2
Daily Review 9-2

 **Two-Minute Math**

Find the ratio of any place value in our system to:
the place to its right. *(10 to 1)*
two places to its right. *(100 to 1)*
three places to its right. *(1,000 to 1)*

1 PREPARE

CONNECTING ACTIVITY

☑ **MATERIALS CHECKLIST:** pattern blocks or Teaching Aid 12 (Pattern Blocks) for each group

Have students work in groups of 4 or 5. Name ratios for students to model with the pattern blocks. Call on different groups to describe their models to the class. For example: **Use the blocks to show a ratio of 3 to 2.** *(Possible description: We have 3 triangles and 2 squares. The ratio of triangles to squares is 3 to 2.)*

WHEN YOUR STUDENTS ASK
★ WHY AM I LEARNING THIS? ★

You can connect this skill to real life through cooking. A chef uses ratios every day. For example, to prepare nut bread, the ratio of flour to chopped walnuts is 16 to 4, or 4 to 1.

 EXPLORE

Exploring Ratios

Refer to the colored pattern block polygons at the right.

The ratio of red to green is 5 to 4. You can also write the ratio using the ratio sign, 5:4, or as a quotient (fraction), $\frac{5}{4}$.

Write the ratio for the polygons at the right as a quotient and using the ratio sign.

1. red to yellow $\frac{5}{3}$; 5:3
2. green to all polygons $\frac{4}{12}$; 4:12

Solve.

3. Which polygons at the right have a ratio of 4:5? 12:5? 3:4? $\frac{3}{12}$? green:red; all:red; yellow:green; yellow:all

4. Is 12 to 5 the ratio of red polygons to all polygons? Why or why not? no; It is 5 to 12.

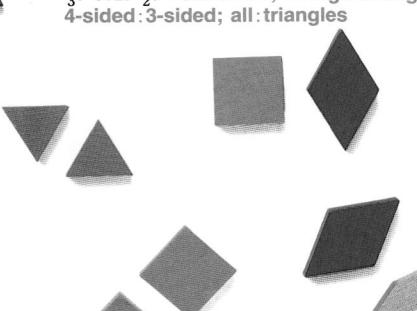

Use the polygons at the left to write the ratio.

5. triangles to squares 2:3

6. squares to all polygons 3:8

7. Which polygons have a ratio of 1:8? $\frac{3}{3}$? 6:2? $\frac{8}{2}$? natural:all; orange:orange 4-sided:3-sided; all:triangles

The triangles and the remaining polygons above have been grouped in sets of 2 at the right.

8. Write the ratio of sets of 2 triangles to all sets of 2. 1:4

Two equally good ways of showing the ratio of triangles to all polygons are 2:8 and 1:4. Such ratios are called **equal ratios**.

276 LESSON 9–2

2 EXPLORE

☑ **MATERIALS CHECKLIST:** pattern blocks or Teaching Aid 12, Pattern Blocks, Math Connection Transparency

Use the blocks on the overhead projector to model several equivalent ratios. For example, display 6 triangles and 9 quadrilaterals. **What is the ratio of triangles to quadrilaterals?** *(6 to 9)* **Can you rearrange the triangles into sets of three?** *(yes)* **the quadrilaterals?** *(yes)* Arrange both into sets of three. **What is another way to describe the ratio of triangles to quadrilaterals?** *(2 to 3)*

Display the transparency. **What math connections can be made to find equal ratios?** *(Finding equal ratios is like finding equivalent fractions.)*

SUMMARIZE/ASSESS Of 14 books you have read, 6 are novels. Write the ratio of novels to books in three different ways. *(6 to 14; 6:14; $\frac{6}{14}$)* **What is the ratio in lowest terms?** *($\frac{3}{7}$)*

Use the 12 rhombuses and the 6 triangles at the right to answer.

9. What is the ratio of triangles
to rhombuses? **6:12**

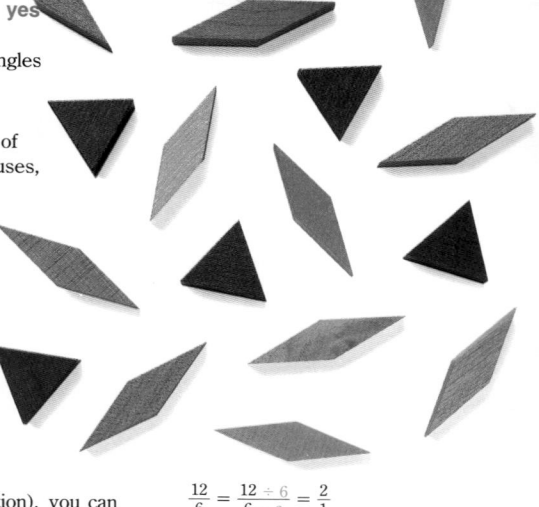

10. Can both the triangles and the
rhombuses be put into sets of 2? **yes**

11. What is the ratio of sets of 2 triangles
to sets of 2 rhombuses? **3:6**

Since $\frac{6}{12}$ and $\frac{3}{6}$ are equally good ways of
stating the ratio of triangles to rhombuses,
they are equal ratios.

12. Arrange the polygons to show
that $\frac{2}{4}$ and $\frac{1}{2}$ can also be used to
describe the ratio of triangles
to rhombuses. **Arrange
in sets of 3, then sets of 6.**

13. The ratio of triangles to all
polygons in the set is $\frac{6}{18}$. Use
the polygons to find three other
equal ratios comparing the
triangles to all polygons.
$\frac{3}{9}, \frac{2}{6}, \frac{1}{3}$

If you write a ratio as a quotient (fraction), you can
divide to find an equal ratio in lowest terms.

$$\frac{12}{6} = \frac{12 \div 6}{6 \div 6} = \frac{2}{1}$$

Write as a ratio in lowest terms.

14. $\frac{12}{4}$ $\frac{3}{1}$ **15.** 8 to 12 $\frac{2}{3}$ **16.** 9:12 $\frac{3}{4}$ **17.** 24 to 36 $\frac{2}{3}$ **18.** 10:100 $\frac{1}{10}$ **19.** 8.5 to 17 $\frac{1}{2}$

> **A _proportion_ is a statement that two ratios are equal.**

Since you know how to multiply or divide to write an equivalent fraction,
you can make a 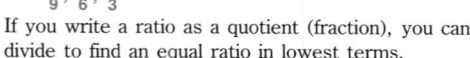 to work with a proportion.

Do the two ratios make a proportion? Choose = or ≠.

20. $\frac{4}{8}$ ▓ $\frac{1}{3}$ ≠   **21.** $\frac{12}{36}$ ▓ $\frac{1}{3}$ =   **22.** $\frac{17}{51}$ ▓ $\frac{1}{3}$ =   **23.** $\frac{4}{8}$ ▓ $\frac{6}{12}$ =

Copy and complete the proportion.

24. $\frac{1}{3} = \frac{\equiv}{12}$ 4   **25.** $\frac{12}{48} = \frac{1}{\equiv}$ 4   **26.** $\frac{10}{50} = \frac{1}{\equiv}$ 5   **27.** $\frac{14}{42} = \frac{\equiv}{6}$ 2

CLASS ACTIVITY **9-2**

Have the students work in groups of four
or five. Give each group a set of index
cards on which you have written questions
such as the following: How many of you
prefer math class to English class? How
many prefer watching football to watching
baseball? How many would prefer a slice
of pizza instead of a sandwich for lunch?
(Or, you may wish to use questions about
current events.) Have the groups compile
answers to each question and record the
results as ratios. For example, $\frac{3}{5}$ prefer
math. Then have the groups combine their
results. Ask each group to tell whether
the group's ratio and the class's ratio
make a proportion.

MEETING INDIVIDUAL NEEDS

For Students Who Are . . .

Acquiring English Proficiency Work with students in a group as
they take turns reading the problems aloud and explaining the
answers.

Gifted and Talented Have students try to find an easy way to tell
if a pair of ratios is a proportion. (Find cross products.) They can use
their method to check answers to Exercises 25–28.

Working 2 or 3 Grades Below Level Have students use pages
36–39 of the Skills Workbook for Equations, Ratio, Proportion, and
Percent.

Having Reading Difficulties Review the meanings of _polygon, triangle, square,_ and _rhombus._

Today's Problem

Harry walked for 3 h 15 min. Eileen walked for 3 h 45 min. What is
the ratio of his time in hours to that of her time in hours? What is
the ratio of his time in minutes to that of hers in minutes?
(_in hours:_ $3\frac{1}{4}/3\frac{3}{4} = \left(\frac{13}{4}\right)/\left(\frac{15}{4}\right) = \frac{13}{15}$; _in minutes:_ $\frac{195}{225} = \frac{13}{15}$)

Lesson Organizer

Objective: Explore proportional thinking.

Prior Knowledge: Students should know the meaning of ratio and equivalent fractions.

Lesson Resources:
Class Activity 9-3
Daily Review 9-3

Two-Minute Math

Write the ratios for your class:
teacher to students;
boys to teacher;
girls to boys;
girls to students.

1 PREPARE

SYMBOLIC ACTIVITY

Present the following problem:
A recipe that makes 3 quarts of fruit punch calls for 2 cups of orange juice. What is the ratio of orange juice to fruit punch? *(2 c to 3 qt.)* **You use 4 c of juice to make 6 qt. of punch. What is the ratio of orange juice to punch?** *(4 c to 6 qt.)* **Do these two ratios make a proportion?** *(Yes.)*

WHEN YOUR STUDENTS ASK
★ WHY AM I LEARNING THIS? ★

You can connect ideas from this lesson to the legislative branch of our government. Proportional thinking and population figures are used to determine how many representatives are sent to the House of Representatives by each state.

Exploring Proportional Thinking

Commuters in China make good use of bicycles. In fact, for every 10 cars in China, there are 2,500 bicycles. That means that for every 1 car there are 250 bicycles.

You are using proportional thinking when you say, "10 cars is to 2,500 bicycles as 1 car is to 250 bicycles."

1. Write the proportion above using two ratio signs. Repeat writing the ratios as quotients.
   $10:2{,}500$; $1:250$; $\frac{10}{2{,}500}$, $\frac{1}{250}$

You use proportional thinking to read and to make graphs. The pictograph shows how students get to school.

Commuters in Beijing, China

2. What ratio of faces to students was used to make the pictograph? $1:25$

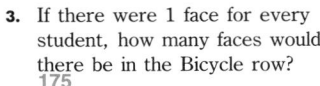

How Students Get to School	
Walk	☺☺☺☺
Bicycle	☺☺☺☺☺☺☺

1 ☺ = 25 students

3. If there were 1 face for every student, how many faces would there be in the Bicycle row? 175

4. How many faces are there in the Walk row? How many students does that represent? 4; 100

You use proportional thinking to compare pairs of ratios. Can the two ratios form a proportion? Write *yes* or *no*.

5. 3 bicycles is to 6 pedals, 1 bicycle is to 2 pedals yes

6. 3 is to 6, 6 is to 9 no   7. 4:5, 28:33 no   8. $\frac{4}{5}$, $\frac{28}{35}$ yes

9. **IN YOUR WORDS** Explain how you compared the ratios in Exercises 7 and 8. Answers will vary. Suggestion given.
   $28 \div 4 = 7$ but $33 \div 5 \neq 7$; $28 \div 4 = 7$ and $35 \div 5 = 7$

2 EXPLORE

Assign students to mixed ability groups of three or four.

Suppose one face represented 10 students. How many walked? rode bicycles? *(40 walked; 70 bicycled)*

After students complete Exercise 8, have them restate the math connection made in the previous lesson and explain how it relates to proportional thinking. *(When ratios are written as quotients you can use equivalent fractions to work with proportions.)*

SUMMARIZE/ASSESS Use proportional thinking to determine who did better shooting baskets at the game: Joan, who scored 8 for 24 attempts, or Jill, who was 5 for 12. *(Write ratios as quotients and compare; Jill did better.)*

Use proportional thinking to rearrange the four numbers into a proportion. **Answers will vary. Suggestions given.**

10. 1, 4, 20, $5\frac{1}{4} = \frac{5}{20}$ **11.** 1, 2, 12, $6\frac{1}{2} = \frac{6}{12}$ **12.** 6, 7, 28, 24 $\frac{6}{24} = \frac{7}{28}$ **13.** 2, 12, 18, 3 $\frac{2}{3} = \frac{12}{18}$

You use proportional thinking to write a proportion equation and make a table.

In rural China, there are about 4 bicycles to every 5 households, or 8 bicycles to every ▥ households. Think: 4 is to 5 as 8 is to ▥? **10**

$\frac{4}{5} = \frac{8}{▥}$ ⟹ Double 4 to get 8, so double the 5. ⟹ $\frac{4}{5} = \frac{8}{10}$

Copy and complete the table.

14.

Households	5	10	20	40
Bicycles	4	8	▥ 16	▥ 32

15.

			30	
Bicycles	1	10	▥	40
Wheels	2	▥ 20	60	▥ 80

In China's cities there are about 8 bicycles to every 5 households. That's a ratio of 8:5.

16. IN YOUR WORDS Are the ratios 8:5 and 40:30 proportional? Explain. **no; $\frac{8}{5} \neq \frac{40}{30}$**

17. Use the 8:5 ratio to make a table for 8, 16, 24, 32, 40, and 48 bicycles.

8	16	24	32	40	48
5	10	15	20	25	30

Yai Yee rode her bicycle for 18 mi in 3 h.

$\frac{18 \text{ mi}}{3 \text{ h}}$ — The ratio, $\frac{18 \text{ mi}}{3 \text{ h}}$, is called a rate because miles are compared to hours.

> **A rate compares two quantities of different kinds.**

You use proportional thinking when you change the ratio to lowest terms and say, "18 mi is to 3 h as 6 mi is to 1 h."

$\frac{18 \text{ mi}}{3 \text{ h}} = \frac{6 \text{ mi}}{1 \text{ h}}$ — The ratio, $\frac{6 \text{ mi}}{1 \text{ h}}$, is called a unit rate. In short form, we write 6 mi/h.

> **A ratio of a quantity to 1 is called a _unit rate_.**

MENTAL MATH Use proportional thinking to solve mentally.

18. A motorbike travels at the rate of 36 mi/gal of gas. At this rate, how many miles would the motorbike travel on 10 gal of gas? **360 mi**

19. In a 20-mi bicycle race, Kim traveled at a speed of 5 mi/h. At that rate, how long did she take to complete the race? **4 h**

> **CLASS ACTIVITY 9-3**

☑ **MATERIALS CHECKLIST:** $8\frac{1}{2} \times 11''$ scratch paper, envelopes, stopwatches

Show the students how to fold a business letter: Fold the bottom third up, then fold the top third down. Place the piece of paper in an envelope and seal the envelope. Have the students work in pairs. Ask one partner to fold as many "letters" and stuff as many envelopes as possible in 20 sec. The other partner is the timer. Have partners trade roles and repeat the activity. Ask them to find the number of envelopes they could stuff in 1 min by using proportional thinking. Have each pair compare its time with those of other pairs.

MEETING INDIVIDUAL NEEDS

For Students Who Are . . .

Acquiring English Proficiency Define the word _commuter_. Ask why there are so many bicycles in China.

Gifted and Talented Have students survey their classmates to obtain a set of data. They can use the data to create a pictograph, writing the ratio used in the pictograph at the bottom of the graph.

Working 2 or 3 Grades Below Level Help students find the patterns in Exercises 14 and 15. Have students use pages 40–43 of the Skills Workbook for Equations, Ratio, Proportion, and Percent.

Having Reading Difficulties Remind students that _mental math_ refers to calculating without paper and pencil.

Today's Problem

Are people's weights proportional to their heights? (_No; if they were then two people of the same height would weigh the same._)

Lesson Organizer

Objective: Solve a proportion.

Prior Knowledge: Students should be able to write proportions and work with equivalent fractions.

Lesson Resources:
Practice Worksheet 9-4
Reteaching Worksheet 9-4
Enrichment Activity 9-4
Daily Review 9-4
Cooperative Problem Solving 1, Chapter 9

Two-Minute Math

Write an equivalent fraction with a denominator of 36.

$\frac{1}{2}$ $\frac{1}{9}$ $\frac{2}{3}$ $\frac{3}{4}$ $\frac{8}{72}$

$\left(\frac{18}{36}, \frac{4}{36}, \frac{24}{36}, \frac{27}{36}, \frac{4}{36}\right)$

1 INTRODUCE

SYMBOLIC ACTIVITY

1. Write $\frac{2}{5} = \frac{n}{20}$. **Solve the equation for** *n*. *(n = 8)* **How can you check that your answer is correct?** *(Substitute 8 for n; $\frac{2}{5}$ and $\frac{8}{20}$ are equivalent)*

2. **Solve these equations:** $\frac{4}{3} = \frac{2}{n}$ **and** $\frac{24}{36} = \frac{2}{n}$. *(n = 1.5; n = 3)*

WHEN YOUR STUDENTS ASK
★ WHY AM I LEARNING THIS? ★

You can use this skill to solve real life problems. For example, to maintain a ratio of 8 to 1 on the front and rear gears of a bicycle, how many teeth are needed on the rear sprocket if the front sprocket has 96?

MATH AND ART

Solving Proportions

In the proportion at the right, the arrows show the **cross products** 4×9 and 6×6.

$$\frac{4}{6} \bowtie \frac{6}{9}$$

THINK ALOUD Multiply the cross products. What do you notice?

> **The *cross products* of a proportion are equal.**

CRITICAL THINKING Can a proportion be written for the two ratios? If so, write it.

$\frac{2}{16}$ and $\frac{3}{24}$ $\frac{2}{16} = \frac{3}{24}$ $\frac{3}{4}$ and $\frac{2}{3}$ **no** $\frac{21}{9}$ and $\frac{14}{6}$ $\frac{21}{9} = \frac{14}{6}$

You use proportional thinking to write a proportion and you use cross products to solve for an unknown.

The purple at the right is a mixture of 8 parts red and 6 parts blue. How many parts red are needed to make this purple if 12 parts blue are used?

Use proportional thinking to set up the proportion. Let *n* represent the number of red parts.

8 red is to 6 blue   as *n* red is to 12 blue.

$$8:6 \text{ as } n:12$$

$$\frac{\text{red}}{\text{blue}} \longrightarrow \frac{8}{6} = \frac{n}{12} \longleftarrow \frac{\text{red}}{\text{blue}}$$

$6n = 8 \times 12$ ⟨ Use the cross products to solve.

$6n = 96$

$\frac{6n}{6} = \frac{96}{6}$

$n = 16$

$\frac{8}{6} = \frac{16}{12}$ ⟨ Check by substituting 16 for *n*.

$8 \times 12 = 6 \times 16$

$96 = 96$ ✔   8 ⊠ 12 ÷ 6 = 16

Sixteen parts red are needed to make the purple.

═══════════ **GUIDED PRACTICE** ═══════════

Use cross products to choose = or ≠.

1. $\frac{4}{7} ▦ \frac{5}{8}$ ≠   2. $\frac{15}{12} ▦ \frac{20}{16}$ =   3. $\frac{7}{9} ▦ \frac{5}{7}$ ≠   4. $\frac{5}{16} ▦ \frac{2}{5}$ ≠

Calculators should be available for tedious calculations.

2 TEACH

✓ MATERIALS CHECKLIST: Calculators

Write $\frac{6}{10} = \frac{12}{n}$ and $\frac{6}{10} = \frac{n}{12}$ on the chalkboard, and have students solve.

Why is the solution to the first proportion the same as the one in the lesson, but the solution to the second proportion different? *(In the second proportion the order is not the same in both ratios.)*

> **Chalkboard Examples**
>
> Solve for *n*.
>
> $\frac{4}{5} = \frac{16}{n}$ *(n = 20)*
>
> $\frac{8}{5} = \frac{n}{30}$ *(n = 48)*
>
> $\frac{51}{17} = \frac{n}{1}$ *(n = 3)*

SUMMARIZE/ASSESS   What math connections help you solve proportions? *(You can solve proportions if you know how to use multiplication and division to solve equations.)*

Solve. Check your answer.

5. $\frac{3}{4} = \frac{x}{20}$ 15   **6.** $\frac{4}{x} = \frac{8}{5}$ 2.5   **7.** $\underset{\text{pounds}}{\text{cost}} \rightarrow \frac{\$5.99}{7} = \frac{x}{12} \leftarrow \underset{\text{pounds}}{\text{cost}}$ $10.27

========================= PRACTICE =========================

Use cross products. Choose = or ≠.

8. $\frac{11}{20} \blacksquare \frac{1}{2}$ ≠   **9.** $\frac{18}{10} \blacksquare \frac{27}{15}$ =   **10.** $\frac{4}{18} \blacksquare \frac{10}{45}$ =   **11.** $\frac{7}{8} \blacksquare \frac{4}{5}$ ≠

Solve the proportion. Use pencil and paper or a calculator.

12. $\frac{3}{8} = \frac{15}{x}$ 40   **13.** $\frac{3}{4} = \frac{r}{16}$ 12   **14.** $\frac{12}{15} = \frac{x}{45}$ 36   **15.** $\frac{7}{15} = \frac{14}{a}$ 30

16. $\frac{m}{10} = \frac{1}{2}$ 5   **17.** $\frac{15}{2} = \frac{x}{8}$ 60   **18.** $\frac{24}{8} = \frac{12}{n}$ 4   **19.** $\frac{6}{12} = \frac{9}{d}$ 18

20. $\frac{14}{16} = \frac{35}{x}$ 40   **21.** $\frac{5}{12} = \frac{c}{30}$ 12.5   **22.** $\frac{4}{6} = \frac{5}{p}$ 7.5   **23.** $\frac{1}{4} = \frac{5}{f}$ 20

24. $\frac{5}{b} = \frac{2}{7}$ 17.5   **25.** $\frac{16}{x} = \frac{2}{3}$ 24   **26.** $\frac{5}{8} = \frac{2}{t}$ 3.2   **27.** $\frac{1}{5} = \frac{q}{16}$ 3.2

CALCULATOR   Solve.

28. $\frac{3.7}{x} = \frac{11.1}{9}$ 3   **29.** $\frac{5.6}{7.2} = \frac{2.8}{t}$ 3.6   **30.** $\frac{4.2}{x} = \frac{9}{10.5}$ 4.9   **31.** $\frac{u}{0.99} = \frac{1.35}{2.43}$ 0.55

===================== PROBLEM SOLVING =====================

Choose the proportion. Solve the problem.

32. The orange color at the right uses 13 parts yellow and 3 parts warm red. How many parts yellow are needed if 24 parts warm red are used?

   a. $\frac{13}{3} = \frac{24}{x}$ **b.** $\frac{13}{3} = \frac{x}{24}$ b; 104

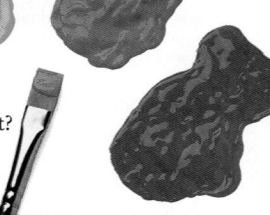

33. Paint costs $3.96/fl oz. At that rate, what does $1\frac{1}{4}$ fl oz cost?

   a. $\frac{\$3.96}{1} = \frac{1.25}{x}$ **b.** $\frac{\$3.96}{1} = \frac{x}{1.25}$ b; $4.95

Estimate

You can use compatible numbers to estimate the unknown in a proportion.

$$\frac{9}{34} = \frac{n}{12} \quad \Rightarrow \quad \frac{1}{4} = \frac{n}{12} \quad \Rightarrow \quad 1 \text{ is to } 4 \text{ as } n \text{ is to } 12. \qquad n \approx 3$$

Accept reasonable estimates.
Use compatible numbers to estimate the value of the variable. **Suggestions given.**

1. $\frac{7}{15} = \frac{x}{2}$ ≈1   **2.** $\frac{8}{13} = \frac{2}{x}$ ≈3   **3.** $\frac{n}{11} = \frac{5}{21}$ ≈2.5   **4.** $\frac{4}{9} = \frac{n}{44}$ ≈20

CHAPTER 9   281

MEETING INDIVIDUAL NEEDS
For Students Who Are . . .

Acquiring English Proficiency   In the Problem Solving exercises, stress that the order in which the ratios are written must be the same.

Gifted and Talented   Have students solve these proportions.
$\frac{4}{5}/0.9 = \frac{x}{8}$ *(40)* $\frac{0.005}{n} = \frac{1.4}{0.28}$ *(0.001)* $n : 2\frac{2}{3} = 12 : \frac{2}{3}$ *(48)*

Working 2 or 3 Grades Below Level   Suggest students draw in the arrows to show the cross products. (✗) Have students use pages 46–49 of the Skills Workbook for Equations, Ratio, Proportion, and Percent.

Having Reading Difficulties   Review the concept of compatible numbers for the Estimate exercises.

Today's Problem

In one day, it is estimated that about two hundred Americans become millionaires. At this rate, how many Americans become millionaires a year? *(about 365 × 200, or 73,000 a year)*

PRACTICE 9-4

Use cross products to choose = or ≠.

1. $\frac{5}{15} \boxed{=} \frac{1}{3}$ **2.** $\frac{5}{42} \boxed{≠} \frac{9}{16}$ **3.** $\frac{5}{7} \boxed{≠} \frac{3}{21}$ **4.** $\frac{21}{90} \boxed{=} \frac{7}{30}$

Solve the proportion. Check your answer.

5. $\frac{2}{5} = \frac{8}{x}$ x = 20   **6.** $\frac{4}{9} = \frac{x}{36}$ x = 16   **7.** $\frac{12}{5} = \frac{x}{10}$ x = 24   **8.** $\frac{x}{9} = \frac{12}{18}$ x = 6

9. $\frac{3}{21} = \frac{x}{7}$ x = 1   **10.** $\frac{12}{32} = \frac{30}{x}$ x = 80   **11.** $\frac{6}{20} = \frac{x}{30}$ x = 9   **12.** $\frac{6}{34} = \frac{9}{x}$ x = 51

13. $\frac{1}{10} = \frac{10}{x}$ x = 100   **14.** $\frac{9}{x} = \frac{18}{50}$ x = 25   **15.** $\frac{x}{7} = \frac{4}{28}$ x = 1   **16.** $\frac{3}{16} = \frac{6}{x}$ x = 32

17. $\underset{\text{hours}}{\text{dollars}} \rightarrow \frac{\$20}{1} = \frac{x}{8} \leftarrow \underset{\text{hours}}{\text{dollars}}$ x = $160   **18.** $\underset{\text{cars}}{\text{people}} \rightarrow \frac{6}{1} = \frac{78}{x} \leftarrow \underset{\text{cars}}{\text{people}}$ x = 13 cars

Use paper and pencil to solve.

19. $\frac{x}{6.5} = \frac{4}{26}$ x = 1   **20.** $\frac{2.8}{x} = \frac{14}{55}$ x = 11   **21.** $\frac{17}{19.5} = \frac{x}{3.9}$ x = 3.4   **22.** $\frac{5.49}{10.2} = \frac{1.83}{x}$ x = 3.4

Solve.

23. A gallon of milk costs $1.60. At that rate, how much does a quart cost? $.40

24. A milk shake can be made with 1 scoop of ice cream and 2 cups of milk. You have 14 cups of milk. How many scoops of ice cream do you need?   7 scoops

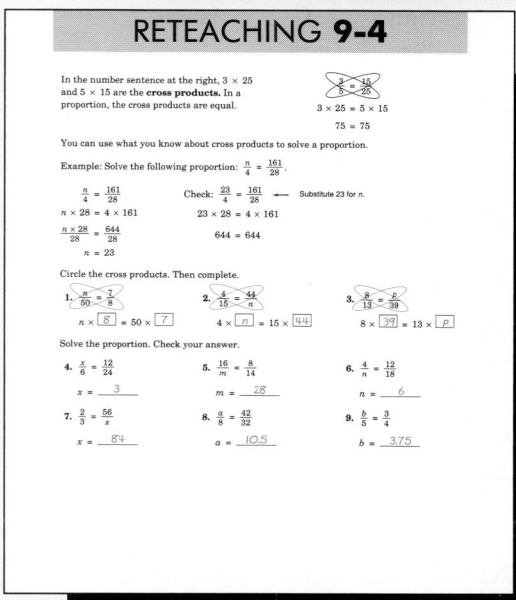

RETEACHING 9-4

In the number sentence at the right, 3 × 25 and 5 × 15 are the **cross products**. In a proportion, the cross products are equal.

$$3 \times 25 = 5 \times 15$$
$$75 = 75$$

You can use what you know about cross products to solve a proportion.

Example: Solve the following proportion: $\frac{n}{4} = \frac{161}{28}$.

$\frac{n}{4} = \frac{161}{28}$ Check: $\frac{23}{4} = \frac{161}{28}$ ← Substitute 23 for n.

$n \times 28 = 4 \times 161$ $23 \times 28 = 4 \times 161$

$\frac{n \times 28}{28} = \frac{644}{28}$ $644 = 644$

$n = 23$

Circle the cross products. Then complete.

1. $\frac{n}{50} = \frac{7}{8}$ $n \times \boxed{8} = 50 \times \boxed{7}$ **2.** $\frac{4}{15} = \frac{44}{n}$ $4 \times \boxed{n} = 15 \times \boxed{44}$ **3.** $\frac{8}{13} = \frac{p}{39}$ $8 \times \boxed{39} = 13 \times \boxed{p}$

Solve the proportion. Check your answer.

4. $\frac{x}{6} = \frac{12}{24}$ x = 3   **5.** $\frac{16}{m} = \frac{8}{14}$ m = 28   **6.** $\frac{4}{n} = \frac{12}{18}$ n = 6

7. $\frac{2}{3} = \frac{56}{x}$ x = 84   **8.** $\frac{a}{8} = \frac{42}{32}$ a = 10.5   **9.** $\frac{b}{5} = \frac{3}{4}$ b = 3.75

ENRICHMENT 9-4

✓ **MATERIALS CHECKLIST:** Index cards

Have the students work in pairs. Provide each pair with a set of cards on which you have written ratios such as $\frac{5}{6}, \frac{25}{30}, \frac{2}{3}, \frac{6}{9}, \frac{12}{7}, \frac{36}{21}, \frac{1}{9}, \frac{4}{36}, \frac{2}{7}, \frac{14}{49}, \frac{5}{12}, \frac{25}{60}, \frac{3}{8}, \frac{18}{48}, \frac{8}{15}, \frac{24}{75}$. Have the students mix the cards and place them face down in a pile. Each partner takes six cards. Tell the students that the winner is the first to get three pairs of ratios that could make a proportion. Player 1 draws a card and begins a discard pile by placing a card from his or her hand face up next to the original pile. Player 2 chooses a card from either pile to continue the game. Players continue drawing and discarding until one has three proportions.

LESSON 9-5

Lesson Organizer

Objective: Write a proportion.

Prior Knowledge: Students should understand the concepts of ratio and equivalent fractions.

Error Analysis and Remediation: See page 303A.

Lesson resources:
Practice Worksheet 9-5
Reteaching Worksheet 9-5
Enrichment Activity 9-5
Daily Review 9-5
Cooperative Investigations, Chapter 9

Two-Minute Math

Decide whether each is a proportion.

$\frac{6}{9} = \frac{9}{12}$ *(no)*

4:6 = 20:36 *(no)*

8 to 2 and 4 to 1 *(yes)*

1 INTRODUCE

CONNECTING ACTIVITY

MATERIALS CHECKLIST: pattern blocks

1. Have students suggest a ratio such as 4:3.
2. Ask a volunteer to use pattern blocks to model the ratio on the overhead projector.
3. **Name some ratios equivalent to the model.** *(Possible answers: 8:6 or 20:15)*

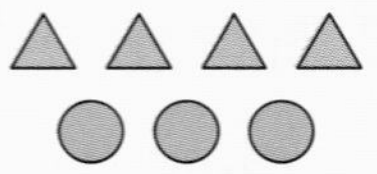

4. Repeat with other ratios.

WHEN YOUR STUDENTS ASK
★ WHY AM I LEARNING THIS? ★

You can use proportions and rates to solve everyday problems. For example, if a car averages 27 mi/gal, about how many gallons would be needed for a 520-mi trip? *(about 20 gal)*

MATH AND HISTORY

Writing Proportions

In 1932, Amelia Earhart became the first woman to fly solo across the Atlantic Ocean. She flew 2,026 mi, from Newfoundland to Ireland, at a speed of 135 mi/h. At that speed, how many hours did her transatlantic flight take?

Let x represent the flight time in hours.

Think: 2,026 mi is to x as 135 mi is to 1 h.

$$2{,}026 : x = 135 : 1$$

$$\frac{\text{miles}}{\text{hours}} \rightarrow \frac{2{,}026}{x} = \frac{135}{1} \leftarrow \frac{\text{miles}}{\text{hours}}$$

Keep the order in each ratio the same.

$$135x = 2{,}026 \times 1$$

Use cross products to solve.

$$\frac{135x}{135} = \frac{2{,}026}{135}$$

$$x = 15.007$$

Amelia Earhart's transatlantic flight took about 15 h.

THINK ALOUD How would you check your answer? **Insert answer in original proportion and cross multiply.**

CRITICAL THINKING Explain why the speed, 135 mi/h, is also called a unit rate. **It is a ratio of 135 mi to 1 h and compares different things, i.e., miles to hours.**

GUIDED PRACTICE

Copy and complete the proportion.

1. The fastest time in which a glider has flown 625 mi is about 7 h. How many miles is that per hour? **≈89**

$$\frac{\text{miles}}{\text{hours}} \rightarrow \frac{625}{7} = \frac{\blacksquare}{1} \leftarrow \frac{\text{miles}}{\text{hour}}$$

2. **CRITICAL THINKING** Which proportion does *not* represent the problem at the right? Why? Now solve the problem.

In 1908, Glen Curtis flew an airplane 5,090 ft at a speed of 50 ft/s. How many seconds did the flight last?

a. $\frac{5{,}090}{1} = \frac{\blacksquare}{50}$ **b.** $\frac{5{,}090}{\blacksquare} = \frac{50}{1}$

a; It is not 5,090 ft/s; 101.8 s

MULTICULTURAL NOTE

Earhart was the first woman to receive the Distinguished Flying Cross, awarded by the U.S. Congress. She attempted to fly around the world, but she disappeared over the Pacific Ocean.

2 TEACH

Why is it important to keep the order the same in both ratios? *(The order must be the same to have a proportion.)*

Write $\frac{12}{120} = \frac{6}{x}$. **What other ways could these ratios be set up to have a proportion?** $\left(\frac{120}{12} = \frac{x}{6}, \frac{12}{6} = \frac{120}{x}, \frac{6}{12} = \frac{x}{120}\right)$ Repeat the question for the ratios related to the Earhart flight.

Chalkboard Examples

Make up a situation for the equation.

$\frac{\text{mi}}{\text{h}}\ \frac{350}{7} = \frac{x}{1}$ $\frac{70}{1} = \frac{x}{8} = \frac{\text{ft}}{\text{s}}$

SUMMARIZE/ASSESS **Explain how to write a proportion to solve a problem. Give an example.** *(Using a variable, set up a proportion that has the ratios in the same order. Solve the proportion using cross products. Examples will vary.)*

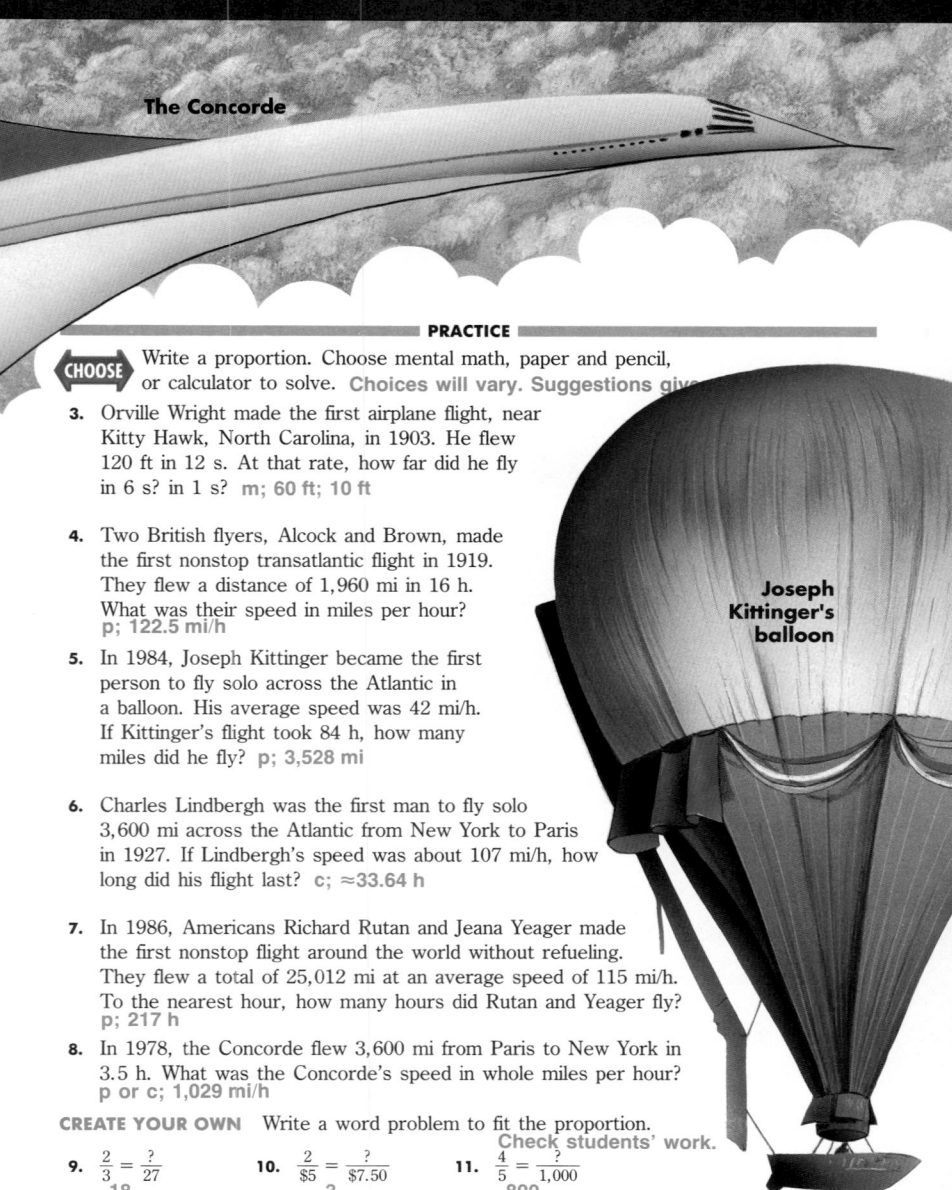

The Concorde

Joseph Kittinger's balloon

PRACTICE

CHOOSE Write a proportion. Choose mental math, paper and pencil, or calculator to solve. **Choices will vary. Suggestions giv[en]**

3. Orville Wright made the first airplane flight, near Kitty Hawk, North Carolina, in 1903. He flew 120 ft in 12 s. At that rate, how far did he fly in 6 s? in 1 s? **m; 60 ft; 10 ft**

4. Two British flyers, Alcock and Brown, made the first nonstop transatlantic flight in 1919. They flew a distance of 1,960 mi in 16 h. What was their speed in miles per hour? **p; 122.5 mi/h**

5. In 1984, Joseph Kittinger became the first person to fly solo across the Atlantic in a balloon. His average speed was 42 mi/h. If Kittinger's flight took 84 h, how many miles did he fly? **p; 3,528 mi**

6. Charles Lindbergh was the first man to fly solo 3,600 mi across the Atlantic from New York to Paris in 1927. If Lindbergh's speed was about 107 mi/h, how long did his flight last? **c; ≈33.64 h**

7. In 1986, Americans Richard Rutan and Jeana Yeager made the first nonstop flight around the world without refueling. They flew a total of 25,012 mi at an average speed of 115 mi/h. To the nearest hour, how many hours did Rutan and Yeager fly? **p; 217 h**

8. In 1978, the Concorde flew 3,600 mi from Paris to New York in 3.5 h. What was the Concorde's speed in whole miles per hour? **p or c; 1,029 mi/h**

CREATE YOUR OWN Write a word problem to fit the proportion. **Check students' work.**

9. $\frac{2}{3} = \frac{?}{27}$ 18

10. $\frac{2}{\$5} = \frac{?}{\$7.50}$ 3

11. $\frac{4}{5} = \frac{?}{1,000}$ 800

CHAPTER 9   283

MEETING INDIVIDUAL NEEDS
For Students Who Are . . .

Acquiring English Proficiency Have students locate Newfoundland and Ireland on a globe. Discuss the meaning of *transatlantic*.

Gifted and Talented Have students research other flying feats. They can create a problem using the information and have a classmate solve it.

Working 2 or 3 Grades Below Level For Exercise 3, have students write the labels to the left before they set up the proportion: $\frac{\text{ft}}{\text{s}} \frac{120}{12} = \frac{n}{6}$.

Today's Problem

If a mile of nickels has a value of $3,696 and a mile of dimes has a value of $8.976, what is the ratio of the number of nickels to the number of dimes? *(3,696 × 20 = 73,920 nickels; 8.976 × 10 = 89,760 dimes; then $\frac{73,920}{89,760} = \frac{154}{187}$)*

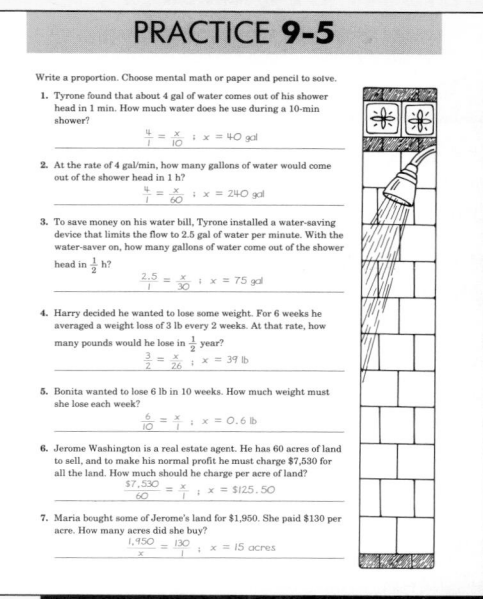

PRACTICE 9-5

Write a proportion. Choose mental math or paper and pencil to solve.

1. Tyrone found that about 4 gal of water comes out of his shower head in 1 min. How much water does he use during a 10-min shower?
$\frac{4}{1} = \frac{x}{10}$; $x = 40$ gal

2. At the rate of 4 gal/min, how many gallons of water would come out of the shower head in 1 h?
$\frac{4}{1} = \frac{x}{60}$; $x = 240$ gal

3. To save money on his water bill, Tyrone installed a water-saving device that limits the flow to 2.5 gal of water per minute. With the water-saver on, how many gallons of water come out of the shower head in $\frac{1}{2}$ h?
$\frac{2.5}{1} = \frac{x}{30}$; $x = 75$ gal

4. Harry decided he wanted to lose some weight. For 6 weeks he averaged a weight loss of 3 lb every 2 weeks. At that rate, how many pounds would he lose in $\frac{1}{2}$ year?
$\frac{3}{2} = \frac{x}{26}$; $x = 39$ lb

5. Bonita wanted to lose 6 lb in 10 weeks. How much weight must she lose each week?
$\frac{6}{10} = \frac{x}{1}$; $x = 0.6$ lb

6. Jerome Washington is a real estate agent. He has 60 acres of land to sell, and to make his normal profit he must charge $7,530 for all the land. How much should he charge per acre of land?
$\frac{\$7,530}{60} = \frac{x}{1}$; $x = \$125.50$

7. Maria bought some of Jerome's land for $1,950. She paid $130 per acre. How many acres did she buy?
$\frac{1,950}{x} = \frac{130}{1}$; $x = 15$ acres

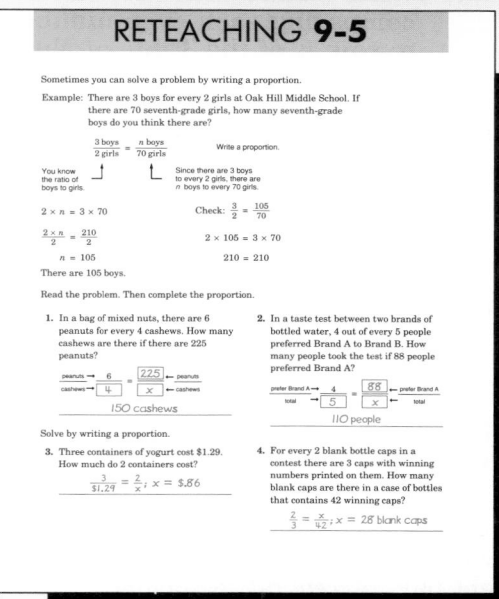

RETEACHING 9-5

Sometimes you can solve a problem by writing a proportion.

Example: There are 3 boys for every 2 girls at Oak Hill Middle School. If there are 70 seventh-grade girls, how many seventh-grade boys do you think there are?

$\frac{3 \text{ boys}}{2 \text{ girls}} = \frac{n \text{ boys}}{70 \text{ girls}}$ Write a proportion.

You know the ratio of boys to girls.   Since there are 3 boys to every 2 girls, there are n boys to every 70 girls.

$2 \times n = 3 \times 70$ Check: $\frac{3}{2} = \frac{105}{70}$

$\frac{2 \times n}{2} = \frac{210}{2}$ $2 \times 105 = 3 \times 70$

$n = 105$ $210 = 210$

There are 105 boys.

Read the problem. Then complete the proportion.

1. In a bag of mixed nuts, there are 6 peanuts for every 4 cashews. How many cashews are there if there are 225 peanuts?
peanuts → $\frac{6}{4}$ = $\frac{225}{x}$ ← peanuts, ← cashews
150 cashews

2. In a taste test between two brands of bottled water, 4 out of every 5 people preferred Brand A to Brand B. How many people took the test if 88 people preferred Brand A?
prefer Brand A → $\frac{4}{5}$ = $\frac{88}{x}$ ← prefer Brand A, total
110 people

Solve by writing a proportion.

3. Three containers of yogurt cost $1.29. How much do 2 containers cost?
$\frac{3}{\$1.29} = \frac{2}{x}$; $x = \$.86$

4. For every 2 blank bottle caps in a contest there are 3 caps with winning numbers printed on them. How many blank caps are there in a case of bottles that contains 42 winning caps?
$\frac{2}{3} = \frac{x}{42}$; $x = 28$ blank caps

ENRICHMENT 9-5

Write the following proportions on the board: $\frac{2}{3} = \frac{x}{225}$, $\frac{3}{\$.87} = \frac{2}{p}$, $\frac{11.8}{368} = \frac{10.5}{g}$. Have the students work in groups of three. Instruct each student to write a realistic problem for each proportion. For example for $\frac{2}{3} = \frac{x}{225}$, a student might write the following: Two out of every 3 people surveyed said that they own a cassette player. How many people out of 225 do you predict own a cassette player? [150] Have group members exchange papers and solve each other's problems. Ask: Is the problem reasonable? Is the answer?

Lesson Organizer

Objective: Determine rates and uses for comparison shopping.

Prior Knowledge: Students should be able to write and solve proportions.

Error Analysis and Remediation: See page 303A.

Lesson Resources:
Practice Worksheet 9-6
Reteaching Worksheet 9-6
Enrichment Activity 9-6
Daily Review 9-6

Two-Minute Math

Write a ratio in lowest terms comparing each even number in row A of the Table of Numbers on the inside back cover to the sum of all the numbers in the row. $\left(\frac{38}{501}; \frac{82}{501}; \frac{8}{167}; \frac{56}{501}\right)$

1 INTRODUCE

SYMBOLIC ACTIVITY

☑ **MATERIALS CHECKLIST:** newspaper ads from different stores for the same product

1. Display the ads. **Compare the items advertised.** *(They are the same size but are priced differently.)*

2. Make a list of things to consider when deciding which of two similar products you might buy. *(Accept all reasonable responses.)*

WHEN YOUR STUDENTS ASK
★ WHY AM I LEARNING THIS? ★

You can use this skill in everyday life to increase your purchasing power. Which is the better buy: 3 lb for $3.49 or 5 lb for $6.29?

Rates and Comparison Shopping

When shopping, you often find different quantities of the same item sold at different prices. In such cases, you can use proportional thinking to find the better buy.

Which is the better buy of Italian plum tomatoes?

75¢/6 oz

$1.85/lb

To decide, find the unit rates, or the cost of 1 oz, for each.

Let x represent the cost per ounce (cost/oz).

75¢ is to 6 oz as x is to 1 oz.

$$\frac{\text{cost}}{\text{ounces}} \rightarrow \frac{\$.75}{6} = \frac{x}{1} \leftarrow \frac{\text{cost}}{\text{ounces}}$$

$$\frac{6x}{6} = \frac{\$.75}{6}$$

$$x = \$.125, \text{ or } 13¢$$

The unit rate is 13¢ for 1 oz, or 13¢/oz.

$1.85 is to 16 oz as x is to 1 oz.

$$\frac{\text{cost}}{\text{ounces}} \rightarrow \frac{\$1.85}{16} = \frac{x}{1} \leftarrow \frac{\text{cost}}{\text{ounces}}$$

$$\frac{16x}{16} = \frac{\$1.85}{16}$$

$$x = \$.115625, \text{ or } 12¢$$

The unit rate is 12¢ for 1 oz, or 12¢/oz.

Which is the better buy? **$1.85/lb**

You can also find the cost per ounce using a calculator.

0.75 ÷ 6 = 0.125   1.85 ÷ 16 = 0.115625

━━━━━━━━━━ **GUIDED PRACTICE** ━━━━━━━━━━

Find the unit rate.

1. 70¢ for 2 oz parsley flakes **35¢/oz**
2. $1.89 for 3 lb onions **63¢/lb**
3. 96¢ for 8 tomatoes **12¢/tomato**
4. $7.50 for $1\frac{1}{2}$ lb Gorgonzola cheese **$5/lb**

Find the unit rate to determine the better buy.

5. Which is the better buy for the Parmesan cheese at the right? **$3.99/9 oz**

$1\frac{1}{2}$ lb $ 3.99

$ 11.98 9 oz

Calculators should be available for lengthy computations with data.

2 TEACH

☑ **MATERIALS CHECKLIST:** calculators

How can you use proportional thinking to determine which of the two quantities of plum tomatoes is the better buy? *(Set up a proportion to find the unit rates.)*

Is it always best to buy the item with the least unit cost? Explain. *(Accept reasonable answers and explanations.)*

Chalkboard Example

Find the unit rate to determine the better buy.
6 pens for $6.89 or 10 pens for $11.29? *($1.148; $1.129; 10 pens)*

SUMMARIZE/ASSESS **Explain how you would use unit rates to choose the better buy if one brand was $2.65 for 28 oz. and the other brand cost $1.60 for 15 oz.** *(The larger size cost about $.09 per oz.; the smaller cost about $.10 per oz. The larger size is the better buy.)*

Find the better buy. Use a calculator, mental math, or pencil and paper.

6. jar of olives, $1.89/12 oz can of olives, $2.29/lb ✓

7. pasta salad, $2.20/8 oz OR pasta salad, $9.38/2 lb

8. lasagna noodles, $3.98/2 lb ✓ OR lasagna noodles, $2.29/lb

9. 1 can olive oil, $13.32/gal ✓ OR two bottles olive oil, $9.38/2 qt

10. ricotta cheese, $3.05/12 oz OR ricotta cheese, $3.29/lb ✓

11. fresh garlic, $.50/4 oz ✓ OR garlic powder, $.60/3 oz

12. mozzarella cheese, $3.29/12 oz OR mozzarella cheese, $2.49/8 oz

13. tomato sauce, $1.29/14 fl oz ✓ OR tomato sauce, $.85/7½ fl oz

14. **CRITICAL THINKING** Suppose you will be serving 3 people 16 fl oz of soup each. Which is the more economical buy, if you do not wish to buy too much more soup than you will need? **4 for $5.16**

14 fl oz Tortellini SOUP

4 cans for $ 5.16
OR
5 cans for $ 5.79

Mental Math

You can use proportional thinking and equivalent fractions to find the better buy mentally.

Which is the better buy for apples, 6 for 74¢ or a dozen for $1.59?

Think: $\frac{6}{0.74} = \frac{12}{?}$.

Double 6 to get 12, so also double 0.74.
$\frac{6}{0.74} = \frac{12}{1.48}$, so it is better to buy 12/$1.48 than 12/$1.59.

Is one a better buy than the other? If so, which one?

1. 4 for 79¢ or 12 for 99¢ **12 for 99¢**
2. 15 for $70 or 3 for $16 **15 for $70**
3. 8 for $1.09 or 4 for $0.49 **4 for $0.49**
4. 10 for $13 or 40 for $50 **40 for $50**

CHAPTER 9   285

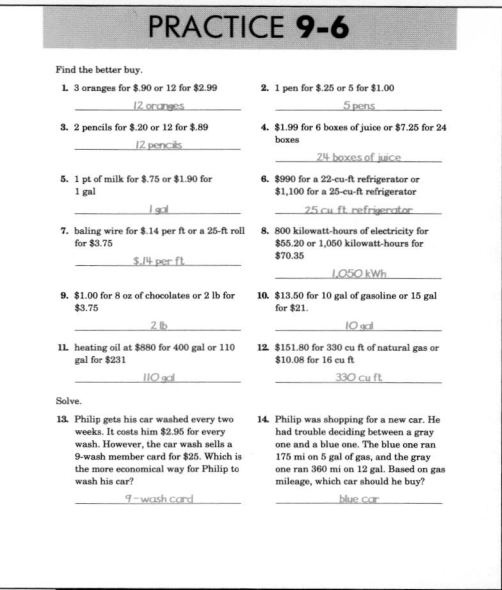

3 FOLLOW-UP

PRACTICE 9-6

Find the better buy.

1. 3 oranges for $.90 or 12 for $2.99
   12 oranges
2. 1 pen for $.25 or 5 for $1.00
   5 pens
3. 2 pencils for $.20 or 12 for $.89
   12 pencils
4. $1.99 for 6 boxes of juice or $7.25 for 24 boxes
   24 boxes of juice
5. 1 pt of milk for $.75 or $1.90 for 1 gal
   1 gal
6. $990 for a 22-cu-ft refrigerator or $1,100 for a 25-cu-ft refrigerator
   25 cu ft refrigerator
7. baling wire for $.14 per ft or a 25-ft roll for $3.75
   $.14 per ft
8. 800 kilowatt-hours of electricity for $55.20 or 1,050 kilowatt-hours for $70.35
   1,050 kWh
9. $1.00 for 8 oz of chocolates or 2 lb for $3.75
   _2 lb_
10. $13.50 for 10 gal of gasoline or 15 gal for $21.
    10 gal
11. heating oil at $880 for 400 gal or 110 gal for $231
    110 gal
12. $151.80 for 330 cu ft of natural gas or $10.08 for 16 cu ft
    _330 cu ft_

Solve.

13. Philip gets his car washed every two weeks. It costs him $2.95 for every wash. However, the car wash sells a 9-wash member card for $25. Which is the more economical way for Philip to wash his car?
    9-wash card
14. Philip was shopping for a new car. He had trouble deciding between a gray one and a blue one. The blue one ran 175 mi on 5 gal of gas, and the gray one ran 360 mi on 12 gal. Based on gas mileage, which car should he buy?
    blue car

RETEACHING 9-6

You can use what you know about unit rates to compare different prices for different quantities of the same item.

Example: Which is the better buy for a T-bone steak: $2.39 for a 6=oz package or $3.65 for a 10-oz package?

$$\frac{2.39}{6 \text{ oz}} = \frac{x}{1 \text{ oz}}$$
$$6 \times x = 2.39 \times 1$$
$$\frac{6 \times x}{6} = \frac{2.39}{6}$$
$$x = 0.3983$$

$$\frac{3.65}{10 \text{ oz}} = \frac{y}{1 \text{ oz}}$$
$$10 \times y = 3.65 \times 1$$
$$\frac{10 \times y}{10} = \frac{3.65}{10}$$
$$y = 0.365$$

Since $y < x$, the better buy is $3.65 for a 10-oz package.

Circle the better buy. If there is no difference, write *same*.

1. hamburger
   ($5.38 for 4.63 lb)
   or
   $4.87 for 4.12 lb
2. hand lotion
   $1.59 for a 20-oz bottle
   or
   ($1.89 for a 22.5-oz bottle)
3. chicken fillets
   ($4.49 for 1.5 lb)
   or
   $8.98 for 2.1 lb
4. cranberry juice
   $1.59 for a 12-oz can
   or
   ($2.06 for a 16-oz can)
5. lemonade
   $.69 for a 12-oz can
   or
   $.92 for a 16-oz can
   same
6. orange juice
   ($1.89 for a 12-oz can)
   or
   $2.99 for a 16-oz can
7. laundry detergent
   136 oz for $11.39
   or
   (39 oz for $2.79)
8. dishwasher detergent
   50 oz for $2.49
   or
   (88 oz for $4.19)
9. bleach
   $.79 for ½ gal
   or
   ($1.19 for 1 gal)

ENRICHMENT 9-6

☑ **MATERIALS CHECKLIST:** Blank spinners, newspapers

Have the students work in groups of four. Provide each group with newspaper advertisements and a spinner labeled *Shampoo, Laundry detergent, Bottled water, Garbage bags, Toothpaste, Pet food.* One student in each group spins the spinner. Using the newspaper ads, the students find as many items as possible in the category indicated. Ask: What is the best buy? When might you choose *not* to buy the item with the lowest cost per unit? [Answers will vary. Suggestion: when a brand name is important to you.]

MEETING INDIVIDUAL NEEDS

For Students Who Are . . .

Acquiring English Proficiency Emphasize that the denominator of the second fraction will always be one, since the ratio is intended to find the unit price.

Gifted and Talented Have students find newspaper ads to compare quantity and cost of the same item. Ask them to find the better buy.

Working 2 or 3 Grades Below Level Review with students that 1 lb = 16 oz and 4 qt = 1 gal. In Exercise 6, remind students to change 1 lb to 16 oz so the same units can be compared. Have students use pages 54–55 of the Skills Workbook for Equations, Ratio, Proportion, and Percent.

Today's Problem

Three $12\frac{3}{4}$ oz cans of Brand A cost $1.56. Two $17\frac{1}{2}$ oz cans of Brand B cost $1.50. Both brands are the same quality. Which is the better buy? *(The unit price of Brand A is about $.040 per oz; the unit price of Brand B is about $.043 per oz. Brand A is the better buy.)*

MIDCHAPTER

Checkup

The midchapter checkup provides a way for you to check students' understanding of the skills taught in the first half of the chapter.

Language and Vocabulary

Some key language and vocabulary ideas from the first half of the chapter are reinforced here.

Quick Quiz

The quiz provides a means of evaluating students' understanding of the objectives for the first half of the chapter. Page references are given so that students can check back to where the skill was taught.

Use the following guide to score the quick quiz.

Score	Percent
10	100%
9	90
8	80
7	70
6	60
5	50
4	40
3	30
2	20
1	10

Use this chart to identify the Management Objectives tested.

Items	Management Objectives	Pages
1–4	**9B** Solve proportions.	280–281
5–9	**9A** Write ratios, proportions, and rates.	282–285
10	**9E** Problem Solving: Use proportions.	282–283

MIDCHAPTER CHECKUP

LANGUAGE & VOCABULARY

Use the term in a sentence to show that you know its meaning. **Accept reasonable answers.**

1. ratio
2. cross products
3. rate
4. unit rate
5. proportion

QUICK QUIZ ✓

Solve the proportion. Check your answer. *(pages 280–281)*

1. $\frac{8}{24} = \frac{x}{36}$ **12**
2. $\frac{a}{17} = \frac{6}{51}$ **2**
3. $\frac{8}{12} = \frac{20}{x}$ **30**
4. $\frac{15}{m} = \frac{3}{8}$ **40**

Find the better buy. *(pages 284–285)*

5. cereal: 10 oz for $1.79 or 13 oz for $2.09
   13 oz
6. paper towels: 50 sheets for $1.09 or 65 sheets for $1.35
   65 sheets
7. light bulbs: 4 for $3.28 or $.85 each
   4 for $3.28
8. oranges: 12 for $1.00 or 15 for $1.50
   12 for $1.00
9. olives: 8 oz for $1.45 or 10 oz for $1.69
   10 oz

Solve. *(pages 276–279, 282–283)*

10. Bamboo, a very fast growing plant, has been known to grow as much as 35 in. in 1 d. Some seaweeds can grow as much as 1 yd in 1 d.

    a. Has a bamboo plant ever been known to grow as much as 1 yd in 1 d? **no**

    b. How could you find the maximum growth for either plant in 1 wk? **multiply growth per day by 7**

    c. If a bamboo plant could continue growing at the rate of 35 in./d, how much would it grow in 1 wk? **245 in**

Write the answers in your learning log.   **Answers will vary. Suggestions given.**
1. Describe two ways you can test to see whether two ratios form a proportion.
   find cross products; simplify to lowest terms
2. Your friend thinks the four numbers in a proportion can be arranged any way. Explain why you agree or disagree with this thinking.   **Arrangements may change as long as cross products remain the same.**

DID YOU KNOW . . . ?   About 3 out of every 10 workers in the United States work in an agricultural career. Poll your classmates. Ask whether anyone in their families works in an agriculture-related job. Compare your reduced ratio to the national ratio. Are the two proportional? What could explain the differences?   **Check students' work.**

BONUS

The menu of the Bet You Can't Buy Just One restaurant includes these items and prices:

Orange juice: 3 for $1.95

Apples: 3 for $.79

Tuna sandwich: 2 for $2.15

Yogurt: 3 for $2.39

Milk: 2 for $.99

Baked potato: 2 for $2.45

Egg salad sandwich: 2 for $1.99

Tea: 2 for $1.27

How much does each order cost? Round to the nearest cent.

1. 5 orange juices   **$3.25**
3. 3 milks   **$1.49**
5. 7 apples   **$1.84**
7. 1 baked potato   **$1.23**

2. 1 tuna sandwich   **$1.08**
4. 3 egg sandwiches   **$2.99**
6. 2 yogurts   **$1.59**
8. 1 tea   **$.64**

Learning Log

These are suggestions for writing about some topics taught so far in the chapter. The students keep their Learning Logs from the beginning of the school year through the end.

Math America

A mathematical skill that students have learned is related to an interesting fact about the United States.

Bonus

Students are given an opportunity to solve a challenge-type problem like a puzzle or nonroutine problem.

Lesson Organizer

Objective: Discuss how to write problems.

Prior Knowledge: Students should be able to organize information in a logical way.

Lesson Resources:
Practice Worksheet 9-7
Reteaching Activity 9-7
Enrichment Worksheet 9-7
Daily Review 9-7

Two-Minute Math

Name a classroom situation that can be represented by the ratio.

2 to 1   5:1   1:10 $\frac{5}{4}$

(Possible answers: 2 shoes to 1 person, 5 fingers to 1 hand, 1 person to 10 toes, 5 pencils for every 4 people.)

1 INTRODUCE

SYMBOLIC ACTIVITY

1. Has anyone heard about a passenger ship called the *Titanic*? Give students a chance to share what they may know.

2. Tell the class that in today's lesson they will learn some additional interesting facts about this ship and then write some math problems based on these facts.

WHEN YOUR STUDENTS ASK
★ WHY AM I LEARNING THIS? ★

You can connect this skill to real life through human resources work. People who determine hiring policies in large companies often must create tests to screen job applications.

288 *Chapter 9 • Lesson 9-7*

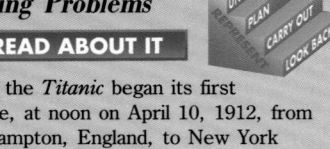
Jot it Down

Problem Solving:
Writing Problems

📖 READ ABOUT IT

When the *Titanic* began its first voyage, at noon on April 10, 1912, from Southampton, England, to New York City, it was the largest ship in the world. It was 882 ft long, weighed 46,328 t, and carried about 2,227 people. Its 3 anchors alone weighed a total of 31 t.

The *Titanic* was nicknamed "The Unsinkable Ship." But at 11:40 P.M. on the night of April 14, it struck an iceberg about 400 mi off the coast of North America and began to sink.

The *Carpathia*, a ship about 60 mi from the *Titanic* at the time, raced to the scene in answer to the *Titanic*'s distress signals. When it arrived on the scene $4\frac{1}{2}$ h later, it found only 705 of the *Titanic*'s passengers and crew in lifeboats.

As the *Titanic* sank 12,460 ft to the ocean floor, it broke into two pieces, which now rest 1,970 ft apart.

MATH AND HISTORY

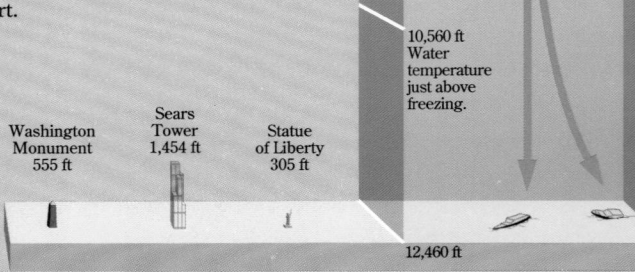

437 ft
Deepest point a scuba diver has gone.

1,500 ft
No light below this depth.

5,280 ft

10,560 ft
Water temperature just above freezing.

Washington Monument 555 ft

Sears Tower 1,454 ft

Statue of Liberty 305 ft

12,460 ft

288   LESSON 9-7

2 TEACH

READ ABOUT IT   Have students read the information about the *Titanic* on page 288.

TALK ABOUT IT   Have students discuss Exercises 1 and 2. **What problem solving approaches did you use to answer these exercises?** *(Possible answers: working backward; identifying needed information, making a table)*

WRITE ABOUT IT   **Which problem that you wrote used addition to solve? Which used subtraction? multiplication? division? Which used multiple steps?**

SUMMARIZE/ASSESS   **What fact about the *Titanic* did you find most interesting? Write a problem related to this fact.** *(Accept reasonable answers and problems.)*

The *Titanic* was thought to be lost forever, but it was located in 1985 by a French and American team. Two years later, Congress moved to make the *Titanic* an international memorial.

■ TALK ABOUT IT

Use the information about the *Titanic* on pages 288 and 289.

1. This proportion was used to solve a problem.

$$\text{miles} \longrightarrow \frac{60}{4\frac{1}{2}} = \frac{x}{1} \longleftarrow \text{hours}$$

The answer was, *The* Carpathia *traveled at a speed of* $13\frac{1}{3}$ *mi in 1 h.* What was the question? **What was the *Carpathia's* average speed?**

2. Work with a partner. Discuss what problem you can write that has the given answer. Tell what information is needed to write the problem. **Answers will vary. Suggestions given.**

   a. about 1,522 people **About how many people were lost?**

   b. about 2.4 mi **About how deep is the *Titanic* now?**

   c. 62,000 lb **What did the three anchors weigh?**

   d. 73 yr **How long after the *Titanic* sank was it located?**

   e. about 0.4 mi **How far apart are the two pieces of wreckage?**

■ WRITE ABOUT IT

Work with a partner. Use the information on pages 288 and 289. **Check students' work.**

3. Devise a math problem that involves ratio.

4. Devise a math problem involving time.

5. Write a problem involving depth.

6. Write a problem that requires division to find its solution.

7. Write a problem in which a unit of measurement is changed to another unit.

8. Write a problem for which the answer cannot be found because not enough information is given.

9. Write a problem that contains too much information.

Now exchange problems with another pair of partners and solve.

MEETING INDIVIDUAL NEEDS

For Students Who Are . . .

Acquiring English Proficiency   Pair students with an English-proficient student to work on the Problem Solving activities.

Gifted and Talented   Have students create two more problems similar to Exercise 2, exchange problems with a classmate, and solve.

Working 2 or 3 Grades Below Level   Have students use pages 16–19 of the Skills Workbook for Problem Solving Strategies.

Having Reading Difficulties   Discuss the meaning of *ratio, depth, solution,* and *unit of measurement* before partners start the Write About It section.

Today's Problem

Planets close to the sun travel around the sun with a greater speed than do planets farther from the sun, but the length of their orbit is less than planets farther from the sun. Do closer planets take longer to circle the sun than do further planets? *(No, first because their speed is greater, and second because their orbit is shorter.)*

---

3 FOLLOW-UP

PRACTICE 9-7

In 1903, the Wright brothers accomplished the first successful airplane flight. They flew 120 ft in 12 s. By 1905, they flew a record distance of 24 mi in a single flight.

Four years later, Glenn Curtiss set the world speed record of 47 mi/h. In 1910, new records were set when Louis Paulhan flew to an altitude of 4,165 ft and Glenn Curtiss achieved 55 mi/h. Later that year, Walter Brookins broke the altitude record with a 4,732-ft height. Also, Ralph Johnstone established an in-flight record of 3 h, 5 min, and 40 s.

By 1911, Lincoln Beachley shattered the altitude record by flying 11,642 ft and pushed the speed record to 78.8 mi/h. In just eight years, aviation had become a soaring success.

Use the information in the passage. Answers will vary. Suggestions are given.

1. Write a math problem that involves a ratio. *Write a ratio comparing the duration of the Wright brothers' first flight to Ralph Johnstone's record flight.*

2. Devise a math problem involving a proportion. *If the Wright brothers had continued their first flight at the same speed, how far would they have flown in 1 min?*

3. Devise a math problem involving time. *How long would it take to fly 1,000 mi traveling at Lincoln Beachley's 1911 speed of 78.8 mi/h?*

4. Write a problem involving distance. *Flying at his 1909 record speed of 47 mi/h, how far would Glenn Curtiss fly in 8 h?*

5. Write a problem in which one unit of measure is changed to another unit. *How many miles high was Lincoln Beachley flying when he broke the altitude record?*

6. Write a problem for which the answer is not possible because not enough information is given. *How far did Ralph Johnstone fly?*

RETEACHING 9-7

Write the following on index cards: ratio, time, depth, division, change unit of measurement, not enough information, too much information. Have pairs of students draw a card and write a math problem that involves what is written on the card. Have students exchange problems and solve. Before writing the problem, have students write a possible answer or a possible step that would be used in the problem to help give them possible numbers to work with.

ENRICHMENT 9-7

Use the facts to write the problem described. Answers will vary. Suggestions are given.

- The Earth's crust is made up of huge slabs, or plates. These plates push against each other and shift at a rate of more than 2.4 in. per year.
- Martha's Vineyard is a small island off the coast of Massachusetts. The island's area is 108 mi². Its cliffs are being eroded by the sea at a rate of 515 ft per year.
- The Sahara desert is the world's largest desert. With an area of about 3.5 million mi², it is larger than the continental United States. The Sahara is growing, too. Every year, the desert's southern border expands by 200 ft.
- Tropical rain forests are home to many valuable plants. However, in many parts of the world, the rain forests are being cleared away for farmland. Despite the fact that the soil in them is often too poor to support agriculture, the rain forests continue to disappear at a rate of 14 acres per minute.

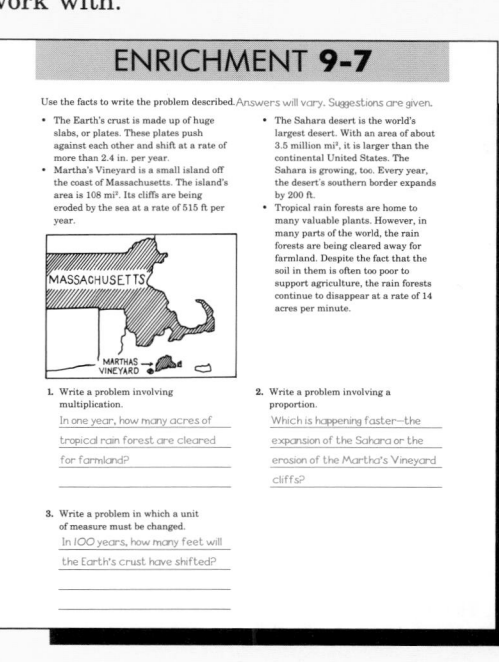

1. Write a problem involving multiplication. *In one year, how many acres of tropical rain forest are cleared for farmland?*

2. Write a problem involving a proportion. *Which is happening faster—the expansion of the Sahara or the erosion of the Martha's Vineyard cliffs?*

3. Write a problem in which a unit of measure must be changed. *In 100 years, how many feet will the Earth's crust have shifted?*

Lesson Organizer

Prior Knowledge: Students should know the meaning of ratio and be able to solve proportions.

Lesson Resources:
Class Activity 9-8
Daily Review 9-8

Two-Minute Math

A tree that is 10 ft. tall is 1 in. tall in a photograph. What is the actual height of a building that is 2 in. tall in the same photo? *(20 ft.)* **of a bush that is $\frac{1}{2}$ in. tall?** *(5 ft.)*

1 PREPARE

CONCRETE ACTIVITY

✓ **MATERIALS CHECKLIST:** Teaching Aid 13 (Tangrams), scissors for each group

Assign students to groups of three or four.

1. Have each group cut out the tangrams and separate the triangles.

2. Assign a capital letter to identify each triangle, and have students label their triangles.

Show two triangles that have congruent angles and congruent sides. Show two triangles that have congruent angles but not congruent sides.

WHEN YOUR STUDENTS ASK
★ WHY AM I LEARNING THIS? ★

You can connect this skill to real life through interior design. Interior designers routinely work with similar polygons when they plan the location of furniture and fixtures in a room.

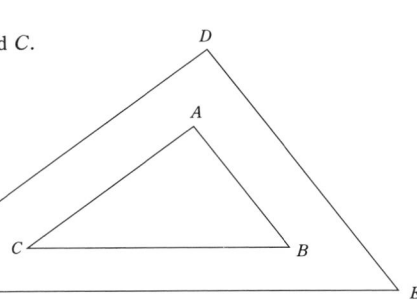

Exploring Similar Polygons

Polygons having the same shape, but not necessarily the same size, are called **similar** polygons.

1. Follow the steps to make a triangle similar to △ABC, but larger.

- Trace △ABC. Label the vertices A, B, and C.
- Place a ruler along $\overline{AB}$. Draw line $\overline{DE}$ parallel to $\overline{AB}$ along the other edge of the ruler.
- Repeat for the other two sides of △ABC. Use a ruler to extend the lines until they intersect and form △DEF.
- Label the vertices of the larger triangle D, E, and F.

If you worked carefully, △DEF should be similar to △ABC.

2. $\overline{DE}$ and $\overline{AB}$ are called corresponding sides of the similar triangles. Why?
because $\overline{AB}$ was used to draw $\overline{DE}$

3. Which side of △ABC corresponds to $\overline{FD}$ of △DEF? Which side corresponds to $\overline{FE}$? $\overline{CA}$; $\overline{CB}$

Use a centimeter ruler to compare the lengths in the diagram above. Write the ratio in lowest terms.

4. length of $\overline{CB}$: length of $\overline{FE}$ 1:2

5. length of $\overline{AB}$: length of $\overline{DE}$ 1:2

6. length of $\overline{AC}$: length of $\overline{DF}$ 1:2

7. What do you notice about the ratios you wrote in Exercises 4–6?
all equal

8. What do you think is true about the corresponding sides of similar figures? **The ratios of their lengths are equal.**

9. Why are ∠ABC and ∠DEF called corresponding angles?
They are equal.

10. Which angle of △DEF corresponds to ∠ACB of △ABC? Which angle corresponds to ∠FDE? ∠DFE; ∠CAB

2 EXPLORE

✓ **MATERIALS CHECKLIST:** centimeter ruler, Teaching Aid 8 (Protractor) or protractor for each group of three or four students

Assign students into mixed ability groups of three or four.

Which angle of △DEF corresponds to ∠CBS of △ABC? *(∠FED)*

SUMMARIZE/ASSESS How can you tell that two or more different-sized triangles are similar? *(Measure the angles and corresponding sides of the triangles to show that their angles are congruent and their corresponding sides are proportional.)*

11. Use a protractor to measure ∠DFE and ∠ACB. How do they compare in size? **equal**

12. Use a protractor to compare ∠CAB and ∠ABC with their corresponding angles. How do they compare in size? **equal**

13. CRITICAL THINKING Use a protractor and a ruler to draw five different pairs of similar triangles. Can you draw a pair of triangles with congruent angles that are not similar? **no**

> Two figures are *similar* when their corresponding angles are congruent and their corresponding sides are in proportion.

The two triangles at the right are similar. The ratio of $\overline{LM}$ to $\overline{RS}$ is 3:2.

14. Without measuring, what is the ratio of $\overline{MN}$ to $\overline{ST}$? the ratio of $\overline{LN}$ to $\overline{RT}$? **3:2; 3:2**

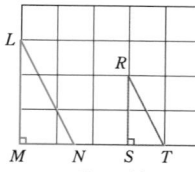

15. IN YOUR WORDS It is easy to find the corresponding sides and angles for the triangles in Exercise 14. For the polygons below it is not so easy. Trace and turn the polygons to find the corresponding sides and angles.

∠A = ∠D
∠B = ∠E
∠C = ∠F

∠F = ∠Q
∠G = ∠R
∠H = ∠S
∠I = ∠T

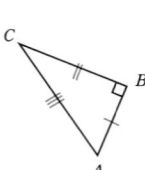
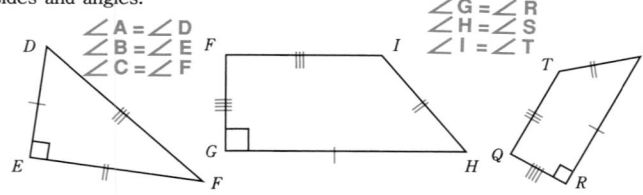

Trace the pairs of similar polygons. Mark the corresponding angles and sides.

16.

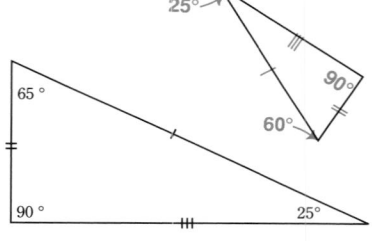

17.

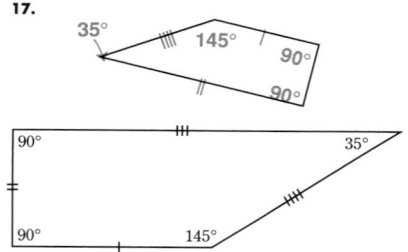

---

3 FOLLOW-UP

CLASS ACTIVITY **9-8**

☑ **MATERIALS CHECKLIST:** Yardsticks, measuring tape

Have the students work in groups of four. Take the students outside on a sunny day. Have one member of each group hold a yardstick at a 90° angle to the ground and ask two other group members to measure the length of the yardstick's shadow. Have the students take turns measuring the length of each other's shadow. Then have the students solve this proportion to find the height of each student in the group:

$$\frac{1 \text{ yd}}{\text{length ydstick/shadow}} = \frac{\text{height of student}}{\text{length student/shadow}}.$$

Instruct the students to change their answers to feet and inches. Ask: How accurate are the measurements?

MEETING INDIVIDUAL NEEDS
For Students Who Are . . .

Acquiring English Proficiency Pair students with an English-proficient student to follow the steps on page 290.

Gifted and Talented Have students draw a triangle with a ruler and protractor. Then have them draw a similar triangle with sides in the proportion of 3:4.

Working 2 or 3 Grades Below Level For Exercises 16 and 17, have students trace the figures so that they face the same direction.

Having Reading Difficulties If necessary, demonstrate how to use a protractor and a centimeter ruler.

Today's Problem

For science, you write a paper of 1,000 lines with no more than 75 letters per line. For English, you write a paper of 1,050 lines with no more than 60 letters per line. Which paper contains more words? *(not enough information to answer)*

Chapter 9 • Lesson 9-8   **291**

Lesson Organizer

> **Objective:** Use proportion with similar polygons.

Prior Knowledge: Students should be able to set up and solve proportions.

Error Analysis and Remediation: See page 303A.

Lesson Resources:
Practice Worksheet 9-9
Reteaching Worksheet 9-9
Enrichment Activity 9-9
Daily Review 9-9

Two-Minute Math

Find two ratios that form a true proportion in row I of the Table of Numbers on the inside back cover. Write the proportion. $\left(\frac{1}{2} = \frac{6}{12}\right)$

1 INTRODUCE

SYMBOLIC ACTIVITY

☑ **MATERIALS CHECKLIST:** Teaching Aid 14 (Rectangular Box) for each student

Pose this problem:
Suppose you want to make a similar but larger pattern for a rectangular box. In the original pattern, the longer dimension is 8 cm; your new pattern will have a corresponding dimension of 12 cm. Other dimensions on the original pattern are all 4 cm. What will the other dimensions of your new pattern be? *(6 cm)*

What ratio compares the longer dimension on the original pattern with the longer dimension on your larger, similar pattern? *(8:12)*

What ratio compares the other dimensions in the original pattern to the dimension of your larger, similar pattern? *(4:n)*

WHEN YOUR STUDENTS ASK
★ WHY AM I LEARNING THIS? ★

You can connect this skill to real life through art. Painters use proportions as they paint portraits, still lifes, and landscapes.

Similar Polygon Applications

Marla is sewing a pillow with an African design. The instructions show a reduced version of the design. If the length of the finished pillow will be 14 in., what will be its width?

Set up a proportion to solve the problem. Let w be the width of the pillow in inches.

$1\frac{3}{4}$ in. is to 2 in. as 14 in. is to w.

Reduced size: Actual size:

$$\frac{\text{length} \rightarrow}{\text{width} \rightarrow} \quad \frac{1.75}{2} = \frac{14}{w} \quad \frac{\leftarrow \text{length}}{\leftarrow \text{width}}$$

$$1.75w = 2 \times 14 \qquad \text{Use cross products.}$$
$$\frac{1.75w}{1.75} = \frac{28}{1.75}$$
$$w = 16$$
$$\frac{1.75}{2} = \frac{14}{16} \qquad \text{Check by substituting 16 for } w.$$
$$1.75 \times 16 = 2 \times 14$$
$$28 = 28 \;✔$$

2 in.

$1\frac{3}{4}$ in.

Traditional African designs

The width of the finished pillow will be 16 in.

The figures in the design are similar. What is the length of side x of the large triangle?

Use corresponding sides to set up the proportion.

$$\frac{\text{large} \rightarrow}{\text{small} \rightarrow} \quad \frac{16}{4} = \frac{x}{3} \quad \frac{\leftarrow \text{large}}{\leftarrow \text{small}}$$

$$4x = 16 \times 3$$
$$\frac{4x}{4} = \frac{48}{4}$$
$$x = 12 \qquad \text{How would you check this answer?}$$

Check the cross-products.
The length of the side x of the large triangle is 12 in.

18 in.   16 in.

4 in.

3 in.   x in.

━━━━━━━━━ **GUIDED PRACTICE** ━━━━━━━━━

The figures are similar. Copy and complete the proportion. Solve for the value of the unknown.

1. $\frac{10}{15} = \frac{x}{\blacksquare}$ **6 in.**   **2.** $\frac{\blacksquare}{4} = \frac{12}{y}$ **8 in.**

12 in.
9 in. [ ] 6 in.
15 in.

x [ ] 4 in.
10 in.

━━━━ **MULTICULTURAL NOTE** ━━━━
Painting dried mud houses with geometric designs in bright colors is a common art form of several African peoples, including the Ndebele of southern Africa. Wall art is one of several African art forms that are created primarily by women.

2 TEACH

Why is the length for the reduced size of the pillow written as a decimal? *(It is sometimes easier, though not necessary, to work with decimal equivalents in proportions.)*

What other way could you correctly set up the proportion for the pillow? *(Example:* $\frac{1.75}{14} = \frac{2}{w}$*; accept any proportion in which the order of both ratios is the same.)* **for the triangular figures?** *(Example:* $\frac{4}{16} = \frac{3}{x}$ *or other proportion in which the order of both ratios is the same.)*

SUMMARIZE/ASSESS
What is the key to making the proportion fit the situation? *(Keeping the order the same in both ratios)*

The figures are similar. Write a proportion to solve for the unknown. **Check students' work.**

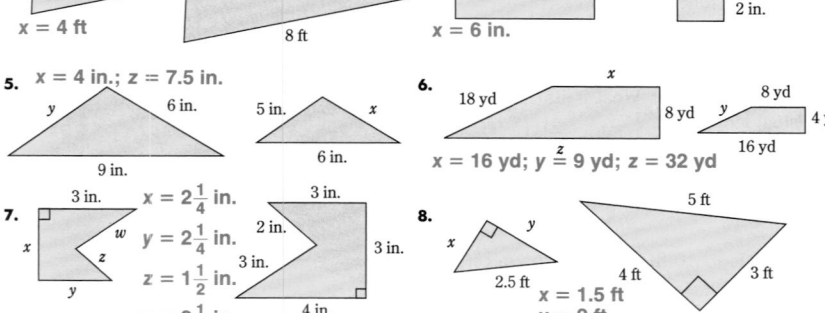

3. x ft, 2 ft, 4 ft, 8 ft, 8 ft
x = 4 ft

4. 9 in., x, 3 in., 2 in.
x = 6 in.

5. **x = 4 in.; z = 7.5 in.**
y, 6 in., 5 in., x, 6 in., 9 in.

6. x, 18 yd, 8 yd, y, 8 yd, 4 yd, z, 16 yd
x = 16 yd; y = 9 yd; z = 32 yd

7. 3 in., $x = 2\frac{1}{4}$ in., $y = 2\frac{1}{4}$ in., $z = 1\frac{1}{2}$ in., $w = 2\frac{1}{4}$ in.
x, w, z, y, 3 in., 2 in., 3 in., 4 in.

8. y, x, 2.5 ft, 4 ft, 5 ft, 3 ft
x = 1.5 ft
y = 2 ft

Write a proportion to solve. **Check students' work.**

9. A slide image is $1\frac{3}{8}$ in. wide and $\frac{7}{8}$ in. high. When the image is projected onto a screen, it is 88 in. wide. How high is the projected image? **56 in.**

10. You want to enlarge the pillow design on page 292 so that the pillow becomes 3 ft wide. How long will it be? **31.5 in.**

11. A photograph that is 8 in. wide and 10 in. long is reduced on a photocopy machine to 3 in. long. How wide is the reduced photograph? **2.4 in.**

12. In some parts of Africa, houses are painted colorfully. A pattern for these painted African houses is shown at the right, on $\frac{1}{4}$ in. grid paper. Measure the height of the front/back piece of the house. To what size square would the grid have to be enlarged to make the actual height of this piece 12 in. tall? **3 in.**

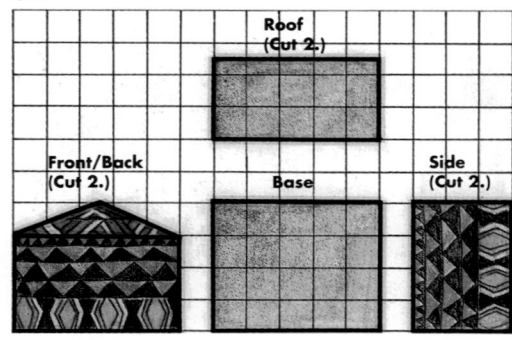

Roof (Cut 2.)
Front/Back (Cut 2.)
Base
Side (Cut 2.)

MEETING INDIVIDUAL NEEDS

For Students Who Are . . .

Acquiring English Proficiency Explain the meaning of *slide image* and *projected image* in Exercise 9.

Gifted and Talented Assign the technology lesson on page 308.

Working 2 or 3 Grades Below Level Have students mark the corresponding sides in the figures in the Guided Practice and Practice exercises.

Today's Problem

There are two square gardens. The large one is four times the area of the small one. A one-foot wide sidewalk lies along the perimeter of each garden. The sidewalks are made of 1 ft² tiles. If 40 tiles are needed for the shorter sidewalk, how many tiles are needed for the longer sidewalk? *(The small square is 11 ft × 11 ft. The large one is 22 ft by 22 ft, or 84 tiles.)*

3 FOLLOW-UP

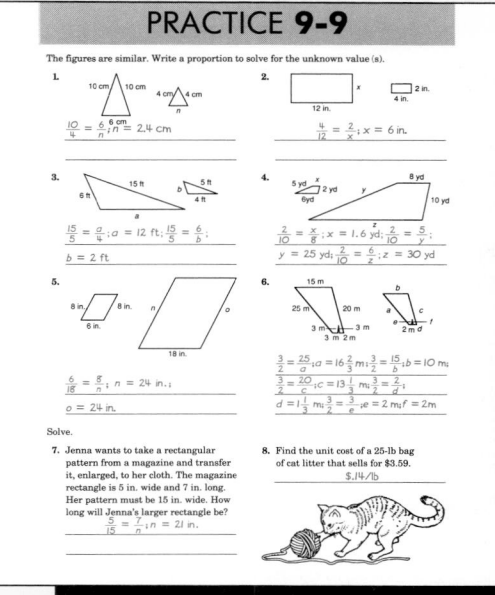

ENRICHMENT 9-9

☑ **MATERIALS CHECKLIST:** 3 × 5 index cards, rulers, measuring tape

Have the students work in groups of three or four. Provide each group with a 3 × 5 index card. Explain that the dimensions of the card approximate the **golden ratio.** Tell the students that objects or buildings that are proportional to the card have long been considered especially pleasing to the eye. Have the students find the ratio of the card's length to its width. Then challenge them to find several similar objects in the classroom.

Lesson Organizer

> **Objective:** Use information from a scale drawing.

Prior Knowledge: Students should know how to write and solve proportions.

Error Analysis and Remediation: See page 303A.

Lesson Resources:
Practice Worksheet 9-10
Reteaching Worksheet 9-10
Enrichment Activity 9-10
Daily Review 9-10
Cooperative Connections, Chapter 9
Cooperative Problem Solving 2, Chapter 9

Two-Minute Math

Explain why proportions would be important if you were drawing an accurate picture of the front of your school. *(The height and width as well as other details should be in proportion to that of the actual building.)*

1 INTRODUCE

SYMBOLIC ACTIVITY

1. How is a scale drawing of a building different from a photograph of the building. *(A scale drawing is made so that one can find the actual measurements of the building.)*

2. Provide this information:
In a scale drawing of a house, 1 in. on the drawing represents 2 ft on the actual house. What ratio compares the measurement on the drawing to the measurement on the house? *(1 in.:2 ft or 1 in.:24 in.)* **What ratio compares the measurement on the house to the measurement on the drawing?** *(2 ft/1 in. or 24 in./1 in.)*

WHEN YOUR STUDENTS ASK
★ WHY AM I LEARNING THIS? ★

You can connect this skill to real life through the work of automobile designers who prepare scale drawings at each stage in the development of their designs.

Scale Drawings and Similarity

Some Kickapoo people live in traditional compounds in parts of Texas, Oklahoma, Kansas, and northern Mexico. Some live in cities and towns.

What is the length along the top side of the scale drawing of the compound? What is its actual length?

Use the scale to set up a proportion. Let x represent the actual length in feet.

0.5 in. is to 10 ft as 2.75 in. is to x ft.

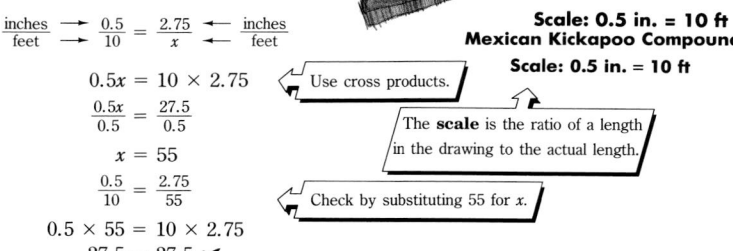

**Scale: 0.5 in. = 10 ft
Mexican Kickapoo Compound**

$$\frac{\text{inches}}{\text{feet}} \longrightarrow \frac{0.5}{10} = \frac{2.75}{x} \longleftarrow \frac{\text{inches}}{\text{feet}}$$

Scale: 0.5 in. = 10 ft

$$0.5x = 10 \times 2.75$$

Use cross products.

$$\frac{0.5x}{0.5} = \frac{27.5}{0.5}$$

The **scale** is the ratio of a length in the drawing to the actual length.

$$x = 55$$

$$\frac{0.5}{10} = \frac{2.75}{55}$$

Check by substituting 55 for x.

$$0.5 \times 55 = 10 \times 2.75$$
$$27.5 = 27.5 \checkmark$$

The actual length across the top of the compound is 55 ft.

GUIDED PRACTICE

Use a ruler and the scale to find the length in miles.   Scale: $\frac{1}{4}$ in. = 150 mi

1. 600 mi   2. 900 mi   3. 225 mi

4. Use a ruler and the scale to find the actual length of a cookhouse in the compound.
10 ft

MULTICULTURAL NOTE

The summer and winter houses shown on the Kickapoo compound are generally built and maintained by Kickapoo women. Traditionally, the oldest female occupant of the home is its owner.

2 TEACH

☑ **MATERIALS CHECKLIST:** inch ruler for each student, calculators

How would the angles of an actual building compare with the angles of a scale drawing of the building? *(They would be congruent.)* **How would the corresponding sides compare?** *(They would be proportional.)* **The scale says 0.5 in. = 10 ft. We know 0.5 in. *is not* equal to 10 ft. What does it mean?** *(Every 0.5 in. on the drawing represents 10 ft.)*

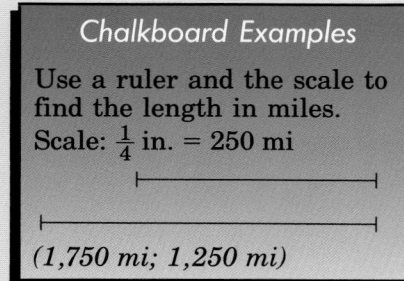

Chalkboard Examples

Use a ruler and the scale to find the length in miles.
Scale: $\frac{1}{4}$ in. = 250 mi

(1,750 mi; 1,250 mi)

SUMMARIZE/ASSESS **Give an example of a scale and how you would use it to tell how much 5 in. in the drawing represents in real-life.**

===== PRACTICE =====

Use a ruler and the scale to find the length in yards.   **Scale: 0.5 in. = 5 yd**

5. 7.5 yd   **6.** 12.5 yd   **7.** 10 yd   **8.** 6.25 yd

Use a ruler and the scale to find the length in miles.   **Scale: $\frac{1}{8}$ in. = 2 mi**

9. 16 mi   **10.** 4 mi   **11.** 18 mi   **12.** 12 mi

===== PROBLEM SOLVING =====

CHOOSE Use a ruler and the scale. Choose estimation, paper and pencil, or a calculator to solve.   Choices will vary. Suggestions given.

Refer to the Kickapoo winter house at the right.

13. What is the actual length (*a*) of the Kickapoo winter house at the right?
p; 20 ft

14. What is the actual size of the opening to the winter house (*b*)? p; $2\frac{1}{2}$ ft

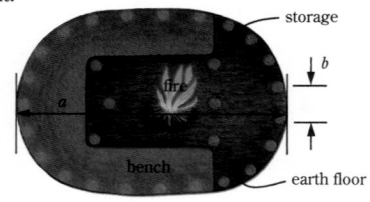

storage
b
a
fire
bench
earth floor

Scale: $\frac{1}{4}$ in. = $2\frac{1}{2}$ ft

Refer to the map.

15. What is the actual distance from Oklahoma City to Tulsa?
e; ≈100 mi

16. What is the actual distance between McLoud, Oklahoma, and San Antonio, Texas?
e; ≈300 mi

17. Find two cities that are about 600 mi apart.
e; El Paso and Tulsa

∗18. Estimate the length of the Oklahoma/Texas border.
p; ≈500 mi

• Tulsa
Oklahoma
Oklahoma City •• McLoud
• Dallas
• El Paso   **Texas**
Houston
San Antonio

Scale: 0.5 in. = 100 Mi

MEETING INDIVIDUAL NEEDS

For Students Who Are . . .

Acquiring English Proficiency Discuss the meaning of *compound*.

Gifted and Talented Have students use a map with a scale to write questions similar to Exercises 15–18. They can exchange papers and solve.

Today's Problem

Imagine looking at the Earth from an altitude of a mile. Now, imagine doubling your altitude to two miles. Do you see twice as much of the area of the Earth as before? *(No, you see about the same area of the Earth, but it looks smaller.)*

---

3 FOLLOW-UP

PRACTICE 9-10

Use a ruler and the scale to find the length in feet. Scale: 0.5 in. = 7 ft

1.   **2.**   **3.**

14 ft   12.25 ft   17.5 ft

4.   **5.**   **6.**

29.75 ft   8.75 ft   19.25 ft

Use a ruler and the scale to find the length in yards. Scale: $\frac{1}{4}$ in. = 5 yd

7.   **8.**   **9.**

15 yd   30 yd   40 yd

10.   **11.**   **12.**

35 yd   7.5 yd   32.5 yd

Solve.

13. The scale on a map of the United States shows that 1 in. equals 135 mi. The distance on the map from Atlanta to Orlando is $3\frac{1}{4}$ in. What is the actual distance?

$\frac{1}{135} = \frac{3.25}{n}$; n = 438.75 mi

14. The distance from Nashville to Atlanta is 250 mi. Using the scale in Problem 13, draw and label in inches a line that represents the distance from Nashville to Atlanta.

$\frac{1}{135} = \frac{n}{250}$; n = 1.85 in.

about 1.85 in.

RETEACHING 9-10

In a **scale drawing** of an item, a small measure (such as 1 in.) is proportional to a larger measure on the actual item. For example, a scale drawing of a car might show that 1 in. on the drawing equals 18 in. on the actual car.

If you know the scale of a drawing or a model, you can find any measure on the actual object from a measure on the drawing or model.

Example: A model of a Navy Curtiss seaplane has the following scale: 1 in. = 10 ft. How long is the wingspan on the model if the actual wingspan is 126 ft?

Use the scale to set up a proportion.

scale model → $\frac{1 \text{ in.}}{10 \text{ ft}} = \frac{n}{126 \text{ ft}}$ ← scale model
actual size →   ← actual size

$10 \times n = 1 \times 126$

$10 \times n = 126$

$\frac{10 \times n}{10} = \frac{126}{10}$

$n = \frac{126}{10}$

$n = 12.6$

The wingspan on the model is 12.6 in.

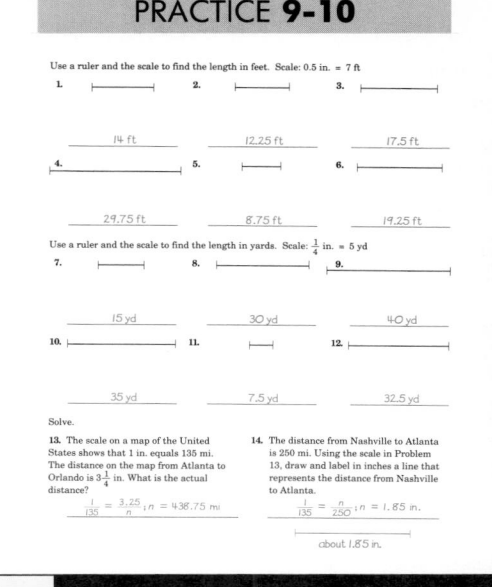

Find the length on the model. Use the scale given.

1. scale: 0.5 in. = 3 ft
You want to show a distance of 240 ft.

$\frac{0.5 \text{ in.}}{3 \text{ ft}} = \frac{n}{240}$

n = 40 in.

2. scale: 0.25 in. = 5 yd
What is the actual size of a piece that is 15 in. long on the model?

$\frac{0.25 \text{ in.}}{5 \text{ yd}} = \frac{15 \text{ in.}}{n}$

n = 300 yd

3. scale: 1 in. = 12 ft
You want to show a distance of 360 ft.

$\frac{1 \text{ in.}}{12 \text{ ft}} = \frac{n}{360}$

n = 30 in.

4. scale: 2 ft = 5 mi
You want to show a distance of 75 mi.

$\frac{2 \text{ ft}}{5 \text{ mi}} = \frac{n}{75 \text{ mi}}$

n = 30 ft

ENRICHMENT 9-10

☑ **MATERIALS CHECKLIST:** Reference books

Have the students work in pairs. Ask them to imagine that they are designing a miniature-golf course. Have them tell what scale they would use to construct models of each of the following: the Sears Tower, a shoe, the Eiffel Tower, a doughnut, a calculator, a pencil, Mt. Everest. Instruct pairs of students to compare their scales with those devised by other pairs.

Lesson Organizer

Objective: Solve problems by using proportions.

Prior Knowledge: Students should be able to set up and solve proportions.

Error Analysis and Remediation: See page 303A.

Lesson Resources:
Practice Worksheet 9-11
Reteaching Activity 9-11
Enrichment Worksheet 9-11
Daily Review 9-11

Two-Minute Math

Set up the proportion in at least three different ways. Solve.
The ratio of boys to girls in a class is 2 to 3. There are 12 girls in the class. How many boys are there?
$\left(\frac{2}{3} = \frac{x}{12}; \frac{3}{2} = \frac{12}{x}; \frac{3}{12} = \frac{2}{x}; \frac{12}{3} = \frac{x}{2}; x = 8; 8 \text{ boys}\right)$

1 INTRODUCE

CONNECTING ACTIVITY

☑ **MATERIALS CHECKLIST:** adding machine tape or tape measure for each group

Have students work in groups of three or four.

1. Use the adding machine tape to find the ratio of your heights to the lengths of your heads. *(Ratio should be close to 8 to 1.)*

2. Use the tape to find the ratio of the circumference of your heads to your heights. *(Ratio should be close to 1 to 3.)*

Each group records a description of their findings.

WHEN YOUR STUDENTS ASK
★ WHY AM I LEARNING THIS? ★

You can connect this skill to history. To the ancient Greeks, the golden ratio, approximately 1.618, was pleasing to the eye. The Greeks incorporated this ratio into their buildings, such as the Parthenon.

296 *Chapter 9 • Lesson 9-11*

Problem Solving Strategy:
Using Proportions

For centuries, artists have worked with proportions. For example, Greek sculptors worked with a body height to head height ratio of 8 to 1.

Suppose you want to make a clay sculpture of a human with a head 2 in. high. Using the Greek sculptors' 8 to 1 ratio, what would be the total height of the sculpture?

THINK ALOUD Does each proportion represent the problem? Explain. **yes**

human body height → $\frac{8}{1} = \frac{x}{2}$ ← sculpture body height
human head height →   ← sculpture head height

human body height → $\frac{8}{x} = \frac{1}{2}$ ← human head height
sculpture body height →   ← sculpture head height

Now solve the problem. **16 in.**

▬ GUIDED PRACTICE ▬

Write a proportion to solve.

1. A sculpture of a human with a head height of 3 in. is made using the 8 to 1 ratio.
   a. What is the head height of the sculpture? **3 in.**
   b. Explain what the 8 to 1 ratio means. **body is 8 times head height**
   c. What is the total body height of the sculpture? **24 in.**

2. For the sculpture described in Exercise 1, what is the height of the figure to the waist? **15 in. (floor to waist)**

▬ PRACTICE ▬

Write a proportion to solve.

3. The most common head shape is oval. In an oval head, the ratio of width to height is about 2:3. For the sculpture described in Exercise 1, about how wide should the head be? **2 in.**

4. The head usually is "five eyes" wide. For the sculpture described in Exercise 1, how wide should each eye be? **0.4 in.**

296   LESSON 9-11

MATH AND ART

← width →
← height →

---

2 TEACH

A sculpture has a body height of 30 in. Using the Greek sculptor's ratio, what is the head height? *(Possible proportion: $\frac{8}{1} = \frac{30}{x}$, $x = 3\frac{3}{4}$ in.)*

Could you use the proportion $\frac{8}{2} = \frac{x}{1}$ to solve the problem at the top of page 296? Explain. *(No; the order of the ratios does not match the problem situation.)*

Chalkboard Example

Write a proportion to solve:
A sculpture of a human with a head 5 in. high is made using the 8:1 ratio. What is the body height of the sculpture? *(Possible proportion: $\frac{8}{1} = \frac{x}{5}$; $x = 40$ in.)*

SUMMARIZE/ASSESS Using the ratio of 8 to 1, what should be the height of the head of the Statue of Liberty if the actual height of the statue is 152 ft? *(19 ft.)*

The images of George Washington, Thomas Jefferson, Theodore Roosevelt, and Abraham Lincoln are on Mount Rushmore, in South Dakota. Each head is about 60 ft high, about the height of a five-story building!

Use the 8:1 or the 2:3 sculptor's ratio to write a proportion and solve.

5. If Washington's whole body had been sculpted, how high would it have been? **480 ft**

6. If Lincoln had been sculpted from the waist to the head, how many stories high would he have been? **15**

7. Together, approximately how wide are all four heads? **160 ft**

8. About what would be the combined width of Jefferson's two eyes? **16 ft**

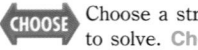 Choose a strategy to solve. **Choices will vary.**

9. **IN YOUR WORDS** Measure your total height and the height of your head. Explain how your body and head height compares to the 8 to 1 ratio described on page 296. **Answers will vary.**

10. The heads on Mount Rushmore were sculpted from models $\frac{1}{12}$ their size. About how high were the models? **5 ft**

11. How many times higher are the heads on Mount Rushmore than your head? **Answers will vary.**

MEETING INDIVIDUAL NEEDS

For Students Who Are . . .

Acquiring English Proficiency Pair students with an English-proficient student to work on the Practice problems.

Gifted and Talented Have students find the meaning of the Golden Ratio.

Working 2 or 3 Grades Below Level Have students use pages 32–33 of the Skills Workbook for Problem Solving Strategies.

Having Reading Difficulties Have students explain to each other the meaning of *body height to head height* ratio.

Today's Problem

Mix a quart of orange juice with a quart of fruit punch. Pour a third of this mixture into a glass. What is the ratio of the amount of orange juice to the amount of fruit punch? *(It is 1:1, no matter how much you pour into a glass.)*

3 FOLLOW-UP

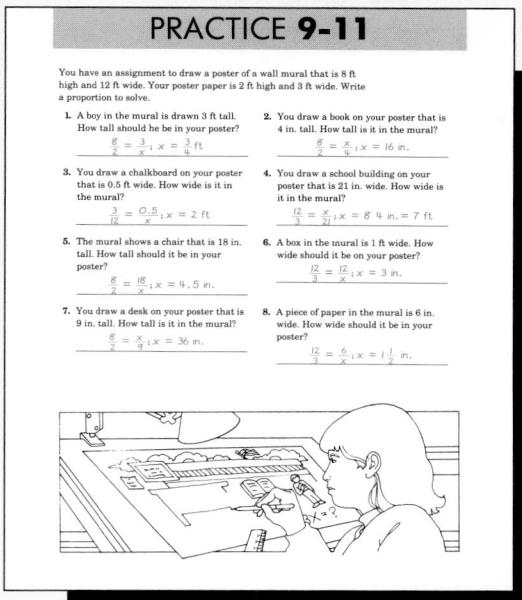

RETEACHING 9-11

Have students bring in recipes. Have them work in pairs and decide how many people they want to serve. Have them write a proportion in words before using numbers to write the amount of ingredients needed to serve that number of people.

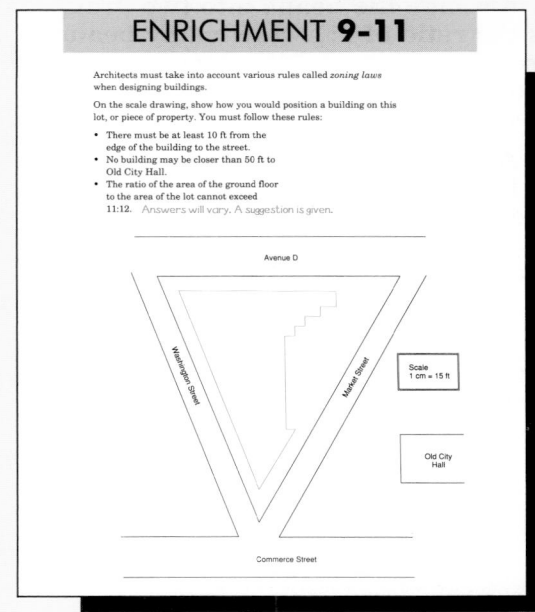

Lesson Organizer

> **Objective:** Solve problems creatively.

Prior Knowledge: Students should have a basic understanding of ratio and be able to multiply and divide whole numbers and money.

Lesson Resources:
Daily Review 9-12

Two-Minute Math

Solve.

$\frac{7}{n} = \frac{1}{19}$ *(133)* $\frac{n}{18} = \frac{2}{3}$ *(12)*

$\frac{5}{6} = \frac{225}{n}$ *(270)* $\frac{12}{39} = \frac{n}{13}$ *(4)*

1 PREPARE

CONNECTING ACTIVITY

☑ **MATERIALS CHECKLIST:** 24 beans or counters for each group

Organize the class into groups of three or four.

1. Arrange the beans into two groups in the ratio of 2:1. How many beans are in each group? Explain your reasoning. *(16 and 8; accept reasonable responses.)*

2. Arrange the beans into three groups in the ratio of 1:1:1. How many beans are in each group? Explain your reasoning. *(8 in each group; accept reasonable responses)*

3. Arrange the beans into three groups in the ratio of 1:2:3. How many beans are in each group? Explain your reasoning. *(4:8:12; accept reasonable responses.)*

WHEN YOUR STUDENTS ASK
★ WHY AM I LEARNING THIS? ★

You can connect this lesson to real life through partnership arrangements of businesses. When there are three or more partners, the costs and profits may be determined on the basis of a given ratio.

CREATIVE PROBLEM SOLVING

Planning a Window-Washing Business

MATH AND ECONOMICS

Imagine that you and some friends want to start a summer business. You decide that washing windows might be a good way to earn money. What kind of planning must you do? Accept reasonable answers.

Work in a small group. Use a calculator when necessary.

1. Decide how much money you will need to start your business. Your start-up costs for this business will be the cost of your cleaning supplies. Make a chart like the one below and fill it in. Check students' charts.

Calculators should be available for complex calculations.

2 EXPLORE

☑ **MATERIALS CHECKLIST:** calculators

Students should continue to work in their groups for this lesson. **Suppose your start-up costs were $30, and three people were sharing in the ratio 1:2:3. How much would each person contribute?** *($5, $10, $15)*

How much less would your group make if each of the three people worked 6 h/wk? *(6 h × 6 windows/h = 36 windows/wk; 36 × $4 = $144/wk; $192 − $144 = $48 less)*

SUMMARIZE/ASSESS   **What mathematics skills did you use to plan a window-washing business?** *(Answers will vary. Example: making a table, multiplication and division.)*

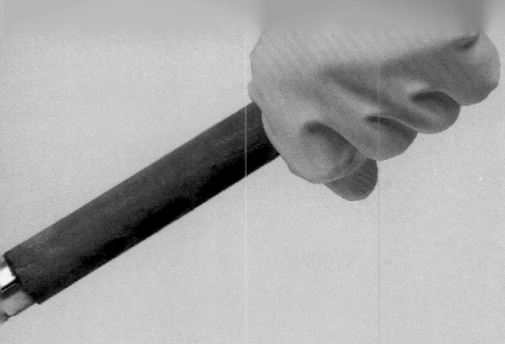

2. Total your start-up costs.
   Check students' work.

3. If the start-up costs are shared equally among all members of your group, how much must each member contribute?
   Accept reasonable answers.

4. Sometimes partners do not share the start-up costs or the profits equally. For example, they might share the start-up costs and the profits in the ratio 1:2:3. If your start-up costs were $18, how much would each person contribute if three people shared the costs in the ratio 1:2:3? Explain.
   $3, $6, $9; Accept reasonable explanations.

Equipment Needed	cost
Total	

5. What are some advantages and disadvantages to business partners of sharing start-up costs equally? of not sharing start-up costs equally? Decide how your group will share the start-up costs for your window-washing business. Write a ratio to show this.
   Check students' work.

6. Suppose you decide to work 8 h/wk. Your group can wash 6 windows in 1 h. You will charge $4.00 per window. How many windows can you wash each week? How much would your group make each week if each of you works 8 h/wk?
   48 windows; $192/wk

7. Use the start-up costs from Exercise 4 and your answer from Exercise 6. If three people shared the start-up costs and the profits in a 1:2:3 ratio, how much would each receive for the first week's work? Remember to subtract your start-up costs from the week's profits. Explain your answer.
   Accept reasonable answers.

8. Suppose that business slows down. To stay in business, how can you vary the services your business provides without adding to your start-up costs? Now suppose business grows so much that there is too much work for you and your partners to handle. What are some things you can do to adjust to this possibility?
   Accept reasonable answers.

9. Exercises 1–9 are based on a window-washing business. List ten other jobs that you could do in the summer to earn money. Be creative. Discuss the advantages and disadvantages of each job.
   Accept reasonable answers.

10. Select one job from Exercise 9. Apply the types of questions asked about the window-washing business to this job. Could you earn money in this business? Explain.
    Accept reasonable answers.

CLASS ACTIVITY 9-12

☑ **MATERIALS CHECKLIST:** grid paper, scissors, tape

Arrange students in groups of two. Provide each student with two sheets of grid paper, scissors, and tape. Have students make two noncongruent rectangles in a ratio of 4 to 3, length to width. Next, have them make a box in the ratio of 4:3:2 for length, width, and height.

MEETING INDIVIDUAL NEEDS

For Students Who Are . . .

Acquiring English Proficiency Discuss the concepts of start-up costs and profits. Explain also that some words, such as *total,* can be used as verbs as well as nouns.

Gifted and Talented Have students write a problem like Exercise 4 using a different start-up amount and ratio. They can exchange papers and solve.

Working 2 or 3 Grades Below Level Explain that when $18 is shared in the ratio 1:2:3, the three amounts must total $18. Have students share $12 in the ratio 1:2:3. *(2:4:6)*

Today's Problem

Three friends started a T-shirt business. Their start-up costs were $195. Ned contributed $135, Jed contributed $45, and Ted contributed $15. In what ratio did they share the start-up costs? *(9:3:1)*

Lesson Organizer

Objective: Review LCM and GCF; operations with whole numbers, decimals, fractions, and mixed numbers; writing equivalent fractions.

Lesson Resources:
Daily Review 9-13

These pages provide students with a review of finding the LCM and GCF of two numbers; writing fractions in lowest terms; adding, subtracting, multiplying, and dividing whole numbers, decimals, fractions and mixed numbers; and choosing the computation method to solve problems. Remind students that these pages review skills covered in previous chapters and will help them to do a self-check to see how well they remember what they have learned.

Mixed Review

Find the LCM.

1. 5, 10 **10**   2. 4, 5 **20**   3. 4, 6 **12**   4. 10, 18 **90**   5. 12, 14 **84**

Find the GCF.

6. 20, 30 **10**   7. 10, 15 **5**   8. 36, 40 **4**   9. 36, 42 **6**   10. 36, 45 **9**

Write the fraction in lowest terms.

11. $\frac{10}{30}$ $\frac{1}{3}$ 12. $\frac{5}{30}$ $\frac{1}{6}$ 13. $\frac{4}{16}$ $\frac{1}{4}$ 14. $\frac{16}{72}$ $\frac{2}{9}$ 15. $\frac{14}{16}$ $\frac{7}{8}$

Compute.

16. $578 + 324$ **902**   17. 23×754 **17,342**   18. $972 - 631$ **341**   19. $5,074 \div 86$ **59**

20. $359,988 \div 524$ **687**   21. $6,627 - 4,738$ **1,889**   22. $11,931 + 12,001$ **23,932**   23. $491 \times 5,561$ **2,730,451**

24. $3.4 + 16.2$ **19.6**   25. 71.6×71.6 **5,126.56**   26. $225.6 \div 56.4$ **4**   27. $89.6 - 9.7$ **79.9**

28. $57.125 + 41.92$ **99.045**   29. $57.125 - 41.92$ **15.205**   30. 14.57×16.2 **236.034**   31. $22.75 + 18.31$ **41.06**

32. $10.73 - 10.67$ **0.06**   33. 378.41×27.8 **10,519.798**   34. $464.16 \div 77.36$ **6**   35. $663.6 \div 55.3$ **12**

Compute. Write the answer in lowest terms.

36. $\frac{3}{4} + \frac{1}{2}$ $1\frac{1}{4}$ 37. $\frac{3}{8} + \frac{5}{16}$ $\frac{11}{16}$ 38. $\frac{11}{12} - \frac{2}{3}$ $\frac{1}{4}$ 39. $\frac{7}{11} \times \frac{1}{4}$ $\frac{7}{44}$

40. $\frac{3}{4} \times \frac{4}{5}$ $\frac{3}{5}$ 41. $\frac{6}{8} \div \frac{1}{2}$ $1\frac{1}{2}$ 42. $12\frac{5}{16} - 10\frac{1}{2}$ $1\frac{13}{16}$ 43. $\frac{8}{9} \div \frac{4}{5}$ $1\frac{1}{9}$

44. $20\frac{5}{16} - 17\frac{1}{2}$ $2\frac{13}{16}$ 45. $2\frac{3}{5} + 8\frac{1}{10}$ $10\frac{7}{10}$ 46. $1\frac{1}{4} \times 2\frac{1}{5}$ $2\frac{3}{4}$ 47. $12\frac{2}{3} \div 2\frac{2}{3}$ $4\frac{3}{4}$

Luzon, Philippines

MATH AND SOCIAL STUDIES

CHOOSE Choose estimation, mental math, **Choices will vary. Suggestions given.** pencil and paper, or calculator to solve.

48. Estimate the part of the Philippine flag that is red.
e; $\approx \frac{5}{12}$

49. Spanish explorers colonized the Philippines in the 1500s. In 1898, Spain gave the Philippines to the United States. On July 4, 1946, the Philippines became independent. For how many years has the Philippines been independent? p; **Answer depends on current year.**

50. There are about 66,156,000 people living in the Philippines, on about 116,000 mi² of land. About how many persons is that per square mile?
c; ≈ 570

51. Nearly half the population of the Philippines live on Luzon, the largest island. About how many people is that? Use the information in Exercise 50.
e; $\approx 33,000,000$

52. Luzon has an area of about 40,000 mi². What is the ratio in lowest terms of the area of Luzon to the total area of the country? Use the information in Exercise 50.
p; 10:29

53. Use an inch ruler to measure along the blue line on the map at right. About how many miles is the distance along the length of the country?
e; ≈ 950 mi

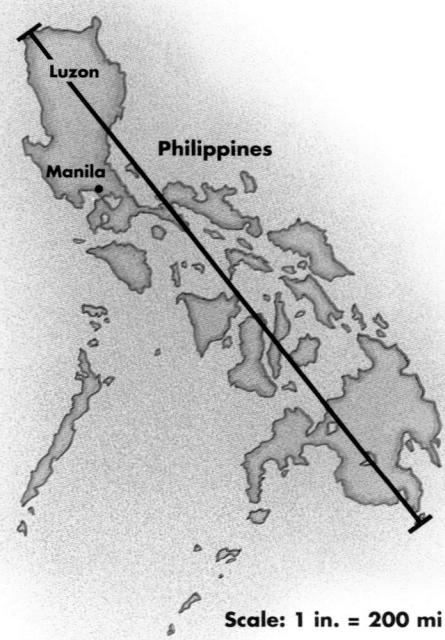

Luzon

Philippines

Manila

Scale: 1 in. = 200 mi

CHAPTER 9   301

MULTICULTURAL NOTE

After first coming to the United States in the 1700s, thousands of Filipinos emigrated while the United States ruled the Philippines. Today Filipinos are the one of the largest Asian-American groups in the United States.

CHAPTER Checkup

This chapter checkup provides a quick language and vocabulary review, a test for the chapter, and suggestions for student Learning Log entries.

Language and Vocabulary

Some key language and vocabulary ideas from this chapter are reinforced here.

Test

This test can be used either as a test or as a review of the chapter prior to your administering the test worksheets found in the Teacher's Resource Book.

The following guide will help you determine percentage scores.

Score	Percent	Score	Percent
19	100%	9	47%
18	95	8	42
17	90	7	36
16	84	6	31
15	79	5	26
14	74	4	20
13	68	3	15
12	63	2	10
11	58	1	5
10	52		

Each test has 3 sections: concepts, skills, and problem solving. These sections provide students with exposure to the formats used on standardized tests.

Use this chart to identify the Management Objectives tested for this chapter.

Items	Management Objectives	Pages
1–10	**9A** Write proportions. **9B** Solve proportions.	280–281; 284–285
11–14	**9C** Use proportions with similar polygons.	292–293
15–16	**9D** Use information from scale drawings.	294–295
17–19	**9E** Problem Solving: Use proportions.	296–297

CHAPTER CHECKUP

LANGUAGE & VOCABULARY

Is the statement *true* or *false*?

1. The only figures that can be similar are polygons. **false**

2. All rectangles are similar. **true**

3. A scale drawing can be smaller than the original. **true**

TEST ✓

CONCEPTS

Use cross products to choose = or ≠. *(pages 280–281)*

1. $\frac{2}{9} \blacksquare \frac{4}{15}$ ≠
2. $\frac{10}{15} \blacksquare \frac{30}{45}$ =
3. $\frac{8}{7} \blacksquare \frac{12}{9}$ ≠
4. $\frac{14}{20} \blacksquare \frac{21}{30}$ =

SKILLS

Solve for the unknown value. Check your answer. *(pages 280–281)*

5. $\frac{3}{9} = \frac{5}{x}$ 15
6. $\frac{7}{12} = \frac{x}{36}$ 21
7. $\frac{1}{8} = \frac{6}{x}$ 48
8. $\frac{r}{12} = \frac{12}{16}$ 9

Find the better buy. *(pages 284–285)*

9. peanut butter: 12 oz for $1.75 or 18 oz for $2.35
   18 oz
10. bread: 24-oz loaf for $1.67 or 32-oz loaf for $2.49
    24-oz

The figures are similar. Write a proportion to solve for the unknown value. *(pages 290–293)* **Check students' work.**

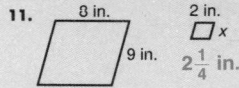

11. 8 in. / 9 in. / 2 in. x / $2\frac{1}{4}$ in.

12. 8 cm / 10 cm / m / 12 cm / 15 cm

13. 27 m / x / y / 60 m / 12 m / 45 m   x = 36 m   y = 7.2 m

14. 15 ft / a / 20 ft / 18 ft / 24 ft

CHAPTER TEST • FORM A

Do the two ratios make a proportion? Choose = or ≠. *(pp. 274–279, 282–283)* 9A

1. $\frac{3}{7} \neq \frac{2}{3}$
2. $\frac{3}{21} = \frac{1}{7}$
3. $\frac{36}{48} = \frac{6}{8}$
4. $\frac{13}{45} \neq \frac{1}{3}$
5. $\frac{3}{8} \neq \frac{1}{3}$

Solve the proportion. *(280–281, 284–285)* 9B

6. $\frac{3}{8} = \frac{x}{32}$ 12
7. $\frac{7}{12} = \frac{35}{x}$ 60
8. $\frac{16}{3} = \frac{x}{12}$ 64
9. $\frac{5}{x} = \frac{2}{3}$ $7\frac{1}{2}$
10. $\frac{x}{24} = \frac{15}{9}$ 40

The figures are similar. Write a proportion to solve for the unknown value. *(pp. 290–293)* 9C

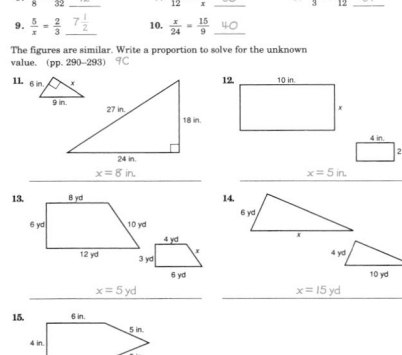

11. 6 in. / x / 9 in. / 27 in. / 18 in. / 24 in.   x = 8 in.

12. 10 in. / x / 4 in. / 2 in.   x = 5 in.

13. 8 yd / 6 yd / 10 yd / 12 yd / 4 yd x / 3 yd / 6 yd   x = 5 yd

14. 6 yd / x / 4 yd / 10 yd   x = 15 yd

15. 6 in. / 4 in. / 5 in. / 5 in. / 6 in. / 2 in. / 3 in.   x = $2\frac{1}{2}$ in.

CHAPTER TEST • FORM A

(pp. 294–295) 9D

Use a ruler and the scale to find the length in yards.   Scale: $\frac{1}{2}$ in. = 5 yd.

16. _____ 15 yd
17. _____ $8\frac{3}{4}$ yd
18. _____ $22\frac{1}{2}$ yd

Use a ruler and the scale to find the length in miles.   Scale: $\frac{1}{8}$ in. = 2 mi

19. _____ 12 mi
20. _____ 22 mi

Use a proportion to solve each problem. *(pp. 288–289, 296–297)* 9E

21. At Woodland Hills Junior High School the ratio of students to teachers is 16 to 1. Find the number of students if there are 45 teachers.   720 students

22. There are 3 seventh graders for every 2 ninth graders. Find the number of ninth graders if there are 477 seventh graders.   318 ninth graders

23. The ratio of girls to boys at Woodland Hills Junior High is 6:5. Find the number of girls if there are 580 boys.   696 girls

24. The ratio of the number of school buses to vans is 11:2. Find the number of vans if there are 88 school buses.   16 vans

25. A farmer planted fruit trees in a ratio of 3 red delicious apple trees to 2 golden delicious apple trees. Find the number of red delicious apple trees that would be planted if 40 golden delicious apple trees are planted.   60 red

Use a ruler and the scale to find the length in feet. *(pages 294–295)*

Scale: $\frac{1}{4}$in. = 3 ft **15.** $\overline{\qquad}$ 15 ft **16.** $\overline{\qquad}$ 30 ft

PROBLEM SOLVING

Write a proportion to solve. *(pages 296–297)*

17. A building is being constructed from a scale model that is 4 ft high. The scale used to construct the building is 1 in. = 10 ft.

a. What is the height of the scale model? **4 ft**

b. What does a scale of 1 in. = 10 ft mean? **Every inch in the scale means ten feet of actual building.**

c. What will the height of the actual building be? **480 ft**

Write a proportion. Solve. *(pages 276–279, 282–283)*

18. David paid $4.83 for 3 gal of gasoline. At that rate, how much will Rosella pay for 8 gal of gasoline? **$12.88**

19. A photograph with dimensions 14 in. by 20 in. is to be enlarged. Will the enlargement have the same shape as the original if its dimensions are 21 in. by 30 in? **yes**

LEARNING LOG

Write the answers in your learning log. **Answers will vary. Suggestions given.**

1. Your friend thinks all pieces of paper are similar. Explain what is wrong with this thinking. **Pieces of paper can be different shapes and colors.**

2. What is important to remember when using proportions to solve problems? **Be sure the ratios are in the right order.**

Note that the same numbers are used in Exercises 4 and 19.

CHAPTER 9 303

Problem Solving

Item 17 has 3 parts:
a. literal—this is a reading comprehension question
b. interpretive—this involves interpretation using the facts given
c. applied—students use a strategy or skill to find an answer

Item 4 in the skill section and item 19 in the problem solving section use the same numbers.

This will help you informally assess how your students transfer from numerical skills to work problems.

For scoring problem solving items you may wish to use partial credit. If a student uses the correct strategy but gets a wrong answer, give the student 2 points toward the total percent score.

Learning Log

These are suggestions for writing about some topics taught in this chapter. The students keep their Learning Logs from the beginning of the school year through the end.

CHAPTER TEST • FORM B

Do the two rations make a proportion? Choose = or ≠. (pp. 274–279, 282–283) 9A

1. $\frac{13}{39} \stackrel{=}{} \frac{1}{3}$ **2.** $\frac{34}{51} \stackrel{=}{} \frac{2}{3}$ **3.** $\frac{1}{7} \stackrel{\neq}{} \frac{5}{49}$ **4.** $\frac{2}{4} \stackrel{=}{} \frac{3}{6}$ **5.** $\frac{9}{12} \stackrel{=}{} \frac{6}{8}$

Solve the proportion. (280–281, 284–285) 9B

6. $\frac{3}{7} = \frac{x}{28}$ *12* **7.** $\frac{5}{12} = \frac{35}{x}$ *84* **8.** $\frac{20}{3} = \frac{x}{12}$ *80*

9. $\frac{5}{x} = \frac{2}{5}$ *$12\frac{1}{2}$* **10.** $\frac{x}{24} = \frac{15}{5}$ *72*

The figures are similar. Write a proportion to solve for the unknown value. (pp. 290–293) 9C

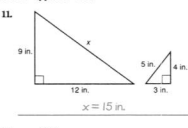

x = 15 in.

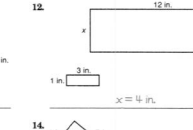

x = 4 in.

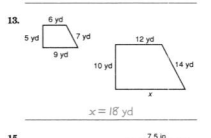

x = 18 yd   x = 8 ft

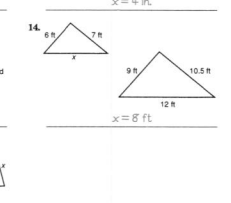

x = 5 in.

CHAPTER TEST • FORM B

(pp. 294–295) 9D

Use a ruler and the scale to find the length in yards. Scale: $\frac{1}{2}$ in. = 5 yd.

16. $\overline{\qquad}$ **17.** $\overline{\qquad}$ **18.** $\overline{\qquad}$
  20 yd   *$11\frac{1}{4}$ yd*   *$17\frac{1}{2}$ yd*

Use a ruler and the scale to find the length in miles. Scale: $\frac{1}{8}$ in. = 2 mi

19. $\overline{\qquad}$ **20.** $\overline{\qquad}$
  34 mi   *20 mi*

Use a proportion to solve each problem. (pp. 288–289, 296–297) 9E

21. At Crest Junior High School the ratio of students to teachers is 15 to 1. Find the number of students if there are 48 teachers. *720 students*

22. At Elk City High School there are 3 sophomores for every 2 seniors. Find the number of seniors if there are 675 sophomores. *450 seniors*

23. The ratio of girls to boys at Elk City High school is 5:4. Find the number of girls if there are 560 boys. *700 girls*

24. The ratio of the length to the width of the swimming pool is 5:2. Find the width of the pool if it is 80 ft long. *32 ft*

25. A farmer planted citrus trees in a ratio of 7 orange trees to 2 lemon trees. Find the number of orange trees that would be planted if 44 lemon trees are planted. *154 orange trees*

Error Analysis and Remediation

Here are some common errors students make when they are working with ratios and proportions. The errors are listed by lesson under the appropriate management objective.

9A • WRITE RATIOS, PROPORTIONS, AND RATES

Source of Error (Lesson 9-1)
Students write the terms of the ratio in the wrong order.

Remediation
Have students first write the ratio in words and then substitute the numbers. For example, the ratio of 20 boys to 30 girls is:

$$\frac{\text{boys}}{\text{girls}} = \frac{20}{30}$$

Source of Error (Lesson 9-5)
Students multiply straight across instead of using cross products.

Remediation
Have students write the proportion with arrows and show the products to indicate cross multiplication.

9B • SOLVE PROPORTIONS

Source of Error (Lesson 9-4)
Students set up proportions incorrectly.

Remediation
Review how to use proportional thinking to write a proportion and cross products to solve for an unknown by having students use two-color counters to model $\frac{3}{2} = \frac{n}{8}$.

Source of Error (Lesson 9-6)
Students divide in the wrong order when finding the unit rate.

Remediation
Give students a simple problem to solve, such as: If 10 pens cost, $3.00, find the cost of one pen. Guide students through each step, emphasizing the correct order in which they should divide.

9C • USE PROPORTION WITH SIMILAR POLYGONS

Source of Error (Lesson 9-9)
Students have difficulty setting up the appropriate proportion.

Remediation
Display two similar right triangles and label them ABC and DEF. Review how to find corresponding sides. Then write $\frac{AB}{DE} = \frac{BC}{EF} = \frac{CA}{FD}$ on the chalkboard to show how the proportions can be written. Have students substitute known values and then solve for unknown values.

9D • USE INFORMATION FROM SCALE DRAWINGS

Source of Error (Lesson 9-10)
Students set up the proportion incorrectly.

Remediation
Strongly suggest that students write the proportion in words first. Stress that the scale is the ratio of the length in the drawing to the actual length.

9E • PROBLEM SOLVING: USE PROPORTIONS

Source of Error (Lesson 9-11)
Students do not use the same order of comparison in setting up the proportion.

Remediation
Tell students to check the terms of their proportions against the problems and to check the reasonableness of their answer. Remind them to focus on the Plan step in the four-part process when solving proportion problems.

Multicultural Notes

Mathematics in the Building of the Pyramids

The building of the pyramids in ancient Egypt was one of the greatest engineering feats of all times. The three pyramids at Giza face perfectly north, south, east, and west. The maximum error in the lengths of the sides and the corner angles of the Great Pyramid is much less than 1%. This precision proves that the Egyptians knew how to construct right angles with great accuracy and had detailed understanding of the sun's movement and its relationship to direction on earth.

The Egyptians knew and used formulas for the volume of a pyramid and the frustum (a part of a solid between two parallel planes cutting the solid, often one of the planes is the base of the solid) of a pyramid. In all, about 2.3 millions blocks of granite and limestone were used to build the Great Pyramid. The average weight of these blocks was about 3,000 lb, but some weighed as much as 32,000 lb.

The engineering within the Great Pyramid is equally amazing. The passages above the chambers of the pyramids are so designed that they distribute the weight of the stones above them. Without these passages the weight of the stones would crush the chambers.

The Great Pyramid served as a landmark for Egyptian surveyors based on its positioning precisely halfway between the boundaries of ancient Egypt. Some Egyptian scholars believe that the very measurements of various parts of the Great Pyramid served essentially as standards of measurement and as representations of mathematical and astronomical ideas.

Measurement in Ancient Egypt

The ancient Egyptians were the first to use standard measures for distances, weights, and time. One of the earliest units of measure was the *cubit*, the length of a forearm from the elbow to the tip of the middle finger. Different ancient peoples had different lengths for the cubit.

The Egyptians had two cubits, the *royal cubit* (about 20.59 in.) and the *short cubit* (about 17.72 in.). The royal cubit was used for measuring when buildings were constructed. Other units of length were the *palm* (one-seventh of a cubit), the *finger* (one-quarter of a palm), and the *double-remen* (the length of the diagonal of a square with a side of 1 cubit).

Measures of volume were important for measuring grain. The ancient Egyptians used the *hekat*, a dry measure that was about one-eighth of a modern bushel. Other measures of volume were the *hinu* (one-tenth of a hekat), the *ro* ($\frac{1}{320}$ of a hekat), and the *khar* (two-thirds of a cubic cubit).

The Egyptian Value of Pi

The Rhind Mathematical Papyrus is one of the few records of ancient Egyptian mathematics that has been found and translated. Copied by a scribe named Ah-mose about 1650 B.C. from some works that had been done about 200 years earlier, it contains mathematical tables and problems. One of the problems discusses finding the area of a circle. The method used can be described this way: Subtract one-ninth of the diameter from the diameter and square this difference to find the area. A formula for the area of a circle using this method would be $A = (\frac{8d}{9})^2$ and the value for pi derived from this formula is about 3.1605. This value of pi is much closer to its real value (about 3.14159) than the Babylonian value of 3.

Ancient Awareness of the Pythagorean Theorem

Credit for determining that the sum of the squares of the lengths of the legs of a right triangle is equal to the square of the length of the hypotenuse has long been given to Pythagoras, who was born on Samos about 560 B.C. and died in Metapontum about 480 B.C. It is known that he traveled to Egypt and to Babylonia when he was a young man and learned the mathematics of both countries. Today we know that both the ancient Babylonians and Egyptians were aware of the relationship expressed in the Pythagorean theorem long before Pythagoras was born.

We know more about the mathematics of the early Babylonians than that of the early Egyptians because the Babylonians did their writing and kept their records on clay tables. The clay tablets were far more durable than the pieces of papyrus used by the Egyptians. But problems of translation made access to the knowledge of both peoples almost impossible for centuries. The hieroglyphic writing of the Egyptians was first deciphered in the middle 1800s and the cuneiform script of the Babylonians was not decoded until the end of the 1800s.

A Babylonian clay tablet written sometime between 1900 and 1600 B.C. was translated in 1945 by O. Neugebauer and A. Sachs. The tablet contains 15 sets of numbers that satisfy the Pythagorean theorem and proves that the Babylonians knew and used this relationship over 1,000 years before Pythagoras was born.

Egyptian references to "rope-stretchers" help to establish that the Egyptians were aware of at least one case of the Pythagorean theorem. The "rope-stretchers" were the officials who laid out the marks for the foundations of new buildings. It is believed that they used ropes with 12 equally spaced knots to form a 3-4-5 right triangle to establish square corners. There are other indicators that the Egyptians knew of this relationship; for example, the cover of the tomb of Ramses IX as shown in the pupil edition on page 454 depicts an Egyptian god and a snake in a design based on a 3-4-5 right triangle. This tomb dates from 1140 B.C.

Extra Practice

This page provides extra practice of all the major chapter objectives. Use this page after the chapter has been taught to reinforce the chapter skills. Page references are provided for each group of items so that students can easily look back at the appropriate lesson for additional support.

Use cross products to choose = or ≠. *(pages 280–281)*

1. $\frac{3}{12} \blacksquare \frac{9}{48}$ ≠
2. $\frac{7}{15} \blacksquare \frac{21}{45}$ =
3. $\frac{20}{12} \blacksquare \frac{16}{10}$ ≠
4. $\frac{9}{25} \blacksquare \frac{3}{8}$ ≠

Solve the proportion. Check your answer. *(pages 280–281)*

5. $\frac{1}{5} = \frac{6}{x}$ 30
6. $\frac{2}{3} = \frac{x}{21}$ 14
7. $\frac{2}{5} = \frac{8}{x}$ 20
8. $\frac{12}{32} = \frac{18}{m}$ 48

9. $\frac{y}{4} = \frac{42}{56}$ 3
10. $\frac{6}{x} = \frac{8}{12}$ 9
11. $\frac{5}{9} = \frac{n}{45}$ 25
12. $\frac{14}{2} = \frac{42}{a}$ 6

Find the better buy. *(pages 284–285)*

13. salt: 16 oz for $.59 or 18 oz for $.75
    16 oz
14. vinegar: 20 oz for $.45 or 32 oz for $.60
    32 oz
15. rice: 32 oz for $1.39 or 48 oz for $1.89
    48 oz
16. frankfurters: 8 for $2.49 or 12 for $2.70
    12

The figures are similar. Write a proportion to solve for the unknown value. *(pages 292–293)*

17. 4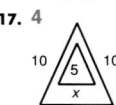

18. 15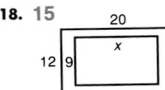

19. 15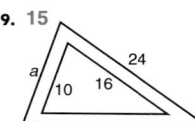

20. 32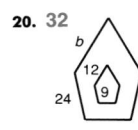

Use a ruler and the scale to find the length. *(pages 294–295)*

21. |———————————| **9 yd** Scale: 0.5 in. = 3 yd

22. |————————————————| **54 ft** Scale: 0.25 in. = 6 ft

23. |————————————| **64 mi** Scale: $\frac{1}{8}$ in. = 4 mi

Solve. *(pages 282–283, 296–297)*

24. A model of an airplane that is 150 ft long is built to a scale of $\frac{1}{8}$ in. = 1 ft. How long will the model be?
    18.75 in.
25. For the airplane described above, the ratio of the wingspan to the length is 3 to 4. How long is the wingspan of the actual plane? of the model? **112.5 ft; 14.06 ft**

304   EXTRA PRACTICE

MAKING A SCALE MODEL DRAWING

Some examples of scale models are blueprints, photographs, maps, dolls, and television pictures. You can make scale model drawings this way.

- Tape several sheets of centimeter graph paper together to use for an enlargement.
- Draw a simple design on another sheet of graph paper.
- Enlarge the design using a 1:2 ratio. For example, make every segment that is 1 cm long in the original 2 cm long in the enlargement.

Try several designs. By doubling the length of each segment, by what ratio does the area of the figure increase? **4:1; Check students' work.**

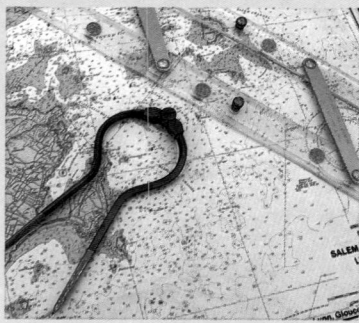

Fast Times

Choose a race. It could be the Boston Marathon, the Indianapolis 500, an Olympic swim meet, or any race you are interested in. Use an almanac to find the winning times for the race over a period of years. Make a graph of the data. See if you can predict from your graph what the winning time may be 10 yr from now. **Check students' work.**

Scales of Squares

Play with a partner. On a piece of paper, make a game board like the one below. Take turns putting your first initial in a circle. The winner is the player whose initials are in 4 circles that, when connected, would make a square.
Check students' work.

$$
\begin{array}{cccc}
\bigcirc & \bigcirc & \bigcirc & \bigcirc \\
\bigcirc & \bigcirc & \bigcirc & \bigcirc \\
\bigcirc & \bigcirc & \bigcirc & \bigcirc \\
\bigcirc & \bigcirc & \bigcirc & \bigcirc
\end{array}
$$

Enrichment

This page contains activities that provide extension and enrichment for all levels of students. Depending on the needs of your students, you may wish to assign an activity from this page at certain points during the chapter, or you may want to use this page when the entire chapter has been completed.

Making a Scale Model Drawing

If students have difficulty starting, suggest they think of polygon figures, which can be used to create interesting designs.

Fast Times

You will need to have several almanacs on hand for this activity. As students look at the group of completed graphs, ask what general trends they observe (for example, winning times generally improve) and have them suggest reasons for these trends.

Scales of Scales
(COOPERATIVE)

After partners play a few rounds of the game, ask if anyone has discovered a way either to win or to prevent the partner from winning.

CHAPTER 9

Cumulative Review

The Cumulative Review focuses on skills covered in previous chapters. All important skills are reviewed on a cyclic basis.

If students are having difficulty with particular groups of exercises, refer to the chart for follow-up work.

Find the answer.

1. $3,459 \times 28 =$ c
   a. 92,282
   b. 34,590
   c. 96,852
   d. none of these

2. $27.09 \times 0.6 =$ d
   a. 162.54
   b. 1.6254
   c. 0.16254
   d. none of these

3. $0.039 \times 0.003 =$ a
   a. 0.000117
   b. 0.00117
   c. 0.0117
   d. none of these

4. $3,843 \div 25 =$ b
   a. 112 R 13
   b. 153 R 18
   c. 152 R 18
   d. none of these

5. $\$16.28 \div 22 =$ c
   a. $7.40
   b. $358.16
   c. $.74
   d. none of these

6. $83.41 \div 0.19 =$ c
   a. 43.9
   b. 4.39
   c. 439
   d. none of these

Solve for x.

7. $\frac{x}{24} = \frac{35}{60}$ a
   a. 14
   b. 16
   c. 20
   d. none of these

8. $\frac{10}{16} = \frac{x}{24}$ b
   a. 12
   b. 15
   c. 18
   d. none of these

9. $\frac{25}{40} = \frac{20}{x}$ b
   a. 30
   b. 32
   c. 36
   d. none of these

Find the best estimate.

10. $418 \div 83 =$ a
    a. 5
    b. 6
    c. 50
    d. none of these

11. $2,421 \div 59 =$ c
    a. 30
    b. 50
    c. 40
    d. none of these

12. $26.8 \div 0.31 =$ a
    a. 90
    b. 9
    c. 900
    d. none of these

Evaluate the expression. Use the value of the given variable.

13. $x^2 - x$ b
    Use $x = 9$.
    a. 0
    b. 72
    c. 90
    d. none of these

14. $3(9 - y)$ c
    Use $y = 2$.
    a. 27
    b. 25
    c. 21
    d. none of these

15. $7 - (m \div 3)$ b
    Use $m = 6$.
    a. $\frac{1}{3}$
    b. 5
    c. 4
    d. none of these

Items	Management Objectives	Where Taught	Reteaching Options	Extra Practice Options
1, 4	**3B** Multiply and divide whole numbers.	64–65; 68–69	TE/RA 3-3 and 3-5	TRB/PW 3-3 and 3-5
2–3; 5–6	**3C** Multiply and divide decimals.	66–67; 70–71; 80–81	TRB/RW 3-4 and 3-6; TE/RA 3-10	TRB/PW 3-4, 3-6, and 3-10
7–9	**9B** Solve proportions.	280–281	TRB/RW 9-4	TRB/PW 9-4
10–12	**3D** Estimate quotients.	82–83	TRB/RW 3-11	TRB/PW 3-11
13–15	**4A** Write and evaluate expressions.	96–99	TE/RA 4-2	TRB/PW 4-2

Problem Solving Review

This page focuses on problem solving strategies and types learned in this chapter and previous chapters. A problem solving checklist lists some of the strategies students may use to solve the problems on this page.

PROBLEM SOLVING REVIEW

Strategies may vary. Suggestions given.
Remember the strategies and types of problems you have done so far. Solve.

> **Problem Solving Check List**
>
> - Too much information
> - Too little information
> - Making a table
> - Multistep problems
> - Using proportions
> - Making a list
> - Using a pattern

1. Lee measured his room and drew a scale model of it. The drawing was a rectangle 6 in. by 9 in. The scale was $\frac{1}{2}$ in. = 1 ft.

   a. What scale did Lee use? $\frac{1}{2}$ in. = 1 ft

   b. How can you find the actual dimensions of the room? **multiply by 2**

   c. What are the dimensions of the room? **multistep; 12 ft by 18 ft**

2. Kim has $2.35 in coins. Her friend has exactly $1.00 more in coins. They combine their money and exchange it for bills. What is the fewest number of bills they can receive?
   table; 1 bill

3. Carla delivers balloon bouquets that come in three sizes: small, for $7.95; medium, for $12.95; and large, for $22.95. She earns $2.00 per delivery. How much does she earn for delivering 3 small, 3 medium, and 4 large bouquets?
   too much information; $20

4. Stan ran the first lap of a race in 2 min 48 s. He ran each of the remaining laps in 3 min 19 s. What was his time for the entire race?
   too little information

5. Mercedes had $10. She bought 1 pen for $2.95, labels for $.59, and envelopes for $2.19. How much more did she spend for the pen than the envelopes?
   too much information; $.76

6. Grover Cleveland served as President of the United States from 1885 to 1889 and from 1893 to 1897. How many years elapsed between the beginning of his first term and the end of his second term?
   too much information; 12 yr

7. Jan traveled from Buffalo to Memphis, from Memphis to New Orleans, and from New Orleans to Mobile. She could choose from 3 flights, 4 trains, and 2 buses. How many choices did Jan have?
   too much information; 9

8. Sun drew a coordinate grid. He plotted the points represented by the ordered pairs: (1, 3), (2, 5), and (3, 7). If he continued the pattern, what are the coordinates of the next ordered pair?
   pattern; (4, 9)

9. A baby weighed 7 lb 4 oz at birth. During the next two months, the baby gained 13 oz, lost 3 oz, and then gained 6 oz. How much did the baby weigh after two months?
   multistep; 8 lb 4 oz

Technology

This page is designed to provide calculator or computer experiences for all levels of students. The calculator or computer logo indicates the type of activity.

You may wish to assign these activities after the chapter has been taught or during the course of the chapter, depending on your needs and those of your students.

Easy as Pi

If students have difficulty starting, suggest that they consider a division in which the dividend is slightly more than three times the divisor. Students may do this activity in pairs if you wish.

Smart Shopping

Be sure students identify the unit *(oz)* before they begin this activity.

What's the Ratio?

If students use guess and check, they should record their "guesses" so as not to repeat them.

Although this is a paper and pencil activity, software that develops the same skill is found in Houghton Mifflin Math Activities Courseware, Grade 7.

TECHNOLOGY

EASY AS PI

On a calculator with eight digits, π equals 3.1415927. Some people use 3.14 to estimate π, while some use $\frac{22}{7}$. Write $\frac{22}{7}$ as a decimal.
3.1428571
Find three nonequivalent fractions that give 3.141 as a quotient when all the decimal places to the right of the thousandths' place are dropped.
Check students' work

WHAT'S THE RATIO?

In the computer activity *Ratio Maze*, you find your way out of a maze by finding equivalent ratios. This pencil-and-paper activity will build your skills at writing equivalent ratios.
See below.
Write three equivalent ratios using the numbers in each box.

1. $\boxed{2\ 3\ 4\ 5\ 6\ 10}$ $\quad \frac{2}{4}; \frac{3}{6}; \frac{5}{10}$

2. $\boxed{6\ 9\ 10\ 12\ 15\ 18}$ $\quad \frac{6}{9}; \frac{10}{15}; \frac{12}{18}$

3. $\boxed{10\ 12\ 15\ 18\ 25\ 30}$ $\quad \frac{10}{12}; \frac{15}{18}; \frac{25}{30}$

4. $\boxed{6\ 12\ 16\ 18\ 32\ 48}$ $\quad \frac{6}{16}; \frac{12}{32}; \frac{18}{48}$

SMART SHOPPING

Which price gives you the most for your money? **XYZ Salt**

Salty Sam's salt: 1 lb $0.60

XYZ Salt: 1 lb, 12 oz $0.89

Salt-o'-the-Earth: 26 oz $0.99

How much would 64 oz of the best buy cost, using the same unit price?
$2.03

Software Activities

Note: To leave the program, students should use the ESCAPE or QUIT command for their computers.

activity 1 • PERCENT OF SHORELINE

MATERIALS: database program, almanacs, calculators, USA maps

Procedure: In this activity, students calculate the percent of shoreline that is coastline. Have students begin by creating a database for the information displayed in the chart along with a field for percent.

Coast	Shoreline	Coastline	Percent
Atlantic	28,673	2,069	
Gulf	17,141	1,631	
Pacific	40,298	7,623	
Arctic	2,521	1,060	

Next, students should find the percent for each region: divide the coastline by the shoreline and multiply by 100. Have students enter the percent into the appropriate field and sort on the percent field to determine the region with the largest percent.

Follow-up: Ask students to look at a map and guess which states have the least and greatest percent of shoreline that is coastline. They should confirm their answer by obtaining the state data in almanacs.

activity 2 • FRACTIONS TO PERCENTS

MATERIALS: BASIC programming

Procedure: This program converts a fraction that is input by the student to a percent. Have students enter this program into the computer and run it.

```
10 PRINT "THIS PROGRAM WILL
   CHANGE ";
20 PRINT "FRACTIONS TO PERCENTS. "
30 PRINT "ENTER THE NUMERATOR AND
   THE ";
40 PRINT "DENOMINATOR AS X , Y "
50 PRINT: INPUT X,Y
60 LET D=X/Y
70 P=INT(100*D +.5)
80 PRINT P; "%": GOTO 30
```

Follow-up: Have students modify the program so it prints the percent to two decimal places.

HOUGHTON MIFFLIN SOFTWARE

Computational Skills Program. Boston, MA: Houghton Mifflin Company, 1988. For Apple II.

Easy Graph. Boston, MA: Houghton Mifflin Company, 1987. For Apple II, Commodore, IBM.

EduCalc. Boston, MA: Houghton Mifflin Company, 1990. For Apple II, Commodore, IBM.

Friendly Filer. Boston, MA: Houghton Mifflin Company, 1989. For Apple II, Commodore, IBM.

Mathematics Activities Courseware. Boston, MA: Houghton Mifflin Company, 1983. For Apple II, IBM.

The Computer Tutor. Boston, MA: Houghton Mifflin Company, 1990. For Apple II, IBM.

OTHER SOFTWARE

Math Skills-Junior High Level. Des Plaines, IL: Looking Glass Learning, 1989. For Apple II.

Microsoft Works. Redmond, WA: Microsoft Corporation, 1989. For IBM, Macintosh.

Ratio and Proportion. Big Spring, TX: Gamco Industries, Inc., 1989. For Apple II, Commodore, IBM, TRS-80.

Ratios and Proportions. Fairfield, CT: Intellectual Software/Queue Software, Inc., 1989. For Amiga, Apple II, IBM, Macintosh.

Super Paint. San Diego, CA: Silicon Beach Software, 1988. For Macintosh.

Percent

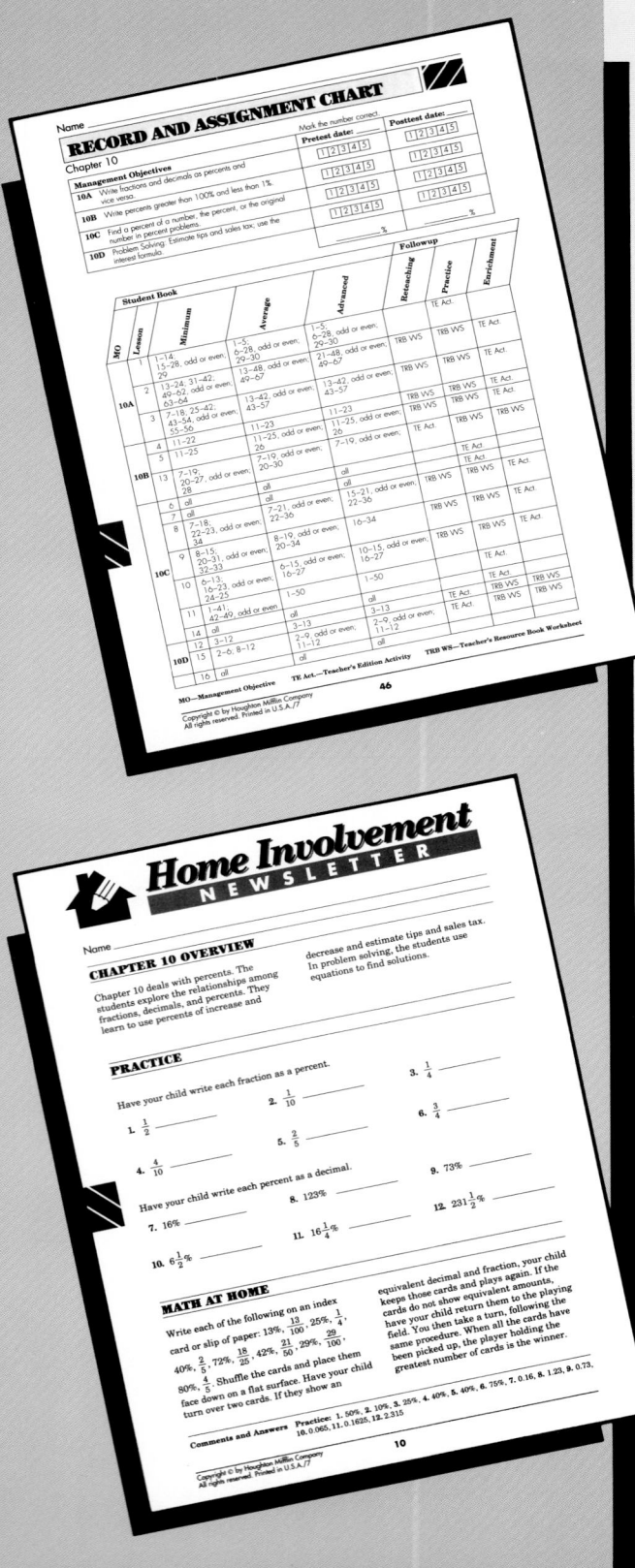

This chapter introduces the concept of percent. It focuses on writing fractions and decimals as percents and percents as fractions and decimals, the uses of percents, and finding the percent of a number, the percent, and the original number.

The concept of percent is expanded into using mental math to find percents and to solving problems by estimating tips and sales tax and using the interest formula.

Management Objectives

10A Write fractions and decimals as percents and percents as fractions and decimals.

10B Write percents greater than 100% and less than 1%.

10C Find the percent of a number, the percent, or the original number in percent problems.

10D Problem Solving: Estimate tips and sales tax. Use the interest formula.

Assignments for different achievement levels are provided on the Record and Assignment Chart in the Teacher's Resource Book.

Vocabulary

percent, page 310
percent of increase, page 336
percent of decrease, page 337
percent of profit, page 337
percent of loss, page 337
interest, page 338
principal, 338
rate, page 338
time, page 338

Home Involvement

As you begin to teach this chapter, give each student a copy of the Home Involvement Newsletter for this chapter.

This newsletter provides parents with
■ an overview of the chapter
■ suggestions for practicing some of the skills in the chapter
■ an at-home activity to do with their child, applying the skills taught in the chapter.

Management Chart

Management Objectives	Lesson/ Pages	Student Not Successful	Student Needs More Practice	Student Successful	Pacing Range
10A Write fractions and decimals as percents and percents as fractions and decimals.	10-1/310-311			TE/CA 10-1	3-4 days
	10-2/312-313	TRB/RW 10-2	TRB/PW 10-2 CSP Percents	TE/EA 10-2	
	10-3/314-315	TRB/RW 10-3	TRB/PW 10-3 CSP Percents	TE/EA 10-3	
10B Write percents greater than 100% and less than 1%.	10-4/316	TRB/RW 10-4/5	TRB/PW 10-4/5	TE/EA 10-4/5	3-4 days
	10-5/317	TRB/RW 10-4/5	TRB/PW 10-4/5	TE/EA 10-4/5	
	10-13/334-335	TE/RA 10-13	TRB/PW 10-13	TRB/EW 10-13	
10C Find the percent of a number, the percent, or the original number in percent problems.	10-6/318-319			TE/CA 10-6	7-8 days
	10-7/320-321			TE/CA 10-7	
	10-8/322-323	TRB/RW 10-8	TRB/PW 10-8 CSP Percents MAC 6 Activity 11	TE/EA 10-8 MAC 6 Activity 11 MAC 6 Activity 10	
	10-9/324-325	TRB/RW 10-9	TRB/PW 10-9 CSP Percents	TE/EA 10-9	
	10-10/326-327	TRB/RW 10-10	TRB/PW 10-10 CSP Percents CT Unit 5 Obj. 4.1	TE/EA 10-10	
	10-11/328-329		MAC 6 Activity 11 MAC 8 Activity 8	TE/CA 10-11 MAC 7 Activity 10	
	10-14/336-337		CT Unit 7	TE/CA 10-14	
10D Problem Solving: Estimate tips and sales tax. Use the interest formula.	10-12/332-333	TE/RA 10-12	TRB/PW 10-12	TRB/EW 10-12	2 days
	10-15/338-339	TE/RA 10-15	TRB/PW 10-15 CT Unit 7 Obj. 3.1	TRB/EW 10-15	
Creative Problem Solving	10-16/340-341				
Chapter Checkups	330-331; 342-343				
Extra Practice	344				
Enrichment	345				
Cumulative Review/Problem Solving Review	346-347				
Technology	348				

TE = Teacher's Edition
TRB = Teacher's Resource Book
RW = Reteaching Worksheet
RA = Reteaching Activity
EA = Enrichment Activity
EW = Enrichment Worksheet
PW = Practice Worksheet
CA = Classroom Activity

*Other Available Items
MAC = Mathematics Activities Courseware
CSP = Computational Skills Program
CT = Computer Tutor

CHAPTER 10

Manipulative Planning Guide

This is a complete list of manipulatives and materials needed for Chapter 10.

Materials for Manipulatives	TE Activities (INTRODUCE)	Student Book Lesson
Newspapers for each pair		Lessons 10-1, 10-6
Teaching Aid 15* for each student		Lesson 10-1
Calculator for each student		Lessons 10-2, 10-3, 10-8, 10-9, 10-10, 10-13, 10-16
Teaching Aid 2* 150 strips, cut and colored	Lesson 10-3 Lessons 10-4/5	Lesson 10-5
Transparencies Math Connection Percent Bar Diagram	Lessons 10-2, 10-8 Lessons 10-7 through 10-10	Lessons 10-2, 10-3, 10-11
Teaching Aid 16* for each group for each student		Lesson 10-7 Lessons 10-8, 10-10, 10-13
Teaching Aid 17* for each student	Lesson 10-14	
Calendar page for each group		
Index cards		
Almanacs or atlases		
Pieces of paper $1'' \times 1''$ and $\frac{1}{2}'' \times \frac{1}{2}''$		

*Teaching Aids are found in the Teacher's Resource Book.

CONCRETE

Learning Stages

The concepts and skills in Chapter 10 are presented through these learning stages.

Using manipulatives and verbalizing about a concept. No symbols.

Teacher Edition Activities	Student Book
At this grade level the skills of this chapter are taught at the connecting and symbolic stages.	

Enrichment	Reteaching	In the Houghton Mifflin Manipulative Kit?	In the Houghton Mifflin Overhead Kit?
Lesson 10-14			
			Yes
			Available separately
			Yes
Lesson 10-2			Yes
			Yes
			Yes
Lesson 10-3			
Lessons 10-4/5, 10-10, 10-11			
Lesson 10-9			
	Lesson 10-13		

CONNECTING

5¢ 9cm^2 $\frac{1}{3}$

Making a connection between manipulatives and symbols.

Teacher Edition Activities	Student Book
Lessons 10-3, 10-4/5, 10-7, 10-8, 10-9, 10-10, 10-13, 10-14, 10-15	Lessons 10-7, 10-8, 10-9, 10-10

SYMBOLIC

$\$.05$ $A = 9\text{cm}^2$ $1 - \frac{2}{3} = \frac{1}{3}$

Using numbers or symbols. No manipulatives or pictures of manipulatives.

Teacher Edition Activities	Student Book
Lessons 10-1, 10-2, 10-6, 10-11, 10-12	Lessons 10-1, 10-2 through 10-6, 10-11 through 10-15

Additional Activities

COOPERATIVE LEARNING RESOURCE ACTIVITIES

Through cooperative learning activities, students learn by interacting with one another in small groups. These cooperative activities provide students with motivating settings for making connections, investigations, and problem solving situations.

The cooperative connections are interdisciplinary problem-solving projects. Each student has a particular job that helps lead the group to complete the project. For the cooperative investigations students work in pairs for investigations involving data collection and analysis. The cooperative problem solving activities encourage the sharing of ideas and information. Students work in groups of four to solve a problem. Students are each assigned a clue and work together to find a common solution.

COOPERATIVE CONNECTIONS
Chapter 10

COOPERATIVE CONNECTIONS / Math and Sports

PROBLEM: The table lists the teams that played in the World Series from 1979 to 1988. Find the percent of victories of the league that won the most World Series titles.

World Series Results: 1979–1988

Year	National League	American League
1979	PITTSBURG	Baltimore
1980	PHILADELPHIA	Kansas City
1981	LOS ANGELES	New York
1982	ST. LOUIS	Milwaukee
1983	Philadelphia	BALTIMORE
1984	San Diego	DETROIT
1985	St. Louis	KANSAS CITY
1986	NEW YORK	Boston
1987	St. Louis	MINNESOTA
1988	LOS ANGELES	Oakland

COOPERATIVE INVESTIGATIONS
Chapter 10

COOPERATIVE INVESTIGATIONS / Telephone Percents

GOAL: Determine what percent of the total number of pages of the telephone book is occupied by listings beginning with each letter of the alphabet.

Materials: telephone book, pencil, paper, calculator (optional)

Work with a partner.

1. Find the total number of residential listings pages in the telephone book. Record the number.

2. Take turns counting the pages for each letter. Record each number. If necessary round to the next whole number.

3. Write a fraction for each letter to represent the part of the total number of residential listings pages it occupies. Express each fraction as a percent. Check you work by finding the sum of the 26 percents. What should the sum be close to?

COOPERATIVE PROBLEM SOLVING 1
Chapter 10

COOPERATIVE PROBLEM SOLVING / Problem 1

If Jennifer keeps exactly the same pressure on the gas pedal, at what rate will her car travel up the hill?

Clue 1: A 100% incline on a road is equivalent to the road turning straight up at an angle of 90°.

If Jennifer keeps exactly the same pressure on the gas pedal, at what rate will her car travel up the hill?

Clue 3: Jennifer's car loses 5% of its speed for every 2.5° of incline of the road.

If Jennifer keeps exactly the same pressure on the gas pedal, at what rate will her car travel up the hill?

Clue 2: The hill that the car must climb is a 10% incline.

If Jennifer keeps exactly the same pressure on the gas pedal, at what rate will her car travel up the hill?

Clue 4: Before starting up the hill, Jennifer was traveling at 50 mi/h.

COOPERATIVE PROBLEM SOLVING 2
Chapter 10

COOPERATIVE PROBLEM SOLVING / Problem 2

What percent of the eighth graders plan to join a club in high school?

Clue 1: There are 56 girls in the eighth grade. Twice as many boys plan to join the Rocket Club as the Drama Club.

What percent of the eighth graders plan to join a club in high school?

Clue 3: There are 64 boys in the eighth grade. Five girls plan to join the Rocket Club.

What percent of the eighth graders plan to join a club in high school?

Clue 2: Ten boys plan to join the Art Club. The same number of girls plan to join the Chess as boys plan to join the Drama Club.

What percent of the eighth graders plan to join a club in high school?

Clue 4: Five times as many girls plan to join the Art Club as plan to join the Rocket Club. Fifteen boys plan to join the Drama Club.

GAMES

MATCH   (For use after Lesson 10-3)

Objective: Name percents as fractions and decimals.

☑ **MATERIALS CHECKLIST:** 40 index cards for each team of players

Write a percent on each of 20 cards and an equivalent common fraction or decimal on each of 20 matching cards. Four students can use the cards to play a matching game.

One player mixes the cards, deals six cards to each player, and places the remaining cards in a pile. Students immediately display any matched cards. Then the first player asks any other player for a decimal, fraction, or percent card depending on the cards he or she holds. If the player receives a card, he or she displays the matched cards and takes another turn. If no card is forthcoming, the player draws a card from the pile, and the player to the left takes a turn. Play continues until all the cards have been matched. The player with the most matched cards at the end wins.

PIZZA DOUGH   (For use after Lesson 10-12)

Objective: Find the amount of a tip.

☑ **MATERIALS CHECKLIST:** two number cubes (1-6; 4-9) and spinner for each group

Assign students to four-member groups. Give each group two number cubes and a spinner divided into four sections. Have students write one of the following on each section: Cold pizza—No tip; 10% tip; 15% tip; 20% tip. Explain that students work for a pizzeria and usually get a tip when they deliver to customers.

To start the game, have a player toss the number cubes and multiply the numbers to figure the customer's bill. For example, a toss of 6 and 3 means a bill of $18. The player spins to find the percentage for the tip and uses mental math to compute it. For instance, with a spin of 20%, the player above would get a tip of $3.60. Group members take turns. Other players check calculations, and correct tips for each player are recorded. The player with the most tips at the end wins.

BULLETIN BOARD

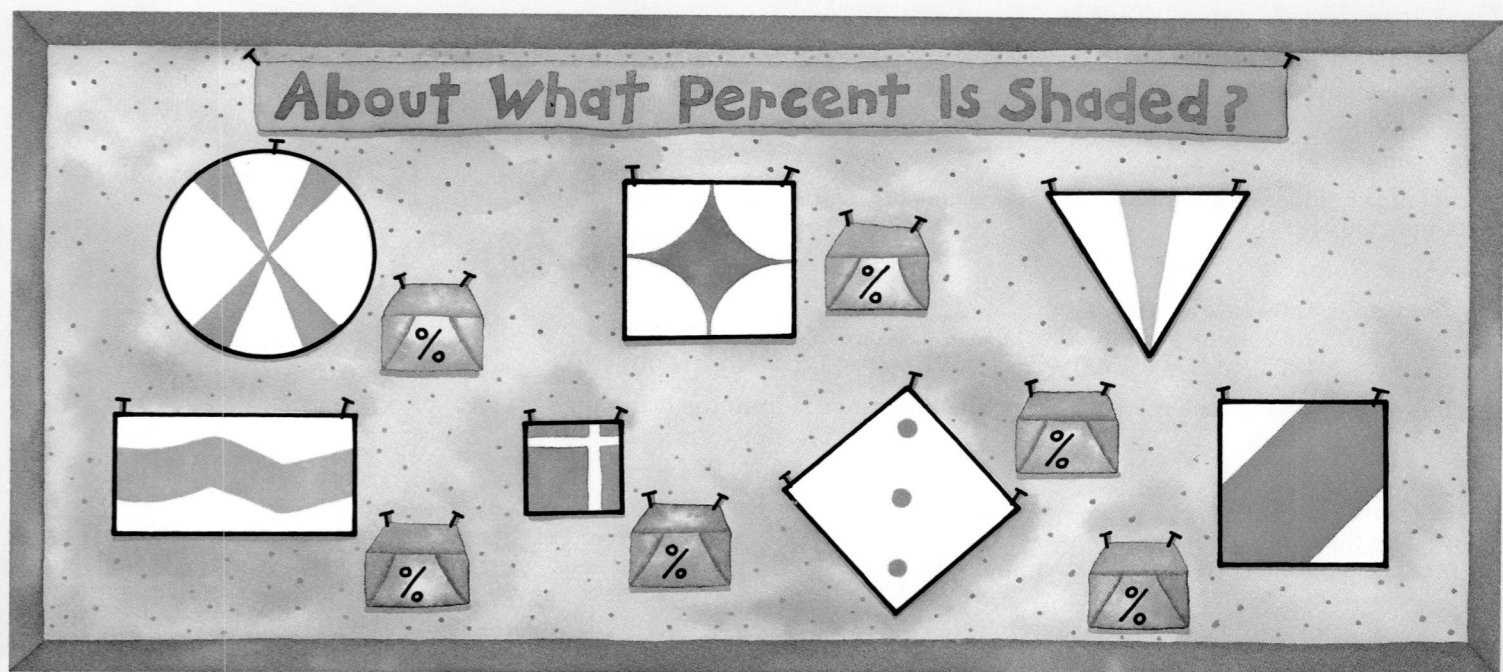

Display geometric shapes or designs that you have partially shaded. Keep a list of the shaded percentages for the figures. Provide an answer envelope next to each figure, and ask students to write what percent of each figure is shaded. They may guess, estimate, and/or measure to arrive at an answer. After all have submitted entries, display your percentages and the closest student responses. Suggest that students make their own designs for others to guess the percent that is shaded.

Alternative Assessment

In addition to the paper and pencil tests available with this program, the following items can help you assess critical thinking as well as your students' ability to solve problems in a wide variety of ways.

Investigation

Use strips of adding machine tape to compare the percent increase and decrease. Example: In 1990, a salesman increased his sales by 25%.

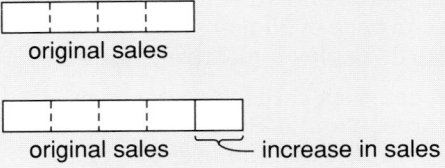

original sales

Fold the strip to find what portion represents 25%. Cut a piece of adding machine tape equal to 25% and add it to the original tape.

original sales   increase in sales

In 1991, sales decreased by 25%. His 1991 sales are less than his original sales.

How could you use the adding machine tape to show this?

Will a percent increase in sales followed by the same percent decrease in sales always result in a smaller number than the original sales? Create other situations to test your conclusion.

Teacher Notes
• Students could fold the longer tape to represent 4 equal segments (25% + 25% + 25% + 25%) and compare the length of 25% + 25% + 25% to the length which represents the original tape. They should explain why they are comparing 75% of the longer tape to 100% of the original tape.

Group Writing Activity (See p. T24.)

(See p. T24.)

Generate a variety of examples that represent an initial percent decrease followed by the same percent increase.

• Students should be encouraged to create situation using numbers (for example, $10,000)

• Students should be encouraged to create situations using different percents (for example, 50%)

Teacher Notes

Example: 1990 sales = $10,000
1991 sales = $10,000 − 25% of $10,000 or 75% of $10,000 = $7,500
1992 sales = $7,500 + 25% of $7,500 or 125% of $10,000 = $9,375

The larger the percent, the more dramatic the difference is from the original.

Individual Writing Activity

Why do you think a percent increase (or decrease) followed by the same percent decrease (or increase) does not produce a quantity equal to the original quantity?

Teacher Notes
The percent of increase or decrease are equal, but the quantities affected by the percent are not, so you do not get back to the original quantity. Since multiplication is commutative and associative, the results are the same whether decrease is followed by increase or vice versa.

Portfolios

The students' work involving the investigation and writing activity suggested on this page along with work on the Critical Thinking feature on page 315, the Write About It exercise on page 319, the Learning Log exercises on pages 331 and 343, and the Creative Problem Solving lesson on pages 340-341 could be included in portfolios. You can use the last Teaching Aid to gain insight about your students' attitudes regarding mathematics and its relevance. This activity will be recommended again in chapter 15. It will help you establish an ongoing dialogue with your students as they progress through the school year.

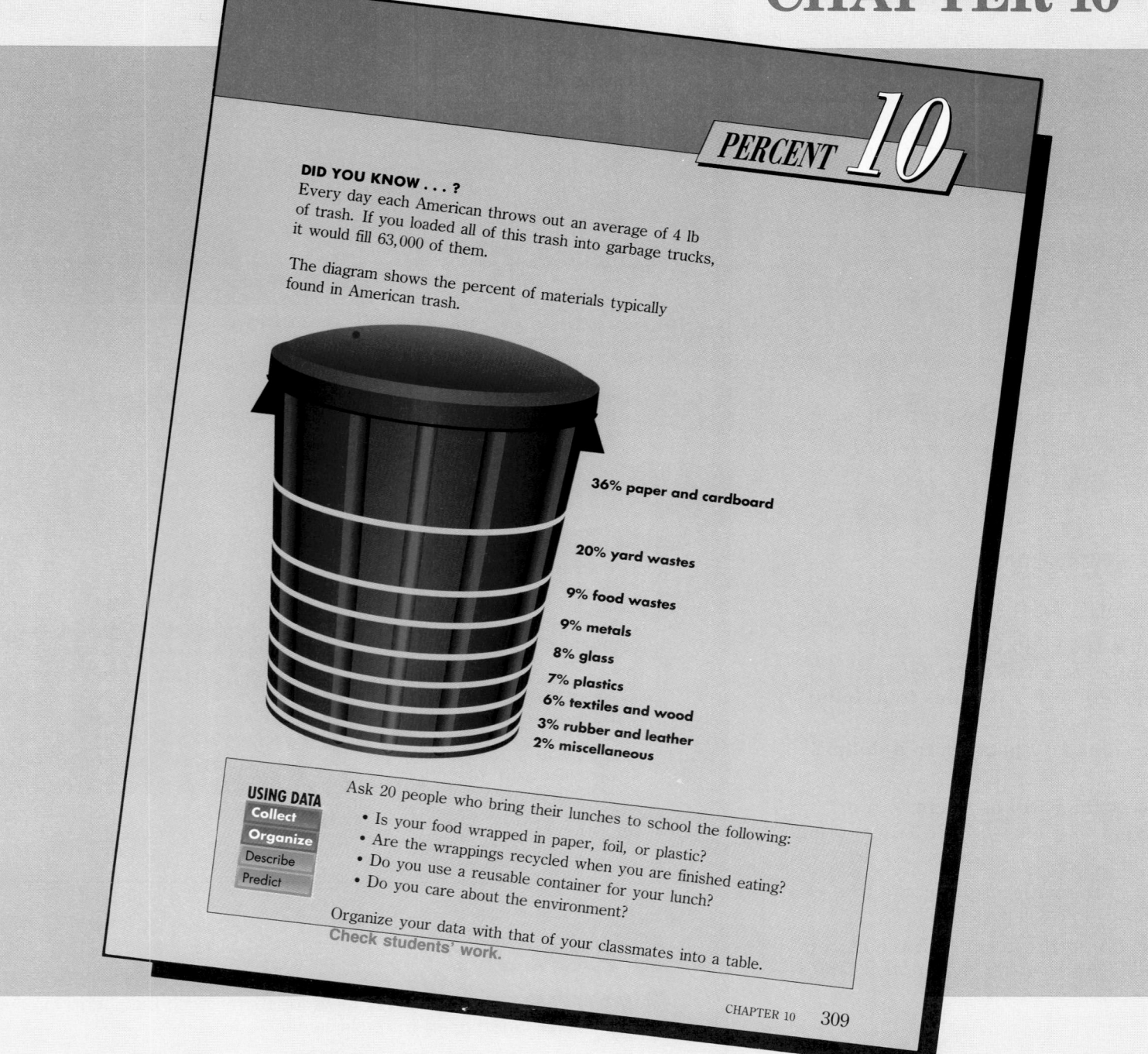

PERCENT **10**

DID YOU KNOW . . . ?

Every day each American throws out an average of 4 lb of trash. If you loaded all of this trash into garbage trucks, it would fill 63,000 of them.

The diagram shows the percent of materials typically found in American trash.

36% paper and cardboard

20% yard wastes

9% food wastes

9% metals

8% glass

7% plastics

6% textiles and wood

3% rubber and leather

2% miscellaneous

USING DATA

Collect

Organize

Describe

Predict

Ask 20 people who bring their lunches to school the following:

- Is your food wrapped in paper, foil, or plastic?
- Are the wrappings recycled when you are finished eating?
- Do you use a reusable container for your lunch?
- Do you care about the environment?

Organize your data with that of your classmates into a table.
Check students' work.

CHAPTER 10   309

Using the Chapter Opener

The purpose of this page is to involve students in the use of real data much like that presented in newspapers and magazines.

To use this page as you begin the chapter, direct students' attention to the data. You may wish to ask questions such as the following:

Which category of materials makes up about one third of American garbage? *(paper and cardboard)*

What percent of American garbage consists of metals, glass, and plastics? *(24%)*

In 1990 there were about 250 million Americans. If each of them threw out an average of about 4 lb of garbage each day, approximately how many pounds of garbage were thrown out each day in the entire United States? *(1,000,000,000 lb)* **How many tons?** *(500,000 t)*

LESSON 10-1

Lesson Organizer

Objective: Explore the meaning of percent.

Prior Knowledge: Students should understand the meaning of ratio.

Error Analysis and Remediation: See page 343A.

Lesson Resources:
Class Activity 10-1
Daily Review 10-1

 **Two-Minute Math**

Complete the proportion.

$\frac{7}{3} = \frac{n}{54}$ *(126)* $\frac{5}{6} = \frac{8}{n}$ *(9.6)*

$\frac{n}{4} = \frac{18}{24}$ *(3)* $\frac{9}{n} = \frac{3}{10}$ *(30)*

1 PREPARE

SYMBOLIC ACTIVITY

What is the ratio of:

8 pennies to a dollar? $\left(\frac{8}{100}\right)$

2 quarters and 7 pennies to a dollar? $\left(\frac{57}{100}\right)$

3 dimes and 19 pennies to a dollar? $\left(\frac{49}{100}\right)$

What is the ratio of 31 cm to a m? $\left(\frac{31}{100}\right)$ **of 43 cm to a m?** $\left(\frac{43}{100}\right)$ **of 5 dm + 9 cm to a m?** $\left(\frac{59}{100}\right)$

What is the ratio of your age to a century? *(Answers may vary.)*

What do all these ratios have in common? *(They compare something to 100.)*

WHEN YOUR STUDENTS ASK
★ **WHY AM I LEARNING THIS?** ★

You can connect understanding the meaning of percent to interpreting various kinds of data encountered in newspapers, magazines, and news reports on radio and television.

310 *Chapter 10 • Lesson 10-1*

 EXPLORE

Exploring the Meaning of Percent

> In about the last 50 yr, 40% of the world's original rain forest cover has been destroyed.
>
> The tropical rain forests support about 50% of the world's species of plants and animals.
>
> It is estimated that about 12% of the 40,000 mi² of tropical forest left in 1980 may be gone by the year 2000.

In each example above, a percent is used to describe a fact about tropical rain forests. **Percent** is a special ratio that compares a number to 100.

1. **IN YOUR WORDS** A percent sign is written at the right. Explain how the sign itself helps you remember the meaning of percent as the ratio of a number to 100, or per hundred.

2. **IN YOUR WORDS** Explain how the word *percent* can help you remember its meaning.

3. Name and define two words that have *cent* as a prefix.

The illustration at the right contains 100 trees. If 20 of them have needles, you can say the ratio of trees with needles to the total number of trees is 20:100, or 20%.

4. The remaining trees are broad-leaved. What percent of the trees are broad-leaved?

5. Suppose 50 of the trees at the right are tropical. What percent of the trees are tropical?

310   LESSON 10-1

MATH AND ECOLOGY

---

2 EXPLORE

☑ **MATERIALS CHECKLIST:** newspapers for each pair, Teaching Aid 15 (Centimeter Grid Paper) for each student

Suppose 30 of the trees in the illustration flower in spring. What percent of the trees flower in spring? *(30%)* **do not flower in spring?** *(70%)*

On a 10-by-10 grid, four rows are shaded. What percent is this? *(40%)*

Have students work with a partner for Exercise 30.

SUMMARIZE/ASSESS How do you name 60% as a ratio? *(60:100)*

The diagram shows 100. What percent of the diagram is shaded?

6.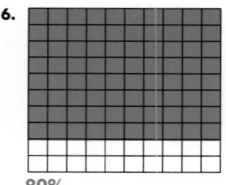
80%

7.
100%

8.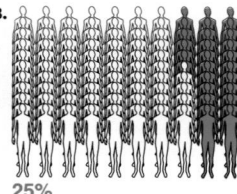
25%

ESTIMATE Estimate the percent that is shaded.
Accept reasonable estimates. Suggestions given.

9.
≈ 80%

10.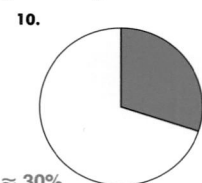
≈ 30%

11.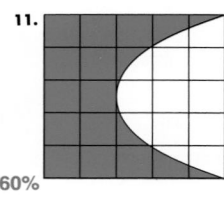
≈ 60%

12. In 1950, 30 acres out of every 100 acres of land on Earth was forest. The ratio of forest to land was 30:100. What percent is this?
30%

13. By the year 2000, about 7 acres out of every 100 acres of land on Earth will be forest. This is a ratio of $\frac{7}{100}$. What percent is this? 7%

14. In some areas, all of the trees are protected. What is the ratio of trees to protected trees in these areas? What percent is this? 1:1; 100%

Write the ratio as a percent.

15. 35 out of 100
35%

16. 9 out of 100
9%

17. $\frac{1}{100}$
1%

18. 5:100
5%

Write the percent as a ratio.

19. 30%
30:100

20. 1%
1:100

21. 100%
100:100

22. 67%
67:100

23. 4.5%
4.5:100

Draw and shade a 10-by-10 grid to represent the percent.

24. 95%
Check students' drawings.

25. 15%

26. 37%

27. 80%

28. 41%

IN YOUR WORDS Explain the meaning of the estimate.

29. It is estimated that over 20% of the rain forest in Brazil has already been destroyed to clear land for settlers. Answers will vary.

30. **IN YOUR WORDS** Work with a partner. Use a newspaper to find three uses of percent. Explain the meaning of each percent you find. Check students' work.

CLASS ACTIVITY 10-1

Have each student write the numbers *1–100* in rows of 10. Then ask the students to express the percent of the numbers in these categories: even numbers [50%]; odd numbers [50%]; numbers with 3 as a factor [33%]; numbers with 5 as a factor [20%]; numbers that contain the digit 0 [10%]; numbers that are prime [25%]; numbers that are factors of 36 [9%]; numbers that are not prime or composite [1%].

MEETING INDIVIDUAL NEEDS

For Students Who Are . . .

Acquiring English Proficiency Explain the meanings of *softwood trees, hardwood trees, needleleaf trees* and *broadleaf trees*. For Exercise 3, make sure students know what a prefix is.

Gifted and Talented Have students research other facts about trees or forests. Then have them write percent problems using these facts.

Working 2 or 3 Grades Below Level Have students use pages 58–61 of the Skills Workbook for Equations, Ratio, Proportion, and Percent.

Having Reading Difficulties Pair students with an able reader for the In Your Words activities.

Today's Problem

The Grand Banks of Newfoundland in Canada are the foggiest place on Earth. There the annual average is one foggy day in three. What percent of the time is it foggy? ($\frac{1}{3} \times 100\% = 33\frac{1}{3}\%$)

Lesson Organizer

Objective: Write fractions as percents and percents as fractions.

Prior Knowledge: Students should know the meaning of percent and how to write equivalent fractions.

Error Analysis and Remediation: See page 343A.

Lesson Resources:
Practice Worksheet 10-2
Reteaching Worksheet 10-2
Enrichment Activity 10-2
Daily Review 10-2

 ***Two-Minute Math***

Write as an equivalent fraction with a denominator of 100.

$\frac{1}{2}$ $\left(\frac{50}{100}\right)$ $\frac{4}{5}$ $\left(\frac{80}{100}\right)$

$\frac{17}{25}$ $\left(\frac{68}{100}\right)$ $\frac{11}{20}$ $\left(\frac{55}{100}\right)$

1 INTRODUCE

SYMBOLIC ACTIVITY

☑ **MATERIALS CHECKLIST:** Math Connection Transparency

Display the transparency. **What is a math connection?** *(Possible answer: connecting a skill that you know to something new that you may not know)*

Give examples of math connections you have made.

WHEN YOUR STUDENTS ASK
★ WHY AM I LEARNING THIS? ★

You can use this skill to solve real life problems. For example, if you answer $\frac{4}{5}$ of the test questions correctly, what will be your score in percent? *(80%)*

Fractions and Percent

In a basketball game, Patrena scored on 1 of the 4 free throws she attempted. On what percent of her free throws did Patrena score?

You can make a **MATH CONNECTION** to change a fraction to a percent.

- You know a percent is a ratio per 100.
- You know how to write equivalent fractions.

What fraction with a denominator of 100 is equivalent to $\frac{1}{4}$?

$\frac{1}{4} = \frac{25}{100} = 25\%$ 1 ⊡ 4 ⊟ 0.25

Patrena scored on 25% of her free throws.

Another example:

Gino's team won 2 of 3 games. What percent is this?

$\begin{array}{r} 0.66\frac{2}{3} \\ 3\overline{)2.00} \end{array} = 66\frac{2}{3}\%$ 2 ⊡ 3 ⊟ 0.6666666

> Basketball statistics often record this as 0.667. Why is it misleading to call this a percent?

THINK ALOUD Does $\frac{2}{3}$ exactly equal 0.6666666, on a calculator? Explain.   **no; repeating decimal**

If you know that *percent* means "per hundred," you can make a **MATH CONNECTION** to change a percent to a fraction.

$20\% = \frac{20}{100} = \frac{1}{5}$ $5\% = \frac{5}{100} = \frac{1}{20}$ $12\frac{1}{2}\% = \frac{12.5}{100} = \frac{125}{1,000} = \frac{1}{8}$

══════════════ **GUIDED PRACTICE** ══════════════

Write in percent form.

1. $\frac{1}{10}$ 10% **2.** $\frac{1}{2}$ 50% **3.** $\frac{3}{8}$ 37.5% **4.** $\frac{7}{25}$ 28% **5.** $\frac{4}{4}$ 100% **6.** $\frac{1}{3}$ $33\frac{1}{3}\%$

Write as a fraction in lowest terms or as a whole number.

7. 80% $\frac{4}{5}$ **8.** 35% $\frac{7}{20}$ **9.** 100% 1 **10.** 72% $\frac{18}{25}$ **11.** 6% $\frac{3}{50}$ **12.** $87\frac{1}{2}\%$ $\frac{7}{8}$

Calculators should be available for tedious calculations.

2 TEACH

☑ **MATERIALS CHECKLIST:** Math Connection Transparency; calculators

Display the transparency. Have students fill in the spaces and discuss the math connection.

How can you name a fraction as a percent? *(Write an equivalent fraction with a denominator of 100; name it as a percent.)* **to name a percent as a fraction?** *(Write the percent as a fraction with a denominator of 100; name the fraction in lowest terms.)*

Why is 100% equal to 1? $\left(\frac{100}{100} = 1\right)$

> **Chalkboard Examples**
>
> Write in percent form:
> $\frac{13}{100}$ *(13%)* $\frac{1}{2}$ *(50%)* $\frac{3}{5}$ *(60%)*

SUMMARIZE/ASSESS **Explain why thinking of a percent as "per hundred" is the key to changing from fractions to percents and vice versa.** *(Students should suggest that this thought connects the idea of percent to a fraction with a denominator of 100.)*

Write in percent form. Use a calculator, mental math, or pencil and paper.

13. $\frac{3}{4}$ 75% 14. $\frac{27}{50}$ 54% 15. $\frac{3}{5}$ 60% 16. $\frac{6}{6}$ 100% 17. $\frac{5}{8}$ 62.5% 18. $\frac{16}{64}$ 25%

19. $\frac{12}{18}$ 66$\frac{2}{3}$% 20. $\frac{7}{20}$ 35% 21. 1 100% 22. $\frac{0}{45}$ 0% 23. $\frac{24}{25}$ 96% 24. $\frac{15}{60}$ 25%

25. $\frac{32}{40}$ 80% 26. $\frac{12}{36}$ 33$\frac{1}{3}$% 27. $\frac{21}{24}$ 87.5% 28. $\frac{3}{8}$ 37.5% 29. $\frac{45}{135}$ 33$\frac{1}{3}$% 30. $\frac{125}{500}$ 25%

Write as a fraction in lowest terms or as a whole number.

31. 56% $\frac{14}{25}$ 32. 43% $\frac{43}{100}$ 33. 2% $\frac{1}{50}$ 34. 18% $\frac{9}{50}$ 35. 70% $\frac{7}{10}$ 36. 17% $\frac{17}{100}$

37. 45% $\frac{9}{20}$ 38. 68% $\frac{17}{25}$ 39. 24% $\frac{6}{25}$ 40. 100% 1 41. 80% $\frac{4}{5}$ 42. 32% $\frac{8}{25}$

43. 1% $\frac{1}{100}$ 44. 72% $\frac{18}{25}$ 45. 31% $\frac{31}{100}$ 46. 95% $\frac{19}{20}$ 47. 5% $\frac{1}{20}$ 48. 8% $\frac{2}{25}$

MIXED REVIEW Compute.

49. $\frac{1}{2} + \frac{3}{8}$ $\frac{7}{8}$ 50. $\frac{3}{5} \times \frac{1}{6}$ $\frac{1}{10}$ 51. 6.2 − 1.004 5.196 52. 180 ÷ $\frac{2}{3}$ 270

53. 15$\frac{1}{3}$ − $\frac{5}{9}$ 14$\frac{7}{9}$ 54. 0.25 + 0.087 0.337 55. $\frac{5}{6}$ ÷ 1$\frac{1}{5}$ $\frac{25}{36}$ 56. 0.7 × 950 665

MENTAL MATH Write as a percent. Compute mentally.

57. $\frac{1}{2}$ 50% 58. $\frac{1}{10}$ 10% 59. $\frac{1}{4}$ 25% 60. $\frac{1}{3}$ 33$\frac{1}{3}$% 61. $\frac{1}{5}$ 20% 62. $\frac{2}{3}$ 66$\frac{2}{3}$%

PROBLEM SOLVING

CHOOSE Use the table to answer to the nearest percent. **Choices will vary.**
Choose mental math, paper and pencil or calculator. **Suggestions given.**

63. What percent of the team's total points were scored by player 1? p; 36%

64. Which player scored 25% of the team's total points? m or p; 4

65. What percent of the total field goals attempted were made? c; 42%

66. Which player scored on 100% of the free throws she attempted? m; 5

67. **CREATE YOUR OWN** Write two math problems using the facts in the table. **Check students' work.**

Basketball Scores

Player	Field Goals Made	Field Goals Attempted	Free Throws Made	Free Throws Attempted	Total Points
1	11	21	5	6	27
2	1	3	1	2	3
3	2	8	2	3	6
4	6	12	7	9	19
5	2	10	2	2	6
6	5	7	3	4	13
7	1	4	0	0	2
8	0	0	0	0	0
9	0	0	0	0	0
10	0	1	0	0	0
Totals	**28**	**66**	**20**	**26**	**76**

CHAPTER 10 313

MEETING INDIVIDUAL NEEDS

For Students Who Are . . .

Acquiring English Proficiency Pair students with an English-proficient student for the Problem Solving section. Reinforce the idea that 100% means all in Exercise 9.

Gifted and Talented Have students create three more percent problems using the information in the table on page 313, trade papers with a partner, and solve.

Working 2 or 3 Grades Below Level Have students use pages 64–65 of the Skills Workbook for Equations, Ratio, Proportion, and Percent.

Today's Problem

The liver is the largest gland in the body. It weighs about 3.5 pounds for a 150-pound person. What percent of the total weight is the weight of the liver? ($\frac{3.5}{150} = 0.02\frac{1}{3} = 2\frac{1}{3}$%)

3 FOLLOW-UP

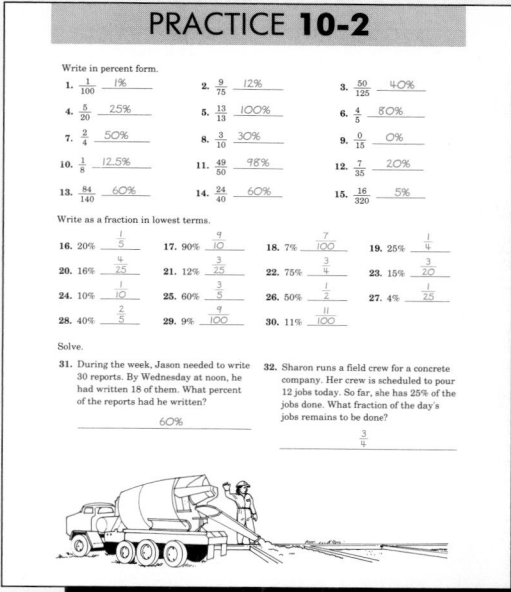

PRACTICE 10-2

Write in percent form.

1. $\frac{1}{100}$ 1% 2. $\frac{9}{75}$ 12% 3. $\frac{50}{125}$ 40%

4. $\frac{5}{20}$ 25% 5. $\frac{13}{13}$ 100% 6. $\frac{4}{5}$ 80%

7. $\frac{2}{4}$ 50% 8. $\frac{3}{10}$ 30% 9. $\frac{0}{15}$ 0%

10. $\frac{1}{8}$ 12.5% 11. $\frac{49}{50}$ 98% 12. $\frac{7}{35}$ 20%

13. $\frac{84}{140}$ 60% 14. $\frac{24}{40}$ 60% 15. $\frac{16}{320}$ 5%

Write as a fraction in lowest terms.

16. 20% $\frac{1}{5}$ 17. 90% $\frac{9}{10}$ 18. 7% $\frac{7}{100}$ 19. 25% $\frac{1}{4}$

20. 16% $\frac{4}{25}$ 21. 12% $\frac{3}{25}$ 22. 75% $\frac{3}{4}$ 23. 15% $\frac{3}{20}$

24. 10% $\frac{1}{10}$ 25. 60% $\frac{3}{5}$ 26. 50% $\frac{1}{2}$ 27. 4% $\frac{1}{25}$

28. 40% $\frac{2}{5}$ 29. 9% $\frac{9}{100}$ 30. 11% $\frac{11}{100}$

Solve.

31. During the week, Jason needed to write 30 reports. By Wednesday at noon, he had written 18 of them. What percent of the reports had he written? 60%

32. Sharon runs a field crew for a concrete company. Her crew is scheduled to pour 12 jobs today. So far, she has 25% of the jobs done. What fraction of the day's jobs remains to be done? $\frac{3}{4}$

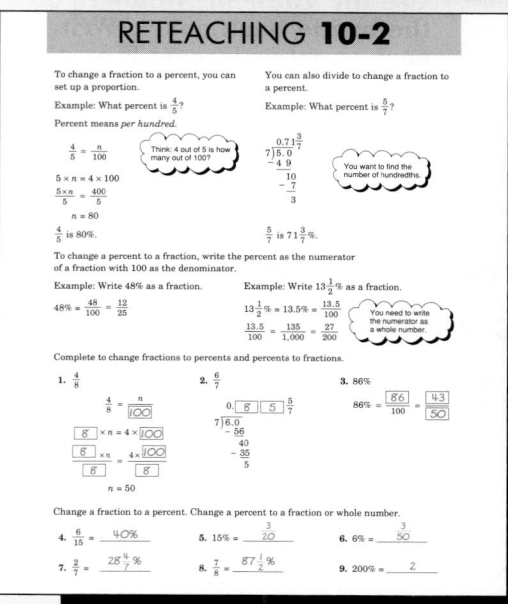

RETEACHING 10-2

To change a fraction to a percent, you can set up a proportion.

Example: What percent is $\frac{4}{5}$?

Percent means *per hundred.*

$\frac{4}{5} = \frac{n}{100}$ Think: 4 out of 5 is how many out of 100?

$5 \times n = 4 \times 100$

$\frac{5 \times n}{5} = \frac{400}{5}$

$n = 80$

$\frac{4}{5}$ is 80%.

You can also divide to change a fraction to a percent.

Example: What percent is $\frac{5}{7}$?

$7)\overline{5.0}^{0.71\frac{3}{7}}$ You want to find the number of hundredths.

$\frac{5}{7}$ is 71$\frac{3}{7}$%.

To change a percent to a fraction, write the percent as the numerator of a fraction with 100 as the denominator.

Example: Write 48% as a fraction.

$48\% = \frac{48}{100} = \frac{12}{25}$

Example: Write 13$\frac{1}{2}$% as a fraction.

$13\frac{1}{2}\% = 13.5\% = \frac{13.5}{100}$ You need to write the numerator as a whole number.

$\frac{13.5}{100} = \frac{135}{1,000} = \frac{27}{200}$

Complete to change fractions to percents and percents to fractions.

1. $\frac{4}{8}$ $\frac{4}{8} = \frac{n}{100}$ $\boxed{8} \times n = 4 \times \boxed{100}$ $\frac{\boxed{8} \times n}{\boxed{8}} = \frac{4 \times \boxed{100}}{\boxed{8}}$ $n = 50$

2. $\frac{6}{7}$ $7)\overline{6.0}^{0.\boxed{8}\ 5\ \boxed{7}}$ -56 40 -35 5

3. 86% 86% = $\frac{\boxed{86}}{100} = \frac{\boxed{43}}{\boxed{50}}$

Change a fraction to a percent. Change a percent to a fraction or whole number.

4. $\frac{6}{15}$ = 40% 5. 15% = $\frac{3}{20}$ 6. 6% = $\frac{3}{50}$

7. $\frac{2}{7}$ = 28$\frac{4}{7}$% 8. $\frac{7}{8}$ = 87$\frac{1}{2}$% 9. 200% = 2

ENRICHMENT 10-2

☑ **MATERIALS CHECKLIST:**
Newspapers, magazines

Have the students work in pairs to find the most common fractions and percents in newspapers and magazines. Find at least 10 examples. Instruct each pair to make a table that shows the fractions and percents, the place where each was found, and the information the fraction or percent tells. Have each pair of students share its work with other pairs.

LESSON 10-3

Lesson Organizer

Objective: Write decimals as percents and percents as decimals.

Prior Knowledge: Students should know the meaning of percent and be able to change fractions to percents.

Error Analysis and Remediation: See page 343A.

Lesson Resources:
Practice Worksheet 10-3
Reteaching Worksheet 10-3
Enrichment Activity 10-3
Daily Review 10-3

Two-Minute Math

Use the Table of Numbers on the inside back cover. Write each number in row F as a fraction with a denominator of 100. ($\frac{30}{100}$, $\frac{80}{100}$, $\frac{90}{100}$, $\frac{71}{100}$, $\frac{60}{100}$, $\frac{34}{100}$, $\frac{79}{100}$, $\frac{20}{100}$, $\frac{65}{100}$)

1 INTRODUCE

CONNECTING ACTIVITY

☑ **MATERIALS CHECKLIST:** Teaching Aid 2 (Decimal Squares)

1. Display a decimal square with $\frac{3}{10}$ shaded. **What part is shaded?** ($\frac{3}{10}$) Then display a decimal square with $\frac{30}{100}$ shaded. **What part is shaded?** ($\frac{30}{100}$) **How do the shaded parts compare in size?** *(They are the same.)* **What is another way of describing the shaded part?** ($0.3 = 0.30 = 30\%$)

2. Write $\frac{3}{10} = \frac{30}{100} = 30\%$ and $0.3 = 0.30 = 30\%$ on the chalkboard.

3. Repeat the activity for $\frac{1}{10}$, $\frac{9}{10}$, and $\frac{10}{10}$.

WHEN YOUR STUDENTS ASK
★ WHY AM I LEARNING THIS? ★

You can use this skill to solve real life problems. For example, if a package of cheese lists the amount of protein per gram as 0.28 g, what percent of the food contains protein? *(28%)*

Decimals and Percent

About 0.8 of all the animals on Earth are insects. About 0.01 of all the animals on Earth are mammals.

These numbers are easier to compare if they are written as percents.

If you know that percent means per hundred, you can make a **MATH CONNECTION** to change decimals to percents.

Start by changing to a fraction with a denominator of 100. Why?

$$0.8 = \frac{8 \times 10}{10 \times 10} = \frac{80}{100} = 80\% \qquad 0.01 = \frac{1}{100} = 1\%$$

About 80% of all the animals on Earth are insects. About 1% are mammals.

> Why are 80% and 1% easier to compare?

easier to see 80 > 1

Other examples:

$$0.75 = \frac{75}{100} = 75\% \qquad 0.453 = \frac{453 \div 10}{1,000 \div 10} = \frac{45.3}{100} = 45.3\%$$

$$20\% = \frac{20}{100} = 0.20 \qquad 37.5\% = \frac{37.5}{100} = 0.375$$

THINK ALOUD Why does the decimal point move when you change a decimal to a percent? a percent to a decimal? **The percent sign is the same as hundredths, so the decimal point moves when changing between percents and decimals.**

GUIDED PRACTICE

Write the decimal as a percent. | Write the percent as a decimal.

1. 0.25	2. 0.02	3. 0.8	4. 70%	5. 7%	6. 12.5%
25%	2%	80%	0.7	0.07	0.125

PRACTICE

Write the percent as a decimal.

7. 10%	8. 19%	9. 42%	10. 36%	11. 27%	12. 99%
0.1	0.19	0.42	0.36	0.27	0.99
13. 66.7%	14. 100%	15. 7.6%	16. 11.9%	17. 6.5%	18. 50%
0.667	1.0	0.076	0.119	0.065	0.5
19. 3.25%	20. 0.9%	21. 1.9%	22. 11.75%	23. 0.5%	24. 3.8%
0.0325	0.009	0.019	0.1175	0.005	0.038

314   LESSON 10–3

Animals on Earth

Mammals

Insects

MATH AND SCIENCE

---

2 TEACH

☑ **MATERIALS CHECKLIST:** Math Connection Transparency, calculators

Display the transparency. Have students fill in the spaces and discuss the math connection. *(See student pages.)*

Write 0.35 and $\frac{35}{100}$. **How are these numbers the same and how are they different?** *(They are read in the same way and they represent the same number, but they are written differently.)*

How is 0.35 written as a percent? *(35%)*

> ### Chalkboard Examples
> Write as a percent.
> 0.73 *(73%)*   0.9 *(90%)*
> 0.07 *(7%)*   0.625 *(62.5%)*

SUMMARIZE/ASSESS Use the fraction $\frac{3}{4}$ to explain how fractions, decimals, and percents are related. ($\frac{3}{4} = \frac{75}{100} = 0.75 = 75\%$)

Write the decimal as a percent.

25. 0.25	**26.** 0.35	**27.** 0.1	**28.** 0.11	**29.** 0.8	**30.** 0.06
25%	35%	10%	11%	80%	6%
31. 0.001	**32.** 0.31	**33.** 0.031	**34.** 0.1667	**35.** 0.991	**36.** 0.121
0.1%	31%	3.1%	16.67%	99.1%	12.1%
37. 0.083	**38.** 0.705	**39.** 0.4567	**40.** 1	**41.** 0.005	**42.** 0.0002
8.3%	70.5%	45.67%	100%	0.5%	0.02%

MIXED REVIEW Write as a decimal.

43. $\frac{1}{2}$ 0.5   **44.** $\frac{3}{5}$ 0.6   **45.** $\frac{35}{100}$ 0.35   **46.** $\frac{7}{8}$ 0.875   **47.** $\frac{9}{9}$ 1.0   **48.** $\frac{1}{20}$ 0.05

MENTAL MATH Name the fraction and the decimal.

49. 25%   **50.** 75%   **51.** 50%   **52.** 10%   **53.** 60%   **54.** 80%
$\frac{1}{4}$; 0.25 $\frac{3}{4}$; 0.75 $\frac{1}{2}$; 0.5 $\frac{1}{10}$; 0.1 $\frac{3}{5}$; 0.6 $\frac{4}{5}$; 0.8

===== PROBLEM SOLVING =====

CHOOSE Choose mental math, paper and pencil, or calculator to solve. **Choices will vary. Suggestions given.**

55. About 0.2 of all insects on Earth are butterflies and moths. What percent of all insects are not butterflies or moths? **m; 80%**

A mammal is a backboned animal that feeds its young on mother's milk.

56. There are about 1,000,000 known insect species on Earth today. Of these, about 112,000 are ants or bees. In lowest terms, what is the ratio of ants or bees to total insects known today?
p or c; 14:125

57. Of the known living species on Earth, 71% are insects, 11% are other animals, and 18% are plants. Model these facts with a 10-by-10 square grid.
Check students' drawings.

Critical Thinking

Work with a partner. Use the diagram to solve.

1. What percent of the insects shown are ants? flies?
   70%; 30%
2. What percent of the insects are either ants or flies?
   100%
3. What percent of the insects are bees? **0%**

MEETING INDIVIDUAL NEEDS

For Students Who Are . . .

Acquiring English Proficiency Discuss the meanings of *insects*, *mammals*, and *species* in this lesson.

Gifted and Talented Have students draw a picture on a grid to represent Exercises 31, 33, and 41.

Working 2 or 3 Grades Below Level Have students annex a zero to decimals like 0.4 so they can read the decimal as hundredths. Then they can write the percent. Remind students that percent means per hundred. 30% means 30 out of 100 or 0.30. Have students use pages 62–63 of the Skills Workbook for Equations, Ration, Proportion, and Percent.

Today's Problem

Is $\frac{2}{3}$ written as a percent equal to $\frac{66}{99}$ written as a percent? Explain.
(Yes; The fractions are equal. $\frac{66}{99}$ is written as $\frac{2}{3}$ in lowest terms.)

3 FOLLOW-UP

PRACTICE 10-3

Write the percent as a decimal.

1. 21% 0.21   **2.** 55% 0.55   **3.** 91% 0.91
4. 25% 0.25   **5.** 37% 0.37   **6.** 85% 0.85
7. 7.5% 0.075   **8.** 61% 0.61   **9.** 95% 0.95
10. 11% 0.11   **11.** 9.9% 0.099   **12.** 12.5% 0.125
13. 32.3% 0.323   **14.** 0.75% 0.0075   **15.** 6.05% 0.0605

Write the decimal as a percent.

16. 0.2 20%   **17.** 0.5 50%   **18.** 0.75 75%
19. 0.19 19%   **20.** 0.66 66%   **21.** 0.89 89%
22. 0.9 90%   **23.** 0.44 44%   **24.** 0.17 17%
25. 0.35 35%   **26.** 0.09 9%   **27.** 0.333 33.3%
28. 0.05 5%   **29.** 0.101 10.1%   **30.** 1.01 101%

Write as a decimal.

31. $\frac{3}{10}$ 0.3   **32.** $\frac{7}{20}$ 0.35   **33.** $\frac{4}{5}$ 0.8

Name the fraction or whole number and the decimal.

34. 20% $\frac{1}{5}$;0.2   **35.** 100% 1; 1.0   **36.** 40% $\frac{2}{5}$;0.4

Solve.

37. At Bloom Middle School, there are 423 boys and 457 girls. Only 11 of the students have red hair. What percent of the students have red hair?   1.25%

38. Of the students at Bloom Middle School, about 45% have brown hair. Write this percent as a fraction in lowest terms. $\frac{9}{20}$

RETEACHING 10-3

To change a decimal to a percent, write the decimal as a fraction. Then, if necessary, write an equivalent fraction with a denominator of 100.

Example: Change 0.6 to a percent.

0.6 is 6 tenths.

$0.6 = \frac{6}{10} = \frac{60}{100}$

0.6 is 60%.

You can also change a decimal to a percent by moving the decimal point two places to the right.

Example: Change 0.27 and 0.575 to percents.

$0.27 = 27\%$

$0.575 = 57.5\%$

To change a percent to a decimal, write the percent as a fraction with a denominator of 100. Then divide.

Example: Change 44% to a decimal.

$44\% = \frac{44}{100} = 0.44$

You can also change a percent to a decimal by moving the decimal point two places to the left.

Example: Change 62% and 18.9% to decimals.

$62\% = 0.62$
$18.9\% = 0.189$

Change the percent to a decimal or whole number.

1. 14% = 0.14   **2.** 28% = 0.28   **3.** 6% = 0.06
4. 56% = 0.56   **5.** 6.1% = 0.061   **6.** 0.2% = 0.002
7. 600% = 6   **8.** 38.5% = 0.385   **9.** 4.67% = 0.0467

Change the decimal to a percent.

10. 0.15 = 15%   **11.** 0.02 = 2%   **12.** 0.67 = 67%
13. 1.63 = 163%   **14.** 0.004 = 0.4%   **15.** 0.72 = 72%
16. 0.048 = 4.8%   **17.** 9.8 = 980%   **18.** 3 = 300%

ENRICHMENT 10-3

☑ **MATERIALS CHECKLIST:** Calendars

Write the following on the board: 1) weekdays; 2) weekend days; 3) days that begin with *T*; 4) days that begin with *S* or *W*; 5) national holidays. Have the students work in pairs. Provide each pair with a different calendar page. Have each pair write a fraction, a decimal, and a percent for each of the five categories. Tell the students to round decimals to the nearest hundredth. Have the pairs share their work. Then ask which month had the highest percent of days in each category.

Lesson Organizer

Objective:
10-4 Write percents greater than 100%.
10-5 Write percents less than 1%.

Prior Knowledge: Students should be able to write ratios as percents.

Lesson Resources:
Practice Worksheet 10-4; 10-5
Reteaching Worksheet 10-4; 10-5
Enrichment Activity 10-4; 10-5
Daily Review 10-4; 10-5

 *Two-Minute Math*

Write the fraction with a denominator of 100.

$\frac{3}{5}$ $\left(\frac{60}{100}\right)$ $\frac{6}{5}$ $\left(\frac{120}{100}\right)$

$\frac{9}{5}$ $\left(\frac{180}{100}\right)$ $\frac{10}{5}$ $\left(\frac{200}{100}\right)$

1 INTRODUCE

CONNECTING ACTIVITY

☑ **MATERIALS CHECKLIST:** 150 strips cut or colored from Teaching Aid 2 (Decimal Squares)

1. Pose this situation: **Last year a stereo tape deck cost $100.** Show 100 strips. **This year it costs $150. How can the increase be represented with paper strips?** *(with 50 more strips)* **Why is it true that this year the cost is 150% of what it was last year?** *(100 strips represents 100%; 50 strips or half a hundred represents 50%; 100% + 50% = 150%)*

2. Repeat for a radio that was $100 last year and is now $125.

3. You have $100. You spend 50 cents. Did you spend 1% of your money? *(No; one percent of $100 is $1.)* **What percent of your money did you spend?** *($\frac{1}{2}$ of $1, $\frac{1}{2}$ of 1%, or 0.5% of the money was spent.)*

4. Repeat for spending 25 cents of $100. *($\frac{1}{4}$ of $1, $\frac{1}{4}$ of 1%, or 0.25%)*

WHEN YOUR STUDENTS ASK
★ **WHY AM I LEARNING THIS?** ★

You can use this skill to understand reports about government finances. For example, if you read that spending for education increased 110% last year, you know that last year 10% more was spent for education than in the previous year.

Writing Percents Greater Than 100%

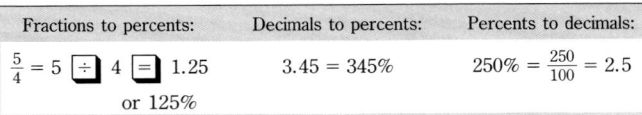

In the year 2000, the population of Alaska is expected to be 119% of what it was in 1990. This means that for every 100 people in Alaska in 1990, there will be 119 in the year 2000. This is a ratio of $\frac{119}{100}$.

You can write this ratio as a percent. $\frac{119}{100} = 119\%$

You can work with percents greater than 100% just like you work with those less than 100%.

Fractions to percents:	Decimals to percents:	Percents to decimals:
$\frac{5}{4}$ = 5 ÷ 4 = 1.25 or 125%	3.45 = 345%	250% = $\frac{250}{100}$ = 2.5

GUIDED PRACTICE

Write as a percent.

1. $\frac{120}{100}$ **120%**   **2.** 1.75 **175%**   **3.** 4 **400%**   **4.** $\frac{3}{2}$ **150%**   **5.** $\frac{5}{3}$ **166$\frac{2}{3}$%**

Write as a decimal.

6. 112% **1.12**   **7.** 350% **3.5**   **8.** 700% **7.0**   **9.** 175% **1.75**   **10.** 250% **2.5**

PRACTICE

Write as a percent.

11. 1.09 **109%**   **12.** 11 **1,100%**   **13.** $\frac{104}{100}$ **104%**   **14.** 8 **800%**   **15.** $\frac{450}{100}$ **450%**

Write as a decimal.

16. 120% **1.2**   **17.** 225% **2.25**   **18.** 500% **5.0**   **19.** 125% **1.25**   **20.** 700% **7.0**

Express the percent as a ratio per 100.

21. Alaska's area is about 219% that of Texas.
219:100

22. Juneau's population is about 110% of Fairbanks's population.
110:100

23. **NUMBER SENSE** In some cases, percents greater than 100 do not make sense. For example, *150% of the cars in the parking lot are black*, does not make sense. Name two other situations where it is not sensible to have a percent greater than 100.
Check students' work.

316   LESSON 10-4

---

2 TEACH   Lesson 10-4

How do you know that all numbers greater than 1 can be named as percents greater than 100% *(1 = $\frac{100}{100}$ = 100%, so any number greater than 1 will be greater than 100%.)*

Name a situation in which it is sensible to have a percent greater than 100%, and one in which it is not sensible. *(Accept reasonable answers.)*

SUMMARIZE/ASSESS   **Use decimal squares to help you explain the meaning of 120%.** *(Accept reasonable explanations.)*

MULTICULTURAL NOTE

Alaska's population density is the least of all the states; however, its population is growing. More than ten percent of the state's population is Native American. The largest groups of Native-American peoples are the Inuit, Tlingit, Haida, Athabaskan, and Aleut.

City Hall, Nome, Alaska

Writing Percents Less Than 1%

In Alaska, about 0.6% of the population lives in Nome. Percents even less than 1% are important. About 0.6% of the 588,000 people in Alaska is 3,500 people!

To work with percents less than 1%, you use the same procedures as working with other percents. For example, we can change from one form to another.

Percents to decimals:

$$0.75\% = \frac{0.75 \times 100}{100 \times 100} = \frac{75}{10,000} = 0.0075$$

$$\frac{1}{2}\% = \frac{0.5 \times 10}{100 \times 10} = \frac{5}{1,000} = 0.005$$

Decimals to percents:

$$0.006 = \frac{6}{1,000} = \frac{6 \div 10}{1,000 \div 10} = \frac{0.6}{100} = 0.6\%$$

Fractions to percents:

$$\frac{1}{500} = \frac{1 \div 5}{500 \div 5} = \frac{0.2}{100} = 0.2\%$$

GUIDED PRACTICE

Write as a decimal.

1. 0.2% **0.002** 2. 0.8% **0.008** 3. 0.25% **0.0025** 4. 0.7% **0.007** 5. $\frac{1}{4}$% **0.0025**

Write as a percent.

6. 0.005 **0.5%** 7. 0.002 **0.2%** 8. 0.0055 **0.55%** 9. $\frac{0.7}{100}$ **0.7%** 10. $\frac{1}{400}$ **0.25%**

PRACTICE

Write as a decimal.

11. 2% **0.02** 12. 0.2% **0.002** 13. 0.02% **0.0002** 14. 0.6% **0.006** *15. $\frac{3}{4}$% **0.0075**

Write as a percent.

16. 0.0075 **0.75%** 17. 0.001 **0.1%** 18. 0.0006 **0.06%** 19. 0.008 **0.8%** 20. 0.0014 **0.14%**

21. $\frac{0.75}{100}$ **0.75%** 22. $\frac{0.1}{100}$ **0.1%** 23. $\frac{0.04}{100}$ **0.04%** *24. $\frac{2}{1,000}$ **0.2%** *25. $\frac{1}{800}$ **0.125%**

26. **IN YOUR WORDS** Think about a quick way of changing 0.6% to a decimal. Write a sentence describing this short cut.
    Move the decimal point 2 places to the left.

LESSON 10–5   317

---

2 TEACH Lesson 10-5

☑ **MATERIALS CHECKLIST:** Teaching Aid 2 (Decimal Squares)

Explain how to name 0.009 as a percent. Use the decimal squares if you wish. $\left(0.009 = \frac{9}{1,000} = \frac{[9 \div 10]}{[1,000 \div 10]} = \frac{0.9}{100} = 0.9\%\right)$

SUMMARIZE/ASSESS   **Explain this statement: The food contains 0.5% fat. Use decimal squares with your explanation if you wish.** *(The food is $\frac{1}{2}$ of 1% fat, or $\frac{1}{2}$% fat.)*

---

3 FOLLOW-UP

PRACTICE 10-4, 10-5

Write as a percent.

1. $\frac{101}{100}$ _101%_   2. 1.25 _125%_   3. $\frac{10}{5}$ _200%_
4. 2 _200%_   5. $\frac{200}{100}$ _200%_   6. 10 _1,000%_
7. $\frac{10}{2}$ _500%_   8. 1.11 _111%_   9. $\frac{110}{100}$ _110%_
10. 7.5 _750%_   11. 0.003 _0.3%_   12. $\frac{0.5}{100}$ _0.5%_
13. 0.007 _0.7%_   14. $\frac{1}{200}$ _0.5%_   15. 0.0035 _0.35%_
16. $\frac{0.25}{100}$ _0.25%_   17. 0.0099 _0.99%_   18. $\frac{0.05}{100}$ _0.05%_
19. 0.0004 _0.04%_   20. $\frac{1}{1,000}$ _0.1%_

Write as a decimal.

21. 115% _1.15_   22. 300% _3.0_   23. 150% _1.5_
24. 110% _1.1_   25. 210% _2.1_   26. 750% _7.5_
27. 101% _1.01_   28. 135% _1.35_   29. 1,000% _10.0_
30. 105% _1.05_   31. 0.4% _0.004_   32. 0.9% _0.009_
33. $\frac{1}{2}$% _0.005_   34. 0.55% _0.0055_   35. 0.22% _0.0022_
36. 0.01% _0.0001_   37. 0.025% _0.00025_   38. $\frac{1}{5}$% _0.002_

Solve.

39. The population of metropolitan Mexico City is about 20 million. Metropolitan Chicago has a population of about 8 million. What percent of the population of Mexico City is the population of Chicago?
    _40%_

40. The population of the world is about 5,000 million. What percent of the world's population lives in metropolitan Chicago?
    _0.16%_

RETEACHING 10-4, 10-5

Treat percents larger than 100% and percents smaller than 1% the same way you treat percents between 1% and 100%.

Example 1: Change these fractions to percents: $\frac{1}{200}$ and $\frac{8}{5}$.

$\frac{1}{200} = \frac{n}{100}$

$200 \times n = 1 \times 100$

$\frac{200 \times n}{200} = \frac{100}{200}$

$n = 0.5$

$\frac{1}{200} = 0.5\%$

$\frac{8}{5} = \frac{m}{100}$

$5 \times m = 8 \times 100$

$\frac{5 \times m}{5} = \frac{800}{5}$

$m = 160$

$\frac{8}{5} = 160\%$

Example 2: Change these decimals to percents: 8.15 and 0.004.

$8.15 = 815\%$

$0.004 = 0.4\%$

Example 3: Change these percents to decimals: 110% and 0.33%.

$110\% = 1.10$

$0.33\% = 0.0033$

Write as a percent.

1. $\frac{7}{2} =$ _350%_   2. 3.8 = _380%_
3. $\frac{1}{1,000} =$ _0.1%_   4. 12 = _1,200%_
5. 0.006 = _0.6%_   6. $\frac{0.25}{100} =$ _0.25%_
7. $\frac{489}{100} =$ _489%_   8. $\frac{5}{1,000} =$ _0.5%_

Write as a decimal.

9. 159% = _1.59_   10. 0.03% = _0.0003_
11. 675% = _6.75_   12. 0.00024% = _0.0000024_
13. $\frac{1}{2}$% = _0.005_   14. 359% = _3.59_
15. 730% = _7.3_   16. $\frac{1}{5}$% = _0.002_

ENRICHMENT 10-4, 10-5

☑ **MATERIALS CHECKLIST:** Index cards

Provide pairs of students with index cards on which you have written 0.02%, $\frac{0.01}{50}$, 0.0002, 200%, $\frac{2}{1}$, 2, $\frac{7}{5}$, 1.4, 140%, $\frac{3}{5}$, 0.6, 60%, 0.005%, $\frac{1}{20,000}$, 0.00005. Have the students mix the cards and place them face down in a pile. Each partner draws six cards and looks for two sets of equivalent fractions, percents, and decimals. Player 1 draws a card and places that card or a card from his or her hand face up next to the original pile. Player 2 then draws from either pile. Play continues until one partner has two complete sets.

Lesson Organizer

Objective: Discuss the uses of percent.

Prior Knowledge: Students should understand the concept of percent.

Lesson Resources:
Class Activity 10-6
Daily Review 10-6

Two-Minute Math

In his will, Mr. Jones left $\frac{1}{5}$ of his estate to each of this three children and $\frac{1}{4}$ to each of his two grandchildren. What is wrong with the will. *(20% + 20% + 20% + 25% + 25% = 110%; this is not possible because 100% represents his entire estate.)*

1 INTRODUCE

SYMBOLIC ACTIVITY

Have students discuss this question: **Percents are really fractions with a denominator of 100. Why do you think percents have been singled out and given a special name?**

WHEN YOUR STUDENTS ASK
★ WHY AM I LEARNING THIS? ★

You can connect using percent to real life through interpreting geography facts. In the United States, there is 20% arable land, 26% meadows and pastures, 29% woodland and forest, and 25% other types of land. What does this suggest about land use in the United States?

Percent Sense

When Do We Use Percent?

READ ABOUT IT

Percents help us to make comparisons. Because *percent* means "per hundred", we can compare very large and small things in terms of 100.

For example, percents make it easy to realize how large the Pacific Ocean is compared to 100% of the ocean water on Earth.

Our Earth's Oceans

Pacific Ocean 47%

TALK ABOUT IT

Working with a partner, discuss what the percent means. Talk about how percent is making a comparison in terms of 100.

Answers will vary.

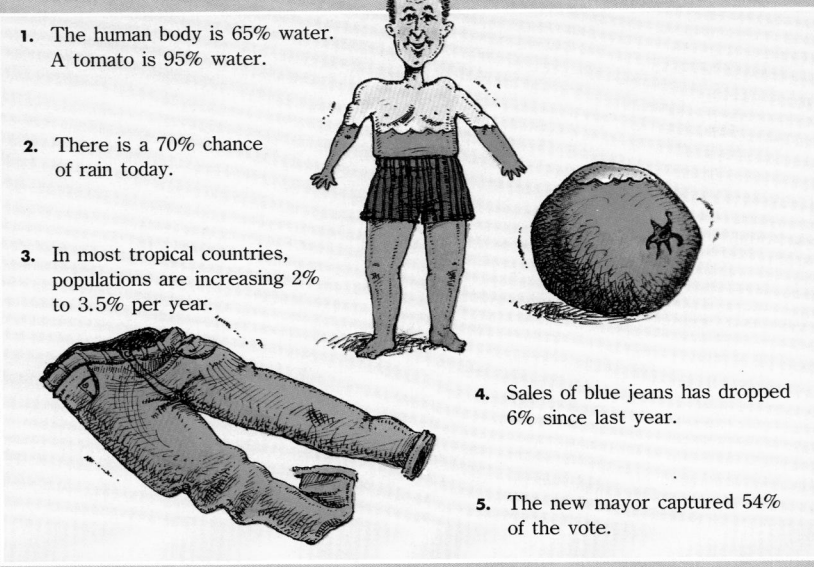

1. The human body is 65% water. A tomato is 95% water.

2. There is a 70% chance of rain today.

3. In most tropical countries, populations are increasing 2% to 3.5% per year.

4. Sales of blue jeans has dropped 6% since last year.

5. The new mayor captured 54% of the vote.

318   LESSON 10–6

---

2 TEACH

✓ **MATERIALS CHECKLIST:** newspaper or magazine for each pair

Have students work with a partner for the activities in this lesson.

READ ABOUT IT   **About 86% of the Earth's land surface is occupied by countries other than the Soviet Union. About what percent is occupied by the Soviet Union?** *(about 14%)* **Is this more or less than $\frac{1}{10}$ of the Earth's surface?** *(more than $\frac{1}{10}$)*

TALK ABOUT IT   **Why is it easy to compare information presented as percents?** *(Percents are fractions with a common denominator, 100.)*

WRITE ABOUT IT   **Suppose you had an article that reported 43% of people surveyed supported the president's policy. What other information could you learn from that fact?** *(Possible answers: less than half the people surveyed supported the policy.)*

SUMMARIZE/ASSESS   **When does it make sense to use percents to describe things? Give examples.**

6.

Pitchers with at least 270 wins

	Wins	Losses	Wins/Total	Percent
Tom Seaver	311	205	0.603	60.3%
Phil Niekro	318	274	0.537	53.7%
Steve Carlton	329	244	0.574	57.4%
Tommy John	288	231	0.555	55.5%
Cy Young	511	313	0.620	62.0%

7. Only 25% of the world's paper is recycled.

8. 50% of the teenagers polled said they study 2 h every evening except on weekends.

9. Paula scored 90% on a test of 50 items.

10. 72% of the people voted to build a community swimming pool.

11. By the year 2000, we could lose 18% of the world's land that is suitable for farming.

◼ WRITE ABOUT IT

Work with a partner.

Cut out a percent example from a newspaper or magazine.
Write a paragraph explaining how the percent is used.
Check students' work.

MEETING INDIVIDUAL NEEDS

For Students Who Are . . .

Acquiring English Proficiency Pair students with an English-proficient student for the Talk About It and Write About It activities.

Gifted and Talented For the Write About It exercise, have partners create a problem using the percent example they cut from a newspaper or magazine.

Working 2 or 3 Grades Below Level Have students use pages 70–73 of the Skills Workbook for Equations, Ratio, Proportion, and Percent.

Having Reading Difficulties Have students read the Talk About It exercises aloud to their partner.

Today's Problem

Ted has 23 books in his library at home. Four of them are science books. To the nearest tenth, what percent of Ted's books are science books? ($\frac{4}{23} = 17.4\%$)

---

3 FOLLOW-UP

CLASS ACTIVITY 10-6

◼ MATERIALS CHECKLIST: Grocery items or labels

Tell the students that humans need to take in more than 40 nutrients every day to maintain good health. Eight of these nutrients are required to appear on food labels. Have the students work in groups of four. Each group examines food labels and then makes a table showing the Recommended Daily Allowance percents for protein, vitamin A, vitamin C, thiamine, riboflavin, niacin, calcium, and iron. Have the students indicate which items are a poor ($< 7\%$), fair (7–10%), very good (10–20%), or excellent ($> 20\%$) source of each nutrient.

Lesson Organizer

Objective: Explore the percent model.

Prior Knowledge: Students should understand the concept of percent.

Lesson Resources:
Class Activity 10-7
Daily Review 10-7

Two-Minute Math

Write as a percent.
0.25 *(25%)*   0.75 *(75%)*
$\frac{1}{5}$ *(20%)* $\frac{3}{20}$ *(15%)*

1 PREPARE

CONNECTING ACTIVITY

☑ **MATERIALS CHECKLIST:** Percent Bar Transparency

1. Present this situation: **On Tuesday, 16 of the 32 members of the soccer team came to practice. This is 50% of the members.**

2. Represent the problem with the transparency.

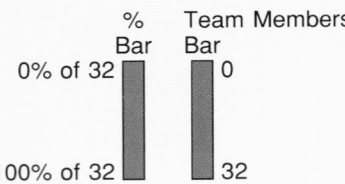

3. **Why are the bottoms of the bars marked 100% and 32?** *(32 players represent 100% of the members of the team.)*

4. Draw a line halfway across the diagram. **How can you label both bars at the line?** *(50%; 16)*. Write: 50% of 32 is 16.

WHEN YOUR STUDENTS ASK
★ WHY AM I LEARNING THIS? ★

You can use percent models to solve real life problems. For example, you can find the number of responses to a questionnaire, given the number of questionnaires sent out and the percent of responses.

The baseball team has won 30 of the 60 games they have played. That is 50% of the games played.

Exploring Percent Models

A percent bar diagram can be used to represent situations involving percent.

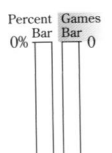

To make percent bar diagrams, you work from the top down. In this situation, each bar represents the games played. One represents the *percent* of games played and the other the *number* of games played.

1. Why is there a 0 on the games bar across from the 0% point on the percent bar? Why are the bottoms of the bars marked 100% and 60? **Both represent no games played. 100% and 60 both represent the total played.**

A line has been drawn across the diagram to show the part of the games the team has won.

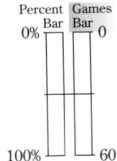

2. How far down the bar was the line drawn? **halfway**

3. How did you know to draw the line at that point? $\frac{1}{2}$ **of 60 or 50%**

The games bar has been labeled.

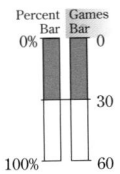

4. Why was the 30 placed at the middle of the games bar? Why were the top halves of the bars shaded? **Half of 60. 30 games or 50% were won.**

5. What should be placed on the percent bar across from the 30? **50%**

The completed bar diagram is shown. The math sentence that represents the situation is shaded.

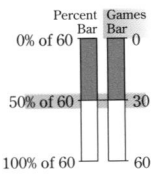

6. What part of the bars would have been shaded if the team had won all 60 games? no games? **100% of 60 = 60; 0% of 60 = 0**

7. How would the diagram change if the team had played 80 games? $\frac{3}{8}$ **of bar shaded, 80 would be on bottom**

---

2 EXPLORE

☑ **MATERIALS CHECKLIST:** Teaching Aid 16 (Percent Bar Diagram, less than 100%) for each group

Assign students into mixed ability groups of three or four.

Encourage students to explain their reasoning as they use the teaching aid for Exercises 9–12 and 16–18.

Complete a percent bar diagram to show: 45% of 140 is 63; 40% of 75 is 30; 3 out of 60 is 5%. Explain your diagram.

SUMMARIZE/ASSESS   **Draw and label a percent bar diagram to represent "25% of 64 is 16."** *(Check students' drawings.)*

The percent bar diagram shows the baseball games in which Melinda got at least one hit.

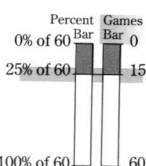

8. a. In how many games did she play? **60**

   b. In how many games did she get at least one hit? What percent is this? **15; 25%**

When making a percent bar diagram to fit a situation, it is helpful to be able to draw the line across the bars in *about* the right place. Knowing these fraction/percent relationships can help: $\frac{1}{4} = 25\%$, $\frac{1}{2} = 50\%$, $\frac{3}{4} = 75\%$.

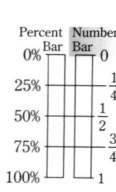

9. Describe where the line would cross the bars for the given percent.
   Answers will vary. Suggestion given.

   a. 80%   **b.** 15%   **c.** 40%
   below 75% mark   **above 25% mark**   **slightly above 50% mark**

Sometimes in a percent problem the percent will not be given. In such cases, the other numbers in the problem will help you draw the line across the bars.

Todd got a hit 15 of the 24 times he came to bat.

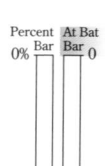

10. What is half of 24? Did Todd get a hit *more than* or *less than* half of his times at bat? Where would you draw the line?
   12; more than; below the 50% mark

Describe where you would draw the line across a percent bar diagram for the situation.

11. 75 stolen bases in 80 attempts   **close to bottom**

12. 2 of 50 games rained out   **close to top**

Julio got a hit 80% of the times he came to bat. If he batted a total of 25 times, how many hits did he get? Use the percent bars at the right to answer.   **20 hits**

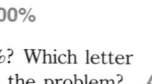
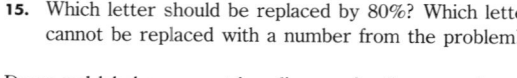

13. What number will replace the *B* on the diagram? **100%** Why will the number in that place always be the same?
   because the whole bar is always 100%

14. Would you say that 25 is *100%* of Julio's times at bat or *80%* of the times Julio got a hit?   **100%**

15. Which letter should be replaced by 80%? Which letter cannot be replaced with a number from the problem? **A; C**

Draw and label a percent bar diagram for the example.
   Check students' drawings.

16. 75% of 80 is 60.   **17.** 40% of 25 is 10.   **18.** 2 out of 20 is 10%.

3 FOLLOW-UP

CLASS ACTIVITY 10-7

☑ **MATERIALS CHECKLIST:** Strips of paper

Have the students work in pairs within groups of four. Give each pair a strip of paper 10 cm long. Have one pair label its strip from 0 to 25 in increments of 4 mm to make a counters bar. Have the other pair label its strip from 0% to 100% in increments of 1 cm to make a percent bar. Ask the pairs to line up the ends of the two bars. Then give each group 25 counters—17 red and 8 white. Ask: How would you show the number of red counters out of the group of 25? [shade the counters bar to show 17 out of 25] How can you tell what percent this is? [draw a line to show where the 17 out of 25 is on the percent bar—68%]

MEETING INDIVIDUAL NEEDS

For Students Who Are . . .

Acquiring English Proficiency Discuss the baseball terminology used in this lesson.

Gifted and Talented Assign the technology lesson on page 348.

Working 2 or 3 Grades Below Level Review the percent equivalents for $\frac{1}{3}$, $\frac{1}{4}$, and $\frac{3}{4}$ and how to show these percents by shading part of a bar. Remind students that in this lesson, 100% means the total number of games played. Have students use pages 74–75 of the Skills Workbook for Equations, Ratio, Proportion, and Percent.

Today's Problem

The PERCENT of the TOTAL is the PART. Of the three words in capital letters, the value of one will be unknown, whereas the value of the other two are known. How many different kinds of problems can there be? *(Three. What PERCENT of the total is the part? A percent of what TOTAL is the part? What PART is the percent of the total?)*

LESSON 10-8

Lesson Organizer

Objective: Find the percent of a number.

Prior Knowledge: Students should be able to multiply decimals and change percents to decimals.

Error Analysis and Remediation: See page 343A.

Lesson Resources:
Practice Worksheet 10-8
Reteaching Worksheet 10-8
Enrichment Activity 10-8
Daily Review 10-8

Two-Minute Math

Write as a decimal.

9% *(0.09)*   82% *(0.82)*

$\frac{1}{2}$% *(0.005)*   114% *(1.14)*

1 INTRODUCE

CONNECTING ACTIVITY

✓ **MATERIALS CHECKLIST:** Percent Bar Transparency

Write "50% of 80 is 40" and display the transparency. With students, work through the diagram to model the example:

1. Write 100% and 0% on the percent bar. **Where should 80 be written?** *(at the bottom of the right-hand bar)* Write it in the appropriate place.

2. Draw a horizontal line dividing both bars in half. **Why is the line drawn here?** *(50% = $\frac{1}{2}$)* Write 50% in the appropriate place. **Where should 40 be written?** *(at the middle of the second bar)*

3. How does the model show that 50% of 80 is 40? *(Possible answer: The model shows that 80 is 100% and 40 is 50%.)*

WHEN YOUR STUDENTS ASK
★ WHY AM I LEARNING THIS? ★

You can connect this skill to real life. For example, if you invited 28 guests to the hockey game but only 75% could go, how many tickets would you need to buy?

Finding the Percent of a Number

From 1889 to 1989, 12% of North Carolina's 25 governors were Republicans. All the others were Democrats. How many governors were Republicans?

Percent bars can model this problem.

Let x be the number of Republican governors.

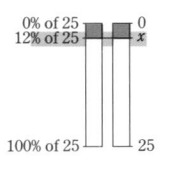

12% of the 25 governors were Republican.

12% of 25 is what number?

$0.12 \times 25 = x$

$3 = x$

If you know how to change a percent to a decimal and how to multiply decimals, you can make a **MATH CONNECTION** to find the percent of a number.

There were three Republican governors.

Another example:

What is 12% of 400?

$12\% \times 400 = x$

$0.12 \times 400 = x$

$48 = x$

State Capitol Building, Raleigh, North Carolina.

Use the percent bars to check.

MATH AND SOCIAL STUDIES

GUIDED PRACTICE

Write an equation and solve.

1. 70% × 200 = x; 140
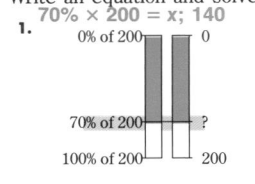

2. 90% × 50 = x; 45
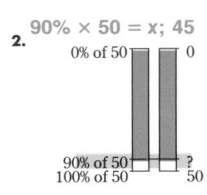

3. 38% × 600 = x; 228
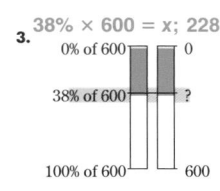

4. What is 60% of 900?
540

5. What is 5% of 120?
6

6. What is $\frac{1}{2}$% of 600?
3

322   LESSON 10–8

---

2 TEACH

✓ **MATERIALS CHECKLIST:** Math Connection Transparency, Teaching Aid 16 (Percent Bar) for each student; calculators

Display the transparency. Have students fill in the spaces and discuss the math connection. *(See student pages.)*

Will 48% of 500 be greater than or less than 192?
(greater than; 48% of 400 is 192, and 500 is greater than 400.)

What equation would you write to find 8% of 40?
(8% × 40 = 0.08 × 40 = 3.2)

Chalkboard Examples

Write an equation and solve.
What is 80% of 500? *(400)*
What is 5% of 140? *(7)*
What is $\frac{1}{2}$% of 800? *(4)*

SUMMARIZE/ASSESS Describe the steps to follow to find 75% of 90. Use the percent bar diagram to model and check. *(Students should write the equation, model it on the percent bars, multiply, and look back at the model to check; 75% of 90 = 67.5)*

Find the percent of the number. Use percent bars to help.

7. 50% of 480   240   **8.** 7% of 84   5.88   **9.** 50% of 9   4.5   **10.** 10% of 450   45

11. 1% of 350   3.5   **12.** 75% of 40   30   **13.** 5% of 80   4   **14.** 0.5% of 80   0.4

15. 0.1% of 80   0.08   **16.** 0.6% of 456   2.736   **17.** 2% of 96   1.92   **18.** 0.05% of 350   0.175

19. 0.5% of 800   4   ***20.** $\frac{1}{2}$% of 1,000   5   ***21.** $37\frac{1}{2}$% of 40   15

MIXED REVIEW   Compute.

22. 0.2×86 17.2   **23.** $\frac{3}{4} \times 96$ 72   **24.** $25\% \times 28$ 7   **25.** $\frac{1}{2} \times 52$ 26

26. $40\% \times 40$ 16   **27.** 0.1×75 7.5   **28.** $\frac{4}{5} \times 55$ 44   **29.** $50\% \times 120$ 60

CALCULATOR   Compute.

30. $62\frac{1}{2}\%$ of 8,440   **31.** 98% of 3,662   **32.** 17% of 5.66   **33.** $\frac{1}{4}\%$ of 228.4
5,275   3,588.76   0.9622   0.571

 Choose mental math, paper and pencil, or calculator to solve.   **Choices will vary. Suggestions given.**

34. About 40% of North Carolina's 53,669 mi² is farmland. How many square miles is that?
p or c; 21,467.6

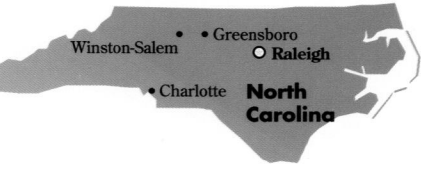

35. There are about 6 million people in North Carolina. About 21% of them are under age 15, and about 11% are 65 or older. About how many people are between the ages of 15 and 65?
p or c; 4,080,000

36. Of about $2\frac{3}{4}$ million workers in North Carolina, about 30% are in manufacturing. How many workers are in manufacturing?
p or c; 825,000

Estimate

Compatible numbers help you estimate the percent of a number.

9% of 105   is close to   ⇨10% × 105 = 10.5   So 9% of 105 is about 10.

Estimate.   **Accept reasonable estimates. Suggestion given.**

1. 11% of 256   **2.** 47% of 600   **3.** 9% of 185   **4.** 24% of 320
≈ 25.6   ≈ 300   ≈ 18.5   ≈ 80

---

3 FOLLOW-UP

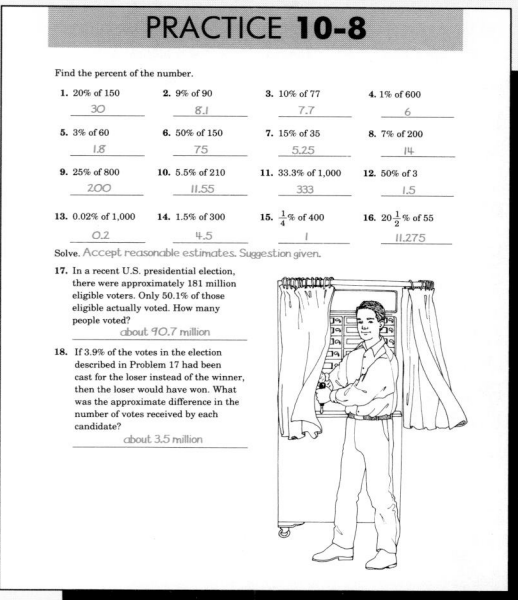

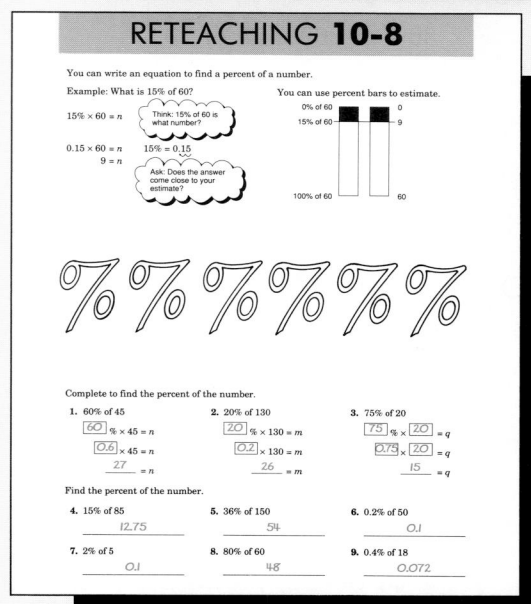

MEETING INDIVIDUAL NEEDS

For Students Who Are . . .

Acquiring English Proficiency   Explain the terms *Republicans, Democrats,* and *governors.* Have students locate North Carolina on a map.

Gifted and Talented   Have students use an almanac or state history to find the political party affiliation of the governors of their state from 1889 to 1989. Then have students calculate the percent that were Republicans and the percent that were Democrats.

Working 2 or 3 Grades Below Level   Review changing percents to decimals, particularly percents less than one. Have students use pages 76–77 of the Skills Workbook for Equations, Ratio, Proportion, and Percent.

Today's Problem

What does twenty-eight percent of 16, plus forty-three percent of 16, plus twenty-nine percent of 16 equal? *(sixteen, because 28% + 43% + 29% = 100%)*

ENRICHMENT 10-8

Ask the students to make a table to record the time in a typical school day they spend on activities besides learning each subject: for example, in homeroom, eating lunch, dressing for gym class, or walking to and from class. Have the students include a category called "other." Tell them to find the numbers of minutes in a typical school day and then to find the percent of the day spent doing each activity. Have the students compare their results.

Lesson Organizer

Objective: Find the percent.

Prior Knowledge: Students should be able to set up a percent bar diagram to model or check a percent problem.

Error Analysis and Remediation: See page 343A.

Lesson Resources:
Practice Worksheet 10-9
Reteaching Worksheet 10-9
Enrichment Activity 10-9
Daily Review 10-9

Two-Minute Math

Solve.

80% of 200   4% of 70

10% of 300   0.5% of 26

(160); (30); (2.8); (0.13)

1 INTRODUCE

CONNECTING ACTIVITY

☑ **MATERIALS CHECKLIST:** Percent Bar Transparency

Write "*n*% of 20 = 7." Model the problem on the percent bars with students. **Assume *n* is less than 100. How should the percent bar be labeled?** *(Write 0% at the top and 100% at the bottom.)*

What should be written at the bottom of the second bar? *(20)* **Explain.** *(20 represents 100% in this problem.)*

Where should the 7 be written? *(a little less than halfway down, because 7 is less than half of 20)*

Draw the line across the two bars. **Will *n* be greater than or less than 50%?** *(less than 50%)*

WHEN YOUR STUDENTS ASK
★ WHY AM I LEARNING THIS? ★

You can connect this skill to real life through careers in market research. For example, knowing what percent of the population prefers white toothpaste can help toothpaste companies design a saleable product.

Finding the Percent

In the northern hemisphere, June 21 has more daylight than any other day. On this day Barrow, Alaska, has daylight for 24 h, while Philadelphia has 15 h of daylight. What percent of the day is daylight in Philadelphia on June 21?

Set up percent bar models for the problem. Are the labels correct?

Let *n* represent the percent of daylight in Philadelphia on June 21.

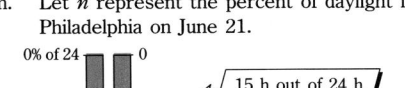

15 h out of 24 h are sunlight.

What percent is 15 out of 24?

$$n \times 24 = 15$$
$$\frac{n \times 24}{24} = \frac{15}{24}$$
$$n = 0.625 \text{ or } 62.5\%$$

On June 21, 62.5% of the day in Philadelphia is daylight.

Another example:
24 is what percent of 96?

$$n \times 96 = 24$$
$$\frac{n \times 96}{96} = \frac{24}{96}$$
$$n = 0.25, \text{ or } 25\%$$

Use a percent bar diagram to check.

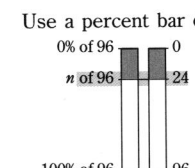

=== **GUIDED PRACTICE** ===

Write an equation and solve.

1. $n \times 80 = 12$; 15%

2. $n \times 600 = 240$; 40%

3. $n \times 200 = 2$; 1%

4. What percent of 12 is 3? 25%

5. 45 is what percent of 360? 12.5%

6. What percent is $\frac{18}{54}$? $33\frac{1}{3}$%

324   LESSON 10-9

MATH AND GEOGRAPHY

---

2 TEACH

☑ **MATERIALS CHECKLIST:** Teaching Aid 16; calculators

Why is 24 written at the bottom of the daylight bar? *(There are 24 hours in a day; 24 represents 100% of the hours in a day.)*

Why is the line drawn below the halfway point? *(15 is more than half of 24.)* **What does this tell us about the answer?** *(It will be greater than 50%.)*

What equation would you use to solve "15 is what percent of 25?" *(n × 25 = 15; n = 0.6 or 60%)*

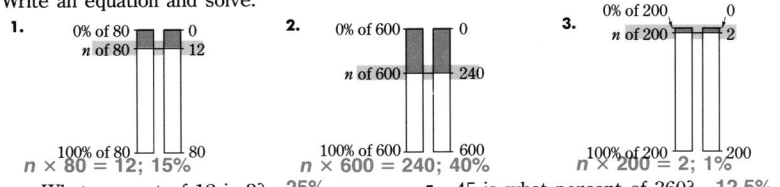

Chalkboard Examples

Write an equation and solve.
What percent is 20 out of 80? *(25%)*
14 is what percent of 42? $(33\frac{1}{3}\%)$
What percent is $\frac{3}{24}$? *(12.5%)*

SUMMARIZE/ASSESS **Explain how to find what percent 15 is of 75.** *(Write an equation, solve, model on percent bars, use the model to check the solution; 15 is 20% of 75)*

PRACTICE

Write an equation and solve. Use percent bars to help.

7. 12 is what percent of 15? **80%**

8. What percent of 40 is 13? **32.5%**

9. What percent is 15 out of 80? **18.75%**

10. 96 is what percent of 120? **80%**

11. What percent of 6 is 2? $33\frac{1}{3}$**%**

12. 15 is what percent of 15? **100%**

13. What percent is 19 out of 76? **25%**

14. 32 is what percent of 128? **25%**

15. What percent is 250 out of 2,000? **12.5%**

16. 1 is what percent of 6? $16\frac{2}{3}$**%**

17. What percent is $\frac{14}{112}$? **12.5%**

18. What percent is $\frac{64}{16}$? **400%**

MIXED REVIEW Compute.

19. $45\% \times 150 = $ � **67.5**

20. 13 out of 65 = ▓% **20**

21. $9\frac{1}{2}\% \times 800 = $ ▓ **76**

22. ▓% $= \frac{72}{360}$ **20**

23. ▓ $= 28\%$ of 1,000 **280**

24. $\frac{54}{162} = $ ▓% $33\frac{1}{3}$

NUMBER SENSE Is the percent *greater than* or *less than* 10%?

25. 2 of 60 **less**

26. 10 of 30 **greater**

27. 2 of 25 **less**

28. 4 of 43 **less**

29. 6 of 58 **greater**

30. 8 of 81 **less**

PROBLEM SOLVING

 Use the percent bars to solve.
Choose mental math, paper and pencil, or calculator.

Choices will vary.
Suggestions given.

31. What percent of the day is daylight in Houston on June 21? **p;** $58\frac{1}{3}$**%**

32. On June 21, which city has daylight for more than 75% of the day? **m; Anchorage; June 21**

33. IN YOUR WORDS Which city has more daylight in the summer? Why?
Answers will vary.

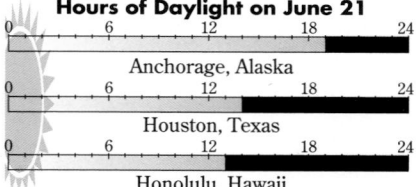

Hours of Daylight on June 21

Anchorage, Alaska

Houston, Texas

Honolulu, Hawaii

Mental Math

Think of a fraction in lowest terms to help you find the percent.

15 of 60 ⇨ $\frac{15}{60}$ ⇨ $\frac{1}{4}$ ⇨ 25%

Compute the percent mentally.

1. 25 of 50 **50%**

2. $50 of $500 **10%**

3. 12 of 48 **25%**

CHAPTER 10 **325**

MEETING INDIVIDUAL NEEDS

For Students Who Are . . .

Acquiring English Proficiency Use a map or globe to define *northern hemisphere*. Have students locate Barrow, Alaska and Philadelphia on a map.

Gifted and Talented Have students write an equation and solve: What percent of 100 is 125? *(125%)* What percent of 12 is 72? *(600%)* What percent of 24 is 54? *(225%)* What percent of 12 is 32? *(266$\frac{2}{3}$%)*

Working 2 or 3 Grades Below Level Review how to change a fraction to a decimal and then how to write the decimal as a percent.

Today's Problem

In 1987, net budget receipts of the federal government were $854,143,000. About 46% of this amount came from individual income taxes. How much money was collected as individual income taxes? *(about 46% of $854,143,000, or $392,905,780)*

---

3 FOLLOW-UP

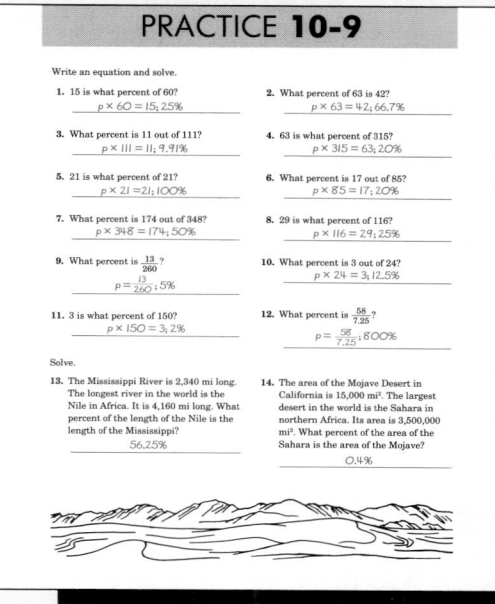

PRACTICE 10-9

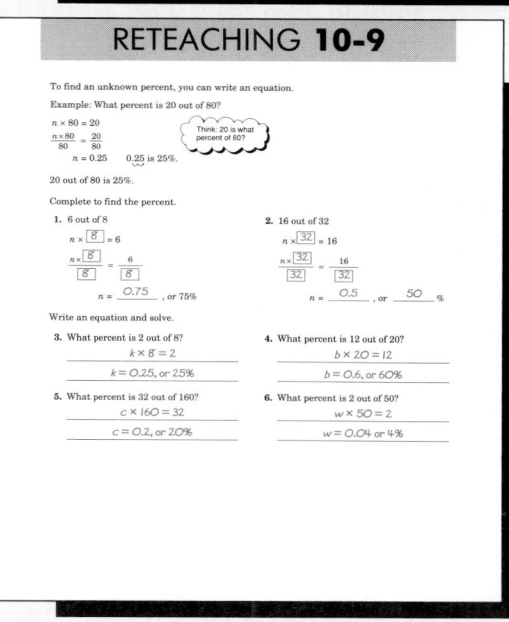

RETEACHING 10-9

ENRICHMENT 10-9

☑ **MATERIALS CHECKLIST:** Almanacs or atlases

Have the students work in pairs. Ask each pair to find the number of national parks in the United States. [48, plus 1 in the U.S. Virgin Islands] Then have the students make a table showing what percent of the total number of national parks each state with a national park has. Instruct the students to round to the nearest hundredth when calculating the percent. You may wish to have the students write the percent for each state within its borders on a blank map of the United States.

Lesson Organizer

Objective: Find the original number.

Prior Knowledge: Students should be able to model finding percents with a percent bar diagram.

Error Analysis and Remediation: See page 343A.

Lesson Resources:
Practice Worksheet 10-10
Reteaching Worksheet 10-10
Enrichment Activity 10-10
Daily Review 10-10

Two-Minute Math

Will the value of n be greater than or less than 195? Explain.

75% of 195 = n $(n < 195)$

75% of n = 195 $(n > 195)$

1 INTRODUCE

CONNECTING ACTIVITY

☑ **MATERIALS CHECKLIST:** Percent Bar Transparency

Display the percent bars and write "50% of n is 40." Write 100% and 0% on the percent bar, and draw a line across the middle of both bars.

Why is the line drawn across the middle of both bars? $(50\% = \frac{1}{2})$

Where should 40 be written? Explain. *(to the right of the second bar at the middle; 40 is 50% of the number.)*

Where should n be written? *(at the bottom of the second bar)*

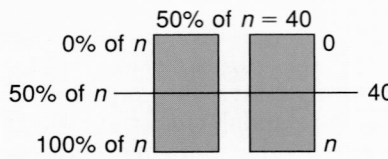

WHEN YOUR STUDENTS ASK
★ WHY AM I LEARNING THIS? ★

You can connect this skill to real life through economics. For example, the fact that 94% or 64 million people are employed is meaningful only if the size of the total work force is known.

MATH AND HISTORY

Finding the Original Number

In the 1984 Presidential election, Ronald Reagan received close to 60% of the popular vote. If he received more than 54 million votes, about how many people voted in the election?

Percent bars can represent this problem.

Why are the labels correct?   Let n represent the total number of votes.

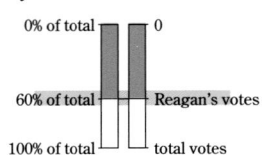
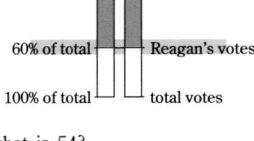

60% of what is 54?

$0.60 \times n = 54$

$\dfrac{0.60 \times n}{0.60} = \dfrac{54}{0.60}$

$n = 90$

About 90 million (90,000,000) people voted in the election.

Another example: Use percent bars to check.

42 is 20% of what number?

$0.2 \times n = 42$

$\dfrac{0.2 \times n}{0.2} = \dfrac{42}{0.2}$

$n = 210$

Use a percent bar diagram to check.

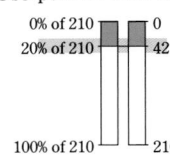

GUIDED PRACTICE

Write an equation and solve.

1. $0.50 \times n = 26$
   $n = 52$

2. $0.10 \times n = 25$
   $n = 250$

3. $0.45 \times n = 162$
   $n = 360$

4. 37 is 20% of what number? 185   5. 80% of what number is 72? 90

326   LESSON 10–10

---

2 TEACH

☑ **MATERIALS CHECKLIST:** Teaching Aid 16 (Percent Bar) for each student, calculators

What equation would you write to solve "36 is 40% of what number?" *($0.4 \times n = 36$; $n = 90$)*

How much greater is the solution to "45 is 20% of what number?" than the solution to "20% of 45 is what number?" *($45 = 20\%$ of 225; 20% of $45 = 9$; $225 - 9 = 216$)*

Chalkboard Examples

Write an equation and solve.
50% of what number is 35?
(70)
45 is 25% of what number?
(180)
5% of what number is 30?
(600)

SUMMARIZE/ASSESS   **Explain the difference between "n is 50% of 80" and "50% of n is 80." Use percent bar diagrams to help you.** *($40 = 50\%$ of 80; 50% of $160 = 80$; responses should include the fact that in the second sentence, n represents the whole amount.)*

Write an equation and solve. Use percent bars to check.

6. 25% of what number is 8? **32**

7. 35 is 20% of what number? **175**

8. 12 is 75% of what number? **16**

9. 40% of what number is 12? **30**

10. 35% of what number is 7? **20**

11. 720 is 18% of what number? **4,000**

12. 75 is 50% of what number? **150**

13. 25% of what number is 14? **56**

14. $37\frac{1}{2}$% of what number is 40? **$106\frac{2}{3}$**

15. 7.2 is 80% of what number? **9**

MIXED REVIEW Write an equation, and then solve for n.

16. n% of 40 is 20? **50**

17. 50% of 80 is n. **40**

18. 9 is 30% of n. **30**

19. 52% of n is 13. **25**

20. n% of 60 is 12. **20**

21. 75% of 300 is n. **225**

MENTAL MATH Find the unknown value mentally.

22. 50% of what number is 60? **120**

23. 25% of what number is 10? **40**

PROBLEM SOLVING

CHOOSE Choose paper and pencil or calculator to solve. **Choices will vary. suggestions given.**

24. In the 1984 Presidential election, Ronald Reagan captured 97% of the 538 electoral college votes. How many electoral votes did he get? **p; 522**

25. Officially, George Bush received 53.37% of the popular vote, or 48,886,097 votes, in 1988. About how many votes were cast in total that year? **c; 91, 592, 458**

26. In the 1960 Presidential election, John Kennedy received about 50.08% and Richard Nixon received about 49.92% of the 68,335,642 votes cast. About how many votes did each candidate receive? **c; Kennedy 34,222,490; Nixon 34,113,152**

27. **CRITICAL THINKING** In 1984, Ronald Reagan received 97% of the electoral college votes but only about 60% of the popular vote. How do you account for such a big difference?
Answers will vary.

CHAPTER 10 327

MEETING INDIVIDUAL NEEDS

For Students Who Are . . .

Acquiring English Proficiency Discuss the meaning of the terms *popular vote, presidential election,* and *electoral college votes.*

Gifted and Talented Have students research the candidates for the 1892 presidential election, find the number of votes for each candidate, and draw a percent bar diagram showing what percent of the popular vote each candidate received.

Working 2 or 3 Grades Below Level Review how to divide a whole number by a decimal and how to write a percent as a decimal.

Today's Problem

Tony is three years older than his 12-year-old brother. Tony's brother's age is what percent of Tony's age? *(n × 15 = 12; n = 80%)*

---

3 FOLLOW-UP

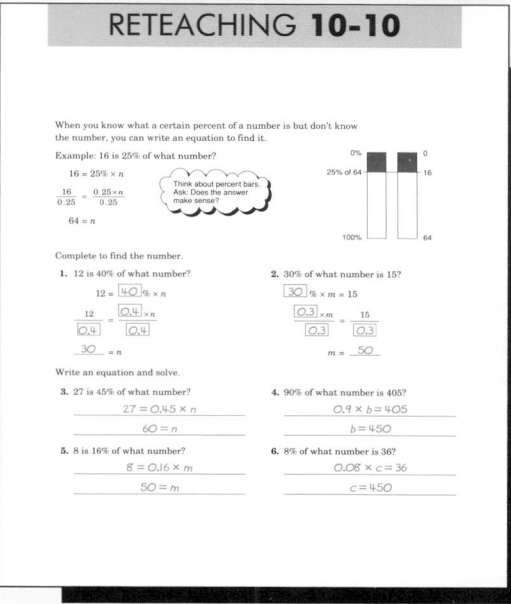
ENRICHMENT 10-10

☑ **MATERIALS CHECKLIST:** Index cards, reference books

Provide small groups with a set of index cards on which you have written the names of all the presidents of the United States. Ask each group to complete each card with this information: birth date, state of birth, age at time of election, and political party. Then have the students mix the cards. Each student selects a card and writes a percent problem. For example, a student might write, Jimmy Carter was born in 1924. What percent of U.S. presidents were born before 1924? [95%] The students solve each other's problems.

Lesson Organizer

Objective: Explore finding percents with mental math.

Prior Knowledge: Students should be able to write percents as fractions.

Lesson Resources:
Class Activity 10-11
Daily Review 10-11

Two-Minute Math

Use the Table of Numbers on the inside back cover. Write each percent in row M as a whole number or as a fraction in lowest terms.

$\left(\frac{1}{2}; \frac{1}{100}; 1; \frac{1}{4}; \frac{1}{20}; \frac{3}{4}; \frac{3}{10}; 2; \frac{4}{5}\right)$

1 PREPARE

SYMBOLIC ACTIVITY

What is $\frac{1}{2}$ of 48 *(24)* **of 53?** *(26.5)* **of 108?** *(54)*

Is 50% another name for $\frac{1}{2}$? How do you know? *(Yes; $50\% = \frac{50}{100} = \frac{1}{2}$.)*

What is 50% of 48? *(24)* **of 53?** *(26.5)* **of 108?** *(54)* **of any number?** *($\frac{1}{2}$ of the number)*

WHEN YOUR STUDENTS ASK
★ WHY AM I LEARNING THIS? ★

You can use this skill in many real life situations. For example, you might decide not to spend the month of April on vacation in a place in which it rained 80% of the days because you know that $\frac{4}{5}$ of 30 is 24!

EXPLORE

Exploring Mental Math and Percent

If you know how to write a percent as a fraction, you can make a **MATH CONNECTION** to find a percent mentally.

Write the fraction and percent that tell what part of the bar is shaded.

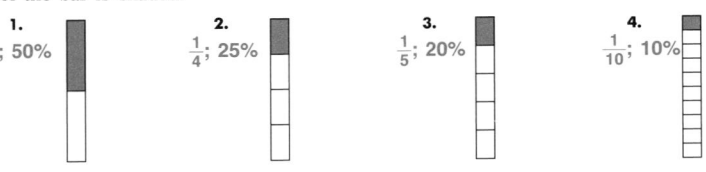

1. $\frac{1}{2}$; 50%   2. $\frac{1}{4}$; 25%   3. $\frac{1}{5}$; 20%   4. $\frac{1}{10}$; 10%

Since $25\% = \frac{1}{4}$, finding 25% of a number is like taking $\frac{1}{4}$ of that number. 25% of 80 $= \frac{1}{4}$ of 80 $= 4\overline{)80} = 20$.

5. Since $20\% = \frac{1}{5}$, what is 20% of 50?   10

Use the fraction equivalent to find the percent of the number mentally.

6. 50% of 60   30   7. 25% of 60   15   8. 20% of 60   12

9. 10% of 60   6   10. 20% of 40   8   11. 10% of 50   5

12. 25% of 120   13. 50% of 360   14. 25% of 360   90
    30   180

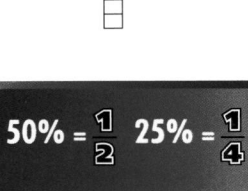
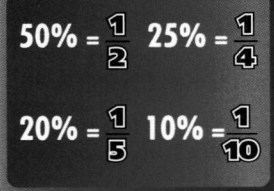

50% of what number is 4? You know that half of the number you want is 4.

If half of a number is 4, you can multiply 4×2 to find the number.
50% of 8 is 4.

15. Since $20\% = \frac{1}{5}$, 20% of ▧ $= 8$?   40

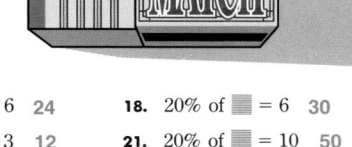
50% are showing. How many in all?

Find the original number mentally.

16. 50% of ▧ $= 6$ 12   17. 25% of ▧ $= 6$ 24   18. 20% of ▧ $= 6$ 30

19. 10% of ▧ $= 6$ 60   20. 25% of ▧ $= 3$ 12   21. 20% of ▧ $= 10$ 50

22. 10% of ▧ $= 15$ 150   23. 50% of ▧ $= 100$ 200   24. 50% of ▧ $= 1,000$
                                                              2,000

---

2 EXPLORE

☑ **MATERIALS CHECKLIST:** Math Connection Transparency

Display the transparency. Have students fill in the spaces and discuss the math connection. *(See student pages.)*

Before students begin Exercise 5, ask: **Why does dividing 80 by 4 give you 25% of 80?** *(Finding $\frac{1}{4}$ of a number is the same as finding the size of one of four equal-sized parts.)*

How would you use mental math to solve: 10% of what number is 13.5? *(Possible answer: If $\frac{1}{10}$ of the number is 13.5, multiply 13.5 × 10 to get 135.)*

SUMMARIZE/ASSESS **Explain how you can think about 25% of 20 to help you find 125% of 20.** *(Possible answer: Find $\frac{1}{4}$ of 20, which is 5; multiply by 5, which is 25. Other explanations are possible.)*

If you can find 25% of a number in your head, you can make a **MATH CONNECTION** to find 75% of a number.

25. How many times larger is 75% than 25%? If 25% of 28 is 7, and 75% is three times larger than 25%, what is 75% of 28? **3; 21**

26. How many times larger is 40% than 10%? If 10% of 30 is 3, what is 40% of 30? **4; 12**

Compute mentally.

27. 25% of 12 **3**   **28.** 75% of 12 **9**   **29.** 20% of 15 **3**   **30.** 40% of 15 **6**

31. 60% of 20 **12**   **32.** 75% of 20 **15**   **33.** 20% of 25 **5**   **34.** 40% of 10 **4**

The members of a school band needed to sell 80 boxes of greeting cards to raise money for a trip. The percent bar diagram shows how they did. By the end of week 4, they had sold 120 boxes. This was more than 100% of their goal.

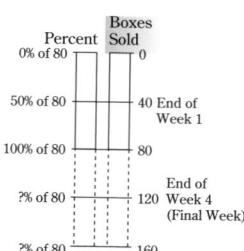

35. How many boxes had to be sold to double their goal? Was the goal doubled? **160; no**

36. If the goal had been doubled, what percent of their goal would have been reached? **200%**

37. What percent of their goal was reached by selling 120 boxes of cards? **150%**

38. To find 150% of 60, think
  a. What is 100% of 60? **60**
  b. What is 50% of 60? **30**
  c. If 100% is 60, and 50% is 30, what is 150% of 60? **90**

39. To find 125% of 40, think:
  a. What is 100% of 40? **40**
  b. What is 25% of 40? **10**
  c. What is 125% of 40? **50**

40. To find 120% of 50, think:
  a. What is 100% of 50? **50**
  b. What is 20% of 50? **10**
  c. What is 120% of 50? **60**

41. To find 110% of 80, think:
  a. What is 100% of 80? **80**
  b. What is 10% of 80? **8**
  c. What is 110% of 80? **88**

Compute mentally.

42. 150% of 10 **15**   **43.** 125% of 12 **15**   **44.** 110% of 40 **44**   **45.** 200% of 10 **20**

46. 125% of 20 **25**   **47.** 100% of 20 **20**   **48.** 175% of 20 **35**   **49.** 160% of 20 **32**

50. **IN YOUR WORDS** Describe how you can think about 1% of 320 to help you find 3% of 320. **Answers will vary.**

3 FOLLOW-UP

CLASS ACTIVITY **10-11**

☑ **MATERIALS CHECKLIST:** Index cards, stopwatches

Provide groups of four with cards on which are written *$2.50, $8, $12, $20*. The backs of the cards contain the following, respectively: *$.30 or 20%; $2.25 or 25%, $5 or 40%; $16 or 75%.* A moderator displays a price and reads the back of the card. A timer announces when 5 seconds have passed, and the two players write which represents the lower price—the amount or the percent. When all cards have been used, students add up their results. The student with the lower total wins. Have group members trade roles and repeat the activity with different cards.

MEETING INDIVIDUAL NEEDS

For Students Who Are . . .

Acquiring English Proficiency To develop the idea of percents greater than 100%, ask: **What percent would represent a goal doubled?** *(200%)* **What does 150% of a value mean?** *($1\frac{1}{2}$ times the value)*

Gifted and Talented Challenge students to find another way to use mental math to find 20%, 30%, or 40% of a number. *(Possible method: find 10% by moving decimal point, then multiply by 2, 3, or 4.)*

Having Reading Difficulties Have students read the paragraph preceding Exercises 33–35 aloud. Remind students that sometimes they must read math problems several times for understanding.

Today's Problem

You scored 95 out of 125 possible points on last week's test. This week you earned 45 out of a possible 50 points. To the nearest percent, what percent of last week's test is this week's test? *(Last week's score was 76%; this week's score was 90%; $\frac{90\%}{76\%} = 118\%$)*

MIDCHAPTER Checkup

The midchapter checkup provides a way for you to check students' understanding of the skills taught in the first half of the chapter.

Language and Vocabulary

Some key language and vocabulary ideas from the first half of the chapter are reinforced here.

Quick Quiz

This quiz provides a means of evaluating students' understanding of the objectives for the first half of the chapter. Page references are given so that students can check back to where the skill was taught.

Use the following guide to score the quiz.

Score	Percent
10	100%
9	90
8	80
7	70
6	60
5	50
4	40
3	30
2	20
1	10

Use this chart to identify the management objectives tested.

Items	Management Objective	Pages
1–4	**10A** Write fractions and decimals as percents and percents as fractions and decimals.	312–315
5–6	**10B** Write percents greater than 100% and less than 1%.	316–317
7–10	**10C** Find the percent of a number, the percent, or the original number in percent problems.	322–327

MIDCHAPTER CHECKUP

LANGUAGE & VOCABULARY

Write a sentence to explain how you would: **Answers will vary. Suggestions given.**
1. change a fraction to a percent   **See below.**
2. change a percent to a fraction   **See below.**
3. change a decimal to a percent   **See below.**
4. change a percent to a decimal   **See below.**
5. find a percent of a number   **See below.**

QUICK QUIZ ✓

Write as a percent. *(pages 312–317)*

1. $\frac{13}{20}$ **65%**   2. $\frac{12}{16}$ **75%**   3. 0.43 **43%**   4. 0.195 **19.5%**
5. 1.32 **132%**   6. 0.0028 **0.28%**

Find the percent of the number. *(pages 322–323)*

7. 3% of 82 **2.46**

Write an equation and solve. *(pages 324–327)*

8. What percent is 24 out of 80? **30%**
9. 40% of what number is 50? **125**

Solve. *(pages 326–327)*

10. Leslie counted birds on a walk in the park. She saw 23 pigeons and 7 robins.
   a. How many robins did Leslie see? **7**
   b. How can you find the percent of the birds that were robins? **divide; 7 ÷ 30**
   c. What percent were robins? **23.3%**

1. Divide the numerator by the denominator.
2. Put percent over 100 and simplify.
3. Multiply by 100.
4. Divide by 100.
5. Change the percent to a decimal or fraction and multiply.

330   MIDCHAPTER CHECKUP

Write the answers in your learning log.   **Answers will vary. Suggestion given.**

1. Write one or more sentences telling what is important to remember when dealing with percents.
   Percents are usually based on a total of 100.
2. Describe a way to find 25% of a number mentally.
   Divide by four.

DID YOU KNOW . . . ? In the 1920's, people in the United States could buy a dozen large eggs for 68¢, a quart of whole milk for 17¢, and a pound of butter for 70¢. By what percentage has the price of each item changed in more than 70 years?   **Check students' work.**

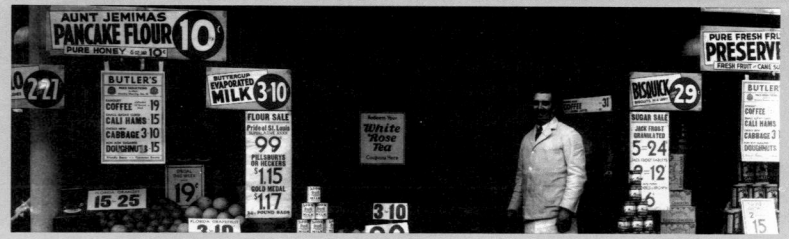

BONUS

In the state in which Marilyn lives, sales tax on restaurant meals is 7%. When a tip is appropriate, Marilyn always leaves exactly 15% of the bill. The past two nights, she has eaten at a self-service restaurant where the bill before tax was $11.55 and at a cafe with waitress service where the bill before tax was $10.15. Which dinner cost more? How much more? Round to the nearest cent. Make up some other restaurant problems.   **cafe; $.02; Accept reasonable answers.**

CHAPTER 10   331

Learning Log

These are suggestions for writing about some topics taught so far in the chapter. The students keep their learning logs from the start of the school year to the end.

Math America

A mathematical skill that students have learned is related to an interesting fact about the United States.

Bonus

Students are given an opportunity to solve a challenge-type problem such as a puzzle or a nonroutine problem.

LESSON 10-12

Lesson Organizer

Objective: Solve problems by estimating tips and sales tax.

Prior Knowledge: Students should be able to find numbers compatible to given numbers and to solve different types of percent problems.

Lesson Resources:
Practice Worksheet 10-12
Reteaching Activity 10-12
Enrichment Worksheet 10-12
Daily Review 10-12

Two-Minute Math

Find 1% and 10% of the amount.

$600 ($6; $60) $300 ($3; $30)

$50 ($.50; $5) $45 ($.45; $4.50)

1 INTRODUCE

SYMBOLIC ACTIVITY

How does 10% compare in size with 5%? *(It is twice as great.)*

If 10% of some number is equal to 8, what is 5% of that number? *(4)* **Explain.** *(5% is half of 10%.)*

If 5% of some amount is equal to $12, what is 10% of that amount? *($24)* **Explain.** *(5% is half of 10%.)*

WHEN YOUR STUDENTS ASK
★ WHY AM I LEARNING THIS? ★

This skill will help you solve real life problems such as computing a tax when you purchase something in a store or figuring a tip when you eat in a restaurant.

Problem Solving:
Estimating Tips and Sales Tax

Jacek has $50 to spend at an international student fair. He is about to buy a hand-embroidered tablecloth for $44.95. If the sales tax is 6%, does he have enough money to buy the tablecloth?

Compatible numbers can help you estimate the sales tax.

- Think: $44.95 is close to $50. The sales tax is about 6% of $50.
- Think: 6% is 6 × 1%. What is 1% of $50? What is 6% of $50? **50¢; $3.00**
- Now estimate the cost including the sales tax on your own. Does Jacek have enough money? **≈$48; yes**

The food bill at the Polish pavilion is $29.45. The usual amount for a tip is about 15% of the bill. About how much should you leave for a tip?

- Think: $29.45 is close to $30. The tip is about 15% of $30.
- Think: 15% is 10% + 5%. What is 10% of $30? What is 5% of $30? What is 15% of $30? **$3; $1.50; $4.50**
- Now estimate a fair tip on your own. **≈$4.50**

■ GUIDED PRACTICE ■

Estimate the solution to the problem.

1. Dahlia wants to buy a hand-crafted belt for $29.95 and a leather handbag for $34.59. The sales tax is 5%.

   a. What is the sales tax? **5%**

   b. Would the cost of the two items be *more than* or *less than* $62? **more than**

   c. Is the total cost, with sales tax, *more than* or *less than* $70? **less than**

2. Luigi bought a $5.75 lunch at the German food stand. He would like to leave a 15% tip. About how much should the tip be? **≈$1.00**

$29.95

---

2 TEACH

You know that $44.95 rounds to $40, not $50. Why did Jacek think of $44.95 as $50 rather than $40? *(to be sure he had enough money)*

Once you have found 10% of $30, how do you find 5% of $30? Explain. *(Divide the first result by 2 because 5% is half of 10%.)*
Once you have found 10% and 5% of $30, how do you find 15%? *(Add.)*

SUMMARIZE/ASSESS   How do you estimate a 15% tip or a 5% sales tax? *(Use compatible numbers. Find 10%, then 5%, and add; find 10% and divide by 2.)*

MULTICULTURAL NOTE

Exercises 3 and 7. The Chinese were the first to discover that silk could be made from the cocoon of a small worm; they guarded this secret for about 3,000 years. In about 550, a foreign emperor sent spies to China to learn how silk was produced. Today the beautiful fabric is produced all over the world.

Estimate the solution to the problem. Accept reasonable estimates. Suggestions given.

3. Ernest bought a windbreaker for $45 and two Chinese silk scarfs for $15 each. The sales tax was 7.8%. About how much did he spend?
≈$80

4. The tax paid on three Italian take-out dinners costing $42 was $4.90. About what percent of the price was tax?
≈12½%

5. Morana and Tony had two Japanese meals for a total of $11.50. The sales tax was 6%. About how much change would Morana and Tony get from a $20 bill if they left a 15% tip?
≈$6

6. Rhonda bought a $64.99 painting, a $14.49 cookbook, and an Egyptian scarf for $19.29. About what was the total cost if the sales tax was 7%?
≈$107

7. Mrs. Thomas wants to buy 4 yd of silk from Thailand to make a dress. The silk costs $9.95/yd plus a 5% sales tax. About how much should Mrs. Thomas expect to spend?
≈$42

8. José buys a $29.50 meal at the East Indian pavilion. The sales tax on the food is 5% and José wants to include a 15% tip. About how much money will José pay for the meal?
≈$36

9. At the Dutch pavilion, $3.50 is charged for 1 lb of Gouda cheese. This price *includes* a sales tax of 21¢. About what percent of the price is the tax?
≈6%

10. In some places, people can use the amount of sales tax they pay to estimate the tip. If you pay $3.42 sales tax, at 8.25%, about how much money would you leave for a 15% tip?
≈$6

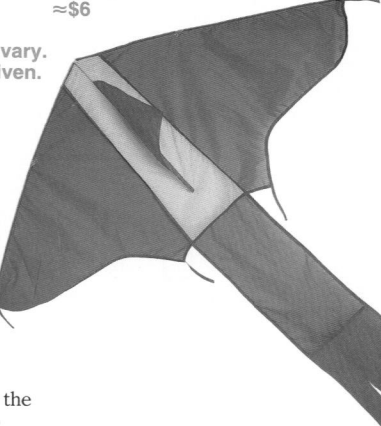

CHOOSE Choose a strategy to solve. Strategies will vary. Suggestions given.

11. Jana wants to buy a $40 Chinese kite on sale at 25% off the regular price. There is an additional 10% off the sale price if you pay cash. What would the cash price for the kite be if the sales tax is 5.2%?
multistep; $28.40

12. Art left a $1.20 tip for his meal. If the tip was about 15% of the cost of the meal, what was the cost of the meal?
read for understanding; $8

13. CRITICAL THINKING Marina estimated the solution to Exercise 8 by multiplying $30 by 1.2. Explain why her method works. Answers will vary. Suggestion given: José paid 100% + 5% + 15%, or 120% of the meal cost.

CHAPTER 10   333

MEETING INDIVIDUAL NEEDS

For Students Who Are . . .

Acquiring English Proficiency Discuss what students might find at an international student fair. Introduce the words *pavilion, hand-embroidered, food stand,* and *Gouda cheese.*

Gifted and Talented Have students solve this problem: Gasoline costs $1.22 a gallon. This price includes a 14-cent tax. To the nearest percent, what is the tax rate? *(about 13%)*

Working 2 or 3 Grades Below Level Review how to find 10% and 5% of a number.

Having Reading Difficulties Pair students with an able reader for the Practice exercises.

Today's Problem

The sales tax is 5% and you want to leave a tip of 15%. Does it make a difference if you add 5% and then add 15% to the bill, or add 15% and then 5%? *(Assume you are going to pay the tax only on the meal and the tip only on the meal, it does not make any difference.)*

3 FOLLOW-UP

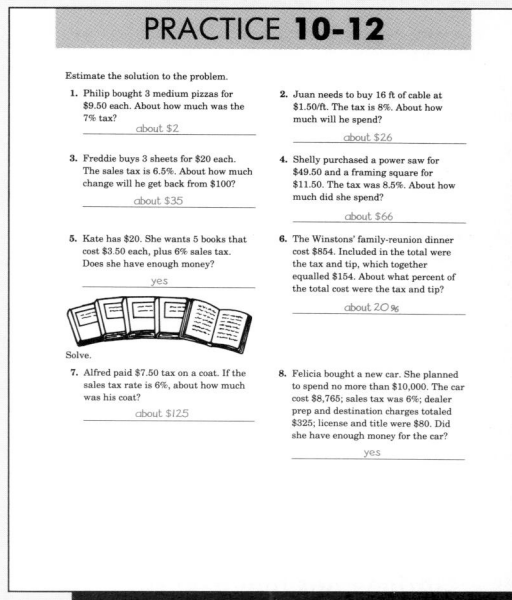

PRACTICE 10-12

Estimate the solution to the problem.
1. Philip bought 3 medium pizzas for $9.50 each. About how much was the 7% tax? *about $2*
2. Juan needs to buy 16 ft of cable at $1.50/ft. The tax is 8%. About how much will he spend? *about $26*
3. Freddie buys 3 sheets for $20 each. The sales tax is 6.5%. About how much change will he get back from $100? *about $35*
4. Shelly purchased a power saw for $49.50 and a framing square for $11.50. The tax was 8.5%. About how much did she spend? *about $66*
5. Kate has $20. She wants 5 books that cost $3.50 each, plus 6% sales tax. Does she have enough money? *yes*
6. The Winstons' family-reunion dinner cost $854. Included in the total were the tax and tip, which together equalled $154. About what percent of the total cost were the tax and tip? *about 20%*
Solve.
7. Alfred paid $7.50 tax on a coat. If the sales tax rate is 6%, about how much was his coat? *about $125*
8. Felicia bought a new car. She planned to spend no more than $10,000. The car cost $8,765; sales tax was 6%; dealer prep and destination charges totaled $325; license and title were $80. Did she have enough money for the car? *yes*

RETEACHING 10-12

Some of the students may have difficulty estimating sales tax and tips. Help a student solve Problem 1, *Practice Worksheet 93,* by asking these questions: What amount that is close to $9.50 would be easier to work with? [$10] How much would the sales tax on $10 be? [$.70] How many times greater than $10 is $30? [3 times] How many times should you multiply the tax on 1 pizza to get the tax on 3 pizzas? [3 times] About how much is this? [about $2]

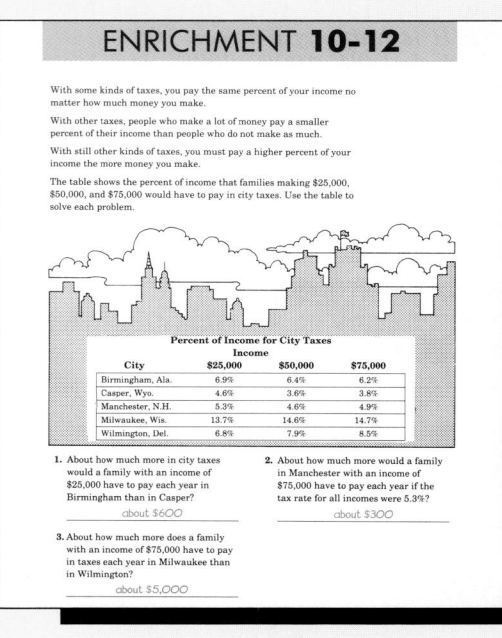

ENRICHMENT 10-12

With some kinds of taxes, you pay the same percent of your income no matter how much money you make.

With other taxes, people who make a lot of money pay a smaller percent of their income than people who do not make as much.

With still other kinds of taxes, you must pay a higher percent of your income the more money you make.

The table shows the percent of income that families making $25,000, $50,000, and $75,000 would have to pay in city taxes. Use the table to solve each problem.

Percent of Income for City Taxes

City	Income $25,000	$50,000	$75,000
Birmingham, Ala.	6.9%	6.4%	6.2%
Casper, Wyo.	4.6%	3.6%	3.8%
Manchester, N.H.	5.3%	4.6%	4.9%
Milwaukee, Wis.	13.7%	14.6%	14.7%
Wilmington, Del.	6.8%	7.9%	8.5%

1. About how much more in city taxes would a family with an income of $25,000 have to pay each year in Birmingham than in Casper? *about $600*
2. About how much more would a family in Manchester with an income of $75,000 have to pay each year if the tax rate for all incomes were 5.3%? *about $300*
3. About how much more does a family with an income of $75,000 have to pay in taxes each year in Milwaukee than in Wilmington? *about $5,000*

Lesson Organizer

Objective: Use percents greater than 100%.

Prior Knowledge: Students should be able to find a percent of a number.

Lesson Resources:
Practice Worksheet 10-13
Reteaching Activity 10-13
Enrichment Worksheet 10-13
Daily Review 10-13

 *Two-Minute Math*

Name a situation in which a percent greater than 100 makes sense and one in which it does not make sense. *(Possible answers: Profits for this year are 115% of last year's; he spent 115% of his income.)*

1 INTRODUCE

CONNECTING ACTIVITY

☑ **MATERIALS CHECKLIST:** Percent Bar Transparency

1. Write "150% of 80 = 120." Display the transparency and draw a line across the bars to show 150%. **Why does the line go here?** *(It is halfway between 100% and 200%.)* Label 0%, 100%, 200%, and 150% on the percent bar.

2. Write *80* across from the 100% point on the second bar. Locate the point on the second bar across from 200%. **What should be written here?** *(Twice 80, or 160)*

3. Write 120 across from the 150% point. **Why is this answer reasonable?** *(It is greater than 80 and less than 160.)*

WHEN YOUR STUDENTS ASK
★ **WHY AM I LEARNING THIS?** ★

You can connect this skill to real life through consumer purchases. For example, you may pay 106% of the cost of a new car when the sales tax is included on the bill of sale.

Using Percents Greater Than 100%

Lori wants to buy a pair of jeans for $34. Sales tax is 8%. What is the total amount of money Lori must pay for the jeans?

Lori has to pay:

$$\begin{array}{rl} 100\% & \text{of the cost of the jeans} \\ + \quad 8\% & \text{sales tax} \\ \hline 108\% \end{array}$$

The percent bars represent this situation. Let n represent the total amount Lori pays.

108% of $34 is what number?
$$1.08 \times 34 = n$$
$$36.72 = n$$

On a calculator: 1.08 ☒ 34 ☐ 36.72

In all, Lori must pay $36.72 for the jeans.

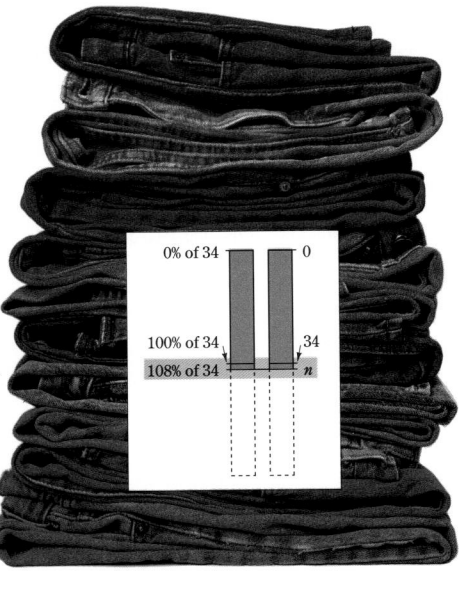

Julio paid $14, including tip, for his dinner at Sparto's restaurant. That was 112% of the price of the dinner on the menu. What was the price of the dinner on the menu?

The percent bars represent this situation. Let x represent the menu price of the dinner.

112% of what number is $14?
$$1.12 \times x = 14$$
$$\frac{1.12 \times x}{1.12} = \frac{14}{1.12}$$
$$x = 12.5$$

On a calculator: 14 ☐ 1.12 ☐ 12.5
The price of Julio's dinner on the menu was $12.50.

================ **GUIDED PRACTICE** ================

What percent of the cost is the total amount paid? Include the percent of tax or tip.

1. $75 with a 6% sales tax
106%

2. $22.50 with a 15% tip
115%

3. $3.95 with a 7% sales tax
107%

Calculators should be available for tedious calculations.

2 TEACH

☑ **MATERIALS CHECKLIST:** calculators, Teaching Aid 16

How would you estimate the total for meal, tax, and tip at a restaurant if the cost of the meal were rounded to $13? *(Find 10% of $13, $1.30, plus 5%, $.65, add to determine 15%, $1.95. Round to $2 and add this amount to $13., to get $15.)*

In some cities a sales tax is added to restaurant bills. If dinner for two costs $28.50 and a sales tax of 8% is charged, what is the cost of the dinner without a tip? *($30.78)* What is the total cost of the dinner with a 15% tip on $28.50? *($35.06)*

Chalkboard Examples

What percent of the cost is the total amount paid?
$85 with a 6% sales tax *(106%)*
$34.50 with a 15% tip *(115%)*

SUMMARIZE/ASSESS   **Explain why 128% of 80 should be greater than 80, less than 160, but closer to 80.** *(128% is greater than 100%, less than 200%, but closer to 100%.)*

Write an equation and solve.   **Check students' work.**

4. What is 105% of $30?
$31.50

5. What percent is $\frac{\$10.35}{\$9}$?
115%

6. 180% of what is 360?
200

===== **PRACTICE** =====

Write an equation and solve. Use percent bars to help. **Check students' work.**

7. What is 120% of 48? **57.6** **8.** 150% of 8 is what? **12** **9.** What percent is $\frac{285}{95}$? **300%**

10. 200% of what is 124? **62** **11.** What is 105% of 90¢? **94.5¢** **12.** 150% of what is 36? **24**

Add a 15% tip to find the amount to be paid for the meal.

13. $9.95 **$11.44**   **14.** $25.17 **$28.95**   **15.** $5.29 **$6.08**   **16.** $8.44 **$9.71**

Add a 5.5% sales tax to find the amount to be paid for the item.

17. sweater: $24 **$25.32**   **18.** jacket: $49 **$51.70**   **19.** boots: $81 **$85.46**

MIXED REVIEW Compute.

20. 20% of what is 15? **75**
21. 45 is what percent of 90? **50%**
22. What is 72% of 300? **216**
23. What percent of 50 is 5? **10%**
24. What is 115% of 85? **97.75**
25. 180% of what is 360? **200**

CALCULATOR Copy and complete the function table.

26.

n	30%	60%	90%	120%	150%
280n	?	?	?	?	?

84 168 252 336 420

27.

n	40%	80%	120%	160%	200%
320n	?	?	?	?	?

128 256 384 512 640

===== **PROBLEM SOLVING** =====

 Choose paper and pencil or calculator to solve. **Choices will vary.**

28. The sales tax in Willis, Texas, is 7% and in New Waverly, Texas, it is 9%. Drew lives in New Waverly. If it takes $1.50 worth of gas to drive to Willis and back, how much would Drew save by driving to Willis to buy a $200 weed eater?
c; $2.50

29. Ruth and Carl ordered 2 Mexican dinners at $8.80 each. A tax of 5% and a 15% tip was paid on the cost of the 2 meals. How much did Ruth and Carl pay in all?
p; $21.12

30. **CREATE YOUR OWN** Make up a math problem involving sales tax or tips. Give it to a friend to solve.
Check students' work.

CHAPTER 10   335

MEETING INDIVIDUAL NEEDS

For Students Who Are . . .

Acquiring English Proficiency Discuss the concept of adding the percent of tax or tip to the cost of the item on the bill (100%); suggest the alternative method of finding the amount of tax or tip and adding it to the cost.

Gifted and Talented Have students research other kinds of taxes, such as social security taxes, income taxes, withholding taxes.

Working 2 or 3 Grades Below Level Review how to change a percent greater than 100% to a decimal.

Having Reading Difficulties Pair students with an able reader for the Create Your Own activity.

Today's Problem

Every day the population in California increases by 1,287 people. The population of California is about 27,663,000. To the nearest tenth, by what percent does the population of California increase each year? *(1,287 × 365 × $\frac{1}{27,663,000}$ or 1.7%)*

3 FOLLOW-UP

PRACTICE 10-13

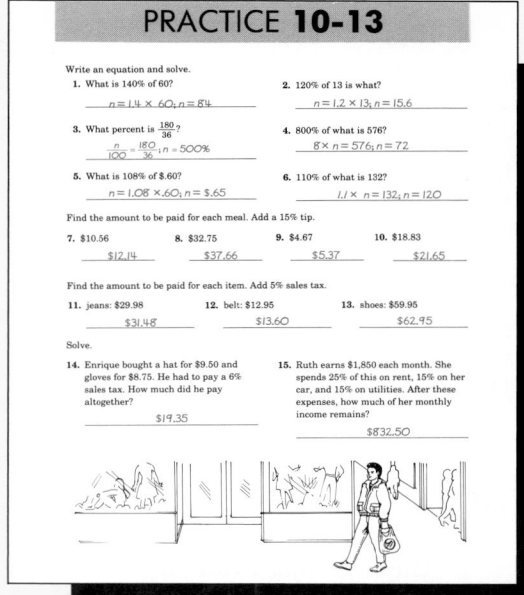

RETEACHING 10-13

☑ **MATERIALS CHECKLIST:** 1 in. × 1 in. and $\frac{1}{2}$ in. × $\frac{1}{2}$ in. pieces of paper

The partners make percent bar diagrams placing the column with the ten 1 in. squares on the left and the $\frac{1}{2}$ in. squares on the right. Tell them that the left bar shows increments of 10% and that the right bar shows the numbers 1, 2, 3 . . . . Ask: What percent does the bottom edge of the left bar show? [100%] What number does the bottom edge of the right bar show? [20] The students shade to show 100% of 20 and add pieces to each bar to find 120% of 20. [24]

ENRICHMENT 10-13

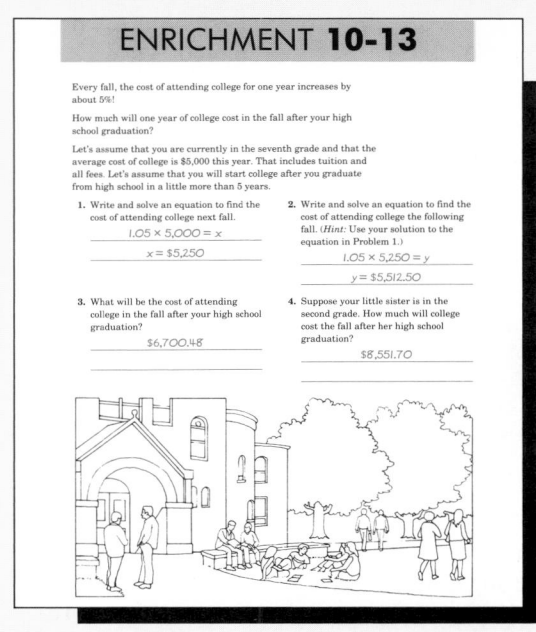

Lesson Organizer

Objective: Explore percent of increase and decrease.

Prior Knowledge: Students should be familiar with percents greater than 100%.

Lesson Resources:
Class Activity 10-14
Daily Review 10-14

 **Two-Minute Math**

Below are the sale prices of three items. Find the original price if each price were reduced $15.

$29.75 ($44.75) $46.59 ($61.59)

$128.29 ($143.29)

1 PREPARE

CONNECTING ACTIVITY

☑ **MATERIALS CHECKLIST:** Teaching Aid 17 (Percent Bar Diagram, greater than 100%) for each student

Label the percent bars for the following examples.

175% of 80 = 140   150% of 400 = 600

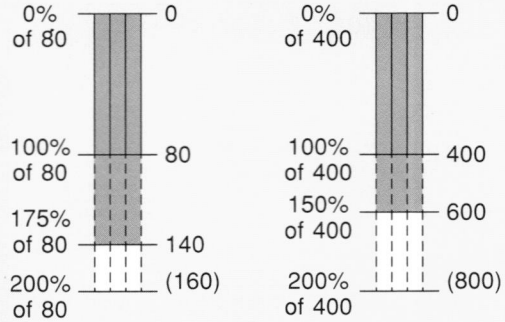

WHEN YOUR STUDENTS ASK
★ WHY AM I LEARNING THIS? ★

You can connect this skill to real life through health records. The number of cases of a given disease is sometimes reported as a percent of increase or decrease compared to a baseline year.

 EXPLORE

Exploring the Percent of Increase and Decrease

Aaron wants to buy a new racing bicycle. Last year the price of the bicycle was $240. Now the price is $360. By what percent did the price of the bicycle increase?

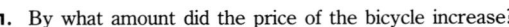

1. By what amount did the price of the bicycle increase?

2. The **percent of increase** is the ratio of the increase to the original amount. Copy and complete the percent of increase ratio for this problem. $\frac{\$120}{\$240} = 50\%$ (increase in price)

$$\frac{\text{amount of increase} \rightarrow}{\text{original amount} \rightarrow} \quad \frac{?}{\$240} = \blacksquare\% \leftarrow \text{percent of increase}$$

The ratio of the amount of increase to the original amount is given. Find the percent of increase.

3. $\frac{\$100}{\$125}$ 80%   4. $\frac{\$20}{\$25}$ 80%   5. $\frac{\$350}{\$700}$ 50%   6. $\frac{\$120}{\$150}$ 80%   7. $\frac{\$15}{\$20}$ 75%

Suppose you know that the price of a three-speed bicycle increased by 12%. Last year the bicycle sold for $150. The percent bar model at the right can help you find this year's price. Let p represent this year's price.

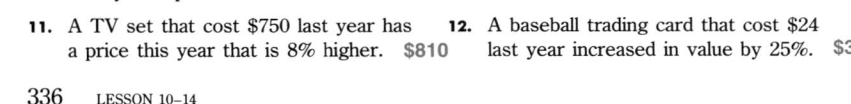

8. Would this year's price be *more than* or *less than* 100% of $150?
   more than

9. What percent of 150 is this year's price? **112%**

10. What is this year's price? **$168**

Find this year's price.

11. A TV set that cost $750 last year has a price this year that is 8% higher. **$810**

12. A baseball trading card that cost $24 last year increased in value by 25%. **$30**

---

2 EXPLORE

Have students work in groups of three or four.

Ask students why this solution to Exercise 22 is *not* correct: 25% of $8,400 is $2,100. $8,400 + $2,100 = $10,500. $10,500 is the original cost. (*Accept reasonable responses; possible answer: 25% of $8,400 is not equal to 25% of the original cost, a number larger than $8,400.*)

SUMMARIZE/ASSESS   **How would you find the percent of increase from $250 to $325?** (*Find the amount of increase, $75; compare it to the original amount to determine the percent:* $\frac{75}{250} = 30\%$)

The present value of Bettina's car is $7,200. Last year the value was $9,600. By what percent did the value of her car decrease?

13. By what amount did Bettina's car decrease in value?
by $2,400

14. The **percent of decrease** is the ratio of the decrease to the original amount. Copy and complete the percent of decrease ratio for this problem. $\frac{\$2,400}{\$9,600}$ = 25% **(decrease in value)**

$$\begin{array}{c}\text{amount of decrease} \rightarrow \\ \text{original amount} \rightarrow\end{array} \frac{?}{\$9,600} = \blacksquare\% \leftarrow \text{percent of decrease}$$

The ratio of the amount of decrease to the original amount is given. Find the percent of decrease.

15. $\frac{\$1.50}{\$6}$ **25%** **16.** $\frac{\$2.40}{\$20}$ **12%** **17.** $\frac{\$.45}{\$3}$ **15%** **18.** $\frac{\$.72}{\$1.80}$ **40%** **19.** $\frac{\$4}{\$6}$ **66$\frac{2}{3}$%**

Bruce knows his jeep has decreased in value by 25% from its original value. If the present value is $8,400, what was the original price of the jeep?

Let p represent the original price.

20. Is the *original price* or the *present value* of the jeep equal to 100% of $8,400?
present value

21. What percent of the original price of Bruce's jeep is $8,400? **75%**

22. What was the original price of the jeep?
$11,200

Find the original price.

23. A sailboat decreased in value by 20%. It is now worth $3,200. **$4,000**

24. A van is now valued at $18,000 after a 40% decrease. **$30,000**

In business, the percent of increase is called the **percent of profit**. The percent of decrease is the **percent of loss**.

Does the situation have a *profit* or a *loss*? Find the percent of profit or loss.

25. A storekeeper pays $4.50 for a book and sells it for $9.
profit; 100%

26. One month, a business has $50,000 in sales and $70,000 in expenses.
loss; 40%

CLASS ACTIVITY **10-14**

☑ **MATERIALS CHECKLIST:**
Newspapers

Ask the students to work in pairs. Provide each group with newspaper advertisements for the same grocery store from two different weeks. Have the students find several products that appear in two ads. Have them make a table and record the price of each product in Week 1 and in Week 2. Have the students calculate the percent of increase or decrease from Week 1 to Week 2. Ask: Why do you think the prices of these products changed? [Answers will vary; suggestion: products went on sale.]

MEETING INDIVIDUAL NEEDS

For Students Who Are . . .

Acquiring English Proficiency Discuss the meanings of *increase* and *decrease* in this lesson. Reinforce concepts of original price, present value, percent of profit, and percent of loss.

Gifted and Talented Have students create four problems using percent of increase, percent of decrease, percent of profit, and percent of loss.

Having Reading Difficulties Be sure students understand the difference between *percent of increase* and *amount of increase (or decrease)*. Discuss the new vocabulary introduced in this lesson.

Today's Problem

At her job, Mary was asked to take on extra work for a short time. During this time she received a higher salary, a 10% increase of her original salary. When she finished the extra work, her employer wanted her back at her former salary, so he decreased the higher salary by 10%. Was this fair? *(No; if her original salary was $100, the higher salary would be $110. Her lower salary would be $99.)*

Lesson Organizer

Objective: Solve problems by using the interest formula.

Prior Knowledge: Students should be able to multiply whole numbers, decimals, and fractions and work with percents.

Error Analysis and Remediation: See page 343A.

Lesson Resources:
Practice Worksheet 10-15
Reteaching Activity 10-15
Enrichment Worksheet 10-15
Daily Review 10-15

Two-Minute Math

Write as a decimal and as a fraction in lowest terms.

6% $(0.06; \frac{3}{50})$ 12% $(0.12; \frac{3}{25})$

12.5% $(0.125; \frac{1}{8})$ 0.4% $(0.004; \frac{1}{250})$

1 INTRODUCE

CONNECTING ACTIVITY

1. Use questions such as the following to help students understand that banks pay less for money they borrow than they charge for money they lend. **How do banks make their money?** *(by charging interest on money they lend; by charging fees for services they perform)* **How can banks afford to pay interest on savings?** *(The interest they pay on savings accounts, for example is less than the interest they charge.)*

2. Discuss the concept of interest as a fee for the use of borrowed money. **Give examples of situations in which interest is charged, and situations in which interest is earned.** *(Possible situations: interest charged: car loan; interest earned: savings account)*

WHEN YOUR STUDENTS ASK
★ WHY AM I LEARNING THIS? ★

You can use this skill to solve real-life problems related to choosing a savings plan, borrowing money for a house or a car, or financing purchases using bank and department store credit cards.

Problem Solving:
Using an Interest Formula

The amount of money borrowed is called the **principal.**

The interest **rate** is usually given as a percent of the principal you pay for a certain period of time, usually 1 yr.

How long you keep the money is called the **time.**

There is a formula that tells how interest, *I*, principal, *p*, rate, *r*, and time, *t*, are related.

$I = p \times r \times t$

> The **interest**, *I*, is what the bank charges you for the loan.

The table shows how the values in the formula depend on each other. As one value changes, so do the others.

$I = p \times r \times t$	Interest (I)	Principal (p)	Rate (r)	Time (t)
$8 = 100 \times 0.08 \times 1$	$8	$100	8%	1 yr
$4 = 100 \times 0.08 \times 0.5$	$4	$100	8%	$\frac{1}{2}$ yr
$17 = 100 \times 0.085 \times 2$	$17	$100	8.5%	2 yr
$6 = 100 \times 0.08 \times 0.75$	$6	$100	8%	9 mo

> Change 9 mo to $\frac{3}{4}$ yr.

Juan borrows $800 from the bank at $8\frac{1}{2}$ % for 2 yr. How much money must Juan pay back to the bank after 2 yr?

- Would the $8\frac{1}{2}$% be substituted for the *I, p, r,* or *t* in the formula?   *r*
- Remember that Juan must pay back the $800 plus the interest charged.
- Now solve the problem. **$936**

338   LESSON 10–15

2 TEACH

Why should the amount of the principal affect how much interest is paid on the loan? *(It should cost more to borrow more money.)*

What is meant by a rate of 15% per year? *(You pay $15 per year for every $100 you borrow.)*

Why should the time determine how much interest is paid? *(It should cost more to borrow money for a longer time.)*

SUMMARIZE/ASSESS   **Explain the meaning of each letter in the interest formula.** *(In the formula, $I = p \times r \times t$, the amount of interest [I] is the product of principal [p] times the rate [r] times the time [t].)*

Use the interest formula to solve.

1. Tanya borrowed $1,000 for 4 yr at $10\frac{1}{2}\%$.

   a. What was the interest rate? $10\frac{1}{2}\%$

   b. What would the $1,000 be substituted for in the interest formula? **p**

   c. How much will Tanya owe the bank after 4 yr? **$1,420**

PRACTICE

Use the interest formula to solve.

2. Riva took out a 5-yr, $8,000 loan to buy a car. If the interest rate is 16%, how much interest will she pay on the loan after 5 yr? **$6,400**

3. Angela borrows $1,000 from the bank at 11% for 6 mo. How much will Angela owe the bank after 6 mo? **$1,055**

4. Sharon paid $95 interest on a 2-yr loan. The interest rate was $12\frac{1}{2}\%$. How much money did she borrow? **$380**

5. Paul paid $135 interest on a 3-yr loan with a principal of $300. What was the interest rate? **15%**

6. How much more interest is paid on a $1,000,000 loan for 1 yr at 12% than at 11.5%? **$5,000 more**

7. **IN YOUR WORDS** How can you work Exercise 6 without figuring the interest on both loans and subtracting?
Answers will vary. Multiply 1,000,000 by 0.005.

8. Antonio borrows $3,200 at a yearly interest rate of 12%. How much will he owe the bank if he keeps the money for only 6 mo? for only 3 mo? **$3,392; $3,296**

9. The Ching family borrows $18,000 at 11.5% to renovate their house. How much money will the Ching family owe the bank after $1\frac{1}{2}$ yr? **$21,105**

10. Suppose you put $1,024 into a savings account that earns 9.5% simple interest per year. How much money will you have in your savings account after 1 yr? **$1,121.28**

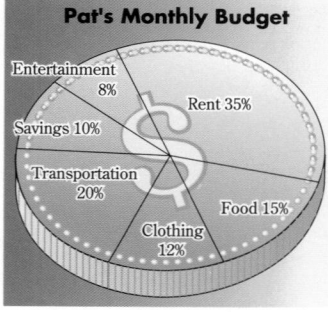

Pat's Monthly Budget

Entertainment 8%
Rent 35%
Savings 10%
Transportation 20%
Food 15%
Clothing 12%

CHOOSE Use the circle graph. Choose any strategy to solve.

11. Pat earns $1,500/mo. How much of that pays her rent? read for understanding; **$525**

12. If Pat does not buy any clothing one month, how much of her $1,500 salary could she save? multistep; **$180**

MEETING INDIVIDUAL NEEDS

For Students Who Are . . .

Acquiring English Proficiency Discuss the meaning of the terms *interest, principal, rate,* and *time* in this lesson. Remind students that time is expressed in years.

Gifted and Talented Have students find the annual rates of interest: $150 for 1 yr, interest = $18 *(12%)*; $2,000 for 3 yr, interest = $600 *(10%)*; $1,600 for 4 yr, interest = $288 *(4.5%)*

Working 2 or 3 Grades Below Level Review how to change 6 months and 3 months to part of a year.

Today's Problem

Simple interest is interest earned only on principal. Compound interest is interest earned on principal plus interest. Compare the effects of the two kinds of interest; find the simple interest and the compound interest paid on $100 at 10% for two years. Assume interest is calculated once a year. *(Simple interest is $100 × 10% × 2 or $20 for two years. Compound interest is $10 for the first year; for the second year it is $110 × 10%, or $11, giving a total of $21 for both years.)*

---

3 FOLLOW-UP

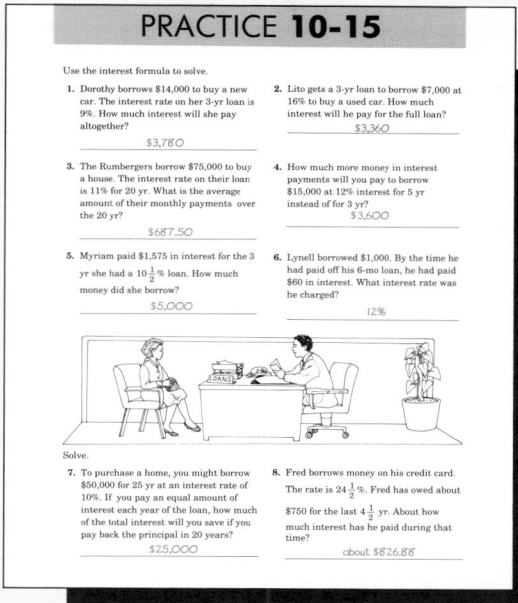

PRACTICE 10-15

Use the interest formula to solve.

1. Dorothy borrows $14,000 to buy a new car. The interest rate on her 3-yr loan is 9%. How much interest will she pay altogether? **$3,780**

2. Lito gets a 3-yr loan to borrow $7,000 at 16% to buy a used car. How much interest will he pay for the full loan? **$3,360**

3. The Rumbergers borrow $75,000 to buy a house. The interest rate on their loan is 11% for 20 yr. What is the average amount of their monthly payments over the 20 yr? **$687.50**

4. How much more money in interest payments will you pay to borrow $15,000 at 12% interest for 5 yr instead of for 3 yr? **$3,600**

5. Myriam paid $1,575 in interest for the 3 yr she had a $10\frac{1}{2}\%$ loan. How much money did she borrow? **$5,000**

6. Lynell borrowed $1,000. By the time he had paid off his 6-mo loan, he had paid $60 in interest. What interest rate was he charged? **12%**

Solve.

7. To purchase a home, you might borrow $50,000 for 25 yr at an interest rate of 10%. If you pay an equal amount of interest each year of the loan, how much of the total interest will you save if you pay back the principal in 20 years? **$25,000**

8. Fred borrows money on his credit card. The rate is $24\frac{1}{2}\%$. Fred has owed about $750 for the last $4\frac{1}{2}$ yr. About how much interest has he paid during that time? **about $826.88**

RETEACHING 10-15

Have students write each variable of the interest formula on an index card.

$$I = p \times r \times t$$

Write these principals on cards and place them in a pile face down: $4,000, $200, $6200, $700, $3800. Do the same for rates and times: 5%, 6%, 10%, 2%, 18%; 1 yr, $1\frac{1}{2}$ yr, 2 yr, $2\frac{1}{2}$ yr, $3\frac{1}{2}$ yr, 5 yr. Have students draw a card from each pile, replace the variables in the formula with the correct card and find the interest.

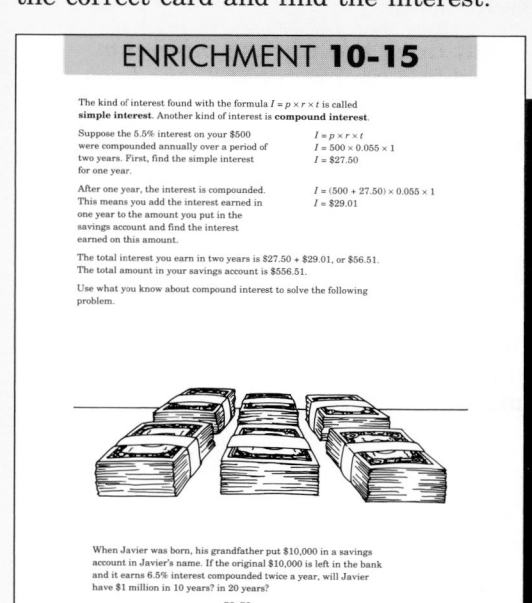

ENRICHMENT 10-15

The kind of interest found with the formula $I = p \times r \times t$ is called **simple interest**. Another kind of interest is **compound interest**.

Suppose the 5.5% interest on your $500 were compounded annually over a period of two years. First, find the simple interest for one year.

$I = p \times r \times t$
$I = 500 \times 0.055 \times 1$
$I = \$27.50$

After one year, the interest is compounded. This means you add the interest earned in one year to the amount you put in the savings account and find the interest earned on this amount.

$I = (500 + 27.50) \times 0.055 \times 1$
$I = \$29.01$

The total interest you earn in two years is $27.50 + $29.01, or $56.51. The total amount in your savings account is $556.51.

Use what you know about compound interest to solve the following problem.

When Javier was born, his grandfather put $10,000 in a savings account in Javier's name. If the original $10,000 is left in the bank and it earns 6.5% interest compounded twice a year, will Javier have $1 million in 10 years? in 20 years? no; no

Lesson Organizer

> **Objective:** Solve problems creatively.

Prior Knowledge: Students should be able to solve percent problems, including finding interest.

Lesson Resources:
Daily Review 10-16

Two-Minute Math

Solve. Use mental math.
10% of $400 *($40)*
30% of $400 *($120)*
5% of $400 *($20)*
1% of $400 *($4)*

1 PREPARE

SYMBOLIC ACTIVITY

What are some advantages and some disadvantages of using a credit card? List student responses in two columns on the chalkboard. Then present this situation:

In March, you buy a $1,200 computer using your credit card. You do not buy anything else with your card. The terms of the card state that the minimum monthly payment is 25% of the balance.

- **What does the phrase *minimum monthly payment* mean?** *(the least amount you must pay)*

- **What does the word *balance* mean?** *(the total amount you owe)*

- **If you make the minimum monthly payment of 25% on your balance of $1,200, what must you pay?** *(25% of $1,200, or $300)*

- **What is your new balance after you make the minimum monthly payment?** *($1,200 − $300 = $900)*

WHEN YOUR STUDENTS ASK
★ WHY AM I LEARNING THIS? ★

You can use this skill in real life to make decisions about which credit card to use and whether or not it is practical for you to pay your entire balance or to finance part of it.

Making Decisions About Credit Cards

CREATIVE PROBLEM SOLVING ▼

Credit cards are convenient because they are easy to carry. People who have credit cards do not need to carry around a lot of money.

Credit cards can also be used to borrow money. For example, if you make a $400 purchase, you do not have to pay the entire amount when the bill comes due. The credit card company adds a finance charge to the unpaid balance. You have "borrowed" from the credit card company the amount of the bill you did not pay. The finance charge is **interest** you must pay for borrowing this money.

Work in a small group. Use the information given for three imaginary credit cards. A calculator or computer will be useful.

MATH AND ECONOMICS

Card Name	CrediCard	BUYER'S *plus*	SavCred
Annual Fee	$20	$25	$0
Minimum Monthly Payment	15% of balance	10% of balance	25% of balance
Interest Rate for Monthly Finance Charge	1.3%	1.4%	1.7%

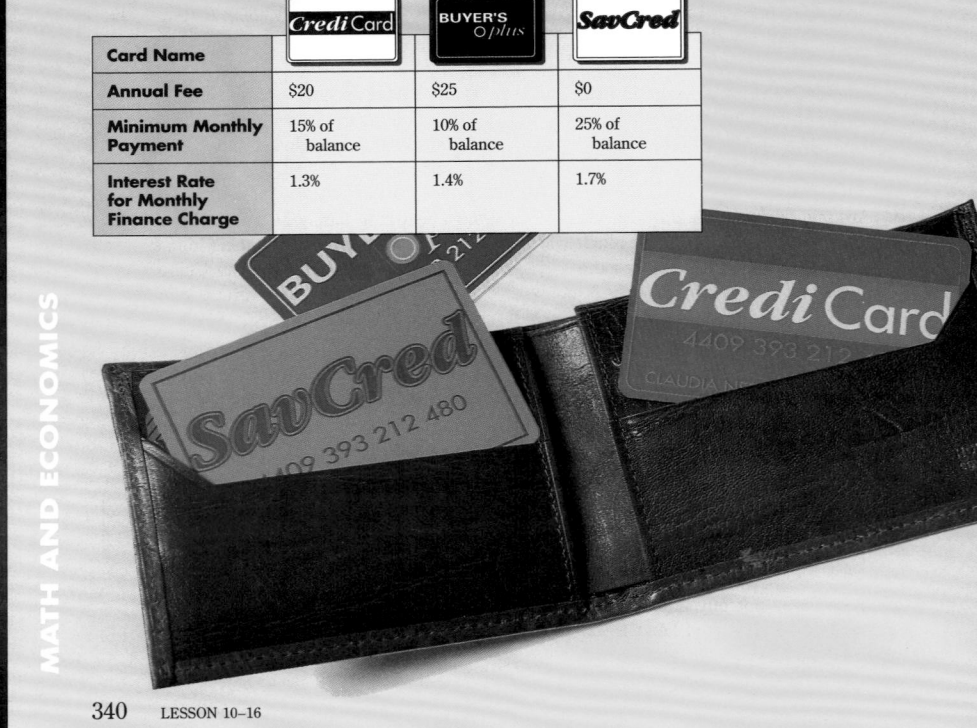

2 EXPLORE

☑ MATERIALS CHECKLIST: calculators

Organize the class into groups of three or four. **If the interest rate for the SavCred card were computed on an annual basis, what would it be?** *(12 × 1.7% = 20.4%)*

Suppose Bill Bateman made the minimum monthly payment on his purchase, using a CrediCard. What would his unpaid balance be the next month? *($2,000 − $300 = $1,700)* **How much interest must he pay on this unpaid balance?** *(1.3% of $1,700 = $22.10)*

SUMMARIZE/ASSESS   **What mathematics skills did you use to make decisions about credit cards?** *(Answers will vary. Example: finding percents, calculating interest.)*

1. Discuss which credit card seems to offer the best terms. What factors might affect your decision to choose one credit card over the others?
annual fee; interest charge; monthly payment

2. Annie Anderson charges about $300/mo on her credit card. She pays the bill in full every month. Which credit card offers the best terms for Annie? Explain.
SavCred; Accept reasonable answers.

3. Bill Bateman plans to use his credit card to buy a $2,000 furnace for his home. He will not use the card for any other purchases. He plans to buy the furnace in September and pay $500 per month. Copy and complete the chart to determine how much Bill will pay per month in finance charges on each of the three cards.

Month		*Credi*Card	BUYER'S *O plus*	*SavCred*
Sept	Amount of Bill	$2,000.00	$2,000.00	$2,000.00
	Amount paid	500.00	500.00	500.00
Oct	Unpaid Balance	$1,500.00	$1,500.00	$1,500.00
	Interest	19.50	21.00	25.50
	Amount paid	500.00	500.00	500.00
Nov	Unpaid Balance	$1,019.50	$1,021.00	$1,025.50
	Interest	13.25	14.29	17.43
	Amount paid	500.00	500.00	500.00
Dec	Unpaid Balance	$ 532.75	$ 535.29	$ 542.93
	Interest	6.93	7.49	9.23
	Amount paid	500.00	500.00	500.00
Jan	Unpaid Balance	$ 39.68	$ 42.78	$ 52.16
	Interest	.52	.60	.89
	Amount paid	40.20	43.38	53.05

4. Use the chart from Exercise 3. Find the total finance charges Bill will pay for the five months for each of the cards. Then add the annual fee to the finance charge total for each card. Which credit card offers the best terms for Bill?
SavCred

5. Clyde Carlyle plans a $4,800 credit card purchase and will not use the card again for any other purpose. He will pay the minimum monthly payment or $400.00 per month, whichever is greater. Create a chart similar to Bill's and decide which card is best. Give reasons for your choice. Do not forget the annual fees.
Check students' work.

6. IN YOUR WORDS Write a paragraph explaining how to decide which of the three credit cards to choose.
Check students' work.

3 FOLLOW-UP

CLASS ACTIVITY 10-16

☑ **MATERIALS CHECKLIST:** set of 20 small cards for each group

Have students work in pairs.

Each pair marks one side of the cards as follows:

borrow $1 (4 cards)
borrow $5 (2 cards)
pay back $1 (5 cards)
pay back $2 (5 cards)
pay back $3 (2 cards)
pay back $5 (2 cards)

Each game begins with both players owing $15. They take turns drawing shuffled cards. After each draw, an adjustment on the amount borrowed is made. The first person to be out of debt wins. If all cards are used before the game ends, cards are reshuffled and used again.

MEETING INDIVIDUAL NEEDS

For Students Who Are . . .

Acquiring English Proficiency Discuss the meanings of *annual fee*, *minimum monthly payment*, and *monthly finance charge*. For Exercises 2 and 5, explain what is meant by *best terms*.

Gifted and Talented Have students solve this problem: The unpaid balance in Art's account is $80. He makes a payment of $25 and buys new clothing for $140. His finance charge is $2.12. What is the new balance in Art's account? *($197.12)*

Working 2 or 3 Grades Below Level Review finding percent of a number.

Today's Problem

Monthly interest on the first $50 of unpaid balance is 1.3%. Interest on the remaining unpaid balance is 1.9%. What is the interest on an unpaid balance of $1,000? *($.65 + $18.05 = $18.70)*

Chapter 10 • Lesson 10-16   **341**

CHAPTER
Checkup

This chapter checkup provides a quick language and vocabulary review, a test for the chapter, and suggestions for student Learning Log entries.

Language and Vocabulary

Some key language and vocabulary ideas from this chapter are reinforced here.

Test

The test can be used either as a test or as a review of the chapter prior to administering the test worksheets found in the Teacher's Resource Book.

The following guide will help you determine percentage scores.

Score	Percent	Score	Percent
26	100%	13	50%
25	96	12	46
24	92	11	42
23	88	10	38
22	85	9	35
21	81	8	31
20	77	7	27
19	73	6	23
18	69	5	19
17	65	4	15
16	62	3	12
15	58	2	8
14	54	1	4

Each test has three sections: concepts, skills, and problem solving.

Use this chart to identify the Management Objectives tested for this chapter.

Items	Management Objectives	Pages
1–5, 20–23	**10A** Write fractions and decimals as percents and percents as fractions and decimals.	312–315
6–8	**10B** Write percents greater than 100% and less than 1%.	316–317, 334–335
9–19	**10C** Find the percent of a number, the percent, or the original number in percent problems.	322–327
24–26	**10D** Problem Solving: Estimate tips and sales tax. Use the interest formula.	332–333, 338–339

CHAPTER CHECKUP

LANGUAGE & VOCABULARY

Tell whether the result will be >, <, or = 100%.

1. the total cost of a purchase, including sales tax, compared to the price of the item **>100%**

2. the value of a share of stock that drops by 50% and then increases by 100% **=100%**

3. the height of Mount St. Helens after its eruption compared to its height before the eruption **<100%**

4. the depth of a lake following a heavy rain compared to its depth before the rain **>100%**

TEST ✓

CONCEPTS

Write as a percent. *(pages 312–317)*

1. $\frac{9}{36}$ **25%**   2. $\frac{35}{105}$ **$33\frac{1}{3}$%**   3. 0.07 **7%**   4. 0.467 **46.7%**

5. $\frac{325}{100}$ **325%**   6. 9 **900%**   7. 0.008 **0.8%**   8. $\frac{1}{400}$ **0.25%**

SKILLS

Find the percent of the number. *(pages 322–323)*

9. 10% of 380 **38**   10. 3% of 82 **2.46**   11. 0.07% of 640 **0.448**

Write an equation and solve. *(pages 324–327, 334–335)*

12. 9 is what percent of 30? **30%**   13. 21 is what percent of 50? **42%**

14. 114 is what percent of 500? **22.8%**   15. 63 is 45% of what number? **140**

16. 80% of what number is 52? **65**   17. 256 is 25% of what number? **1,024**

18. What number is 130% of 27? **35.1**   19. 108% of what number is 108? **100**

Write the percent as a decimal and as a fraction in lowest terms. *(pages 312–314)*

20. 6% **0.06, $\frac{3}{50}$**   21. 42% **0.42, $\frac{21}{50}$**   22. 75% **0.75, $\frac{3}{4}$**   23. 98% **0.98, $\frac{49}{50}$**

CHAPTER TEST • FORM A

(pp. 310–315) *10A*

Write in percent form.

1. $\frac{12}{60}$ *20%*   2. 0.05 *5%*

Write as a fraction in lowest terms and as a decimal.

3. 40% *$\frac{2}{5}$, 0.4*   4. 55% *$\frac{11}{20}$, 0.55*   5. 2.5% *$\frac{1}{40}$, 0.025*

(pp. 316–317, 334–335) *10B*

Write as a decimal

6. 150% *1.5*   7. 0.6% *0.006*   8. 300% *3*

Write as a percent.

9. 5 *500%*   10. $\frac{0.3}{100}$ *0.3%*

(pp. 318–327, 336–337) *10C*

Find the percent of the number.

11. 10% of 350 *35*   12. 2% of 86 *1.72*

Write an equation and solve.

13. 20% of what number is 8? *$0.2 \times n = 8; 40$*   14. 12 is 50% of what number? *$12 = 0.5 \times n; 24$*

15. What percent of 96 is 24? *$n \times 96 = 24; 25\%$*

CHAPTER TEST • FORM A

(pp. 332–333, 338–339) *10D*

Estimate the solution to the problem.

16. Luigi bought a $4.95 lunch at a pizza parlor. The sales tax is 6%. About how much did he spend? *about $5.30*

17. The sales tax paid on three submarine sandwiches for $12 was $.90. About what was the sales tax rate? *about 7.5%*

18. Elton buys a $29.95 steak and lobster dinner. The sales tax on the food is 8% and Elton wants to include a 15% tip. About how much money should Elton pay for the meal? *about $37*

Use the interest formula to solve.

19. LuAnn took out a 4-yr $9,000 loan to buy a car. If the interest is 15%, how much interest will she pay on the loan after 4 yr? *$5,400*

20. Gordon paid $216 interest on a 3-yr loan with a principle of $600. What was the interest rate? *12%*

═══════ **PROBLEM SOLVING** ═══════

Estimate the solution to the problem. *(pages 332–333)*

24. The food bill for Patricia's dinner was $12.05. Sales tax was
5% and she left a 15% tip.

   a. What percent was the sales tax? What percent was the
tip? **5%; 15%**

   b. About how many times greater was the tip than the tax? **3 times**

   c. Estimate the total of the tax and tip on the dinner. **$2.40**

Use the interest formula to solve. *(pages 338–339)*

25. Which will cost Alberto more in interest payments: $2,000
borrowed for 1 yr at 6%, or $3,000 borrowed for 2 yr at 3%?
How much more? **$3,000; $60 more**

26. On her last science test, Chartia scored 80% by answering 52
questions correctly. How many questions were on the test? **65 questions**

═══════  **LEARNING LOG** ═══════

Write the answers in your learning log. **Answers will vary. Suggestions given.**

1. What does "percent sense" mean to you?
Accept reasonable answers.

2. A bank advertises that it will pay 8% interest on deposits.
What does that mean? **For every $100 deposited,
the bank pays $8/yr in interest.**

Item 16 in the skill section and item 26 in
the problem solving section use the same
numbers.

Problem Solving

Item 20 has three parts:
a. literal—this is a reading comprehension question.
b. interpretive—this involves interpretation using the facts given.
c. applied—students use a strategy or skill to find an answer.

Item 16 in the skill section and item 26 in the problem solving section use the same numbers.

This will help you informally assess how your students transfer from numerical skills to word problems.

For scoring problem solving items, you may wish to use partial credit. If a student uses the correct strategy but gets a wrong answer, give the student two points toward the total percent score.

Learning Log

These are suggestions for writing about some topics taught in the chapter. The students keep their learning logs from the start of the school year through the end.

CHAPTER TEST • FORM **B**

(pp. 310–315)

Write in percent form.

1. $\frac{14}{56}$ _____   **2.** 0.08 _____

Write as a fraction in lowest terms and as a decimal.

3. 60% _____   **4.** 48% _____   **5.** 3.5% _____

(pp. 316–317, 334–335)

Write as a decimal.

6. 175% _____   **7.** 0.4% _____   **8.** 200% _____

Write as a percent.

9. 3 _____   **10.** $\frac{0.6}{100}$ _____

(pp. 318–327, 336–337)

Find the percent of the number.

11. 20% of 250 _____   **12.** 4% of 85 _____

Write an equation and solve.

13. 25% of what number is 9? _____

14. 15 is 75% of what number? _____

15. What percent of 85 is 17? _____

CHAPTER TEST • FORM **B**

(pp. 332–333, 338–339)

Estimate the solution to the problem.

16. Cellini bought a $5.95 lunch at the Chinese Palace. The sales tax
is 7%. About how much did Cellini spend? _____

17. The sales tax paid on three burgers and fries was $.50. The
burgers and fries cost $9.00. About what was the sales tax rate? _____

18. Vincent buys a $19.95 dinner. The sales tax on the food is 7% and
Vincent wants to include a 15% tip. About how much money
should he pay for the meal? _____

Use the interest formula to solve. *(pp. 338–339)*

19. Louisa took out a 3-yr $6,000 loan to buy a boat. If the interest is
12%, how much interest will she pay on the loan after 3 yr? _____

20. Gilbert paid $4,800 interest on a 4-yr loan with a principle of
$8,000. What was the interest rate? _____

CHAPTER 10

Error Analysis and Remediation

Here are some common errors students make when working with percents.

10A • WRITE FRACTIONS AND DECIMALS AS PERCENTS AND PERCENTS AS FRACTIONS AND DECIMALS

Source of Error (Lessons 10-1, 10-2)
When writing the fractional equivalent of a percent, students include a percent sign.

For example: $\frac{17}{100}\%$

Remediation
Demonstrate to students that they have written $\frac{17}{100} \times \frac{1}{100}$, which is not the same as 17 per hundred. Emphasize this by showing that *percent* means "per hundred" or $\frac{1}{100}$, and so 17 percent means $17 \times \frac{1}{100}$.

Source of Error (Lesson 10-3)
Students write decimals such as 0.3 as 3% and percents such as 1% as 0.1.

Remediation
Have students write the intermediate step: $0.3 = 0.30 = \frac{30}{100} = 30\%$ and $1\% = \frac{1}{100} = 0.01$.

10B • WRITE PERCENTS GREATER THAN 100% AND LESS THAN 1%

Source of Error (Lessons 10-4, 10-5, 10-13)
Students place the decimal point incorrectly when writing percents greater than 100% and less than 1%.

Remediation
Review decimal place value with students. Emphasize the importance of performing the intermediate steps.

10C • FIND THE PERCENT OF A NUMBER, THE PERCENT, OR THE ORIGINAL NUMBER IN PERCENT PROBLEMS

Source of Error (Lessons 10-8, 10-10)
Students write the equation for a verbal statement incorrectly.

Remediation
Remind students to replace "what number" with a variable, "of" with a multiplication sign, and "is" with the equals sign.

Source of Error (Lesson 10-9)
Students place the decimal point incorrectly when changing the decimal to a percent or when multiplying.

Remediation
Emphasize that *percent* means hundredths or two decimal places. Review the steps for writing a decimal as a percent and for multiplying by decimals.

10D • PROBLEM SOLVING: ESTIMATE TIPS AND SALES TAX. USE THE INTEREST FORMULA.

Source of Error (Lesson 10-12)
Students forget to add the price to the sales tax to determine the total cost.

Remediation
Remind students to check that their answers are reasonable. Stress that most sales tax problems have two steps: (1) multiply the percent and the price, and then (2) add the price and the tax.

Source of Error (Lesson 10-15)
Students make mistakes when calculating a fractional part of a yearly rate.

Remediation
For example, if the time is 9 months, students may multiply the principal and the rate by 9 instead of $\frac{9}{12}$ or $\frac{3}{4}$. Remind students to think of a period of time less than a year as a fractional part of a year.

Notes

Extra Practice

This page provides extra practice of all the major chapter objectives. Use this page after the chapter has been taught to reinforce the chapter skills. Page references are provided for each group of items so that students can easily look back at the appropriate lesson for additional support.

EXTRA PRACTICE

Write as a percent. *(pages 312–317)*

1. $\frac{18}{36}$ **50%**   **2.** $\frac{8}{40}$ **20%**   **3.** $\frac{7}{8}$ **87.5%**   **4.** $\frac{12}{12}$ **100%**   **5.** $\frac{16}{24}$ **66.$\overline{6}$%**

6. 0.75 **75%**   **7.** 0.1 **10%**   **8.** 0.375 **37.5%** **9.** 0.87 **87%** **10.** 0.08 **8%**

11. 0.075 **7.5%** **12.** 0.603 **60.3%** **13.** 0.210 **21%** **14.** 0.012 **1.2%** **15.** 0.15 **15%**

16. 2 **200%** **17.** $\frac{147}{100}$ **147%** **18.** $\frac{9}{5}$ **180%** **19.** 2.65 **265%** **20.** 1.03 **103%**

21. 0.009 **0.9%** **22.** 0.0078 **0.78%** **23.** 0.0081 **0.81%** **24.** $\frac{1}{200}$ **0.5%** **25.** $\frac{1}{250}$ **0.4%**

Find the percent of the number. *(pages 322-323)*

26. 2% of 28 **0.56**   **27.** 85% of 190 **161.5**   **28.** 0.25% of 80 **0.2**

29. 0.8% of 150 **1.2**   **30.** $\frac{1}{2}$% of 200 **1**   **31.** 0.03% of 96 **0.0288**

Write an equation and solve. *(pages 324–327, 334–335)*

32. 18 is what percent of 45? **40%**   **33.** 48 is what percent of 200? **24%**

34. 9 is what percent of 54? **16.$\overline{6}$%**   **35.** 16 is 40% of what number? **40**

36. 54 is 75% of what number? **72**   **37.** 70% of what number is 63? **90**

38. 20% of what number is 2.2? **11**   **39.** What number is 150% of 18? **27**

40. What number is 115% of 32? **36.8**   **41.** 175% of what number is 42? **24**

Solve. *(pages 332–333, 338–339)*

42. Jackson bought a sandwich for $3.50 and a fruit drink for $1.25. If the tax was 7%, how much did he pay, to the nearest cent? **$5.08**

43. Roberto borrowed $1,600 for $1\frac{1}{2}$ yr from a bank charging 14% yearly interest. How much did he have to repay the bank at the end of the time of the loan? **$1,936**

MORTGAGE RATES

A mortgage is a loan, usually made by a bank, that is used to buy a home. Talk with an adult in your home or visit a bank to talk with a loan officer to answer these questions.

1. Why is the interest rate lower if the time of the loan is shorter?

2. Why is the "annual" rate sometimes different from the "annual percentage rate"?

3. Why would a home buyer choose an adjustable interest rate mortgage (one whose rate changes) rather than one with an interest rate that remains the same for the time of the loan?
Accept reasonable answers.

NONSENSE PERCENTS

Percents are used often in everyday conversation. However, some of the uses do not reflect an understanding of what percent really means. Read the statement and think about why, although it may sound good, it really does not make sense.

1. "He always tries his best. He makes a 110% effort."

2. "I agree with you 1,000%."

3. "There is a 100% chance of rain tomorrow."

4. "Prices reduced almost 100%!"

Comparison Shopping

Different states throughout the United States charge different sales tax rates. Some states charge no sales tax. As a result, the same item can cost a consumer different prices, depending on where the item is bought.

Work with a partner. Find sales tax rates in an almanac. Then use a calculator to determine the difference in cost of the item bought in each location.

- a $219 bicycle bought in Alabama or Florida
- a $500 television set bought in Nebraska or Ohio
- a $12,000 car bought in Montana or Wyoming

Make up some comparisons. Some cities or counties also charge a sales tax. Find the sales tax where you live. To what items does it apply?
Check students' work.

Enrichment

This page contains activities that provide extension and enrichment for all levels of students. Depending on the needs of your students, you may wish to assign an activity from this page at certain points during the chapter, or you may wish to use this page when the entire chapter has been completed.

Mortgage Rates

You may wish to have students visit local banks in pairs. Suggest that they prepare a question of their own that they can ask the loan officer.

Nonsense Percents

Discuss the first statement as class activity. Make sure students understand that "110% effort" is impossible and merely an exaggeration used to make a point.

Comparison Shopping (COOPERATIVE)

Have students find out how much each item would cost if it were purchased in their city or county. Tell students they can add the state sales tax rate and the local sales tax rate, if any, to find the combined sales tax rate.

CHAPTER 10

Cumulative Review

The Cumulative Review focuses on skills covered in previous chapters. All important skills are reviewed on a cyclic basis.

If students are having difficulty with particular groups of exercises, refer to the chart below for follow-up work.

CUMULATIVE REVIEW

Find the answer.

1. Which number is less, **c** than 82,097?
   a. 82,107
   b. 82,709
   c. 81,970
   d. none of these

2. Which number is **a** greater than 7.060?
   a. 7.6
   b. 7.059
   c. 7.010
   d. none of these

3. 17.04 is between **a** which two numbers?
   a. 17.00 and 17.05
   b. 17.05 and 17.10
   c. 16.95 and 17.00
   d. none of these

4. $38 - r = 19$ **b**
   a. 38
   b. 19
   c. 57
   d. none of these

5. $g - 8 = 26$ **c**
   a. 16
   b. 18
   c. 34
   d. none of these

6. $107 - d = 68$ **d**
   a. 41
   b. 175
   c. 49
   d. none of these

7. $47m = 282$ **a**
   a. 6
   b. 60
   c. 13,254
   d. none of these

8. $11.3 - x = 6.5$ **b**
   a. 5.2
   b. 4.8
   c. 17.8
   d. none of these

9. $\frac{y}{7} = 58$ **b**
   a. 8.3
   b. 406
   c. 0.12
   d. none of these

10. A solution to $b - 8 < 17$ is ? **d**
    a. 25
    b. 26
    c. 27
    d. none of these

11. A solution to $x + 9 > 13$ is ? **c**
    a. 4
    b. 3
    c. 22
    d. none of these

12.

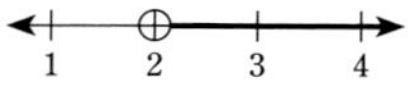

The graph shows ? **a**
    a. $x > 2$
    b. $x = 2$
    c. $x < 2$
    d. none of these

13. What are the prime factors of 72? **a**
    a. 3, 3, 2, 2, 2,
    b. 2, 2, 3, 3, 3,
    c. 3, 3, 8
    d. none of these

14. 54 is divisible by what numbers? **b**
    a. 2, 3, 5, 6, 9
    b. 2, 3, 6, 9,
    c. 2, 3, 5, 9
    d. none of these

15. Which number is a prime number? **c**
    a. 49
    b. 57
    c. 59
    d. none of these

346 CUMULATIVE REVIEW

Items	Management Objectives	Where Taught	Reteaching Options	Extra Practice Options
1–3	**1B** Compare and order whole numbers and decimals.	pp. 8–9	TRB/RW 1-4	TRB/PW 1-4
4–9	**4B** Solve equations using inverse operations.	pp. 102–105	TRB/RW 4-4 and 4-5	TRB/PW 4-4 and 4-5
10–12	**4C** Solve and graph inequalities.	pp. 110–113	TRB/RW 4-7, TE/RA 4-8	TRB/PW 4-7 and 4-8
13–15	**5A** Determine divisibility, primes and composites, and write prime factorizations.	pp. 130–133		TRB/PW 52

346 Chapter 10 • Cumulative Review

Strategies may vary. Suggestions given.
Remember the strategies and types of problems you've
had so far. Solve.

1. Jen was trying to make a train. She left
   her home at 3:30 P.M. for the 45-min trip
   to the station. This should have left her
   15 min to find and board the train. **3:30 P.M.**

   a. At what time did Jen leave her home?

   b. What time was her train scheduled
      to leave? **4:30 P.M.**

   c. The trip to the station took 1h 10 min.
      By how much did she miss her train?
      Multistep; 10 min

2. During a baseball game, one team had
   12 hits. The opponents had $1\frac{1}{2}$ times as
   many hits. How many hits did the
   teams have altogether?
   equation; 30 hits

3. Alex bought two pieces of electronic
   equipment advertised for $200 and
   $300. The store took 8% off because
   he paid cash. How much did he pay?
   equation; $460

4. The greatest depth of the Pacific
   Ocean is 36,198 ft. Mount Everest is
   29,028 ft tall. How much greater are
   the combined heights of Mount
   Everest and 7,965-ft Mount Olympus
   than the depth of the deepest part of
   the Pacific? **multistep; 795 ft**

5. A recipe for 4 people uses 1 lb
   spaghetti, $1\frac{1}{2}$ lb tomatoes, 1 tsp garlic
   powder, and other ingredients. If the
   recipe were increased to serve 6, how
   many pounds of tomatoes would be
   needed? **multistep; $2\frac{1}{4}$ lb**

6. To make her purchases, Adrienne
   borrowed $400 at 14% interest for 1
   yr. How much must she repay the
   bank? **formula; $456**

7. A bicycle is on sale for $232. If this is
   80% of its original price, what was its
   price before the sale?
   proportion; $290

8. Paolo bought 1 lb peppers, twice as
   much asparagus, and $\frac{1}{4}$ lb less beans
   than asparagus. How many pounds of
   beans did he buy? **multistep; $1\frac{3}{4}$ lb**

9. Use each digit from 2 through 9 once
   to form two 4-digit numbers that
   have the greatest possible difference.
   guess and check; 9,876 and 2,345

10. An airline ticket that usually sells for
    $220 can be purchased in advance for
    $187. What percent of the usual price
    is saved with advance purchase?
    proportion; 15%

11. Niabi has $3.75 in dimes and nickels.
    She has twice as many dimes as
    nickels. How many nickels does she
    have?
    guess and check; 30 dimes, 15 nickels

CHAPTER 10   347

Problem Solving Review

This page focuses on problem solving
strategies and types learned in this and
previous chapters. A problem solving
checklist lists some of the strategies students may use to solve the problems on
this page.

CHAPTER 10

Technology

This page is designed to provide calculator or computer experiences for all levels of students. The calculator or computer logo indicates the type of activity.

You may wish to assign these activities after the chapter has been taught or during the course of the chapter, depending on your needs and those of your students.

Oops!

After students have determined the correct bill, ask them to suggest a tip of about 15% for the server. *(about $5.50 if tax is included in amount; about $5.15 if tax is not included)*

Taxi Tippers

To get started, suggest that students determine the value of a 15% tip for the fare of $7.45 and compare that amount to the clues about how much each rider tipped.

Quick Way
(COOPERATIVE)

If necessary, review how to multiply by 10% or 0.1, by moving the decimal point one place to the left.

The computer activity uses Houghton Mifflin software, which is found in Houghton Mifflin Math Activities Courseware, Grade 7.

TECHNOLOGY

OOPS!

Find the mistakes that the waiter made when he wrote up the bill. Figure the correct bill.

dinner for 3	$30.85
3 milks	+ 2.25
	33.10
6% tax	+ 1.99
	35.09
1 ice cream	+ 1.20
	37.29
6% tax	+ 2.24
total	$39.53

$36.36

TAXI TIPPERS

Reggie, Maria, Jack, and Eli took a taxi to the airport. Each fare was $8.

The first rider left the lowest tip. Only two riders left the customary tip of 15%. Reggie, the last rider, paid a total of $9.50. Jack gave the cab driver a 10% tip. Maria took the cab immediately after Eli.

Tell the order of the riders and how much each paid for the ride. **Jack, $8.80; Eli, $9.20; Maria, $9.20; Reggie, $9.50**

QUICK WAY

In the computer activity *Making Sense of Percents*, you use estimation to guess the percent of a number. This pencil-and-paper activity will help you become familiar with one of the estimation techniques used in that game. **See below.**

You can use the 10% method when a percent is close to a multiple of 10%. For example, 61% of 2,986 is about 60% of 3,000.

10% of 3,000 = 300
6 × 300 = 1,800   so, 61% of 2,986 ≈ 1,800.

Compete with a friend. See how many seconds it takes each of you to estimate all the problems using the 10% method.

1. 41% of 2,977 **1,200**
2. 69% of 8,012 **5,600**
3. 71% of 48,904 **35,000**
4. 19% of 20,086 **4,000**
5. 38% of 41,101 **16,000**
6. 89% of 98,900 **90,000**

348   TECHNOLOGY   **This activity is available on computer disk in Houghton Mifflin *Mathematics Activities Courseware*.**

348   *Chapter 10 • Technology*

Software Activities

Note: To leave the program, students should use the ESCAPE or QUIT command for their computers.

activity 1 • INTEREST ON MONEY

MATERIALS: spreadsheet program

Procedure: This activity has students create a spreadsheet that calculates simple interest. Ask students to prepare the following spreadsheet and then enter the formula in the *Interest* column that calculates the interest for the various time periods identified.

	A	B	C	D
	Interest	Principal	Fixed Rate	Time
1				
2		$1000	0.07	5
3		$1000	0.07	10
4		$1000	0.07	15

Follow-up: Have students research the current interest rates. Using those rates, they should determine if the $1,000 principal plus interest would provide them with enough money to attend trade school or college by the time they graduate.

activity 2 • PRICE PLUS TAX

MATERIALS: This program will compute the total bill, including tax. Have students enter the program and run it.

```
10  PRINT "THIS PROGRAM WILL
    COMPUTE ";
20  PRINT "THE TOTAL COST OF ";
30  PRINT "SOMETHING YOU BUY. "
40  INPUT "WHAT WAS YOUR BILL
    WITHOUT TAX? ";B
50  INPUT "WHAT PERCENT IS YOUR TAX
    RATE? ";R
60  LET Z=R/100
70  LET T= (1+Z)*B*100
80  LET N=INT(T)/100
90  LET N=INT (T+.05)/100
100 PRINT "YOUR TOTAL BILL
    INCLUDING TAX IS $";N
110 GOTO 40
```

Follow-up: Challenge students to change the program so it prints the tax amount as well as the total bill.

HOUGHTON MIFFLIN SOFTWARE

Computational Skills Program. Boston, MA: Houghton Mifflin Company, 1988. For Apple II.

Easy Graph. Boston, MA: Houghton Mifflin Company, 1987. For Apple II, Commodore, IBM.

EduCalc. Boston, MA: Houghton Mifflin Company, 1990. For Apple II, Commodore, IBM.

Friendly Filer. Boston, MA: Houghton Mifflin Company, 1989. For Apple II, Commodore, IBM.

Mathematics Activities Courseware. Boston, MA: Houghton Mifflin Company, 1983. For Apple II, IBM.

Mathematics: Solving Story Problems. Boston, MA: Houghton Mifflin Company, 1985. For Apple II, IBM.

The Computer Tutor. Boston, MA: Houghton Mifflin Company, 1990. For Apple II, IBM.

OTHER SOFTWARE

Basic Skills Math Series: Fractions, Decimals and Percent. State College, PA: Courses by Computers, 1989. Apple II, IBM.

Conquering Percents. St. Paul, MN: MECC, 1989. For Apple II.

Microsoft Works. Redmond, WA: Microsoft Corporation, 1989. For IBM, Macintosh.

Percent. Big Spring, TX: Gamco Industries, Inc., 1989. For Apple II, Commodore, IBM, TRS-80.

Percent Word Problems. Big Spring, TX: Gamco Industries, Inc., 1991. For Apple II, Commodore, IBM, TRS-80.

Percents. Fairfield, CT: Media Materials/Queue Software, Inc., 1989. For Apple II.

Percent Applications

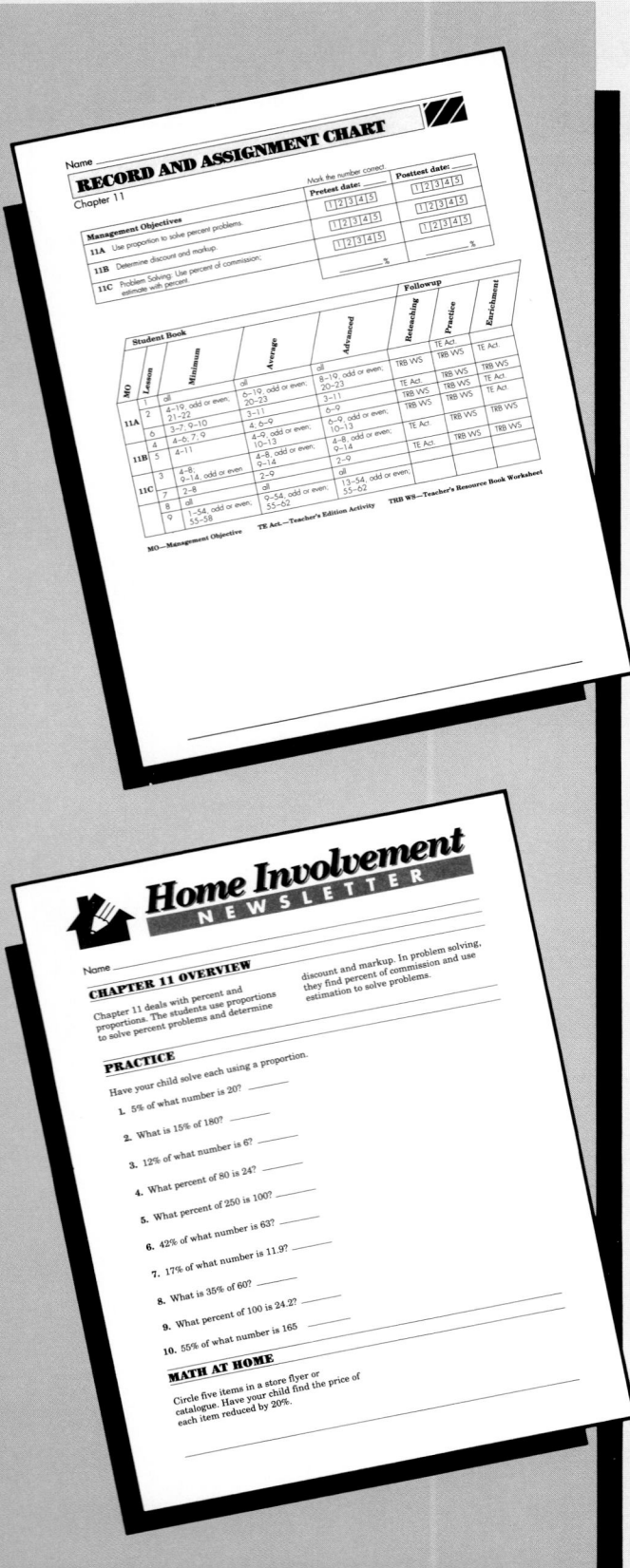

This chapter involves percents and applications. It focuses on using proportions to solve percent problems and to interpret circle graphs, determining discount and markup, and solving problems by using percent of commission and estimating with percents.

Management Objectives

11A Use proportion to solve percent problems.
11B Determine discount and markup.
11C Problem Solving: Use percent of commission. Estimate with percent.

Assignments for different achievement levels are provided on the Record and Assignment Chart in the Teacher's Resource Book.

Vocabulary

commission, page 354
discount, page 358
markup, page 359

Home Involvement

As you begin to teach this chapter, give each student a copy of the Home Involvement Newsletter for this chapter.

This newsletter provides parents with
■ an overview of the chapter
■ suggestions for practicing some of the skills in the chapter
■ an at-home activity to do with their child, applying the skills taught in the chapter.

Management Chart

	Management Objectives	Lesson/ Pages	Student Not Successful	Student Needs More Practice	Student Successful	Pacing Range
11A	Use proportion to solve percent problems.	11-1/350-351			TE/CA 11-1	3-5 days
		11-2/352-353	TRB/RW 11-2	TRB/PW 11-2 MAC 6 Activity 11	TE/EA 11-2	
		11-6/360-361	TE/RA 11-6	TRB/PW 11-6	TRB/EW 11-6 MAC 7 Activity 11	
11B	Determine discount and markup.	11-4/358	TRB/RW 11-4/5	TRB/PW 11-4/5 CT Unit 7 Obj. 2.3, 2.4	TE/EA 11-4/5	2-3 days
		11-5/359	TRB/RW 11-4/5	TRB/PW 11-4/5 CT Unit 7 Obj. 2.1, 2.2	TE/EA 11-4/5	
11C	Problem Solving: Use percent of commission. Estimate with percent.	11-3/354-355	TE/RA 11-3	TRB/PW 11-3	TRB/EW 11-3	2 days
		11-7/362-363	TE/RA 11-7	TRB/PW 11-7 MAC 6 Activity 11 MAC 7 Activity 10	TRB/EW 11-7 MAC 7 Activities 10, 11 MAC 6 Activity 11	
	Creative Problem Solving	11-8/364-365				
	Mixed Review	11-9/366-367				
	Chapter Checkups	356-357; 368-369				
	Extra Practice	370				
	Enrichment	371				
	Cumulative Review/Problem Solving Review	372-373				
	Technology	374				

TE = Teacher's Edition
TRB = Teacher's Resource Book
RW = Reteaching Worksheet
RA = Reteaching Activity
EA = Enrichment Activity
EW = Enrichment Worksheet
PW = Practice Worksheet
CA = Classroom Activity

*Other Available Items
MAC = Mathematics Activities Courseware
CT = Computer Tutor

Manipulative Planning Guide

This is a complete list of manipulatives and materials needed for Chapter 11.

Materials for Manipulatives	TE Activities (INTRODUCE)	Student Book Lesson
Teaching Aid 16* for each pair		Lesson 11-1
Calculator for each student		Lessons 11-2, 11-6, 11-8
Manila price tags		

*Teaching Aids are found in the Teacher's Resource Book.

Learning Stages

The concepts and skills in Chapter 11 are presented through these learning stages.

CONCRETE

Using manipulatives and verbalizing about a concept. No symbols.

Teacher Edition Activities	Student Book
At this grade level, the skills of this chapter are taught at the connecting and symbolic stages.	

Enrichment	Reteaching	In the Houghton Mifflin Manipulative Kit?	In the Houghton Mifflin Overhead Kit?
			Yes
			Available separately
Lessons 11-4/5			

CONNECTING

🏛 ▦ ▭ ➡ 5¢ ⑨cm² ⅓

Making a connection between manipulatives and symbols.

Teacher Edition Activities	Student Book
Lessons 11-2, 11-4, 11-5	Lessons 11-1, 11-2, 11-4, 11-5

SYMBOLIC

$.05 A=⑨cm² $1-\frac{2}{3}=\frac{1}{3}$

Using numbers or symbols. No manipulatives or pictures of manipulatives.

Teacher Edition Activities	Student Book
Lessons 11-3, 11-6, 11-7, 11-8	Lessons 11-3, 11-6, 11-7, 11-8

Additional Activities

COOPERATIVE LEARNING RESOURCE ACTIVITIES

Through cooperative learning activities, students learn by interacting with one another in small groups. These cooperative activities provide students with motivating settings for making connections, investigations, and problem solving situations.

The cooperative connections are interdisciplinary problem-solving projects. Each student has a particular job that helps lead the group to complete the project. For the cooperative investigations students work in pairs for investigations involving data collection and analysis. The cooperative problem solving activities encourage the sharing of ideas and information. Students work in groups of four to solve a problem. Students are each assigned a clue and work together to find a common solution.

COOPERATIVE CONNECTIONS

COOPERATIVE CONNECTIONS / Math and Conservation   Chapter 11

Problem: How can you reduce your electric bill by 25% and at the same time conserve energy?

Electrical energy use is measured in kilowatt-hours (kW.h). Household appliances use different amounts of energy. One hour of usage does not always equal 1 kilowatt-hour. For example, an electric blanket uses 0.08 kW.h in one hour, while a room air conditioner uses 1.13 kW.h of energy in one hour.

Appliance	Kilowatt Usage	
Refrigerator/	5.5	kW.h per day
freezer	0.34	kW.h per hour
Color TV		
room air	1.13	kW.h per hour
conditioner	0.6	kW.h per load
dishwasher	0.4	kW.h per hour
stereo	0.2	kW.h per load
washing machine	2.9	kW.h per slice
dryer	0.03	kW.h per hour
toaster	0.66	kW.h per pot
vacuum cleaner	0.15	kW.h per hour
coffee maker	0.09	kW.h per hour
100-watt light bulb	0.09	
60-watt light bulb	0.06	

Work in a group of 4 students.
Estimate the energy cost for each appliance for one week to determine the approximate cost of your electric bill. Assume that each kilowatt-hour costs 10.5¢.

COOPERATIVE INVESTIGATIONS

COOPERATIVE INVESTIGATIONS / Commissions   Chapter 11

GOAL: Explore using percents to find real estate commissions.

Materials: real estate ads, pencil, paper, ruler

Work with a partner.
1. Research information on selling real estate by contacting a local real estate agency. Find out about these terms:
   listing broker   asking price   selling broker
   selling price   selling agent   commission
2. Also find the following information: What percent of the selling price is charged by a broker as a real estate commission? What percent of the real estate commission goes to the selling broker? How much goes to the listing broker and how much goes to the selling agent? Record the information.

HOUSE for SALE

COOPERATIVE PROBLEM SOLVING 1

COOPERATIVE PROBLEM SOLVING / Problem 1   Chapter 11

What is Mrs. Chan's commission on the sale of the Parker's house?

Clue 1: The broker's fee on the house is 6.5% of the selling price. Sunrise Realty is the broker.

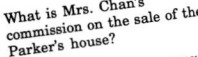

What is Mrs. Chan's commission on the sale of the Parker's house?

Clue 3: Mrs. Chan gets 35% of the fee her company, Sunrise Realty, receives on the sale.

What is Mrs. Chan's commission on the sale of the Parker's house?

Clue 2: The Parker's house was listed with Sunrise Realty, so Sunrise will receive half of the broker's fee.

What is Mrs. Chan's commission on the sale of the Parker's house?

Clue 4: Mrs. Chan sold the Parker's house for $136,500.

COOPERATIVE PROBLEM SOLVING 2

COOPERATIVE PROBLEM SOLVING / Problem 2   Chapter 11

Ashley compared prices and bought a stereo in the store with the lowest price. Where did Ashley buy the stereo? How much did she pay?

Clue 1: The wholesaler sold the stereo for $100 to Doreen's Discount Store, Benny's Bargain Basement, and Quality Corner.

Ashley compared prices and bought a stereo in the store with the lowest price. Where did Ashley buy the stereo? How much did she pay?

Clue 3: Benny's Bargain Basement discounted the stereo 20% after a mark-up of 65% on the wholesale price.

Ashley compared prices and bought a stereo in the store with the lowest price. Where did Ashley buy the stereo? How much did she pay?

Clue 2: Doreen's Discount Store marked up the wholesale price by 80%. The stereo was then put on sale at a 25% discount.

Ashley compared prices and bought a stereo in the store with the lowest price. Where did Ashley buy the stereo? How much did she pay?

Clue 4: At Quality Corner, the mark-up on the wholesale price was 100%, but then they discounted the stereo 30%.

GAMES

COMMISSION BOARD   (For use after Lesson 11-3)

Objective: Use percent of commission.

✓ **MATERIALS CHECKLIST:** 6 x 4 grid, number cube, spinner, two game markers for each pair of students

Assign partners. Prepare or have each pair prepare the grid and spinner as shown:

GO	$770	$3,600	$975	$4,000	$650
$96	$810	$1,850	$440	$3,625	$200
$80	$125	$1,000	$333	$5,500	$500
Finish	$75	$600	$775	$7,000	$50

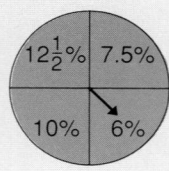

To start the game, players place their markers at GO and in turn toss the number cube to determine the number of spaces to move. After landing on an amount of money, a player spins to get the rate of commission and multiplies the amount by the rate. A correctly computed commission is recorded as the player's score for that turn. The player with the greater total when a player crosses Finish wins.

DISCOUNT STORE   (For use after Lesson 11-4)

Objective: Find the percent of discount.

✓ **MATERIALS CHECKLIST:** two pages of sales advertisements, six index cards, and calculator for each pair

Assign partners, and distribute two pages of sales advertisements and six index cards to each pair. Ask students to write the original price and the sale price of an item of their choice on each card. Explain that all prices above $10 should be rounded to the nearest dollar. Collect all cards and mix them.

To start the game, give each pair six new cards and a calculator. Cards should be placed face down. One player chooses a card and computes the percent of discount. Remind students they will have to find the value of the discount before they can find the percent of discount. Players check each other. A correct answer is worth five points. Pairs can exchange cards after partners have had six turns. The pair with the most points at the end is the winner.

BULLETIN BOARD

Discuss with students various ways people use percents in their lives. Mention occupations, such as real estate brokers; information displays and percents, for example, circle graphs; shopping with markups and discounts; and banking, especially savings accounts, credit cards, and other loans. Ask students to bring in illustrations, articles, and problems that illustrate the importance of percents in everyday life. Make a display of the materials, including an envelope of percent problems for students to solve.

Alternative Assessment

In addition to the paper and pencil tests available with this program, the following items can help you assess critical thinking as well as your students' ability to solve problems in a wide variety of ways.

Open-ended Problem

The results of a recent survey indicate that 30% of the students study Spanish and 20% of the students study French. Does this mean that 50% of the students study a foreign language? When is the 50% true and when may it be false?

Teacher Notes
Some students may study Spanish and French. If this is the case, less than 50% of the students study a foreign language.

If other foreign languages are available, the percent of students studying a foreign language may be greater than 50%.

The statement will be true if students can study only one language and the school offers only Spanish and French.

Group Writing Activity (See p. T24.)

A new student in your school solves percent problems in a different way. Explain what the student is doing.

$$\frac{25}{100} = \frac{n}{36}$$

Step 1: $(4 \times 25 \times 9) \times \frac{25}{100} = (4 \times 25 \times 9) \times \frac{n}{36}$

Step 2: $(4 \times 25 \times 9) \times \frac{25}{100} = (4 \times 25 \times 9) \times \frac{n}{36}$

Step 3: $9 \times 25 = 25n$

Step 4: $\frac{9 \times 25}{25} = \frac{25n}{25}$

Solution: $9 = n$

Teacher Notes
- The new student is factoring the denominators and finding the least common multiple (the LCM of 100 and 36 is 900 or $4 \times 25 \times 9$).
- The student keeps the equation balanced by multiplying both sides by the same product.
- The student avoids computational errors by keeping the products in factored form.
- The student simplifies the fractions by canceling common factors.
- The student keeps the equation balanced by dividing both sides by the same factor.

Individual Writing Activity

Does $\frac{1}{2}\%$ equal 50%? Include a diagram with your answer.

Teacher Notes

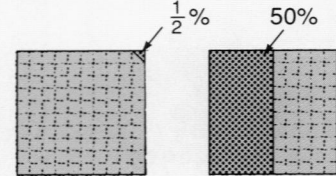

- $\frac{1}{2}\% = \frac{1}{2} \times \frac{1}{100} = \frac{1}{200}$ and
  $50\% = 50 \times \frac{1}{100} = \frac{50}{100}$ or $\frac{100}{200}$
- 50% is 100 times $\frac{1}{2}\%$ ($50\% = \frac{1}{2}\% \times 100$)
- $\frac{1}{2}\% = 0.005$ and $50\% = 0.5$

Portfolios

Portfolios can provide information about a student's growth in mathematical understanding over a period of time. They can help you make instructional decisions as well as become a vehicle for communicating with parents. The students' work involving the open-ended problem and writing activity suggested on this page along with work on the Write Your Own exercise on page 353, the Create Your Own exercise on page 355, the Learning Log exercises on pages 357 and 369, the Critical Thinking feature on page 363, and the Creative Problem Solving lesson on pages 364-365 could be included in portfolios.

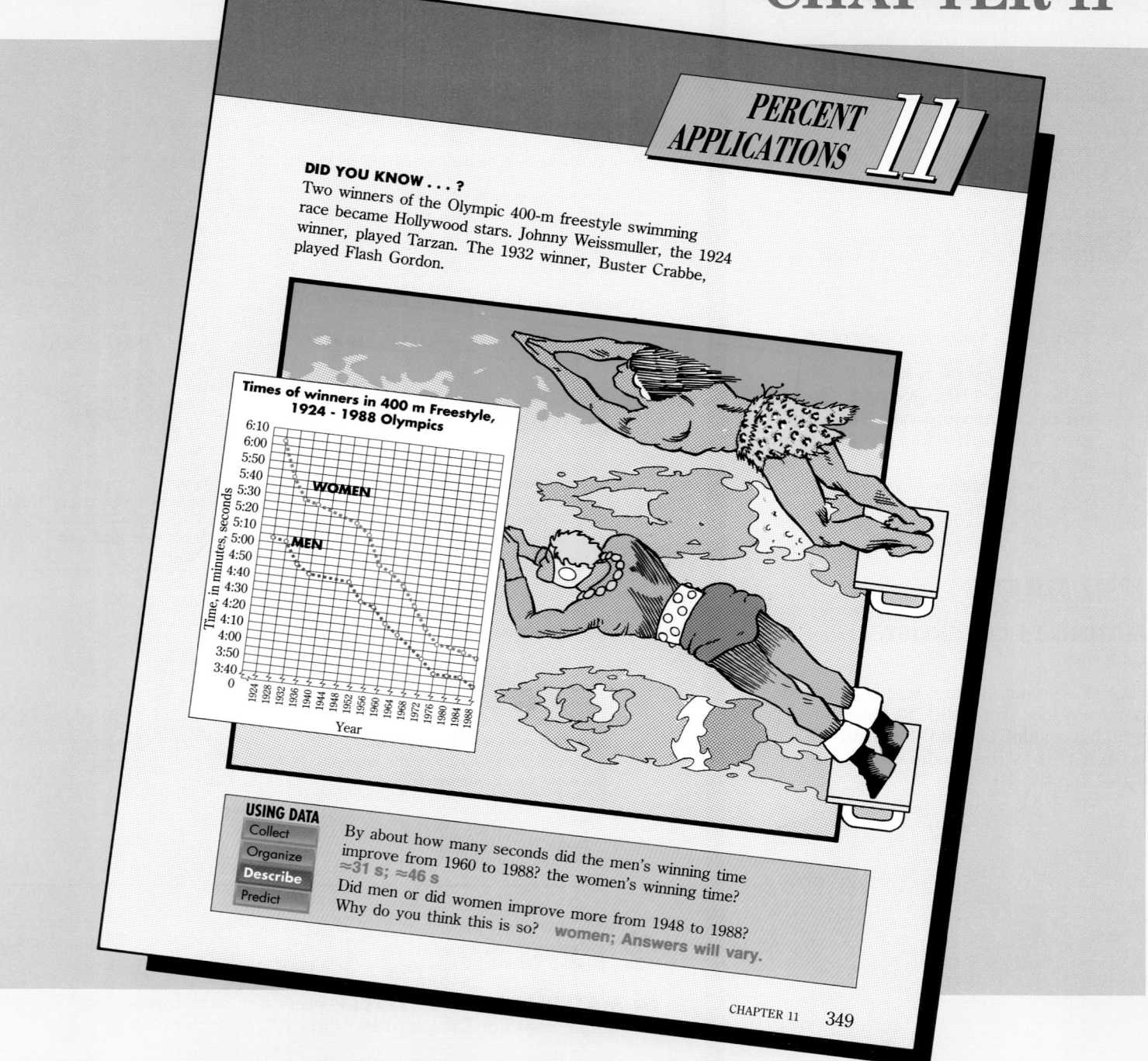

PERCENT APPLICATIONS **11**

DID YOU KNOW . . . ?
Two winners of the Olympic 400-m freestyle swimming race became Hollywood stars. Johnny Weissmuller, the 1924 winner, played Tarzan. The 1932 winner, Buster Crabbe, played Flash Gordon.

Times of winners in 400 m Freestyle, 1924 - 1988 Olympics

WOMEN

MEN

Time, in minutes, seconds

Year

USING DATA
Collect
Organize
Describe
Predict

By about how many seconds did the men's winning time improve from 1960 to 1988? the women's winning time? ≈31 s; ≈46 s
Did men or did women improve more from 1948 to 1988? Why do you think this is so? women; Answers will vary.

CHAPTER 11   349

Using the Chapter Opener

The purpose of this page is to involve students in the use of real data much like that presented in newspapers and magazines.

To use this page as you begin the chapter, direct students' attention to the double-line graph. You may wish to ask questions such as the following:

Can you think of a reason why no data are displayed for the years 1940 and 1944? *(The Olympic games were not held during World War II.)*

How many seconds better was the 1960 winning time for the women's 400-m freestyle than the 1956 winning time? *(4 seconds)*

During which three years were the men's winning times about the same? *(1976, 1980, and 1984)* **How do you know?** *(The line remains horizontal.)*

Compare the men's times to that of the women's in 1924 and in 1988. What conclusions can you make? *(In 1924, the men were 58 s faster than the women. In 1988, the men were 16.9 s faster than the women. Both men and women gained in speed, but women's gains were relatively greater.)*

LESSON 11-1

Lesson Organizer

Objective: Explore proportional thinking and percent.

Prior Knowledge: Students should know the meaning of percent and how to solve proportions.

Lesson Resources:
Class Activity 11-1
Daily Review 11-1

Two-Minute Math

A school gives a sports award called the 110% Award. Do you think an athlete can actually give 110% effort? Explain your answer.
(It is not physically possible to give more than 100% effort.)

1 PREPARE

☑ **MATERIALS CHECKLIST:** Percent Bar Transparency

Display the transparency, using the model for percents less than 100. Review how the percent bar model is used. Remind students that this is the model which they used in Chapter 10.

WHEN YOUR STUDENTS ASK
★ WHY AM I LEARNING THIS? ★

You can use this skill to solve real life problems. For example, if a newspaper survey showed that 40% of 685 people surveyed voted for an energy tax, you can use proportional thinking to determine how many people this represents. *(274 people)*

Exploring Proportional Thinking and Percent

The percent bar diagram can be used to set up proportions to solve percent problems. Here is a completed diagram for 75% of 68.

The ratio for the percent bar is $\frac{75}{100}$. What is the equal ratio for the number bar? $\frac{51}{68}$

The ratios on the left and on the right of the diagram give us the proportion $\frac{75}{100} = \frac{51}{68}$.

Write the proportion that fits the diagram.

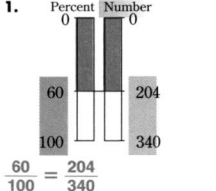
1.
$$\frac{60}{100} = \frac{204}{340}$$

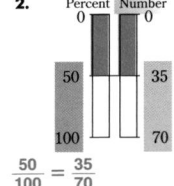
2.
$$\frac{50}{100} = \frac{35}{70}$$

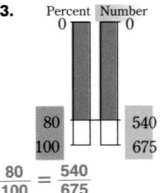
3.
$$\frac{80}{100} = \frac{540}{675}$$

4. What number is found in each of the proportions in Exercises 1–3? Why will this be true for all percent problems? **100; percent means per hundred**

> A survey of 360 seventh graders revealed that 80% made their own breakfasts. How many students is that?

You can complete the percent bar because the 80% is given. Use the answers to Exercises 5–8 to copy and complete the number bar.

5. Does 100% represent the *total number* of students in the survey or the *number who make their own breakfasts*?
total number

6. Does 80% represent the *total number* of students in the survey or the *number who make their own breakfasts*?
number who make their own breakfast

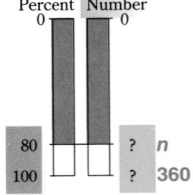

---

2 EXPLORE

☑ **MATERIALS CHECKLIST:** Percent Bar Transparency and Teaching Aid 16 (Percent Bar Diagrams less than 100%) for each pair

Have students work with a partner for Exercises 9–18. For Create Your Own, partners can exchange the problems they have written to be sure that each problem matches a diagram.

After Exercise 4, display the transparency. **Describe how the diagram can be filled out for each of these examples:**

50% of 60 = 30	25% of 80 = 20
10% of 50 = 5	80% of 40 = 32

SUMMARIZE/ASSESS **Explain why 100 is a part of every proportion that you use to solve a percent problem.** *(It is always the denominator of the ratio for the percent bar.)*

7. Is 360 the *total number* of students in the survey or the *number who make their own breakfasts?* **total number**

8. Why does the proportion below fit this problem? **both ratios represent:** $\frac{80}{100} = \frac{n}{360}$ make own breakfast / total

Copy the percent bar diagram. Set up a $\frac{a}{100} = \frac{c}{d}$ proportion for the problem. Do not solve.

9. Of 60 students who play baseball after school, 25% ride the bus. How many students ride the bus? $\frac{25}{100} = \frac{c}{60}$

10. Of 90 students who take Spanish, 30% also study music. How many Spanish language students study music? $\frac{30}{100} = \frac{c}{90}$

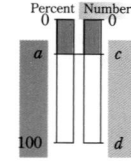

A student survey showed that 17 out of the 25 students who have gym during last period of the day have math during first period. What percent is that?

---

11. Is the 17 represented by the *c* or by the *d* on the percent bar diagram? Which letter represents the 25? **c; d**

12. What represents the unknown percent? **a**

13. Write a proportion for the percent problem. $\frac{a}{100} = \frac{17}{25}$

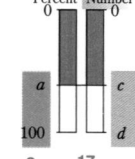

Draw a percent bar diagram. Then write a proportion and solve. **Check students' drawings.**

14. 14% of 150 = ■.   **21**   **15.** ■% of 48 is 18.   **37.5**   **16.** 27 out of ■ is $37\frac{1}{2}$%.   **72**

17. Of 52 girls asked, 39 preferred track and field to volleyball. What percent of the girls preferred track and field? **75%**

18. In a survey, 65%, or 78 students, asked to have science class in the morning. How many students were surveyed? **120**

CREATE YOUR OWN   Write a problem to fit the percent bar diagram. **Check students' work.**

19. 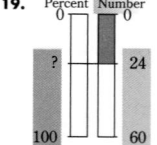   **20.** 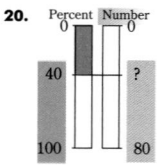   **21.**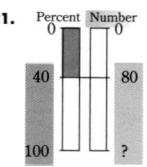

CLASS ACTIVITY **11-1**

☑ **MATERIALS CHECKLIST:** 2-in. by 10-in. strips of paper, index cards, rulers

Divide a strip of paper into 20 equal sections. Label the sections from 0% to 100% in increments of 5% and place the strip on the bulletin board. Have small groups work together to divide another strip of paper into 20 sections. Each group then selects a card containing a question such as *Do you eat pizza at least once a week? Have you visited a museum in the past year?* Each group asks 20 people the survey question and shades the bar to show how many answer yes. Each group aligns its shaded bar with the percent bar to find the percent of those surveyed who answered yes.

MEETING INDIVIDUAL NEEDS

For Students Who Are . . .

Acquiring English Proficiency   Describe concepts of proportion and ratio in terms of equivalent fractions. Relate these ideas to construction of percent bar diagrams.

Gifted and Talented   Have students choose five characteristics and conduct a survey to determine the extent of these characteristics among their classmates. Students should describe survey results in proportional terms and construct percent bar diagrams to show results.

Having Reading Difficulties   Call attention to the reading clues provided by the phrases in italics and the sentences in the boxes.

Today's Problem

Two hundred eighty-five pennies weigh one pound. How much would 285 nickels weigh? *(Not enough information is given to determine the answer. A more sensible question would be: How much value would 285 nickels have? The answer is $14.25.)*

LESSON 11-2

Lesson Organizer

Objective: Use proportion to solve percent problems.

Prior Knowledge: Students should know the meaning of percent and how to write and solve proportions.

Error Analysis and Remediation: See page 369A.

Lesson Resources:
Practice Worksheet 11-2
Reteaching Worksheet 11-2
Enrichment Activity 11-2
Daily Review 11-2

 *Two-Minute Math*

Solve the proportion.

$\frac{14}{3} = \frac{n}{9}$ *(42)* $\frac{45}{48} = \frac{9}{n}$ *(9.6)*

1 INTRODUCE

CONNECTING ACTIVITY

☑ **MATERIALS CHECKLIST:** Percent Bar Transparency

1. Write 150% of 60 = 90. **Does 90 make sense as the answer? Explain.** *(Yes; 100% of 60 is 60, 50% of 60 is 30, and so 150% of 60 is 60 + 30, or 90.)*

2. Display the percent bar diagram. **Where should the line for 150% be drawn?** *(halfway between 100% and 200%)*
Where should 60 be written? 90? *(next to 100%; next to 150%)*

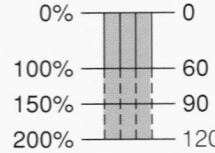

3. Write the proportion $\frac{100}{150} = \frac{60}{90}$ and relate it to the diagram.

WHEN YOUR STUDENTS ASK
★ WHY AM I LEARNING THIS? ★

You can connect this skill to real life through economics. If economists assume 1980 figures to be equal to 100%, then the figures for 1995, which may be higher, will be represented as percents greater than 100.

MATH AND SOCIAL STUDIES

Using Proportion and Percent

It has been projected that by the year 2000 the population of Florida will be 120% of what it was in 1990. If the 1990 population was about 12.8 million, about what will it be by the year 2000?

NUMBER SENSE Will the answer be *greater than* or *less than* 12.8 million? Why? **greater than; 120% > 100%**

Write and solve the proportion. Let n represent the population in the year 2000.

When the percent is greater than 100%, you may want to read the diagram upward and write the ratios so that 100 is a denominator.

$\frac{120}{100} = \frac{n}{12.8}$
$100n = 12.8 \times 120$
$\frac{100n}{100} = \frac{1,536}{100}$
$n = 15.36$

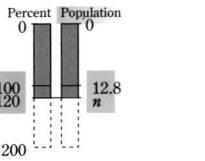

$\frac{100}{120} = \frac{12.8}{n}$
$100n = 12.8 \times 120$
$\frac{100n}{100} = \frac{1,536}{100}$
$n = 15.36$

THINK ALOUD Why was the 12.8 million placed opposite the 100?
both represent 1990 population
By the year 2000, Florida's population will be about 15.36 million.

Other examples:

24 is 8% of what number?

$\frac{8}{100} = \frac{24}{n}$
$8n = 100 \times 24$
$\frac{8n}{8} = \frac{2,400}{8}$
$n = 300$

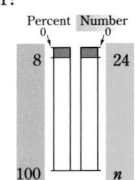

What percent of 192 is 48?

$\frac{n}{100} = \frac{48}{192}$
$192n = 100 \times 48$
$\frac{192n}{192} = \frac{4,800}{192}$
$n = 25$ (%)

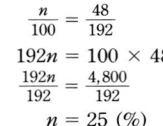
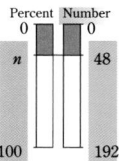

━━━━━━━━━ **GUIDED PRACTICE** ━━━━━━━━━

Use a proportion to solve. Use percent bars to help.

1. 40% of 60 is what number? **24**

2. What percent of 30 is 24? **80%**

3. What percent of 24 is 30? **125%**

352 LESSON 11-2

MULTICULTURAL NOTE

St. Augustine, Florida, founded in 1565 by Don Pedro Menendez de Aviles, is the oldest permanent settlement established in the U.S. by Europeans. A stone fort there, built in 1672, is now a national monument.

2 TEACH

☑ **MATERIALS CHECKLIST:** Percent Bar Transparency, calculators

You may wish to display the transparency and guide students through the example step by step.

Where should the 120% line be drawn? *(below 100% and less than halfway between 100% and 200%)*

Is 12.8 million 100% or 120% of the 1990 population? *(100%)*

If n represents the population in the year 2000, where should n be placed? *(next to 120%)*

Chalkboard Examples

Solve using a proportion.

150% of □ = 60 *(40)*
150% of 60 = □ *(90)*
□% of 20 = 30 *(150)*

SUMMARIZE/ASSESS **Explain how using a percent bar diagram helps you write the proportion for a percent problem.** *(Students should indicate that the diagram helps them visualize the proportional relationships.)*

Use a proportion to solve.

4. 30% of what number is 7.5? **25**

5. 5% of what number is 10? **200**

6. What percent of 75 is 15? **20%**

7. What percent of 18 is 6? **33$\frac{1}{3}$%**

8. 18 is what percent of 6? **300%**

9. What percent of 60 is 6? **10%**

10. 23% of what number is 20.7? **90**

11. What percent of 300 is 9? **3%**

12. 6% of what number is 15? **250**

13. What percent of 8 is 3? **37.5%**

14. 52% of n is 33.8. **$n = 65$**

15. 40% of n is 36. **$n = 90$**

Write a problem to fit the question. **Check students' work.**

16. 12 is 30% of what number?

17. 9 is what percent of 45?

18. 0.6% of what number is 2.4?

19. What percent of 5.2 is 3.9?

20. **IN YOUR WORDS** Why is the word *percent* a good name for fractions with a denominator of 100? **Answers will vary. Suggestion given. Percent means per 100.**

  Choose paper and pencil or calculator to solve.

21. The Everglades are about 2,746 mi^2 and Lake Okeechobee covers about 25.5% of the Everglades. About how many square miles is Lake Okeechobee? **c; 700.23 mi^2**

22. About 580 mi of Florida's 1,350-mi coastline is on the Atlantic Ocean and the rest is on the Gulf of Mexico. About what percent of Florida's coastline is on the Gulf of Mexico? **p; ≈57%**

23. **WRITE YOUR OWN** In 1513, Juan Ponce de León landed on Florida's east coast and claimed the region for Spain. In 1565, Pedro Menéndez de Avilés of Spain founded St. Augustine, now the oldest city in the United States. Use these facts to write a problem. **Check students' work.**

MEETING INDIVIDUAL NEEDS

For Students Who Are . . .

Acquiring English Proficiency Have students work in groups to model the Guided Practice exercises with percent bar diagrams.

Gifted and Talented Have students research at least two Spanish explorers who reached America, find the distance and travel time for each, and calculate each explorer's travel speed in mi/hr. Describe the data as a percent of today's air travel speed of about 450 mi/hr.

Working 2 or 3 Grades Below Level Remind students that when percent is greater than 100%, they should read the percent bar diagram upward.

Today's Problem

There are 15 members in the brass section of a school orchestra, and this section makes up 12% of the entire orchestra. How many members of the orchestra are there? ($\frac{15}{n} = \frac{12}{100}$; *There are 125 members.*)

3 FOLLOW-UP

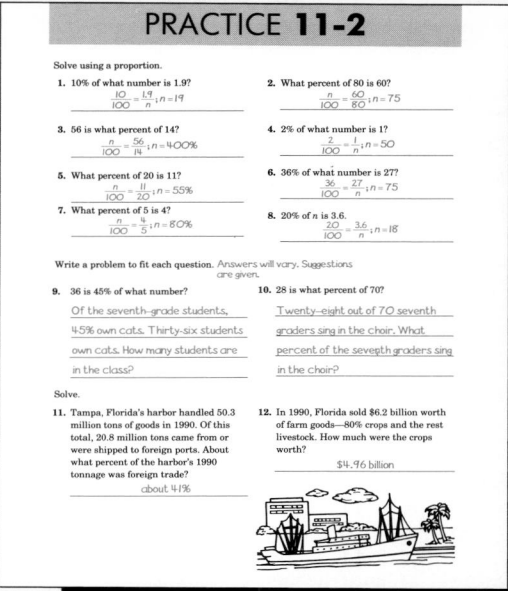

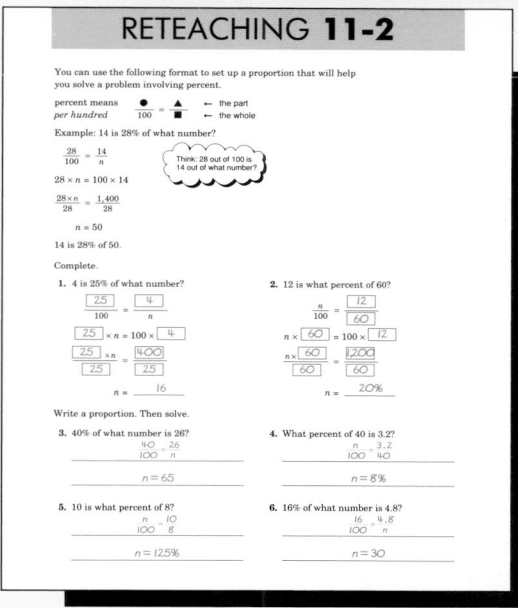

ENRICHMENT 11-2

Write these equations on the board: $n\%$ of $x = y$; $x\%$ of $n = y$; $x\%$ of $y = n$. Explain to students that they are to make generalizations about the variables in these equations. Ask: **In the first equation, what can you say about n when $x > y$?** ($n < 100$) **In the second equation, what is the relationship between y and n when $x > 100$?** ($n < y$) **In the third equation, what is the relationship between y and n when $x > 100$?** ($n > y$) **when $x < 100$?** ($n < y$) **What is the value of n in the first equation when $x = y$?** ($n = 100$) **in the second?** ($n = 100$)

Lesson Organizer

Objective: Solve problems using percent of commission.

Prior Knowledge: Students should know how to use proportions to solve percent problems.

Error Analysis and Remediation: See page 369A.

Lesson Resources:
Practice Worksheet 11-3
Reteaching Activity 11-3
Enrichment Worksheet 11-3
Daily Review 11-3
Cooperative Investigations, Chapter 11
Cooperative Problem Solving 1, Chapter 11

Two-Minute Math

List three situations in which people use percents in daily life.
(Accept reasonable answers; possible answers: to calculate taxes, to see which store offers the greater discount, to understand newspaper articles.)

1 INTRODUCE

SYMBOLIC ACTIVITY

Discuss the meaning of commission as a percent of total sales. Emphasize that commissions are powerful incentives to sell, because the more one sells, the more one earns in commissions.

WHEN YOUR STUDENTS ASK
★ WHY AM I LEARNING THIS? ★

You can connect this skill to real life through careers in real estate. A person who sells a house for $67,500 may earn a 6% commission. How much is this? *($4050)*

Problem Solving:
Using Percent of Commission

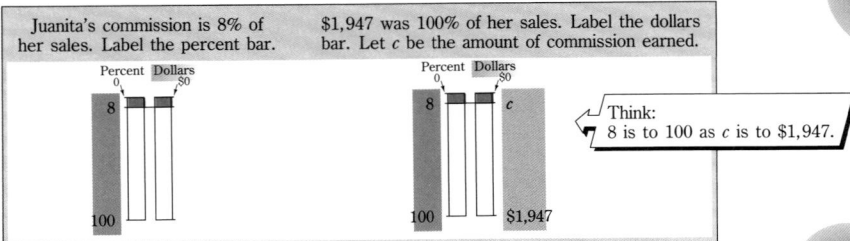

A salesperson is often paid a **commission**, which is a percent of the total sales the person makes.

Juanita sells computers and earns 8% commission on her sales. One day she sold a computer for $1,947. How much commission did she earn that day?

Juanita's commission is 8% of her sales. Label the percent bar.	$1,947 was 100% of her sales. Label the dollars bar. Let *c* be the amount of commission earned.

Percent Dollars
0        $0
8

100

Percent Dollars
0        $0
8   c

Think:
8 is to 100 as *c* is to $1,947.

100      $1,947

What proportion represents this problem? Now solve the problem. $\frac{8}{100} = \frac{c}{1,947}$; **c = $155.76**

CRITICAL THINKING   Why do you think a person who sells expensive items is often paid a commission?   **Answers will vary. Suggestion given. It's an incentive to work harder.**

━━━━━━━━━━ **GUIDED PRACTICE** ━━━━━━━━━━

Write a proportion to solve.

1. Lap-Cheung sells computers and earns $12\frac{1}{2}\%$ commission on his sales. He would like to earn $5,000 in commission in the next month.
   a. What percent of his sales is Lap-Cheung's commission? $12\frac{1}{2}\%$
   b. To get $5,000 in commission, would Lap-Cheung have to sell *less than* or *more than* $5,000 worth of computers?   more than
   c. How much in total computer sales must Lap-Cheung have in order to make $5,000 in commission?   **$40,000**

2. Alicia received a commission of $120 for selling a printer worth $2,000. What percent of total sales is her commission?   **6%**

3. Jason earns a 15% commission selling jewelry. One week he sold 2 necklaces at $450 each, 5 rings at $799 each, and 15 bracelets at $150 each. How much commission did he earn that week?   **$1,071.75**

354   LESSON 11–3

MULTICULTURAL NOTE

An Wang, a Chinese immigrant to the United States, helped develop today's computers. Wang invented a memory device for computers and founded Wang Laboratories, an important computer company.

2 TEACH

☑ **MATERIALS CHECKLIST:** Percent Bar Transparency

Instead of using the completed diagram on page 354, you may wish to display the transparency and have students explain how to represent the problem. Then ask: **What proportion can be written to find how much Juanita earned in commission?** $\left(\frac{8}{100} = \frac{c}{1,947}\right)$ **How much did Juanita earn?** *($155.76)*

SUMMARIZE/ASSESS   **How much in total sales would a person need to make in order to earn $3,000, when the percent of commission is 12%?** $\left(\frac{12}{100} = \frac{3,000}{c}\right)$; *c = $25,000)*

Use a proportion to solve.

4. Norma earns a 6% commission on sales, plus a base salary of $400/mo. Last month, she earned a total of $1,300. What were her total sales? **$15,000**

5. Angie earned $78 in commission for selling a $600 pair of gold earrings. What percent is her commission? **13%**

6. What would Hiroshi earn for selling 3 Egyptian paintings for $12,500 each, if his commission is 5.2% of his total sales? **$1,950**

7. Rosa is paid a base salary of $1,800/mo plus commission. One month she made $10,000 in sales and her total income was $3,000. What percent is her commission? **12%**

8. Errol earns a 15% commission for selling African art. For the sale of 1 wood carving, he earned $120 in commission. What was the value of the carving he sold? **$800**

CHOOSE Choose a strategy to solve. **Choices will vary.**

9. Last year, Renete earned $36,000 in commission. Owing to more sales this year, she will earn 125% of that amount. What will she earn this year? **$45,000**

10. The Art and Jewelry Shoppe requires a down payment of 20% of the price of any item purchased on credit. What is the price of a wall hanging that requires a down payment of $120? **$600**

*11. Enzo bought a $230 suit on credit, paying $24.50/mo for 12 mo. How much would Enzo have saved had he paid for the suit all at once? **$64**

CREATE YOUR OWN Create your own commission problem to fit the percent bar diagram. **Check students' work.**

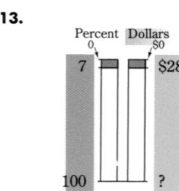
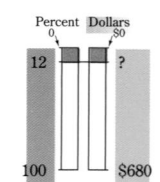

12.
Percent Dollars
0 $0
? $15
100 $350

13.
Percent Dollars
0 $0
7 $28
100 ?

14.
Percent Dollars
0 $0
12 ?
100 $680

MEETING INDIVIDUAL NEEDS

For Students Who Are . . .

Acquiring English Proficiency Discuss the concept of commission. Pair students with an English-proficient student for the Practice activities.

Gifted and Talented Have students choose several properties advertised for sale in the newspaper, then calculate the amounts earned by three real estate agents who sell these properties and are paid 8%, 13%, and 17% commissions.

Today's Problem

Bob gets a salary of $15,000 a year plus a 5% commission on all car sales. Jim gets no salary, but earns 7% commission on the first $300,000 of car sales and 12% commission on sales over $300,000. Last year, each person sold $500,000 worth of cars. Who made more money? How much more? *(Bob made $15,000 + 5% of $500,000, or $40,000. Jim made 7% of $300,000 + 12% of $200,000 or $45,000. Jim made $5,000 more than Bob.)*

3 FOLLOW-UP

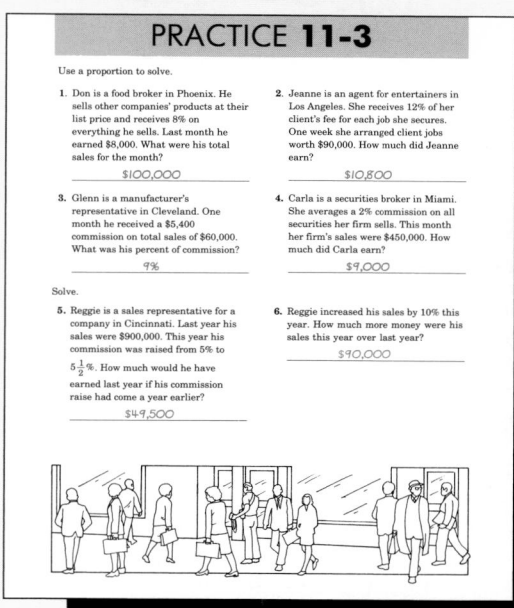

RETEACHING 11-3

Some students may have difficulty with the concept of commission. Explain that commission encourages people to sell more. Because it is a percent, the more you sell the more you earn in commission. Help a student solve Problem 1, *Practice Worksheet 97*, by asking these questions: **What is the percent of the commission?** *(8%)* **How do you write this as a ratio?** $\left(\frac{8}{100}\right)$ **What is the amount of the commission earned?** *($8,000)* **How do you write a ratio showing the amount of commission to the total sales?** $\left(\frac{8,000}{n}\right)$ **What proportion will you write?** $\left(\frac{8}{100} = \frac{8,000}{n}\right)$ **What is the solution?** *(n = $100,000)*

MIDCHAPTER Checkup

The midchapter checkup provides a way for you to check students' understanding of the skills taught in the first half of the chapter.

Language and Vocabulary

Some key language and vocabulary ideas from the first half of the chapter are reinforced here.

Quick Quiz

This quiz provides a means of evaluating students' understanding of the objectives for the first half of the chapter. Page references are given so that students can check back to where the skill was taught.

Use the following guide to score the quiz.

Score	Percent
10	100%
9	90
8	80
7	70
6	60
5	50
4	40
3	30
2	20
1	10

Use this chart to identify the management objectives tested for this chapter.

Items	Management Objectives	Pages
1–9	**11A** Use proportion to solve percent problems.	352–353
10	**11C** Problem Solving: Use percent of commission.	354–355

MIDCHAPTER CHECKUP

LANGUAGE & VOCABULARY

Match the situation with the appropriate expression.

1. 15% of the 40 students joined the club. **b**   **a.** 40% of 150

2. Of 150 books on a reading list, 40% **a**   **b.** 15% of 40
   were fiction.

3. The length of the photo is 150% of its **d**   **c.** 150% of 40
   15 cm width.

4. 40% of the 15-mi trip is complete. **e**   **d.** 150% of 15

5. 150% more than last year's 40 voters **c**   **e.** 40% of 15
   are expected to vote this year.

QUICK QUIZ

Solve using a proportion. *(pages 352–353)*

1. 40% of what number is 56? **140**   2. 75% of what number is 48? **64**

3. What percent of 50 is 45? **90%**   4. What percent of 35 is 28? **80%**

5. 24 is what percent of 8? **300%**   6. What percent of 125 is 55? **44%**

7. 27 is what percent of 18? **150%**   8. 48 percent of *x* is 18. **37.5**

9. 165% of what number is 42.9? **26**

Use a proportion to solve. *(pages 354–355)*

10. Last month, Arthur earned a commission of 7% on sales of $15,000 in addition to his base salary of $500.

    a. What was Arthur's rate of commission? **7%**

    b. Were Arthur's total earnings for the month less than or greater than $15,000? **less than**

    c. What were Arthur's total earnings for the month? **$1,550**

Write the answers in your learning log. **Answers will vary. Suggestions given.**

1. When using a proportion to find a percent, what is an important thing to remember? **Be sure the numbers are placed in the correct order.**

2. You have learned two ways to solve percent problems. Describe the two ways and tell which way you prefer and why. **Accept reasonable answers.**

DID YOU KNOW . . . ? The United States Capitol stands on Capitol Hill in Washington, D.C. The building has 540 rooms and 658 windows. How many rooms and windows does your state capitol have? See whether you can write proportions to compare the two sets of numbers. **Check students' work.**

The Mark Down Clothing Store deducts 15% from the selling price of a garment at the end of each week it remains unsold. If a $249 coat goes on sale and remains unsold, how many weeks will it take for the price to drop below $150? **after 4 wk**

CHAPTER 11   357

Learning Log

These are suggestions for writing about some topics taught so far in the chapter. The students keep their learning logs from the start of the school year to the end.

Math America

A mathematical skill that students have learned is related to an interesting fact about the United States.

Bonus

Students are given an opportunity to solve a challenge-type problem such as a puzzle or a nonroutine problem.

Lesson Organizer

Objectives:
11-4 Determine discount.
11-5 Determine markup.

Prior Knowledge: Students should be able to solve problems involving percents less than and greater than 100%.

Error Analysis and Remediation: See page 369A.

Lesson Resources:
Practice Worksheet 11-5
Reteaching Worksheet 11-5
Enrichment Activity 11-5
Daily Review 11-4, 11-5
Cooperative Connections, Chapter 11
Cooperative Problem Solving 2, Chapter 11

Two-Minute Math

Determine whether n will be less than or greater than 100.
$n\%$ of $37 = 20$ *(less than)*
135% of $100 = n$ *(greater than)*
125% of $n = 100$ *(less than)*
$n\%$ of $34 = 65$ *(greater than)*

1 INTRODUCE

CONNECTING ACTIVITY

☑ **MATERIALS CHECKLIST:** Percent Bar Transparency

1. Display the transparency. Use the model for percents less than 100 and have students complete the diagram to model this problem:
Jack works part-time. He puts 25% of his weekly salary of $120 into his savings account. How much does he save each week? *($30)* **How much does he have left?** *($90)*

2. Use the models on the transparency for percents greater than 100. Have students explain how the diagram can be used to model this problem:
Jill received a raise from $4.50 to $4.95 per hour. What percent of her former hourly rate is her new hourly rate? *(110%)*

Discount

A **discount** is a *decrease* in the regular price of an item. A discount of 20% tells you that you save 20¢ on every dollar of the regular price.

The discount on a pair of roller skates is 20%. How much would you save on a pair of roller skates that regularly sells for $49? What is the sale price?

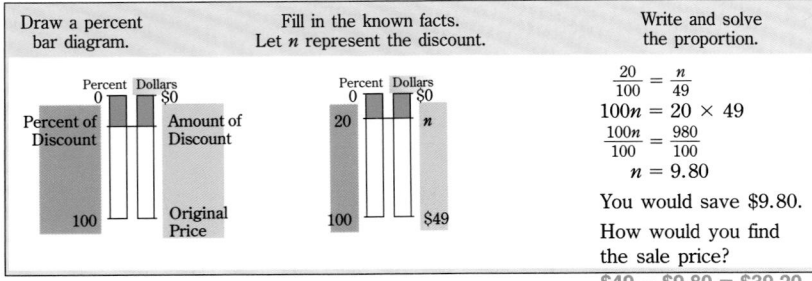

Draw a percent bar diagram.	Fill in the known facts. Let n represent the discount.	Write and solve the proportion.
		$\frac{20}{100} = \frac{n}{49}$
		$100n = 20 \times 49$
		$\frac{100n}{100} = \frac{980}{100}$
		$n = 9.80$
		You would save $9.80.
		How would you find the sale price?
		$49 - 9.80 = 39.20

CRITICAL THINKING The shaded part of the dollars bar is the amount of the discount. What does the unshaded part represent? How can you use this information to find the sale price?
sale price; sale price = 80% of $49

━━━━━━━━━━━━━━━ **GUIDED PRACTICE** ━━━━━━━━━━━━━━━

Find the amount of discount and the sale price.

1. original price: $125
   discount: 15%
   $18.75; $106.25

2. original price: $23
   discount: 5%
   $1.15; $21.85

3. original price: $65
   discount: 50%
   $32.50; $32.50

━━━━━━━━━━━━━━━ **PRACTICE** ━━━━━━━━━━━━━━━

Find the amount of discount and the sale price.

4. original price: $43.50
   discount: 30%
   $13.05; $30.45

5. original price: $49.88
   discount: 50%
   $24.94; $24.94

6. original price: $1,230
   discount: 20%
   $246; $980

7. A $59.99 skateboard now costs $54.
   What is the percent of discount? 10%

8. Which is cheaper, a $49.99 skateboard with a 20% discount, or a $54.99 skateboard with a 25% discount?
   $49.99 skateboard

*9. If a skateboard is on sale for $49 which is a 30% discount, what was the original price? $70

358   LESSON 11–4

---

2 TEACH   Lesson 11-4

Does finding n give you the solution to the problem? Explain. *(No; to find the sale price, you subtract n, $9.80, from the original price, $49, to obtain $39.20.)*

Discuss the percent bar model as it relates to the Critical Thinking questions. **How can you find the sale price in one step?** *(Find 80% of $49 to obtain $39.20.)*

SUMMARIZE/ASSESS   Demonstrate how to use a percent bar model to find the amount of a discount. *(Model should show*
$\frac{\text{percent of discount}}{100} = \frac{\text{amount of discount}}{\text{original price}}$*.)*

Markup

Stores buy goods and then sell them at increased prices. The amount of the price increase is called the **markup**.

Dino's Sports buys volleyballs for $14.99 each. If a volleyball is marked up by 40%, what is its selling price?

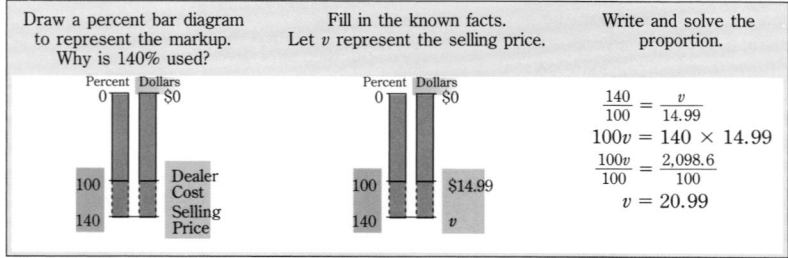

Draw a percent bar diagram to represent the markup. Why is 140% used?	Fill in the known facts. Let v represent the selling price.	Write and solve the proportion.
		$\frac{140}{100} = \frac{v}{14.99}$
		$100v = 140 \times 14.99$
		$\frac{100v}{100} = \frac{2{,}098.6}{100}$
		$v = 20.99$

Dino's selling price of a volleyball is $20.99.

GUIDED PRACTICE

Find the missing value.

1. cost to store: $52.50
   markup: 50%
   selling price: ▓
   $78.75

2. cost to store: $25
   markup: ▓%
   selling price: $45
   80%

3. cost to store: ▓
   markup: 40%
   selling price: $32.55
   $23.25

PRACTICE

The cost to Dino's Sports is given. Find the selling price.

4. baseball bat: $12.00
   markup: 45% **$17.40**

5. baseball: $9.50
   markup: 100% **$19**

6. soccer ball: $3.25
   markup: 80% **$5.85**

7. swim goggles: $5.30
   markup: 120% **$11.66**

8. sport bag: $7.99
   markup: 60% **$12.78**

9. fishing pole: $15.99
   markup: 65% **$26.38**

10. Dino's buys a shirt for $15.99, marks it up 50%, and sells it at a 25% discount. What is the profit? **$2**

11. Dino's sells a bicycle for $280. The markup was 40%. What did Dino's pay for the bike? **$200**

*12. A dozen junior tennis rackets are bought for a total of $96. Dino's marks them up by 40%. What is the selling price of *each* racket? **$11.20**

*13. **IN YOUR WORDS** If Dino's marks up an item by 50% and then sells it at a 50% discount, do they make a profit? Explain. **no; 100% + 50% = 150%, 50% of 150% = 75%, 75% < 100%**

LESSON 11-5   359

2 TEACH Lesson 11-5

✓ **MATERIALS CHECKLIST:** Percent Bar Transparency

After students work through the example, display the transparency and have them explain how to fill in the percent bar diagram for each of these problems:

What is the percent of markup if a store owner sells an item that cost $80 for $100? *(25%)*

What was the original price of an item if the selling price of $105 includes a markup of 40%? *($75)*

SUMMARIZE/ASSESS   **How much profit does a store make on 1,000 swim caps if it buys the caps at $1.50 each, marks them up 50%, and sells them all?** *(The amount of markup is $.75 per cap; $.75 × 1,000 = $750 profit.)*

3 FOLLOW-UP

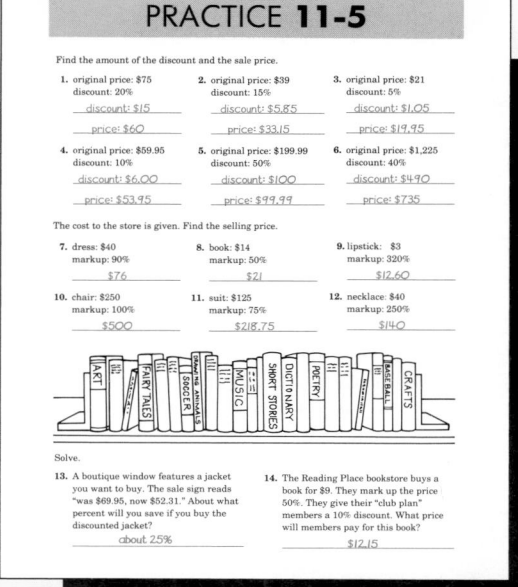

PRACTICE 11-5

Find the amount of the discount and the sale price.

1. original price: $75
   discount: 20%
   discount: $15
   price: $60

2. original price: $39
   discount: 15%
   discount: $5.85
   price: $33.15

3. original price: $21
   discount: 5%
   discount: $1.05
   price: $19.95

4. original price: $59.95
   discount: 10%
   discount: $6.00
   price: $53.95

5. original price: $199.99
   discount: 50%
   discount: $100
   price: $99.99

6. original price: $1,225
   discount: 40%
   discount: $490
   price: $735

The cost to the store is given. Find the selling price.

7. dress: $40
   markup: 90%
   $76

8. book: $14
   markup: 50%
   $21

9. lipstick: $3
   markup: 320%
   $12.60

10. chair: $250
    markup: 100%
    $500

11. suit: $125
    markup: 75%
    $218.75

12. necklace: $40
    markup: 250%
    $140

Solve.

13. A boutique window features a jacket you want to buy. The sale sign reads "was $69.95, now $52.31." About what percent will you save if you buy the discounted jacket? **about 25%**

14. The Reading Place bookstore buys a book for $9. They mark up the price 50%. They give their "club plan" members a 10% discount. What price will members pay for this book? **$12.15**

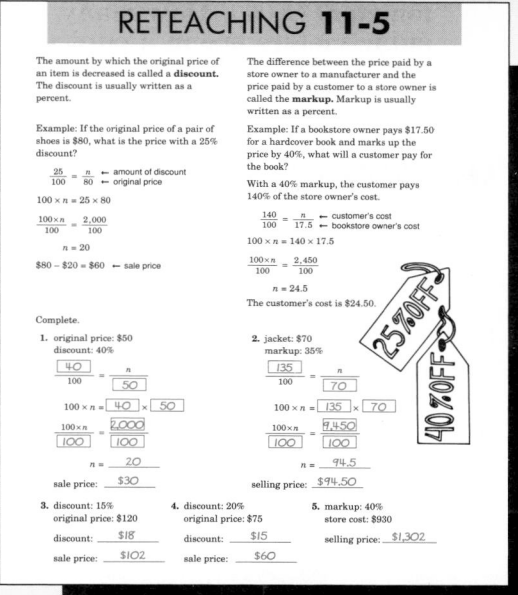

RETEACHING 11-5

The amount by which the original price of an item is decreased is called a **discount**. The discount is usually written as a percent.

Example: If the original price of a pair of shoes is $80, what is the price with a 25% discount?

$\frac{25}{100} = \frac{n}{80}$ ← amount of discount
                    ← original price

$100 \times n = 25 \times 80$

$\frac{100 \times n}{100} = \frac{2{,}000}{100}$

$n = 20$

$80 - 20 = 60$ ← sale price

The difference between the price paid by a store owner to a manufacturer and the price paid by a customer to a store owner is called the **markup**. Markup is usually written as a percent.

Example: If a bookstore owner pays $17.50 for a hardcover book and marks up the price by 40%, what will a customer pay for the book?

With a 40% markup, the customer pays 140% of the store owner's cost.

$\frac{140}{100} = \frac{n}{17.5}$ ← customer's cost
                      ← bookstore owner's cost

$100 \times n = 140 \times 17.5$

$\frac{100 \times n}{100} = \frac{2{,}450}{100}$

$n = 24.5$

The customer's cost is $24.50.

Complete.

1. original price: $50
   discount: 40%
   $\frac{40}{100} = \frac{n}{50}$
   $100 \times n = 40 \times 50$
   $\frac{100 \times n}{100} = \frac{2{,}000}{100}$
   $n = 20$
   sale price: $30

2. jacket: $70
   markup: 35%
   $\frac{135}{100} = \frac{n}{70}$
   $100 \times n = 135 \times 70$
   $\frac{100 \times n}{100} = \frac{9{,}450}{100}$
   $n = 94.5$
   selling price: $94.50

3. discount: 15%
   original price: $120
   discount: $18
   sale price: $102

4. discount: 20%
   original price: $75
   discount: $15
   sale price: $60

5. markup: 40%
   store cost: $930
   selling price: $1,302

ENRICHMENT 11-5

✓ **MATERIALS CHECKLIST:** price tags

Provide each student with several price tags on which you have written and crossed out one price, such as $12.50, and on which you have written a lower sale price such as $10.00. Mark some of the tags with a red dot and explain that an additional 10% discount will be taken on these items. Mark other tags with a blue dot and explain that an additional 25% will be taken on these items. Ask: **What percent of the original price is the sale price?** *(90%; 75%)* **Which is the better deal: a 10% discount and then a 15% discount or a 25% discount?** *(25% discount)*

Lesson Organizer

Objective: Use proportion with circle graphs.

Prior Knowledge: Students should know how to solve all types of percent problems.

Error Analysis and Remediation: See page 369A.

Lesson Resources:
Practice Worksheet 11-6
Reteaching Activity 11-6
Enrichment Worksheet 11-6
Daily Review 11-6

 **Two-Minute Math**

How many meters are in a kilometer? *(1,000)* How many cubic meters are in a cubic kilometer (km³)? *(1,000³)*

1 INTRODUCE

SYMBOLIC ACTIVITY

Help students sketch a circle graph for the following data from a survey on favorite kinds of fruit: Apples—25%, Oranges—20%, Pears—11%, Grapefruit—9%, and Bananas—35%.

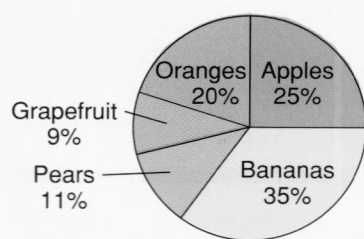

If 100 people were surveyed, how many chose oranges as their favorite fruit? *(20)* grapefruit? *(9)* What other fact or facts do you notice about the graph? *(Answers will vary. Possible answer: The sum of percents = 100%.)*

WHEN YOUR STUDENTS ASK
★ WHY AM I LEARNING THIS? ★

You can use this skill to solve real life problems. Suppose you want to make a circle graph to show how the athletic budget is spent. If you know the amount in the budget and how much is spent in each category, you can create the graph.

Proportions and Circle Graphs

The circle graph shows what happens to the precipitation that falls each year on the land over Earth. About how much precipitation evaporates back into the air each year?

You can use the percents in the circle graph to set up a proportion. Let e represent the precipitation that evaporates, in cubic kilometers.

What Happens to Precipitation on Earth's Land Area

On average, about 96,000 km³ of precipitation fall every year.

$62\frac{1}{2}$ is to 100 as e is to 96,000.

$$\frac{62.5}{100} = \frac{e}{96,000}$$

$$100e = 62.5 \times 96,000$$

$$\frac{100e}{100} = \frac{6,000,000}{100}$$

$$e = 60,000$$

About 60,000 km³ of precipitation evaporates each year.

CRITICAL THINKING What are two ways of finding out how much precipitation runs off the land on Earth in a year? $\frac{37.5}{100} = \frac{r}{96,000}$ or $96,000 - 60,000 = r$

■ **GUIDED PRACTICE** ■

Use the information in the circle graph below to set up a proportion and solve for n.

1. The circle represents 4,200 people.
   a. How many is 25% of the people? **1,050**
   b. How many people are represented by n? **3,150**

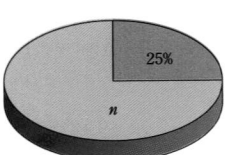

2. The circle represents 180 mi.
   a. How many is 60% of the miles? **108 mi**
   b. How many miles are represented by n? **72 mi**

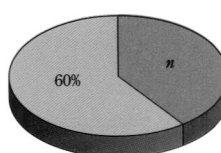

MATH AND SCIENCE

---

2 TEACH

☑ **MATERIALS CHECKLIST:** calculators

What does the unshaded area of the second bar represent? *(It represents the amount of water that runs off.)*

What proportion can be written to find the amount of precipitation, r, that runs off? $\left(\frac{375}{100} = \frac{r}{96,000}\right)$

> ### Chalkboard Example
>
> A circle graph showing the results of a survey of 3,000 people has a section labeled 28.5%. How many people are represented by that section? *(855 people)*

SUMMARIZE/ASSESS With what percent would you label a section on a circle graph representing 640 out of 4,000 people surveyed? $\left(\frac{x}{100} = \frac{640}{4,000}; x = 16;$ *the section should be labeled 16%.)*

Use the information in the circle graph to set up a proportion and solve.

3. On average, about how much precipitation in the United States returns unused to the sea each day?
3.84 km³

4. About how much precipitation in the United States evaporates each day?
11.2 km³

5. About how much precipitation in the United States is used by people each day?
0.96 km³

What Happens to Precipitation in the United States

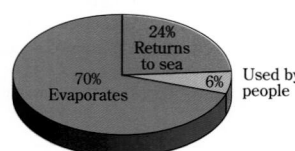

On average, about 16 km³ of precipitation fall every day in the United States.

How Water is Used in the United States

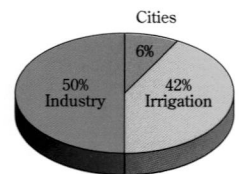
Cities

On average, about 280 billion gallons of water are used each day.

6. About how many gallons of water are used daily for irrigation?
117.6 billion gallons

7. About how many gallons of water do United States industries use each day?
140 billion gallons

8. IN YOUR WORDS How can you find the amount of water used by cities without using percents?
(280 − 117.6 − 140) = 22.4 billion gallons

━━━━━━━━━ PROBLEM SOLVING ━━━━━━━━━

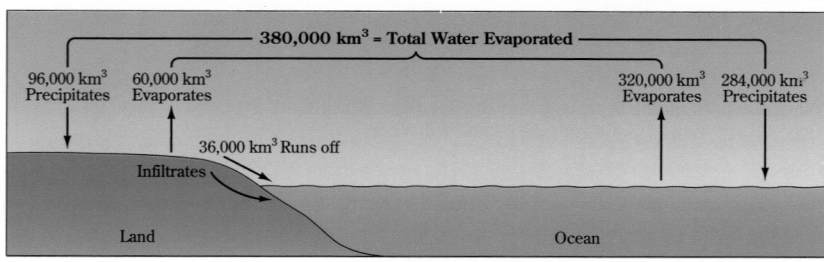

380,000 km³ = Total Water Evaporated

96,000 km³ Precipitates   60,000 km³ Evaporates   320,000 km³ Evaporates   284,000 km³ Precipitates

36,000 km³ Runs off

Infiltrates

Land   Ocean

CHOOSE Use the diagram above. Choices will vary. Suggestions given.
Choose paper and pencil or calculator to solve.

9. What percent of the water that evaporates comes from the oceans?
C; 84.2%

10. What percent of the total precipitation falls on land?
C; 25.3%

*11. IN YOUR WORDS With nearly 320,000 km³ of water evaporating each year from our oceans, why are the water levels not dropping? **The evaporated water returns to the oceans as precipitation and run off.**

MEETING INDIVIDUAL NEEDS

For Students Who Are . . .

Acquiring English Proficiency Discuss the meanings of *precipitation, evaporation,* and *run off.* Remind students that a cubic kilometer may be written km³.

Gifted and Talented Have each student find a circle graph in a science or social studies book and write two questions about the graph that can be solved using proportions. Students can trade, study the graphs, and answer the questions.

Today's Problem

Why aren't concentric circles (one within the other sharing the same center point) used instead of sections to show categories in a circle graph? If you wanted to divide a circle with a radius of 8 cm into four equal areas, what would be the radius of the smallest circle? *(With concentric circles, it is too difficult to compare areas; area largest circle = $\pi(8)^2 = 64\pi$; area smallest circle = $\frac{1}{4}(64\pi) = 16\pi$, the smallest radius is equal to 4 cm, since $16\pi = \pi(4)^2$.)*

---

3 FOLLOW-UP

PRACTICE 11-6

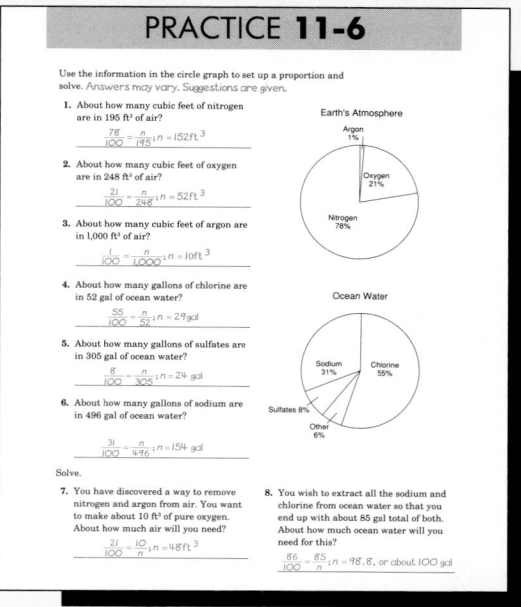

Use the information in the circle graph to set up a proportion and solve. *Answers may vary. Suggestions are given.*

1. About how many cubic feet of nitrogen are in 195 ft³ of air?
$\frac{78}{100} = \frac{n}{195}$; $n = 152$ ft³

2. About how many cubic feet of oxygen are in 248 ft³ of air?
$\frac{21}{100} = \frac{n}{248}$; $n = 52$ ft³

3. About how many cubic feet of argon are in 1,000 ft³ of air?
$\frac{1}{100} = \frac{n}{1,000}$; $n = 10$ ft³

4. About how many gallons of chlorine are in 52 gal of ocean water?
$\frac{55}{100} = \frac{n}{52}$; $n = 29$ gal

5. About how many gallons of sulfates are in 305 gal of ocean water?
$\frac{8}{100} = \frac{n}{305}$; $n = 24$ gal

6. About how many gallons of sodium are in 496 gal of ocean water?
$\frac{31}{100} = \frac{n}{496}$; $n = 154$ gal

Solve.

7. You have discovered a way to remove nitrogen and argon from air. You want to make about 10 ft³ of pure oxygen. About how much air will you need?
$\frac{21}{100} = \frac{10}{n}$; $n = 48$ ft³

8. You wish to extract all the sodium and chlorine from ocean water so that you end up with about 85 gal total of both. About how much ocean water will you need for this?
$\frac{86}{100} = \frac{85}{n}$; $n = 98.8$, or about 100 gal

RETEACHING 11-6

Present a circle graph titled "Where I Like to Spend My Vacation" that has sections labeled 25%, ocean; 40%, city; 20%, lake; 15% stay home. Tell students that 120 people were surveyed. **You can set up a proportion to find how many people liked each type of vacation spot.** Give students the following "frame" for the proportion:

$$\frac{\text{part of percent}}{\text{whole \%}} = \frac{\text{part surveyed}}{\text{total surveyed}}$$

Have students write the appropriate numbers in the frame to set up and solve proportions that will help find the number that preferred each type of spot. (ocean: 30; city: 48; lake: 24; home: 8)

ENRICHMENT 11-6

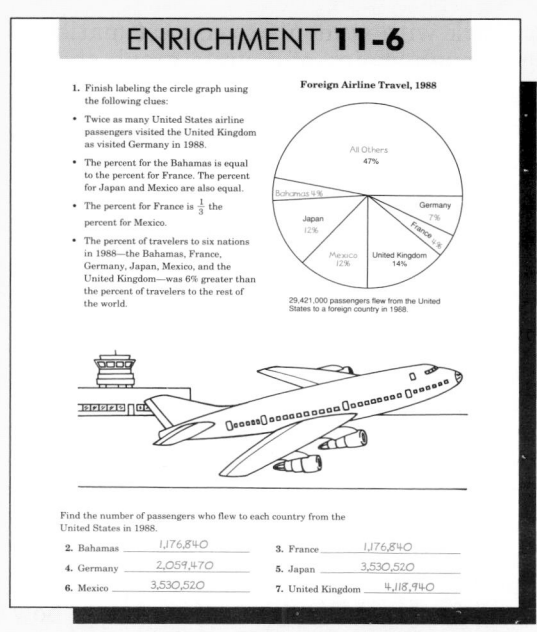

1. Finish labeling the circle graph using the following clues:

- Twice as many United States airline passengers visited the United Kingdom as visited Germany in 1988.
- The percent for the Bahamas is equal to the percent for France. The percent for Japan and Mexico are also equal.
- The percent for France is $\frac{1}{3}$ the percent for Mexico.
- The percent of travelers to six nations in 1988—the Bahamas, France, Germany, Japan, Mexico, and the United Kingdom—was 6% greater than the percent of travelers to the rest of the world.

Foreign Airline Travel, 1988

29,421,000 passengers flew from the United States to a foreign country in 1988.

Find the number of passengers who flew to each country from the United States in 1988.

2. Bahamas _1,176,840_
3. France _1,176,840_
4. Germany _2,059,470_
5. Japan _3,530,520_
6. Mexico _3,530,520_
7. United Kingdom _4,118,940_

Lesson Organizer

Objective: Solve problems by estimating with percent.

Prior Knowledge: Students should know how to solve all types of percent problems.

Lesson Resources:
Practice Worksheet 11-7
Reteaching Activity 11-7
Enrichment Worksheet 11-7
Daily Review 11-7

Two-Minute Math

Does a store owner make money on a $50 item that is marked up 50% and then sold for 50% off?
(No, the markup price is $75; at 50% off, the sale price is $37.50. Owner loses $50 − $37.50 or $12.50.)

1 INTRODUCE

SYMBOLIC ACTIVITY

1. On the chalkboard, list the music categories from the circle graph on page 362.

2. Do a similar survey for your students and record the numbers. (Each student should select only one kind of music.)

3. Work with students to use estimation to do a rough sketch of a circle graph showing the results.

4. Have students compare the sketch with the circle graph on page 362 and discuss any similarities and differences.

WHEN YOUR STUDENTS ASK
★ WHY AM I LEARNING THIS? ★

You can use this skill to interpret real life data. For example, if a circle graph shows that 28% of the 500 people surveyed eat cereal for breakfast, you can estimate how many people are being described. *(140 people)*

Problem Solving:
Estimating with Percents

A survey was made recently in Houston, Texas, of the music preferences of 990 teen-agers. The circle graph shows the results.

About how many teen-agers preferred rock and roll?
all teen-agers surveyed

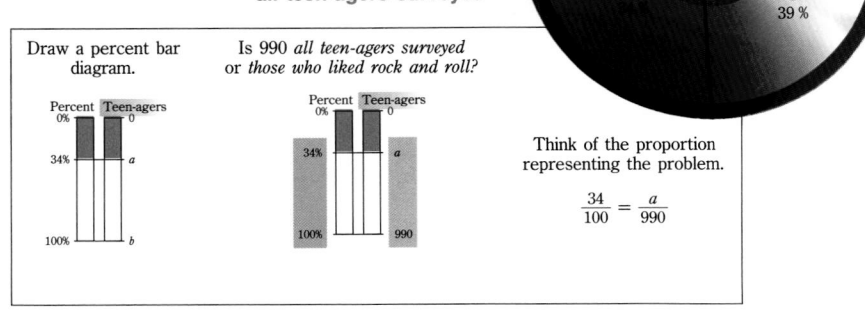

Draw a percent bar diagram.

Is 990 *all teen-agers surveyed* or *those who liked rock and roll?*

Think of the proportion representing the problem.

$$\frac{34}{100} = \frac{a}{990}$$

There are two ways to estimate the solution.

Method 1: Since 34% is close to $33\frac{1}{3}\%$, or $\frac{1}{3}$, think:

$$\frac{1}{3} = \frac{\equiv}{990}.$$

Method 2: Since 990 is close to 1,000, think:

$$\frac{34}{100} = \frac{\equiv}{1,000}.$$

Now use both methods to estimate the solution. Which method was easier? Why?   **330; 340; Answers will vary.**

■■■■■■■■■■■■■■■■■■■■■■■■■■ **GUIDED PRACTICE** ■■■■■■■■■■■■■■■■

Use the circle graph above to answer.

1. **a.** What percent of the teen-agers preferred country-and-western music?   **5%**

   b. What is 1% of 990? 5% of 990?   **9.9; 49.5**

   c. Estimate the number of teen-agers who preferred country-and-western music.   **50**

   d. If you can estimate 5% of 990 how can you use it to estimate the number of teen-agers who preferred new-wave music (17%)?   **Multiply 5% of 990 by 3.**

---

2 TEACH

Emphasize that the numbers in a problem situation are often a factor in deciding which method will be easier to use.

What are two ways to estimate the number of teenagers who prefer rap music? *(Since 39% is close to 40% or $\frac{2}{5}$, think: $\frac{2}{5} = \frac{n}{990}$; since 990 is close to 1,000, think: $\frac{39}{100} = \frac{n}{1,000}$.)*

How can knowing 10% of 990 help you estimate the number of teenagers who prefer country and western? *(Find half of that number, or 5%.)*

SUMMARIZE/ASSESS   Estimate the solution to 19% of 990.
(20% or $\frac{1}{5}$ of 990 = 198; $\frac{19}{100} = \frac{190}{1,000}$; or 10% + 10% of 990 = 99 + 99 = 198; all answers are estimates.)

PRACTICE

Use the circle graph to estimate the solution.
Accept reasonable estimates. Suggestions given.

Age Preference of 990 Seventh Grade Students

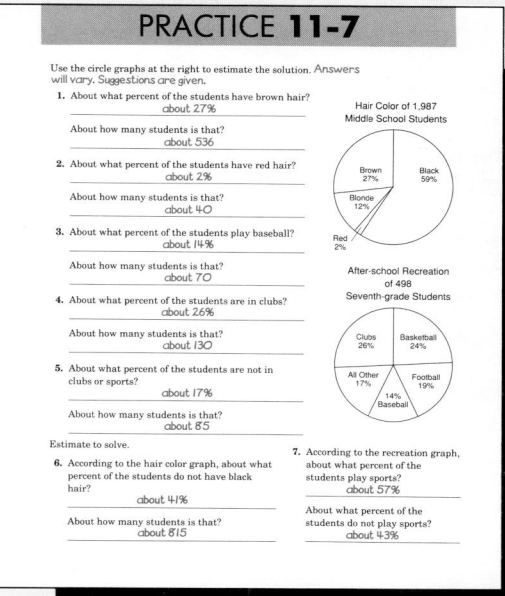

To be older 63%
To be younger 10%
To be same age 27%

2. About what percent of students prefer to be the same age as they are? About how many students is that?
27%; ≈270

3. About what percent of students would prefer to be older? About how many students is that?
63%; ≈630

4. About what percent of students would prefer to be younger? About how many students is that?
10%; 99

 CHOOSE Choose any strategy to estimate the solution. **Choices will vary. Suggestions given.**

5. The Longhorn Music Shop made $17,946 during a recent sale. If their profit was 15% of their total sales, about how much profit was made during the sale? **≈$2,700**

6. A local radio station plays country-and-western music for 21 min of every hour. About what percent of each hour is country-and-western music played? **≈33⅓%**

7. A rock-and-roll CD is on sale for $3.05 less than its regular price. If the discount is 25%, about what is the regular price of the CD? **≈$12**

8. To buy a $595 CD player, Jake makes an 18% down payment. About how much is the down payment? **≈$120**

*9. Lucia saves 50% of her weekly paycheck and spends 50% of what is left on audio tapes. About how much did Lucia earn one week if she bought $14.98 worth of audio tapes? **≈$60**

Critical Thinking

Work with a partner.
1. How many quarters are there in $2.75? **11**

2. $2.75 \div 0.25$ **11**   3. $275 \div 25$ **11**   4. $2\frac{3}{4} \div \frac{1}{4}$ **11**

• How did you solve Exercise 1? Did you use a different method to solve Exercises 2–4? **Answers will vary.**

• Which method is easier? Defend your choice.

MEETING INDIVIDUAL NEEDS

For Students Who Are . . .

Acquiring English Proficiency Discuss the meaning of *music preferences, preferred,* and *survey.*

Gifted and Talented Assign the technology lesson on page 374.

Having Reading Difficulties Pair students with an able reader for the Problem Solving exercises.

Today's Problem

Rob works in a supermarket. He was asked to create a display of canned goods by stacking the cans in the shape of a triangle, with the bottom row having ten cans. A case contains 24 cans. About how many cases will Rob need? *(Since each row of cans is reduced by one as you go up, the display is ten rows high. The number of cans is 55. The number of cases is 55 ÷ 24 = 2.3, so Rob needs 3 cases.)*

---

3 FOLLOW-UP

PRACTICE 11-7

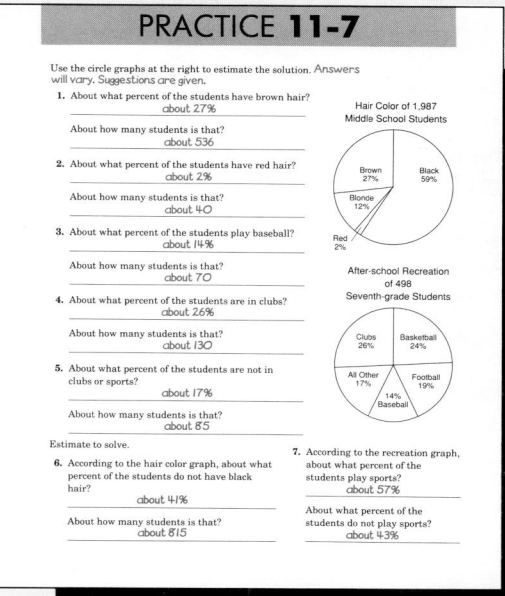

Use the circle graphs at the right to estimate the solution. Answers will vary. Suggestions are given.

1. About what percent of the students have brown hair?
about 27%

About how many students is that?
about 536

2. About what percent of the students have red hair?
about 2%

About how many students is that?
about 40

3. About what percent of the students play baseball?
about 14%

About how many students is that?
about 70

4. About what percent of the students are in clubs?
about 26%

About how many students is that?
about 130

5. About what percent of the students are not in clubs or sports?
about 17%

About how many students is that?
about 85

Estimate to solve.

6. According to the hair color graph, about what percent of the students do not have black hair?
about 41%

About how many students is that?
about 815

7. According to the recreation graph, about what percent of the students play sports?
about 57%

About what percent of the students do not play sports?
about 43%

Hair Color of 1,987 Middle School Students
Brown 27% Black 59% Blonde 12% Red 2%

After-school Recreation of 498 Seventh-grade Students
Clubs 26% Basketball 24% All Other 17% Football 19% Baseball 14%

RETEACHING 11-7

Have students work in small groups. Survey the class to find out how many buttons each student has on his or her clothing that day. Ask them to set up a proportion to find the percent with no buttons. For example, in a class of 29, they may write $\frac{x}{100} = \frac{19}{29}$. Have the students solve the proportion. Repeat for the other categories. Make a circle graph on the board to show the percent with no buttons, with 1–5, with 6–10, and with 10 or more.

ENRICHMENT 11-7

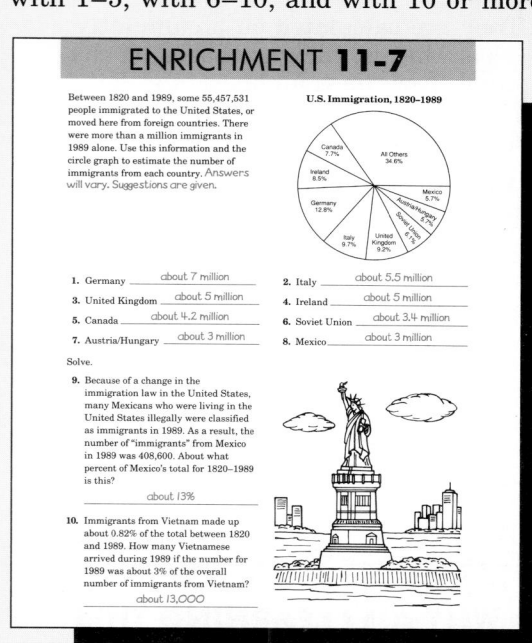

Between 1820 and 1989, some 55,457,531 people immigrated to the United States, or moved here from foreign countries. There were more than a million immigrants in 1989 alone. Use this information and the circle graph to estimate the number of immigrants from each country. Answers will vary. Suggestions are given.

U.S. Immigration, 1820–1989
Canada 7.7% All Others 34.6% Ireland 8.5% Mexico 5.7% Germany 12.8% Italy 9.7% United Kingdom 9.2% Soviet Union

1. Germany ___ about 7 million   **2.** Italy ___ about 5.5 million

3. United Kingdom ___ about 5 million   **4.** Ireland ___ about 5 million

5. Canada ___ about 4.2 million   **6.** Soviet Union ___ about 3.4 million

7. Austria/Hungary ___ about 3 million   **8.** Mexico ___ about 3 million

Solve.

9. Because of a change in the immigration law in the United States, many Mexicans who were living in the United States illegally were classified as immigrants in 1989. As a result, the number of "immigrants" from Mexico in 1989 was 408,600. About what percent of Mexico's total for 1820–1989 is this?
about 13%

10. Immigrants from Vietnam made up about 0.82% of the total between 1820 and 1989. How many Vietnamese arrived during 1989 if the number for 1989 was about 3% of the overall number of immigrants from Vietnam?
about 13,000

Objective: Solve problems creatively.

Prior Knowledge: Students should be able to interpret and apply a formula.

Lesson Resources:
Daily Review 11-8

Two-Minute Math

Use the Table of Numbers on the inside back cover. Divide each number in row G by 0.3. Write answers to the nearest tenth. *(16.0; 32.3; 1.8; 3.7; 11.7; 5.3; 24.0; 9.7; 8.0)*

1 PREPARE

SYMBOLIC ACTIVITY

Tell students that in 1990, George Brett of the Kansas City Royals baseball team had a batting average of .382. **Can anyone explain what a batting average is?** *(Possible answer: a number obtained by dividing the number of hits by the number of times a player is at bat.)*

Discuss other aspects of batting averages:

- They are calculated on a cumulative basis; that is, they are based on the number of times a player is at bat during the whole season, not only during a single game.

- They are customarily expressed as decimals to the thousandths place.

WHEN YOUR STUDENTS ASK
★ WHY AM I LEARNING THIS? ★

You can relate this lesson to real life through the sports pages of newspapers. Batting averages show how statistics can be used to evaluate or compare teams and players.

PROBLEM SOLVING

Investigating Batting Averages

Next time you watch or listen to a baseball game, notice what different statistics are mentioned. A player's batting average is the ratio of the number of hits the player gets to the number of times the player is at bat. It can be computed using this formula:

$$B = \frac{h}{a} \text{ (written as a decimal rounded to thousandths)}$$

where h = number of hits
a = number of times at bat

The table has batting data for a baseball team that plays 20 games a season.

Player	First half of season		Second half of season		Entire season	
	At–bats	Hits	At–bats	Hits	At–bats	Hits
Mario	60	20	70	12	130	32
Jack	75	24	50	8	125	32
Rita	58	12	68	7	126	19
Ana	73	15	48	5	121	20
Yoko	62	13	72	8	134	21
Omar	72	16	52	6	124	22
Julia	60	10	60	10	120	20
Jason	58	11	58	11	116	22
Takashi	55	9	55	8	110	17
Lani	72	10	74	10	146	20
Kate	30	6	35	4	65	10
David	37	8	25	3	62	11

Calculators should be available for lengthy computations with data.

2 EXPLORE

☑ MATERIALS CHECKLIST: calculators

Assign students to work with a partner for these activities.

What does a batting average of .500 mean? *(one hit out of every two times at bat)* **When would this type of average be most likely to occur?** *(Possible answer: It is most likely during the first game of the season; a player may frequently have one hit out of two times at bat.)*

How would you estimate the batting average of a player who had 9 hits out of 29 times at bat? *(Possible answer: $\frac{9}{29}$ is close to $\frac{9}{27}$, which is $\frac{1}{3}$ or a batting average of .333; $\frac{9}{29}$ would be a little less than .333.)*

SUMMARIZE/ASSESS   **What mathematics skills did you use to investigate batting averages?** *(Answers will vary. Example: division, using a formula.)*

☑ **MATERIALS CHECKLIST:** $7.41 in play money to make these denominations: 78¢, 64¢, 93¢, 81¢, 92¢, 68¢, 96¢, 87¢ and 82¢

Let students work with play money to find averages. Give nine volunteers the play money designated above. Put students with 78¢, 64¢, 93¢ and 81¢ into one group and the rest of the students in another. Explain that sharing money equally is like finding the average of the money. Have students in each group share the money equally. Ask: If we share equally, will each student have exactly 80¢? Explain. *(No, there will be one extra penny because the sizes of the groups are not the same).*

Work with a partner. Use the table on page 364 and a calculator.

1. Find each player's batting average for the first half of the season, the second half of the season, and the entire season.   See page 369b.

2. Who had the highest batting average for the entire season?
   Jack

3. Did that person have the highest batting average in the first half of the season? in the second half?
   no; no

4. Compare Mario's and Jack's batting averages for the first half of the season, the second half of the season, and the entire season. Try to explain why such a situation can happen.
   Accept reasonable answers.

5. Compare the first half, second half, and season batting averages for Mario, Ana, and David. Does it seem as if you can find the seasonal batting average by averaging the batting averages for the two halves of the season?
   no

6. Compare the first half, second half, and season batting averages for Julia, Takashi, and Lani. Does it seem as if you can find the seasonal batting average by averaging the batting averages for the two halves of the season?
   yes

7. Do your answers to Exercises 5 and 6 agree? Look for differences between the two groups of batting averages that might explain the reason.
   Accept reasonable answers.

CHAPTER 11   365

MEETING INDIVIDUAL NEEDS

For Students Who Are . . .

Acquiring English Proficiency Pair students with an English-proficient student for Exercises 1–7. Encourage students to read the problems aloud to each other.

Gifted and Talented Have pairs of students use almanacs or other references to compile a list of outstanding batting averages for the last ten years. Students can display this data as a bar graph.

Working 2 or 3 Grades Below Level Review division and rounding decimals to the thousandths place.

Today's Problem

What number does each letter in this problem stand for?

$$
\begin{array}{r}
B3 \\
1A\overline{)3BB} \\
\underline{BC} \\
AB \\
\underline{AB} \\
\end{array}
\qquad (A = 4,\ B = 2,\ C = 8)
$$

Lesson Organizer

Objective: Review operations with whole numbers, decimals, fractions and mixed numbers; fraction concepts; solving proportions; percents.

Lesson Resources:
Daily Review 11-9

These pages provide students with a review of computing with whole numbers, decimals, fractions, and mixed numbers; writing fractions in lowest terms and as percents; finding percents; solving proportions; and choosing a computation method to solve problems involving whole numbers, fractions, and percents. Remind students that these pages review skills covered in previous chapters and will help them to do a self-check to see how well they remember what they have learned.

Mixed Review

Compute.

1. $17{,}340 \div 68$ **255**
2. $922 + 211$ **1,133**
3. $6{,}741 - 5{,}630$ **1,111**
4. 412×42 **17,304**
5. $895.43 - 312.44$ **582.99**
6. $73.01 + 147.77$ **220.78**
7. $431.6 - 1.27$ **430.33**
8. $2{,}344.8 \div 586.2$ **4**
9. $\frac{7}{8} \div \frac{1}{2}$ $1\frac{3}{4}$
10. $5\frac{1}{4} \times 5\frac{1}{4}$ $27\frac{9}{16}$
11. $9\frac{5}{6} + 2\frac{3}{4}$ $12\frac{7}{12}$
12. $2\frac{1}{3} - 1\frac{1}{2}$ $\frac{5}{6}$
13. $\frac{7}{8} \times 1\frac{1}{3}$ $1\frac{1}{6}$
14. $1\frac{5}{8} \div \frac{1}{2}$ $3\frac{1}{4}$
15. $6\frac{8}{12} + \frac{5}{6}$ $7\frac{1}{2}$
16. $4\frac{1}{2} - 3\frac{7}{8}$ $\frac{5}{8}$

Write as a percent.

17. $\frac{3}{4}$ **75%**
18. $\frac{2}{3}$ $66\frac{2}{3}\%$
19. 0.35 **35%**
20. 0.7 **70%**
21. 0.005 **0.5%**
22. $\frac{9}{4}$ **225%**

Write as a fraction in lowest terms.

23. 0.4 $\frac{2}{5}$
24. 0.04 $\frac{1}{25}$
25. 45% $\frac{9}{20}$
26. 6% $\frac{3}{50}$
27. 120% $1\frac{1}{5}$
28. 0.5% $\frac{1}{200}$

Write as a decimal.

29. $\frac{3}{8}$ **0.375**
30. $\frac{4}{5}$ **0.8**
31. 16% **0.16**
32. 4% **0.04**
33. 0.25% **0.0025**
34. 105% **1.05**

Find the missing number.

35. 30% of ▦ is 54. **180**
36. ▦% of 35 is 14. **40**
37. 180% of 320 is ▦. **576**
38. 30% of 423 is ▦. **126.9**
39. 1% of ▦ is 80. **8,000**
40. ▦% of 20 is 40. **200**
41. 16% of ▦ is 36. **225**
42. ▦% of 56 is 28. **50**
43. 150% of 400 is ▦. **600**
44. $33\frac{1}{3}\%$ of 423 is ▦. **141**
45. 0.5% of ▦ is 80. **16,000**
46. ▦% of 30 is 45. **150**

Create a true proportion by solving for n.

47. $\frac{3}{4} = \frac{15}{n}$ **20**
48. $\frac{2}{3} = \frac{n}{108}$ **72**
49. $\frac{35}{20} = \frac{5}{n}$ $2\frac{6}{7}$
50. $\frac{9}{5} = \frac{n}{100}$ **180**
51. $\frac{3}{4} = \frac{n}{15}$ $11\frac{1}{4}$
52. $\frac{24}{36} = \frac{n}{108}$ **72**
53. $\frac{3.5}{20} = \frac{5}{n}$ $28\frac{4}{7}$
54. $\frac{9}{4} = \frac{n}{100}$ **225**

366   LESSON 11-9

MATH AND SOCIAL STUDIES

> **CHOOSE** Choose estimation, mental math, paper and pencil, or calculator to solve. **Choices will vary. Suggestions given.**

55. Of China's working population of over 520 million people, 70% are farmers. How many people is that?
p; 364 million people

56. About 78 million of China's 520 million workers are in manufacturing or mining. What percent of China's workers is that?
p; 15%

57. The Qin dynasty, which completed the Great Wall of China, ruled from 221 B.C. to 206 B.C. For how many years was the Qin dynasty in power?
m; 15 yr

58. The Great Wall covers 4,000 mi of the northern border of China. In 1794, the Great Wall celebrated its 2,000th birthday. How old is it today?
m; Answer depends on current year.

59. Eastern China contains 50% of the land area but only 10% of the population of the country. If about 110 million people live in eastern China, about what is the country's total population?
e; 1,100,000,000

60. About $\frac{1}{5}$ of the world's population live in China. If China recently had a population of about 1,098,000,000, about what was the population of the world at that time?
e; ≈5,500,000,000

61. In 1990, China produced goods valued at $225 billion.

a. About how much money came from agricultural goods? **c; $92.25 billion**

b. About how much money came from nonagricultural sources? **c; $132.75 billion**

62 **CREATE YOUR OWN** Write a math problem about China. Give it to a friend to solve. **Check students' work.**

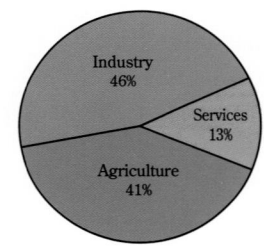

CHAPTER 11 367

MULTICULTURAL NOTE

The Great Wall of China is the longest structure ever built, and was once as long as 6,200 miles. The wall was built by the Chinese between 400 B.C. and 1600 A.D. as protection from northern invaders.

CHAPTER Checkup

This chapter checkup provides a quick language and vocabulary review, a test for the chapter, and suggestions for student Learning Log entries.

Language and Vocabulary

Some key language and vocabulary ideas from this chapter are reinforced here.

Test

The test can be used either as a test or as a review of the chapter prior to administering the test worksheets found in the Teacher's Resource Book.

The following guide will help you determine percentage scores.

Score	Percent	Score	Percent
22	100%	11	50%
21	95	10	45
20	91	9	41
19	86	8	36
18	82	7	32
17	77	6	27
16	73	5	23
15	68	4	18
14	64	3	14
13	59	2	9
12	55	1	5

Each test has three sections: concepts, skills, and problem solving. These sections provide students with exposure to the format used on standardized tests.

Use this chart to identify the Management Objectives tested for this chapter.

Items	Management Objectives	Pages
1–6, 17–19	**11A** Use proportion to solve percent problems.	352–353, 360–361
7–16	**11B** Determine discount and markup.	358–359
20–22	**11C** Problem Solving: Use percent of commission. Estimate with percent.	354–355, 362–363

CHAPTER CHECKUP

LANGUAGE & VOCABULARY

Write *true* or *false*. If false, give a counterexample.

1. If one store discounts an item 20% and another store discounts the same item 30%, you will save money by shopping at the second store. **false; depends on original price**

2. A store offering no discount can have a lower price than a store selling the same item at a 15% discount. **true**

3. A store marks up prices in order to make a profit. **true**

4. A large markup followed by a large discount can result in the same selling price as a small markup followed by a small discount. **true**

5. A 30% discount on an original price of $150 is a smaller discount than a 15% discount on an original price of $150. **false; the discount is doubled.**

TEST

CONCEPTS

Solve using a proportion. *(pages 352–353)*

1. 40% of what number is 8.6? **21.5**
2. 80% of what number is 27? **33.75**
3. 16 is what percent of 50? **32%**
4. 4.2 is what percent of 12? **35%**
5. What percent of 30 is 72? **240%**
6. 2% of what number is 55? **2,750**

SKILLS

Find the amount of the discount and the sale price. *(page 358)*

7. Original price: $29.95
   Discount: 20% **$5.99; $23.96**

8. Original price: $38.50
   Discount: 25% **$9.63; $28.87**

9. Original price: $175.40
   Discount: 15% **$26.31; $149.09**

10. Original price: $1,860
    Discount: 35% **$651; $1,209**

CHAPTER TEST • FORM A

Solve using a proportion. (pp. 350–353, 360–361) IIA

1. 20% of what number is 6.5? _32.5_
2. What percent of 8 is 5? _62.5%_
3. What percent of 80 is 16? _20%_
4. 40% of *n* is 24? _n = 60_

5. The circle represents 3,600 students.
   a. How many is 40% of the students? _1,440 students_
   b. How many students are represented by *n*? _2,160 students_

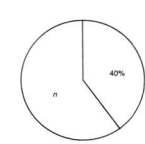

Find the missing value. (pp. 358–359) IIB

6. original price: $64.60
   discount: 25%
   amount of discount: _$16.15_

7. original price: $1,220
   discount: 15%
   selling price: _$1,037_

8. cost to store: $92
   mark-up: 35%
   selling price: _$124.20_

9. cost to store: $7.50
   mark-up: 50%
   amount of mark-up: _$3.75_

10. cost to store: $48.75
    mark-up: _60%_
    selling price: $78

CHAPTER TEST • FORM A

(pp. 354–355, 362–363) IIC

Use a proportion to solve.

11. Olga earns an 8% commission on sales plus a base salary of $1,200/mo. Last month she earned a total of $2,500. What were her total sales? _$16,250_

12. Charlene earns a 6% commission for selling furniture. For selling furniture to one family, she earned $570 in commission. What was the value of the furniture she sold? _$9,500_

13. Chris earned $3,300 in commission for selling a $22,000 building lot. What percent is his commission? _15%_

Use the circle graph below to estimate the solution. Accept reasonable estimates.

14. What percent of students prefer to watch team sports? _52%_
    About how many students is that? _about 425 students_

15. What percent of students prefer to watch individual competitions? _38%_
    About how many students is this? _about 340 students_

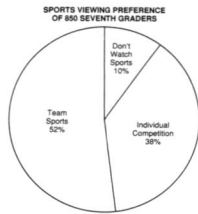

SPORTS VIEWING PREFERENCE OF 850 SEVENTH GRADERS

The cost to the store and the markup are given. Find the selling price. *(page 359)*

11. Coat: $45 **$78.75**

Markup: 75%

12. Computer: $525 **$945**

Markup: 80%

13. Game: $15 **$31.50**

Markup: 110%

14. Book: $9 **$14.85**

Markup: 65%

15. Shoes: $35 **$61.25**

Markup: 75%

16. Glasses: $38.50 **$77**

Markup: 100%

Use the information in the circle graph to set up a proportion and solve. *(pages 360–361)*

17. How many students chose spring vacation as their favorite?
138 students

18. How many students chose summer?
270 students

19. How many students chose winter?
192 students

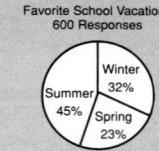

Favorite School Vacations
600 Responses

Winter 32%
Summer 45%
Spring 23%

━━━━━━━ **PROBLEM SOLVING** ━━━━━━━

Use a proportion to solve. *(pages 354–355)*

20. Sally earned $3,000 in salary and commission one month. Of this, $1,800 was commission on $22,500 in sales.

  a. How much did Sally earn in commission? **$1,800**

  b. What proportion will give Sally's percent of commission? $\frac{x}{100} = \frac{1,800}{22,500}$

  c. What percent of sales is Sally's commission? **8%**

Estimate. *(pages 362–363)* **Accept reasonable estimates. Suggestion given.**

21. During one January, it rained 9 d. About what percent of the days did it rain? **about 30%**

22. At a sale, a discount of 35% was offered on all computers. How much would you save on a computer that regularly sells for $1,860? What is the sale price? **$651; $1,209**

LEARNING LOG

Write the answers in your learning log. **Answers will vary. Suggestions given.**

1. A newspaper advertisement says "Up to 50% off." Explain what this means to you. **Prices could be reduced between 0% and 50%.**

2. A toy store is having a 20% off everything sale. How would you estimate the sale price of items in the store? **Divide by five and subtract.**

Note that the same numbers are used in Exercises 10 and 22.

CHAPTER 11 369

Problem Solving

Item 20 has three parts:
a. literal—this is a reading comprehension question.
b. interpretive—this involves interpretation using the facts given.
c. applied—students use a strategy or skill to find an answer.

Item 10 in the skill section and item 22 in the problem solving section use the same numbers.

This will help you informally assess how your students transfer from numerical skills to word problems.

For scoring problem solving items, you may wish to use partial credit. If a student uses the correct strategy but gets a wrong answer, give the student two points toward the total percent score.

Learning Log

These are suggestions for writing about some topics taught in the chapter. The students keep their learning logs from the start of the school year through the end.

CHAPTER TEST • FORM **B**

Solve using a proportion. (pp. 350–353, 360–361) IIA

1. 40% of what number is 4.5? __11.25__

2. What percent of 16 is 2? __12.5%__

3. 25 is what percent of 5? __500%__

4. 30% of n is 18? __n = 60__

5. The circle represents 4,500 people.

  a. How many is 30% of the people?
  __1,350 people__

  b. How many people are represented by n? __3,150 people__

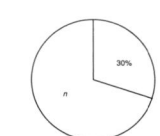

30%

n

Find the missing value. (pp. 358–359) IIB

6. original price: $51.50

discount: 20%

amount of discount: __$10.30__

7. original price: $1,380

discount: 15%

selling price: __$1,173__

8. cost to store: $65

mark-up: 25%

selling price: __$81.25__

9. cost to store: $8.50

mark-up: 50%

amount of mark-up: __$4.25__

10. cost to store: $25.50

mark-up: __40%__

selling price: $35.70

CHAPTER TEST • FORM **B**

(pp. 354–355, 362–363) IIC

Use a proportion to solve.

11. Ivan earns a 6% commission on sales plus a base salary of $1,050/mo. Last month he earned a total of $2,205. What were his total sales? __$19,250__

12. Phyllis earns a 4% commission for selling real estate. For selling a house she earned $9,000 in commission. What was the value of the house she sold? __$225,000__

13. Steve earned $1,500 in commission for selling a $25,000 car. What percent is his commission? __6%__

Use the circle graph below to estimate the solution. Accept reasonable estimates.

14. What percent of students would prefer to own a 2-door sedan? __30%__

About how many students is that? __about 300 students__

15. What percent of students would prefer to own a sport car? __46%__

About how many students is that? __about 450 students__

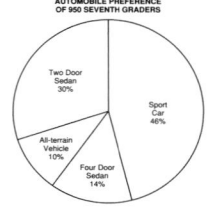

AUTOMOBILE PREFERENCE
OF 950 SEVENTH GRADERS

Two Door Sedan 30%
Sport Car 46%
All-terrain Vehicle 10%
Four Door Sedan 14%

Chapter 11 • Chapter Checkup **369**

Error Analysis and Remediation

Here are some common errors students make when they are working with percents. The errors are listed by lesson under the appropriate management objective.

11A • USE PROPORTION TO SOLVE PERCENT PROBLEMS

Source of Error (Lesson 11-2 and 11-6)
Students set up the proportion incorrectly.

Remediation
Remind students that a percent is a ratio of a number compared to one hundred and that a proportion is an equation showing that two ratios are equal. Then review how to set up a proportion.

11B • DETERMINE DISCOUNT AND MARKUP

Source of Error (Lesson 11-4 and 11-5)
Students forget to subtract the discount or add the markup to find the sale price.

Remediation
Stress that a discount is a decrease and a markup is an increase. Remind students of the two steps, each involving the original price, that can help them find the sale price: write and solve a proportion, and then subtract or add to find the sale price.

11C • PROBLEM SOLVING: USE PERCENT OF COMMISSION. ESTIMATE WITH PERCENT.

Source of Error (Lesson 11-3)
Students use the wrong proportion to represent a problem.

Remediation
Use percent bar models to show that the amount of sales is 100% and that the commission is a percent of the amount of sales. Then guide students to set up the proportion that represents the problem.

Answers

Page 365

1.

Player	1st half	2nd half	Entire season
Mario	.333	.171	.246
Jack	.320	.160	.256
Rita	.207	.103	.151
Ana	.205	.104	.165
Yoko	.210	.111	.157
Omar	.222	.115	.177
Julia	.167	.167	.167
Jason	.190	.190	.190
Takashi	.164	.145	.155
Lani	.139	.135	.137
Kate	.200	.114	.154
David	.216	.120	.177

Extra Practice

This page provides extra practice of all the major chapter objectives. Use this page after the chapter has been taught to reinforce the chapter skills. Page references are provided for each group of items so that students can easily look back at the appropriate lesson for additional support.

EXTRA PRACTICE

Solve using a proportion. *(pages 352–355)*

1. What percent of 38 is 9.5? **25%**
2. 68 is 34% of what number? **200**
3. What percent of 126 is 44.1? **35%**
4. What percent of 14 is 42? **300%**
5. 4% of what number is 25? **625**
6. 32% of what number is 22? **68.75**
7. What percent of 17 is 22.1? **130%**
8. 456 is 120% of what number? **380**
9. What percent of 8 is 27.2? **340%**
10. What percent of 16 is 52? **325%**

Find the amount of the discount and the sale price. *(page 358)*

11. Original price: $75
    Discount: 15% **$11.25; $63.75**
12. Original price: $36
    Discount: 20% **$7.20; $28.80**
13. Original price: $120
    Discount: 35% **$42; $78**
14. Original price: $79
    Discount: 50% **$39.50; $39.50**
15. Original price: $5,600
    Discount: 25% **$1,400; $4,200**
16. Original price: $885
    Discount: 45% **$398.25; $486.75**

Find the selling price for the given cost and markup. *(page 359)*

17. TV: $300 **$570**
    Markup: 90%
18. Phone: $20 **$43**
    Markup: 115%
19. Radio: $17.50 **$31.50**
    Markup: 80%
20. Shirt: $15.75 **$31.50**
    Markup: 100%
21. Lamp: $23.10 **$48.51**
    Markup: 110%
22. Rug: $55 **$101.75**
    Markup: 85%

Use the information in the circle graph to set up a proportion and solve. *(pages 360–361)*

23. The graph represents 3,400 students.

    a. How many students is 40% of the students? **1,360 students**
    b. How many students are represented by x? **2,040 students**

24. The graph shows how one student spends her time.

    a. How much time does she spend studying? **96 min**
    b. How much time does she spend reading? **60 min**

The graph represents 8 h of a day.

Solve. *(pages 354–355, 362–363)*

25. Roberto earned $3,920 in commission on sales of $24,500. What percent is his commission? **16%**

26. Angela was absent from school 11 out of 180 school days last year. About what percent of the school year was she absent? **6%**

International Percents

Choose a country other than the United States. Do research to learn about its money.

- What is the monetary unit called?
- What denominations are used?
- What is the current value of one unit of the country's currency in United States money?

You can set up and solve a proportion to determine the value in United States money of each unit of the country's money. For example, in France, the monetary unit is the French franc. One denomination of the French franc is the 50-franc note. If 1 French franc has a value equal to $.23, you can use the following proportion to determine the value in United States money of a 50-franc note:

$$\frac{1}{.23} = \frac{50}{x}$$

Use proportions to determine the value in United States money of each denomination used in the country you have chosen. **Check students' work.**

Comparison Shopping

Supermarkets compete for business in many ways. One goal of supermarkets is to convince consumers that they have the lowest prices. But is one supermarket really less expensive than another?

Work with a group. Make a list of about 15 or 20 common items and their most common size. Have members of your group visit at least two supermarkets to record the prices of the items.

- List the items and prices in both stores in a table.
- Can you see a pattern?
- Are prices in one store consistently lower than those in another? If the answer is *yes*, what might explain the fact that people continue to shop in the more expensive store? Is price the only concern of consumers?

Check students' work.

Math Scavenger Hunt

Look through a newspaper for these examples of percents. **Check students' work.**

- a percent greater than 100%
- a percent that refers to a population
- a percent that refers to time
- a percent less than 100%
- a percent that refers to money
- a percent used in a graph

Enrichment

This page contains activities that provide extension and enrichment for all levels of students. Depending on the needs of your students, you may wish to assign an activity from this page at certain points during the chapter, or you may wish to use this page when the entire chapter has been completed.

International Percents

Tell students that they can find the information that they need in an almanac and in the financial section of a major newspaper. After students complete the activity, you may wish to have volunteers share their research and proportions with the class.

Comparison Shopping
(COOPERATIVE)

Have students comparison shop in groups of three or four. After they compile their list of items, suggest that they each take five items and prepare a table before setting out to gather prices.

Math Scavenger Hunt

Tell students that advertisements are a good source for some of the examples of percents given.

CHAPTER 11

Cumulative Review

The Cumulative Review focuses on skills covered in previous chapters. All important skills are reviewed on a cyclic basis.

If students are having difficulty with particular groups of exercises, refer to the chart below for follow-up work.

CUMULATIVE REVIEW

Find the answer.

1. What is the LCM of 9 and 15?　**d**
   a. 3
   b. 30
   c. 135
   d. none of these

2. What is the LCM of 3, 5, and 6?　**b**
   a. 15
   b. 30
   c. 90
   d. none of these

3. What is the GCF of 18 and 27?　**a**
   a. 9
   b. 18
   c. 36
   d. none of these

4. $\frac{15}{35} = \blacksquare$　**b**
   a. $\frac{3}{5}$
   b. $\frac{3}{7}$
   c. $\frac{5}{7}$
   d. none of these

5. $\frac{7}{12} = \blacksquare$　**c**
   a. $\frac{14}{21}$
   b. $\frac{14}{36}$
   c. $\frac{21}{36}$
   d. none of these

6. $\frac{7}{8}$ is greater than $\blacksquare$.　**a**
   a. $\frac{5}{6}$
   b. $\frac{9}{10}$
   c. $\frac{11}{12}$
   d. none of these

7. $\frac{5}{8} + \frac{7}{10} = \blacksquare$　**b**
   a. $\frac{12}{18}$
   b. $1\frac{13}{40}$
   c. $1\frac{1}{4}$
   d. none of these

8. $\frac{12}{16} - \frac{1}{4} = \blacksquare$　**b**
   a. $\frac{11}{12}$
   b. $\frac{1}{2}$
   c. $\frac{1}{4}$
   d. none of these

9. $2\frac{1}{3} + 5\frac{2}{5} = \blacksquare$　**c**
   a. $7\frac{1}{5}$
   b. $7\frac{3}{8}$
   c. $7\frac{11}{15}$
   d. none of these

10. All squares are $\blacksquare$.　**c**
   a. trapezoids
   b. kites
   c. rectangles
   d. none of these

11. All parallelograms are $\blacksquare$.　**a**
   a. quadrilaterals
   b. rectangles
   c. squares
   d. none of these

12. All trapezoids are $\blacksquare$.　**d**
   a. parallelograms
   b. rhombuses
   c. rectangles
   d. none of these

13. $\frac{14}{27} = \frac{x}{81}$　**b**
   a. 28
   b. 42
   c. 56
   d. none of these

14. $\frac{15}{8} = \frac{75}{x}$　**c**
   a. 45
   b. 32
   c. 40
   d. none of these

15. 7 oranges: $1.33　**c**
   1 orange: x
   a. $9.31
   b. $.13
   c. $.19
   d. none of these

Items	Management Objectives	Where Taught	Reteaching Options	Extra Practice Options
1–3	**5B** Identify factors and multiples; GCF; LCM.	pp. 134–137	TRB/RW 5-3 and 5-4	TRB/PW 5-3 and 5-4
4–6	**5C** Write equivalent fractions, and compare and order fractions.	pp. 142–145, 150–151	TRB/RW 5-7, TE/RA 5-8, TRB/RW 5-10	TRB/PW 5-7, 5-8, 5-10
7–8	**6B** Add and subtract fractions, different denominators.	pp. 174–175	TE/RA 6-3	TRB/PW 6-3
9	**6C** Add and subtract mixed numbers, different denominators.	pp. 178–179	TRB/RW 6-5	TRB/PW 6-5
10–12	**8F** Problem Solving: Use Venn diagrams; Make generalizations.	pp, 242–243	TE/RA 8-6	TRB/PW 8-6
13–15	**9B** Solve proportions.	pp. 280–281, 284–285	TRB/RW 9-4 and 9-6	TRB/PW 9-4 and 9-6

Strategies may vary. Suggestions given.
Remember the strategies and types of
problems you've had so far. Solve.

Problem Solving Check List

- Too much information
- Too little information
- Using a simpler problem
- Making a table
- Using equations

1. A school district owns a 40-seat bus, a 15-seat minibus, and two station wagons, one with 9 seats and one with 7 seats.

   a. How many seats does the bus have? **40 seats**

   b. How can you find out the total number of ways students can be transported using 1, 2, 3, or 4 vehicles? **Make a table**

   c. How many different ways can students be transported using 1, 2, 3, or 4 vehicles?
   15 ways

2. A parade begins at 10:45 A.M. Each band takes 2 min to pass the reviewing stand. If the parade lasts 2 h 25 min, at what time does it end?
   too much information; 1:10 P.M.

3. A juice machine dispenses 10 oz bottles. There is a total of 1 gal 12 oz of juice in the machine. How many bottles are in the machine?
   multistep; 14 bottles

4. Of 20 students asked, 12 said they liked the school lunch. At that rate, how many of 200 students would probably say they liked the lunch?
   equation; 120 students

5. Ruth bought a pair of jeans that were priced at $39.95. She received a 10% employee's discount. How much did the jeans cost her? **multistep; $35.96**

6. If Corey lived 4 blocks closer to school, he would live twice as far from school as Jorge. If Jorge lives 3 blocks from school, how far from school does Corey live?
   simpler problem; 10 blocks

7. Five friends shared a dinner check evenly. The check was $65.50 and they decided to give the waiter a 15% tip. To the nearest dollar, how much did each friend pay? **multistep; $15**

8. A $2\frac{1}{2}$ h film has 2 reels: one $1\frac{1}{3}$ h long and one $1\frac{1}{6}$ h long. An intermission comes between the reels. If the reels are played in reverse order, how much earlier would the intermission be?
   equation; 10 min

9. Apples are 5 for $1.00 and oranges are 3 for $1.00. Arthur spent $7.00 and came home with 29 pieces of fruit. What did he buy?
   equation; 20 apples and 9 oranges

10. A school lunchroom offered a choice of chicken, tuna, or pizza. Seventy-five more students had pizza than chicken, and 60 more students had chicken than tuna. If 165 tunas were served, how many lunches were served in all? **work backward; 690 lunches**

Problem Solving Review

This page focuses on problem solving strategies and types learned in this and previous chapters. A problem solving checklist lists some of the strategies students may use to solve the problems on this page.

Technology

This page is designed to provide calculator or computer experiences for all levels of students. The calculator or computer logo indicates the type of activity.

You may wish to assign these activities after the chapter has been taught or during the course of the chapter, depending on your needs and those of your students.

Thinking in Circles

Tell students to use proportional thinking to solve the problem. You may want to point out that each of the three remaining categories must have the same relationship to 100% in the new circle graph as it has to 68% in the circle graph shown.

Zeroing In

Suggest that students use a guess-and-check strategy. Students should record each guess in a list, and use earlier guesses and results to help them to "zero in" on the percent.

Getting Interested

(COOPERATIVE)

You may want to have students work in groups of two or four as they set up the tables and compute compound interest. Make certain that students understand compound interest by having them first work through the given table.

The computer activity uses Houghton Mifflin software, which is found in Houghton Mifflin Math Activities Courseware, Grade 7.

TECHNOLOGY

THINKING IN CIRCLES

The circle graph gives the budget breakdown for the drama club this year. How would the graph change if someone donated rehearsal space to the club for free? Give the new percentages. **Accept reasonable answers.**

32 % Rehearsal
17.5 % Scripts
Costumes 21.5 %
29 % Scenery & Lights

ZEROING IN

Use a calculator to find a percent of 893 that is within the given range. **Answers will vary. Range given:**

	Range	
1.	50–100	5.5991%–11.1982%
2.	70–95	7.8388%–10.6383%
3.	71.5–72.5	8.0068%–8.1187%
4.	71.9–72.2	8.0516%–8.0851%
5.	71.93–71.97	8.0549%–8.0593%

GETTING INTERESTED

In *EduCalc*, you learn to use a computer spreadsheet to compute compound interest—that is, interest earned on interest. This pencil-and-paper activity will help you become familiar with how compound interest works. **See below.**

This spreadsheet shows how much interest a deposit of $500 will earn after 4 yr in an account that pays 5% interest compounded annually.

End of Year	Principal x Interest Rate = Interest			Total
1	500.00	0.05	25.00	525.00
2	525.00	0.05	26.25	551.25
3	551.25	0.05	27.56	578.81
4	578.81	0.05	28.94	607.75

Set up a similar table, and use a calculator to compute the compound interest and the new totals. Use the annual compound interest shown.

1. $1,200; 5%; 6 yr
$1,608.11

2. $800; 6%; 10 yr
$1,432.68

3. $985; 6%; 6 yr
$1,397.24

4. $1,420; $6\frac{1}{4}$%; 4 yr
$1,809.69

5. $1,340; $5\frac{1}{2}$%; 5 yr
$1,751.33

6. $800; $9\frac{3}{4}$%; 5 yr
$1,273.83

Software Activities

activity 1 • DOUBLING FIGURES

MATERIALS: draw program

Procedure: Have students create a rectangle with a draw program. They should make a copy of the figure and use the scaling function to double both the length and width. Next, they should duplicate and move the original shape onto the expanded one. Ask students, *How many copies of the original figure will it take to completely cover the larger figure?*

Follow-up: Have students repeat the activity using a triangle instead of a rectangle. How many original triangles does it take to cover the larger triangle? Discuss with students why it takes four of the original shapes to cover the larger figure.

activity 2 • ARE THEY EQUAL?

MATERIALS: BASIC programming

Procedure: This program determines if two ratios that are input by the student are equal. The student should type the program into the computer and run it several times.

```
10 PRINT "THIS PROGRAM WILL TELL
   IF TWO RATIOS "
20 PRINT "FORM A PROPORTION, OR
   WHICH IS LARGER. "
30 PRINT: PRINT
40 PRINT "WHAT ARE THE NUMERATOR
   AND DENOMINATOR "
50 INPUT "OF YOUR FIRST RATIO
   ";N,D
60 PRINT "WHAT ARE THE NUMERATOR
   AND DENOMINATOR "
70 INPUT "OF YOUR SECOND RATIO
   ";M,E
80 LET Y=N*E: LET Z=M*D
90 IF Y=Z THEN 120
100 IF Y > Z THEN PRINT "YOUR RATIO
    "N"/"D ">"M "/"E:GOTO 130
110 IF Y<Z THEN PRINT "YOUR RATIO
    "N"/"D "<"M "/"E:GOTO 130
120 PRINT "RATIOS: "N "/"D " &
    "M"/"E "ARE EQUAL."
130 END
```

Follow-up: Challenge students to write other computer programs to check if ratios are equal.

HOUGHTON MIFFLIN SOFTWARE

EduCalc. Boston, MA: Houghton Mifflin Company, 1990. For Apple II, Commodore, IBM.

Mathematics Activities Courseware. Boston, MA: Houghton Mifflin Company, 1983. For Apple II, IBM.

Mathematics: Solving Story Problems. Levels 7–8, Boston, MA: Houghton Mifflin Company, 1985. For Apple II, IBM.

The Computer Tutor. Boston, MA: Houghton Mifflin Company, 1990. For Apple II, IBM.

OTHER SOFTWARE

Basic Skills Math Series: Fractions, Decimals and Percent. State College, PA: Courses by Computers, 1989. For Apple, IBM.

Conquering Percents. St. Paul, MN: MECC, 1989. For Apple II.

Math Football: Percent. Big Spring, TX: Gamco Industries, Inc., 1988. For Apple II, Commodore, IBM, TRS-80.

Microsoft Works. Redmond, WA: Microsoft Corporation, 1989. For IBM, Macintosh.

Percentage Panic. Las Vegas, NV: Unicorn Software, 1989. For Apple II, Commodore, IBM.

Statistics and Probability

This chapter involves the concept of probability as it relates to statistics. It focuses on finding the mean and median for a set of data, making a double bar graph and a double line graph, recognizing equally likely outcomes, finding the probability of an event, and solving problems by choosing an appropriate graph and by using simulation.

Management Objectives

12A Find the mean and median.
12B Make and interpret a double bar graph and a double line graph.
12C Recognize equally likely outcomes.
12D Find the probability of an event.
12E Problem Solving: Choose an appropriate graph. Use simulation.

Assignments for different achievement levels are provided on the Record and Assignment Chart in the Teacher's Resource Book.

Vocabulary

population, sample, page 378
representative sample, page 378
random sample, page 378
mode, page 380
mean, median, page 382
relative frequency, page 388
probability, page 392
equally likely outcomes, page 394
actual and experimental probability, page 396
Law of Large Numbers, page 399
simulation, page 400

Home Involvement

As you begin to teach this chapter, give each student a copy of the Home Involvement Newsletter for this chapter.

This newsletter provides parents with
■ an overview of the chapter
■ suggestions for practicing some of the skills in the chapter
■ an at-home activity to do with their child, applying the skills taught in the chapter.

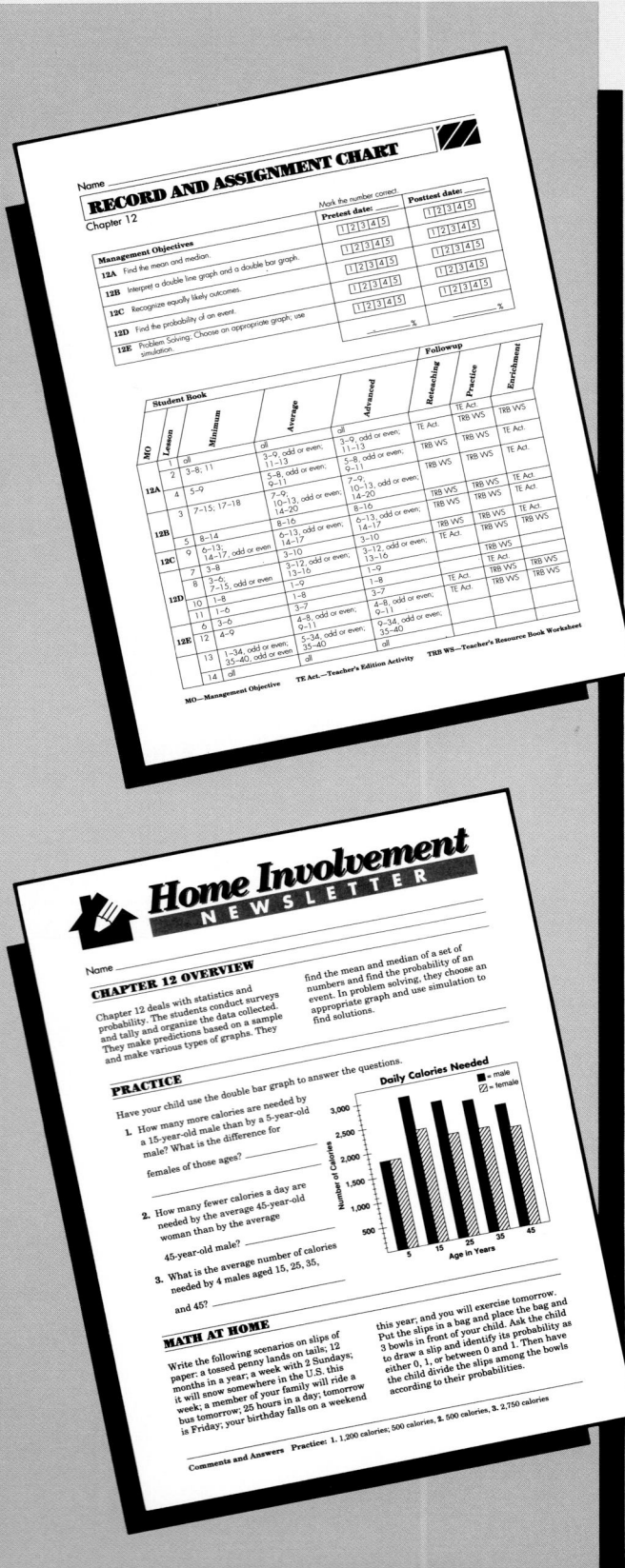

Management Chart

Management Objectives	Lesson/ Pages	Student Not Successful	Student Needs More Practice	Student Successful	Pacing Range
12A Find the mean and median.	12-1/376-377	FF	FF	TE/CA 12-1 FF	3 days
	12-2/378-379	TE/RA 12-2 FF	TRB/PW 12-2 FF	TRB/ 12-2 FF	
	12-4/382-383	TRB/RW 12-4	TRB/PW 12-4	TE/EA 12-4 MAC 8 Activity 11	
12B Make and interpret a double bar graph and a double line graph.	12-3/380-381	TRB/RW 12-3	TRB/PW 12-3 CT Unit 6 Obj. 2.1	TE/EA 12-3	2 days
	12-5/384-385	TRB/RW 12-5	TRB/PW 12-5 CT Unit 6 Obj. 2.2	TE/EA 12-5	
12C Recognize equally likely outcomes.	12-9/394-395	TRB/RW 12-9	TRB/PW 12-9	TE/EA 12-9	1 day
12D Find the probability of an event.	12-7/388-389	TRB/RW 12-7	TRB/PW 12-7	TE/EA 12-7	4-5 days
	12-8/392-393	TE/RA 12-8	TRB/PW 12-8	TRB/EW 12-8	
	12-10/396-397		TRB/PW 12-10		
	12-11/398-399			TE/CA 12-11 MAC 8 Activity 14B	
12E Problem Solving: Choose an appropriate graph. Use simulation.	12-6/386-387	TE/RA 12-6 EG	TRB/PW 12-6 EG	TRB/EW 12-6 EG	2 days
	12-12/400-401	TE/RA 12-12	TRB/PW 12-12	TRB/EW 12-12	
Mixed Review	12-13/402-403				
Creative Problem Solving	12-14/404-405				
Chapter Checkups	390-391; 406-407				
Extra Practice	408				
Enrichment	409				
Cumulative Review/Problem Solving Review	410-411				
Technology	412				

TE = Teacher's Edition
TRB = Teacher's Resource Book
RW = Reteaching Worksheet
RA = Reteaching Activity
EA = Enrichment Activity
EW = Enrichment Worksheet
PW = Practice Worksheet
CA = Classroom Activity

*Other Available Items
MAC = Mathematics Activities Courseware
CSP = Computational Skills Program
CT = Computer Tutor
FF = Friendly Filer
EG = Easy Graph

Manipulative Planning Guide

This is a complete list of manipulatives and materials needed for Chapter 12.

Materials for Manipulatives	TE Activities (INTRODUCE)	Student Book Lesson
Teaching Aid 15* for each pair for each student	Lesson 12-3 Lesson 12-5	Lessons 12-3, 12-5, 12-6
Calculator for each student		Lessons 12-3, 12-4, 12-7, 12-11
Ruler for each pair for each student	Lesson 12-3 Lesson 12-5	Lessons 12-3, 12-5, 12-6
Colored pencils or markers for each student		Lessons 12-3, 12-5
Cubes, six blue and two green	Lesson 12-10	Lesson 12-10
Paper bag for each group for each student	Lesson 12-10	Lesson 12-10
Slips of paper		
Assorted marbles, five for each pair		Lesson 12-10
Tagboard squares, six for each pair	Lesson 12-11	Lesson 12-11
Marker for each pair	Lesson 12-11	
One coin	Lesson 12-12	
Phone books		
Index cards		
Probability Spinners transparency		Lesson 12-10
Counters		
Calorie charts		
Blank spinners		

*Teaching Aids are found in the Teacher's Resource Book.

Learning Stages

The concepts and skills in Chapter 12 are presented through these learning stages.

CONCRETE

Using manipulatives and verbalizing about a concept. No symbols.

Teacher Edition Activities	Student Book
Lesson 12-10	

Enrichment	Reteaching	In the Houghton Mifflin Manipulative Kit?	In the Houghton Mifflin Overhead Kit?
Lessons 12-3, 12-5, 12-7			Yes
Lesson 12-7			Available separately
Lessons 12-5, 12-7		Yes	
		Yes	
	Lessons 12-2, 12-12		
	Lessons 12-2, 12-12		
	Lesson 12-2		
Lessons 12-3, 12-4	Lesson 12-8		
Lesson 12-3			Yes
Lesson 12-11			
Lesson 12-5			
Lesson 12-9		Yes	

CONNECTING

5¢ 9cm² 1/3

Making a connection between manipulatives and symbols.

Teacher Edition Activities	Student Book
Lessons 12-1, 12-2, 12-3, 12-5, 12-7, 12-8, 12-9, 12-11, 12-12	Lessons 12-10, 12-11

SYMBOLIC

$.05   A=9cm² $1 - \frac{2}{3} = \frac{1}{3}$

Using numbers or symbols. No manipulatives or pictures of manipulatives.

Teacher Edition Activities	Student Book
Lessons 12-4, 12-6	Lessons 12-1 through 12-9, 12-11, 12-12, 12-14

Additional Activities

COOPERATIVE LEARNING RESOURCE ACTIVITIES

Through cooperative learning activities, students learn by interacting with one another in small groups. These cooperative activities provide students with motivating settings for making connections, investigations, and problem solving situations.

The cooperative connections are interdisciplinary problem-solving projects. Each student has a particular job that helps lead the group to complete the project. For the cooperative investigations students work in pairs for investigations involving data collection and analysis. The cooperative problem solving activities encourage the sharing of ideas and information. Students work in groups of four to solve a problem. Students are each assigned a clue and work together to find a common solution.

COOPERATIVE CONNECTIONS

Chapter 12

COOPERATIVE CONNECTIONS / Math and Genetics

GOAL: Make a chart showing the number of people who have inherited each trait.

Materials: tagboard, rulers

Genetics is the study of how traits are inherited. Some traits are dominant and some are recessive. According to the laws of genetics, dominant traits are the ones most likely to appear. Recessive traits must be inherited from both parents and only appear when the dominant trait does not appear.

Conduct a survey of 60 students and teachers to determine which of the traits listed in the chart each of them possesses. Present your results in a chart. Based on your survey, which traits do you think are dominant?

Inherited Traits	
Can roll tongue into a U	Cannot roll tongue into a U
Cleft chin	No cleft chin
Straight hair line	Widow's peak

COOPERATIVE INVESTIGATIONS

Chapter 12

COOPERATIVE INVESTIGATIONS / Double-line Graph

GOAL: Draw a double-line graph that illustrates the average monthly normal temperatures for two cities.

Materials: almanac, grid paper, pencil, paper, ruler, colored pencils (2 colors)

Work with a partner.

1. In the almanac, find the chart that displays the average monthly normal temperatures for cities in the United States. Find your city or the one closest to your community. Then choose a place you would like to visit. Use the information on the chart to compare the change in average monthly temperatures during the year.

2. Draw a double-line graph. Determine the appropriate interval for the temperatures. Complete the graph, using a different color line for each city. A ruler can help you read across the columns.

COOPERATIVE PROBLEM SOLVING 1

Chapter 12

COOPERATIVE PROBLEM SOLVING / Problem 1

What is the mean score for Friday's Math test?

Clue 1: On Friday's Math test 11 students scored below 90%.

What is the mean score for Friday's Math test?

Clue 2: Two students scored 95% and twice that number scored 92%.

What is the mean score for Friday's Math test?

Clue 3: One student scored 85%. This was the median. Two other students scored 87%.

What is the mean score for Friday's Math test?

Clue 4: The remaining students each scored 80% on the test.

COOPERATIVE PROBLEM SOLVING 2

Chapter 12

COOPERATIVE PROBLEM SOLVING / Problem 2

Four students take turns drawing colored cards at random. They do not return the cards after they make each choice. How many cards of each color were there at the start?

Clue 1: The first student drew a red card. The probability of drawing a red card was $\frac{1}{4}$.

Four students take turns drawing colored cards at random. They do not return the cards after they make each choice. How many cards of each color were there at the start?

Clue 3: The third student drew a yellow card. The probability of drawing a yellow card was $\frac{1}{3}$.

Four students take turns drawing colored cards at random. They do not return the cards after they make each choice. How many cards of each color were there at the start?

Clue 2: The second student drew a blue card. The probability of drawing a blue card was $\frac{3}{7}$.

Four students take turns drawing colored cards at random. They do not return the cards after they make each choice. How many cards of each color were there at the start?

Clue 4: After the fourth student drew a green card, there were four cards left.

GAMES

DATA HUNT (For use after Lesson 12-4)

Objective: Find the mean and median of a group of data.

☑ **MATERIALS CHECKLIST:** almanac or similar resource book, two index cards for each pair of students; calculator for each team in the game

Partners can use an almanac or similar source to generate data for this game. Suggest that students find data about rainfall, temperatures, population growth, and the like, and write the data on an index card. The data in each case should be eight or fewer items. You may want to have students collect the data over a one-week period.

Ask students to form two or four teams for the game. A player chooses a card, which is displayed or read for all teams. All teams calculate the mean and median. At a signal from you, teams compare answers and correct any errors. Correct answers earn five points. The team with the greatest number of points at the end is the winner.

TOSS SIX (For use after Lesson 12-9)

Objective: Recognize when events are equally likely.

☑ **MATERIALS CHECKLIST:** number cube and number cards (1-6) for each pair of students

Assign partners, and give each pair a number cube and a set of number cards. Tell students to mix the cards and place them face down. The first player draws a number card and tosses the cube until he or she gets that number. The score recorded for the player is the sum of the number on the card and the total number of tosses needed to get that number. The second player repeats the process with a new card. Play alternates in this manner until all six cards are used. Have students record their total scores, noting who had the lower score, and play another round.

After the second round, discuss with students whether skill was involved in this game *(no)* and whether both players had an equally likely chance of having the lower score *(yes)*.

BULLETIN BOARD

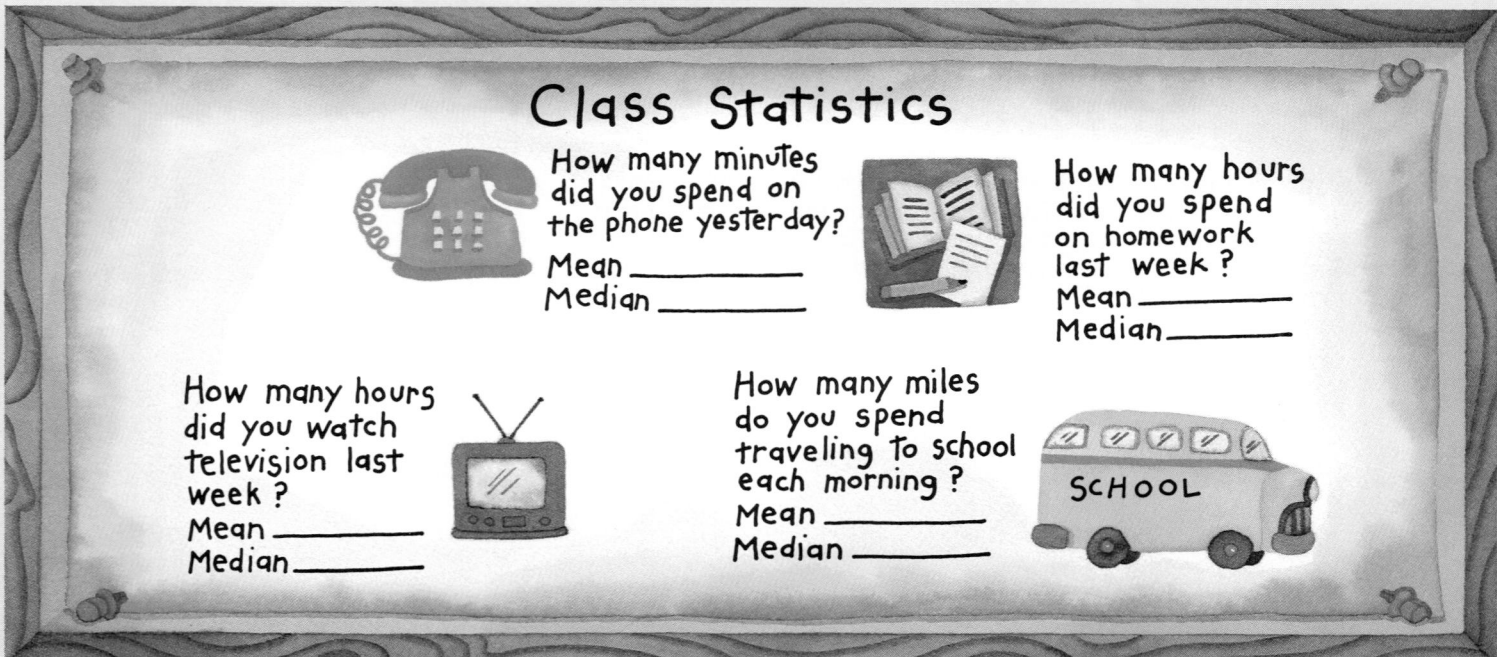

Ask students to prepare a survey to generate data about their class. After students have obtained their data, they should organize the information and determine the mean and median for each set of data. Have students display their results, including appropriate pictures or drawings to illustrate each question. Discuss with students whether mean or median better describes each set of data.

Alternative Assessment

In addition to the paper and pencil tests available with this program, the following items can help you assess critical thinking as well as your students' ability to solve problems in a wide variety of ways.

Open-ended Problem

Two students designed a game as a math project for the school's Math Fair.
GAME: They used a blank spinner and shaded one half red and the other half blue. Student A would win if two consecutive spins resulted in the same color. Student B would win if two consecutive spins resulted in different colors.

They ran a simulation by playing the game 50 times. In the simulation, student A won 37 times and student B won 13 times. They decided that the game was not fair because in a fair game both students would win the same number of times. How would you decide if the game is fair?

Teacher Notes
• If the game is played many more times, the results should approximate the actual probability.

• The outcomes for the games are red/red, red/blue, blue/red, and blue/blue. Each of these four outcomes is equally likely.

• The probability of either student winning on a turn is $\frac{1}{4} + \frac{1}{4}$ or $\frac{1}{2}$.

• If both students have the same probability of winning, the game is fair.

Group Writing Activity (See p. 24T.)

Write as many examples as possible of the use of probability and facts that you know about probability.

Individual Writing Activity

What does probability mean to you?

Portfolios

Portfolios can provide information about a student's growth in mathematical understanding over a period of time. They can help you make instructional decisions as well as become a vehicle for communicating with parents. The students' work involving the open-ended problem and writing activity suggested on this page along with work on the Explore lesson on pages 376-377, the In Your Words exercises on pages 381, 387, and 393, the Learning Log exercises on pages 391 and 407, the Critical Thinking feature on page 395, and the Creative Problem Solving lesson on pages 404-405 could be included in portfolios.

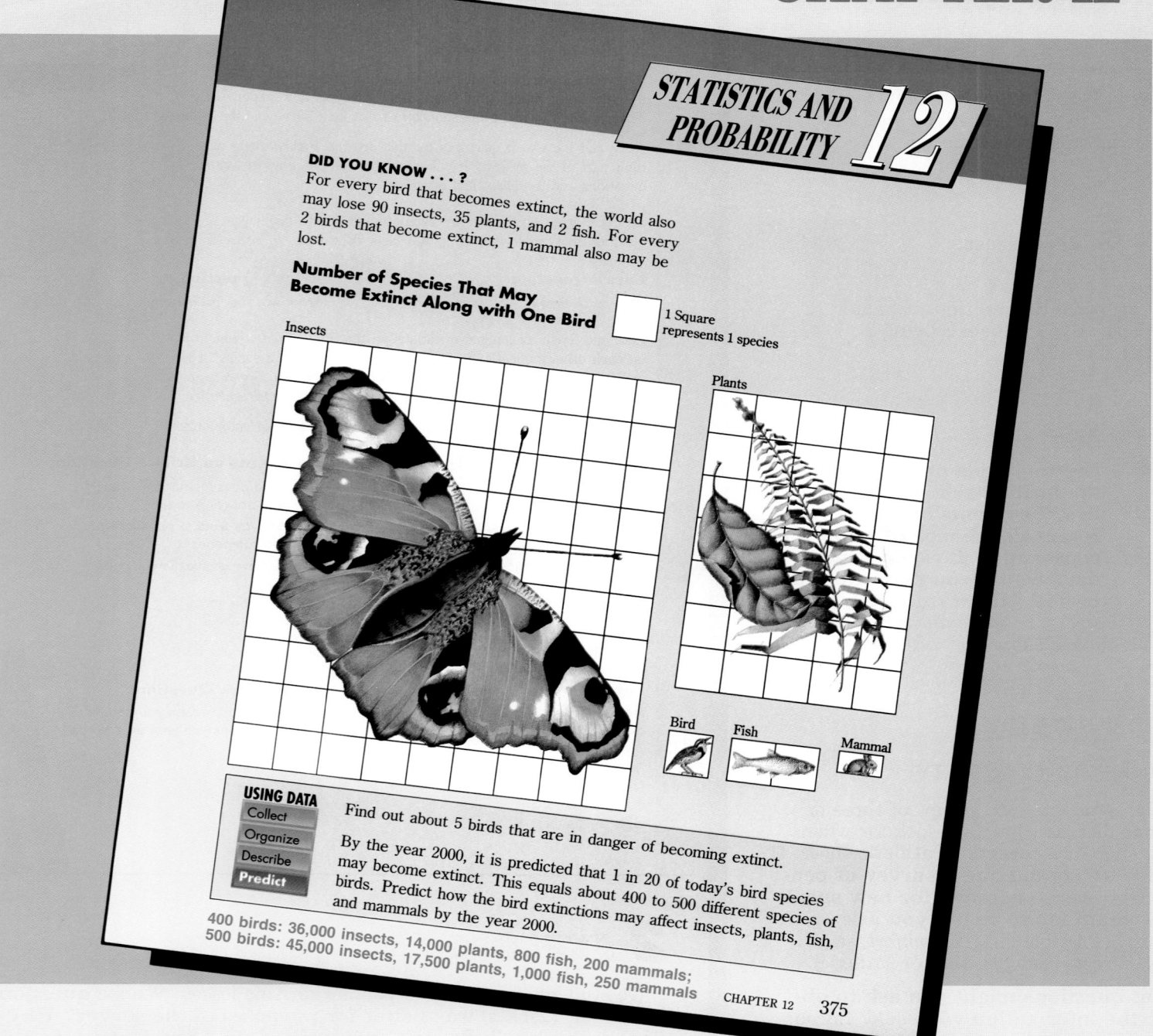

STATISTICS AND PROBABILITY 12

DID YOU KNOW . . . ?

For every bird that becomes extinct, the world also may lose 90 insects, 35 plants, and 2 fish. For every 2 birds that become extinct, 1 mammal also may be lost.

Number of Species That May Become Extinct Along with One Bird

Insects

☐ 1 Square represents 1 species

Plants

Bird   Fish   Mammal

USING DATA

Collect
Organize
Describe
Predict

Find out about 5 birds that are in danger of becoming extinct.

By the year 2000, it is predicted that 1 in 20 of today's bird species may become extinct. This equals about 400 to 500 different species of birds. Predict how the bird extinctions may affect insects, plants, fish, and mammals by the year 2000.

400 birds: 36,000 insects, 14,000 plants, 800 fish, 200 mammals;
500 birds: 45,000 insects, 17,500 plants, 1,000 fish, 250 mammals

CHAPTER 12   375

Using the Chapter Opener

The purpose of this page is to involve students in the use of real data much like that presented in newspapers and magazines.

To use this page as you begin the chapter, direct students' attention to the data. You may wish to ask questions such as the following:

What is the unit in this diagram? *(the square that is associated with the loss of one species of birds)*

What is the area of the rectangle that represents insects? *(90 square units)* **plants?** *(35 square units)*

How is the relationship between birds and mammals shown? *(The rectangle that represents mammals is about half the area of the square that represents birds, since one mammal is lost for every two birds.)*

Lesson Organizer

Objective: Explore making a survey.

Prior Knowledge: Students should be able to write questions and tally and categorize information.

Lesson Resources:
Class Activity 12-1
Daily Review 12-1
Cooperative Connections, Chapter 12
Cooperative Problem Solving 1,
   Chapter 12

Two-Minute Math

Use the Table of Numbers on the inside back cover. If the first 7 percents in row M represent the chance of rain on 7 consecutive days, on which days would you carry an umbrella? *(Accept reasonable answers. Possible answer: Days when chance of rain was 50% or greater.)*

1 PREPARE

CONNECTING ACTIVITY

Assign students into groups of three or four to discuss what they look for when they shop for sneakers or athletic shoes. **If you were conducting a survey of people who were shopping for new sneakers, what factors would you ask about?** *(Possible factors: comfort, sturdiness, design, color, fashion or status)*

What questions might you ask to obtain the information you seek? Encourage students to comment on questions that are suggested.

WHEN YOUR STUDENTS ASK
★ WHY AM I LEARNING THIS? ★

You can connect conducting surveys to careers in market research and advertising. People who work in these fields often use results from surveys to persuade people to buy particular products or services.

EXPLORE

Exploring Surveys

A seventh grade class was writing a story about the graduating eighth grade class for the school newspaper. They decided to use a questionnaire to make a survey of the eighth graders.

Erick and Lara were partners for this project. Follow along on their part of the project. It will give you ideas on how to write questions and to collect and organize data.

To get started on the survey each student had to develop a question that would help to gather clear data about an interesting topic.

Lara's Question:
How much time do you spend studying?

Erick's Question:
What was the last important item you bought?

Lara and Erick exchanged questions so that they could comment on each other's questions. They could ask about the meaning of an unclear question, point out data that would be hard to organize, or mention anything to help the other person write a better question.

Erick and Lara exchanged questions and received these comments.

Comments on Lara's Question:
* Do you include studying during school hours?
* Will students really know in general how much time they spend studying?

Comments on Erick's Question:
* What does "important" mean? New socks? A radio?
* Will you want to put the responses into categories?
* Or have choices in categories?

1. **THINK ALOUD** What other comments might be made about their questions? **Answers will vary. Suggestion given Their questions are too broad.**

Then they rewrote their own questions to make the questions better.

Lara's New Question:
How much time did you spend studying after school yesterday?
(a) 0–15 min
(b) 16–60 min
(c) more than 60 min

Erick's New Question:
What was the last item you bought for $10 or more with your own money?

MATH AND LANGUAGE ARTS

---

2 EXPLORE

Have students work with a partner for this lesson. **Whose question, Lara's or Erick's, was better for purposes of the survey? Why do you think so?** *(Possible answer: Lara's question, because the responses were easier to organize)*

What categories did you use to sort Erick's data? *(Possible answers: sport equipment, clothing, electronic equipment, entertainment)*

SUMMARIZE/ASSESS   **Rewrite the following question: What is the most important thing you look for when buying a new pair of athletic shoes? Then explain how the data could be collected and organized.** *(Possible answer: Did you buy your last pair of sneakers because of comfort, sturdiness, color, design, or brand-name?; list choice, then tally choices.)*

2. **THINK ALOUD** How did Erick and Lara respond to the comments on their questions? **Answers will vary. Suggestion given. They made their questions more specific.**

3. **CREATE YOUR OWN** Choose an interesting topic and write a question. Exchange questions with a partner. Give helpful comments. Then rewrite your own question. **Check students' work.**

The students put all the questions together into one questionnaire. Then they discussed how they would collect the data.

4. Lara didn't want her question to be asked on a Monday. Can you tell why? **Sunday wasn't a school night.**

Once the questionnaires had been filled out by the eighth graders, each seventh grade student tallied and organized the raw data for his or her question.

Lara's Tallied Data:		Lara's Organized Data:	
		Minutes	Number of Responses
0–15 min ~~HH~~ ~~HH~~ ~~HH~~ ~~HH~~ ~~HH~~ ~~HH~~ ////		0–15	34
16–60 min ~~HH~~ ~~HH~~ ~~HH~~ ~~HH~~ ~~HH~~ ///		16–60	28
more than 60 min ~~HH~~ ~~HH~~ ~~HH~~ ///		more than 60	18

Erick's Tallied Data			
CD ~~HH~~ ~~HH~~ //	record album ~~HH~~ ///	shorts //	video movie ~~HH~~
blouse ////	audio tape ~~HH~~ ~~HH~~ ~~HH~~	software ////	soccer ball /
T-shirt ~~HH~~ /	clock /	radio /	CD player /
book ~~HH~~ /	cassette player //	purse ///	pizza /
jeans ////	video game //	football /	guitar strings /

5. Work with a partner to sort Erick's data by putting similar objects into a category. For instance, you could put the football and the soccer ball into a category called Sports Equipment. Then make a table of organized data like Lara's. **Check students' work.**

Your class may want to make a survey and write a story about the results for the school newspaper. You can collect and organize data for the questions you wrote in Exercise 3.

CLASS ACTIVITY 12-1

Have the students work in pairs. Instruct each pair to conduct a survey of at least ten adults to determine their favorite subject when they were in school. The students make tables showing the results for age groups such as 20–29, 30–39, and so on, and then for men and women. Ask: Were there differences among the different age groups? Were there differences between men and women?

MEETING INDIVIDUAL NEEDS

For Students Who Are . . .

Acquiring English Proficiency Explain the meaning of *questionnaire*. Discuss how the phrases *tallied* and *raw data* are used.

Gifted and Talented Have students write to the local newspaper or to a national polling organization. Find out what steps are taken in conducting surveys and report their findings to the class.

Working 2 or 3 Grades Below Level Help students rewrite a question such as "How much time did you spend playing sports last week?"

Today's Problem

A survey of 50 students gave these results: 4 were born in Jan., 5 in Feb., 2 in Mar., 0 in Apr., 4 in May, 6 in June, 7 in July, 4 in Aug., 3 in Sept., 4 in Oct., 6 in Nov., and 5 in Dec. If there were an equal chance of being born on any particular day, for which month would you expect the least number of births? Why? *(February, because it has the fewest number of days)*

Lesson Organizer

Objective: Sample and predict.

Prior Knowledge: Students should be familiar with Venn diagrams.

Lesson Resources:
Practice Worksheet 12-2
Reteaching Activity 12-2
Enrichment Worksheet 12-2
Daily Review 12-2
Cooperative Connections, Chapter 12

 *Two-Minute Math*

Name a collection that is contained entirely within the larger collection. *(Possible answers are given.)*
all cities in the United States *(state capitals)*
all cars on the road. *(sports cars)*

1 INTRODUCE

CONNECTING ACTIVITY

How would you define the student population of your school? *(Possible answers: students in grades 6–8, or 10- to 14-year-olds)* **What are some groups within the school population?** *(Possible answer: boys, French Club members, seventh graders)*

Which group would you question if you wanted to find out

- **how many students liked 8th grade science?** *(people in eighth grade)*
- **how many students wanted to try out for girls' sports teams** *(girls)*
- **how many students liked the cafeteria lunches** *(people in each of the groups)*

WHEN YOUR STUDENTS ASK
★ WHY AM I LEARNING THIS? ★

You can connect this skill to real life through professional pollsters, who design questions about a variety of issues and analyze and publish data collected from samples that represent particular populations.

Sampling and Predicting

The sales manager of Smart Sporting Goods wants to predict the number of students at Carver High School who might purchase school jackets. The manager can use a sample to predict the percent of students who are likely jacket buyers.

A **population** is an entire group about whom information is wanted. The population in this example is students at Carver High School.

A **sample** is a part, or subset, of the population. You collect information about the sample in order to make a prediction about the population. To do this you use proportional thinking to draw conclusions about the population from the sample.

> All students at Carver High School
>> Some students at Carver High School

When a sample has characteristics that are very similar to the population, it is called a **representative sample.** The best chance to ensure representativeness is to use a **random sample.**

Random selections are made when every member of the population has an equally likely chance of being selected. One way to get a random sample of students at the high school is to put separate slips with each student's name into a box, mix the name slips, and draw some name slips.

THINK ALOUD   Suppose the sales manager asks students at the junior after-school volleyball game whether they would buy the jacket. Would the results of this sample group give a good prediction for the entire student body? Would this be a representative sample?
no; no

━━━━━━━━━━━━━━ **GUIDED PRACTICE** ━━━━━━━━━━━━━━

Use the diagram.

1. Name the population and the sample.
   All students at Carver; music club
2. Explain why this sample is neither representative nor random.
   Check students' work.

> Students at Carver High School
>> Carver High School Music Club

378   LESSON 12-2

---

2 TEACH

If you were the sales manager, how might you select a representative sample? *(Possible answers: Ask every tenth student who leaves school; ask every third student who enters the cafeteria.)*

What are some ways the sales manager would select an unrepresentative sample? *(Accept reasonable answers.)*

> **Chalkboard Example**
>
> List samples for the population of car owners in your community. *(Possible samples: women, people between the ages of 25 and 40)*

SUMMARIZE/ASSESS   **Suppose you wanted to predict how people in various sections of your community would respond to a proposed recycling plant. From which sample of the population would you expect a response that was not representative?** *(Possible answer: people who live near the site of the proposed plant.)* **How could you attempt to obtain a representative sample?** *(Possible answer: question every 100th person listed in the community phone book.)*

■ PRACTICE ■

Name the population and the sample in Exercises 3–8.   See page 407b.

3.

Students in
Homeroom 303

10 Students whose names
were drawn from a hat

4.

People in Indiana

Girls at a high
school in Indiana

5. A magazine subscription company wants information about all the people in the United States.
They survey the people in a nursing home in California.

6. The manager of a restaurant leaves customer surveys at the entrance to the restaurant one evening. He wants to know how all his customers feel about the service at the restaurant.

7. You want to select 10 members of the band to complete a survey about uniforms. You pick names of band members from a hat.

8. A research company wants information about high school students across the country. They interview students at one high school in Florida.

9. Which samples in Exercises 3–8 are random samples of the population? Explain.   **3 and 7; Each member of the population had an equal chance for selection.**

10. CRITICAL THINKING Sometimes it's very difficult to obtain random samples. Use the examples in Exercises 4, 5, 6, and 8 to discuss why. **Answers will vary. Suggestion given: 4 and 8; the populations are large, diverse, and spread out. Random sample is time consuming and costly.**

■ PROBLEM SOLVING ■

11. A principal wants to know how many students in her school are interested in attending a field trip to the modern art museum. How might she get a representative sample of 80 students from the population of 1,200 students? **Pick every 150th student from alphabetical listing.**

Answers will vary. Suggestions given.

12. The seventh grade class at Washington School wants to have a committee of eight typical students represent them at an all-school meeting. How might the students be selected? **Put names in box and select eight.**

13. A town wants to build a swimming pool. How could you sample 100 out of 2,500 townspeople to find out how many would buy season swimming passes? **Computer picks at least 100 random addresses; survey sent to each address.**

MEETING INDIVIDUAL NEEDS

For Students Who Are . . .

Acquiring English Proficiency Discuss the extensive vocabulary in this lesson. Have students give examples of populations and samples.

Gifted and Talented Have students create a problem similar to Exercises 11–13 using representative samples.

Today's Problem

Every year, the Athletic Association has a party for the entire school of 500. To determine the menu, club members took a survey. Out of 10 students, 3 wanted pizza, 2 wanted salads, 1 wanted chili, 2 wanted sandwiches, and 2 wanted cheese and crackers. The members decided to serve pizza. What do you think of their decision? *(The sample was too small, and the results of the survey were too close to predict accurately what the entire school would like.)*

---

3 FOLLOW-UP

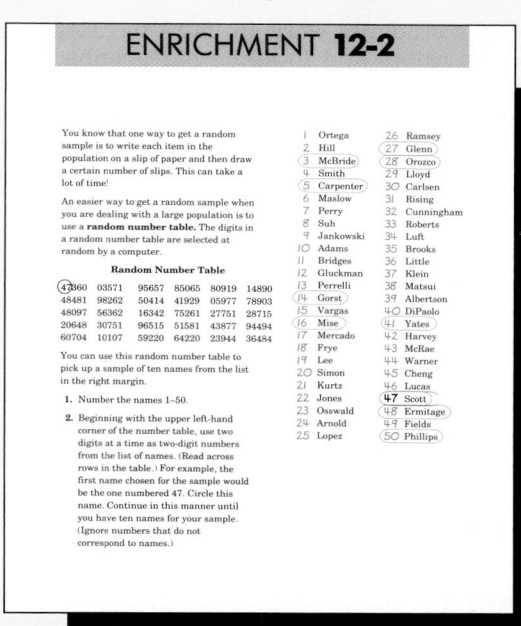

Lesson Organizer

Objective: Make a double bar graph.

Prior Knowledge: Students should know how to make and interpret single bar graphs.

Error Analysis and Remediation: See page 407A.

Lesson Resources:
Practice Worksheet 12-3
Reteaching Worksheet 12-3
Enrichment Activity 12-3
Daily Review 12-3

Two-Minute Math

Estimate. Which of the following percents is about twice the given percent?
21%: 48% 64% 32% 43% (43%)
17%: 30% 39% 24% 45% (30%)
44%: 83% 71% 91% 58% (91%)

1 INTRODUCE

CONNECTING ACTIVITY

☑ **MATERIALS CHECKLIST:** Teaching Aid 15 (Centimeter Grid Paper) and ruler for each pair

1. Ask: **What is your favorite color?** Survey the boys and girls separately. Show the results in a table for each group on the chalkboard.

2. Have students work in pairs to categorize the colors and to make bar graphs for each group. **Is it easy to use your bar graph to make comparisons for boys and girls? Explain.** (*No, the data are on two separate graphs.*)

WHEN YOUR STUDENTS ASK
★ **WHY AM I LEARNING THIS?** ★

In real life, meteorologists often use double bar graphs to compare the high and low temperatures over a period of days.

Double Bar Graphs

The single bar graphs below show the types of injuries received by students playing high school basketball during one year.

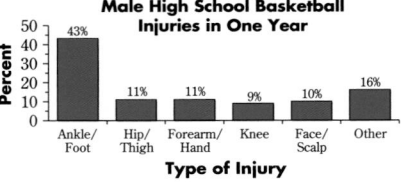

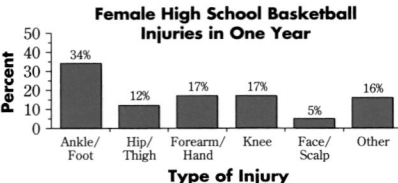

THINK ALOUD How do the injuries for males and for females compare? The **mode** is the event that occurs most frequently. What injury is the mode for males? for females? ankle/foot; ankle/foot

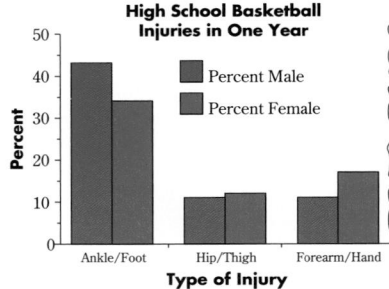

You can compare injuries for males and for females more easily on a double bar graph.

STEPS Label the horizontal axis as Injury.

Label the vertical axis as Percent.

Since the greatest percent on either single bar graph is 43%, the vertical axis can stop at 50%. Each division can represent 5%.

Use separate and distinct bars for males and for females.

GUIDED PRACTICE

Copy and complete the double bar graph by using facts from the single bar graphs. Use the graph to answer the question. Check students' work.

1. Which injuries occurred more often for males than for females?
ankle/foot; face/scalp

2. Which injury occurred most often overall?
ankle/foot

3. **ESTIMATE** Which injury occurred about twice as often for females as for males? How can you tell?
knee; 9 × 2 is close to 17

4. **CRITICAL THINKING** Which type of injury will probably be the mode for females in the year after the one graphed?
ankle/foot

5. **THINK ALOUD** How do you think this data was obtained?
Discuss the sample, the population, and the survey question(s).
See page 407b.

380   LESSON 12-3

---

2 TEACH

☑ **MATERIALS CHECKLIST:** Teaching Aid 15 (Centimeter Grid Paper), ruler, two colored pencils or markers for each student; calculators

Why is it easy to compare two sets of data on a double bar graph? (*Possible answer: The bars are side-by-side so data can be visually compared.*)

What is another situation that would be best represented with a double bar graph? (*Example: heights of boys and girls over a period of years*)

SUMMARIZE/ASSESS   **With a partner, make a double bar graph from the single bar graphs you made in the Introduce activity.** (*Check students' graphs.*)

Players in High School Sports		
Sport	Players	Players Injured
Football	1,021,685	374,678
Wrestling	273,334	82,987
Basketball	697,907	162,981

This table shows the number of players injured at least once during one year in three different high school sports.

Graph the information. Write the names of the sports in alphabetical order on the horizontal axis. Make 11 divisions on the vertical axis, each representing 100,000 players.

6. Draw a single bar graph showing the total number of players in each sport. **Check students' work.**

7. Draw a single bar graph showing the number of players injured playing each sport. **Check students' work.**

8. Use your two single bar graphs. Draw a double bar graph comparing the total number of players to the number of players injured for each sport. **Check students' work.**

Is the statement *true* or *false*? Explain.

9. Based on the number of players, football was the mode. **true**

10. There were fewer players than injured players in each sport. **false**

11. For each sport, over half the players were injured. **false**

12. Wrestling had fewer injured players than did basketball. **true**

ESTIMATE About what was the percent of players injured that year?

13. football **about 40%**
14. basketball **about 25%**
15. wrestling **about 30%**

Solve. Use the data in the table.

16. **CALCULATOR** Find the percent of players who were injured in each sport. **F: 37%; W: 30%; B: 23%**

17. Which sport had the greatest risk of injury? Explain. **Football; highest percent of injuries.**

18. Make a single bar graph showing the percent of injury in each of the three sports in the table above. **Check students' work.**

19. **IN YOUR WORDS** Compare your single bar graph of the percent of injury to your single bar graph of the number of injuries. Discuss how the two graphs are alike. Tell how and why they are different. **Accept reasonable answers.**

MEETING INDIVIDUAL NEEDS

For Students Who Are . . .

Acquiring English Proficiency Have students use the pictures in the lesson to show the meaning of *horizontal axis, vertical axis, separate distinct bars,* and *mode.*

Gifted and Talented Have students create a problem using information in the graph on page 380.

Working 2 or 3 Grades Below Level Have students use pages 70–71 of the Skills Workbook for Problem Solving Strategies.

Today's Problem

Create a double bar graph that shows the percent of the population according to age that voted in the 1980 and 1984 presidential elections. Use the data in the table. Check students' graphs.

	18–24	25–44	45–64	65 and Older
1980	40.8	58.4	69.8	67.7
1984	39.9	58.7	69.3	65.1

3 FOLLOW-UP

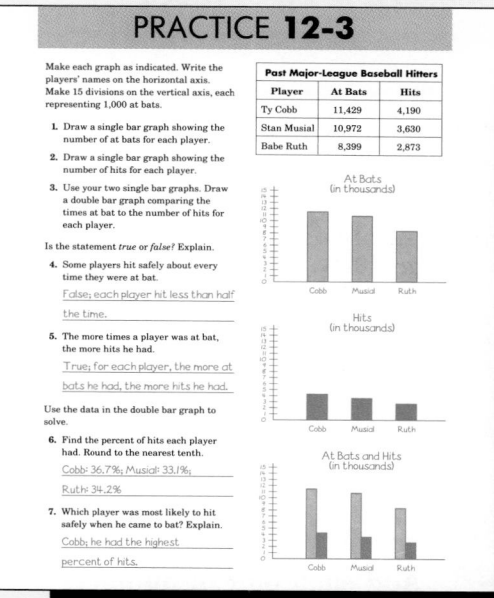

PRACTICE 12-3

Make each graph as indicated. Write the players' names on the horizontal axis. Make 15 divisions on the vertical axis, each representing 1,000 at bats.

Past Major-League Baseball Hitters		
Player	At Bats	Hits
Ty Cobb	11,429	4,190
Stan Musial	10,972	3,630
Babe Ruth	8,399	2,873

1. Draw a single bar graph showing the number of at bats for each player.

2. Draw a single bar graph showing the number of hits for each player.

3. Use your two single bar graphs. Draw a double bar graph comparing the times at bat to the number of hits for each player.

Is the statement *true* or *false*? Explain.

4. Some players hit safely about every time they were at bat. **False; each player hit less than half the time.**

5. The more times a player was at bat, the more hits he had. **True; for each player, the more at bats he had, the more hits he had.**

Use the data in the double bar graph to solve.

6. Find the percent of hits each player had. Round to the nearest tenth. **Cobb: 36.7%; Musial: 33.1%; Ruth: 34.2%**

7. Which player was most likely to hit safely when he came to bat? Explain. **Cobb; he had the highest percent of hits.**

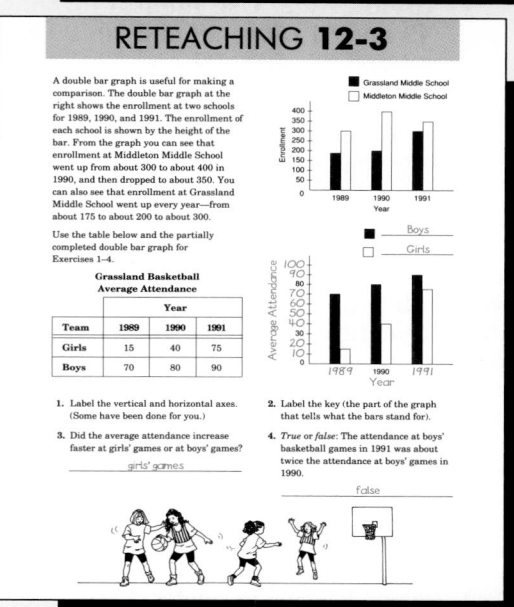

RETEACHING 12-3

A double bar graph is useful for making a comparison. The double bar graph at the right shows the enrollment at two schools for 1989, 1990, and 1991. The enrollment of each school is shown by the height of the bar. From the graph you can see that enrollment at Middleton Middle School went up from about 300 to about 400 in 1990, and then dropped to about 350. You can also see that enrollment at Grassland Middle School went up every year—from about 175 to about 200 to about 300.

Use the table below and the partially completed double bar graph for Exercises 1–4.

Grassland Basketball Average Attendance			
	Year		
Team	1989	1990	1991
Girls	15	40	75
Boys	70	80	90

1. Label the vertical and horizontal axes. (Some have been done for you.)

2. Label the key (the part of the graph that tells what the bars stand for.)

3. Did the average attendance increase faster at girls' games or at boys' games? **girls' games**

4. *True* or *false*: The attendance at boys' basketball games in 1991 was about twice the attendance at boys' games in 1990. **false**

ENRICHMENT 12-3

✓ **MATERIALS CHECKLIST:** Index cards, reference books, grid paper

On the board, write the names of five or so cities in the United States. Then give pairs of students one card apiece; each card contains the name of one of the cities on the board. Ask them to research the 1990 and 1970 populations of the city on the card and to draw a double bar graph on grid paper comparing the populations. Tell them to leave their graphs unlabeled, and display them in random order along the chalk rail under the city names. Have partners guess which graphs belong with which city, and reorder them.

Lesson Organizer

Objective: Find the mean and median.

Prior Knowledge: Students should be able to compare and order large whole numbers.

Error Analysis and Remediation: See page 407A.

Lesson Resources:
Practice Worksheet 12-4
Reteaching Worksheet 12-4
Enrichment Activity 12-4
Daily Review 12-4

Two-Minute Math

Add each pair of numbers and divide by 2. Use mental math.
49 and 51 *(50)*   29 and 30 *(29.5)*
48 and 52 *(50)*   27 and 32 *(29.5)*

1 INTRODUCE

SYMBOLIC ACTIVITY

Ask the class:
How much money did you each spend on lunch yesterday? Write each student's amount on the board in rank order. **Estimate the average cost of lunch for students in our class.** *(Accept reasonable answers.)* **What does the "average" describe?** *(Answers may vary. Possible answers: the mean, the usual cost of lunch, the center amount in the order listed)*

WHEN YOUR STUDENTS ASK
★ WHY AM I LEARNING THIS? ★

You can use this skill to plan a budget when you live on your own. For example, since electric bills vary each month, you can use the mean and/or median as a regular monthly expense in your budget.

MATH AND SOCIAL STUDIES

Mean and Median

Over the last 200 years the population of the New England states has grown dramatically, as you can see in the chart below. (The populations are rounded to the nearest thousand.)

	1790	1890	1990
Maine	97,000	661,000	1,212,000
New Hampshire	142,000	377,000	1,412,000
Vermont	85,000	332,000	562,000
Massachusetts	379,000	2,239,000	5,880,000
Rhode Island	69,000	346,000	1,002,000
Connecticut	238,000	746,000	3,279,000
Total	1,010,000	4,701,000	13,347,000

You can represent the "average" population for the New England states in 1790 by the mean or the median.

The **mean** is the sum of the data items divided by the number of data items.

$$\frac{\text{total population}}{\text{number of states}} \Rightarrow \frac{1,010,000}{6} \Rightarrow 168,333.33$$

The mean population of the six states in 1790 was about 168,000.

The **median** is the middle number in a set of data arranged in order.

After putting the state populations in order, you will find *two* middle numbers, 97,000 and 142,000. When you have an even number of data items, the median is the mean of the two middle numbers.

$$\frac{97,000 + 142,000}{2} = 119,500$$

The median population in 1790 was 119,500.

THINK ALOUD Since the 1790 population of Massachusetts was so much greater than the other states, the median may be a better representation of the average population than the mean. Explain. *See right.*

Since the mean is affected more by extreme numbers, the large population of Massachusetts has a big effect on the mean. The median depends only on order and middle number(s) and so is less affected by extremes.

Calculators should be available for tedious calculations.

2 TEACH

☑ MATERIALS CHECKLIST: calculators

When does the median rather than the mean better represent a set of data? *(when there is an extreme that affects the mean.)*

How do the mean and median compare when there is an extremely high value in the data set? *(The median is likely to be less.)*

When do you think both the mean and median of a data set should be reported? *(Possible answer: when the two are quite different and you want to demonstrate the existence of extreme values)*

> ### Chalkboard Examples
>
> Find the mean and the median for this set of data:
> 600; 500; 700; 1,200; 500
> *(mean: 700; median: 600)*

SUMMARIZE/ASSESS   Why do you think the "average" cost of a house in the United States is reported as a median? *(Because costs of houses vary from reasonable to very expensive, the median better represents the data.)*

Use the chart on page 382 for Exercises 1–9.
Suppose the population of Massachusetts in 1790
had been 250,000.

1. Find the new mean population for the
New England states for that year.
146,833

2. Find the new median population for the
New England states for that year. (*Hint:*
Remember to put the state populations in order.)
119,500

3. Did both the mean and the median change
with the changed population? Why or why not?
See page 407b.

4. CRITICAL THINKING Why did the mean get
closer to the median? Which would you use to best
show the "average"?
**Answers will vary. Suggestion given.
There is less range.**

PRACTICE

Find the mean of the population.

5. the New England states in 1890
783,500

6. the New England states in 1990
2,224,500

Find the median of the population.

7. the New England states in 1890
519,000

8. the New England states in 1990
1,312,000

Newfane, Vermont

PROBLEM SOLVING

Solve. Use pencil and paper or a calculator.

9. Change the 1890 population of Massachusetts to 750,000. See page 407b.

   a. Find the mean (to the nearest thousand). Did it change
with the changed population? Why or why not?

   b. Find the median (to the nearest thousand). Did it change
with the changed population? Why or why not?

10. IN YOUR WORDS When do you think the average should
be reported as the median? as either the mean or the median?
See page 407b.

11. Chris calculated the median population of the New England
states in 1990 this way: $\frac{562,000 + 5,880,000}{2}$. What was his error?
See page 407b.

MEETING INDIVIDUAL NEEDS

For Students Who Are . . .

Acquiring English Proficiency Have students locate the six New
England states on a map. Discuss the phrase *even number.*

Gifted and Talented Have students find each New England state's
percent of the total United States population in 1990.

Working 2 or 3 Grades Below Level Review ordering numbers
from least to greatest and dividing to the nearest thousand.

Today's Problem

Find the mean and the median of the following math test scores to
the nearest tenth: two 9's, four 7's, three 8's, and two 10's.
$[\frac{18 + 28 + 24 + 20}{11}$, or about 8.2; the ordered scores are 7, 7, 7, 7, 8, 8,
8, 9, 9, 10; median is the sixth score, or 8.0.]

3 FOLLOW-UP

PRACTICE 12-4

Use the chart at right to solve. Find the
mean.

1. the population of the seven largest
cities in the United States in 1980
2,629,429

2. the population of the seven largest
cities in the United States in 1990
2,733,857

Population of the 7 Largest Cities in the United States		
City	**1990**	**1980**
New York	7,352,000	7,072,000
Los Angeles	3,353,000	2,967,000
Chicago	2,977,000	3,005,000
Houston	1,698,000	1,595,000
Philadelphia	1,647,000	1,688,000
San Diego	1,075,000	876,000
Detroit	1,035,000	1,203,000
Total	19,137,000	18,406,000

Find the median.

3. the population of the seven largest
cities in the United States in 1980
1,688,000

4. the population of the seven largest
cities in the United States in 1990
1,698,000

Use the data in the chart to solve.

5. a. New York has more than twice the
population of the next largest city in
the United States. Which of the
measures (mean or median) does
New York's population affect the
most?
mean

   b. Find the mean and median in 1990,
not counting New York, to prove
your answer.
**mean = 1,964,167 – almost 2
million less
median = 1,672,500 – only
about 20,000 less**

6. Why did the mean change so
drastically compared to the median?
**The mean involves finding the
sum, so extreme amounts influence
the average greatly. The median
is simply the center of the data.**

RETEACHING 12-4

Look at the following set of data:

$$13, 45, 29, 37, 40, 31$$

The **mean** of a set of data is found by
dividing the sum of the numbers in the
set of data by the number of items in the
set.

$$\frac{13 + 45 + 29 + 37 + 40 + 31}{6} = \begin{matrix} \text{numbers in set} \\ \text{items in set} \end{matrix}$$

$$\frac{195}{6} = 32.5 \leftarrow \text{mean}$$

The **median** of a set of data is the
middle number when the items are
arranged in order from least to greatest.
To find the middle number when there is
an even number of items in a set of data,
you divide the sum of the two middle
numbers by 2.

$$13, 29, \mathbf{31, 37}, 40, 45$$

$$\frac{31 + 37}{2} = \frac{68}{2} = 34 \leftarrow \text{median}$$

Find the mean and the median for each set of numbers. Round to the
nearest tenth.

1. 65, 87, 91, 75, 82
mean **80**
median **82**

2. 9, 11, 18, 6, 7, 5, 4
mean **8.6**
median **7**

3. 30, 41, 29, 50, 36, 37
mean **37.2**
median **36.5**

4. 23, 28, 23, 24, 29, 23
mean **25**
median **23.5**

5. 96, 109, 115, 89, 92
mean **100.2**
median **96**

6. 14, 56, 38, 40, 19, 36, 38, 32, 21, 16
mean **31**
median **34**

ENRICHMENT 12-4

☑ **MATERIALS CHECKLIST:** Index cards

Have the students work in pairs. Provide
each partner with an index card on which
you have written the mean and median of
a set of data, as well as the number of
items in each set. For example, a card
might contain the following: *mean: 17;
median: 17; items in set: at least 5.* The
partners then write on the card a set of
data that fits the conditions specified (for
the above, for example: 20, 18, 17, 16, 14).
The partners exchange cards and check
each other's work. Repeat the activity as
time permits.

Lesson Organizer

> **Objective:** Make a double line graph.

Prior Knowledge: Students should be able to make and interpret single line graphs.

Error Analysis and Remediation: See page 407A.

Lesson Resources:
Practice Worksheet 12-5
Reteaching Worksheet 12-5
Enrichment Activity 12-5
Daily Review 12-5

Two-Minute Math

Name the first ten multiples of:
25 *(0, 25, 50, 75, 100, 125, 150, 175, 200, 225)*
40 *(0, 40, 80, 120, 160, 200, 240, 280, 320, 360)*
60 *(0, 60, 120, 180, 240, 300, 360, 420, 480, 540)*

1 INTRODUCE

CONNECTING ACTIVITY

☑ **MATERIALS CHECKLIST:** Teaching Aid 15 (Centimeter Grid Paper) and ruler for each student

Show students how to find their pulse, either in the wrist or neck.

1. Count and record your heart rate (number of beats per minute) for 3 minutes.

2. Make a line graph of the results.

3. Why do you think your graph does not form a smooth line? *(Possible answer: Heartbeats have a certain amount of natural variation.)*

WHEN YOUR STUDENTS ASK
★ WHY AM I LEARNING THIS? ★

Double line graphs are published daily in newspapers and magazines. These graphs display trends in sales of consumer products, changes in interest rates, and changes in weather over time.

Double Line Graphs

The table shows two heart rates for a 12 year-old girl.

Minutes	1	2	3	4	5	6	7	8	9	10
Heart Rate at Rest	86	88	87	89	90	87	87	90	88	87
Heart Rate After Exercise	190	185	147	117	103	105	98	90	92	89

You can show the after-exercise heart rate with a line graph.

STEPS Draw the horizontal and the vertical axes on grid paper.

Label the horizontal axis as minutes.

Label the vertical axis as heart rate. Use multiples of 20 from 0 to 200, since the highest rate is 190.

Plot the after-exercise heart rates and join with segments to make a line graph.

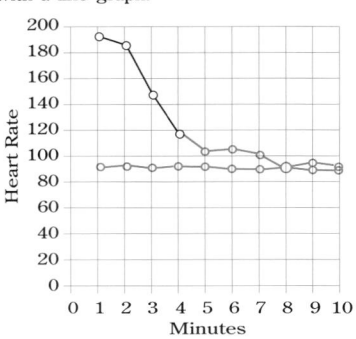

4. (1, 86); (2, 88); . . . ; (9, 88); (10, 87)

GUIDED PRACTICE

1. Copy the graph started above.
   Check students' work.
2. What is the next point you should show?
   (5, 103)
3. Complete the graph using the after-exercise heart rates shown.
   See above.
4. What points would you plot to show at-rest heart rates?
   See above.
5. On the same grid, make a line graph of the at-rest heart rates. Use a different colored pencil.
   See above.
6. What would you title this graph?
   Answers will vary.
7. **CRITICAL THINKING** About how long does it take heart rate after exercise to return to heart rate at rest? What factors could influence this recovery time?
   9–10 min; fitness level

MATH AND HEALTH

384   LESSON 12-5

2 TEACH

☑ **MATERIALS CHECKLIST:** Teaching Aid 15 (Centimeter Grid Paper), ruler, 2 different colored pencils for each student

What other scale could be used for the vertical axis? *(Possible answer: A scale with intervals of 10 or 25 would also work.)*

Why does the vertical scale go to 200? *(The greatest heart rate in the table is 190.)*

What happened when you plotted the data for 8 minutes and drew the line segments? *(The two lines met at the same point; a heart rate of 90.)*

SUMMARIZE/ASSESS   **A double line graph showed the growth rate of two bean sprouts under different scientific conditions. What would you expect the graph to look like?** *(Possible answer: Both lines would start at the same point, then separate.)*

Use this table, showing heart-rate data for an adult man, for Exercises 8–13.

Minutes	1	2	3	4	5	6	7	8	9	10
Heart Rate at Rest	50	48	60	51	54	52	55	53	56	58
Heart Rate After Exercise	111	104	80	81	72	64	65	57	53	57

8. Make a line graph for the man's heart rate after exercise.
   Check students' work.

9. **NUMBER SENSE** What would you expect the man's heart rate to be 15 min after exercise?
   54; the average heart rate at rest

10. Make another line graph on the same grid showing the man's heart rate at rest for 10 min. Use a different colored pencil.
   Check students' work.

Is the statement *true* or *false*? Explain.

11. The man's heart rate rapidly decreases for the first 5 min after exercise.
   true; drops from 111 to 72.

12. The man's heart rate after exercise will probably gradually slow down to 0 beats/min.
   false; His heart will not stop beating.

13. The man's heart rate after exercise will probably level off to about 55 beats/min if he continues to rest.
   true; That is about his average resting rate.

Solve. Use your line graphs of the heart rates of the girl and of the man.

14. About how long does it take for the man's heart rate to return to "normal" after exercising?
   8–10 minutes

15. **IN YOUR WORDS** Compare the after-exercise and at-rest heart rates of the 12-year-old girl and the adult man. What similarities and differences do you see?
   Check students' work.

16. A doctor looked at the line graphs for the girl and the man and remarked that they both appeared to be in good physical condition. The graph of another person's after-exercise and at-rest rates is shown at right. What physical condition do you think the person is in? Why?
   Answers will vary. Suggestion given: Not good; after 10 minutes heart rate remains high

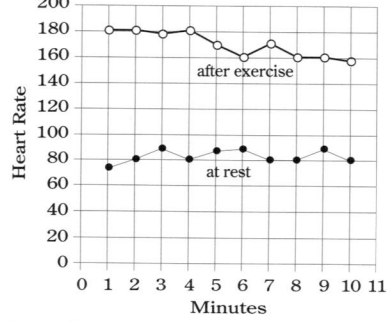

CHAPTER 12 385

MEETING INDIVIDUAL NEEDS

For Students Who Are . . .

Acquiring English Proficiency Explain that heart rate is the number of heartbeats per minute. Review the meanings of the words *multiples* and *segments*.

Gifted and Talented Have students make a table and a double line graph showing their own heart rates at rest and after exercise.

Working 2 or 3 Grades Below Level Have students use pages 72–73 of the Skills Workbook for Problem Solving Strategies.

Today's Problem

Below are the average weekly earnings of production workers in five major industries during 1986 and 1987. Make a graph of the data. Describe what you observe. *(Earnings increased in 1987.)*

	Mining	Construction	Manufac-turing	Transportation/Public Utilities	Wholesale Trade
1986	$525.81	$466.75	$396.01	$458.64	$358.11
1987	$530.85	$479.68	$406.31	$471.89	$365.38

---

3 FOLLOW-UP

PRACTICE 12-5

Use the table at right to make and label line graphs as indicated to show the calories used per minute.

Calories Used per Minute At 100 lb of Body Weight	
Activity	**Calories**
Standing	1
Walking (3 mph)	3
Walking (4 mph)	4
Jogging (5.5 mph)	6
Running (7.5 mph)	9.5

1. Use a solid line to show Andy running a 1-mi race in 8 min, jogging for 1 min to slow down, then walking slowly for 1 min to stand and receive his first-place medal.

2. On the same graph, use a broken line to show what Betty was doing while Andy was running the race: standing at the starting line to take pictures for 4 min, jogging about 1 min to a better position, standing to take pictures there for another 3 min, then walking quickly for 2 min to get shots of Andy accepting his medal.

Is the statement *true* or *false*? Explain.

3. Betty used more calories than Andy during the 10 min.
   False; Andy used many more.

4. Andy used more than 9 calories per minute for most of the 10 min.
   True; he used 9.5 cal/min for the 8 min he jogged.

5. At one point during the 10 min, both Andy and Betty were using the same number of calories.
   False; they never did the same thing at the same time.

6. During the ninth minute, Betty had increased and Andy had decreased the calories each used per minute.
   true, per graph

Solve.

7. During the first minute, how many calories were Andy and Betty using together?
   10.5 cal

8. During what minute was Betty using more calories than Andy?
   during the tenth minute

RETEACHING 12-5

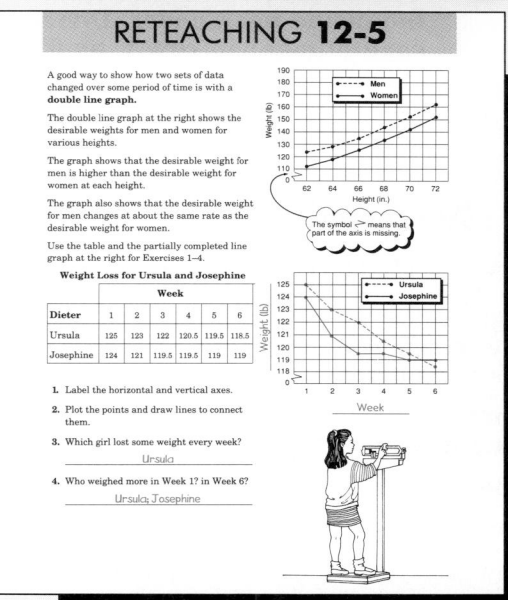

A good way to show how two sets of data changed over some period of time is with a **double line graph**.

The double line graph at the right shows the desirable weights for men and women for various heights.

The graph shows that the desirable weight for men is higher than the desirable weight for women at each height.

The graph also shows that the desirable weight for men changes at about the same rate as the desirable weight for women.

The symbol ⌇ means that part of the axis is missing.

Use the table and the partially completed line graph at the right for Exercises 1–4.

Weight Loss for Ursula and Josephine						
Week						
Dieter	1	2	3	4	5	6
Ursula	125	123	122	120.5	119.5	118.5
Josephine	124	121	119.5	119.5	119	119

1. Label the horizontal and vertical axes.
2. Plot the points and draw lines to connect them.
3. Which girl lost some weight every week?
   Ursula
4. Who weighed more in Week 1? in Week 6?
   Ursula; Josephine

ENRICHMENT 12-5

☑ **MATERIALS CHECKLIST:** Calorie charts, grid paper, rulers

Have the students work in pairs. Each partner thinks about the foods he or she has eaten for lunch over the last five days. The partners estimate the amount of food eaten and use a calorie chart to find the number of calories. Each pair then makes a bar graph on grid paper showing the number of calories consumed for each of the last five days. You may wish to have the students use reference books to determine whether they are getting the right amount of calories.

LESSON | 12-6

Lesson Organizer

> **Objective:** Solve problems by choosing an appropriate graph.

Prior Knowledge: Students should be able to interpret bar and line graphs.

Error Analysis and Remediation: See page 407A.

Lesson Resources:
Practice Worksheet 12-6
Reteaching Activity 12-6
Enrichment Worksheet 12-6
Daily Review 12-6

Two-Minute Math

Use the Table of Numbers on the inside back cover. Divide each number in row F by 0.2. *(1.5; 4; 4.5, 3.55; 3; 1.7; 3.95; 1; 3.25)*

1 INTRODUCE

SYMBOLIC ACTIVITY

Begin a discussion to help students recognize the value of using graphs and of choosing appropriate graphs.

What are some experiments you have done in your science class?

What was being compared?

How did you collect the data?

How did you make your conclusions?

WHEN YOUR STUDENTS ASK
★ **WHY AM I LEARNING THIS?** ★

When you write reports for social studies or science class, you may need to show information in a graph. This skill will help you choose the appropriate graph to represent a particular situation.

MATH AND SCIENCE

Problem Solving:
Choosing an Appropriate Graph

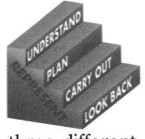

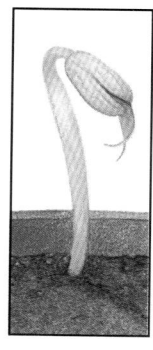

A science class grew bean seedlings under three different conditions. Students watered some of the seedlings with tap water, some with bleach water, and some with salt water. Each day the students measured the heights of the seedlings and calculated an average height for each type of watering.

THINK ALOUD How would an average height for several seedlings be calculated? **Measure all; Add their heights; Divide by the number of seedlings measured.**
The table below has the data for the average heights of the seedlings for the first five days of the experiment.

Average Height of Seedlings					
	Day 1	Day 2	Day 3	Day 4	Day 5
Tap water	0.2 cm	1.3 cm	2.5 cm	3.8 cm	5.2 cm
Bleach water	0.2 cm	0.5 cm	0.5 cm	0.5 cm	0.5 cm
Salt water	0.2 cm	1.0 cm	1.9 cm	2.3 cm	2.8 cm

The two graphs below are from students' reports about their experiment.

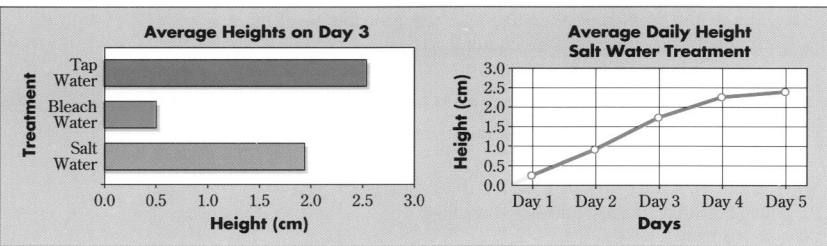

THINK ALOUD Which of the graphs above is a bar graph? a line graph? Use the line graph to estimate the heights at $2\frac{1}{2}$ d of the seedlings treated with salt water. **graph 1; graph 2; 1.5 cm**

> **When data are organized by nonnumerical categories, you can use bar graphs or pictographs.**
>
> **When data are organized numerically, you can use bar graphs, pictographs, or line graphs.**

THINK ALOUD The data in the first graph should not be shown as a line graph. Discuss why.
Left axis is of nonnumerical data.

---

2 TEACH

☑ **MATERIALS CHECKLIST:** Teaching Aid 15 (Centimeter Grid Paper) and ruler for each student

On the table, what do the individual data items represent? *(the average height in cm of the seedlings each day, under different conditions)*

Would it be correct to turn the bar graph on page 386 into a line graph by simply connecting the tops of the bars with lines and erasing the bars? Explain. *(No; non-numerical categories can be put in any order, so it makes no sense to connect them in a particular order. In addition, the points on the line segments connecting the bars would have no meaning.)*

SUMMARIZE/ASSESS
Why was a bar graph used to show the average height of the seedlings on day 3 and a line graph used to show the average daily heights for the salt water-treated seedlings? *(Possible answer: A bar graph can be used to show data for comparing nonnumerical categories; a line graph can be used to show change over a period of time.)*

1. Use the information in the box at the bottom of page 386.

   a. What kind of graphs can you use for data that is organized by numerical categories? **bar, line, or pictographs**

   b. Are types of watering treatments numerical or nonnumerical data? **nonnumerical**

   c. Ruth has a record of her height on each of her birthdays. What kind of graph would you use to show the data?
   Answers will vary. Suggestion given. bar, line, or pictograph

PRACTICE

Use the table on page 386. What types of graph can be used to represent the data set?

2. the average heights for five days of the seedlings treated with salt water
bar, line, and pictograph

3. the average height on day 5 for seedlings treated all three ways
bar and pictograph

4. CREATE YOUR OWN Use the data in the table to make a line graph for the average daily growth of seedlings under bleach water treatment for five days.
Check students' work.

5. IN YOUR WORDS Find several graphs in newspapers or magazines. Write an explanation for each graph of why the graph makers may have chosen the type of graph they did.
Check students' work.

 CHOOSE Choose any strategy to solve. **Strategies may vary.**

6. A recipe calls for 3 c of milk. You have a 1-qt container of milk. What fraction of the container will you use? $\frac{3}{4}$

7. Laura has 9 coins that equal $1. What coins might she have?
Answers will vary. Suggestion given: 2Q, 3D, 4N.

8. What is the total cost of a coat priced at $99.98 with 5% sales tax? **$104.98**

Estimate

When several data items are close to the same number, you can round them to that number to make a mental estimate of the mean.

Example: 57, 58, 60, 62, 64, 90, 100
Round 57, 58, 60, 62, and 64 to 60; multiply 60 by 5 (300), add the other numbers to 300 (490), and divide 490 by 7 to get a mean of 70.

Estimate the mean mentally.
1. 31, 30, 29, 30, 36 **31** **2.** 60, 76, 77, 81, 83, 100 **80** **3.** 39, 49, 47, 52, 51, 61 **50**

MEETING INDIVIDUAL NEEDS

For Students Who Are . . .

Acquiring English Proficiency Discuss the phrase *non-numerical categories*. Pair students with an able reader for Exercises 6 and 7.

Gifted and Talented Have students find the percent of growth for the seedlings from day 1 to day 5 for each treatment.

Having Reading Difficulties Remind students that mental math refers to calculating without pencil and paper.

Today's Problem

On a bar graph, the bar for week 1 is $\frac{1}{3}$ the height of the bar for week 2. The bar for week 2 is twice the height of the bar for week 3 and $\frac{3}{4}$ the height of the bar for week 4. If the bar for week 4 represents 16 h, how many hours are represented by the bars for weeks 1, 2, and 3? *(week 1: 4 h; week 2: 12 h; week 3: 6 h)*

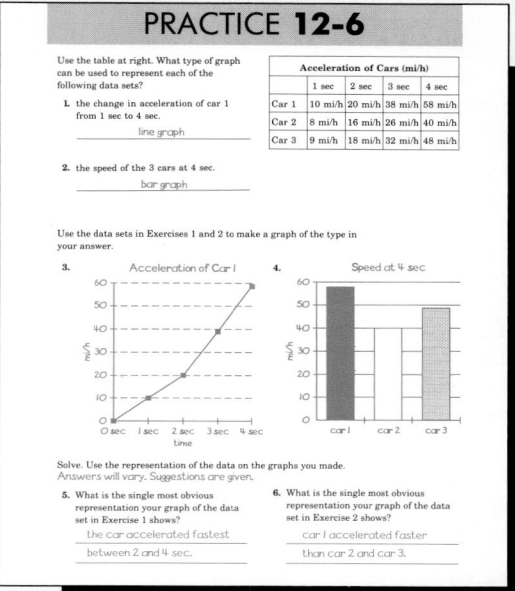

PRACTICE 12-6

Use the table at right. What type of graph can be used to represent each of the following data sets?

Acceleration of Cars (mi/h)				
	1 sec	2 sec	3 sec	4 sec
Car 1	10 mi/h	20 mi/h	38 mi/h	58 mi/h
Car 2	8 mi/h	16 mi/h	26 mi/h	40 mi/h
Car 3	9 mi/h	18 mi/h	32 mi/h	48 mi/h

1. the change in acceleration of car 1 from 1 sec to 4 sec.
   line graph

2. the speed of the 3 cars at 4 sec.
   bar graph

Use the data sets in Exercises 1 and 2 to make a graph of the type in your answer.

3. Acceleration of Car 1

4. Speed at 4 sec

Solve. Use the representation of the data on the graphs you made.
Answers will vary. Suggestions are given.

5. What is the single most obvious representation your graph of the data set in Exercise 1 shows?
   the car accelerated fastest
   between 2 and 4 sec.

6. What is the single most obvious representation your graph of the data set in Exercise 2 shows?
   car 1 accelerated faster
   than car 2 and car 3.

RETEACHING 12-6

Some students may have difficulty choosing the appropriate graph for a given set of data. Have them make this checklist.

Type of Data	Type of Graph to Use		
	Bar	Picto	Line
Numerical	X	X	X
Nonnumerical	X	X	—

ENRICHMENT 12-6

The table shows the number of records, compact discs, and cassettes that were produced in the United States for the years 1975–1989.

Record, CD, and Cassette Production (in thousands)			
Year	Records	CDs	Cassettes
1975	421,000	–	16,200
1976	463,000	–	21,800
1977	534,000	–	36,900
1978	531,800	–	61,300
1979	513,800	–	82,800
1980	487,100	–	110,200
1981	449,900	–	137,000
1982	381,100	–	182,300
1983	334,400	800	236,800
1984	336,100	5,800	332,000
1985	287,700	22,600	339,100
1986	219,100	53,000	344,500
1987	189,000	102,100	410,000
1988	138,000	149,700	450,000
1989	71,200	207,200	446,200

1. Make a graph to show the changes in these music formats between 1975 and 1989. (*Hint:* What units are the figures for each format given in?)

   Check students' graphs.

2. Describe the trends shown in the graph you made. Include any thoughts you have on the reasons for the changes. Answers will vary. A suggestion is given.
   Production of records peaked in the late 1970s. Because
   of the introduction of CDs in 1983 and the popularity of
   portable cassette players in 1984, production of records
   started to diminish about that time.

Lesson Organizer

Objective: Make frequency and relative frequency tables.

Prior Knowledge: Students should be able to find percents and understand bar graphs and tables.

Error Analysis and Remediation: See page 407A.

Lesson Resources:
Practice Worksheet 12-7
Reteaching Worksheet 12-7
Enrichment Activity 12-7
Daily Review 12-7

Two-Minute Math

Write each decimal as a percent.
0.02 *(2%)*   0.17 *(17%)*
0.3 *(30%)*   0.009 *(.9%)*

1 INTRODUCE

CONNECTING ACTIVITY

1. Ask a volunteer to use a chart to record and tally students' responses to this question: **How did you get to school this morning: By walking? On a bus? In a car? On a bike?**

2. **Estimate the percent of students who used each method of transportation**

3. **Based on the data, what plans should be made for the school's parking lot and entrance?**

WHEN YOUR STUDENTS ASK
★ WHY AM I LEARNING THIS? ★

You can connect this skill to real life through the work of consumer "watchdogs" who rate different products and goods by finding the relative frequency of complaints and the need for repairs.

Relative Frequency

Middle schools are organized in different ways. The bar graph allows you to compare different types of middle schools that existed in 1970–71. For example, you can see there were over twice as many schools for grades 6–8 as for grades 5–8.

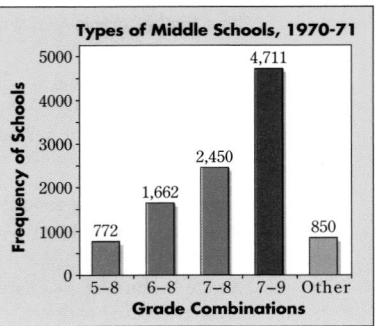

THINK ALOUD Why can't you see how many schools for grades 5–8 there were compared to all the middle schools?
There is no bar for that category.

To make such a comparison, you need to find a relative frequency. A **relative frequency** is a ratio that compares a part to the whole.

THINK ALOUD How can you find the whole, or the *total,* number of middle schools?
Add all of the sections together.

You can construct a **relative frequency table** from the information in the bar graph.

STEPS Make a chart with three columns. Put the grade combinations in the first column.

Show each grade combination's frequency (the part) in the second column. Find the total number of schools (the whole).

Find the relative frequency by using a calculator to divide the part by the whole. Round the quotient to the nearest hundredth.

Types of Middle Schools, 1970-71		
Grade Combination	Frequency (Part)	Relative Frequency (Part ÷ Whole)
5–8	772	0.07 or 7%
6–8	1,662	☐ or ☐
7–8	2,450	☐ or ☐
7–9	☐	☐ or ☐
Other	☐	☐ or ☐
Total (whole)	10,445	

The relative frequency of middle schools for grades 5–8 is about 0.07. In 1970–71, about 7% of all middle schools were for grades 5–8.

THINK ALOUD What grade combination does your school have? In 1970–71 what percent of middle schools had that combination?
Answers may vary.

GUIDED PRACTICE

1. **CALCULATOR** Copy and complete the relative frequency table above. Round the relative frequencies to hundredths. Then write them as percents. Check students' graphs.

Calculators should be available for lengthy computations with data.

2 TEACH

✓ MATERIALS CHECKLIST: calculators

What does the word *frequency* mean? *(how often an event or outcome occurs)*

How are percents and relative frequencies related? *(Percents compare parts to wholes; relative frequencies compare the frequency of desired events to the number of all events)*

Why can relative frequencies be represented by fractions, decimals, or percents? *(They all can be used to compare parts to wholes.)*

Chalkboard Example

Have students make a relative frequency table for the data collected in the Introduce activity.

SUMMARIZE/ASSESS **What do relative frequencies tell you that bar graphs using frequencies do not?** *(Possible answer: They compare parts to wholes, not just part to parts.)*

2. **THINK ALOUD** How do you think the data on page 388 about middle schools was obtained? Discuss the sample, the population, and the question(s) that may have been asked. See page 407b.

PRACTICE

Refer to your relative frequency table.

3. **ESTIMATE** Find a grade combination that
   a. occurred about twice as often as did grades 7–8. 7–9
   b. occurred almost half as often as didgrades 6–8. Other
   c. occurred in about 1 out of every 4 middle schools. 7–8

4. **IN YOUR WORDS** Explain why the sum of the relative frequencies should always be close to 1.00, or 100%. 100% is the total sample.

5. What is the sum of the relative frequencies in percents? Is it close to 1.00, or 100%? 99%; yes

PROBLEM SOLVING

Refer to the bar graph at right.

6. **CALCULATOR** Make a relative frequency table for types of middle schools in 1986–87. Round the relative frequencies to hundredths. Then write each relative frequency as a percent. See page 407b.

7. **ESTIMATE** Find a grade combination for 1986–1987 that fits the description.
   a. occurred about twice as often as did grades 7–9? 6–8
   b. occurred in about 1 out of every 10 middle schools? 5–8
   c. occurred in about $\frac{1}{4}$ of all middle schools? 7–8

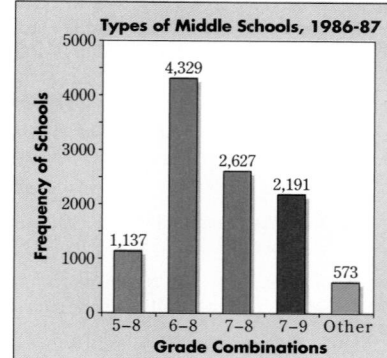

8. What is the mode for the grade combinations? 6–8

9. **IN YOUR WORDS** Explain how to find the mode by using either the bar graph or your relative frequency table. Accept reasonable answers.

10. **CREATE YOUR OWN** Make a double bar graph of the relative frequencies for 1970–1971 and 1986–87. Use it to predict which grade combination will be most common in 1997–98. Check students' work.

MEETING INDIVIDUAL NEEDS

For Students Who Are . . .

Acquiring English Proficiency Help students set up the relative frequency table for Exercise 6. Remind them to find the whole (number of combinations) in the second column of their table.

Gifted and Talented Assign the technology lesson on page 412.

Working 2 or 3 Grades Below Level Review rounding quotients to the nearest hundredth and changing decimals to percents.

Today's Problem

Because relative frequency is frequency divided by total frequency, its value is always greater than or equal to what number and always less than or equal to what number? *(Relative frequency is always greater than or equal to zero, and it is always less than or equal to one.)*

3 FOLLOW-UP

PRACTICE 12-7

Refer to the relative frequency table at right.

1. Estimate which grade average occurred
   a. about half as often as a C B
   b. about twice as often as a D B
   c. in about one out of every 50 grades F

Middle School Student Grade Averages		
Grade	Frequency	Relative Frequency
A	49	4%
B	337	27%
C	675	54%
D	162	13%
F	26	2%
Total	1,249	100%

Refer to the bar graph.

2. Make a relative frequency table for the high school student grade averages.

High School Student Grade Averages		
Grade	Frequency	Relative Frequency
A	28	1%
B	451	19%
C	1,187	49%
D	589	25%
F	145	6%
Total	2,400	100%

3. Estimate which grade average occurred
   a. about twice as often as a D C
   b. in about 1 out of every 5 grade averages B
   c. in about one hundredth of all grade averages A

4. What is the mode of the grade averages? C
   Explain how you found the mode. identified the most frequently occurring grade

RETEACHING 12-7

The **relative frequency** tells what percent of the whole is accounted for by a part. Finding the relative frequencies of the parts makes it easier to compare them.

The table at the right shows the frequency of each hair color in Ms. Stein's class. The frequency column tells you that there are 14 students with brown hair—more than with any other color hair. The relative frequency column tells what percent of the whole class this is.

Hair Color in Ms. Stein's Class		
Color	Frequency	Relative Frequency
Red	2	0.08 or 8%
Blond	6	0.24 or 24%
Brown	14	0.56 or 56%
Black	3	0.12 or 12%
Total	25	1.00 or 100%

relative frequency = $\frac{\text{part}}{\text{whole}} = \frac{14}{25} = 0.56$, or 56%

The results of a survey have been tallied. Complete the table.

If necessary, round the relative frequency to the nearest hundredth.

1. Foreign Travel in Mr. Cooper's Class

Country Visited	Tally	Frequency	Relative Frequency		
Mexico	𝍸	5	0.25	or	25 %
United Kingdom	||||	4	0.2	or	20 %
France	||	2	0.1	or	10 %
Other	|||	3	0.15	or	15 %
None	𝍸 |	6	0.3	or	30 %
Total	20	20	1.0	or	100 %

2. School Transportation Survey

Primary Method of Transportation	Frequency	Relative Frequency		
Automobile	18	0.3	or	30 %
Bus	34	0.57	or	57 %
Walking	6	0.1	or	10 %
Train/other	2	0.03	or	3 %
Total	60	1.0	or	100 %

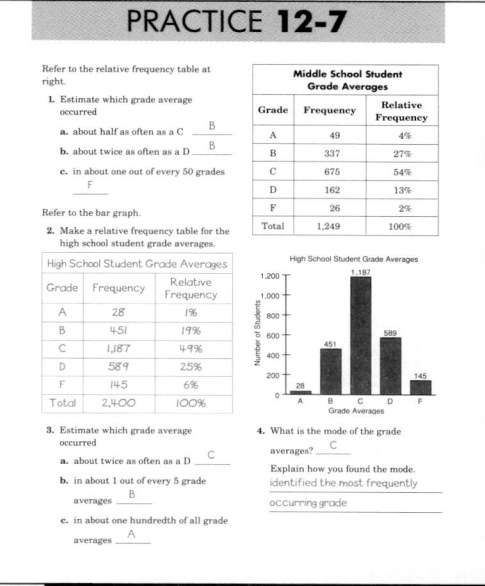

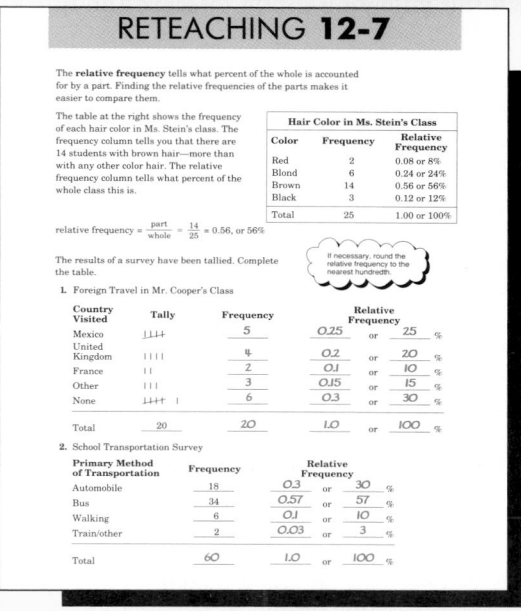

ENRICHMENT 12-7

☑ MATERIALS CHECKLIST: Small box of raisins for each student, self-stick removable notes

Have students guess how many raisins are in one box and write their guesses on self-stick notes. Have them make the bars for a histogram (a bar graph showing frequency) with their notes using intervals of 2 starting at 30 (30–31, 32–33, and so on). Then have students count the number of raisins in their boxes and put the number on their self-stick notes. Make another histogram. Compare the two histograms. What is the range of data? Is there a mode? Change the histograms using intervals of 3 or 4. Discuss changes in the graphs.

MIDCHAPTER
Checkup

The midchapter checkup provides a way for you to check students' understanding of the skills taught in the first half of the chapter.

Language and Vocabulary

Some key language and vocabulary ideas from the first half of the chapter are reinforced here.

Quick Quiz

This quiz provides a means of evaluating students' understanding of the objectives for the first half of the chapter. Page references are given so that students can check back to where the skill was taught.

Use the following guide to score the quick quiz.

Score	Percent
6	100%
5	83
4	66
3	50
2	34
1	17

Use this chart to identify the management objectives tested.

Items	Management Objective	Pages
1–2; 4	**12A** Find the mean and median.	378–379, 382–384
3	**12B** Make a double bar graph and a double line graph.	380–381, 384–385
5	**12D** Find the probability of an event.	388–389
6	**12E** Problem Solving: Choose an appropriate graph.	386–387

MIDCHAPTER CHECKUP

LANGUAGE & VOCABULARY

Write a sentence describing the relationship between the two terms.
Accept reasonable answers.

1. sample, population
2. data items, mean
3. middle number, median
4. time, line graph

QUICK QUIZ ✓

Name the population and the sample. *(pages 378–379)*

1. A national mail order clothing company wants to know how customers feel about the quality of their products. They send questionnaires to customers in 5 states. **all customers; customers in 5 states**

2. A TV game show hostess asks each viewer to send in a post card. The producer wants to determine the age range of the audience. Those who send in cards may win a prize. On a later show, the hostess draws 100 post cards from a drum. **all game show viewers; viewers who sent a post card**

Use the data from the table. *(pages 380–385, 388–389)*

The table shows Parent-Teacher Association membership in two schools for 4 years.

	Fillmore	Coolidge
1988	85	112
1989	96	115
1990	108	130
1991	110	135

3. Make a double bar graph of this data. **Check students' graphs.**
4. Find the mean and the median of the Coolidge membership. **123; 122.5**
5. In what year was the Fillmore membership about $\frac{3}{4}$ of the 1991 Fillmore membership? **1988**

Solve. *(pages 386–387)*

6. The table shows the average price of gasoline during a 4-wk period.

Week	Regular	Premium
1	$1.09	$1.28
2	$1.15	$1.25
3	$1.17	$1.39
4	$1.21	$1.43

   a. What was the average price of regular gasoline during week 3? **$1.17**
   b. How can you compare the average prices of the gasoline? **Draw a graph.**
   c. What type of graph can be used to represent the average prices of both gasolines? **double bar graph**

LEARNING LOG

Write the answers in your learning log.   **Answers will vary. Suggestions given.**

1. Explain the advantage of having a large sample when attempting to make predictions.   **A larger sample should be more representative.**

2. Your math test grades are 42, 100, 85, 82, and 88. Would you rather have your teacher use the mean or the median to represent your final grade? Explain.   **Mean = 79.4; Median = 85**

MATH AMERICA

DID YOU KNOW . . . ? In 1976, the United States celebrated its bicentennial, or 200th, birthday. What birthday will your city or town celebrate this year? Express your city or town's age in centuries. Use fractions if necessary. **Check students' work**

BONUS

Conduct a survey. Choose a representative sample of students from your grade. Ask them to name their favorite news broadcaster.

Consider these questions in conducting your survey:

- How will you get a representative sample?
- How many students will you need to ask?
- How can you best display your data?

Predict the results of your survey. How do the results compare with your prediction? Are they what you expected? How can you explain the results?   **Accept reasonable answers.**

Learning Log

These are suggestions for writing about some topics taught so far in the chapter. The students keep their learning logs from the start of the school year to the end.

Math America

A mathematical skill that students have learned is related to an interesting fact about the United States.

Bonus

Students are given an opportunity to solve a challenge-type problem such as a puzzle or a nonroutine problem.

Lesson Organizer

Objective: Measure chance.

Prior Knowledge: Students should understand that there are an infinite number of numbers between 0 and 1.

Lesson Resources:
Practice Worksheet 12-8
Reteaching Activity 12-8
Enrichment Worksheet 12-8
Daily Review 12-8
Cooperative Problem Solving 2,
    Chapter 12

Two-Minute Math

Which of the following numbers are between 0 and 1?
0.4   1.009   2% $\frac{2}{3}$ 0.992   ⁻0.5
(All except 1.009 and ⁻0.5)

1 INTRODUCE

CONNECTING ACTIVITY

1. Have students work in pairs to write three lists: certain events, impossible events, and uncertain events.

2. Then have students rank-order the uncertain events from most likely to least likely and share their lists with the class.

WHEN YOUR STUDENTS ASK
★ **WHY AM I LEARNING THIS?** ★

You can use this skill in everyday life to make decisions based on uncertain circumstances. Mathematically analyzing chance will help you make the best possible decision.

Measuring Chance

What do you think is the chance that one of your classmates will become President of the United States tomorrow?

If you answered *no chance,* you are right. Mathematically, the probability of this happening is 0.

Probability (*P*) is a measure of chance.

- Events that are impossible have a probability of 0. The probability that a car traveling under its own power down the highway has no wheels is 0.
- Events that are certain to happen have a probability of 1. For example, the probability that the day after next Tuesday will be a Wednesday is 1.
- Events that are uncertain have a probability between 0 and 1. The probability of getting a head when tossing a penny is $\frac{1}{2}$, or 0.5.

GUIDED PRACTICE

1. THINK ALOUD   Give one example of the event.   **Answers will vary. Suggestions given.**
  a. an event that has a probability of 0   **October will have 40 days.**
  b. an event that has a probability of 1   **Sunday will follow Saturday.**
  c. an event that has a probability between 0 and 1   **The sun will shine tomorrow.**

2. Could the number represent a probability? Write *yes* or *no.*
a. 5 **no** **b.** $\frac{6}{10}$ **yes** **c.** 0.04 **yes** **d.** $1\frac{1}{5}$ **no** **e.** 45% **yes** **f.** 95 **no** **g.** 150% **no**

PRACTICE

Is the probability *0, 1,* or *between 0 and 1?*
3. You toss a nickel and it will land heads up.
  between 0 and 1
4. You will drive a car to school tomorrow.
  0
5. It will rain tomorrow.
  between 0 and 1
6. It will snow somewhere in the Rocky Mountains next year.
  1

---

2 TEACH

What is the probability that a newborn human will not be a boy or a girl? *(0)* **that a leap year will occur within the next five years?** *(1)* **that you will see a rainbow tomorrow?** *(between 0 and 1)*

Use your rank-ordered list of uncertain events. Identify those events that you think have a probability greater than one-half. *(Examples: tossing a number greater than 2 on a number cube, being right-handed.)*

Chalkboard Example

Which numbers would not represent a probability?
7   $\frac{9}{10}$ 0.35 $1\frac{1}{9}$ 16%
(7 and $1\frac{1}{9}$)

SUMMARIZE/ASSESS   How is the range from 0 to 1 used to represent chance? *(Since an impossible event has a probability of 0 and a certain event has a probability of 1, a number greater than 0 but less than 1 is used to represent the probability of an uncertain event.)*

Write the probability of the event. Then rewrite the sentence so that the probability is 0. **See page 407b.**

7. There will be at least one full moon in the spring. **1**
There will be no full moon in the spring.

8. March will follow February. **1**
March will not follow February.

Write the probability of the event. Then rewrite the sentence so that the probability is between 0 and 1. **See page 407b.**

9. A cat will fly to the top of a tree to escape a dog. **0**
A cat will run to the top of a tree to escape a dog.

10. Someone will be born in the United States today. **1**
Someone will be born in Chicago Ridge today.

Is the probability statement close to the truth? Write *yes* or *no*. Explain your answer.

11. The probability that the next person you see will be a twin is 0.9.
no; 9 out of 10 people are not twins.

12. The probability a new teacher will be left handed is $\frac{1}{6}$.
yes.

━━━━━━━━━━━━━ **PROBLEM SOLVING** ━━━━━━━━━━━━━

Use your number sense and the graph to solve.

13. In which city is the chance of rain closest to 0 for any random day?
Los Angeles

14. In which city is the chance of rain greater than 50% on any random day?
Juneau

15. List the cities in order from the least to the greatest according to the chance of rain on any random day.
See page 407b.

16. **IN YOUR WORDS** Tell why probabilities range from 0 to 1.
Answers will vary. Suggestion given: If it is certain that an event will occur, its probability is 1. If it is certain that an event will not occur, its probability is 0.

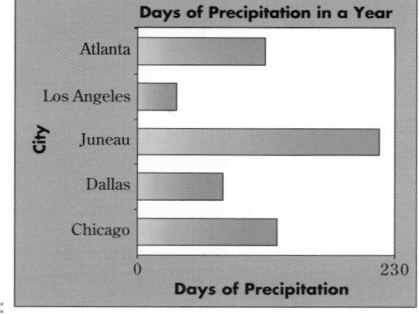

Days of Precipitation in a Year

City: Atlanta, Los Angeles, Juneau, Dallas, Chicago

Days of Precipitation: 0 — 230

CHAPTER 12   393

MEETING INDIVIDUAL NEEDS

For Students Who Are . . .

Acquiring English Proficiency Discuss the meanings of *chance, probability, certain,* and *uncertain.*

Gifted and Talented Have students write sentences in which the probability is 0, 1, or close to 0 or 1.

Working 2 or 3 Grades Below Level Reinforce the concept that probability is a number between 0 and 1.

Today's Problem

Many states in the United States run lotteries. In some states, when more people than usual buy lottery tickets the number of prizes remains the same but the size of the prizes becomes larger. When an unusually large number of lottery tickets is sold, what is the effect on a person's chance of winning? *(A person's chance of winning decreases.)*

---

3 FOLLOW-UP

PRACTICE 12-8

Is the probability 0, 1, or between 0 and 1?

1. The sun will come up in the east tomorrow. _1_

2. You will find a dollar on the floor later today. _between 0 and 1_

3. You will get a cold within a year. _between 0 and 1_

4. The sun will not come up tomorrow. _0_

Write the probability of the event. Then rewrite the sentence so the probability is 0.

5. You will be 1 day older tomorrow. _1; You will be 1 day younger tomorrow._

6. You know someone who is younger than you are. _1; You know no one who is younger than you are._

Is the probability statement close to the truth? Write *yes* or *no*. If no, tell why. *Answers will vary. Suggestions are given.*

7. The probability that a tossed coin will land on heads is 0.1. _No; the probability is 0.5._

Solve.

8. Which of the following numbers could be probabilities?
1.5%, 0.5, 50%, 500%, $\frac{5}{10}$, $\frac{10}{5}$
1.5%, 0.5, 50%, $\frac{5}{10}$

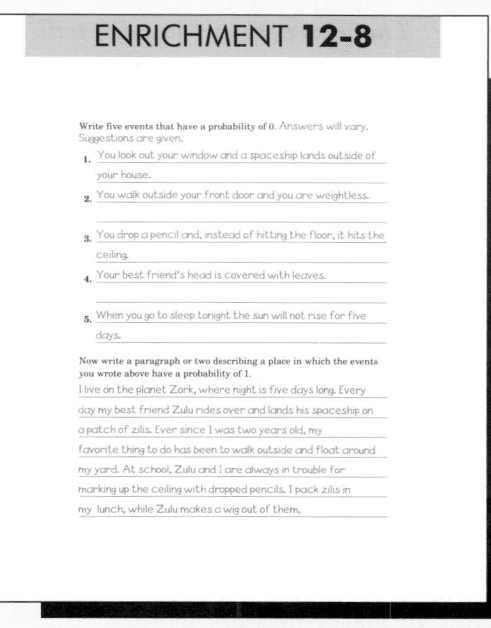

RETEACHING 12-8

☑ **MATERIALS CHECKLIST:** Index cards

Provide small groups with a set of cards on which you have written events such as the following: One member of your group will become Queen of England tomorrow; The year after 1999 will be 2000; It will be cloudy tomorrow. Each group discusses the likelihood that the event will occur. The students then write *certain, possible,* or *impossible* on each card. Have them show probability by writing *0* on the *impossible* cards, *1* on the *certain* cards, and *between 0 and 1* on the *possible* cards. Have the groups exchange cards and repeat the activity.

ENRICHMENT 12-8

Write five events that have a probability of 0. *Answers will vary. Suggestions are given.*

1. You look out your window and a spaceship lands outside of your house.

2. You walk outside your front door and you are weightless.

3. You drop a pencil and, instead of hitting the floor, it hits the ceiling.

4. Your best friend's head is covered with leaves.

5. When you go to sleep tonight the sun will not rise for five days.

Now write a paragraph or two describing a place in which the events you wrote above have a probability of 1.

I live on the planet Zork, where night is five days long. Every day my best friend Zulu rides over and lands his spaceship on a patch of zilis. Ever since I was two years old, my favorite thing to do has been to walk outside and float around my yard. At school, Zulu and I are always in trouble for marking up the ceiling with dropped pencils. I pack zilis in my lunch, while Zulu makes a wig out of them.

LESSON | 12-9

Lesson Organizer

Objective: Recognize equally likely outcomes.

Prior Knowledge: Students should be familiar with gameboard spinners and the probability of an event.

Error Analysis and Remediation: See page 407A.

Lesson Resources:
Practice Worksheet 12-9
Reteaching Worksheet 12-9
Enrichment Activity 12-9
Daily Review 12-9

 *Two-Minute Math*

What must be added to the number to make a sum of 1?

$\frac{1}{3}$ $\left(\frac{2}{3}\right)$ $\frac{4}{5}$ $\left(\frac{1}{5}\right)$

$\frac{2}{7}$ $\left(\frac{5}{7}\right)$ $\frac{9}{10}$ $\left(\frac{1}{10}\right)$

1 INTRODUCE

CONNECTING ACTIVITY

Suppose you toss a coin. What outcomes are possible? *(heads, tails)* **Are heads or tails equally likely to occur?** *(yes)*
What is meant by the phrase "equally likely"? *(Possible answer: There is as good a chance for heads to occur as for tails.)*
What are some examples of situations that are not equally likely? *(Possible answer: The next person you meet will be left-handed.)*

WHEN YOUR STUDENTS ASK
★ WHY AM I LEARNING THIS? ★

Many situations in real life have equally likely outcomes. For example, tomato seeds grown in a hothouse under the same controlled conditions have the same chance of maturing into healthy, fruit-bearing plants.

Equally Likely Outcomes

Do you think the chances of spinning a 1, 2, 3, or 4 are the same, or equal, on each of these spinners?

Yes, the chances are the same, because the regions are the same size. This spinner has equally likely outcomes.

No, the chances are not equal because the regions are not the same size.

Suppose you closed your eyes and drew one card from the hat. Does each card have an equally likely chance of being drawn?

No, each card does not have an equally likely chance because the folded card would feel different. The difference probably would be noticed by the person who is drawing.

A situation has **equally likely outcomes** when each result has the same chance of occurring.

▬▬▬ **GUIDED PRACTICE** ▬▬▬

Write *yes or no.* Explain.

1. Are heads and tails equally likely outcomes in a penny toss?
   yes; both have $\frac{1}{2}$ chance
2. You reach into your lunch bag with your eyes closed. Is the selection of the sandwich or of the orange equally likely?
   no; The shape makes them different.
3. Are even numbers and odd numbers equally likely outcomes on the toss of a 1–6 number cube?
   yes; There are three of each.
4. Three different sandwiches, peanut butter, jelly, and peanut butter and jelly, are made with bread from the same loaf, wrapped in wax paper, and put in a bag. Is the selection of any one by reaching into the bag without looking equally likely?
   yes; They would look and feel identical.
5. Without looking, are you equally likely to draw a blue marble as a red marble from a bag that contains 6 red marbles and 3 blue marbles that are all the same size?
   no; There are more red marbles.

394   LESSON 12-9

2 TEACH

Suppose you have ten pairs of rolled socks in a drawer. Half of them are solid colors and half are patterns. Without looking, you grab a pair from the drawer. Is it equally likely that the pair of socks you grabbed is solid-colored or patterned? Explain. *(Yes; there are the same number of each kind of socks.)*

Suppose that one sock has a hole in the toe. Is it equally likely that the pair of socks you grab without looking includes or does not include the sock with the hole? Why? *(No; each result does not have the same chance of occurring.)*

> ### Chalkboard Example
>
> When you toss a cube numbered 1 to 6, is it equally likely that the number on top is or is not a factor of 6? Explain.

SUMMARIZE/ASSESS   **The letters M, A, T, and H are written on separate cards all the same size and placed in a box. Is it equally likely that the letter drawn without looking is M, A, T, or H?** *(yes)* **is a vowel?** *(no)* **Explain.**

PRACTICE

Write *equally likely* or *not equally likely* for the outcomes.

6. an even number
or an odd number
not equally likely

7. red, blue, or green
not equally likely

8. green or yellow
not equally likely

9. rolling a 1, 2, 3, 4, 5, or 6
on a 1–6 number cube
equally likely

10. rolling a composite number or a
prime number on a 1–6 number cube
not equally likely

11. having 3, 4, 5, 6, or 7 letters
in a person's first name
not equally likely

12. Either a male or a female will be the
next new student to join your class.
equally likely

13. The next person you meet will be
left-handed or right-handed.
not equally likely

PROBLEM SOLVING

Blue and red are equally likely
outcomes on the spinner at right.
Is it likely that the data set comes
from this spinner? Explain.

14. blue: 492
red: 508
yes; close to 1:2

15. blue: 249
red: 751
no; not close to 1:2

16. blue: 36
red: 41
yes; close
to 1:2

17. blue: 912
red: 948
yes; close
to 1:2

Critical Thinking

1. You ask a person to select one of the
numbers, 1, 2, 3, or 4. Do you think that
all four outcomes are equally likely?
yes

2. Work in a group of four. Each of you should
ask 25 people to select one of the numbers
1, 2, 3, or *4.* Compile your data on one tally
sheet. Does it appear that each of the choices
was equally likely? Why or why not?
Check students' work.

3. If you asked another 100 people the same
question, do you think your results would
change greatly? Explain. Accept reasonable answers.

SURVEY
1. lll
2. llll lll
3. llll llll
4. llll

CHAPTER 12   395

MEETING INDIVIDUAL NEEDS

For Students Who Are . . .

Acquiring English Proficiency Point out that the word *drawing*
as used in this lesson means choosing or selecting.

Gifted and Talented Have students write examples of outcomes
that are equally likely and those that are not equally likely.

Working 2 or 3 Grades Below Level Review the meaning of even
and odd numbers, and prime and composite numbers.

Today's Problem

You have two cubes, each numbered from 1 to 6, and you roll both at
once. Consider the two events of rolling a total of 2 and of rolling a
total of 5. Are they equally likely events? Explain. *[No, because there
is only one way to roll a total of 2 (1 + 1), but there are four ways of
rolling a total of 5 (1 + 4, 2 + 3, 3 + 2, 4 + 1).]*

---

3 FOLLOW-UP

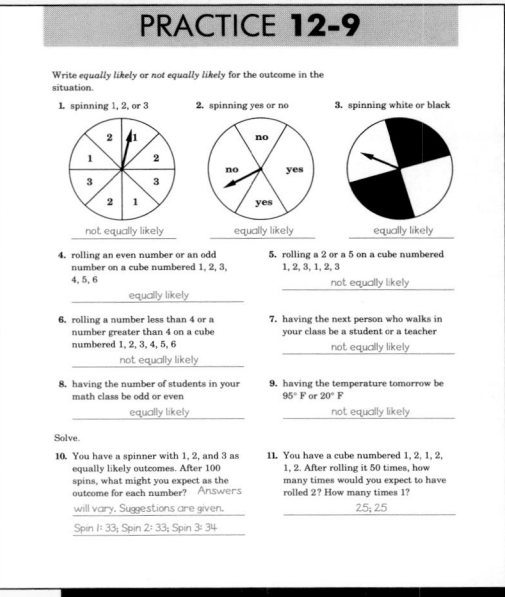

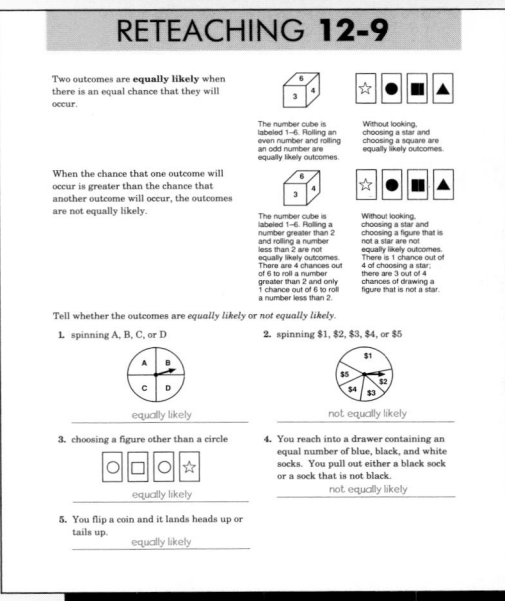

ENRICHMENT 12-9

☑ **MATERIALS CHECKLIST:** Blank
spinners

Have the students work in pairs. Then
instruct each pair to create a fair game
involving the spinner and equally likely
outcomes and an unfair game involving
the spinner and outcomes that are not
equally likely. Be sure that the students
tell how points are to be awarded. Have
pairs of students exchange spinners and
game rules. Each pair then decides which
game is fair and which game is unfair.

Chapter 12 • Lesson 12-9   **395**

Lesson Organizer

Objective: Explore finding the experimental probability and the actual probability of a single event.

Prior Knowledge: Students should understand ratio and the concept of measuring chance.

Error Analysis and Remediation: See page 407A.

Lesson Resources: Practice Worksheet 12-10 Daily Review 12-10

Two-Minute Math

Write the fraction in lowest terms.

$\frac{8}{12}$ $\left(\frac{2}{3}\right)$ $\quad$ $\frac{9}{18}$ $\left(\frac{1}{2}\right)$

$\frac{11}{22}$ $\left(\frac{1}{2}\right)$ $\quad$ $\frac{3}{6}$ $\left(\frac{1}{2}\right)$

1 PREPARE

CONCRETE ACTIVITY

☑ **MATERIALS CHECKLIST:** 6 blue cubes and 2 green cubes of the same size; paper bag

1. There are 8 cubes in the paper bag, some blue and some green. Your job is to guess the number of each color.

2. Ask a student to draw a cube, and re-place it. Keep a record of the color drawn. Have a volunteer record the results of the colors drawn. Repeat the steps until students have enough information to make a "good" guess.

3. Display the cubes so that students can see how "good" their guesses were.

You may also wish to use the Probability Spinners transparency from the Overhead Kit when teaching this lesson.

WHEN YOUR STUDENTS ASK
★ WHY AM I LEARNING THIS? ★

You can connect this skill to real life through the use of experimental probability to predict the fairness of a new game being developed by a computer company.

EXPLORE

Exploring the Meaning of Probability

Mrs. Foy ran an experiment with her class. She put 12 cubes of the same size and shape in a bag. Some cubes were green. Some were blue.

THINK ALOUD Is the probability of drawing a blue cube *0, 1,* or *between 0 and 1*? **between 0 and 1**

Each of her 25 students took 2 turns drawing a cube from the bag without looking. After each draw, the cube was returned to the bag and the bag was shaken. Each cube in the bag had an equally likely chance of being drawn.

The results of the 50 draws in this experiment were tallied as shown.

Blue	ℍ ℍ ℍ ℍ ℍ ℍ ‖	32
Green	ℍ ℍ ℍ ‖‖	18

The relative frequency of an outcome is its **experimental probability.** For blue, it was 32 out of 50, or $\frac{32}{50}$. For green, it was 18 out of 50, or $\frac{18}{50}$.

With a large number of trials, the experimental probability gives a good estimate of the **actual probability**. Sometimes you can tell the actual probability by looking at the possible outcomes. Then you would use the following ratio.

Probability (P) of an event $= \frac{\text{number of favorable outcomes}}{\text{total number of possible outcomes}}$

Mrs. Foy emptied the bag so that the students could look at the cubes and find the actual probabilities.

$P \text{ (blue)} = \frac{\text{number of blue cubes}}{\text{total number of cubes}} = \frac{8}{12}, \text{ or } \frac{2}{3}$

$P \text{ (green)} = \frac{\text{number of green cubes}}{\text{total number of cubes}} = \frac{4}{12}, \text{ or } \frac{1}{3}$

You write P (blue). You say, "the probability of blue."
You write P (green). You say, "the probability of green."

1. THINK ALOUD How close was the experimental probability to the actual probability for drawing a blue cube? a green cube? **very close for both; $\frac{2}{3}$; $\frac{1}{3}$**

---

2 EXPLORE

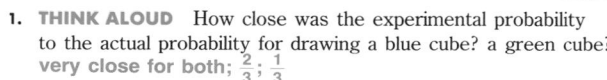

☑ **MATERIALS CHECKLIST:** number cube, blank spinner, one for each pair; 5 assorted marbles and a paper bag for each group

Have students work in pairs for Exercises 4 and 8; then have two pairs form a group for Create Your Own.

Why is relative frequency used to find experimental probability? *(Both compare the actual occurrence of an event to the total number of trials.)*

How are actual probability and experimental probability different? *(Actual probability is found by looking at the situation and imagining what would happen; experimental probability is found by running trials and gathering data.)*

SUMMARIZE/ASSESS **In situations in which the actual probability cannot be found, how can experimental probability help determine the chances?** *(When a large enough number of trials is run, a good estimate of the actual probability can be obtained.)*

You may also use the Probability Spinners Transparency during this lesson.

Some students experimented with tossing a 1–6 number cube 60 times. The table shows the tally for the frequency of each number tossed.

1:	﹩ ﹩ ﹩ |||	4:	﹩ ﹩ ﹩ ﹩ ﹩ ﹩
2:	﹩ ﹩ ﹩ ﹩ ﹩ ﹩ ||	5:	﹩ ﹩ ﹩ ﹩ ﹩ ﹩
3:	﹩ ﹩ ﹩ ﹩ ﹩ ﹩		6:	﹩ ﹩ ﹩ ||||

2. Use the data table. Write the experimental probability as a fraction and as a decimal.
   a. tossing a 4 $\frac{1}{6}$; 0.1$\overline{6}$ b. tossing a 3 $\frac{11}{60}$; 0.18$\overline{3}$

3. Look at the 1–6 cube. Find the actual probability as a fraction and as a decimal.
   a. tossing a 4 $\frac{1}{6}$; 0.1$\overline{6}$ b. tossing a 3 $\frac{1}{6}$; 0.1$\overline{6}$

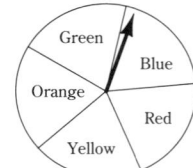

4. Use a number cube to do a probability experiment. Work with a partner. Toss the cube 80 times. Tally your results. What experimental probabilities do you find for each outcome in Exercise 3?
   Check students' work.

Some students spun a spinner like the one at right 100 times and recorded the results below.

5. Find the experimental probability and the actual probability for the event. Write each as a fraction, as a decimal, and as a percent.
   a. spinning red   b. spinning green
   c. spinning yellow   d. spinning red or yellow
   See below.

Red	17
Yellow	21
Orange	18
Green	19
Blue	25

6. **THINK ALOUD** How do you think the experimental probability and the actual probability for each of the events in Exercise 5 will compare after 20 spins? after 500 spins?
   not close; very close

7. Work with a partner. Use a five-section spinner like the one above. Complete 100 trials. How do your experimental probabilities compare to those in Exercise 5?
   Check students' work.

8. **CREATE YOUR OWN** Work in a small group. Design a probability experiment using different-colored objects of the same size, such as marbles or pencils. Find the experimental probability and the actual probability for the event(s) in your experiment. **Check students' work.**

5. Experimental: a. $\frac{17}{100}$, 0.17, 17%; b. $\frac{25}{100}$, 0.25, 25%; c. $\frac{21}{100}$, 0.21, 21%; d. $\frac{38}{100}$, 0.38, 38%; actual: a., b., c. $\frac{1}{5}$, 0.20, 20%; d. $\frac{2}{5}$, 0.40, 40%

CHAPTER 12   397

PRACTICE 12-10

Sam has a bag with 2 yellow, 3 blue, 4 green, and 6 red marbles. He mixed the marbles, took one out, recorded its color, and replaced it. He repeated the experiment 200 times. These are the results.

Color	Tally	Frequency
Yellow	﹩﹩﹩﹩﹩ |||	28
Blue	﹩﹩﹩﹩﹩﹩﹩		36
Green	﹩﹩﹩﹩﹩﹩﹩﹩﹩﹩ ||||	54
Red	﹩﹩﹩﹩﹩﹩﹩﹩﹩﹩﹩﹩﹩﹩﹩﹩ ||	82

Use the data table above to answer Exercises 1–8. Write the experimental probability as a fraction and a decimal.

1. P(yellow) = $\frac{28}{200}$ 0.14
2. P(blue) = $\frac{36}{200}$ 0.18
3. P(green) = $\frac{54}{200}$ 0.27
4. P(red) = $\frac{82}{200}$ 0.41

Write the actual probability as a fraction and a decimal.

5. P(yellow) = $\frac{2}{15}$ 0.1$\overline{3}$
6. P(blue) = $\frac{3}{15}$ 0.2
7. P(green) = $\frac{4}{15}$ 0.2$\overline{6}$
8. P(red) = $\frac{6}{15}$ 0.4

Divide a blank spinner into 4 equal parts. Label them 1, 2, 3, and 4. Spin the spinner 100 times. Complete the table. Answers will vary for experiment.

Spinner Number	Tally	Frequency	Actual Probability			Experimental Probability		
			Fraction	Decimal	%	Fraction	Decimal	%
1			$\frac{1}{4}$	0.25	25%			
2			$\frac{1}{4}$	0.25	25%			
3			$\frac{1}{4}$	0.25	25%			
4			$\frac{1}{4}$	0.25	25%			

MEETING INDIVIDUAL NEEDS

For Students Who Are . . .

Acquiring English Proficiency Make sure students understand what favorable outcomes are in the probability ratio.

Gifted and Talented Have students find the relative frequency of each number using the information in the chart at the top of page 397.

Working 2 or 3 Grades Below Level Review how to change a fraction to a decimal and a decimal to a percent.

Today's Problem

Find four consecutive numbers and three consecutive numbers that add up to 186. *(45 + 46 + 47 + 48; 61 + 62 + 63)* Explain why you cannot find two consecutive numbers that add up to 186. *(186 is an even number. The sum of any two consecutive numbers must equal an odd number.)*

Lesson Organizer

Objective: Explore relative frequency as a good estimate of probability.

Prior Knowledge: Students should understand relative frequency and probability and be able to estimate fraction-decimal equivalencies.

Lesson Resources:
Class Activity 12-11
Daily Review 12-11

Two-Minute Math

Which of the following could reasonably be rounded by $\frac{1}{3}$? to $\frac{2}{3}$?

0.37   0.13   0.62   0.31   0.23
0.031   0.066   0.3   0.65
($\frac{1}{3}$; 0.37, 0.31, 0.3; $\frac{2}{3}$; 0.62, 0.65)

1 PREPARE

CONNECTING ACTIVITY

☑ **MATERIALS CHECKLIST:** 6 tagboard squares, a marker per pair

Assign students to work in pairs.

1. Mark three squares X and three squares O.

2. How might you find the experimental probability of picking a square marked X if these squares were shuffled and placed face down? *(Possible answer: Do the experiment 20, 50 or a greater number of times.)*

3. Do the experiment 20 times. What is the experimental probability?

4. If these squares were shuffled and placed face down, what would be the actual probability of picking a square marked X? *[$P(X) = \frac{3}{6}$]*

5. How do the two probabilities compare?

WHEN YOUR STUDENTS ASK
★ **WHY AM I LEARNING THIS?** ★

The skill in this lesson provides you with experience in deciding when you have enough information to make a "good" guess or an informed decision.

 EXPLORE

Exploring Good Estimates of Probability

Playing the Guess $P(X)$ game with a partner will help you explore some ideas about probability. Player 1 will know the actual probability of selecting an X from looking at the squares. Player 2 will try to determine the probability by using experimental data.

GUESS P(X)

Materials: 6 small squares (3 labeled with X, 3 labeled with O).
a calculator
a record sheet like this one for each player:

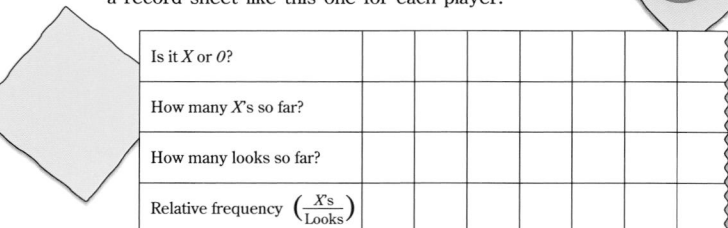

Is it X or O?					
How many X's so far?					
How many looks so far?					
Relative frequency $\left(\frac{X's}{\text{Looks}}\right)$					

Rules:

1. Player 1 turns all the squares face down and mixes them. Player 2 points to three squares.

2. Player 1 looks at the three squares, places them face down in a row, and puts the others aside.

3. Player 2 chooses one of the squares, looks at it, answers the three questions on the record sheet, calculates and writes the relative frequency, and puts back the square face down.

4. Player 1 mixes the three squares again.

5. Player 2 repeats the steps in rule 3.

6. Play continues until Player 2 wants to guess the probability of turning over an X. (Choices are 0, $\frac{1}{3}$, $\frac{2}{3}$, or 1.)

7. Both players look at the three squares and calculate the actual probability. If the guess is correct, Player 2 receives 1 point for each look. If not, Player 2 receives 25 points.

8. Players change roles for the next round. After four rounds, the player with the lower score wins.

---

2 EXPLORE

 Calculators should be available for lengthy computations with data.

☑ **MATERIALS CHECKLIST:** 6 marked tagboard squares and a record sheet for each pair; calculators

What are the possible probabilities for uncovering an X?
(0, $\frac{1}{3}$, $\frac{2}{3}$, and 1)

What are the decimal equivalents of the possible probabilities?
0, $0.\overline{3}$, $0.\overline{6}$, 1.0)

As you continue to play the game, why do you think it is easier to guess the probability? *(Possible answer: The relative frequency "settles down" close to one of the possible probabilities.)*

SUMMARIZE/ASSESS   **Explain the Law of Large Numbers.**
(The larger the numbers of trials, the closer the experimental probability will be to the actual probability.)

1. **THINK ALOUD** What happens to the relative frequency as you take more looks?
The relative frequency tends to stabilize.

2. **CRITICAL THINKING** What is the highest relative frequency possible? What would it indicate? What is the lowest relative frequency possible? What would it indicate?
See page 407b.

3. **THINK ALOUD** How is the relative frequency used to estimate the probability of choosing a square with an X?
See page 407b.

4. Use your record sheet from a game. Change the relative frequencies to decimals. Write the decimals for each round in a row in the order of play. Look for patterns that describe how the relative frequency changes in the earlier part of a round as compared with how it changes in the later part of a round.
Check students' work.

5. **CRITICAL THINKING** When you play a round of this game, the first relative frequencies usually vary greatly. Later in a round, they tend to stabilize. Why do you think this happens? See page 407b.

> **The Law of Large Numbers says that if you run a large number of experiments, the experimental probability you find will be close to the actual probability.**

6. During a round of the Guess $P(X)$ game, a player turned over these squares in 16 looks: O, O, X, X, X, O, X, X, O, X, O, X, X, X, O, O. Make a relative frequency table for the data. Change the relative frequencies to decimals and write them in order of play. What pattern do you see?
See page 407b.

7. **CRITICAL THINKING** How would you change the rules to play this game with ten squares?
See page 407b.

8. **NUMBER SENSE** Suppose you are playing this game with 100 squares, 50 with X's and 50 with O's. Fifty squares have been turned over and you are Player 2. About how many looks would you want to take before you would guess the probability using the Law of Large Numbers? Explain.
See page 407b.

CLASS ACTIVITY 12-11

☑ **MATERIALS CHECKLIST:** Red and white counters, paper bags

Give pairs of students a paper bag containing 3 white counters and 2 red counters. The partners take turns drawing, recording the color, and replacing a counter from the bag for 100 turns. Ask each pair to write the relative frequency of choosing a white counter and of choosing a red counter. Then have the pairs of students combine their results and record the resulting relative frequencies. Ask: What do you think the probability of drawing a red counter is? of drawing a white counter? Have the students find the actual probabilities. [red: 0.4; white: 0.6]

MEETING INDIVIDUAL NEEDS

For Students Who Are . . .

Acquiring English Proficiency Make sure students understand the rules of the game. Discuss Rule 6: why the possibilities for the probability are 0, $\frac{1}{3}$, $\frac{2}{3}$, and 1.

Gifted and Talented Have students work in a group to create another game that would verify the Law of Large Numbers.

Today's Problem

In baseball, why would it be inappropriate to say that the probability of a player hitting the ball is .258793? *(Probability already is an estimate of the possibility of an event happening, so a probability of that many decimal places suggests an unrealistic precision.)*

Lesson Organizer

Objective: Solve problems by using simulation.

Prior Knowledge: Students should understand the concept of outcomes and the relationship between experimental and actual probability.

Lesson Resources:
Practice Worksheet 12-12
Reteaching Activity 12-12
Enrichment Worksheet 12-12
Daily Review 12-12

 *Two-Minute Math*

Find the sum. Use mental math.
65 + 59 + 62 + 66 + 65 + 62 + 61 + 60 *(500)*

1 INTRODUCE

CONNECTING ACTIVITY

☑ **MATERIALS CHECKLIST:** a coin

1. Ask students to analyze what they are doing when they play a computer simulation game. Generalize that they are using the computer as a battlefield or spaceship and are imitating events that might occur.

2. Display a coin and ask students to think about how the coin could be used to imitate the number of girls and boys in a family. *(Assign heads [H] for girls and tails [T] for boys.)*

3. Toss the coin three times, and call out whether a girl (H) or a boy (T) was tossed each time. Record the results. Ask two or three volunteers to repeat the activity.

WHEN YOUR STUDENTS ASK
★ **WHY AM I LEARNING THIS?** ★

You can connect this skill to real life through computer simulations. For example, simulation programs have been designed that predict the results of space flights under varying conditions.

Simulation Outcomes
T = Boys   H = Girls

Coin 1	Coin 2	Coin 3
H	T	T
T	H	H
H	T	H
T	T	T
T	T	H
H	T	H
T	H	T
H	H	T
H	H	H
H	H	T
T	T	H
H	T	H
H	T	T
H	T	H
T	H	T
H	H	T
T	T	T
T	H	H
T	H	T
H	H	H
T	T	T
T	H	T
H	H	H
T	T	H
H	T	T
T	H	H
T	T	T
T	T	T
H	H	H
T	T	T
T	H	H
T	H	T
H	T	T
T	H	H
H	T	H
H	T	T
T	H	T
H	H	T
T	T	T
T	H	T
H	T	T
H	H	H
H	H	T
T	T	T
T	H	T
T	H	H
H	T	H
H	H	H
T	H	T
H	T	T

Problem Solving:
Simulation

Some probability problems are solved using an experiment that imitates the problem. This kind of experiment is called a **simulation**. A simulation gives a good estimate of the actual probability of an event.

Mr. and Mrs. Otero have no children yet. What is the probability that the three children they want to have will all be boys?

You can simulate this problem with a random device.

STEPS Select a random device. The toss of a coin could represent a child's position in a family. Tails (T) could represent a boy. Heads (H) could represent a girl.

Design the event. A family of three children could be simulated by tossing three coins.

Find the desired event. Having three coins land tails up (T, T, T) could represent a three-boy family.

Use the Law of Large Numbers. Run 500 events. The relative frequency of three tails will be a good estimate of the probability of a three-boy family.

These were the results after 500 tosses of three coins.

Event	Frequency	Event	Frequency
(T, T, T)	65	(H, H, T)	65
(T, T, H)	59	(H, T, H)	62
(T, H, T)	62	(T, H, H)	61
(H, T, T)	66	(H, H, H)	60

NUMBER SENSE Why do these events all represent different types of families? **They represent the number of boys and girls and the order of their birth.**

THINK ALOUD Use the data to find the relative frequency of three-boy families. What is the experimental probability that a couple's three children will all be boys? $\frac{65}{500}$; 0.13

GUIDED PRACTICE

1. Look at the frequency table to answer.
   a. How many different types of families are possible? **8**
   b. How many of these family types are all boys? **1**
   c. What is the actual probability of a three-boy family? $\frac{1}{8}$ **or 0.125**

---

2 TEACH

What is the event in this stimulation? *(the birth of three children, which is represented by three consecutive coin tosses)*

How does the first simulated event describe a real family? *(HTT represents a family that has a girl as the oldest child followed by two boys.)*

In this experiment, how many families had a boy as the oldest child followed by two girls? *(61)*

SUMMARIZE/ASSESS **How can a simulation be used to solve a probability problem?** *(A simulation applies the Law of Large Numbers in an experiment that runs enough events to yield a good estimate of the actual probability of an event.)*

2. **THINK ALOUD** Discuss how the experimental probability and the actual probability compare for a family in which all three children are boys.
0.13 is slightly greater than 0.125.

3. Consider a family with a girl born first and then two boys born later.

   a. Which event represents this kind of family? HTT

   b. How many times did this event occur in the simulation? 66

   c. What is the relative frequency of this event as a percent? 13.2%

   d. What is the experimental probability of this event as a percent? 13.2%

▬▬▬▬▬▬▬ PRACTICE ▬▬▬▬▬▬▬

Use the frequency table on page 400 to answer.

4. Which event represents a three-girl family? HHH
   What is the frequency of this event? $\frac{60}{500}$ or 0.12

5. What is the relative frequency of a three-girl family as a percent? 12%

6. What is the experimental probability of a three-girl family? $\frac{3}{25}$ or 0.12

7. What is the actual probability of a three-girl family? 0.125
   How does this compare with the experimental probability? very close

8. Which event represents a family with two girls born first and then a boy? What are the experimental probability and the actual probability for this event? HHT; 0.13; 0.125

CHOOSE Choose any strategy to solve. Strategies may vary.

9. The number of different ways that three coins can be tossed is eight. How many different ways can four coins be tossed?
   16 ways

10. Jorge told his brother to walk 4 blocks north of their house, to turn left and walk 2 blocks, to turn left again and walk 3 more blocks, and to turn left one more time and walk 3 blocks to find their meeting place. After his brother left, Jorge cut across one block to get to the meeting place. In what direction did he go?
    Northeast

11. Marta gave her sister Juana 60¢. She gave her at least one quarter, one dime, one nickel, and one penny. How many different ways could Marta have given Juana 60¢?
    6 ways

MEETING INDIVIDUAL NEEDS

For Students Who Are . . .

Acquiring English Proficiency Explain that a *random device* refers to a way to model or represent a problem. Review the phrases *event, relative frequency,* and *experimental and actual probability.*

Gifted and Talented Challenge students to discover a pattern for the number of different ways coins can be tossed. (*n = number of coins; 2^n = number of ways*)

Having Reading Difficulties Pair students with an able reader for the Practice exercises.

Today's Problem

Consider the problem of tossing a number cube 1,000 times and adding the total of all the numbers that appear. A computer can quickly find the solution. One line of the computer program could be D = INT(6*RND(1) + 1). What do you think this line simulates?
(*This line simulates tossing the cube, with D becoming either 1, 2, 3, 4, 5, or 6.*)

---

3 FOLLOW-UP

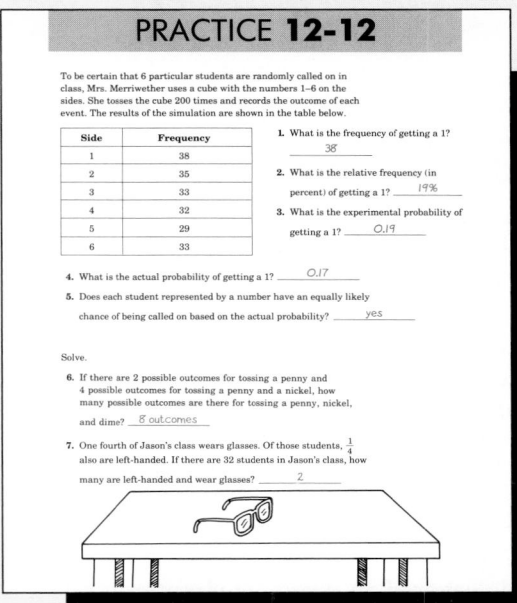

PRACTICE 12-12

To be certain that 6 particular students are randomly called on in class, Mrs. Merriwether uses a cube with the numbers 1–6 on the sides. She tosses the cube 200 times and records the outcome of each event. The results of the simulation are shown in the table below.

Side	Frequency
1	38
2	35
3	33
4	32
5	29
6	33

1. What is the frequency of getting a 1? 38

2. What is the relative frequency (in percent) of getting a 1? 19%

3. What is the experimental probability of getting a 1? 0.19

4. What is the actual probability of getting a 1? 0.17

5. Does each student represented by a number have an equally likely chance of being called on based on the actual probability? yes

Solve.

6. If there are 2 possible outcomes for tossing a penny and 4 possible outcomes for tossing a penny and a nickel, how many possible outcomes are there for tossing a penny, nickel, and dime? 8 outcomes

7. One fourth of Jason's class wears glasses. Of those students, $\frac{1}{4}$ also are left-handed. If there are 32 students in Jason's class, how many are left-handed and wear glasses? 2

RETEACHING 12-12

✓ **MATERIALS CHECKLIST:** Slips of paper, bags

Provide this problem to pairs of students having difficulty using simulations to find experimental probability: What is the probability that a team will win its first three games? (No ties are allowed.) Ask: What are the possible outcomes of Game 1? Game 2? Game 3? [for each, win or lose] Write *win* or *loss* on slips of paper, place the slips in a bag and take turns drawing strips three times, recording the results. Each pair conducts the experiment 100 times. Ask: How many times did you draw *win* three times in a row? What is the experimental probability?

ENRICHMENT 12-12

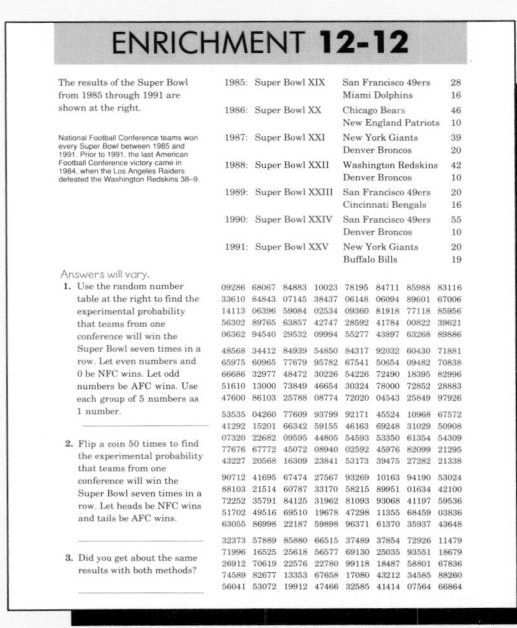

The results of the Super Bowl from 1985 through 1991 are shown at the right.

1985:	Super Bowl XIX	San Francisco 49ers	28
		Miami Dolphins	16
1986:	Super Bowl XX	Chicago Bears	46
		New England Patriots	10
1987:	Super Bowl XXI	New York Giants	39
		Denver Broncos	20
1988:	Super Bowl XXII	Washington Redskins	42
		Denver Broncos	10
1989:	Super Bowl XXIII	San Francisco 49ers	20
		Cincinnati Bengals	16
1990:	Super Bowl XXIV	San Francisco 49ers	55
		Denver Broncos	10
1991:	Super Bowl XXV	New York Giants	20
		Buffalo Bills	19

National Football Conference teams won every Super Bowl between 1985 and 1991. Prior to 1991, the last American Football Conference victory came in 1984, when the Los Angeles Raiders defeated the Washington Redskins 38–9.

Answers will vary.

1. Use the random number table at the right to find the experimental probability that teams from one conference will win the Super Bowl seven times in a row. Let even numbers and 0 be NFC wins. Let odd numbers be AFC wins. Use each group of 5 numbers as 1 number.

2. Flip a coin 50 times to find the experimental probability that teams from one conference will win the Super Bowl seven times in a row. Let heads be NFC wins and tails be AFC wins.

3. Did you get about the same results with both methods?

Lesson Organizer

Objective: Review operations with whole numbers, decimals, fractions, and mixed numbers; fraction concepts; solving proportions; percents.

Lesson Resources:
Daily Review 12-13

These pages provide students with a review of computing with whole numbers, decimals, fractions, and mixed numbers; solving proportions; writing decimals as percents and vice versa; finding percents; and using a map and a graph to solve problems.

Remind students that these pages review skills covered in previous chapters and will help them to do a self-check to see how well they remember what they've learned.

MATH AND SOCIAL STUDIES

Mixed Review

Carnival **in Rio de Janiero, Brazil**

Compute.

1. 694×36
24,984

2. $674 - 433.76$
240.24

3. $87.89 + 268.54$
356.43

4. $1,627.5 \div 2.5$
651

5. $\frac{6}{8} \div \frac{3}{4}$
1

6. $6\frac{2}{3} \times 5\frac{1}{2}$
$36\frac{2}{3}$

7. $2\frac{1}{6} + 2\frac{1}{4}$
$4\frac{5}{12}$

8. $5\frac{1}{4} - 2\frac{1}{2}$
$2\frac{3}{4}$

Make a true proportion by solving for *n*.

9. $\frac{6}{8} = \frac{9}{n}$
$n = 12$

10. $\frac{n}{21} = \frac{1}{3}$
$n = 7$

11. $\frac{8}{n} = \frac{14}{56}$
$n = 32$

12. $\frac{12}{16} = \frac{n}{36}$
$n = 27$

Write as a percent.

13. 0.16
16%

14. 0.95
95%

15. 1
100%

16. $\frac{3}{4}$
75%

17. 0.04
4%

Write as a decimal.

18. $\frac{1}{2}$
0.5

19. 100%
1.0

20. $37\frac{1}{2}\%$
0.375

21. 50%
0.5

22. 19.1%
0.191

Find the unknown.

23. What percent is 15 out of 60?
25%

24. What is 80% of 60?
48

25. 75% of what number is 48?
64

26. What percent is 17 out of 68?
25%

27. What is 40% of 75?
30

28. 65% of what number is 156?
240

29. What percent is 72 out of 300?
24%

30. What is 25% of 496?
124

31. 20% of what number is 105?
525

32. What percent is 232 out of 400?
58%

33. What is 12.5% of 2?
0.25

34. 35% of what number is 210?
600

402   LESSON 12–13

Use the graph and the map. Choose pencil and paper, calculator, or estimation to solve.

Choices will vary.
Suggestions are given.

35. Every spring, in Rio de Janeiro's famous *Carnival*, neighborhoods compete to have the showiest costumes and parades. *Carnival* lasts for 4 days and 4 nights. For about what percent of 1 wk does it last?
c or p; 57%

36. About how many times greater was Brazil's population in 1900 than in 1800?
e; about 4 times

37. About how many times greater will Brazil's population be in the year 2000 than it was in 1900?
e; about 10 times

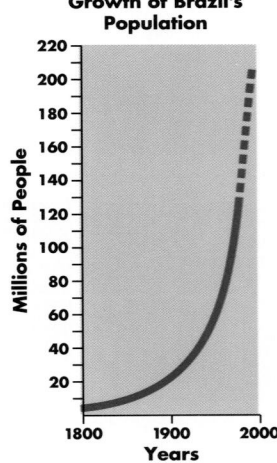

Growth of Brazil's Population

38. In 1960, Brazil's capital was moved from Rio de Janeiro to Brasilia. Use the scale and a ruler to find the approximate distance between Rio de Janeiro and Brasilia.
e; about 600 mi

39. When swollen by rain, the Amazon River flows at about 3 mi/h, which is about 200% of its average speed. About what is its average speed?
e; 1.5 mi/h

40. From 1930, when the competition was first held, to 1990, soccer's World Cup has been played 14 times and Brazil has won it 3 times. About what percent of the time has Brazil won the World Cup?
e; 20%

CHAPTER 12   **403**

MULTICULTURAL NOTE

Brazil has the sixth largest population in the world. It is made up of people of European ancestry, African ancestry, Native-American ancestry, and mixed ancestry. The nation's official language is Portuguese, though some Native-American groups in the Amazon area use traditional languages.

Lesson Organizer

Objective: Creative Problem Solving.

Prior Knowledge: Students should be able to interpret a chart.

Lesson Resources:
Daily Review 12-14

 **Two-Minute Math**

You work one day a month. You earn $1 the first month, and double the previous month's pay each month after that. How much would you earn in a year? *($4,095)*

1 PREPARE

SYMBOLIC ACTIVITY

Have students work in groups of three or four.

How do you make a decision? Work together to compile a list of the steps you follow in making a decision and the order in which you follow them.

After a short time, bring the class together to compare lists. Write the steps that are common to all lists on the chalkboard. Examples:

• identify the goal

• list alternatives or options

• evaluate each option

Point out that rank-ordering options is an essential part of evaluating them.

WHEN YOUR STUDENTS ASK
★ WHY AM I LEARNING THIS? ★

You can relate this lesson to many real life decisions that must be made every day. Examples include deciding how to spend time or money, or how to prepare for a test or a job interview.

 CREATIVE PROBLEM SOLVING

Making Decisions About After-School Activities

How do you go about making decisions? You can use a chart in the decision-making process.

In the chart below, Alice analyzed three after-school activities according to four factors. A score of *1*, *2*, or *3* shows the rank, or importance, of each factor, with 3 being the *most important* for a factor and 1 being the *least important.*

FACTOR	SCHOOL NEWSPAPER	SWIM TEAM	GUITAR LESSONS
COST	3	2	1
TIME	2	1	3
STATUS	2	3	1
FUN	2	1	3

For example, Alice ranked the cost factor because she wants to spend as little money as possible. Taking guitar lessons gets a score of 1 because it is the most expensive choice. Joining the swim team gets a score of 2 because it is less expensive than guitar lessons. Working on the school newspaper gets a score of 3 because it is free.

---

2 EXPLORE

Assign students to work with a partner for these activities.

Suppose Alice gave the cost factor a weight of 10, but did not change the weighted value of the other factors. Which activity is now valued most? *(school newspaper, which now has a weighted score of 62)*

SUMMARIZE/ASSESS **What mathematics skills did you use to investigate making decisions?** *(Answers will vary. Example: multiplication, addition, ordering numbers.)*

Work with a partner. Use the data on page 404 to solve.

1. Alice did not want to spend a lot of time on after-school activities. According to the ranking, which activity is the least time consuming? the most time consuming?
   Swim Team; Guitar Lessons

2. Which activity does Alice consider the most fun? the least fun?
   Guitar Lessons; Swim Team

3. Total the scores for each activity. Which activity received the highest score? Would you rank these activities in the same way? Explain.
   newspaper; Accept reasonable answers.

The factors themselves in a decision-making chart may be weighted to show the value assigned to them by the chart maker. In this expanded chart, Alice has weighted the factors according to her personal preferences. Her weighted scores range from 10 (*most important*) to 1 (*least important*).

FACTOR	WEIGHT	SCHOOL NEWSPAPER		SWIM TEAM		GUITAR LESSONS	
		SCORE	WEIGHTED SCORE	SCORE	WEIGHTED SCORE	SCORE	WEIGHTED SCORE
COST	6	3	18	2	12	1	6
TIME	5	2	10	1	5	3	15
STATUS	1	2	2	3	3	1	1
FUN	10	2	20	1	10	3	30

4. According to the chart, which factor, the time involved or the amount of fun, is more important to Alice? Explain.
   Fun; Accept reasonable answers.

5. Copy and complete the chart. Find the total of the weighted scores for each activity. Which activity is now valued most?
   50; 30; 52; Guitar Lessons

6. When you create a decision-making chart, you can include any factors. For example, in the chart above you might include *Friends involved* and assign a score of 3 if there are many friends participating in the activity. What other factors might you add to the chart?
   Accept reasonable answers.

7. You must also decide upon the scoring and weighting system you will use. What are some advantages of scoring an activity from 10 to 1 instead of from 3 to 1? What are some disadvantages?
   Accept reasonable answers.

8. Working alone, create your own decision-making chart for out-of-school activities. Share your chart with the class.
   Check students' work.

CHAPTER 12   405

MEETING INDIVIDUAL NEEDS

For Students Who Are . . .

Acquiring English Proficiency Discuss the concepts of rank ordering and weighted scores. Have students list and rank order five foods they like.

Gifted and Talented Have students find a newspaper article in which someone has made a decision. Ask them to use the article to write a lesson about rank ordering alternatives in decision making.

Today's Problem

In the number puzzle, each letter represents a number from 0–9. No two letters represent the same number. The F or the E do not represent zero. What number does each letter represent? (*Answers may vary. A suggestion is given.*)

$$\begin{array}{rr} \text{FOUR} & 8,532 \\ + \text{FOUR} & + 8,532 \\ \hline \text{EIGHT} & 17,064 \end{array}$$

3 FOLLOW-UP

CLASS ACTIVITY **12-4**

☑ **MATERIALS CHECKLIST:** two number cubes marked 1 to 6 for each group of 4 students

Say: I am going to give you a sum. Have each student guess and write how many times that sum might appear if the cubes are rolled 100 times. Give the sum of 7. Have students roll 100 times to see who has the best estimate. Repeat using the sum of 5. Then use the sum of 2. Ask: What observations do you make? (*The 7 will probably appear most often and 2 the least often*).

CHAPTER
Checkup

This chapter checkup provides a quick language and vocabulary review, a test for the chapter, and suggestions for student Learning Log entires.

Language and Vocabulary

Some key language and vocabulary ideas from this chapter are reinforced here.

Test

The test can be used either as a test or as a review of the chapter prior to administering the test worksheets found in the Teacher's Resource Book.

The following guide will help you determine percentage scores.

Score	Percent
11	100%
10	91
9	82
8	73
7	64
6	55
5	46
4	37
3	28
2	19
1	10

Each test has three sections: concepts, skills, and problem solving. These sections provide students with exposure to the format used on standardized tests.

Use the chart on page 407 to identify the Management Objectives tested for this chapter.

CHAPTER CHECKUP

LANGUAGE & VOCABULARY

Write *true* or *false*. If *false*, tell why.

1. Every event has a probability of at least 0 and at most 1. **true**

2. If a situation has 2 equally likely outcomes and 20 trials are done, the results will always be 10 of each outcome. **false; The experimental probability will be close to the actual probability.**

3. A simulation with a large number of trials will always give the actual probability of the event. **false; It should be very close to the actual probability.**

TEST

CONCEPTS

Name the population and the sample. *(pages 378–379)*

1. A guidance counselor wants to know how many seventh graders want to start a class newspaper. She asks the seventh grade students with whom she meets on Monday. **all seventh graders; seventh graders in Monday class**

2. A radio station wants to know how its audience feels about an issue. Listeners are asked to call and express their opinions. **all listeners; listeners who call**

Use the data in the table. *(pages 394–397)*

3. If you randomly choose 1 student from class 7-315, what is the probability that the student was absent in September? **0**

4. Each month, one student with perfect attendance is honored by selecting a name at random. During which month was there an equally likely chance that the student chosen was from either class? **October**

Students with Perfect Attendance

	Class 7-305 (20 students)	Class 7-315 (18 students)
September	15	18
October	13	13
November	8	11
December	12	13

SKILLS

Use the data from the table above. *(pages 382–383, 388–389)*

5. Find the mean number of students in class 7-305 with perfect attendance from September through December. **12 students**

406   CHAPTER CHECKUP

CHAPTER TEST • FORM A

Find the mean and median. (pp. 376–379, 382–383) 12A

1. Points scored: 64, 74, 80, 101, 78, 89, 95 _83, 80_

2. Cost of calculators: $18, $36, $28, $41, $11, $85, $180 _$57, $36_

3. Cloudy days each month: 8, 11, 6, 12, 6, 3, 2, 8, 11, 2, 9, 6 _7, 7_

4. Daily phone calls: 110, 84, 77, 68, 81 _84, 81_

5. Student absences: 27, 38, 23, 29, 18 _27, 27_

Use the graph to answer the questions. (pp. 380–381, 384–385) 12B

6. Which town had the lesser amount of rain in November? _Cary_

7. What was the average rainfall for Spiro in October? _about 3½ in._

8. What was the average rainfall for Cary in December? _about 4 in._

9. During which month was the difference in the amount of rainfall the greatest? _September_

10. For the four month period, how much more rain did Spiro receive than Cary? _about 5½ in._

AVERAGE RAINFALL
(bar graph: Spiro, Cary — Sept. Oct. Nov. Dec.)

Write equally likely or not equally likely for the outcome in the situation. Use the spinner for Exercises 11–13. (pp. 394–395) 12C

11. spinning an even or odd number _equally likely_

12. spinning a number less than 4 or a number greater than 4 _not equally likely_

13. spinning a prime or composite number _equally likely_

14. The next person you meet will be a male or female. _equally likely_

15. The next car you see will be a hard top or a convertible. _not equally likely_

(spinner showing 8, 9, 2, 3, 5, 4, 6, 7)

CHAPTER TEST • FORM A

(pp. 388–389, 392–393, 396–399) 12D

Is the probability 0, 1, or between 0 and 1?

16. You roll a number cube and a 2 is face up. _between 0 and 1_

17. Someone in your school will eat lunch on Tuesday. _1_

Some students spun the spinner at the right 80 times. The table shows the tally for the frequency of each spin.

18. Use the data table. Write as a fraction the experimental probability of spinning a 5. _23/80_

(spinner showing 5, 4, 6, 6, 5, 6)

Look at the spinner. Find the actual probability as a fraction.

19. spinning a 6 _5/8_

20. spinning a 5 _¼ or 2/8_

4	卌 III	8
5	卌 卌 卌 卌 III	23
6	卌 卌 卌 卌 卌 卌 卌 卌 卌 IIII	49

(pp. 386–387, 400–401) 12E

Tell which graph(s) can best be used to represent the data set. (Choose *bar graph, pictograph,* or *line graph.*)

21. The heights of the teachers in your school. _bar graph_

22. The number of books in the library at Duke University. _bar graph or pictograph_

To be certain that 4 part-time announcers are chosen on a random basis, each announcer is represented by a number 1–4. A spinner with the numbers 1 through 4 was spun 200 times. The results of the simulation are shown in the chart.

Number	Number of Times Spun
1	46
2	51
3	50
4	53

23. What is the experimental probability of getting a 4? _53/200_

24. What is the actual probability of getting a 4? _¼_

25. Does each announcer represented by a number have an equally likely chance of being selected on the basis of the actual probability? _yes_

6. In class 7-305, during which month was the relative frequency of students with perfect attendance 65%? **October**

Is the probability *0, 1,* or *between 0 and 1*? *(pages 392–393)*

7. May 1998, will follow July 1998. **0**

8. Monday, May 17, will follow Sunday, May 16. **1**

===== **PROBLEM SOLVING** =====

9. Use the data from the table on page 406. *(pages 386–387)*

  a. During which month was the total number of students with perfect attendance the lowest? **Nov.**

  b. What type of graphs can be used to compare the number of students with perfect attendance during the 4 mo? **double bar graph**

  c. Why would a line graph not be appropriate to compare the number of students absent in September? **does not include change over time**

Use a simulation. *(pages 400–401)*

10. One of 8 different posters is packed inside a music magazine. Stanley wants to predict the number of magazines he would have to buy in order to collect all 8 posters. He ran a simulation using the spinner and tallied his results.

  Poster 1: ||| Poster 2: | Poster 3: |||| Poster 4: ~~||||~~

  Poster 5: ||| Poster 6: ||| Poster 7: |||| Poster 8: ||

How many magazines did Stanley's simulation tell him he would need to buy? **25 magazines**

11. During 4 consecutive weeks a ski resort had the following amounts of snow: 15 in., 13 in., 8 in., and 12 in. What was the mean weekly amount of snow? **12 in.**

LEARNING LOG

Write the answers in your learning log.
  1. Describe what is meant by "chance."
  Accept reasonable answers.
  2. When you roll two number cubes, how would you determine what sums are equally likely to occur? **Accept reasonable answers.**

Note that the same numbers are used in Exercises 5 and 11.

Problem Solving

Item 9 has three parts:
a. literal—this is a reading comprehension question.
b. interpretive—this involves interpretation using the facts given.
c. applied—students use a strategy or skill to find an answer.

Item 5 in the skills section and item 11 in the problem solving section use the same numbers.

This will help you informally assess how your students transfer from numerical skills to word problems.

For scoring problem solving items, you may wish to use partial credit. If a student uses the correct strategy but gets a wrong answer, give the student two points toward the total percent score.

Learning Log

These are suggestions for writing about some topics taught in the chapter. The students keep their learning logs from the start of the school year through the end.

Items	Management Objective	Pages
1–2; 5; 11	**12A** Find the mean and median.	378–379; 382–383
4	**12C** Recognize equally likely outcomes.	394–395
3; 6–8	**12D** Find the probability of an event.	388–389; 392–393; 396–397
9–10	**12E** Problem Solving: Choose an appropriate graph. Use simulation.	386–387; 400–401

CHAPTER TEST • FORM B

Find the mean and median. (pp. 376–379, 382–383) 12A

1. Points scored: 62, 70, 83, 103, 76, 88, 92 _82, 83_
2. Cost of sweaters: $38, $58, $48, $41, $96, $62, $70 _$59, $58_
3. Snow levels at ski lodges: 29 in., 41 in., 86 in., 74 in., 50 in. _56 in., 50 in._
4. Cars leased: 42, 50, 61, 58, 47, 60 _53, 54_
5. Overdue books: 32, 40, 50, 38, 45 _41, 40_

Use the graph to answer the questions. (pp. 380–381, 384–385) 12B

6. Which town had the greater amount of snow in February? _Micro_

7. What was the average snowfall for Micro in January? _about 3½ in._

8. During which month did Lewis have 4 in. of snowfall? _February_

9. During which month was the difference in snowfall the greatest? _March_

10. For the four month period, how much snowfall did Micro receive than Lewis? _about 4½ in._

Write equally likely or not equally likely for the outcome in the situation. Use the spinner for Exercises 11–13. (pp. 394–395) 12C

11. spinning an odd or even number _equally likely_

12. spinning a number less than 3 or a number more than 3 _not equally likely_

13. spinning a prime or composite number _not equally likely_

14. The next student you see will be a male or a female. _equally likely_

15. The next vehicle you see will be a motorcycle or a car. _not equally likely_

CHAPTER TEST • FORM B

(pp. 388–389, 392–393, 396–399) 12D

Is the probability *0, 1,* or *between 0 and 1*?

16. You roll a number cube and a 3 is face up. _between 0 and 1_

17. Someone in your school will write their name on Monday. _1_

Some students spun the spinner at the right 100 times. The table shows the tally for the frequency of each spin.

18. Use the data table. Write as a fraction the experimental probability of spinning a 3. _29/50_

Look at the spinner. Find the actual probability as a fraction.

19. spinning a 2 _1/3_ | 1 | ||| ||| || | 12 |
20. spinning a 3 _1/2_ | 2 | ||| ||| ||| ||| ||| ||| | 30 |
                                | 3 | ||| ||| ||| ||| ||| ||| ||| ||| ||| ||| ||| ||| ||| | 58 |

(pp. 386–387, 400–401) 12E

Tell which graph(s) can best be used to represent the data set. (Choose *bar graph*, *pictograph*, or *line graph*.)

21. The heights of the students in your school. _bar graph_
22. The number of cars in your state. _bar graph or pictograph_

To be certain that five particular cars are randomly used, each car is represented by a number 1–5. A spinner with the numbers 1 through 5 was spun 200 times. The results of the simulation are shown in the chart.

Number	Number of Times Spun
1	34
2	43
3	40
4	36
5	47

23. What is the experimental probability of getting a 2? _43/200_

24. What is the actual probability of getting a 2? _1/5_

25. Does each car represented by a number have an equally likely chance of being selected on the basis of the actual probability? _yes_

Error Analysis and Remediation

Here are some common errors students make when they are finding the mean and the median; making a double bar graph and a double line graph; recognizing equally likely outcomes; and finding the probability of an event. The errors are listed by lesson under the appropriate management objective.

12A • FIND THE MEAN AND MEDIAN

Source of Error (Lesson 12-4)
Students do not put the data in order when finding the median.

Remediation
Remind students that they can find the median only after they have arranged the data from least to greatest.

12B • MAKE A DOUBLE BAR GRAPH AND A DOUBLE LINE GRAPH

Source of Error (Lesson 12-3)
Students use inappropriate divisions on the vertical axis.

Remediation
Review how to determine divisions for the vertical axis. Point out that they should consider multiples of 10, 100, and so on depending on the size of the data they are displaying.

Source of Error (Lesson 12-5)
Students have difficulty locating the correct values for a given point on the graph.

Remediation
Suggest that students use a sheet of paper as a guide: (1) place the corner of the paper on the given point; (2) position the right edge of the paper with the appropriate number on the horizontal axis; and (3) align the top edge of the paper with the correct value on the vertical scale.

12C • RECOGNIZE EQUALLY LIKELY OUTCOMES

Source of Error (Lesson 12-9)
Students mistake outcomes that are not equally likely as equally likely.

Remediation
Display a spinner with three different-color regions, two that are equal and one that is larger than the other two. Point out that the outcomes would not be equally likely because one region is so much larger than the other two. Stress that outcomes are equally likely only when each outcome has an equal chance of occurring.

12D • FIND THE PROBABILITY OF AN EVENT

Source of Error (Lesson 12-7)
Students do not distinguish between the frequency and the relative frequency.

Remediation
Remind students that the relative frequency is a ratio that compares a part to a whole and that it is expressed as a percent.

Source of Error (Lesson 12-10)
Students do not distinguish between an actual probability and an experimental probability.

Remediation
Remind students that an actual probability concerns possible outcomes of an event. Experimental probability is based on the results of a particular experiment.

12E • PROBLEM SOLVING: CHOOSE AN APPROPRIATE GRAPH. USE SIMULATION.

Source of Error (Lesson 12-6)
Students choose a line graph to display data that are not organized numerically.

Remediation
Tell students that once they have drawn a few of the points on their line graph, they should examine the line segments connecting the points and see if they have any meaning. If the students can use them to predict values between the amounts on the horizontal axis, then a line graph makes sense. If the line segment has no meaning between the points it is connecting, it is better to use a bar graph.

Answers

Page 379

3. students in Homeroom 303; 10 random names

4. people in Indiana; girls in high school in Indiana

5. people in the United States; residents in a California nursing home.

6. customers of a restaurant; customers who choose to take a survey

7. band members; 10 random names

8. high school students in the United States; high school students in one Florida school

Page 380

5. **Think Aloud:** Answers will vary. Suggestion given: Sample could have been selected high school basketball coaches across the United States; the population must have been male and female players on high school basketball teams; questions could have been about the nature and number of injuries that season.

Page 383

3. Answers will vary. Suggestion given: no; The median was unchanged because Massachusetts would still be the state with the greatest population.

9. a. 535,000; yes; The numbers used to calculate it changed.
   b. 519,000; no; 750,000 remained the greatest population

10. **In Your Words:** Answers will vary. Suggestion given: The average should be reported as the median where there is one number that is much greater or smaller than the others. It can be reported as either when there is not a great difference between one number and all the others.

11. Answers will vary. Suggestions given: He did not arrange the numbers in order first.

Page 388

1. 6–8; 0.16; 16%
   7–8; 0.23; 23%
   7–9; 4,711; 0.45; 45%
   Other; 850; 0.08; 8%

Page 389

2. **Think Aloud:** Answers will vary. Suggestion given: The sample may have been principals from some middle schools in every state; The population may have been principals of all middle schools; questions may have been about the number of grades in the principal's school.

6.

Types of Middle Schools 1986–87		
Grade Combination	Frequency (part)	Relative Frequency (part ÷ whole)
5–8	1,137	0.10 or 10%
6–8	4,329	0.40 or 40%
7–7	2,627	0.24 or 24%
7–9	2,191	0.20 or 20%
Other	573	0.05 or 5%
Total (whole)	10,857	0.99 or 99%

Page 393

15. Los Angeles, Dallas, Atlanta, Chicago, Juneau

Page 399

2. **Critical Thinking:** The highest relative frequency, 1, would indicate that all squares had X's. The lowest relative frequency, 0, would mean that all squares had O's.

3. **Think Aloud:** Answers will vary. Suggestion given: As more looks are made, the relative frequency should come closer to the actual probability.

5. **Critical Thinking:** Answers will vary. Suggestion given: More data (from all of the looks) are included in the calculation of the relative frequency later in the game.

6. See below.

7. **Critical Thinking:** Answers will vary. Suggestion given: Player 2 could choose 5 squares in rule 1 and could look at 2 squares each time.

8. **Number Sense:** Answers will vary. Suggestion given: For guessing the probability with 3 squares, it takes at least 9 looks for the experimental probability to begin to stabilize, so it might take at least 150 looks for the experimental probability to stabilize if you look at only one of the 50 squares each look.

6.

X or O	O	O	X	X	X	O	X	X	O	X	O	X	X	X	O	O
X's so far	0	0	1	2	3	3	4	5	5	6	6	7	8	9	9	9
Number of looks	1	2	3	4	5	6	7	8	9	10	11	12	13	14	15	16
Relative frequency $(\frac{X's}{looks})$	0	0	$\frac{1}{3}$	$\frac{2}{4}$	$\frac{3}{5}$	$\frac{3}{6}$	$\frac{4}{7}$	$\frac{5}{8}$	$\frac{5}{9}$	$\frac{6}{10}$	$\frac{6}{11}$	$\frac{7}{12}$	$\frac{8}{13}$	$\frac{9}{14}$	$\frac{9}{15}$	$\frac{9}{16}$
Decimals	0.00	0.00	0.33	0.50	0.60	0.50	0.57	0.63	0.56	0.60	0.55	0.58	0.62	0.64	0.60	0.56

Extra Practice

This page provides extra practice of all the major chapter objectives. Use this page after the chapter has been taught to reinforce the chapter skills. Page references are provided for each group of items so that students can easily look back at the appropriate lesson for additional support.

EXTRA PRACTICE

Name the population and the sample. *(pages 378–379)*

1. A college wants to know about the interests of its freshman students. A questionnaire is sent to all students whose last name begins with the letter *S*. **freshman students at the college; those with last names beginning with the letter S.**

2. To learn about their customers' tastes, a music store questions every tenth person who enters the store. **all customers; every tenth customer**

Use the data from the table. *(pages 380–385, 388–389)*

3. Make a double bar graph of the data. **Check students' graphs.**

4. Find the mean weekly sales for each store. **Tunetown–69.25; Sounds–81.25**

5. During which week did Sounds sell about 40% of its monthly total of CD players? **June 17**

CD Players Sold in Two Stores

Week of	Tunetown	Sounds
June 3	38	29
June 10	52	72
June 17	102	128
June 24	85	96

6. Find the relative frequency of Tunetown's June 3 weekly sales compared to its monthly total. **14%**

Is the probability *0, 1,* or *between 0 and 1*? *(pages 392–393)*

7. Humans will walk on Mars this year. **0**

8. Humans will walk on Mars during the 21st century. **between 0 and 1**

Write *equally likely* or *not equally likely* for the outcomes in the situation. *(pages 394–395)*

9. Rolling an even or odd number on a cube numbered 1 through 6.
equally likely

10. Tossing 1 coin and the results being 1 head.
not equally likely

Solve. *(pages 386–387, 400–401)*

11. What type of graph can be used to represent the data set? The average daily temperature in Seattle, Washington during July. **bar or line graph**

12. Sandy has 6 sweaters she wants to wear, but she wants to vary the order in which she wears them. She ran a simulation using a number cube and got these results:

    3   1   4   3   6   5   1   3   2

    If each number represents a different sweater, how many days would it take for her to wear all 6 sweaters? **9 d**

GRAPHS IN ADS

Companies often use graphs in their advertisements. When used properly, a graph can make information clear to the reader. However, sometimes graphs are included only because they look official and the information in the graph may have little to do with the claim being made for the product.

Work with a group. Find several advertisements in newspapers or magazines that use graphs. Write a short paragraph summarizing your feelings about the effectiveness of the graphs you have found. **Check students' work.**

WHATS NORMAL

Words like *normal*, *typical*, and *average* are used in conversation, in the written media (newspapers, magazines), and on radio and television every day. Some examples are references to *normal* rainfall for a day, the height of the *typical* person, or the *average* price of shares of stock. These words may refer to the mean, median, or mode of a set of data.

Find references using the words *normal*, *typical*, or *average*. For each one decide whether it refers to the mean, median, or mode of the data being considered. You may not be able to determine which was intended. If you cannot tell, make a note of that also. Decide which of the three, mean, median, or mode, is used most commonly. **Check students' work.**

Pizza Pieces

You can slice a pizza into 2 pieces with 1 cut. You can slice a pizza into 4 pieces with 2 cuts. Show how you can slice a pizza into 7 pieces with 3 cuts. What is the greatest number of pieces you can slice with 4 cuts?

11 pieces

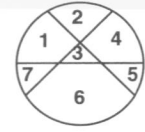 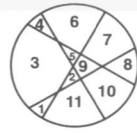

Enrichment

This page contains activities that provide extension and enrichment for all levels of students. Depending on the needs of your students, you may wish to assign an activity from this page at certain points during the chapter, or you may wish to use this page when the entire chapter has been completed.

Graphs in Ads
(COOPERATIVE)

Have groups of three or four visit the library to look in major newspapers and magazines for examples of ads that use graphs to advertise products.

What's Normal

Suggest that students look for at least three uses of each word. Encourage the class to create a bulletin board display of their findings.

Pizza Pieces

Suggest that students use a compass to draw several circles to use for this activity. Remind them that there are 360 degrees in a circle.

CHAPTER 12

Cumulative Review

The Cumulative Review focuses on skills covered in previous chapters. All important skills are reviewed on a cyclic basis.

If students are having difficulty with particular groups of exercises, refer to the chart below for follow-up work.

CUMULATIVE REVIEW

Find the answer.

1. $3\frac{1}{5} \times 1\frac{7}{8}$ **c**
   a. $3\frac{7}{40}$
   b. $4\frac{7}{40}$
   c. 6
   d. none of these

2. $\frac{3}{8} \div 4$ **a**
   a. $\frac{3}{32}$
   b. $1\frac{1}{2}$
   c. $\frac{3}{8}$
   d. none of these

3. $12\frac{1}{2} \div \frac{2}{3}$ **c**
   a. $8\frac{1}{3}$
   b. $25\frac{2}{3}$
   c. $18\frac{3}{4}$
   d. none of these

4. An angle less than 90° is **b**
   a. obtuse
   b. acute
   c. straight
   d. none of these

5. An angle of exactly 180° is **d**
   a. acute
   b. right
   c. obtuse
   d. none of these

6. Circumference of **a** circle: $d = 9$m, $\pi \approx$ 3.14
   a. 28.26 m
   b. 14.1 m
   c. 63.6 m
   d. none of these

7. $\frac{3}{20} = \underline{\ ?\ }$ **c**
   a. 30%
   b. 20%
   c. 15%
   d. none of these

8. $0.062 = \underline{\ ?\ }$ **b**
   a. 0.62%
   b. 6.2%
   c. 62%
   d. none of these

9. $18.5\% = \underline{\ ?\ }$ **b**
   a. 0.0185
   b. $\frac{185}{1000}$
   c. 18.5
   d. none of these

10. $3.72 = \underline{\ ?\ }$ **a**
   a. 372%
   b. 37.2%
   c. 0.372%
   d. none of these

11. $\frac{207}{100} = \underline{\ ?\ }$ **d**
   a. 20.7%
   b. 0.207%
   c. 2.07%
   d. none of these

12. $0.8\% = \underline{\ ?\ }$ **c**
   a. 0.8
   b. 0.08
   c. 0.008
   d. none of these

Find the matching value.

13. 2 yd 3 in. **b**
   a. 27 in.
   b. 75 in.
   c. 39 in.
   d. none of these

14. 1 gal 2 pt **a**
   a. 20 c
   b. 16 c
   c. 12 c
   d. none of these

15. 3 lb 1 oz **b**
   a. 17 oz
   b. 49 oz
   c. 97 oz
   d. none of these

410   CUMULATIVE REVIEW

Items	Management Objectives	Where Taught	Reteaching Options	Extra Practice Options
1	**7A** Multiply fractions and mixed numbers.	pp. 208–209	TRB/RW 7-3	TRB/PW 7-3
2–3	**7B** Divide fractions and mixed numbers.	pp. 214–215 218–219	TRB/RW 7-5 and 7-7 TE/RA 7-6	TRB/PW 7-5, 7-7
4–5	**8A** Measure and classify angles.	pp. 234–235	TRB/RW 8-2	TRB/PW 8-2
6	**8D** Find the circumference and area of a circle.	pp. 254–255	TRB/RW 8-11	TRB/PW 8-11
7–9	**10A** Write fractions and decimals as percents and percents as fractions and decimals.	pp. 312–315	TRB/RW 10-2 and 10-3	TRB/PW 10-2 and 10-3
10–12	**10B** Write percents greater than 100% and less than 1%.	pp. 316–317	TRB/RW 10-4/5	TRB/PW 10-4/5
13–15	**6D** Determine the appropriate customary units of length, capacity, and weight.	pp. 188–193	TRB/RW 6-9 to 6-11	TRB/PW 6-9 to 6-11

Strategies may vary. Suggestions given.

Remember the strategies and types of problems you've had so far. Solve.

Problem Solving Check List

- Too much information
- Too little information
- Multistep problems
- Using guess and check
- Using percents
- Using estimation
- Drawing a picture

1. One hundred students were asked to name their favorite pet. Twenty eight percent chose a cat, 23% a parrot, and 7% a lizard. The rest chose a dog.

   a. What percent of the students chose a cat as their favorite? **28%**

   b. Which pet was preferred by the most students? **dog**

   c. How many more students chose a dog than a lizard? **multistep; 35 more students**

2. After filling her car's gas tank, Shirley went on a 300-mi trip. The gas tank holds 12 gal and the car averages 42 mi/gal. To the nearest gallon, how much gas was left after the trip? **multistep; 5 gal**

3. Oak Street is 16 blocks long. A traffic signal is to be placed at every other intersection along Oak Street and at both ends. How many traffic signals are needed? **picture; 9 signals**

4. A phone call costs $.25 for the first 3 min and $.10 for each additional minute, but on weekends, the first 3 min are $.20 and each extra minute is $.07. How much cheaper is a 15-min call on the weekend? **multistep; $.41**

5. After math class, $\frac{1}{3}$ of the students went to gym. Of those that were left, $\frac{1}{2}$ went to lunch and the rest of the students stayed to talk with their teacher. How many went to the gym? **too little information**

6. Vivian and Richard were running for class president. A total of 347 votes were cast. Vivian received 79 votes more than Richard. How many votes did each candidate receive? **guess and check; V–213; R–134**

7. A spinner has 8 equal sections. Six sections are green and two are red. In 500 spins, about how many times would you expect the spinner to stop on green? **percents; 375 times**

8. Four boys determine that the mean of their heights is 60 in. If a 5th boy joins them, how tall must he be if the mean height of the 5 boys is 61 in.? **guess and check; 65 in.**

9. A rectangular picture measuring 5 in. by 8 in. is in a rectangular frame that measures 9 in. by 12 in. What is the area of the border? **picture; 68 in.²**

10. Last week, Jason's after-school job paid him $24.00 plus a 15% bonus. What were his total earnings for the week? **percents; $27.60**

Problem Solving Review

This page focuses on problem solving strategies and types learned in this and previous chapters. A problem solving checklist lists some of the strategies students may use to solve the problems on this page.

Technology

This page is designed to provide calculator or computer experiences for all levels of students. The calculator or computer logo indicates the type of activity.

You may wish to assign these activities after the chapter has been taught or during the course of the chapter, depending on your needs and those of your students.

I'll Take $7\frac{1}{2}$

Suggest that students use proportional thinking to answer the first question. You may also want to discuss how the company could ensure that the sample was representative.

Starting Salaries

If necessary, review how students determine the median and the mean of a set of data.

Simply Circular

Remind students that the every change in the numerator, the number of white or black circles, also affects the denominator, the total number of circles.

The computer activity uses Houghton Mifflin software, which is found in Houghton Mifflin Math Activities Courseware, Grade 7.

TECHNOLOGY

I'LL TAKE $7\frac{1}{2}$

A large insurance company employs 40,580 people. A sample was taken of 1,250 of those employees. Of those sampled, 500 were in favor of an 8-h workday, instead of the $7\frac{1}{2}$-h workday they currently have.

How many of the 40,580 would you expect to be in favor of the longer work day? How many more hours will be worked for the company in one day if the company goes to an 8-h work day? **16,232; 20,290 hr**

STARTING SALARIES

The annual salaries of the 20 employees of a company are:

$14,280; $15,490; $15,575; $16,280;

$16,575; $17,200; $17,485; $20,450;

$26,475; $32,571; $32,890; $32,927;

$33,100; $33,250; $34,800; $34,956;

$35,103; $36,428; $36,792; $50,211

Sam joined the company, and will earn $\frac{1}{2}$ the sum of the median plus the mean. What is Sam's salary? **$30,186.20**

SIMPLY CIRCULAR

In the computer activity *Animal Farm*, you must shift two types of animals in and out of a pen until you reach a target ratio of one type of animal to the total number of animals. This activity will help you work with ratios in this way. **See below.**

Look at the initial ratio in each problem below. Try to change this to the target ratio in exactly the number of steps indicated by the spaces. At each step you add or subtract just one black or white circle.

		Initial Ratio	Steps				Target
1.		$\frac{\text{white circles}}{\text{circles in all}}$ $\frac{3}{4}$	$\frac{2}{3}$	$\frac{2}{4}$	$\frac{1}{3}$	$\frac{1}{4}$	$\frac{1}{4}$
2.		$\frac{\text{black circles}}{\text{circles in all}}$ $\frac{5}{6}$	$\frac{4}{5}$ $\frac{3}{4}$ $\frac{3}{5}$	$\frac{3}{6}$ $\frac{3}{7}$ $\frac{3}{8}$			$\frac{3}{8}$

Software Activities

Note: Students should enter commands as single lines. They must not hit RETURN within a command.

activity 1 • TV TIME

MATERIALS: database and spreadsheet programs

Procedure: This activity will have students collect data about their television viewing. Ask students to keep a log of their TV viewing for a week, recording the exact time they watched TV each evening between 4 PM and 9 PM and all day Saturday and Sunday. They should also record the type of program (cartoons, drama, specials, and sports).

Next, have students create a spreadsheet, with headings for the days of the week. Under each day, students should record the length of time they watched TV that day. Students should then calculate the percent of total time they watched TV on each day of the week. Have students compare results to see if there are trends in television watching. Discuss the effects on students.

Follow-up: Students should use the data they collected above to devise a TV schedule for a fictitous station.

activity 2 • BUILD A BAR GRAPH

MATERIALS: Logo program

Procedure: This program draws a bar graph. Have students enter the program and run it with data such as 30, 50, 100, 120, and 200. Students should run the program several more times using small numerical data.

```
TO BARGRAPH
  PU SETX -100 SETY -89 PRINT
[ENTER DATA. WE'LL DRAW A GRAPH.]
GRAPH
END
TO GRAPH
  HT MAKE "X FIRST READSLISTCC
REPEAT 2[PD FD:X
  RT 90 FD 8 RT 90] RT 90 FD 15 LT
90 GRAPH
END
```

Follow-up: Challenge students to modify the program so that the width of the bars depends on the number of pieces of data entered.

HOUGHTON MIFFLIN SOFTWARE

Computational Skills Program. Boston, MA: Houghton Mifflin Company, 1988. For Apple II.

Easy Graph. Boston, MA: Houghton Mifflin Company, 1987. For Apple II, Commodore, IBM.

EduCalc. Boston, MA: Houghton Mifflin Company, 1990. For Apple II, Commodore, IBM.

Friendly Filer. Boston, MA: Houghton Mifflin Company, 1989. For Apple II, Commodore, IBM.

Mathematics Activities Courseware. Boston, MA: Houghton Mifflin Company, 1983. For Apple II, IBM.

The Computer Tutor. Boston, MA: Houghton Mifflin Company, 1990. For Apple II, IBM.

OTHER SOFTWARE

Microsoft Works. Redmond, WA: Microsoft Corporation, 1989. For IBM, Macintosh.

Probability Lab. St. Paul, MN: MECC, 1990. For Apple II.

Special Topics in Math: Logic, Permutations, Probability. State College, PA: Courses by Computers, 1989. For Apple II, IBM.

TABS Math Probability, "Pete's Probability Raffle," "Probability Games," "What is Random," "Spinners," Des Plaines, IL: Looking Glass Learning, 1989. For Apple II.

What's the Chance? Danbury, CT: EME, 1987. For Apple II.

Integers and Coordinate Graphing

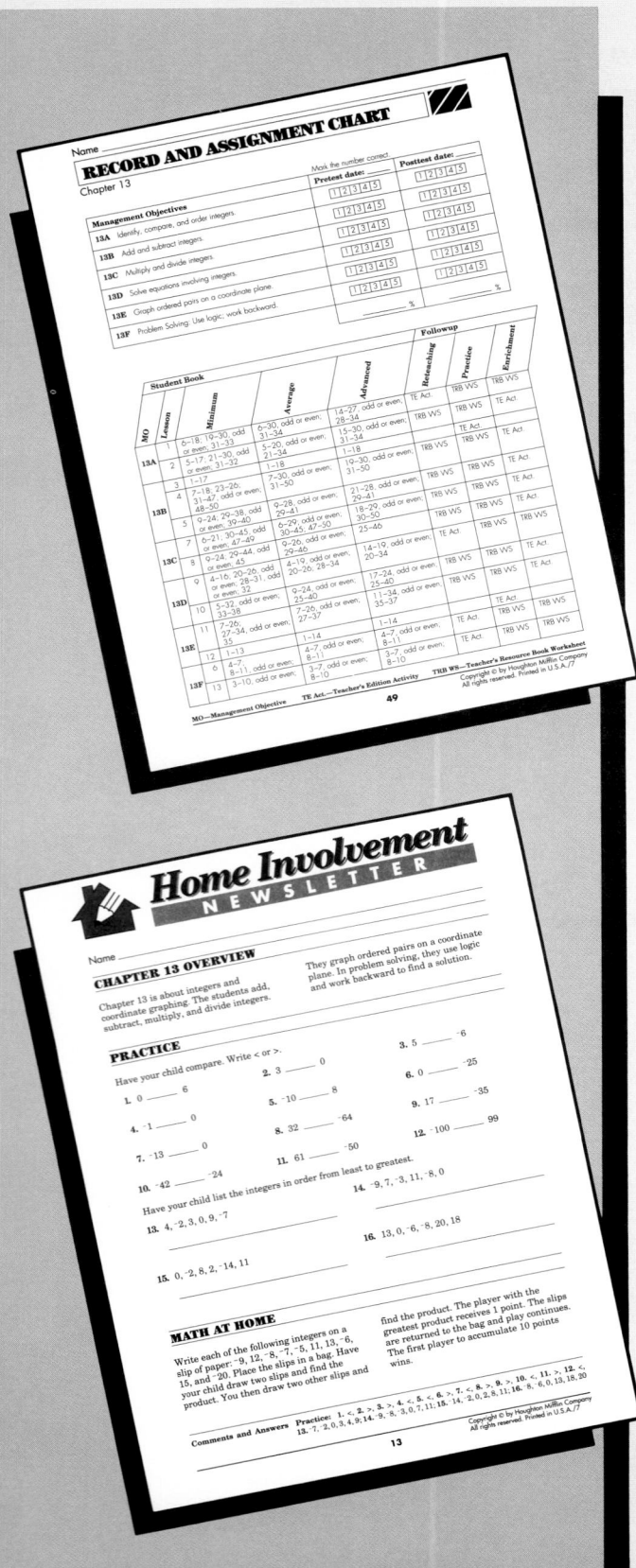

This chapter involves the concepts of integers. It focuses on ordering and comparing integers; and adding, subtracting, multiplying, and dividing integers.

The concept of using inverse operations to solve equations, introduced in Chapter 4, is expanded to include integers. Using integers to locate points on a coordinate plane is introduced and then extended to include the translation and rotation of an ordered pair within a coordinate plane. Problem solving is extended to include using logic and the strategy of working backward to solve a problem.

Management Objectives

13A Identify, compare, and order integers.
13B Add and subtract integers.
13C Multiply and divide integers.
13D Solve equations involving integers.
13E Graph ordered pairs on a coordinate plane.
13F Problem Solving: Use logic. Work backward.

Assignments for different achievement levels are provided on the Record and Assignment Chart in the Teacher's Resource Book.

Vocabulary

integers, opposites, page 414
absolute value, page 414
degrees Celsius (°C), page 416
charged particles, page 418
coordinate plane, page 436
x-axis, page 436
y-axis, page 436
origin, page 436
graph, page 436
ordered pair, page 436
coordinates, page 436
translation image, page 438
line of reflection, page 439
reflection image, page 439

Home Involvement

As you begin to teach this chapter, give each student a copy of the Home Involvement Newsletter for this chapter.

This newsletter provides parents with
- an overview of the chapter
- suggestions for practicing some of the skills in the chapter
- an at-home activity to do with their child, applying the skills taught in the chapter.

Management Chart

	Management Objectives	Lesson/ Pages	Student Not Successful	Student Needs More Practice	Student Successful	Pacing Range
13A	Identify, compare, and order integers.	13-1/414-415	TE/RA 13-1	TRB/PW 13-1	TRB/EW 13-1	2 days
		13-2/416-417	TRB/RW 13-2	TRB/PW 13-2 CT Unit 11 Obj. 1.1	TE/EA 13-2	
13B	Add and subtract integers.	13-3/418-419			TE/CA 13-3	3-4 days
		13-4/420-421	TRB/RW 13-4	TRB/PW 13-4 CT Unit 11 Obj. 2.1	TE/EA 13-4	
		13-5/422-423	TRB/RW 13-5	TRB/PW 13-5 CT Unit 11 Obj. 2.2	TE/EA 13-5	
13C	Multiply and divide integers.	13-7/426-427	TRB/RW 13-7	TRB/PW 13-7 CT Unit 11 Obj. 4.1	TE/EA 13-7	2-3 days
		13-8/428-429	TRB/RW 13-8	TRB/PW 13-8 CT Unit 11 Obj. 4.2	TE/EA 13-8	
13D	Solve equations involving integers.	13-9/432-433	TE/RA 13-9	TRB/PW 13-9	TRB/EW 13-9	2-3 days
		13-10/434-435	TRB/RW 13-10	TRB/PW 13-10	TE/EA 13-10 MAC 8 Activity 5 MAC 8 Activity 8	
13E	Graph ordered pairs on a coordinate plane.	13-11/436-437	TRB/RW 13-11	TRB/PW 13-11 MAC 6 Activity 13	TE/EA 13-11 MAC 7 Activity 14A MAC 7 Activity 8	2 days
		13-12/438-439		MAC 6 Activity 12A MAC 7 Activity 13	TE/CA 13-12 MAC 6 Activity 12A MAC 8 Activity 12B	
13F	Problem Solving: Use logic. Work backward.	13-6/424-425	TE/RA 13-6	TRB/PW 13-6	TRB/EW 13-6	2 days
		13-13/440-441	TE/RA 13-13	TRB/PW 13-13	TRB/EW 13-13	
	Chapter Checkups	430-431; 442-443				
	Extra Practice	444				
	Enrichment	445				
	Cumulative Review/Problem Solving Review	446-447				
	Technology	448				

TE = Teacher's Edition
TRB = Teacher's Resource Book
RW = Reteaching Worksheet
RA = Reteaching Activity
EA = Enrichment Activity
EW = Enrichment Worksheet
PW = Practice Worksheet
CA = Classroom Activity

*Other Available Items
MAC = Mathematics Activities Courseware
CT = Computer Tutor

Manipulative Planning Guide

This is a complete list of manipulatives and materials needed for Chapter 13.

Materials for Manipulatives	TE Activities (INTRODUCE)	Student Book Lesson
Teaching Aid 1*	Lesson 13-1	
Celsius thermometer	Lesson 13-2	

Teaching Aid 18*
  for each student
  for each pair
	Lesson 13-3
	Lessons 13-4, 13-5
		Lessons 13-4, 13-5
		Lesson 13-3

Workmat
  for each student
  for each pair
	Lesson 13-3
	Lessons 13-4, 13-5
		Lessons 13-4, 13-5
		Lesson 13-3

Calculator for each student		Lessons 13-4, 13-5, 13-7, 13-8
Math Connection Transparency		Lesson 13-10
Metric ruler, teaching Aid 15* for each student	Lesson 13-11	
Coordinate Plane transparency	Lesson 13-11	

Teaching Aid 19*
  for each student
  for demonstration
  two for each student
	Lesson 13-12	Lesson 13-11
		
		Lesson 13-12

Tagboard triangle	Lesson 13-12	
Tracing paper, scissors for each student		Lesson 13-12
Blank spinner for each pair		

*Teaching Aids are found in the Teacher's Resource Book.

Learning Stages

The concepts and skills in Chapter 13 are presented through these learning stages.

CONCRETE

Using manipulatives and verbalizing about a concept. No symbols.

Teacher Edition Activities	Student Book
Lesson 13-3	Lesson 13-3

Enrichment	Reteaching	In the Houghton Mifflin Manipulative Kit?	In the Houghton Mifflin Overhead Kit?
			Yes
			Available separately
			Yes
Lessons 13-11, 13-12			Yes
			Yes
Lessons 13-2, 13-5, 13-10		Yes	Yes

CONNECTING

5¢ 9cm^2 $\frac{1}{3}$

Making a connection between manipulatives and symbols.

Teacher Edition Activities	Student Book
Lessons 13-1, 13-2, 13-4, 13-5, 13-6, 13-11, 13-12	Lessons 13-1, 13-2, 13-4, 13-5, 13-6, 13-11, 13-12

SYMBOLIC

$\$.05$ $A = 9\text{cm}^2$ $1 - \frac{2}{3} = \frac{1}{3}$

Using numbers or symbols. No manipulatives or pictures of manipulatives.

Teacher Edition Activities	Student Book
Lessons 13-7, 13-8, 13-9, 13-10, 13-13	Lessons 13-7, 13-8, 13-9, 13-10, 13-13

Additional Activities

COOPERATIVE LEARNING RESOURCE ACTIVITIES

Through cooperative learning activities, students learn by interacting with one another in small groups. These cooperative activities provide students with motivating settings for making connections, investigations, and problem solving situations.

The cooperative connections are interdisciplinary problem-solving projects. Each student has a particular job that helps lead the group to complete the project. For the cooperative investigations students work in pairs for investigations involving data collection and analysis. The cooperative problem solving activities encourage the sharing of ideas and information. Students work in groups of four to solve a problem. Students are each assigned a clue and work together to find a common solution.

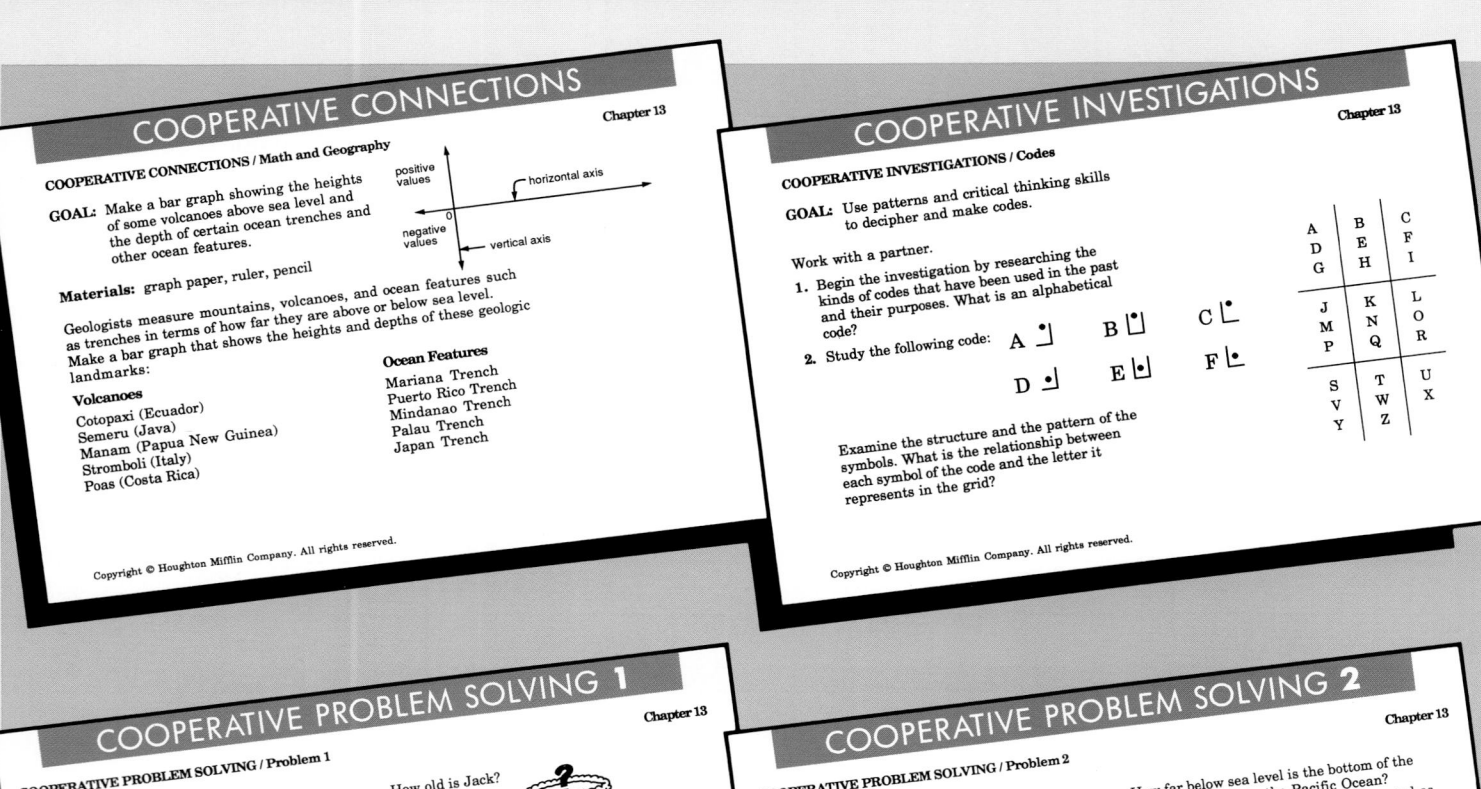

COOPERATIVE CONNECTIONS — Chapter 13

COOPERATIVE CONNECTIONS / Math and Geography

GOAL: Make a bar graph showing the heights of some volcanoes above sea level and the depth of certain ocean trenches and other ocean features.

Materials: graph paper, ruler, pencil

Geologists measure mountains, volcanoes, and ocean features such as trenches in terms of how far they are above or below sea level. Make a bar graph that shows the heights and depths of these geologic landmarks:

Volcanoes
Cotopaxi (Ecuador)
Semeru (Java)
Manam (Papua New Guinea)
Stromboli (Italy)
Poas (Costa Rica)

Ocean Features
Mariana Trench
Puerto Rico Trench
Mindanao Trench
Palau Trench
Japan Trench

Copyright © Houghton Mifflin Company. All rights reserved.

COOPERATIVE INVESTIGATIONS — Chapter 13

COOPERATIVE INVESTIGATIONS / Codes

GOAL: Use patterns and critical thinking skills to decipher and make codes.

Work with a partner.
1. Begin the investigation by researching the kinds of codes that have been used in the past and their purposes. What is an alphabetical code?
2. Study the following code:

A, B, C, D, E, F

Examine the structure and the pattern of the symbols. What is the relationship between each symbol of the code and the letter it represents in the grid?

Copyright © Houghton Mifflin Company. All rights reserved.

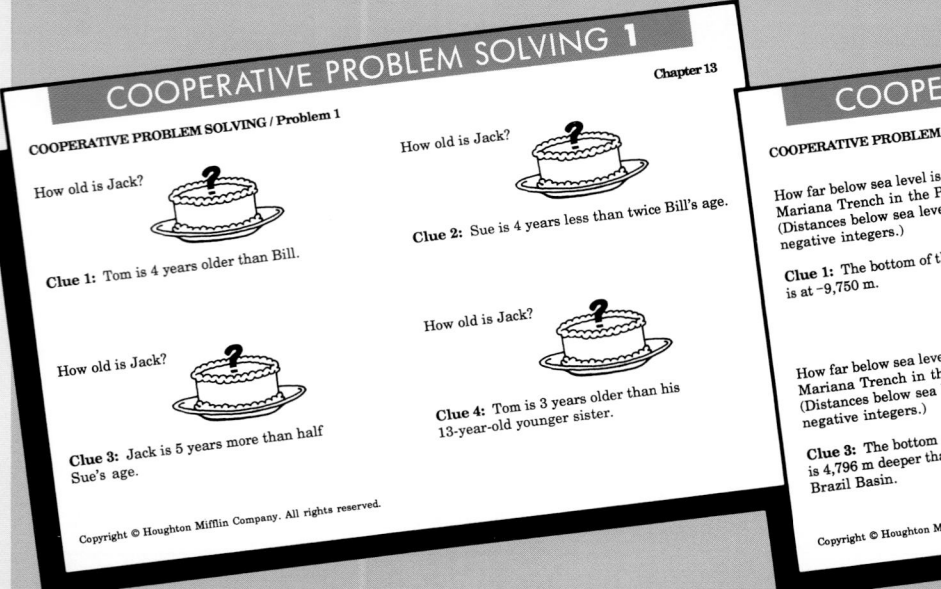

COOPERATIVE PROBLEM SOLVING 1 — Chapter 13

COOPERATIVE PROBLEM SOLVING / Problem 1

How old is Jack?

Clue 1: Tom is 4 years older than Bill.

How old is Jack?

Clue 2: Sue is 4 years less than twice Bill's age.

How old is Jack?

Clue 3: Jack is 5 years more than half Sue's age.

How old is Jack?

Clue 4: Tom is 3 years older than his 13-year-old younger sister.

Copyright © Houghton Mifflin Company. All rights reserved.

COOPERATIVE PROBLEM SOLVING 2 — Chapter 13

COOPERATIVE PROBLEM SOLVING / Problem 2

How far below sea level is the bottom of the Mariana Trench in the Pacific Ocean? (Distances below sea level are represented as negative integers.)

Clue 1: The bottom of the Kuril Trench is at -9,750 m.

How far below sea level is the bottom of the Mariana Trench in the Pacific Ocean? (Distances below sea level are represented as negative integers.)

Clue 3: The bottom of the Mariana Trench is 4,796 m deeper than the bottom of the Brazil Basin.

How far below sea level is the bottom of the Mariana Trench in the Pacific Ocean? (Distances below sea level are represented as negative integers.)

Clue 2: The bottom of the Kuril Trench is deeper than the bottom of the Japan Trench by 1,338 m.

How far below sea level is the bottom of the Mariana Trench in the Pacific Ocean? (Distances below sea level are represented as negative integers.)

Clue 4: The bottom of the Japan Trench is 2,293 m deeper that the bottom of the Brazil Basin.

Copyright © Houghton Mifflin Company. All rights reserved.

GAMES

PRODUCT SPIN (For use after Lesson 13-7)

Objective: Add and multiply integers.

☑ **MATERIALS CHECKLIST:** two spinners for each group of four students

Divide the class into groups of four. The members in each group form two teams of two. Distribute two spinners to each group, labeled as shown.

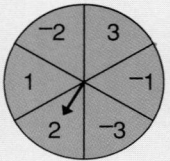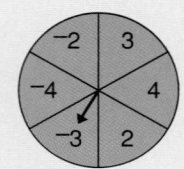

Teams alternate turns. For each turn the player spins both spinners to determine the factors to be multiplied. A correct product is recorded as the team's score. Each succeeding team member's score is added to the team score. When time is called, the team with the score farther from zero (the score with the greater absolute value) is the winner.

SATELLITE SEARCH (For use after Lesson 13-11)

Objective: Graph ordered pairs on coordinate plane.

☑ **MATERIALS CHECKLIST:** Teaching Aid 3 (Grid Paper) for each student

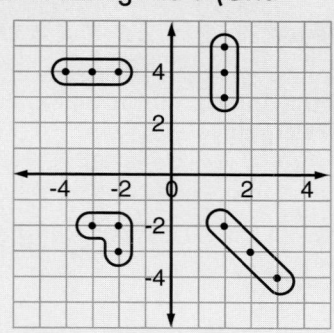

Students play this game in pairs. Have each student prepare two coordinate planes and secretly draw four "satellites" on one. Possible positions, which cover three points having integer coordinates, are shown at right. Players take turns trying to locate each other's satellites by naming a number pair. If a satellite point is named, the opposing player must say "On Course." When all points for a satellite are located, it becomes "inoperative." A player uses the blank grid to record all points he or she named and to indicate which were "on course." The first player to locate all opposing satellites wins.

BULLETIN BOARD

Display a map of the United States, and provide small pieces of paper in an envelope. Assign one to three states to each student so that all 50 states are accounted for. Ask students to research the highest and lowest recorded temperatures for their states in an almanac. They should give each temperature and the weather station where it was recorded. Students can use a pushpin to show the approximate location of the weather station when they hang the data on the map.

Alternative Assessment

In addition to the paper and pencil tests available with this program, the following items can help you assess critical thinking as well as your students' ability to solve problems in a wide variety of ways.

Open-ended Problem

A mat with a +10 charge can become a mat with a 0 charge using any of the following computations. Choose two of the examples and explain why they are equal.

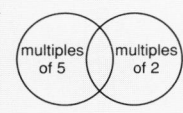

1) $+10 - +10 = 0$
2) $+10 + -10 = 0$
3) $+10 + (5 \times -2) = 0$
4) $+10 + (2 \times -5) = 0$
5) $+10 - (2 \times 5) = 0$
6) $+10 - (5 \times 2) = 0$

You may use a diagram with your answer.

Teacher Notes
- Adding 10 negatives is the same as subtracting 10 positives.
- 5 groups of $-2 = -10$ and 2 groups of $-5 = -10$.
- Multiplication is commutative, so $2 \times 5 = 5 \times 2$; both equal $+10$.

Group Writing Activity (See p. T24.)

Copy the Venn diagram on your paper. Write as many numbers as you can in each section of the diagram. Describe the numbers in the intersection.

multiples of 5   multiples of 2

Teacher Notes
- The numbers in the intersection are the common multiples of 2 and 5.
- The numbers in the intersection all end in 0.
- The numbers in the intersection are the multiples of 10.

Individual Writing Activity

Sometimes the intersection of two sets is said to be empty because the sets have no common elements. Draw a Venn diagram representing two sets whose intersection is empty. Explain why you think there are no numbers in the intersection.

Teacher Notes
Possible examples:

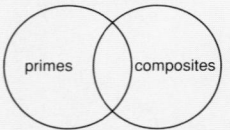 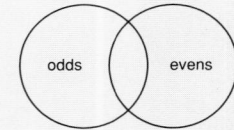 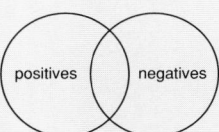

Portfolios

Portfolios can provide information about a student's growth in mathematical understanding over a period of time. They can help you make instructional decisions as well as become a vehicle for communicating with parents. The students' work involving the open-ended problem and writing activity suggested on this page along with work on the Create Your Own exercise on pages 419 and 437, the Learning Log exercises on pages 431 and 443, and the Explore lesson on pages 438–439 could be included in portfolios.

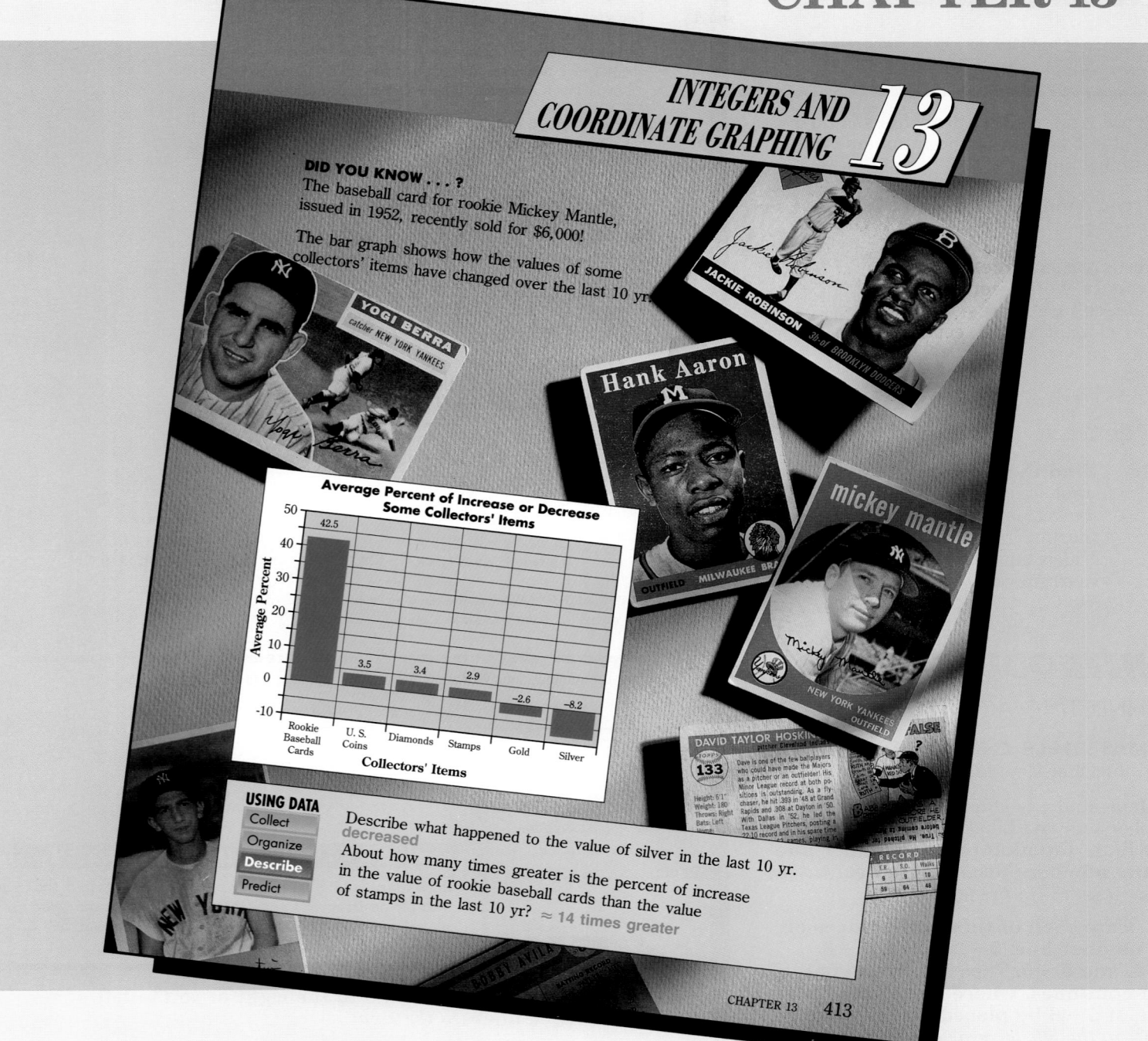

INTEGERS AND COORDINATE GRAPHING 13

DID YOU KNOW . . . ?

The baseball card for rookie Mickey Mantle, issued in 1952, recently sold for $6,000!

The bar graph shows how the values of some collectors' items have changed over the last 10 yr.

Average Percent of Increase or Decrease Some Collectors' Items

Collectors' Items	Average Percent
Rookie Baseball Cards	42.5
U.S. Coins	3.5
Diamonds	3.4
Stamps	2.9
Gold	−2.6
Silver	−8.2

USING DATA

Collect

Organize

Describe

Predict

Describe what happened to the value of silver in the last 10 yr. *decreased*

About how many times greater is the percent of increase in the value of rookie baseball cards than the value of stamps in the last 10 yr? *≈ 14 times greater*

CHAPTER 13   413

Using the Chapter Opener

The purpose of this page is to involve students in the use of real data much like that presented in newspapers and magazines.

To use this page as you begin the chapter, direct students' attention to the data. You may wish to ask questions such as the following:

Which two items experienced about the same average percent of increase or decrease in value over the past 10 yr? *(coins, diamonds)*

What was the percent of increase in the value of rookie baseball cards over the last ten years? *(42.5%)* **Write that percent as a decimal.** *(0.425)* **If you bought a "rookie" baseball card for $4 ten years ago, what would it be worth now?** *($5.70)*

Suppose you invested $10,000 in silver ten years ago. If you use the graph as a guide, how much is the silver worth today? *(only $9,180)*

Lesson Organizer

Objective: Identify integers on a number line.

Prior Knowledge: Students should be able to graph whole numbers on a number line.

Error Analysis and Remediation: See page 443A.

Lesson Resources:
Practice Worksheet 13-1
Reteaching Activity 13-1
Enrichment Worksheet 13-1
Daily Review 13-1

 *Two-Minute Math*

Find the price to the nearest cent.
Jacket: original price, $63; markup rate, 60% *($100.80)*
Video tape: original price, $12.95; markup rate, 85% *($23.96)*

1 INTRODUCE

CONNECTING ACTIVITY

☑ **MATERIALS CHECKLIST:** Teaching Aid 1 (Number Line) for each student

1. Have students start in the middle of a number line and label points 0 through 8. **In which direction on the number line do the numbers become greater?** *(to the right)* **lesser?** *(to the left)*

2. Locate each of these differences on the number line: 5 − 1, 5 − 2, 5 − 3, 5 − 4, and 5 − 5. Then ask: If the pattern continues, where would the difference of 5 − 6 be placed on the number line? *(to the left of zero)*

3. Explain that numbers located to the left of zero answer questions such as 5 − 6 = ? Locate and label ⁻1, and then ask volunteers to locate ⁻2, ⁻3, ⁻4, and ⁻5 on the number line.

WHEN YOUR STUDENTS ASK
★ WHY AM I LEARNING THIS? ★

In real life you can use integers to describe distances above and below sea level and a gain or a loss of yards in football.

MATH AND GEOGRAPHY

Integers

Pensacola, Florida, is about 5 m above sea level, and New Orleans, Louisiana, is about 1 m below sea level.

Distances above and below sea level can be recorded using positive and negative numbers. To record Pensacola's altitude you can write ⁺5 or 5. For the altitude of New Orleans, you can write ⁻1.

The numbers ⁺5 and ⁻1 are called **integers**. The set of integers is made up of the counting numbers (1, 2, 3, . . .), their opposites (⁻1, ⁻2, ⁻3, . . .), and 0.

THINK ALOUD Why is 5 the same as ⁺5?
The absence of a negative sign means it is positive.
Integers can be graphed on a number line. Numbers to the left of 0 are negative and those to the right of 0 are positive.

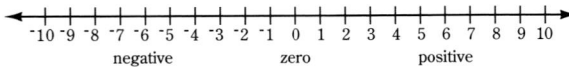

The numbers 7 and ⁻7 are opposites. **Opposite numbers** are on opposite sides of 0 but are the same distance from 0. The distance an integer is from 0 is called its **absolute value**.

The absolute value of 7 is 7. We write: |7| = 7.
The absolute value of ⁻7 is 7. We write: |⁻7| = 7.

Other examples:

Number	Opposite
15° below zero (⁻15°)	15° above zero (15°)
8 s before liftoff (⁻8 s)	8 s after liftoff (8 s)

THINK ALOUD What is the absolute value of ⁻15? of 15?
Do opposites have the same absolute value? **15; 15; yes**

━━━━━━━ **GUIDED PRACTICE** ━━━━━━━
Use the number line. Write the integer, its opposite, and its absolute value.

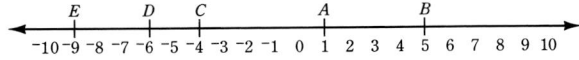

1. *A* 1; ⁻1; 1 **2.** *B* 5; ⁻5; 5 **3.** *C* ⁻4; 4; 4 **4.** *D* ⁻6; 6; 6 **5.** *E* ⁻9; 9; 9

┃ **MULTICULTURAL NOTE** ┃

More than 2,000 years ago the Chinese recognized the need for positive and negative numbers and used two-colored rods to represent them: red rods for positive numbers and black rods for negative numbers.

2 TEACH

Is the opposite of ⁻8 located to the right or to the left of zero on a number line? *(to the right)*

Which has the greater absolute value: ⁻4 or 3? *(⁻4, because on a number line, it is farther from 0 than is 3)*

Why is ½ not an integer? *(Integers are 0, 1, 2, 3, . . . and their opposites.)*

Chalkboard Examples

Name the integer that corresponds to each letter.

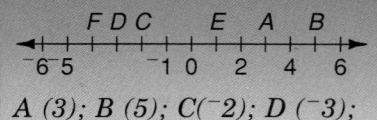

A (3); *B* (5); *C* (⁻2); *D* (⁻3); *E* (1); *F* (⁻4)

SUMMARIZE/ASSESS **Name the opposite of ⁻4, and explain why both integers have the same absolute values.** *(4; both integers are the same distance from zero on a number line.)*

Name the opposite in words. Write the original number and its opposite as integers.

5 mi south; 5; ⁻5

6. You owe $6.　　**7.** 5 mi north　　**8.** The temperature is 5° below 0.
You are owed $6; 6; ⁻6;　　　　　　　5° above zero; 5; ⁻5

Name the opposite of the integer.

9. 1　⁻1　　**10.** 6　⁻6　　**11.** ⁻6　6　　**12.** ⁻9　9　　**13.** 5　⁻5

Write the absolute value of the integer.

14. ⁻3　3　　**15.** ⁻12　12　　**16.** 45　45　　**17.** ⁻62　62　　**18.** ⁻100　100

19. NUMBER SENSE What number is its own opposite?　0

20. NUMBER SENSE Name the opposite of the opposite of ⁻2.　⁻2

Copy the number line. Graph the integer and name its opposite.

-10 -9 -8 -7 -6 -5 -4 -3 -2 -1　0　1　2　3　4　5　6　7　8　9　10

21. 6　⁻6　　**22.** ⁻6　6　　**23.** 8　⁻8　　**24.** ⁻4　4　　**25.** ⁻2　2

26. Name two integers that are 7 units from 0.　7, ⁻7

27. Name two integers that have an absolute value of 7.　7, ⁻7

28. CRITICAL THINKING Tell the value(s) of n.

　a. $n = |23|$　　**b.** $|n| = 23$　　**c.** $|-n| = 23$
　　23　　　　　23, ⁻23　　　　　23, ⁻23

MENTAL MATH Name the next three integers in the pattern.

29. ⁻8, ⁻5, ⁻2, ▧, ▧, ▧　　**30.** 18, 10, 2, ▧, ▧, ▧
　　　　　1　4　7　　　　　　　　　　⁻6 ⁻14 ⁻22

■■■■■■■■■■■■■ PROBLEM SOLVING ■■■■■■■■■■■■■

Use the graph.

31. How far (in meters) is Death Valley below sea level?　≈ 85 m

32. How far (in meters) above sea level is Shreveport, Louisiana?　≈ 62 m

33. Name the listed city that is the least above sea level.　New Haven, CT

34. Denver, Colorado, is called the mile-high city. Write its altitude as an integer.
5,280 ft, or 1 mi

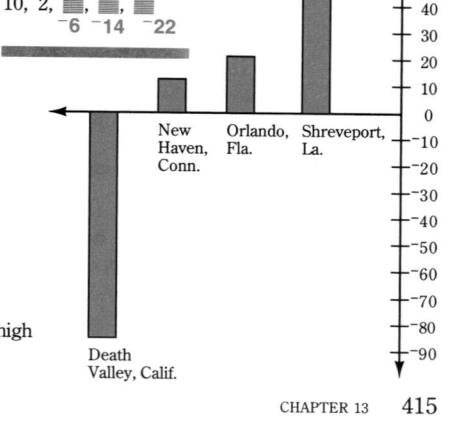

New Haven, Conn.　Orlando, Fla.　Shreveport, La.
Death Valley, Calif.

70
60
50
40
30
20
10
0
-10
-20
-30
-40
-50
-60
-70
-80
-90

CHAPTER 13　　415

MEETING INDIVIDUAL NEEDS

For Students Who Are . . .

Acquiring English Proficiency Discuss the meanings of *sea level* and *altitude*. Have students locate the places in the lesson on a map.

Gifted and Talented Have students find the altitude of five additional places and graph them on a number line. At least one place should be below sea level.

Working 2 or 3 Grades Below Level Remind students to think of 0 as the center of the number line; if a number is 5 places to the left of 0, its opposite will be 5 places to the right.

Today's Problem

The formula for changing a Fahrenheit temperature to a Celsius temperature is $C = (F - 32)\frac{5}{9}$. What is the Celsius temperature when it is 50°F? *(10°C)*

---

3 FOLLOW-UP

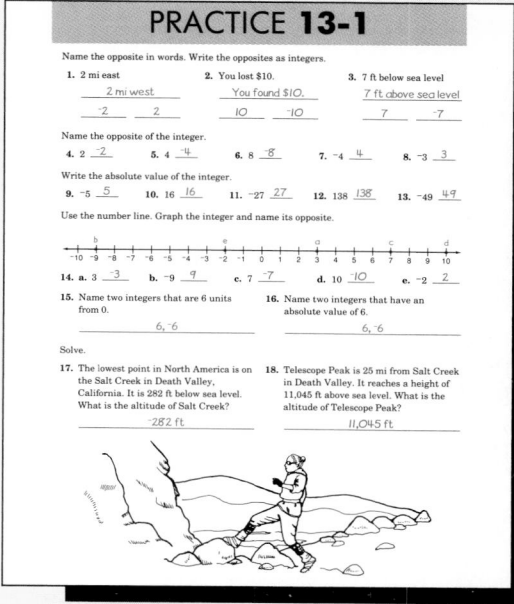
RETEACHING 13-1

☑ **MATERIALS CHECKLIST:** Tagboard, colored markers, index cards, counters

Provide pairs of students with tagboard on which you have drawn a line with 21 evenly-spaced tick marks. Label the middle tick mark *0*. Use a different color for each positive integer tic mark. Use the same colors for the negative side. Have the students take turns drawing cards on which you have written the colors used on the number line. Each partner places a counter on the positive value and the negative value for the color selected. Help students see that the distance from zero, or the absolute value is the same.

ENRICHMENT 13-1

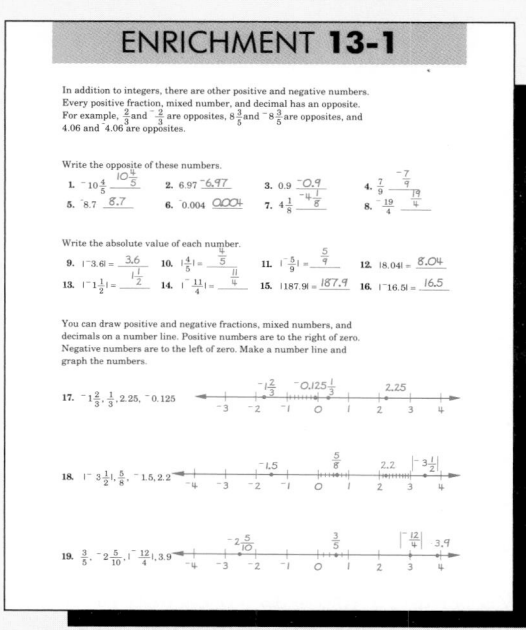

LESSON 13-2

Objective: Compare and order integers.

Prior Knowledge: Students should know how to compare and order whole numbers.

Error Analysis and Remediation: See page 443A.

Lesson Resources:
Practice Worksheet 13-2
Reteaching Worksheet 13-2
Enrichment Activity 13-2
Daily Review 13-2

 **Two-Minute Math**

Are the ratios a proportion?
5:8 as 7:8   3:4 as 18:21
(no)/(no)
5:8 as 20:32   4:9 as 4:13
(yes)/(no)

1 INTRODUCE

CONNECTING ACTIVITY

☑ **MATERIALS CHECKLIST:** Celsius thermometer

1. Display the thermometer. Point out temperatures less than zero.

2. Draw the following number line on the chalkboard to compare with the thermometer scale.

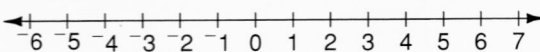

Which is true: 5 > 0 or 5 < 0 *(5 > 0)*
How can you tell by looking at the number line? *(5 is to the right of zero.)*

Which is true: ⁻4 > 0 or ⁻4 < 0? *(⁻4 < 0)*
How can you tell? *(⁻4 is to the left of 0.)*

3. Have students write expressions comparing other numbers to 0.

WHEN YOUR STUDENTS ASK
★ WHY AM I LEARNING THIS? ★

In real life you can use integers to compare temperatures. For example, if Tuesday's temperature was ⁻3°C, and Monday's temperature was 2°C, which day was colder?

Comparing and Ordering Integers

Temperature is measured in degrees Celsius (°C) in the metric system. The weather map shows some expected high temperatures for some Michigan cities on a day in February.

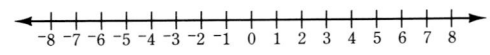

Since numbers above 0 are greater than numbers below 0, they represent a warmer temperature than those below 0.

5°C is warmer than ⁻14°C
5°C > ⁻14°C

A number line is often used to compare integers.

$$\overset{\longleftarrow}{\underset{⁻8\ ⁻7\ ⁻6\ ⁻5\ ⁻4\ ⁻3\ ⁻2\ ⁻1\ \ 0\ \ 1\ \ 2\ \ 3\ \ 4\ \ 5\ \ 6\ \ 7\ \ 8}{|\ \ |\ \ |\ \ |\ \ |\ \ |\ \ |\ \ |\ \ |\ \ |\ \ |\ \ |\ \ |\ \ |\ \ |\ \ |\ \ |}}\overset{\longrightarrow}{}$$

5 is to the right of ⁻3. ⟶ 5 > ⁻3 *or* ⁻3 < 5
⁻8 is to the left of 6. ⟶ ⁻8 < 6 *or* 6 > ⁻8

THINK ALOUD Locate any two integers on the number line. Is the integer to the left always less than the integer to the right? yes

━━━━━━━━━ **GUIDED PRACTICE** ━━━━━━━━━

Use the number line to compare. Write *left* or *right* for the first blank, and choose < or > for the second blank.

1. 4 is to the ▓ of 3. 4 ▓ 3 Rt; >   **2.** ⁻1 is to the ▓ of 0. ⁻1 ▓ 0 Lt; <

3. ⁻5 is to the ▓ of ⁻4. ⁻5 ▓ ⁻4 Lt; <   **4.** ⁻3 is to the ▓ of ⁻6. ⁻3 ▓ ⁻6 Rt; >

2 TEACH

On a number line, *x* is to the left of zero. Is *x* greater than or less than zero? *(less than 0)*

How can you use a number line to show that ⁻15 is less than ⁻8? *(Locate both points, and show that ⁻15 is to the left of ⁻8.)*

What integer is five to the left of zero? *(⁻5)* **seven to the right of zero?** *(7)*

> ### Chalkboard Examples
> Compare. Write >, <, or =.
> ⁻1 ☐ 5 *(<)*   ⁻3 ☐ ⁻8 *(>)*
> 5 ☐ ⁻5 *(>)* |⁻8| ☐ 8 *(=)*

SUMMARIZE/ASSESS **Explain how the number line can help you compare two or more integers.** *(The integer on the left is always less than the integer located to its right.)*

Name the integer.

5. two to the left of 0   ⁻2

6. five to the right of 0   5

7. three to the left of ⁻1   ⁻4

8. six to the right of ⁻3   3

Compare. Choose >, <, or =.

9. 2 ▨ 4   <

10. ⁻2 ▨ ⁻4   >

11. 4 ▨ ⁻2   >

12. ⁻4 ▨ 2   <

13. ⁻6 ▨ ⁻8   >

14. ⁻14 ▨ ⁻6   <

15. ⁻7 ▨ 0   <

16. ⁻3 ▨ 5   <

17. |⁻5| ▨ |3| >

18. |⁻6| ▨ |⁻4| >

19. |⁻12| ▨ |8| >

20. |⁻3| ▨ |3| =

MENTAL MATH   Write in order from the least to the greatest.

21. ⁻8, 4, ⁻7, 2   ⁻8, ⁻7, 2, 4

22. 5, ⁻7, ⁻10, 3   ⁻10, ⁻7, 3, 5

23. ⁻12, 4, ⁻9, 6   ⁻12, ⁻9, 4, 6

24. 0, ⁻2, 4, ⁻3, 2   ⁻3, ⁻2, 0, 2, 4

25. ⁻8, 6, |⁻2|, ⁻4   ⁻8, ⁻4, |⁻2|, 6

26. 0, |⁻1|, 6, |2|, ⁻4   ⁻4, 0, |⁻1|, |2|, 6

NUMBER SENSE   Write the next three integers in the pattern.

27. 5, 3, 1, ⁻1, ⁻3, ⁻5, ⁻7

28. ⁻8, ⁻6, ⁻4, ⁻2, 0, 2

29. 10, 5, 0, ⁻5, ⁻10, ⁻15, ⁻20

30. 10, ⁻10, 20, ⁻20, 30, ⁻30, 40, ⁻40

PROBLEM SOLVING

Use the table to solve.

31. Which state had the highest record temperature? the lowest record temperature?
No. Dakota; Alaska

32. Record the low temperatures in order from least to greatest.
⁻62; ⁻51; ⁻46; ⁻37; ⁻34; ⁻19

33. What is the difference between the least and greatest record low temperatures?   **43°C**

34. For which state does the absolute value of the record high and the record low differ by 1°C?
Michigan

Record Lowest and Highest Temperature to Nearest °C

State	Lowest	Highest
Alaska	⁻62	38
Florida	⁻19	43
Indiana	⁻37	47
Michigan	⁻46	45
North Dakota	⁻51	49
Virginia	⁻34	43

MEETING INDIVIDUAL NEEDS

For Students Who Are . . .

Acquiring English Proficiency   Pair students with an English proficient student for Exercises 31–34.

Gifted and Talented   Have students create three more problems like those in the Problem Solving section.

Today's Problem

In a Northeast city during one week in February, the low temperatures in degrees Fahrenheit were 18, 6, ⁻2, ⁻7, 4, ⁻3, and 10. Order these temperatures from least to greatest. (⁻7, ⁻3, ⁻2, 4, 6, 10, 18)

3 FOLLOW-UP

PRACTICE 13-2

Name the integer.

1. three to the right of 4   7
2. one to the left of 0   ⁻1
3. four to the left of ⁻2   ⁻6
4. four to the right of ⁻2   2

Compare. Write >, <, or =.

5. 3 < 5
6. ⁻3 > ⁻5
7. ⁻5 < 3
8. 1 > ⁻2
9. 1 > 0
10. 0 > ⁻1
11. |⁻8| > ⁻7
12. |⁻15| > |3|
13. |⁻9| = 9

Write in order from least to greatest.

14. 4, ⁻2, 6, ⁻8   ⁻8, ⁻2, 4, 6
15. ⁻6, 5, 3, ⁻2   ⁻6, ⁻2, 3, 5
16. 0, ⁻1, 2, |⁻3| ⁻1, 0, 2, |⁻3|
17. |⁻7|, |3|, 0, ⁻7, 4   ⁻7, 0, |3|, 4, |⁻7|

Write the next three integers in the pattern.

18. 4, 3, 2, 1, 0, ⁻1, ⁻2
19. ⁻20, ⁻40, ⁻60, ⁻80, ⁻100, ⁻120, ⁻140
20. 3, 0, ⁻3, ⁻6, ⁻9, ⁻12, ⁻15
21. ⁻4, ⁻2, 0, 2, 4, 6, 8

Solve.

22. Russell and Ted went to the baseball throw at the carnival. Each received 3 balls to knock down 10 bottles. When they finished, Ted had 3 bottles left standing and Russell had 4 left standing. Who had the better score?
_____ Ted

23. Susan was on a 10-h trip. She first looked at her watch when she started her trip. The second time that she looked at her watch was 2 h after she left. The third time was 2 h before she was to arrive. How much time passed between her second and third looks?
_____ 6 h

RETEACHING 13-2

You can use a number line to order and compare integers. The numbers increase as you move to the right. The numbers decrease as you move to the left.
Example: Compare 5 and ⁻1.

⁻10 ⁻9 ⁻8 ⁻7 ⁻6 ⁻5 ⁻4 ⁻3 ⁻2 ⁻1 0 1 2 3 4 5 6 7 8 9 10

The integer 5 is to the right of ⁻1 on the number line. Therefore, 5 > ⁻1.
Use a number line to compare. Write > or <.

1. ⁻2 < 3
2. 14 > ⁻16
3. ⁻6 < 0
4. 2 > ⁻5
5. ⁻4 < 2
6. ⁻3 > ⁻6
7. ⁻11 > ⁻13
8. 6 < 9
9. 0 > ⁻16
10. ⁻117 < ⁻24
11. ⁻87 < 67
12. ⁻10 < 10
13. 56 > ⁻34
14. ⁻6 > ⁻2,341
15. 0 > ⁻489
16. ⁻13 < ⁻7

Write these integers in order from least to greatest.

17. ⁻3, 2, 0, ⁻6   ⁻6, ⁻3, 0, 2
18. ⁻18, ⁻3, ⁻10, ⁻6   ⁻18, ⁻10, ⁻6, ⁻3
19. 4, ⁻1, 0, 3   ⁻1, 0, 3, 4
20. 6, ⁻2, 9, 0   ⁻2, 0, 6, 9
21. ⁻15, ⁻18, ⁻6, 4   ⁻18, ⁻15, ⁻6, 4
22. 9, 3, ⁻19, ⁻21   ⁻21, ⁻19, 3, 9

Write the next three integers in the pattern.

23. ⁻4, ⁻2, 0, 2   4, 6, 8
24. ⁻1, 1, ⁻2, 2   3, 3, ⁻4
25. 20, 10, 0, ⁻10   ⁻20, ⁻30, ⁻40
26. 3, 2, 1, 0   ⁻1, ⁻2, ⁻3

ENRICHMENT 13-2

☑ **MATERIALS CHECKLIST:** Blank spinners

Have students work in pairs. Provide each pair with a spinner labeled ⁻10, ⁻8, ⁻6, ⁻4, ⁻2, and 0. Each partner spins the spinner. Then one partner names a number that is between the two numbers spun. The other partner names a number between his or her partner's number and the lowest number spun. Play continues in this manner until each partner has named several numbers. Have students draw a number line if they need help. **How many numbers can you name between two numbers on a number line?** (an infinite number)

LESSON | 13-3

Objective: Explore representing integers as charged particles.

Prior Knowledge: Students should understand that two integers the same distance from zero are opposites.

Lesson Resources:
Class Activity 13-3
Daily Review 13-3

Two-Minute Math

Use the Table of Numbers on the inside back cover. Order the integers in row N from greatest to least.
(8, 6, 3, 0, ⁻1, ⁻2, ⁻3, ⁻4, ⁻5)

1 PREPARE

CONCRETE ACTIVITY

☑ **MATERIALS CHECKLIST:** Teaching Aid 18 (Charged Particles), workmat for each student; Overhead Charged Particle Models

Have students examine the charged particles, and explain that ⊞ represents 1 and the ⊟ represents its opposite, the integer ⁻1. Display the Charged Particle Models on the overhead projector as students work on their workmats.
Show how to represent ⁻3 with the charged particles. *(Show three negative charges.)*
Show how to represent 5 with the charged particles. *(Show 5 positive charges.)*

WHEN YOUR STUDENTS ASK
★ WHY AM I LEARNING THIS? ★

You can use this model to describe real life situations. For example, a skin diver 12 m below sea level rises 8 m. What is the new depth?

Exploring a Model for Integers

Benjamin Franklin discovered many properties of electricity. He suggested calling opposite electrical charges positive and negative. The idea of charged particles can be used to help you understand operations with integers.

You can use cubes or models to represent charged particles. Choose one color to represent positively charged particles, or positive integers, and a different color to represent negatively charged particles, or negative integers. Use a sheet of paper as a workmat.

Let ⊞ represent the integer 1. Let ⊟ represent the integer ⁻1.

The workmat at right contains 3 ⊞ charges. The integer represented is 3.

1. Place 4 ⊟ on your workmat. What integer is represented? ⁻4

2. Clear your workmat. Put 5 ⊞ on it. What integer is represented? 5

3. Represent the integer with charged particles.
   a. ⁻2   **b.** ⁻5   **c.** ⁻8   **d.** ⁺6
   Check students' work.

The ⊞ and the ⊟ are opposite charges. When you combine a ⊞ and a ⊟ , a zero charge results.

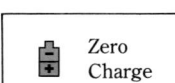
Zero Charge

Show 7 ⊞ on your workmat. Then place 3 ⊟ on it.

4. How many ⊟ charges can you make? 3

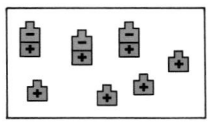

5. Make the zero charges. What integer is represented? Remove the zero charges. What integer is represented now? 4; 4

6. **IN YOUR WORDS** Explain why removing the 3 zero charges doesn't change the integer represented.
   7 − 3 = 4 + (3 + ⁻3); Because I subtracted zero.

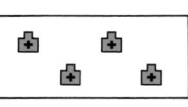

418   LESSON 13–3

---

2 EXPLORE

☑ **MATERIALS CHECKLIST:** Teaching Aid 18 (Charged Particles) and workmat for each pair

Have students work with a partner to complete Exercises 1–5 and 7–17. **A workmat has 6 zero charges and 3 negative charges. What integer is represented?** *(⁻3)*

A workmat has 4 positive charges and 2 negative charges. How many zero charges can you make? *(2)*

SUMMARIZE/ASSESS   **What integer is represented when you put 9 positive charges and 5 negative charges on a workmat?** *(4)*

7. Show 5 ➕ on your workmat. Put on 3 ➖. Make as many zero charges as you can and then remove them. What integer is represented by the remaining charges? **2**

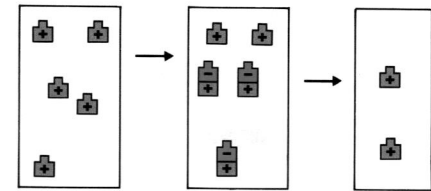

Follow the directions. Tell what integer is represented.

8. Show 4 ➕. Put on 3 ➖. **1**

9. Show 3 ➕. Put on 8 ➖. ⁻5

10. Show 7 ➕. Put on 5 ➖. **2**

11. Show 2 ➕. Put on 6 ➖. ⁻4

12. THINK ALOUD Show 3 ➕. on your workmat. What could you do to take out 2 ➖?

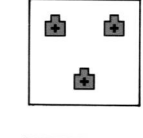

a. Put 2 zero charges on the workmat. Does this change the integer represented on the workmat? **No**

b. Can you take out 2 ➖ now? **Yes**

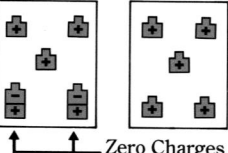

Zero Charges

c. What integer is represented after you take out 2 ➖? **5**

13. Show 2 ➕ on your workmat. Can you take out 5 ➕? **No**

a. How many zero charges must be placed on the workmat? **3**

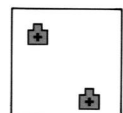

b. What integer is represented after you take out 5 ➕? ⁻3

How many zero charges do you need to place on the workmat to take out the given charge? What is the integer represented?

14. Show 6 ➖. Take out 4 ➕. **0; ⁻2**

15. Show 3 ➕. Take out 5 ➕. **2; ⁻2**

16. Show 4 ➖. Take out 1 ➕. **1; ⁻5**

17. Show 2 ➖. Take out 8 ➖. **6; 6**

18. CREATE YOUR OWN Write a charged particle problem using positive charges and negative charges. Challenge a friend to name the integer you represented.
Check students' work.

CHAPTER 13   419

☑ **MATERIALS CHECKLIST:** Index cards

Have the students work in small groups. Explain that, like positive and negative charges, yes and no responses to a survey question cancel each other out. Provide each group with several "controversial" survey questions, such as *Should everyone with a birthday between January 1 and May 31 be given an extra week of vacation?* Have one person in each group record the response of each group member by writing *Yes* or *No* on a card. Each group then spreads out the response cards, removing each pair of *Yes* and *No* cards. **How many responses are left? Are they positive or negative? What integer is represented?**

MEETING INDIVIDUAL NEEDS

For Students Who Are . . .

Acquiring English Proficiency Discuss positive and negative charges, relating them to electricity and the concept of opposites.

Gifted and Talented Have students illustrate a charged particle problem by drawing charges on a paper. Have them trade papers, and translate the drawing into a word problem.

Working 2 or 3 Grades Below Level Remind students they can add zero to or subtract zero from any number without changing the value of the number.

Today's Problem

State the rule and name the next three integers in this pattern: 2, ⁻3, ⁻5, 7, ⁻11, ⁻13, 17, ⁻19, ⁻23, . . . *(The next integers are 29, ⁻31, ⁻37. The rule is prime, the opposite of the next prime, the opposite of the next prime, and then repeat.)*

LESSON 13-4

Lesson Organizer

Objective: Add integers.

Prior Knowledge: Students should be able to add and subtract whole numbers.

Error Analysis and Remediation: See page 443A.

Lesson Resources
Practice Worksheet 13-4
Reteaching Worksheet 13-4
Enrichment Activity 13-4
Daily Review 13-4

 *Two-Minute Math*

Write the integer and its opposite.
8°C below zero. ($^-8$, 8)
a loss of $15 ($^-15$, 15)
12 m above sea level (12, $^-12$)
a gain of 9 yd (9, $^-9$)

1 INTRODUCE

CONNECTING ACTIVITY

✓ **MATERIALS CHECKLIST:** Teaching Aid 18 (Charged Particles) and workmat for each pair

1. Have students work with a partner to follow these directions: **Display four ⊞ charges. What integer is represented?** *(4)* **Place two more ⊞ charges on the workmat. What integer is represented now?** *(6)*

2. **Repeat the activity with two ⊟ charges and three more ⊟ charges.**

3. **Ask students to show 5 ⊞ charges and 2 ⊟ charges. How many zero charges can you make?** *(2)* **Remove the two zero charges. What is the value of the remaining charges?** *(3)*

WHEN YOUR STUDENTS ASK
★ **WHY AM I LEARNING THIS?** ★

You can connect this skill to real life through football. For example, if a running back lost 4 yd and then gained 12 yd, you could add integers to find the net gain on the play.

Adding Integers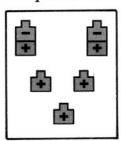

In the Game of Twelve, players take turns spinning positive and negative integers. They keep track of their spins and totals on a sheet like this one. The first player to reach 12 points wins.

Dana's first spin is $^-2$. Her second spin is $+5$. How many points does she have? **3**

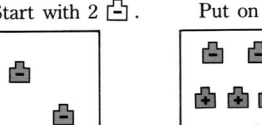 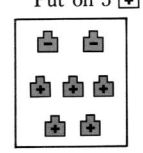 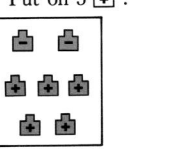

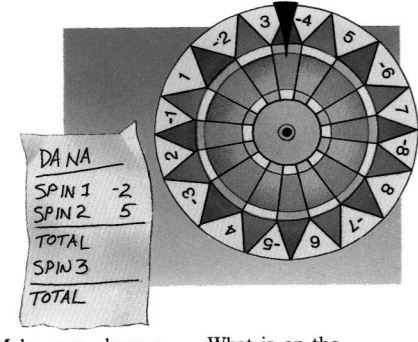

You can use charged particles to represent her spins of $^-2$ and 5 on your workmat.

Start with 2 ⊟ .   Put on 5 ⊞ .   Make zero charges, if possible.   What is on the workmat? **3**

Dana has 3 points after two spins.

THINK ALOUD Look at the examples at right.

What can you say about the sum if all the charges are positive? if all are negative?
positive; negative
What can you say about the sum if there are more negative charges than positive? if there are more positive charges than negative?
negative; positive
Notice that in b, c, d, and e the sign of the sum is the same as the sign of the integer with the greater absolute value.

a. $5 + 8 = 13$
b. $6 + ^-9 = ^-3$
c. $12 + ^-5 = 7$
d. $8 + ^-2 = 6$
e. $^-15 + 9 = ^-6$
f. $^-2 + ^-6 = ^-8$

> **The sum of two positive integers is positive.**
> **The sum of two negative integers is negative.**
> **The sum of a positive integer and a negative integer will have the same sign as the integer with the greater absolute value.**

CALCULATOR Use the ⟦±⟧ to change an integer to its opposite. To enter a negative integer, first enter its absolute value and then press ⟦±⟧.
For $^-6 + 2$, press 6 ⟦±⟧ ⟦+⟧ 2 ⟦=⟧. $^-6 + 2 = ^-4$
For $^-5 + ^-3$, press 5 ⟦±⟧ ⟦+⟧ 3 ⟦±⟧ ⟦=⟧. $^-5 + ^-3 = ^-8$
For $14 + ^-32$, press 14 ⟦+⟧ 32 ⟦±⟧ ⟦=⟧. $14 + ^-32 = ^-18$

---

2 TEACH

✓ **MATERIALS CHECKLIST:** calculators; Teaching Aid 18 (Charged particles) and workmat for each student

When you add 8 + 2, what is the sign of the sum? *(positive)*
When you add $^-8 + ^-2$, what is the sign of the sum? *(negative)*

When you add $^-8 + 14$, why will the sum be positive? *(because 14, the integer with the greater absolute value, is positive)*

What calculator keys would you press to find 12 + $^-36$? *(Press 12 ⟦+⟧ 36 ⟦±⟧ ⟦=⟧)*

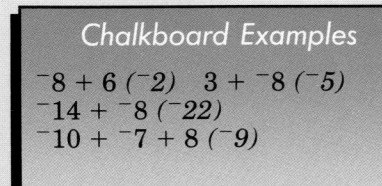

Chalkboard Examples
$^-8 + 6$ ($^-2$) $3 + ^-8$ ($^-5$)
$^-14 + ^-8$ ($^-22$)
$^-10 + ^-7 + 8$ ($^-9$)

SUMMARIZE/ASSESS **Explain why $^-3 + 8 = 5$.** *(Possible answer: When zero charges have been made, 5 ⊞ charges remain; other explanations are possible.)*

GUIDED PRACTICE

Add. Think of charged particles.

1. ⁻8 + 14 **6**   2. 16 + ⁻9 **7**   3. 19 + ⁻7 **12**   4. ⁻15 + 15 **0**   5. ⁻9 + ⁻21 **⁻30**

6. **CRITICAL THINKING** What is the sum of any integer and its opposite? **0**

PRACTICE

Decide whether the sum will be positive or negative. Then add.

7. ⁻9 + 4 **⁻5**   8. ⁻7 + 6 **⁻1**   9. ⁻6 + ⁻9 **⁻15**   10. 3 + ⁻7 **⁻4**

11. 10 + ⁻8 **2**   12. ⁻9 + ⁻5 **⁻14**   13. 6 + ⁻12 **⁻6**   14. ⁻7 + ⁻4 **⁻11**

15. 6 + ⁻15 **⁻9**   16. ⁻8 + ⁻17 **⁻25**   17. ⁻9 + 9 **0**   18. 5 + ⁻6 **⁻1**

19. ⁻10 + ⁻3 **⁻13**   20. 28 + ⁻25 **3**   21. 15 + ⁻35 **⁻20**   22. ⁻50 + 25 **⁻25**

Add. Use charges if necessary.

23. ⁻4 + ⁻2 + ⁻3 **⁻9** 24. 5 + ⁻2 + ⁻1 **2**   25. ⁻6 + ⁻2 + 4 **⁻4** 26. ⁻7 + ⁻9 + ⁻3 **⁻19**

27. 9 + 2 + ⁻9 **2**   28. ⁻1 + ⁻6 + 4 **⁻3** 29. 6 + ⁻12 + 6 **0**   30. ⁻5 + ⁻3 + 2 **⁻6**

MIXED REVIEW Compute.

31. 6.2×0.3 **1.86**   32. $\frac{3}{4} \times \frac{4}{5}$ **$\frac{3}{5}$**   33. $15 \div 0.5$ **30**   34. $\frac{1}{5} + \frac{3}{4}$ **$\frac{19}{20}$**

35. $3.8 - 2.02$ **1.78**   36. $\frac{4}{7} - \frac{2}{3}$ **$\frac{-2}{21}$**   37. $0.3 + 4.9$ **5.2**   38. $7 \div \frac{2}{3}$ **$10\frac{1}{2}$**

CALCULATOR Name the sum.

39. ⁻38 + 78 **40**   40. ⁻83 + 138 **55**   41. 197 + ⁻139 **58**   42. ⁻182 + 423 **241**

MENTAL MATH Make the sum with a positive and a negative integer. **Answers will vary.**

43. 8 **11, ⁻3**   44. ⁻7 **⁻8, 1**   45. 15 **20, ⁻5**   46. ⁻12 **⁻15, 3** 47. 0 **⁻1, 1**

PROBLEM SOLVING

Dick Chamberlain uses his own method of keeping score in golf. Par is zero. One over par is 1, one under par is ⁻1, two over par is 2, two under par is ⁻2, and so on. Remember, the *low* score in golf wins.

48. Which player had the lowest score? the highest? **Ron; Roya**

49. Arrange the players by name from the lowest score to the highest score.
Ron, Rob, Ruth, Roya

50. If Rob and Ruth were partners and played Ron and Roya, which team won?
Ron and Roya

Hole	Rob	Ruth	Ron	Roya
1	⁻2	1	⁻1	2
2	⁻1	2	0	1
3	0	⁻1	1	1
4	2	3	⁻2	2
5	3	0	1	⁻1
6	⁻1	1	⁻1	2
7	0	⁻1	1	⁻1
8	1	2	2	2
9	2	1	⁻1	3

CHAPTER 13   421

MEETING INDIVIDUAL NEEDS

For Students Who Are . . .

Acquiring English Proficiency Pair students with an English-proficient student for the Problem Solving activities. Discuss the words *golf* and *par*.

Gifted and Talented Have students create two additional problems from the table on page 421.

Today's Problem

Credits or assets (earnings) can be represented by positive integers and debits or liabilities (debts) by negative integers. Suppose Tom's Aunt Nora gave him $10 for his birthday. However, Tom owed $5 to May, $7 to Kim, and $4 to Sandy. What is his financial situation? *(His credits are 10, and his liabilities are ⁻5 + ⁻7 + ⁻4, or ⁻16; 10 + ⁻16 = ⁻6; he still has liabilities of $6.)*

PRACTICE 13-4

Decide whether the sum will be positive or negative. Then add.

1. ⁻2 + 6 = __4__   2. 3 + ⁻4 = __⁻1__   3. ⁻5 + ⁻5 = __⁻10__

4. ⁻8 + ⁻4 = __⁻12__   5. 7 + ⁻1 = __6__   6. 9 + ⁻3 = __6__

7. ⁻10 + 4 = __⁻6__   8. ⁻3 + 4 = __1__   9. 2 + ⁻1 = __1__

10. ⁻6 + ⁻2 = __⁻8__   11. ⁻5 + 6 = __1__   12. ⁻17 + 7 = __⁻10__

13. 20 + ⁻21 = __⁻1__   14. ⁻40 + ⁻40 = __⁻80__   15. ⁻29 + 19 = __⁻10__

Add. Use charges if you need to.

16. ⁻3 + ⁻2 + ⁻1 = __⁻6__   17. 4 + ⁻1 + 2 = __5__   18. ⁻3 + 4 + ⁻1 = __0__

19. ⁻5 + ⁻4 + ⁻6 = __⁻15__   20. 9 + ⁻3 + ⁻4 = __2__   21. ⁻7 + 4 + ⁻7 = __⁻10__

Find a positive and negative integer whose sum is Answers will vary.

22. 4 __4, 8__   23. ⁻6 __⁻7, 1__   24. 9 __⁻1, 10__   25. ⁻15 __1, ⁻16__

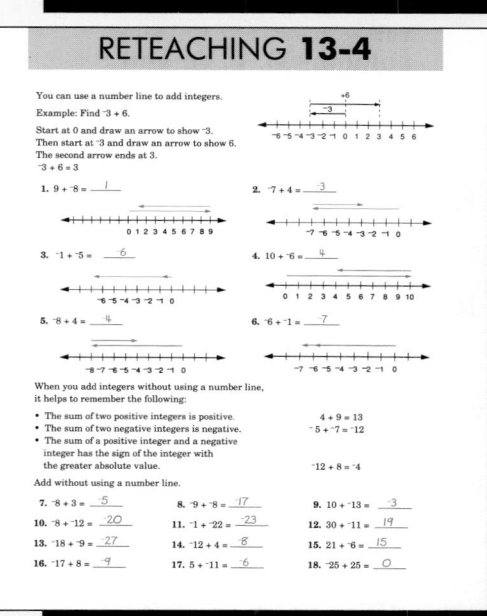

Solve.

26. At the end of the year, Geoff and Jeanne figured out how much money they had lost or gained on the five stocks they had owned since the beginning of the year: $275, ⁻$150, $0, $800, ⁻$37. What was the sum of their gains and losses? __$888__

27. Rance sells ice cream cones for $2. In the morning, he started with $50 in the cash drawer. He sold 50 cones. He spent $5 on lunch. How much does he now have in his cash drawer? __$145__

RETEACHING 13-4

You can use a number line to add integers.

Example: Find ⁻3 + 6

Start at 0 and draw an arrow to show ⁻3.
Then start at ⁻3 and draw an arrow to show 6.
The second arrow ends at 3.
⁻3 + 6 = 3

1. 9 + ⁻8 = __1__

2. ⁻7 + 4 = __⁻3__

3. ⁻1 + ⁻5 = __⁻6__

4. 10 + ⁻6 = __4__

5. ⁻8 + 4 = __⁻4__

6. ⁻6 + ⁻1 = __⁻7__

When you add integers without using a number line, it helps to remember the following:

- The sum of two positive integers is positive.   4 + 9 = 13
- The sum of two negative integers is negative.   ⁻5 + ⁻7 = ⁻12
- The sum of a positive integer and a negative integer has the sign of the integer with the greater absolute value.   ⁻12 + 8 = ⁻4

Add without using a number line.

7. ⁻8 + 3 = __⁻5__   8. ⁻9 + ⁻8 = __⁻17__   9. 10 + ⁻13 = __⁻3__

10. ⁻8 + 12 = __20__   11. ⁻1 + ⁻22 = __⁻23__   12. 30 + ⁻11 = __19__

13. ⁻18 + ⁻9 = __⁻27__   14. ⁻12 + 4 = __⁻8__   15. 21 + ⁻6 = __15__

16. ⁻17 + 8 = __⁻9__   17. 5 + ⁻11 = __⁻6__   18. ⁻25 + 25 = __0__

ENRICHMENT 13-4

☑ **MATERIALS CHECKLIST:** Blank cubes, two-sided counters

Have the students work in pairs. Provide each pair with two cubes labeled *1–6* and a two-sided counter. Have the partners determine which color will stand for negative integers and which color will stand for positive integers. Player 1 flips the counter, rolls both number cubes, and writes the greatest number possible. Player 2 repeats the procedure. The partners play ten rounds and then add the results of each round. The partner with the greatest sum wins.

Lesson Organizer

Objective: Subtract integers.

Prior Knowledge: Students should know how to add integers.

Error Analysis and Remediation: See page 443A.

Lesson Resources:
Practice Worksheet 13-5
Reteaching Worksheet 13-5
Enrichment Activity 13-5
Daily Review 13-5

Two-Minute Math

In row N of the Table of Numbers on the inside back cover, name the sum of the integers in:
columns O, P, Q, and S (⁻2)
columns T, U, V, and W (4)

1 INTRODUCE

CONNECTING ACTIVITY

☑ **MATERIALS CHECKLIST:** Teaching Aid 18 (Charged Particles), workmat for each pair

Have students work with a partner to follow these directions:

1. Put 5 ⊕ charges on your workmat. Remove 2 ⊕ charges. How many are left? *(3)*

2. Show 6 ⊖ charges. Remove 4 ⊖ charges. How many are left? *(2)* What integer represents this difference? *(⁻2)*

3. Show 5 ⊕ charges. Can you think of a way to remove 2 ⊖ charges? Allow students time to come up with a solution; if necessary, ask: If 2 ⊕ and 2 ⊖ charges are added to the 5 positive charges, does the value change? Why? *(No; same as adding zero.)* Now you can remove 2 ⊖ charges. What is the value of the remaining charges? *(7)*

WHEN YOUR STUDENTS ASK
★ WHY AM I LEARNING THIS? ★

You can use this skill to solve real life problems. For example, if the temperature at 6:00 P.M. is ⁻4°C and it drops to ⁻17°C by midnight, how many degrees did it fall?

Subtracting Integers

A hot-air balloonist noticed that the air temperature at an altitude of 1,050 m was ⁻2°C while the air temperature at ground level was 5°C. What was the difference between the air temperatures?

You can use charged particles to represent the subtraction 5 − ⁻2.

Show 5 ⊕.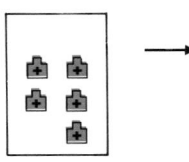

To take out 2 ⊖, put in 2 zero charges.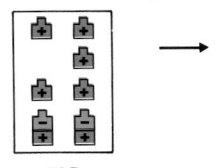

What do you have left?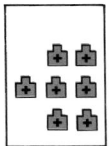

The difference between the air temperatures was 7°C.

THINK ALOUD The pairs of equations below show examples of subtracting an integer and adding its opposite. Instead of subtracting an integer, what can you do? **Add its opposite.**

⁻4 − 7 = ⁻11	3 − ⁻2 = 5	6 − 9 = ⁻3	⁻6 − ⁻14 = 8
⁻4 + ⁻7 = ⁻11	3 + 2 = 5	6 + ⁻9 = ⁻3	⁻6 + 14 = 8

To subtract an integer, add its opposite.

CALCULATOR You can use the ⌊±⌋ key when you want to find the difference between two integers.

For 32 − ⁻59, press 32 ⌊−⌋ 59 ⌊±⌋ ⌊=⌋.
For ⁻67 − ⁻95, press 67 ⌊±⌋ ⌊−⌋ 95 ⌊±⌋ ⌊=⌋.
For ⁻59 − 23, press 59 ⌊±⌋ ⌊−⌋ 23 ⌊=⌋.

━━━━━━━━━ **GUIDED PRACTICE** ━━━━━━━━━

Use charged particles on your workmat to find the difference.

1. 5 − ⁻3 8   **2.** ⁻8 − ⁻2 ⁻6   **3.** ⁻2 − 8 ⁻10   **4.** ⁻11 − ⁻5 ⁻6

Subtract the integer by adding its opposite.

5. 7 − ⁻3 10   **6.** ⁻9 − ⁻12 3   **7.** 5 − 11 ⁻6   **8.** ⁻2 − 10 ⁻12

---

2 TEACH

☑ **MATERIALS CHECKLIST:** Teaching Aid 18 (Charged Particles) and workmat for each student; calculators

Use the charged particles to represent 12 − ⁻6. *(Show 12 ⊕ charges; in order take out 6 ⊖ charges, put in 6 zero charges. The difference is the remaining 18 ⊕ charges.)*

When you subtract a negative integer from a positive integer will the difference be positive or negative? Give an example: *(Positive; example: 4 − ⁻4 = 8)* when you subtract a positive integer from a negative integer? *(Negative; example: ⁻6 − 5 = ⁻11)*

> **Chalkboard Examples**
>
> Subtract.
> ⁻13 − 6 (⁻19)
> ⁻7 − ⁻3 (⁻4)
> 3 − ⁻9 (12)
> 15 − ⁻12 (27)

SUMMARIZE/ASSESS How do you subtract ⁻50 from ⁻15?
(Possible answer: Add the opposite of ⁻50 to ⁻15; the difference is 35; students may also demonstrate with charged particles.)

Solve. Use a calculator, mental math, or pencil and paper.

9. ⁻5 − 2 ⁻7   **10.** 3 − ⁻8 11   **11.** 4 − ⁻6 10   **12.** 2 − 11 ⁻9

13. ⁻2 − 9 ⁻11   **14.** ⁻4 − ⁻7 3   **15.** ⁻6 − 13 ⁻19   **16.** 10 − ⁻4 14

17. 0 − 6 ⁻6   **18.** 0 − ⁻6 6   **19.** 3 − ⁻11 14   **20.** ⁻7 − ⁻12 5

21. ⁻5 − 6 ⁻11   **22.** ⁻3 − 8 ⁻11   **23.** 14 − ⁻5 19   **24.** 2 − 9 ⁻7

25. ⁻3 + ⁻4 − 2 ⁻9   **26.** 7 − ⁻3 + 2 12   **27.** ⁻5 − 1 + ⁻4 ⁻10   **28.** 5 − 6 − ⁻9 8

MIXED REVIEW Compare. Choose >, <, or =.

29. 6 + ⁻2 ▇ 3 − ⁻5 <   **30.** ⁻6 + ⁻4 ▇ ⁻2 − 8 =   **31.** ⁻5 − ⁻1 ▇ 0 − 6 >

32. 2 − ⁻6 ▇ ⁻7 + 3 >   **33.** 5 − ⁻2 ▇ ⁻4 + 1 >   **34.** ⁻7 + ⁻1 ▇ ⁻3 − ⁻5 <

CALCULATOR Name the missing integer that makes the equation true.

35. 2 ⊞ ⊞ ▇ ⊟ 7 9   **36.** 4 ⊞ ⊞ ▇ ⊞ ⊟ ⁻12 8

37. ▇ ⊟ 5 ⊞ +6 ⊟ 13 2   **38.** 7 ⊞ ⊞ ▇ ⊟ 5 ⊟ ⁻4 8

Write the problem as the difference between two integers. Then solve.

39. The greatest recorded temperature change in the United States occurred in Browning, Montana, when the temperature dropped from 7°C to ⁻49°C in 24 h. What is the difference between these two temperatures? **56°C**

40. The greatest recorded temperature change in the world occurred in Verkhoyansk, USSR. Temperatures changed from −70°C to 37°C. What is the difference between these two temperatures? **107°C**

41. Garopan, Saipan, located in the Mariana Islands in the Pacific Ocean, during a nine-year period recorded the least change in temperature on record. The temperature ranged from a high of 31°C to a low of 20°C. What is the difference between these two temperatures? **11°C**

MEETING INDIVIDUAL NEEDS

For Students Who Are . . .

Acquiring English Proficiency If students are working in a group, read Exercises 39–41 aloud and call on students to state the problem in their own words.

Gifted and Talented Have students use an almanac to find the high and low temperatures of five cities last year. Students can write problems using this information, exhange with a classmate, and solve.

Working 2 or 3 Grades Below Level Review ordering integers. Have students represent temperature ranges on a number line.

Today's Problem

On Sunday the high temperature was 14°F and the low temperature was ⁻3°F. On Monday the high temperature was 22°F and the low temperature was ⁻1°F. On which day was the difference in temperature greater? What is the difference between Sunday's low temperature and Monday's high temperature? *(Monday; 25°F)*

3 FOLLOW-UP

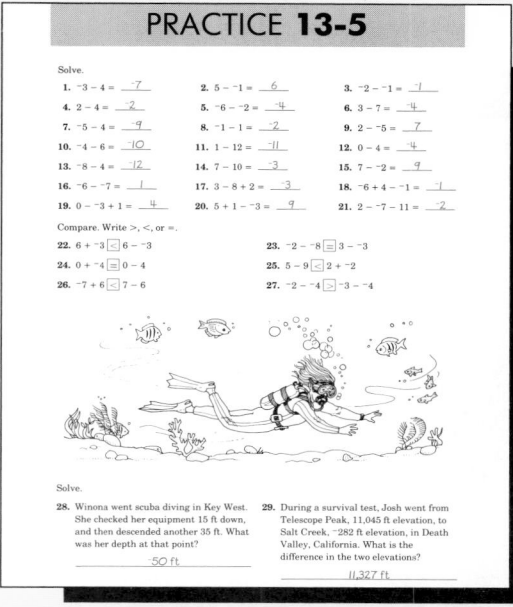

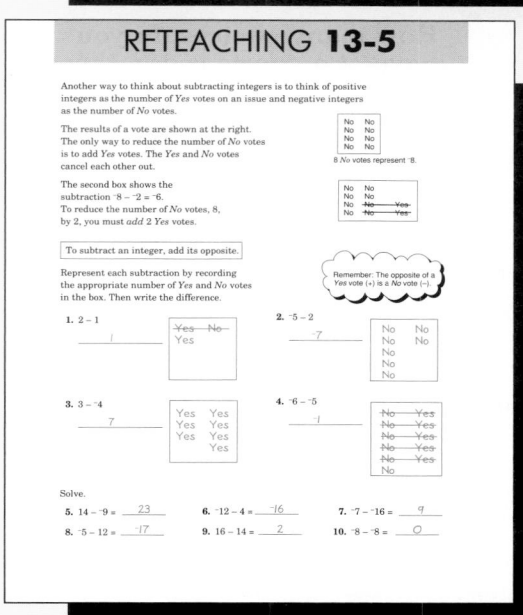

ENRICHMENT 13-5

☑ **MATERIALS CHECKLIST:** Tagboard, blank spinners, counters

Have the students work in pairs in groups of four. On tagboard draw two bars; divide them into 20 equal parts. Label the leftmost boxes *Start* and the rightmost, *Finish*. Give each group this game board, and a spinner labeled ⁻1, ⁻2, ⁻4, ⁻6, ⁻8, ⁻10, 4, and 6. Each pair places a counter on *Start*. The partners each spin once, and subtract the second number from the first. The result is the number of squares backward or forward the pair's counter moves. The first pair to reach *Finish* wins.

Lesson Organizer

Objective: Solve problems by using logic.

Prior Knowledge: Students should be able to use the four-part process.

Lesson Resources:
Practice Worksheet 13-6
Reteaching Activity 13-6
Enrichment Worksheet 13-6
Daily Review 13-6
Cooperative Investigations,
   Chapter 13

Two-Minute Math

How many choices do you have of a sports sedan that comes in 6 colors, with 2 or 4 doors, and with standard or automatic transmission? *(24)*

1 INTRODUCE

CONNECTING ACTIVITY

Display the following Venn diagram.

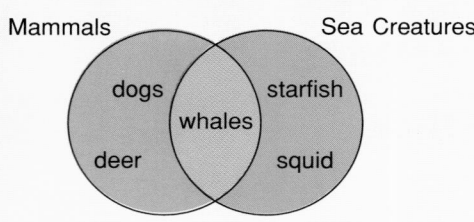

Mammals — Sea Creatures
dogs / whales / starfish
deer / squid

Have students use the diagram to explain why each of the following statements is true or false.

• **Some sea creatures are whales.** *(true)*

• **No whales are sea creatures.** *(false)*

• **Some squid are mammals.** *(false)*

• **No dogs are sea creatures.** *(true)*

WHEN YOUR STUDENTS ASK
★ WHY AM I LEARNING THIS? ★

You can use logic in real life to make personal decisions. For example, you can select which colleges to apply to based on their locations, available financial aid, their reputations, and the courses they offer.

Problem Solving:
Using Logic

The city health department wants to send a pamphlet about free vaccines to all families with children and to all teachers. There are 25,000 families with children in the city. Of the city's 1,500 teachers, 1,000 have children. How many pamphlets does the health department need to print?

The solution to problems often requires organizing and examining data. A Venn diagram is one way to organize the data.

Start by entering the available information.

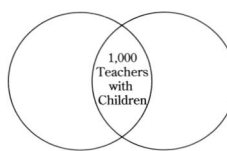

1,000
Teachers
with
Children

25,000 families   1,500 teachers
with children

Now you can see how to complete the Venn diagram.

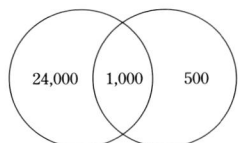

24,000 | 1,000 | 500

Families with   Teachers without
children;   children:
no one is a teacher: 1,500 − 1,000
25,000 − 1,000

The health department needs to print 25,500 pamphlets.

─────────── **GUIDED PRACTICE** ───────────

1. Use the Venn diagram at right to tell whether the statements are *true* or *false*.

   a. There are more car owners than home owners. **true**

   b. All car owners are home owners. **false**

   c. If there are 25,000 car owners and 1,000 home owners, then there are 24,000 car owners who do not own homes. **true**

Car Owners

Home
Owners

Use the Venn diagram. Fill in the blanks with *All, Some,* or *No*.

2.

Home
Owners

Students

   a. _No_ home owners are students.

   b. _No_ students are home owners.

3.

Students / Car
Owners

   a. _Some_ students are car owners.

   b. _Some_ car owners are students.

---

2 TEACH

Have students use the Venn diagram to tell whether each of the following statements is true or false.

• **Some families have members who are teachers.** *(true)*

• **No teachers have children.** *(false)*

GUIDED PRACTICE   Discuss questions such as: Could some car owners not be home owners? *(Yes)*

SUMMARIZE/ASSESS   **Draw a Venn diagram to show that all students take math.** *(Check students' drawings. Drawing should show one circle inside another.)*

Solve. Make a Venn diagram to help.

4. In a class, 13 students went to a doctor last year, 18 went to a dentist, and 5 went to both. If all the students saw either a doctor or dentist, how many students are in the class?
26 students

5. Amy is taller than Beth but shorter than Tom. Who is the tallest? **Tom**

6. A politician claims that all home owners and all skilled workers will vote for him since he has supported them in the past. How many votes will he get if there are 15,000 home owners, 3,000 skilled workers, and 1,800 skilled workers who own homes?
16,200 votes

7. A salesperson made calls to 20 homes with dogs, 28 homes with cats, and 18 homes with birds. Five of the homes with dogs also had birds, 11 homes with cats also had birds, and 3 homes with dogs also had cats. One home had all three kinds of animals. How many homes were called? **45 homes**

 Choose any strategy to solve. **Strategies may vary. Suggestions given.**

8. On a recent math test, Sally scored higher than Dennis and Kelleen but lower than Vincent. Kelleen had a lower score than Dennis. Name the students in order from the highest score to the lowest.
diagram; Vincent, Sally, Dennis, Kelleen

9. In a class, 11 students have one or more sisters, 16 have one or more brothers, 4 have one or more brothers and sisters, and 5 have neither a brother nor a sister. How many students are in the class? **Venn diagram; 28 students**

10. Earl spent $4.20 for 1 milk, 2 hamburgers, and an apple. Enid bought 2 milks, one hamburger, and 2 apples for $3.30. If Eric bought 1 milk, 1 hamburger, and 1 apple, how much did his meal cost?
use equation; $2.50

11. If a lawn-mowing service can mow a lawn 100 m by 100 m in 1 h, how long should it take to mow a lawn 50 m by 50 m?
use proportion; 15 min

MEETING INDIVIDUAL NEEDS

For Students Who Are . . .

Acquiring English Proficiency Discuss the meanings of *vaccines* and *pamphlets*. Pair students with an English proficient student to solve Exercises 4–11.

Gifted and Talented Have students determine who is shortest: Billy is taller than Willy and shorter than Milly. Milly is taller than Tilly and shorter than Dilly. Tilly is taller than Willy. Billy is shorter than Dilly. Tilly is taller than Billy. *(Willy)*

Working 2 or 3 Grades Below Level Review Venn diagrams as a way to determine whether two collections have all in common, some in common, or none in common.

Today's Problem

Garry is older than Barry. Harry is younger than Larry. Garry is younger than Larry. Barry is older than Harry. Who is the youngest? *(Harry)*

---

3 FOLLOW-UP

PRACTICE 13-6

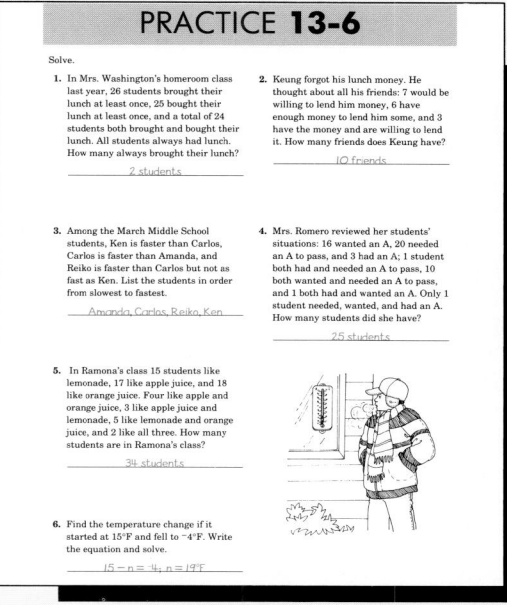

Solve.

1. In Mrs. Washington's homeroom class last year, 26 students brought their lunch at least once, 25 bought their lunch at least once, and a total of 24 students both brought and bought their lunch. All students always had lunch. How many always brought their lunch?
2 students

2. Keung forgot his lunch money. He thought about all his friends: 7 would be willing to lend him money, 6 have enough money to lend him some, and 3 have the money and are willing to lend it. How many friends does Keung have?
10 friends

3. Among the March Middle School students, Ken is faster than Carlos, Carlos is faster than Amanda, and Reiko is faster than Carlos but not as fast as Ken. List the students in order from slowest to fastest.
Amanda, Carlos, Reiko, Ken

4. Mrs. Romero reviewed her students' situations: 16 wanted an A, 20 needed an A to pass, and 3 had an A; 1 student both had and needed an A to pass, 10 both wanted and needed an A to pass, and 1 both had and wanted an A. Only 1 student needed, wanted, and had an A. How many students did she have?
25 students

5. In Ramona's class 15 students like lemonade, 17 like apple juice, and 18 like orange juice. Four like apple and orange juice, 3 like apple juice and lemonade, 5 like lemonade and orange juice, and 2 like all three. How many students are in Ramona's class?
34 students

6. Find the temperature change if it started at 15°F and fell to −4°F. Write the equation and solve.
15 − n = −4, n = 19°F

RETEACHING 13-6

Present this situation: Last weekend, 17 students in a class watched a movie at home, 9 saw a movie in a theater, and 4 did both. If every student saw at least one movie, how many are in the class? Have the students draw two overlapping circles, shading the overlapping region. **To which circle does an item in the shaded area belong?** *(both)* Have students label the circles *Home* and *Theater*, and represent each student with an X. **How many Xs go in the shaded area?** *(4)* How many Xs go in the *Home* circle outside the shaded area? (13) in the unshaded portion of the Theater circle? *(5)* How many Xs are there in all? *(22)*

ENRICHMENT 13-6

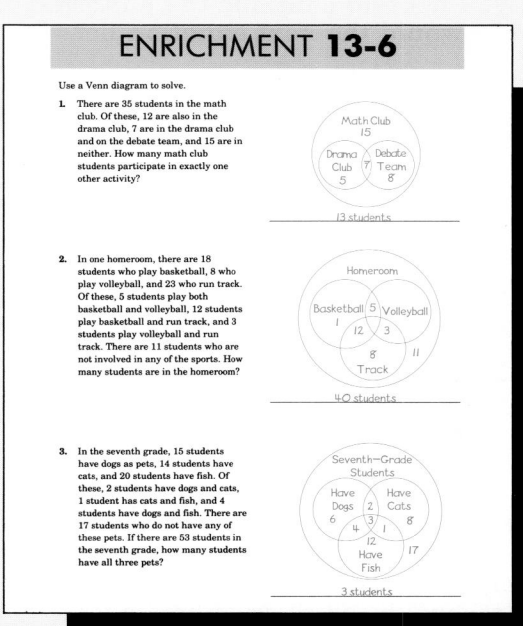

Use a Venn diagram to solve.

1. There are 35 students in the math club. Of these, 12 are also in the drama club, 7 are in the drama club and on the debate team, and 15 are in neither. How many math club students participate in exactly one other activity?
13 students

2. In one homeroom, there are 18 students who play basketball, 8 who play volleyball, and 23 who run track. Of these, 5 students play both basketball and volleyball, 12 students play basketball and run track, and 3 students play volleyball and run track. There are 11 students who are not involved in any of the sports. How many students are in the homeroom?
40 students

3. In the seventh grade, 15 students have dogs as pets, 14 students have cats, and 20 students have fish. Of these, 2 students have dogs and cats, 1 student has cats and fish, and 4 students have dogs and fish. There are 17 students who do not have any of these pets. If there are 53 students in the seventh grade, how many students have all three pets?
3 students

Lesson Organizer

Objective: Multiply integers.

Prior Knowledge: Students should be able to multiply whole numbers.

Error Analysis and Remediation: See page 443A.

Lesson Resources:
Practice Worksheet 13-7
Reteaching Worksheet 13-7
Enrichment Activity 13-7
Daily Review 13-7

Two-Minute Math

Write the next three numbers in the series.

$^-20$, $^-15$, $^-10$, ___, ___, ___
$(^-5, 0, 5)$
6, 3, 0, ___, ___, ___ $(^-3, ^-6, ^-9)$
$^-12$, $^-8$, $^-4$, ___, ___, ___ $(0, 4, 8)$

1 INTRODUCE

SYMBOLIC ACTIVITY

Write the following equations on the chalkboard for students to complete orally:

$4 \times 3 = $ *(12)*
$4 \times 2 = $ *(8)*
$4 \times 1 = $ *(4)*
$4 \times 0 = $ *(0)*

What pattern do you see? *(The second factor in each equation decreases by 1; the product in each equation decreases by 4.)*
If you were to continue the pattern, what would the next equation be? *(4 × $^-1$ = $^-4$)*
How could you use the charged particles to show that 4 × $^-1$ = $^-4$? *(4 × $^-1$ = $^-1$ + $^-1$ + $^-1$ + $^-1$ = $^-4$)*

WHEN YOUR STUDENTS ASK
★ WHY AM I LEARNING THIS? ★

You can connect this skill to real life through engineering. For example, if the elevation of a highway decreases 2 m for every kilometer of length, an engineer can determine the necessary decrease for a 12-km stretch by multiplying $^-2 \times 12$.

Multiplying Integers

In chemistry, an electrically charged atom or group of atoms is called an ion. The charge on an ion may be either positive or negative. The table at right gives the names and charges of some common ions.

Name	Charge
Tin (Stannic)	$^+4$
Carbonate	$^-2$
Mercury	$^+2$
Phosphate	$^-3$
Fluoride	$^-1$
Sodium	$^+1$

If there are 5 carbonate ions, what is the total charge?

You can write the expression $5 \times {}^-2$ to represent the situation.

You multiply positive integers as you do whole numbers. You can use patterns to name the product of $5 \times {}^-2$.

$$5 \times 2 = 10$$
$$5 \times 1 = 5$$
$$5 \times 0 = 0$$
$$5 \times {}^-1 = {}^-5$$
$$5 \times {}^-2 = {}^-10$$

> To continue the pattern, these products must be negative.

The charge on 5 carbonate ions is $^-10$.

NUMBER SENSE Since $5 \times {}^-2$ means $^-2 + {}^-2 + {}^-2 + {}^-2 + {}^-2$, tell how you could use charged particles to show that $5 \times {}^-2 = {}^-10$.

To multiply two negative integers, look at the pattern.

$$^-5 \times 2 = {}^-10$$
$$^-5 \times 1 = {}^-5$$
$$^-5 \times 0 = 0$$
$$^-5 \times {}^-1 = 5$$
$$^-5 \times {}^-2 = 10$$

> To continue the pattern, these products must be positive.

The product of two positive integers or two negative integers is a positive integer.

The product of a positive integer and a negative integer is a negative integer.

THINK ALOUD What is the product of any integer and 0? **0**

Other examples:

$^-3 \times {}^-5 = 15$ $^-3 \times 5 = {}^-15$
$3 \times 5 = 15$ $3 \boxed{\times} 5 \boxed{\pm} \boxed{=} {}^-15$

Atomium
Sculpture,
Brussels, Belgium

MATH AND SCIENCE

Calculators will be an effective teaching tool for this lesson.

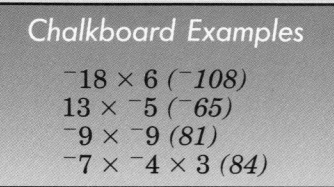

2 TEACH

☑ **MATERIALS CHECKLIST:** calculators

If you know that 3 × $^-4$ = $^-12$, what multiplication property can help you name the product of $^-4$ × 3? *(commutative property of multiplication)*

If the product of x and a positive integer is a negative integer, is x positive or negative? *(negative)*

Will the product of an even number of integers always be positive or negative? Give examples. *(It could be either. For example, 7 × $^-30$ = $^-210$; 4 × 4 × 4 × 1 = 48; $^-4$ × 4 × $^-4$ × $^-1$ = $^-48$.)*

Chalkboard Examples

$^-18 \times 6$ *($^-108$)*
$13 \times {}^-5$ *($^-65$)*
$^-9 \times {}^-9$ *(81)*
$^-7 \times {}^-4 \times 3$ *(84)*

SUMMARIZE/ASSESS **What two steps are required to find the product of two integers?** *(Multiply the factors involved, then use the correct sign—positive or negative.)*

State whether the product is *positive*, *zero*, or *negative*.

1. $8 \times {}^-2$
negative

2. ${}^-3 \times {}^-6$
positive

3. ${}^-6 \times 4$
negative

4. ${}^-12 \times 0$
zero

5. THINK ALOUD Explain why the product of ${}^-1 \times {}^-2 \times {}^-3$ is ${}^-6$.
${}^-1 \times {}^-2 = 2; 2 \times {}^-3 = {}^-6$

PRACTICE

Simplify. Use a calculator, mental math, or pencil and paper.

6. $3 \times {}^-2$ ${}^-6$

7. ${}^-5 \times 8$ ${}^-40$

8. ${}^-4 \times {}^-3$ 12

9. ${}^-6 \times 0$ 0

10. ${}^-2 \times 7$ ${}^-14$

11. 6×9 54

12. ${}^-6 \times {}^-7$ 42

13. $4 \times {}^-9$ ${}^-36$

14. ${}^-7 \times {}^-4$ 28

15. ${}^-2 \times 5$ ${}^-10$

16. 5×0 0

17. ${}^-9 \times {}^-8$ 72

18. $5 \times {}^-7$ ${}^-35$

19. ${}^-6 \times 8$ ${}^-48$

20. ${}^-7 \times {}^-7$ 49

21. ${}^-12 \times 2$ ${}^-24$

22. ${}^-3 \times 5 \times {}^-4$ 60

23. ${}^-5 \times {}^-2 \times {}^-1$ ${}^-10$

24. $3 \times {}^-2 \times 2$ ${}^-12$

25. ${}^-6 \times 2 \times 4$ ${}^-48$

26. ${}^-3 \times |{}^-8|$ ${}^-24$

27. $|{}^-3| \times {}^-8$ ${}^-24$

28. $|{}^-3| \times |{}^-8|$ 24

29. ${}^-3 \times {}^-8$ 24

MIXED REVIEW Compute.

30. ${}^-5 + 1$ ${}^-4$

31. ${}^-3 - {}^-6$ 3

32. $5 + {}^-8$ ${}^-3$

33. $8 - {}^-3$ 11

34. ${}^-6 - {}^-6$ 0

35. $3 + {}^-9$ ${}^-6$

36. ${}^-17 - 3$ ${}^-20$

37. ${}^-14 + {}^-8$ ${}^-22$

ESTIMATE Estimate. Be sure the sign is correct. Accept reasonable estimates. Suggestions given.

38. $2 \times {}^-396$
${}^-800$

39. ${}^-247 \times {}^-4$
$1,000$

40. ${}^-117 \times 5$
${}^-600$

41. ${}^-8 \times 412$
${}^-3,200$

42. ${}^-104 \times {}^-81$
$8,000$

43. ${}^-212 \times 197$
${}^-40,000$

44. ${}^-48 \times 402$
${}^-20,000$

45. ${}^-203 \times {}^-23$
$4,600$

46. CALCULATOR Name four pairs of integers that have a product of ${}^-558$. Answers will vary. Suggestions given.
$(31)({}^-18); ({}^-31)(18); ({}^-9)(62); (9)({}^-62)$

PROBLEM SOLVING

Use the chart on page 426 to find the total charge.

47. 3 tin ions and 6 carbonate ions 0

48. 7 sodium ions and 4 phosphate ions ${}^-5$

49. 10 mercury ions and 8 fluoride ions 12

50. CRITICAL THINKING A molecule is formed by 2 or more ions whose total charge is 0. Could 3 mercury ions and 2 phosphate ions form a molecule? Yes

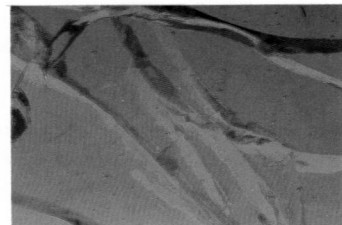

MEETING INDIVIDUAL NEEDS

For Students Who Are . . .

Acquiring English Proficiency Discuss the meaning of *atom* and *ion*. Explain the Think Aloud activity in Guided Practice, relating it to the product of an odd number of negative factors.

Gifted and Talented Have students write three original problems based on the chart on page 428, exchange with a classmate, and solve.

Working 2 or 3 Grades Below Level Remind students that multiplication can be thought of as repeated addition. Have students represent $3 \times {}^-4$ and $6 \times {}^-3$ with the charged particles.

Today's Problem

It took 24 hours for a snail to get home. If the snail crawled at a rate of 3 inches every hour, what negative integer represents the distance in feet the snail was from home?
$({}^-3 \times 24 = {}^-72; -\frac{72}{12} = {}^-6 \text{ feet})$

---

3 FOLLOW-UP

PRACTICE 13-7

Simplify.

1. $2 \times {}^-4$ ${}^-8$

2. ${}^-4 \times 4$ ${}^-16$

3. ${}^-7 \times {}^-3$ 21

4. ${}^-2 \times 0$ 0

5. ${}^-3 \times 9$ ${}^-27$

6. 2×8 16

7. ${}^-6 \times {}^-3$ 18

8. $4 \times {}^-3$ ${}^-12$

9. ${}^-1 \times {}^-8$ 8

10. ${}^-5 \times 6$ ${}^-30$

11. $3 \times {}^-7$ ${}^-21$

12. $6 \times {}^-6$ ${}^-36$

13. ${}^-9 \times {}^-7$ 63

14. ${}^-7 \times {}^-8$ 56

15. ${}^-12 \times {}^-5$ 60

16. ${}^-4 \times {}^-5$ 20

17. ${}^-2 \times 4 \times 2$ 16

18. ${}^-5 \times {}^-6 \times 1$ 30

19. ${}^-2 \times {}^-2 \times {}^-2$ ${}^-8$

20. ${}^-2 \times 4 \times {}^-6$ 48

21. ${}^-2 \times |{}^-5|$ ${}^-10$

22. $|{}^-4| \times {}^-5$ ${}^-20$

23. $|{}^-2| \times |{}^-6|$ 12

24. $|{}^-3| \times {}^-|{}^-3|$ ${}^-9$

Estimate. Be sure the sign is correct.

25. ${}^-201 \times 3$ ${}^-600$

26. ${}^-249 \times {}^-2$ 500

27. $5 \times {}^-198$ ${}^-1,000$

28. ${}^-503 \times {}^-4$ $2,000$

29. ${}^-59 \times {}^-203$ $12,000$

30. ${}^-397 \times 204$ ${}^-80,000$

31. ${}^-29 \times {}^-301$ $9,000$

32. $11 \times {}^-196$ ${}^-2,000$

33. ${}^-19 \times {}^-498$ $10,000$

Solve.

34. A shark was swimming at a depth of 2 m. Startled by a boat, the shark increased its depth by 5 times. What was its new depth? 10 m

If you represented the surface as 0, how would you represent the shark's initial depth? ${}^-2 \text{ m}$

35. While on a diet, Bessie's weight loss averaged 8 lb per month for 4 months. What was the absolute value of the number of pounds she lost? 32

RETEACHING 13-7

If two integers have the same sign, their product is positive.

$2 \times 8 = 16$
Both integers are positive. The product is positive.

${}^-2 \times {}^-8 = 16$
Both integers are negative. The product is positive.

If two integers have different signs, their product is negative.

${}^-2 \times 8 = {}^-16$
The integers have different signs. The product is negative.

Simplify.

1. $8 \times {}^-5 =$ ${}^-40$

2. ${}^-7 \times 7 =$ ${}^-49$

3. ${}^-10 \times {}^-2 =$ 20

4. $0 \times 3 =$ 0

5. $4 \times {}^-12 =$ ${}^-48$

6. ${}^-11 \times {}^-5 =$ 55

7. ${}^-6 \times 7 =$ ${}^-42$

8. ${}^-2 \times 9 =$ 18

9. ${}^-12 \times 9 =$ ${}^-108$

To multiply more than two integers, multiply two integers at a time. Then multiply the product by the next integer.

Example: ${}^-2 \times 5 \times {}^-3 = ({}^-2 \times 5) \times {}^-3$
$= {}^-10 \times {}^-3$
$= 30$

Simplify.

10. ${}^-5 \times {}^-5 \times {}^-5 =$ ${}^-125$

11. $4 \times {}^-3 \times 2 =$ ${}^-24$

12. ${}^-8 \times 3 \times 2 =$ ${}^-48$

13. $6 \times {}^-3 \times 2 =$ ${}^-36$

14. ${}^-2 \times {}^-7 \times {}^-3 =$ ${}^-42$

15. ${}^-7 \times 3 \times 8 =$ ${}^-168$

ENRICHMENT 13-7

☒ MATERIALS CHECKLIST: Index cards, stopwatch

Provide pairs of students with two sets of cards on which you have written sums and products and differences and products, such as "difference: ${}^-3$; product: 40" and "sum: ${}^-2$; product: ${}^-99$." Player 1 reads one card at a time to Player 2, who names two numbers that meet the conditions on the card. $({}^-5, {}^-8; 9, {}^-11)$ Player 1 records the time it takes Player 2 to finish the set of cards. The partners then trade roles and use the other set of cards. Students earn 1 point for each correct response; 10 seconds are added to a student's time for an incorrect answer. The student with the highest score and lowest time wins.

LESSON | 13-8

Prior Knowledge: Students should be able to divide whole numbers.

Error Analysis and Remediation: See page 443A.

Lesson Resources:
Practice Worksheet 13-8
Reteaching Worksheet 13-8
Enrichment Activity 13-8
Daily Review 13-8

 *Two-Minute Math*

Use the Table of Numbers on the inside back cover. Multiply each number in row N by ⁻8. *(24; 40; ⁻64; 0, 16, ⁻24; 8; ⁻48; 32)*

1 INTRODUCE

SYMBOLIC ACTIVITY

1. Ask students to summarize the rules for multiplying two integers. *(The product of two positive or two negative integers is positive; the product of a negative and a positive integer is negative.)*

2. Use the rules of multiplying integers to complete each equation:
$5 \times n = 40$ *(n = 8)*
$^-5 \times n = 40$ *(n = ⁻8)*
$5 \times n = ^-40$ *(n = ⁻8)*
$^-5 \times n = ^-40$ *(n = 8)*

WHEN YOUR STUDENTS ASK
★ WHY AM I LEARNING THIS? ★

You can use this skill to describe real life situations. For example, if you were skin diving and you descended 14 m in 2 min, you could say that your average descent per minute was ⁻14 ÷ 2 or ⁻7 m/min.

428 *Chapter 13 • Lesson 13-8*

Dividing Integers ▦

During a 5-d period, the stock market index decreased 20 points. What was the average daily change in the stock market index?

You can use a related multiplication fact to divide.

$^-20 \div 5 = $ ▤ — What number multiplied by 5 gives ⁻20?

▤ $\times 5 = ^-20 \longrightarrow ^-4 \times 5 = ^-20$

So, $^-20 \div 5 = ^-4$.

The average daily change was a loss of 4 points.

Other examples:

Divide.	Related Multiplication Fact	Conclude.
$^-20 \div ^-5 = $ ▤	$4 \times ^-5 = ^-20$	$^-20 \div ^-5 = 4$
$20 \div ^-5 = $ ▤	$^-4 \times ^-5 = 20$	$20 \div ^-5 = ^-4$
$20 \div 5 = $ ▤	$4 \times 5 = 20$	$20 \div 5 = 4$

> **The quotient of two positive integers or two negative integers is a positive integer.**
> **The quotient of a positive integer and a negative integer is a negative integer.**

CALCULATOR $35 \div ^-5$; 35 ⊡ 5 ± = ⁻7 $^-48 \div ^-6$; 48 ± ÷ 6 ± = 8

The quotient of 0 divided by any other integer is 0.
$0 \div ^-8 = 0$ $0 \div 5 = 0$

CRITICAL THINKING Use the relationship between multiplication and division to explain why you cannot divide an integer by 0. **See page 443b.**

▬▬▬▬▬ **GUIDED PRACTICE** ▬▬▬▬▬

Is the quotient *positive, negative,* or *zero*?
1. $^-24 \div ^-3$ +   **2.** $^-36 \div 9$ −   **3.** $^-27 \div ^-3$ +   **4.** $0 \div 4$ 0

Find the quotient by writing a related multiplication fact.
5. $^-10 \div 5$ ⁻2   **6.** $14 \div ^-7$ ⁻2   **7.** $^-15 \div ^-3$ 5   **8.** $18 \div 6$ 3

428   LESSON 13–8

Calculators will be an effective teaching tool for this lesson. ▦

2 TEACH

☑ MATERIALS CHECKLIST: calculators

What related multiplication can help you divide ⁻39 by 13? *(13 × ⁻3 = ⁻39)*

For every multiplication fact such as ⁻9 × 3 = ⁻27, how many related division facts can you name? *(two; ⁻27 ÷ 3 = ⁻9 and ⁻27 ÷ ⁻9 = 3)*

What division is expressed by pressing the following calculator keys:
45 ± ÷ 9 ± =
(⁻45 ÷ ⁻9 = ?)

> *Chalkboard Examples*
>
> Divide.
> 40 ÷ ⁻5 *(⁻8)*   ⁻84 ÷ ⁻4 *(21)*
> ⁻46 ÷ 2 *(⁻23)*   ⁻48 ÷ ⁻3 *(16)*

SUMMARIZE/ASSESS **Explain why the rules for dividing integers are similar to the rules for multiplying integers.** *(Multiplication and division are inverse operations.)*

PRACTICE

Divide. Use a calculator, mental math, or pencil and paper.

9. ⁻64 ÷ 8 ⁻8
10. ⁻48 ÷ 6 ⁻8
11. 54 ÷ ⁻9 ⁻6
12. 20 ÷ ⁻2 ⁻10

13. ⁻72 ÷ ⁻8 9
14. ⁻35 ÷ 7 ⁻5
15. ⁻18 ÷ ⁻9 2
16. ⁻50 ÷ 5 ⁻10

17. 0 ÷ ⁻9 0
18. 16 ÷ ⁻2 ⁻8
19. ⁻66 ÷ ⁻11 6
20. ⁻30 ÷ ⁻5 6

21. ⁻70 ÷ 10 ⁻7
22. ⁻7 ÷ 1 ⁻7
23. ⁻28 ÷ 7 ⁻4
24. ⁻24 ÷ ⁻2 12

25. 51 ÷ 17 3
26. 84 ÷ |⁻4| 21
*27. |⁻46| ÷ ⁻2 ⁻23
*28. |⁻45| ÷ |⁻3| 15

MIXED REVIEW Compute.

29. ⁻8 + 3 ⁻5
30. ⁻5 × ⁻8 40
31. 12 − ⁻9 21
32. 15 + ⁻7 8

33. ⁻3 × 7 ⁻21
34. ⁻6 − ⁻4 ⁻2
35. ⁻4 − ⁻6 2
36. ⁻12 + ⁻8 ⁻20

CALCULATOR Multiply or divide.

37. 756 ÷ ⁻21
⁻36
38. ⁻1,316 ÷ ⁻47
28
39. ⁻153 × ⁻209
31,977
40. ⁻82,804 ÷ ⁻254
326

41. 4,293 ÷ 81
53
42. 198 × ⁻278
⁻55,044
43. 115,116 ÷ ⁻318
⁻362
44. ⁻125,697 ÷ ⁻429
293

PROBLEM SOLVING

45. Over 7 business days a stock dropped 14 points. What was its average drop per day? **2 points**

46. Five days ago the ABC Corporation's stock was 30 points lower. Did the stock rise or fall in the last 5 days? By how much did it rise or fall on average each day? **Rise; 6 points**

Critical Thinking

You can use four ⁻2's to write an equation equal to 1.

$$(⁻2 + ⁻2) ÷ (⁻2 + ⁻2) = 1$$

Use only the integer ⁻2 exactly four times and the operations of addition, subtraction, multiplication, and division to write an equation that equals the number. **See page 443b.**

1. 0
2. 2
3. 3
4. 4
5. 5
6. 6

7. CREATE YOUR OWN Use four ⁻2's to write equations that equal other integers. **Check students' work.**

CHAPTER 13 429

MEETING INDIVIDUAL NEEDS

For Students Who Are . . .

Acquiring English Proficiency Discuss the terms *stock market index, stock,* and *corporation.* Pair students with an English-proficient student for the Critical Thinking activities.

Gifted and Talented Have students use only the integer ⁻4 exactly four times and addition, subtraction, multiplication, and division to write an equation that equals 0, 1, and 2.

$$\left(\text{Possible answers: } \frac{⁻4 - ⁻4}{⁻4 × ⁻4} = 0; \frac{⁻4 + ⁻4}{⁻4 + ⁻4} = 1; \frac{⁻4}{⁻4} + \frac{⁻4}{⁻4} = 2\right)$$

Today's Problem

The following temperatures in degrees Celsius were observed in a laboratory: ⁻10, 6, 18, ⁻3, ⁻5, and 6. What was the average temperature for these readings?

(⁻10 + 6 + 18 + ⁻3 + ⁻5 + 6 = 12; 12 ÷ 6 = 2°C)

PRACTICE 13-8

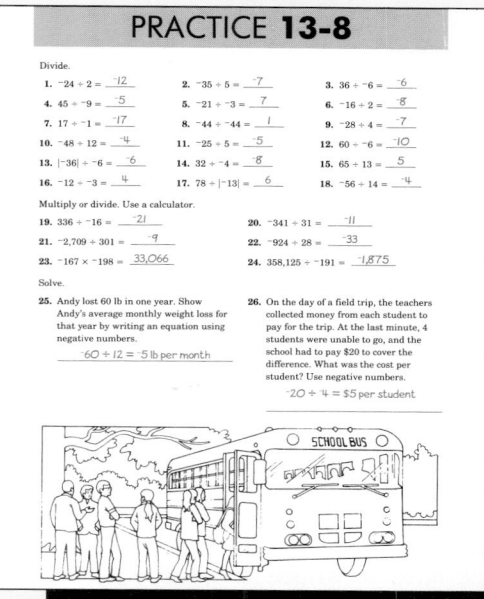

Divide.

1. ⁻24 ÷ 2 = ⁻12
2. ⁻35 ÷ 5 = ⁻7
3. 36 ÷ ⁻6 = ⁻6

4. 45 ÷ ⁻9 = ⁻5
5. ⁻21 ÷ ⁻3 = 7
6. ⁻16 ÷ 2 = ⁻8

7. 17 ÷ ⁻1 = ⁻17
8. ⁻44 ÷ ⁻44 = 1
9. ⁻28 ÷ 4 = ⁻7

10. ⁻48 ÷ 12 = ⁻4
11. ⁻25 ÷ 5 = ⁻5
12. 60 ÷ ⁻6 = ⁻10

13. |⁻36| ÷ ⁻6 = ⁻6
14. 32 ÷ ⁻4 = ⁻8
15. 65 ÷ 13 = 5

16. ⁻12 ÷ ⁻3 = 4
17. 78 ÷ |⁻13| = 6
18. ⁻56 ÷ 14 = ⁻4

Multiply or divide. Use a calculator.

19. 336 × ⁻16 = ⁻21
20. ⁻341 ÷ 31 = ⁻11

21. ⁻2,709 ÷ 301 = ⁻9
22. ⁻924 ÷ 28 = ⁻33

23. ⁻167 × ⁻198 = 33,066
24. 358,125 ÷ ⁻191 = ⁻1,875

Solve.

25. Andy lost 60 lb in one year. Show Andy's average monthly weight loss for that year by writing an equation using negative numbers.
⁻60 ÷ 12 = ⁻5 lb per month

26. On the day of a field trip, the teachers collected money from each student to pay for the trip. At the last minute, 4 students were unable to go, and the school had to pay $20 to cover the difference. What was the cost per student? Use negative numbers.
⁻20 ÷ 4 = ⁻$5 per student

RETEACHING 13-8

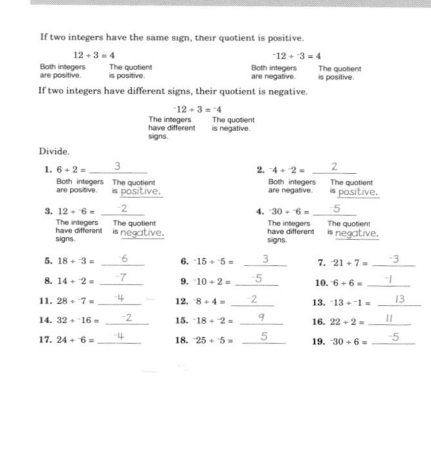

If two integers have the same sign, their quotient is positive.

12 ÷ 3 = 4
Both integers are positive. The quotient is positive.

⁻12 ÷ ⁻3 = 4
Both integers are negative. The quotient is positive.

If two integers have different signs, their quotient is negative.

⁻12 ÷ 3 = ⁻4
The integers have different signs. The quotient is negative.

Divide.

1. 6 ÷ 2 = 3
Both integers are positive. The quotient is positive.

2. ⁻4 ÷ ⁻2 = 2
Both integers are negative. The quotient is positive.

3. 12 ÷ ⁻6 = ⁻2
The integers have different signs. The quotient is negative.

4. ⁻30 ÷ 6 = ⁻5
The integers have different signs. The quotient is negative.

5. 18 ÷ 3 = 6
6. ⁻15 ÷ ⁻5 = 3
7. ⁻21 ÷ 7 = ⁻3

8. 14 ÷ 2 = 7
9. ⁻10 ÷ 2 = ⁻5
10. ⁻6 ÷ 6 = ⁻1

11. 28 ÷ 7 = 4
12. ⁻8 ÷ 4 = ⁻2
13. ⁻13 ÷ ⁻1 = 13

14. 32 ÷ 16 = 2
15. ⁻18 ÷ ⁻2 = 9
16. 22 ÷ 2 = 11

17. 24 ÷ 6 = 4
18. ⁻25 ÷ ⁻5 = 5
19. ⁻30 ÷ 6 = ⁻5

ENRICHMENT 13-8

☑ **MATERIALS CHECKLIST:** Reference books

The cost to run the country often exceeds the amount of money the United States government collects in taxes. When this happens, the government goes into debt. As of 1990, the government's debt was more than $3.1 trillion. Ask the students to find the most recent estimate of the federal debt, and to write the debt as a negative number. Then have them find the latest population figure for the U.S. How much would each person in the United States have to contribute to eliminate the federal government's debt?

MIDCHAPTER Checkup

The midchapter checkup provides a way for you to check students' understanding of the skills taught in the first half of the chapter.

Language and Vocabulary

Some key language and vocabulary ideas from the first half of the chapter are reinforced here.

Quick Quiz

This quiz provides a means of evaluating students' understanding of the objectives for the first half of the chapter. Page references are given so that students can check back to where the skill was taught.

Use the following guide to score the quick quiz.

Score	Percent
10	100%
9	90
8	80
7	70
6	60
5	50
4	40
3	30
2	20
1	10

Use this chart to identify the management objectives tested for this chapter.

Items	Management Objectives	Pages
1–4	**13A** Identify, compare, and order integers.	414–417
5–6	**13B** Add and subtract integers.	418–423
7–9	**13C** Multiply and divide integers.	426–429
10	**13F** Problem Solving: Use logic.	424–425

MIDCHAPTER CHECKUP

LANGUAGE & VOCABULARY

Tell whether the situation can most clearly be represented by *addition, subtraction, multiplication,* or *division* of integers.

1. determining your location after driving 9 mi west, then driving 12 mi east addition

2. finding your depth in a cave after descending 25 m/h for 5 h. multiplication

3. determining the number of minutes needed for a plane to climb to 2,400 ft if it climbs at the rate of 600 ft/min division

4. finding the difference in temperature between two cities, one whose temperature is 15°C and the other whose temperature is $^-4$°C subtraction

5. finding the total loss in value for a share of stock whose value has dropped $4/wk for each of the past 3 wk multiplication

QUICK QUIZ ✓

Name the opposite. *(pages 414–415)*

1. You walk up 3 flights of stairs. walking down 3 flights

2. $^-14$ 14

Compare. Write $>$, $<$, or $=$. *(pages 416–417)*

3. $2 \blacksquare ^-18$ $>$

4. $^-11 \blacksquare 11$ $<$

Solve. *(pages 418–423, 426–429)*

5. $^-12 + 7$ $^-5$

6. $0 - ^-9$ 9

7. $^-8 \times 6$ $^-48$

8. $^-56 \div 7$ $^-8$

9. $^-81 \div ^-9$ 9

Solve. *(pages 424–425)*

10. In one apartment building, all apartments have at least 1 telephone. There are regular telephones in 32 apartments, cordless telephones in 10 apartments, and both kinds in 8 apartments.

   a. How many apartments have both kinds of telephones? 8 apartments

   b. Are there more regular or more cordless telephones? regular

   c. What is the fewest number of apartments that can be in the building? Draw a Venn diagram to verify your answer. 34 Check students' drawings.

Write the answers in your learning log.   Accept reasonable answers.

1. Your friend was absent yesterday. Explain how to draw a number line that includes positive and negative numbers. Describe how to tell where the smallest and largest numbers are located.

2. Explain how adding positive charges and negative charges represents adding integers.

DID YOU KNOW . . . ? The Pony Express delivered letters from St. Joseph, Missouri, to Sacramento, California, covering 1,966 miles in about 10 days. Estimate how long it would have taken to send a letter from your school to Sacramento by Pony Express. How long does it take today to send a letter from your school to Sacramento? **Check students' work.**

This magic square uses only the first 9 counting numbers. What is the sum of each row, column, and diagonal?

8	1	6
3	5	7
4	9	2

15; 15; 15

You can create other magic squares this size using other numbers as long as you keep the relative positions of the numbers constant. In this magic square, 2 has been added to the number in each cell above. What is the sum? **21**

10	3	8
5	7	9
6	11	4

2	⁻5	0
⁻3	⁻1	1
⁻2	3	⁻4

Make another magic square. Use the integers: ⁻5, ⁻4, ⁻3, ⁻2, ⁻1, 0, 1, 2, 3.

Does the "magic" still work? Does every row, column, and diagonal have the same sum? **See above; yes; yes, ⁻3**

Learning Log

These are suggestions for writing about some topics taught so far in the chapter. The students keep their learning logs from the start of the school year to the end.

Math America

A mathematical skill that students have learned is related to an interesting fact about the United States.

Bonus

Students are given an opportunity to solve a challenge-type problem such as a puzzle or a nonroutine problem.

Lesson Organizer

Objective: Solve addition and subtraction equations with integers.

Prior Knowledge: Students should be able to solve addition and subtraction equations with whole numbers.

Lesson Resources:
Practice Worksheet 13-9
Reteaching Activity 13-9
Enrichment Worksheet 13-9
Daily Review 13-9
Cooperative Problem Solving 1,
  Chapter 13

Two-Minute Math

Evaluate.
$^-8 + 5 - {}^-6 + 3 + 2$ *(8)*
$7 + {}^-4 - {}^-3 - 1 + 5$ *(10)*
$^-24 + 3 - {}^-9 - 16 + {}^-4$ *(⁻32)*

1 INTRODUCE

SYMBOLIC ACTIVITY

1. **Name each value:**
Start with 5. Add 3, subtract 3. *(5)*
Start with ⁻9. Subtract 8, add 8. *(⁻9)*
Start with 4. Subtract ⁻5, add ⁻5. *(4)*

When the same number is added and then subtracted from a given number, what is the result? *(the original number)*
Adding and then subtracting the same number is the same as adding what number? *(zero)*

WHEN YOUR STUDENTS ASK
★ WHY AM I LEARNING THIS? ★

You can use this skill to solve real life problems. For example, if you spent $8 and had $3 left, how much money did you start with? Solving the equation $x - 8 = 3$ will answer your question.

Solving Addition and Subtraction Equations with Integers

One of the most freakish changes in temperature occurred in Spearfish, South Dakota, in 1943. In just two minutes, the temperature increased 27°C to reach a high of 7°C.

To find the original temperature, let t represent the original temperature. Then write and solve the equation, $t + 27 = 7$.

THINK ALOUD What operation can you use to get t by itself on one side of the equation? Explain. **Subtract 27 from both sides.**

$$t + 27 = 7$$ — Subtraction is the inverse of addition.
$$t + 27 - 27 = 7 - 27$$ — Subtract 27 from both sides.
$$t + 0 = {}^-20$$
$$t = {}^-20$$ — The solution is ⁻20.

Check: $t + 27 = 7$
$^-20 + 27 = 7$ ✔

The original temperature was ⁻20°C.

Another example:

$$n - 4 = 15$$
$$n - 4 + 4 = 15 + 4$$ — Add 4 to both sides.
$$n + 0 = 19$$
$$n = 19$$ — The solution is 19.

Check: $n - 4 = 15$
$19 - 4 = 15$ ✔

> **You can add or subtract the same integer on both sides of an equation.**

432   LESSON 13–9

---

2 TEACH

Calculators should be available for lengthy computations with data.

☑ **MATERIALS CHECKLIST:** Calculators

What math connections help you to solve addition and subtraction equations with integers? *(Responses should include knowing how to solve equations with whole numbers, knowing that addition and subtraction are inverses of each other.)*

How can a solution be checked? Demonstrate your answer by solving and checking the equation $n - 18 = -12$. *(Substitute the solution in the original equation; $n = 6$, and $6 + {}^-18 = {}^-12$.)*

> **Chalkboard Equations**
>
> Solve and check.
> $p - 4 = {}^-5$ *(p = ⁻1)*
> $x + 6 = {}^-8$ *(x = ⁻14)*
> $t - 14 = {}^-8$ *(t = 6)*

SUMMARIZE/ASSESS **Explain how to solve and check $p - {}^-3 = {}^-2$.** *(Add ⁻3 to both sides of the equation; $p = {}^-5$; substitute ⁻5 for p in the original equation.)*

MATH AND SCIENCE

Solve and check the equation. Explain how you did it.

1. $x + 8 = 27$
$x + 8 - 8 = 27 - 8$
$x = 19$

2. $y - 14 = 32$
$y - 14 + 14 = 32 + 14$
$y = 46$

3. $t - 8 = {}^-12$
$t - 8 + 8 = {}^-12 + 8$
$t = {}^-4$

4. $z + 12 = {}^-16$
$z + 12 - 12 = {}^-16 - 12$
$z = {}^-28$

PRACTICE

Solve and check. Use a calculator, mental math, or pencil and paper.

5. $n + 6 = 2$ ⁻4
6. $x + 8 = {}^-7$ ⁻15
7. $y + 15 = 5$ ⁻10

8. $n - 6 = {}^-3$ 3
9. $t - 8 = {}^-11$ ⁻3
10. $t - 14 = {}^-16$ ⁻2

11. $8 = 2 + m$ 6
12. $n + {}^-5 = {}^-6$ ⁻1
13. ${}^-7 + k = {}^-7$ 0

14. $r - 5 = {}^-6$ ⁻1
15. $y + 3 = {}^-10$ ⁻13
16. $t - 5 = {}^-8$ ⁻3

17. $p + {}^-7 = {}^-12$ ⁻5
18. $m - {}^-5 = {}^-5$ ⁻10
19. $h - 9 = {}^-4$ 5

MIXED REVIEW Evaluate. Use $a = {}^-2$, $b = 6$, and $c = {}^-5$.

20. $a + 8$ 6
21. $7 + a$ 5
22. $b + {}^-8$ ⁻2
23. $c - {}^-4$ ⁻1

24. $a + {}^-b$ ⁻8
25. $c - b$ ⁻11
26. $b - a$ 8
27. $a - b - c$ ⁻3

NUMBER SENSE Name the integer if it exists.

28. the least positive integer 1
29. the least integer cannot be determined
30. the greatest positive integer cannot be determined
31. the greatest negative integer ⁻1

PROBLEM SOLVING

In the troposphere, the lowest part of the earth's atmosphere, temperatures drop about 5.6°C for every kilometer of altitude.

The formula below gives the temperature (t) at a point in the troposphere if you know the ground temperature (g) and the altitude of the point in kilometers (k).

$$t = g - 5.6k$$

Use the formula to complete the table.

	Ground level temperature	Temperature at 5 km	Temperature at 20 km	Temperature at 50 km	Temperature at 75 km
32.	18°C	⁻10°C	⁻94°C		
33.	6°C	⁻22°C	⁻106°C		
34.	⁻5°C	⁻33°C	⁻117°C		

MEETING INDIVIDUAL NEEDS

For Students Who Are . . .

Acquiring English Proficiency Discuss the science words in this lesson: *troposphere, atmosphere, ground temperature.* Explain the formula on page 433.

Gifted and Talented Assign the technology lesson on page 448 at the end of this chapter.

Working 2 or 3 Grades Below Level Review addition and subtraction with integers and solving addition and subtraction equations with whole numbers.

Today's Problem

MULTICULTURAL NOTE

Near Spearfish, North Dakota is an isolated, eroded volcanic cone known as Bear Butte. It was a holy place for the Cheyenne people and plays a part in some of their myths. The Sioux, who later lived in the region, also prayed and fasted at Bear Butte.

3 FOLLOW-UP

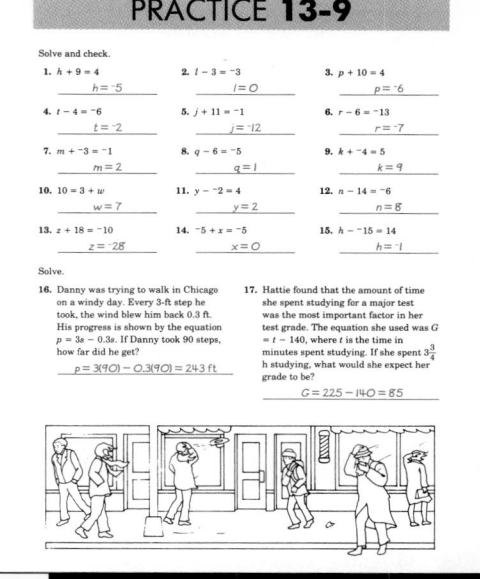

PRACTICE 13-9

Solve and check.

1. $h + 9 = 4$ $h = {}^-5$
2. $l - 3 = {}^-3$ $l = 0$
3. $p + 10 = 4$ $p = {}^-6$

4. $t - 4 = {}^-6$ $t = {}^-2$
5. $j + 11 = {}^-1$ $j = {}^-12$
6. $r - 6 = {}^-13$ $r = {}^-7$

7. $m + {}^-3 = {}^-1$ $m = 2$
8. $q - 6 = {}^-5$ $q = 1$
9. $k + {}^-4 = 5$ $k = 9$

10. $10 = 3 + w$ $w = 7$
11. $y - {}^-2 = 4$ $y = 2$
12. $n - 14 = {}^-6$ $n = 8$

13. $z + 18 = {}^-10$ $z = {}^-28$
14. ${}^-5 + x = {}^-5$ $x = 0$
15. $h - {}^-15 = 14$ $h = {}^-1$

Solve.

16. Danny was trying to walk in Chicago on a windy day. Every 3-ft step he took, the wind blew him back 0.3 ft. His progress is shown by the equation $p = 3s - 0.3s$. If Danny took 90 steps, how far did he get?
$p = 3(90) - 0.3(90) = 243$ ft

17. Hattie found that the amount of time she spent studying for a major test was the most important factor in her test grade. The equation she used was $G = t - 140$, where t is the time in minutes spent studying. If she spent $3\frac{3}{4}$ h studying, what would she expect her grade to be?
$G = 225 - 140 = 85$

RETEACHING 13-9

Write the first equation in each pair in a column on the board, then write the other equations in random order in a second column: $x + {}^-3 = 9$, $x + {}^-3 + 3 = 9 + 3$; $n - {}^-3 = 12$, $n + 3 + {}^-3 = 12 + {}^-3$; ${}^-4 + m = {}^-11$, $4 + {}^-4 + m = {}^-11 + 4$; $a + {}^-6 = 13$, $a + {}^-6 + 6 = 13 + 6$; $b - {}^-2 = 4$, $b + 2 + {}^-2 = 4 + {}^-2$. Have students come to the board in turn and draw a line between an equation and the first step in its solution. Ask each student to explain his or her choice. Then have students finish solving the equation.

ENRICHMENT 13-9

You know that you can add or subtract the same integer on both sides of an equation. You can also add or subtract the same positive or negative fraction, mixed number, or decimal on both sides of an equation.

Example 1: $x - 0.8 = {}^-4.3$
$x - 0.8 + 0.8 = {}^-4.3 + 0.8$ Addition is the inverse of subtraction. Add 0.8 to both sides.
$x = {}^-3.5$

Example 2: $y + {}^-1\frac{2}{3} = {}^-\frac{1}{3}$
$y - 1\frac{2}{3} + 1\frac{2}{3} = {}^-\frac{1}{3} + 1\frac{2}{3}$ Rewrite the equation. The inverse of adding ${}^-1\frac{2}{3}$ is subtracting $1\frac{2}{3}$.
$y = 1\frac{1}{3}$

Solve for n.

1. $n + 1.6 = 6.7$ $n = 5.1$
2. $n + 1\frac{5}{8} = {}^-\frac{1}{8}$ $n = {}^-1\frac{3}{4}$
3. $n + {}^-8.06 = {}^-3.42$ $n = 4.62$

4. ${}^-2\frac{3}{4} + n = {}^-1\frac{7}{8}$ $n = \frac{7}{8}$
5. $n + {}^-\frac{1}{2} = \frac{5}{2}$ $n = 3$
6. $n - 0.217 = {}^-3.468$ $n = {}^-3.251$

7. ${}^-3.2 + 6.1 + n = {}^-1.5$ $n = {}^-4.4$
8. $n + {}^-0.3 + 0.2 = 0.5$ $n = 1$
9. $\frac{1}{2} + {}^-\frac{1}{2} + n = 4$ $n = 4$

Lesson Organizer

> **Objective:** Solve multiplication and division equations with integers.

Prior Knowledge: Students should be able to solve multiplication and division equations with whole numbers.

Error Analysis and Remediation: See page 443A.

Lesson Resources:
Practice Worksheet 13-10
Reteaching Worksheet 13-10
Enrichment Activity 13-10
Daily Review 13-10

Two-Minute Math

Find the missing number.
$9 \times \square = 63$ *(7)*
$\square \div 8 = 9$ *(72)*
$\square \times 9 = 108$ *(12)*
$96 \div \square = 12$ *(8)*

1 INTRODUCE

SYMBOLIC ACTIVITY

Write the following expressions on the chalkboard: $3x$; $\frac{y}{7}$; ^-9z; $\frac{w}{^-5}$

What is being done to each variable? *(x is multiplied by 3; y is divided by 7; z is multiplied by $^-9$, and w is divided by $^-5$.)*
What inverse operation is needed to undo each operation used above? *(division, multiplication, division, multiplication)*

WHEN YOUR STUDENTS ASK
★ WHY AM I LEARNING THIS? ★

In real life, stock analysts use this skill to determine price changes of stock traded during a given time. For example, a loss of 27 points over 3 consecutive days can be written as the equation $3n = ^-27$ to find the average price change per day.

Solving Multiplication and Division Equations with Integers

During a recent 7-d drought in the Southwest, the water level in a reservoir decreased 14 cm. About how much did the water level change each day during this period?

Let n represent the average daily change in centimeters.

$7n$ represents the change in 7 d.
$7n = ^-14$

Since you know how to solve addition and subtraction equations with integers, you can use a MATH CONNECTION to solve this equation.

Cracked earth near Beatty, Nevada

THINK ALOUD   What operation can you use to get n by itself on one side of the equation? Explain.
division; It is the inverse of multiplication.

$7n = {}^-14$ ⟵ Division is the inverse of multiplication.
$\frac{7n}{7} = \frac{^-14}{7}$ ⟵ Divide both sides by 7.
$n = {}^-2$ ⟵ The solution is $^-2$.

Check:
$7n = {}^-14$
$7(^-2) = {}^-14$ ✔

The water level changes about $^-2$ cm each day.

Another example:

$\frac{x}{^-3} = 2$
$\frac{x}{^-3} \times {}^-3 = 2 \times {}^-3$ ⟵ Multiply both sides by $^-3$.
$x = {}^-6$ ⟵ The solution is $^-6$.

Check:
$\frac{x}{^-3} = 2$
$\frac{^-6}{^-3} = 2$ ✔

> **You can multiply or divide both sides of an equation by the same nonzero integer.**

434   LESSON 13–10

2 TEACH

☑ **MATERIALS CHECKLIST:** Math Connection Transparency

Display the transparency. Have students explain how to fill in the spaces and discuss the math connection. *(See student pages.)*

What is the purpose of using the inverse operation to solve equations? *(It allows you to isolate the variable on one side of the equation sign and the answer on the other side.)*

> ### *Chalkboard Equations*
>
> Solve and check each equation.
> $\frac{b}{15} = {}^-5$ *(b = $^-75$)*
> $\frac{s}{^-4} = {}^-11$ *(s = 44)*
> $12\,m = {}^-144$ *(m = $^-12$)*
> $\frac{t}{^-7} = {}^-14$ *(t = 98)*

SUMMARIZE/ASSESS   **Explain how to solve and check the equation $^-14n = ^-70$.** *(Divide both sides of the equation by $^-14$; n = 5. Substitute 5 for n in the original equation.)*

Explain how you would solve and check the equation.
First name the operation you would use.

1. $3n = {}^-12$
division; $^-4$

2. $\frac{x}{4} = {}^-2$
multiplication; $^-8$

3. $^-3t = 24$
division; $^-8$

4. $\frac{n}{5} = {}^-4$
multiplication; $^-20$

PRACTICE

Solve.

5. $\frac{x}{5} = {}^-7$ $^-35$

6. $^-3k = 27$ $^-9$

7. $9b = {}^-54$ $^-6$

8. $\frac{n}{^-9} = 8$ $^-72$

9. $^-12x = 60$ $^-5$

10. $\frac{t}{^-4} = {}^-8$ 32

11. $\frac{y}{4} = 10$ 40

12. $^-6y = {}^-30$ 5

13. $\frac{m}{12} = {}^-4$ $^-48$

14. $6z = {}^-48$ $^-8$

15. $\frac{x}{8} = {}^-15$ $^-120$

16. $^-7n = {}^-56$ 8

17. $^-8x = 80$ $^-10$

18. $\frac{p}{13} = {}^-11$ $^-143$

19. $^-4b = 52$ $^-13$

20. $\frac{x}{^-7} = 23$ $^-161$

21. $^-8z = 96$ $^-12$

22. $\frac{r}{^-21} = {}^-6$ 126

23. $^-14a = {}^-168$ 12

24. $^-15n = {}^-180$ 12

MIXED REVIEW Give the answer in lowest terms.

25. $\frac{2}{3} + \frac{3}{5}$ $1\frac{4}{15}$

26. $\frac{4}{5} - \frac{2}{3}$ $\frac{2}{15}$

27. $\frac{21}{30} \times \frac{4}{7}$ $\frac{2}{5}$

28. $\frac{3}{7} \div \frac{7}{12}$ $\frac{36}{49}$

29. $5\frac{2}{3} + 2\frac{1}{6}$ $7\frac{5}{6}$

30. $7\frac{1}{3} \div 3\frac{2}{3}$ 2

31. $2\frac{3}{4} \times 1\frac{5}{7}$ $4\frac{5}{7}$

32. $6\frac{1}{2} - 2\frac{3}{8}$ $4\frac{1}{8}$

NUMBER SENSE Solve the equation. Look for a pattern.

33. $2a = 2$ 1

34. $3a = {}^-9$ $^-3$

35. $4a = 36$ 9

36. $5a = {}^-135$ $^-27$

37. Write the next two equations that continue the pattern begun in Exercises 33–36. $6a = 486; 7a = {}^-1701$

PROBLEM SOLVING

Write the equation and solve.

38. If an irrigation pond is being filled at the rate of 10 L/s, how long will it take to increase the amount of water in the pond by 500 L? $10n = 500; 50s$

39. If water is pumped from an irrigation pond at the rate of 8 L/s, how long will it take to decrease the amount of water in the pond by 512 L? $8n = 512; 64s$

40. An irrigation pond was being filled at the rate of 11 L/s. Water was being drained out simultaneously at the rate of 9 L/s. How many minutes did it take to increase the water in the pond by 600 L ? $2n = 600; 5 min$

CHAPTER 13 **435**

MEETING INDIVIDUAL NEEDS

For Students Who Are . . .

Acquiring English Proficiency Discuss the meanings of *drought*, *water level*, *reservoir*, and *irrigation*.

Gifted and Talented Have students solve these equations, then find the difference between the greatest and least solution:
$5a = {}^-135$ ($^-27$); $\frac{s}{19} = {}^-28$ ($^-532$); $^-7c + 16 - 16 = {}^-98$ (14; the difference between 14 and $^-532$ is 546.)

Working 2 or 3 Grades Below Level Review using inverse operations to solve multiplication and division equations with whole numbers.

Today's Problem

Explain how you would locate the following quotients on a number line: $\frac{^-200}{^-2}$, $\frac{^-400}{4}$, $\frac{600}{^-6}$, $\frac{800}{8}$. ($\frac{^-400}{4} = \frac{600}{^-6} = {}^-100$; $\frac{^-200}{^-2} = \frac{800}{8} = 100$. *Even though one is positive and one is negative, $^-100$ and 100 are located the same distance from zero.*)

---

3 FOLLOW-UP

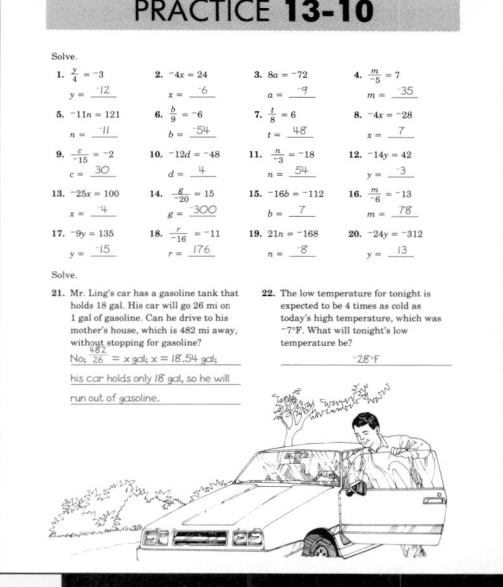

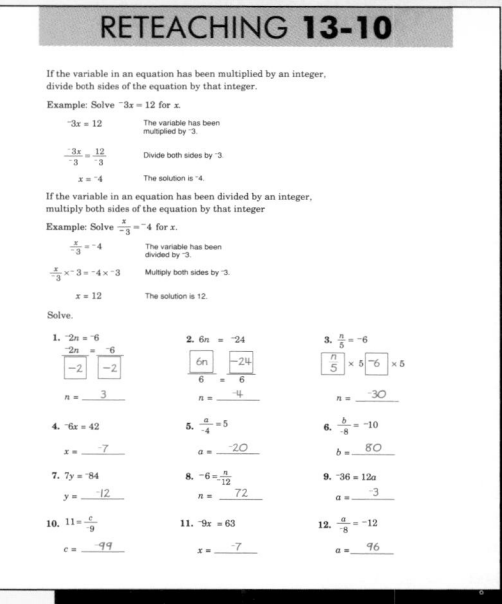

ENRICHMENT 13-10

☑ **MATERIALS CHECKLIST:** Blank spinners

Have the students work in pairs. Provide each pair with one spinner labeled $^-15$, $^-4$, 13, $^-20$, 36, $^-2$, and another spinner labeled *Multiplication* and *Division*. Explain that the numbers are solutions to equations that involve either multiplication or division. Each pair spins the spinners and writes an equation based on the spins. For example, spins of $^-15$ and *Division* might result in the following: $\frac{x}{^-5} = 3$. Tell the students to make their equations as challenging as possible. When students have written several equations, have them exchange with another group and solve.

Lesson Organizer

Objective: Graph ordered pairs on a coordinate plane.

Prior Knowledge: Students should know how to graph integers on a number line.

Error Analysis and Remediation: See page 443A.

Lesson Resources:
Practice Worksheet 13-11
Reteaching Worksheet 13-11
Enrichment Activity 13-11
Daily Review 13-11
Cooperative Connections, Chapter 13

Two-Minute Math

Compare. Write > or <.

$^-5$ ☐ $^-3$ *(<)* 0 ☐ $^-2$ *(>)*

$^-2$ ☐ 1 *(<)* 3 ☐ $^-1$ *(>)*

1 INTRODUCE

CONNECTING ACTIVITY

☑ **MATERIALS CHECKLIST:** Teaching Aid 15 (Centimeter Grid Paper) and metric ruler for each student, Coordinate Plane transparency

1. Display the transparency. **Draw a horizontal line at the middle of the grid.** Explain that this is called the *x*- axis on a coordinate plane. **Label the *x*- axis as you would a number line, from $^-6$ to 6.**

2. **Draw a vertical line through the 0 of the *x* axis.** Explain that this line is called the *y*- axis, and that the place where the *x*- and *y*- axes intersect is called the origin.

3. **Mark the origin (0, 0). Label the *y*- axis 1 through 6 moving up from the origin, and $^-1$ through $^-6$ moving down from the origin.**

WHEN YOUR STUDENTS ASK
★ **WHY AM I LEARNING THIS?** ★

You can connect this skill to real life through air traffic control. Coordinates showing the location of aircraft are displayed electronically on computer terminals, allowing controllers to guide the planes safely along their routes.

Coordinate Plane

The map of Washington, D.C., at right is on a number grid called a **coordinate plane.**

In the coordinate plane, the horizontal number line is called the ***x*-axis.** The vertical number line is called the ***y*-axis.** The two lines meet at a point called the **origin** (0, 0).

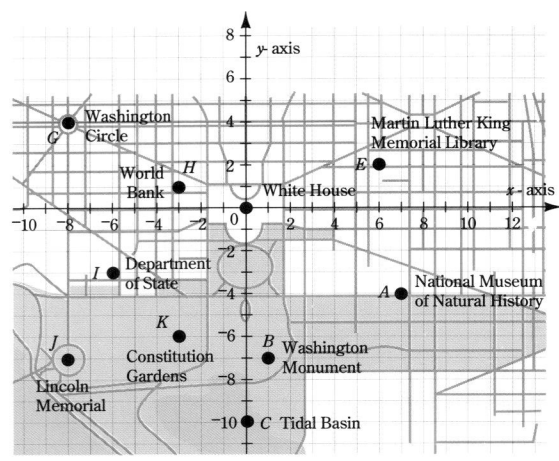

- On the map, what is located at (0, 0)? **White House**

Point *A* is called the **graph** of the ordered pair (7, $^-4$). You can locate point *A* by starting at origin (0, 0) and moving 7 units to the right and 4 units down. The numbers 7 and $^-4$ are called the **coordinates** of *A*.

- What is located at (7, $^-4$)? **National Museum of Natural History**
- What are the coordinates of *I*, the Department of State? **($^-6$, $^-3$)**

THINK ALOUD Do (7, $^-4$) and ($^-4$, 7) name the same point? **No**
Why is the order of naming the coordinates important?
Tells you which "direction" to go first.

━━━━━━ **GUIDED PRACTICE** ━━━━━━

Use the grid above. Name the ordered pair.

1. *E*(▦, 2)
6

2. *I*($^-6$, ▦)
$^-3$

3. *C*(▦, ▦)
0, $^-10$

Name the landmark located at the given coordinates. Use the grid above.

4. ($^-3$, 1)
World Bank

5. ($^-8$, $^-7$)
Lincoln Memorial

6. (1, $^-7$)
Washington Monument

436   LESSON 13–11

MATH AND GEOGRAPHY

2 TEACH

☑ **MATERIALS CHECKLIST:** Teaching Aid 19 (Quadrant Grid) for each student

What is the difference between graphing ($^-5$, 2) and (2, $^-5$)? *[For ($^-5$, 2) the point is graphed 5 units to the left of (0, 0) along the x-axis and 2 units up; for (2, $^-5$) the point is graphed 2 units to the right of (0, 0) along the x- axis and 5 units down.]*

What can you say about the second coordinates of all points on the x- axis? *(They are 0.)*

Chalkboard Examples

Graph the points on a coordinate grid: $A = (0, 2)$; $B = (2, 0)$ $C = (2, ^-1)$; $D = (^-2, ^-2)$
(Check students' graphs.)

SUMMARIZE/ASSESS   **How do the numbers in an ordered pair explain the location of a point?** *(The first coordinate gives the distance on the x- axis from the point of origin; the second coordinate gives the distance on the y-axis from the point of origin.)*

Write the letter of the point named by the ordered pair.

7. ($^-$3, 4) W   **8.** (3, 5) Q

9. (5, $^-$2) K   **10.** ($^-$7, $^-$2) A

11. (2, 7) S   **12.** ($^-$1, 1) E

13. ($^-$3, 1) D   **14.** (1, $^-$2) H

Name the ordered pair for each point.

15. Z ($^-$7, 5) **16.** B ($^-$5, $^-$2) **17.** N (5, 5)

18. G (0, $^-$2) **19.** X ($^-$5, 4) **20.** T ($^-$2, 7)

21. L (7, $^-$2) **22.** I (1, 1) **23.** R (2, 5)

24. V ($^-$3, 5) **25.** C ($^-$5, 1) **26.** M (7, 5)

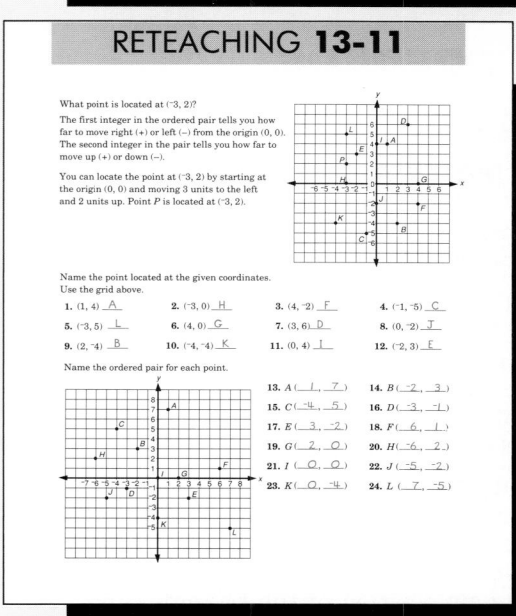

The White House

Find the distance between the pair of points.

27. M and L 7   **28.** J and K 3   **29.** C and E 4   **30.** S and T 4

31. X and P 8   **32.** M and Z 14 **33.** C and I 6   **34.** F and L 8

35. Draw and label an x-axis and a y-axis on graph paper. Graph and label each ordered pair:

$A($$^-$2, 6), B(0, 10), C(2, 6), D(3, $^-$9), E(0, $^-$10), F($^-$3, $^-$9),$ and $G(0, 5).$

Connect the points:

A to B, B to C, C to D, D to E, E to F, F to A, A to G, C to G, and B to E.   See page 443b.

36. **CREATE YOUR OWN** Plot and connect ordered pairs to create a figure. See whether a classmate can draw your figure. Give her or him the ordered pairs for the points and tell her or him which points to connect.
Check students' work.

37. **CRITICAL THINKING** Graph any three ordered pairs such that each x-coordinate is 2 more than each y-coordinate.
Answers will vary. Check students' work.
  a. Draw a line through these points.

  b. Name the coordinates of any other two points on this line.

  c. What do you notice about the coordinates of these points? $x = y + 2$

MEETING INDIVIDUAL NEEDS

For Students Who Are . . .

Acquiring English Proficiency Discuss the words *vertical* and *horizontal*, relating them to the *x*-axis and the *y*-axis. Pair students with an able reader for the Critical Thinking activities.

Gifted and Talented Have students use a ruler to draw a hexagon on a grid. Ask them to label each vertex with a capital letter, then name the ordered pair for each point. Students can trade to check each other's work.

Working 2 or 3 Grades Below Level Remind students that on the *x*-axis, negative integers are located to the left of (0, 0); on the *y*-axis, they are located below (0, 0).

MULTICULTURAL NOTE

In 1791 surveyors Andrew Ellicott and Benjamin Banneker, an African American, began working with the French engineer Charles L'Enfant to design Washington, D.C. When L'Enfant left the project, Banneker and Ellicott completed the job on their own.

---

3 FOLLOW-UP

PRACTICE 13-11

Using the graph below, write the letter of the point named by the ordered pair.

1. (3, 2) _____ D   **2.** ($^-$4, 1) ___ C
3. ($^-$1, $^-$2) ___ F   **4.** (5, $^-$5) ___ H
5. (0, 4) _____ E   **6.** ($^-$3, 0) ___ B
7. ($^-$6, 4) _____   **8.** ($^-$4, 6) ___

Using the graph below, name the ordered pair for each point.

9. A ___ (2, $^-$3)   **10.** B ___ (1, 1)
11. C ___ ($^-$3, 3)   **12.** D ___ (0, 3)
13. E ___ (5, 5)   **14.** F ___ (4, $^-$3)
15. G _____   **16.** H _____

17. Graph and label each ordered pair at the right:
$A($$^-$6,1), B($$^-$5,0),$
$C($$^-$4,0), D($$^-$3,2),$
$E($$^-$1,3), F(0,2),$
$G(3,2),\ H(4,1),$
$I(5,$$^-$3),\ J(4,$$^-$3),$
$K(3,$$^-$1), L(3,$$^-$3),$
$M(2,$$^-$3), N(2,$$^-$1),$
$O(0,$$^-$1),\ P(0,$$^-$3),$
$Q($$^-$1,$$^-$3), R($$^-$1,$$^-$1),$
$S($$^-$3,$$^-$3), T($$^-$4,$$^-$3),$
$U($$^-$2,$$^-$1), V($$^-$3,0),$
$W($$^-$4,$$^-$1), X($$^-$5,$$^-$1),$
$Y($$^-$6,0)$
Connect the points in order.

18. A survey showed that 70% of the 500 students at Central High School plan to attend college. Of these students, 10% did not take the college entrance exam. How many students took the exam?

RETEACHING 13-11

What point is located at ($^-$3, 2)?
The first integer in the ordered pair tells you how far to move right (+) or left ($^-$) from the origin (0, 0). The second integer in the pair tells you how far to move up (+) or down ($^-$).

You can locate the point at ($^-$3, 2) by starting at the origin (0, 0) and moving 3 units to the left and 2 units up. Point P is located at ($^-$3, 2).

Name the point located at the given coordinates. Use the grid above.

1. (1, 4) _A_   **2.** ($^-$3, 0) _H_   **3.** (4, $^-$2) _F_   **4.** ($^-$1, $^-$5) _C_
5. ($^-$3, 5) _L_   **6.** (4, 0) _G_   **7.** (3, 6) _D_   **8.** (0, $^-$2) _J_
9. (2, $^-$4) _B_   **10.** ($^-$4, $^-$4) _K_   **11.** (0, 4) _I_   **12.** (2, 3) _E_

Name the ordered pair for each point.

13. A (_1_, _7_)   **14.** B (_$^-$2_, _3_)
15. C (_$^-$4_, _5_)   **16.** D (_$^-$3_, _$^-$1_)
17. E (_3_, _$^-$2_)   **18.** F (_6_, _1_)
19. G (_2_, _3_)   **20.** H (_$^-$6_, _2_)
21. I (_0_, _0_)   **22.** J (_$^-$5_, _$^-$2_)
23. K (_0_, _$^-$4_)   **24.** L (_7_, _$^-$5_)

ENRICHMENT 13-11

☑ **MATERIALS CHECKLIST:** Teaching Aid 3 (Grid Paper), straightedges

Have students work in pairs. Instruct one partner to graph the points (1, 1), (8, 6), (6, 12), and (2, 10) and to draw line segments to form a figure. Then have the other partner divide the *x*-coordinate by 2, graph the resulting ordered pairs, and draw a figure. **What happened to the original figure?** (*moved to the left and became narrower*) Ask the partners to divide both original *x*- and *y*- coordinates by 2, graph the resulting coordinates, and draw a figure. **What happened to the original figure?** (*moved down and left and decreased in size by $\frac{1}{2}$*)

Lesson Organizer

Objective: Explore coordinate transformations.

Prior Knowledge: Students should know how to name points on a coordinate plane and how to slide and flip a figure.

Lesson Resources:
Class Activity 13-12
Daily Review 13-12

Two-Minute Math

Add.

$^-5 + 2$ *($^-3$)* $6 + ^-5$ *(1)*
$^-4 + 8$ *(4)* $^-2 + ^-15$ *($^-17$)*

1 PREPARE

CONNECTING ACTIVITY

☑ **MATERIALS CHECKLIST:** Teaching Aid 19 (Coordinate Grid); tagboard triangle with sides 6 cm, 3.2 cm, and 7.5 cm, Coordinate Grid transparency

1. On an overhead projector place the triangle on the coordinate grid so that its vertices are at the points (6, 2), ($^-$1, 5), and (3, 1). Trace the triangle and ask students to name the coordinates of the vertices.

2. Replace the triangle and slide it 3 units to the left. **This is a translation; how did it change the triangle?** *(Did not change the shape, only the position.)* Trace the new position of the triangle, and have students name the coordinates of the vertices. *[(3, 2), ($^-$4, 5), (0, 1)]*

3. Repeat the activity, sliding the triangle down 2 units.

WHEN YOUR STUDENTS ASK
★ WHY AM I LEARNING THIS? ★

You can connect this skill to real life through architecture. Architects often use translations and flips to alter building and design plans when changing the locations of windows and doors.

Exploring Coordinate Transformations

A translation (slide) of a figure in the coordinate plane does not change its size or shape, only its location. The result of a translation is called the translation image.

Trace and cut out △ABC.
Copy the table.

1. Record the coordinates for points *A*, *B*, and *C*.

Start with your triangle on △ABC. Perform the translation. Record the coordinates of the translation image.

2. 5 units to the right, 0 units up or down

3. 2 units to the right, 3 units up

4. 1 unit left, 2 units down

5. **CREATE YOUR OWN** Start with △ABC. Make any translation you wish. Record the coordinates of the translation image.

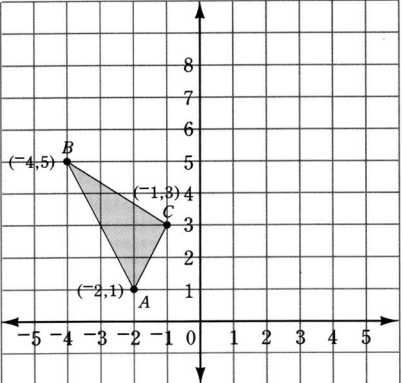

Triangle	Coordinates			
	A	*B*	*C*	
ABC	(-2, 1)	(-4, 5)	(-1, 3)	1.
Image after 5*R*,0	(3, 1)	(1, 5)	(4, 3)	2.
Image after 2*R*,3*U*	(0, 4)	(-2, 8)	(1, 6)	3.
Image after 1*L*,2*D*	(-3, 1)	(-5, 3)	(-2, 1)	4.
Your Image	Check students' work.			5.

6. How do the translation images compare to the original triangle?
Images are the same size and shape, but their locations have moved.

7. **IN YOUR WORDS** Explain how you would find the *x*- or *y*-coordinates for the translation image resulting from the translation.

   a. 3 units to the right
      add 3 to x coordinate
   c. 6 units down
      subtract 6 from y
   e. 1 unit to the left, 2 units up
      subtract 1 from x, add 2 to y

   b. 4 units up
      add 4 to y
   d. 1 unit down
      subtract 1 from y
   f. 2 units to the right, down 3 units
      add 2 to x, subtract 3 from y

2 EXPLORE

☑ **MATERIALS CHECKLIST:** Teaching Aid 19 (Coordinate Grid) (two per student); tracing paper, and scissors for each student

Have students work with a partner for these activities.
How would the coordinates of the translation image change in Exercise 3 if you moved the triangle 2 units to the left? *[The coordinates of the translation image would be A ($^-$4, 1); B ($^-$6, 5), and C ($^-$3, 3).]*

If students have difficulty with Exercise 7, suggest that they perform the actual slide several times so that they see the resulting change.

For Exercises 8–10, you may wish to suggest that students fold the coordinate plane along the *x*-axis and the *y*-axis to see the actual flip.

SUMMARIZE/ASSESS **The coordinates for points *A*, *B*, and *C* of a triangle are (3, 2), (3, $^-$2), and (0, 0). What are the coordinates for these points after a move 2 units to the left, 1 unit up?** *[(1, 3), (1, $^-$1), and ($^-$2, 1); encourage students to demonstrate on the grid.]*

A reflection (flip) of a figure in the coordinate plane also does not change the shape or size of the figure. The line over which a figure is reflected is called the **line of reflection** and the result of a reflection is called the **reflection image**.

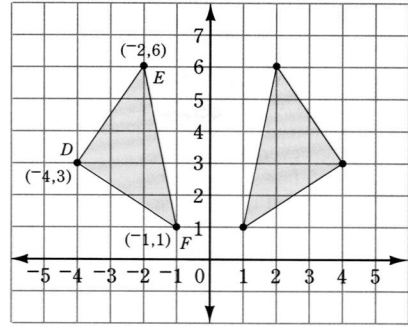

Trace $\triangle DEF$. Cut it out. Copy the table.

8. Record the coordinates for points D, E, and F.

Start with your triangle on $\triangle DEF$. Perform the reflection. Record the coordinates of the reflection image.

9. reflection over the y-axis

10. reflection over the x-axis

Triangle	Coordinates			
	D	E	F	
DEF	(⁻4, 3)	(⁻2, 6)	(⁻1, 1)	8.
Reflection Image over *y*-axis	(4, 3)	(2, 6)	(1, 1)	9.
Reflection Image over *x*-axis		(⁻2, ⁻6)	(⁻1, ⁻1)	10.

11. **CRITICAL THINKING** How do the coordinates of the reflection image compare to the original coordinates?
    same absolute values

12. Copy the coordinate system and $\triangle TUV$ on a sheet of grid paper.

    a. Reflect $\triangle TUV$ over the y-axis $T(-2, -4)$; $U(-6, -6)$; $V(-4, -1)$

    b. Translate the reflection image of $\triangle TUV$ 6 units to the left. What are the coordinates of the vertexes of the image? $T(-8, -4)$; $U(-12, -6)$; $V(-10, -1)$

13. Copy the coordinate system and the original $\triangle TUV$ on a sheet of grid paper. See page 443b.

    a. Translate $\triangle TUV$ 6 units to the left.

    b. Reflect the translation image of $\triangle TUV$ over the y-axis. What are the coordinates of the vertexes of the image?

    c. Compare your results with Exercise 12.

14. **CRITICAL THINKING** Are translation and reflection commutative operations? **no**

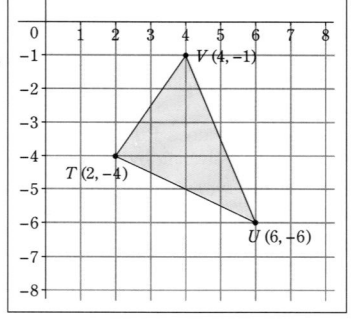

MEETING INDIVIDUAL NEEDS

For Students Who Are . . .

Acquiring English Proficiency Review the concepts of *translation* and *reflection*. Explain that the *image* is what results after the triangle has been moved.

Gifted and Talented Have students draw a triangle on a quadrant grid and write a set of directions for a translation. Students can exchange papers and name the x- and y-coordinates for the translation image.

Working 2 or 3 Grade Below Level Review writing and naming coordinate points on a grid. Name three points and help students locate them on a grid; then show students what happens when a point is moved up, down, left, or right.

Today's Problem

Through which vertex of triangle ABC should the triangle be reflected so that the figure with its reflection looks like a bow tie? *(through B)*

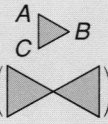

---

3 FOLLOW-UP

CLASS ACTIVITY 13-12

☑ **MATERIALS CHECKLIST: Grid paper**

Review the concept of opposites and how they can be represented on horizontal and vertical number lines.

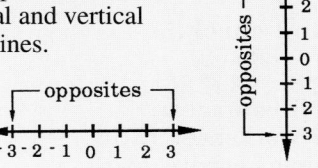

Have students make a coordinate grid on grid paper. Have them draw an array to the right of the y-axis that represents $3 \times 2 = 6$. Have them write $3 \times 2 = 6$ above the array.

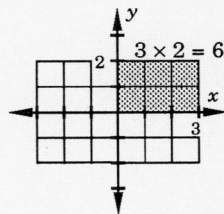

Have students draw an array for $^-3 \times 2$ by drawing the array to the left of the y-axis. By comparing the coordinate grid to a number line, the product is $^-6$ because the array is opposite the first array that was drawn. The same can be shown with the array for $3 \times ^-2$.

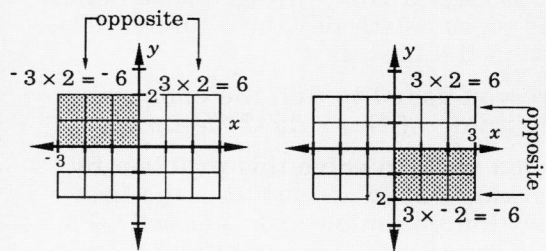

Have students discuss how they would draw an array for $^-3 \times ^-2$ and what the product would be. *(Since the array is opposite both the array for $3 \times ^-2$ and the array for $^-3 \times 2$, the product would be 6 because 6 is the opposite of $^-6$.)*

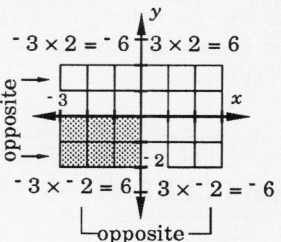

LESSON 13-13

Lesson Organizer

Objective: Solve problems by working backward.

Prior Knowledge: Students should know the four-part process.

Solve and check.
$^-41 = y - 39$ $(^-2)$
$h + ^-12 = ^-98$ $(^-86)$

Lesson Resources:
Practice Worksheet 13-13
Reteaching Activity 13-13
Enrichment Worksheet 13-13
Daily Review 13-13
Cooperative Problem Solving 2,
    Chapter 13

Two-Minute Math

Solve and check.
$^-41 = y - 39$ $(^-2)$
$h + ^-12 = ^-98$ $(^-36)$

1 INTRODUCE

SYMBOLIC ACTIVITY

Pose this problem:
Gus the gorilla was on a special diet for 6 days. Each day he was given twice as many bananas as on the previous day. If Gus were given 96 bananas on the sixth day, how many did he get on the first day?

Are you asked to find the end or the beginning of Gus's diet? *(beginning)*

If you were to solve this problem by working backward, what is the first question you might ask yourself? *(Possible answer: If Gus got 96 bananas on the sixth day, how many did he receive the day before?)* **What would you do to answer your question?** *(divide 96 by 2 to get 48 bananas.)*

What is the relationship between the multiplication suggested by the "twice as many" in the problem and the division you did to answer your question? *(inverse operations)*

WHEN YOUR STUDENTS ASK
★ WHY AM I LEARNING THIS? ★

You can connect this skill to investigative work. For example, detectives often work backward to uncover the conditions leading to an event.

Problem Solving:
Working Backward

Most problem solving situations present you with information and ask you to determine a solution. Sometimes, however, you know the solution and how it was found, but you need to find the beginning condition. A strategy used to solve this kind of problem is working backward.

Marcia is flying from Detroit to Los Angeles. Her plane leaves at 9:45 A.M. and she wants to be at the airport $\frac{3}{4}$ h before departure. She can drive to the airport in 50 min and she needs $1\frac{1}{2}$ h to dress and have breakfast. For what time should she set her alarm clock?

THINK ALOUD What do you want to know? What facts do you know? How can you work backward to answer the question? **Accept reasonable answers.**

Marcia's plane leaves at 9:45 A.M. She wants to arrive $\frac{3}{4}$ h before this.　She will take about 50 min to drive to the airport.　She needs $1\frac{1}{2}$ h to dress and eat before she leaves.

9:45 A.M. $- 0:45 = 9:00$ A.M.　9:00 A.M. $- 0:50 = 8:10$ A.M.　8:10 A.M. $- 1:30 = 6:40$ A.M.

Marcia should set the alarm clock for 6:40 A.M.

GUIDED PRACTICE

1. Read the story to answer the questions.

   Ruth is thinking of a number. If she multiplies the number by 3 and divides by 2, she gets 6.

   a. What does Ruth get after multiplying her number by 3 and dividing by 2?　**6**

   b. To work backward, what is the first step to take?　mult. by 2

   c. What is the number Ruth is thinking of?　**4**

2. Dick is thinking of a number. If he divides the number by 2, then multiples it by 3, and finally divides by 0.9, the result is $^-5$. What is the number?　$^-3$

---

2 TEACH

Suppose Marcia's plane leaves at 10:30, and she needs to be at the airport 50 minutes before departure. The drive to the airport takes 45 minutes, and she needs an hour and a half to get ready. When should she begin her preparations? *(10:30 − 0:50 = 9:40; 9:40 − 0:45 = 8:55; 8:55 − 1:30 = 7:25)*

> **Chalkboard Example**
>
> A number is divided by 2 and multiplied by $^-6$ to give a result of 30. What is the number? $(^-10)$

SUMMARIZE/ASSESS
Describe how to work backward to solve a problem. *(Start with the final result and work in reverse order until you reach the first of a chain of events.)*

Solve.

3. Annie's plane leaves at 10:35 A.M. It takes $1\frac{1}{2}$ h to get to the airport from her house. If she allows 30 min to check in and get to the gate, what time should she leave the house?
8:35 A.M.

4. Willie was thinking of a number. If he adds 8 to it, subtracts $\frac{1}{2}$ and then subtracts 5, he gets 1. What number was Willie's number? **⁻1.5**

5. Mary bought a cassette player with half of her money. Then she spent $15 more. After that, she spent half of her remaining money on tapes. Then she spent $18 on head phones. If she had $12 left, how much did she have before she bought the cassette player?
$150

6. Sandy paid $14.90 for taxi fare from the airport to the hotel, including a $2.00 tip. Sky Cab charges $1.90 for the first mile plus $.20 for each additional $\frac{1}{5}$ mi. How many miles did Sandy travel from the airport to the hotel? **12 mi**

7. Carlos deposited his paycheck in a new savings account on Monday. On Tuesday, he withdrew $25.00 to buy a concert ticket. He deposited $37.50 on Wednesday and then withdrew $20.00 on Thursday to spend at the concert. On Friday, he withdrew $18.75 to buy a shirt. If his savings account then contained $56.25, what amount did Carlos deposit on Monday?
$82.50

 CHOOSE Choose any strategy to solve. **Strategies may vary. Suggestions given.**

8. Name the simplest value of the continuous fraction.
working backward; $\frac{8}{13}$

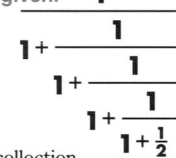

$$1 + \cfrac{1}{1 + \cfrac{1}{1 + \cfrac{1}{1 + \frac{1}{2}}}}$$

9. Mr. Ryan divided his stamp collection among his children. Roger got $\frac{1}{2}$ of the stamps, Rose got $\frac{1}{4}$ of the stamps, Ray got $\frac{1}{5}$ of the stamps, and Ruth got 1,000 stamps. How many stamps did Mr. Ryan have in his collection?
multistep; 20,000 stamps

10. Think of a number. Add 4, multiply by 3, subtract 4, and multiply by 3. Add together the digits of the result. If the answer has more than 1 digit, keep adding digits until it is a single-digit number. Is it 6? Try other numbers.
yes

CHAPTER 13   441

MEETING INDIVIDUAL NEEDS

For Students Who Are . . .

Acquiring English Proficiency Emphasize the relationship between inverse operations and working backward. In problem 5, note that the word *half* indicates multiplying by $\frac{1}{2}$ or dividing by 2.

Gifted and Talented Have students write two additional problems that can be solved by working backward. Have them exchange papers and solve.

Working 2 or 3 Grades Below Level Have students use pages 102–105 of the Skills Workbook for Problem Solving Strategies.

Having Reading Difficulties Pair students with an able reader for the Practice section.

Today's Problem

A number is divided by ⁻7, multiplied by 8, and added to 25. Finally 200 is subtracted from it. If the result is 81, what is the number?
(200 + 81 = 281, 281 − 25 = 256, 256 ÷ 8 = 32, 32 × ⁻7 = ⁻224)

---

3 FOLLOW-UP

PRACTICE 13-13

Solve.

1. Arlo needs to be in school by 8:00 A.M. He has a 5-min walk to the bus and a 20-min bus ride. He also needs 45 min to eat and dress. For what time should he set his alarm?
_____ **6:50 A.M.**

2. Ayo shared the prize money he won in a raffle with some friends. He gave $\frac{1}{2}$ of the money to Eli, and $\frac{1}{2}$ of the remainder to Joel. He kept the $250 remainder for himself. How much money did Ayo win?
_____ **$1,000**

3. Verona spent $15 on tickets to a concert. She then spent $11 on cushions to sit on the ground and $8 for a special bus to the concert. She had $14 left to spend on food. How much did she have to start?
_____ **$48**

4. George played a game with his friend Jake. He said, "I am thinking of a number. If I divide it by 2, add 3 to the result, and then multiply by 4, the result is 36. What is the number?" Jake said, "The number is _____."
12

5. A number is doubled, then 18 is subtracted from it. The number is then divided by 4, resulting in 32. What was the starting number?
_____ **73**

6. Melanie's grades in algebra class were 85, 93, 96, 90, 82. What was her average score? **89.2**
What grade does she need on her next test to have a 90 average?
_____ **94**

RETEACHING 13-13

Some students may not understand that you can solve a problem by working backward. Help a student solve Problem 1, *Practice Worksheet 13-13*, by asking these questions: By what time must Ricardo arrive at school? [8 A.M.] How long is Ricardo's bus ride? [20 min] What time must he board the bus to arrive at school on time? [8:00 A.M. − 20 min, or 7:40 A.M.] How long is Ricardo's walk to the bus stop from home? [5 min] When must he leave home to arrive at the bus stop at 7:40 A.M.? [7:40 A.M. − 5 min, or 7:35 A.M.] How much time does Ricardo need to dress and eat? [45 min] When must he get up to start walking at 7:35 A.M.? [7:35 − 45 min, or 6:50 A.M.]

ENRICHMENT 13-13

Work backward to solve.

1. Jody wants a 92 average in her history class. Her grades so far are 80, 95, 93, and 88. There are 2 more major tests she must take. What range of grades may she get in order to have a 92 average? **97 – 100**

2. I'm thinking of a number. When I triple the number, then divide it by 4, and finally subtract 26, the result is 28. What is my number? **72**

3. Write a problem similar to Exercise 2. Exchange problems with a classmate and solve each other's problem. **Answers will vary.**

4. Joyce needs to be in Los Angeles, California, by July 23. She will leave from Cincinnati, Ohio, and drive 350 mi per day at an average speed of 50 mi/h. She also wants to arrive at her motel each day by 4:00 P.M. The road distance from Cincinnati to Los Angeles is about 2,100 mi.

   a. On what date should Joyce leave? **July 17**

   b. If Joyce needs $1\frac{1}{2}$ h for gas and food breaks each day, what time each morning must she leave in order to be at her motel by 4:00 P.M.? **7:30 A.M.**

5. In June, Tamara tripled the amount in her savings account, and then withdrew $10 from the account. She did this each month. At the end of September she had $45.50 left in the account. How much did Tamara have in the account at the beginning of June? **$5.50**

This chapter checkup provides a quick language and vocabulary review, a test for the chapter, and suggestions for student Learning Log entries.

Language and Vocabulary

Some key language and vocabulary ideas from this chapter are reinforced here.

Test

The test can be used either as a test or as a review of the chapter prior to administering the test worksheets found in the Teacher's Resource Book.

The following guide will help you determine percentage scores.

Score	Percent	Score	Percent
26	100%	13	50%
25	96	12	46
24	92	11	42
23	88	10	38
22	85	9	35
21	81	8	31
20	77	7	27
19	73	6	23
18	69	5	19
17	65	4	15
16	62	3	12
15	58	2	8
14	54	1	4

Each test has three sections: concepts, skills, and problem solving. These sections provide students with exposure to the format used on standardized tests.

Use this chart to identify additional lesson resources for this chapter.

Items	Management Objectives	Pages
1–11	**13A** Identify, compare, and order integers.	414–417
16–17	**13B** Add and subtract integers.	418–423
18–19	**13C** Multiply and divide integers.	426–429
20–23	**13D** Solve equations involving integers.	432–435
12–15	**13E** Graph ordered pairs on a coordinate plane.	436–439
24–26	**13F** Problem Solving: Use logic. Work backward.	424–425; 440–441

CHAPTER CHECKUP

LANGUAGE & VOCABULARY

Each situation can be represented by an equation. Without solving the equation, tell whether the solution will be *positive* or *negative*.

1. If a number y is increased by 5, the result is $^-9$. **negative**
2. A number b multiplied by $^-3$ equals $^-21$. **positive**
3. Dividing a number x by 8 gives a quotient of $^-7$. **negative**
4. If 24 is subtracted from a number q, the difference is 8. **positive**
5. When a number m is subtracted from 10 the result is $^-3$. **positive**

TEST ✓

CONCEPTS

Name the opposite of the integer. *(pages 414–415)*

1. $^-2$ **2**
2. 18 **$^-18$**
3. 1 **$^-1$**
4. 0 **0**
5. $^-25$ **25**

Write the absolute value of the integer. *(pages 414–415)*

6. $^-6$ **6**
7. $^-47$ **47**
8. 36 **$^-36$**

Compare. Write >, <, or =. *(pages 416–417)*

9. 0 ▮ $^-3$ **>**
10. $^-15$ ▮ 8 **<**
11. $|^-9|$ ▮ $|9|$ **=**

Name the ordered pair for the point. *(pages 436–439)*

12. A **(3, 0)**
13. B **($^-3$, 2)**
14. C **(1, $^-4$)**
15. D **($^-4$, $^-2$)**

SKILLS

Solve. *(pages 418–423, 426–429, 432–435)*

16. $^-4 + 17$ **13**
17. $31 - {}^-14$ **45**
18. $^-16 \times 4$ **$^-64$**
19. $48 \div {}^-6$ **$^-8$**
20. $x + 14 = 5$ **$^-9$**
21. $y - 8 = {}^-3$ **5**
22. $^-4k = 36$ **$^-9$**
23. $\frac{m}{7} = {}^-9$ **$^-63$**

442   CHAPTER CHECKUP

CHAPTER TEST • FORM A

(pp. 414–417) 13A

Write the opposite of the integer.

1. $^-16$ __16__
2. 34 __$^-34$__

Compare. Write >, <, or =.

3. 3 __>__ $^-6$
4. $^-5$ __>__ $^-7$
5. $^-2$ __<__ 2

Solve. (pp. 418–423) 13B

6. $^-5 + 2 =$ __$^-3$__
7. $^-6 + {}^-5 =$ __$^-11$__
8. $3 - {}^-7 =$ __10__
9. $6 - 10 =$ __$^-4$__
10. $^-1 - 9 =$ __$^-10$__

Solve. (pp. 426–429) 13C

11. $^-4 \times 7 =$ __$^-28$__
12. $^-5 \times {}^-8 =$ __40__
13. $6 \times {}^-3 =$ __$^-18$__
14. $^-18 \div {}^-3 =$ __6__
15. $^-40 \div 5 =$ __$^-8$__

Solve the equation. (pp. 432–435) 13D

16. $n + 7 = 1$ __$n = {}^-6$__
17. $t - 10 = {}^-18$ __$t = {}^-8$__
18. $^-6y = {}^-24$ __$y = 4$__
19. $\frac{m}{13} = {}^-10$ __$m = {}^-130$__
20. $x + 6 = {}^-9$ __$x = {}^-15$__

Use the graph. (pp. 436–439) 13E

Write the ordered pair for the point.

21. L __(2, 1)__
22. Q __($^-2$, 1)__
23. S __($^-1$, $^-2$)__

Write the letter of the point named by the ordered pair.

24. (2, $^-1$) __T__
25. ($^-1$, 3) __P__

CHAPTER TEST • FORM A

Solve. (pp. 424–425, 440–441) 13F

26. In a classroom, 15 students study a foreign language, 20 play a musical instrument, and 6 do both. If all students in the class study a foreign language or play a musical instrument, how many students are in the class? __29 students__

27. In a recent 10 km race, Sidney finished before Donna and Karla, but behind Vera. Karla finished behind Donna. Name their finishing order from first to fourth. __Vera, Sidney, Donna, Karla__

28. Craig's plane leaves at 1:10 P.M. It takes $1\frac{1}{4}$ h to get to the airport from his house. If he allows 45 min for parking, check-in and getting to the gate, what time should he leave home? __11:10 A.M.__

29. Julio was thinking of a number. If he subtracts 4 from it, adds $\frac{1}{2}$, and then adds 7, he gets 3. What number was Julio thinking of? __$^-\frac{1}{2}$__

30. Sandra deposited last week's pay check on Tuesday. On Wednesday she wrote a check for $35.00 to pay for dinner. She deposited $48.50 on Thursday and wrote a $23.95 check on Friday to pay her water bill. On Saturday she wrote a check for $62.45 to buy groceries. If her checking account then contained $271.40, how much did Sandra deposit on Tuesday? __$344.30__

Problem Solving

Item 24 has three parts:
a. literal—this is a reading comprehension question.
b. interpretive—this involves interpretation using the facts given.
c. applied—students use a strategy or skill to find an answer.

Item 21 in the skill section and item 26 in the problem solving section use the same numbers.

This will help you informally assess how your students transfer from numerical skills to word problems.

For scoring problem solving items, you may wish to use partial credit. If a student uses the correct strategy but gets a wrong answer, give the student two points toward the total percent score.

Learning Log

These are suggestions for writing about some topics taught in the chapter. The students keep their learning logs from the start of the school year through the end.

PROBLEM SOLVING

Use a Venn diagram. *(pages 424–425)*

24. In a survey, 21 students liked gym class, 44 liked library period, and 9 liked both.

  a. How many students liked library period?   **44 students**

  b. Did more students like gym than library?   **no**

  c. What is the smallest number of students that could have been surveyed? Draw a Venn diagram to verify your answers.   **56 students; Check students' drawings.**

Solve. *(pages 440–441)*

25. If you subtract 6 from a number, then divide by 3, and finally add 2, the result is 16. What is the number?
48

26. Overnight a temperature of $y°C$ dropped 8°C to $^-3°C$. What was the temperature before the drop?   **5°C**

LEARNING LOG

Write the answers in your learning log.   **Answers will vary. Suggestions given.**

1. Describe two inverse operations used in mathematics and two inverse operations that are not mathematical.
$+$; $-$; climbing up stairs; going downstairs

2. You just graphed the point (4, 5). Now explain to your friend how to graph the point $(^-4, ^-5)$.   **Accept reasonable answers.**

Note that the same numbers are used in Exercises 21 and 26.

CHAPTER 13   443

CHAPTER TEST • FORM B

(pp. 414–417) 13A

Write the opposite of the integer.

1. 24 $^-24$

2. $^-39$ 39

Compare. Write >, <, or =.

3. $^-3$ $<$ 6

4. $^-7$ $>$ $^-11$

5. $^-10$ $<$ 10

Solve. *(pp. 418–423)* 13B

6. $^-7 + 3 =$ $^-4$

7. $^-4 + ^-6 =$ $^-10$

8. $4 - ^-5$ 9

9. $5 - 11 =$ $^-6$

10. $^-2 - 7 =$ $^-9$

Solve. *(pp. 426–429)* 13C

11. $^-5 \times 6 =$ $^-30$

12. $^-6 \times ^-7 =$ 42

13. $8 \times ^-2 =$ $^-16$

14. $^-21 \div ^-7 =$ 3

15. $^-42 \div 6 =$ $^-7$

Solve. *(pp. 432–435)* 13D

16. $n + 8 = 2$ $n = ^-6$

17. $t - 6 = ^-16$ $t = ^-10$

18. $^-7y = ^-28$ $y = 4$

19. $\frac{m}{24} = ^-10$ $m = ^-240$

20. $x + 8 = ^-14$ $x = ^-22$

Use the graph. *(pp. 436–439)* 13E

Write the ordered pair for the point.

21. R $(^-2, ^-1)$

22. P $(^-1, 3)$

23. T $(2, ^-1)$

Write the letter of the point named by the ordered pair.

24. (2, 1) L

25. $(^-3, ^-1)$ U

CHAPTER TEST • FORM B

Solve. *(pp. 424–425, 440–441)* 13F

26. In a classroom, 16 students study Spanish, 20 are in the band, and 7 do both. If all students in the class study Spanish or play in the band, how many students are in the class?
29 students

27. In a recent stock car race, Tim finished before Ernie and Lou, but behind Will. Lou finished behind Ernie. Name their finishing order from first to fourth.
Will, Tom, Ernie, Lou

28. Ron's plane leaves at 8:20 A.M. It takes $1\frac{1}{2}$ h to get to the airport from his house. If he allows 30 min for check-in and getting to the gate, what time should he leave home?
6:20 A.M.

29. Kelli was thinking of a number. If she subtracts 5 from it, adds $\frac{1}{2}$, and then adds 9, she gets 4. What number was Kelli thinking of?
$^-\frac{1}{2}$

30. Wendy deposited her last week's pay on Monday. On Tuesday, she wrote a check for $45.00 to pay her phone bill. She deposited $54.30 on Wednesday and wrote a $32.75 check on Thursday to pay her water bill. On Friday she wrote a check for $61.85 to buy groceries. If her checking account then contained $281.20, how much did Wendy deposit on Monday?
$366.50

Error Analysis and Remediation

Here are some common errors students make when they are working with integers. The errors are listed by lesson under the appropriate management objective.

13A • IDENTIFY, COMPARE, AND ORDER INTEGERS

Source of Error (Lesson 13-1)
Students identify the absolute value of an integer as the opposite of the integer.

Remediation
Help students by reviewing the definition of *absolute value* and how integers are graphed on a number line. Demonstrate by graphing 8 and −8 on a number line and asking students to count the number of units between 0 and 8 to find |8|.

Source of Error (Lesson 13-2)
Students ignore the negative symbol when comparing integers.

Remediation
Have students locate the integers on a number line. Remind them that the integer to the right is the greater integer and that the integer to the left is the lesser integer.

13B • ADD AND SUBTRACT INTEGERS

Source of Error (Lesson 13-4)
Students find a positive sum for two negative integers.

Remediation
Display a number line to demonstrate that adding two negative integers results in a negative integer.

Source of Error (Lesson 13-5)
Students make errors when subtracting a positive integer from a lesser positive integer.

Remediation
Write 2 − 9 on the chalkboard, and use a number line to demonstrate that the change from 9 to 2 is a move to the left of 7 units, or ⁻7. Then show the subtraction, 2 − 9 = 2 + ⁻9 = ⁻7, pointing that to subtract 9, you added its opposite.

13C • MULTIPLY AND DIVIDE INTEGERS

Source of Error (Lesson 13-7)
Students confuse the rules for multiplication of integers with the rules for addition of integers.

Remediation
For example, students remember that ⁻3 + 9 is a positive integer and then assume that ⁻3 × 9 is a positive integer. Review and distinguish the rules for adding and multiplying integers. Then give students examples to show on a number line.

Source of Error (Lesson 13-8)
Students forget to apply the rules for determining when the quotient is positive or negative.

Remediation
Review the rules for dividing integers. Then give students several examples. Have them perform each division as if there were no negative signs and then apply the rule to determine whether the quotient is negative.

13D • SOLVE EQUATIONS INVOLVING INTEGERS

Source of Error (Lesson 13-9 and 13-10)
Students do not use the inverse operation to solve an equation.

Remediation
Remind students that equations are solved by using the inverse operation. Then suggest that students ask themselves, What operation do I use to get the variable by itself on one side of the equation?

13E • GRAPH ORDERED PAIRS ON A COORDINATE PLANE

Source of Error (Lesson 13-11)
Students do not locate ordered pairs correctly.

Remediation
Remind students that the first coordinate is located by referring to the *x*-axis and the second by referring to the *y*-axis. Point out that *x* comes before *y* in the alphabet.

Answers

Page 428

Critical Thinking: Answers will vary. Suggestion given: Multiplication and division are inverse relationships: $4 \times 2 = 8$; $8 \div 2 = 4$. Because there is no number by which you can multiply zero to get an integer, you cannot divide an integer by zero.

Page 429

Critical Thinking: Answers will vary. Suggestions given:

1. $(^-2 - {}^-2) + (^-2 - {}^-2) = 0$
2. $\frac{^-2}{^-2} + \frac{^-2}{^-2} = 2$
3. $\frac{^-2 + {}^-2 + {}^-2}{^-2} = 3$
4. $\frac{(^-2)(^-2)(^-2)}{^-2} = 4$
5. $^-2(^-2) + \frac{^-2}{^-2} = 5$
6. $^-2 - (^-2)(^-2)(^-2) = 6$

Page 437

35.

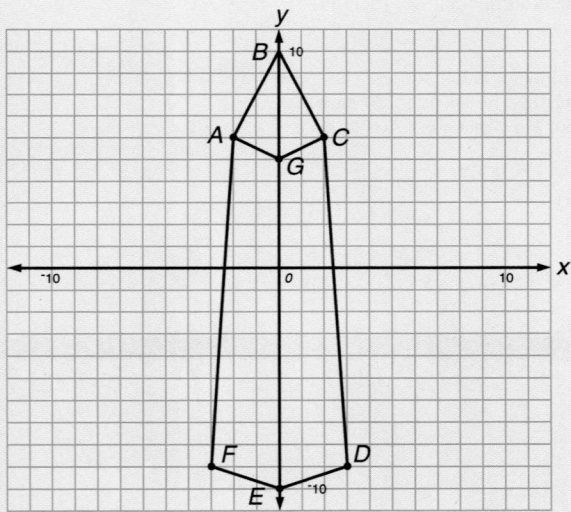

Page 439

13. **a.** T($^-4$, $^-4$); U(0, $^-6$); V($^-2$, $^-1$)
    b. T(4, $^-4$); U(0, $^-6$); V(2, $^-1$)
    c. triangle in exercise 13b is 12 units to the right of the triangle in exercise 12b

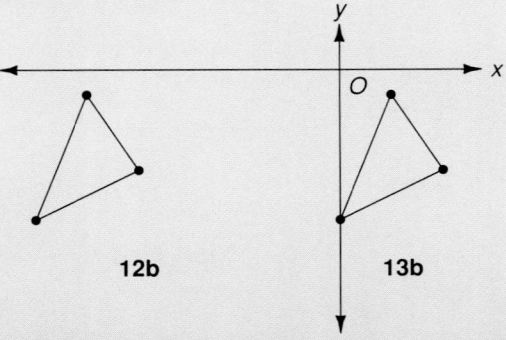

12b   13b

Extra Practice

This page provides extra practice of all the major chapter objectives. Use this page after the chapter has been taught to reinforce the chapter skills. Page references are provided for each group of items so that students can easily look back at the appropriate lesson for additional support.

Name the opposite of the integer. *(pages 414–415)*

1. $^-3$ 3   **2.** 8 $^-8$ **3.** 0 0   **4.** $^-100$ 100   **5.** 15 $^-15$

Write the absolute value of the integer. *(pages 414–415)*

6. 21 21   **7.** $^-2$ 2   **8.** 150 150   **9.** $^-81$ 81   **10.** $^-14$ 14

Compare. Write >, <, or =. *(pages 416–417)*

11. $^-3$ ▓ 4 <   **12.** 12 ▓ $^-15$ >   **13.** 0 ▓ 9 <   **14.** $^-8$ ▓ $^-4$ <

15. $^-23$ ▓ 0 <   **16.** $^-5$ ▓ $^-10$ >   **17.** $|^-6|$ ▓ $|6|$ =   **18.** 6 ▓ $^-16$ >

Solve. *(pages 418–423, 426–429, 432–435)*

19. $^-2 + ^-8$ $^-10$ **20.** $^-9 - 3$ $^-12$ **21.** $0 - ^-8$ 8   **22.** $13 + ^-13$ 0

23. $^-9 \div ^-3$ 3   **24.** $^-15 \times 2$ $^-30$ **25.** $14 \times ^-5$ $^-70$ **26.** $^-40 \div 10$ $^-4$

27. $25 + ^-27$ $^-2$ **28.** $18 - ^-12$ 30   **29.** 0×7 0   **30.** $^-81 \div 9$ $^-9$

31. $a + 16 = 4$ $^-12$ **32.** $c - 4 = ^-9$ $^-5$ **33.** $e - ^-2 = 15$ 13   **34.** $\frac{g}{6} = ^-6$ $^-36$

35. $m + ^-8 = ^-21$ $^-13$ **36.** $^-7p = ^-35$ 5   **37.** $\frac{r}{8} = 2$ 16   **38.** $\frac{t}{^-3} = 21$ $^-63$

39. $\frac{x}{5} = ^-35$ $^-175$ **40.** $n - ^-3 = ^-8$ $^-11$ **41.** $x + ^-9 = 13$ 22   **42.** $x - 3 = 9$ 12

Name the ordered pair for the point. *(pages 436–439)*

43. A (0, 4)   **44.** B ($^-2$, 3)

45. C ($^-4$, 0)   **46.** D (3, 3)

47. E ($^-3$, $^-5$)   **48.** F (1, $^-4$)

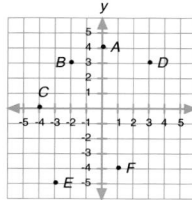

Solve. *(pages 424–425, 440–441)*

49. In one farming community, soybeans are grown on 7 farms, corn is grown on 7 farms, and both crops are grown on 3 farms. What is the smallest number of farms that can be in the community? **11 farms**

50. Arnold left home with some money in his pocket. He spent half of what he had on lunch, then he spent $1.20 on a magazine, and still had $1.50. How much did Arnold have when he left home? **$5.40**

444   EXTRA PRACTICE

GUESS MY POLYGON

Play this game with a group. You will need a geoboard, rubber band, and centimeter graph paper. One player is the Polygon Placer and the others are the guessers.

1. Using the geoboard as a coordinate grid, the Polygon Placer makes a polygon with a rubber band. The polygon must fit in the first quadrant and no coordinate can exceed 4. The polygon shown has vertexes with coordinates A (1, 0), B (2, 1), C (3, 1), D (3, 3), and E (1, 3).

2. The guessers draw a coordinate grid on their sheets of graph paper. The x and y axes need only go 4 units each in the positive direction.

3. The Guessers take turns naming the coordinates of a point. The Placer must tell whether the point named is a vertex of the polygon.

4. On any turn a Guesser can show his or her figure to the Placer. The first player who correctly copies the Placer's polygon wins the round.

5. Play until each player has been the Polygon Placer.

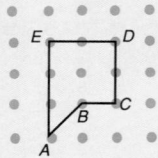

Large Number Estimates

We often hear statements about the size of populations that seem too large to count. For example, you might read that 250,000 people watched a parade. Do you think that is an exact number or an estimate? How is a number like that obtained? One way to estimate crowds is to count the number of people within a small area and multiply by the number of similar areas.

You can use this principle to make a large number estimate in your school. Look around your classroom. Is either the floor or the ceiling covered with tiles? If either is, work with a partner to estimate the number of tiles that are in the entire building. If your building doesn't have this, estimate the number of pencils in the school. **Check students' work.**

Six in a Row

Find six consecutive integers that add up to 369. After you find the answer, think about how you would make up a question like this one. Then make up two or three "In a Row" questions and share them with a friend.

$59 + 60 + 61 + 62 + 63 + 64$

Check students' work.

Enrichment

This page contains activities that provide extension and enrichment for all levels of students. Depending on the needs of your students, you may wish to assign an activity from this page at certain points during the chapter, or you may wish to use this page when the entire chapter has been completed.

Guess My Polygon
(COOPERATIVE)

Have students place a small piece of tape along one edge of the geoboard. Holding the geoboard with the taped edge at the bottom, identify the x-axis (the horizontal row of pegs directly above the taped edge) and the y-axis. Caution the Polygon Placer not to rotate the geoboard during the game.

Large Number Estimates
(COOPERATIVE)

Before partners actually begin any estimation work, suggest that they discuss the following questions. How do you choose a small area to count? How do you determine how many similar areas there are in the entire building?

Six in a Row
(COOPERATIVE)

Make certain that everyone understands the meaning of *consecutive integer*. Remind students that incorrect answers can help to guide them closer to the solution.

Cumulative Review

The Cumulative Review focuses on skills covered in previous chapters. All important skills are reviewed on a cyclic basis.

If students are having difficulty with particular groups of exercises, refer to the chart below for follow-up work.

Find the answer. c

1. 30% of 86
 a. 2.58
 b. 258
 c. 25.8
 d. none of these

2. 18 is what percent b
 of 96?
 a. 187.5%
 b. 18.75%
 c. 1.875%
 d. none of these

3. 40% of what number b
 is 24?
 a. 9.6
 b. 60
 c. 96
 d. none of these

4. $\frac{23}{100} = \frac{x}{56}$ a
 a. 12.88
 b. 1.288
 c. 128.8
 d. none of these

5. $\frac{0.3}{100} = \frac{n}{42}$ d
 a. 1.26
 b. 12.6
 c. 126
 d. none of these

6. $\frac{160}{100} = \frac{y}{89}$ c
 a. 1.424
 b. 14.24
 c. 142.4
 d. none of these

7. original price: $95 c
 discount: 15%
 selling price:
 a. $14.25
 b. $80
 c. $80.75
 d. none of these

8. original price: $23 a
 discount: 7%
 selling price:
 a. $21.39
 b. $16
 c. $1.61
 d. none of these

9. cost: $38 c
 markup: 70%
 selling price:
 a. $108
 b. $54.29
 c. $64.60
 d. none of these

10. 81, 76, 82, 94 b
 mean =
 a. 333
 b. 83.25
 c. 82.5
 d. none of these

11. 1, 8, 3, 7, 8 a
 median =
 a. 7
 b. 8
 c. 5.4
 d. none of these

12. 6, 9, 7, 8, 9, 11 a
 median =
 a. 8.5
 b. 8
 c. 9
 d. none of these

13. $^-7$ is between b
 a. $^-6$ and 0
 b. $^-10$ and $^-6$
 c. $^-4$ and 0
 d. none of these

14. $^-23$ is greater than c
 a. 0
 b. 15
 c. $^-36$
 d. none of these

15. $^-8$ is less than b
 a. $^-35$
 b. $^-2$
 c. $^-15$
 d. none of these

Items	Management Objectives	Where Taught	Reteaching Options	Extra Practice Options
1–3	**10C** Find the percent of a number, the percent, or the original number in percent problems.	pp. 322–327	TRB/RW 10-8 to 10-10	TRB/PW 10-8 to 10-10
4–6	**11A** Use proportion to solve percent problems.	pp. 350–353	TRB/RW 11-2	TRB/PW 11-2
7–9	**11B** Determine discount and markup.	pp. 358–359	TRB/RW 11-4/5	TRB/PW 11-4/5
10–12	**12A** Find the mean and median.	pp. 382–383	TRB/RW 12-4	TRB/PW 12-4
13–15	**13A** Identify, compare, and order integers.	pp. 416–417	TRB/RW 13-2	TRB/PW 13-2

Strategies may vary. Suggestions given.
Remember the strategies and types of
problems you've had so far. Solve.

Problem Solving Check List

- Too much information
- Too little information
- Multistep problems
- Making a graph
- Using a pattern
- Using an equation
- Using percents

1. A staircase is made with 5 bricks in the bottom row, 4 in the next, then 3, 2, and 1. Another staircase follows the same pattern, but has 2 additional rows of bricks.

   a. How many bricks are in the bottom row of the smaller staircase?   5 bricks

   b. How many bricks are needed to build the smaller staircase?   15 bricks

   c. How many more bricks does the larger staircase need than the smaller one?   pattern; 13 bricks

2. An elevator runs between $^-2$s (subbasement) to + 7 (7th floor). Edgar rode from the main floor (0), up to the 5th floor, then to the subbasement. How many floors did he pass by?
   draw a picture; 10 floors

3. A racing bicycle has 2 gear positions in front and 6 in the rear. If a rider must select a combination of a front gear and a back gear, how many choices does the rider have?
   equation; 12 choices

4. Arizona became the 48th state in 1912. Delaware became the first state 125 yr earlier. In what year did Delaware become a state?
   equation; 1787

5. An airline ticket that normally sells for $362 can be bought at discount for $248. Estimate the total savings for a family buying 5 tickets.
   multistep; about $600

6. A car maker guarantees its cars for 7 yr or 70,000 mi, whichever comes first. If an owner has had her car 5 yr and has driven 57,328 mi, which is likely to come first, 7 yr of ownership or 70,000 mi?
   pattern; 70,000 mi

7. A driver is making a trip of 250 mi in desert and 150 mi in mountains. His car averages 25 mi/gal in the desert, but only 18 in mountains. What is the fewest whole number of gallons of gas the driver should expect to use?
   multistep; 19 gal

8. Scientists estimate that 6,500 objects are orbiting the Earth. About 21% are dead satellites and about 6% are live satellites. About how many more satellites are dead than are live?
   multistep; about 975 more satellites

9. In 1986, Brook Junior High School raised $120 from a plant sale. By 1988, the amount increased to $165. In 1990, it was $210. If the pattern continues, predict how much the school will earn in 1994. Make a graph.
   graph; 300

Problem Solving Review

This page focuses on problem solving strategies and types learned in this and previous chapters. A problem solving checklist lists some of the strategies students may use to solve the problems on this page.

Technology

This page is designed to provide calculator or computer experiences for all levels of students. The calculator or computer logo indicates the type of activity.

You may wish to assign these activities after the chapter has been taught or during the course of the chapter, depending on your needs and those of your students.

Give Me a Sign
(COOPERATIVE)

Point out that operational signs do not include the raised minus sign used to designate negative integers. Review order of operations with students.

Give Me the Truth

Suggest that students make a list of any arrangements they try and the results in order to avoid duplicates. Remind them to follow order of operations, performing calculations within parentheses first.

Off the Board
(COOPERATIVE)

Ask students to explain the rules in their own words. If necessary, model one or two rounds before they begin play.

The computer activity uses Houghton Mifflin software, which is found in Houghton Mifflin Math Activities Courseware, Grade 7.

GIVE ME A SIGN

Change one operational sign in each problem so that a true statement is formed.

$(98 \overset{\times}{+} 121) \div 11 + {}^-78 = 1{,}000$

$({}^-40 + {}^-6) \overset{+}{-} (8 \div {}^-2) = {}^-50$

${}^-120 \div (36 + {}^-30) \overset{-}{+} ({}^-420 \div 21) = 0$

Make up two more problems like these for a classmate to solve.
Check students' work.

GIVE ME THE TRUTH

Insert one or two pairs of parentheses so that a true statement is formed.

$98 + {}^-27 + 84 - {}^-85 = {}^-48$

${}^-79 \times 56 \div {}^-8 \times 34 - {}^-17 = {}^-9{,}401$

$91 + 43 + 117 + 125 = {}^-6$

$246 \div {}^-41 + 846 - {}^-126 = 714$

OFF THE BOARD

In the computer activity *Operation Integer*, you move spaceships on a coordinate plane by adding or subtracting integer values for x or y coordinates. This pencil-and-paper activity will help you become familiar with moving a point on the coordinate plane.
See below.
Work with a partner. You will need a graph labeled from ${}^-15$ to 15 on both the x- and y-axes. You will also need a number cube and a coin. Each player places a marker at (0, 0). Move the marker according to these rules. Take turns.

1. Flip the coin. Heads means "add to x-coordinate." Tails means "add to y-coordinate."

2. Roll the number cube. This is the absolute value of the number to be added to the appropriate coordinate. Add a positive integer on the first turn, then alternate between positive and negative on the other turns.

Play until one player's marker has moved off the graph.
Check students' work.

Software Activities

Note: Students should enter commands as single lines. They must not hit RETURN within a command.

activity 1 • ADDING INTEGERS

MATERIALS: spreadsheet program

Procedure: In this activity, students create a spreadsheet which adds integers. Students begin by entering the integer ⁻3 into cell C2 of a spreadsheet and continue to label the cells across the row with the integers ⁻2, ⁻1 . . . 2, 3. In the third row, students enter expressions adding the integer in the cell above and the integer in cell A2. For example, students enter the integer 3 in cell A2 and watch the integers appear in row 3. Have students describe the pattern if negative integers are entered.

	A	B	C	D
1	Enter Integer in A2			
2	?		⁻3	⁻2
3			⁻3 + A2	⁻2 + A2
4				
5				
6				

E	F	G	H	I
⁻1	0	1	2	3
⁻1 + A2	0 + A2	1 + A2	2 + A2	3 + A2

Follow-up: Have students change the expressions in row 3 to show the addition of the integer in cell A2 and the integer in the above cell. Students should describe the new rule and how the commutative property of addition applies.

activity 2 • NUMBER LINE ADDITION

MATERIALS: Logo program

Procedure: This program allows students to explore the meaning of addition of integers by viewing a problem on a number line. Students should enter the program into the computer and run it several times.

```
TO NLINE
  CG CT PRINT[WHAT IS THE FIRST
VALUE?]
  MAKE "X READLISTCC PRINT [WHAT IS
  THE SECOND VALUE?] MAKE "Y
  READLISTCC RT 90 FIR FIRST :X SEC
  FIRST :Y PRINT (SE[THE SUM IS: ]
  XCOR)
END
TO FIR :X
  IFELSE :X > 0 [FD :X] [BK −1*:X]
END
TO SEC :Y
  PU SETY 5 IFELSE :Y > 0 [FD :Y]
  [BK −1*:Y]
END
```

Follow-up: Help students to modify the program to accomodate subtraction of integers.

HOUGHTON MIFFLIN SOFTWARE

EduCalc. Boston, MA: Houghton Mifflin Company, 1990. For Apple II, Commodore, IBM.

Mathematics Activities Courseware. Boston, MA: Houghton Mifflin Company, 1983. For Apple II, IBM.

The Computer Tutor. Boston, MA: Houghton Mifflin Company, 1990. For Apple II, IBM.

OTHER SOFTWARE

Bumble Plot. Fremont, CA: The Learning Company, 1989. For Apple II, Commodore, IBM.

Integers/Equations. Dimondale, MI: Hartley Courseware, 1988. For Apple II, IBM.

Logo Writer 2.0. Montreal, Quebec: Logo Computer Systems, Inc., 1988. For Apple II, IBM, Macintosh.

Math Blaster Mystery. Torrance, CA: Davidson and Associates, 1989. For Apple II, IBM, Macintosh.

Geometry and Measurement

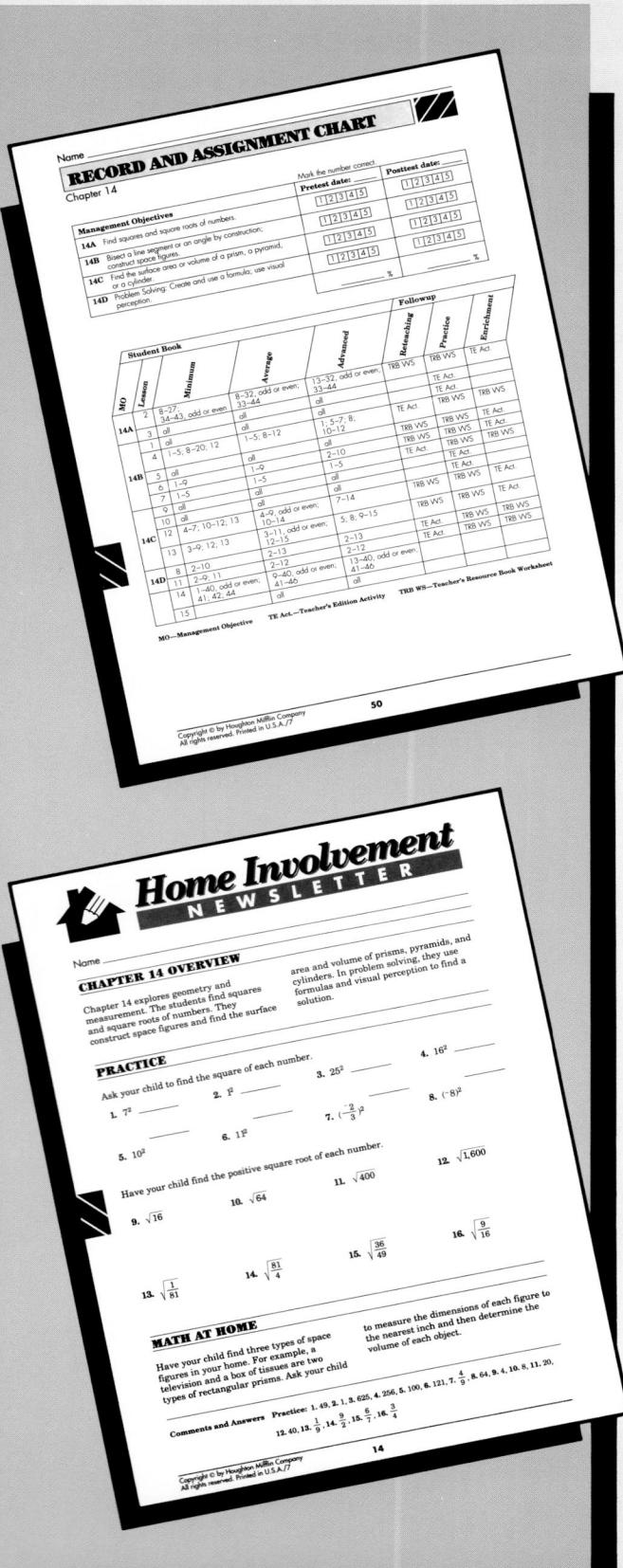

This chapter involves space figures, surface area, and volume. It focuses on finding squares and square roots; exploring the Pythagorean theorem; constructing arcs, perpendicular lines, line and angle bisectors, triangles, and several Platonic solids; exploring surface area relations; and finding volumes of prisms, pyramids, and cylinders. Problem solving is extended to include the strategy of creating and using a formula to solve a problem and using visual perception.

Management Objectives

14A Find squares and square roots of numbers.
14B Bisect a line segment or an angle by construction; construct space figures.
14C Find the surface area or volume of a prism, a pyramid, or a cylinder.
14D Problem Solving: Create and use a formula. Use visual perception.

Assignments for different achievement levels are provided on the Record and Assignment Chart in the Teacher's Resource Book.

Vocabulary

square, page 452
square root, page 452
hypotenuse, page 452
legs, page 454
Pythagorean theorem, page 455
bisect, page 458
side-by-side rule (SSS), page 460
cube, page 462
space figures, page 462
solid, Platonic solids, page 462

edge, vertexes, page 462
prisms, page 468
surface area, page 468
pyramid, page 469
sphere, page 470
cylinder, page 470
cone, page 470
cross section, page 472
volume, page 474

Home Involvement

As you begin to teach this chapter, give each student a copy of the Home Involvement Newsletter for this chapter.

This newsletter provides parents with
■ an overview of the chapter
■ suggestions for practicing some of the skills in the chapter
■ an at-home activity to do with their child, applying the skills taught in the chapter.

Management Chart

Management Objectives	Lesson/ Pages	Student Not Successful	Student Needs More Practice	Student Successful	Pacing Range
14A Find squares and square roots of numbers.	14-2/452-453	TRB/RW 14-2	TRB/PW 14-2 MAC 8 Activity 13A	TE/EA 14-2 MAC 8 Activity 13A	3 days
	14-3/454-455			TE/CA 14-3	
14B Bisect a line segment or an angle by construction; construct space figures.	14-1/450-451			TE/CA 14-1	5-6 days
	14-4/456-457	TE/RA 14-4	TRB/PW 14-4 MAC 7 Activities 12, 13	TRB/EW 14-4 MAC 7 Activities 12, 13	
	14-5/458-459	TRB/RW 14-5	TRB/PW 14-5 MAC 7 Activity 12	TE/EA 14-5 MAC 7 Activity 12	
	14-6/500-501	TRB/RW 14-6	TRB/PW 14-6 MAC 8 Activity 12A	TE/EA 14-6 MAC 8 Activity 12A	
	14-7/502-503	TE/RA 14-7	TRB/PW 14-7	TRB/EW 14-7	
14C Find the surface area or volume of a prism, a pyramid, or a cylinder.	14-9/468-469			TE/CA 14-9	4-6 days
	14-10/470-471			TE/CA 14-10	
	14-12/474-475	TRB/RW 14-12 ED	TRB/PW 14-12 ED	TE/EA 14-12 ED	
	14-13/476-477	TRB/RW 14-13 ED	TRB/PW 14-13 ED	TE/RA 14-13 ED	
14D Problem Solving: Create and use a formula. Use visual perception.	14-8/466-467	TE/RA 14-8	TRB/PW 14-8	TRB/EW 14-8	2 days
	14-11/472-473	TE/RA 14-11	TRB/PW 14-11	TRB/EW 14-11	
Mixed Review	14-14/478-479				
Creative Problem Solving	14-15/480-481				
Chapter Checkups	464-465; 482-483				
Extra Practice	484				
Enrichment	485				
Cumulative Review/Problem Solving Review	486-487				
Technology	488				

TE = Teacher's Edition
TRB = Teacher's Resource Book
RW = Reteaching Worksheet
RA = Reteaching Activity
EA = Enrichment Activity
EW = Enrichment Worksheet
PW = Practice Worksheet
CA = Classroom Activity

*Other Available Items
MAC = Mathematics Activities Courseware
ED = EduCalc

Manipulative Planning Guide

This is a complete list of manipulatives and materials needed for Chapter 14.

Materials for Manipulatives	TE Activities (INTRODUCE)	Student Book Lesson
Teaching Aid 15*	Lessons 14-2, 14-3, 14-6	Lessons 14-9, 14-10
Calculator for each student		Lessons 14-2, 14-3
Math Connection Transparency		Lesson 14-2
Scissors	Lessons 14-3, 14-6, 14-8, 14-9, 14-10, 14-12	Lessons 14-7, 14-9, 14-10
Centimeter or inch ruler	Lessons 14-3, 14-15	Lessons 14-3, 14-15
Compass	Lessons 14-4, 14-5, 14-6	Lessons 14-4, 14-5, 14-6, 14-7, 14-10, 14-11
Straightedge	Lessons 14-5, 14-6	Lessons 14-4, 14-5, 14-6, 14-7, 14-9, 14-11
Chalkboard compass		Lessons 14-4, 14-5, 14-6
Construction paper or oaktag for each student		Lesson 14-7
Tape	Lessons 14-8, 14-9, 14-10, 14-12	Lessons 14-8, 14-10, 14-12
Teaching Aid 20* for each group	Lessons 14-8, 14-9, 14-12	
Teaching Aid 21*	Lessons 14-8, 14-9, 14-12	
Teaching Aid 22*	Lesson 14-10	
Teaching Aid 23* for each pair	Lesson 14-10	
Knife and orange	Lesson 14-11	
Rice or beans in a paper cup	Lesson 14-12	
Can or cylinder-shaped object	Lesson 14-13	

*Teaching Aids are found in the Teacher's Resource Book.

CONCRETE

Learning Stages

The concepts and skills in Chapter 14 are presented through these learning stages.

Using manipulatives and verbalizing about a concept. No symbols.

Teacher Edition Activities	Student Book
Lessons 14-4, 14-5, 14-6, 14-11	Lessons 14-4, 14-5, 14-6, 14-7

Enrichment	Reteaching	In the Houghton Mifflin Manipulative Kit?	In the Houghton Mifflin Overhead Kit?
			Yes
Lesson 14-2			Available separately
			Yes
Lessons 14-3, 14-10, 14-13			
Lesson 14-13	Lesson 14-4	Yes	
Lessons 14-5, 14-6	Lesson 14-4	Yes	
Lessons 14-5, 14-6			
Lesson 14-13			
Lesson 14-13			

CONNECTING

  ➡ 5¢ cm² ⅓

Making a connection between manipulatives and symbols.

Teacher Edition Activities	Student Book
Lessons 14-2, 14-3, 14-7, 14-8, 14-9, 14-10, 14-12, 14-13	Lessons 14-3, 14-5, 14-6, 14-9 through 14-12

SYMBOLIC

$.05 $A = 9\text{cm}^2$ $1 - \frac{2}{3} = \frac{1}{3}$

Using numbers or symbols. No manipulatives or pictures of manipulatives.

Teacher Edition Activities	Student Book
Lessons 14-1, 14-7, 14-11, 14-12	Lessons 14-1, 14-2, 14-8, 14-12, 14-13

CHAPTER 14

Additional Activities

COOPERATIVE LEARNING RESOURCE ACTIVITIES

Through cooperative learning activities, students learn by interacting with one another in small groups. These cooperative activities provide students with motivating settings for making connections, investigations, and problem solving situations.

The cooperative connections are interdisciplinary problem-solving projects. Each student has a particular job that helps lead the group to complete the project. For the cooperative investigations students work in pairs for investigations involving data collection and analysis. The cooperative problem solving activities encourage the sharing of ideas and information. Students work in groups of four to solve a problem. Students are each assigned a clue and work together to find a common solution.

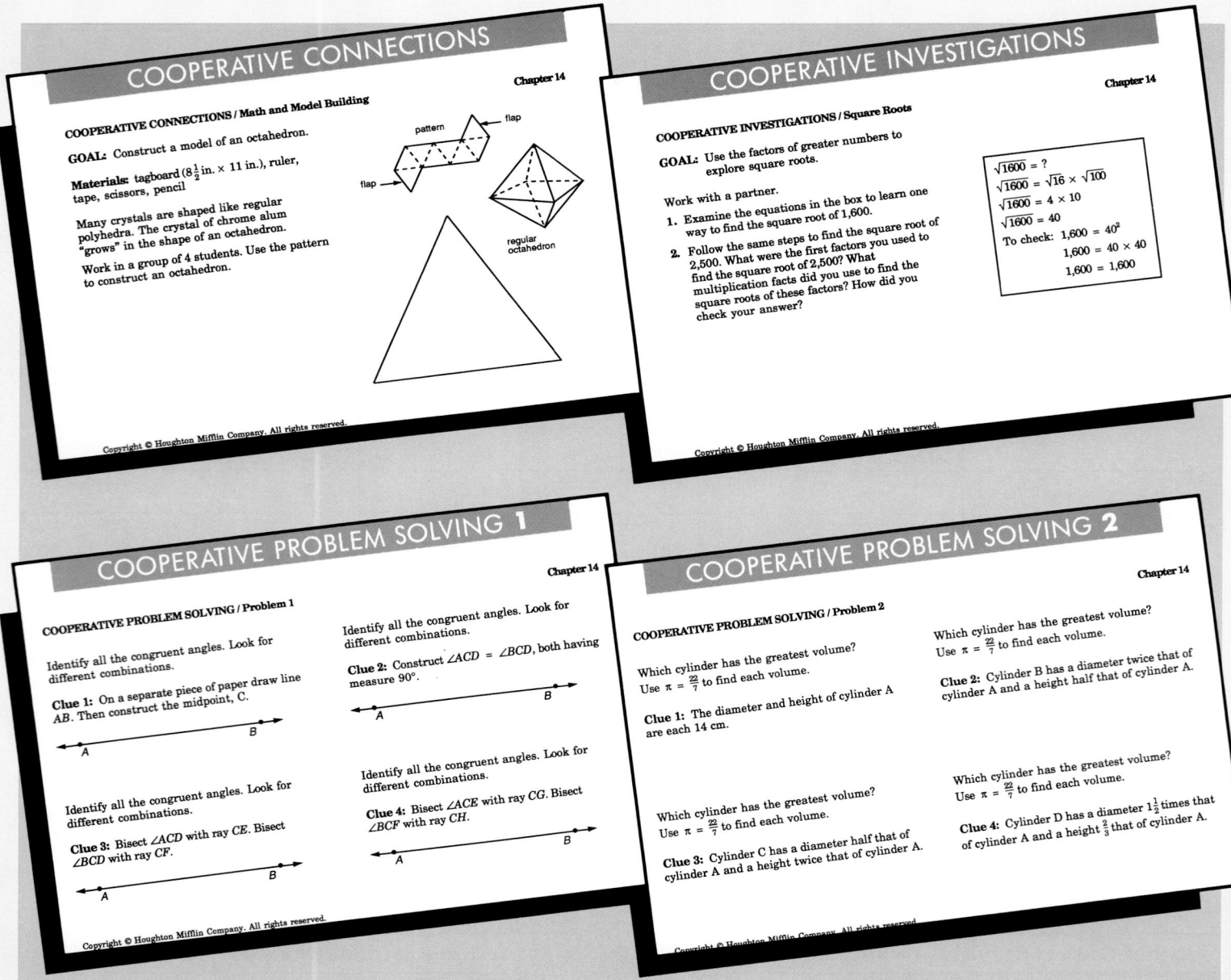

COOPERATIVE CONNECTIONS

COOPERATIVE CONNECTIONS / Math and Model Building

Chapter 14

GOAL: Construct a model of an octahedron.

Materials: tagboard ($8\frac{1}{2}$ in. × 11 in.), ruler, tape, scissors, pencil

Many crystals are shaped like regular polyhedra. The crystal of chrome alum "grows" in the shape of an octahedron.

Work in a group of 4 students. Use the pattern to construct an octahedron.

COOPERATIVE INVESTIGATIONS

COOPERATIVE INVESTIGATIONS / Square Roots

Chapter 14

GOAL: Use the factors of greater numbers to explore square roots.

Work with a partner.
1. Examine the equations in the box to learn one way to find the square root of 1,600.
2. Follow the same steps to find the square root of 2,500. What were the first factors you used to find the square root of 2,500? What multiplication facts did you use to find the square roots of these factors? How did you check your answer?

$$\sqrt{1600} = ?$$
$$\sqrt{1600} = \sqrt{16} \times \sqrt{100}$$
$$\sqrt{1600} = 4 \times 10$$
$$\sqrt{1600} = 40$$
To check: $1{,}600 = 40^2$
$1{,}600 = 40 \times 40$
$1{,}600 = 1{,}600$

COOPERATIVE PROBLEM SOLVING 1

COOPERATIVE PROBLEM SOLVING / Problem 1

Chapter 14

Identify all the congruent angles. Look for different combinations.

Clue 1: On a separate piece of paper draw line AB. Then construct the midpoint, C.

Identify all the congruent angles. Look for different combinations.

Clue 2: Construct ∠ACD = ∠BCD, both having measure 90°.

Identify all the congruent angles. Look for different combinations.

Clue 3: Bisect ∠ACD with ray CE. Bisect ∠BCD with ray CF.

Identify all the congruent angles. Look for different combinations.

Clue 4: Bisect ∠ACE with ray CG. Bisect ∠BCF with ray CH.

COOPERATIVE PROBLEM SOLVING 2

COOPERATIVE PROBLEM SOLVING / Problem 2

Chapter 14

Which cylinder has the greatest volume? Use $\pi = \frac{22}{7}$ to find each volume.

Clue 1: The diameter and height of cylinder A are each 14 cm.

Which cylinder has the greatest volume? Use $\pi = \frac{22}{7}$ to find each volume.

Clue 2: Cylinder B has a diameter twice that of cylinder A and a height half that of cylinder A.

Which cylinder has the greatest volume? Use $\pi = \frac{22}{7}$ to find each volume.

Clue 3: Cylinder C has a diameter half that of cylinder A and a height twice that of cylinder A.

Which cylinder has the greatest volume? Use $\pi = \frac{22}{7}$ to find each volume.

Clue 4: Cylinder D has a diameter $1\frac{1}{2}$ times that of cylinder A and a height $\frac{2}{3}$ that of cylinder A.

GAMES

SQUARE ROOT BINGO (For use after Lesson 14-2)

Objective: Find the square root of a perfect square.

☑ **MATERIALS CHECKLIST:** 16 index cards, 4 × 4 grid, game markers for each student

Write the squares of the numbers from 1 through 16 on the index cards. Ask students to write numbers from 1 through 16 randomly in the squares on their grids without repeating any number. Students will use grids and markers in a game of bingo.

To begin the game, mix the cards and place them face down in a pile. Choose the top card, and write the perfect square found on the card, say 225, on the chalkboard. Students should cover the corresponding square root, 15, with a marker. Repeat with the next square. The first player to cover four square roots across, down, or on a diagonal is the winner.

VOLUME CHALLENGE (For use after Lesson 14-13)

Objective: Find the volume of a prism and cylinder.

☑ **MATERIALS CHECKLIST:** four different-sized rectangular prisms, four different-sized cylinders, centimeter ruler

Arrange four seats in the front of the classroom, and select four class members as the first contestants in the game. Remind each to bring paper and pencil. Give contestants the first prism or cylinder, and ask each to write an estimate of the volume in cubic centimeters. At the same time, the members of the audience also write their estimates on paper.

When you signal, the contestants announce their estimates, which you record on the chalkboard. Then give the contestants a ruler, and ask them to measure the container, announce the measurements, and calculate the volume. Students in the audience also perform the computation. The contestant whose estimate was closest to the calculated volume plays in the next round with three new contestants.

BULLETIN BOARD

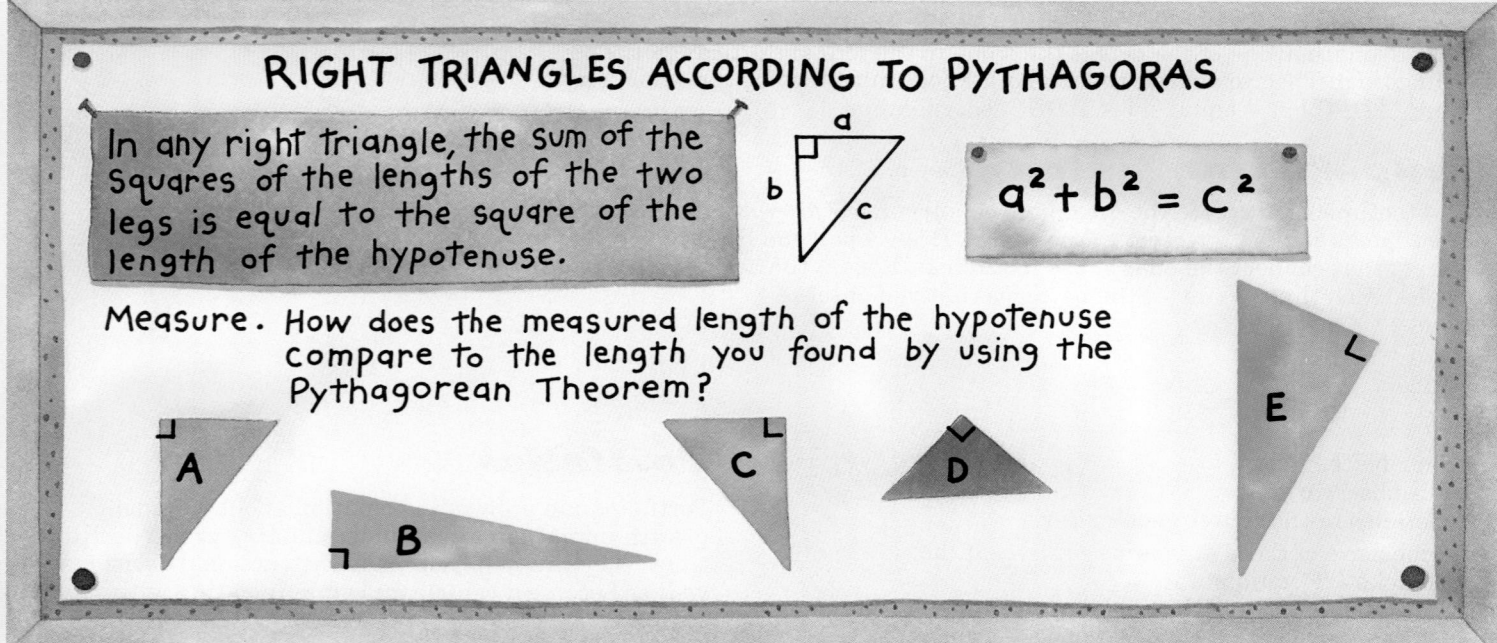

Prepare a display of the Pythagorean Theorem similar to that shown above. Cut out and display right triangles whose legs have lengths that are whole number centimeters. Hang the triangles with pushpins or thumbtacks so that students can easily remove the triangles. First have students measure only the legs of the triangles and use the Pythagorean Theorem to find the length of the hypotenuse. Then they can check their result by measuring the hypotenuse.

CHAPTER 14

Alternative Assessment

In addition to the paper and pencil tests available with this program, the following items can help you assess critical thinking as well as your students' ability to solve problems in a wide variety of ways.

Open-ended Problem

Use the steps to construct a perpendicular.
1. Draw a circle with center P.
2. Draw diameter $\overline{AB}$.
3. With the compass opening larger than the length from P to B, place the compass point at A. Strike two marks, one above and one below the circle.
4. With the same compass opening, repeat at B so that the marks intersect. Label the points where they intersect C and D.
5. Draw $\overleftrightarrow{CD}$.

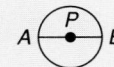
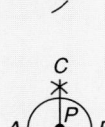

Now join the points to draw $\overline{AC}$, $\overline{BC}$, $\overline{AD}$, and $\overline{BD}$.
Describe the triangles and the relationship of their sides.

Teacher Notes
Possible responses:
• Triangles CDA and CDB are isosceles because $\overline{AC} \cong \overline{AD}$, and $\overline{BC} \cong \overline{BD}$.
• Triangles ABC and ABD are isosceles because $\overline{AC} \cong \overline{BC}$ and $\overline{AD} \cong \overline{BD}$.
• $\triangle CDA \cong \triangle CDB$ and $\triangle ABC \cong \triangle ABD$ because the three sides of one triangle are congruent to the three sides of the other triangle.
• Triangles APC, BPC, APD, and BPD are right triangles because $\overline{AB}$ and $\overleftrightarrow{CD}$ are perpendicular.
• $\triangle APC \cong \triangle BPC \cong BPD \cong \triangle APD$ because the three sides of each triangle are congruent to the three sides of the other triangles. (The length of the hypotenuse is the same and the length of one of the legs is the same in the four right triangles. The Pythagorean Theorem shows that the other legs must also be the same length.)
• Figure $ADBC$ has 4 equal sides. $ADBC$ is a rhombus.

Group Writing Activity (See p. T24.)

Use 14 toothpicks to create the diagonals of polygons. Start with 2 toothpicks. Place the toothpicks so they intersect at the center. Draw a polygon by drawing the line segments that connect the ends of the toothpicks. Repeat the activity adding one toothpick each time. Write all the patterns that you observe.
Example:

Teacher Notes
Possible observations:
• The angles in the center get smaller.
• The measure of those angles $= \dfrac{360°}{\# \text{ of sides}}$ if the toothpicks are equidistant.
• The number of sides of the polygons increases by 2.
• The number of sides of the polygons is 2 times the number of toothpicks.
• The area increases from one polygon to the next.
• If you could use an infinite number of toothpicks you would get a circle with radius $= \frac{1}{2}$ toothpick.

Individual Writing Activity

Explain how observing patterns could be a helpful skill.

Portfolios

Portfolios can provide information about a student's growth in mathematical understanding over a period of time. They can help you make instructional decisions as well as become a vehicle for communicating with parents. The students' work involving the open-ended problem and writing activity suggested on this page along with the Critical Thinking feature on page 453, the Create Your Own exercise on page 463, the In Your Words exercise on page 469, the Learning Log exercises on pages 465 and 483, and the Creative Problem Solving lesson on pages 480-481 could be included in portfolios.

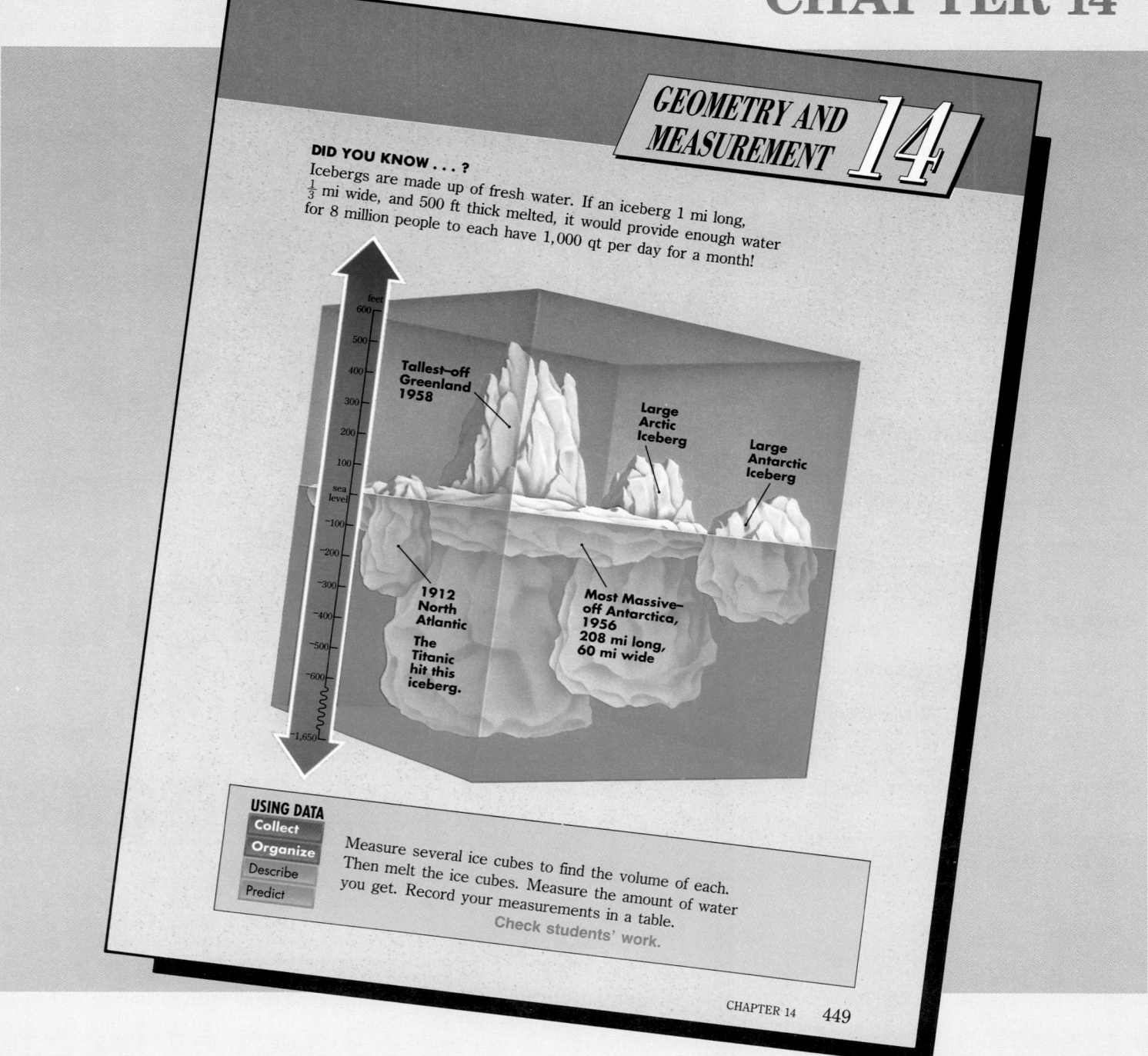

GEOMETRY AND
MEASUREMENT 14

DID YOU KNOW . . . ?

Icebergs are made up of fresh water. If an iceberg 1 mi long, $\frac{1}{3}$ mi wide, and 500 ft thick melted, it would provide enough water for 8 million people to each have 1,000 qt per day for a month!

Tallest–off
Greenland
1958

Large
Arctic
Iceberg

Large
Antarctic
Iceberg

1912
North
Atlantic

The
Titanic
hit this
iceberg.

Most Massive–
off Antarctica,
1956
208 mi long,
60 mi wide

USING DATA
Collect
Organize
Describe
Predict

Measure several ice cubes to find the volume of each. Then melt the ice cubes. Measure the amount of water you get. Record your measurements in a table.
Check students' work.

CHAPTER 14   449

Using the Chapter Opener

The purpose of this page is to involve students in the use of real data much like that presented in newspapers and magazines.

To use this page as you begin the chapter, direct students' attention to the data. You may wish to ask questions such as the following:

Calculate about how many gallons of water in all would be provided by the melted iceberg described in the first paragraph. Use 30 days for 1 month. *(about 60 billion gal)*

What was the approximate total height of the tallest iceberg sighted in 1958 off Greenland? *(about 2,000 ft)*

How does the area of the top surface of the massive iceberg observed off Antarctica in 1956 compare with the area of the state of West Virginia, which is 24,181 mi²? *(about half the area of West Virginia)*

Lesson Organizer

Objective: Discuss geometry in the world around us.

Prior Knowledge: Students should understand rotations and symmetry.

Lesson Resources:
Class Activity 14-1
Daily Review 14-1
Cooperative Connections, Chapter 14

Two-Minute Math

If you rotate around a point and stop at every 45°, how many stops will you make if the last stop returns you to the original position? *(8)* If you stop at every 20°? *(18)*

1 INTRODUCE

Have students look at the pictures of the pottery on pages 450–451. Explain that today we have many reproductions of original works of art that were created centuries ago.

Has anyone ever seen pottery being made?

Does anyone have dishes at home that look like the pieces in the book?

WHEN YOUR STUDENTS ASK
★ WHY AM I LEARNING THIS? ★

Artists use geometry to create shapes. An old saying by artists is that "Form follows function." The form refers to the shape. The shape helps create the beauty of the piece of art.

LET'S TALK
MATH

Shaping Our World

Geometry Around Us

▢ READ ABOUT IT

The influence of the Chinese and the Japanese on the art of Europe and other parts of the world came about in part through the trade of cobalt blue and white pottery.

Japanese dish, Late 17th century

Chinese vase, Early 15th century

Pottery can be built up by hand, made from molds, or thrown (formed) on a pottery wheel. Master craftspeople throw clay into cylinders or other round pots on a rotating pottery wheel. The artist begins with a piece of clay, exerts the right amount of pressure, and forms the shape.

Chinese vase, Middle 14th century

MULTICULTURAL NOTE

Porcelain, the hardest ceramic product, is often called *china* because it was first made in China. The Chinese learned to make it during the T'ang dynasty (618–907). Since the 1600s, many other countries have developed ways of making porcelain in their own styles.

2 TEACH

READ ABOUT IT　Have students read about the influence of Chinese and Japanese art on European art. Tell them that they will use this information as they do the next page.

TALK ABOUT IT　**How is the Japanese dish on page 450 different from the one on page 451?** *(Possible answer: six versus five rotations; center design with line symmetry versus no line symmetry.)*

Why do you think there are more rotations than line symmetries? *(The shapes of the objects are circular; circles lend themselves to rotations.)*

WRITE ABOUT IT　Have students complete Exercises 6–9 independently, then compare and discuss their explanations.

SUMMARIZE/ASSESS　**Explain some ways that these artists used geometry.** *(Possible answers: Shapes are circular; rotations and line symmetry were used for designs; potter wheels form cylindrical shapes; slabs resemble prisms.)*

7. Chinese vase, Middle 14th century; accept reasonable explanations.

▣ TALK ABOUT IT

1. Designs on many early works of art did not follow the shape, or contour, of the potteries. Which piece of art on these pages shows this kind of design?
   Chinese vase; Middle 14th century

2. Repeated designs can be created by rotations. The dish at right has five equally spaced designs made from rotations. What is the measure of the angle of rotation?   72°

3. Discuss the rotations and angles of rotation on the Japanese dish on page 450.   Border stripes rotate 60°; border designs rotate 120°.

4. Are there repeated designs or rotations on the vases? Discuss them. See page 483b.

5. Do you see any line symmetry on the dishes? Explain.   yes; Answers will vary. Suggestions given: outline of coat of arms, bands in borders.

Chelsea plate
Middle 18ᵗʰ century

▣ WRITE ABOUT IT

Use the three vases on pages 450 and 451 as examples.

6. Which vases were thrown on a wheel?   the first two

7. Which vase was probably made by combining different parts, each thrown on a wheel? Explain.   See above.

8. Which vase was made from several flat slabs like prisms? Explain.   the Dutch tulip vase; flat faces

9. Do you see any Asian influences in the Dutch tulip vase? Explain.   yes; Accept reasonable answers. Suggestions given: the feet, the decorative designs.

Dutch Tulip vase,
Late 17ᵗʰ century

CHAPTER 14   451

---

3 FOLLOW-UP

CLASS ACTIVITY 14-1

Take the students on a walking tour of the school and school property. Encourage them to find designs made by the repetition of one or more figures. Examples might include patterned floor tiles, lines on the gym floor, or the spots on a ladybug's wings. Have them sketch the designs along the way and indicate their locations. In the classroom, have the students examine their sketches and tell whether the design could be made by rotating, reflecting, or translating a figure. Also have them find any lines of symmetry. Have students share their work with the rest of the class.

MEETING INDIVIDUAL NEEDS

For Students Who Are . . .

Acquiring English Proficiency Pair students with an English-proficient student to write responses to the Write About It questions.

Gifted and Talented Have students find pictures of other examples of repeated designs or rotations on pieces of art.

Today's Problem

A soccer ball is made from a pattern of two different regular polygons sewn together. Study the picture and identify these two polygons. *(hexagons and pentagons)*

Lesson Organizer

Objective: Find squares and square roots of numbers.

Prior Knowledge: Students should know how to multiply whole numbers and decimals.

Error Analysis and Remediation: See page 483A.

Lesson Resources:
Practice Worksheet 14-2
Reteaching Worksheet 14-2
Enrichment Activity 14-2
Daily Review 14-2

Two-Minute Math

What number multiplied by itself results in each product?
49 *(7)*   81 *(9)*   100 *(10)*
36 *(6)*   16 *(4)*   121 *(11)*

1 INTRODUCE

CONNECTING ACTIVITY

☑ **MATERIALS CHECKLIST:** Teaching Aid 15 (Centimeter Grid Paper), 3 for each student

Have students draw a 9-cm square on the grid paper. **What is the area of this square?** *(81 cm²)* **If you did not count squares, how could you determine the area?** *(9 × 9 = 81)*

What is the length of each side of a square that has an area of 64 cm². **Expain how you know.** *(Possible answer: All sides of a square are the same length; they must be 8 cm because 8 × 8 is 64.)* Have students check their answer by drawing a square with a side of 8 cm.

WHEN YOUR STUDENTS ASK
★ WHY AM I LEARNING THIS? ★

You can connect this skill to real life through surveying. A surveyor needs to determine the relationships between different dimensions of a yard or field.

Squares and Square Roots

In ancient times, people used geometry to understand numbers. You can, too, by making a **MATH CONNECTION**

What is the area of the square at right? **9**

What is 3^2? **9**

How does 3^2 relate to the length of a side and the area of the square? **They are the same.**

The **square** of any number is that number multiplied by itself. $3^2 = 3 \times 3 = 9$
You read: *The square of 3, or 3 squared, is 3 times 3, or 9.*

If you know that the area of a square is 9 cm², then each side is 3 cm. Similarly, if you know that 9 is the square of a number, then 3 is the number because $3^2 = 9$.

The symbol for a positive square root is $\sqrt{}$. You write $\sqrt{9} = 3$. You read: *The positive square root of 9 is 3.*

THINK ALOUD Remember what you learned about multiplying integers. What is $^-3 \times {}^-3$, or $(^-3)^2$? Is $^-3$ also a square root of 9? **9; yes**

CALCULATOR Other examples:

$29^2 = 841$ $\sqrt{55,696} = 236$

$30^2 = 900$ $\sqrt{56,169} = 237$

Estimate, then find 29.2^2.   Estimate, then find $\sqrt{56,000}$.
900; 852.64   **240; 236.643**

■ **GUIDED PRACTICE** ■

Read the exercise aloud. Then explain how to find the square or square root, and tell what it is.

1. 6^2 **36**   **2.** 4.1^2 **16.81**   **3.** $\sqrt{16}$ **4**   **4.** $\sqrt{\frac{4}{9}}$ **$\frac{2}{3}$**   **5.** $\sqrt{\frac{36}{9}}$ **2**   **6.** $\left(\frac{1}{3}\right)^2$ **$\frac{1}{9}$**

7. What solutions does $x^2 = 25$ have? What is the positive value of x?   **5; −5; 5**

Calculators should be available for tedious calculations.

2 TEACH

☑ **MATERIALS CHECKLIST:** Math Connection Transparency; calculators

Display the transparency. Have students fill in the spaces and discuss the math connection.

How many square roots does 25 have? What are they? *(2; 5, −5)* **100?** *(2; 10, −10)* **0?** *(1; 0)*

Is the square root of 17 closer to 4 or 5? How do you know? *(4; because $4^2 = 16$ and $5^2 = 25$, and 17 is closer to 16 than it is to 25.)*

> **Chalkboard Examples**
> $37^2 = (1,369)$ $18^2 = (324)$
> $24^2 = (576)$ $\sqrt{169} = (13)$
> $\sqrt{225} = (15)$
> $\sqrt{10,000} = (100)$

SUMMARIZE/ASSESS **Explain how to find the square and square root of a number.** *(Multiply a number by itself; find the number that when multiplied by itself gives that number.)*

Find the square of the number.

8. 9^2 81   **9.** 1^2 1   **10.** 10^2 100   **11.** 0^2 0   **12.** 12^2 144

13. $(^-2)^2$ 4   **14.** $\left(\frac{1}{2}\right)^2$ $\frac{1}{4}$ **15.** $\left(\frac{1}{10}\right)^2$ $\frac{1}{100}$ **16.** $(^-5)^2$ 25   **17.** 25^2 625

Find the positive square root of each number.

18. $\sqrt{25}$ 5   **19.** $\sqrt{36}$ 6   **20.** $\sqrt{0}$ 0   **21.** $\sqrt{100}$ 10   **22.** $\sqrt{121}$ 11

23. $\sqrt{225}$ 15   **24.** $\sqrt{81}$ 9   **25.** $\sqrt{1}$ 1   **26.** $\sqrt{900}$ 30   **27.** $\sqrt{49}$ 7

28. $\sqrt{\frac{4}{16}}$ $\frac{1}{2}$ **29.** $\sqrt{\frac{1}{4}}$ $\frac{1}{2}$ **30.** $\sqrt{\frac{1}{25}}$ $\frac{1}{5}$ **31.** $\sqrt{\frac{49}{81}}$ $\frac{7}{9}$ **32.** $\sqrt{\frac{64}{9}}$ $\frac{8}{3}$

33. a. Write the squares of each whole number from 1 to 10.
    1; 4; 9; 16; 25; 36; 49; 64; 81; 100
  b. Write the numbers whose square roots are the whole
    numbers from 1 to 10. What do you observe?
    1; 4; 9; 16; 25; 36; 49; 64; 81; 100; same list

CALCULATOR Find a number with a square between
the given numbers. **Answers will vary. Suggestions given.**

34. 6 and 7 **2.5**   **35.** 9,000 and 10,000 **95**   **36.** 0.1 and 0.2 **0.4**

37. 600 and 700 **26**   **38.** 90 and 100 **9.7**   **39.** 0.7 and 0.8 **0.85**

Use = or ≠ to make *true* sentences.

40. $5^2 \times 7^2$ ▦ $(5 \times 7)^2$ =   **41.** $5^2 + 7^2$ ▦ $(5 + 7)^2$ ≠

42. $8^2 \times 9^2$ ▦ $(8 \times 9)^2$ =   **43.** $8^2 + 9^2$ ▦ $(8 + 9)^2$ ≠

44. CREATE YOUR OWN Create and solve other examples like those
  in Exercises 40–43. What conclusions can you reach?
  Check students' work.

Critical Thinking

Work with a partner. The figures below show that 1, 4, and 9
are square numbers. Find the next three square numbers. **16; 25; 36**

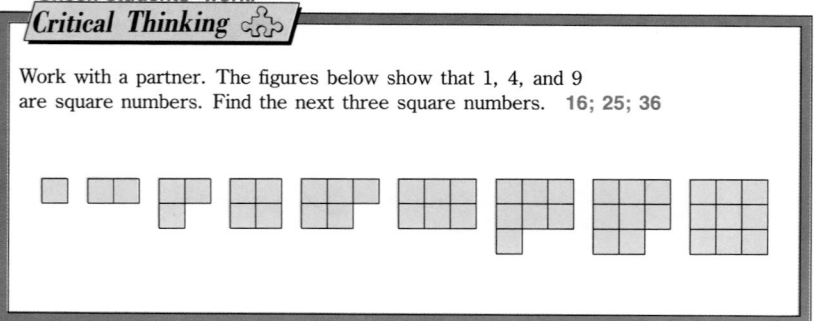

CHAPTER 14   453

MEETING INDIVIDUAL NEEDS

For Students Who Are . . .

Acquiring English Proficiency Discuss the meanings of *symbol,
area, observe, conclusion,* and *figures.*

Gifted and Talented Have students make up a word problem to go
with one of the Exercises 8–12.

Working 2 or 3 Grades Below Level Have students draw squares
to find the answers to Exercises 8–12.

Today's Problem

What is the approximate area of a washer with an outside radius of
2 in. and an inside radius of 1 in.? *(The answer is the difference of
the areas of the two circles: $2 \times 2\pi - 1 \times 1\pi = 3\pi$; about 9.4 in.²)*

3 FOLLOW-UP

PRACTICE 14-2

Find the square of the number.
1. 7^2 _49_   2. 2^2 _4_   3. 11^2 _121_   4. 6^2 _36_
5. $(^-3)^2$ _9_   6. $(\frac{1}{4})^2$ _$\frac{1}{16}$_   7. $(^-8)^2$ _64_   8. 30^2 _900_
Find the positive square root of each number.
9. $\sqrt{64}$ _8_   10. $\sqrt{4}$ _2_   11. $\sqrt{9}$ _3_   12. $\sqrt{196}$ _14_
13. $\sqrt{289}$ _17_   14. $\sqrt{256}$ _16_   15. $\sqrt{400}$ _20_   16. $\sqrt{\frac{4}{9}}$ _$\frac{2}{3}$_
17. $\sqrt{\frac{1}{49}}$ _$\frac{1}{7}$_   18. $\sqrt{\frac{9}{36}}$ _$\frac{1}{2}$_   19. $\sqrt{\frac{25}{100}}$ _$\frac{5}{10}$_   20. $\sqrt{\frac{81}{16}}$ _$\frac{9}{4}$_
Use = or ≠ to make *true* sentences.
21. $2^2 \times 11^2$ ≠ $(2 + 11)^2$ 22. $(6 + 12)^2$ ≠ $6^2 + 12^2$
23. $3^2 \times 7^2$ = $(3 \times 7)^2$ 24. $4^2 + 8^2$ ≠ $(4 + 8)^2$
Solve.
25. Barbara and Bob bought a square piece of land that is 410 ft on a side. How many square feet is this land? _168,100 ft²_
26. The floor of Barbara and Bob's square living room measures 484 ft². What are the dimensions of the room? _Each side measures 22 ft._

RETEACHING 14-2

You can **square** a number by multiplying the number by itself.

Example 1: Find 2^2.   Example 2: Find $(^-5)^2$.   Example 3: Find $\left(\frac{3}{5}\right)^2$.
$2^2 = 2 \times 2$ $(^-5)^2 = ^-5 \times ^-5$ $\left(\frac{3}{5}\right)^2 = \frac{3}{5} \times \frac{3}{5}$
  $= 4$ $= 25$ $= \frac{9}{25}$
Find the square of the number.
1. $6^2 =$ _36_   2. $11^2 =$ _121_   3. $1.2^2 =$ _1.44_
4. $\left(\frac{1}{4}\right)^2 =$ _$\frac{1}{16}$_   5. $15^2 =$ _225_   6. $7.3^2 =$ _53.29_
7. $18^2 =$ _324_   8. $100^2 =$ _10,000_   9. $(^-4)^2 =$ _16_
10. $21^2 =$ _441_   11. $8.6^2 =$ _73.96_   12. $50^2 =$ _2,500_
13. $(^-8)^2 =$ _64_   14. $16^2 =$ _256_   15. $\left(\frac{2}{7}\right)^2 =$ _$\frac{4}{49}$_

You can find the **square root** of a given number by finding a number
that, when multiplied by itself, produces the given number. The
symbol for a positive square root is $\sqrt{\ }$.

Example 1: Find $\sqrt{16}$.   Example 2: Find $\sqrt{\frac{9}{16}}$.
Think: $4 \times 4 = 16$ Think: $\frac{3}{4} \times \frac{3}{4} = \frac{9}{16}$
  $\sqrt{16} = 4$ $\sqrt{\frac{9}{16}} = \frac{3}{4}$
Find the positive square root of the number.
16. $\sqrt{64} =$ _8_   17. $\sqrt{169} =$ _13_   18. $\sqrt{\frac{1}{16}} =$ _$\frac{1}{4}$_   19. $\sqrt{441} =$ _21_
20. $\sqrt{\frac{4}{25}} =$ _$\frac{2}{5}$_   21. $\sqrt{144} =$ _12_   22. $\sqrt{576} =$ _24_   23. $\sqrt{\frac{9}{49}} =$ _$\frac{3}{7}$_
24. $\sqrt{256} =$ _16_   25. $\sqrt{676} =$ _26_   26. $\sqrt{324} =$ _18_   27. $\sqrt{\frac{36}{25}} =$ _$\frac{6}{5}$_

ENRICHMENT 14-2

☑ **MATERIALS CHECKLIST:** Calculators

Have the students work in pairs. Ask:
What is the area of a square with a 4-in.
side? [16 in.²] a 3-in. side? [9 in.²] What do
you know about a 15-in.² square? [each
side is between 3 in. and 4 in. long] One
partner adds 3 and 4 and divides by 2 to
get the first estimate of $\sqrt{15}$. [3.5] The
other partner divides 15 by this result.
[about 4.3] The first partner adds the quotient rounded to the nearest tenth to the
first estimate of $\sqrt{15}$ and divides by 2 to
get the second estimate of $\sqrt{15}$. [about
3.9] The students continue in the same
manner to get a third estimate. [15 ÷
3.9 = 3.85; (3.9 + 3.9) ÷ 2 = 3.9] Ask:
What is $\sqrt{15}$? [about 3.9]

LESSON 14-3

Lesson Organizer

Objective: Explore the Pythagorean Theorem.

Prior Knowledge: Students should be able to find squares of numbers and know the meaning of a right triangle.

Lesson Resources:
Class Activity 14-3
Daily Review 14-3

Two-Minute Math

Find the square.
14 *(196)*   22 *(484)*   16 *(256)*
35 *(1,225)*   47 *(2,209)*

1 PREPARE

CONNECTING ACTIVITY

☑ **MATERIALS CHECKLIST:** Teaching Aid 15 (Centimeter Grid Paper), 5 per group; scissors and cm ruler for each group

Assign students to work in groups of three or four. Have each group prepare the following materials from the grid paper:

- four strips that are 3 cm, 4 cm, 5 cm, and 6 cm long

- eight squares with sides of these lengths: 3 cm, 4 cm, 5 cm, 8 cm, 10 cm, 12 cm, and 13 cm

---

WHEN YOUR STUDENTS ASK
★ **WHY AM I LEARNING THIS?** ★

You can connect this skill to real life through carpentry. A carpenter can measure the lengths of two sides of a triangle to find the length of the third side.

EXPLORE

Exploring the Pythagorean Theorem

Early Egyptian surveyors were called *harpedonaptai,* or "rope stretchers." They used ropes with 12 equally spaced knots to make right angles when they were laying out the boundaries of pieces of land.

THINK ALOUD Why are right angles important in surveying land?

Use centimeter graph paper, scissors, and a centimeter ruler.

1. Cut strips of paper of four different lengths: 3 cm, 4 cm, 5 cm, and 6 cm. Which three can be put together to form a right triangle?

2. In a right triangle, the side opposite the right angle is called the **hypotenuse**. The other sides are called **legs**.
   a. How long is the hypotenuse of your right triangle?
   b. How long are the legs?

3. Cut out eight squares with sides of the following lengths: 3 cm, 4 cm, 5 cm, 6 cm, 8 cm, 10 cm, 12 cm, and 13 cm. On each square, mark the length of one side and mark the area of the square.

4. Experiment to see how many ways you can arrange three of your squares to make a right triangle as shown.

List the lengths of sides and areas of squares that can be arranged to form right triangles.

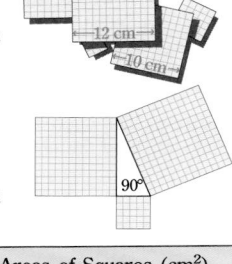

The tomb of Ramses IX of Egypt, built about 1140 B.C. near Thebes. It shows a 3-4-5 right triangle.

	Lengths of Sides (cm)	Areas of Squares (cm²)
Triangle 1		
Triangle 2		
Triangle 3		

MATH HISTORY

454   LESSON 14-3

---

2 EXPLORE

☑ **MATERIALS CHECKLIST:** strips of paper and squares from Prepare section; calculators

Have students continue working in their groups.

For Exercise 4, make sure students are placing squares correctly to form right triangles. Tell students to discount triangles that do not form right triangles.

How do you know that a triangle with sides 15 in., 20 in., and 25 in. is a right triangle? *($15^2 + 20^2 = 625$; the square root of 625 is 25.)*

SUMMARIZE/ASSESS   **What does the Pythagorean theorem state?** *(In a right triangle the square of the length of the hypotenuse equals the sum of the square of the lengths of the legs.)*

5. Make a list of some squares that form triangles that are not right triangles.   **Answers will vary. Suggestion given.**

	Lengths of Sides (cm)	Areas of Squares (cm²)
Triangle 1	3, 4, 6	9, 16, 36
Triangle 2		
Triangle 3		

6. Look at your lists from Exercises 4 and 5. Can you discover any relationships between the areas? (*Hint*: Think about adding squares on the legs and comparing the sums of their areas with the area of a square added on the hypotenuse.)   **the sum of the areas of squares on the legs = area of square on hypotenuse**

7. If you did not discover a relationship in Exercise 6, work through this example.

area of square on hypotenuse	$(5 \text{ cm})^2 \longrightarrow 25 \text{ cm}^2$
area of square on one leg	$(3 \text{ cm})^2 \longrightarrow 9 \text{ cm}^2$
area of square on other leg	$(4 \text{ cm})^2 \longrightarrow 16 \text{ cm}^2$

Notice that $25 \text{ cm}^2 = 9 \text{ cm}^2 + 16 \text{ cm}^2$.

The relationship in Exercises 6 and 7 is known as the **Pythagorean Theorem.** It was named for Pythagoras, a Greek mathematician who studied in Babylonia, Egypt, and Italy about 2,500 y ago.

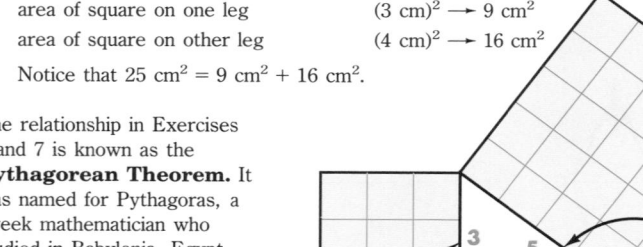

The Pythagorean Theorem states that for a right triangle, the square of the length of the hypotenuse equals the sum of the squares of the lengths of the legs.

8. Look at your lists from Exercises 4 and 5. Does the Pythagorean Theorem work for right triangles? for other triangles?
yes; no

9. **CALCULATOR**   Is a triangle with sides of these lengths a right triangle?

   a. 7 cm, 24 cm, 25 cm **yes b.** 8 cm, 11 cm, 14 cm **no**

CLASS ACTIVITY **14-3**

☑ **MATERIALS CHECKLIST:** Drinking straws, metric rulers, scissors

Provide pairs of students with long drinking straws and ask them to cut the straws into these lengths: 13 cm, 6 cm, 4 cm, 15 cm, 10 cm, 3 cm, 5 cm, 9 cm, 8 cm, and 12 cm. Remind students that in a right triangle the sum of the squares of the lengths of the legs equals the square of the hypotenuse. Ask each pair to create four right triangles with the straw lengths and to record the lengths. Tell them that they may use a straw length in more than one right triangle. [3 cm, 4 cm, 5 cm; 6 cm, 8 cm, 10 cm; 9 cm, 12 cm, 15 cm; 5 cm, 12 cm, 13 cm]

MEETING INDIVIDUAL NEEDS

For Students Who Are . . .

Acquiring English Proficiency   Review the meaning of *right angle* and *right triangle*.

Gifted and Talented   Have students draw a right triangle with legs 5 cm and 12 cm on grid paper. Have them draw the squares on the legs and then cut out the square to fit on the hypotenuse.

Working 2 or 3 Grades Below Level   Have students practice naming the sides opposite given angles and angles opposite given sides of different right triangles.

Today's Problem

When you draw a line segment connecting the upper-lefthand corner of a square to the midpoint of the base of the square and draw a diagonal from the same corner, three triangles are formed. Compare the areas of these triangles. *(All three triangles have the same height. The bases of the two small triangles are equal. The base of the large triangle is twice that of the small triangles. Therefore, the areas are in a proportion of 1:1:2.)*

Lesson Organizer

Objective: Construct an arc and perpendicular lines with a compass and straightedge.

Prior Knowledge: Students should know how to use a compass to draw a circle and know the meaning of *center, radius,* and *perpendicular lines.*

Error Analysis and Remediation: See page 483A.

Lesson Resources:
Practice Worksheet 14-4
Reteaching Activity 14-4
Enrichment Worksheet 14-4
Daily Review 14-4
Cooperative Problem Solving 1, Chapter 14

Two-Minute Math

Find the diameter, given a radius of: 16 cm *(32 cm)*   25 cm *(50 cm)*

Find the radius, given a diameter of: 15 in. *(7.5 in.)*   1.5 in. *(0.75 in.)*

1 INTRODUCE

CONCRETE ACTIVITY

☑ **MATERIALS CHECKLIST:** compass for each pair

Have students work with a partner.

1. Have partners take turns constructing different-size circles using a compass.

2. Have each student draw two different-size circles that share the same center.

WHEN YOUR STUDENTS ASK
★ WHY AM I LEARNING THIS? ★

You can connect this skill to real life through graphic design. Graphic designers frequently construct circles when they create logos or designs for packaging.

Construction: Designs

Many designs can be made using only a compass and a straightedge. A straightedge is a ruler without numbers or units.

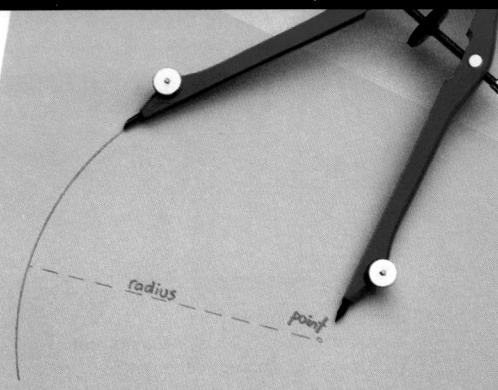

1. Practice the construction. Then use it for Exercises 2–7. **Check students' drawings.**

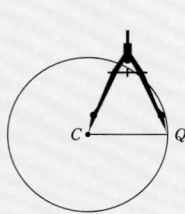

Construction: Arcs of a circle

Use a compass to draw a circle with center C and radius $\overline{CQ}$.	Do not change the compass opening. Place the compass point at Q. Strike a mark on the circle.	Place the compass point on the mark. Strike again. Repeat around the circle.

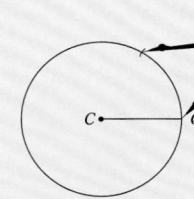

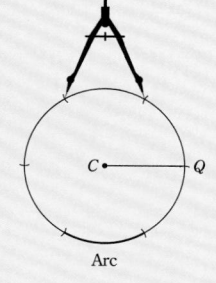

Arc

Use the construction above to make the figure. Then, construct the design or create a new one of your own.   **Check students' drawings.**

2. a regular hexagon   **3.** an equilateral triangle   **4.** a trapezoid

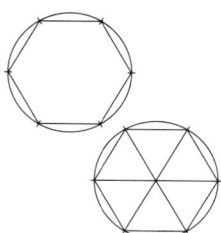

MATH AND ART

---

2 TEACH

☑ **MATERIALS CHECKLIST:** compass and straightedge for each student; chalkboard compass

In the first construction, into how many arcs did you divide the circle? *(6)* **What can you say about these arcs?** *(They are the same shape and size, or congruent.)*

In Exercise 8, what is meant by the statement, "$\overleftrightarrow{CD}$ and $\overline{AB}$ are perpendicular."? *(They meet at right angles.)*

Chalkboard Examples

Have volunteers use a chalkboard compass to construct: a circle with a radius of 1 ft; a circle with a diameter of $1\frac{1}{2}$ ft.

SUMMARIZE/ASSESS   **Explain how to draw a line perpendicular to a line segment.** *(Students should explain the steps for the second construction, page 457.)*

Construct the design. **Check students' drawings.**

5.
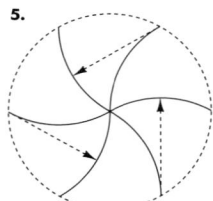

6.
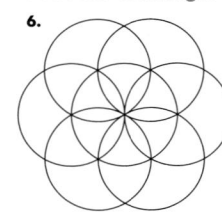

7.

8. Practice the construction. Then use it for Exercises 9–12. **Check students' drawings.**

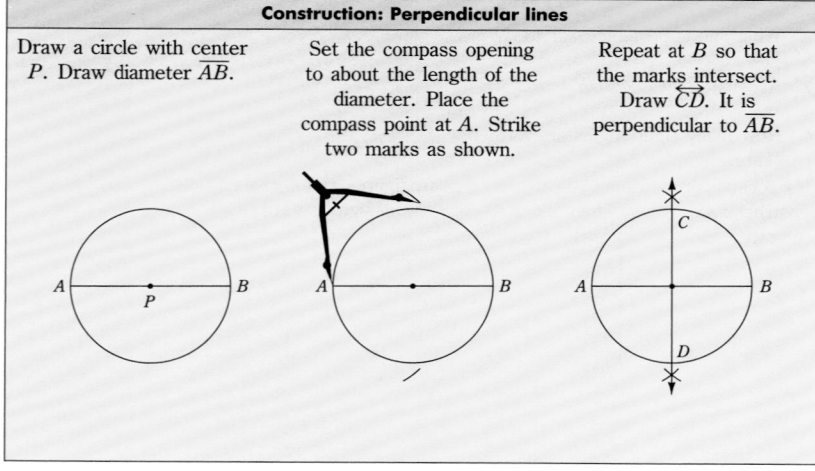

Construction: Perpendicular lines

Draw a circle with center P. Draw diameter $\overline{AB}$.

Set the compass opening to about the length of the diameter. Place the compass point at A. Strike two marks as shown.

Repeat at B so that the marks intersect. Draw $\overleftrightarrow{CD}$. It is perpendicular to $\overline{AB}$.

Construct the design. **Check students' drawings.**

9.
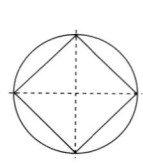

10.

11.
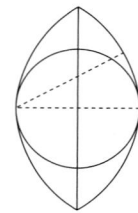

12. CREATE YOUR OWN Use the constructions to make a design of your own.
Check students' work.

CHAPTER 14   457

MEETING INDIVIDUAL NEEDS

For Students Who Are . . .

Acquiring English Proficiency Have students work with an English-proficient student to make the constructions.

Gifted and Talented Assign the technology lesson on page 488.

Today's Problem

A plane tesselation is a complete covering of a plane by one or more figures in a repeating pattern with no overlapping of figures. Explain (or show) why you cannot create a tesselation with just regular octagons. (*Each angle of a regular octagon is 135° [$\frac{(n-2)180°}{n}$]. When octagons are fitted next to one another, there is no whole number multiple of 135° that equals 360°. Accept a demonstration.*)

3 FOLLOW-UP

PRACTICE 14-4

Construct each design. Use only a compass and straightedge.

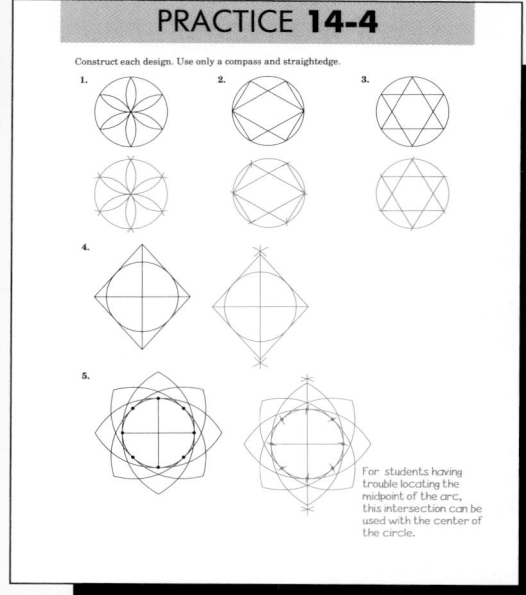

1. **2.** **3.**

4.

5.

For students having trouble locating the midpoint of the arc, this intersection can be used with the center of the circle.

RETEACHING 14-4

☑ **MATERIALS CHECKLIST:** Sharp pencil, Mira, flat surface

Have students draw a segment $\overline{AB}$ the length of a Mira. Place the Mira perpendicular so that the reflection of point A is on top of point B. Draw the line of reflection. Label the intersection C. With the Mira on point C, reflect point B onto the perpendicular line. Label the reflection D. With the Mira on points B and D, reflect point C and label point E. Draw $\overline{DE}$ and $\overline{EB}$. What shape have you drawn? [a square] Have students use the Mira to find the 4 lines of symmetry.

ENRICHMENT 14-4

Follow the directions to construct the design on a separate sheet of paper. Answer art is not actual size. Figure is drawn to scale.

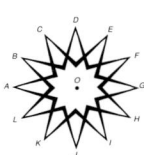

1. Use a compass to make a circle with a radius of $2\frac{1}{4}$ inches. Mark the center O.

2. Mark point A on the circle. Close the compass to one half the radius and place the compass point at point A. Now mark out 12 equal arcs around the circumference.

3. Label these points of intersection in order with B–L.

4. Lightly draw all diameters to connect points A–L. (A to G, B to H, etc.)

5. Find one half of each radius and mark this location on each radius.

6. Connect the midpoint of radius $\overline{BO}$ with point A and then with C. Similarly, connect the midpoint of radius $\overline{CO}$ with point B and then to point D. Continue around the circle.

7. Connect all points that are 5 arcs apart such as A to F, B to G, and C to H. Continue around the circle, connecting I to B, J to C, etc, ending with H to A.

8. Shade the area as shown above.

9. Erase any extra lines.

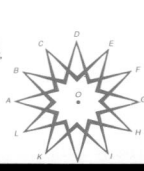

Chapter 14 • Lesson 14-4   **457**

Lesson Organizer

Objective: Bisect line segments and angles by construction.

Prior Knowledge: Students should know how to draw a line perpendicular to a line segment and identify congruent line segments and angles, right angles, and vertices.

Error Analysis and Remediation: See page 483A.

Lesson Resources:
Practice Worksheet 14-5
Reteaching Worksheet 14-5
Enrichment Activity 14-5
Daily Review 14-5

Two-Minute Math

What is the measure of a line segment congruent to a line segment 4 in. long? *(4 in.)* **What is the measure of an angle congruent to an angle of 40°?** *(40°)*

1 INTRODUCE

CONCRETE ACTIVITY

☑ **MATERIALS CHECKLIST:** compass and straightedge for each student

Assign students to work in pairs to review the construction from Lesson 14-4 for a line perpendicular to a line segment.

1. Draw a line segment $\overline{AB}$ about 3 in. long.

2. Use your compass and straightedge to construct a line perpendicular to the segment.

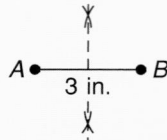

3. Have students compare constructions.

WHEN YOUR STUDENTS ASK
★ **WHY AM I LEARNING THIS?** ★

You can use this skill to design a cover for a school project or create a poster for a math or science fair.

Construction: Bisecting Segments and Angles

When you construct a perpendicular line by placing the compass point at the ends of a line segment, you also bisect the segment, or divide it into two congruent parts. In the construction at right, $\overleftrightarrow{DE} \perp \overline{AB}$ and $\overleftrightarrow{DE}$ bisects $\overline{AB}$.

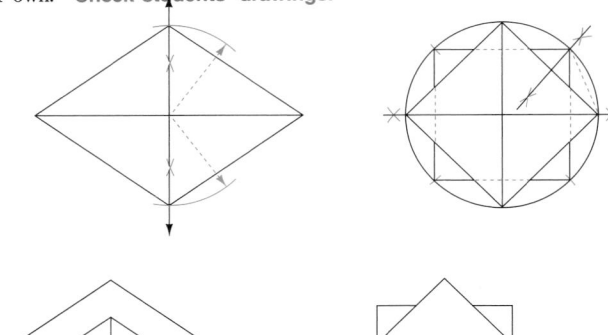

1. What are the two congruent segments on $\overline{AB}$?
   AC; CB
2. What line is perpendicular to $\overline{AB}$?
   $\overleftrightarrow{DE}$
3. At what point does $\overleftrightarrow{DE}$ bisect $\overline{AB}$?
   C
4. How many right angles are formed? Name them. **4; ∠ACD; ∠BCD; ∠ACE; ∠BCE**

This construction enables you to create many figures and designs. Construct each figure. Then use it to copy the design or to make your own. **Check students' drawings.**

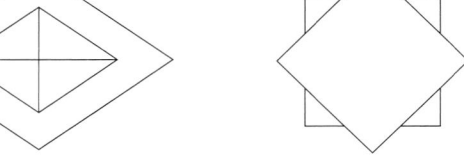

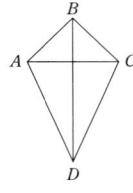

5. **THINK ALOUD** In the kite at right there are two pairs of congruent sides. Name them. What property do you think the diagonals of a kite have? Construct a kite.
   $\overline{AB} \cong \overline{BC}$; $\overline{AD} \cong \overline{CD}$; diagonals are perpendicular; Check students' work.

---

2 TEACH

☑ **MATERIALS CHECKLIST:** compass and straightedge for each student; chalkboard compass

Compare the words *bisect* and *bicycle*. Why do you think the prefix *bi-* is in the word *bisect*? *(Possible answer: When you bisect a line segment or an angle, you divide it into two congruent segments or angles.)*

Why do you think the bisection of an angle works? *(Possible answers: The marks on corresponding parts were made the same distance apart; the bisector is the line of symmetry, so the angles are congruent.)*

Chalkboard Examples

Draw a segment and angle on the board. Have volunteers use a chalkboard compass or string to bisect the segment and angle.

SUMMARIZE/ASSESS Draw any angle and explain how to bisect it. *(Students should explain the steps given in the lesson for constructing an angle bisector.)*

To bisect an angle, you divide it into two congruent angles.

Construction: Bisecting of an angle

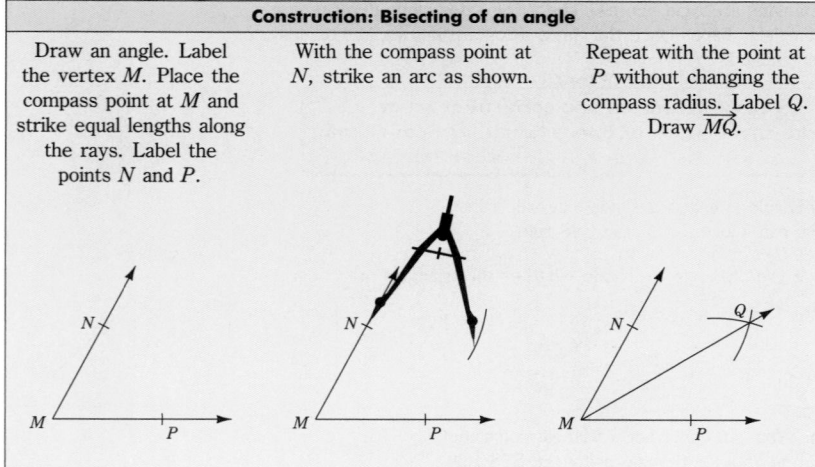

| Draw an angle. Label the vertex M. Place the compass point at M and strike equal lengths along the rays. Label the points N and P. | With the compass point at N, strike an arc as shown. | Repeat with the point at P without changing the compass radius. Label Q. Draw $\overrightarrow{MQ}$. |

6. Use the construction above.

   a. What angle was bisected? ∠NMP

   b. What ray bisected the angle? $\overrightarrow{MQ}$

   c. Name the two congruent angles. ∠NMQ ≅ ∠PMQ

   d. Copy the construction on a sheet of paper.
      Check students' drawings.

7. Trace the triangle at right.

   a. Bisect the three angles carefully.
      What do you observe?
      bisectors meet at same point

   b. Draw another triangle of your own.
      Bisect the three angles. What do you observe?
      Check students' drawings; bisectors
      meet at same point

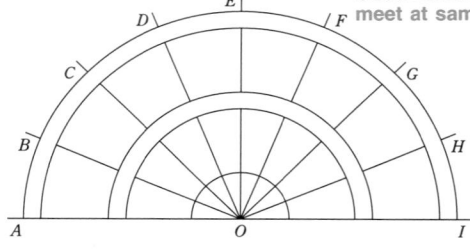

8. **IN YOUR WORDS** Use angle bisectors to construct the design at the left on a sheet of paper.
   Check students' drawings.

9. Write a paragraph explaining how you did the construction in Exercise 8. Tell what angle measures you made.
   Accept reasonable answers.

CHAPTER 14   459

MEETING INDIVIDUAL NEEDS

For Students Who Are . . .

Acquiring English Proficiency Discuss the meaning of *bisect*. Ask students to name other words that begin with the prefix *bi-*.

Gifted and Talented Challenge students to construct an octagon within a circle.

Working 2 or 3 Grades Below Level When students bisect an angle, remind them not to change the opening of their compass.

Today's Problem

Draw a triangle. Then draw a line segment joining a vertex to the midpoint of the side opposite the vertex. Is the triangle divided into two equal areas? *(Yes, the two areas are triangles having equal bases and the same heights.)* Draw another triangle. Construct an angle bisector of one of the angles to the side opposite the angle. Is the triangle divided into two congruent triangles? *(not necessarily)*

---

3 FOLLOW-UP

PRACTICE 14-5

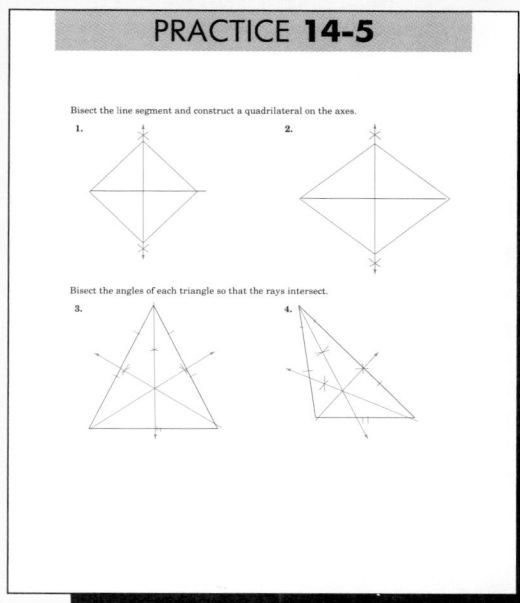

Bisect the line segment and construct a quadrilateral on the axes.

1.   2.

Bisect the angles of each triangle so that the rays intersect.

3.   4.

RETEACHING 14-5

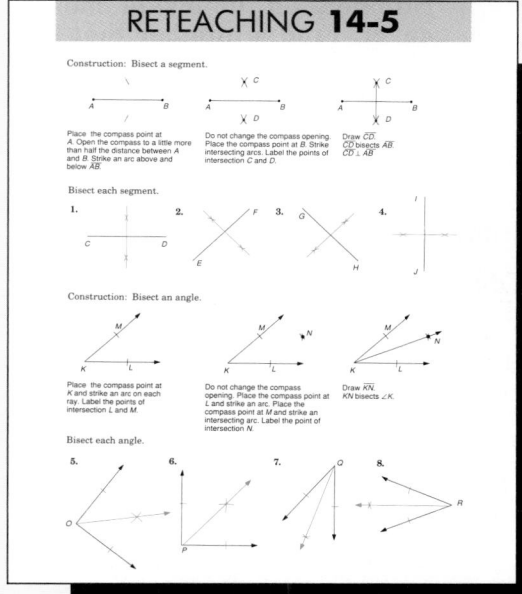

Construction: Bisect a segment.

Bisect each segment.
1.   2.   3.   4.

Construction: Bisect an angle.

Bisect each angle.
5.   6.   7.   8.

ENRICHMENT 14-5

☑ **MATERIALS CHECKLIST:** Compasses, straightedges

On the board write the following steps: Step 1: Draw a large circle. Step 2: Use the radius of the circle and any point on the circle to construct an arc. Repeat around the circle. Step 3: Bisect a radius to get the compass setting. Then bisect each arc to make 12 equal arcs. Step 4: Draw line segments that connect every third arc. Step 5: Find the midpoint of a side of the square to determine the radius of an inscribed circle, or a circle inside the square that touches each side. Step 6: Construct an inscribed circle.

Chapter 14 • Lesson 14-5   **459**

Lesson Organizer

Objective: Construct a triangle.

Prior Knowledge: Students should understand the meaning of *triangle, congruent triangle, right triangle, legs,* and *perpendicular lines.*

Error Analysis and Remediation: See page 483A.

Lesson Resources:
Practice Worksheet 14-6
Reteaching Worksheet 14-6
Enrichment Activity 14-6
Daily Review 14-6

Two-Minute Math

Use row A of the Table of Numbers on the inside back cover. Find a number that has a factor of 7 but not factors of 8 and 11. Then find a prime number. *(49; 19)*

1 INTRODUCE

CONCRETE ACTIVITY

☑ **MATERIALS CHECKLIST:** Teaching Aid 15 (Centimeter Grid Paper), compass, straightedge, and scissors for each student

Have students work in groups of three

1. Cut out three strips of grid paper: 4 cm long, 6 cm long, and 7 cm long.

2. Make a triangle that looks different from the other group members' triangles.

3. Are any of the triangles you made congruent? *(Students should discover that all the triangles are congruent. If they cannot tell, have them carefully lift a triangle and place it on top of another one.)*

WHEN YOUR STUDENTS ASK
★ WHY AM I LEARNING THIS? ★

You can use this skill to copy figures from books or magazines. For example, you can use a compass and straightedge to measure segments and angles and construct triangles and other figures.

Construction: Triangles

Triangles are rigid figures. The three sides alone determine a triangle's shape. Once the three sides are known, the angles are determined.

> **Two triangles are congruent when the three sides of one triangle are congruent to the three sides of the other triangle.**

This rule is called the side-side-side rule.
You can shorten it to the SSS rule.

Use the SSS rule to decide whether the triangles are congruent.

1. yes 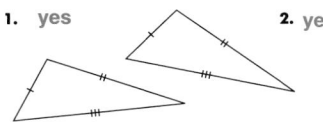 **2.** yes 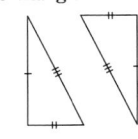 **3.** yes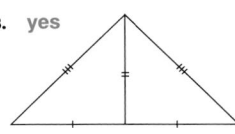

4. You can construct a triangle congruent to another triangle using the SSS rule. Copy this construction.
Check students' drawings.

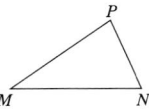

Construction: △ABC congruent to △MNP using the SSS rule	
Measure $\overline{MN}$ with a compass as shown.	Draw a line. Use the open compass to mark the length of $\overline{MN}$ along it. Call the segment $\overline{AB}$.
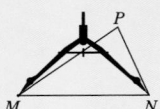	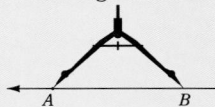
Measure $\overline{MP}$ on △MNP using the compass. With the same compass opening and compass point at A, strike an arc as shown.	Measure $\overline{NP}$ on △MNP using the compass. With the compass point at B and the same opening, strike an arc crossing the first arc at C. Draw △ABC.
	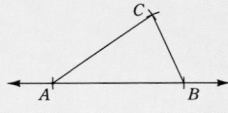

---

2 TEACH

☑ **MATERIALS CHECKLIST:** compass and straightedge for each student; chalkboard compass

If the side-side-side rule holds, what can you say about the angles of two triangles? *(Since the three sides are congruent, corresponding angles are also congruent.)*

When you construct a right triangle, why do you construct perpendicular lines in the first step? *(Perpendicular lines form right angles; a right triangle has one right angle.)*

In the construction for Exercise 8, could you make legs $\overline{GH}$ and $\overline{GI}$ longer and still have a right triangle? *(Yes, however, the two triangles would not be congruent.)*

> ### Chalkboard Example
> Draw a triangle on the chalkboard. Have a volunteer use a chalkboard compass to copy the triangle.

SUMMARIZE/ASSESS **Explain how to construct a congruent triangle using SSS.** *(Students should explain the steps on page 460.)*

Use the SSS rule to construct a congruent figure. **Check students' drawings.**

5.

6.

7.

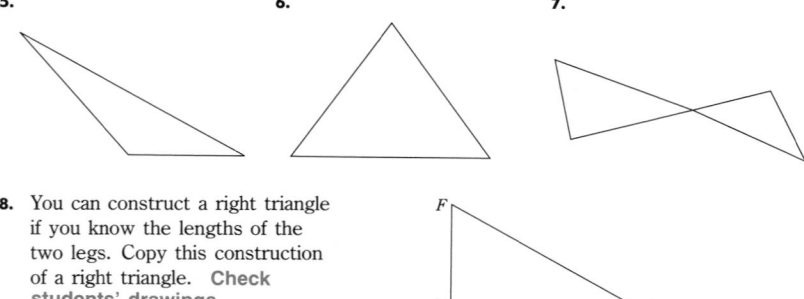

8. You can construct a right triangle if you know the lengths of the two legs. Copy this construction of a right triangle. **Check students' drawings.**

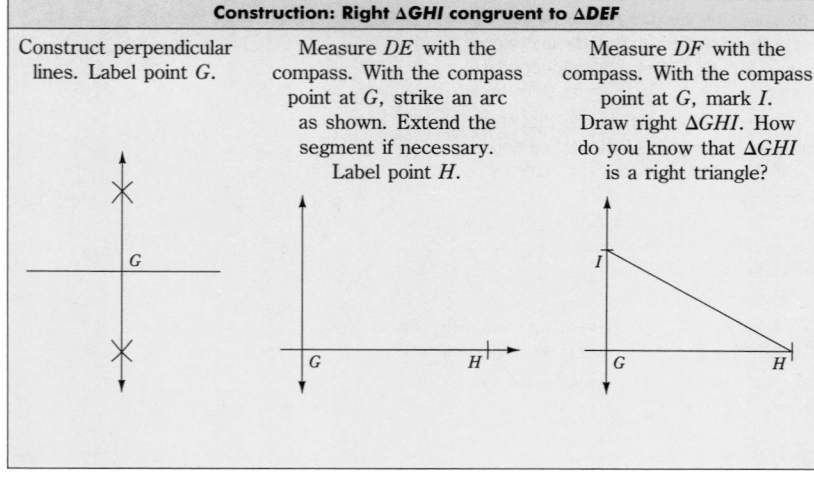

Construction: Right △GHI congruent to △DEF		
Construct perpendicular lines. Label point *G*.	Measure *DE* with the compass. With the compass point at *G*, strike an arc as shown. Extend the segment if necessary. Label point *H*.	Measure *DF* with the compass. With the compass point at *G*, mark *I*. Draw right △*GHI*. How do you know that △*GHI* is a right triangle?

Construct the figures. **Check students' drawings.**

9.

10.

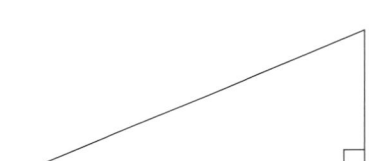 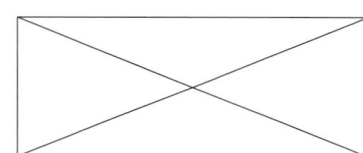

MEETING INDIVIDUAL NEEDS

For Students Who Are . . .

Acquiring English Proficiency Have students draw two congruent triangles, then label and name the vertices and congruent sides.

Gifted and Talented Have students draw a triangle, trade papers and construct a triangle (with compass and straightedge) congruent to the one on their partner's paper.

Working 2 or 3 Grades Below Level Remind students to make their first line long enough to mark off one side of the triangle they are constructing.

Today's Problem

How can you divide a triangle into four equal areas? *(Bisect a side of the triangle into two equal segments. Then bisect each segment into two more equal segments, producing four equal segments. Draw three lines from the vertex opposite the bisected side to the points that divide the side, thus forming four triangles of equal area.)*

3 FOLLOW-UP

PRACTICE 14-6

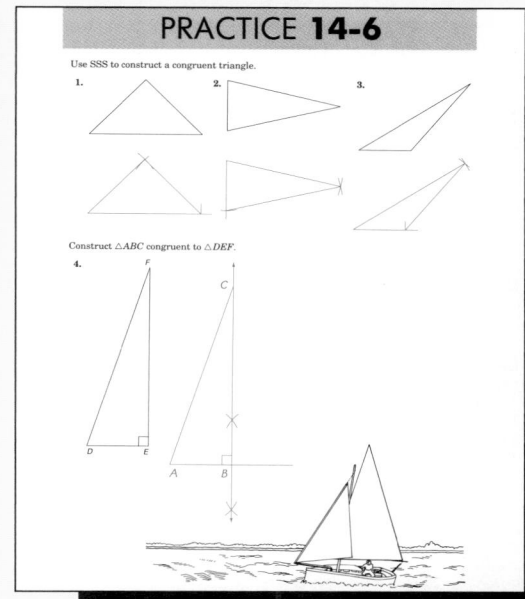

RETEACHING 14-6

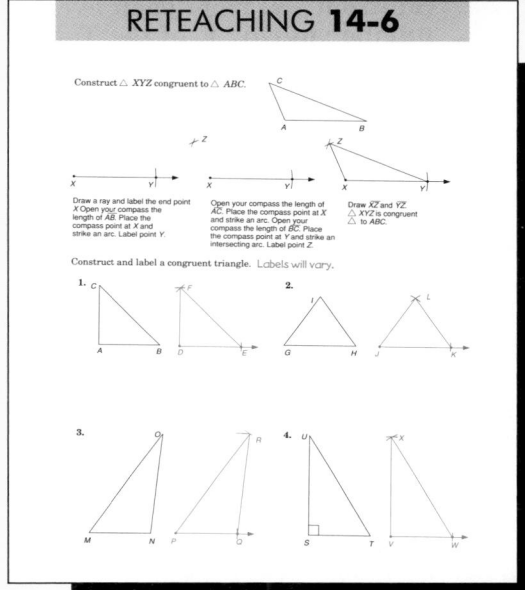

ENRICHMENT 14-6

☑ **MATERIALS CHECKLIST:** Magazines or newspapers, blank spinners, compasses, straightedges

Have the students work in pairs. Each partner finds several examples of triangles in photographs or illustrations and constructs congruent triangles. The partners then exchange triangles. For each triangle, each partner spins a spinner labeled ×2 and ÷2 in equal sections and, based on the spin, constructs a triangle with sides that are either twice as long or half as long as the sides of the original triangles.

Lesson Organizer

Objective: Construct space figures.

Prior Knowledge: Students should know the meanings of *regular polygons, congruent figures, triangles, squares, pentagons, segments*, and how to do six-arc construction.

Error Analysis and Remediation: See page 483A.

Lesson Resources:
Practice Worksheet 14-7
Reteaching Activity 14-7
Enrichment Worksheet 14-7
Daily Review 14-7

Two-Minute Math

Subtract 189 from each even number in row E of the Table of Numbers on the inside back cover. *(6,427; 2,129; 643)*

1 INTRODUCE

CONNECTING ACTIVITY

Have students work with a partner.

Have partners sketch a regular triangle, a regular quadrilateral, a regular pentagon, and a regular hexagon. **What is a regular triangle?** *(a three-sided figure that has congruent sides and angles.)* **a regular quadrilateral?** *(a four-sided figure that has congruent sides and angles.)* **What is true of all regular polygons?** *(All angles and sides are congruent.)*

WHEN YOUR STUDENTS ASK
★ WHY AM I LEARNING THIS? ★

You can connect this skill to real life through games. If you toss a cube, tetrahedron, or other Platonic solid, each face has an equal chance of landing on the table.

Construction: Space Figures

Many beautiful crystals have faces that are regular polygons. A salt crystal is shaped like a **cube**. A diamond crystal is shaped like an **octahedron**. Cubes and octahedrons are called **space figures**. A space figure has three dimensions—length, width, and height.

There are exactly five regular space figures. They have faces that are congruent regular polygons. See the drawings at right.

A space figure with its interior is a **solid**. The solids of the five regular space figures are called **Platonic solids** and were named for the Greek philosopher Plato.

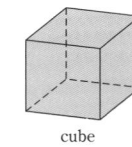

Salt crystals (sodium chloride)

The ancient Greeks believed that the universe was made of these five solids. They thought the earth was made of cubes, fire was of tetrahedrons, air of octahedrons, and water of icosahedrons. For them, the dodecahedron represented the entire universe.

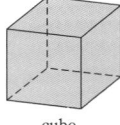

cube   tetrahedron

1. Which of the five regular space figures has this figure for its faces? **See below.**
   a. a triangle   **b.** a square
   c. a pentagon

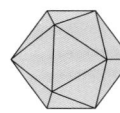

octahedron

2. Two faces meet at a line segment called an **edge**. Tell how many edges the figure has.
   a. a cube   **b.** a tetrahedron
      12   6

3. Edges meet in points called **vertexes**. Tell how many edges meet at each vertex.
   a. a tetrahedron 3   **b.** an octahedron 4
   c. an icosahedron 5   **d.** a dodecahedron 3

icosahedron   dodecahedron

462   LESSON 14-7   1. a. tetrahedron; octahedron; icosahedron
                                b. cube; c. dodecahedron

---

2 TEACH

☑ **MATERIALS CHECKLIST:** compass, straightedge, construction paper or oaktag, scissors, tape for each student

Are there other space figures in addition to these? Explain. *(Yes; there are many space figures such as spheres and cylinders; these are only the convex space figures whose faces are regular polygons.)*

Which Platonic solids have more than eight faces? *(icosahedrons and dodecahedrons)*

Which Platonic solids have more than four triangular faces? *(octahedrons and icosahedrons)*

SUMMARIZE/ASSESS   **What are Platonic solids?** *(They are the solids of exactly five space figures with faces that are congruent regular polygons.)*

4. Copy this construction to make a model of a tetrahedron.
Check students' drawings.

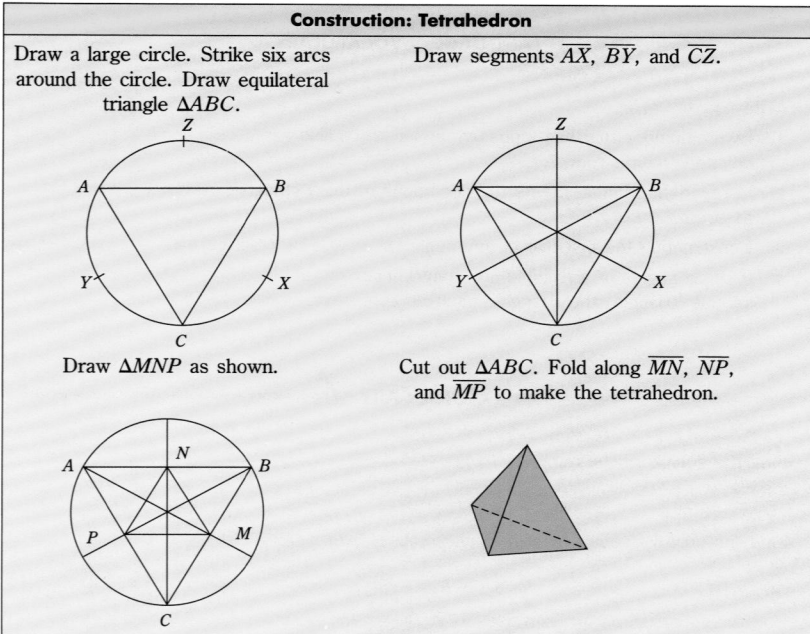

Construction: Tetrahedron

Draw a large circle. Strike six arcs around the circle. Draw equilateral triangle △*ABC*.

Draw segments $\overline{AX}$, $\overline{BY}$, and $\overline{CZ}$.

Draw △*MNP* as shown.

Cut out △*ABC*. Fold along $\overline{MN}$, $\overline{NP}$, and $\overline{MP}$ to make the tetrahedron.

5. A tetrahedron can be used to construct an octahedron. *Check students' drawings.*

   a. Make a copy of the construction for the tetrahedron.

   b. Trace it twice so that the parts match at $\overline{ST}$ as shown.

   c. Cut along the outside edges. Fold along other segments. Construct the octahedron.

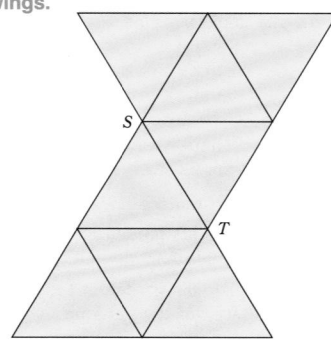

6. **CREATE YOUR OWN** Describe a plan you could follow to construct a cube. Try your plan. *Check students' work.*

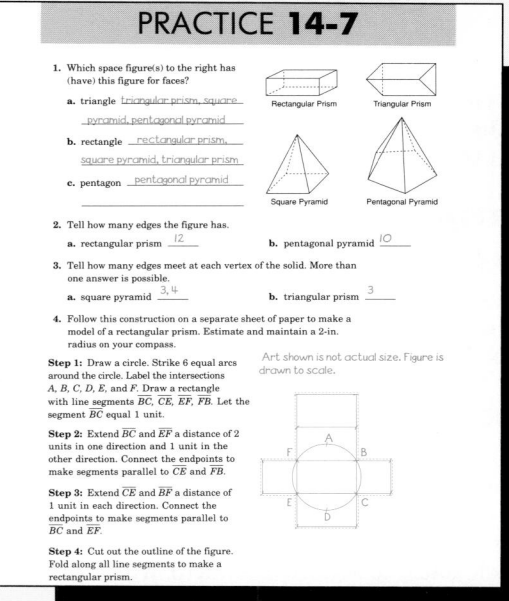

PRACTICE 14-7

1. Which space figure(s) to the right has (have) this figure for faces?

   a. triangle   <u>triangular prism, square</u>
      <u>pyramid, pentagonal pyramid</u>

   b. rectangle   <u>rectangular prism,</u>
      <u>square pyramid, triangular prism</u>

   c. pentagon   <u>pentagonal pyramid</u>

Rectangular Prism   Triangular Prism   Square Pyramid   Pentagonal Pyramid

2. Tell how many edges the figure has.

   a. rectangular prism <u>12</u>
   b. pentagonal pyramid <u>10</u>

3. Tell how many edges meet at each vertex of the solid. More than one answer is possible.

   a. square pyramid <u>3, 4</u>
   b. triangular prism <u>3</u>

4. Follow this construction on a separate sheet of paper to make a model of a rectangular prism. Estimate and maintain a 2-in. radius on your compass.

Art shown is not actual size. Figure is drawn to scale.

Step 1: Draw a circle. Strike 6 equal arcs around the circle. Label the intersections *A, B, C, D, E,* and *F*. Draw a rectangle with line segments $\overline{BC}$, $\overline{CE}$, $\overline{EF}$, $\overline{FB}$. Let the segment $\overline{BC}$ equal 1 unit.

Step 2: Extend $\overline{BC}$ and $\overline{EF}$ a distance of 2 units in one direction and 1 unit in the other direction. Connect the endpoints to make segments parallel to $\overline{CE}$ and $\overline{FB}$.

Step 3: Extend $\overline{CE}$ and $\overline{BF}$ a distance of 1 unit in each direction. Connect the endpoints to make segments parallel to $\overline{BC}$ and $\overline{EF}$.

Step 4: Cut out the outline of the figure. Fold along all line segments to make a rectangular prism.

RETEACHING 14-7

☑ **MATERIALS CHECKLIST:** Sharp pencil, Mira, scissors, flat surface

Have students draw a segment $\overline{AB}$, about 4 in. long, in the lower righthand corner of a piece of paper. Draw the perpendicular bisector. Label the intersection *C*. With the Mira on point *C*, reflect point *B* onto the perpendicular line. Label the reflection point *D*. With the Mira on points *B* and *D*, reflect point *C* and label point *E*. Draw $\overline{DE}$ and $\overline{EB}$. Reflect the square to make the pattern at right. Cut out the pattern and fold along the lines to make a cube.

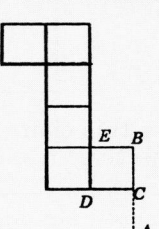

ENRICHMENT 14-7

A **net** is a flattened pattern that is used to make a space figure.

1. What space figure can be made using the net to the right?
   <u>a cube</u>

2. Draw another net that can be used to form the same space figure as above.
Answers will vary. Suggestions are given.

A dodecahedron is a polyhedron with 12 regular pentagons as faces.

3. What polygon makes up each face of a dodecahedron?
   <u>a pentagon</u>

4. What is the measure of each angle of a regular pentagon? <u>108°</u>

5. On another piece of paper, draw a net that will form a dodecahedron.

MEETING INDIVIDUAL NEEDS

For Students Who Are . . .

Acquiring English Proficiency Use patterns or models to point out faces, edges, and vertexes of space figures. Explain the word *interior*.

Gifted and Talented Challenge students to construct at least two different patterns that can be used to make a cube.

Working 2 or 3 Grades Below Level Have students identify the polygon face of each Platonic solid on page 462. Have them point to a face, an edge, and a vertex.

Today's Problem

Imagine 8 cubes glued together to form a supercube. How many individual cubes have 1 face showing? *(none)* 2 faces showing? *(none)* 3 faces showing? *(8)*

MIDCHAPTER
Checkup

The midchapter checkup provides a way for you to check students' understanding of the skills taught in the first half of the chapter.

Language and Vocabulary

Some key language and vocabulary ideas from the first half of the chapter are reinforced here.

Quick Quiz

This quiz provides a means of evaluating students' understanding of the objectives for the first half of the chapter. Page references are given so that students can check back to where the skill was taught.

Use the following guide to score the quiz.

Score	Percent
10	100%
9	90
8	80
7	70
6	60
5	50
4	40
3	30
2	20
1	10

Use this chart to identify the management objectives tested.

Items	Management Objectives	Pages
1–6	**14A** Find squares and square roots of numbers.	452–455
7–10	**14B** Bisect a line segment or an angle by construction; construct space figures.	456–463

MIDCHAPTER CHECKUP

═ LANGUAGE & VOCABULARY ═

Write *true* or *false*.

1. Every number that has a positive square root also has a negative square root. **true**
2. Every right triangle meets the conditions of the Pythagorean theorem. **true**
3. Constructing the bisector of any angle requires a protractor.
4. If three angles of a triangle are congruent to three angles of   **false** another triangle, the triangles must be congruent. **false**

═ QUICK QUIZ ✓ ═

Find the square of the number. *(pages 452–455)*

1. 7^2 **49**
2. $(^-4)^2$ **16**
3. $\left(\frac{1}{3}\right)^2$ $\frac{1}{9}$

Find the positive square root of each number. *(pages 452–455)*

4. $\sqrt{64}$ **8**
5. $\sqrt{625}$ **25**
6. $\sqrt{\frac{1}{16}}$ $\frac{1}{4}$

Use the construction for exercises 7–9. *(pages 456–463)*

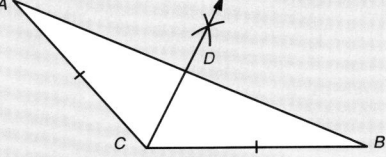

7. Name the bisected angle.
   ∠ACB
8. Name the angle bisector.
   CD
9. Name the congruent angles created by the angle bisector.
   ∠ACD ≅ ∠DCB

10. Mr. Salazar wants to enclose a plot of land to use as a vegetable garden. He has 52 ft of fencing to use.

    a. How much fencing does Mr. Salazar have available? **52 ft**
    b. If he builds his garden in the shape of a square, how long can each side be? **13 ft**
    c. If he builds his garden in the shape of a square, what will be the area of the garden? **169 ft²**

Write the answers in your learning log. **Answers will vary. Suggestions given.**
1. Your friend thinks that the Pythagorean Theorem will work for all triangles. What is wrong with this thinking? **It works only for right triangles.**
2. Explain what will be true if you correctly bisect a line segment or angle. **The line segments or angles formed will be congruent.**

DID YOU KNOW . . . ? In 1960 Americans generated an average of 2.5 lb/d of garbage per person. Twenty-five years later, we were generating about 3.5 lb/d. How much garbage is collected in your city or town in a week? About how many pounds is that per person per day? **Check students' work.**

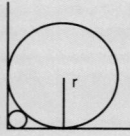

In the drawing at right, r is the radius of the large circle that fits in the corner. The corner is a right angle. Tell how you could find the radius of the smaller circle in the corner. $\frac{r\sqrt{2}-r}{2}$ or $\frac{1}{2}$ the difference of $r\sqrt{2}$ and r

Learning Log

These are suggestions for writing about some topics taught so far in the chapter. The students keep their learning logs from the start of the school year to the end.

Math America

A mathematical skill that students have learned is related to an interesting fact about the United States.

Bonus

Students are given an opportunity to solve a challenge-type problem such as a puzzle or a nonroutine problem.

Lesson Organizer

Objective: Solve problems by creating and using formulas.

Prior Knowledge: Students should know the meanings of *faces, edges,* and *vertices* of space figures and have a basic understanding of circumference and area of a circle.

Lesson Resources:
Practice Worksheet 14-8
Reteaching Activity 14-8
Enrichment Worksheet 14-8
Daily Review 14-8
Cooperative Investigations,
    Chapter 14

Two-Minute Math

Find the circumference and area of a circle with:
a radius of 10 cm
$(C \approx 62.8 \text{ cm}; A \approx 314 \text{ cm}^2)$
a diameter of 30 cm
$(C \approx 94.2 \text{ cm}; A \approx 706.5 \text{ cm}^2)$

1 INTRODUCE

CONNECTING ACTIVITY

✔ **MATERIALS CHECKLIST:** Teaching Aids 20 and 21 (Cube and Rectangular Pyramid), scissors, tape for each group

Have students work in groups of three or four.

1. Cut out each shape. Then fold along the lines and tape the sides together.

2. Count and record the total number of faces, edges, and vertices for each model.

3. Have groups save their models and information for use later in this lesson and in Lesson 14-9.

WHEN YOUR STUDENTS ASK
★ WHY AM I LEARNING THIS? ★

In real life, computer programmers create and use formulas that tell the computer which steps to follow to produce certain responses.

Problem Solving Strategy:
Creating and Using Formulas

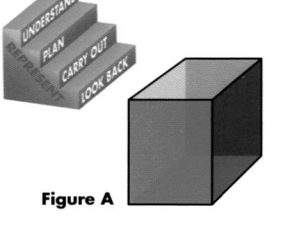

A formula uses symbols to show relationships. Creating a formula for a relationship lets you work with the relationship more easily.

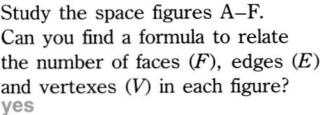

Figure A   Figure B

Study the space figures A–F. Can you find a formula to relate the number of faces (*F*), edges (*E*), and vertexes (*V*) in each figure?
yes

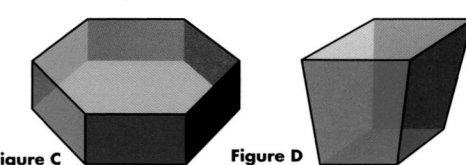

Figure C   Figure D

You can count faces, edges, and vertexes and collect information in a chart like this one.

Space Figure	F	E	V
A	6	12	8
B	4	6	4
C	8	18	12

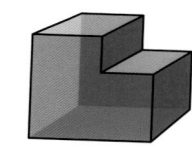

Figure E   Figure F

Which formula is correct for all of the space figures? b
a. $F + V = E$ **b.** $F + V = E + 2$ **c.** $F + E = V - 1$

Check the formula you chose using this space figure. If the relationship you chose is not correct, you may need to count again.

THINK ALOUD Explain the formula in your own words. **The sum of all faces and vertices is equal to the number of edges plus two.**

■■■■■■■■ **GUIDED PRACTICE** ■■■■■■■■

1. Use the formula $F + V = E + 2$ and Figures G and H to answer.
  a. What three variables are related by the formula? *F; V; E*
  b. Do the space figures at right satisfy the formula? yes
  c. If $F = 5$ when $V = 5$, what is E? 8

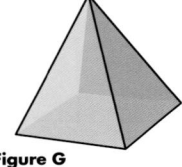
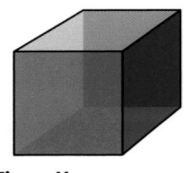

Figure G   Figure H

466   LESSON 14-8

---

2 TEACH

Look at the information you recorded for the models you made. Does the formula work for these solids? *(Yes, if the counting was accurate)*

Do you think this formula will work for any Platonic solid? *(Yes)*

A regular tetrahedron has 6 edges and 4 vertices. How many faces does it have? *(4; F + 4 = 6 + 2)*

What is a different way to write this formula? *(Possible answers: F + V − E = 2; F + V − 2 = E)*

SUMMARIZE/ASSESS   **What formula explains how the faces, edges, and vertices of the space figures that you studied are related?** *(F + V = E + 2)*

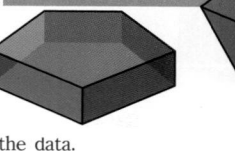

Use the formula to find the missing variable.

2. $F = 7$ $V = 10$ $E = ?$ **15**

3. $F = 6$ $V = ?$ **6** $E = 10$

4. Use the chart to write a formula that relates the data.

C	D
12.56 cm	4 cm
21.98 cm	7 cm
35.17 cm	11.2 cm

C = circumference of a circle
d = diameter
$\pi \approx 3.14$
$C = \pi D$

5. Use the formula from Exercise 4 to show that when the diameter of a circle is 6.8 cm, the circumference is about 21.35 cm.
$6.8 \times 3.14 \approx 21.352$

6. Use the chart to write a formula that relates the data.

A	r
3.14 cm²	1 cm
12.56 cm²	2 cm
78.5 cm²	5 cm

A = area of circle
r = radius
$\pi \approx 3.14$
$A = \pi r^2$

7. Use the formula from Exercise 6 to show that when the radius of a lid is 8 cm, the area is about 200.96 cm².
$(8)^2 \times 3.14 \approx 200.96$

Solve. Tell what formula you used.

8. The first Ferris wheel was built in 1893 in Chicago. Its diameter was about 75 m. After the Ferris wheel revolved 20 times, about how far did the passengers travel?
4,710 m

9. Four years later, a Ferris wheel was built in London with an area of about 6,400 m². Did this Ferris wheel have a greater diameter than the one built in Chicago?
yes

CHOOSE Choose any strategy to solve. **Strategies may vary. Suggestions given.**

10. What is the next number in the pattern: 1, 5, 3, 7, 5, 9, 7, . . . ?
pattern; 11

11. A 1-L bottle of orange juice costs $1.25. A 2-L bottle of the same juice costs $2.39. Only three 2-L bottles are left. How much will 10-L of orange juice cost?
multistep; $12.17

12. Rosa gave half of her baseball card collection to Sam. He gave half of what Rosa gave him to Harold. Harold gave half of the cards he got from Sam to Herman. Herman already had 8 baseball cards. The cards he got from Harold doubled his collection. How many baseball cards does Rosa now have?
working backward; 32 cards

MEETING INDIVIDUAL NEEDS

For Students Who Are . . .

Acquiring English Proficiency   Reinforce the meanings of *faces, edges,* and *vertices.*

Gifted and Talented   Have students create a chart like those in Exercises 4 and 6. Then have them exchange papers and write a formula to relate the data in each other's chart.

Having Reading Difficulties   For Exercise 9, explain what a Ferris wheel is and define the word *revolve.*

Today's Problem

A square piece of metal is 5 in. on a side. A hole with a diameter of 2 in. was cut into the square. What is the area of the metal that is left? (Area left; $5^2 - \pi r^2$ or $25 - \pi$ or about $25 - 3.14 = 21.86$ sq. in.)

3 FOLLOW-UP

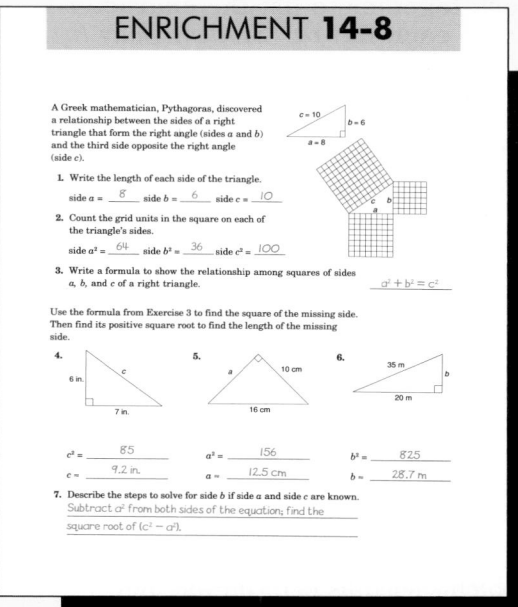

PRACTICE **14-8**

Use the formula $A = \frac{1}{2} bh$ to find the missing variable.

1. $A = 30$, $b = 12$, $h = \boxed{5}$ **2.** $A = 44$, $b = \boxed{8}$, $h = 11$

3. On what type(s) of triangles can you use this formula to find the area?
     all types of triangles

4. Use the chart to write a formula that relates the data.

A	s
9 cm²	3 cm
25 cm²	5 cm
64 cm²	8 cm

A = area of a square
s = length of a side

$A = s^2$

5. Use the formula from Exercise 4 to show that when the side of a square is 5.9 cm, the area is 34.81 cm².

$A = s^2$
$A = 5.9^2$
$A = 34.81$ cm²

6. Use the chart to write a formula that relates the data.

A	l	w
20 cm²	10 cm	2 cm
60 cm²	10 cm	6 cm
100 cm²	10 cm	10 cm

A = area of a rectangle
l = length (10 cm)
w = width

$A = l \times w$

7. Use the formula from Exercise 6 to show that when the width of a rectangle is 7.5 cm and the area is 75 cm², the length is 10 cm.

$A = l \times w$
$75 = l \times 7.5$
$l = 10$

Solve.

8. The Garcias bought a piece of land measuring 95 ft on each side to build their new store. The price of the land was $12 per ft². What was the total cost of the land?
$108,300

9. The Garcias passed up an opportunity to buy a piece of land measuring 120 ft by 75 ft at a cost of $135,000. What was the price per square foot of the land?
$15 per ft²

RETEACHING **14-8**

☑ **MATERIALS CHECKLIST:** Geometric solids

Provide each student with a square pyramid. On the board write *Find the number of vertices.* Also write *Faces + Vertices = Edges + 2.* Ask: How many flat surfaces are there? [5] What are flat surfaces called? [faces] Ask a volunteer to write 5 on the board under *Faces.* Tell the students to find the number of edges, or all the places where the faces meet. Ask: How many edges are there? [8] Another volunteer writes 8 under *Edges.* A third volunteer solves the equation. [$V = 5$] The other students count the vertices to check the work on the board.

ENRICHMENT **14-8**

A Greek mathematician, Pythagoras, discovered a relationship between the sides of a right triangle that form the right angle (sides a and b) and the third side opposite the right angle (side c).

$c = 10$, $b = 6$, $a = 8$

1. Write the length of each side of the triangle.
side a = 8   side b = 6   side c = 10

2. Count the grid units in the square on each of the triangle's sides.
side a^2 = 64   side b^2 = 36   side c^2 = 100

3. Write a formula to relate the relationship among squares of sides a, b, and c of a right triangle. $a^2 + b^2 = c^2$

Use the formula from Exercise 3 to find the square of the missing side. Then find its positive square root to find the length of the missing side.

4.   6 in., 7 in., c
c^2 = 85
c = 9.2 in.

5.   10 cm, 16 cm, a
a^2 = 156
a = 12.5 cm

6.   35 m, 20 m, b
b^2 = 825
b = 28.7 m

7. Describe the steps to solve for side b if side a and side c are known.
Subtract a^2 from both sides of the equation; find the square root of ($c^2 - a^2$).

Lesson Organizer

Objective: Explore the surface area of a prism and a pyramid.

Prior Knowledge: Students should know how to find areas of rectangles and triangles and be familiar with basic plane and space figures.

Lesson Resources:
Class Activity 14-9
Daily Review 14-9

Two-Minute Math

Find the area.
rectangle: length = 16 cm;
width = 11 cm $(A = 176 cm^2)$
triangle: base = 14 cm;
height = 8 cm $(A = 56 cm^2)$

1 PREPARE

CONNECTING ACTIVITY

✔ **MATERIALS CHECKLIST:** Teaching Aids 20 and 21 (Cube and Rectangular Pyramid), scissors, tape for each group

Have students work in groups of three.

Students can use the models of a cube and a rectangular pyramid they made for Lesson 14-8, or you can have them make new models using Teaching Aids 20 and 21.

Work together to list the characteristics of each figure. *(Students may list: number of faces, edges, and vertices; formula that relates faces, edges, and vertices; flat sides, shapes of faces, dimensions of models.)*

Have groups exchange and compare lists.

WHEN YOUR STUDENTS ASK
★ WHY AM I LEARNING THIS? ★

You can use this skill to solve real life problems such as determining how much gift wrap you need to cover a gift box.

Exploring Surface Area of Prisms and Pyramids

A cube is a special example of a prism. All **prisms** have two bases that are congruent polygons on parallel planes.

cube   triangular prism

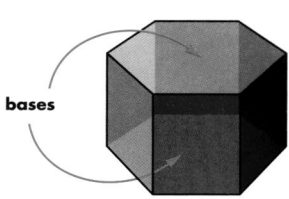

rectangular prism

1. For any prism, what are the shapes of the faces that are not bases?
   rectangles

2. What is the name of a rectangular prism with square bases and square faces?
   cube

The **surface area** of a space figure is the sum of the areas of the faces. To find the surface area, you can use a pattern.

3. What is the surface area of this rectangular prism? Answer these questions to help you find out.
   a. How do you find the area of face E? $A = b \times h$
   b. What other face has the same area? **F**
   c. Is there a face with the same area as face B? face A?
      yes; yes

4. Draw the pattern on centimeter graph paper. Cut it out to make the rectangular prism. What pairs of faces have the same areas?
   A, C; B, D; E, F

5. **IN YOUR WORDS** Write a paragraph explaining how to find the surface area of any rectangular prism.
   Accept reasonable answers.

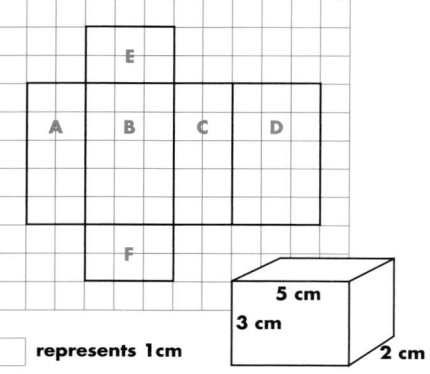

⬜ represents 1cm

5 cm
3 cm
2 cm

---

2 EXPLORE

✔ **MATERIALS CHECKLIST:** Teaching Aid 15 (Centimeter Grid Paper), scissors, straightedge, and tape for each group

Students should continue to work in their groups.

How might you find the surface area of a cube? *(Possible answers: Make a cube pattern on the grid paper and count the number of squares; find the area of each square face; then add all the areas.)*

How might you use centimeter grid paper to find the surface area of a hexagonal prism? *(Possible answer: Cover the prism carefully with the grid paper, then count the number of squares. Accept reasonable answers.)*

SUMMARIZE/ASSESS **What is the surface area of a prism or a pyramid?** *(the sum of the areas of all the faces)*

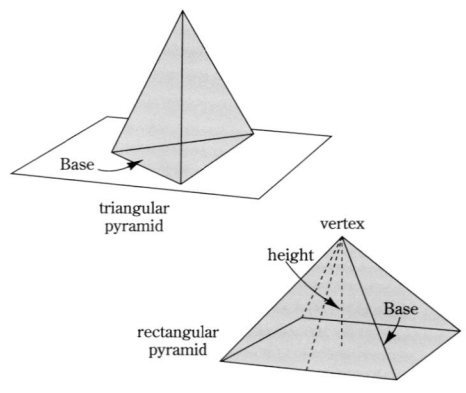

triangular
pyramid

A **pyramid** has only one base and is named according to the shape of the base. A segment from a vertex perpendicular to the base is called the height of the pyramid. The height is not related to surface area, but to the volume of the pyramid.

vertex

height

Base

rectangular
pyramid

6. For a pyramid, what are the shapes of the faces that are not the base? **triangles**

7. What is the name of a triangular pyramid with all faces congruent? **tetrahedron**

8. a. What is the surface area of the pyramid at right? Count squares or use formulas. Remember: The area of a triangle $= \frac{1}{2}(b \times h)$. **56 cm²**

   b. Draw the pattern on centimeter graph paper. Cut it out to make the pyramid. Describe the positions of the faces with the same areas. **See below.**

   c. **IN YOUR WORDS** Write a paragraph explaining how you found the surface area. **Accept reasonable answers.**

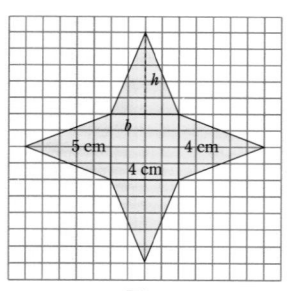

h

b

5 cm   4 cm

4 cm

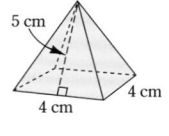

5 cm

4 cm

4 cm

☐ represents 1 cm²

Find the surface area.

9. **232 cm²**

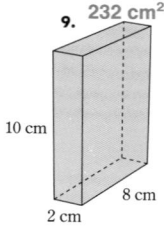

10 cm

8 cm

2 cm

10. **297 cm²**

square base

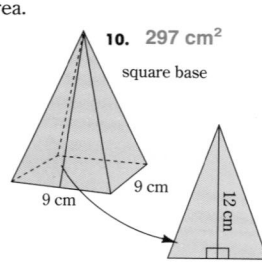

9 cm   9 cm

12 cm

11. **92 in.²**

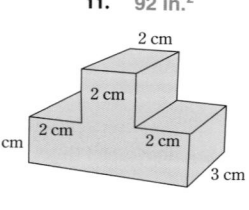

2 cm

2 cm

2 cm   2 cm

2 cm

3 cm

12. a triangular pyramid with the area of each face equal to 24 cm² **96 cm²**

*13. a cube with the lengths of each side equal to m **6 m²**

8b. **Answers will vary. Suggestion given: The faces slant and meet at a common vertex.**

CLASS ACTIVITY **14-9**

☑ **MATERIALS CHECKLIST:** Boxes, scissors, rulers

Have the students work in pairs. Instruct each pair to find the surface area of a cereal (or similar) box. The partners cut the box so that it can be unfolded and laid flat on a desk. They then measure the length and width of each rectangular section that was visible before the box was cut apart, and find the areas of these sections. Tell them that the sum of the rectangular areas is the total surface area of the box. Have each pair share its work with the other pair.

MEETING INDIVIDUAL NEEDS

For Students Who Are . . .

Acquiring English Proficiency Review the meanings of *bases*, *congruent polygons*, and *parallel planes*. Display a model of a prism and have students identify the bases.

Gifted and Talented Challenge students to write a formula for finding the surface area of a rectangular prism. (SA = 2 lw + 2 lh + 2 wh)

Working 2 or 3 Grades Below Level Review finding the area of a rectangle, square, and triangle.

Today's Problem

The pyramid of Khufu at Giza, Egypt, has a square base 755 ft on a side. Its height is 482 ft, and its slant height is 612 ft. Which is greater, the area of the base or the area of a triangle. *(Base: 755 ft × 755 ft; triangle: $\frac{755}{2} \times 612$; the area of the base is greater.)*

LESSON 14-10

Lesson Organizer

Objective: Explore the surface area of curved surfaces.

Prior Knowledge: Students should know the meanings of *polygon, congruent, base,* and *face* and the formulas for the area and circumference of a circle.

Lesson Resources:
Class Activity 14-10
Daily Review 14-10

Two-Minute Math

Find the area and circumference of a circle that has a radius of 15 cm. *(A ≈ 706.5 cm²; C ≈ 94.2 cm)*

1 PREPARE

CONNECTING ACTIVITY

☑ **MATERIALS CHECKLIST:** Teaching Aids 22 (Cylinder) and 23 (Cone), scissors, and tape for each pair

Assign students to work with a partner.

Have students cut out the patterns of a cylinder and a cone and use tape to build each model.

Which space figure has two flat circular faces and one curved surface? What is this figure called? *(cylinder)* **Which space figure has one flat circular face and one curved surface? What is this figure called?** *(cone)*

WHEN YOUR STUDENTS ASK
★ WHY AM I LEARNING THIS? ★

You can connect this skill to real life through the manufacture of cans. When a company makes cans to hold fruit and vegetables, a model or prototype of the can is made to make sure it can hold the intended amount of food.

EXPLORE

Exploring Surface Area of Curved Surfaces

All faces of prisms and pyramids are polygons. However, some space figures have faces that cannot be contained in a plane. These faces are called curved surfaces. Many of these surfaces are found in nature.

Spheres The Sun, the Moon, and the planets resemble **spheres**. All points on the surface of a sphere are the same distance from the center.		
Cylinders A tree trunk resembles a cylinder. The two bases of the cylinder are congruent and on parallel planes.		
Cones An erupting volcano looks like a cone. A cone has one base.		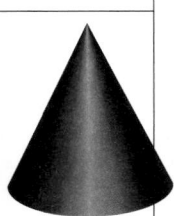

1. Which figure above has these qualities?
   a. one circular base and one curved surface   cone
   b. all points equidistant from one point   sphere
   c. two flat faces and one curved surface   cylinder
   d. exactly one curved surface   sphere

470   LESSON 14-10

MATH AND SCIENCE

---

2 EXPLORE

☑ **MATERIALS CHECKLIST:** Teaching Aid 15 (Centimeter Grid Paper), 2 per student; compass, scissors, and tape for each student

Have students read the material at the top of page 470 and as a class identify the figures for Exercise 1.

For Exercises 2–9, have students work in small groups to compare the patterns they each make independently and to discuss the questions.

For Exercise 4, have students demonstrate that the length of the rectangle forms the circumference of the circular base.

SUMMARIZE/ASSESS   **What are two ways to find the surface area of a cylinder?** *(Estimate by counting square units; use formulas to find the areas of the faces and then find the sum of the areas.)*

To find the surface area of a cylinder, you can use a pattern.

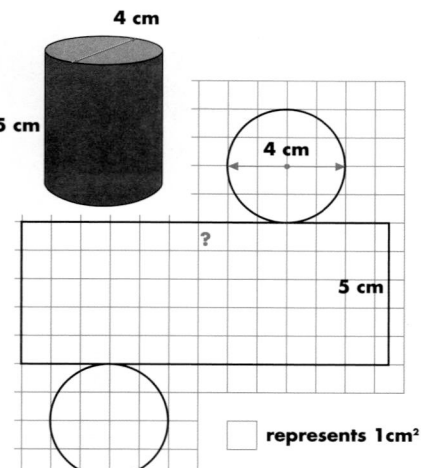

2. Estimate the surface area of the cylinder by counting and piecing together squares.   **Accept reasonable estimates; about 90 cm²**

3. Draw the pattern. How long is the rectangle? Cut out the pattern and make the cylinder.
12–13 cm
(*Hint:* How does the length of the rectangle relate to the circumference of the circle? If you know the radius or diameter, how can you find the circumference?)
same; $C = \pi D$; $C = 2\pi r$

4. What other method could you use to find the surface area? Choose a method and use it.   **Answers will vary.**

   (*Hint 1:* Use the formula for the area of a circle to find the area of each base. $A = \pi \times r^2$.)

   (*Hint 2:* The length of the rectangle is the same as the circumference of the circular base. $C = \pi \times d$. What is the area of the rectangle?)   **$C \times h$**
   Suggestion given: $2(\pi r^2) + C(h)$

5. Compare your estimates for the surface area obtained in Exercises 2 and 4.   **Check students' work.**

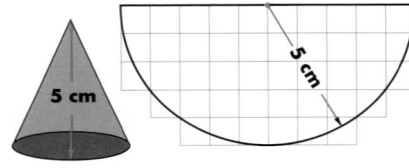

This is a pattern for the curved surface of a cone.

6. Estimate the surface area of this part of the cone.   **Accept reasonable estimates; about 40 cm²**

7. Draw the pattern on centimeter graph paper. Cut it out and bend it to make the curved surface.
   Check students' drawings.

8. Draw the flat face.
   Check students' drawings.

★ 9. Estimate the surface area of the cone.   **Accept reasonable estimates; about 60 cm²**

CHAPTER 14   471

CLASS ACTIVITY **14-10**

☑ **MATERIALS CHECKLIST:** Cans, rulers

Have the students work in pairs. Give each pair a can or cylindrical container. Ask them to trace one base. Then have them cut a rectangular piece of paper that can be wrapped to fit exactly around the can or container. Have the partners find the area of the rectangle and of the circle they drew. Have them multiply the area of the circle by 2 and then add the area of the rectangle to find the surface area. Ask: Why did you multiply the area of the circle by 2? [2 bases]

MEETING INDIVIDUAL NEEDS

For Students Who Are . . .

Acquiring English Proficiency   Cooperatively discuss how to find the surface area of curved surfaces. Have students demonstrate with cans or other models.

Gifted and Talented   Have students create their own patterns for a cylinder and a cone on grid paper. Then have them estimate the surface area of each figure.

Today's Problem

What happens to the surface area of a cube with $s = 2$ when s is doubled? *($6 \times 2^2 = 24$; $6 \times 4^2 = 96$; the surface area is multiplied by 4.)* Is this relationship true for cubes of other sizes? *(Yes, for example, $s = 3$; $6 \times 3^2 = 54$; $6 \times 6^2 = 216$; $4 \times 54 = 216$.)*

Lesson Organizer

Objective: Solve problems by using visual perception.

Prior Knowledge: Students should be familiar with the sphere and basic figures.

Error Analysis and Remediation: See page 483A.

Lesson Resources:
Practice Worksheet 14-11
Reteaching Activity 14-11
Enrichment Worksheet 14-11
Daily Review 14-11

Two-Minute Math

Use row M of the Table of Numbers on the inside back cover. Use mental math to find each percent of 100 and of 500. *(50, 1, 100, 25, 5, 75, 30, 200, 80; 250, 5, 500, 125, 25, 375, 150, 1,000, 400)*

1 INTRODUCE

CONCRETE ACTIVITY

☑ **MATERIALS CHECKLIST:** blank paper for each student, knife, orange

1. Have the class watch as you cut an orange in half as shown below.

2. Before showing the inside, ask students to draw what they think the part along which you cut will look like.

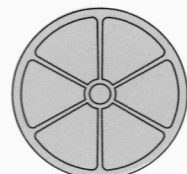

3. Show the inside and have students check their drawings.

WHEN YOUR STUDENTS ASK
★ **WHY AM I LEARNING THIS?** ★

You can connect this skill to real life through assembling different objects, such as a gas grill, a model airplane, or furniture. Assembly instructions often show cross sections that help you visualize the interior parts.

472 *Chapter 14 • Lesson 14-11*

MATH AND INDUSTRIAL ARTS

Problem Solving:
Visual Perception

A drafter draws designs or plans to construct tools, utensils, cars, and other objects. For some objects, it is necessary to draw a **cross section** of the object so you can see a hidden part.

To make a cross section of this faucet handle, you would cut through the handle along a plane. The shape of the figure the plane cuts is called the **cross section**.

The picture at the left shows a cross section of an object you often use. What is the object? Answer these questions to help you decide.

> What could a cross section look like from a different direction?
> Answers will vary.

> Is the object's shape more like a prism, cylinder, or sphere?
> cylinder

> What is contained within the object? It holds liquid.

▬▬ **GUIDED PRACTICE** ▬▬

1. Use the diagram at right to answer.
   a. What does the diagram show? plane through center of sphere
   b. What is the shape of the cross section? circle
   c. What is the shape of the cross section of a sphere when the plane does not pass through the center of the sphere? always a circle

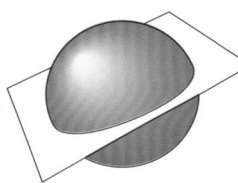

472   LESSON 14–11

---

2 TEACH

☑ **MATERIALS CHECKLIST:** compass, straightedge

Why are cross sections made? *(to see parts hidden from view from the outside)*

If the shape of a cross section is a rectangle, does this mean that the object has flat sides? *(No; the cross section of a cylinder can appear to be a rectangle; a cross section does not always show the curve of a surface.)*

SUMMARIZE/ASSESS   **What is a cross section?** *(It is the shape of a figure that a plane cuts.)*

┌─────────────────────────────────┐
│   **MULTICULTURAL NOTE**   │
└─────────────────────────────────┘

One important drafter in the 1800s was Lewis Latimer, an African American. He worked with Alexander Graham Bell and made the patent drawings for the first telephone. After inventing a new filament for light bulbs, Latimer became chief drafter for two early electric companies.

Which shapes can be cross sections of the figure on the left?

2. a, b

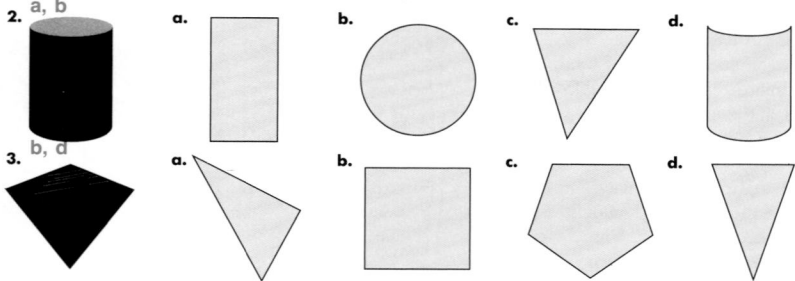

a. b. c. d.

3. b, d

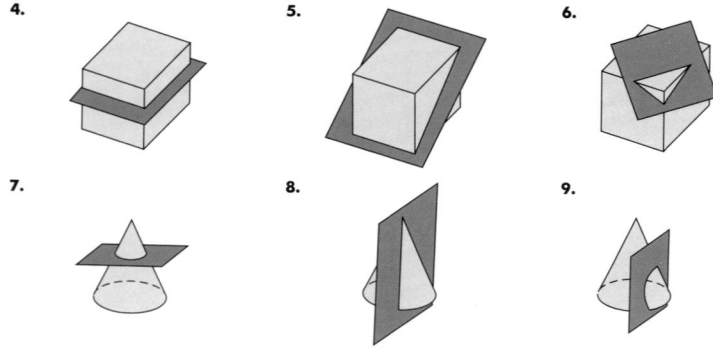

a. b. c. d.

Draw the shape of the cross section. Use a compass if necessary.   Check students' drawings.

4.   **5.**   **6.**

7.   **8.**   **9.**

CHOOSE Choose any strategy to solve.   Strategies may vary. Suggestions given.

10. Judith bought a pair of jeans at an outlet sale. The original price was $50.00. She received the regular 20% outlet discount and, in addition, a 25% discount on the first discounted price because of the sale. How much did she pay for the jeans?
multistep; $30

11. Roger made 5 model cars and wants to put them on a shelf. He is trying to decide how to arrange them and wants to try every possible way. How many different ways can he arrange the cars on a shelf?
picture or pattern; 120 ways

12. About how many days in all will there be in the 21st century? (*Hint:* It begins January 1, 2001 and ends December 31, 2100.)
estimation; about 36,500 days

MEETING INDIVIDUAL NEEDS

For Students Who Are . . .

Acquiring English Proficiency   Pair students with an English-proficient student for the Practice exercises.

Gifted and Talented   Have students sketch a figure similar to those in Exercises 4–9. They can give their sketch to a classmate to draw the shape of the cross section.

Working 2 or 3 Grades Below Level   For cones and cubes, have students cut paper models to see the cross section.

Today's Problem

A three-dimensional tic-tac-toe consists of planes at three heights, each with three columns and three rows. You win if you place 3X's or 3 O's in a straight line in any column, row, or diagonal on any one plane or in different planes. How many possibilities for winning are there? *(8 for each of the three planes at different heights, plus 8 for each of three planes parallel to the front of the game, plus 8 for each of the three planes parallel to the side of the game, plus 4 diagonals for a total of 76.)*

3 FOLLOW-UP

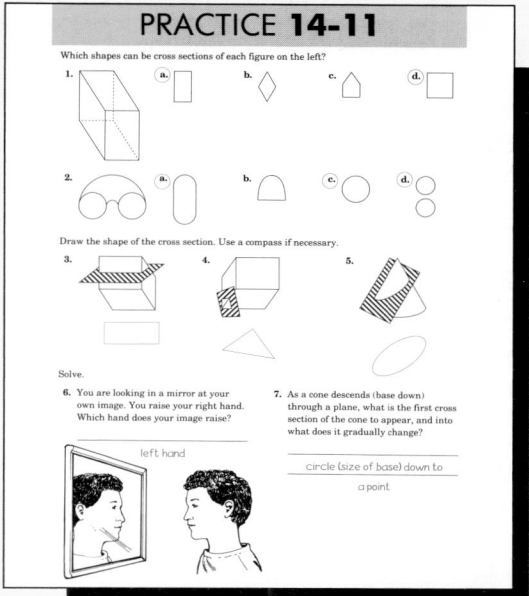

PRACTICE 14-11

Which shapes can be cross sections of each figure on the left?

1.   a.   b.   c.   d.

2.   a.   b.   c.   d.

Draw the shape of the cross section. Use a compass if necessary.

3.   4.   5.

Solve.

6. You are looking in a mirror at your own image. You raise your right hand. Which hand does your image raise?   left hand

7. As a cone descends (base down) through a plane, what is the first cross section of the cone to appear, and into what does it gradually change?
circle (size of base) down to a point

RETEACHING 14-11

Some students may have difficulty visualizing cross sections. Help a student solve Problem 1, *Practice Worksheet 14-11*, by asking these questions: Which polygons make up the faces of the space figure shown? [rhombuses and rectangles] If you make a thin slice parallel to one of the rectangular faces, what polygon would the slice resemble when viewed straight on? [rectangle] If you sliced the figure vertically close to the base that is visible in the drawing, what polygon would the slice resemble when viewed straight on? [rhombus] Which letters show a rectangle and a rhombus? [**a** and **b**] Is there any way to slice the figure to get a pentagon or a square? [no]

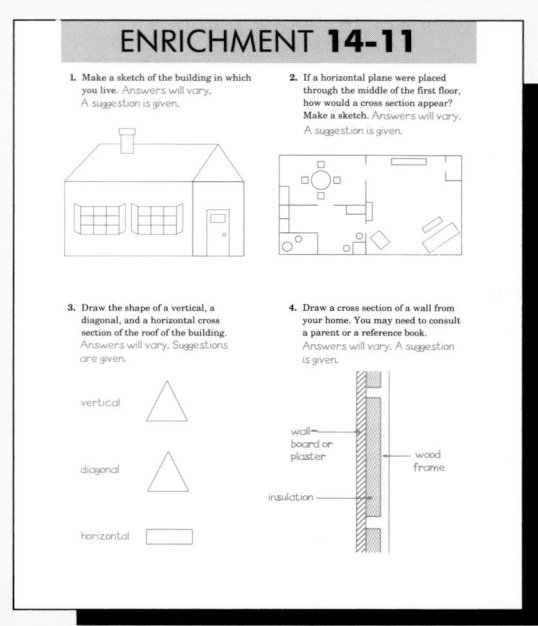

ENRICHMENT 14-11

1. Make a sketch of the building in which you live. Answers will vary. A suggestion is given.

2. If a horizontal plane were placed through the middle of the first floor, how would a cross section appear? Make a sketch. Answers will vary. A suggestion is given.

3. Draw the shape of a vertical, a diagonal, and a horizontal cross section of the roof of the building. Answers will vary. Suggestions are given.

vertical

diagonal

horizontal

4. Draw a cross section of a wall from your home. You may need to consult a parent or a reference book. Answers will vary. A suggestion is given.

wall-board or plaster

insulation

wood frame

Lesson Organizer

> **Objective:** Find the volume of a prism and a pyramid.

Prior Knowledge: Students should know the meanings of *prism* and *pyramid* and how to find the areas of a rectangle and a triangle.

Error Analysis and Remediation: See page 483A.

Lesson Resources:
Practice Worksheet 14-12
Reteaching Worksheet 14-12
Enrichment Activity 14-12
Daily Review 14-12

Two-Minute Math

Find the area.
rectangle: $l = 16$ ft, $w = 10$ ft
square: $s = 9$ m
triangle: $b = 12$ in., $h = 8$ in.
(160 ft^2; 81 m^2; 48 in.^{2})

1 INTRODUCE

CONCRETE ACTIVITY

✓ **MATERIALS CHECKLIST:** Teaching Aids 20 and 24 (Cube and Square Pyramid), scissors, tape, and paper cupful of rice or beans for each pair

Have students work with a partner to make the two space figures, leaving a base open in each. **How are the two figures alike?** (*Both have rectangular bases and the heights are the same length.*)

Carefully fill the pyramid with rice (beans). If you pour rice (beans) from the pyramid into the prism, how much of the prism do you think will be filled? (*Correct answer is $\frac{1}{3}$.*)

Have students check their estimates by pouring. **What can you say about the volume of a pyramid?** (*It is $\frac{1}{3}$ the volume of a prism with the same base and height.*)

WHEN YOUR STUDENTS ASK
★ WHY AM I LEARNING THIS? ★

You can connect this skill to real life through outdoor camping. The interior space of a tent is measured in cubic feet, and you would select a tent based on your particular needs.

Volume: Prism and Pyramid

This refrigerator holds 18 cubic feet (18 ft^3) of food. Estimate the size of a cubic foot and show it using your hands.

The **volume** of a space figure measures the amount of space inside of it. The volume of the rectangular prism at right is 18 ft^3. Its dimensions are 3 ft by 3 ft by 2 ft, or 18 ft^3.

The volume (V) of any prism is the product of the area of the base (B) and the height (h).	The volume (V) of a pyramid is one third of the volume of a prism with the same base (B) and height (h).
$V = Bh$	$V = \frac{1}{3}(Bh)$

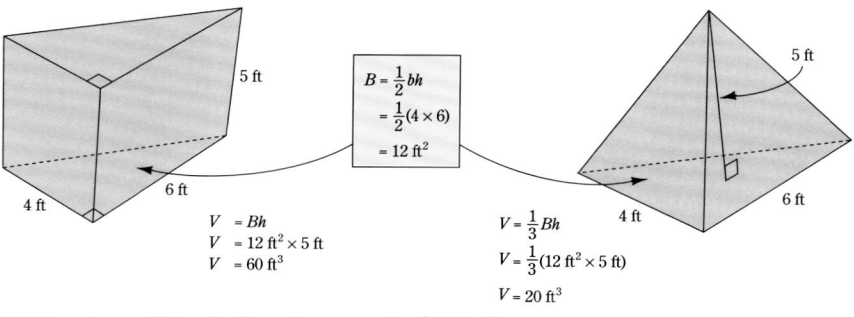

$B = \frac{1}{2}bh$
$= \frac{1}{2}(4 \times 6)$
$= 12$ ft^2

$V = Bh$
$V = 12$ ft$^2 \times 5$ ft
$V = 60$ ft^3

$V = \frac{1}{3}Bh$
$V = \frac{1}{3}(12$ ft$^2 \times 5$ ft$)$
$V = 20$ ft^3

Find the volume. Write the formula you used. See below.

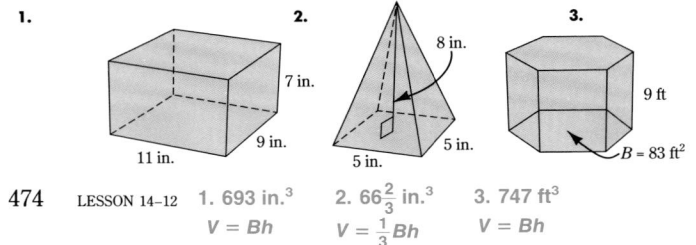

1.   2.   3.

1. 693 in.^{3} 2. $66\frac{2}{3}$ in.^{3} 3. 747 ft^3
$V = Bh$ $V = \frac{1}{3}Bh$ $V = Bh$

2 TEACH

How many cubic feet will fit into a cubic yard? Explain how you know. (*Students should reason that there will be 3 ft in a row, with 3 rows on the base, or 9 ft^3 in the bottom layer. There are three layers, or 27ft^3 in a cubic yard.*)

Look at the prism in Exercise 1. What is the volume of a pyramid with the same base and height? (*The volume of that prism is 693 in.^{3}; the volume of a pyramid with the same base and height is $\frac{1}{3}$ (693 in.^{3}), or 231 in.^{3}*)

> ### Chalkboard Examples
>
> Find the volume of a prism and a pyramid with, $B = 72$ yd^2, $h = 8$ yd. (*prism: $V = 576$ yd^3; pyramid: $V = 192$ yd^3*)

SUMMARIZE/ASSESS **What is the formula for the volume of a prism?** ($V = Bh$) **a pyramid?** [$V = \frac{1}{3}(Bh)$]

PRACTICE

Find the volume.

4. 240 ft³ 6 ft, 8 ft, 5 ft

5. 48 in.³ Area = 24 in.² 2 in.

6. $26\frac{2}{3}$ yd³ 10 yd Area = 8 yd²

7. 72 in.³ 9 in., 8 in., 2 in.

8. 192 in.³ 9 in., 8 in.

9. 6 in., 12 in., 6 in., 8 in. 480 in.³

10. a cube with length of side:
  a. 10 in.   **b.** 11 ft   **c.** s feet
     1,000 in.³   1,331 ft³   s³ft³

Find the height.

11. a prism with a volume of 308 in.³ and a base area of 28 in.²
11 in.

12. a pyramid with a volume of 255 in.³ and a base area of 45 in.²
17 in.

PROBLEM SOLVING

13. Name one possible set of dimensions for an 18 ft³ freezer.
Accept reasonable answers.

14. **IN YOUR WORDS** You want to buy a freezer. Use the ad below to write two questions you should ask yourself before buying it.
Answers will vary. Suggestions given. How much will it hold? What is the price per cubic foot?

10 ft³ HOLDS 350 lb $339

16 ft³ HOLDS 560 lb $399

21 ft³ HOLDS 735 lb $499

FREEZER

CHAPTER 14   475

MEETING INDIVIDUAL NEEDS

For Students Who Are . . .

Acquiring English Proficiency Review how to find the area of a triangle and a rectangle. Have students identify models for prisms in the classroom.

Gifted and Talented Challenge students to find the side of a cube whose volume is 729 mm³. *(9 mm)*

Working 2 or 3 Grades Below Level Reinforce the idea that B in the formula refers to the area of the base. For a rectangular prism, have students write the formula $l \times w \times h$.

Today's Problem

The prism shown is 10 in. high, and its square base is 2 in. on a side. The pyramid is 6 in. tall. What is the total volume of the solid? *(The volume is $10 \times 2 \times 2 + \frac{1}{3} \times 6 \times 2 \times 2 = 40 + 8$ or 48 in.³)*

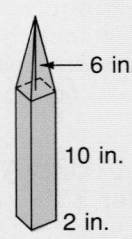

6 in.
10 in.
2 in.

---

3 FOLLOW-UP

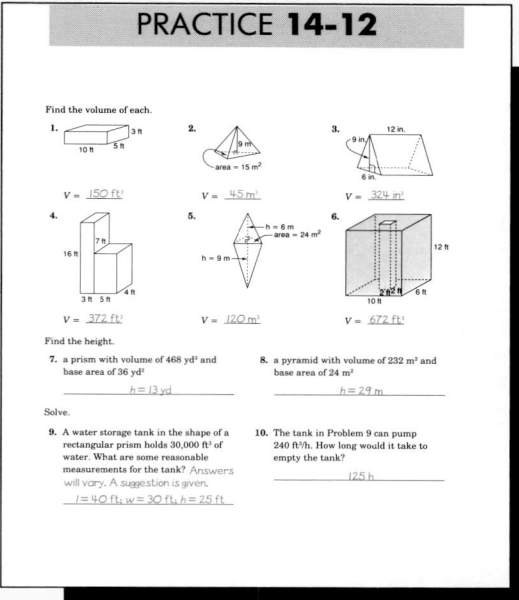
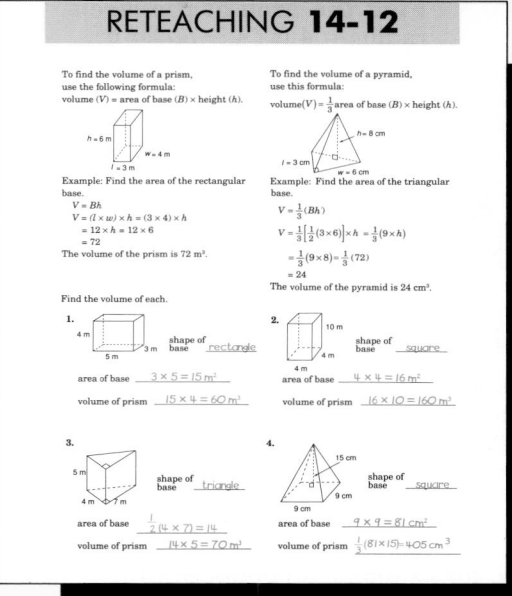
ENRICHMENT 14-12

☑ **MATERIALS CHECKLIST:** Gram cubes

Have the students work in pairs. Provide each partner with a large handful of centimeter cubes (gram cubes). Ask the students to use the cubes to model at least four rectangular prisms that have a volume of 60 cm³. [Suggestions: 5 cm × 2 cm × 6 cm; 3 cm × 2 cm × 10 cm; 10 cm × 1 cm × 6 cm; 3 cm × 5 cm × 4 cm] Then have them find the surface area of each space figure. [104 cm², 112 cm², 152 cm², 94 cm²] Have each pair share its work with the other pairs. Ask: Which figures had less surface area?

Lesson Organizer

> **Objective:** Find the volume of a cylinder.

Prior Knowledge: Students should know how to find the area of a circle.

Error Analysis and Remediation: See page 483A.

Lesson Resources:
Practice Worksheet 14-13
Reteaching Worksheet 14-13
Enrichment Activity 14-13
Daily Review 14-13
Cooperative Problem Solving 2, Chapter 14

 *Two-Minute Math*

Find the area of the circle.
radius = 4 ft *(A ≈ 50.24 ft²)*
radius = 10 ft *(A ≈ 314 ft²)*
diameter = 8 ft *(A ≈ 50.24 ft²)*

1 INTRODUCE

CONNECTING ACTIVITY

☑ **MATERIALS CHECKLIST:** empty can and cupful of beans for each group

Assign students to work in groups of four. **Guess the number of beans the can will hold and write your guess on a piece of paper.**

Use the beans to check your guess. Point out that it isn't necessary to fill the can; for example, students can fill $\frac{1}{10}$ of the can and multiply by 10.

Whose guess was closest to the estimate? Ask each group to write a summary of their method of estimating to present to the class. Compare methods and estimates.

WHEN YOUR STUDENTS ASK
★ WHY AM I LEARNING THIS? ★

This skill will help you become a better shopper. For example, you need to know how much food is in a can, which may be labeled by volume, before you make a purchase.

MATH AND HOME ECONOMICS

Volume: Cylinder

A springform pan used for baking has a removable rim fastened with a spring. When the rim is removed, the sides of the cake look perfect. One standard size for a springform pan is 10 in. in diameter and $2\frac{1}{2}$ in. in height. What is its volume?

First, you find the area of the circular base and multiply by a height of 1 in.

For the volume of one layer:
$V = (\pi \times r^2) \times 1$
$V \approx (3.14 \times 5^2) \times 1$, or
78.50 in.³

Then for the entire cylinder, multiply by a height of $2\frac{1}{2}$ in.

$V \approx 78.5$ in.³ × 2.5, or 196.25 in.³

The pan holds about 200 in.³.

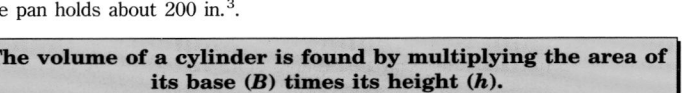
Remember: Area (A) of circle = $\pi \times r^2$
$\pi \approx 3.14$ $d = 2 \times r$

10 in. $2\frac{1}{2}$ in.

> **The volume of a cylinder is found by multiplying the area of its base (B) times its height (h).**
> **Volume (V) = Area of Base (B) × height (h)**
> $V = B \times h$

THINK ALOUD For what other space figure is the same formula used to find its volume? **prism**

CALCULATOR Could you multiply this way—3.14 × 2.75 × 16—to find the volume of the cylinder? Explain your answer.
yes; using commutative property

8 ft   2.75 ft

━━━ **GUIDED PRACTICE** ━━━

Find the volume. Explain how you used the formula.

1.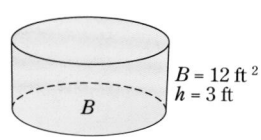
$B = 12$ ft²
$h = 3$ ft
B

2.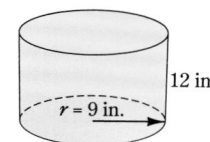
12 in.
$r = 9$ in.

476   LESSON 14-13   1. 36 ft³; **V = Bh**
2. 3,052.08 in.³; **V = Bh**

---

2 TEACH

☑ **MATERIALS CHECKLIST:** calculators

How does finding the volume of a cylinder compare to finding the volume of a rectangular prism? *(After you use different formulas to find the area of the different-shaped bases, you use the same formula to find the volume of both space figures.)*

Why do you think that the volume formulas for the prism and cylinder are the same, but the formula for the pyramid is different? *(Possible answer: Prisms and cylinders have parallel and congruent bases, but pyramids do not.)*

> ### Chalkboard Example
> Find the volume of a cylinder with a diameter of 14 cm and a height of 12 cm. Use $\frac{22}{7}$ for π. *(V ≈ 1,848 cm³)*

SUMMARIZE/ASSESS Explain how to find the volume of a cylinder. *(Find the area of the base; then multiply the area by the height.)*

PRACTICE

Find the volume of the cylinder. Use 3.14 for π.

3. $r = 3$ ft
$h = 7$ ft
197.82 ft³

4. $r = 9$ ft
$h = 3$ ft
763.02 ft³

5. $r = 17$ yd
$h = 11$ yd
9,982.06 yd³

6. $d = 19$ in.
$h = 17$ in.
4,817.545 in.³

7. $d = 82$ ft
$h = 25$ ft
131,958.5 ft³

8. $d = 3\frac{1}{2}$ yd
$h = 2\frac{1}{4}$ yd
21.637 yd³

Find the volume.   See below.

9. 18.84 in.³

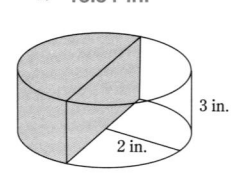

10. 769.3 ft³

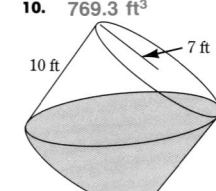

11. 604.24 in.³

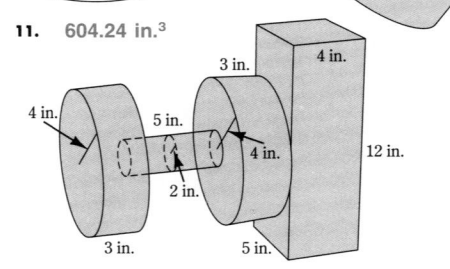

12. **CALCULATOR** Find the radius and the height of two different cylinders, each with a volume between 50 in.³ and 60 in.³
Answers will vary. Suggestion given. $r = 2$ $h = 4$

PROBLEM SOLVING

13. Springform pans come in two standard sizes with diameters of 7 in. and 10 in. Both pans have the same height. Compare their volumes.
volume of 10 in. is about double the 7 in.

14. **CRITICAL THINKING** Why do you think the two sizes of pans in Exercise 13 are the standard sizes? Answers will vary. Suggestion given. So that recipes can be doubled, or halved.

15. Some springform pans look like the one at right. What is its volume?

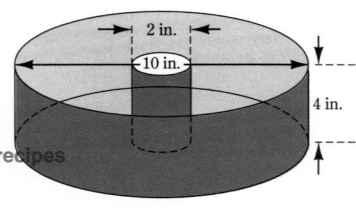

9. 678.24 in.³   **10.** 769.3 ft³   **11.** 604.24 in.³

CHAPTER 14   **477**

MEETING INDIVIDUAL NEEDS

For Students Who Are . . .

Acquiring English Proficiency Use a can or other model to help students differentiate between a radius and a diameter. Emphasize that the radius is used to find the volume of a cylinder.

Gifted and Talented Challenge students to find the area of the base of a cylinder if the volume is 192 cm³ and the height is 16 cm. *(12 cm²)*

Working 2 or 3 Grades Below Level In finding the volume of a cylinder, have students first square the radius, then multiply by the height, and finally multiply by pi.

Today's Problem

A concrete sewer pipe in the shape of a hollow cylinder is 20 in. long. Its outside diameter is 10 in., and the thickness of the concrete is 1 in. About how many cubic inches of concrete are there? *(The volume is about $(\pi \times 5^2 \times 20) - (\pi \times 4^2 \times 20) = (\pi \times 500) - (\pi \times 320) = \pi(500 - 320) = \pi(180)$ or about 565.2 in.³)*

---

3 FOLLOW-UP

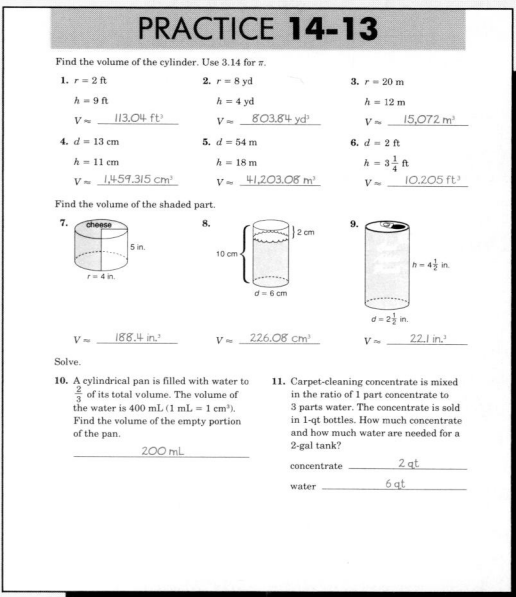

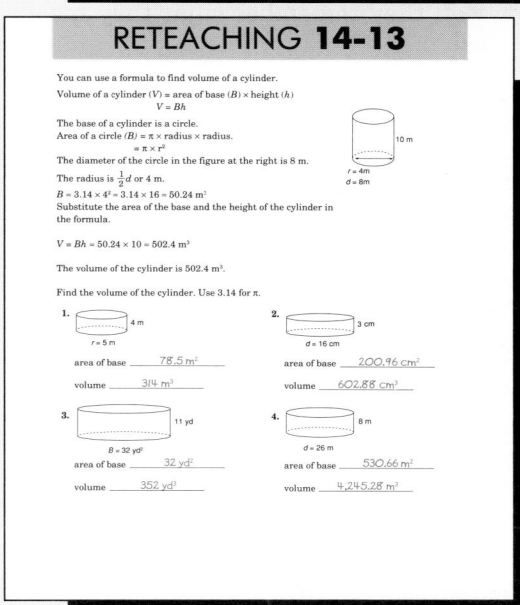

ENRICHMENT **14-13**

☑ **MATERIALS CHECKLIST:** Cylindrical containers, construction paper, scissors, tape, beans

Provide small groups with a cylindrical object, such as an empty oatmeal container or can of baking powder. Ask each group to make a cone with the same height and base as the cylinder. Each group fills its cone with beans and then pours the beans into the cylinder. Ask: About how full is the container? [about $\frac{1}{3}$ full] Ask: How do you think the volume of a cone compares to the volume of a cylinder? [volume of cone = $\frac{1}{3}$ volume of cylinder] What formula would you use to find the volume of a cone? [$V = \frac{1}{3}Bh$]

Lesson Organizer

Objective: Review operations with whole numbers, integers, decimals, and mixed numbers; fraction concepts; solving proportions; percents.

Lesson Resource:
Daily Review 14-14

These pages provide students with a review of computing with whole numbers, integers, decimals, and mixed numbers; using fraction concepts; solving proportions; finding percents; and solving problems using a map and a table.

Remind students that these pages review skills covered in previous chapters and will help them to do a self-check to see how well they remember what they have learned.

MATH AND SOCIAL STUDIES

Mixed Review

Compute.

1. $28,182 \div 77$ 366
2. $913 + 302$ 1,215
3. $7,650 - 4,721$ 2,929
4. $613.4 - 1.58$ 611.82

5. $\frac{5}{8} \times 2\frac{1}{6}$ $1\frac{17}{48}$
6. $4\frac{5}{8} \div \frac{1}{4}$ $18\frac{1}{2}$
7. $10\frac{11}{12} + \frac{10}{24}$ $11\frac{1}{3}$
8. $9\frac{3}{8} - 3\frac{7}{8}$ $5\frac{1}{2}$

Solve for n in the proportion.

9. $\frac{n}{35} = \frac{12}{60}$ 7
10. $\frac{8}{20} = \frac{n}{45}$ 18
11. $\frac{9}{15} = \frac{33}{n}$ 55
12. $\frac{14}{n} = \frac{8}{24}$ 42

Find the unknown.

13. 75% of what number is 90? 120
14. What is 80% of 385? 308
15. What is 60% of 610? 366
16. 25% of what number is 111? 444
17. What percent is 258 out of 516? 50%
18. What is 50% of 270? 135
19. 90% of what number is 198? 220
20. What percent is 161 out of 460? 35%

Compute.

21. $9 + {}^-3$ 6
22. $1 - 5$ $^-4$
23. $2 \times {}^-4$ $^-8$
24. $^-4 \div 2$ $^-2$
25. $^-1 - 6$ $^-7$
26. $7 + {}^-4$ 3
27. $4 \div {}^-2$ $^-2$
28. $^-7 \times {}^-3$ 21
29. $^-5 \times 2$ $^-10$
30. $^-4 \div {}^-2$ 2
31. $^-12 + {}^-8$ $^-20$
32. $5 - {}^-3$ 8
33. $^-16 \div 4$ $^-4$
34. $4 \times {}^-6$ $^-24$
35. $^-2 - {}^-12$ 10
36. $^-15 + 15$ 0
37. $^-20 + {}^-10$ $^-30$
38. $^-12 - 21$ $^-33$
39. $^-4 \times {}^-4$ 16
40. $20 \div {}^-10$ $^-2$

Niamey, Niger

478   LESSON 14–14

Use the map and the table. Choose estimation, mental math, pencil and paper, or calculator to solve.

Choices will vary. Suggestions are given.

41. About 6,894,000 people live in Niger.
Accept reasonable estimates.
   a. About 1 person out of every 23 people in Niger owns a radio. About how many people own radios? e; ≈300,000 people

   b. Less than 1% of the population owns a television. About how many people, at most, own televisions? c; 68,940 people

   c. About 4 out of every 5 people live in rural areas. About how many people live in urban areas? c; 1,378,800 people

42. The Niger River is the third largest river in Africa. It is about 252 mi longer than the 2,348-mi Mississippi River. About how long is the Niger River?
m; 2,600 mi

43. Niger's capital, Niamey, is located at about 13° N latitude and 2° W longitude. What is the latitude and longitude of Mount Gréboun, Niger's highest point?
e; 20°N and 9°W

44. *Sahara* comes from an Arabic word meaning "desert." The United States, which has an area of about 3,619,000 mi², is only about 119,000 mi² larger than the Sahara. About how large is the Sahara?
m; 3,500,000 mi²

45. Estimate the distance from Mount Gréboun to Niamey.
e; about 600 mi

46. Draw a double bar graph of the average monthly high and low temperatures for Niamey.
Check students' drawings.

Niamey's Average High and Low Temperatures		
January	93°F	61°F
February	91°F	64°F
March	102°F	72°F
April	106°F	79°F
May	106°F	81°F
June	100°F	77°F
July	93°F	75°F
August	90°F	72°F
September	93°F	73°F
October	97°F	73°F
November	99°F	66°F
December	93°F	59°F

CHAPTER 14　479

MULTICULTURAL NOTE

Niger is a landlocked country in West Africa. Its area is larger than the combined area of Arkansas, Louisiana, Mississippi, Oklahoma, and Texas, but its population is only half that of Texas. Much of the country is desert or semidesert, and farming is only possible in the extreme southwest, near the Niger River.

Lesson Organizer

> **Objective:** Solve problems creatively.

Prior Knowledge: Students should be able to compute volume of a rectangular prism and a cylinder.

Lesson Resources:
Daily Review 14-15

Two-Minute Math

Find the volume of the cylinder.

$B = 75$ cm^2, $h = 10$ cm *(750 cm³)*

$B = 314$ in.^{2}, $h = 15$ in. *(4,710 in.³)*

$B = 50.24$ m^2, $h = 0.9$ m *(45.216 m³)*

1 PREPARE

CONNECTING ACTIVITY

☑ **MATERIALS CHECKLIST:** plastic beaker or cylindrical container, water, inch ruler for each group

Assign students to work in groups of three or four.

Find the area of the base of the container. Pour water into that container to a height of $5\frac{1}{2}$ in. What is the approximate volume of water in the container?

Tell students to keep the container of water to use in the next part of the lesson.

WHEN YOUR STUDENTS ASK
★ WHY AM I LEARNING THIS? ★

You can relate the ideas in this lesson to the work of mechanical engineers. When bridges and roads are designed, engineers must allow for expansion and contraction of materials under changing weather conditions.

CREATIVE PROBLEM SOLVING

Investigating Water and Ice

Ice is water that has frozen solid. Raindrops are water, but snow, sleet, frost, and hail are ice. Ice has many uses because it is cold. It helps to keep foods fresh, to chill beverages, and to treat injuries.

Pure water changes to ice, or freezes, when it is cooled to 32°F. This temperature is the freezing point of water.

Almost all substances contract, or grow smaller, as they cool. Water contracts as it cools to 39°F. Then it begins to expand, or grow larger. When water freezes, it increases in volume by about $\frac{1}{11}$.

When the temperature around ice becomes warmer than 32°F, ice begins to melt into water. The temperature of the ice and the melted water will stay at 32°F until all the ice has melted.

Work with a partner. You will need nonglass containers, some water, a ruler, packaging materials, and a freezer. A thermometer may be helpful.

MATH AND SCIENCE

2 EXPLORE

☑ **MATERIALS CHECKLIST:** plastic beaker or cylindrical container (identical to that used in Introduce), water, a ruler, and packaging materials for each pair; a freezer should be available

Have groups separate into pairs.

After students have followed the instruction in Exercise 1, have them find the volume of the ice. **Estimate; about how much greater is the volume of the ice than the volume of the water?**

What is the volume of each ice block shown on page 481? *(Each is 125 in.³)* **How would you change the dimensions so that the volume would be doubled?** *(Possible answer: For each block, double one 5 in. dimension to 10 in.)*

SUMMARIZE/ASSESS   **What mathematics skills did you use to investigate water and ice?** *(Answers will vary. Example: measuring, computing volume)*

1. Use a tall container. Pour water in it to a depth of at least $5\frac{1}{2}$ in., but don't fill the container. Freeze the water in the container. Measure the height of the ice.
   Check students' work.

2. Did the ice increase in volume? If so, by what fraction did it increase? Do your results agree with the information given on page 480?
   Check students' work.

3. Use your results from Exercises 1 and 2 to explain the situations.
   a. Water pipes may burst in very cold weather.
   b. Ice floats in water.
   Accept reasonable answers.

4. Imagine that you have the blocks of ice shown below. If all three are placed on a sidewalk on a warm day, which do you think will completely melt first? Explain.
   third; Accept reasonable answers.

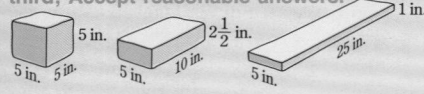

5. For most uses of ice, it is important to keep it so cold that it doesn't melt or that it melts very slowly. List some ways to keep ice cold.
   Check students' work.

6. Can you think of a better way to keep ice from melting? List your ideas.
   Check students' work.

7. Have a contest. Make several blocks of ice using the same amount of water and the same kind of container. Use whatever materials you like (but nothing involving electricity) to "package" the ice. See whose packaging best keeps the ice from melting.
   Check students' work.

8. In Exercise 7, how can you determine when the ice has completely melted without opening the "packages" of ice? (*Hint*: Read the fourth paragraph on page 480.)
   Accept reasonable answers.

CHAPTER 14   481

☑ **MATERIALS CHECKLIST:** Three thermometers, a heating pot, three containers with different size bases (all plastic or all metal); measuring cup

Fill the pot with water and let it boil. Pour equal amounts of water into the three containers. After one minute, place a thermometer in each container. Have students record the temperatures on a chart. Repeat every five minutes until the temperatures are constant. Are the rates of change of temperature the same or different for the three containers? Discuss.

MEETING INDIVIDUAL NEEDS

For Students Who Are . . .

Acquiring English Proficiency You may wish to display a Fahrenheit thermometer and have students identify the freezing point of water. You can discuss the words *temperature* and *melted*, and explain the notation for "degrees Fahrenheit."

Gifted and Talented Have students use science books or other references to compile a list of freezing points for other substances.

Working 2 or 3 Grades Below Level Remind students that the area of the circular base represents the B in the formula for the volume of a cylinder. They should find the area of the base first, then multiply by the height of the cylinder.

Today's Problem

If a circular clock face has a radius of 10 in., what area of the clock face is enclosed by the hour and minute hands at 11:45? (*The hour hand is close to 12:00 and the minute hand is at 9:00, enclosing about $\frac{1}{4}$ of the circle. The area of the circle is 3.14×10^2, or about 314 in.; $\frac{1}{4}$ of 314 is $78\frac{1}{2}$ in.*)

This chapter checkup provides a quick language and vocabulary review, a test for the chapter, and suggestions for student Learning Log entries.

Language and Vocabulary

Some key language and vocabulary ideas from this chapter are reinforced here.

Test

The test can be used either as a test or as a review of the chapter prior to administering the test worksheets found in the Teacher's Resource Book.

The following guide will help you determine percentage scores.

Score	Percent	Score	Percent
23	100%	11	48%
22	96	10	43
21	91	9	39
20	87	8	35
19	83	7	30
18	78	6	26
17	74	5	22
16	70	4	17
15	65	3	13
14	61	2	9
13	57	1	4
12	52		

Each test has three sections: concepts, skills, and problem solving. These sections provide students with exposure to the format used on standardized tests.

Use this chart to identify the Management Objectives tested for this chapter.

Items	Management Objectives	Pages
1–10	**14A** Find squares and square roots of numbers.	452–455
11–12	**14B** Bisect a line segment or an angle by construction; construct space figures.	458–461
13–20; 23	**14C** Find the surface area or volume of a prism, a pyramid, or a cylinder.	468–471; 474–477
21–22	**14D** Problem Solving: Create and use a formula. Use visual perception.	466–467; 472–473

CHAPTER CHECKUP

LANGUAGE & VOCABULARY

Match the figure with its description.

1. a figure with two congruent triangular bases **b**
2. a figure with six congruent faces **d**
3. a figure with one square base and four congruent triangular faces **e**
4. a figure with one base and no polygon faces **a**
5. a figure with two circular bases **c**

a. cone
b. triangular prism
c. cylinder
d. cube
e. square pyramid

TEST ✓

CONCEPTS

Find the square of the number. *(pages 452–455)*

1. 11^2 121
2. 23^2 529
3. 1^2 1
4. 4^2 16
5. $(^-6)^2$ 36

Find the positive square root of each number. *(pages 452–455)*

6. $\sqrt{169}$ 13
7. $\sqrt{400}$ 20
8. $\sqrt{1}$ 1
9. $\sqrt{\frac{25}{64}}$ $\frac{5}{8}$
10. $\sqrt{\frac{1}{36}}$ $\frac{1}{6}$

Use the construction. Points Q and X were found by striking arcs from points M and N. Line QX is to be drawn. Complete each statement. *(pages 458–461)*

11. QX and MN will be __perpendicular__ .

12. Segments MO and ON are __congruent__ .

SKILLS

Find the volume. Use 3.14 for π. *(pages 468–471, 474–477)*

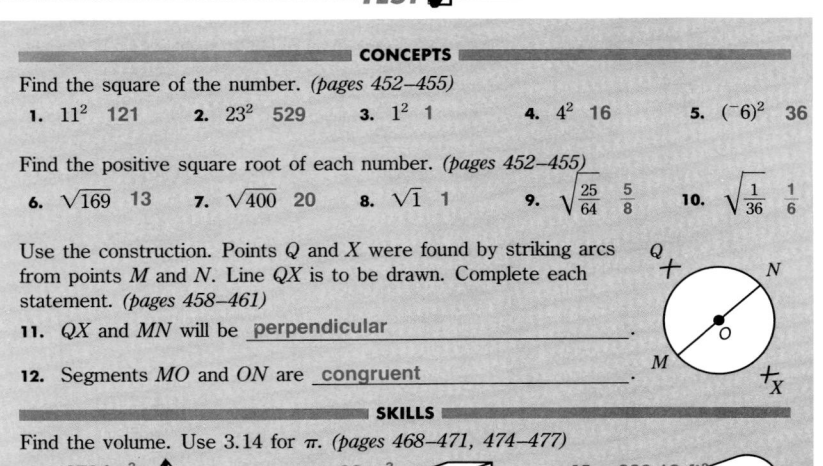

13. 270 in.³ $h = 10$ in. $A = 81$ in.²
14. 96 m³   4m   6m   4m
15. 339.12 ft³ $r = 3$ ft $h = 12$ ft

16. A cube with length of side 15 in.   3,375 in.³
17. A pyramid with base area 100 m² and height 12 m.   400 m³
18. A cylinder with diameter 12 yd and height 12 yd.   1,356.48 yd³

For Exercises 14 and 15 find the surface area also.

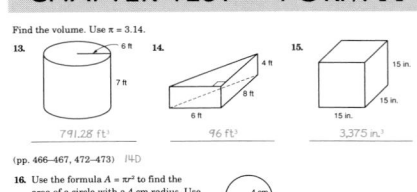

CHAPTER TEST • FORM A

(pp. 452–455) 14A
Find the square of the number.
1. 11^2 ___121___
2. $\left(\frac{1}{5}\right)^2$ ___$\frac{1}{25}$___
3. $(^-6)^2$ ___36___

Find the positive square root of each number.
4. $\sqrt{900}$ ___30___
5. $\sqrt{\frac{36}{49}}$ ___$\frac{6}{7}$___

(pp. 450–451, 456–463) 14B
6. Construct a regular hexagon
7. Bisect $\angle QRS$.
8. Construct perpendicular lines
9. Use SSS to construct a congruent triangle.
10. Construct an equilateral triangle.

(pp. 468–471, 474–477) 14C
Find the surface area.
11. ___436 ft²___   4 ft   9 ft   14 ft
12. ___384 in.²___   10 in.   12 in.   12 in.

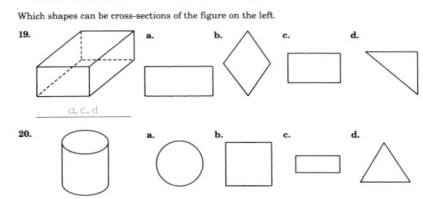

CHAPTER TEST • FORM A

Find the volume. Use π = 3.14.
13. 6 ft   7 ft   ___791.28 ft³___
14. 4 ft   8 ft   6 ft   ___96 ft³___
15. 15 in.   15 in.   15 in.   ___3,375 in³___

(pp. 466–467, 472–473) 14D
16. Use the formula $A = \pi r^2$ to find the area of a circle with a 4 cm radius. Use 3.14 for π.   ___50.24 cm²___   4 cm
17. Use the formula $F + V = E + 2$ to find the missing variable: $F = 7$, $E = 15$, $V =$ ___10___
18. Use the formula $C = \pi d$ to find the circumference of a circle with a 6 cm diameter. Use 3.14 for π.   ___18.84 cm___   6 cm

Which shapes can be cross-sections of the figure on the left.
19.   a.   b.   c.   d.   ___a, c, d___
20.   a.   b.   c.   d.   ___a, b___

Find the height. *(pages 474–475)*

19. A prism with volume of 539 in.³ and base area of 77 in.²
   7 in.

20. A pyramid with volume of 405 in.³ and base area of 135 in.²
   9 in.

■■■■■■■■■■ **PROBLEM SOLVING** ■■■■■■■■■■

Solve. *(pages 472–473, 466–467, 476–477)*

21. Use the space figure.

   a. What is the shape of the figure?   prism

   b. How many faces (*F*), vertexes (*V*), and edges (*E*) does
      the figure have?   8; 12; 18

   c. Does the figure satisfy the formula $F + V = E + 2$?   yes

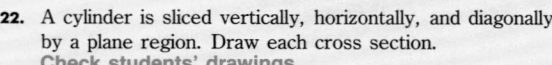

22. A cylinder is sliced vertically, horizontally, and diagonally
   by a plane region. Draw each cross section.
   Check students' drawings.

23. A cylindrical oil tank has a radius of 3 ft for its base and a
   height of 12 ft. What is the volume of the tank? Use 3.14 for π.
   ≈339.12 ft³

─────── 📖 **LEARNING LOG** 📖 ───────

Write the answers in your learning log.   **Answers will vary. Suggestion given.**

1. Describe in your own words what is meant by surface area.
   Accept reasonable answers.

2. Explain how you would make a cylinder using a flat piece of
   paper.   **Roll the paper into a cylinder.**

Note that the same numbers
are used in Exercises 15 and 23.

CHAPTER 14   **483**

CHAPTER TEST • FORM **B**

(pp. 452–455) 14A

Find the square of the number.

1. 15² 225   **2.** $\left(\frac{1}{6}\right)^2$ $\frac{1}{36}$ **3.** (⁻8)² 64

Find the positive square root of each number.

4. √400 20   **5.** $\sqrt{\frac{49}{64}}$ $\frac{7}{8}$

(pp. 450–451, 456–463) 14B

6. Construct a trapezoid.   **7.** Bisect $\overline{AB}$.

8. Construct perpendicular lines   **9.** Use SSS to construct a congruent triangle.

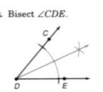

10. Bisect ∠CDE.

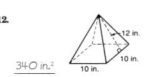

(pp. 468–471, 474–477) 14C

Find the surface area.

11.   458 ft²

12.   340 in.²

CHAPTER TEST • FORM **B**

Find the volume. Use π = 3.14.

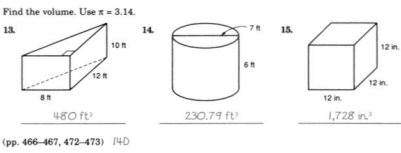

13.   480 ft³   **14.**   230.79 ft³   **15.**   1,728 in.³

(pp. 466–467, 472–473) 14D

16. Use the formula $C = \pi d$ to find the circumference of a circle with an 8 cm diameter. Use 3.14 for π.   25.12 cm

17. Use the formula $F + V = E + 2$ to find the missing variable: $F = 6$, $V = 4$, $E =$ ___   8

18. Use the formula $A = \pi r^2$ to find the area of a circle with a 5 cm radius. Use 3.14 for π.   78.5 cm²

Which shapes can be cross-sections of the figure on the left?

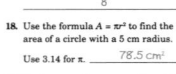

19.   a.   b.   c.   d.
   a, c

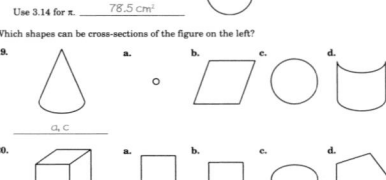

20.   a.   b.   c.   d.
   a, b

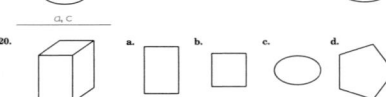

Error Analysis and Remediation

Here are some common errors students make when they find the squares and square roots of numbers; bisect line segments and angles; and find the surface areas and volumes of prisms, pyramids, and cylinders. The errors are listed by lesson under the appropriate management objective.

14A • FIND SQUARES AND SQUARE ROOTS OF NUMBERS

Source of Error (Lesson 14-2)
Students give the wrong answer when finding the square or square root of a fraction.

Remediation
Remind students that the square of any number is that number multiplied by itself and that therefore $(\frac{1}{4})^2 = \frac{1}{4} \times \frac{1}{4} = \frac{1}{16}$. Then write $\sqrt{\frac{1}{4}}$ on the chalkboard and ask: What number multiplied by itself is $\frac{1}{4}$? ($\frac{1}{2}$)

14B • BISECT A LINE SEGMENT OR AN ANGLE BY CONSTRUCTION; CONSTRUCT SPACE FIGURES

Source of Error (Lessons 14-4, 14-5, 14-6, and 14-7)
Students make errors because they do not use a compass correctly.

Remediation
Remind students that a compass is not used by holding its legs but by rotating it by the stem at the top of the compass.

Source of Error (Lessons 14-4, 14-5, 14-6, and 14-7)
Students make errors because they do not follow the steps in order.

Remediation
Have students make "cue" cards for each construction and refer to them as they work through the exercises.

14C • FIND THE SURFACE AREA OR VOLUME OF A PRISM, A PYRAMID, OR A CYLINDER

Source of Error (Lesson 14-12)
Students make errors when finding the volume of a triangular prism because they incorrectly calculate the area of the base or cannot find the height.

Remediation
Remind students that they must first find the area of the triangle and then multiply that area by the height of the prism. Suggest that students mentally flip the figure to help see the height in a different position.

Source of Error (Lesson 14-13)
Students make errors because they find the area of the base by multiplying $(3.14 \times r)$ and then squaring the product.

Remediation
Remind students to follow the rules for the order of operations.

14D • PROBLEM SOLVING: CREATE AND USE A FORMULA. USE VISUAL PERCEPTION

Source of Error (Lesson 14-11)
Students have difficulty visualizing the different cross sections of an object.

Remediation
Have students use play dough to mold various three-dimensional shapes. Then have them make vertical, horizontal, and diagonal cuts; place the cut surfaces on paper; and trace the outlines.

Answers

4. Answers will vary. Suggestions given. In the 14th century vase, the flower design is repeated. In the 15th century vase, there are repeated designs and rotations in the top and bottom borders. There are repeated designs in the borders of the Tulip vase.

CHAPTER 14

Extra Practice

This page provides extra practice of all the major chapter objectives. Use this page after the chapter has been taught to reinforce the chapter skills. Page references are provided for each group of items so that students can easily look back at the appropriate lesson for additional support.

Find the square of the number. *(pages 452–455)*

1. 3^2 9
2. 9^2 81
3. 16^2 256
4. 13^2 169
5. 24^2 576
6. $(^-16)^2$ 256
7. $(^-2)^2$ 4
8. $\left(\frac{3}{8}\right)^2$ $\frac{9}{64}$
9. 0^2 0
10. $\left(\frac{2}{3}\right)^2$ $\frac{4}{9}$

Find the positive square root of each number. *(pages 452–455)*

11. $\sqrt{16}$ 4
12. $\sqrt{144}$ 12
13. $\sqrt{256}$ 16
14. $\sqrt{961}$ 31
15. $\sqrt{289}$ 17
16. $\sqrt{0}$ 0
17. $\sqrt{100}$ 10
18. $\sqrt{\frac{4}{9}}$ $\frac{2}{3}$
19. $\sqrt{\frac{16}{9}}$ $\frac{4}{3}$
20. $\sqrt{\frac{81}{36}}$ $\frac{9}{6}$

Constructions. *(pages 456–463)*

21. Draw line segment PQ. Construct the perpendicular bisector of $\overline{PQ}$. Label the point of intersection O. How many right angles are formed? What can you say about segments PO and OQ?
    4; They are congruent

22. Draw $\angle ABC$. Construct the bisector of $\angle ABC$ with ray BD. What can you say about $\angle ABD$ and $\angle CBD$?
    They are congruent.

23. Draw obtuse triangle FGH. Construct triangle JKL congruent to triangle FGH. What can you say about the corresponding sides and angles of the two triangles? **They are all congruent**

Find the volume. Use 3.14 for π. *(pages 468–471, 474–477)*

24. **28 yd³**

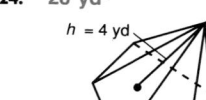

h = 4 yd

Area = 21 yd²

25. **1,620 in.³**

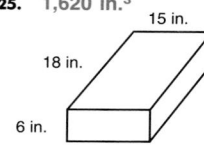

15 in.

18 in.

6 in.

26. **28,260 cm³**

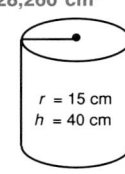

r = 15 cm
h = 40 cm

Solve. *(pages 466–467)*

27. Use the table to write a formula that relates the data.   **c = 0.15m + 1**

C	M
$1.15	1
$1.30	2
$1.45	3
$1.60	4

C = cost of a train ride

M = number of miles ridden

28. Can the intersection of a plane region and a cube be a point? a line segment? Explain.   **yes; at a vertex; yes; at an edge**

484   EXTRA PRACTICE

What is the Volume of a Rock

Can you find the volume of an irregularly shaped object, such as a rock? One way is to measure the amount of water it displaces. You will need a liter container with markings and several rocks that will fit into the container.

Work with a partner. First estimate the volume of each rock. Remember a liter container has a volume of 1,000 mL or 1,000 cm³ Then measure the volume of each rock,

- Put water in the container to the 300 mL line.
- Place a rock in the container, making sure it is completely submerged. If it is not completely under water, remove it and add 100 ml of water. Replace the rock and check whether the water covers it. Continue if necessary.
- Read the level of the water in the container. Subtract the amount that was in the container before the rock was submerged. The difference is the volume of the rock.
- Repeat with the other rocks.

How do your estimates compare with your findings?
Check students' work.

Are Volume and Surface Area Related?

What happens to the ratio of surface area to volume as the size of a figure increases? You will need at least 64 small cubes.

Build or draw cubes with different edge lengths—1 unit, 2 units, 3 units, 4 units, and so on. Make a table showing the length of the edge, the surface area, the volume, and the surface area to volume ratio. Check students' work.

What do you notice about the ratio as the size of the figure increases?
The ratio decreases.

NUMBERS FROM NUMBERS

Try to make every number from 1 through 25 this way. Use each of the last 4 digits of a telephone number just once with any operation (addition, subtraction, multiplication or division) and with parentheses.

Example: 1237 Answers will vary.

$$7 - (3 + 2 + 1) = 1$$
$$(7 - 3) \div (2 \times 1) = 2$$
$$7 - ((3 - 1) \times 2) = 3$$

ENRICHMENT 485

Enrichment

This page contains activities that provide extension and enrichment for all levels of students. Depending on the needs of your students, you may wish to assign an activity from this page at certain points during the chapter, or you may wish to use this page when the entire chapter has been completed.

What Is the Volume of a Rock?
(COOPERATIVE)

Some students may want to measure the rock with a centimeter ruler or tape measure in order to estimate the volume. Stress the relationship between cubic centimeters and milliliters.

Are Volume and Surface Area Related?

Ask students to continue the table through cubes with edge lengths of 8 units. You may want to relate the results to the formulas for the volume and surface area of a cube: $V = s^3$ and $SA = 6s^2$.

Numbers From Numbers

You may want to have students work in groups of two to four for this activity. Tell students to choose telephone numbers whose last four digits are all different and do not include 0.

Cumulative Review

The Cumulative Review focuses on skills covered in previous chapters. All important skills are reviewed on a cyclic basis.

If students are having difficulty with particular groups of exercises, refer to the chart below for follow-up work.

CUMULATIVE REVIEW

A green cube numbered 1–6 is tossed once. Find the probability.

1. $P(3) =$ **d**
a. $\frac{1}{3}$
b. $\frac{1}{2}$
c. $\frac{3}{6}$
d. none of these

2. $P(\text{odd}) =$ **a**
a. $\frac{1}{2}$
b. $\frac{1}{4}$
c. $\frac{1}{8}$
d. none of these

3. $P(\text{green}) =$ **c**
a. $\frac{1}{3}$
b. $\frac{3}{4}$
c. 1
d. none of these

Find the answer.

4. $(^-3) - (^-8) =$
a. 5   **a**
b. $^-11$
c. $^-5$
d. none of these

5. $12 \times (^-4) =$
a. 48   **b**
b. $^-48$
c. $^-16$
d. none of these

6. $(^-56) \div (^-7) =$
a. 9   **b**
b. 8
c. $^-8$
d. none of these

7. $m - 9 = ^-4$
a. $^-5$ **c**
b. $^-13$
c. 5
d. none of these

8. $x + ^-3 = 14$
a. 11   **b**
b. 17
c. $^-11$
d. none of these

9. $\frac{t}{15} = ^-5$
a. $^-3$ **c**
b. 75
c. $^-75$
d. none of these

10. $\sqrt{324} =$
a. 32   **b**
b. 18
c. 24
d. none of these

11. $\sqrt{9} =$
a. 6   **c**
b. 9
c. 3
d. none of these

12. $36^2 =$
a. 1,296   **a**
b. 906
c. 1,196
d. none of these

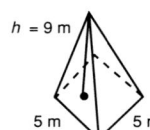

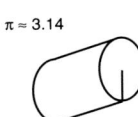

13. Volume =
a. 26 in.^{3} **d**
b. 78 in.^{3}
c. 446 in.^{3}
d. none of these

14. Volume =
a. 225 m^3 **c**
b. 90 m^3
c. 75 m^3
d. none of these

15. Volume =
a. 188.4 ft^3 **d**
b. 754 ft^3
c. 94.2 ft^3
d. none of these

Items	Management Objectives	Where Taught	Reteaching Options	Extra Practice Options
1–3	**12D** Find the probability of an event.	pp. 396–397		TRB/PW 12-10
4	**13B** Add and subtract integers.	pp. 418–423	TRB/RW 13-4 to 13-5	TRB/PW 13-4 to 13-5
5–6	**13C** Multiply and divide integers.	pp. 426–429	TRB/RW 13-7 to 13-8	TRB/PW 13-7 to 13-8
7–9	**13D** Solve equations involving integers.	pp. 432–435	TE/RA 13-9 TRB/RW 13-10	TRB/PW 13-9 to 13-10
10–12	**14A** Find squares and square roots of numbers.	pp. 452–453	TRB/RW 14-2	TRB/PW 14-2
13–15	**14C** Find the surface area or volume of a prism, a pyramid, or a cylinder.	pp. 474–477	TRB/RW 14-12 to 14-13	TRB/PW 14-12 to 14-13

PROBLEM SOLVING REVIEW

Strategies may vary. Suggestions given.
Remember the strategies and types of
problems you've had so far. Solve.

1. A copying machine is used 8 h/d.
   During the first hour, 50 copies were made;
   75 copies during the second; 105 during
   the third; and 140 during the fourth hour.

   a. How many copies are made
      during the first hour? **50 copies**

   b. If the pattern continues, how
      many copies will be made
      during the fifth hour? **180 copies**

   c. If the pattern continues, how many copies
      will be made during the day? **patterns;
      1,380 copies**

2. The letters of the word EASTERNER
   are each written on a tile and placed in
   a bag. What is the probability that a tile
   drawn randomly will contain either
   an E or an A?
   formula; $\frac{4}{9}$

3. Each row in the design on an Acoma
   Indian bowl contains a rectangle
   alternating with 4 triangles.
   There are 6 rows and each row has
   8 rectangles. What is the total
   number of triangles?
   pattern; 192 triangles

4. The formula for the total cost (C)
   of a visit to an amusement park is
   $C = 3N + 1.25R$ where N is the
   number of people and R is the number
   of rides. What would it cost a family of
   3 to go on 11 rides?
   formula; $22.75

5. Five friends visit the park in Exercise
   4. When they left they noticed that the
   total cost of the rides was exactly
   twice what they paid for admission.
   How many rides had they gone on?
   multistep; 24 rides

6. To determine the monthly service
   charge of a checking account, a bank
   uses the formula $C = 5 + 0.25N$.
   If N is the number of checks above
   10, what is the service charge for
   20 checks?
   multistep; $7.50

7. A board game spinner is 50% red and
   25% blue. The rest of the spinner is
   green. Of 160 spins, how many would
   you expect to be green?
   formula; 40 spins

8. The desks in room 325 are arranged in
   5 rows of 6 desks. One day, a different
   number of students were absent in
   each row, but no row was empty.
   What is the largest number that could
   have been present?
   guess and check; 15 students

9. A carpenter cuts boards from planks
   using the formula $B = \frac{P}{2} - 1$, where
   B is the length of a board
   and P is the length of the plank.
   If the carpenter has a 12-ft board,
   how long was the plank?
   formula; 26 ft

CHAPTER 14 487

Problem Solving Review

This page focuses on problem solving
strategies and types learned in this and
previous chapters. A problem solving
checklist lists some of the strategies students may use to solve the problems on
this page.

Technology

This page is designed to provide calculator or computer experiences for all levels of students. The calculator or computer logo indicates the type of activity.

You may wish to assign these activities after the chapter has been taught or during the course of the chapter, depending on your needs and those of your students.

Two by Two by Two

Caution that there is more to the problem than only finding the volume of the large box and that of each cube, and dividing. Students have to determine how many cubes of each size will fit along each dimension of the box.

Buy the C-Side

Review how to find the areas of a triangle and a trapezoid. Suggest that students divide the C-region into smaller regions whose areas they know how to calculate.

Making It Fit

If students are having difficulties, tell them to trace the triangles, cut out the traced figures, and then try to place them on the coordinate grid. Students can make their final drawings on centimeter grid paper (Teaching Aid 15).

The computer activity uses Houghton Mifflin software, which is found in Houghton Mifflin Math Activities Courseware, Grade 7.

TECHNOLOGY

TWO BY TWO BY TWO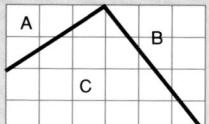

A large box measures 126 cm by 144 cm by 286 cm. How many cubes can you place in the box, if each cube measures:

1. 2 cm × 2 cm × 2 cm? 648,648
2. 4 cm × 4 cm × 4 cm? 81,081
3. 8 cm × 8 cm × 8 cm? 10,135.125

BUY THE C-SIDE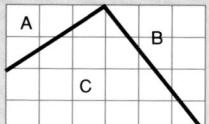

In the grid below, each square represents 35 mi². Each square mile costs $10. How much does each region cost?   A – $1,050; B – $2,100; C – $5,25(

MAKING IT FIT 💻

In the computer activity *Congruent Triangles*, you must be able to create a triangle congruent to another triangle, placing it on a coordinate grid so that the vertices are at points on the grid. This activity, which does not require a computer, will help you develop skills at placing a triangle on a coordinate grid.
See below.
Using a metric ruler, measure the sides of each triangle. Then measure the coordinate grid. How can you draw the triangles on the grid so that each vertex is at a point on the grid? You may flip or turn the triangles.   **Check students' drawings.**

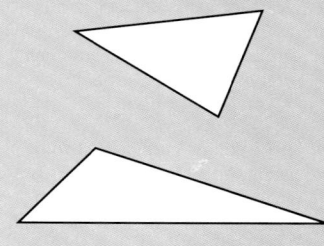

Software Activities

activity 1 • THE GOLDEN RECTANGLE

MATERIALS: draw program with a scale selection function

Procedure: The Golden Rectangle is a rectangle whose one side is 1.62 the length of the other. With a draw program, students can discover one of the features of this special proportion. Have students draw a very small square. They then make a duplicate, scale it up by 1.62 and move it beside the original square. They then duplicate the larger square, scale it up by 1.62, and continue as shown below. Each rectangle is a Golden Rectangle.

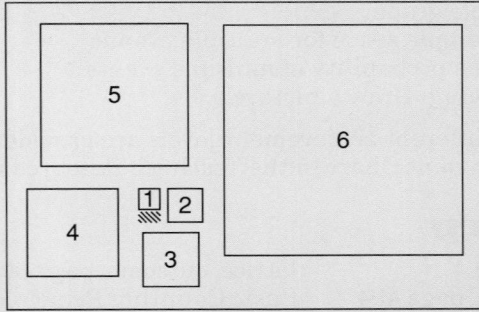

Follow-up: Have students search for Golden Rectangles by measuring all the rectangles they can find and calculating the ratio of the long side to the shorter side. Places to look include books, basketball courts, buildings, and windows.

activity 2 • A FUNCTION

MATERIALS: BASIC programming

```
10 PRINT "THIS PROGRAM WILL MAKE A
   TABLE ";
20 PRINT "FOR THE FUNCTION Y=2X+3"
30 INPUT "WHAT IS YOUR BEGINNING
   VALUE: ";N
40 PRINT " X        2X+3"
50 PRINT "---------------"
60 FOR I=N TO N+5
70 PRINT N"        "2*N+3
80 LET N=N+1
90 PRINT
100 NEXT I
```

Follow-up: Challenge students to modify the program to use the function $Y = 2X - 3$.

HOUGHTON MIFFLIN SOFTWARE

EduCalc. Boston, MA: Houghton Mifflin Company, 1990. For Apple II, Commodore, IBM.

Mathematics Activities Courseware. Boston, MA: Houghton Mifflin Company, 1983. For Apple II, IBM.

Mathematics: Solving Story Problems, Levels 7–8. Boston, MA: Houghton Mifflin Company, 1985. For Apple II, IBM.

The Computer Tutor. Boston, MA: Houghton Mifflin Company, 1990. For Apple II, IBM.

OTHER SOFTWARE

Basic Skills Math Series: Geometry and Measurement. Courses by Computers, State College, PA: 1989. For Apple II, IBM.

Building Perspective. Pleasantville, NY: Sunburst Communications, 1990. For Apple II, IBM.

Elastic Lines: The Electronic Geoboard. Pleasantville, NY: Sunburst Communications, 1989. For Apple II.

Graphics Calculator. Iowa City, IA: Conduit, 1989. For Apple II.

The Geometric PreSupposer: Problems and Projects. Pleasantville, NY: Sunburst Communications, 1990. For Apple II, IBM.

Statistics and Probability

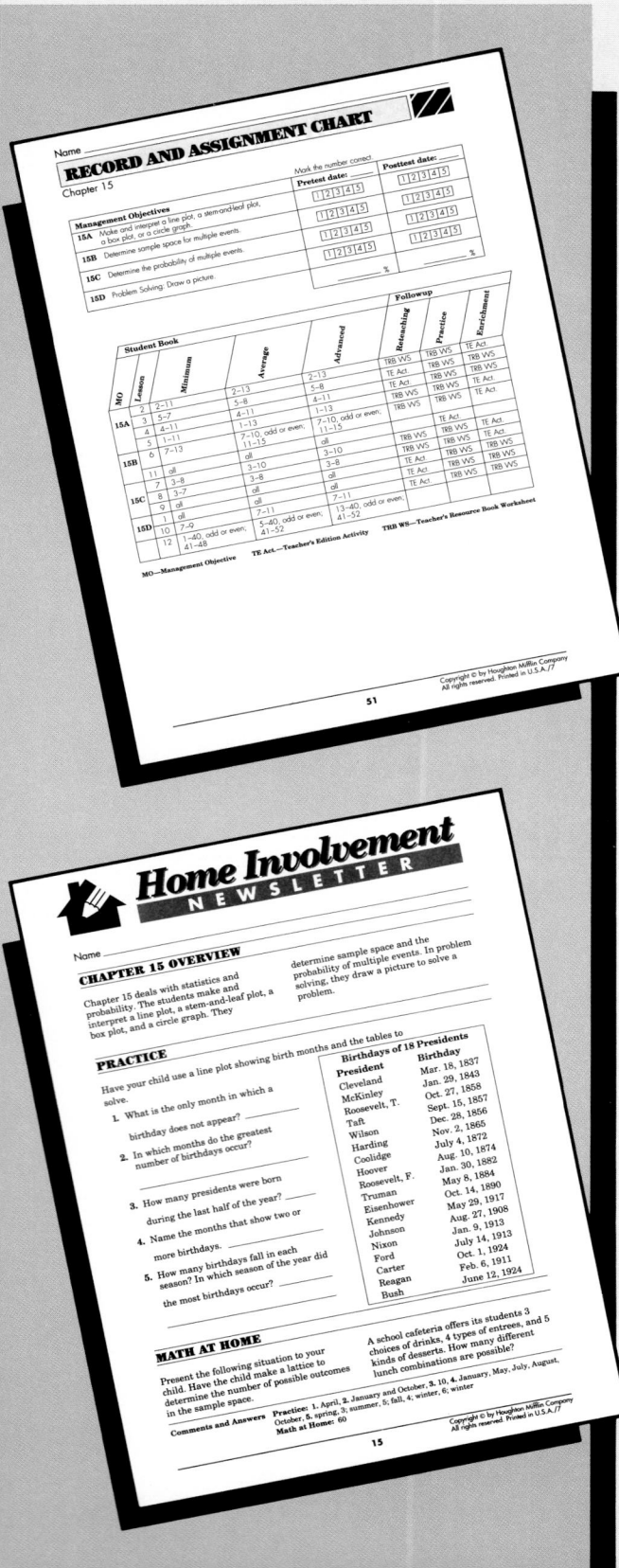

This chapter involves probability and displaying statistical data. It focuses on making and interpreting a line plot, a stem-and-leaf plot, a box plot, and a circle graph; determining a sample space for multiple events; and determining the probability of multiple events, independent events, and dependent events.

The concept of probability is expanded to include combinations and permutations, and problem solving is extended to include recognizing a misleading graph and the strategy of drawing a picture to solve a problem.

Management Objectives

15A Make and interpret a line plot, a stem-and-leaf plot, a box plot, or a circle graph.
15B Determine sample space for multiple events.
15C Determine the probability of multiple events.
15D Problem Solving: Draw a picture.

Assignments for different achievement levels are provided on the Record and Assignment Chart in the Teacher's Resource Book.

Vocabulary

line plot, page 492
stem-and-leaf plot, page 494
box plot, page 496
quartiles, page 496
extremes, page 496
outlier, page 497
organized list, page 502
sample space, page 502
tree diagram, page 502

lattice, outcome, page 502
Basic Counting Principle, page 502
independent events, page 506
Multiplication Principle, page 506
complementary events, page 507
dependent events, page 508
odds, page 509
combinations, page 512
permutations, page 512

Home Involvement

As you begin to teach this chapter, give each student a copy of the Home Involvement Newsletter for this chapter.

This newsletter provides parents with
■ an overview of the chapter
■ suggestions for practicing some of the skills in the chapter
■ an at-home activity to do with their child, applying the skills taught in the chapter.

Management Chart

	Management Objectives	Lesson/ Pages	Student Not Successful	Student Needs More Practice	Student Successful	Pacing Range
15A	Make and interpret a line plot, a stem-and-leaf plot, a box plot, or a circle graph.	15-2/492-493	TRB/RW 15-2	TRB/PW 15-2 MAC 7 Activity 8	TE/EA 15-2 MAC 7 Activity 8	4-6 days
		15-3/494-495	TE/RA 15-3	TRB/PW 15-3	TRB/EW 15-3	
		15-4/496-497	TE/RA 15-4	TRB/PW 15-4	TRB/EW 15-4	
		15-5/498-499	TRB/RW 15-5 EG	TRB/PW 15-5 EG MAC 7 Activity 11 CT Unit 6 Obj. 1.1	TE/EA 15-5 EG MAC 7 Activity 11	
15B	Determine sample space for multiple events.	15-6/502-503	TRB/RW 15-6	TRB/PW 15-6	TE/EA 15-6	2 days
		15-11/512-513		MAC 7 Activity 12	TE/CA 15-11 MAC 7 Activity 12	
15C	Determine the probability of multiple events.	15-7/504-505	TRB/RW 15-7	TRB/PW 15-7	TE/EA 15-7	3-4 days
		15-8/506-507	TRB/RW 15-8	TRB/PW 15-8	TE/EA 15-8	
		15-9/508-509	TE/RA 15-9	TRB/PW 15-9 MAC 8 Activity 10	TRB/EW 15-9 MAC 8 Activity 10	
15D	Problem Solving: Draw a picture.	15-1/490-491	TE/RA 15-1	TRB/PW 15-1	TRB/EW 15-1	2 days
		15-10/510-511	TE/RA 15-10	TRB/PW 15-10	TRB/EW 15-10	
	Mixed Review	15-12/514-515				
	Chapter Checkups	500-501; 516-517				
	Extra Practice	518				
	Enrichment	519				
	Cumulative Review/Problem Solving Review	520-521				
	Technology	522				

TE = Teacher's Edition
TRB = Teacher's Resource Book
RW = Reteaching Worksheet
RA = Reteaching Activity
EA = Enrichment Activity
EW = Enrichment Worksheet
PW = Practice Worksheet
CA = Classroom Activity

*Other Available Items
MAC = Mathematics Activities Courseware
CT = Computer Tutor
EG = Easy Graph

Manipulative Planning Guide

This is a complete list of manipulatives and materials needed for Chapter 15.

Materials for Manipulatives	TE Activities (INTRODUCE)	Student Book Lesson
Teaching Aid 15* or grid paper for each student two per student	Lesson 15-1	Lesson 15-1
Straightedge for each student	Lesson 15-5	Lessons 15-1, 15-5
Centimeter ruler for each student		Lesson 15-2
Calculator for each student	Lesson 15-3	Lesson 15-3
Compass, protractor for each student		Lesson 15-5
Stem and Leaf/Box Plot transparency		Lesson 15-5
Two blank spinners divided into two equal regions	Lesson 15-6	
Blank spinners divided into four equal regions, two per pair	Lesson 15-7	
Colored markers—red, green, blue, and yellow	Lesson 15-6	
Four index cards	Lesson 15-9	
Paper bag		
8.5 in. × 11 in. paper, one sheet per student	Lesson 15-10	

*Teaching Aids are found in the Teacher's Resource Book.

Learning Stages

The concepts and skills in Chapter 15 are presented through these learning stages.

CONCRETE

Using manipulatives and verbalizing about a concept. No symbols.

Teacher Edition Activities	Student Book
	Lessons 15-2, 15-3, 15-5, 15-6, 15-10

Enrichment	Reteaching	In the Houghton Mifflin Manipulative Kit (yes/no)	In the Houghton Mifflin Overhead Kit?
	Lesson 15-1		Yes
		Yes	
			Available separately
Lesson 15-5		Yes	Yes
			Yes
		Yes	
Lesson 15-7		Yes	
	Lesson 15-9		

CONNECTING

🏛 ▦ ▭ ➡ 5¢ ⌀cm² ⅓

Making a connection between manipulatives and symbols.

Teacher Edition Activities	Student Book
Lessons 15-1 through 15-5, 15-6 through 15-10	Lessons 15-2, 15-3, 15-5, 15-10

SYMBOLIC

$.05 $A = 9cm^2$ $1 - \frac{2}{3} = \frac{1}{3}$

Using numbers or symbols. No manipulatives or pictures of manipulatives.

Teacher Edition Activities	Student Book
Lessons 15-3, 15-4, 15-11	Lessons 15-1, 15-4, 15-6 through 15-9, 15-11

Additional Activities

COOPERATIVE LEARNING RESOURCE ACTIVITIES

Through cooperative learning activities, students learn by interacting with one another in small groups. These cooperative activities provide students with motivating settings for making connections, investigations, and problem solving situations.

The cooperative connections are interdisciplinary problem-solving projects. Each student has a particular job that helps lead the group to complete the project. For the cooperative investigations students work in pairs for investigations involving data collection and analysis. The cooperative problem solving activities encourage the sharing of ideas and information. Students work in groups of four to solve a problem. Students are each assigned a clue and work together to find a common solution.

COOPERATIVE CONNECTIONS — Chapter 15

COOPERATIVE CONNECTIONS / Math and Insurance

PROBLEM: When an outdoor event is planned, an organization needs to consider how the weather might affect the plans. For example, rain might cause an event to be cancelled or it might reduce attendance. To protect themselves against financial loss, organizations might choose to purchase weather insurance.

When an insurance company decides whether or not to write a policy for an organization, they consider the probability of the event taking place.

Suppose your group owns an insurance company. Which of these events would you insure?

June 17 — Concert – if it rains the concert will be cancelled

July 3–9 — Carnival – needs 4 days without rain to be profitable

August 21–22 — Horse Show – if it rains attendance will be reduced

September 15–19 — Art Show – if it rains the show cannot be held

Long Range Weather Forecast			
	Type of Weather		
Month	Sun	Rain	Clouds
June	10 days	16 days	4 days
July	14 days	12 days	5 days
August	17 days	11 days	3 days
September	6 days	14 days	10 days

COOPERATIVE INVESTIGATIONS — Chapter 15

COOPERATIVE INVESTIGATIONS / Circle Graphs

GOAL: Make circle graphs to compare the percent of different kinds of advertisements in news magazines.

Materials: three weekly news magazines

Work with a partner.

1. Examine three weekly news magazines. One partner finds what percent of all the advertisements in each magazine are for cars and food products. The other partner finds what percent are for electronic items and travel.

2. Combine your data for each magazine. Then work together to make a circle graph for each magazine. Show the four types of advertisements in each graph and label each percent.

COOPERATIVE PROBLEM SOLVING 1 — Chapter 15

COOPERATIVE PROBLEM SOLVING / Problem 1

Unknown to the others, Ayanna, Tracy, Yoko, and Rita each bought exactly the same school lunch. What is the probability of this happening?

Clue 1: Each girl bought one item from each choice. List the possible lunch combinations for Ayanna.

Unknown to the others, Ayanna, Tracy, Yoko, and Rita each bought exactly the same school lunch. What is the probability of this happening?

Clue 3: The girls could choose either milk or orange drink. List the possible lunch combinations for Yoko.

Unknown to the others, Ayanna, Tracy, Yoko, and Rita each bought exactly the same school lunch. What is the probability of this happening?

Clue 2: The girls could choose either pizza or a hamburger. List the possible lunch combinations for Tracy.

Unknown to the others, Ayanna, Tracy, Yoko, and Rita each bought exactly the same school lunch. What is the probability of this happening?

Clue 4: The choice for dessert is either fresh strawberries or fruit cup. List the possible lunch combinations for Rita.

COOPERATIVE PROBLEM SOLVING 2 — Chapter 15

COOPERATIVE PROBLEM SOLVING / Problem 2

Three boys were finishing a board game. Who probably won and why?

Clue 1: The winner must spin the exact number. The winner won on his third spin.

Three boys were finishing a board game. Who probably won and why?

Clue 3: Use a tree diagram to show the possible combinations for each winning number.

Three boys were finishing a board game. Who probably won and why?

Clue 2: The spinner was divided into four equal sections numbered 1, 2, 3, and 4.

Three boys were finishing a board game. Who probably won and why?

Clue 4: Tim needed a 9 to win the game. Jonas needed a 7 and Enrico needed a 5.

GAMES

TOSS AND SPIN   (For use after Lesson 15-9)

Objective: Explore probability of dependent events.

☑ **MATERIALS CHECKLIST:** two spinners and two coins for each pair

Assign partners. Give each pair of students two coins and two spinners divided into four sections. For Spinner A use 1, 1, 1, 2; for Spinner B use 1, 2, 3, 4.

For the first part of the activity, have each player in turn toss a coin. If the coin lands heads up, the players spins Spinner A and records the number spun as his or her score. Tails means that the player spins B and records 1, 2, 3, or 4 as the score. Scoring is cumulative. Have players toss and spin fifteen times.

Explain that there will be one change in the second part of the activity. Partners will toss two coins before they spin. If they toss two heads, they should use Spinner A; otherwise, they will use B. Before partners begin, ask them to predict their scores for the second part. Then have them toss and spin for fifteen times. The partner whose prediction is closer to his or her actual score in this part is the winner.

LETTER RACE   (For use after Lesson 15-11)

Objective: Explore permutations.

Write the word *car* on the chalkboard, and ask students for all other arrangements of the letters *c, a,* and r (*acr, arc, cra, rac, rca*). Then divide the class into teams of four or five students. Tell teams that you are going to write another word on the board and they should use the letters from your word to write all the different letter arrangements they can.

Begin with the word *math*, and give teams three to five minutes to write as many different letter arrangements as possible (there are 24). Have teams exchange papers to confirm the number of different arrangements, which becomes the team's score. Give teams a few minutes to discuss strategy before you write the next word. Repeat with the words *down, eight, spring, even,* and *noon*. There are 24 arrangements for *down*, 120 for *eight* and *spring*, 12 for *even*, and 6 for *noon*. The team with the highest score at the end is the winner.

BULLETIN BOARD

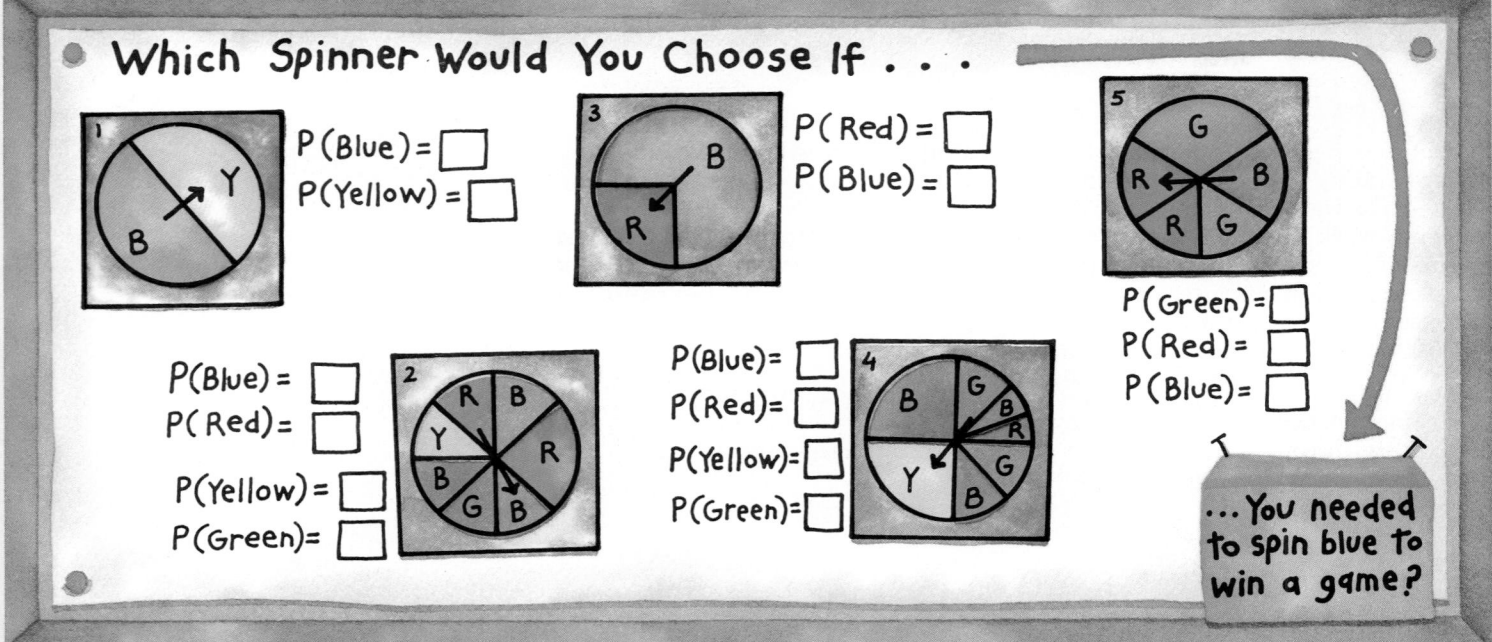

Prepare spinners similar to those shown above using poster board. Number them as a reference, and attach them to the bulletin board. Include a question about the spinners; students can place their answers inside the envelope. You can change the question regularly. Also have students fill in the boxes with actual probabilities. Encourage students to prepare similar spinners and perform simple experiments, comparing experimental probabilities to actual probabilities. (The answer to the given question is Spinner 3.)

Alternative Assessment

In addition to the paper and pencil tests available with this program, the following items can help you assess critical thinking as well as your students' ability to solve problems in a wide variety of ways.

Open-ended Problem

A group of students wants the school to sell t-shirts to raise funds for a school project. They want you to help them conduct a survey to decide what kind of t-shirts to buy. What kind of questions do you think they should include in the survey and why?

Teacher Notes
Possible responses:
• What size t-shirts do you wear? (to estimate how many of each size to order)
• What color t-shirts do you like to wear? (to decide on the color)
• What do you think is a fair price for a t-shirt? (to help you decide what price t-shirts to buy and to help you set the sale price)
• Do you like to wear t-shirts?
• Would you buy a school t-shirt?
• Would you prefer that the school sold something else as a fund raiser? If so, what?
(The last three questions are to determine if this is the best item to sell in a fund raiser.)

Group Writing Activity (See p. 24T.)

Write everything that the members of your group have learned about probability and statistics.

Teacher Notes
See chapter summary for possible answers.
Newspapers often use surveys to predict the percent of voters that will support certain election issues or candidates.

Individual Writing Activity

How do you think the newspapers use statistics and probability to predict the outcome of an election?

Portfolios

Portfolios can provide information about a student's growth in mathematical understanding over a period of time. They can help you make instructional decisions as well as become a vehicle for communicating with parents. The students' work involving the open-ended problem and writing activity suggested on this page along with work on the Write About It exercises on page 491, the Create Your Own exercises on pages 493, 495, 503, and 513, the Learning Log exercises on pages 501 and 517, and the Critical Thinking features on pages 507 and 509 could be included in portfolios.

You can use the last Teaching Aid to gain insight about your students' attitudes regarding mathematics and its relevance. It will help you establish an ongoing dialogue with your students as they progress through the school year.

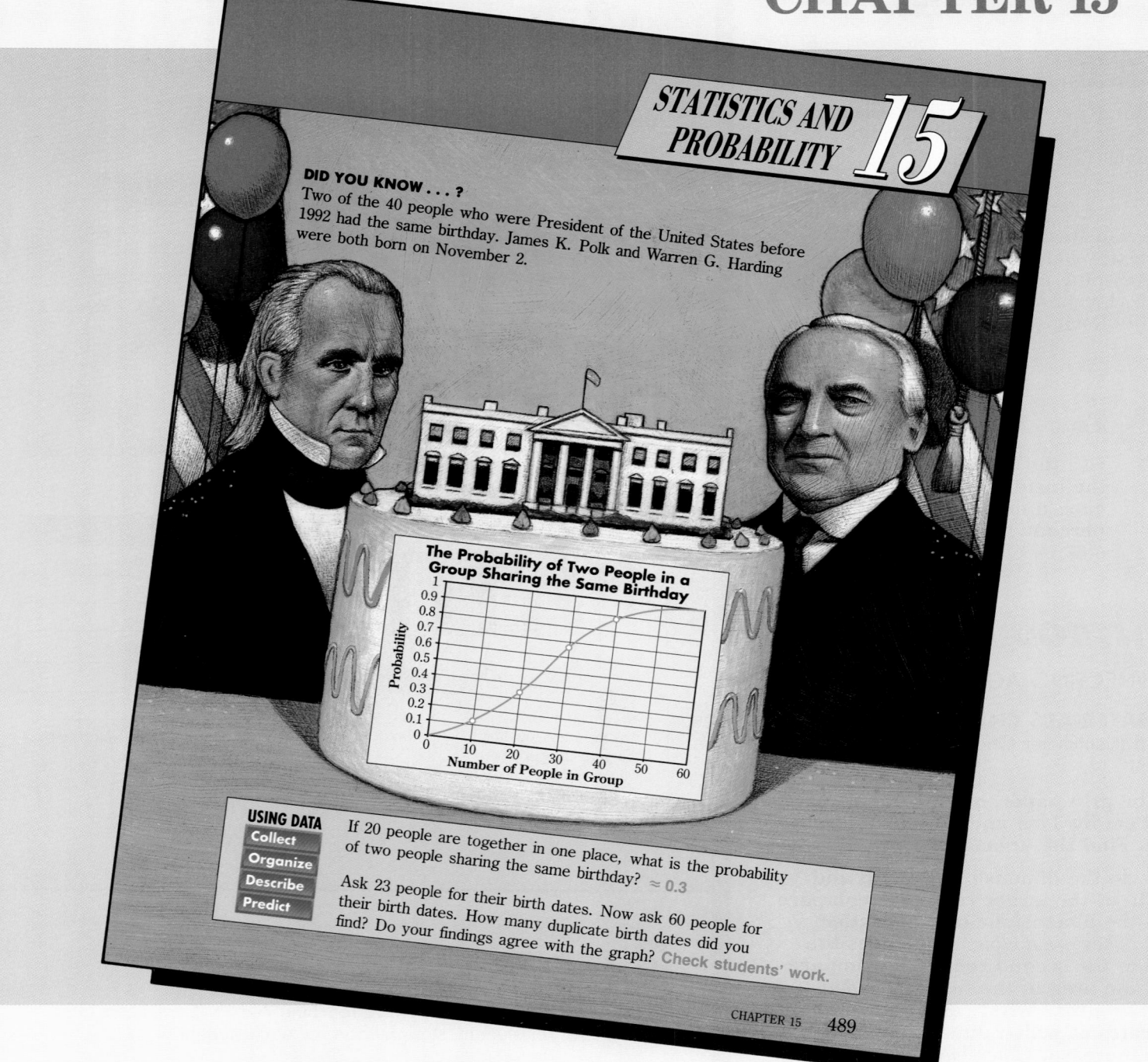

Using the Chapter Opener

The purpose of this page is to involve students in the use of real data much like that presented in newspapers and magazines.

To use this page as you begin the chapter, direct students' attention to the data. You may wish to ask questions such as the following:

According to the graph, is it surprising that President Polk and President Harding shared the same birthday? (*No, the probability of two people in group of 40 sharing the same birthday is about 0.9*)

What is the probability that two students in your mathematics class have the same birthday? (*Answers will vary depending on class size.*)

According to the graph, about how many people must be in a group to be almost certain that two of them definitely share the same birthday? (*about 55 people*)

Lesson Organizer

Objective: Discuss misleading graphs.

Prior Knowledge: Students should be able to interpret tables and bar graphs.

Lesson Resources:
Practice Worksheet 15-1
Reteaching Activity 15-1
Enrichment Worksheet 15-1
Daily Review 15-1

Two-Minute Math

Use the Table of Numbers on the inside back cover. Write each number in row F as a percent. *(30%, 80%, 90%, 71%, 60%, 34%, 79%, 20%, 65%)*

1 INTRODUCE

CONNECTING ACTIVITY

☑ **MATERIALS CHECKLIST:** Teaching Aid 15 (Centimeter Grid Paper) for each student

On the grid paper, outline one rectangle 2 cm by 3 cm and another 4 cm by 6 cm. Find the areas.

How do the dimensions (length and width) of the larger rectangle compare with the dimensions of the smaller one? *(They are double.)* How does the area of the second rectangle compare with the area of the first? *(It is four times as great.)* What can you say about the rates at which dimensions and area increase? *(They increase at very different rates.)*

WHEN YOUR STUDENTS ASK
★ WHY AM I LEARNING THIS? ★

Advertisers sometimes use exaggerations to persuade you to buy their products. Understanding how graphs can be misleading will help you become a wiser consumer.

More Than Meets the Eye

Problem Solving:
Misleading Graphs

📖 **READ ABOUT IT**

Graphs are sometimes used to give misleading impressions.

The data in the table at right have been used to make the two different graphs below.

Year	Persons per Household
1930	4.11
1960	3.33
1990	2.60

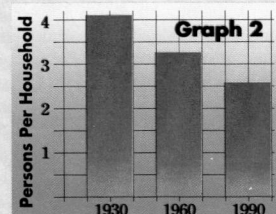

The table and graph show the number of skiers during some recent ski seasons as reported by the United States ski industry.

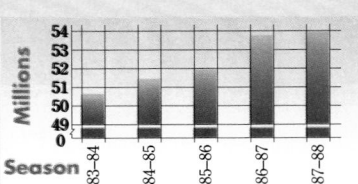

Season	Skiers (in millions)
'83–'84	50.6
'84–'85	51.4
'85–'86	51.9
'86–'87	53.7
'87–'88	53.9

The graph at right was used to show how the percent of adults who have high school diplomas has increased over time.

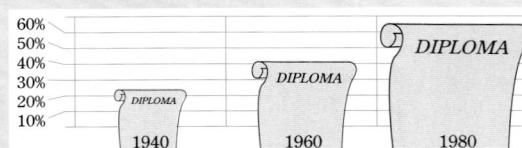

---

2 TEACH

☑ **MATERIALS CHECKLIST:** Teaching Aid 15 (Centimeter Grid Paper), two per student; straightedge for each student

Which dimension of a bar graph should be changed to show increases or decreases in the data? *(height of bars)* **Which dimension should remain the same, and why?** *(Width of bars should be constant so that they do not appear to exaggerate changes in the data.)*

Why are changes in data exaggerated on a bar graph by leaving out part of the scale beginning with zero? *(because you see only the tops of the bars)*

GUIDED PRACTICE   Do Exercise 1 as a class activity. Have students work in pairs for Exercise 2.

SUMMARIZE/ASSESS   **How can you tell that a bar graph is not misleading?** *(Possible answer: Check that the scale begins at zero, the graph presents all data, and differences in data are not exaggerated by bars that vary in width.)*

Use the graphs and the data table for the number of persons per household to answer Exercises 1 and 2.

1. In the data table, how do the number of persons per household in 1930 and in 1990 compare? How does the area covered by the 1930 bar compare with the area covered by the 1990 bar in the two graphs? **fewer persons per household in 1990; 1990 bar is one third the size of the 1930 bar.**

2. Why might someone incorrectly use Graph 1 in an article titled, "The Shrinking American Family"? **The width of the bars differs which makes the change seem greater than it is.**

Use the graph and the data table for the number of skiers per season to answer Exercises 3 and 4.

3. How many skiers were there in the 1983–84 season? in the 1987–88 season? By how much did the number of skiers increase from the 1983–84 season to the 1987–88 season? **50.6 million; 53.9 million; by 3.3 million**

4. Does the graph or the table give a stronger impression that the popularity of skiing is rising rapidly? Explain. **graph; increase seems greater**

Use the graph for the number of adults with high school diplomas to answer Exercises 5 and 6.

5. Look at the heights of the diplomas. About how many times more people completed high school in 1980 as in 1940? **about 3 times**

6. Compare the areas of the diplomas for 1940 and 1980 on the graph. About how many times larger is the area of the 1980 diploma than the area of the 1940 diploma? **between 5 1/2 and 6 times**

Accept reasonable answers. Suggestions given.

7. Write a paragraph explaining why Graph 1 showing the change in size of households gives a false impression. **bars are different widths**

8. Redraw the graph of the ski industry statistics so that the horizontal scale starts at zero. Use divisions of 10 (for millions). Explain why this graph gives a more accurate impression. **Check students' graphs.**

9. Explain why the areas of the diplomas make the graph for adults with diplomas misleading. Is it the width or the height of the diplomas that accurately reflects the increase in the number of people completing high school? **diplomas shown in different widths; height accurate reflection**

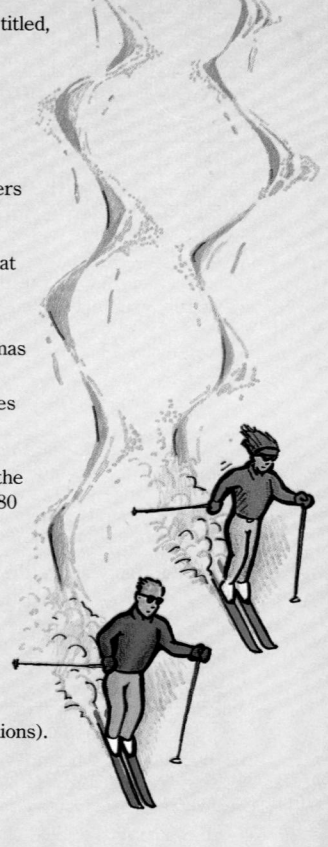

CHAPTER 15   491

MEETING INDIVIDUAL NEEDS

For Students Who Are . . .

Acquiring English Proficiency Pair students with a partner to work on this lesson.

Gifted and Talented Have students look in newspapers and magazines for examples of misleading graphs. They can share these graphs with the class.

Having Reading Difficulties If necessary, demonstrate how to read the graphs in the lesson.

Today's Problem

Why might it be easy to misinterpret a bar graph in which the vertical scale does not begin with zero? (*When only the tops of the bars are shown, the differences between the different subsets of data are exaggerated.*)

---

3 FOLLOW-UP

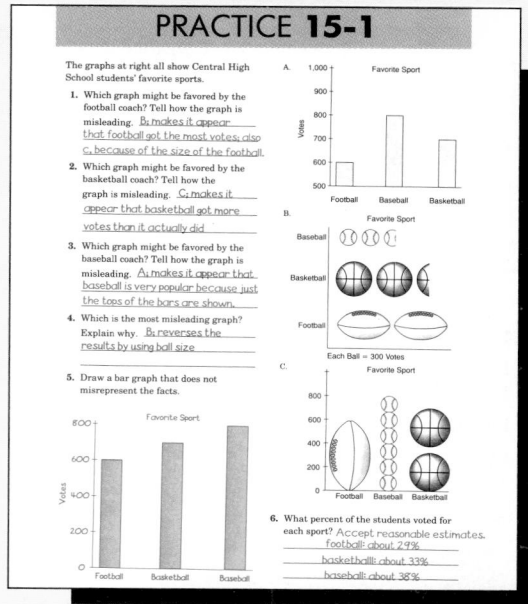

PRACTICE 15-1

RETEACHING 15-1

☑ MATERIALS CHECKLIST: Grid paper

School Year	Students
1986–87	55
1987–88	57
1988–89	58
1989–90	60
1990–91	61

Have students work in groups of two. Each makes a bar graph for the data. One student labels the y-axis from 55 through 63 with 55 starting near zero. The other uses the scale 0–100 for the y-axis. Which graph shows a rapid increase? (*first*) Very little change? (*second*) Which graph is misleading? (*first*)

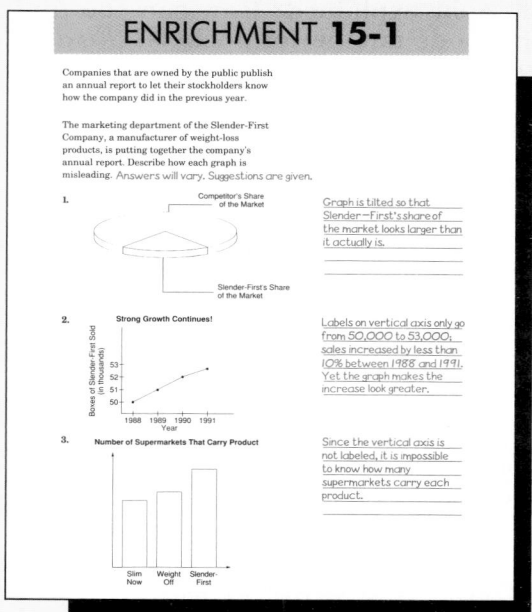

ENRICHMENT 15-1

LESSON 15-2

Lesson Organizer

Objective: Make and interpret a line plot.

Prior Knowledge: Students should be able to find the range and graph points on a number line.

Lesson Resources:
Practice Worksheet 15-2
Reteaching Worksheet 15-2
Enrichment Activity 15-2
Daily Review 15-2

Two-Minute Math

Subtract. Use mental math.
190 − 165 *(25)*   73 − 59 *(14)*
34 − 28 *(6)*   54 − 33 *(21)*
243 − 124 *(119)*   80 − 64 *(16)*

1 INTRODUCE

CONNECTING ACTIVITY

☑ **MATERIALS CHECKLIST:** "Post-its," 1 per student

1. Draw a number line from 0 to 12 on the chalkboard. Ask each student to report the number of pockets they have by sticking their "Post-it" over the corresponding number on the number line.

Help students examine the results. **Are there clusters? Are there gaps? Can these be explained? How can you find the mode number of pockets?** *(Find the number of pockets that occurred the most.)* **How can you find the median?** *(Find the middle number when the numbers of pockets are arranged in order from least to greatest.)*

WHEN YOUR STUDENTS ASK
★ WHY AM I LEARNING THIS? ★

You can connect this skill to real life through teaching. Teachers who want to look at the overall performance of a class on a particular test can make a line plot to obtain a visual impression of the whole set of test data.

Line Plots

Some facts, or statistics, about the players on a recent United States soccer team are listed in the table below.

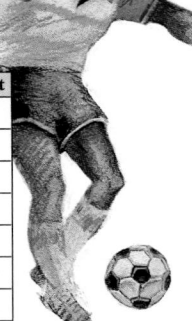

Player	Age	Height	Weight	Player	Age	Height	Weight
Sonny Askew	25	6'1"	175 lb	Paul Hammond	29	6'1"	195 lb
Chico Borja	23	5'11"	155 lb	Hayden Knight	25	6'1"	175 lb
Dan Canter	22	6'1"	175 lb	Arnold Mausser	28	6'2"	185 lb
Tony Crescitelli	25	5'11"	180 lb	Alan Merrick	32	5'10"	170 lb
Pedro Debrito	23	6'1"	170 lb	Rob Olson	23	6'1"	175 lb
Jeff Durgan	21	6'1"	175 lb	Bruce Savage	21	5'9"	155 lb
Rudy Glenn	24	6'2"	185 lb	Perry VanDerBeck	23	5'10"	155 lb

You can graph the ages of the players on a **line plot**. Line plots are usually used only when you are plotting fewer than 25 data items.

You can make a line plot by following these steps.

STEPS Identify the range by subtracting the smallest number from the largest. The smallest number is 21 and the largest is 32.

Range = 32 − 21 = 11

Make a horizontal line and label it with numbers. Because the range is 11, there should be at least 12 numbers on the line. The lowest number should be 21 or less and the highest number should be 32 or more to cover the whole age range.

Mark an *x* above the line for each player's age.

Ages of Soccer Players

```
        x
        x        x
 x      x        x
 x  x   x   x    x           x   x           x
21  22  23  24  25  26  27  28  29  30  31  32
```

THINK ALOUD What does the line plot tell you about the data? *Most players are under 26 yr old.*

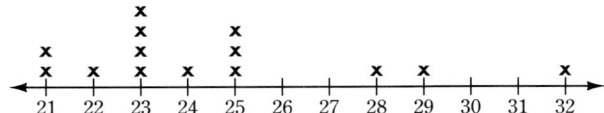
— GUIDED PRACTICE —

Use the data in the table above.

1. What is the oldest player's age? What is the youngest player's age?
32; 21

MULTICULTURAL NOTE

Soccer, the world's most popular sport, is played in over 140 countries. Many countries developed similar games, but soccer as presently played began in England in the 1800s. Recent winners of soccer's World Cup Championship include West Germany, Argentina, and Italy.

2 TEACH

☑ **MATERIALS CHECKLIST:** metric ruler for each student

Which four soccer players are represented by the "x's" over the 23? *(Chico Borja, Pedro Debrito, Rob Olson, Perry VanDerBeck)*

What would the line plot look like if it ranged from 20 to 33? *(The data would be spread out over the length.)* **from 10 to 40?** *(No data would be located on the ends.)*

What does an *x* mean on a line plot? *(a frequency of 1)*

Chalkboard Exercise

What is the weight of the heaviest player? *(195 lb)* How many players weigh less than 170 lb? *(3)*

SUMMARIZE/ASSESS **Explain how to make a line plot.** *(Students should explain the three steps given on page 492.)*

Use the data in the table on page 492.

2. Where do the players' ages seem to cluster? What is the range of heights in inches? **23; 5 in.**

3. **IN YOUR WORDS** What ages would you expect most soccer players to be?
between 21 and 25 yr old

4. Where are the gaps in the ages? Why do you think this is so?
26-27; 30-31, Only one team is listed.

5. Make a line plot of the players' heights. Convert each height to inches.
Check students' drawings.

6. Are there clusters? Are there gaps? What conclusions can you make by looking at the line plot of the players' heights?
yes; yes; Most are 73 in.

7. **THINK ALOUD** By using the line plots, how could you find the mode? the median? In each case, explain.
See page 517b.

8. **CRITICAL THINKING** Why do you think that a line plot is usually used only for sets of data with fewer than 25 entries?
More than 25 makes plot too long.

9. Make a line plot of the players' weights. Use multiples of 5 lb on the scale.
Check students' drawings.

10. Can the conclusion be drawn just by looking at your line plot of the players' weights? Write *yes* or *no*. If *no*, tell why.

 a. Most of the players are between 170 lb and 185 lb. **yes**
 b. The total weight of the players is more than 1 t. **no; must add weights**
 c. Some of the players are a little too heavy for their height. **no; heights not plotted**
 d. Three of the players are quite a bit lighter than the others. **yes**
 e. The light players tend to be the short players. **no; heights not plotted**
 f. The mode for the weights of the players is 175 lb. **yes**

Suppose that a 23-year-old player who is 5′11″ tall and weighs 165 lb and a 26-year-old player who is 6′ tall and weighs 170 lb joined the soccer team.

11. Add these data to your line plots for weights and heights.
Check students' drawings.

12. What conclusions would you now make about the players' heights? the players' weights?
Modes and medians remain the same.

13. **CREATE YOUR OWN** Choose data from a newspaper or magazine. Make a line plot. Use fewer than 25 entries. Be sure some of the statistics are repeated so that a line plot is a sensible way to organize the data.
Check students' work.

MEETING INDIVIDUAL NEEDS

For Students Who Are . . .

Acquiring English Proficiency Discuss the meanings of *clusters* and *gaps*. Have students work in groups for the Create Your Own activity.

Gifted and Talented Have students record the heights of class-mates and make a line plot to show the data.

Working 2 or 3 Grades Below Level Review changing feet to inches for Exercises 2 and 5.

Today's Problem

To test the fairness of a coin, you can toss it until "heads" appears and then record how many times you tossed it to get your first "heads." After many trials, find the average number of tosses needed to obtain "heads." *(2)* How many tosses do you expect to make to obtain "heads"? Why?

3 FOLLOW-UP

PRACTICE 15-2

Use the data in the table on the right.

1. Make a line plot of the temperatures.

x		x		x	x	
70	71	72	73	74	75	76

Average Temperature and Precipitation During August

City	T	P
Albany	70°F	3.3 in.
Boston	72	3.7
Chicago	72	3.5
Cleveland	70	3.4
Columbus	72	3.7
Detroit	71	3.3
Grand Rapids	70	3.5
Indianapolis	73	3.5
Moline	73	3.8
Newark	76	3.9
New York	75	3.9
Pittsburgh	71	3.3
Syracuse	70	3.8
Wilmington	75	3.9

2. Make a line plot showing amounts of precipitation.

x	x		x	x	x	
3.3	3.4	3.5	3.6	3.7	3.8	3.9

3. Find the cluster(s) for

temperature ___70°–73°___
precipitation ___3.3 – 3.5, 3.7 – 3.9___

4. What temperature is most likely to occur? ___70°___

5. What amount of precipitation is most likely to fall? ___3.3, 3.5, or 3.9___

6. Where are the gaps in the temperature and the precipitation? ___74°; 3.6___

Solve.

7. In August, you visit a city in the geographic center of the cities listed in the table. What would you expect the temperature and precipitation to be for the month? Why? ___Answers will vary. Suggestions are given. 70°F; 3.3, 3.5, or 3.9 in.; these numbers appear more times than others in the table.___

8. Add these data to your line plots for temperatures and precipitation: Hartford—71°, 3.9 in.; Philadelphia—75°, 3.9 in.; Providence—71°, 3.9 in. What conclusions would you now make about the temperatures and precipitation? ___The most likely temperature now is 70°–71°F; the most likely amount of precipitation now is 3.9 in.___

RETEACHING 15-2

The table below shows the average temperatures recorded in a midwestern city.

Date	Temperature	Date	Temperature	Date	Temperature
Jan. 1	25°F	Jan. 5	22°F	Jan. 9	22°F
Jan. 2	19°F	Jan. 6	26°F	Jan. 10	19°F
Jan. 3	10°F	Jan. 7	29°F	Jan. 11	16°F
Jan. 4	17°F	Jan. 8	17°F	Jan. 12	17°F

Use the line below for Exercises 1–3. Then use your line plot for Exercises 4–7.

Temperatures from January 1 through January 12

| | | | | | X | | | | | | | | | | | | | | |
| X | | | | | X | X | X | | X | | | | | X | X | | X | | |

10 11 12 13 14 15 16 17 18 19 20 21 22 23 24 25 26 27 28 29

1. You need to label the line with numbers. To find out how many numbers to write under the line, find the range by subtracting the lowest temperature from the highest temperature. What is the lowest temperature? ___10°___ What is the highest temperature? ___29°___ What is the range of the temperatures? ___19°___ Add 1 to the range. How many tick marks should the line have? ___20___

2. Label the line with numbers. Start with the lowest temperature and end with the highest temperature.

3. Use the table to plot each temperature. Mark an X above the appropriate tick mark for each temperature.

4. How can you be sure that you plotted each temperature? ___The number of X's should equal the number of temperatures.___

5. During this time period, where are most temperatures clustered? ___16°–19°___

6. What temperature occurred most frequently? ___17°___

7. Where is the largest gap in the temperatures? Why do you think this is so? ___11°–15° (or 10°–16°) There was one unusually cold day.___

ENRICHMENT 15-2

☑ **MATERIALS CHECKLIST:** Blank cubes

Have the students work in pairs. Give each pair two blank cubes. Have them label both cubes *1–6*. They then make a line plot showing the possible results when the cubes are tossed and the numbers are added. [2, 3, 4, 5, 6, 7, 8, 9, 10, 11, 12] The partners take turns tossing the number cubes 25 times, recording each sum with an *X* above the appropriate number on the line plot. Ask: Were certain sums more frequent than others? Have the pairs compare their results.

Lesson Organizer

Objective: Make and interpret a stem-and-leaf plot.

Prior Knowledge: Students should be able to interpret data from a table.

Error Analysis and Remediation: See page 517A.

Lesson Resources:
Practice Worksheet 15-3
Reteaching Activity 15-3
Enrichment Worksheet 15-3
Daily Review 15-3

Two-Minute Math

How many tens are in each number?

27 *(2)*   142 *(14)*
58 *(5)*   259 *(25)*
63 *(6)*   136 *(13)*

1 INTRODUCE

CONNECTING ACTIVITY

You may wish to use the Stem-and-Leaf transparency in the Overhead Kit.

1. Ask students to report their heights in inches. Write each height on the chalkboard.

2. Ask volunteers to: list the heights in order; identify the median; identify the mode.

3. What is the range of the tens digits? Use the response to set up a stem-and-leaf plot that includes all the tens between the largest and smallest value. Put each height on the plot by recording all the ones digits.

4. Help students examine the results. **Are there clusters? gaps? Can these be explained?**

WHEN YOUR STUDENTS ASK
★ WHY AM I LEARNING THIS? ★

You can connect this skill to real life through the career of historian. Historians use stem-and-leaf plots to show the distribution of ages of United States presidents when they take office.

Stem-and-Leaf Plots

All states are trying to increase the graduation rate for high school students. The table below shows the high school graduation rates for each state and the District of Columbia. Each rate is rounded to the nearest percent.

Ala......... 67%	Fla..........62%	La.......... 63%	Nebr....... 88%	Ohio....... 80%	Tex.........64%
Alaska.....68%	Ga..........63%	Maine......77%	Nev.........65%	Okla........72%	Utah........80%
Ariz.........63%	Hawaii 71%	Md..........77%	N.H.........73%	Oreg.......74%	Vt.......... 78%
Ark.........78%	Idaho...... 79%	Mass.......77%	N. J.........78%	Pa..........79%	Va..........74%
Calif........67%	Ill...........67%	Mich.......68%	N. Mex.....72%	R. I......... 67%	Wash.......75%
Colo........73%	Ind......... 72%	Minn.......91%	N. Y........64%	S. C........ 64%	W. Va.......75%
Conn....... 90%	Iowa....... 89%	Miss........63%	N. C. 70%	S. Dak......82%	Wis.........86%
Del......... 71%	Kans....... 82%	Mo......... 76%	N. Dak..... 90%	Tenn....... 67%	Wyo........81%
D.C.........57%	Ky.......... 69%	Mt..........87%			

You can make a **stem-and-leaf plot** to organize this data. Think of each data item as a *stem* and a *leaf*. For these numbers, the stems will be the tens' digits and the leaves will be the ones' digits.

Stem	Leaf
9	
8	
7	
6	
5	

STEPS Find the stems. They are all the tens' digits between the smallest and largest values.

List the stems vertically with a line to their right.

Now go through the list, separating each value into its stem and its leaf. The first value is 67% for Alabama.

Stem	Leaf
9	
8	
7	
6	7
5	

Put the leaf for each item to the right of the stem. The leaf for Alabama, 7, goes to the right of the stem 6.

Continue plotting this way until all the data have been listed.

Stem	Leaf
9	010
8	927802061
7	8311962777638202498455
6	7837239383547474
5	7

THINK ALOUD What can be done now to organize the data better? **Arrange the leaves from smallest to greatest.**

---

2 TEACH

Why is it important to show all consecutive values for tens, even when there are no leaves to go with the stem? *(If a set of ten values is skipped, the visual impact of the distribution over all numbers is distorted and inaccurate.)*

How are line plots and stem-and-leaf plots alike? *(Both show distribution of data and both preserve the individual items.)* **How are they different?** *(The line plot is intended for a smaller range of data (less than 25) than the stem-and-leaf plot, which can display larger sets of data with wider ranges.)*

> ### *Chalkboard Examples*
> Identify the stems you would use for this data: 26, 34, 28, 45, 32, 48, 56, 67, 54, 49, 61, 42 *(2, 3, 4, 5, 6)*

SUMMARIZE/ASSESS   How does a stem-and-leaf plot help in finding the range and median? *(It is easy to see the least and greatest values and where the middle number is.)*

1. Make a new stem-and-leaf plot of the data by arranging the leaves for each stem from smallest to largest.
Check students' drawings.

2. Are there any clusters or gaps in this data?
Yes

3. In which stem would you expect to find the median value?
7

4. **THINK ALOUD** How are a bar graph and a stem-and-leaf plot alike? How are they different?
See page 517b.

PRACTICE

5. Make a stem-and-leaf plot for the high school dropout rate for each state and the District of Columbia.
(*Hint:* Each high school dropout rate can be found by subtracting the graduation rate from 100%.)
Check students' drawings.

6. **CRITICAL THINKING** How does the stem-and-leaf plot for the dropout rate compare with that for the graduation rate?
basically the same distribution of points

PROBLEM SOLVING

Imagine you are writing a story for your school newspaper about the dropout rates in the United States based on the information from Exercise 5. Use the stem-and-leaf plot to complete the news story.

7. Many educators are concerned about the high school dropout rate in the United States. More than half the states have a dropout rate of __a.__ or higher. The highest dropout rate is __b.__ . The place with the lowest dropout rate is Minnesota, with a rate of __c.__ .
25%; 43%; 9%

8. **IN YOUR WORDS** Add to the news story by writing one more sentence that contains a factual statement.
Check students' work.

9. **CREATE YOUR OWN** Find data in a magazine or newspaper appropriate for a stem-and-leaf plot. Then plot the data.
Check students' work.

CHAPTER 15   495

MEETING INDIVIDUAL NEEDS

For Students Who Are . . .

Acquiring English Proficiency Use pictures or actual branches with leaves to help students understand the relationship between stem and leaf.

Gifted and Talented Have students attempt to make a line plot for the data on page 494 and discuss which type is more appropriate

Working 2 or 3 Grades Below Level Review how to find the median. For Exercise 1, have students cross out each number as they put it in order.

Today's Problem

The following stem-and-leaf plot represents test grades. What is the median grade?
(80)

```
9 | 1 3 4 4 8
8 | 0 0 1 5
7 | 2 6 6 6
6 |
5 | 8 9
```

---

3 FOLLOW-UP

PRACTICE 15-3

1. Make a stem-and-leaf plot for the test score averages at right.

Stem	Leaf
6	8 5
7	3 5 2 4 4 5 6
8	1 5 9 5 6 5 3 2 2 4 5 7 8
9	1 1 2 7 0 2 3
10	0

Test Score Averages	
Bill	81
Susan	85
Candice	73
Carlos	91
Nancy	68
Maria	75
Rita	89
Sam	72
Patel	88
Wilma	86
Dottie	91
Sandy	85
Fred	74
Mary	83
Leon	92
Letitia	97
Miriam	74
Ramon	65
Mark	90
Vanessa	82
Doreen	75
Marvin	82
Jeff	100
Bev	84
Jan	85
Consuela	76
Jerry	87
Corinne	92
Martha	88
Don	93

2. Make a new stem-and-leaf plot of the same data by arranging the leaves for each stem from least to greatest.

Stem	Leaf
6	5 8
7	2 3 4 4 5 5 6
8	1 2 2 3 4 5 5 5 6 7 8 8 9
9	0 1 1 2 2 3 7
10	0

Solve.

Imagine you are writing a summary about the test scores in the class based on the information in Exercise 2. You don't have enough room to include the table, but you can include the stem-and-leaf plot. Complete the summary.

3. Most students scored __85__ , which is the __mode__ . The mean score was __83.4__ . All but three test score averages fell within the range __72–97__ .

4. Write one more sentence with another conclusion to add to the summary. Answers will vary. A suggestion is given.
The median score was 85.

RETEACHING 15-3

Write these numbers on the board: 7, 28, 19, 24, 50, 32, 24, 51, 28, 46, 10, 8, 14, 32, 22, and 6. Have a volunteer put a vertical line to the left of the ones place in each number. (Examples: 0|7, 2|8) Explain that the leaves are the numbers in the ones place and the stems are the numbers of tens. **What is the greatest number of 10s in these numbers?** *(5)* **The least number of tens?** *(0)* Have students list the stems from 5 to 0 vertically, and draw a vertical line to the right. Then have students write, in order, the digit or digits in the ones place for each stem. **Which stem has the most leaves?** *(2)* **Do all stems have leaves?** *(yes)*

ENRICHMENT 15-3

Bridgette and Bud investigated the study habits of the students in their school. They recorded for six weeks the number of students who left the east exit of the school with one or more books. There are 150 students who use the east exit.

	Week 1		Week 2		Week 3		Week 4		Week 5		Week 6	
	students	percent	students	percent	students	percent	students	percent	students	percent	students	percent
Mon.	101	67%	121	81%	110	73%	141	94%	62	41%	87	58%
Tues.	97	65%	63	42%	115	77%	139	93%	59	39%	95	63%
Wed.	85	57%	94	63%	121	81%	128	85%	73	49%	97	65%
Thurs.	98	65%	97	65%	136	91%	120	80%	58	39%	93	62%
Fri.	81	54%	86	57%	102	68%	111	74%	70	47%	89	59%

1. Make a stem-and-leaf plot of the number of students by arranging the leaves for each stem from least to greatest.

Stem	Leaf
14	1
13	6 9
12	0 1 1 8
11	0 1 5
10	1 2
9	3 4 5 7 7 7 8
8	1 5 6 7 9
7	0 3
6	2 3
5	8 9

2. Use the stem-and-leaf plot to find the
   a. range __83__   b. median __97__
   c. mode __97__

3. Find the percent of the students who use the east exit that took books home each day. Write each percent in the table.

4. On average, what percent of the students who used the east exit took books home? (*Hint:* Use the median from Exercise 2.)
__65%__

5. Do you think that there is a relationship between taking books home, studying, and grades? Explain your answer.
Answers will vary. Yes; students probably need their books to study, and most students get better grades when they study.

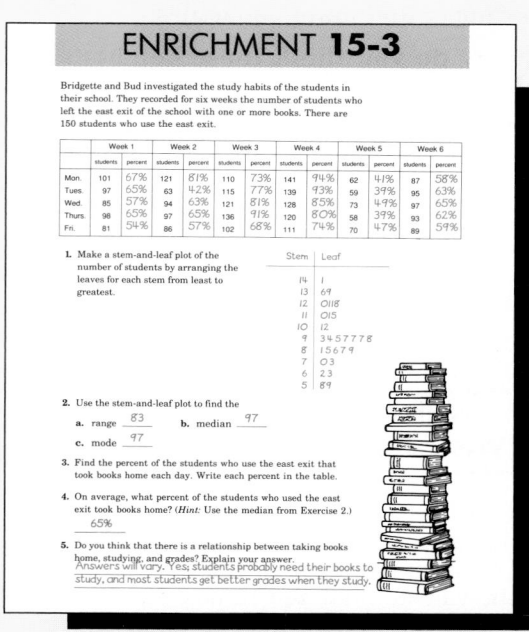

Lesson Organizer

> **Objective:** Read box plots.

Prior Knowledge: Students should be able to read and interpret scaled number lines.

Error Analysis and Remediation: See page 517A.

Lesson Resources:
Practice Worksheet 15-4
Reteaching Activity 15-4
Enrichment Worksheet 15-4
Daily Review 15-4

Two-Minute Math

Use mental math. Find the difference.

1,300 − 900 *(400)*
2,400 − 1,800 *(600)*
1,100 − 700 *(400)*
2,600 − 1,800 *(800)*

1 INTRODUCE

CONNECTING ACTIVITY

1. Have students give their heights in inches.

2. Arrange the heights in order from least to greatest. Identify the median height, and separate the heights into two groups.

3. Identify the middle height in each group. Tell students that these points are the "upper and lower" quartiles.

4. Why do you think these heights are called quartiles? *(They separate the set of heights into fourths or quarters.)*

WHEN YOUR STUDENTS ASK
★ WHY AM I LEARNING THIS? ★

In real life box plots are used in reports to summarize and display data. For example, the performance of eighth-grade U.S. students was summarized in box plots published in the *Second International Mathematics Study.*

Box Plots

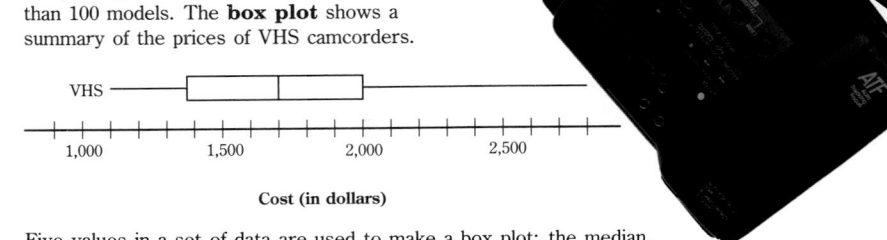

Recently, an estimated 2.5 million camcorders were sold in a year. That year a buyers' guide reported the prices of more than 100 models. The **box plot** shows a summary of the prices of VHS camcorders.

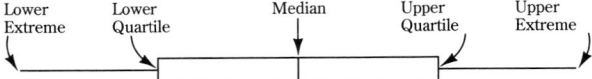

Cost (in dollars)

Five values in a set of data are used to make a box plot: the median, the upper and lower quartiles, and the upper and lower extremes.

The median is the middle number of the data set and separates it into an upper and a lower half.

The quartiles are the middle numbers of the upper half and the lower half; they separate the data into quarters, or fourths.

The extremes are the largest and the smallest values.

You can see these values clearly in a box plot

| Lower Extreme | Lower Quartile | Median | Upper Quartile | Upper Extreme |

THINK ALOUD A box plot is sometimes called a "box-and-whiskers" plot. Which parts make up the box? Which parts are the whiskers?
lower quartile to upper quartile; lower extreme and upper extreme
CRITICAL THINKING The data are separated into fourths in a box plot. What part of the data is in the box? What part of the data is in the whiskers? Why is the right whisker longer than the left one?
middle half; lower $\frac{1}{4}$ and upper $\frac{1}{4}$; upper $\frac{1}{4}$ of data is more spread out.

GUIDED PRACTICE

Estimate the range of prices. Accept reasonable estimates. Suggestions given.

1. the middle 50% of the VHS camcorders $1,375 to $2,000

2. the lower half of the VHS camcorders $1,100 to $1,700

3. the lower quarter of the VHS camcorders $1,100 to $1,375

---

2 TEACH

Which is easiest to see in a box plot: mean, median, or mode? Explain. *(The median, is easiest because the vertical line in the box shows where it is.)*

Why aren't the median and the quartiles all the same distance apart? *(Data in different sections may be bunched up or spread out.)*

SUMMARIZE/ASSESS **What information is communicated by box plots?** *(Responses should include ideas of spread and range: the median, the quartiles, the ranges of the upper and lower halves and quarters)*

You may also want to use the Box Plot transparency from the Overhead Kit when teaching this lesson.

PRACTICE

The buyers' guide described three types of camcorders: high quality super VHS and Hi8, compact, and standard VHS. The prices for these types are shown in the box plots.

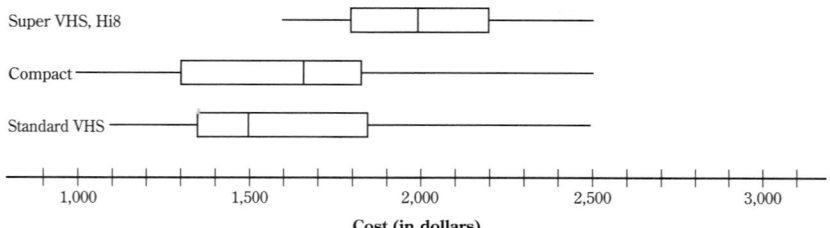

Cost (in dollars)

Use the box plots to answer the question for each kind of camcorder.

4. Estimate the value of the lower extreme.
   See page 517b.
5. Describe the range of the lower quarter.
   See page 517b.
6. Describe the range of the lower half.
   See page 517b.
7. Estimate the median price.
   See page 517b.
8. Estimate the range of the middle 50%.
   See page 517b.
9. Estimate the range of the upper quarter.
   See page 517b.

PROBLEM SOLVING

Refer to the box plots for the three kinds of camcorders.

10. **IN YOUR WORDS** Compare the prices of the compact, the standard VHS, and the super *Super is more* VHS camcorders. *expensive than the others.*

11. The middle 50% of the prices for the compact and the standard VHS camcorders are about the same, but the medians are different. Explain.
    See page 517b.

Critical Thinking

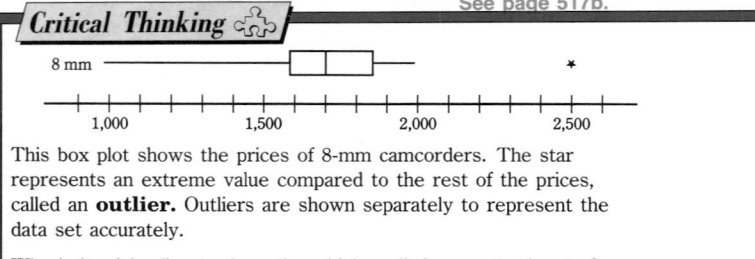

This box plot shows the prices of 8-mm camcorders. The star represents an extreme value compared to the rest of the prices, called an **outlier**. Outliers are shown separately to represent the data set accurately.

Why is it misleading to draw the whisker all the way to the star?

There are no models in the space between the end of the whisker and the star.

MEETING INDIVIDUAL NEEDS

For Students Who Are . . .

Acquiring English Proficiency Review the meanings of *range*, *extremes*, *median*, and *quartiles*.

Gifted and Talented Challenge students to find data for a box plot in a magazine or other resource. Then have them work in pairs to make a box plot from their data.

Working 2 or 3 Grades Below Level Review how to find middle numbers for the median and quartiles.

Today's Problem

During a two-week period, Derek spent the following number of minutes per day speaking on the telephone:

| Week 1 | 65 | 30 | 22 | 18 | 28 | 10 | 52 |
| Week 2 | 32 | 20 | 25 | 15 | 30 | 12 | 28 |

Write a problem about the data. *(Check students' work.)*

---

3 FOLLOW-UP

PRACTICE 15-4

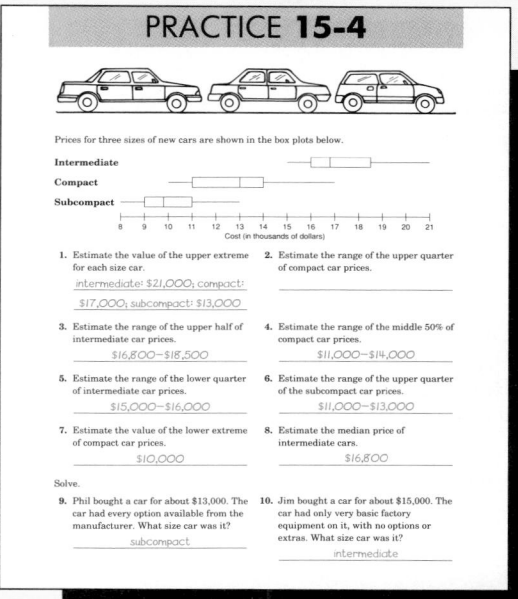

Prices for three sizes of new cars are shown in the box plots below.

Cost (in thousands of dollars)

1. Estimate the value of the upper extreme for each size car.
   intermediate: $21,000; compact: $17,000; subcompact: $13,000

2. Estimate the range of the upper quarter of compact car prices.

3. Estimate the range of the upper half of intermediate car prices.
   $16,800–$18,500

4. Estimate the range of the middle 50% of compact car prices.
   $11,000–$14,000

5. Estimate the range of the lower quarter of intermediate car prices.
   $15,000–$16,000

6. Estimate the range of the upper quarter of the subcompact car prices.
   $11,000–$13,000

7. Estimate the value of the lower extreme of compact car prices.
   $10,000

8. Estimate the median price of intermediate cars.
   $16,800

Solve.

9. Phil bought a car for about $13,000. The car had every option available from the manufacturer. What size car was it?
   subcompact

10. Jim bought a car for about $15,000. The car had only very basic factory equipment on it, with no options or extras. What size car was it?
    intermediate

RETEACHING 15-4

Write these heights in inches on the chalkboard: 55, 56, 57, 58, 59, 60, 61, 62, 63. Have a student circle the median *(59)* and put a box around the middle numbers in the lower and upper halves. *(57, 62)* These are called lower and upper quartiles. Next, have another student underline the extremes values. *(55 and 62)* Finally, draw the box plot below on the chalkboard, have students identify these 5 values and give their names.

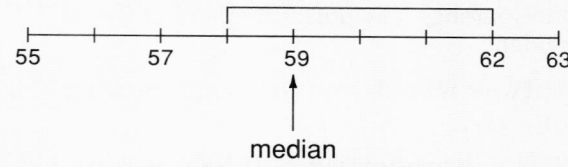

median

ENRICHMENT 15-4

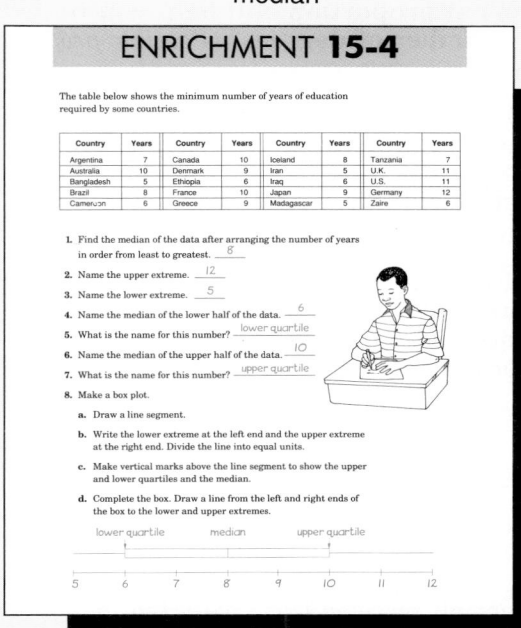

The table below shows the minimum number of years of education required by some countries.

Country	Years	Country	Years	Country	Years	Country	Years
Argentina	7	Canada	10	Iceland	8	Tanzania	7
Australia	10	Denmark	9	Iran	5	U.K.	11
Bangladesh	5	Ethiopia	6	Iraq	6	U.S.	11
Brazil	8	France	10	Japan	9	Germany	12
Cameroon	6	Greece	9	Madagascar	5	Zaire	6

1. Find the median of the data after arranging the number of years in order from least to greatest. ___8___
2. Name the upper extreme. ___12___
3. Name the lower extreme. ___5___
4. Name the median of the lower half of the data. ___6___
5. What is the name for this number? ___lower quartile___
6. Name the median of the upper half of the data. ___10___
7. What is the name for this number? ___upper quartile___
8. Make a box plot.
   a. Draw a line segment.
   b. Write the lower extreme at the left end and the upper extreme at the right end. Divide the line into equal units.
   c. Make vertical marks above the line segment to show the upper and lower quartiles and the median.
   d. Complete the box. Draw a line from the left and right ends of the box to the lower and upper extremes.

   lower quartile   median   upper quartile

Chapter 15 • Lesson 15-4   **497**

LESSON 15-5

Lesson Organizer

Objective: Make and interpret a circle graph.

Prior Knowledge: Students should know how to solve proportions and use a compass and a protractor.

Lesson Resources:
Practice Worksheet 15-5
Reteaching Worksheet 15-5
Enrichment Activity 15-5
Daily Review 15-5
Cooperative Investigations, Chapter 15

Two-Minute Math

Use mental math. Solve.

$\frac{5}{36} = \frac{n}{360}$ (n = 50)

$\frac{50}{180} = \frac{n}{360}$ (n = 100)

$\frac{3}{4} = \frac{n}{360}$ (n = 270)

1 INTRODUCE

CONCRETE ACTIVITY

☑ **MATERIALS CHECKLIST:** Teaching Aid 8 (Protractor) or protractor, protractor transparency, compass, straightedge for each student

1. **How would you go about showing $\frac{1}{9}$ of a circle?** (Accept all responses.)

2. **What proportion will help you find the number of degrees?** (Possible proportion: $\frac{1}{9}:n = \frac{9}{9}:360$; n = 40)

3. **Draw a circle with your compass. Draw a radius with your straightedge. Use your protractor to construct a 40° angle inside the circle. Does it appear to be about $\frac{1}{9}$ of the circle?**

You may wish to demonstrate this on an overhead projector by using the Protractor transparency from the Houghton Mifflin Overhead Kit.

WHEN YOUR STUDENTS ASK
★ **WHY AM I LEARNING THIS?** ★

Circle graphs can be used to display real data such as the percentages of paper, plastic, metal, and glass that together represent all recycled trash collected in a community.

Construction: Circle Graph

In the 1988 Olympics, the USSR won the most medals. Its athletes received 132 medals. Of these, 55 were gold, 46 were silver, and 31 were bronze.

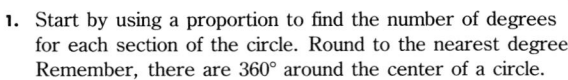

You can show these data in a circle graph that represents the proportions of gold, silver, and bronze medals.

1. Start by using a proportion to find the number of degrees for each section of the circle. Round to the nearest degree. Remember, there are 360° around the center of a circle.

Medals	Gold	Silver	Bronze
Part / Whole	$\frac{55}{132}$	$\frac{46}{132}$	$\frac{31}{132}$
Proportion	$\frac{55}{132} = \frac{n}{360}$	$\frac{46}{132} = \frac{p}{360}$	$\frac{31}{132} = \frac{q}{360}$
	$55 \times 360 = 132 \times n$	$46 \times 360 = 132 \times p$	$31 \times 360 = 132 \times q$
	$n = \frac{55 \times 360}{132}$	$p = \frac{46 \times 360}{132}$	$q = \frac{31 \times 360}{132}$
	$n = 150°$	$p = 125°$	$q = 85°$

2. You can use a compass, a protractor, and a straightedge to construct the circle graph.
Check students' graphs.

STEPS Draw a circle with a radius.

Use the protractor to measure the degrees needed to represent the gold medals (150°).

Draw the second side of the central angle. Write "gold" as a label for the section.

Use the protractor to measure the degrees needed to represent the silver medals (125°). Draw the angle. Label the section "silver."

The remaining section will be for the bronze medals. Check the angle measure with your protractor. It should be 85°. Label the section.

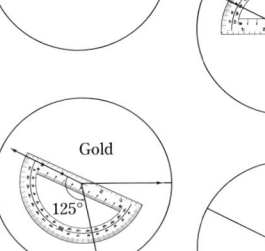

---

2 TEACH

☑ **MATERIALS CHECKLIST:** compass, protractor, and straightedge for each student

Estimate the fractional part of the USSR's medals that were gold, silver, and bronze. (gold: almost $\frac{1}{2}$; silver: more than $\frac{1}{3}$; bronze: less than $\frac{1}{4}$; accept reasonable estimates.)

What does 360 represent in each proportion? (the number of degrees in a whole circle)

What does the variable represent? (the number of degrees needed to represent a particular color medal)

SUMMARIZE/ASSESS **With what types of data should circle graphs be used?** (with data that represent parts of a known whole)

3. Look at your circle graph. Estimate the fractional part of the circle graph represented by each section.

4. About what fraction of the medals were gold? bronze? silver?

5. **ESTIMATE** About what percent of the medals were gold? bronze? silver?

The chart shows the number of gold, silver, and bronze medals won by East Germany and the United States in the 1988 Olympics.

	Gold	Silver	Bronze
East Germany	37	30	35
United States	36	27	31

6. For East Germany, how many degrees of a circle would be needed to represent the gold medals? the silver medals? the bronze medals?

7. Draw a circle graph to show the proportions of gold, silver, and bronze medals won by East Germany.

8. **ESTIMATE** What fractional part of the East Germany circle graph is each section?

9. For the United States, how many degrees of a circle would be needed to represent the gold medals? the silver medals? the bronze medals?

10. Draw a circle graph to show the proportions of gold, silver, and bronze medals won by the United States.

11. **ESTIMATE** What fractional part of the United States circle graph is each section?

CRITICAL THINKING Use your three circle graphs to answer.

12. If you referred to nothing other than the graphs, would you be able to tell which country—the USSR, East Germany, or the United States—won the most medals in 1988? Explain.

13. By looking at just the graphs, what comparisons can you make between the countries' athletes?

MEETING INDIVIDUAL NEEDS
For Students Who Are . . .

Acquiring English Proficiency Pair students with an English proficient student to construct the circle graphs.

Gifted and Talented Have students use the almanac to find the number of gold, silver, and bronze medals won by the United States in the 1988 Winter Olympics. Students can make circle graphs displaying the information.

Working 2 or 3 Grades Below Level Review solving proportions and rounding to the nearest whole number in division.

Today's Problem

Estimate your weekly budget. About what percent do you spend on food, entertainment, and so on. Use a calculator, compass, and protractor to make a circle graph that illustrates your weekly spending habits.

---

3 FOLLOW-UP

PRACTICE 15-5

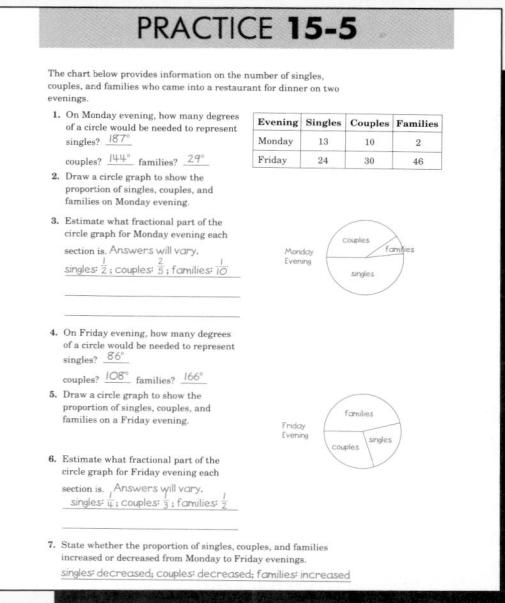

The chart below provides information on the number of singles, couples, and families who came into a restaurant for dinner on two evenings.

1. On Monday evening, how many degrees of a circle would be needed to represent singles? _187°_ couples? _144°_ families? _29°_

Evening	Singles	Couples	Families
Monday	13	10	2
Friday	24	30	46

2. Draw a circle graph to show the proportion of singles, couples, and families on Monday evening.

3. Estimate what fractional part of the circle graph for Monday evening each section is. Answers will vary. singles: $\frac{1}{2}$; couples: $\frac{2}{5}$; families: $\frac{1}{10}$

4. On Friday evening, how many degrees of a circle would be needed to represent singles? _86°_ couples? _108°_ families? _166°_

5. Draw a circle graph to show the proportion of singles, couples, and families on a Friday evening.

6. Estimate what fractional part of the circle graph for Friday evening each section is. Answers will vary. singles: $\frac{1}{4}$; couples: $\frac{1}{3}$; families: $\frac{1}{2}$

7. State whether the proportion of singles, couples, and families increased or decreased from Monday to Friday evenings. singles: decreased; couples: decreased; families: increased

RETEACHING 15-5

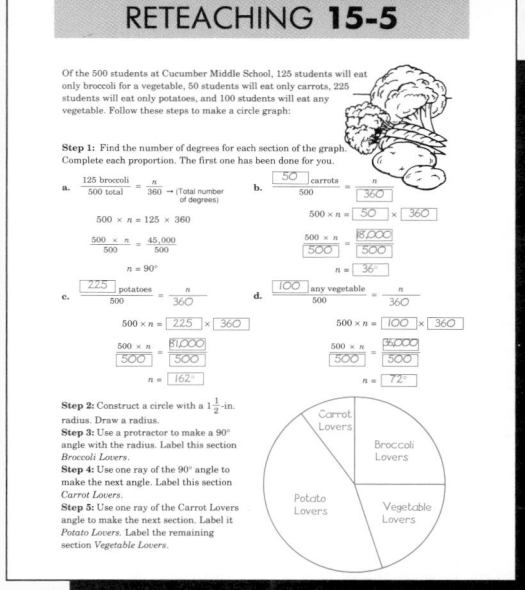

Of the 500 students at Cucumber Middle School, 125 students will eat only broccoli for a vegetable, 50 students will only eat carrots, 225 students will eat only potatoes, and 100 students will eat any vegetable. Follow these steps to make a circle graph:

Step 1: Find the number of degrees for each section of the graph. Complete each proportion. The first one has been done for you.

a. $\frac{125 \text{ broccoli}}{500 \text{ total}} = \frac{n}{360} \rightarrow$ (Total number of degrees)

$500 \times n = 125 \times 360$

$\frac{500 \times n}{500} = \frac{45,000}{500}$

$n = 90°$

b. $\frac{50 \text{ carrots}}{500} = \frac{n}{360}$

$500 \times n = 50 \times 360$

$\frac{500 \times n}{500} = \frac{18,000}{500}$

$n = 36°$

c. $\frac{225 \text{ potatoes}}{500} = \frac{n}{360}$

$500 \times n = 225 \times 360$

$\frac{500 \times n}{500} = \frac{81,000}{500}$

$n = 162°$

d. $\frac{100 \text{ any vegetable}}{500} = \frac{n}{360}$

$500 \times n = 100 \times 360$

$\frac{500 \times n}{500} = \frac{36,000}{500}$

$n = 72°$

Step 2: Construct a circle with a $1\frac{1}{2}$-in. radius. Draw a radius.
Step 3: Use a protractor to make a 90° angle with the radius. Label this section *Broccoli Lovers*.
Step 4: Use one ray of the 90° angle to make the next angle. Label this section *Carrot Lovers*.
Step 5: Use one ray of the Carrot Lovers angle to make the next section. Label it *Potato Lovers*. Label the remaining section *Vegetable Lovers*.

ENRICHMENT 15-5

☑ **MATERIALS CHECKLIST:** Compasses, protractors

Have the students estimate the amount of time they spend during a typical weekend doing activities such as eating, sleeping, studying, watching television, playing sports, performing household chores, or babysitting. (They may have an "other" category if they wish.) Tell them to assume that a weekend is 48 hr long. The students draw a circle graph showing their weekend activities and then share their work with each other. Were there any surprising results?

MIDCHAPTER Checkup

The midchapter checkup provides a way for you to check students' understanding of the skills taught in the first half of the chapter.

Language and Vocabulary

Some key language and vocabulary ideas from the first half of the chapter are reinforced here.

Quick Quiz

This quiz provides a means of evaluating students' understanding of the objectives for the first half of the chapter. Page references are given so that students can check back to where the skill was taught.

Use the following guide to score the quiz.

Score	Percent
6	100%
5	83
4	67
3	50
2	33
1	17

Use this chart to identify the management objectives tested.

Items	Management Objectives	Pages
1–5	**15A** Make and interpret a line plot, a stem-and-leaf plot, a box plot, or a circle graph.	492–499
6	**15D** Problem Solving: Draw a picture.	490–491

MIDCHAPTER CHECKUP

LANGUAGE & VOCABULARY

Write *true* or *false*.

1. A line plot makes the mode of a set of data easily visible? **true**

2. The middle stem in a stem-and-leaf plot will always have the largest number of leaves. **false**

3. In a box plot, the upper and lower extremes must be equidistant from the median. **false**

QUICK QUIZ ✓

The table shows the number of tickets to the school play sold by students in room 212. Use the data. *(pages 492–499)*

Bill 34	Sally 29	Eddie 28
Donna 24	Arnold 24	Paul 22
Winnie 24	Sue 29	Wanda 22
Johnny 24	Mike 27	Julio 40
Michael 35	Michelle 20	Charlene 28

1. What is the range of the data? **20**

2. Make a line plot of the data. **Check students' work.**

3. Name the stems you would use to make a stem-and-leaf plot. **2; 3; 4**

4. Name the median and upper and lower quartiles you would use to make a box plot. **median: 27; quartiles: 24, 29**

5. Tell how to make a circle graph. **Accept reasonable answers.**

Solve. *(pages 490–491)*

6. The graph shows the number of books in one class library.

   a. About how many novels are in the library? **90**

   b. What impression does the graph give about the number of novels compared to the number of biographies? **twice as many**

   c. About how many more novels are there than biographies? **20 more novels**

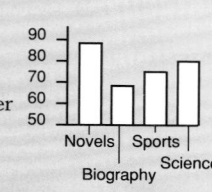

Answers will vary. Suggestions given.
Write the answers in your learning log.
1. In what ways can a graph not tell the real truth. **Accept reasonable answers.**
2. Explain what is meant by the range of ages of the members of your family. **the difference between oldest and youngest**
3. When you look at a circle graph, what does the whole circle represent? **100%; everything; all of the data**

DID YOU KNOW . . . ? Refined sugar is the only known food that provides only calories and no nutrients. The average American consumes nearly 100 lb of sugar/yr. 36% is eaten directly and the rest is eaten as an ingredient in prepared foods. If each member of your class consumes the average amount, how many pounds of sugar would the class eat in a year? Of that, how many pounds would come from prepared foods? **Check students' work.**

"In what year is your birthday?" In China people can answer this question with the name of an animal. Find out what animals the Chinese years are named for. Then answer the question.
Check students' work.

CHAPTER 15   501

Learning Log

These are suggestions for writing about some topics taught so far in the chapter. The students keep their learning logs from the start of the school year to the end.

Math America

A mathematical skill that students have learned is related to an interesting fact about the United States.

Bonus

Students are given an opportunity to solve a challenge-type problem such as a puzzle or a nonroutine problem.

LESSON 15-6

Lesson Organizer

Objective: Determine the sample space for multiple events.

Prior Knowledge: Students should know how to make and interpret organized lists.

Error Analysis and Remediation: See page 517A.

Lesson Resources:
Practice Worksheet 15-6
Reteaching Worksheet 15-6
Enrichment Activity 15-6
Daily Review 15-6

Two-Minute Math

List as many real and nonsense words as you can using the letters M A T H. *(MATH, MAHT, MTHA, MTAH, MHAT, MHTA, ATHM, ATHM, AHTM, AHMT, AMTH, AMHT, THAM, THMA, TAMH, TAHM, TMAH, TMHA, HMAT, HMTA, HTMA, HTAM, HAMT, HATM)*

1 INTRODUCE

CONNECTING ACTIVITY

☑ **MATERIALS CHECKLIST:** two blank spinners; red, green, blue, and yellow markers for each pair

Have students work with a partner.

1. Divide each spinner into halves. Shade half of the first spinner red and half green. Shade half the second spinner yellow and the other half blue.

2. Have partners spin the first spinner, then the second. **Record the color pair obtained from each pair of spins.**

3. Have students repeat the spins until they think they have obtained every color pair possible. Report the color pairs back to the class.

WHEN YOUR STUDENTS ASK
★ **WHY AM I LEARNING THIS?** ★

Suppose you were packaging nuts and bolts. You would have to plan packaging that combined the various sizes together.

502 *Chapter 15 • Lesson 15-6*

Sample Space

Leah works at the Salty Seafood Shop. Her uniform includes 3 skirts (blue, white, and striped) and 2 blouses (blue and striped). How many different outfits can she make?

Each outfit can be thought of as an **outcome**. There are several ways to figure out the number of all possible outcomes.

• Use an organized list.

Blue blouse with each skirt		Striped blouse with each skirt	
blue blouse, blue skirt	(b,b)	striped blouse, blue skirt	(s,b)
blue blouse, white skirt	(b,w)	striped blouse, white skirt	(s,w)
blue blouse, striped skirt	(b,s)	striped blouse, striped skirt	(s,s)

This list of all possible outcomes is called the **sample space**. There are 6 possible outcomes in the sample space.

• Use a tree diagram.

List the blouses.	Connect to the skirts.	Sample Space	
blue	blue	(blue, blue)	(b, b)
	white	(blue, white)	(b, w)
	striped	(blue, striped)	(b, s)
striped	blue	(striped, blue)	(s, b)
	white	(striped, white)	(s, w)
	striped	(striped, striped)	(s, s)

There are 6 possible outcomes in the sample space.

• Use a lattice.

List the skirts across the top and the blouses down the side. Write the outfits in the cells.

Blouses	Skirts		
	blue	white	striped
blue	b, b	b, w	b, s
striped	s, b	s, w	s, s

There are 6 possible outcomes in the sample space.

• Use the basic counting principle.

2 blouses, 3 skirts → 2 × 3 = 6 outcomes

> **When you know the number of outcomes for each event, you can multiply those numbers to find the number of outcomes in the sample space for the multiple event.**

502   LESSON 15–6

---

2 TEACH

How are the organized list method and the tree diagram alike? *(Both methods pair up each blouse with the three different skirts.)*

How does the lattice method help you understand why the basic counting principle uses multiplication? *(The lattice method shows that there are 2 rows of 3, which means there are 2 × 3 cells, or outcomes.)*

SUMMARIZE/ASSESS   **What are three methods of listing the sample space? Which do you prefer, and why?** *(Students can describe the lattice method, the tree diagram, or the organized list; answers will vary.)*

Eric can choose from 4 types of shirts and 3 types of slacks for his park district uniform. Find the number of different outfits he can wear.

1. Use an organized list.

2. Use a tree diagram.

3. Use a lattice.

4. Use the basic counting principle.

5. What is the sample space for the above problem?

6. How many outcomes are there in the sample space?

PRACTICE

Jason bought 2 pairs of shorts (yellow and blue) and 4 T-shirts (yellow, blue, green, and red). Find the total number of possible outfits.

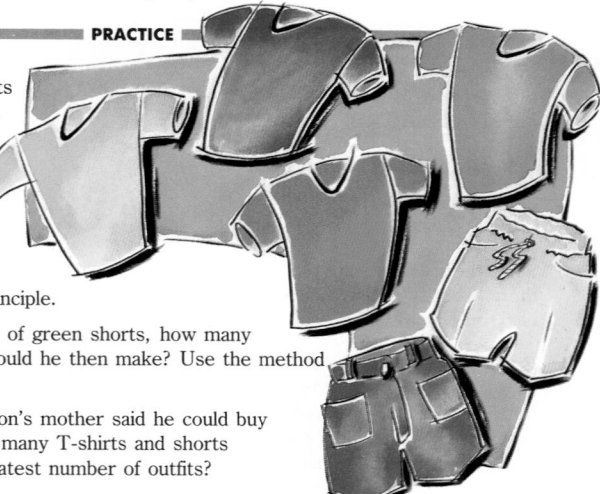

7. Use an organized list.

8. Use a tree diagram.

9. Use a lattice.

10. Use the basic counting principle.

11. If Jason also bought a pair of green shorts, how many combinations of clothing could he then make? Use the method of your choice.

12. **CRITICAL THINKING** Jason's mother said he could buy 6 pieces of clothing. How many T-shirts and shorts are needed to get the greatest number of outfits?

PROBLEM SOLVING

Identify a situation for the sample space.

13.

```
              heads   (H, H)
      heads
              tails   (H, T)
              heads   T, H)
      tails
              tails   (T, T)
```

14.

	1	2	3	4	5	6
1	1, 1	2, 1	3, 1	4, 1	5, 1	6, 1
2	1, 2	2, 2	3, 2	4, 2	5, 2	6, 2
3	1, 3	2, 3	3, 3	4, 3	5, 3	6, 3
4	1, 4	2, 4	3, 4	4, 4	5, 4	6, 4
5	1, 5	2, 5	3, 5	4, 5	5, 5	6, 5
6	1, 6	2, 6	3, 6	4, 6	5, 6	6, 6

15. **CREATE YOUR OWN** Describe a situation that has a sample space of 24 outcomes.

MEETING INDIVIDUAL NEEDS

For Students Who Are . . .

Acquiring English Proficiency Discuss the meaning of *outcomes, sample space, lattice, cells,* and *multiple event.*

Gifted and Talented Have students make a sample space similar to that in the Problem Solving section. They can exchange papers and describe a situation in the partner's sample space.

Working 2 or 3 Grades Below Level For Exercise 7, remind students to list the shorts first and the T-shirts second.

Today's Problem

You can choose one of three different-size servings of frozen yogurt: small, medium, or large. You can choose one of two flavors: vanilla or mixed berry. You can choose one of three toppings: wheat germ, chopped nuts, or fresh fruit. How many possible choices do you have? *(sample space: 3 × 2 × 3 = 18; 18 possible choices)*

---

3 FOLLOW-UP

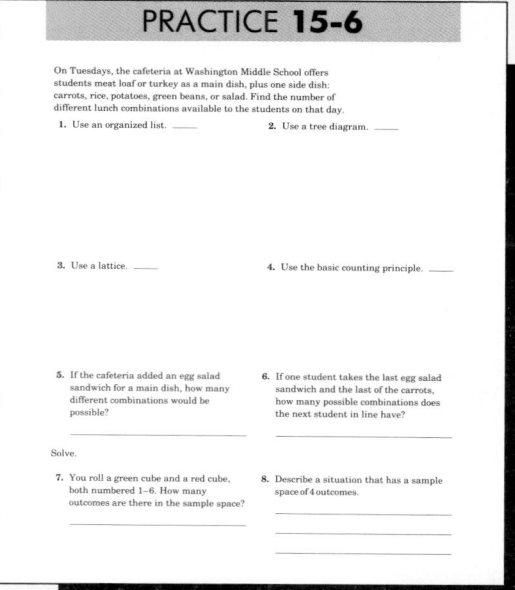

ENRICHMENT 15-6

☑ **MATERIALS CHECKLIST:** Reference books

Explain that the U.S. Postal Service uses ZIP codes to help sort and deliver mail more efficiently. Write the ZIP code for your school's city or town on the board. (The first digit indicates the general geographical area; the first three digits indicate sectional centers; and the last two digits indicate local post offices.) Have the students find the greatest possible number of local post offices within a sectional center. [99] Ask: Have you ever seen a nine-digit ZIP code? Have them research the history of ZIP codes and be able to explain the need for a nine-digit code.

Lesson Organizer

Objective: Find the probability of multiple events.

Prior Knowledge: Students should be able to list sample spaces and find simple probabilities.

Error Analysis and Remediation: See page 517A.

Lesson Resources:
Practice Worksheet 15-7
Reteaching Worksheet 15-7
Enrichment Activity 15-7
Daily Review 15-7
Cooperative Problem Solving 1, Chapter 15

Two-Minute Math

Use the Table of Numbers on the inside back cover. Round each number in row C to the nearest 25. *(100, 100, 700, 75, 475, 275, 75, 550, 325)*

1 INTRODUCE

CONNECTING ACTIVITY

☑ **MATERIALS CHECKLIST:** blank spinners divided into four equal regions, two for each pair

1. Label each region *A*, *B*, *C*, or *D*. Mark one spinner #1 and the other #2.

2. Spin both spinners 50 times to find the experimental probability of spinning *B* on #1 and *D* on #2. Combine the class data to determine the experimental probability.

3. Find the actual probability.

• **List the sample space.**

• **Identify the desirable outcomes.**

• **Describe the actual probability.** $\left(\frac{1}{16}\right)$

4. Compare the two probabilities.

WHEN YOUR STUDENTS ASK
★ **WHY AM I LEARNING THIS?** ★

You can connect this skill to real life through computer technology. Software designers use probability of multiple events when they develop computer simulations that show the effects of earthquakes on tall buildings.

Probability of Multiple Events

The swim team members couldn't decide among three choices—the Dolphins, the Porpoises, and the Pisces—for a new name. They also had a tie in the vote for swim suit colors between purple and blue.

So the coach put cards with the names in one box and cards with the colors in another. A card from each box would be picked without looking.

Vicki wanted the team name to be the Porpoises and the suit color to be purple. She listed the sample space.

Porpoises, blue	Porpoises, purple
Dolphins, blue	Dolphins, purple
Pisces, blue	Pisces, purple

Since the outcomes are equally likely, the probability of her choice was 1 out of 6, or $\frac{1}{6}$.

Eric's choice was the Dolphins with blue suits. He used the basic counting principle to match each name with each color. There were 2 × 3, or 6, possibilities. The probability of his choice was 1 out of 6, or $\frac{1}{6}$.

THINK ALOUD Explain how you could use a tree diagram or a lattice to find the probability of a name and color choice. See page 517b.

GUIDED PRACTICE

1. Find the probability of the choice *Dolphins, purple* from the names Dolphins, Porpoises, Pisces, and Waves and the colors purple, blue, and green. Use an organized list, a tree diagram, a lattice, or the basic counting principle to list the sample space.
$\frac{1}{12}$

2. **IN YOUR WORDS** Why did you choose the method you used to list the sample space? Accept reasonable answers.

504   LESSON 15–7

---

2 TEACH

Combine pairs of students into groups of four for this lesson. **What steps do you follow to find the probability of multiple events?** *(First, list the sample space to find the number of possible outcomes. Second, identify the desired outcomes. Third, set up the ratio comparing the number of desired events to the number of possible events.)*

GUIDED PRACTICE   Have each group report the method chosen and the reason for the choice.

SUMMARIZE/ASSESS **How are finding the probability of single events and the probability of multiple events alike? different?** *(Possible answer: Both compare the number of desired outcomes to the number of possible outcomes; with multiple events you first have to determine all possible outcomes.)*

At the swim meet, the swimmers picked sweat pants and sweat shirts from two team boxes. By the time Benjy got to the box, there were only 2 sweat shirts (1 small and 1 medium) and 3 sweat pants (1 small, 1 medium, and 1 large) left.

3. List the sample space for all the possible combinations of sweat shirts and sweat pants.
(s,s); (s,m); (s,l) (m,s); (m,m); (m,l)

4. Use your favorite method to find the probability that Benjy selected a medium sweat shirt and medium sweat pants by reaching into the boxes without looking. $\frac{1}{6}$

5. What is the probability that Benjy picked out both a small sweat shirt and small sweat pants? $\frac{1}{6}$

The coach can assign swimmers to lane 1, lane 2, lane 3, or lane 4. The coach always has the swimmers pick lane numbers out of a hat.

6. Jenny is going to swim in two races. Find the probability that Jenny will get lane 4 for both races if she gets to pick first from the hat for each race. Solve by listing the sample space. $\frac{1}{16}$

7. Alissa is going to swim in only two races. She likes lane 3 and lane 4 equally well. Find the probability that she will get in a lane she likes for both races if she gets to pick first for each race. $\frac{1}{4}$

8. Alex likes even numbers. Find the probability that he will draw even-numbered lanes for both of his two races if he gets to pick first. $\frac{1}{4}$

9. Hamid is going to swim in three races. What is the probability that he will swim in lane 4 for all three races if he gets to pick first for each? $\frac{1}{64}$

10. Maria is the star of the team. She will swim in four races. What is the probability that she will swim in lane 4 for all four races if she picks first for each race? $\frac{1}{256}$

MEETING INDIVIDUAL NEEDS
For Students Who Are . . .

Acquiring English Proficiency Explain the meaning of *lane* and *lane numbers*. Pair students with an English proficient student for the Practice and Problem Solving exercises.

Gifted and Talented Challenge students to create a problem with multiple events and write a probability question. They can exchange papers and answer each other's question.

Today's Problem
A spinner is divided into two equal areas. One area is marked 0, and the other is marked 1. Which of the following outcomes seems most probable if the spinner is spun many times?

   A. 0111110010000111000
   B. 1001001001001100100
   C. 1100001000001100100

(They all have equally likely chances of occurring.)

3 FOLLOW-UP

PRACTICE 15-7

The Applegate family had a unique way of deciding where to go on vacation. The parents and each child filled out one slip of paper for location and one for lodging and put the slips in boxes marked the same way. The parents wrote "lake" on one slip and "camper" on the other. The daughter wrote "seashore" and "hotel." The son wrote "mountains" and "tent." They mixed the slips in each box, and then drew one slip from each box without looking.

1. List the sample space for all the possible combinations of locations and lodgings.

	camper	hotel	tent
lake	l,c	l,h	l,t
seashore	s,c	s,h	s,t
mountains	m,c	m,h	m,t

2. Use the multiplication principle to find the probability that the son's choices will be selected.
$3 \times 3 = 9$; $\frac{1}{9}$

3. What is the probability that at least one of the parents' choices for location or lodging will be selected?
$\frac{5}{9}$

Solve.
The daughter convinces the son to change his location slip to "seashore"; the parents convince him to change his lodging to "camper."

4. List the new sample space for all possible combinations of locations and lodgings.

	camper	camper	hotel
lake	l,c	l,c	l,h
seashore	s,c	s,c	s,h
seashore	s,c	s,c	s,h

5. What is the probability that the family will go to a lake and stay in a camper?
$\frac{2}{9}$

6. What is the probability that the family will go to the seashore and stay either in a hotel or in a camper?
$\frac{2}{3}$

RETEACHING 15-7

The probability that an event will occur tells how likely it is that the event will occur.

Look at the two bags at the right. One bag contains a quarter and a half-dollar coin. The other bag contains a dime, a nickel, and a penny. What is the probability of drawing a penny and a quarter (p, q)?

Make a tree diagram to find the possible outcomes. Then write the sample space.

Sample Space

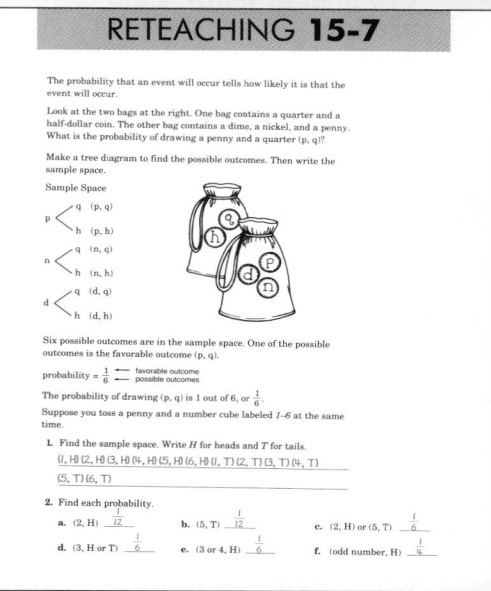

$$p \begin{cases} q & (p, q) \\ h & (p, h) \end{cases}$$
$$n \begin{cases} q & (n, q) \\ h & (n, h) \end{cases}$$
$$d \begin{cases} q & (d, q) \\ h & (d, h) \end{cases}$$

Six possible outcomes are in the sample space. One of the possible outcomes is the favorable outcome (p, q).

probability = $\frac{1}{6}$ ← favorable outcome
                ← possible outcomes

The probability of drawing (p, q) is 1 out of 6, or $\frac{1}{6}$.

Suppose you toss a penny and a number cube labeled 1–6 at the same time.

1. Find the sample space. Write *H* for heads and *T* for tails.
(1, H) (2, H) (3, H) (4, H) (5, H) (6, H) (1, T) (2, T) (3, T) (4, T)
(5, T) (6, T)

2. Find each probability.

  a. (2, H) $\frac{1}{12}$ **b.** (5, T) $\frac{1}{12}$ **c.** (2, H) or (5, T) $\frac{1}{6}$

  d. (3, H or T) $\frac{1}{6}$ **e.** (3 or 4, H) $\frac{1}{6}$ **f.** (odd number, H) $\frac{1}{4}$

ENRICHMENT 15-7

☑ **MATERIALS CHECKLIST:** Blank spinner, and a penny for each pair of students

Have students work in pairs. Provide each pair with a spinner and a penny. On the spinner have students mark off four equally-spaced regions shaded red, blue, green, and yellow. One student spins the spinner while the other tosses the coin. List the outcome. Example: (red, heads). Repeat 100 times. **How many different outcomes are there?** *(8)* **Do they appear to be equally likely? What is the probability of (red, heads)?** *(Answers will vary, depending on experimental results.)*

LESSON | 15-8

Lesson Organizer

Objective: Determine the probability of independent events.

Prior Knowledge: Students should be able to multiply fractions and to find probabilities of multiple events.

Error Analysis and Remediation: See page 517A.

Lesson Resources:
Practice Worksheet 15-8
Reteaching Worksheet 15-8
Enrichment Activity 15-8
Daily Review 15-8

Two-Minute Math

Use mental math. Find the product.

$\frac{2}{3} \times \frac{2}{3}$ $\left(\frac{4}{9}\right)$ $\frac{1}{2} \times \frac{2}{3}$ $\left(\frac{1}{3}\right)$

$\frac{3}{4} \times \frac{1}{2}$ $\left(\frac{3}{8}\right)$ $\frac{2}{5} \times \frac{2}{3}$ $\left(\frac{4}{15}\right)$

1 INTRODUCE

CONNECTING ACTIVITY

✔ **MATERIALS CHECKLIST:** index cards and a hat

1. Present the following situation: **Two prizes will be given at the first two meetings. Names will be drawn from a hat containing cards with each member's name.**

2. Write *Sue, Maria, Don, Julio,* and *Al* on each of the index cards. Mix them in the hat. Imitate the contest by drawing one winner, returning the card, and drawing the second winner.

3. Have students work in pairs to list the sample space using two different methods.

4. Find the probability that:
- **two girls will win the prizes.** $\left(\frac{4}{25}\right)$
- **Don will win both prizes.** $\left(\frac{1}{25}\right)$
- **two boys will win the prizes.** $\left(\frac{9}{25}\right)$

WHEN YOUR STUDENTS ASK
★ WHY AM I LEARNING THIS? ★

In real life, understanding independent events will help you recognize instances when one situation causes or influences another.

Independent Events

The Oakton Middle School Volunteer Club has 5 members, 2 boys and 3 girls. Whenever there is a request for help, the club members draw 1 of their 5 names out of a hat to see who will give the help. All 5 names go back into the hat at the end of the day.

Mr. Buono is recovering from an illness and has asked to have his lawn mowed on two Fridays.

On the first Friday, 1 of the 5 names is drawn. On the second Friday, 1 of the 5 names is drawn.

The two drawings are called **independent events** because the name drawn on the first Friday has no effect on the name drawn on the second Friday.

What is the probability that a girl's name will be chosen both times?

You could use a lattice to find the sample space. You would find that the probability that a girl's name will be chosen both times is 9 out of 25, or $\frac{9}{25}$.

You also could reason that the probability of a girl being chosen is 3 out of 5, or $\frac{3}{5}$, on the first Friday and 3 out of 5, or $\frac{3}{5}$, on the second Friday. When you find the probability this way, you are using the **multiplication principle**.

You could use a lattice to find the sample space.

	g	g	g	b	b
g	gg	gg	gg	gb	gb
g	gg	gg	gg	gb	gb
g	gg	gg	gg	gb	gb
b	bg	bg	bg	bb	bb
b	bg	bg	bg	bb	bb

The probability of a girl's name being chosen both times is 9 out of 25, or $\frac{9}{25}$.

> **Multiplication Principle: To find the probability of two independent events occurring at the same time, find the product of the individual probabilities.**
>
> $$P(A \text{ and } B) = P(A) \times P(B)$$

First Friday: $P(g)$		Second Friday: $P(g)$		Both Fridays: $P(g \text{ and } g)$
$\frac{3}{5}$	$\times$	$\frac{3}{5}$	$=$	$\frac{9}{25}$

GUIDED PRACTICE

The club had a request from Mrs. Wells at its last meeting. She needed someone to pick up her mail on Monday and Friday of this week.

1. Will the drawings for the names of the helpers on the two days be independent events? Explain. **Yes; All names returned to hat at end of day.**

2. What is the probability that a boy will be chosen on both days? $\frac{4}{25}$

---

2 TEACH

How do you know that the drawing on the first Tuesday will have no effect on the drawing for the second Tuesday? *(Because all the names are replaced at the end of each day, the first drawing will have no effect on the second.)*

Why do the *g*'s and *b*'s have to be listed so many times on the axes of the lattice? *(because each one represents a different girl or a different boy)*

SUMMARIZE/ASSESS   **How are the lattice method and the multiplication principle related?** *(The product of the numerators tells the number of spaces in the lattice that represent the desired event. The product of the denominators tells the number of spaces in the whole lattice.)*

Remember, there are 2 boys and 3 girls in the Volunteer Club.
What is the probability of the event?

3. A girl will be selected on both days to pick up mail
   for Mrs. Wells. $\frac{9}{25}$

4. A girl will pick up Mrs. Wells's mail on the first day and a boy
   will pick it up on the second day. $\frac{6}{25}$

PROBLEM SOLVING

The homeless shelter needs someone to help serve dinner on each
of two Saturday nights. The Volunteer Club consists of 1 eighth grader,
2 seventh graders, and 2 sixth graders.

5. What is the probability that the two volunteers selected
   will be seventh graders? $\frac{4}{25}$

6. What is the probability that an eighth grader will be selected
   the first week and a seventh grader will be selected the next? $\frac{2}{25}$

7. What is the probability that a boy will be selected the first
   week and a girl will be selected the second week? $\frac{6}{25}$

8. What is the probability that the eighth grader will be picked
   twice? Explain your answer. $\frac{1}{25}$; $\frac{1}{5} \times \frac{1}{5} = \frac{1}{25}$

Critical Thinking

Use this pet fact: 57 out of 100 households have pets.

How many households out of 100 do not have pets?

The two events, households with pets and households without
pets, cover all the possibilities. They are **complementary events.**

Name the complementary event.

1. In the United States, 4 out of 5 dog
   owners give their dogs table scraps.
   1 out of 5 do not give scraps.

2. Table scraps are not given to their cats
   by 69 out of 100 cat owners.
   31 out of 100 give cats scraps.

3. Snakes are disliked by 3 out of 11 people.

8 out of 11 people like snakes.

CHAPTER 15   507

MEETING INDIVIDUAL NEEDS

For Students Who Are . . .

Acquiring English Proficiency Review the concept of an independent event. Have students give original examples to reinforce this idea.

Gifted and Talented Ask students to find newspaper advertisements like those in the Critical Thinking section. Then have them find the complementary event.

Working 2 or 3 Grades Below Level Review multiplying fractions.

Today's Problem

A box contains 10 plastic buttons of the same size. Six of these buttons are black and 4 are white. Without looking, you draw a button and record the color. You return the button to the box and draw another button. Find the probability of drawing a white button both times. $[P(W \text{ and } W) = P(W) \times P(W) = \frac{4}{10} \times \frac{4}{10} = \frac{16}{100} = \frac{4}{25}]$

---

3 FOLLOW-UP

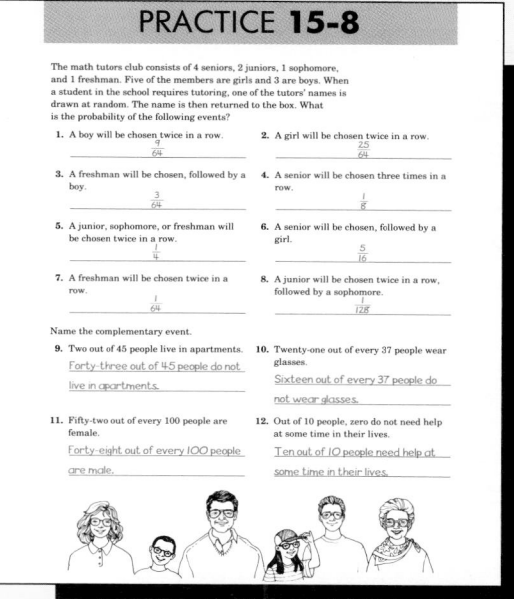

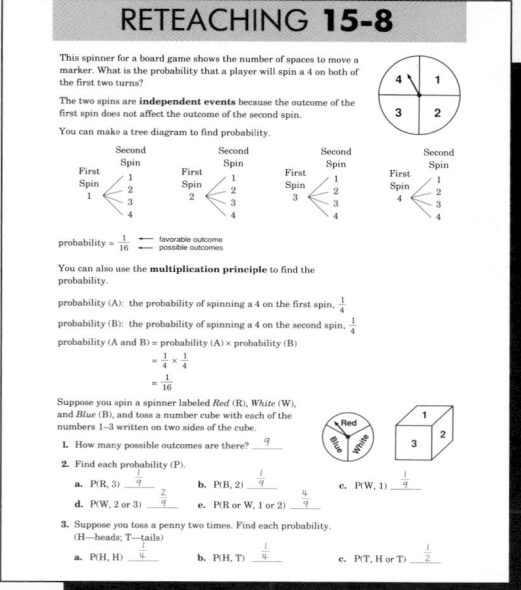

ENRICHMENT 15-8

☑ **MATERIALS CHECKLIST:** Blank spinners, blank cubes

Provide each pair of students with a spinner divided equally into *Red, White,* and *Blue* sections, and a number cube labeled *1–6.* Have one partner spin the spinner while the other partner tosses the number cube. When they get a result, ask: What is the probability of spinning this color? $[\frac{1}{3}]$ of tossing this number? $[\frac{1}{6}]$ of spinning this color and tossing this number in the same turn? $[\frac{1}{3} \times \frac{1}{6} = \frac{1}{18}]$ Have the students find the experimental probability that the color and the number will occur in the same turn by spinning and tossing at least 100 times.

Lesson Organizer

Objective: Determine the probability of dependent events.

Prior Knowledge: Students should be able to multiply fractions and find probabilities using the multiplication principle.

Lesson Resources:
Practice Worksheet 15-9
Reteaching Activity 15-9
Enrichment Worksheet 15-9
Daily Review 15-9
Cooperative Problem Solving 2, Chapter 15

 **Two-Minute Math**

Write a situation for which the probability would be found by multiplying $\frac{1}{2}$ and $\frac{1}{3}$.

1 INTRODUCE

CONNECTING ACTIVITY

☑ **MATERIALS CHECKLIST:** 4 index cards and a hat

Two boys are needed to help pack the car for a field trip. Two names will be drawn from a hat.

1. With the class, write four names on the cards and put them in the hat. What is the probability that any one name will be selected? ($\frac{1}{4}$) Draw a name and write it on the chalkboard.

2. Should the first name drawn be returned to the hat? (*No.*) **What is the probability that any one of the remaining names will be selected?** ($\frac{1}{3}$)

3. Did the outcome of the first draw affect the probability of the second draw? Explain. (*Yes; it changed the probability from $\frac{1}{4}$ to $\frac{1}{3}$.*)

WHEN YOUR STUDENTS ASK
★ WHY AM I LEARNING THIS? ★

You can connect this lesson to real life through sociology. Understanding whether two events are dependent or independent helps a sociologist decide how one event may be causing another.

Dependent Events

Sometimes the Oakton Middle School Volunteer Club has more than one request for help on a given day, as shown in the notice at right.

Remember, there are 2 boys and 3 girls in the club and they draw names to select the helper.

To select the first helper, 1 of the 5 names is drawn. To select the second helper, 1 of the 4 names *remaining* is drawn.

The two drawings are called **dependent** events because the second selection is influenced by the first selection.

What is the probability that two boys' names will be selected? The probability of selecting a boy's name on the first draw is $\frac{2}{5}$.

THINK ALOUD Suppose that a boy's name was drawn on the first draw. What is the probability that a boy's name will be selected on the second draw?

You can use the multiplication principle to find the probability of selecting a boy's name on both draws.

$$P(\text{boy, 1st draw}) \times P(\text{boy, 2nd draw}) = P(\text{boy, both draws})$$
$$\frac{2}{5} \times \frac{1}{4} = \frac{2}{20}$$

> **When two events are dependent, the outcome of one event influences the outcome of the other event. To use the multiplication principle for dependent events, you must think about how the first event affects the second event.**

■ **GUIDED PRACTICE** ■

Jenny Johnson asked for volunteers to deliver breakfast and lunch to her handicapped mother on Thursday.

1. Are these selections dependent or independent events?

2. What is the probability that a boy will be selected to deliver breakfast and a girl will be selected to deliver lunch?

508   LESSON 15-9

2 TEACH

Why was the first name drawn not returned to the hat? (*Because two helpers were needed, the possibility of picking the same name twice had to be eliminated.*)

Not putting a name back in the hat before drawing again is called drawing "without replacement." What does this phrase mean? (*Once the first selection of a name is made, that name is not replaced or put back in the hat.*)

SUMMARIZE/ASSESS   **When repeated drawings are made, sometimes they are done "with replacement" and sometimes "without replacement." Which type of repeated drawing would be independent events?** (*with replacement*) **which would be dependent events?** (*without replacement*)

PRACTICE

Refer to the situation in Guided Practice. Find the probability.

3. Two girls will be selected to deliver the meals. $\frac{6}{20}$ or $\frac{3}{10}$

4. A girl will be selected to deliver breakfast and a boy will be selected to deliver lunch. $\frac{6}{20}$ or $\frac{3}{10}$

PROBLEM SOLVING

Remember, the Volunteer Club consists of 1 eighth grader, 2 seventh graders, and 2 sixth graders. There are 2 boys and 3 girls in the club.

The nursing home needs two helpers to serve dinner on Saturday night this week.

5. Are the selections of the two helpers independent or dependent events? Explain.
dependent; first choice from 5; second from 4

6. What is the probability that the two helpers are both sixth graders?
$\frac{2}{20}$ or $\frac{1}{10}$

7. What is the probability that the two helpers are both girls?
$\frac{6}{20}$ or $\frac{3}{10}$

The homeless shelter needs one person to pick up donation packages at the park on each of the next two Sundays.

8. The club selects a volunteer each week by drawing a name from the hat containing the five names. Are the selections independent or dependent events? Explain.
independent; all names in hat each week

9. What is the probability that the two volunteers are both seventh graders? $\frac{4}{25}$

10. What is the probability that a boy is selected the first week and a girl is selected the second week? $\frac{6}{25}$

Critical Thinking

Odds are ratios that compare favorable outcomes to unfavorable outcomes. If the probability that it will snow today is 4 out of 10, the odds in favor of it snowing are 4 to 6 and the odds against it are 6 to 4.

What are the odds in favor of and against the event?

1. thunderstorm when the probability of a storm is 3 out of 5
3:2; 2:3

2. sunny day when the probability of a cloudy day is 74%
26:74; 74:26

3. fog when the forecast for clear air is 50% 1:1

PRACTICE 15-9

There are 3 red, 5 blue, and 4 yellow marbles in a bag. When a marble is selected, it is not replaced. What is the probability of each event?

1. Two reds will be selected. $\frac{1}{22}$

2. One red and 1 yellow will be selected. $\frac{1}{5}$

3. One blue and 1 yellow will be selected. $\frac{5}{33}$

4. One red, 1 blue, and 1 yellow will be selected. $\frac{2}{22}$

5. Two blues and 1 yellow will be selected. $\frac{2}{33}$

6. Four reds will be selected. 0

Petula's Pet Store had a special on rabbits. To buy a rabbit at the sale price, customers had to take the rabbit that a store employee selected at random from the rabbits' cage. There were 2 white, 3 brown, 4 spotted, and 1 black rabbit.

7. Customers chose rabbits until all were sold. Were these dependent or independent events? dependent

8. The first customer, who wanted two rabbits, got the black rabbit and a white rabbit. What was the probability? $\frac{1}{45}$

9. The second customer got a brown rabbit and a spotted rabbit. What was the probability? $\frac{3}{14}$

10. The third customer got a white rabbit. What was the probability? $\frac{1}{6}$

Solve.

Ronnie threw all his pencils into his book bag: his 2 favorite white pencils, 4 old yellow pencils, 3 stubby blue pencils, and 6 red pencils.

11. What is the probability that Ronnie will choose a blue pencil, then a white, then a yellow, without replacing any? $\frac{1}{455}$

12. What percent of the pencils are
white? 13%
blue? 20%
yellow? 27%
red? 40%

RETEACHING 15-9

☑ **MATERIALS CHECKLIST:** Counters, paper bags

Give each small group 3 white counters, 2 red counters, and a bag. Put the counters in the bag. Ask: How many counters are there? [5] How many are white? [3] What would be the probability of drawing a white counter? $[\frac{3}{5}]$ Have a student take out one white counter. Ask: How many counters are there now? [4] How many are white? [2] What is the probability of drawing a white counter? $[\frac{1}{2}]$ Ask them to find the probability of drawing 2 whites in a row. $[\frac{3}{10}]$ Would these events be independent or dependent? [dependent]

ENRICHMENT 15-9

D E P E N D E N T

Suppose you put the nine slips shown above in a container. You drew one slip at random from the container and did not replace it. Then you drew another slip.

Find each probability (P).

1. P(D, D) $\frac{2}{9} \times \frac{1}{8} = \frac{2}{36}$
2. P(E, E) $\frac{3}{9} \times \frac{2}{8} = \frac{1}{12}$
3. P(P, P) $\frac{1}{9} \times \frac{0}{8} = 0$
4. P(N, N) $\frac{2}{9} \times \frac{1}{8} = \frac{1}{36}$
5. P(D, E) $\frac{2}{9} \times \frac{3}{8} = \frac{1}{12}$
6. P(P, E) $\frac{1}{9} \times \frac{3}{8} = \frac{1}{24}$
7. P(E, N) $\frac{3}{9} \times \frac{2}{8} = \frac{1}{12}$
8. P(N, E) $\frac{2}{9} \times \frac{3}{8} = \frac{1}{12}$
9. P(T, E) $\frac{1}{9} \times \frac{3}{8} = \frac{1}{24}$
10. P(P, T) $\frac{1}{9} \times \frac{1}{8} = \frac{1}{72}$

Write the letters *DEPENDENT* on nine slips of paper as shown and place them in a container.

11. In the table to the right, list each possible outcome. Answers will vary. A suggestion is given.

12. Without looking, draw one slip from the container and do not replace it. Then draw another slip. Tally the result in the table.

13. Replace both slips. Repeat the experiment 100 times.

14. After 100 times, write the probability of each event based on your experiment.

15. Are the experimental probabilities and the probabilities you calculated in Exercises 1–10 the same? Why or why not?
Answers will vary. No; performing the experiment 100 times is not enough to approach the theoretical probability.

Outcome	Tally	Probability
(D, D)		
(D, E)		
(D, P)		
(D, N)		
(E, D)		
(E, E)		
(E, P)		
(E, N)		
(E, T)		
(P, D)		
(P, E)		
(P, N)		
(P, T)		
(N, D)		
(N, E)		
(N, P)		
(N, N)		
(N, T)		
(T, D)		
(T, E)		
(T, P)		
(T, N)		

MEETING INDIVIDUAL NEEDS

For Students Who Are . . .

Acquiring English Proficiency Have students explain the difference between independent and dependent events in their own words.

Gifted and Talented Have students write a problem similar to those in the Critical Thinking section. Students can exchange problems with a partner and solve.

Today's Problem

One cube is numbered 1, 1, 1, 5, 5, and 5. Another cube is numbered 0, 0, 4, 4, 4, and 4. In a game using these cubes, two people each roll a cube and the person who rolls the higher number wins. Which cube would you choose to win? Explain. *(The person who rolls the cube with the 1's and 5's is more likely to win because there are more winning events in the sample space.)*

Lesson Organizer

Objective: Solve problems by drawing a picture.

Prior Knowledge: Students should be able to identify parts of regions as fractions.

Error Analysis and Remediation: See page 517A.

Lesson Resources:
Practice Worksheet 15-10
Reteaching Activity 15-10
Enrichment Worksheet 15-10
Daily Review 15-10
Cooperative Connections, Chapter 15

Two-Minute Math

Write as a fraction in lowest terms.

2 out of 12 $\left(\frac{1}{6}\right)$ 3 out of 6 $\left(\frac{1}{2}\right)$

4 out of 10 $\left(\frac{2}{5}\right)$ 3 out of 9 $\left(\frac{1}{3}\right)$

5 out of 15 $\left(\frac{1}{3}\right)$ 4 out of 6 $\left(\frac{2}{3}\right)$

1 INTRODUCE

CONCRETE ACTIVITY

✔ **MATERIALS CHECKLIST:** 8.5 in. × 11 in. paper, one sheet per student

1. Fold the piece of paper into eighths.

2. Fold it back to show half of the whole. Fold it back again to show half of the half. What fraction of the whole is this? $\left(\frac{1}{4}\right)$

3. Fold it again to show one-fourth of a half. What fraction of the whole is this? $\left(\frac{1}{8}\right)$

4. Fold it to show one-half of a fourth. What fraction of the whole is this? $\left(\frac{1}{8}\right)$

WHEN YOUR STUDENTS ASK
★ WHY AM I LEARNING THIS? ★

You can use this skill to solve real life problems involving chance. Using a whole sheet of paper to illustrate probability can often be easier than figuring out the computational rules.

Problem Solving Strategy: Draw a Picture

Students in Mr. Sosa's math class use calculators often. Sometimes calculators get broken. Alicia needs a calculator. There are 3 calculators in the left drawer and 2 calculators in the right drawer.

One of the calculators in the right drawer is not working, but the students don't know that. What is the probability that Alicia will select the broken calculator?

A good strategy for solving this problem is to draw and use fractional areas of a unit square, like the one at right. Into how many sections is this square cut up? The area of each section is what fraction of the area of the square? **12; $\frac{1}{12}$**

First, you can show the probability of selecting each of the drawers. Since the probability for selecting each drawer is $\frac{1}{2}$, draw a vertical line dividing the unit square into two equal parts.

Second, show the probability of selecting each calculator within each drawer. Label each section "working" or "broken."

The probability of selecting each calculator in the left drawer is $\frac{1}{3}$. Draw two horizontal lines to divide the left half of the square into thirds.

Left	Right
working	
working	
working	

The probability of selecting each calculator in the right drawer is $\frac{1}{2}$. Draw a horizontal line to divide the right half of the square in half.

Left	Right
working	working
working	
	broken
working	

Next, identify what portion of the whole square is labeled as broken. Three of the 12 small sections represent the probability of selecting a broken calculator. The probability that Alicia will select a broken calculator is $\frac{3}{12}$, or $\frac{1}{4}$.

2 TEACH

What fractional part of the unit square is represented by each of the small sections? $\left(\frac{1}{12}\right)$

Why was the left side cut into three parts, each with two small sections? *(Because the probability of selecting a calculator from the box on the left is $\frac{1}{3}$, the three major sections had to be represented.)*

How many small sections represent broken calculators? *(3 out of 12)*

GUIDED PRACTICE   Have students work with a partner to do the exercises.

SUMMARIZE/ASSESS   **How does drawing a picture show equally likely outcomes?** *(Using parts of equal area illustrates equally likely outcomes.)*

1. Use the unit square and the story to answer.

Huong needs a calculator. There are 2 calculators in one box and 4 calculators in another box. Each box contains one calculator that is not working properly.

a. Into how many parts is the square divided? What fraction of the area of the square is each part? $8; \frac{1}{8}$

b. Divide the unit square into parts that represent the probability of selecting each box. Then divide each part into sections that represent the probability of selecting each calculator. Label each section as "working" or "broken." What portion of the square represents working calculators? $\frac{5}{8}$

c. What is the probability that Huong will select a working calculator? $\frac{5}{8}$

	working
working	working
	working
broken	broken

PRACTICE

Show your work by sketching a copy of the unit square and its fractional parts. Use it to solve the problem.

2. Ian needs a timer. There are 2 timers in the left drawer and 5 timers in the right drawer. In the right drawer 3 of the timers are not working.

a. What is the probability that Ian will select a working timer? $\frac{14}{20}$ or $\frac{7}{10}$

b. What is the probability that he will select a timer that is not working? $\frac{6}{20}$ or $\frac{3}{10}$

		W
		W
W	W	N
		N
		N

3. Ina needs a stopwatch. There are 3 stopwatches in the left drawer and only 1 in the right drawer. The one in the right drawer is broken, but the three in the left drawer are working.

a. What is the probability that Ina will select a working stopwatch? $\frac{3}{6}$ or $\frac{1}{2}$

b. What is the probability that she will select a broken stopwatch? $\frac{3}{6}$ or $\frac{1}{2}$

W	
W	B
W	

 CHOOSE Choose any strategy to solve. **Strategies may vary. Suggestions given.**

4. A sweater with an original price of $50 has been marked down 10% 3 times. What is its price now? **multistep; $36.45**

5. How many times are the hour hand and the minute hand of a clock lined up together in one day? **patterns; 24 times**

6. How many ways can the 5 letters, *l, e, a, r,* and *n,* be arranged? **multistep; 120**

CHAPTER 15   **511**

MEETING INDIVIDUAL NEEDS
For Students Who Are . . .

Acquiring English Proficiency Work with the students as they do the Practice section. They can take turns reading the problems aloud and paraphrasing them.

Gifted and Talented Assign the technology lesson on page 522.

Working 2 or 3 Grades Below Level Have students use pages 46–53 of the Skills Workbook for Problem Solving Strategies.

Having Reading Difficulties Review strategies that may be used to solve Exercises 9–11.

Today's Problem

A cube with a different number from 1 to 6 printed on each side is rolled twice. What are the odds for the event that at least one of the rolls yields a number less than 3? [$P(event) = \frac{20}{36} = \frac{5}{6}$ and the odds for the event are 5:1.]

---

3 FOLLOW-UP

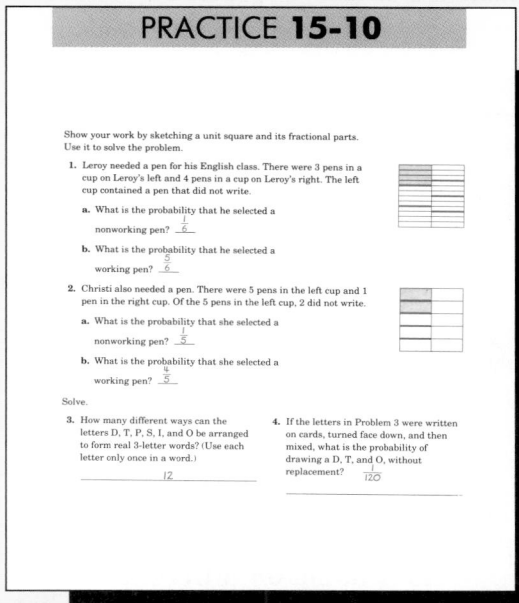

PRACTICE 15-10

Show your work by sketching a unit square and its fractional parts. Use it to solve the problem.

1. Leroy needed a pen for his English class. There were 3 pens in a cup on Leroy's left and 4 pens in a cup on Leroy's right. The left cup contained a pen that did not write.

a. What is the probability that he selected a nonworking pen? $\frac{1}{6}$

b. What is the probability that he selected a working pen? $\frac{5}{6}$

2. Christi also needed a pen. There were 5 pens in the left cup and 1 pen in the right cup. Of the 5 pens in the left cup, 2 did not write.

a. What is the probability that she selected a nonworking pen? $\frac{2}{5}$

b. What is the probability that she selected a working pen? $\frac{4}{5}$

Solve.

3. How many different ways can the letters D, T, P, S, I, and O be arranged to form real 3-letter words? (Use each letter only once in a word.) _12_

4. If the letters in Problem 3 were written on cards, turned face down, and then mixed, what is the probability of drawing a D, T, and O, without replacement? $\frac{1}{120}$

RETEACHING 15-10

Present the following problem: Jena wants to build a fence around a 25-yd by 40-yd piece of land. The type of fence she is building needs a special support post at corners and at least every 10 ft. How many support posts does she need for this fence?

Have students work in groups of two to draw a picture that will help them solve the problem. Encourage students to build a model with concrete materials if they need to.

ENRICHMENT 15-10

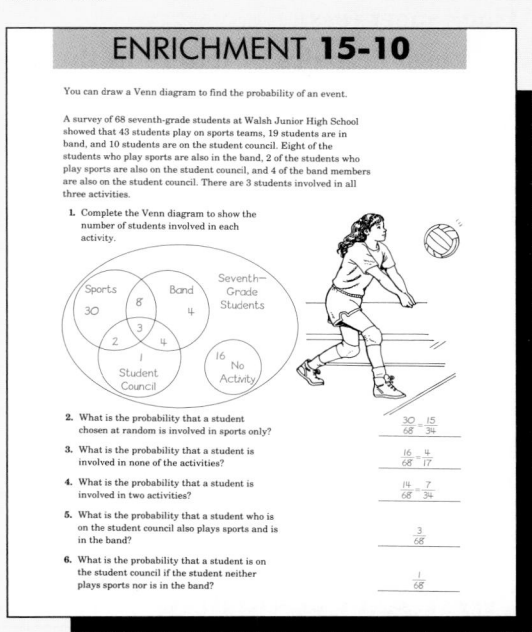

You can draw a Venn diagram to find the probability of an event.

A survey of 68 seventh-grade students at Walsh Junior High School showed that 43 students play on sports teams, 19 students are in band, and 10 students are on the student council. Eight of the students who play sports are also in the band, 2 of the students who play sports are also on the student council, and 4 of the band members are also on the student council. There are 3 students involved in all three activities.

1. Complete the Venn diagram to show the number of students involved in each activity.

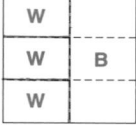

2. What is the probability that a student chosen at random is involved in sports only? $\frac{30}{68} = \frac{15}{34}$

3. What is the probability that a student is involved in none of the activities? $\frac{16}{68} = \frac{4}{17}$

4. What is the probability that a student is involved in two activities? $\frac{14}{68} = \frac{7}{34}$

5. What is the probability that a student who is on the student council also plays sports and is in the band? $\frac{3}{68}$

6. What is the probability that a student is on the student council if the student neither plays sports nor is in the band? $\frac{1}{68}$

Lesson Organizer

Objective: Explore combinations and permutations.

Prior Knowledge: Students should know how to make organized lists of possible outcomes.

Lesson Resources:
Class Activity 15-11
Daily Review 15-11

Two-Minute Math

If you write the letters of your first name on different index cards, put the cards into a hat, and draw a card without looking, what is the probability of drawing a vowel? a consonant?

1 PREPARE

SYMBOLIC ACTIVITY

In each situation below, is the order important?

- **All possible pairs of runners who can come in first and second at a track meet** *(yes)*

- **All possible pairs of letters in the word *TILE* that can form real words** *(yes)*

- **All possible pairs of people who can sit in the two remaining seats in the theater?** *(no)*

WHEN YOUR STUDENTS ASK
★ WHY AM I LEARNING THIS? ★

In real life, combinations and permutations of available telephone numbers are used to assign telephone numbers to new customers.

EXPLORE

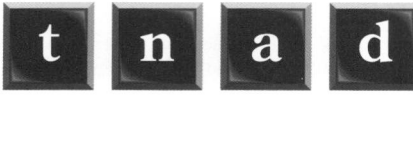

Exploring Combinations and Permutations

Jenny, Amir, and some friends were playing a word game with tiles that had letters on one side.

Four tiles remained. They were placed face down.

On Amir's turn he was to pick three tiles. He could get these different sets of letters:

These four sets of possibilities are called **combinations**. There were four combinations of three letters that Amir could get.

It turned out that Amir picked the first combination: t n a . He then listed all the possible arrangements using the three letters:

1. **THINK ALOUD** How many arrangements made real words? How many arrangements made nonsense words? **2:4**

These different arrangements of the three letters are called **permutations**. In a permutation, the order, or arrangement, is important. Amir found 6 permutations using all three letters.

2. What combinations could Jenny pick if she were to select two of the four letters without looking? **tn, td, ta, na, nd, ad**

3. If Jenny had picked b and a for her two letters, what would be all the permutations using both letters? **ab, ba**

---

2 EXPLORE

Suppose five letter tiles were left (*t, n, a, d, and e*), and Amir picked four tiles. What combinations could he get? *[(tnad), (tnae), (tade), (tnde), (nade)]*

Suppose Amir had picked the letters *t, n, d, e*. How many real and nonsense words could he make? *(24)*

SUMMARIZE/ASSESS **When would you look for a combination and when you would look for a permutation?** *(Look for a combination when the order or arrangement is unimportant; look for a permutation when the order of every outcome is important.)*

When listing all possible outcomes, it is important to know whether you are looking for all combinations or all permutations. In combinations, the arrangement, or order does not matter. In permutations, the order of every outcome is important.

Some friends were playing a word game. Tell whether you would look for a *combination* or a *permutation* to answer the question.

4. Pierre was to select three of the letters at random. What possible sets might he have picked if he picked without looking?
combinations

5. Pierre was to make real and nonsense words with his three letters. What words could he make?
permutations

6. Alexis already had picked four letters. What arrangements of these letters could she make?
permutations

7. Sue was to pick two letters on her turn. Three letters were left. What sets of letters might she have picked without looking?
combinations

During another game, the last five tiles had these letters: *b, a, u, k, c.*

8. Pierre was to select three of the letters without looking. List all the combinations he might have picked.
See page 517b.

9. Pierre picked *b, a,* and *c.* List all the possible permutations.
See page 517b.

10. Alexis picked *b, a, k,* and *c.* List all the possible permutations.
See page 517b.

11. Sue was to pick two letters on her turn. List all the combinations she might have picked.
See page 517b.

Carmen and Adelita were playing the same word game. The last four tiles had these letters: *a, e, n, t.*

12. What are all the possible combinations for two letters?
ae, an, at, en, et, nt

13. What are all the possible combinations for three letters?
aen, aet, ant, ent

14. Adelita picked *a* and *n.* What are the permutations of these two letters?
an, na

15. Carmen picked *e, n,* and *t.* What are the permutations of these three letters?
ent, etn, net, nte, ten, tne

16. How many of the permutations in Exercise 15 are real words?
2

17. CREATE YOUR OWN Make cards for six different letters. Choose different numbers of letters and find all possible combinations and permutations.
Check students' work.

CHAPTER 15   513

MEETING INDIVIDUAL NEEDS

For Students Who Are . . .

Acquiring English Proficiency Give other examples of permutations and combinations to reinforce the idea that order does not matter for combinations but is the basis for permutations.

Gifted and Talented Have students create a combination and a permutation problem, exchange papers, and solve.

Working 2 or 3 Grades Below Level When listing all possible permutations, have students start with one letter and list all possibilities using that letter first; then continue in the same manner with other letters.

Today's Problem

You have a quarter, a nickel, a dime, and a penny in your pocket. Without looking, you pull out three coins. What different amounts of money might you have selected? *(Q,N,D = 40¢; Q,N,P = 31¢; Q,D,P = 36¢; N,D,P = 16¢)*

---

3 FOLLOW-UP

CLASS ACTIVITY **15-11**

Set up a row of three chairs facing the class. Invite four volunteers to come forward and to stand behind the chairs. Ask: In how many different ways can these four students be arranged in these three chairs? [24] Ask the rest of the students to write each permutation as it is modeled by the four volunteers and to suggest ways for making other permutations when the volunteers can't think of one or when they repeat themselves. Have the students find the combinations of four students in three chairs by crossing out duplicate arrangements of the same students. [there are four combinations]

Lesson Organizer

Objective: Review operations with decimals, fractions, mixed numbers, and integers; solving proportions; percents.

Lesson Resource:
Daily Review 15-12

These pages provide students with a review of computing with decimals, fractions, mixed numbers, and integers; solving proportions; finding percents; and solving problems using a map.

Remind students that these pages review skills covered in previous chapters and will help them to do a self-check to see how well they remember what they've learned.

MATH AND SOCIAL STUDIES

Mixed Review

Perth, Australia

Compute.

1. $240.72 \div 68$
3.54

2. $0.677 + 87.4$
88.077

3. $65.39 - 454.6$
⁻389.21

4. 8.2×0.52
4.262

5. $\frac{5}{6} \times 3\frac{1}{8}$
$2\frac{29}{48}$

6. $8\frac{3}{8} \div \frac{1}{4}$
$33\frac{1}{2}$

7. $7\frac{5}{6} + \frac{5}{12}$
$8\frac{1}{4}$

8. $19\frac{1}{6} - 3\frac{5}{12}$
$15\frac{3}{4}$

Solve for n in the proportion.

9. $\frac{n}{90} = \frac{14}{20}$ 63

10. $\frac{8}{24} = \frac{n}{15}$ 5

11. $\frac{8}{17} = \frac{24}{n}$ 51

12. $\frac{6}{n} = \frac{9}{12}$ 8

Find the unknown.

13. 85% of what number is 595?   700

14. What is 55% of 165?   90.75

15. What is 25% of 360?   90

16. 20% of what number is 30?   150

17. What percent of 80 is 12?   15%

18. What is 10% of 600?   60

19. 35% of what number is 217?   620

20. What percent of 400 is 260?   65%

Compute.

21. $4 + ^-1$ 3

22. $3 - 8$ ⁻5

23. $^-3 \times 4$ ⁻12

24. $^-6 \div 3$ ⁻2

25. $1 - ^-5$ 6

26. $^-6 + ^-4$ ⁻10

27. $^-14 \div 7$ ⁻2

28. $^-3 \times ^-3$ 9

29. $^-1 \times ^-1$ 1

30. $^-10 \div 5$ ⁻2

31. $6 + ^-5$ 1

32. $^-4 - ^-10$ 6

33. $^-8 \div ^-2$ 4

34. $3 \times ^-5$ ⁻15

35. $^-7 - ^-12$ 5

36. $^-12 + ^-7$ ⁻19

37. $^-5 + ^-1$ ⁻6

38. $9 - 14$ ⁻5

39. $12 \times ^-20$ ⁻240

40. $^-24 \div ^-6$ 4

514   LESSON 15–12

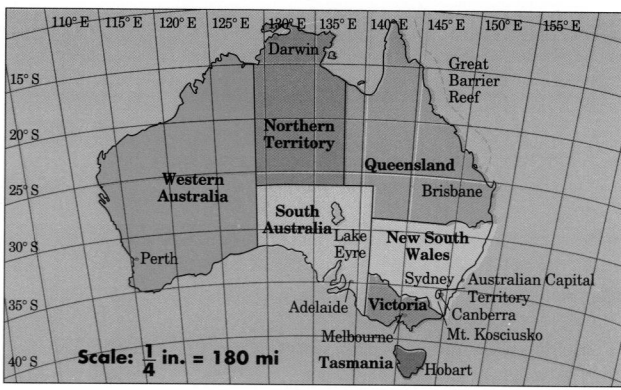

110°E 115°E 120°E 125°E 130°E 135°E 140°E 145°E 150°E 155°E

Darwin

Great
Barrier
Reef

15° S

Northern
Territory

20° S

Queensland

Western
Australia

25° S

Brisbane

South
Australia

Lake
Eyre

New South
Wales

30° S

Perth

Sydney / Australian Capital
Territory

Adelaide   Victoria   Canberra

35° S

Melbourne   Mt. Kosciusko

40° S   **Scale:** $\frac{1}{4}$ **in. = 180 mi**   Tasmania   Hobart

CHOOSE Choose estimation, mental math, pencil **Choices will vary. Suggestions given.**
and paper, or calculator to solve.

Use the map to match each state or territory to its area.   **m; See below.**

| **a.** 920 mi² | **b.** 26,200 mi² | **c.** 87,900 mi² | **d.** 309,500 mi² |
| **e.** 380,070 mi² | **f.** 519,770 mi² | **g.** 666,900 mi² | **h.** 975,100 mi² |

41. Northern Territory   f   **42.** South Australia   e   **43.** Queensland   g

44. New South Wales   d   **45.** Victoria   c   **46.** Tasmania   b

47. Western Australia   h   **48.** Australian Capital Territory   a

49. In 1851, gold was discovered in Australia. As a result, the
population rose from about 400,000 in 1850 to about 1,100,000
in 1860. By about what percent did the population rise during
this time period?   **p; about 175%**

50. Use the map scale to estimate the flying distance
in miles between the cities.   **Accept reasonable estimates. Suggestions given.**

   a. Brisbane and Adelaide   **b.** Sydney and Perth   **c.** Darwin and Hobart
   1,000 mi   **1,800 mi**   **2,000 mi**

51. Lake Eyre in South Australia is completely dry most of the
year. The lake, 52 ft below sea level, is Australia's lowest point.
Mt. Kosciusko in New South Wales, 7,310 ft high, is Australia's
highest point. What is the difference between these two points?   **m; 7,362 ft**

52. What is the approximate latitude and longitude of Perth? of
Australia's capital city, Canberra?   **m; about 33°S; 116°E; 36°S and 149°E**

MULTICULTURAL   NOTE

Australia, the sixth largest country in the world, is the
only country that occupies an entire continent. Its name
comes from the Latin *australis,* meaning "southern." It
is famous for its open spaces, bright sunshine, large
numbers of sheep and cattle, and unusual wildlife.

CHAPTER
Checkup

This chapter checkup provides a quick language and vocabulary review, a test for the chapter, and suggestions for student Learning Log entries.

Language and Vocabulary

Some key language and vocabulary ideas from this chapter are reinforced here.

Test

The test can be used either as a test or as a review of the chapter prior to administering the test worksheets found in the Teacher's Resource Book.

The following guide will help you determine percentage scores.

Score	Percent	Score	Percent
11	100%	5	45%
10	91	4	36
9	82	3	27
8	73	2	18
7	64	1	9
6	55		

Each test has three sections: concepts, skills, and problem solving. These sections provide students with exposure to the format used on standardized tests.

Use the chart on page 516 to identify the management objectives tested for this chapter.

Items	Management Objectives	Pages
1–5	**15A** Make and interpret a line plot, a stem-and-leaf plot, a box plot, or a circle graph.	492–499
6	**15B** Determine sample space for multiple events.	502–503; 512–513
7–8	**15C** Determine the probability of multiple events.	504–509
9–11	**15D** Problem Solving: Draw a picture.	490–491; 510–511

CHAPTER CHECKUP

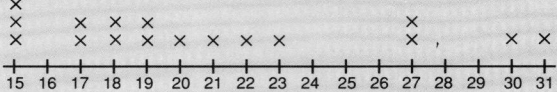

LANGUAGE & VOCABULARY

Complete each sentence with the appropriate expression from this list: *sample space, basic counting principle, independent events, dependent events.*

1. Two events whose probabilities do not influence one another are **independent events** .

2. Multiplying outcomes to find total possible outcomes is one use of the **basic counting principle** .

3. The list of all possible outcomes of an event is the **sample space** .

4. Two events, the second of which is influenced by the first, are **dependent events** .

TEST ✔

CONCEPTS

The line plot shows the number of officially sanctioned 300 games bowled by the top 17 bowlers. *(pages 492–497)*

```
×
×      × × ×                        ×
×    × × × × × × ×            ×  ,    × ×
+---+---+---+---+---+---+---+---+---+---+---+---+---+---+---+---+
15  16  17  18  19  20  21  22  23  24  25  26  27  28  29  30  31
```

1. What is the range of the data? **16**
   Check students' work.
2. Make a stem-and-leaf plot of the data.
   Check students' work.
3. What is the median? **19**
4. What is the upper extreme of the data?
   Check students' work.

Construct a circle graph of the data. *(pages 498–499)*

5. A marketing research company needs to make a graph of the number of visitors, in millions, to 3 cities in a recent year. The data from these cities is: Los Angeles, 45, San Diego, 30, and New York City, 15. **Check students' graphs.**

CHAPTER TEST • FORM A

(pp. 492–499) *15A*

Use the line plot to answer questions 1–3.

HEIGHTS OF BASKETBALL PLAYERS
```
                  X
            X   X XX
X           XX  XX XX XX     X
+--+--+--+--+--+--+--+--+
70 72 74 76 78 80 82 84
       inches
```

1. What is the shortest player's height?
   _70 in._

2. What is the tallest player's height?
   _84 in._

3. What is the range of the players' heights?
   _14 in._

Use the circle graph to answer questions 4 and 5.

RECORDING SALES
(in millions of dollars)
Total Sales: $125

```
Compact Disks
$52
Singles      Cassettes
$13           $25
Albums
$35
```

4. What fractional part of the circle is used to represent compact disks?
   _52/125_

5. How many degrees of the circle are used to represent cassettes?
   _72°_

Solve. (pp. 502–503, 512–513) *15B*

6. Jon can choose from three types of shirts and 5 types of slacks to wear to school. How many different outfits can he wear?
   15 outfits

7. Virginia is shopping for a TV. She can choose from 4 screen sizes and 3 cabinet styles. How many different TVs can she buy?
   12 TVs

8. Jamal is shopping for a music system. He can choose from 4 different receivers, 3 speakers, and 2 CD players. How many choices does he have?
   24 choices

9. Helga rolls a number cube and tosses a coin. How many different outcomes can occur?
   12 outcomes

10. Loretta is choosing a dinner from 5 main courses, 4 vegetables, and 3 salads. How many different dinners could she choose?
    60 dinners

CHAPTER TEST • FORM A

Solve. (pp. 504–509) *15C*

11. Cassie rolls a number cube and records the number on top. She rolls the number cube again and records the number on top. Find the probability that she rolls a 3 on both rolls.
    _1/36_

12. Sylvia tosses a coin and rolls a number cube. Find the probability she tosses heads and rolls a 5.
    _1/12_

13. Doug tosses a coin five times. Find the probability he tosses tails all five times.
    _1/32_

There are 5 quarters, 4 dimes, and 3 nickels in a box. If you draw a coin from the box without looking, then draw another coin from the box without looking, find the probability:

14. Two dimes will be drawn.
    _1/11_

15. A quarter and a dime will be drawn.
    _5/33_

(pp. 510–511) *15D*

Use the unit square to solve problems 16–19.

Darla needed to use a calculator. There is 1 calculator in the left box and 6 calculators in the right box. Three of the calculators in the right box are broken, but she doesn't know this.

16. What is the probability she will select a working calculator?
    _3/6_

17. What is the probability she will select a broken calculator?
    _1/4_

Two of the three broken calculators in the right box are repaired.

18. What is the probability she will select a working calculator?
    _11/12_

19. What is the probability she will select a broken calculator?
    _1/12_

Solve.

20. A tour bus left a hotel and drove 4 blocks due south, turned east and drove 6 blocks. From there it drove 4 blocks due north. At this point, how far and in what direction was the bus from the hotel?
    6 blocks due east

SKILLS

Solve. (pages 502–509, 512–513)

Bill has 4 books (3 novels and 1 play) and 5 magazines (2 sports and 3 news). He wants to take a book and a magazine on a trip.

6. Find the number of different combinations he can take. **20**

7. What is the probability that if Bill picks without looking, he will select a novel and a sports magazine? $\frac{6}{20}$ or $\frac{3}{10}$

8. If Lawrence decides to take only 2 books, what is the probability that if he picks without looking, he will choose a novel followed by a play? $\frac{3}{12}$ or $\frac{1}{4}$

PROBLEM SOLVING

9. Use the graph to answer. (pages 490–491)

   a. What was the average family size in 1960? **3.6**

   b. Does the graph make it seem that the average family size in 1988 is half that in 1960? **yes**

   c. By how much did the average family size decrease from 1960 to 1988? **about 11%; 0.4**

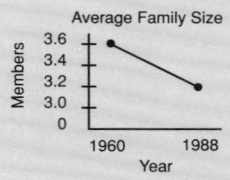

Solve. (pages 510–511)

10. Maria has 2 boxes of eggs, one with 3 eggs and one with 4 eggs. One egg in each box is bad, but she doesn't know it. She needs 1 egg. What is the probability that she will pick a bad one? $\frac{7}{24}$

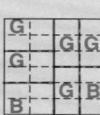

11. Four girls and 5 boys are on a baseball team. A captain and a co-captain are to be chosen. If one must be a girl and one a boy, how many different combinations are possible? **20**

LEARNING LOG

Write the answers in your learning log.

1. Dan says the letters of his name have more permutations than the letters of Ann's name. Do you agree with him? Explain.
   Accept reasonable answers.

2. The odds are 4 to 3 you have English, math, social studies, or science at any given period during the day. Explain.
   Accept reasonable answers.

CHAPTER 15   517

Note that the same numbers are used in Exercises 6 and 11.

Problem Solving

Item 9 has three parts:
a. literal—this is a reading comprehension question.
b. interpretive—this involves interpretation using the facts given.
c. applied—students use a strategy or skill to find an answer.

Item 6 in the skill section and item 11 in the problem solving section use the same numbers.

This will help you informally assess how your students transfer from numerical skills to word problems.

For scoring problem solving items, you may wish to use partial credit. If a student uses the correct strategy but gets a wrong answer, give the student two points toward the total percent score.

Learning Log

These are suggestions for writing about some topics taught in the chapter. The students keep their learning logs from the start of the school year through the end.

CHAPTER TEST • FORM B

(pp. 592–599) 15A

Use the line plot to answer questions 1–3.

AGES OF BASKETBALL PLAYERS

1. What is the youngest player's age?
   21

2. What is the oldest player's age?
   32

3. What is the range of the players' ages?
   11

Use the circle graph to answer questions 4 and 5.

ATHLETIC SHOE SALES
(in millions of dollars)
Total Sales: $80

4. What fractional part of the circle is used to represent canvas low-tops?
   $\frac{11}{80}$

5. How many degrees of the circle are used to represent leather low-tops?
   126°

Solve. (pp. 502–503, 512–513) 15B

6. Dottie can choose from 4 brands and 3 body styles. How many different cars can she choose?
   12 cars

7. Doug is shopping for a camera. He can choose from 6 different brands and 2 different sizes. How many different cameras can he choose?
   12 cameras

8. Kathryn is shopping for a music system. She can choose from 4 different receivers, 3 speakers, and 3 CD players. How many choices does she have?
   36 choices

9. George tosses a coin and rolls a number cube. How many different outcomes can occur?
   12 outcomes

10. Josie is choosing a dinner from 5 main courses, 3 vegetables, and 4 salads. How many different dinners could she choose?
    60 dinners

CHAPTER TEST • FORM B

Solve. (pp. 504–509) 15C

11. Duane rolls a number cube and records the number on top. He rolls the number cube again and records the number on top. Find the probability that he rolls a 6 on both rolls.
    $\frac{1}{36}$

12. Lorrie tosses a coin and rolls a number cube. Find the probability she tosses heads and rolls a 2.
    $\frac{1}{12}$

13. Duane tosses a coin four times. Find the probability he tosses heads all four times.
    $\frac{1}{16}$

There are 5 quarters, 3 dimes, and 4 nickels in a box. If you draw a coin from the box without looking in the box, then draw another coin from the box without looking, find the probability:

14. Two quarters will be drawn.
    $\frac{5}{33}$

15. A quarter and a dime will be drawn.
    $\frac{5}{44}$

(pp. 510–511) 15D

Use the unit square to solve problems 16–19.
Ron needs to use a calculator. There are 2 calculators in the left box and 3 calculators in the right box. Two of the calculators in the right box are not working, but he doesn't know this.

16. What is the probability he will select a working calculator?
    $\frac{2}{3}$

17. What is the probability he will select a broken calculator?
    $\frac{1}{3}$

One of the two broken calculators in the right box is repaired.

18. What is the probability he will select a working calculator?
    $\frac{5}{6}$

19. What is the probability he will select a broken calculator?
    $\frac{1}{6}$

Solve.

20. A tour bus left a hotel and drove 6 blocks north, turned west and drove 8 blocks. From there it drove 6 blocks due south. At this point, how far and in what direction was the bus from the hotel?
    8 blocks due west

Error Analysis and Remediation

Here are some common errors students make when they make stem-and-leaf plots and box plots; determine sample spaces and the probability of multiple events; and draw a picture to solve a problem. The errors are listed by lesson under the appropriate management objective.

15A • MAKE AND INTERPRET A LINE PLOT, A STEM-AND-LEAF PLOT, A BOX PLOT, OR A CIRCLE GRAPH

Source of Error (Lesson 15-3)
Students do not include values that occur more than once in a set of data.

Remediation
Emphasize that every value should be included as a leaf on the plot. Suggest that students count the values to make sure that they are shown on the stem-and-leaf plot.

Source of Error (Lesson 15-4)
Students have difficulty distinguishing the five values used to make a box plot.

Remediation
Display the box plot from page 496 on an overhead projector. Label the upper and lower quartiles, the upper and lower extremes, and the median. Guide students to interpret the data by examining the lengths of the boxes and whiskers.

15B • DETERMINE SAMPLE SPACE FOR MULTIPLE EVENTS

Source of Error (Lesson 15-6)
Students omit a factor when using the Basic Counting Principle.

Remediation
Have students use a tree diagram to find the sample space. Then ask them to identify the factor for each section of the diagram. Relate this to the Basic Counting Principle to reinforce the importance of using each factor to find the sample space.

15C • DETERMINE THE PROBABILITY OF MULTIPLE EVENTS

Source of Error (Lesson 15-7)
Students think that outcomes written in different orders are the same outcomes.

Remediation
Emphasize by pointing out that H occurs first in (H, T) and that T occurs first in (T, H), and thus they are different outcomes.

Source of Error (Lesson 15-8)
Students misinterpret the word *and* in a statement when finding the probability of two independent events.

Remediation
For example, when finding the P(H and H) on two tosses of a coin, they incorrectly add $\frac{1}{2}$ and $\frac{1}{2}$ and get 1 instead of multiplying $\frac{1}{2}$ and $\frac{1}{2}$ to get $\frac{1}{4}$. Have students use a tree diagram to check the possible outcomes.

15D • PROBLEM SOLVING: DRAW A PICTURE.

Source of Error (Lesson 15-10)
Students misinterpret information and draw the incorrect picture to represent a problem.

Remediation
Tell students to read the problem slowly and carefully and then to list the key information needed to find the information. Remind them that their pictures should represent the problem and aid them in finding the answer. Have them compare their pictures and the problem to make sure.

Answers

Page 493

7. Think Aloud: Answers will vary. Suggestion given: Find the mode by finding the column with the most marks. To find the median, you count down from the right end of the plot and up from the left end of the plot until you find the middle value.

Page 497

4. Accept reasonable estimates. Suggestions given. Super: $1,600; Compact: $1,000; Standard: $1,075

6. Super: $1,600 to $2,000; Compact: $1,000 to $1,650; Standard: $1,075 to $1,500

8. Accept reasonable estimates. Suggestions given. Super: $1,800 to $2,200; Compact: $1,325 to $1,800; Standard: $1,360 to $1,825

11. Answers will vary. Suggestion given: The prices of the models in the lower half are clustered closer together.

Page 503

For Exercises 1–4, answers may vary. Suggestions given. Use 1, 2, 3, 4 for the shirts. Use a, b, c for the slacks.

1. Organized list:

Shirt 1 with all the slacks	Shirt 3 with all the slacks
shirt 1, slacks a (1, a)	shirt 3, slacks a (3, a)
shirt 1, slacks b (1, b)	shirt 3, slacks b (3, b)
shirt 1, slacks c (1, c)	shirt 3, slacks c (3, c)
Shirt 2 with all the slacks	Shirt 4 with all the slacks
shirt 2, slacks a (2, a)	shirt 4, slacks a (4, a)
shirt 2, slacks b (2, b)	shirt 4, slacks b (4, b)
shirt 2, slacks c (2, c)	shirt 4, slacks c (4, c)

4. Basic counting principle:
4 shirts, 3 slacks → 4 × 3 = 12

For Exercises 7–10, answers may vary. Suggestions given. Use y, b, g, r for the T-shirts. Use y, b for the shorts.

7. Organized list:

T-shirt y with all the shorts	T-shirt g with all the shorts
T-shirt y, shorts y (y, y)	T-shirt g, shorts y (g, y)
T-shirt y, shorts b (y, b)	T-shirt g, shorts b (g, b)
T-shirt b with all the shorts	T-shirt r with all the shorts
T-shirt b, shorts y (b, y)	T-shirt r, shorts y (r, y)
T-shirt b, shorts b (b, b)	T-shirt r, shorts b (r, b)

10. Basic counting principle:
4 T-shirts, 2 shorts → 4 × 2 = 8

Page 504

Think Aloud: Answers will vary. Suggestion given: Use the tree diagram or the lattice to find the sample space. Use the sample space to find the probability.

Page 513

8. abc, abk, abu, ack, acu, aku, bck, bcu, bku, cku

10. bakc, bkca, bcak, back, bkac, bcka, abkc, abck, akcb, akbc, ackb, acbk, kabc, kacb, kbca, kbac, kcab, kcba, ckab, ckba, cbka, cbak, cakb, cabk

Page 495

4. Think Aloud: Answers will vary. Suggestion given: The shapes of both kinds of graphs are similar, but you can see individual values in the stem-and-leaf plot.

5. Super: $1,600 to $1,800; Compact: $1,000 to $1,325; Standard: $1,075 to $1,360

7. Accept reasonable estimates. Suggestions given. Super: $2,000; Compact: $1,650; Standard: $1,500

9. Accept reasonable estimates. Suggestions given. Super: $2,200 to $2,500; Compact: $1,800 to $2,500; Standard: $1,825 to $2,500

2. Tree diagram should include 4 shirts, 3 slacks, and should generate 12 outcomes.

3. Lattice:

		Shirts			
		1	2	3	4
	a	a, 1	a, 2	a, 3	a, 4
Slacks	b	b, 1	b, 2	b, 3	b, 4
	c	c, 1	c, 2	c, 3	c, 4

5. With all 4 ways of finding the sample space, it is 12: a, 1; a, 2; a, 3; a, 4; b, 1; b, 2; b, 3; b, 4; c, 1; c, 2; c, 3; c, 4. The students should see that they can use whatever method they choose to find the sample space.

8. Tree diagram should include 4 shirts, 2 shorts, and generate 8 outcomes.

9. Lattice:

		T-shirts			
		y	b	g	r
	y	y, y	y, b	y, g	y, r
Shorts	b	b, y	b, b	b, g	b, r

9. bac, bca, abc, acb, cba, cab

11. ab, ac, ak, au, bc, bk, bu, ck, cu, ku

Extra Practice

This page provides extra practice of all the major chapter objectives. Use this page after the chapter has been taught to reinforce the chapter skills. Page references are provided for each group of items so that students can easily look back at the appropriate lesson for additional support.

Use the data. *(pages 492–497)*

The chart shows the ages of various Presidents of the United States when they were inaugurated.

Washington 57	Polk 49	Hoover 54
Jefferson 57	Lincoln 52	Truman 60
Madison 57	Grant 46	Kennedy 43
Jackson 61	Arthur 50	Nixon 56
Tyler 51	Taft 51	Carter 52

1. Make a line plot of the data.   **Check students' work.**

2. Make a stem-and-leaf plot of the data.   **Check students' work.**

3. What is the lower extreme of the data?   **Check students' work.**

Construct a circle graph. *(pages 498–499)*

4. Of 85 phone calls made one month, 52 were local, 28 were long distance, and 5 were international. Construct a circle graph showing the percent of the calls of each type. Round to the nearest percent.   **Check students' graphs.**

Solve. Use a sample space. *(pages 502–507, 512–513)*

Robin has 2 coats (black and green) and 4 sweaters (green, red, brown, and orange).

5. In how many different ways can she wear a coat and a sweater?   **8 ways**

6. What is the probability that if Robin picks a coat and sweater at random, she will select a black coat and red sweater? $\frac{1}{8}$

Solve. *(pages 490–491, 510–511)*

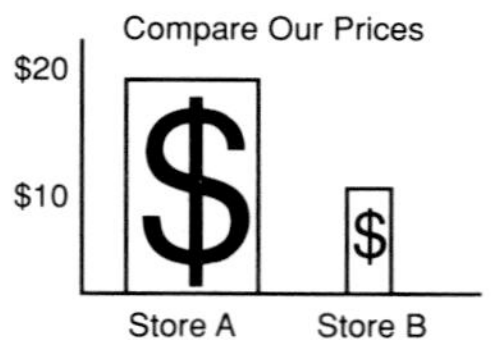

7. The graph at right was used in an advertisement by Store B to compare its prices to Store A. What impression does the graph give about the comparison of prices?
A is four times more expensive than b.

8. Jackie has two holders with pens on her desk. One holder has 5 pens and the other has 4 pens. One pen in each holder is out of ink. What is the probability that Jackie will select a pen that is out of ink if she randomly picks a pen from either of the holders? $\frac{9}{40}$

Compare Our Prices

518   EXTRA PRACTICE

Statistical Claims

Statistics, like graphs, are frequently used in advertising to help convince consumers of a claim. All statistical claims ought to be examined, not only for their honesty and accuracy, but for their relevance to the claim being made. For example, you may read or hear that 90% of a car maker's automobiles sold within the past 10 years are still on the road. You may wonder what "still on the road" means and how this makes the cars reliable.

Work with a group. Each member should look for ads making statistical claims. Discuss each ad with the group, especially how the statistic being used helps support the claim? **Check students' work.**

Palindromes

RADAR is a palindrome. It is spelled the same forward and backward. Numbers can also be palindromes. The time, 10:01 is a palindrome; so is 234,432.

You can generate number palindromes. Take any number and add the reverse of the number to the number. If you don't get a palindrome keep going. Sometimes you get a palindrome right away; sometimes it takes a while. **Answers will vary.**

Examples:

$$\begin{array}{r} 123 \\ + 321 \\ \hline 444 \end{array} \qquad \begin{array}{r} 138 \\ + 831 \\ \hline 969 \end{array} \qquad \begin{array}{r} 372 \\ + 273 \\ \hline 645 \\ + 546 \\ \hline 1191 \\ + 1911 \\ \hline 3102 \\ + 2013 \\ \hline 5115 \end{array}$$

The Connection Game

Play with a partner. You'll need dot paper. Mark off the game area. Start with 5 dots by 5 dots.

Connect any 2 dots that are next to each other: above, below, or side-by-side. You may not connect more than 2 dots. The player who makes the last connection wins. **Check students' work.**

Enrichment

This page contains activities that provide extension and enrichment for all levels of students. Depending on the needs of your students, you may wish to assign an activity from this page at certain points during the chapter, or you may wish to use this page when the entire chapter has been completed.

Statistical Claims
(COOPERATIVE)

Assign students to groups of three to five. Ask group members to look in magazines and newspapers for appropriate advertisements. They may also want to examine television and radio advertisements that make statistical claims. Groups can report their findings to the class.

The Connection Game
(COOPERATIVE)

Dot paper is available as Teaching Aid 11. Encourage students to look for a strategy that can help them to win.

Palindromes

Have students choose five different three-digit numbers and use the method described to generate number palindromes. There are also sentence palindromes, for example: Was it a cat I saw?

CHAPTER 15

Cumulative Review

The Cumulative Review focuses on skills covered in previous chapters. All important skills are reviewed on a cyclic basis.

If students are having difficulty with particular groups of exercises, refer to the chart below for follow-up work.

CUMULATIVE REVIEW

Find the answer.

1. 3 shirts **c**
   5 sweaters
   number of outfits =
   a. 8
   b. 2
   c. 15
   d. none of these

2. 1 coat **b**
   4 shirts
   number of outfits =
   a. 3
   b. 4
   c. 5
   d. none of these

3. 3 pants **a**
   3 shirts
   number of outfits =
   a. 9
   b. 6
   c. 3
   d. none of these

4. $3.9 + 2.07 + 0.34$ **b**
   a. 2.80
   b. 6.31
   c. 28.0
   d. none of these

5. $8,000 - 784$ **c**
   a. 8,784
   b. 7,116
   c. 7,216
   d. none of these

6. $7 - 4.308$ **c**
   a. 3.308
   b. 11.308
   c. 2.692
   d. none of these

7. 28×964 **a**
   a. 26,992
   b. 26,492
   c. 9,140
   d. none of these

8. 402×0.93 **d**
   a. 3.7386
   b. 37.386
   c. 3,738.6
   d. none of these

9. 2.57×0.08 **b**
   a. 0.02056
   b. 0.2056
   c. 2.056
   d. none of these

10. $x - 13 = 2.5$ **c**
   a. 10.5
   b. 11.5
   c. 15.5
   d. none of these

11. $r + 7 = 23$ **a**
   a. 16
   b. 30
   c. 14
   d. none of these

12. $m + {}^-9 = {}^-2$ **b**
   a. $^-7$
   b. 7
   c. 11
   d. none of these

13. The prime factors of **a**
   72 are
   a. 2, 2, 2, 3, 3
   b. 2, 4, 3, 3
   c. 2, 2, 2, 9
   d. none of these

14. 75 is divisible **c**
   by
   a. 2, 3
   b. 2, 3, 5
   c. 3, 5
   d. none of these

15. Which is a prime **d**
   number?
   a. 57
   b. 77
   c. 91
   d. none of these

520   CUMULATIVE REVIEW

Items	Management Objectives		Where Taught	Reteaching Options	Extra Practice Options
1–3	**15B**	Determine sample space for multiple events.	pp. 502–503; 512–513	TRB/RW 15-6	TRB/PW 15-6
4	**2B**	Add whole numbers and decimals.	pp. 40–43	TRB/RW 2-4 to 2-5	TRB/PW 2-4 to 2-5
5–6	**2C**	Subtract whole numbers and decimals.	pp. 46–49	TRB/RW 2-6 TE/RA 2-7	TRB/PW 2-6 to 2-7
7	**3B**	Multiply and divide whole numbers.	pp. 64–65	TE/RA 3-3	TRB/PW 3-3
8–9	**3C**	Multiply and divide decimals.	pp. 66–67	TRB/RW 3-4	TRB/PW 3-4
10–11	**4B**	Solve equations using inverse operations.	pp. 102–103	TRB/RW 4-4	TRB/PW 4-4
12	**13D**	Solve equations involving integers.	pp. 432–433	TE/RA 13-9	TRB/PW 13-9
13–15	**5A**	Determine divisibility, primes, and composites, and write prime factorization.	pp. 130–133		TRB/PW 5-2

Strategies may vary. Suggestions given.
Remember the strategies and types of
problems you've had so far. Solve.

1. Gerald does not have a ruler, but he
   needs to measure some lengths. He does
   have strips of wood that he knows are
   1 in., 2 in., 4 in., and 10 in. long.

   a. How long are the strips of wood that Gerald
   has? **1 in., 2 in., 4 in., 10 in.**

   b. How can he measure a length of 7 in?
   4 in. + 2 in. + 1 in.
   c. What whole number lengths between
   1 in. and 17 in. can he measure?
   guess and check; all

2. Jack rolled two cubes numbered 1
   through 6 and added the face numbers.
   What fraction of the possible outcomes
   are prime numbers?
   table; $\frac{15}{36}$ or $\frac{5}{12}$

3. Jan is 5 yr older than Bob. Bob is 3 yr
   younger than Louise. List the friends
   from youngest to oldest.
   list; Bob, Louise, Jan

4. Norma, Olive, and Petra study as a
   group. Each has a favorite subject:
   math, history, or English. Olive does
   not like math or history. Petra does not
   like history. What is each girl's
   favorite subject? **table; Norma:
   history; Olive: English; Petra: Math**

5. The Wright Brothers' first flight
   covered approximately 120 ft. There
   are 5,280 ft in one mi. Estimate the
   number of flights the Wright Brothers
   would have had to make to cover one
   mile.
   estimation; between 40 and 45

6. Training for a 15 mi race, Karen ran
   6 mi in 42 min. If she ran the entire
   15 mi at the same pace, how long would
   it take her to complete the race?
   multistep; 105 min

7. Mrs. Roman takes one medicine every
   2 h and another every 5 h. If she took
   both medicines at 11:00 A.M., when
   will she next take them together?
   list; 9:00 P.M.

8. Danny has 5 kinds of juice. He wants
   to make a fruit drink by mixing 3 of
   them. How many different fruit drinks
   can Danny make?
   list; 60 fruit drinks

9. Roberto's average on his first 4 tests
   was 92. After 5 tests his average
   dropped to 88. What was his grade on
   his fifth test?
   guess and check; 72

10. Toward the end of a day, a letter carrier
    had 25 pieces of mail left. She had
    delivered 95% of the pieces she started
    with. With how many pieces of mail
    did she start?
    equation; 500 pieces

Problem Solving Review

This page focuses on problem solving
strategies and types learned in this and
previous chapters. A problem solving
checklist lists some of the strategies students may use to solve the problems on
this page.

Technology

This page is designed to provide calculator or computer experiences for all levels of students. The calculator or computer logo indicates the type of activity.

You may wish to assign these activities after the chapter has been taught or during the course of the chapter, depending on your needs and those of your students.

Retake!

If necessary, review how to find the median and the mean of a set of data. Some students may determine the lowest possible score that would result in a median of 72 and then use a guess-and-check strategy to find the score that results in a mean of 72. Others may first determine the lowest possible missing score that would result in a mean of 72 and then consider the median.

Math America

If students have difficulties, remind them that the area of a square is found by squaring the length of a side.

A Piece of the Pie

Ask students to name fractions for the shaded sections of the circles used as guides. ($\frac{1}{8}$, $\frac{1}{4}$, $\frac{3}{8}$, $\frac{1}{2}$, $\frac{5}{8}$, $\frac{3}{4}$, and $\frac{7}{8}$)

The computer activity uses Houghton Mifflin software, which is found in Houghton Mifflin Math Activities Courseware, Grade 7.

TECHNOLOGY

RETAKE!

Miss Rhodes has an unusual testing system in her math class. If the median *or* the mean of the lowest 6 scores on a quiz falls below 72, the whole class has to take the quiz again. Here are 5 of the lowest 6 scores.

73 60 81 75 69

If the class did not have to retake the quiz, what is the lowest possible missing score?   **74**

DID YOU KNOW . . . ?

Juneau, Alaska, is the capital of our 49th state. With an area of 3,108 mi^2, it is the largest city in area in the United States.

If the area were in the shape of a square, between what two whole numbers would be the length of   **55 and 56**
each side of the square?

A PIECE OF THE PIE

In the computer activity *Pie Graphics*, you must estimate what percent of the circle each pie slice represents. This pencil-and-paper activity will help you develop skills estimating what percent of the pie a certain slice represents. Use these circles as guides.   **See below.**

| 12.5% | 25% | 37.5% | 50% | 62.5% | 75% | 87.5% |

Estimate the percent of each circle that is shaded.   **Accept reasonable estimates.**

1. **80%**   2. **40%**   3. **10%**   4. **25%**

5. **10%; 20%**   6. **90%**   7. **15%; 50%**   8. **20%; 65%**

522   TECHNOLOGY   **This activity is available on computer disk in Houghton Mifflin *Mathematics Activities Courseware*.**

Software Activities

activity 1 • RECORD LOW AND HIGH TEMPERATURES

MATERIAL: database program, almanacs, calculators, maps of US

Procedure: Have students enter the following into their database file.

State	Low	High
Alabama	⁻27	112
Alaska	⁻80	100
California	⁻45	134
Colorado	⁻60	118
Florida	⁻2	109
Hawaii	14	100
Louisiana	⁻16	114
Missouri	⁻40	118
New York	⁻52	108

Ask students to place states in order by low temperatures and then by high temperatures. Have them use calculators to see which state has the largest and smallest range of temperatures.

Follow-up: Have students add other states to the database and then write problems for their classmates to answer, using the database's tools and calculators.

activity 2 • COIN TOSS

MATERIALS: Logo program

Procedure: This program simulates the tossing of a coin. Have students enter the program and run it.

```
TO PLAY :N
   HT MAKE "H 0 MAKE "T 0 TOSS :N
   PRINT (SE[THERE WERE ]:N
      [ TOSSES])
   PRINT (SE:H [WERE HEADS])
   PRINT (SE:T [WERE TAILS])
END
TO TOSS :N
   MAKE "F RANDOM 2 IFELSE :F=0
   [PRINT [HEADS] MAKE "H :H+1]
   [PRINT [TAILS] MAKE "T :T+1]
   MAKE "N :N -1 IFELSE :N=0
      [STOP][TOSS :N]
END
```

Follow-up: Have students collect the results for the entire class. Draw a bar graph of these results. Discuss with the class how these results compare with theory.

HOUGHTON MIFFLIN SOFTWARE

Easy Graph. Boston, MA: Houghton Mifflin Company, 1987. For Apple II, Commodore, IBM.

EduCalc. Boston, MA: Houghton Mifflin Company. For Apple II, Commodore, IBM.

Friendly Filer. Boston, MA: Houghton Mifflin Company, 1989. For Apple II, Commodore, IBM.

Mathematics Activities Courseware. Boston, MA: Houghton Mifflin Company, 1983. For Apple II, IBM.

The Computer Tutor. Boston, MA: Houghton Mifflin Company, 1990. For Apple II, IBM.

OTHER SOFTWARE

LogoWriter 2.0. Montreal, Quebec: Logo Computer Systems, Inc., 1988. For Apple II, IBM, Macintosh.

Probability Lab. St. Paul, MN: MECC, 1990. For Apple II.

Super Paint. San Diego, CA: Silicon Beach Software, 1988. For Macintosh.

Understanding Charts and Graphs. Chicago, IL: Society for Visual Education, 1989. For Apple II.

GAMES

pages 523 and 524

This section contains some games you can play at school or at home with your friends or family. You will need only a few simple materials to play most of these games. This list tells you what these items are and how you can substitute if you don't have them.

Number cubes (1–6) or numbered slips of paper in a box
A spinner (1–10) or numbered slips in a box
Different color markers, buttons, or small circles cut from paper
Small index cards or pieces of construction paper

Find the Missing Number

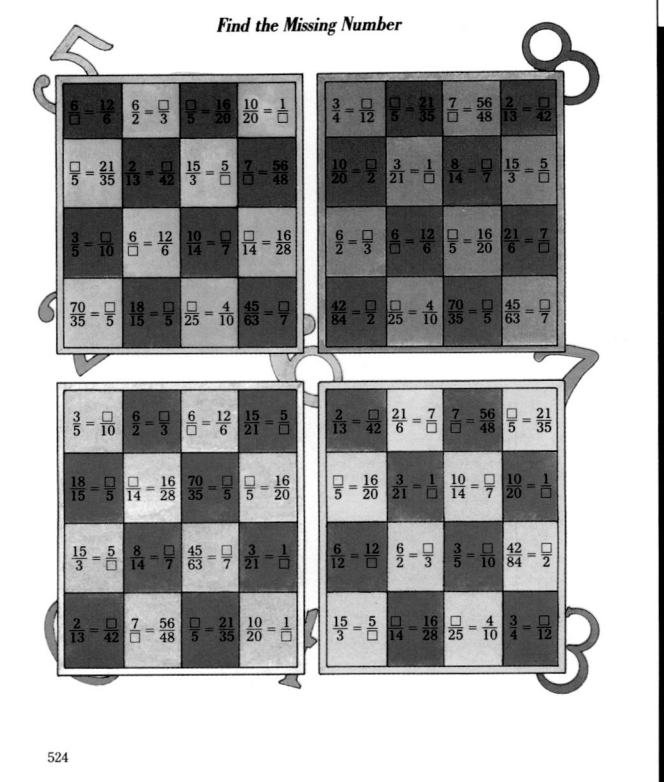

523

524

pages 525 and 526

Find the Missing Number

Goal: To cover all the squares in a row, column, or diagonal
Number of Players: 2–4
Skills: Chapters 5, 6, 7
Materials: Markers, a spinner (1–10)

Rules
1. Choose one of the missing number boards.
2. Take turns spinning the spinner.
3. If the number on the spinner is the answer to one of the problems on your board, place a marker on that square.
4. The player who covers all the squares in a row, column, or diagonal is the winner.

Variations Make up your own missing number boards and use other spinners. Be sure to write problems whose answers will be one of the numbers on the spinner you use.

Contact 7

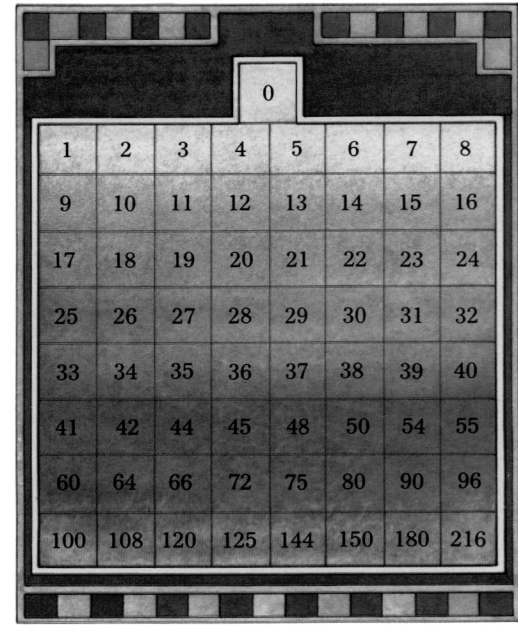

525

526

pages 527 and 528

Contact 7

Goal: To get the most points for touching boxes
Number of Players: 2 (or 1)
Skills: Chapters 2, 3, 4
Materials: 24 different color markers for each player, 3 number cubes

Rules for Playing with a Partner

1. Take turns rolling the 3 cubes. Make a number by adding, subtracting, multiplying, dividing, taking the square root of, or using as an exponent the numbers on the cubes. Put one of your markers on the box with your number, but don't cover another marker.

2. If the box you put the marker on touches other boxes with markers, you get a point for each box with a marker. The boxes may touch on a side or at a corner. After each turn, record the number of points you got on that turn.

3. Play until each player has had 8 turns.

4. The winner is the player who has more points. You may use a calculator to add your total points.

Rules for Playing Alone

1. Roll the 3 cubes. Make a number by adding, subtracting, multiplying, dividing, taking the square root of, or using as an exponent the numbers on the cubes. Put one of your markers on the box with your number, but don't cover another marker.

2. If the box you put the marker on touches other boxes with markers, you get a point for each box with a marker. The boxes may touch on a side or at a corner. After you put down a marker, record the number of points you got with that marker. Roll the cubes 8 times.

3. Find your total score. Use a calculator if you want. Play again. Try to get a higher total.

527

Probability Bingo

528

pages 529 and 530

Probability Bingo

Goal: To cover all the squares in a row, column, or diagonal
Number of Players: 2–4
Skills: Chapter 12
Materials: Markers, 30 index cards marked in 2 sets with the following numbers: $0, 1, \frac{1}{5}, \frac{2}{5}, \frac{3}{5}, \frac{4}{5}, \frac{1}{4}, \frac{1}{3}, \frac{1}{2}, \frac{2}{3}, \frac{1}{6}, \frac{5}{6}, \frac{1}{8}, \frac{3}{8}$, a number cube (1–6)

Rules

1. Mix up the cards and place them face down on the table.

2. Choose one of the bingo boards.

3. Take turns rolling the number cube. The player with the least number begins by turning over the top card.

4. If the number on the card shows the probability for one of the events on your board, place a marker on that square.

5. The next player turns over the next card, and play continues until someone covers all the squares in a row, column, or diagonal. That person is the winner.

529

Shady Squares

Goal: To shade more of a given square than anyone else
Number of Players: 2–4
Skills: Chapters 10, 11
Materials: Graph paper, 10 pennies, paper cup

Rules

1. Each player draw a 10×10 square on a sheet of graph paper.

2. Players take turns putting the 10 pennies in the paper cup, shaking them, then spilling them onto the table.

3. After each toss, the player shades the percent of the square equal to either:

   a. the ratio of the number of heads to the number of tails
   b. the ratio of the number of tails to the number of heads
   c. the ratio of the number of heads to the total number of coins
   d. the ratio of the number of tails to the total number of coins

4. A player can decide to stop tossing coins and shading parts of the square before any turn. Play continues for 4 rounds. After 4 rounds, the player whose square is most completely filled in is the winner. A player who is forced to shade more than 100% of the square loses.

530

Arithmetic Roundup

Goal: To make a problem with the desired goal
Number of Players: 2 or more
Skills: Chapter 3
Materials: Pencil and paper, 0–9 spinner

Problem Forms

Greatest Product   Least Remainder

___ . ___ ___ × ___ . ___   ___ ___ ___ ÷ ___ ___

Rules

1. Choose a problem form. Each player draws the problem form on a sheet of paper. After you play with these problem forms, make up your own problem forms.

2. Take turns spinning a number. After each number is selected, write it in one of the blanks. Once you put a number in a blank, you can't move it.

3. After all the blanks have been filled in, the winner is the player closest to the goal. Use estimation to decide. Calculate the exact answers only if you can't tell by estimating.

4. The winner of each round gets 1 point. If there is a tie, each of those players gets 1 point.

Make a Percent

Goal: To make fractions equal to a chosen percent
Number of Players: 2 or more
Skills: Chapters 10 and 11
Materials: Paper and pencil, 2 number cubes (1–6), 10 markers for each player

Sample Game Form

Rules

1. Each player makes a game form like the sample above.

2. Fill in each box with a percent. You may use the same percent more than once and you may used percents greater than 100%.

3. Take turns rolling the 2 cubes. On each roll, make a fraction. If the percent that is equivalent to the fraction is in your box, place a marker on that box. You may put only one marker on a box.

4. Play for 10 rounds. The winner is the player who has covered more boxes.

Variations Fill in the game form only with percents less than 100% or only with percents greater than 100%.

531   532

526

CALCULATORS

pages 533 and 534

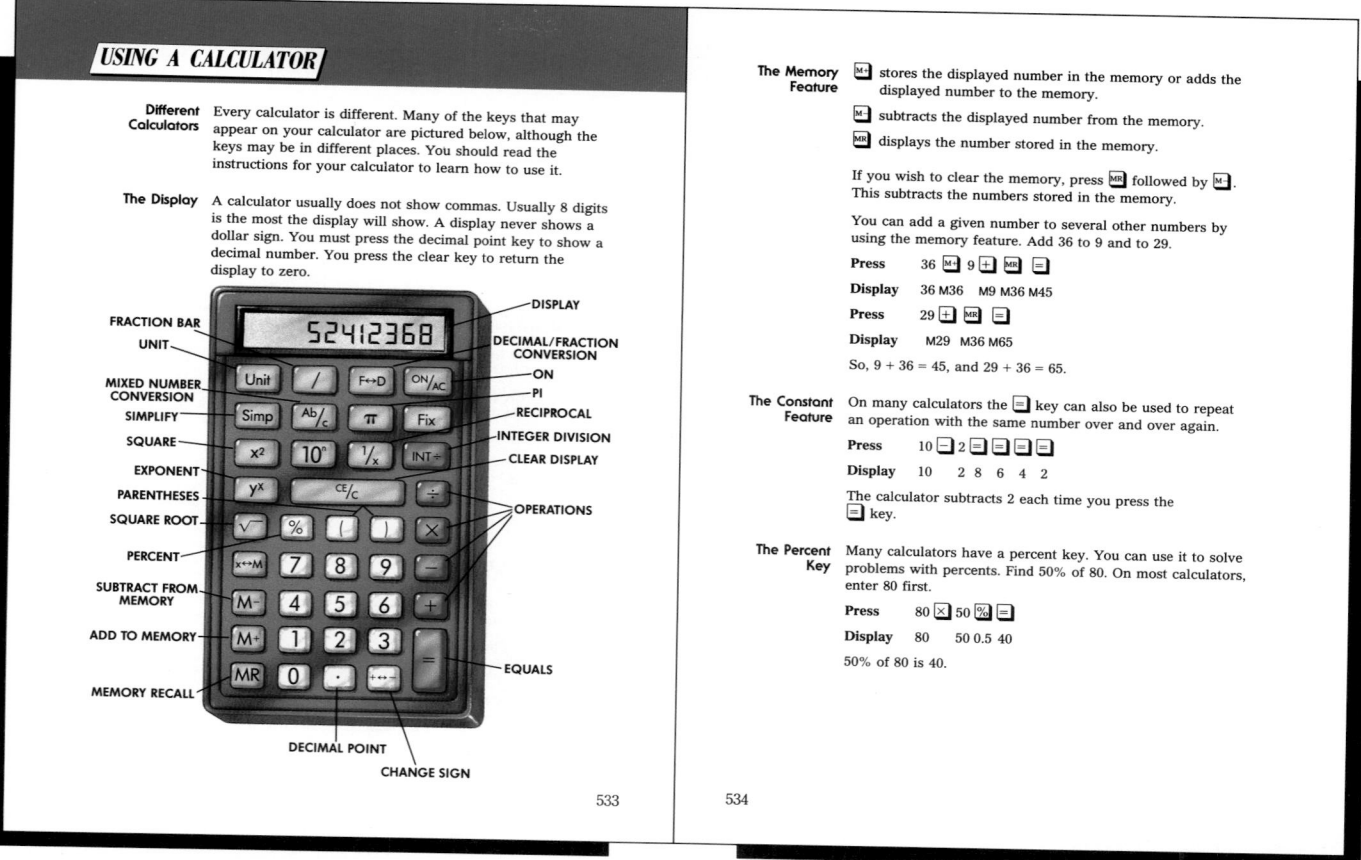

USING A CALCULATOR

Different Calculators Every calculator is different. Many of the keys that may appear on your calculator are pictured below, although the keys may be in different places. You should read the instructions for your calculator to learn how to use it.

The Display A calculator usually does not show commas. Usually 8 digits is the most the display will show. A display never shows a dollar sign. You must press the decimal point key to show a decimal number. You press the clear key to return the display to zero.

FRACTION BAR
UNIT
MIXED NUMBER CONVERSION
SIMPLIFY
SQUARE
EXPONENT
PARENTHESES
SQUARE ROOT
PERCENT
SUBTRACT FROM MEMORY
ADD TO MEMORY
MEMORY RECALL

DISPLAY
DECIMAL/FRACTION CONVERSION
ON
PI
RECIPROCAL
INTEGER DIVISION
CLEAR DISPLAY
OPERATIONS
EQUALS

DECIMAL POINT
CHANGE SIGN

The Memory Feature [M+] stores the displayed number in the memory or adds the displayed number to the memory.

[M-] subtracts the displayed number from the memory.

[MR] displays the number stored in the memory.

If you wish to clear the memory, press [MR] followed by [M-]. This subtracts the numbers stored in the memory.

You can add a given number to several other numbers by using the memory feature. Add 36 to 9 and to 29.

Press 36 [M+] 9 [+] [MR] [=]

Display 36 M36   M9 M36 M45

Press 29 [+] [MR] [=]

Display M29 M36 M65

So, 9 + 36 = 45, and 29 + 36 = 65.

The Constant Feature On many calculators the [=] key can also be used to repeat an operation with the same number over and over again.

Press 10 [-] 2 [=] [=] [=] [=]

Display 10   2 8 6 4 2

The calculator subtracts 2 each time you press the [=] key.

The Percent Key Many calculators have a percent key. You can use it to solve problems with percents. Find 50% of 80. On most calculators, enter 80 first.

Press 80 [×] 50 [%] [=]

Display 80   50 0.5 40

50% of 80 is 40.

pages 535 and 536

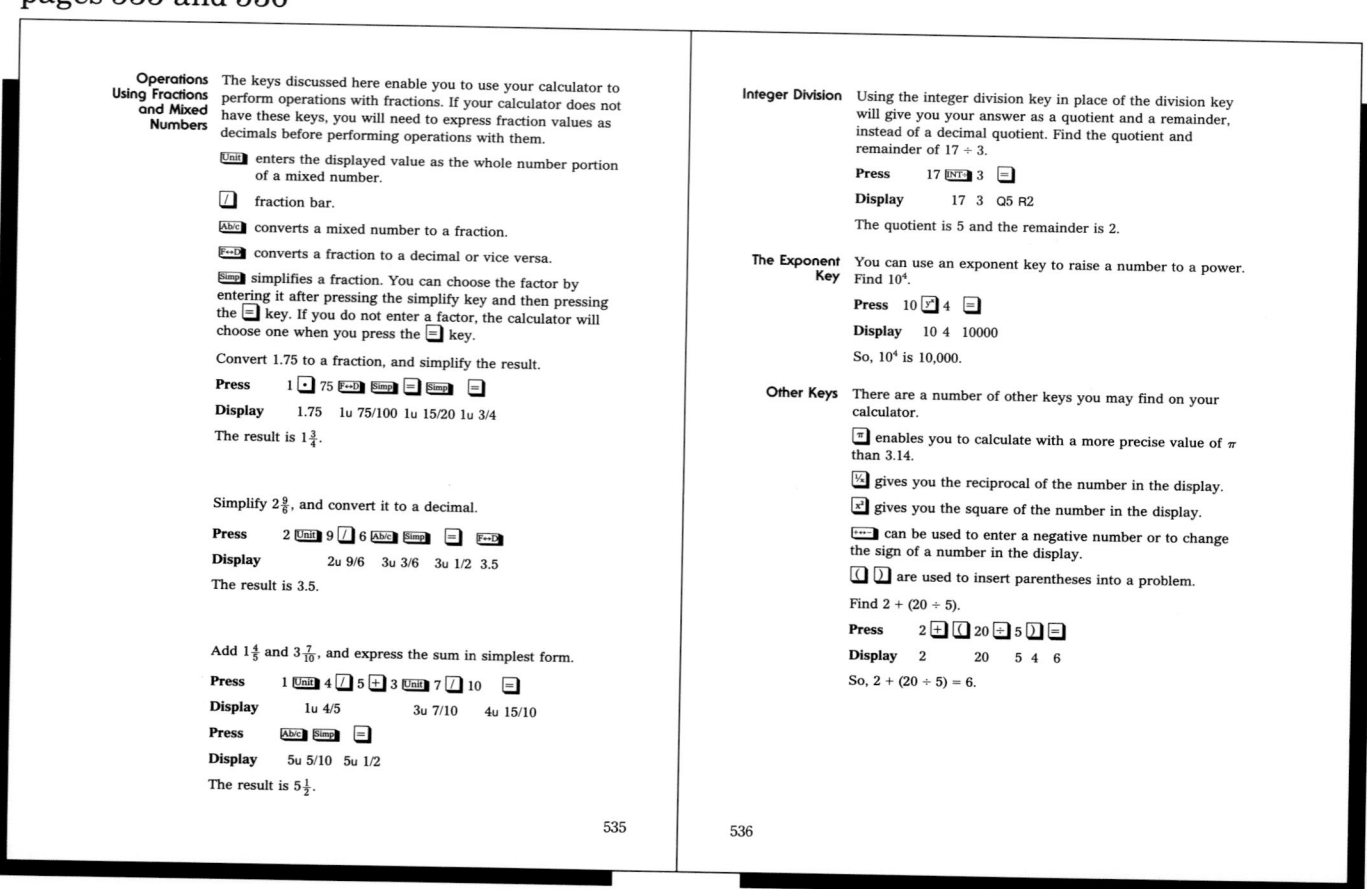

Operations Using Fractions and Mixed Numbers The keys discussed here enable you to use your calculator to perform operations with fractions. If your calculator does not have these keys, you will need to express fraction values as decimals before performing operations with them.

[Unit] enters the displayed value as the whole number portion of a mixed number.

[/] fraction bar.

[Ab/c] converts a mixed number to a fraction.

[F↔D] converts a fraction to a decimal or vice versa.

[Simp] simplifies a fraction. You can choose the factor by entering it after pressing the simplify key and then pressing the [=] key. If you do not enter a factor, the calculator will choose one when you press the [=] key.

Convert 1.75 to a fraction, and simplify the result.

Press 1 [.] 75 [F↔D] [Simp] [=] [Simp] [=]

Display 1.75   1u 75/100 1u 15/20 1u 3/4

The result is $1\frac{3}{4}$.

Simplify $2\frac{9}{6}$, and convert it to a decimal.

Press 2 [Unit] 9 [/] 6 [Ab/c] [Simp] [=] [F↔D]

Display 2u 9/6   3u 3/6   3u 1/2   3.5

The result is 3.5.

Add $1\frac{4}{5}$ and $3\frac{7}{10}$, and express the sum in simplest form.

Press 1 [Unit] 4 [/] 5 [+] 3 [Unit] 7 [/] 10 [=]

Display 1u 4/5   3u 7/10   4u 15/10

Press [Ab/c] [Simp] [=]

Display 5u 5/10 5u 1/2

The result is $5\frac{1}{2}$.

Integer Division Using the integer division key in place of the division key will give you your answer as a quotient and a remainder, instead of a decimal quotient. Find the quotient and remainder of 17 ÷ 3.

Press 17 [INT÷] 3 [=]

Display 17 3 Q5 R2

The quotient is 5 and the remainder is 2.

The Exponent Key You can use an exponent key to raise a number to a power. Find 10^4.

Press 10 [yˣ] 4 [=]

Display 10 4 10000

So, 10^4 is 10,000.

Other Keys There are a number of other keys you may find on your calculator.

[π] enables you to calculate with a more precise value of π than 3.14.

[1/x] gives you the reciprocal of the number in the display.

[x²] gives you the square of the number in the display.

[+/-] can be used to enter a negative number or to change the sign of a number in the display.

[(] [)] are used to insert parentheses into a problem.

Find 2 + (20 ÷ 5).

Press 2 [+] [(] 20 [÷] 5 [)] [=]

Display 2   20   5 4 6

So, 2 + (20 ÷ 5) = 6.

GLOSSARY/TABLE OF MEASURES

pages 537 and 538

GLOSSARY

A

absolute value (p. 414) The distance an integer is from 0 on the number line.
actual probability (p. 396) The number of favorable outcomes divided by the total of possible outcomes.
acute angle (p. 234) An angle measuring less than 90°.
acute triangle (p. 244) A triangle with all acute angles.
adjacent angles (p. 236) Angles with a common vertex and side.
angle (p. 233) Two rays with the same endpoint.
angle bisector (p. 458) A ray that divides an angle into two congruent parts.
arc (p. 456) A part of a circle.
area (p. 256) The measure of a surface of a plane figure.
Associative Property (pp. 36, 60) Changing the grouping of the addends or factors does not change the sum or product.
average (p. 8) The quotient found by dividing the sum of a group of numbers by the number of addends.

B

base [of a geometric shape] (p. 468) The face of a pyramid or a cone opposite the vertex. One of two congruent parallel faces of a prism or a cylinder.
base [of a power] (p. 4) One of equal factors in a product.
basic counting principle (p. 502) A principle that states that when you know the number of outcomes for each event you can multiply those numbers to find the number of outcomes in the sample space for the multiple events.
bisector (p. 458) A line that divides a line segment or an angle into two equal parts.
box plot (p. 496) A graphic display that divides the data into four parts, the middle two parts shown by a box from the lowest to highest quartile, the means and extremes shown by line segments.
budget (p. 339) A plan you make to be sure your income will cover your expenses.

C

capacity (p. 22) The amount of fluid a container will hold.
centimeter (cm) (p. 20) A metric unit of length. 1 cm = 10 mm
circle (p. 254) The set of all points in a plane that are at the same distance from a point in the plane.
circle graph (p. 498) A circle divided into parts to show data.
circumference (p. 254) The distance around a circle.
clustering (p. 71) A process used to estimate a sum of numbers in close proximity by multiplying a representative addend by the number of addends.
combinations (p. 512) An arrangement of things in which the order does not matter.
commission (p. 354) A percent of the total sales a person makes.
common factor (p. 134) A number that is a factor of two or more numbers.
Commutative Property (pp. 36, 60) Changing the order of addends or factors does not change the sum or product.
compatible numbers (p. 61) Numbers close to given numbers that make estimation easier.
complementary angles (p. 236) Angles the sum of whose measures is 90°.
complementary events (p. 507) Two events that together make up the sample space.
composite number (p. 132) A number that has more than two factors.
cone (p. 470) A space figure with one circular base and one vertex.
congruent angles (p. 236) Angles with the same measure.
congruent figures (p. 250) Figures that have the same size and shape.

537

congruent line segments (p. 232) Two line segments with the same length.
congruent triangles (p. 250) Triangles whose corresponding sides and angles are congruent.
coordinate plane (p. 436) A grid on a plane with two perpendicular number lines.
coordinates (p. 436) The numbers in an ordered pair associated with a point on a graph.
corresponding angles (p. 250) The angles at matching vertexes of congruent figures.
corresponding sides (p. 250) The matching sides of congruent figures.
count on (p. 43) A means of adding, by starting with one addend and counting up the amount of the next addend.
cross products (p. 151) Products used to check if two fractions are equivalent.
cross section (p. 472) The figure formed when a space figure is sliced by a plane.
cubic centimeter (cm^3) (p. 25) The amount of space contained in a cube with all edges 1 cm long.
cylinder (p. 470) A space figure with two parallel congruent circular bases.

D

data (p. 129) Numbers that give information.
degree (p. 234) The unit of measure used to measure angles.
degrees Celsius (°C) (p. 416) the metric unit for measuring temperature.
denominator (p. 142) The bottom number in a fraction.
dependent events (p. 508) Two events in which the result of the first affects the result of the second.
diagonal (p. 102) A line segment that joins two vertexes of a polygon and is not a side of the polygon.
diameter (p. 254) The distance from the points on a circle through the center.
discount (p. 358) A decrease in the price of an item.
discount rate (p. 358) A reduction that is a percent of the original price.
Distributive Property (p. 60) The product of a factor and a sum is equal to the sum of the products.
divisible (p. 130) Capable of being divided evenly with a remainder.
dodecahedron (p. 462) A space figure made of 12 faces, each a regular pentagon.
double bar graph (p. 380) A graph that uses bars to compare two sets of data.
double line graph (p. 384) A graph that uses lines to compare the change over time of two sets of data.

E

edge (p. 462) The intersection of two faces or two sides of a space figure.
elapsed time (p. 65) The time that passes between the start and end of an event.
equation (p. 34) A mathematical sentence stating that two quantities are equal.
equally likely outcomes (p. 394) When each result has the same chance of occurring.
equilateral triangle (p. 244) A triangle with all sides and angles congruent.
equivalent fractions (p. 144) Fractions that have the same value.
estimate (p. 16) A number close enough to an exact number that permits you to make a correct decision.
evaluate (p. 98) To substitute a number for each variable in an expression and then do the indicated arithmetic.
expanded form (p. 6) The representation of a number as the sum of products of each digit and a power of 10.
experimental probability (p. 396) The relative frequency of an outcome.
exponent (p. 4) The number showing how many times a base is used as a factor.
exponential form (p. 4) The form of a number written as a base with a power. The exponential form for 100 is 10^2.

F

faces (p. 462) The flat surfaces that form space figures.
factors (p. 4, 130) Any of two or more numbers that are multiplied to obtain a product.
factor tree (p. 133) A diagram showing the prime factorization of a product.

538

pages 539 and 540

fathom (p. 70) Unit of water depth measuring 6 ft.
formula (p. 466) A short way of stating a rule.
fraction (p. 142) A number in the form $\frac{a}{b}$, where b is not zero, that compares part of an object or a set with the whole.
frequency (p. 388) The number of times a given item appears in a set of data.
front-end estimation. (p. 42) An estimation method using the left digits of the numbers involved.
function (p. 114) A set of ordered pairs (x, y) such that for each value of x there is one and only one value of y.
function rule (p. 116) A rule that states how two variables are related to form a function.

G

geometric transformations (p. 248) Changes in the position of a figure while the size and shape remain the same.
gram (g) (p. 24) A metric unit of mass. 1 g = 1,000 mg
graph of a number (p. 110) The point paired with a number on a number line.
greatest common factor (GCF) (p. 134) The greatest of the common factors of two or more numbers.

H

height (h) (p. 256) The length of a segment that is perpendicular to the base.
hypotenuse (p. 454) The side opposite the right angle in a right triangle.

I

icosahedron (p. 462) A space figure with 20 faces, all equilateral triangles.
Identity Property (p. 36, 60) The sum of any number and zero is that number; the product of one and any other number is that number.
inequality (p. 110) A statement formed by placing an inequality symbol between two expressions.
integers (p. 414) The positive numbers 1, 2, 3, . . ., the negative numbers −1, −2, −3, . . ., and zero.
independent events (p. 506) Events that have no effect on each other.
interest (p. 338) The money the bank charges you for a loan.
interest rate (p. 338) A percent of the principal you pay for a certain period of time.
intersecting lines (p. 233) Lines that cross each other.
inverse operations (p. 100) One operation that "undoes" the other.
isosceles triangle (p. 244) A triangle with two congruent sides and two congruent angles.

K

kilogram (kg) (p. 24) A metric unit of mass. 1 kg = 1,000 g
kilometer (km) (p. 20) A metric unit of length. 1 km = 1,000 m

L

lattice (p. 502) A chart with columns and rows used for listing all outcomes in the sample space.
Law of Large Numbers (p. 399) If you run a large number of experiments, the experimental probability you find will be close to the actual probability.
least common denominator (LCD) (p. 150) The LCM of two or more denominators.
least common multiple (LCM) (p. 136) The least of the common multiples of two nonzero numbers.
legs of a right triangle (p. 454) The sides of a right triangle that are not the hypotenuse.
line (p.232) A set of points that extends without end in opposite directions.
line of reflection (p. 248) The line over which a figure is reflected.
line of symmetry (p. 252) A line through a figure so that if the figure were folded on the line, the two parts of the figure would be congruent.

539

line plot (p. 492) A method of displaying a small set of data by showing the data along a segment and marking each frequency.
line segment (p. 232) A part of a line with two endpoints.
liter (L) (p. 22) A metric unit of capacity. 1 L = 1,000 mL
lowest terms (p. 146) A fraction is in lowest terms if the GCF of the numerator and the denominator is 1.

M

markup (p. 359) An increase in the price of an item.
mass (p. 24) The quantity of matter in an object.
mathematical expression (p. 96) A combination of numbers, variables, and operation symbols.
mean (p. 382) The sum of the data items divided by the number of data items.
median (p. 382) The middle number in a set of data arranged in order.
meter (m) (p. 20) A metric unit of length. 1,000 m = 1 km
milligram (mg) (p. 24) A metric unit of mass. 1,000 mg = 1 g
milliliter (mL) (p. 22) A metric unit of capacity. 1,000 mL = 1 L
millimeter (mm) (p. 20) A metric unit of length. 1 mm = 0.1 cm
mixed number (p. 148) A number that has a whole number part and a fractional part.
mode (p. 380) The number or numbers that appear most frequently in a set of data.
multiple (p. 136) The product of a given number and any whole number.
multiplication principle (p. 506) To find the probability of two independent events occurring at the same time, find the product of the individual probabilities.

N

negative numbers (p. 418) Numbers less than zero.
number line (p. 8) A line in which numbers have been paired with points.
numerator (p. 142) The top number in a fraction.

O

obtuse angle (p. 234) An angle that has a measure greater than 90° and less than 180°.
obtuse triangle (p. 244) A triangle with one obtuse angle.
octahedron (p. 462) A space figure with 8 faces, all equilateral triangles.
opposites (p. 414) Two numbers that are the same distance from 0 but on opposite sides of 0.
ordered pair (p. 436) A pair of numbers in which the order shows the location of a point on a grid. (4, 3) is an ordered pair.
origin (p. 436) The point where the x-axis and the y-axis meet.
outcome (p. 502) The result of a probability experiment.
outlier (p. 497) An extreme value compared to the other values.

P

parallel lines (p. 233) Lines that never intersect and are in the same plane.
parallelogram (p. 240) A quadrilateral with opposite sides parallel.
pentagon (p. 240) A five-sided polygon.
percent (p. 310) The ratio of a number to 100. The symbol % means per hundred.
percent of decrease (p. 337) The ratio of the decrease to the original amount.
percent of increase (p. 336) The ratio of the increase to the original amount.
percent of loss (p. 337) The percent of decrease.
percent of profit (p. 337) The percent of increase.
perimeter (p. 16) The total distance around.
permutation (p. 512) An arrangement of things in which the order of the things is important.
perpendicular (p. 234) Two lines, line segments, or rays that form a right angle.
perpendicular bisector (p. 458) The bisector of a line segment that is also perpendicular to the line segment.
pi (π) (p. 254) The ratio of the circumference of a circle to its diameter.

540

pages 541 and 542

perimeter (p. 16) The total distance around.

permutation (p. 512) An arrangement of things in which the order of the things is important.

perpendicular (p. 234) Two lines, line segments, or rays that form a right angle.

perpendicular bisector (p. 458) The bisector of a line segment that is also perpendicular to the line segment.

pi (π) (p. 254) The ratio of the circumference of a circle to its diameter.

plane (p. 232) A flat surface that goes on and on without end.

point (p. 232) An exact location.

polygon (p. 240) A closed, plane figure made from three or more line segments.

population (p. 378) The entire group about whom information is wanted.

positive numbers (p. 418) Numbers greater than zero.

prime factorization (p. 133) The product of prime factors that name a given number, such as $2 \times 2 \times 3 \times 5$ to name 60.

prime number (p. 132) A number that has exactly 2 factors, namely 1 and the number itself.

principal (p. 338) The amount of money you borrow.

prism (p. 468) A space figure with two bases that are congruent polygons and are on parallel planes.

probability (p. 392) A number describing the chance that an event will happen.

proportion (p. 277) Two equal ratios.

pyramid (p. 469) A space figure with only one base.

Pythagorean theorem (p. 455) If a triangle is a right triangle, the square of the hypotenuse is equal to the sum of the squares of the other two sides.

Q

quadrilateral (p. 240) A four-sided polygon.

quartiles (p. 496) The values at the median, and at the median of the upper and lower half of the set of data.

R

radius (r) (p. 254) The distance from the center to any point on a circle.

random sample (p. 378) A sampling made ensuring every member of the population has an equally likely chance of being selected.

range (p. 492) The difference between the greatest number and the least number in a list of data.

rate (p. 279) A ratio that compares two quantities of different kinds. A rate may be expressed as a ratio, a decimal, or a percent.

ratio (p. 274) A quotient of two numbers that is used to compare one quantity to another.

ray (p. 233) A part of a line with one endpoint.

reciprocals (p. 208) Two numbers whose product is one.

rectangle (p. 241) A parallelogram with all angles right angles.

reflection (p. 248) A geometric transformation that changes the position of a figure through the motion of a flip.

reflection image (p. 248) In a coordinate plane, the result of a reflection.

regular polygon (p. 240) A polygon in which all sides and angles are congruent.

relative frequency (p. 388) A ratio that compares a part to the whole.

relative frequency table (p. 388) A table that organizes information to enable one to find relative frequency.

repeating decimals (p. 154) A decimal in which the last digit or block of digits repeats without end.

representative sample (p. 378) A sample with characteristics similar to the population.

rhombus (p. 241) A parallelogram with all sides congruent.

right angle (p. 234) An angle with a measure of 90°.

right triangle (p. 244) A triangle with a right angle.

541

rotation (p. 248) A geometric transformation that changes the position of a figure through the motion of a turn.

S

sample (p. 378) A part or subset of a population.

sample space (p. 502) List of all possible outcomes.

scale (p. 294) The ratio of the size of a drawing to the size of the actual object.

scale drawing (p. 294) A sketch of an object with all lengths in proportion to corresponding actual lengths.

scalene triangle (p. 244) A triangle with no congruent sides or angles.

scientific notation (p. 78) A way of naming numbers. There are two factors. One factor is a number greater than or equal to 1 but less than 10. The other factor is a power of 10.

similar figures (p. 291) Two figures whose corresponding angles are congruent and whose corresponding sides are in proportion.

similar polygons (p. 291) Polygons having the same shape, but not necessarily the same size.

similar triangles (p. 290) Triangles that have the same shape but not always the same size.

solution (p. 34) The number that replaces a variable to form a true equation.

space figures (p. 462) Figures that have 3 dimensions, length, width, and height.

  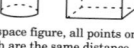

sphere (p. 470) A space figure, all points on the surface of which are the same distance from the center.

square (p. 241) A parallelogram with all sides congruent and only right angles.

square (p. 452) The product of two equal factors.

square root (p. 452) One of two equal factors of a number.

standard form (p. 6) The usual, short form of a number. 573 is the standard form for 5 hundreds, 7 tens, 3 ones.

standard unit (p. 186) Units of measure that are the same everywhere.

straight angle (p. 234) An angle with a measure of 180°.

substitution (p. 98) To replace the variable with numbers.

supplementary angles (p. 236) Two angles whose measures add up to 180°.

surface area (p. 468) The sum of the areas of the faces of a space figure.

symmetry (p. 252) A property that a figure has when parts match on opposite sides of a line.

T

terminating decimal (p. 154) A decimal with a limited number of nonzero digits.

tessellation (p. 249) Fills a plane with figures that touch but do not overlap.

translation (p. 249) A geometric transformation that changes the position of a figure through the motion of a slide.

trapezoid (p. 240) A quadrilateral with exactly one pair of parallel sides.

tree diagram (p. 502) A picture showing possible outcomes of an activity.

U

unit rate (p. 279) The ratio of a quantity to 1.

unit price (p. 284) The cost per unit of a product.

V

variable (p. 34) An unknown number.

542

pages 543 and 544

Venn diagram (p. 238) A diagram that helps organize and classify numbers and objects. Usually made with ovals and circles.

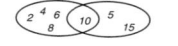

vertex (p. 233) The common endpoint of two rays or two segments.

vertical angles (p. 236) Opposite angles formed by two intersecting lines.

volume (p. 474) The amount of space inside a space figure.

W

word form (p. 6) The long, written form for a number in words.

X

x-axis (p. 436) The horizontal number line in a coordinate plane.

Y

y-axis (p. 436) The vertical number line in a coordinate plane.

Z

Zero Property of Multiplication (p. 60) The product of zero and any other number is zero.

543

TABLE OF MEASURES

Time

60 seconds (s) = 1 minute (min)	
60 minutes (min) = 1 hour (h)	
24 hours = 1 day (d)	
7 days = 1 week	

365 days, 52 weeks, 12 months = 1 year

10 years = 1 decade
100 years = 1 century

Metric

LENGTH

10 millimeters (mm) = 1 centimeter (cm)
10 centimeters = 1 decimeter (dm)
10 decimeters, 100 centimeters = 1 meter
10 meters = 1 dekameter (dam)
10 dekameters = 1 hectometer (hm)
10 hectometers, 1000 meters = 1 kilometer (km)

AREA

100 square millimeters = 1 square centimeter (mm²) (cm²)
10,000 square centimeters = 1 square meter (m²)
10,000 square meters = 1 hectare (ha)

VOLUME

1000 cubic millimeters = 1 cubic centimeter (mm³) (cm³)
1,000,000 cubic centimeters = 1 cubic meter (m³)

MASS

1000 milligrams (mg) = 1 gram (g)
1000 grams = 1 kilogram (kg)

CAPACITY

1000 milliliters (mL) = 1 liter (L)

United States Customary

LENGTH

12 inches (in.) = 1 foot (ft)
3 feet, 36 inches = 1 yard (yd)
5280 feet, 1760 yards = 1 mile (mi)

AREA

144 square inches (in.²) = 1 square foot (ft²)
9 square feet = 1 square yard (yd²)
4840 square yards = 1 acre (A)

VOLUME

1728 cubic inches = 1 cubic foot (ft³)
27 cubic feet = 1 cubic yard (yd³)

WEIGHT

16 ounces (oz) = 1 pound (lb)
2000 pounds = 1 ton (t)

CAPACITY

8 fluid ounces (fl oz) = 1 cup (c)
2 cups = 1 pint (pt)
2 pints = 1 quart (qt)
4 quarts = 1 gallon (gal)

544

529

BIBLIOGRAPHY

This bibliography lists contemporary publications. Unless otherwise indicated, all books were in print at the time the list was compiled. An asterisk indicates that a book was not in print. These titles may be obtainable through your public or school library.

Literature and Stories

Briggs, Carole S. *Women in Space: Reaching the Last Frontier.* Lerner, 1988.
   Biographical profiles of women astronauts. Math was an essential part of training for these remarkable careers.

Dolan, Edward F. *Famous Firsts in Space.* Cobblehill, 1989.
   Accounts of the first American and Russian ventures into space. Science and math.

Herzig, Alison C., and Jane L. Mali. *The Ten-Speed Babysitter.* Dutton, 1987.
   A fourteen year old boy has his first summer job and wants to save money for a bike. Money, economics.

Ireland, Karin. *Albert Einstein.* Silver Burdett, 1989.
   Biography. Describes his early life as a difficult student, first great discoveries, early career changes and more. Photos.

James, Elizabeth, and Carol Barkin. *What Do You Mean By Average?* Lothrop, 1978. *
   Jill is running for Student Council president and wants to prove that she is "the most average person" in school. In their efforts to come up with the proof, her campaign committee learns about mean, median and modal averages as well as sampling and percentages. Introduction to statistical concepts.

Juster, Norton. *The Phantom Tollbooth.* Knopf, 1988.
   Milo drives through the Phantom Tollbooth into a strange land. In Digitopolis, he meets the Dodecahedron and the Mathemagician. Sense and nonsense with words and numbers.

Kramer, Stephen, P. *How to Think Like a Scientist: Answering Questions by the Scientific Method.* Crowell, 1987.
   An introduction to the scientific method. A book about questions and how we get answers. Uses stories about ordinary things and events to show how we answer questions every day. Reasoning. Problem Solving.

Leroe, Ellen W. *Robot Raiders.* HarperCollins, 1987.
   Science Fiction. The problems and adventures of a 16 year old computer genius who created a humanoid.

Macaulay, David. *Pyramid.* Houghton Mifflin, 1975.
   Explains the step-by-step construction process of an imaginary pyramid. Detailed illustrations.Geometry. Also by D. Macaulay: *Castle, Cathedral, City, Unbuilding, Underground.*

O'Conner, Karen. *Sally Ride and the New Astronauts: Scientists in Space.* Watts, 1983.
   Non-fiction. Narrative with photos.Science and math.

Ott, Virginia and Gloria Swanson. *Man With a Million Ideas: Fred Jones, Genius Inventor.* Lerner, 1977.
   Biography. The story of Frederick McKinley Jones, 1893-1961, whose work contributed to the growth of the frozen food industry. Science and math.

Pelta, Kathy. *Alexander Graham Bell.* Silver Burdett , 1989.
   Biography. Very readable narrative. Photos.

Pelta, Kathy. *Bridging the Golden Gate.* Lerner, 1987.
   Everyone said the Golden Gate couldn't be bridged. The story of Joseph Strauss who dared to dream and the challenging task of building an amazing structure.

Robertson, Keith. *Henry Reed's Think Tank.* Viking, 1986.
   When Henry and Midge start a "think tank" to help people solve problems they get more excitement than they bargained for. Money, business.

Ross, Frank, Jr. *Oracle Bones, Stars, and Wheelbarrows: Ancient Chinese Science and Technology.* Houghton Mifflin, 1982.
   Describes many Chinese contributions to mathematics as well as astronomy, medicine, engineering and more.

Tolan, Stephanie, S. *The Great Skinner Enterprise.* Puffin, 1988.
   The zany Skinner family starts a successful home business. Money, business.

Other Books for Students

Abdelnoor, R.E. Jason. *The Silver Burdett Mathematical Dictionary.* Silver Burdett , 1986.

Anno, Mitsumasa. *Anno's Sundial.* Philomel, 1987.

Asimov, Isaac. *How Did We Find Out About Computers?* Walker, 1984.

Burns, Marilyn. *The I Hate Mathematics!* Book. Little, 1975.

Burns, Marilyn. *Math for Smarty Pants: Or Who Says Mathematicians Have Little Pig Eyes.* Little, 1982.

Diggins, Julia E. *String, Straightedge, and Shadow; The Story of Geometry.* Viking, 1965. *

Fekete, Irene and Jasmine Denyer. *Mathematics.* Facts on File, 1985.

Fisher, Leonard E. *Calendar Art: Thirteen Days, Weeks, Months, and Years from Around the World.* Four Winds, 1987.

Fisher, Leonard E. *Number Art: Thirteen 123's from Around the World.* Four Winds, 1982.

Gardner, Martin. *Perplexing Puzzles and Tantalizing Teasers.* Dover, 1969. *

Garland, Trudi H. *Fascinating Fibonaccis: Mystery and Magic in Numbers.* Seymour, 1987.

Grater, Michael. *Make It In Paper: Creative Three-Dimensional Paper Projects.* Dover, 1983.

Perl, Lila. *Junk Food, Fast Food, Health Food: What America Eats and Why.* Clarion, 1979.

Smullyan, Raymond. *Alice in Puzzle-Land.* Quill, 1990.

Stwerka, Albert. *Recent Revolution in Mathematics.* Watts, 1987.

Trease, Geoffery. *Timechanges: The Evolution of Everyday Life.* Warwick, 1986.

Resource Books for Teachers

Banks, James A., and Cherry A. Banks, eds. *Multicultural Education: Issues and Perspectives.* Allyn and Bacon. 1989.

Cooney, Thomas J., and Christian R. Hirsch, eds. *Teaching and Learning Mathematics in the 1990s: 1990 Yearbook.* National Council of Teachers of Mathematics. 1990.

Dahlke, Richard, and Roger Verhey. *What Expert Teachers Say About Teaching Mathematics.* Seymour. 1986.

Duke, Daniel, L. ed. *Helping Teachers Manage Classrooms.* Association for Supervision and Curriculum Development. 1982.

Fuys, David, et al. *The Van Hiele Model of Thinking in Geometry Among Adolescents* (Journal for Research in Math Education Monograph No. 3) National Council of Teachers of Mathematics. 1988.

Hayes, John R. *The Complete Problem Solver.* 2nd rev. ed. Lawrence Erlbaum. 1989.

Johnson, David W., et al. *Circles of Learning.* Association for Supervision and Curriculum Development. 1984.

Kidder, Tracy. *Among Schoolchildren.* Houghton Mifflin. 1989.

Marzano, Robert J., et al. *Dimensions of Thinking: A Framework for Curriculum and Instruction.* Association for Supervision and Curriculum Development. 1988.

McKnight, Curtis C., et al. *The Underachieving Curriculum: Assessing U. S. School Mathematics from an International Perspective.* Stipes. 1987.

Murnane, Richard J., and Senta A. Raizen, eds. *Improving Indicators of the Quality of Science and Mathematics Education in Grades K-12.* National Academy Press. 1988.

National Council of Teachers of Mathematics. *Curriculum and Evaluation Standards for School Mathematics.* National Council of Teachers of Mathematics. 1989.

National Council of Teachers of Mathematics. *Professional Standards for Teaching Mathematics.* National Council of Teachers of Mathematics. 1991.

National Research Council. *Everybody Counts.* National Academy. 1989.

National Research Council. *Reshaping School Mathematics.* National Academy Press. 1990.

Paulos, John Allen. *Innumeracy.* Hill and Wang. 1988.

Polya, G. *How to Solve It.* 2nd rev. ed. Anchor Books. 1957.

Resnick, Lauren B., and Leopold E. Klopfer, eds. *Toward the Thinking Curriculum: Current Cognitive Research: 1989 Yearbook.* Association for Supervision and Curriculum Development. 1989.

Rico, Barbara Roche, and Sandra Mano. *American Mosaic.* Houghton Mifflin. 1991.

Skemp, Richard R. *The Psychology of Learning Mathematics.* Lawrence Erlbaum. 1987.

Steen, Lynn Arthur, ed. *On the Shoulders of Giants.* National Academy Press. 1990.

Tobias, Sheila. *Overcoming Math Anxiety.* W. W. Norton. 1978.

Trafton, Paul R., and Albert P. Shulte, eds. *New Directions for Elementary School Mathematics: 1989 Yearbook.* National Council of Teachers of Mathematics. 1989.

Whimbey, Arthur, and Jack Lochhead. *Beyond Problem Solving and Comprehension.* Lawrence Erlbaum Associates. 1984.

Willoughby, Stephen S. *Mathematics Education for a Changing World.* Association for Supervision and Curriculum Development. 1990.

INDEX

CREDITS

Credits

Series design Pronk & Associates

Cover and title page design Sheaff Design, Inc.

Cover and title page photography Schlowsky Photography

Art production of openers Pronk & Associates

Technical Art Pronk & Associates and Morgan Slade & Associates

ILLUSTRATIONS
Meg Kelleher Aubrey 165
Rudy Backart 57, 93 (top)
David Bathurst 1, 84, 85, 174, 175, 186, 187
Nancy Bernard 199, 373
Thach Bui 6, 7, 97, 432, 474, 475, 497, 506, 507, 508
Scott Cameron 104, 105
Ian Carr 16, 17, 190, 191, 207, 220
Doug Cushman 411
Chris Demerest 345
Greg Douglas 180, 181, 314, 315, 386, 452, 457, 467
Rodney Dunn 169
Catherine Farley 46, 48, 78, 79, 95
Ruth Flanigan 19 (right), 127
Raffeala Gal 188, 292, 293
Don Gauthier 392, 393, 440, 510
Bill Gilgannon 64, 65
Donna Gordon 282, 283, 296, 352, 358, 420
David Graves 31
Lois Green 502, 503
Chris Griffin 192
Walt Gunthardt 273, 418, 489
Tim Halstrom 375
Nancy Jackson 148, 149
Gary Lagendyk 349
Joe Lepiano 324
Scott MacNeill 93 (bottom), 109 (right), 519
Maryland CartoGraphics 479
Paul McCuster, 492, 493
Valerie McKeown 167
Jack McMaster 33, 70, 73, 102, 103, 146, 147
Susan Meddaugh 19 (left)
Margery Mintz 30, 91
Tomio Nitto 59
Cheryl Kirk Noll 55
Carol O'Malia 109 (left)
Diane Palmisciano 308, 487

Jun Park/Turning Point 42, 76, 77, 100, 101, 178, 309, 310, 353, 354, 401, 429, 459, 466, 468, 471
Carol Paton 222, 223, 262
Andrew Plewes 20, 26, 27, 62, 63, 116
Stephen Quinlan 36, 112, 113, 144, 145, 208, 209, 217, 318, 319, 335, 338, 416
Paul Rivoche xii–xv, 336, 504
Valerie Spain 125
Margo Stahl 8, 9, 24, 25, 39, 61, 152, 250, 260
Don Stuart 409
Craig Terlson 2, 3
Angela Vaculik 12, 13, 252, 294, 295, 301, 394, 395
Peter Venemen 472
Carl Wiens 422, 423, 491
Andreas Zaretzki 449
Paul Zwolak 120, 121

PHOTOGRAPHY
Ian Crysler 86, 87, 263, 298, 299, 340, 362, 364, 365, 384, 404, 480
Colin Erricson 134, 136, 137
Greg Holman 40, 41, 312
Keith Gabriel 210, 284, 332, 333, 363, 380, 381, 396, 506, 508, 509
Birgitte Nielsen 498, 499
Dan Paul 66, 67, 80, 118, 119, 130, 142, 143, 185, 206, 214, 215, 218, 276, 277, 280, 281, 301, 326, 327, 334, 376, 377, 378, 413, 456, 458, 476, 496

4, 5 Dallas and John Heaton/Miller Comstock; 10 David W. Hamilton/The Image Bank; 14, 15 Buck Ennis/Stock Boston; 22 Santi Vasalli/The Image Bank; 39 Joseph Szkodzinski/The Image Bank; 50, 51 M. Burgess/Miller Comstock; 68, 69 Miller Comstock; 73 Harald Sund/The Image Bank; 75 Jas. Blank/The Stock Market; 82 Derek Caron/Masterfile; 83 Whitney Lane/The Image Bank; 94 Jon Feingersh/The Stock Market; 95 Gary Cralle/The Image Bank; 96 Aram Gesar/The Image Bank; 98 Steve Leonard/Masterfile; 106, 107 Martha Swope Assoc./Carol Rose; 110 Guiliano Colliva/The Image Bank; 114 Birgitte Nielsen; 129 G. Fritz/H. Armstrong Roberta/Miller Comstock; 141 Bryan Peterson/The Stock Market; 156 (top) Johnson Wax Co./Ursula Charaf; 156 IBM Corp/Thomas Way; 157 (top) Johnson Wax Co./Ursula Charaf; 157 2) David Scharf, 1977 All rights reserved; 158 NASA; 159 Georg Gerster/Miller Comstock; 160 Kul Bhatia/The Image Bank; 161 Luis Padilla/The Image Bank; 176 Viesti Associates Inc.; 179 Stephen Marks/Stockphotos Inc.; 183 Superstock; 194 James Davis/International Stock Photo;

195 David Klutho/Sports Illustrated; 204 (top) Larry Fisher Photography/Masterfile; 204 (bottom) Cesar Lucas/The Image Bank; 210, 211 Qualla Arts & Crafts; 213 North Wind Picture Archives; 215 Vicky Elson; 231 Barb & Ron Kroll/Miller Comstock; 231 Macleans/Canapress; 247 Superstock; 254 Georg Gerster/Miller Comstock; 265 Juergen Schmitt/The Image Bank; 275 Milton Feinberg/Stock Boston; 278 Tadao Kimura/The Image Bank; 297 Alvis Upitis/The Image Bank; 300 H. Armstrong Roberts Inc./Miller Comstock; 305 Richard Pasley/Stock Boston; 305 Tony Henshaw/Tony Stone Worldwide; 310 Gary Braasch; 317 The Alaskan Tourist Office; 322 Patti McConville/The Image Bank; 331 Brown Brothers; 357 Pete Saloutos/The Stock Market; 366 Guido Alberto Rossi/The Image Bank; 367 Mecel Isy-Schwart/The Image Bank; 383 John Lewis Stage/The Image Bank; 391 H. Armstrong Roberts; 402 Robert Ostrowski/The Image Bank; 426 Pete Turner/The Image Bank; 427 Roberto Valladares/The Image Bank; 428 Curtis Willocks/The Image Bank; 431 The Granger Collection; 434 Weinberg-Clark/The Image Bank; 445 Mike Kirkpatrick/Profiles West; 450, 451 Courtesy of Christie's, London, and The Victoria and Albert Museum, London; 454 Marburg/Art Resource; 462 Bruce Iverson; 465 Phil Lauro/Profiles West; 470 (top) John Stuart/The Image Bank; 470 (middle) Larry Dale Gordon/The Image Bank; 470 (bottom) Philip M. DeRenzis/The Image Bank; 472 Kay Chernush/The Image Bank; 478 Mecel Isy-Schwart/The Image Bank; 501 Cammermann International; 514 Michael Coyne/The Image Bank

Bulletin Board Illustrations: Pat Wong   T23, 32G, 58G, 94G, 128G, 168G, 202G, 230G, 272G, 308G, 348G, 374G, 412G, 448G, 488G
Design and Production: Textart Inc.
Cover Design: Sheaff Design, Inc.
Cover and Title Page Photography: Ken Karp Photography